THE EARLY
ENGLISH CAROLS

The Carole of the Shepherds at the Nativity
Bodleian Library, MS. Douce 93, f. 28r. Lower Rhineland, fifteenth century

The Early English Carols

EDITED BY

RICHARD LEIGHTON GREENE

Second edition, revised and enlarged

OXFORD
AT THE CLARENDON PRESS
1977

Oxford University Press, Walton Street, Oxford, OX2 6DP

OXFORD LONDON GLASGOW NEW YORK
TORONTO MELBOURNE WELLINGTON CAPE TOWN
IBADAN NAIROBI DAR ES SALAAM LUSAKA ADDIS ABABA
KUALA LUMPUR SINGAPORE JAKARTA HONG KONG TOKYO
DELHI BOMBAY CALCUTTA MADRAS KARACHI

ISBN 0 19 812715 4

First published 1935
Second Edition 1977

*Printed in Great Britain
at the University Press, Oxford
by Vivian Ridler
Printer to the University*

TO THE MEMORY OF
MY PARENTS
JAMES GEREAU GREENE
AND
RUTH LEIGHTON GREENE

PREFACE TO THE SECOND EDITION

THE Preface to the first edition of this work is here reprinted without change, for the basic plan of the book remains unchanged, and the gratitude there expressed to teachers, scholars, library authorities, owners of manuscripts, and friends (categories not at all mutually exclusive) has only deepened with the lapse of four decades. Many of these gifted and generous people must now be honoured *in memoriam*, like the devoted parents to whom the first edition was dedicated. I owe a special mention to the late Kenneth Sisam, former Secretary to the Delegates of the Clarendon Press, who requested that his name should not appear in the list, but who gave both encouragement and vigilance to a young and inexperienced editor. Neither he nor I expected that there would ever be a second edition, and I alone remain to offer apologies to the many would-be owners of the book who have complained to me of its out-of-print status over so many years.

The definition of the medieval English carol put forward in the first edition may now without immodesty be said to have stood the test of time and much scholarly scrutiny and to be generally accepted by historians and critics of medieval literature. In 1935 the study of the music preserved with about one-quarter of the extant carols was in a state that can only be called primitive, and the researches of several brilliant musicologists since that time have most gratifyingly supported my definition of the poetic form and established the carol as a recognized genre of medieval music in England. A good statement of the received definition of the genre in music may be found in Alec Harman, *Mediaeval and Early Renaissance Music* (London, 1958), pp. 214–15.

The Introduction and Notes will be found to contain many substantive additions and, of course, many added references in exposition and footnotes, but the basic positions set forth in the first edition have required very little change. Some of the material which has been added will be recognized as having appeared in the introduction and apparatus of *A Selection of English Carols*, published by the Clarendon Press in 1962 as a volume in its Clarendon Medieval and Tudor Series. In particular that smaller work presented and dealt with the English texts of the most important carol-manuscript discovered in the interim, British Museum Egerton 3307, a collection even more interesting for its music than for its verbal contents. The present edition incorporates most of the new historical and critical material offered in *A Selection*, but it is hoped that 'the little book' will not be entirely overlooked by students and other readers, though now out of print like its parent volume.

The carol-texts which are now added to this second edition are treated in complete accordance with the practices explained in the Preface to the first. The numbers assigned to all pieces in the first edition are retained. Each completely new piece is inserted in what seems to be the most appropriate place in the sequence of subject-matter and assigned the number of the piece which it follows modified by a decimal, e.g. 418.1, 418.2. New texts which are variant versions of carols already in the first edition are assigned distinguishing letters in accordance with the existing scheme, e.g. 23 C, 142 B a. References to 'British Museum' have not been changed to 'British Library', since all but the most recent citations in print use the older name.

All the texts have been rechecked with the original manuscripts or printed sources, except for No. 456.1 from a photocopy kindly supplied by the Huntington Library, No. 95 b, in a manuscript now in Japan, Nos. 79 B and 112, in the manuscript destroyed in 1879, and the numerous and not very significant variant stanzas of Nos. 263 and 309. The resulting changes in the text are mostly trifling, and in only a few cases do they affect the sense of a verse. The re-examination, nevertheless, gave the editor the double pleasure of seeing old manuscript-friends again and finding that his young eye had been nothing to be ashamed of in point of accuracy.

The Bibliography of Original Sources has been thoroughly revised by re-inspection of the manuscripts and early prints. Modern printed works are not included. The entries for new sources generally follow the form and scale of those in the first edition. A number of manuscripts have been subjected since 1935 to expert and highly detailed bibliographical analysis and description by cataloguers and others. I have used their research but have not attempted to rival its bulk and its detail.

Many scholars and associates beside those mentioned in the earlier Preface have given me assistance of various kinds in the preparation of this edition. My thanks are due to the mostly cordial reviewers of both the edition of 1935 and *A Selection of Carols*, who pointed to some errors which I had committed and some which I had not. Among those whose contributions have been particularly valuable I name with pleasure Professor J. A. W. Bennett of Magdalene College, Cambridge; Professor Rossell Hope Robbins of the State University of New York at Albany; Professor Norman Davis of Merton College, Oxford; Douglas Gray of Pembroke College, Oxford; Professor William Ringler of the University of Chicago; N. R. Ker, Fellow Emeritus of Magdalen College, Oxford; R. W. Hunt of the Bodleian Library; Professor Robert R. Raymo of New York University; Stephen Parks of the Osborn Collection at Yale University; Dr. Felix Hull, Kent County Archivist; A. Hyatt King of the British Museum; Dame Gertrude Brown of Stanbrook Abbey, Worcester; John Veale of the Clarendon Press. I acknowledge the special courtesy of James M. Osborn of Yale

University and of Toshiyuki Takamiya of Tokyo, Japan, the new owner of a manuscript formerly belonging to Lord Tollemache.

My work has benefited immeasurably from the knowledge and generosity of musicologists who have dealt expertly with the preserved music of the carols. The late Manfred F. Bukofzer was as enthusiastic as learned, and a most valued friend. John Stevens of Magdalene College, Cambridge, the editor of all the extant music in his *Mediaeval Carols* and *Early Tudor Songs and Carols* (Musica Britannica, iv and xxxvi), has superbly and completely carried out the musical presentation of the genre of the carol for which I could never have become qualified. Frank Ll. Harrison of the Etnomusicologisch Centrum 'Jaap Kunst', Amsterdam, has made important contributions to the study of the medieval carol-music in his *Music in Medieval Britain* and elsewhere. Margaret Bent of the University of London has sent me useful information and joined with other scholars to make enjoyable and profitable my participation in the seminar on the English carol at the Tenth Congress of the International Musicological Society at Ljubljana, Yugoslavia, in 1967.

It is a pleasure to thank the directors and staffs of various libraries in which I have worked during the preparation of this revision. In addition to the institutions named in the earlier Preface these include the Pepysian Library at Magdalene College, Cambridge, the Henry E. Huntington Library and Art Gallery, the New York Public Library, the libraries of Wesleyan, Princeton, Yale, Harvard, and Cornell Universities, and those of the Universities of London, Glasgow, Rochester, Chicago, and California at Berkeley.

I acknowledge with thanks the special permissions to publish material given by the Dean and Chapter of Canterbury Cathedral, the Kent County Council, the Lady Abbess of Stanbrook Abbey, Worcester, and the Huntington Library.

The first edition of this work was published with the aid of a subvention from the University of Rochester, for which I had chiefly to thank the then President, my friend and benefactor, the late Rush Rhees. The research for this second edition has been repeatedly supported by the generous provision of sabbatical leaves and supplementary research funds made by Wesleyan University during the years of my membership in its faculty. A considerable amount of the research took place during my tenure of appointments as Visiting Fellow at Princeton University in 1963 and 1968.

For much assistance not merely clerical but of a kind involving extensive learning and fine scholarly judgement I am earnestly grateful to my former student Joy Day Buel.

R. L. G.

New Haven, Connecticut
April 1974

PREFACE TO THE FIRST EDITION

THE Middle and Early Modern English texts here collected comprise all those lyrics extant and accessible in manuscript or printed sources of date earlier than 1550 to which, in the editor's judgement, the term 'carol' can properly be applied. These texts have been selected on the basis, not of their subject-matter, but of their metrical form. They include only poems intended, or at least suitable, for singing, made up of uniform stanzas and provided with a burden which begins the piece and is to be repeated after each stanza. The reasons for the adoption of this basis of selection and the historical justification for this limitation of the term 'carol' are given at some length in the Introduction.

The year 1550 is chosen as a downward limit for the reason that the carol form appears at about that time to have lost its great popularity with some suddenness. The burst of poetical progress and the accompanying change of metrical fashion which are associated with the Elizabethan period relegated the characteristically medieval carol form to the infrequent and socially undistinguished use claimed by an outmoded style. New musical developments, notably the madrigal, replaced among the cultivated the simple pattern of the carol. New dances imported from the Continent caused the medieval carole to become the amusement almost entirely of children and rustics. As a consequence the term 'carol' lost its definite medieval meaning, already weakened, of 'dance-song' and became the vague synonym for 'song in general' which it remains in common usage today.

It would be profitless and pedantic, as well as historically unjustified, when applying the word to songs of Elizabethan or later times, to insist on the limitation of meaning observed in this collection of songs from the time when 'carol' still held associations with the dance. The familiar instance of the word 'ballad' is a case in point. One may speak of a modern ballad or a ballad opera without prejudice to the technical and historical use of the word to designate a narrative folk-song from oral tradition. The present volume is simply an attempt to present the medieval carol as a definite metrical type, recognized as such by those who sang and wrote it in the England of the later Middle Ages.

No detailed treatment of the musical settings preserved for many of the carols is here undertaken, although the evidence of such music has been used wherever possible in determining the metrical form of the lyrics. From such sources as the bass part-book with British Museum press-mark K.1.e.1, and MS. Addit. 31922 some pieces which resemble carols in arrangement of words have not been included, since the music varies from stanza to stanza and is not repeated as in the true carol. Discussions and transcriptions of the music of some of the carols are available to the reader in Stainer's *Early Bodleian Music*, Fuller Maitland's *Fifteenth Century Carols*, Sir Richard Terry's *A Medieval Carol Book*, and other works to which reference is made in the notes.

The arrangement of the carols by subject-matter calls for some explanation. The two most obvious and usual methods of classifying carols, a division into 'Christmas' and 'other' carols and a division into 'religious' and 'secular' carols, are also the most misleading. If 'Christmas carol' be taken to mean a song explicitly celebrating the Nativity, an English *noël*, the term is arbitrarily narrowed in a way unknown before 1800 at the earliest. If it be taken to mean any song suitable for singing at Christmas (from a modern editor's point of view), it ceases to have any objective value and excludes many songs which certainly *were* sung at Christmas, the loose and profane ones, for example. To the question 'Which of these pieces are Christmas carols?' one can only answer, 'Any, or all.' Probably most of them were felt to be suitable for singing at Christmastide. Quite as probably most of them, including some of those on the Nativity itself, were sung on other occasions, or *ad placitum*, as a heading frequent in one manuscript has it. A few are definitely occasional, especially those for the feast-days following Christmas Day, but there is no reason to assume that most of them, once in a singer's repertory, were disused from one year's end to the other as is the case with the modern 'Christmas carols'.

The division into 'religious' and 'secular' carols is likewise based on a modern rather than a medieval attitude. The distinctive charm of many carols is just that they do belong to two worlds; they were written in days when one could be pious and merry at the same time. Especially has the process of giving wordly or trivial songs a new devotional dress produced many carols which it would be equally misguided to class with *Hymns Ancient and Modern* as 'religious' or even with Herrick's *Hesperides* as 'secular'.

A chronological arrangement of the carols is impracticable for the reason that the relative priority of the texts, as apart from the manuscripts in which they are preserved, cannot in many cases be determined.

The arrangement here adopted is one designed to serve the convenience of the reader without grouping the texts in rigid and unmeaning categories. It adopts a middle course between the care-free arrangement of the compilers of the manuscripts and an unhistorical and arbitrary segregation by types. The order is designed to bring together pieces on the same or similar dominant themes. The reader will quickly perceive the relationship between carols which lie near each other, and the running titles of the pages are to be regarded as guide-posts rather than as designations having ultimate critical validity. The titles given the separate carols in the notes are likewise dictated by considerations of convenience. To attempt to impose them on the texts with any air of finality would be impertinent.

Subject to these reservations, the order of the texts is as follows:

Carols of Advent, the Nativity, the feasts of the Twelve Days, the Purification.

Carols of the infant Christ and His mother.

Carols of the Passion, including *planctus Mariae*.

Devotional carols to or of the Virgin, including those on the Annunciation.

Devotional carols to or of the Trinity, God the Father, and Christ, including appeals of Christ to mankind.

Carols of the Saints.

Carols of the Mass and the Eucharist.

Carols of religious and moral counsel.

Carols of doomsday and mortality.

Carols of satirical tendency.

Carols on persons or events of political significance.

Amorous carols, refined and gross.

Humorous carols.

The notes are designed rather to be of service to those who may wish to study the texts further than to provide exhaustive commentary on each piece. Glossarial notes are provided only for words which might present some difficulty to those readers having a slight acquaintance with Middle English. They do not include linguistic discussions. For each of the many carols by James Ryman with their hundreds of verbal resemblances to each other, a single reference to the full and laborious notes of Zupitza has been made. The work of previous editors has been freely drawn upon without detailed reference, and acknowledgement of indebtedness to all such commentary is gladly made here. A special notice is called for of the present editor's debt to Professor Carleton Brown's *Register of Middle English Religious and Didactic Verse*, without which the task of selecting and locating texts would have been far more difficult.

The Introduction of this volume incorporates, with minor revisions, the greater part of a dissertation submitted, under the title *The English Carol before 1550*, in partial fulfilment of the requirements of the degree of Doctor of Philosophy, and accepted by the faculty of Princeton University in 1929. The corpus of texts now included corresponds in general to that upon which the dissertation was based.

The editing of the texts from the original sources and the preparation of the notes and bibliography were done in England during my tenure of a Research Fellowship of the American Council of Learned Societies for the academic year 1931–2.

Grateful acknowledgement is made to the authorities of the following libraries, who have permitted the transcription and publication of the texts in this volume: The British Museum; The College of Arms; Lambeth Palace; The Public Record Office; Lincoln's Inn; Westminster Abbey; The Bodleian Library; Balliol College, Oxford; New College, Oxford; The University Library, Cambridge; Corpus Christi College, Cambridge; Gonville & Caius College, Cambridge; Jesus College, Cambridge; St. John's College, Cambridge; Trinity College, Cambridge; Chapter Library, Canterbury Cathedral; The John Rylands Library, Manchester; National Library of Scotland; Trinity College, Dublin; Bridgwater Corporation Muniments; Henry E. Huntington Library and Art Gallery, San Marino, California.

My thanks are also offered to the following private owners of manuscripts, who have shown me particular courtesy in permitting the transcription and publication of texts: The Most Honourable the Marquess of Bath; the Right Honourable Lord Harlech; the Right Honourable Lord Tollemache and the Trustees of the Estate of the late Lord W. F. Tollemache; the Honourable Mrs. R. Douglas Hamilton. The text of No. 322 C is included by permission of Messrs. Stainer & Bell, Ltd., owners of the copyright, the texts of Nos. 79 B and 112 by permission of Professor Hardin Craig of Stanford University.

It is a further pleasure to record my gratitude to a number of other persons who have assisted me in various ways. Mr. Geoffrey B. Riddehough of the University of British Columbia very kindly communicated to me some results of his independent search for texts of carols in the British Isles. In particular he first called my attention to the existence and location of Nos. 36 c, 114 c, 147, and 170. Mr. Godfrey Davies of the Huntington Library sent me the necessary bibliographical and other information concerning MS. HM. 147 in that institution. My friends Professors Harvey A. Eagleson of the California Institute of Technology, Henry L. Savage of Princeton University, Edward B. Ham of Yale University, and Mr. Owen E. Holloway of Oxford, have furnished me with useful information. Mr T. Bruce Dilks, F.R.Hist.Soc., made easy and pleasant my access to the archives of the Corporation of Bridgwater. Mrs. D. R. Dalton, Executive Secretary of the American University Union in London, gave me much practical help in my search for carols in English libraries.

For their generous interest and encouragement I owe more than a formal acknowledgement can express to my friends and former teachers at Princeton University, Dean Robert K. Root, Professor Charles G. Osgood, Professor Gordon H. Gerould, who suggested the enlargement of my dissertation into an inclusive edition, and Professor Morris W. Croll, who first suggested a study of the carol, and under whose kindly and understanding direction I wrote my dissertation.

R. L. G.

Rochester, New York
August 1935

CONTENTS

ABBREVIATIONS
USED IN INTRODUCTION AND NOTES

Anal. Hym.   Dreves, Guido Maria, and Clemens Blume, eds., *Analecta Hymnica Medii Aevi*. Leipzig, 1886–1922.

Anglia   *Anglia. Zeitschrift für englische Philologie*. Halle, 1877– .

Archiv   *Archiv für das Studium der neueren Sprachen und Literaturen*. Elberfeld, 1846–9; Brunswick, 1849– .

Babees Book   Furnivall, F. J., ed., *The Babees Book*. Early English Text Society, Original Series, No. 32, 1868.

B. J. W., *Proverbs*   Whiting, Bartlett Jere and H. W., eds., *Proverbs, Sentences and Proverbial Phrases from English Writings Mainly before 1500*. Cambridge, Massachusetts, 1968.

Bliss   Bliss, Philip, ed., *Bibliographical Miscellanies*. Oxford, 1815.

B.M.   British Museum.

Bodl.   Bodleian Library.

Brougham   Brougham, Eleanor M., ed., *Corn from Olde Fieldes, an Anthology of English Poems from the XIVth to the XVIIth Century*. London, [1918].

B.–R.   Brown, Carleton, and Rossell Hope Robbins, eds., *The Index of Middle English Verse*. N.Y., 1943.

B.–R. *Supp.*   Robbins, Rossell Hope, and J. L. Cutler, eds., *Supplement to the Index of Middle English Verse*. Lexington, Kentucky, 1965.

Brown, *R.L. 14 C.*   Brown, Carleton, ed., *Religious Lyrics of the XIVth Century*. 2nd edn., Oxford, 1952.

Brown, *R.L. 15 C.*   Brown, Carleton, ed., *Religious Lyrics of the XVth Century*. Oxford, 1939.

Br. Sar.   Proctor, Francis, and Christopher Wordsworth, eds., *Breviarium ad Usum Insignis Ecclesiae Sarum*. Cambridge, 1879–86.

Bukofzer   Bukofzer, Manfred F., *Studies in Medieval and Renaissance Music*. New York, 1950.

Bullen   Bullen, A. H., ed., *A Christmas Garland : Carols and Poems from the Fifteenth Century to the Present Day*. London, 1885.

C. & S.   Chambers, [Sir] E. K., and Frank Sidgwick, eds., *Early English Lyrics, Amorous, Divine, Moral, & Trivial*. London, 1926.

C. & S., *M.L.R.*   Chambers, [Sir] E. K., and Frank Sidgwick, eds., 'Fifteenth-Century Carols by John Audelay', *The Modern Language Review*.

Chambers, *M.S.*   Chambers, [Sir] E. K., *The Mediaeval Stage*. Oxford, 1903.

Child   Child, Francis James, ed., *The English and Scottish Popular Ballads*. Boston and New York, 1882–98.

C.U. Lib.   Cambridge University Library.

Daniel, *Thes. Hym.*   Daniel, Hermann Adalbert, ed., *Thesaurus Hymnologicus*. Leipzig, 1855–6.

Davies	Davies, R. T., ed., *Medieval English Lyrics*. London, 1963.
Dyboski	Dyboski, Roman, ed., *Songs, Carols, and Other Miscellaneous Poems*. Early English Text Society, Extra Series, No. ci. 1908
E.B.M.	Stainer, Sir John, ed., *Early Bodleian Music*. London, 1901.
E.D.D.	Wright, Joseph, ed., *The English Dialect Dictionary*. London, 1898–1905.
E.E.C.	Greene, Richard Leighton, ed., *The Early English Carols*. Oxford, 1935.
E.E.T.S.	Early English Text Society.
Englische Studien	*Englische Studien. Organ für englische Philologie*, etc. Heilbronn, 1877–89; Leipzig, 1890– .
Ex. Ser.	Extra Series.
facs.	Reproduced in facsimile.
Fehr	Fehr, Bernhard, ed., 'Die Lieder der Hs. Add. 5665', *Archiv für das Studium der neueren Sprachen und Literaturen*, cvi (1901).
Flügel, *Fest.*	Flügel, Ewald, ed., 'Englische Weihnachtslieder aus einer Handschrift des Balliol College zu Oxford', *Forschungen zur deutschen Philologie. Festgabe für Rudolf Hildebrand*. Leipzig, 1894.
Flügel, 'Lieder.'	Flügel, Ewald, 'Liedersammlungen', *Anglia*, xxvi (1903).
Flügel, *N.L.*	Flügel, Ewald, ed., *Neuenglisches Lesebuch*, i. Halle, 1895.
Frost	Frost, Leslie, ed., *Come Christmas*. New York, 1935.
Fuller Maitland	Fuller Maitland, J. A., and W. S. Rockstro, eds., *English Carols of the Fifteenth Century*. London, [1891].
Gray, *Lyrics*	Gray, Douglas, ed., *A Selection of Religious Lyrics*. Clarendon Medieval and Tudor Series. Oxford, 1975.
Gray, *Themes and Images*	Gray, Douglas, *Themes and Images in the Medieval English Religious Lyric*. London, 1972.
Greene, *Selection*	Greene, Richard Leighton, ed., *A Selection of English Carols*. Clarendon Medieval and Tudor Series. Oxford, 1962.
Grigson	Grigson, Geoffrey, ed., *The Faber Book of Popular Verse*. London, 1971.
Guide	Dean-Smith, Margaret, *A Guide to English Folk Song Collections, 1822–1952*. Liverpool, 1954.
Hym. S.	*Hymnarium Sarisburiense*. London, 1851.
James & Macaulay	James, M. R., and G. C. Macaulay, eds., 'Fifteenth Century Carols and Other Pieces', *The Modern Language Review*, viii (1915).
J.A.M.S.	*Journal of the American Musicological Society*. Princeton, New Jersey, etc., 1948– .
Jeffrey	Jeffrey, David L., *The Early English Lyric and Franciscan Spirituality*. Lincoln, Nebraska, 1975.
J.F.S.S.	*Journal of the Folk-Song Society*. London, 1899–1931.
Kaiser, *Anth.*	Kaiser, Rolf, ed., *Alt- und mittelenglische Anthologie*. Berlin, 1955.
Kaiser, *Med. Engl.*	Kaiser, Rolf, ed., *Medieval English* (3rd edn. of *Anth.*). Berlin West, 1958.
MacCracken	MacCracken, Henry N., ed., *The Minor Poems of John Lydgate*, parts i, ii. Early English Text Society, Extra Series, No. cvii, Original Series, No. 192. 1911, 1934.

Mayer   [Mayer, L. S.], ed., *Music Cantelenas Songs Etc.* London, privately printed, 1906.

M.L.R.   *The Modern Language Review.* Cambridge, 1906– .

Mus. Ant.   Stafford Smith, J., ed., *Musica Antiqua.* [London, 1812].

Nat. Lib. Scot. The National Library of Scotland.

Nat. Lib. W.   The National Library of Wales.

N. & Q.   *Notes and Queries.* London, 1850– .

New Ser.   New Series.

O.B.C.   Dearmer, Percy, R. Vaughan Williams, and Martin Shaw, eds., *The Oxford Book of Carols.* London, 1928.

O.E.D.   Murray, [Sir] James A. H., *et al.*, eds., *A New English Dictionary on Historical Principles* [*The Oxford English Dictionary*]. Oxford, 1888–1928.

Oliver   Oliver, Raymond, *Poems Without Names: The English Lyric 1200–1500.* Berkeley, California, 1970.

Or. Ser.   Original Series.

Padelford   Padelford, Frederick Morgan, ed., 'English Songs in Manuscript Selden B. 26', *Anglia*, xxxvi (1912).

Pat. Lat.   Migne, J. P., ed., *Patrologiae Cursus Completus* [*Patrologia Latina*]. Paris, 1842–80.

Patterson   Patterson, Frank A., ed., *The Middle English Penitential Lyric.* Columbia University Studies in English. New York, 1911.

Pollard   Pollard, Alfred William, ed., *An English Garner: Fifteenth Century Prose and Verse.* Westminster, 1903.

pr.   printed.

P.S.   *Percy Society Publications.* London, 1840–52.

Reed   Reed, Edward Bliss, ed., *Christmas Carols Printed in the Sixteenth Century.* Huntington Library Publications. Cambridge, Massachusetts, 1932.

Rel. Ant.   Wright, Thomas, and J. O. Halliwell[-Phillipps], eds., *Reliquiae Antiquae.* London, 1841–3.

repr.   reprinted.

R.E.S.   *The Review of English Studies.* London, 1925–46; Oxford, 1947– .

Rickert   Rickert, Edith, ed., *Ancient English Christmas Carols.* London, 1914.

Ritson, *Ancient Songs*   (1790) Ritson, Joseph, ed., *Ancient Songs from the Time of King Henry the Third to the Revolution.* London, 1790.
(1829) Ritson, Joseph, ed., *Ancient Songs and Ballads from the Reign of King Henry the Second to the Revolution.* London, 1829.
(1877) Ritson, Joseph, ed., *Ancient Songs and Ballads from the Reign of King Henry the Second to the Revolution* (re-ed. W. C. Hazlitt). London, 1877.

Robbins, *Christmas Carols*   Robbins, Rossell Hope, ed., *Early English Christmas Carols.* New York, 1961.

Robbins, *Hist. Poems*   Robbins, Rossell Hope, ed., *Historical Poems of the XIVth and XVth Centuries.* New York, 1959.

Robbins, *Secular Lyrics*   Robbins, Rossell Hope, ed., *Secular Lyrics of the XIVth and XVth Centuries.* 2nd edn., Oxford, 1955.

Sandison	Sandison, Helen E., *The 'Chanson d'Aventure' in Middle English*. Bryn Mawr College Monographs, Monograph Series, xii. Bryn Mawr, Pennsylvania, 1913.
Sandys, *Carols*	Sandys, William, ed., *Christmas Carols, Ancient and Modern*. London, 1833.
Sandys, *Christmas-tide*	Sandys, William, *Christmastide*. London, 1852.
Sar. Miss.	Wickham Legg, J., ed., *The Sarum Missal*. Oxford, 1916.
Silverstein	Silverstein, Theodore, ed., *Medieval English Lyrics*. York Medieval Texts. London, 1971.
Sisam	Sisam, Celia and Kenneth, eds., *The Oxford Book of Medieval English Verse*. Oxford, 1970.
Sitwell, *Atlantic Book*	Sitwell, [Dame] Edith, ed., *The Atlantic Book of British and American Poetry*. Boston, 1958.
Stemmler	Stemmler, Theo, ed., *Medieval English Love-Lyrics*. Tübingen, 1970.
Stevens, *Early Tudor Songs*	Stevens, John, ed., *Early Tudor Songs and Carols*. Musica Britannica, xxxvi. London, 1975.
Stevens, *Henry VIII*	Stevens, John, ed., *Music at the Court of Henry VIII*. Musica Britannica, xviii. London, 1962.
Stevens, *M. & P.*	Stevens, John, *Music and Poetry in the Early Tudor Court*. London, 1961.
Stevens, *Med. Carols*	Stevens, John, ed., *Mediaeval Carols*. Musica Britannica, iv. 2nd edn. London, 1958.
S.T.S.	Scottish Text Society.
Stud. in Phil.	*Studies in Philology*. Chapel Hill, North Carolina, 1907– .
T.C.C.	Trinity College, Cambridge.
T.C.D.	Trinity College, Dublin.
Terry	Terry, Sir Richard R., ed., *A Medieval Carol Book*. London, [1931].
Tydeman	Tydeman, William, ed., *English Poetry 1400–1580*. London, 1970.
Utley	Utley, Francis Lee, *The Crooked Rib*. Ohio State University Contributions in Language and Literature, No. 10. Columbus, 1944.
V.C.H.	*The Victoria County History*.
Wart. Club	*Publications of the Warton Club*. London, 1855–6.
Whiting	Whiting, Ella Keats, ed., *The Poems of John Audelay*. Early English Text Society, Original Series, No. 184. 1931.
Woolf	Woolf, Rosemary, *The English Religious Lyric in the Middle Ages*. Oxford, 1968.
Wright, *P.S.* iv, 'Christmas Carols'	Wright, Thomas, ed., 'Specimens of Old Christmas Carols, etc.', *Percy Society Publications*, iv. London, 1841.
Wright, *P.S.* xxiii	Wright, Thomas, ed., 'Songs and Carols of the Fifteenth Century', *Percy Society Publications*, xxiii. London, 1847.
Wright, *Wart. Club*	Wright, Thomas, ed., *Publications of the Warton Club*, iv. London, 1856.
Zupitza	Zupitza, Julius, ed., 'Die Gedichte des Franziskaners Jakob Ryman', *Archiv für das Studium der neueren Sprachen und Literaturen*, lxxxix (1892).

INTRODUCTION

CHAPTER I

THE CAROL AS A GENRE

1. *The Meaning of 'Carol'*

IN the mass of existing literature which professes to deal with the English carol the term is applied to lyrics differing widely in date, form, and spirit. Two popular works on the subject designate as the first carol the *Gloria in excelsis Deo* of the New Testament narrative, and proceed to apply the term as well to such later and less inspired compositions as eighteenth-century doggerel on Pekoe tea or these complacent lines from *Poor Robin's Almanack* for 1700:

> Now that the time has come wherein
> Our Saviour Christ was born,
> The larder's full of beef and pork,
> The garner's filled with corn.[1]

Small wonder that these treatises, like some more learned ones,[2] modestly eschew any attempt to define a carol in so many words. Comparison of such definitions as have been put forward by various authorities does not reveal any close agreement among them or any clear statement of the difference between what may be properly called a carol and any other song. Julian says:[3]

> A carol is a song of joy originally accompanying a dance ... Under the term *Carol* we may thus include a large class of popular songs, the first of which were characterised by dance-measures, both of time and action ... It has come eventually to be used to designate a kind of lyrical poem, usually, but not exclusively, on sacred subjects, intended to be sung, with or without musical accompaniment ...

He further suggests that the essential difference between hymns and carols may be that the latter

> ... deflect (as do the Psalms themselves) from direct addresses to God into

---

[1] Edmondstoune Duncan, *The Story of the Carol* (London, 1911), pp. 6, 197; William J. Phillips, *Carols : Their Origin, Music, and Connection with Mystery-Plays* (London, [1921]), pp. 1, 118.

[2] e.g. Edith Rickert, *Ancient English Christ-mas Carols* (London, 1914), or Edward Bliss Reed, *Christmas Carols Printed in the Sixteenth Century* (Cambridge, Mass., 1932).

[3] *A Dictionary of Hymnology* (London, 1915), s.v. 'Carols'.

historical references to His miraculous works and providential interpositions in behalf of His people; or into subjective, contemplative admiration of the Divine dealings with His faithful servants as individuals, thereby indirectly promoting His glory, but not directly ascribing glory to Him, and thus 'praising Him'.

The author grants that this leaves a wide borderland between hymn and carol, and the distinction on the basis of 'directness' of worship is plainly of no application to many lyrics which have long borne the name of carol.

The *Encyclopaedia Britannica* describes a carol as 'a hymn of praise, especially such as is sung at Christmas in the open air'.[1] *Grove's Dictionary of Music and Musicians* defines the carol in modern usage as 'a kind of popular song appropriated to some special season of the ecclesiastical or natural year',[2] and Jeffrey Pulver states that it has meant variously a song with text connected with the Nativity, a part of a miracle play, a jovial drinking-song, and a dance like the German *Reigen* or the French *branle*.[3] A much-quoted definition is that by one of the editors of *The Oxford Book of Carols*, who opens his preface with the concise statement:[4]

Carols are songs with a religious impulse that are simple, hilarious, popular, and modern.

This is quoted with warm approval by the reviewer of *The Times Literary Supplement*, who adds:

And it is not really possible to get much nearer to a precise definition; for like so many other names of musical forms (*e.g.*, motet and even symphony) the term means different things at different periods, and yet through all variations it has always managed to embody the same fundamental idea . . . a song (not a hymn) with a religious impulse sung from a warm heart whether solemn or gay.[5]

There is some wisdom in the comment, and it is probably necessary to resign ourselves to this vagueness in modern popular usage, but such resignation in regard to the carol before, roughly, the reign of Elizabeth is both unnecessary and undesirable. A fairly close examination of the history of the word itself will show that in the later Middle Ages, when the carol was most flourishing, it bore a more exact meaning and was, in fact, the accepted name of a definite lyric type.

The *Oxford English Dictionary* lists the following principal senses of the word:[6]

I. A ring-dance, and derived senses.

†1. A ring-dance with accompaniment of song; ? a ring of men or women holding hands and moving round in dancing step. *arch.*

---

[1] Eleventh edition (Cambridge, 1911), s.v. 'Carol'.

[2] (Philadelphia, 1922), s.v. 'Carol'.

[3] *A Dictionary of Old English Music and Musical Instruments* (London, 1923), s.v. 'Carol'.

[4] (London, 1928). The preface is by Percy Dearmer.

[5] 22 November 1928, p. 891.

[6] Condensed from the article 'Carol'. See also for the somewhat obscure etymology of the

b. Diversion or merry-making of which such dances formed a leading feature. *Obs.* (So in mod. F. dial. = 'fête, joie'.)
2. A song; originally, that to which they danced. Now usually, a song of a joyous strain; often *transf.* to the joyous warbling of birds.
3. a. A song or hymn of religious joy.
  †b. *esp.* A song or hymn of joy sung at Christmas in celebration of the Nativity. Rarely applied to hymns on certain other festal occasions.
II. A ring, and related senses.

It will be seen from the definitions previously quoted and from an examination of the pieces included in almost any popular collection of carols[1] that senses 2 and 3b are those in which the word has been most often understood for the last century and a half at least, and that a confusion of the two has been accepted by those who deal with the subject.[2] To modern editors a carol may be either any song dealing with Christmas material or designed for Christmas festivities or worship, or a song, not necessarily connected with Christmas, which is vaguely felt to have some connection with a dance. In any case the term has been far from having any such limits of application as those now recognized for the words 'ballad' or 'ode', let alone any such restricted metrical connotation as is possessed by 'sonnet', 'ballade', or 'roundel'.

It is, however, just such a restriction of meaning, with particular reference to the form of the lyrics, which characterizes the use of the word before the middle of the sixteenth century. It will be seen to be no arbitrary convention, but the natural result of the close association of a certain metrical structure with the round dance.

The word seems first to occur in extant English literature about 1300 in the *Cursor Mundi*, where it has the exact sense of Old French *carole*, that is, a ring-dance in which the dancers themselves sing the governing music:[3]

To ierusalem þat heued bare þai.
þer caroled wiues be þe way.
of þair carol suche was the sange.
atte þai for ioy had ham amange.

word. Further consideration is given it by Rudolf Haberl in *Zeitschrift für romanische Philologie*, xxxvi (1912), 309, by Urban T. Holmes in *Language*, iv (1912), 28–30, and (with Max Förster), ibid., pp. 200–3. The important fact for the present discussion is the direct derivation from Fr. *carole*. The attempt of Dr. Margit Sahlin (*Étude sur la carole médiévale*, Uppsala, 1940) to derive the French word from the Greek exclamation of the Latin liturgy, *Kyrie eleison*, has not met with the general approval of Romance philologists, and an ultimate derivation from Greek *choraules*, flute-player, through the Latin is still regarded as the most probable.

See the important reviews by Paul Falk, *Studia Neophilologica*, xiii (1940–1), 134–9, and Leo Spitzer, *Modern Language Notes*, lvi (1941), 222–5.
  [1] e.g. *The Oxford Book*, or William Sandys, *Christmas Carols, Ancient and Modern* (London, 1833).
  [2] So by Reed, *Christmas Carols Printed in the Sixteenth Century*, Introduction. This begins promisingly, but proceeds to ignore the conclusions indicated by the quoted material.
  [3] Ed. R. Morris, E.E.T.S., Or. Ser., Nos. 57, etc., 1874–93, Fairfax text, ll. 7599–602.

The *Handlyng Synne* of Robert Mannyng takes over and expands from its French original the famous medieval legend of the sacrilegious dancers of Kölbigk, who, for disturbing Mass, were condemned to continue their round for a year without stopping. Both the dance and the accompanying song are designated by 'carol':

> þese wommen ȝede and tolled here oute
> wyþ hem to karolle þe cherche aboute.
> Beune ordeyned here karollyng;
> Gerlew endyted what þey shuld syng:
> þys ys þe karolle þat þey sunge,
> As telleþ þe latyn tunge,
> 'Equitabat Beuo per siluam frondosam,
> Ducebat secum Merswyndam formosam,
> Quid stamus, cur non imus?'[1]

This last is translated as

> 'By þe leued wode rode Beuolyne,
> wyþ hym he ledde feyre Merswyne;
> why stonde we? why go we noght?'

The same poem, in a passage not found in the French source, condemns those woman who 'borwe cloþes yn carol to go'.[2]

In the works of Chaucer 'carol' is used consistently in the sense of 'dance with song', repeatedly in *The Romance of the Rose* (Fragment A) where he is translating the French *carole* of his original[3] and a few times in his independent compositions. In Text G of the prologue to *The Legend of Good Women* (the passage is not in Text F) the great crowd of loyal women kneel to the daisy,

> And after that they wenten in compas,
> Daunsynge aboute this flour an esy pas,
> And songen, as it were in carole-wyse,
> This balade, which that I shal yow devyse.[4]

It is to be observed that the ballade, 'Hyd, Absolon, thy gilte tresses clere', is not called a carol; it is merely indicated as being sung in the manner of carolling. Other lines in which the word occurs show that Chaucer observed a distinction between carolling, which was singing *and* dancing, and mere dancing or mere singing. For example:

> That nevere wakynge, in the day or nyght,
> Ye nere out of myn hertes remembraunce,
> For wele or wo, for carole or for daunce.[5]

[1] Ed. F. J. Furnivall, E.E.T.S., Or. Ser., Nos. 119, 123, 1901–3, ll. 9039–51.
[2] Ibid., l. 3458. Cf. also ll. 985–6, 4684–97.
[3] Ed. F. N. Robinson, *The Works of Geoffrey Chaucer*, 2nd edn. (Boston, 1957).
[4] Ed. Robinson, ibid., ll. 199–202.
[5] *The Legend of Good Women*, ibid., ll. 685–7.

Or:

> I sawgh hir daunce so comlily,
> Carole and synge so swetely,
> Laughe and pleye so womanly.[1]

Among the devices figured on the wall of the Temple of Venus in the *Knight's Tale* are:

> Festes, instrumentz, caroles, daunces,
> Lust and array, and alle the circumstaunces
> Of love . . .[2]

It is said of the 'sotted preest' of the *Canon's Yeoman's Tale* that

> Was nevere noon [nightingale] that luste bet to synge;
> Ne lady lustier in carolynge.[3]

Gower's use of the word appears in some cases to be the same as Chaucer's, as in the following passages from the *Confessio Amantis*:[4]

> . . . whanne hir list on nyhtes wake
> In chambre as to carole and daunce.

> And if it nedes so betyde,
> That I in compainie abyde,
> Wher as I moste daunce and singe
> The hovedance and carolinge,
> Or forto go the newefot.

> Ther was Revel, ther was daunsinge,
> And every lif which coude singe
> Of lusti wommen in the route
> A freissh carole hath sunge aboute.

But in other passages there are signs that the word's implications of actual dancing are weakening, and that Gower means simply a song which may be sung with or without dancing, as when he writes:

> Bot Slowthe mai no profit winne,
> Bot he mai singe in his karole
> How Latewar cam to the Dole.[5]

Or:

> And if it so befalle among,
> That sche carole upon a song,
> Whan I it hiere I am so fedd,
> That I am fro miself so ledd,
> As thogh I were in paradis.[6]

[1] *The Book of the Duchess*, ibid., ll. 848–50.
[2] Ibid., ll. (A) 1931–3.
[3] Ibid., ll. (G) 1344–5.
[4] Ed. G. C. Macaulay, E.E.T.S., Ex. Ser.,

Nos. lxxxi–ii, 1900–1), Bk. IV, ll. 2778–9; Bk. VI, ll. 141–5; Bk. V, ll. 3143–6.
[5] Ibid., Bk. IV, ll. 250–2.
[6] Ibid., Bk. VI, ll. 867–71.

It is definitely applied to such songs as a lyric type in the list of Vain-Glory's accomplishments:

> And ek he can carolles make,
> Rondeal, balade and virelai.[1]

Similarly in the Lover's account of his own poetical efforts:

> And also I have ofte assaied
> Rondeal, balade and virelai
> For hire on whom myn herte lai
> To make, and also forto peinte
> Caroles with my wordes qweinte
> To sette my pourpos alofte;
> And thus I sang hem forth fulofte
> In halle and ek in chambre aboute,
> And made merie among the route.[2]

In the fourteenth-century *Stanzaic Life of Christ* the word 'ring' is used to indicate a closed round dance. This word persists for at least four centuries as the regular term for a circle of carollers. A passage from St. Bernard, who represents Christ as speaking, contrasts the stretched arms of the dancers with his own:

> Thow in þo ryng of carolyng
> spredis þin armes furth from the.
> And I on croice have hom spredyng
> schamely, as men movn see.[3]

It occurs in Lydgate's poem 'The Order of Fools':

> The tenthe fooll may hoppe vpon the ryng,
> Foote al afforn, and lede of riht the daunce.[4]

One of the most sustained pieces of context for the word 'carol' in the fifteenth century is the rhymed ecclesiastical calendar written, or possibly only reworked, by Lydgate:[5] It presents the whole company of saints listed in it as engaged in dancing a carole, 'al on a rowe', and the petition of the faithful is to be taken into that heavenly dance, and to 'escape þe wikked fendes braule (Fr. *branle*, round dance)'. It is no church procession that is in the poet's mind here, but a 'mery' carole like that of lovers with their 'valentines', in which the 'heuenly lepars' 'both hoppe and syng' to instrumental minstrelsy and the poet prays, 'Seynt Apollinaire, teche me ȝoure

---

[1] *Confessio Amantis*, Bk. I, ll. 2708–9.
[2] Ibid., Bk. I, ll. 2726–34.
[3] Frances A. Foster, ed., E.E.T.S., Or. Ser., No. 166, 1926, ll. 5937–40.

[4] ll. 25–6, MacCracken, part ii, p. 450.
[5] MacCracken, part i, pp. 363–76. Two manuscripts weaken the dance-imagery here and there by minor verbal changes.

games', and asks SS. Margaret, Praxed, and Magdalene to let him bear their trains. The calendar ends with a prayer to Christ that he will

> Graunt us for to be with Thomas of ynde,
> A curyous [in some manuscripts 'careles'] caral þis Crystemasse
> As to syng nowel when þat we hens passe,

and with a change of the figure of the carole, naturally enough, to that of a feast:

> That we may sitte at Innocentes borde.[1]

A conclusion with a form of prayer, found in a great many carols, is not a sign that the piece is designed for use in church rather than for a social gathering in a hall.[2] A benediction or a prayer for salvation of the company is the standard conclusion for a piece of medieval poetry of almost any kind, narrative as well as lyric, and often for a song or tale of completely secular or even coarse nature. It usually implies no connection whatever with a church service. A good example is No. 418. The matter needs emphasis because of such astonishing statements as those of Dr. Margit Sahlin that 'les plus anciens *carols* sont souvent de véritables litanies populaires' and 'Ces *carols* ne sont souvent que des litanies populaires, destinées, nous semble-t-il, à être chantées aux processions et aux danses sacrées des fêtes ecclésiastiques.'[3] It is well to point out once for all that there is only one carol out of the five hundred to which the term 'litany' can with any real accuracy be applied, No. 309 a, which adds to the one-stanza prayer 'Jhesus, for thi holy name', found entirely dissociated from any carol in several other manuscripts, a burden and eight stanzas which follow in general the list of saints in a York litany. The carol does not resemble the litany in its form and is found only in Bodleian Library MS. Eng. poet. e. 1, of which the convivial character is obvious. As a carol it is definitely a 'sport' and in no sense typical.

---

[1] Many more examples could be given. It seems worth while to cite a few because of the amazing conclusion of Dr. Margit Sahlin (op. cit., p. 34) that '. . . tous ces examples de caroles arrondies n'assurent guère que le mouvement circulaire fût un élément constitutif de la "carole", et les définitions de la "carole" comme "danse en rond", que donnent tant de savants, manquent de fondement réel'.

[2] Singing in the hall after dinner or supper on religious holidays is explicitly sanctioned in the medieval statutes of Oxford colleges as 'reputable amusement', e.g. Magdalen, Corpus Christi, and All Souls (G. R. M. Ward, trans., *The Statutes of Magdalen College, Oxford*, Oxford, 1840, p. 131; *The Foundation Statutes of Bishop Fox for Corpus Christi College . . .*, A.D. 1512 . . . , London, 1843, p. 164; *The Statutes of All Souls College, Oxford*, London, 1841, p. 164).

[3] Op. cit., pp. 203, 56, cited with approval by R. H. Robbins, *Stud. in Phil.*, lvi (1959), 571. Ryman's carols to the Virgin are in content something like a litany of Mary, but the regular carol-form is used (Nos. 220–6). Robbins mentions only No. 309 a. A good antidote to the confusion of carol with litany is found in the valuable short article by Curt Sachs, 'Primitive and Medieval Music: A Parallel', *J.A.M.S.*, xiii (1960), 43–9. Sachs writes: 'The secular forms of the Middle Ages are well known and easily recorded. In Gothic times, the French musicians distinguished four principal types of forms: (1) hymn or stanza; (2) litany; (3) sequence; (4) round-dance, refrain. . . . The litany type provided one short melody, to cover the first poetic line and to be repeated for every following line. . . . The *rondeau*, round-dance, or refrain form was built on the consistent alternation of a soloist or *precentor* and an answering chorus.'

Neither does a burden in the form of a prayer imply that the carol is intended for a choir rather than a dining-hall, e.g. No. 21 A and B:

> To blis God bryng vs all and sum,
> Christe redemptor omnium.

The mixture, completely congruous to a medieval Christian, of devotional sentiment and 'mirth' in its special sense of 'cheerfulness resulting from the knowledge of one's salvation', is one secret of the carol's special nature, and attempts at interpretation of the 'religious' carol which are not based on an understanding and acceptance of this mixture lead to strange results. A grace before and another after meat do not make of a meal a religious service, nor in a Christian household do they impair the merriment and good fellowship of the table.

The carols mentioned in *Sir Gawain and the Green Knight* are of particular interest, for they are definitely associated with the Christmas season. The word seems usually to mean for the author of *Sir Gawain*, as for Chaucer, the combined song and dance of the carole. The action of social dancing is implied in the following lines:[1]

> þer tournayed tulkes by tymez ful mony,
> Justed ful jolilé þise gentyle kniȝtes,
> Syþen kayred to þe court caroles to make.

> Wel bycommes such craft vpon Christmasse,
> Laykyng of enterludez, to laȝe and to syng,
> Among þise kynde caroles of knyȝtez and ladyez.

> (On St. John's Day)
> Forþy wonderly þay woke, and þe wyn dronken,
> Daunsed ful dreȝly wyth dere carolez.

> And syþen he mace hym as mery among þe fre ladyes,
> With comlych caroles and alle kynnes ioye,
> As neuer he did bot þat daye, to þe derk nyȝt,
>   with blys.

In one passage, however, the term is unmistakably applied to songs which are sung for their own sake:

> Much glam and gle glent vp þerinne
> Aboute þe fyre vpon flet, and on fele wyse
> At þe soper and after, mony aþel songez,
> As coundutes of Krystmasse and carolez newe.[2]

---

[1] Ed. J. R. R. Tolkien and E. V. Gordon, 2nd edn., revised by Norman Davis (Oxford, 1967), ll. 41–3, 471–3, 1025–6, 1885–8. An erroneous interpretation of the second passage is given by the note in the edition of the poem by Sir Israel Gollancz, E.E.T.S., Or. Ser., No. 210, 1940, p. 103: 'kynde caroles: carols rightly belonging to knights and ladies, hence noble. The head-chopping episode is contrasted with these, as on a level with a comic interlude by professional entertainers.' The meaning of 'kynde' is close to that of 'dere' and 'comlych'.

[2] Ibid., ll. 1652–5. See the reviser's note on this passage. It is not justifiable to call a 'con-

A 'coundute', Latin *conductus*, originally a song accompanying a change of position by a liturgical celebrant, was a two-, three-, or four-part piece of which not all the parts were furnished with words. Its distinctive feature was that the melody of the tenor, if not an original theme, was taken from popular song and not from ecclesiastical music as in most other part-songs such as rotas or motets.[1] It was a thoroughly cultured and sophisticated sort of composition, appealing to those who were musically educated. The *conductus* was old-fashioned and passing out of favour by the time that *Sir Gawain* was written, a fact which gives point to the description of the carols as new. The adjective may also have been chosen to distinguish these carols without dancing from the older carols which were only sung in the dance. At any rate the carol is here again mentioned in connection with another kind of lyric which is distinguished by its *form*.

In the fifteenth century the use of 'carol' to designate song not actually accompanied by dancing becomes well established and the association with Christmas more frequent. In the *Promptorium Parvulorum* (1440) the noun and verb appear as 'Carole, songe', and 'Carolyn, or syng carowlys'.[2] An account preserved by Leland of a royal Twelfth Night feast at Greenwich in the third year of Henry VII (1487) records that 'At the Table in the Medell of the Hall sat the Deane and thoos of the Kings Chapell, whiche incontynently after the Kings first Course sange a Carall.'[3] The older meaning of the word is still met with, however, particularly in the North.[4] The *Catholicon Anglicum* (as written probably of the East Riding of Yorkshire, 1483) glosses 'caralle' as *corea, chorus, pecten*, the first two of which significations are likewise given among the equivalents for 'dawnce'.[5] *The Oxford English Dictionary* notes its occurrence in this sense as late as 1616.

In the sixteenth century 'song' is the ordinary meaning of 'carol', and the phrase 'Christmas carols' appears in print in the little books from the presses of Wynkyn de Worde and Richard Kele.[6] In the second half of the century the looseness of usage which remains to the present day makes itself apparent, and 'carol' sometimes implies a connection with Christmas, sometimes is simply interchangeable with 'song'.[7]

---

duit', as does S. O. Andrew (*Sir Gawain and the Green Knight*, London, 1929, p. 102), 'any song in honour of the Christmas season'.

[1] *Grove's Dictionary of Music and Musicians*, 5th edn. (London, 1954), s.v. 'Conductus'; Leonard Ellinwood, *Musical Quarterly*, xxvii (1941), 165–204; *The New Oxford History of Music* (London, 1955), ii. 171–4.

[2] Ed. A. L. Mayhew, E.E.T.S., Ex. Ser., No. cii, 1908, cols. 71, 107.

[3] *Joannis Lelandi Antiquarii de Rebus Britannicis Collectanea* (London, 1770), iv. 237.

[4] So in *The Poetical Works of Gavin Douglas*, ed. John Small (Edinburgh, 1874), iii. 109,

ll. 29–30; *The Poems of Robert Henryson*, ed. G. Gregory Smith, iii, S.T.S., No. 58, 1908, 'The Testament of Cresseid, ll. 431, 443–4; *The Kingis Quhair*, ed. W. W. Skeat, S.T.S., No. 1, 1884, stanza 121.

[5] Ed. Sidney J. H. Herrtage, E.E.T.S., Or. Ser., No. 75, 1881.

[6] Compare also the designations of various carol-collections not now extant but entered in the *Stationers' Register*, 1562–87, quoted by Reed, *Christmas Carols Printed in the Sixteenth Century*, p. xviii.

[7] John Palsgrave's *L'esclaircissement de la langue françoyse* (1530) glosses the word both

The passages cited show that for a late medieval writer or singer the carol was distinguished from other lyrics by its form rather than by its subject. The essential features of that form can only be determined from those texts to which the name was explicitly applied at the time of their writing down. These are not many, but they suffice for the purpose. The most important group consists of twenty-six which appear with the other poems of John Audelay in a unique manuscript, Bodleian Library Douce 302.[1] All but one of these lyrics follow a rubric which reads:

> I pray yow, syrus, boothe moore and las,
> Syng these caroles in Cristemas.

In three of these the word 'carol' is found in the text itself. At the close of a piece invoking a blessing on the youthful Henry VI Audelay makes this appeal:

> I pray youe, seris, of your gentre,
> Syng this carol reuerently,
> Fore hit is mad of Kyng Herre;
> Gret ned fore him we han to pray.[2]

In the course of another, on the 'timor mortis' theme, he tells us:

> As I lay seke in my langure,
> With sorow of hert and teere of ye,
> This caral I made with gret doloure;
> Passio Christi conforta me.[3]

In a third, in honour of St. Francis, he again asks:

> I pray youe, seris, pur charyte,
> Redis this caral reuerently,
> Fore I mad hit with wepyng eye,
> Your broder, Jon, the blynd Awdlay.[4]

The twenty-sixth piece, a narrative of St. Winifred, has not usually been counted among Audelay's carols, but he definitely calls it one:

> I pray youe al, pur charyte
> Redis this carol reuerently,
> Fore I hit mad with wepyng ye;
> Mi name hit is the blynd Awdlay.[5]

as Christmas song and as dance-song: 'Carole—a song *chancon de noel* s.f.: *carolle* s.f.' (ed. F. Genin, Paris, 1852, p. 203). In the *Manipulus Vocabulorum* of Peter Levins (1570) it appears simply as equivalent to song in general: 'A CÁRIL, *canticum*, *i*' (ed. Henry B. Wheatley, E.E.T.S., Or. Ser., No. 27, 1867, col. 124).

[1] For Audelay's other works see *The Poems of John Audelay*, ed. Ella K. Whiting, E.E.T.S. Or. Ser., No. 184, 1931.
[2] No. 428, stanza 15.
[3] No. 369, stanza 8.
[4] No. 310, stanza 13.
[5] No. 314, stanza 30.

In British Museum Additional MS. 31042 is a song in honour of the rose as the symbol of an English champion, probably Henry V. It is in the hand of Robert Thornton, scribe of the famous collection of poems preserved at Lincoln Cathedral, and is marked 'A Carolle for Crystynmesse'.[1] There is no mention of the Nativity in the text, nor indeed any explicit religious reference.

Another piece, written down in 1500 in a collection of Welsh poems, British Museum Additional MS. 14997, uses the word in an especially interesting context. It is a hearty and festive song, not at all pious like Audelay's. The third and fifth stanzas run as follows:

> Therefore euery mon that ys here
> Synge a caroll on hys manere;
> Yf he con non we shall hym lere,
>   So that we be mere allway.

> Mende the fyre, and make gud chere!
> Fyll the cuppe, Ser Botelere!
> Let euery mon drynke to hys fere!
>   Thys endes my caroll with care away.[2]

In a still different style is a laboured and theologically argumentative poem on the Incarnation of which the two stanzas appearing in MS. Takamiya 6 are headed by the hand that wrote them down about 1531 'A carolle'.[3]

The variety of subjects treated by the poems in Richard Hill's commonplace book of about the same time, now Balliol College, Oxford, MS. 354, is well known. A good number of these poems are listed as carols by the contemporary table of contents:

> dyuers carolles . . . ff. CLXXVIII
> Item dyuers good carolles ff. IICIII
> Item dyuers mery carolles ff. IICXXVI
> Item ye iiij complexions of man with diuerys carolles ff. CLXXVIII.[4]

The lyrics which have just been noticed differ among themselves in almost all possible respects except two, in which they are in striking agreement. All are in stanzas, the form of which is not changed in the course of the poem, and all have prefixed a group of lines which forms a *burden* or chorus, to be sung (or considered as sung by a reader) before the first stanza and repeated after that and all succeeding stanzas. It would seem that these two characteristics of form were those which the writers of the manuscripts recognized as the marks of the carol type.

---

[1] No. 427.
[2] No. 10. See also p. lxxx.
[3] No. 95 b.
[4] Printed by E. Flügel, *Anglia* xxvi (1903), 97 ff. The groups of lyrics indicated are those which begin, by the modern foliation of the manuscript, on ff. 176ʳ, 219ᵛ, 248ʳ, 250ʳ, respectively.

This conclusion is strengthened by a closer consideration of the meaning assigned to 'carol' by the compiler of the *Promptorium Parvulorum*. This Galfridus Grammaticus, a Dominican friar of Norfolk, was a man of some learning[1] and distinguished with care a considerable number of musical terms.[2] 'Carole, songe', he glosses as *palinodium*, 'carolyn, or syng carowlys', as *pallinodio*, and 'carowlynge' as *palinadinacio*.[3] As he can hardly have taken 'carol' as equivalent to 'retraction',[4] he must have had in mind the other meaning of *palinodia*, that is, the repetition of part of a song, a sense warranted by a literal interpretation of the word's etymology. Du Cange records an application of *palinodia* to vocal music with an element of repetition, specifically to the *Te Deum* sung antiphonally.[5] A sixteenth-century French theorist applies *palinod* to a recurrent refrain:

> Kyrielle a este appellée la ryme, en laquelle en fin de chaque couplet vn mesme vers est toujours repeté: qu'ils ont appelé Refrain, és Balades et Chans royaux, et l'ont icy nommé Palinod, c'est à dire Rechanté. Et est ce nom de Palinod bien seant en ceste Kyrielle, laquelle se commet le plus souvent en Chans lyriques ou Odes, ou ce Palinod est plusieurs fois rechanté . . .[6]

It appears as the name of a lyric genre in the title of a French volume of about 1525: 'Palinodz, chants royaux, ballades, rondeaux et epigrammes à l'honneur de l'Immaculée Conception de la toute belle mère de Dieu (patronne des Normans), presentez au puy à Rouen . . .'[7] The *palinode* in French is differently described by different authorities, but the characteristic and necessary element involved is always a repeated phrase, a refrain.[8] It is safe to assume that the learned Galfridus glossed 'carol' as he did because to him it meant a song with such a repeated member.

The definition of a carol to which all this points as the one actually accepted before about 1550 is 'a song on any subject, composed of uniform stanzas

---

[1] See the introduction to Mayhew's edition, pp. xi–xvii.

[2] e.g. the following terms for songs of different kinds:

Soong: *Cantus -vs;* . . . *Canticum -i.*

Soong in a halle or in a chambyr: *Cantilena, -e.*

Song of a man alone: *Monodia, -e.*

Song of ii men: *Bicinium, -ij* (etc.).

[3] He gives as his authority for the noun, 'vgucio', i.e. the Latin dictionary of Huguitio Pisanus (d. 1210), and for the verb the *Catholicon* of Johannes de Janua. The *Oxford English Dictionary* prints *psalmodio* for the verb, presumably after Way's edition (London, 1843–65).

[4] Gr. παλιν-ῳδία, a recantation.

[5] *Glossarium Mediae et Infimae Latinitatis*, ed. L. Favre, reprint, Graz, 1954, s.v. 'Palinodia Dei': 'Sic canticum *Te Deum laudamus* vulgo S. Augustino adscriptum vocat Abbo Floriac. in

Epist. ad monachos Anglos apud Mabill. tom. 4 Annal. pag. 30. laudata, ubi idem canticum S. Hilario Pictavensi Episcopo tribuit. Laurentio in Amalth. *Palinodia* est *iter reciprocum. Item, recantatio seu retractatio, contrarius cantus.* Unde patet vocis origo, quod scilicet canticum illud divisis choris soleat decantari.'

[6] Thomas Sibillet, *Art poëtique françois* (Lyon, 1556), 12, pp. 145–6, quoted by Ferdinand Wolf, *Über die Lais, Sequenzen und Leiche* (Heidelberg, 1841), p. 204.

[7] Quoted, Wolf, loc. cit.

[8] Pierre Larousse, *Grand Dictionnaire universel* (Paris, 1866, etc.), s.v. 'Palinod': 'Pièce dans laquelle le même vers revenait à la fin de chaque strophe. . . . [Le puy] de Rouen exigeait que toute pièce de vers qui lui était présentée se terminât par l'éloge de la Vierge.' Compare E. Stengel, *Zeitschrift für romanische Philologie*, xxviii (1904), 372.

and provided with a burden'. This definition is the one which is adopted throughout the present volume and made the basis for the inclusion or rejection of a given text. In the few instances where a rigid application of it seems inadvisable due explanation is given in the notes.

The adoption of this definition, which has been suggested before, but without emphasis,[1] is not a mere attempt to impose verbal pedantry upon what is, or should be, one of the most light-hearted of medieval genres. The importance which it gives to the burden will find its justification in the central role played by that choral element, not in criticism, but in the real, the vocal life of the carols. The definition recognizes this type of song as being in direct descent from the vocally accompanied dance, the carole.

Furthermore, this recognition of the carol as a lyric genre distinguished by form, and not by some specialized content or vaguely defined 'spirit', eliminates for the period to which it applies the confusion now besetting so many of the editors and critics of so-called 'Christmas carols'. Its application involves denying the title of carol to a few, but only a few, well-known and charming pieces which have often borne it, such as the exquisite 'I sing of a maiden', a brilliant derivative of a longer thirteenth-century poem.[2] This song has no burden, though Carleton Brown astonishingly prints one.[3] This denial is in most cases clear gain. The narrative piece, for example, beginning 'Seynt Steuene was a clerk in kyng Herowdes halle', is simply a ballad, very properly included in Child's collection; there is no need to call it anything else.[4] Middle English lyrics of the Nativity which lack a burden it is better to call merely 'songs', or 'Christmas songs' if you will.[5] The term 'carol' can then claim its proper meaning and usefulness as the designation of those lyrics which bear, in their regularly repeated burdens, the mark of their descent from the dancing circle of the carole.[6]

---

[1] Notably by Sir Edmund Chambers, *Early English Lyrics* (London, 1926), p. 291. Compare *Encyclopaedia Britannica*, 11th edn., s.v. 'Carol'.

[2] British Museum, MS. Sloane 2593, f. 10ᵛ. Often printed, e.g. *Early English Lyrics*, p. 107. It has been heavily commented upon, e.g. by Stephen Manning, *Wisdom and Number* (Lincoln, Nebraska, 1962), pp. 158–67, and at length by Leo Spitzer ('*Explication de Texte* Applied to Three Great Middle English Poems', *Archivum Linguisticum*, iii, 1951, 152–63), who treats the poem as referring to the Nativity instead of the Annunciation, in spite of 'his moderes bowr' and the repeated 'Aprylle'.

[3] *R.L. 15 C.*, No. 81, p. 119.

[4] *English and Scottish Popular Ballads*, No. 22.

[5] e.g. 'As I went throw a gardyn grene', MS. Sloane 2593, f. 18ᵛ, included in Rickert, p. 174

(another version in National Library of Scotland, MS. Advocates 19. 3. 1, f. 94ᵛ, *pr.* Brown, *R.L. 15 C.*, No. 78); Brown, *R.L. 14 C.*, Nos. 57, 58.

[6] The articles 'carole', 'carolen', and 'caroling' in the *Middle English Dictionary* present good collections of citations, but the first two are marred by the inclusion in each of a definition which can hardly be supported. The article 'carole n.,' gives two correct meanings, '(a) A kind of round dance accompanied by singing; a group of people dancing and singing in a circle; (b) a song used by carolers; a song'; but then adds '(c) a religious poem or song; a psalm'. This alleged meaning is supported by three citations, two from John Audelay's colophonstanzas, which are misinterpreted (see p. xxx), and the entry in one manuscript of the *Promptorium Parvulorum*, 'Synge carowlys: Psalmodio', which is almost certainly a scribal

2. *The Carol and the Noël*

The modern use of the word 'carol' as equivalent to 'Christmas song' has frequently led to a more or less complete identification of the carol with the type of French popular song known as the *noël*. Such identification, unless carefully qualified, is productive of little but confusion and misunderstanding, particularly when it is applied to the early history of the two genres. For the period before 1550, at least, it is invalid, as a glance at the history of the *noël* will show.[1]

The *noël*, from its first appearance as a recognized type to the present day, has been distinguished from other song by the fact that its subject-matter is specifically concerned with the Nativity. It has never been, like the early carol, a genre recognized by its metrical form. A *noël* may have any verse-form which its author fancies, with or without burden or refrain. It has no historical connection as a type with the round dance, although individual *noëls* have often been written to dance-tunes. In fact, a long stanza is rather characteristic of the *noël*, and long stanzas are rare in medieval dance-song. The essential feature is the Christmas material; a 'May-*noël*' would be a contradiction in terms, whereas a 'May carol' is not.

The heading of one of the two earliest large collections of *noëls* expressly states their common feature: 'S'ensuiuent aucuns ditez et chancons faitz en l'onneur de la natiuite Jhesu Crist commencans par noel.'[2] The only piece not connected with the Nativity in this collection is a Latin song to St. Catherine; in the other, that of Tisserant, there are only three, a song to St. Catherine, a *quête* song for the New Year, and a drinking-song.

The generally overestimated antiquity attributed to the *noël* has been responsible for some of the confusion with the early carol. Instead of dating from the twelfth century or earlier, as it has often been said to do, the *noël* does not emerge as a genre until the late fifteenth century, some time, that is,

error for the 'pallinodio' of the other manuscript, as shown by the occurrence of 'palinodium' for the noun and 'palinadinacio' for the gerund 'carowlynge'. This alleged third definition unfortunately confuses the issue: it is not until after the Reformation that 'carol' unmodified has any religious implications. And I know of no application of 'carol' as noun or verb to a psalm or psalm-singing before the Commonwealth. The article on the verb 'carolen', after giving '(a) To dance and/or sing in a carole; (b) to sing for (the dancers in a carole)' —'to sing as a dancer in a carole' would have been more accurate—adds a figurative meaning '(c) to spend one's time noisily or unprofitably', for which the only citation is from '(a. 1456) Shirley *Death Jas.* 18: "The spows is foundon, wherfore we bene cumne, and all this nyght

haf carold here." ' The context of this sentence shows that the meaning is rather: 'We have been going in circles', as in carolling. (*Here Folowing Begynnythe a Cronycle of the Dethe and False Murdere of James Stewarde, Kyng of Scotys*, Miscellanea Scotica 2 (Glasgow, 1818), pt. 3, art. 1, pp. 5–29.

[1] The difficulties of this identification and the attempt to base a history of the carol on it are exemplified in Reed, Introduction.

[2] Bibliothèque de l'Arsenal, MS. 3653, f. 2ʳ. The observations on this manuscript and that of Tisserant's collection, Bibliothèque Nationale, MS. français 2368, are based on rotograph copies, Modern Language Association Deposit, Library of Congress, Washington, Nos. 97 and 101.

after the carol has been well established in English.[1] It grew in favour rapidly from that time forward, and many volumes of *noëls* were printed and circulated in the sixteenth and following centuries.[2] But in the fourteenth and early fifteenth centuries, when the carol was flourishing in England, the *noël* had not yet been developed.[3]

This does not mean that there were no songs in French which were connected with the religious or festal aspects of the Christmas season. Such there were, but they belonged to recognized medieval genres and did not form a class by themselves. An often-quoted piece is the twelfth-century Anglo-Norman song which begins:[4]

> Seignors, or entendez a nus:
> De loing sumes venuz a vous
>   Quere Noël,
> Car l'em nus dit que en cest hostel
> Soleit tenir sa feste anvel
>   A hicest jur.

This piece, written in England, has been claimed as an early *noël* by French writers and as an early carol by English. Actually, as Gastoué points out,[5] it is an *aguillannée*, or *quête* song, an appeal for entrance to the feasting-hall made by singers in search of largess. The birth of Christ is not alluded to. The burden of the piece does give it a resemblance to the carol, but it is not sung at the beginning, like a true carol-burden, and it is replaced by another couplet at the close of the song. This Norman poet's work is a cousin to the English carol, if you like, but hardly a progenitor.

A much closer parallel is provided by a fifteenth-century *chanson picuse* preserved in a manuscript now in Gonville & Caius College, Cambridge, and hitherto unpublished.[6] It is an exact counterpart of many English carols in form and in substance:

> Aue *virgo* regina,
> D*ei* plena gra*ti*a.
>
> V*os* q*ui* N*os*tre Dame aymez,
> A mo*n* reson entendez;

---

[1] Amédée Gastoué, *Le Cantique populaire en France* (Lyon, 1924), pp. 109–30, 231–321. This work neatly exposes the lack of evidence for the existence of the *noël* at the early dates to which its origin has often been referred.

[2] A good collection, with a somewhat diffuse introduction, is that of Henry Poulaille, *La Grande et belle Bible des noëls anciens du XIIᵉ au XVIᵉ siècle* (Paris, 1942).

[3] Frank Ll. Harrison in his important comments on the probable use of English carols as *Benedicamus* substitutes in some services suggests that vernacular *noëls* of earlier date than 1500 may have been the

models for certain Latin *cantilenae* so used, but he offers no vernacular texts ('Benedicamus, Conductus, Carol: A Newly-Discovered Source', *Acta Musicologica*, xxxvii, 1965, 35–48). See also his *Music in Medieval Britain* (London, 1958), pp. 124, 416–17.

[4] Ed. A. Jeanroy and A. Långfors, *Chansons satiriques et bachiques du XIIIᵉ siècle* (Paris, 1921), p. 80.

[5] *Le Cantique populaire*, p. 115. On *chansons de l'aguilaneuf* see Julien Tiersot, *Histoire de la chanson populaire en France* (Paris, 1889), pp. 187–94.

[6] MS. 383, p. 210.

Q*ui* est a di*r*e si escotez
De *vir*gi*n*e M*a*ria.

Le seynt angel Gab*r*i*e*l,
Q*ui* decendist de ciel,
A Marie p*a*role*s* dit tiele*s*:
    'Aue, plena gr*atia.*

'*V*n fant s*e*ra de toi nee
Q*ui* Jhesu*s* s*e*ra appellee,
Q*ui* tout le monde p*ur* sa pité
    Saluab*i*t a miseria.'

Qu*ant* le douce fant fust nee
Et de Seynt Joh*a*n baptyze
In Jordano flumine:
    Laua n*os*tra cri*mi*n*a*.

Les trois reis d'orientz,
Il ven*e*ront *i*ngnelement
A Bedlem oué lour p*r*esent;
    St*r*icta sunt itin*e*ra.

N*os*tre Dame *et* Emp*e*res,
Si el a*u*ra no*s* p*r*omeez,
Qu'*e*l p*r*iera a son Filz
    P*r*o sua familia.

But the fact that it is written in the manuscript between two English carols[1] and in dubious French point to its being the work of an Englishman in imitation of the English carols then current rather than an instance of 'French influence'.

One reason for the confusion of carol and *noël* as well as for overestimation of the contribution of French poetry to the carol is the frequent occurrence in carol-burdens of the word 'noël'. This is the only French word which seems to be thoroughly at home in the carols; very few include other French phrases of even the simplest kind.[2] In some pieces 'nowel' forms the entire burden, either the whole word or its final syllable being repeated as often as demanded by the music.[3] More often it is combined with an English sentence or so, as:[4]

Nowell, nowell, nowell, nowell,
Tydynges gode Y thyngke to telle.

The word is an interesting one because of the related yet distinct character of its three principal meanings, some notice of which will help to explain

---

[1] Nos. 441, Appendix, No. ii.
[2] Nos. 6, 89, 235, 310, 314, 417, 420, 421, 448.
[3] e.g. Nos. 30, 122 A, 366, 157 C, 236.
[4] No. 133; similarly Nos. 6, 18, 21 C, 29, 41, 122 B, 183, 239, 240, 242, 261.

the occurrences of 'noël' in carols (and traditional folk-songs for Christmas) which contain no other French. It is used in that language as an exclamation of joy, as the name of the Feast of the Nativity, and as the name of a type of Christmas song. The second meaning, *jour de Noël*, seems to be the original one, as implied by the derivation of the word from Latin *natalis*.[1] In this sense it occurs now and then in late Middle English, for example, in the English *Rewle of Sustris Menouresses Enclosid*[2] and Lovelich's *Merlin*,[3] as well as in the earlier *Sir Gawain*.[4] But it was also used by the English as well as the French as an interjection to express rejoicing. This might be at New Year's time, as in Chaucer's *Franklin's Tale*,[5] or on any great occasion, as when companies of virgins sang 'nowell' to welcome Henry V home from Agincourt.[6] This use was plainly adopted from the French custom to which Étienne Pasquier devotes a chapter in his *Les Recherches de la France*.[7] It is as such an interjection, and not as the name of the feast of Christmas that it makes its way into the carols. The fact that it is also used both in this way and as the name of the holiday in the popular Christmas songs of France in no way implies (what is yet often said) that the carol developed from the *noël*.

This is emphasized by the occasional use of 'Nowell' in the burdens of carols on other subjects than the Nativity. It is attached to one version of a carol which is a *planctus Mariae*[8] and to another on mortality,[9] as well as to Annunciation pieces.[10] Incidentally, it is one of the few vernacular words to be incorporated into sacred Latin song, as in the following lines of a *cantilena* of German origin:

> Noel, Noel, iterando,
> Noel triplicando, Noel,
> Ah, Noel, psallite.[11]

The meaning which 'noël' does not possess in Middle English or in the carols before 1550 is that of 'Christmas song'. The line from the *Franklin's Tale* already alluded to,

> And 'Nowel' crieth every lusty man,

does not mean, as Skeat's note in his edition would have it mean, that every lusty man sings a Christmas song, for in Chaucer's time the French them-

---

[1] A. Brachet, *Dictionnaire étymologique de la langue française*, 5th edn. (Paris, 1868), s.v. 'Noël'.

[2] Walter W. Seton, ed., *A Fifteenth-century Courtesy Book and Two Fifteenth-century Franciscan Rules*, E.E.T.S., Or. Ser., No. 148, 1914, p. 108.

[3] l. 6870, cited by *O.E.D.*, s.v. 'Nowel'.

[4] Ed. Tolkien and Gordon, l. 65.

[5] Ed. F. N. Robinson, l. 1255.

[6] Chambers, [Sir] E. K., *The Mediaeval Stage* (Oxford, 1903), i. 272 n. 4; ii. 168.

[7] (Paris, 1643), Bk. IV, chap. xvi: 'D'vne Coustume ancienne qui estoit en France de crier Noüel pour signification de ioye publique.' See also Du Cange, *Glossarium*, s.v. 'Natale 3'. For the custom of loudly crying 'Nouel!' in connection with the singing of the *Te Deum* in celebration of the Nativity of the Virgin see Alexandre Tuetey, ed., *Journal d'un bourgeois de Paris 1405–1499* (Paris, 1881), p. 200.

[8] No. 157 C.   [9] No. 366.

[10] Nos. 239, 240, 242.

[11] *Analecta Hymnica*, xx. 114.

selves, let alone the English, were not using the word in this sense. It means that he shouts the medieval equivalent of 'hurrah!' and 'Merry Christmas!' at once.

3. *The Carol at Feasts and Banquets*

Beyond all question the principal use of the kind of carol which predominates in this collection was at celebrations involving feasting or social dining. The chief habitat of the manuscript carol was the hall, whether of a castle or manor house or of a monastery or cathedral.[1] This was the place above all others where religious and laity, men and women, and, within limits, great and humble, most frequently met to form a common audience and to indulge a taste in lyric entertainment that varied less from group to group than is often thought. Since these gatherings were more concentrated in the twelve days of Christmas than at any other time of year, it is only to be expected that a very large number of carols will deal directly with the Nativity and with the events and personages connected with the other feast days that conclude with the Epiphany. This close connection with holiday feasting may well be the explanation of the strikingly small number of carols dealing with Easter as a holiday or with the Resurrection. There was less feasting at Eastertide for one excellent practical reason which, obvious as it is, seems rarely to be mentioned: the lack of available provisions for lavish meals at the end of the long winter, when any establishment was lucky if its larder had no shortage of everyday food.

Out of an abundance of evidence for the singing of carols at dinners and feasts a few specially interesting records may be noticed. The royal court knew them well.

In the Black Book of Edward IV there is a special note at the end of the section concerned with 'Chapleyns and Clerkes of Chapell':

MEMORANDUM that the king hath a song before hym in his hall or chambre vppon All Halowen-day at the later graces, by some of thes clerkes and children of chapell, in remembraunce of Cristmasse, and so of men and children in Cristmasse thorow-oute; but after the song on All Halowen-day is don, the steward and thesaurer of houshold shall be warned where hit likith the king to kepe his Cristmasse.[2]

Carolling as a routine pastime between meals is mentioned by Duke Neymes in reply to a question by King Lucafere in *The Sowdone of Babylone*, a romance of about 1400:

'But saye me, felow, what is your vse,
To do in contr[é] aftyr the none.

---

[1] It is rather striking that there are no carols extant from before 1550 which imply a *quête* or any sort of outdoor visitation for begging or collecting, in view of the frequency of such use of the later 'Christmas carol'.

[2] A. R. Myers, *The Household of Edward IV*, (Manchester, 1959), p. 136.

> And what is the custome of your hous,
> Tille men to souper shalle gone?'
> 'Sir, somme men iouste with sper[e] and shelde,
> And somme men Carol and singe gode songes,
> Some shote with dartis in the feelde,
> And somme play at Chesse amonge.'[1]

Many passages in the romances and other literature make it plain that carols, sung both in the dance and apart from it, were an expected feature of feasts in hall. One of the most interesting is the account in the North Midland romance of about 1400 of Sir Cleges's sadness on Christmas Eve as he recollects how he has spent all his estate on the great feasts that he held at Christmas, where he would reward generously all the minstrels who came. He has a vision in a kind of walking swoon:

> Sore syȝthyng, he hard a sovne
>   Of dyvers mynstrelsé:
> Of trompus, pypus, and claraneris,
> Of harpis, luttis, and getarnys,
>   A sitole and sawtré,
> Many carellys and gret davnsyng:
> On euery syde he harde syngyng,
>   In euery place, trewly.[2]

A wedding-feast as well as a Christmas banquet would quite naturally include carolling among the musical and athletic entertainments:

> At the fest was harpyng,
> And pipyng and tabournyng,
> And sitollyng and trumpyng,
> Knijf-pleyeyng and syngyng,
> Carolyng and turneieyng,
> And wrestlyng and skirmyng.[3]

It was a diversion for summer as well as for winter:

> Mery it is in June and hoot firmament;
> Fair is þe karole of maydens gent,
> Boþe in halle and ek in tente.[4]

A vivid impression of the kind of feast that an officer of a large monastic house would hold in the holiday season is given by the matter-of-fact

---

[1] Ed. Emil Hausknecht, E.E.T.S., Ex. Ser., No. xxxviii, 1881, p. 57, ll. 1987–94.

[2] *Sir Cleges*, ll. 98–105, ed. Walter Hoyt French and Charles Brockway Hale, *Middle English Metrical Romances* (New York, 1930), pp. 880–1; see also ll. 481–98, pp. 892–3.

[3] *Kyng Alisaunder*, ed. G. V. Smithers, i, E.E.T.S., No. 227, 1952, B-text, ll. 1039–44,

pp. 59, 61.

[4] Ibid., ll. 1843–5, p. 105. Many similar references might be adduced, e.g. *King Ponthus and the Fair Sidone*, ed. Frank Jewett Mather Jr., chaps. xviii, xx, *PMLA*, xii (1897), 48, 61; Barbour, *The Buik of Alexander*, ll. 5835–40, 5849–62, ed. R. L. Graeme Ritchie, S.T.S., No. 19, iii. 273–4.

accounts of disbursements contained in the journal of William More, last Prior of Worcester, who gave a Christmas feast each year to officials of the city of Worcester.[1] Among the most frequent items of expense in the years 1518 to 1532 are malmsey and other wines, minstrels and other entertainers, and singers of carols. It is plain that all of these are regarded as regular components of a large holiday dinner for which a whole ox was bought, and it is equally plain that 'minstrels' and 'singers of carols' are quite separate people, as witness two entries of 1527:

> Item for syngyng of carrolls on cristmas day &
>   to mynstrells 2 *s.* 6 *d.* 16 *d.*
> Item to mynstrells & syngers of carralls 12 *d*/4 *d.*

Carol-singers are also distinguished from a lute-player who sang (and was not paid for some reason) and from players at the Christmas season of 1520:

> Item rewards for caralls on cristmas day
>   dynar 14 d./ at supper 8 *d*
> Item to carrolds a pon seynt Johns Day 8*d.* 2*d.*/8*d.*
> Item rewarded to William ye Lewter for his syngyng &
>   pleyng in ye cristamas wycke nil hic
> Item rewarded to iiij pleyers of glowceter a pon
>   sonday when ye balyffs & ye xxiiij[ti] dyned
>   with me in ye grete hall   3*s.* 4*d.*

There were songs and dances and minstrelsy in the spring as well, when Prior More was enjoying country life at the Priory's manors of Battenhall and Crowle.[2] Those who would put churchmen and popular merry song into separate worlds are advised to look further into these good times at Worcester Priory, not to mention the entertainments paid for through many decades at Selby Abbey in Yorkshire, Winchester College, and Magdalen College, Oxford, and through almost three centuries at Durham Priory.[3] Fountains Abbey appears to have been both hospitable and generous to entertainers, distinguishing in its accounting among minstrels, fools, players, and 'fabulatores', or story-tellers.[4]

The feasting known as a 'Grand Christmas' in the Temple continued into Elizabethan times the same sort of proceedings. The custom was to hold a 'parliament' on the eve of St. Thomas the Apostle (20 December) and, if the celebration was decided upon, to mark it by a speech in the hall from 'the eldest Butler', who announced to the whole society the names of the appointed officers; 'and then in token of joy and good-liking, the Bench

[1] Ethel S. Fegan, ed., Worcestershire Historical Society, 1914. See also the fine chapter on More in David Knowles, *The Religious Orders in England*, iii (Cambridge, 1959), 108–26.
[2] Ibid., pp. 367, 373, 385.
[3] Glynne Wickham, *Early English Stages* *1300–1500* (London, 1959), i. 332–9; Chambers, *Mediaeval Stage*, ii. 246–50, 240–4.
[4] Bursar's accounts, in John Richard Walbran, ed., *Memorials of the Abbey of St. Mary of Fountains*, ii, Surtees Society Publications, lxvii (1878), 89, 90.

and company pass beneath the harth, and sing a carol, and so to boyer'. The custom indicated in No. 10 of calling for a carol from each guest in turn was observed from Christmas Eve through the Twelve Days: 'The antientest Master of the Revels is, after dinner and supper, to sing a caroll or song; and command other gentlemen then there present to sing with him and the company; and so it is very decently performed.'[1]

It is interesting to see the same custom at Christmas dinner in the hall after Mass insisted upon by Squire George Gamwell of Gamwell Hall, Notts., in the ballad *Robin Hood's Birth, Breeding, Valor and Marriage* (Child, No. 149 a, stanzas 15, 16; text from 1716):

> And in comes the squire, and makes a short speech,
> It was, Neighbours, you're welcome all.

> But not a man here shall taste my March beer
> Till a Christmas carrol he sing:
> Then all clapt their hands, and they shouted and sung
> Till the hall and the parlour did ring.

There are many other carols which are shown by the internal evidence of their own texts to be designed for convivial use, especially at holiday feasting. It is well to remember that monasteries and bishops' palaces held many such celebrations and that there is no reason to be surprised at the frequency of such lyrics in connections which a modern reader would classify as 'religious'. Among the examples in this collection are Nos. 10, 11, 31, 79, 120, 121, 133, 136, 141, 316, 341, 421, 422. Many of the references are very explicit, for example:

> No. 311: 'Good men that stondyn and syttyn in this halle.'

The same custom of singing in turn by guests who are not professional performers is clearly implied in an amusing little piece in the carol-manuscript B.M. Sloane 2593.[2] Robbins entitles it 'An Unwilling Minstrel', but it is plainly the excuse of an unskilled singer in the general company, not the plea of a professional on an off day or 'perhaps because of a cold'. By mistranslating 'tey vp ȝour ky' as 'tune up your instrument' instead of 'tie up your cows' (who would think they were being called) Robbins misses the rather hackneyed rustic joke.[3]

In his translation of Erasmus's *The Praise of Folie* Sir Thomas Chaloner in 1577 includes carols among the 'knackes' or 'scoffes' that are used 'to put awaie the sadde stylnesse of the feast'. His examples include '*to chose a kynge*

[1] John Nichols, *The Progresses and Public Processions of Queen Elizabeth*, new edn. (London, 1823), i. 136, 138.

[2] Rossell Hope Robbins, ed., *Secular Lyrics of the XIVth and XVth Centuries*, 2nd edn. (Oxford, 1955), p. 4.

[3] R. L. Greene, 'If I Sing, Tie Up Your Cows', *N. & Q.* ccix (1964), 88–9.

by lottes, to plaie at tables, to bringe good lucke, to quasse about the bourde, to synge carolles'.[1]

[1] Ed. Clarence H. Miller, E.E.T.S., No. 257, 1965, p. 25. That the same custom of singing carols in turn also prevailed in Scotland is shown by a passage in the robust carol in the Bannatyne Manuscript (1568) which has the burden 'Quhy sowld not allane honorit be?':

In ȝule quhen ilk man singis his carrell
gud allane lyis in to ane barrell

(W. Tod Ritchie, ed., *The Bannatyne Manuscript*, ii, S.T.S., New Ser., xxii (1928), 286, ll. 36–7).

Compare Pierre Jean Baptiste Le Grand d'Aussy, *Histoire de la vie privée des François*, nouvelle édition, ed. J. B. B. de Roquefort (Paris, 1815), iii. 366: 'Mais ce qui mérite de l'être [i.e. regretté] c'est l'usage qu'avoient nos Pères, lors qu'ils se rassembloient dans un festin, de s'égayer au dessert par une chanson joyeyse, dont le refrein se répétoit en chœur. Tour-à-tour chacun disoit la sienne . . .'

CHAPTER II

THE CAROL AS DANCE-SONG

1. *The Carole and its Songs*

THAT the carol had its origin in the dance, or that at least the two were at some time closely associated, has been repeatedly affirmed by various writers. The basis for the statement has ordinarily been little more than the etymology of the word 'carol' itself; in only a very few instances has an attempt been made to indicate in any detail the nature of the connection.[1] The neglect of this point is hardly to be wondered at in view of the long-prevailing mode of regarding the carol as distinguished from other lyrics, not by its form, but by its subject-matter or its spirit. For it is on the metrical form of poetry that the influence of the dance has principally operated and left more or less easily discernible traces. The eighteenth-century writer who hazarded the unfortunate suggestion that the word 'carol' was derived from 'Carolus' (because of the great popularity of Christmas songs in the days of King Charles) is hardly to be blamed for failing to see points of contact between a medieval dance and such a piece, say, as Herrick's *A Christmas Caroll, sung to the King in the Presence at White-Hall*, set to music by Henry Lawes, and beginning:

> What sweeter musick can we bring
> Then a Caroll, for to sing
> The Birth of this our heavenly King?
> Awake the Voice! Awake the String!
> Heart, Eare, and Eye, and every thing,
> Awake! the while the active Finger
> Runs division with the Singer.[2]

But when a carol is understood, as it appears to have been in the fifteenth century, to be a song, on whatever subject you please, written in stanzas and having a burden, its character as a possible accompaniment to the dance can be readily grasped. It should be helpful to such understanding to consider some of the evidence for the association of dance and song in medieval Europe.[3]

The carol is only one of a number of lyric forms to be designated by a term suggesting a dance. *Ballette* and *rondel* have passed, with the verse-forms

[1] This is done for Audelay's carols by Chambers and Sidgwick, in *M.L.R.* v (1910), 473–8.
[2] Ed. L. C. Martin (Oxford, 1956), p. 364.
[3] A clear and authoritative account of the widespread and persistent use of the round dance is given by Violet Alford and Rodney Gallop, *The Traditional Dance* (London, 1935), chap. iv.

which they denote, from French into English, the former word undergoing two distinct developments into 'ballade' and 'ballad'. Provençal has its *ballada* and its *dansa*, Italian its *canzoni a ballo*, from which developed various types of *ballata*. Volumes of songs appeared in Germany in the sixteenth century with such titles as *Geistliche Ringeltenze*[1] and *Vier geistliche Reyenlieder*.[2] In Iceland the imported word *danz* was early applied to song.[3] The occurrence of such names indicates that in each of the languages mentioned there exists lyric poetry which is closely connected with the dance and hence in greater or less degree analogous to the carol.

The value and interest which the history of these and related forms holds for the study of the carol are increased by the relative scarcity of direct evidence concerning the dance and the dance-song in England itself, a circumstance which forces the student of the English genre to have frequent recourse to the more abundant material from continental sources. Nor has there been any critical treatment of the connection between song and dance in England comparable for acuteness and comprehensiveness to M. Alfred Jeanroy's classic work on the origins of the French lyric.[4] It is true that the influence of the dance in the shaping of the narrative ballad has been a prominent landmark on the battlefield of ballad-scholarship, and that such zealous collectors and preservers of traditional folk-song as the late Cecil Sharp have been keenly conscious of the importance of the folk-dance for their chosen study. But only brief and general treatment has been given to the connection of the dance with English poetry not classed as folk-song or ballad.

There can be no question of the enormous vogue of the carole as a social pastime. It figures repeatedly in the medieval French romances, among others *Le Roman de la Rose*,[5] *Guillaume de Dole*,[6] and *Le Roman de la Violette*.[7] The descriptions of the carole in literature, together with graphic

---

[1] Magdeburg, 1550.

[2] Nürnberg, 1535. See Franz M. Böhme, ed., *Altdeutsches Liederbuch* (Leipzig, 1877), pp. 369–70.

[3] Francis B. Gummere, ed., *Old English Ballads* (Boston, 1894), p. lxxv n. 1.

[4] *Les Origines de la poésie lyrique en France au moyen âge*, 3rd edn. (Paris, 1925). With it should be used Gaston Paris's important review published with the same title (Paris, 1892).

[5] See the citations from Chaucer's translation, above, p. xvi n. 5.

[6] Ed. G. Servois (Paris, 1893). A carole is described in ll. 504–18:

Les dames et les compegnons
L'empereor s'en issent hors,
Main a main em pur lor biau cors.
Devant le tref, en .j. pré vert,
Les puceles et li vallet

Ront la carole commenciée.
Une dame s'est avanciée,
Vestue d'une cotele en graine;
Si chante ceste premeraine:
  C'est tot la gieus enmi les prez.
Vos ne sentez mie les maus d'amer.
  Dames i vont por caroler.
  Remirez vos bras,
Vos ne sentez mie les maus d'amer,
  Si com ge faz . . .

[7] Ed. Douglas L. Buffum (Paris, 1928), ll. 92–104:

Apriés mangier les envïa
Tous ensamble de caroler.
Qui dont veïst dames aler
En chambres por apparillier.
Chascune prent un chevalier
Pur commenchier l'envoisement.
Commenche tout premierement

representations, especially miniatures in manuscripts,[1] indicate with reasonable exactness the essential features of this dance, which, although the favourite, was by no means the only one known to medieval society.[2] According to M. Bédier's description, it consisted of a chain, open or closed, of male and female dancers, who moved to the accompaniment of the voice or (less frequently) of instruments.[3] The movement was ordinarily three steps in measure to the left, followed by some kind of marking time in place. It was usual for the dancers to join hands, but gestures seem frequently to have been introduced which would require the clasp to be broken.[4] The whole procedure was under the direction of a leader. It was the duty of this leader, *coryphée*, or *Vorsänger*, to sing the stanzas of the song to which the carole was being danced.[5] During the time of such singing the

A chanter ma dame Nicole;
Suer fu l'evesque de Nicole,
Contesse estoit de Besenchon.
Lors commenche ceste canchon
Sans felonnie et sans orguel:

 Alés bielement que d'amer me duel.

Froissart has given a charming glimpse of his youthful pleasure in dancing the carole with his 'fair lady' ('Froissart's Youth', translated from the autobiographical poem *Espinette Amoureuse* in G. G. Coulton, *Social Life in Britain*, Cambridge, 1918, p. 88).

[1] See frontispiece from Bodl. MS. Douce 93, f. 28ʳ. A fifteenth-century representation of the carole is printed in Cecil J. Sharp and A. P. Oppé, *The Dance* (London, 1924), plate xiii, from British Museum MS. Harley 4425 of *The Romance of the Rose*. Three instrumental musicians are shown. Plate ix of the same work reproduces a miniature of a carole from the fourteenth-century Bodleian Library MS. Bodley 264 of the Alexander romance. A carole is the subject of the carving on a mirror-case now in the Louvre, of which a photograph appears in Charles V. Langlois, *La Vie en France au moyen âge d'après des romans mondains du temps* (Paris, 1926), i, plate v.

[2] Compare Joseph Bédier's interesting and ingenious article, 'Les plus anciennes danses françaises', in *Revue des deux mondes*, pér. v, xxxi (1906), 398–424. Various types of dance current in medieval Germany are described in detail by Wilhelm Angerstein, *Volktänze im deutschen Mittelalter* (Sammlung gemeinverständlicher wissenschaftlicher Vorträge, Ser. 3, lviii, Berlin, 1868), and Franz M. Böhme, *Geschichte des Tanzes in Deutschland* (Leipzig, 1886).

[3] There are many references to the carole, in both its popular and its more aristocratic use, which show that it was often danced by women alone. According to Jeanroy (*Origines*, p. 391), the mixed carole was introduced in the thirteenth century.

[4] So in the romance of *Le Châtelain de Coucy* one lady

 prist entour soy sà et là
 par les mains dames, chevaliers,
 pour caroller.

(Quoted by Jeanroy, *Origines*, p. 391 n. 3.) Compare the allusion to the joining of arms in the sermon on 'Bele Aelis' discussed below, p. cxlv and n. 3: '. . . in tripudio tria sunt necessaria, scilicet, vox sonora, nexus brachiorum, et strepitus pedum.' Gestures of various sorts figure, for example, in the account of a very lively carole danced in the vision of 'maître Mahieu', *Lamenta*, ll. 3561–70 (quoted in Charles V. Langlois, *La Vie en France au moyen âge d'après des moralistes du temps* (Paris, 1926), p. 284:

Quidam cum lepido citharam pede concomitante
Vadunt et redeunt, surgunt residentque plicante
In talos cervice sua. Nimis ingeniose
Ducunt se simulantque minas pugneque jocose
Instar habent, sese fugiunt seseque secuntur,
Et verbis, plausu, digitis signisque locuntur.
Aptant se ludo digiti modicumque quiescit
Infurcata manus lateri que sistere nescit,
Dum jubet ipsa lira; subtiles et quasi fixos
Furantur motus humeri cernentibus ipsos.

[5] This leader was very often a woman. Jacques de Vitry compares her to the bell-cow of a herd, with the devil for master. See exemplum

ring moved to the left. At the close of the stanza the entire company of dancers would respond with the refrain or burden of the song, dancing in place the while. Then, as the circle revolved again, the leader would sing the following stanza, and so on. Obviously the leader was the only one of the group who needed to know all the words of a song; the burden, being invariable or nearly so, could be quickly learned and easily remembered by the chorus. Some sort of cue in words or music would serve to notify the chorus of its time for beginning the burden.

The passage already quoted[1] from the *Handlyng Synne* admirably illustrates this manner of dancing. The two narrative lines

> By þe leued wode rode Beuolyne,
> wyþ hym he ledde feyre Merswyne,

are what the leader, Beune, who 'ordeyned here karollyng' would sing, the exclamatory

> why stonde we? why go we noght?

forming a burden for the chorus, highly appropriate if we picture them as singing the line while marking time as if impatient to resume the circular movement.[2]

This legend of the cursed carollers of Kölbigk in Saxony, well known throughout Western Europe, has been discussed until its interpretation has become a literature in itself. In Middle English it is well told in Robert Mannyng's *Handlyng Synne*, but a very brief summary of its contents can best be made from the Latin version recorded by Goscelin, a monk of Wilton and of St. Augustine's, Canterbury, in his *Life of St. Edith*.[3] It is there told in the first person by the pilgrim Theodoric, who was one of the carollers:

On Christmas Eve [in 1020 or thereabout] twelve of us gathered at the church of St. Magnus in Kölbigk. Gerleuus was our leader, and the others were Maeinoldus, Odbertus, Bovo, Gerardus, Wetzelo, Azelinus, Folpoldus, Hildebrandus, Aluuardus, Benna, Odricus. The two girls Mersuind and Wibecyna seized and brought from the church Ava, the priest's daughter. We joined hands and danced in the churchyard; Gerleuus, as *Vorsänger*, gave out the fatal song:

> Equitabat Bouo   per siluam frondosam;
> Ducebat sibi   Mersuindem formosam:
> Quid stamus?   Cur non imus?

No. cccxiv in Thomas F. Crane, ed., *The Exempla of Jacques de Vitry* (London, 1890): 'Sicut vacca que alias precedit in collo campanam gerit, sic mulier que prima cantat coream ducit quasi campanam dyaboli ad collum habet ligatam.'

[1] Above, p. xxiv.

[2] In an admirable survey of the European dance-song Peter Dronke points out that the opposite sort of alternation is also found: 'The circular movement in the dance can coincide with the strophe, or with the refrain, or again with an instrumental or vocal *reprise* between them—depending on the rhythm, nature and content of the particular song' (*The Medieval Lyric*, London, 1968, pp. 189–90).

[3] André Wilmart, ed., 'La Légende de Ste Édith en prose et vers par le moine Goscelin', *Analecta Bollandiana*, lvi (1938), 5–101, 265–307.

When the priest called to us to stop dancing and come to the service, we refused, and the priest invoked the wrath of God through the influence of St. Magnus. The curse took effect, and we found that we could not break the circle or stop dancing for a whole year. The priest's son Azo attempted to pull his sister Ava out of the ring but only tore away her arm, which did not bleed.

Meanwhile we danced and leapt and clapped, mocking our own pain with the refrain of our song, 'Quid stamus? Cur non imus?' We neither ate nor drank nor slept, and our hair and nails did not grow. People flocked to see us, and the Emperor Henry attempted to have a shelter built over us, but each night the work was thrown down. Finally on the next Christmas Eve the curse was lifted, and we went into the church and slept three days, but Ava died and her father soon after. Now we wander separately through all countries, marked by the agitation of our limbs.

The importance of this story is twofold. It shows that as early as 1080 in England a Flemish-born monk who had lived in France could present to an English audience, without feeling the need of any explanation, the text of a carole (whether translated into Latin from French or not really does not matter much) divided into stanza and burden, the burden expressing in its very words the change from rest to motion which comes with the choral part. He writes not at all as if the carole were an unknown foreign phenomenon, and there is no reason to doubt that secular dance-song with a burden was known in England immediately after the Norman Conquest, if not before. Dom Wilmart has demonstrated that Goscelin's version of the legend is the nearest to the presumed common original of all its English, French, and German recordings and has the fullest account of the fatal carole. He explains why, in this part of the *Handlyng Synne*, Robert abandons the poorer version found in the *Manuel des Pechiez*, the French original for most of his work, and utilizes a version like that of Goscelin. In reporting the event, the fourteenth-century English poem consistently uses 'carol' for both the dance and its song. The carol-text is thus translated:

> By þe leued wode rode Beuolyne,
> wyþ hym he ledde feyre Merswyne;
> why stonde we? why go we noght?[1]

The occurrence in the song of the names of the dancers themselves has been given various interpretations, but it is not a difficulty. Game-songs in which the actual names of participants are inserted are still sung by children.

R. H. Robbins attempts to dismiss this bit of song as 'not valid evidence for fifteenth-century England', for it is a serious embarrassment to his thesis of the carol's origin in processional hymns, but he follows Paul Verrier in declaring it to be 'a translation of twelfth-century French' and ignores Dom Wilmart's conclusive criticism of Verrier.[2] There can be no

---

[1] Frederick J. Furnivall, ed., E.E.T.S., Or. Ser., No. 119, 1901-4, p. 285, ll. 9049-51.

[2] *Stud. in Phil.* lvi (1959), 577, referring to

Verrier, 'La plus vieille citation de carole', *Romania*, lviii (1932), 380-421.

serious question that in England in the late eleventh century and in the fourteenth, let alone the fifteenth, a song divided into burden and stanza was recognized as what could be sung in a carole, and that carolling in its origin had no odour of sanctity, but the reverse. The matter would seem to be settled by Robert's proceeding to make it explicit that his English listeners need the warning. Moreover, he emphatically locates the episode in England itself:

> And fyl þys chauncë yn þys londe,
> Yn Ingland, as y vndyrstonde;
> Yn a kynges tyme þat hyght Edward.[1]

The wholly secular processional dance which accompanies the singing of the Padstow 'May Song' retains an association of burden with movement and stanza with standing. As long as the 'hobby horse' and his companion dancers advance along the street or whirl about in it, the crowd of villagers sings the burden over and over again. The instant the dancers pause for breath, the singers change without other signal to the stanza, at the conclusion of which the dance is resumed. One of the company assured the writer in 1932 that this procedure was never varied.[2]

It is not possible to speak with certainty of all details of the carole or to regard it as of invariable form. Its wide dissemination in various countries of Europe must have involved differences of one kind or another in the method of dancing. But the essential elements, the circular motion and the division of the group into leader and chorus, were the same in many lands and centuries. Likewise in many lands and centuries were to be heard songs which owed their form to the fact that they were sung in such dances. The essential characteristic of such dance-songs is their sharp division into stanza and burden, the former to be sung by a leader, the latter by the chorus, the former constantly changing its content, the latter repeated over and over again without change. It is a structure of poetry which has persisted long after its almost complete separation from the conditions which gave it birth. The body of texts here collected gives evidence of that persistence in the period of the decline of the carole.

Before an attempt is made to show the influence of the dance on these English texts, it may be well to assemble some of the scanty gleanings which are available for the early history of the round dance in England. There was a great deal of song-accompanied dance on the continent of Europe in the centuries before the Norman Conquest, as the repeated decrees issued against it by ecclesiastical authorities bear witness,[3] and the silence of Old English

---

[1] Furnivall, op. cit., p. 283, ll. 9011–13.

[2] That the Padstow dance-and-song is a survival of a round dance as well as of an open procession is clear from the first lines of the chorus of the 'Morning Song': 'With the merry ring, adieu the merry spring' (*Padstow Hobby Horse* [pamphlet], Padstow, 1901, p. 1).

[3] A number of these, from A.D. 589 on, are quoted by L. Gougaud, 'La danse dans les églises', in *Revue d'histoire écclésiastique*, xv, (1914), 5–22, 229–45. See below, p. cxl.

literature on the subject is not to be taken as implying that the maidens of
Saxon England did not foot it in the meadows in spring or around a fire at
Yule as did their cousins across the water. Gaston Paris points out that it was
in a 'milieu sans doute purement saxon' that women sang of Hereward in
their dances.[1] The famous boat-song of Canute is said by the twelfth-century
chronicler, Thomas of Ely, to have been composed by the king as he heard
from his boat on the Ouse the singing of the monks:

> Merie sungen ðe muneches binnen Ely
> ða Cnut cning reu ðer by;
> Roweþ, cnites, noer the land,
> And here wve þes muneches saeng.[2]

Gummere would regard this as the burden of what had become in the
twelfth century a dance-song, for Thomas adds, 'et caetera, quae sequuntur,
quae usque hodie in choris publice cantantur et in proverbis memorantur'.[3]
The occurrence of refrains associated with rowing is not unknown in later
dance-song.[4] But at what precise date the boat-song, whether by Canute or
not, passed into such use, Thomas does not tell us.

There was certainly dancing in England soon after the coming of the
Normans. It is probably of ring-dances that William Fitzstephen speaks in
his description of London in the twelfth century when he says (in the language of Horace), 'puellarum Cytherea ducit choros usque imminente luna,
et pede libero pulsatur tellus'.[5] The anecdote extracted by Ritson[6] from
Lambarde's *Dictionary of England*, which gives the couplet

> Hoppe Wylikin, hoppe Wyllykin,
> Ingland is thyne and myne, etc.

as that to which the 'gallantes' of Robert, Earl of Leicester, danced upon the
heath to their own undoing, is of slight significance, as these dancers were
'a rabble of Flemings and Normanes'. The couplet itself cannot be of the
date ascribed to it (1173), but it may very possibly represent a dance-burden
current at some later time. A far more valuable bit of evidence for song-
accompanied dancing in England is contained in a southern manuscript
of the early thirteenth century,[7] for which, as for so much of the records of

---

[1] *Origines*, p. 47 n.
[2] Trinity College, Cambridge, MS. O. 2. 1,
ff. 87ᵛ, 88ʳ.
[3] Quoted in part by Gummere, *Beginnings*,
p. 275. Liebermann's objection to taking
'choros' as meaning 'dances' (*Archiv für das
Studium der neueren Sprachen*, cxl, 1920, 262)
like that of Louise Pound (*Modern Language
Notes*, xxxiv, 1919, 163) is hardly valid in view of
such use of the word as appears in the quotation from William Fitzstephen just below.
[4] Gummere, loc. cit.
[5] Quoted by Chambers, *M.S.* i. 164, n. 2. The

passage is composed of tags from *Odes*, I. iv. 5,
and I. xxxvii. 1, 2.
[6] *Ancient Songs and Ballads*, ed. W. C. Hazlitt (London, 1877), p. xxxv.
[7] Trinity College, Cambridge, B. 1. 45,
f. 41ᵛ. Printed by Max Förster in *Anglia*, xlii
(1919), 152–4. In another manuscript a second
couplet follows:

> allas þat he so sorefel;
> wy nadde he stonde better, vile gorel?

(Cambridge University Library, I. 3. 8, f. 87ʳ,
pr. Robbins, *Secular Lyrics*, p. xxxix).

the medieval dance, we have to thank a moralizing cleric. This particular churchman made the lines here quoted his text for a sermon of the same type as that on the *chanson* of 'Bele Aelis'.[1] The discourse begins:

> 'Atte wrastlinge my lemman i ches,
> and atte ston-kasting i him for-les.'

... Mi leue frend, wilde wimmen & golme i mi contreie, wan he gon o þe ring, among manie oþere songis, þat litil ben wort þat tei singin, so sein þei þus: 'Atte wrastli[n]ge mi lemman etc.'

Förster rightly notes the significance of the passage.[2]

Wir haben hier ... ein stück aus einem vielgesungenen volkstümlichen reigenlied vor uns, das also im chorgesang (*o þe ring*) vorgetragen wurde.

These allusions to the dance imply that in each case it was an amusement of the common people, not the courtly carole of a select aristocratic company, performed perhaps after a noble banquet, or in a retired garden. Such dances were, of course, directly imported from France with other fashions and customs. But, apart from a presumably greater stateliness and restraint of movement, the carole of knights and ladies probably had little to distinguish it from the ring-dances of the folk. It was from the latter that their betters originally borrowed the sport, without at all impairing its popularity with the less-favoured class. The essential division into leader and chorus, with the resulting division of the dance-song into stanza and burden, was to be found in ring-dances of high and low alike. Hardly otherwise could the burden have maintained itself as such a prominent feature of both the songs of the people and of the courtly *chanson à carole*. The aristocratic carole gave way centuries ago to newer figures, though the round dances of the folk have a cheerful survival in the ring-games of children.

Sir John Davies in his ambitious and philosophical *Orchestra, or A Poem of Dancing* (1596), treats the simple round and serpentine as a primitive form of dance, replaced by more restrained types as culture advances:

> Thus when at first Love had them marshalled,
>   As erst he did the shapeless mass of things,
> He taught them rounds and winding hays to tread,
>   And about trees to cast themselves in rings;
>   As the two Bears, whom the first mover flings
> With a short turn about heaven's axletree,
> In a round dance for ever wheeling be.
>
> But after these, as men more civil grew,
>   He did more grave and solemn measures frame.[3]

---

[1] See below, p. cxlvii.
[2] Förster, op. cit., p. 152 n.
[3] [Sir] E. K. Chambers, ed., *The Oxford*

Book of Sixteenth Century Verse (Oxford, 1932), p. 755.

The scraps of song which have been quoted are in no case adequate for an understanding of the form of the early dance-song in England. In spite of this handicap of the almost complete absence of English texts an attempt may be made to reconstruct such a form by consulting the richer records of French poetry, e.g. in the acute work of Jeanroy, for which reconstruction the similarity of the dance itself in the two countries may be the warrant. Jeanroy says:

'La forme [de la chanson à danser] la plus simple et la plus ancienne de toutes était composée de couplets que chantait un soliste et que suivait un refrain repris par le chœur . . . le couplet des deux vers devait être le plus ancien de tous, et . . . il avait dû bientôt céder le pas à celui de trois; vers le commencement du XIIᵉ siècle, dans la poésie latine, les couplets de trois vers non pourvus de refrain se font rares et sont habituellement remplacés par ceux de quatre. Mais les couplets suivis de refrains sont plus souvent de trois vers que de quatre, sans doute parce qu'il y avait là une forme traditionelle qui s'imposait.'[1]

This results in the form of a a a X or a a a X X.[2] But the practical measure of advising the chorus of the moment for it to begin its singing by means of a rhyme common to stanza and burden resulted in the form a a a b B. Jeanroy gives the following as an example:

> Kant li vilains vai(n)t a marchiet,
> il n'i vait pas por berguignier,
> mais por sa feme a esgaitier,
> ke nuns ne li forvoie.
>
> Au cuer les ai les jolis malz, coment en guariroie?[3]

English poetry of the twelfth and thirteenth centuries does not exhibit anything of like form that can be connected with the dance. But a casual jotting of the first half of the fourteenth century in a small collection of written fragments challenges attention by its invitation to the dance.[4] Is it actually a dance-song; is it burden or verse? In the words of Sir Edmund Chambers, 'We would dance gladly did we but know the tune'.[5] As Sir Edmund prints it, it appears to be of a somewhat nondescript metre; but, with the form of the primitive dance-song as guide, inspection will show that the little piece

---

[1] *Origines*, p. 397 and n.

[2] In the notation of verse-forms here used, the rhymes of a stanza are indicated by lower-case letters, those of a burden by capitals. The numeral prefixed to each letter indicates the number of measures or accents normally found in the line.

[3] *Origines*, p. 399, quoted from Karl Bartsch, *Altfranzösische Romanzen und Pastourellen* (Leipzig, 1870), p. 21.

[4] Bodleian Library, MS. Rawlinson D. 913, f. 1ᵛ.

[5] *Early English Lyrics*, p. 279.

divides very easily into a burden and a stanza, the former written first, as it was sung first:

> Icham of Irlaunde,
> Ant of the holy londe
> Of Irlande.

> Gode sire, pray ich þe,
> For of saynte charité,
> Come ant daunce wyt me
> In Irlaunde.[1]

There is the typical stanza, three rhyming lines, and the fourth line linking them to the burden, in this case by the use of the same end-word. If the song was not danced to, at least it could have been. It should also be noted that it appears to be either genuine folk-song or something closely modelled upon genuine folk-song, as is the case with the other bits of verse on the same leaf.[2]

It is reasonable to expect, when we turn to the more abundant texts of the pieces for which the name of carol is claimed, that if these are true products of the carole or even imitations of such true products, we shall find traces of this stanza-form which is so definitely associated with the dance in French. Nor is such evidence lacking. The four-line stanza rhymed a a a b with a burden in B or B B is by far the most frequent metrical scheme of all. No fewer than 195 of the more than 500 carols here collected use it in one or another of its combinations of lines of varying numbers of accents, and of refrain-lines. A few of the more common specializations of this type of stanza may be illustrated by quotations which will also show how nearly the English carol often approaches the metrical pattern of a French song derived from the dance. The form 4a 4a 4a 4b 4B 4B is one of the two most frequently used for the carol, as it is in No. 339:

> (Burden)   Man, bewar, bewar, bewar,
> And kepe the that thou haue no car.

> (Stanza 1)   Thi tunge is mad of fleych and blod;
> Euele to spekyn it is not good;
> But Cryst, that deyid vpon the rood,
> So yyf us grace our tunges to spare.

> (Burden repeated)

---

[1] Text from Kenneth Sisam, ed., *Fourteenth Century Verse and Prose* (Oxford, 1921), p. 166.

[2] Printed by W. Heuser, 'Fragmente von unbekannten Spielmannsliedern des 14. Jahr-hunderts', in *Anglia* xxx (1907), 173–9. For improved readings of some of the verses see Peter Dronke, 'The Rawlinson Lyrics', *N. & Q.* ccvi (1961), 245–6.

(Stanza 2)   Thi lyppis arn withoute bon;
              Spek non euyl of thi fon;
              Man, I rede be Seynt Jon,
                  Of euyl speche that thou be war.

              (Burden repeated)
                                      (etc.)

This exact arrangement of rhymes is not equally common in the French
lyric, but it does occur. Jeanroy[1] refers to the following piece as an example:

(Stanza 1)   An Hachecourt l'autre jour chivauchoie,
              les un aunoi desduisant m'en alloie,
              trovai pastoure seant sus la codroie;
                  an haut s'escria ansi

(Burden)   'enmi enmi enmi!
                  lasse, je n'ai point d'ami.'

(Stanza 2)   Cant j'antendi le cri la simple et coie,
              vers li tornai, de son anuit m'anoie;
              je la saluai, mais se diex me voie,
                  ainz respons je n'oi de li

(Burden)   k' 'ainmi enmi enmi!
                  lasse, je n'ai point d'ami.'[2]
                  (etc.)

More often when the two lines of a French burden rhyme together, they
are not linked to the stanza by this same rhyme.[3] This is also the case with
a considerable number of English carols, No. 60 for example:

(Burden)   In the honour of Christes byrth
                  Syng we al with joye and myrthe.

(Stanza 1)   In this tyme of Chrystmas,
              Bytwyxte an oxe and an asse,
              A mayden delyuered was
                  Of Christ, her dere Son dere.
                      (etc.)

But the early French dance-song did not confine itself to the stanza in
a a a b alone. It retained the clearly separated burden, not assimilating it to
the stanza in the form of text-lines as was done later in forms which were
developed further after their practical connection with the dance began to be
disregarded.[4] The fourth line of a four-line stanza might rhyme with the
first three instead of with the burden, giving a monorhyme stanza not linked
to the burden. Such is the case with the *chanson* of 'Bele Yolanz'.[5]

[1] *Origines*, p. 399 n. 1.
[2] Bartsch, *Romanzen*, pp. 167–8.
[3] Jeanroy, *Origines*, p. 399 n. 1.
[4] Ibid., p. 401.
[5] Bartsch, *Romanzen*, p. 9.

(Stanza 1)   Bele Yolanz en chambre koie
                 sor ses genouz pailes desploie:
                 co'st un fil d'or, l'autre de soie.
                 sa male mere la chastoie.

(Burden)   'chastoi vos en, bele Yolanz.'
                    (etc.)

A similar form, but with the ubiquitous English couplet-burden, is found in five carols, including No. 158:[1]

(Burden)   'Mary moder, cum and se
                 Thy swet Son nayled on a tre.

(Stanza 1)   'Thys blessyd babe that thou hast born,
                 Hys blessyd body ys all to-torne
                 To bye vs agayn, that were forlorne;
                 Hys hed ys crownyd with a thorn.'
                    (etc.)

Or the French dance-song may content itself with three monorhymed lines in the stanza:[2]

(Stanza 1)   Lou samedi a soir, fat la semainne,
                 Gaiete et Oriour, serors germainnes,
                 main et main vont bagnier a la fontainne.

(Burden)   vante l'ore et li raim crollent:
                 ki s'antraimment soweif dorment.
                  (etc.)

And so may the English carol:[3]

(Burden)   What, hard ye not? The Kyng of Jherusalem
                 Is now born in Bethelem.

(Stanza 1)   I shall you tell a gret mervayll:
                 How an angell, for owr avayll,
                 Com to a mayd, and said, 'All hayll!'
                  (etc.)

Instances could be multiplied, but the comparisons already made show the essential identity of principle in the construction of the French dance-songs of the twelfth and thirteenth centuries and the English carols pre-served in manuscripts of two to three hundred years later. That identity of principle is the best possible evidence of their common parentage in the dance, the carole.

    There is, on the other hand, great dissimilarity between the English carol and the courtly French lyric of the period when the carol was flourishing,

---

[1] The others are Nos. 21, 315, 331, 399.   [2] Bartsch, *Romanzen*, p. 8.   [3] No. 241.

a dissimilarity of form as well as of spirit. This may be strikingly shown by a comparison between the texts here collected and the so-called *caroles* written in the fifteenth century and on English soil by Charles d'Orléans during his long captivity. The first of these three *caroles* is rhymed as follows, with lines of varying length:[1]

A b b a c d c d a b b a A e f e f a b b a A

Charles's verses are artificial and literary, the products of a talent schooled in the conventions of the aristocratic poetry of the fourteenth century. They are written, moreover, in a form which no longer preserves the duality of stanza and burden which is the mark of near relationship to the round dance. Thereby they illustrate the change which earlier dance-song underwent at the hands of writers like Guillaume de Machaut and Eustache Deschamps: the originally choral burden, preserved as a literary convention, tended to be absorbed into the structure of the stanza itself as a mere refrain-line. The number of stanzas, indefinite in older dance-songs, as in the English carol, was limited, as in the three-stanza forms of *ballade* and *virelai*. Longer and more elaborate stanzas were devised, with ingenious rhyme-schemes and lines of varying length. In short, the simple periodicity of the dance gave way to the inventive power of the individual poet (or musician) as the shaping influence of song.

A similar tendency can be seen at work in the carol in the fifteenth century, resulting in the more elaborate verse-forms. But its effects are evident in comparatively few pieces; only twenty-two carols are written in stanzas of more than seven lines.[2] These more complicated rhyme-patterns are re-presented as a rule by only one or two carols apiece, and may pass as isolated experiments with the general carol-type. The standard of the carol-writers remained the simpler stanza with separate burden which is characteristic of song where the influence of the round dance is still felt.

The form in French courtly poetry which retains most of the aspect of primitive dance-song is the *virelai*, and hence this may be regarded as the nearest of kin to the English carol. It does not appear, however, to have exerted any direct influence on the carol. The two moved in different circles of literary society. But the analysis made by Jeanroy of the essential structure of the *virelai* shows that it is a sister, or at least a cousin, to the carol.[3] The

[1] Charles d'Héricault, ed., *Poésies complètes de Charles d'Orléans* (Paris, 1896), ii. 73. The English translation of this poem in British Museum MS. Royal 16. F. ii, f. 122ᵛ begins: 'Alas Fortune alas myn hevynes.' (Paul Sauerstein, *Charles d'Orléans und die englische Übersetzung seiner Dichtungen*, Halle a / S., 1899, p. 37.)

[2] Nos. 77, 107, 218, 230, 263, 304, 376, 424, 439, 440 (8 ll.); 44, 95, 161, 464 (9 ll.); 37, 146 B, 150, 434 (10 ll.); 165 (11 ll.); 147 (12 ll.); 146 A (18 ll.), 308 (varying).

[3] *Origines*, p. 427. The name *virelai* recalls the ultimately popular origin of the form, according to Paul Meyer (*Romania*, xix, 1890, 26): '*Virelai*, plus souvent *vireli*, désigne originairement un air populaire, un *dorenlot*, comme *valuru, valura, valuraine*', etc.

fundamental parts of the *virelai* are four: (1) a burden placed at the head of
the piece; (2) a part of the stanza independent of the burden; (3) a second
part of the stanza corresponding (in rhymes and accents) to the burden; (4)
the burden repeated. The texts which Jeanroy cites exhibit this structure
perhaps less clearly than some others which might be chosen. A *virelai* from
Bodleian Library MS. Douce 308, as arranged by Gennrich, will show the
likeness of the type to the carol.[1] The marginal numbers indicate the four
divisions:

1. *Bien doit merci recovreir,*
   qui loialment vuelt ameir.

2. Amors qui tant ait pooir
   por amans faire valoir
   m'ait mis an un dous espoir.

3. ki me semont de chanteir:

4. *Bien doit merci recovre[i]r,*
   qui loialment vuelt ameir.
   (etc.)

This is an early specimen, and except for the limitation to three stanzas is
the same as the primitive dance-song already discussed. A specimen from
the pen of Deschamps will show the refinements which had been introduced
into the *virelai* of the later fourteenth century:[2]

Or a mon cuer ce qu'i vouloit,
Or a mon cuer ce qu'i queroit,
Or a mon cuer son vray desir,
Or a mon cuer tout son plesir,
Or a tout ce qu'i desiroit,

La bonté, la beauté, l'onnour,
La rose, la fresche coulour,
La plus plaisant, la plus amee,
La mieulx garnie de douçour,
Et la plus amoreuse flour
Qui onques fust au monde nee;

Celle de qui nulz ne saroit
Descripre les biens, ne pourroit
Ancre, papier ne plume offrir,
Ne langue ne pourroit souffrir
De la louer selon son droit.

Or a mon cuer *etc.*

---

[1] Friedrich Gennrich, ed., *Rondeaux, Virelais und Balladen*, i (Gesellschaft für romanische Literatur, xliii, Dresden, 1921), 107.

[2] Paul Studer and E. R. G. Waters, eds., *Historical French Reader* (Oxford, 1924), p. 234.

C'est Pallax, deesse d'amour,
Et mon refuge et mon demour;
C'est ma joye et paix ordonnee,
C'est la fin de tout mon labour,
C'est ma vie et ce que j'aour,
C'est ma joyeuse destinee,

C'est celle que mon cuer conoit,
C'est celle que mon cuer servoit,
C'est celle qui fait repartir
Mon cuer d'amour, et remerir;
Folz est qui plus demanderoit.

Or a mon cuer *etc.*

It will be observed that it preserves the burden repeated between stanzas but remaining external to them. In this respect it is still analogous to the carol.

The carol is not an aristocratic genre, however, and the conventions of courtly love touch it hardly at all. We have seen that the development in the aristocratic poetry of France led it away from the simplicity of form which the carol preserved. What of the so-called 'popular' songs of France contemporary with the carol? It might be expected that they would have retained the same simplicity. This is exactly the case with many French songs of the fifteenth century, which are 'popular', not necessarily folk-songs current in oral tradition, but songs composed for the common people away from the influence of court or *puy*. Such pieces as the following present a striking similarity of form to the carol:[1]

(Burden)   Ne l'oseray-je dire
             Se j'ayme par amours?
             Ne l'oseray-je dire?

(Stanza 1)   Mon père m'y maria,
             Vng petit devant le jour;
             A vng villain m'y donna,
             Qui ne sçait bien ne honour,
             Ne l'oseray-je dire?
                  (etc.)

Another, very popular in Normandy in a number of versions, begins in one of these as follows:[2]

(Burden)   Las, il n'a nul mal qui n'a le mal d'amour.

(Stanza 1)   La fille du Roy est aupres de la tour,
             Qui pleure et soupire meine grand doulour,

---

[1] A. Gasté, ed., *Chansons normandes du XVe siècle* (Caen, 1866), p. 28.

[2] Théodore Gérold, ed., *Chansons populaires des XVe et XVIe siècles* (Strasbourg, [1913]), p. 6.

(Burden)   Las, il n'a nul mal qui n'a le mal d'amour.
                  (etc.)

A third Norman song is more elaborate in its structure, but still shows the same arrangement of a burden external to the stanza, although linked to it by rhyme:[1]

(Burden)   Mon cueur vit en esmoy:
                  Las qu'il a de souci!
                  Point ne voy mon amy,
                  Il est trop loing de moy.

(Stanza 1)   Bientost de vos nouvelles
                  Certaines rescripray,
                  Se honte ne craignoie;
                  Et, j'eusse ceste loy,
                  Bientost l'iroye chercher,
                  Sans moy deshonorer,
                  Tant l'ayme, sur may foy!
                    (etc.)

These few examples will suffice to show that popular song of metrical structure essentially like that of the English carol was to be heard in the lands on the other side of the Channel whither so many young Englishmen followed their lords in the fifteenth century.[2] An English gentleman travelling in Normandy under more peaceful conditions would likewise be certain to make the acquaintance of the dance-song of France in its own surroundings. A diverting manual of conversational Norman French of the late fourteenth century, written by an Englishman for Englishmen, describes the very liberal hospitality enjoyed by such a traveller at a Norman inn.[3] After a good dinner, 'Doncques viennent avant ou presence du signeur les corneours et clariouers, ou leur fretielles et clarions, et se comencent a corner et clariouer tres fixt, et puis le signeur ou ses escuiers se croulent, balent, dancent, houvent et chantent de biaux karoles sanz cesser jusques a mynuyt.'

One of the best descriptions of a carole in Middle English is to be found in Lovelich's *Merlin*. In the Forest of Brioque Merlin elects to show to Nimiane as an example of his magic a magnificent 'ryng' of men and ladies dancing to the accompaniment of many different instruments. Nimiane can-

---

[1] Gasté, *Chansons normandes*, p. 111.

[2] The Normans pay their compliments to 'les godons' in some of the pieces in Gasté's volume, e.g. Nos. iii, xxxv *bis*, lxi, lxxxvi; in No. xxxviii as follows:

Nous priron Dieu de bon cueur fin,
Et la doulce Vierge Marie,

Qu'il doint aux Engloys malle fin.
Dieu le Père si les mauldye!

[3] Printed from B.M. MS. Harley 3988 by Paul Meyer, *Revue critique d'histoire et de littérature*, année v, semestre 2 (1870), pp. 382–408.

not make out the meaning of the whole song that the dancers are singing, but she clearly understands the burden or 'refret':

> a joye, a joye ET amours
> et sen issent a dolours![1]

From medieval Germany, too, come dance-songs which show the clear division into burden and stanza like the carol. A thirteenth-century specimen appears among the *Carmina Burana*:

(Burden)   Ich sage dir, ih sage dir,
                  min geselle, chum mit mir.

(Stanza 1)   Ich wil truren varen lan,
                 vf die heide sul wir gan,
                 vil liebe gespilen min!
                 da seh wir der blumen schin.
                      (etc.)[2]

In an old German folk-song to accompany a ring-dance for St. John's Day the stanza is a simple couplet.

(Burden)   Blau, blau Blumen auf mein Hut
                  Hätt ich Geld und das wär gut,
                  Blumen auf mein Hütchen.

(Stanza 1)   Nimm sie bei der schneeweissen Hand,
                 Und führ sie in den Rosenkranz.
                     (etc.)[3]

The part taken by the soloist or *Vorsänger* seems to have left rather less lasting effect on the German lyric than on the French, to judge from the specimens preserved. Dance-songs of the type just quoted are less frequent than those which seem to have been designed for singing throughout by the entire company.[4] Of this latter kind is another 'Abendreihen' for St. John's Day:

> Kommt her, ihr lieben Schwesterlein,
> an diesen Abendtanz!
> Lasst uns ein geistlich Liedelein
> singen um einen Kranz,
> singen um einen Kranz.[5]

---

[1] Part iii, ed. Ernst A. Kock, E.E.T.S., Or. Ser., No. 185 (1932), pp. 569–73. In the corresponding passage in the prose *Merlin* the burden goes: 'Vraiement comencent amours en ioye, et fynissent en dolours' (vol. ii, ed. Henry B. Wheatley, E.E.T.S., Or. Ser., No. 36, pp. 309–10). In both cases the verse is undoubtedly preserved from the French original of the romance.

[2] Ed. Carl Fischer (Zürich, 1974), p. 540, burden and stanza here rearranged.

[3] Franz M. Böhme, *Geschichte des Tanzes in Deutschland* (Leipzig, 1886), i. 239.

[4] Only a small proportion of the texts in Böhme's *Altdeutsches Liederbuch* (Leipzig, 1877) have burdens of the type found in the carol.

[5] Böhme, *Geschichte des Tanzes*, ii. 12.

The dance left its impression on the poetry of the south of Europe as well as on that of the north. The Provençal *dansa* has been alluded to, and deserves a word more, although there is nothing to indicate any direct Provençal influence on the English carol.[1] The *dansa*, in spite of its name, is rather farther removed from the dance itself than either carol or *virelai*. This is shown by the absence of a real burden; its place at the end of each stanza is taken by a *tornada* corresponding to the prefixed 'burden' in rhymes and length of lines, but not repeating its words. An example (of the thirteenth century) will make the arrangement clear:[2]

('Burden') Bos sabers, joyos
      Me faytz e baudos,
      D'amor agradiva.

(Stanza 1) Bos sabers me fay lo cor gay,
      Quar veray pretz ha d'onor.
      Belazor non say, don morray
      S'ieu non hay breumen s'amor.

(*Tornada*) Ay! cor gracios,
      Lunh' autra ses vos.
      No m'es agradiva.
       (etc.)

But another related Provençal form does preserve the verse-form which has been seen to be closely derived from the dance, a a a b B B, as the burden and first stanza of one specimen will show.[3] This is the *ballada*:[4]

(Burden)   Coindeta sui, si cum n'ai greu cossire,
      per mon marit, quar ne·l voil ne·l desire.

(Stanza)   Qu'eu be·us dirai per que son aissi drusa:
      quar pauca son, joveneta e tosa,
      e degr' aver marit, dont fos joiosa,
      ab cui toz temps pogues jogar e rire.
       (etc.)

The burden is also repeated within the stanza as a refrain.

The same name is applied in its Italian form to a type of the Italian lyric which presents in some respects the most striking analogy to the carol to be

[1] For a discussion of the influence of the troubadours on earlier Middle English poetry see Jean Audiau, *Les Troubadours et l'Angleterre* (Paris, 1927).

[2] Quoted by Paul Meyer, 'Des rapports de la poésie des trouvères avec celle des troubadours', *Romania*, xix (1890), 21.

[3] Karl Bartsch, ed., *Chrestomathie provençale* 6th edn. (Marburg, 1904), revised Eduard Koschwitz, col. 269.

[4] The historical relations of *dansa*, *ballada*, and *virelai* are discussed with somewhat different conclusions by Paul Meyer, *Romania*, xix (1890), 11 ff., and E. Stengel, 'Ableitung der provenzalisch-französischen Dansa- und der französischen Virelay-Formen', in *Zeitschrift für französische Sprache und Litteratur*, xvi, part i (1894), 94–101.

found in the literature of continental Europe. The *ballata* is also by origin a dance-song. That it was not a 'literary' genre, that it was emphatically a song to be sung and accompanied by physical movement, we are told by no less an authority than Dante himself. He writes in the *De Vulgari Eloquentia* (soon after 1300):[1]

> Moreover, whatever produces by its own power the effect for which it was made, appears nobler than that which requires external assistance; but *Canzoni* produce by their own power the whole effect they ought to produce, which *Ballate* do not, for they require the assistance of the performers [*plausoribus*: dancers, those who clap their hands or stamp their feet] for whom they are written; it therefore follows that *Canzoni* are to be deemed nobler than *Ballate* . . .

Dante's attitude towards these *ballate* suggests that of his English emulator, the author of *The Art of English Poesie*, towards the 'Carols and rounds and such light or lasciuious Poemes' and other 'small and popular Musickes' which are the concern of strolling singers.[2] Unfortunately Dante's treatise breaks off before it has taken up the *ballata* in detail.

There is no difficulty, however, in recognizing the *ballata* as a product of folk-song and folk-dance, with a form resulting from the physical conditions of performance and not from mere literary convention. Rising and flourishing in central Italy, it was independent of the arts of the early Sicilian school of verse, and, although it came to be employed by the most sophisticated poets, it still kept its place as a vehicle of popular, *volkstümliche*, song.[3]

The oldest and fundamental rhyme-scheme of the *ballata* was the following:

B B (*ritornello*) a a a b (stanza) B B (*rit.*), etc.[4]

This is obviously identical with that of the French 'primitive dance-song' and of many English carols. Flamini quotes an example of such an early *ballata*, which he calls 'coarsely plebeian':

(*Rit.*)   Pur bèi del vin, comadre, e no lo temperare:
           ché lo vin è forte, la testa fa scaldare.

[1] Lib. II, cap. iii: 'Adhuc: quicquid per se ipsum efficit illud ad quod factum est, nobilius esse videtur quam quod extrinseco indiget: sed cantiones per se totum quod debent efficiunt, quod ballate non faciunt (indigent enim plausoribus, ad quos edite sunt); ergo cantiones nobiliores ballatis esse sequitur extimandas...' ed. Pio Rajna, (Florence, 1896), pp. 45–6. The translation is that of A. G. Ferrers Howell, *Dante's Treatise 'De Vulgari Eloquentia'* (London, 1890), p. 53.

[2] George Puttenham [?], ed. Gladys Doidge Willcock and Alice Walker (Cambridge, 1936], pp. 83–4.

[3] Gaspary, Adolf, *Geschichte der italienischen Literatur* (Berlin, 1885), i. 93. An interesting and important discussion of the relation of carole and *ballata* occurs in Angeline H. Lograsso, 'From the *Ballata* of the *Vita Nuova* to the Carols of the *Paradiso*', *Eighty-third Annual Report of the Dante Society* (Cambridge, Mass., 1965), pp. 23–48.

[4] Francesco Flamini, *Notizia Storica dei Versi e Metri italiani* (Livorno, 1919), p. 24

(St. 1)   Gièrnosen le comadri 'ntrambe ad una masone,
            cercòr del vin sotile se l'era de sasone,
            bèvenon cinque barili et erano desone,
            et un quartier de retro per bocca savorare.
(*Rit.*)   Pur bèi del vin, comadre, e no lo temperare:
            ché lo vin è forte, la testa fa scaldare.
            (etc.)[1]

From this beginning in popular song the *ballata* grew, under the hands of cultivated poets, including Gerolamo Savonarola, into a number of longer and more elaborate forms, all of which retained, however (as the French *ballade* did not), the burden external to the stanza, the *ripresa*.[2] The simple four-line stanza with two-line burden, as above, was retained with especial frequency in the Italian lyrics known as *laude*, which, in their association of religious praise with the language and song-measures of the common people, so much resemble the English religious carol.[3] Of the 102 pieces ascribed to the greatest of all writers of *laude*, Fra Jacopone da Todi,[4] 92 are cast in one form or another of the *ballata*,[5] and of these 47 exhibit the fundamental scheme B B a a a b B B, etc.,[6] either with short lines or with long lines divided by a caesura (and rhyming a–b a–b a–b b–c, etc.) as in *Lauda* xcviii:

            Amor, tu m'hai creata—per la tua cortesia,
            ma so villana stata—per la mia gran follia,
            fuor de la mia contrata—smarrita aggio la via,
            la vergine Maria—me torni all'amor mio.
            (etc.)[7]

The persistence of this type of stanza, the foundation of which is three lines rhyming together, may be explained, in the *laude* as in songs of the other languages, by regarding them as written for airs constructed on the model of popular dance-tunes, if not for such dance-tunes themselves. For such a stanza-form grew naturally out of a type of dance with a thrice-

[1] Loc. cit.

[2] A *ballata* fell into one of several categories according to the number of lines in this *ripresa*, as follows: one hendecasyllable, *piccola*, one septenary, *minima*, two lines, *minore*, three lines, *mezzana*, four lines, *grande*, more than four lines, *stravagante* (ibid., pp. 27–8).

[3] See below, pp. cxlix–cl. A good account of the similarities and differences of English carol and Italian *lauda* is the contribution of John Stevens to a symposium of the Tenth Congress of the International Musicological Society at Ljubljana, Yugoslavia, in 1967. It is published in the *Report* of the Congress, ed. Dragotin Cvetko (Basel, Paris, London, Ljubljana, 1970), pp. 207–9. On the *lauda* itself David

L. Jeffrey offers a valuable and comprehensive chapter, 'The Earliest Lyrics in Italy', in *The Early English Lyric and Franciscan Spirituality* (Lincoln, Nebraska, 1975), pp. 118–68.

[4] In the edition of the *Laude* by Giovanni Ferri (Bari, 1915).

[5] Those not in *ballata* form are Nos. xxii, xliii, xlvii, lvi, lxiii, lxix, lxxi, lxxx, lxxxviii, xcv.

[6] Nos. ii, iii, viii, xi, xii, xv, xvi, xvii, xviii, xix, xx, xxi, xxiii, xxv, xxviii, xxix, xxxii, xxxiii, xxxvi, xxxviii, xlv, xlvi, xlviii, li, lii, liii, liv, lv, lviii, lix, lx, lxii, lxviii, lxx, lxxii, lxxv, lxxviii, lxxix, lxxxi, lxxxiv, lxxxv, lxxxvi, lxxxix, xciii, xcvii, xcviii, c.

[7] Ferri, op. cit., p. 242, stanza 1.

repeated movement. A verse for such song would require three lines to the same musical phrase, and hence rhyming,[1] plus a line corresponding to the coda of the music and giving, by its new rhyme, a cue to the chorus, whose burden would end with this new rhyme. The songs to which the young people of Boccaccio's *Decameron* dance for recreation have the *ballata* structure of initial burden and stanzas which give a cue for the burden by rhyme or by ending with the first word of the burden, for example, the songs of the first and second days: 'Lauretta having thus made an end of her ballad, in the burden of which all had blithely joined . . . divers other rounds were danced and a part of the short night being spent, it pleased the queen to give an end to the first day.'[2]

The dominance of this type of stanza in the English carol indicates that the genre may properly be regarded as the English representative of a European family of lyric forms originating in the carole or a round dance very much like it. The corresponding type in French is the *chanson à danser* with a burden (in its courtly development, the *virelai*); in Provençal the *ballada*, in Italian the *ballata*, in German one type of *Reigenlied*. That direct influence was exerted on the English song by the French may be taken for granted; there must have been many a popular dance-song of which 'the note, I trowe, maked was in Fraunce'. Immediate influence from Italy or Germany is inherently less likely, but further investigation will be needed to justify a positive statement. If the same type of round dance was established in all these countries, there is no reason why an analogous but independent process in each should not have given to the language the lyric types which have just been discussed.

In the language of sixteenth-century Scotland the word 'carol' usually keeps the long-established meaning of 'dance accompanied by song', and its frequent association with the word 'ring' shows that a dance in a carole is definitely referred to. Gavin Douglas uses it thus in his translation of the *Aeneid* in telling of Queen Amata's ecstatic worship of Bacchus (translating 'choro'):

> To the scho led ryng sang*is* in caralyng.[3]

And again he writes of the Trojan horse (translating 'sacra canunt funemque manu contingere gaudent'):

> And *th*arabout ran child*er and* madis 3yng
> Syngand karrellis *and* dansand in a ryng.[4]

---

[1] The principle that in Old French lyrics derived from the dance rhyming lines were generally sung to the same musical phrase is demonstrated by Friedrich Gennrich, *Musikwissenschaft und romanischen Philologie* (Halle a/S., 1918).

[2] *The Decameron of Giovanni Boccaccio*, trans. John Payne (New York, n.d.), p. 79.

[3] Book VII, cap. vi, l. 115, ed. David F. C. Coldwell (S.T.S., 3rd Ser., No. 27, iii, 1959, 88).

[4] Book II, cap. iv, ll. 69–70, ibid. ii, 1957, 77.

He also gives us the phrase 'to lead the ring' for the action of the person who directs a *carole* (translating 'pedibus plaudunt choreas'):

> As forto dansyng, and to leid *th*e ryng,
> To syng ballat*is*, and go in karalyng.[1]

That this form of song was actually sung in a round dance in New England in 1627 by the wifeless young men of New Canaan appears in Thomas Morton's account of the famous maypole of Merrymount (Ma-re Mount):

There was likewise a merry song made, which, (to make their Revells more fashionable,) was sung with a Corus, every man bearing his part; which they performed in a daunce, hand in hand about the Maypole, whiles one of the Company sung and filled out the good liquor, like gammedes and Iupiter.

THE SONGE.

Cor. Drinke and be merry, merry, merry boyes;
　　　Let all your delight be in the Hymens ioyes;

[burden] Jô to Hymen, now the day is come,
　　　　　About the merry Maypole take a Roome.

[stza. 1] Make greene garlons, bring bottles out
　　　　　And fill sweet Nectar freely about.
　　　　　Vncover thy head and feare no harme,
　　　　　For hers good liquor to keepe it warme.

[burden] Then drinke and be merry, &c.
　　　　　Iô to Hymen, &c.
　　　　　　　[etc., 4 stzas. in all].

This harmeles mirth . . . was much distasted of the precise Separatists, that keepe much a doe about the tyth of M[i]nt and Cummin . . .[2]

2. *The Carol and the Ballad*

The carol is not the only genre of English poetry for which an ultimate origin in the dance has been claimed. The traditional narrative ballad has often been regarded as a development from folk-song associated with communal dancing. The obvious derivation of the word 'ballad' itself from the late Latin verb 'ballare' has leant much strength to this theory. That narrative ballads have been danced to in Scandinavian countries is known, and in particular the survivals of the practice in the Faroe Islands have been frequently referred to by writers on ballad-origins.[3] In recent years there has

---

[1] Book VI, cap. x, ll. 39–40, ibid. iii. 42.

[2] Thomas Morton, *The New English Canaan of Thomas Morton*, ed. Charles Francis Adams, Jr., The Publications of the Prince Society, Boston, 1883, pp. 279–80.

[3] See Johannes C. H. R. Steenstrup, *The Medieval Popular Ballad*, trans. Edward Godfrey Cox (Boston, 1914), chap. ii; Gummere, *Beginnings*, *passim*, *Old English Ballads*, introduction, *passim*.

been a marked increase in scepticism about the association of dance and ballad in England and Scotland. F. Liebermann maintained that it had not been proved that ballads were so sung in England, and that, on the contrary, the English dance was accompanied only by instrumental music.[1] Louise Pound was a strong opponent of theories connecting dance and ballad.[2] The many American and Canadian survivals of the ballads of the British Isles which have been collected and studied in the last three decades are overwhelmingly instances of solo singing without any dancing by either singer or audience, and the opinion that this was the older as well as the modern method of presenting ballads has put the older view of the ballad as dance-song into almost total eclipse. This evolution has naturally accompanied the rise to dominance of the belief in composition by an individual author rather than by any communal process. But some of the circumstances in the background of the carol which have been considered here have also been studied by workers on the ballad and interpreted this way or that according to the particular theory in support of which they have been invoked. There has also been a considerable confusion of ballad and carol, due to the use of the latter term to designate any Christmas poem, which has led to its being applied to such unquestionable ballads as Nos. 22, 54, 55 in Child's collection and the more recently authenticated folk-ballad 'The Bitter Withy'.[3] Plainly a clear distinction between ballad and carol and a formulation of the relation, if any, between them is of service for the understanding of both genres. An attempt at such a distinction is made here.[4]

The three principal points of difference between the pieces in Child's *English and Scottish Popular Ballads* and those here collected concern method of transmission, narrative quality, and metrical form. The ballad is by definition a narrative poem: with those combinations of ellipsis and repetition which characterize its peculiar style, it tells a tale and there makes an end. The interest is in the tale; none is diverted to the emotions of the teller or of his hearers, or to his relations with them. The objectivity of the ballad is one of the touchstones of its authenticity. Now neither complete objectivity nor narrative content is essential or even usual in the carol, although both may be present. Nor are the carols the product, like the ballads and all other true folk-song, of a sustained process of oral transmission. These contrasts are dealt with in more detail in Chapter IV, below. The third point of difference, that of metrical form, commands attention here because it may be regarded as a reflection of a difference between the respective backgrounds

---

[1] 'Zu Liedrefrain und Tanz im englischen Mittelalter', *Archiv für das Studium der neueren Sprachen*, cxl (1920), 261–2.

[2] *Poetic Origins and the Ballad* (New York, 1921), pp. 67–86; 'The Ballad and the Dance', *PMLA*, xxxiv (1919), 360–400.

[3] See the article on this ballad by Gordon

H. Gerould in *PMLA*, xxiii (1908), 141–67.

[4] Eric Routley's chapter entitled 'The Ballad Carol' in his work *The English Carol* (London, 1958) tends on the whole to dim rather than illuminate the distinction, though the whole book has much in it that is lively and stimulating.

of ballad and carol. It argues a difference between the type of dance associated with the early narrative poetry of England and Scotland, and that
associated with the more purely lyric poetry represented by the carol. The
key to the distinction lies in that important member, the burden.

The burden characteristic of the carol-form is a line or group of lines,
most often a couplet, repeated after every stanza, often linked to the stanza
by rhyme, but essentially independent of and external to it. Such a burden
or any part of it does not ordinarily appear *within a stanza*, although one
of the burden-lines will often be found as the *last* line of a stanza, as a refrain.[1]
The carol, then, consists of an alternation of two organic units, stanza and
burden, the first changing its text, the second invariable.

The ballads, or rather some of the ballads, also include in their structure
repeated choral elements, the ballad-refrains, about which much has been
written. Whatever its historical importance, the refrain is not the essential
feature of the extant ballads that the burden is of the extant carols. Of the
1,250 ballad-versions in Child's collection, only about 300, or less than
a fourth, are provided with refrains.[2] Whether all ballads originally had
refrains or not is an arguable question; the important thing for the present
discussion is that the refrains which are preserved are almost invariably of
one type, and that a type different from the carol-burden. The characteristic
arrangement of stanza-text and refrain in the English ballad is one of alternating lines: a line of narrative text, then a refrain-line; another line of
narration, then another refrain-line, different from the first, but often
rhyming with it. For example:

> Ae king's dochter said to anither,
> *Broom blooms bonnie an grows sae fair*
> We'll gae ride like sister and brither.
> *But we'll neer gae down to the brume nae mair*[3]

This form may be expanded by repetition, as in 'The Three Ravens', but
the same principle persists, of a choral element introduced at two or more
separate points in the stanza and actually forming part of the organic structure of the stanza itself:

> There were three rauens sat on a tree,
> *Downe a downe, hay down, hay downe*
> There were three rauens sat on a tree,
> *With a downe*

---

[1] The only exceptions to this rule are to be found in Nos. 189, 204, 285, all the work of James Ryman, a conscious experimenter with verse-forms, in No. 117, where the influence of the learned music is responsible, and in Nos. 44, 180, 446, 461, 461.1.

[2] Friedrich G. Ruhrmann, *Studien zur Geschichte und Charakteristik des Refrains in der englischen Literatur* (Anglistische Forschungen, Heft 64, Heidelberg, 1927), p. 16.

[3] Child, No. 16 D, stanza 1.

> There were three rauens sat on a tree,
> They were as blacke as they might be.
> *With a downe derrie, derrie, derrie, downe, downe*[1]

This sort of choral element, which I call a refrain inasmuch as it forms part of the stanza, is found in folk-song of other countries. The Danish medieval ballad sometimes uses it, although less often than the refrain at the end of a stanza.[2] It marks the delightful little French *chanson* 'En passant par la Lorraine':

> En passant par la Lorraine
> *Avec mes sabots,*
> Ils m'ont appelé vilaine,
> *Avec mes sabots dondaine,*
> *oh, oh, oh!*
> *Avec mes sabots.*[3]

It appears to have been a common arrangement in songs of ring-dances in Germany, as in the old May-game song of monk and nun:

> Et ging en Paterke langs de Kant
> *Hei, 'twas in de Mei!*
> He nahm en Nönneke bei de Hand.
> *Hei 'twas in de Mei, Mei, Mei,*
> *hei, 'twas in de Mei.*[4]

Another German example is a religious parody of an older secular dance-song:

> Solo: Wolt ir hörn ein news gedicht?
> Chorus: *das singen wir euch mit frewden,*
> Solo: was Gott an uns hat ausgericht,
> Chorus: *das singen wir euch und springen auf mit frewden.*[5]

But, as already noted, this manner of inserting refrain-lines between lines of stanza-text is all but unknown in the English carol.

Nor, on the other hand, is the burden of the type external to the stanza to be met with in the English ballads, except in rare instances. In a text of 'The Elfin Knight' taken from a seventeenth-century broadside such a burden appears superadded to a refrain of the ordinary ballad-type:[6]

> (Burden)   My plaid awa, my plaid awa,
>   And ore the hill and far awa,
>   And far awa to Norrowa,
>   My plaid shall not be blown awa.

---

[1] Child, No. 26, stanza 1.
[2] Johannes C. H. R. Steenstrup, *The Medieval Popular Ballad*, trans. Edward Godfrey Cox, University of Washington Publications in English (Boston, 1914), p. 31, Nos. 129, 146; p. 81.
[3] Gérold, *Chansons populaires*, p. 79, stanza 1.
[4] Böhme, *Geschichte des Tanzes*, ii. 196, stanza 1.

[5] Ibid. ii. 11.
[6] Child, No. 2 A. For full discussion of the variants of this ballad see Bertrand H. Bronson, *The Traditional Tunes of the Child Ballads*, i (Princeton, 1959), 9–16. He has elsewhere effectively demonstrated that the burden in this version is a late addition of no organic relation to the narrative text (*The Ballad as Song*, Berkeley, California, 1969, pp. 257–9).

(Stanza 1) 　　　　　　The elphin knight sits on yon hill,
　　　　　　　　　　　　Ba, ba, ba, lilli ba
　　　　　　　　　　　He blaws his horn both lowd and shril.
　　　　　　　　　　　　The wind hath blown my plaid awa
　　　　　　　　　　　　　(etc.)

In one text of 'Captain Car' a burden of the same form as the ballad stanza is associated with stanzas having no refrain:[1]

(Stanza 1) 　　　　　　　It befell at Martynmas,
　　　　　　　　　　　　　When wether waxed colde,
　　　　　　　　　　　Captaine Care said to his men,
　　　　　　　　　　　　We must go take a holde.

(Burden) 　　　　　　　Syck, sike, and to-towe sike,
　　　　　　　　　　　　And sike and like to die;
　　　　　　　　　　　The sikest nighte that euer I abode,
　　　　　　　　　　　　God lord haue mercy on me!
　　　　　　　　　　　　　(etc.)

But throughout Child's texts only about one in sixty can show a burden of this external type.[2]

It is hardly possible that this almost complete mutual exclusiveness is the result of chance. It indicates rather that there existed two sharply differentiated forms of choral element, one of which was definitely associated with the ballad, while the other was as definitely associated with the carol (and the popular prototypes of the carol). The difference implies different methods of performance in a dance or game, both forms of song being found labelled *Reihetanz* or *Ringeltanz* in German. It is a two-part refrain inserted into a stanza, and not a carol-burden, which Fabyan reports as made and sung in the round dances of the North after Bannockburn:

Than the Scottis enflamyd with pryde, in derysyon of Englysshe men, made this ryme as foloweth.

　　　　　　　Maydens of Englonde, sore maye ye morne.
　　　　　　　For your lemmans ye haue loste at Bannockisborne,
　　　　　　　　With heue a lowe.
　　　　　　　What wenyth the kynge of Englonde,
　　　　　　　So soone to haue wonne Scotlande
　　　　　　　　With rumbylowe.

This songe was after many dayes sungyn, in daunces, in carolis of ye maydens

---

[1] Child, No. 178 A. Bronson has likewise an important note on this ballad which indicates that the burden here appears to have been casually borrowed from another piece, perhaps along with a borrowed air. Thus this text also appears to be a 'sport' of no historical significance for verse-form (op. cit. iii, 1966, 156).

[2] It is found in Nos. 2 A, 44 (two different burdens; another is probably lost), 82 (burden becoming stanza 11), 110 K, 115, 178 A, 192, 200 J, 209 E, 217 M, 222 D, 231 B, D, E, 289 B, C, D, E, 299 A. See Gordon H. Gerould, *The Ballad of Tradition* (Oxford, 1932), pp 122–4.

& mynstrellys of Scotlande, to the reproofe and dysdayne of Englysshe men, w[i]t[h] dyuerse other which I ouer passe.[1]

Unreliable though Fabyan may be, this passage is one of the few bits of external evidence actually connecting a given early English song-text with the dance. It does not matter much if the song be considerably later than Bannockburn, or even of Fabyan's own time, about 1500. The refrain is one which has persisted in popular song into modern times.[2] It is to be found in a narrative song printed in *The Forsaken Lover's Garland* (Newcastle [?], 1750 [?]):

> 'Tis of a ragged beggar man, came tripping o'er the plain,
> He came unto a farmer's door, a lodging good to gain.
> *Rom-below, zin-garee, Rom-be-low, below-below.*[3]

Fabyan does not win our thanks for 'ouer passing' the 'dyuerse other'.

It is plain that it would be no difficult matter to adapt a song cast in one of the two characteristic patterns, ballad or carol, to fit music and action associated with the other. This would be particularly easy in the case of a song in two-line stanzas: the couplet would be sung continuously and followed by a burden in the one case, and in the other divided by the insertion of refrain-lines. Just this variation is shown by some texts of traditional folk-song recently collected in the United States. The two illustrations which follow are selected from versions taken down in the Appalachian Mountains by the late Cecil Sharp. The first comprises two variants of 'The Golden Vanity'. One of these has the inserted refrain, as in Child's versions:

> There was a ship sailed from the North Amerikee,
> *Crying O the lonesome lowlands low,*
> There was a ship sailed from the North Amerikee,
> And she went by the name of the Green Willow Tree,
> *And she sailed from the Lowlands Low.*[4]

But another singer gave it thus, with an external burden (for which the tempo was changed):

> There was a ship a-sailing on the North Amerikee,
> And it went by the name of the Green Willow Tree.
>
> Sailing O the lonesome lowland low,
> So level lands so low.[5]

[1] Robert Fabyan, *The New Chronicles of England and France* (London, 1811, after Pynson's edition of 1516), p. 420.

[2] See Gummere, *Beginnings*, p. 274.

[3] Reprinted by Sabine Baring-Gould and H. Fleetwood Sheppard, eds., *A Garland of Country Song* (London, 1895), p. 53.

[4] Sharp's No. 3968, from MS. *Songs Collected in the Southern Appalachian Mountains*, rotograph copy. Child, No. 286.

[5] Sharp's No. 3909 in MS., No. 41 F in *English Folk Songs from the Southern Appalachians* (London, 1932), i. 288.

The same difference is to be observed between two variants of 'The Farmer's Curst Wife':[1]

> An old man went to the field to plough,
> *Te ole dum diddle dum day,*
> Along comes an old devil, peeps over his horse,
> *Te ole dum diddle dum day.*

> There was an old man who lived under the hill,
> If he ain't moved out he's living there still.
>> Sing dow, dow, diddle a diddle,
>> Sing dow a diddle, a diddle a day.

It is improbable that these variants, recorded in the same section of the country, preserve faithfully two distinct arrangements of the song, each of considerable antiquity. They show rather, that in the oral tradition in which they are now preserved, unconnected with the dance, the change from one form to the other is made without compunction.[2] But, as the comparison of the earlier recorded texts of Child and of the manuscript carols indicates, such a change was not common in the late Middle Ages, the heyday of the carol and the time of the earlier records of the ballad.

Something of the kind has apparently been attempted with two pieces preserved in manuscripts containing numerous carols. One is No. 322 A, the famous 'Corpus Christi Carol', which is conspicuous among the few pieces written in carol form in a manuscript earlier than 1550 and also preserved in oral tradition and recorded by modern collectors of folk-song. It is also one of the few carols with a stanza of two short, four-accent lines.[3] The manuscript text shows clearly that the burden was to be sung first in regulation carol fashion.

(Burden)	Lully, lulley; lully, lulley; The fawcon hath born my mak away.
(Stanza 1)	He bare hym vp, he bare hym down; He bare hym into an orchard brown.
(Burden)	Lully, lulley; lully, lulley; The fawcon hath born my mak away
(Stanza 2)	In that orchard ther was an hall, That was hangid with purpill and pall.

---

[1] Sharp's No. 3889 in MS., No. 40 E, op. cit. i. 279. Child, No. 278. Sharp's No. 3580 in MS., No. 40 D, op. cit. i. 278.

[2] Joseph W. Hendren has very kindly communicated to me the interesting fact that in the variant texts of ballads collected since Child's activity the alternating refrain is much less frequent and the end-refrain (not always easy to distinguish from an external burden) more so. Mr. Hendren suggests that end-refrains may more often have been disregarded by the earlier ballad-collectors.

[3] The others are Nos. 449, 463.

(Burden)
Lully, lulley; lully, lulley;
The fawcon hath born my mak away.
(etc.)

In the three versions recorded from oral tradition in the last hundred years or so, what is recognizably the same piece appears with no burden but with a two-part refrain inserted after the manner of the ballad:

No. 322 B

(Stanza 1)
Over yonder's a park, which is newly begun,
All bells in Paradise I heard them a-ring,
Which is silver on the outside, and gold within,
And I love sweet Jesus above all things.

(Stanza 2)
And in that park there stands a hall,
All bells in Paradise I heard them a-ring,
Which is covered all over with purple and pall,
And I love sweet Jesus above all things.
(etc.)

No. 322 C

(Stanza 1)
Down in yon forest there stands a hall,
The bells of Paradise I heard them ring,
It's covered all over with purple and pall,
And I love my Lord Jesus above anything.
(etc.)

No. 322 E

(Stanza 1)
Down in yon forest be a hall,
Sing May, Queen May, sing Mary,
Its coverlidded over with purple and pall,
Sing all good men for the new-born baby.
(etc.)

The version recorded by Hogg (D) has neither burden nor refrain. The fact that the couplet stanza of this piece, while common enough in the ballads, is seldom found in carols, suggests that the traditional versions really preserve an older form of the song, which was adapted by the addition of a 'lullay' burden, quite probably topical, to be sung as a carol.[1]

Some attempt at adaptation of ballad to carol may be responsible for the rather puzzling piece 'Robyn and Gandelyn'.[2] The poem occurs only in the Sloane MS., which is composed for the most part of regular carols but also contains the ballad of 'St. Stephen and Herod'.[3] The line 'Robynn lyth in grene wode bowndyn', which Child takes to be a burden, is written at the

[1] There is no evidence to support the statement of David C. Fowler that 'The first line of refrain or burden in the A text, in fact, suggests that the song was originally conceived as a "lullaby" carol, traditionally associated with Christmas from time immemorial' (*A Literary History of the Popular Ballad*, Durham, N.C., 1968, p. 61). See the fuller discussion of No. 322 in the Notes. [2] Child, No. 115.
[3] British Museum, MS. Sloane 2593.

very beginning and again at the very end of the piece, but its repetition a
any point is not indicated. If the line was intended as a burden, the piece
could, of course, be sung as a carol, but the narrative content and style, and
its use of the ballad-stanza with first and third lines unrhymed, mark it as
not a carol by origin. The scribe apparently recognized its unlikeness to its
companion poems, for it is the only one in the entire manuscript written
as prose and not marked off into stanzas.

However the evidence of these two pieces may be interpreted, it does
appear that, in the days when the dance and its song had recently parted
company, there was a reluctance to make the change in a given song from
one manner of singing to another. Roughly, the external burden is associated
with songs of a lyric nature, the inserted refrain with narrative. In view
of the extent to which the carole has been seen to condition the form of songs
to which it was danced, is it too much to infer that the ballad with internal
refrain derives from a social dance of a different character, the details of
which still await discovery? There may be an important clue to such a difference in the account of Scottish schoolgirls' singing games set down by
Willa Muir from her own experience. In addition to the games that involved
ring-dances essentially the same as the medieval caroles there were dramatic
games based on rapidly alternating dialogue between 'mothers' and 'daughters'. In these Mrs. Muir records: '. . . we did not seclude ourselves in a dancing
ring; we linked arms in two lines that faced each other, advancing and re-
treating with a processional dancing step, a formation that could be called
the classical embodiment of two opposing forces.'[1]

The tendency of the northern part of the island to preserve both the
custom of dancing in a round to a sung accompaniment and the stanzaic
song with an initial burden associated with such dancing is even stronger on
the Scottish side of the border. Caroles and their songs certainly abounded in
medieval Scotland. There are many references to them, although there are
few preserved texts.

Of pre-Reformation poems in carol form and in Scots we have but three,
two of them by Dunbar. One of Dunbar's is occasional and personal, his
plea to the King for a holiday gift of new clothing, its burden repeating
after each stanza its initial request:

> Schir, lett it nevir in toun be tald
> That I suld be an Yuillis yald.[2]

The other is in the full medieval tradition of moralizing on the contrast of
age and youth and of fleshly and spiritual love with another couplet burden
that bears the required repetition very well:

> Now cumis aige quhair yewth hes bene,
> And trew luve rysis from the splene.[3]

---

[1] *Living with Ballads* (New York, 1965),
pp. 20–1.

[2] No. 121.1.
[3] No. 330.1.

The third is another begging carol, for the New Year, by William Stewart, the tireless translator of Hector Boece's history of Scotland.[1] It is wittily satirical at the expense of the penurious great ones of the court and must have been circulated with discretion at the time of its writing. But surely Scotland knew many others, for we find one by Sir Richard Maitland no later than 1559 which has all the speed and lilt of the best medieval carols:

> In this new 3eir I sie bot weir,
>   Na caus to sing;
> In this new 3eir I sie but weir,
>   Na caus thair is to sing.

> I can not sing for þe vexatioun
> Of Frenchemen and the congregatioun,
> That hes maid trowbill in this natioun
> And mony baire biging.[2]

The Catholic Church in Scotland had the same problem with secular song and dance that troubled English and continental churches, and it adopted the same attitude of opposition. This situation is established beyond question by two passages in the *Catechism* of 1552 issued by John Hamilton, Archbishop of St. Andrews and a staunch papist until his death on the gallows in 1571. The most significant injunction comes under the head of the 'Third Command':

And abone all this, all men and wemen with delegens, nocht only suld forbeir vice and syn on the Sunday and all other dayis, bot specially on the sunday, suld eschew all ydilnes, vaine talking, bakbyting, sclandering, blasphemation of the name of God, and contentioun and also all occasions of syn, as dansyng, unnecesarie drinking, wantones, lecherous sangis and tweching, hurdome, cartyng and dysing, and specially carreling and wanton synging in the kirk, and all uthir vice quhilk commonly has bein maist usit on the sunday.[3]

The Protestant reformers found the caroles of song and dance together, which they regarded as lingering remnants of papistry, quite as difficult to extirpate as had the Catholic Church in earlier times and in more southerly lands. The association, real or supposed, of the carole and its songs with sexual misbehaviour appears to have been as strong in the new order of religion in Scotland as in the old. Abundant evidence is given in the highly interesting documents published by Anna Jean Mill in her *Mediaeval Plays in Scotland*. The authorities were certainly vigorous in their attempts to put down the abuse. In 1574, according to the Aberdeen Kirk Session

---

[1] No. 121.2.

[2] [Sir] W. A. Craigie, ed., *The Maitland Quarto Manuscript*, S.T.S., New Ser. ix, 1920, 26, burden and stanza 1, capitalization and punctuation supplied.

[3] Ed. T. G. Law (Oxford, 1884), p. 68, quoted in part by Anna Jean Mill, *Mediaeval Plays in Scotland* (Edinburgh and London, 1927), p. 86.

Records, fourteen women were charged with 'plaing, dansin and singin off fylthe carrolles on Yeull Day, at evin, and on Sunday, at even, thaireafter'.[1] At Haddington in 1588 an 'obligation' of the Provost, Bailies, and Council was made for the proper observance of Sundays:

> also to abolische and remoue the *con*uenementis of superstitious Observation of festuall dais callit of 3ule pasche witsonday and the pasche of maj plaijs of robe*n* hude litle Iohne abitis of vnresoun setting furth of banefyris singing of carrell*is* wi*th*in or about the kirk or ellis at *c*ertane seasonis of the 3eir togith[er] w*ith* geving of anie significatioun of the fostering þair*of* in apperell or banketting but specially in dais dedicate in time of papestrie to sanctis sumtimes namit patronis . . .[2]

The parish of Errol was even fiercer in its attitude, as an unfortunate sinner named Thomas Loony discovered a few days after the Christmas of 1593:

> Comperit tho loony being su*m*monit for singing off carrellis at þe thornes, and confessing his offence pr*o*misit amendement. It is ordanit þat carrelleris in all tym cu*m*ing be punissit as fornicatou*r*is.[3]

That the carols about which there was such concern included the round dance is made plain by another action taken at Errol a little over a year later on 8 February 1594/5, when two men and four women confessed 'þair going about in ringis and carrelling vpon þe day callit 3oull day And allegit þaj knew no *comma*nd aganis it. Promising to absten in tymes cu*m*ing.'[4] Even as late as 1618 the Kirk Session of Elgin was still struggling with the problem:

> Insolenceis—It is ordenit that the superstitious obseruation of auld reitis and ceremoneis expresly forbidden during the tyme callit Yool that they be altogidder awodit and eschewit, viz. that na persoun within burgh or landward within this parosche pas in gwysing, dansing, singing carallis, play at the fut ball, throch the town, nor about the Chanonrie kirk and kirkyeard, nather wemen to be cled in mens apparrell nor men in womens apparrell, casting of snaw ballis, hurling with stoolis in the streitis . . .[5]

Nevertheless the change in the usual meaning of the word 'carol' from 'dance and song' to 'song for Christmas' takes place in Scotland as in England, though later, and, as any celebration of the holiday comes more firmly under ban, the word comes to be avoided altogether. The change can be conveniently illustrated from no less distinguished a source than the *Gude and Godly Ballatis*. A piece which in the 1567 edition is headed 'Followis ane carrell contrair Idolatrie' appears in the editions of 1578 and 1621 with the word 'carrell' changed to 'Sang', and the piece next after it, headed in 1567 'Ane Carrell of the Epistill on Zule Euin', appears in the same two later editions as 'Ane Ballat of the Epistill on [omitted 1621] Christinmes Euin'.[6]

[1] Mill, op. cit., p. 162.
[2] Ibid., p. 253.
[3] Ibid., p. 243.
[4] Loc. cit.
[5] Ibid., p. 242.
[6] *A Compendious Book of Godly and Spiritual Songs*, ed. A. F. Mitchell, S.T.S., No. 39, 1897, pp. 71, 72.

In spite of this changing usage of the word 'carol' both the medieval verse-form and the practice of circulating religious parody of widely known secular song are very much alive in the Scotland of the later sixteenth century. The two are combined in the 'spiritualized' version of the extremely popular 'Go from my window', a song known in a variety of forms and still to be heard in the twentieth century in the folk-song 'Go 'way from my window'. The burden (not recognized as such by the Scottish Text Society editors) goes:

> Quho is at my windo, quho, quho?
> Go from my windo, go, go.
> Quha callis thair, sa lyke ane stranger,
>   Go from my windo, go.[1]

The form of the stanzas, the regular a a a b of the carols without the internal rhyme of the third line of the burden, and the pious temper of the long composition can be shown by the first stanza:

> Lord I am heir, ane wratcheit mortall,
> That for thy mercy dois cry and call,
> Unto thé my Lord Celestiall,
>   Sé quho is at my windo, quho.

Another carol in the *Ballatis* with a couplet burden obviously from a secular song (this one not identified elsewhere) and couplet-rhymed stanzas shows the same survivals from medieval practice:

> Till our gud man, till our gud man,
> Keip faith and lufe, till our gud man.

> For our gude man in heuin dois regne
> In gloir and blis without ending,
> Quhar Angellis singis euer *Osan*
> In laude and pryse of our gude man.[2]

The Aberdeen *Cantus, Songs and Fancies* of 1662, the first book of secular music printed in Scotland, presents no carols along with its ayres and other pieces showing English and Italian influence. But more than a hundred years later, in the collecting and editing of old songs by Robert Burns for the two Edinburgh publishers John Johnson and George Thomson, we are able to see the clear evidence that the old medieval carol-form had lived on in Scotland as it had largely failed to do in the South. Kenneth Elliott and Helena Mennie Shire, the editors of *Music of Scotland 1500–1700*, state the matter succinctly:

The 'native air' of lowland Scotland, a rich tradition of dance-song drawing on Celtic and Scandinavian influences, was enjoyed at all levels of society during these

---

[1] Ibid., pp. 132–3.   [2] Ibid., p. 198.

two hundred years, but it touches written record only fleetingly in the sixteenth century. Later it is delicately and vigorously recorded for instrumental playing, for lute, cittern, keyboard, lyra-viol and fiddle. . . .

[About 1700] The older music is in eclipse, the native air is in fashion.

For more than two hundred years this wealth of folk-music nourished a live tradition of song-writing, and it came to be claimed that the idiom of the 'native air' was the sole music of Scotland. Today, though interest in the music of the dance is vigorously pursued, song-writing in Scots is withered, unrefreshed by the Lallans poets.[1]

The carol-form appears in songs which are still sung communally in dances of various kinds as well as in pieces which are for performance at the tavern table or in other situations not involving dancing. The true initial burden is frequent and often unmistakable in spite of some editors' lack of understanding of it. So accustomed are modern singers in England and the United States to the practice of singing a chorus only after stanzas that there may be some scepticism about the importance of the initial burden and even about the fact of its performance as the opening words of a song. Reliable musical records of the actual singing of humble and rustic performers are rare before the days of Cecil Sharp, and silent editorial mistreatment of initial burdens is often hard to detect. But the test of sense and syntax which can be applied in some cases would convince everyone that in Burns's Scotland the beginning of many songs with their burdens was not only customary but necessary. For example, here is one of the best known, with anonymous burden and stanzas by Burns:

> O whistle an' I'll come to ye, my lad,
> O whistle, and I'll come to ye, my lad;
> Tho' father, and mother, an' a' should gae mad,
> Thy JEANIE will venture wi' ye, my lad.

> But warily tent when ye come to court me,
> And come nae unless the back-yett be a-jee;
> Syne up the back-style, and let naebody see,
> And come as ye were na comin to me [*bis*].[2]

Or consider a slighter piece which has been only 'corrected', that is, edited and made less frank by the poet:

> The lang lad they ca' jumpin John
> Beguil'd the bonie lassie,
> The lang lad they ca' jumpin John
> Beguil'd the bonie lassie.

---

[1] Musica Britannica, xv (London, 1957), pp. xv, xviii.

[2] *The Poems and Songs of Robert Burns*, ed. James Kinsley (Oxford, 1968), ii. 700.

> Her Daddie forbad, her Minnie forbad;
>   Forbidden she wadna be:
> She wadna trow't, the browst she brew'd
>   Wad taste sae bitterlie![1]

No student of Burns's activities in collecting, editing, and imitating folk-song can suspect him of ignorance of or indifference to the actual mode of its performance among those who learned it from oral tradition. His letter of September 1793 to the publisher Thomson about the treatment to be given some twenty-five songs would by itself establish his lively concern. In another letter to Thomson written on 3 July 1795 Burns is explicit about the initial burden of 'This Is No My Ain House'; he refers to 'the first, or chorus part of the tune'.[2]

This survival into the nineteenth century of the carol-form with initial burden cannot be dismissed as a phenomenon of south-west Scotland alone, as is made clear, not only by Burns's own travel and collecting of songs from other parts, but also by Peter Buchan's *Ancient Ballads and Songs of the North of Scotland Hitherto Unpublished*, which appeared at Edinburgh in 1828. In a manuscript of Buchan's which lies behind the printed collection (British Museum MS. Addit. 29408) there are a number of songs in this form, some of them variants of songs used by Burns, such as 'Hey, Tuttie, Tattie'. The burden and first stanza of a drinking-song of Buchan's will provide an example, independent of Burns, of the necessity of the burden's coming first:

> Up in the morning, up in the morning,
>   Up in the morning early;
> Frae night till morn our squires they sat,
>   And drank the juice o' the barley.

> Some they spent but ae hauf crown,
>   An some six crowns sae rarely;
> In the alewife's pouch the siller did clink
>   She got in the morning early.[3]

It is plain that the Middle English carol-form, derived from dance-song and in places still used to accompany the dance itself, though almost completely merged in the south of England into a generalized mass of stanzaic

---

[1] Ibid. i. 388. Kinsley prints the 'chorus' after the first stanza.

[2] He remarks in his letter to Thomson of 19 November 1794: 'As to the chorus going first, you know it is so with "Roy's Wife" also.' *The Letters of Robert Burns*, ed. J. De Lancey Ferguson (Oxford, 1931), ii. 276. In the Oxford Edition of the *Poetical Works* (ed. J. Logie Robertson, London, 1919) some twenty-two songs retain the initial burden.

[3] f. 187ᵛ.

song, has been preserved into modern times by oral tradition north of the Border, and preserved with remarkable richness and vitality.[1] Its exploitation for Christian didactic purposes, not as widespread as in medieval England because of the Reformed Kirk's tendency to disapprove of the carol in itself, seems to have caused little diversion of its course. That the carol was so preserved, not only independently of the custom of celebrating the Nativity with song but in a society for a long time indifferent or even hostile to that custom, establishes beyond question that the 'Christmas carol' is only a specialization of and derivative from the fundamental carol genre.

It seems clear that the medieval carole lost most of its status as a courtly recreation during the later fifteenth and early sixteenth centuries, but its persistence in rustic surroundings is testified to by many Elizabethan references to ring-dances and to 'carolling' as a characteristic activity of shepherds in more or less realistic pastoral literature. The carole and its songs in fundamental form are by no means completely dead today. It has been danced by millions now alive when they were children and cheerfully unaware that they were doing something that was already venerable in the Middle Ages. The student of children's songs and games in France will find the carole flourishing. But there is no need to leave England to find it, and people whose ancestors once left England have taken it with them. The game-song of 'Looby Loo' has been sung and danced by many who will read this book. It is still known across the ocean in the rocky hill-pastures of New England. Mrs. Flanders recorded it in 1930 as sung for her by Mrs. John Anderson, once of Windsor, Vermont, in a text learned from her mother. The song has not only the barest minimum of intellectual content and the repetitive formula which are found in the most primitive songs for the *carole*, but like the burden of the cursed carollers of the eleventh century it takes what little content it has from the accompanying physical action. The first stanza goes:

> I put my right foot in,
> I put my right foot out,
> I shake it a little, a little,
> And turn myself about.

---

[1] It survives even in nineteenth-century American versions of Scottish song. One example will show how the sense of the piece requires that the burden be sung first:

(Burden) Roy's wife of Aldivalloch
          Roy's wife of Aldivalloch.
          Wat you how she cheated me,
          As I came o'er the braes of
              Balloch[?]

(Stanza 1) She vow'd she swore she
            would be mine,

She said she loe'd me best
    of any;
But ah! the fause, the fickle
    queen
She's ta'en the carle and left
    her Johnnie.
        Roy's wife, etc.

(Broadside of 1860, published by H. De Marsar, 38860 Chatham Street, New York; copy in Brown University Library, Harris Collection, S6981 v. 3, No. 176.)

All that we need to know of the other stanzas is that they successively substitute 'left foot, right hand, left hand, head, myself'. The burden is singable, if not profound:

> Oh! here we go looby low
> Here we go looby light
> Here we go looby low
> All on a Saturday night.

And here is the action which goes with the song: 'Join in circle and dance about during chorus, and then stop to put foot in and out of circle. Dance around again during chorus.'[1]

Willa Muir, a learned and sensitive student of folk-poetry, has given, in the fascinating first chapter of her *Living with Ballads*, an important account of the survival of the carole in the games of modern schoolchildren. It is interesting that in the game-songs in which she took part the Scottish girls sang English and not Scots texts.

The elder girls pushed us into place and left us to learn the words and actions. Round and round we went in a circle with joined hands, moving clockwise, till a protagonist was chosen from among the seniors and set in the middle of the ring. Then the game was under way. Here is one of them, a typical specimen. The girl in the middle sings to the dancing circle:

> 'Father, Mother, may I go?
> May I go? May I go?
> Father, Mother, may I go,
> On a cold, cold frosty morning?'
>
> .   .   .

The answer comes from the circle, still dancing round:

> 'Yes, my darling, you may go,
> You may go, you may go.
> Yes, my darling, you may go,
> On a cold, cold frosty morning.'[2]

There were no systematic collectors of game-songs or folk-songs in medieval England, or, if there were, their anthologies, unlike Richard Hill's, have not survived. The probability is that most of the pieces included in this volume were meant to be sung, at the time they were written down, much as they would be today, not in an actual dancing-ring but in a company gathered for conviviality or for religious purposes, or for both. They preserve,

---

[1] Helen Hartness Flanders and George Brown, *Vermont Folk-Songs and Ballads*, 2nd edn. (Brattleboro, Vermont, 1932), pp. 192–3. For many texts and an account of this game-song in Britain see Alice Bertha [Lady] Gomme, *The Traditional Games of England, Scotland, and Ireland* (London, 1894–8), i. 352–61.

[2] pp. 14–15. See above, p. lxxii.

however, and it is the secret of much of their charm, the atmosphere of general participation which the round dance engenders:

> Therefore euery mon that ys here
> Synge a caroll on hys manere;
> Yf he con non we schall hym lere.

The companionship of the dance remained associated with the form of verse which had the dance-song for its pattern, even when the singers no longer stepped 'hand by hand'.

CHAPTER III

THE LATIN BACKGROUND OF THE CAROL

1. *The Latin Lines of the Carols*

IN the years when the literary lyric was coming to light in the vernacular tongues of medieval Europe, there existed another important tradition of lyric poetry which must not be overlooked because of its almost complete disappearance in modern times. This was the tradition of accentual Latin verse, which had risen during the turbulent centuries from the low estate of labourer's chant or soldier's marching-song to the highest possible use, the service of God.[1] Like the other expressions of medieval Latinity, it took little heed of boundary lines or of national cultures; it shared the universality of the Church by whose servants it was mainly fostered. It could, and did, flourish undisturbed in England while the Germanic speech of the island was assimilating huge doses of Roman vocables and rhythms. There need be no surprise, therefore, in the realization that the background of the English carol includes more than the idyllic picture of maidens dancing in the daisy fields, and that a place is claimed by the cloistered scriptorium and the flagstoned choir.

The most obvious point of contact between the carol and medieval Latin poetry is to be found in the scraps of actual Latin with which the carol-texts are so plentifully larded. English poetry, at least, has no other province in which macaronic construction plays so large, so earnest, and so happy a part. Of the 502 carols here collected, 210 include Latin lines or phrases.[2] With a few exceptions,[3] the carols in this large group are of religious or moral content, and the Latin which they contain is naturally for the most part in the idiom of the Church. If, instead of being dismissed with a word or

---

[1] For three important histories of medieval Latin poetry see F. J. E. Raby, *A History of Christian-Latin Poetry* (Oxford, 1927) and *A History of Secular Latin Poetry in the Middle Ages*, 2nd edn. (Oxford, 1957), and Peter Dronke, *Medieval Latin and the Rise of European Love-Lyric*, 2nd edn. (Oxford, 1968).

[2] Nos. 1, 2, 3, 9, 14, 19–21, 23, 24, 26, 29, 31, 33–6, 38, 39, 39.1, 45, 46, 49, 51, 52, 56, 58, 59, 60.1, 62, 64–6, 68–70, 72, 75–8, 79 A, 80–2, 86, 88, 91, 92–6, 98–100, 101 B, 103–5, 109, 110, 114–16, 118, 119, 122, 125 A, 125.1, 125.2, 126, 127, 130–2, 138, 140, 148, 152, 157 A, 168, 169, 172 a, 173, 176, 178, 179, 179.1, 185–91, 194–202, 204, 206–18, 220–30, 232, 234, 237–45, 248, 253, 258, 262, 265–7, 273–9, 279.1, 284–9, 289.1, 290–305, 307, 311–13, 319, 322 A, 330, 333–5, 351–3, 358, 364, 366, 367, 369, 370, 372, 375, 378, 399, 410, 426, 429, 457, 461, 461.1, 474.

[3] Nos. 132, 399, 410, 457, 461, 461.1, 474.

two, as has often been done,[1] these lines and phrases are considered a little more closely, they may serve as guides to a better understanding of the relations of the carol and medieval Latin literature.

The English–Latin carols are in general the work of authors who had the real knack of macaronic verse. In most cases the sense of the lines is continuous, English and Latin carrying forward the same subject-matter. The joinings are often very neatly made, and the Latin verses come in decidedly pat, as in Ryman's carol of the shepherds:

> Vpon a nyght an aungell bright
>   Pastoribus apparuit,
> And anone right thurgh Goddes myght
>   Lux magna illis claruit.
>   For loue of vs (Scripture seith thus)
>   Nunc natus est Altissimus.
>
> And of that light that was so bright
>   Hii valde timuerunt;
> A signe of blis to vs it is,
>   Hec lux quam hii viderunt.
>   For loue of vs (etc.)[2]

It is rare, however, to find Latin and English alternating so frequently as in the following carol on the 'timor mortis' theme:

> Illa iuventus that is so nyse
> Me deduxit into vayn devise;
> Infirmus sum; I may not rise;
>   Terribilis mors conturbat me.
>
> Dum iuvenis fui, lytill I dred,
> Set semper in sinne I ete my bred;
> Iam ductus sum into my bed;
>   Terribilis mors [conturbat me.][3]

Nothing but a desire for novelty seems to be responsible for the unusual arrangement of the Latin lines in No. 31 a:

> A Patre vnigenitus
> Thorw a maiden is com to vs.
> Synge we to here and sey, 'Welcome!
> Veni redemptor gencium.'

[1] e.g. the paragraph in *The Oxford Book of Carols*, p. xii, or Dyboski's *Songs, Carols and other Miscellaneous Poems*, p. xviii: '. . . they [the Latin lines] can all be traced back to Latin church-hymns in old collections'. William O. Wehrle in *The Macaronic Hymn Tradition in*

Medieval English Literature (Washington, D.C., 1933), attempts some analysis and classification of macaronic lyrics and comments on many of the carols.

[2] No. 75, stanzas 1, 2.

[3] No. 372, stanzas 1, 2.

> Agnoscat omne seculum:
> A bryght sterre thre kynges [made] come
> For to seke with here presens
> Verbum supernum prodiens.

Latin lines used as the *caudae* of tail-rhyme stanzas are of two general types. When they are not repeated from stanza to stanza, they ordinarily carry on the argument of the piece like the other lines which precede them, as in this carol in honour of St. Thomas of Canterbury:

> Lestenytgh, lordynges, bothe grete and smale;
> I xal you telyn a wonder tale,
> How Holy Cherche was brow[t] in bale
>   Cum magna iniuria.

> The greteste clerk of al this lond,
> Of Cauntyrbery, ye vnderstond,
> Slawyn he was [with] wykkyd hond,
>   Demonis potencia.[1]

When the same line is used for the *caudae* of all stanzas, forming a refrain, it is usually one which does not require any particular immediate context; it is exclamatory, or sententious, or directly addressed to God, the Virgin, or a saint. Like the burden, of which such a refrain usually forms one line, it serves as a kind of text or theme-line for the whole composition. The vocative use of such lines is illustrated by the following carol to St. John the Evangelist:

> Prey for vs the Prynce of Pees,
>   Amice Cristi Johannes.

> To the now, Cristes dere derlyng,
> That were a maydyn bothe eld and yyng,
> Myn herte is set to the to syng,
>   Amice Christi Johannes.

> For thou were so clene a may,
> The preuytes of heuene forsothe thou say
> Qwan on Crystys brest thov lay,
>   Amice Christi Johannes.[2]

Their use as pious exclamations is to be seen in a piece for the Epiphany season:

> Alleluya, alleluia,
>   Deo Patri sit gloria.

> Ther ys a blossum sprong of a thorn
> To saue mankynd, that was forlorne,
> As the profettes sayd beforne;
>   Deo Patri sit gloria.

[1] No. 114 a, stanzas 1, 2.   [2] No. 103 A a, burden and stanzas 1, 2.

> Ther sprong a well at Maris fote
> That torned all this world to bote;
> Of her toke Jhesu flesshe and blod;
> Deo Patri [sit gloria.][1]

Almost never are the bits of Latin inserted in a really inconsequential fashion. It is exceptional even to find lack of syntactical agreement between Latin and English, such as occurs in one of the holly–ivy group of carols where third and second personal forms are confused:

> Ivy, chefe off treis it is;
> Veni, coronaberis.

> The most worthye she is in towne—
> He that seyth other do amysse—
> And worthy to bere the crowne;
> Veni, coronaberis.[2]

Even in the highly irreverent song of Jankyn, the Latin phrases are inserted in a way that emphasizes the character of the piece, not quite as a parody of the Mass, but as a kind of sacrilegious trope of bits of its text:

> 'Kyrie, so kyrie,'
> Jankyn syngyt merie,
> With 'aleyson'.
>
> . . . .
>
> Jankyn began the Offys on the Yol Day,
> And yyt me thynkyt it dos me good, so merie gan he say,
> 'Kyrieleyson'.
>
> . . . .
>
> Benedicamus Domino: Cryst fro schame me schylde;
> Deo gracias therto: alas, I go with chylde!
> K[yrieleyson.][3]

Many of the Latin lines in the carols are of a type which, while having little claim to originality, hardly allows us to speak of a 'source' for the individual phrase. Any clerk with some fluency in Latin would have at his command any number of such clichés, not always preserved verbatim, like texts of Scripture, but subject to slight variations in wording which in no way lift them out of the class of pious commonplace. It would be as useless as it would be dull to reproduce here the catalogue of these Latin expressions

---

[1] No. 123 A, burden and stanzas 1, 2.

[2] No. 138, burden and stanza 1.

[3] No. 457, burden and stanzas 2, 7. Other stanzas tell of Jankyn's part in the 'Pystyl', the 'Sanctus', and the 'Angnus'. The principle of interpolation is much like that of a genuine trope. Compare the burden of 'Jankyn' with the following opening lines from a trope of the Kyrie:

> Kyrie,—Rex pie,—Da nobis hodie,—
> Veniae—Munus et gratiae: Eleison.

(Quoted by Léon Gautier, *Histoire de la poésie liturgique au moyen âge. Les Tropes*, i, Paris, 1886, p. 148 n. II. E.)

found in the carols, but a few may be cited as typical. '"Aue" fit ex "Eva"'
(No. 238) is merely the simplest possible way of expressing that favourite of all
medieval anagrams. Hymns to the Virgin are strewn with it, in various word-
ings, the best known being that of the 'Ave Maris Stella'.[1] Phrases of similar
currency and lack of distinction are 'Infernali pena' (No. 179), 'Magnificantes
Dominum' (No. 75), 'Ne cademus sustine' (No. 274), 'O rex noster Emanuel'
(No. 92), 'Pro peccante homine' (No. 24), 'Tria ferentes munera' (No. 127),
and many others. The great store of epithets applied to the Virgin by her
devotees is levied upon for many of these uninspired lines, e.g. 'Mater Dei
electa' (No. 179), 'O virgo summe decora' (No. 198), 'Maria, spes nostra,
salue' (No. 215), 'Dei genitrix pia' (No. 194).

Other lines of Latin appear to have been composed for the particular
place in which we find them, the author of the carol having simply shifted
languages at the appointed place—no difficult matter, and, it may be added,
one that has given the world no very luminous gems of Latin verse. The discovery of a verbal similarity to any one of these lines in some Latin piece
on the same subject, say in the *Analecta Hymnica*, need not imply anything
more than that two writers of verse of much the same background and way
of thought have chanced to use the same expression. Among the many lines
and phrases of this sort are the following: 'Per tua sancta merita' (No. 104),
'Quem gens seua crucifixit' (No. 218), 'Vllo sine crimine' (No. 24), 'Gentibus
in Judea' (No. 68).

2. *The Hymn and the Carol*

Apart from commonplaces of clerkly Latin and connective phrases
especially composed for a particular carol, there are to be found a considerable number of lines which are directly taken from some part of the
service of the Church. As these were borrowed for incorporation without
change into the verses of song, it is not surprising that most of them
are drawn from those parts of the ritual which are metrical, or at least
rhythmical, units, that is, the hymns, the proses or sequences, and the
antiphons. Of these three types the hymn is that which presents the nearest
likeness of form to the carol, being divided into stanzas, each of which is sung
to a repetition of the same musical setting.[2] It is also that which contributes
the greatest number of Latin lines to the carol-texts, as the following table
will show.[3]

---

[1] H. A. Daniel, *Thesaurus Hymnologicus*
(Leipzig, 1855), i. 204, stanza 2:
    Sumens illud Ave
    Gabrielis ore,
    Funda nos in pace,
    Mutans nomen Evae.

[2] Throughout the present discussion the
term 'hymn' will be applied only to stanzaic
pieces in metre, excluding other forms like

proses and tropes which are often classed as
hymns under the broader meaning of the word:
'any song or song-like poem of praise to God'.
See the classification of hymns in *The Catholic
Encyclopedia* (New York, 1910), s.v. 'Hymn'.

[3] This and the similar tables which follow
make no claim to exhaustiveness. Further dili-
gent search in hymn-collections would doubtless reveal further borrowings.

Table of Hymn-Lines Used in the Carols[1]

Line	Carol No.	Use[2]	Text
A Patre Unigenitus	31	Epiphany, Lauds	B.S. i, col. cccxxix
A solis ortus cardine	21, 31, 39.1, 52, 122 B	Christmas, Lauds	B.S. i, col. clxxxix
Adam parens quod polluit (Adam vetus quod polluit)	31 a, b	York, Christmas, Nones	Hym. S., p. 14
Adesto nunc propicius	86	See 'Salvator mundi, Domine' below.	
Aeterne rex altissime	273	Vigil of Ascension, I Vespers	B.S. i, col. dcccclviii
Agnoscat omne saeculum	31	York, Christmas, Prime	Hym. S., p. 13
Aurora lucis rutilat	273	First Sunday after Easter, Matins	B.S. i, col. dccclviii
Aurum, thus, myrrham, offerunt	125 A	See 'Reges de Saba' below.	
Ave, plena gratia	232 B		See Rep. Hym. Nos. 2030–3, 23740–8, 35658–60.
Christe, redemptor omnium	9, 21 A, B, D, 122 A, 273	Christmas, Matins	B.S. i, col. clxxi
Circumfultus undique	99	See 'Protomartyr Stephane' below.	
Conditor alme siderum	273	Advent, First Sunday, Vespers	B.S. i, col. v
Consors paterni luminis	23 B, C, 31 a, b	Tuesday after Octave of Epiphany, Matins	Hym. S., p. 47
Deo patri sit gloria	86 A, B, 123 A	Frequent at end of hymns, e.g. Sunday Lauds	B.S. ii, col. 34
Deus creator omnium	122 A	First Sunday after Octave of Epiphany, I Vespers	B.S. i, col. cccciii
Effusione sanguinis	275	Non-Sarum, Common of a Martyr	Dan. i, p. 109
Enixa est puerpera	39.1, 52, 191 A, 232	See 'A solis ortus' above.	

[1] Abbreviations:

A.H. G. M. Dreves and C. Blume, eds., Analecta Hymnica Medii Aevi (Leipzig, 1886–1922).

B.S. Francis Proctor and Christopher Wordsworth, eds., Breviarium ad Usum Insignis Ecclesiae Sarum (Cambridge, 1879–86).

Dan. H. A. Daniel, ed., Thesaurus Hymnologicus (Leipzig, 1855–6).

Hym. S. Hymnarium Sarisburiense (London, 1851).

Mone. Franz J. Mone, ed., Lateinische Hymnen des Mittelalters (Freiburg, 1853–5).

Rep. Hym. Ulysse Chevalier, ed., Repertorium Hymnologicum (Louvain, 1892–1920).

Sar. Mis. J. Wickham Legg, ed., The Sarum Missal (Oxford, 1916).

[2] References, unless otherwise noted, are to the Sarum Use. In many cases the service cited is only one of several for which the same hymn is prescribed, ordinarily the first recorded occurrence of the hymn in the liturgical year.

Line	Carol No.	Use	Text
Ex illibata virgine	39.1, 127	See 'Christe, redemptor omnium' above.	
Exultet coelum laudibus	21 A, B, C, E, 33	Common of an Apostle	B.S. ii, col. 368
Fili Mariae virginis	275, 276	Non-Sarum, Service of B.V.M. in Advent, Nones	Mone, ii, p. 133
Gaude, mater gloriosa	202		See Rep. Hym. No. 6865
Gloria tibi, Domine	24, 29, 31 a, b, 35, 38.1, 52, 86, 168, 187 B	The 'Gloria', first said Christmas, Matins	B.S. i, col. clxxi
Hostis Herodes impie	21 A, C, D, 122 A	Vigil of Epiphany, Vespers	B.S. i, col. cccxix
Iam lucis orto sidere	21 B, 122 A, C, 273	Advent, First Sunday, Prime	B.S. ii, col. 37
Illuminare Jerusalem	125.2		Dan. ii, p. 192
Jesu, nostra redemptio	122 A	Vigil of Ascension, Compline	B.S. ii, col. 235
Jesu, Salvator saeculi	21, A, D, 122 A, C, 273	a. First Sunday after Easter, Compline	B.S. ii, col. 234
		b. All Saints, I Vespers	B.S. iii, col. 961
Laus, honor, virtus, gloria	33	A doxology	Dan. iv, p. 20 n.
Magnae Deus potentiae	122 A	Thursday after Octave of Epiphany, Vespers	Hym. S., p. 53
Mane nobiscum, Domine	33, 38, 367	See 'A Patre Unigenitus' above.	
Maria ventre concepit	31 a, b	York, Christmas, Terce	Hym. S., p. 13
Mundum pugillo continens	33	Annunciation, Matins	B.S. iii, col. 235
Mysterium mirabile	176	Non-Sarum, Eastertide, Terce	Dan. i, p. 49
Ne mentem somnus opprimat	86 A	See 'Salvator mundi, Domine' below.	
Non ex virili semine	24	See 'Veni, redemptor gentium' below.	
O lux beata Trinitas	21, 31 a, b	First Sunday after Trinity, I Vespers	B.S. i, col. mclxvii
Pastor creator omnium	23	See 'A solis ortus' above.	
Processit ex virgine	49	See 'Verbum Patris hodie' below.	
Protomartyr Stephane	99	St. Stephen's Day, Lauds	B.S. i, col. ccxi
Quem genuit puerpera	127	Non-Sarum, Feasts of B.V.M.	Dan. i, p. 79

Line	Carol No.	Use	Text
Qui creavit omnia	68		See *Rep. Hym.*, No. 16388.
Qui natus es de virgine	35 A, 52, 279.1	See 'Gloria tibi, Domine' above.	
Reges de Saba veniunt	125 A	Non-Sarum, Christmas	Dan. i, p. 334
Resultet terra gaudiis	33	See 'Exultet coelum' above.	
Salvator mundi, Domine	86, 122 A	Advent, First Sunday	*B.S.* ii, col. 226
Secreta quae non noverat	52	See 'A solis ortus' above.	
Sine virili semine	23 A, 58	Non-Sarum, Christmas	Dan. i, pp. 327, 334
Solvit a poena miseros	33	See 'Aurora lucis rutilat' above.	
Succurre nobis miseris	229, 275	Non-Sarum, Compline	Dan. i, p. 34
Summi largitor praemii	273	Lent, First Sunday, Matins	*Hym. S.*, p. 66
Te reformator sensuum	86	See 'Salvator mundi, Domine' above.	
Tu Trinitatis Unitas	122 A, C	Friday after Octave of Epiphany, Matins	*B.S.* ii, col. 149
Veni, Creator Spiritus	122	Whitsunday, Terce (also first words of Ordinary of Mass)	*B.S.* i, col. mviii
Veni, redemptor gentium	23, 31, 69	Vigil of Christmas, I Vespers	*B.S.* i, col. clxvi
Venter puellae baiulat	52	See 'A solis ortus' above.	
Verbo concepit filium	52	See 'A solis ortus' above.	
Verbum Patris altissimi	33	See 'Jesu, salvator saeculi' above.	
Verbum Patris hodie	49	Christmas, Lauds	*B.S.* i, col. cxc
Verbum supernum prodiens	31 a, b	Advent, First Sunday, Matins	*B.S.* i, col. xviii
Vexilla Regis prodeunt	265	Passion Sunday, Vespers	*Hym. S.*, p. 79
Vox clara, ecce, intonat	273	Advent, First Sunday, Lauds	*B.S.* i, col. xxxi

The hymns in the above table include some of the finest and best-known which the Middle Ages produced. It is interesting to observe the manner in which carol-writers made use of their lines.

Often one carol incorporates a number of lines from the same hymn. This is not necessarily a sign that the carol is in any sense a partial translation or even an imitation of that hymn, although often it celebrates the same occasion. It may merely indicate that the lines of the particular hymn were fresher or firmer in the memory of the carol-writer than were others. Such is the case with No. 52, most of the Latin lines of which are taken from the Christmas hymn 'A solis ortus cardine', one of the two hymns made from a fifth-century alphabetical poem by Caelius Sedulius.[1] The carol reads:

> Now syng we, syng we,
>   'Gloria tibi, Domine.'
>
> Cryst kepe vs all, as he well can,
>   *A solis ortu[s] cardine;*
> For he ys both God and man
>   Qui natus est de virgine.
>
> As he ys Lord both day and nyght,
>   *Venter puelle baiulat;*
> So ys Mary moder of myght,
>   *Secreta que non noverat.*
>
> The holy brest of chastyte
>   *Verbo consepit Filium,*
> So browght before the Trinite
>   Vt castytatis lyllyum.
>
> Betwen an ox and an asse
>   *Enixa est puerpera;*
> In pore clothyng clothed he was
>   [Q]ui regnat super ethera.

The italicized lines are all taken from the hymn[2] and occur in the same order in both hymn and carol, but the English text is in no way modelled upon the Latin, as a comparison will quickly show. The following is the older text of the hymn, that in the modern Roman Breviary having undergone some changes:[3]

> A solis ortus cardine
> Ad usque terrae limitem
> Christum canamus principem
> Natum Maria virgine.
>
> Beatus auctor saeculi
> Servile corpus induit,
> Ut carne carnem liberans
> Ne perderet quos condidit.
>
> Clausa parentis viscera
> Coelestis intrat gratia,
> Venter puellae baiulat
> Secreta quae non noverat.

---

[1] It comprises the stanzas beginning with the letters A to G; the stanzas beginning with the letters H, I, L, N form the Epiphany hymn 'Hostis Herodes impie'.

[2] The lines 'Gloria tibi, Domine' and 'Qui natus es[t] de virgine' are from the Gloria used with this hymn, but not peculiar to it alone.

'Castitatis lilium' is conventional; the author may have had in mind the prose for the Mass of the B.V.M., which has the phrase 'O castitatis lilium'. 'Qui regnat super aethera' occurs in the second Lectio for Lauds in the Hours of the Blessed Virgin Mary.

[3] Daniel, *Thesaurus Hymnologicus*, i. 143–4.

Domus pudici pectoris
Templum repente fit Dei;
Intacta, nesciens virum
Verbo concepit filium.

Enixa est puerpera
Quem Gabriel praedixerat,
Quem matris alvo gestiens
Clausus Ioannes senserat.

Foeno iacere pertulit,
Praesepe non abhorruit,
Parvoque lacte pastus est
Per quem nec ales esurit.

Gaudet chorus coelestium
Et angeli canunt Deo
Palamque fit pastoribus
Pastor creator omnium.

Yet in no case does any carol borrow a greater number of lines from one hymn than does this No. 52 from Sedulius's work.

A far more usual procedure on the part of carol-writers was to cull lines here and there for insertion into an English piece. In such a case imitation of a particular hymn is hardly to be expected, nor is it found. A carol so constructed is No. 31 a. As may be seen from the preceding table, for the eleven Latin lines of this piece eight different hymns from various seasons of the year are laid under contribution.[1] In the beginning of the first stanza[2] the author follows the Latin hymn whence his first line is taken, for one line of English, 'Thorw a maiden is com to vs' from 'A Patre Unigenitus, Ad nos venit per virginem', but the remainder of the piece is merely a potpourri of the first lines of hymns.[3] The same momentary following of the Latin text whence a line is taken is to be seen in No. 265, which takes half of its burden from the great Passiontide hymn ascribed to Fortunatus. The first stanza may be regarded as a very free reworking of the opening lines of the hymn:

Now synge we, as we were wont:
'Uexilla Regis prodeunt.'

[1] 'A solis ortus cardine', 'A Patre Unigenitus', 'Veni, redemptor gentium', 'Agnoscat omne saeculum', 'Consors paterni luminis', 'O lux beata Trinitas', 'Verbum supernum prodiens', 'Maria ventre concepit', and the 'Gloria tibi, Domine' used with various hymns.

[2] Quoted above, pp. lxxxii, lxxxiii.

[3] The hymn begins:

Vexilla regis prodeunt,
Fulget crucis mysterium,

Quo carne carnis conditor
Suspensus est patibulo.

Confixa clavis viscera,
Tendens manus, vestigia,
Redemptionis gratia
Hic immolata est hostia.

(Daniel, *Thesaurus Hymnologicus*, i. 160. The older version of this hymn also differs from that in the modern Roman Breviary.)

The Kinges baner on felde is playd;
The crosses mistry can not be nayd,
To whom our Sauyour was betrayd,
    And for our sake,
Thus sayth he:
'I suffre for the;
    My deth I take.'

But, as the 'Thus sayth he' promises, the body of the carol is an address
of the crucified Christ to sinful man, having nothing in common with the
hymn.[1]

As these typical instances indicate, the direct contribution of the hymns
of the Office to the subject-matter of the English text of the carols is extremely
slight.[2] This is hardly to be attributed to lack of interest in the hymns themselves or in their possibilities as subjects of translation. James Ryman, prolific as a carol-writer, translated into English a number of the very hymns
most quoted in the carols, and another collection of such translations made
in the late fifteenth century is largely composed of the hymns which have
been cited.[3] Ryman's translations are the more interesting, as they retain
the four-stress line and four-line stanza of their originals, whereas the
anonymous hymnal is written in rhyme-royal with five-stress lines. Ryman
also occasionally allows a line of Latin to remain, as in the following translation of 'Christe, redemptor omnium':[4]

Crist, that ayene hast made man free,
Ex patre patris vnice,
Onely borne, or this worlde began,
Whose birth dyuyne no tunge tell can.

.   .   .   .   .   .

This day berith witnesse, that now is come
Currens per anni circulum,
That thou art come fro blis an hye,
The welthe of this worlde alone only.
        (etc.)

[1] For the source of the remainder of the
carol, pointed out by Reed, see Notes.

[2] The carols which paraphrase and quote
from the *Te Deum laudamus* (Nos. 96, 285–305)
form a somewhat exceptional group. They show
no particular influence from the rhythmical
form of their great source.

[3] Ed. Frank A. Patterson, 'Hymnal from MS.
Additional 34,193 British Museum', in Roger S.
Loomis, ed., *Medieval Studies in Memory of
Gertrude Schoepperle Loomis* (Paris–New York,
1927), pp. 443–88.

[4] Stanzas 1, 4. Cambridge University
Library, MS. Ee. 1. 12, f. 30^r, printed J.
Zupitza, *Archiv für das Studium der neueren
Sprachen*, lxxxix (1892), 194. Other hymns
translated by Ryman and published from the
same manuscript are: 'Conditor alme siderum'
(ibid., p. 190), 'Verbum supernum prodiens'
(ibid., p. 191), 'Vox clara, ecce, intonat' (ibid.,
p. 192), 'A solis ortus cardine' (divided and
translated as two, ibid., pp. 192, 193), 'A Patre
Unigenitus' (ibid., p. 195), 'Christe, qui lux
es et dies' (ibid., p. 196), 'Salvator mundi,
Domine' (ibid., p. 197), 'Hostis Herodes impie'
(ibid., p. 223).

More probably the carols' independence of the hymns' subject-matter is due to the recognition by those who produced the carols that the master-pieces of church song were in a more exalted strain than was fitting for pieces modelled on popular song.

Metrically the carol and the hymn have more in common. They show similarities in form of both stanza and line which seem to indicate influence of the Latin poetry on the English. The likenesses of stanza-form are perhaps the more obvious.

One of the predominating forms of the Latin hymn through many centuries was a four-line stanza of four-measure lines. This form is found both in quantitative verse and in accentual, as well as in pieces showing the transition from one type of rhythm to the other. Most of the hymns to which reference is made in the table above are written in this stanza. Some, particularly those written in the earlier Middle Ages, are unrhymed, e.g. 'Aeterne rerum conditor'. Others use rhyme in various arrangements. A monorhyme stanza like that found in a few carols[1] is one of these:

> Conditor alme siderum:
> Aeterna lux credentium,
> Christe, redemptor omnium,
> Exaudi preces supplicum.

Six carols[2] use couplet rhyme like that in the following hymn-stanza:

> Chorus novae Ierusalem
> Novam meli dulcedinem
> Promat, colens cum sobriis
> Paschale festum gaudiis.

Other rhyme-schemes occur in the hymns which the carols do not use, e.g. 4a 4b 4c 4b, and 4a 4b 4b 4a. In fact it is usual for the hymns of the Office which have been repeatedly cited here to introduce rhyme somewhat capriciously, omitting it altogether in some stanzas, and varying the rhyme scheme in others. This is to be expected in view of the early date of most of them, as rhyme was seldom applied consistently throughout a Latin piece before the eleventh century.[3] But in hymns which were composed in the centuries immediately preceding the period of the carol's appearance, regular and often ingenious rhyme is constantly used. The fact that the hymns from which lines for macaronic carols were taken do not themselves show rhyme similar to that of the carols is therefore no evidence against the influence of Latin versification.

The four-line cross-rhyme carol stanza, as well as the monorhyme and the couplet-rhyme, appears to be for the most part a product of Latin

---

[1] Nos. 21, 157 C, 158, 315 (in part), 331, 333, 374, 379, 399.

[2] Nos. 31, 88, 178, 380, 438, 460.1.

[3] Raby, *Christian-Latin Poetry*, p. 25.

influence. The ballad-stanza, whether written as the two long lines which it actually is, or in the form 4a 3b 4c 3b, is little used by the carol-writers.[1] When a stanza of four- and three-measure lines in alternation is used, the first and third lines are rhymed, as in the fifteenth-century hymn containing these lines:[2]

> O adoranda deitas,
> te invoco in fide,
> o admiranda bonitas
> nunc audi me et vide![3]

But the largest group of cross-rhyme carol-stanzas is made up of those having all their lines of four measures. This stanza may be regarded as the result of applying internal rhyme to long lines of eight measures,[3] but such lines are not common in early English lyric verse. The much-used form 4a 4b 4a 4b is rather to be regarded in the carols as due to the influence of the isometric Latin hymn-stanza. This is plainly shown by such a piece as No. 23 A, where the b-lines are actually taken from hymns:[4]

> When he was borne that made all thyng,
> Pastor creator omnium,
> Angelles thei began to syng,
> 'Veni, redemptor gencium.'

No. 122 A seems to show a transitional stage in the process of adaptation, one of the b-lines of each stanza being Latin, the other English:[5]

> Ther is a babe born of a may
> In saluacion of vs;
> That he be heryd in this day,
> Vene, Creatore Spiritus.
>
> In Bedlem, in that fayre plas,
> This blessid barne borne he was;
> Him to serue God grawnt vs grace,
> Tu Trinetatis Vnitas.

The example of the Latin hymn-stanza of four four-measure lines is probably responsible for a specialized form of the stanza in a a a b which has been shown to have such an intimate connection with the dance. In vernacular dance-songs using this form, the line in b, forming a transition from the first three lines of the stanza to the burden, is usually shorter than the lines which precede it; often it is only a 'tag' of one or two measures. In some of the carols it has this shorter form, but in a far greater number it has four measures. That this preference for a four-measure *cauda* is the result

[1] Nos. 25, 135 (in part), 136 A, 143, 162, 444.1, 465.
[2] Mone, *Lateinische Hymnen*, i. 287.
[3] As by Jakob Schipper, *Englische Metrik* (Bonn, 1881–8), i. 343.
[4] Stanza 5.
[5] Stanzas 1, 2.

of acquaintance with the isometric hymn-stanza is attested by the large number of such *caudae* which appear in Latin, often directly quoted from a hymn. No. 24 provides a good example:[1]

> Blyssid be that mayde Mary;
> Born he was of here body,
> Godis Sone that syttit on hy,
> Non ex uirili semine.

> .   .   .   .   .

> Man and chyld, bothe eld and ying,
> Now in his blysful comyng
> To that chyld mow we syng,
> 'Gloria tibi, Domine.'

The introduction of internal rhyme into four-measure lines, occasionally met with in the carols, particularly in the lullaby carols, is evidently an imitation of the leonine rhyme so prevalent in later medieval hymns and other Latin poems. No. 75 shows the use of leonine rhymes in English lines.[2] A Latin example follows:[3]

> Christum ducem, qui per crucem
>   redemit nos ab hostibus,
> laudet laetus noster coetus,
>   *Exultet coelum laudibus.*

> Poena fortis tuae mortis
>   et sanguinis effusio
> corda terant, ut te quaerant,
>   *Jesu nostra redemptio.*

These Latin lines also serve to illustrate a practice of medieval hymnody which is reflected in the macaronic verses of the English carol and of various religious lyrics in other languages. Lines from well-known hymns were often incorporated into new Latin hymns precisely as they were into the carol.[4] This principle of providing a new context for a well-known phrase is that which underlies the production of the tropes and *épîtres farcies* in vogue in the period from the ninth to the twelfth centuries. It is distinctly a 'monkish' literary device, and such carols as No. 31 were doubtless inspired by acquaintance with hymns like that just quoted.

3. *The Prose and the Carol*

The principal use of the hymns just discussed is in the Office of the Canonical Hours, as contained in the Breviary. The prose, or sequence, on the contrary, belongs essentially to the ceremony of the Mass. Although the

---

[1] Stanzas 1, 4.
[2] Quoted above, p. lxxxii.
[3] Mone, *Lateinische Hymnen*, i. 112.

[4] For further examples see ibid., pp. 113, 176, 177.

words of many proses present a superficial likeness to those of a hymn, the structural principles of the two forms are radically different, a fact which must be kept in mind in any consideration of the relations of prose and carol. Proper understanding of this difference involves some acquaintance with the early history of the prose, which may be very briefly reviewed here.[1]

The place of the prose in the Mass is between the Gradual and the Gospel on feast-days. In the early Middle Ages the Gradual (an anthem sung between the Epistle and the Gospel, so named because it was sung from the steps of the altar or ambo) ended with an 'Alleluia' of which the last syllable was sung to a prolonged series of notes (*melisma* or *sequentia*). So long, indeed, was this passage in some settings that it was necessary to divide it in order to allow the singers to take breath. Each of these divisions was then called a *sequentia*. Then arose the practice, so important for the future development of the prose, of having each of these musical phrases sung twice, once by each of two opposed choirs, usually of men and boys respectively. The prose as a form of liturgical poetry began when, about the eighth century, in circumstances not fully known, Latin words, at first unmetrical, were fitted to these long musical passages.[2] Such a composition with its words was designated as *sequentia cum prosa*, whence the two terms, now often used synonymously, of 'prose' and 'sequence'.

The earliest proses were written to already existing melodies and were made to correspond to these absolutely, a syllable for every note. Such are the productions of Notker Balbulus of St. Gall, which may be regarded as typical of the first period of prose-writing, lasting into the twelfth century and often called after him 'Notkerian'. The following prose in honour of St. John the Evangelist, attributed to Notker, will illustrate the parallel construction which is the distinctive feature of the form. The first and last strophes were sung by both choirs together, the remainder by the choirs in alternation, strophes here set opposite each other being sung to the same musical phrase:[3]

1. Iohannes, Iesu Christo
   multum dilecte virgo,

2. Tu eius amore   3. In navi parentem
   carnalem   liquisti.

---

[1] In accordance with the authoritative short account of the prose and its development by Clemens Blume, S.J., in *The Catholic Encyclopedia* (New York, 1911), s.v. 'Prose or Sequence'. This article is still a good introduction to the subject, but it should now be used with the corresponding article by B. Leahy in the *New Catholic Encyclopedia* (New York, 1927), s.v. 'Sequence.'

[2] The long-accepted story of the development of the prose by Notker at St. Gall, whither refugee monks from Jumièges had brought the

idea of fitting words to a *sequentia*, is discredited by recent scholarship. Notker was influential in spreading the vogue of the prose in Germany, but its ultimate point of origin appears to have been in French territory. See *Analecta Hymnica*, liii. x–xxx, and for a more recent authoritative statement, Willi Apel, *Gregorian Chant* (Bloomington, Indiana, 1958), pp. 442–64. Another detailed account is that by Bruno Stäblein in *Die Musik in Geschichte und Gegenwart*, s.v. 'Sequenz', xii (1965), cols. 522–50.

[3] Ibid., p. 276.

4. Tu leve coniugis
   pectus respuisti
   Messiam secutus,

5. Ut eius pectoris
   sacra meruisses
   fluenta potare.

· · · · · · · · ·

10. Tute carcere
    flagrisque fractus
    testimonio
    pro Christi es gavisus;

11. Idem mortuos
    suscitas inque
    Iesu nomine
    venenum forte vincis.

12. Tibi summus tacitum
    ceteris Verbum suum
    pater revelat.

13. Tu nos omnes precibus
    sedulis apud Deum
    semper commenda,

14. Iohannes, Christi care.

Proses of this type are far enough removed, to be sure, from metrical, stanzaic song like hymns or carols. But the next stage of development brought proses in which principles of accentual rhythm and rhyme asserted themselves more and more.[1] A prose of this transitional sort is the famous, 'Victimae paschali laudes', attributed to Wipo the Burgundian, and beginning:[2]

1. Victimae paschali laudes
   immolent christiani.

2. Agnus redemit oves,
   Christus innocens patri
   reconciliavit
   peccatores.

3. Mors et vita duello
   conflixere mirando;
   dux vitae mortuus
   regnat vivus.

4. Dic nobis, Maria,
   quid vidisti in via?
   'Sepulcrum Christi viventis
   et gloriam vidi resurgentis;

5. Angelicos testes,
   sudarium et vestes.
   Surrexit Christus, spes mea;
   praecedet suos in Galilaea.'

(etc.)

Greater uniformity of rhythm will be noticed, as well as the introduction of rhyme.

The final result of these tendencies was the 'regular' or 'Adamian' prose, so called after Adam of St. Victor, its principal exponent. In these compositions the twin strophes are rhymed throughout and have a rhythm based on word-accent and with a regular caesura. As the regular prose usually

---

[1] Many early proses ended all their strophes in -a, a reminiscence of the final a of 'Alleluia'. The energetic researches of Peter Dronke lead him to question 'the widely held view that the sequence originated in the liturgy and was first developed out of Alleluia melodies'. His strong suggestion is 'that at its beginnings the sequence was linked with secular and vernacular song at least as much as with a sacred Latin tradition' (*The Medieval Lyric*, London, 1968, pp. 38–44, and 'The Beginnings of the Sequence', *Beiträge zur Geschichte der deutschen Sprache und Literatur* (Tübingen, 1965), lxxxvii. 45–73). Dronke's views, if accepted, do not affect the account given here of the connection between prose and carol. [2] *Analecta Hymnica*, liv. 12.

omitted the opening strophe for the combined choirs, the likeness of its text to that of a hymn is often complete, as in the celebrated 'Verbum bonum et suave':[1]

1. Verbum bonum et suave
   Personemus, illud *Ave*,
   Per quod Christi fit conclave
   Virgo, mater, filia;

2. Per quod *Ave* salutata
   Mox concepit fecundata
   Virgo, David stirpe nata,
   Inter spinas lilia.

(etc.)

But the musical setting for such a prose remained like that for the older type, each phrase of melody being sung only twice, once with each of two paired strophes, and not repeated for each strophe of the entire composition like a hymn-tune. Regular proses like the 'Laetabundus',[2] in which not all the strophe-pairs have the same form, show more clearly the difference in construction between even the latest proses and stanzaic pieces like hymns and carols.

It is plain that the prose is a highly specialized development of the art of song, produced by learned composers in the artificial environment of monastic schools and intended for singing by trained performers. Nevertheless it has repeatedly been asserted that it has a close connection with popular poetry.[3] This fact and certain evident similarities in form and subject-matter between Latin proses and English carols necessitate some scrutiny of the actual relationship between the two. As in the case of the hymns, the lines actually quoted by the carols from the proses claim first attention.

These appear to be fewer in number than the lines taken from hymns. The following Latin passages are probably quoted by the carol-writers directly from the sources indicated:

Table of Prose-Lines Used in the Carols

Line	Carol No.	Use	Text
Amice Christi Johannes	103, 104	St. John the Baptist's Day	*Sar. Mis.*, p. 477
Clangat pastor in tuba cornea Ut libera sit Christi vinea (adapted)	116	Holy Innocents, Vespers, Procession to altar of St. Thomas of Canterbury	*B.S.* i, col. ccxlv
Johannes Christi care	105	St. John the Evangelist's Day	*Sar. Mis.*, p. 463
Nato canunt omnia	179	Christmas, Mass at Cockcrow	*Sar. Mis.*, p. 462
O castitatis lilium, tuum precare filium	196	Mass of B.V.M.	*Sar. Mis.*, p. 480

[1] Ibid., p. 343.
[2] See below, pp. xcix–civ.
[3] e.g. Ferdinand Wolf, *Über die Lais, Sequenzen und Leiche* (Heidelberg, 1841), p. 32 and n. 40; Giovanni Ippoliti, *Dalle Sequenze alle Laudi* (Osimo, 1914).

Line	Corol No.	Use	Text
Sacra fluenta potare	105	St. John the Evangelist's Day	*Sar. Mis.*, p. 463
Salve, regina gloriae	207–11	Non-Sarum, Mass of B.V.M.	*A.H.* ix, p. 74

The carols in which these lines are used in no way show further indebtedness to the proses for their subject-matter. In fact the phrase 'Amice Christi Johannes', the concluding line of a prose in honour of St. John the Baptist, is adopted for the burden of two carols on St. John the Evangelist. 'Johannes, Christi care' is indeed applied to the same saint in both prose and carol, and the phrase 'Sacra fluenta potare' in No. 105 seems to be adapted from strophe 5 of the same prose,[1] but there the likeness ends. Neither do these carols exhibit any similarity of form to the proses whence their Latin is drawn. The two proses for the two St. Johns are of the older, non-rhythmical type, as is the 'Nato canunt omnia'. The prose of the Virgin is in the Adamian form, but none of its strophes suggests the stanza used in the carol which borrows its Latin.

There is one famous prose, however, from which a number of English poems derive subject-matter, Latin tags, and, to some extent, metrical form. This is the 'Laetabundus' attributed to St. Bernard of Clairvaux. The English renderings of the 'Laetabundus' which have been preserved illustrate several stages in the process by which this prose (the only one so treated in surviving texts) was made over into a carol. The original Latin text is as follows:[2]

1. Laetabundus
exsultet fidelis chorus,
Alleluia;

2. Regem regum
intactae profudit thorus;
Res miranda.

3. Angelus consilii
natus est de virgine,
Sol de stella,

4. Sol occasum nesciens,
stella semper rutilans,
Semper clara.

5. Sicut sidus radium,
profert virgo filium
Pari forma:

6. Neque sidus radio,
neque mater filio
Fit corrupta.

7. Cedrus alta Libani
conformatur hyssopo
Valle nostra;

8. Verbum, mens altissimi,
corporari passum est
Carne sumpta.

9. Isaias cecinit;
synagoga meminit,
nunquam tamen desinit
Esse caeca;

10. Si non suis vatibus,
credat vel gentilibus
Sibyllinis versibus
Haec praedicta.

[1] See above, p. xcvii.   [2] *Analecta Hymnica*, liv 5.

11. Infelix propera,
   crede vel vetera;
   cur damnaberis, gens misera?

12. Quem docet litera,
   natum considera;
   ipsum genuit puerpera.

The closest translation of this prose in fifteenth-century English is in Bodleian Library MS. Arch. Selden B. 26.[1] It is rhymed throughout, but preserves the original form of each strophe:

Glad and blithe mote ye be,
All that euer Y here nowe se;
   Alleluya.

           Kynge of Kyngys, Lorde of alle,
           Borne he is in oxe stalle,
              Res miranda.

The Angel of Counsel now borne he is
Of a maide ful clene, ywis,
   Sol de stella;

           The sunne that euer shyneth bryght,
           The sterre that euer yeueth his lyght,
              Semper clara.

Ryght as the sterre bryngth forth his beme,
So the maide here barn-teme,
   Pari forma.

           Nother the sterre for his beme,
           Nother the maide for here barne-teme,
              Fit corrupta.

The cedur of Liban that growyth so hye,
Vnto the ysape is made lye,
   Valle nostra:

           Godys Sone of heuen bryght
           Vntyl a maide is he lyght
              Carne sumpta.

Ysaye saide by prophecie—
The sinagoge hath hit in memorye
Yyt neuer he lynneth maliciusly—
   Esse ceca.

           Yf they leue not here profetys,
           Then lete hem leue ethen metrys
           In sibylinys versiculys
              Hec predicta.

Unhappy Jewe, come thou nere,
Byleue ellys thyne eldere.
Why wolt thou, wrecche, ydampned be?

           Whomme techeth the letter
           Byholde the childe the better;
           Hym bare a maide moder Marye.

[1] f. 19ᵛ, printed Frederick M. Padelford, *Anglia*, xxxvi (1912), 105. Music in *Early Bodleian Music*, Nos. lxx, lxxi.

The editor of *Early Bodleian Music* labels this piece a carol, but it is no carol, as the music plainly shows. It is simply a prose in English, the music being arranged exactly as for a Latin prose; that is, the first pair of strophes are to be sung to the same melody, the next pair to a different one, and so on, except that in this setting each of the last two strophes has its own separate melody.

James Ryman has left two versions of the 'Laetabundus' in English which approach the carol in that they have been cast in uniform stanzas, although they lack the burden necessary for a true carol.[1] The first of the two uses the Latin tags of the original prose, and is in a stanza of two lines plus *cauda* probably suggested by the dominant form of strophe in Bernard's poem:[2]

> The incorrupt wombe virginall
> Hath borne the king of kingis alle,
> Res miranda.

> The aungell of counseill full of myght
> Is borne of a virgyne pure and bright,
> Sol de stella.

> This son of lyght is not fading
> Ne this sterre bright, but is shynyng
> Semper clara.

> As the sterre bright bringith furth his light,
> A mayde hath borne the king of myght
> Pari forma.
> (etc.)

His second version shows plainly that the above lines have been turned into three-line stanzas simply for the sake of having them in that form; the reworking consists merely of adding a weak, redundant line to each stanza:[3]

> The incorrupt wombe virginall
> Hath borne the king of kingis alle
> For to make vs free, that were thrall,
> Res miranda.

> The aungell of counsell full of myght
> Is borne of a virgyne pure and bright
> For to bringe vs ayene to light,
> Sol de stella.

---

[1] Although no music is preserved to give certain evidence, the first strophe of the Latin prose which Ryman puts at the head of his English words is hardly to be regarded as a burden; he quotes similarly the first stanzas of the Latin hymns which he translates.

[2] Cambridge University Library, MS. Ee. 1. 12, f. 35ᵛ, printed J. Zupitza, *Archiv für das Studium der neueren Sprachen*, lxxxix (1892), 201, stanzas 1–4.

[3] MS. cited, f. 76ᵛ, printed Zupitza, op. cit., p. 276, stanzas 1–4.

The son of light is not fadyng
Ne this sterre bright, but is shynyng
With beames of light resplending
    Semper clara.

As a sterre bright bringith furth hir light,
A mayde hath borne the son of right,
Bothe god and man, that Ihesus hight,
    Pari forma.
        (etc.)

Another handling of the 'Laetabundus' material in stanzas of three lines plus *cauda*, with more of the Latin retained, is to be found in Bodleian Library MS. Ashmole 189 of the fifteenth century and apparently from London.[1] As it is hitherto unpublished, it may be here quoted entire:

Regem regum a mayde hath borne
To sawe mankynde, that was forlorne,
And yyt ys sche as sche was beforne;
    Res miranda.

Angelus consilii
Was borne of this blessyd ladye
Virilis ignara consorcii,
    Sol de stella.

Cedrus alta Libani
That yrewe on this hylle so hye,
Yne oure valey he doyth aplye,
    Carne sumpta.

Verbum ens altissimi,
Persaywynge mischefe so nye,
For our synnes he cam to dye
    Valle nostra.[2]

Ysayas cecinit
That a chylde schalle be borne;
Synagoga meminit
Therof longe tyme beforne.

Si[3] non suis vatibus
Therof thay take no affiawns,
Sibilinis[4] versibus
That borne was of oure aliawns.

Infelix, propera, to the Y saye,
Leste thou be dampned a domysdaye;
Thane shalt thou synge welawaye
But thou belyve hec predicta.

[1] ff. 104ᵛ, 105ʳ, text from manuscript. [3] MS. S3.
[2] MS. nostram. [4] MS. Sibilimis.

This piece is not a carol, for it has no burden, and the stanza form does not remain constant, but the form of the first four stanzas indicates the working of some influence besides that of the prose itself.

Finally, in No. 14 b, we have the 'Laetabundus' completely transformed into a carol, as the music shows.[1] The 'Alleluia' becomes a burden, and all the stanzas are to be sung to the same melody. The two-line-plus-tag strophe predominant in the prose has become the favourite three-line-plus-*cauda* stanza of the carol, the Latin tags being retained as the *caudae*:

Alleluya

Now wel may we merthis make,
For vs Jhesus manhode hath take
Only for our synnes sake.
Alleluya, alleluya.

A Kynge of Kynges now forth is brought
Of a maide that synned nought,
Nother in dede, nother in thought,
Res miranda.
(etc.)

The Latin tags of the 'Laetabundus' are used by one carol not otherwise based on Bernard's prose. The burden of this carol has the same words as the first stanza, but lacks the *cauda*:[2]

[T]her is [n]o rose of swych vertu
As is the rose that bare Jhesu.

Ther is no ro[se of] swych vertu
As is the rose that bar Jhesu;
Alleluya.

For in this rose conteynyd was
Heuen and erthe in lytyl space,
Res miranda.
(etc.)

At first glance the texts just quoted might seem to justify an assertion that the prose 'Laetabundus' exerted a considerable influence upon the English carol. The important part assigned to the prose in the shaping of the Italian *laude* by Professor Ippoliti[3] and the recognition of the prose-line of the 'Laetabundus' as a source of the tail-rhyme stanza by Wolf[4] and Schipper[5] further suggest this. But consideration will show that it is hardly the case.[6]

---

[1] *Early Bodleian Music*, No. li, burden and stanzas 1, 2.

[2] No. 173, stanzas 1, 2. Compare No. 338 a from the same manuscript.

[3] *Dalle Sequenze alle Laudi*, pt. i, chap. ii, pt. ii, chap. ii.

[4] *Über die Lais*, pp. 30–6.

[5] *Englische Metrik*, i. 356–7.

[6] It is not surprising to find so many English pieces modelled to some extent on the 'Laetabundus', for the prose was widely imitated in various languages. Karl Bartsch, (*Die lateini-*

The English stanza-form which results from imitation of a pair of long lines of the type found in the first four strophes of the 'Laetabundus' is that in the form a a b a a b. This can hardly be said to occur in the carols at all, the only instances being the single stanza of No. 373 and two stanzas of No. 12. Even if this be divided (as it is not in the proses, where double strophes are essential), the resulting form a a b is to be found in only eight carols. Some of these may indeed be granted to have undergone influence from the prose.[1] The tail-rhyme stanza having three lines rhymed together followed by a *cauda*, a a a b, is by far the most frequent of all in the carols, and has been explained as a form developed by the conditions of the popular dance. But it is a form also to be found in the proses; the fifth strophe-pair of this same 'Laetabundus' suggests it, and it occurs throughout the 'Verbum bonum et suave'.[2] Is it perhaps in imitation of this type of prose rather than of dance-song that the carols use it? Professor Ippoliti regards it as deriving from the prose in those *laude* where it occurs.[3] But this form of tail-rhyme stanza is frequent in other medieval Latin poetry besides the proses, e.g. the *cantilena* 'Bonum vinum cum sapore', quoted below,[4] and in the proses themselves it is less used than the form a a b. There would seem to be more warrant for holding that its occurrence in the proses is the result of an influence exerted upon them by secular song. The entire history of the prose, in fact, shows a process of development from a Gregorian chant, quite unlike anything in popular poetry, to a song in the accentual rhythm borrowed from non-literary verse, and in strophes which are like the stanzas of popular song in their uniformity.[5]

What the fifteenth-century English texts of the 'Laetabundus' actually

---

schen Sequenzen des Mittelalters, Rostock, 1868, pp. 224–5) lists twenty-six other Latin proses to the same melody, many of which imitate the words as well. Typical of these is the prose in honour of St. Francis, 'Laetabundus Francisco decantet clerus: Alleluia' (text in Daniel, *Thesaurus Hymnologicus*, ii. 193), which Ryman translated into English stanzas of two lines plus *cauda* (text in *Archiv für das Studium der neueren Sprachen*, lxxxix, 1892, 237). Bernard's prose was also imitated in German and French. Heinrich von Loufenberg was the author of a fifteenth-century version which follows exactly the form of the original (text in Philipp Wackernagel, ed., *Das deutsche Kirchenlied*, Leipzig, 1864, etc., ii. 586). The Latin tags are preserved in two Old French pieces, one a translation keeping the strophic form of the 'Laetabundus' throughout (text in Alfred Jeanroy and A. Långfors, eds., *Chansons satiriques et bachiques du XIIIᵉ siècle*, Paris, 1921, p. 84). The other, more famous, is a capital Anglo-Norman drinking-song, which varies from the form of

its original only in the third and seventh verses of strophe vi. It begins (ibid., p. 78):

> Or hi parra:
> La cerveyse nos chauntera
> Alleluia!
> Qui que en beyt,
> Si tele seyt com estre deyt,
> Res miranda!

[1] In No. 422 the first two lines of a stanza so rhymed are of seven measures, in no event derived from such lines. No. 173, just quoted, preserves tags from the prose, and the combination of an 'Alleluia' refrain with the non-religious content of holly and ivy in No. 137 suggests a similar relation. The others are Nos. 53, 148 (in part), 418.2, 445, 474.

[2] Quoted above, p. xcviii.

[3] Op. cit., pp. 135–8.   [4] p. cx.

[5] Cf. Wolf, *Über die Lais*, p. 31: '. . . und zwar gerade in dieser Gattung des Kirchengesanges [prose], als der volksmässigsten, wird der Einfluss der volksthümlichen Poesie auch am sichtbarsten.'

show is the effect of the already existing carol-*form*, popular by origin, upon the *material* of a prose, ecclesiastical by origin. The English text obtained by translating the Latin was put into uniform stanzas of three lines plus *cauda*, and provided with a burden so that it might be sung carol-fashion, and in that process the distinctive features of the prose-form were discarded.[1]

4. *The Antiphon and the Carol*

A third form of church-song upon which the carols drew for their Latin phrases was the antiphon. The ordinary antiphons, the verses sung before and after the psalms to Gregorian melodies suggesting those of the psalms, are the sources of the following lines:

Table of Antiphon-Lines Used in the Carols

Line	Carol No.	Use	Text
Ave, rex gentis Anglorum	312	St. Edmund's Day, I Vespers	B.S. iii, col.1073
De fructu ventris	29	Christmas, II Vespers	B.S. i, col. cxciv
Exortum est	29	Christmas, II Vespers	B.S. i, col. cxciv
Ipse invocavit me	474	Christmas, II Nocturn	B.S. i, col.clxxvii
Lapidaverunt Stephanum	9, 100	St Stephen's Day, Lauds	B.S. i, col. ccx
Mirabile mysterium	56, 94, 319	Circumcision, Lauds	B.S. i, col.ccxciii
Missus est angelus Gabriel	246	Advent, Third Wednesday, Lauds	B.S. i, col. cxix
Notum fecit Dominus	474	Christmas, III Nocturn	B.S. i, col. clxxxi
O clavis David	2	Advent, Vespers	B.S. i, col. clv
O radix Jesse	1	Advent, Vespers	B.S. i, col. clv
Ortus est sol iustitiae	127	Purification, Processional	Sar. Mis., p. 249
Pastor caesus in gregis medio pacem emit cruoris pretio	115	Holy Innocents, Vespers	B.S. i, col. ccxlvi
Veritas de terra orta est	77	Christmas, II Nocturn	B.S. i, col.clxxvii

The four Antiphons of the Blessed Virgin Mary, originally connected with psalms, but since the thirteenth century sung as separate chants,[2] contribute Latin lines to the carols as follows:

---

[1] The so-called 'Prose of the Ass', beginning 'Orientis partibus' and with its vernacular burden, represents an extreme in the intrusion of popular ways of song into Latin liturgical poetry. It is actually no prose at all, as the music shows, all stanzas being sung to the same melody. (See *Analecta Hymnica*, xx. 257.) The real prose used in the ritual of Sens for the Feast of the Ass preserves the strophe-pairs characteristic of the type (ibid., p. 217).

[2] See *The Catholic Encyclopedia* (New York, 1907), s.v. 'Antiphon'.

Table of Lines from the Antiphons of B.V.M. used in the Carols

Line	Carol No.	Use	Text
Alma redemptoris mater	234	Service of B.V.M., Advent to Purification, Compline	Dan. ii, p. 318
Pro nobis Christum exora (from 'Ave, regina coelorum')	198	Service of B.V.M., Purification to Septuagesima, Compline	Dan. ii, p. 319
Regina coeli, laetare	185, 186, 189, 204, 218, 237	Service of B.V.M., Eastertide	Dan. ii, p. 319
Quem meruisti portare	204, 218 }	From 'Regina coeli'	
Resurrexit, sicut dixit	218 }		
Salve regina, mater misericordiae	206, 207, 208, 209, 210, 211, 213	Service of B.V.M., Trinity to Advent	Dan. ii, p. 321
O clemens, O pia, O dulcis Maria	199, 228 }	From 'Salve, regina'	
Vita dulcedo et spes	213, 214 }		

The 'Ave, regina celorum' of No. 201 is taken, not from the Antiphon of the Blessed Virgin Mary which so begins, but from a shorter antiphon which begins with the same phrase but continues: 'Mater Regis angelorum'.[1] This had various uses, as a bidding prayer in connection with the *Ave Maria*, as a grace after meat, and, most interestingly, in the services on the vigils of the five feasts of the Virgin in the University Church of St. Mary the Virgin at Oxford, attendance at which was compulsory for scholars living in the various halls.[2] The antiphon has six lines, and to arrive after the beginning of the fifth brought a fine of a farthing. A change of only half the lines of this composition produced the antiphon in honour of St. Edmund, 'Ave, rex gentis Anglorum', which is quoted in the burden of the only known carol to this saint (No. 312) and which was in frequent use at his monastery in Bury. All the lines are used in carols as follows:

	Nos.
Ave, regina celorum	201
Mater Regis angelorum	201
O Maria, flos virginum	201
Velut rosa vel lilium	201, 218
Funde preces ad filium	201, 218
Pro salute fidelium	62, 201, 218

The 'Alma redemptoris mater' of No. 243 b is taken, not from the Antiphon of the Blessed Virgin Mary which so begins, but, as shown by the line

[1] Text in *Horae Eboracenses*, Publications of the Surtees Society, cxxxii, 1920, 29.

[2] Frank Ll. Harrison, *Music in Medieval Britain* (London, 1958), p. 85.

following it in 243 a, 'Quem de celis misit Pater', from a processional anti-phon used from the Octave of Trinity to Advent.[1]

The antiphons seem to have been used merely as sources for Latin phrases and not to have had any part in shaping the form of the carols which quote them.

Some recent attempts to derive the English carol from the specifically processional hymn of the medieval church and to regard the carols themselves (with a wholly artificial distinction between 'religious' and 'non-religious') as hymns performed in liturgical processions into and within the church need no long consideration.[2] The processional hymns for use in the services were very definitely prescribed and were invariably in Latin. Professor Frank Ll. Harrison delivers the verdict of musicology on this point very succinctly: 'The theory ... that carols were sung in ritual processions is untenable, since the ordinals laid down the chants to be sung for processions throughout the year.'[3] There is no piece in the entire body of English carols which is marked with the rubric *ad processionem* or its equivalent, and there is no indication in any known service-book that a carol in English is to be used as a processional hymn.[4] The attempt by Dr. Miller to interpret the headings of British Museum MS. Addit. 5665 (*In die nativitatis, De innocentibus, In die circumcisionis*, etc.) as implying processional use does not survive comparison with similar rubrics in Audelay's manuscript, Bodleian Library Douce 302.[5] She ignores the presence in the manuscript of pieces like No. 6, with its invitation to the 'company' to drink well and make good cheer, the totally secular No. 348, which praises the mean estate with no religious reference, and No. 133, which is clearly meant to be sung, like the better-known Queen's College carol, by those actually bearing a boar's head into a feast. None of these would by any stretch of assumption be suitable for use in a procession within or into a church service.

The characteristic processional hymn used in England is a Latin one built closely upon the pattern and in the classical quantitative metre of the

---

[1] Text in Daniel, *Thesaurus Hymnologicus*, v. 133.

[2] For example, Margit Sahlin, op. cit.; Catharine Keyes Miller, 'A Fifteenth Century Record of Choir Repertory' (Unpublished dissertation, Yale University, 1948, on B.M. MS. Addit. 5665) and 'The Early English Carol', *Renaissance News*, iii (1950), 61–4; R. H. Robbins, 'Middle English Carols as Proces-sional Hymns', *Stud. in Phil.* lvi (1959), 559–82. Bukofzer (pp. 149–50) is very cautious on this point, and recognizes the objections. Stevens (*Mediaeval Carols*, p. xiv) qualifies his state-ments carefully and has no evidence that can stand against Harrison's verdict.

[3] *Music in Medieval Britain*, p. 417 n. 4.

[4] Even a brief study of the comprehensive

work by Terence Bailey, *The Processions of Sarum and the Western Church*, Pontifical Insti-tute of Mediaeval Studies, Studies and Texts, xxi (Toronto, 1971), will make plain the lack of connection between the English carol and liturgical processions.

[5] *Renaissance News*, iii (1950), 63. In her re-view of Stevens, *Mediaeval Carols*, Dr. Miller appears to accept the position that the carol is not essentially a processional hymn: 'Dr. Stevens is quite justified (pp. xiv–xv) in insist-ing that the idea of the carol-as-processional-music is too narrow a concept in which to con-fine the form—that it should be thought of, in a larger sense, as ceremonial ornament' (*Musical Quarterly*, xxxix, 1953, 460).

one great prototype, the *Salve, festa dies* attributed to Fortunatus, a cento made from a sixth-century poem on Easter. The unlikeness of its stately measures to the characteristic four-beat accentual line of the carol is apparent to anyone who hears it read or sung, and there is no preserved carol which imitates or even suggests its content. John Skelton, rector of Diss, who could have written English processional hymns had they been in use, produced instead as choral thanksgivings for the victories of Flodden and the Battle of the Spurs Latin hymns beginning like their model with *Salve, festa dies*.[1]

In the processions of lay folk, which were a feature of many festivals in medieval England and which, of course, were outside the liturgy, the texts which are referred to as being sung are always in Latin. Neither is there any reliable record of a modern custom of singing Christmas carols processionally in church which can be traced back to the Middle Ages. The artificial association of procession and carol found in recent 'carol services' appears to be entirely a matter of supposed revival influenced by nineteenth-century movements within the English Church.

An interesting example is provided by the records of the London church of St. Mary at Hill. The accounts of the church contain, in addition to many entries concerning the purchase of holly and ivy for Christmas decoration, a payment in 1537 of 3s. 4d. to 'sir marke' for 'carolles for cristmas and for v square bookes', and an inventory of 1553 lists 'a gospell boke & x bokes of song to be sovng at mas in parchement, with v Caroll bokes'. But a note added by the churchwardens to the 1486 copy of the will made in 1431 by William Cambrugge, citizen and grocer, makes it plain that not English carols but parts of the Latin service and an anthem were used at that Christmas evensong:

Also it hathe bene acustomyd that vppon Cristmas day at the magnificat in the Evensong, be ordeyned for euerye preste, clark & childe xv small candelles waying all ij lb di. And euery persone hauyng a surplise shall haue one of thise smale candelles brennyng in their handes & so go on processyon to the tombe of Mr. Cambryge syngyng a Respond of Seynte Stephen with the prose therto; that done, a versicle with the colet of S3 Stephen, And in goyng into the Queer a Antempne

---

[1] *Chorus de Dis Contra Scottos cum Omni Processionali Festivitate Solemnisavit Hoc Epitoma* [etc.] and *Chorus de Dis, etc. Super Triumphali Victoria Contra Gallos, etc. Cantavit Solemniter Hoc Elogium* [etc.] in *The Complete Poems of John Skelton Laureate*, ed. Philip Henderson, 3rd edn. (London, 1959), pp. 436–7. And in a service of thanksgiving in St. Paul's for Queen Mary's supposed pregnancy, after the sermon '*Te Deum* was sunge, and solemne procession was made of *Salve, festa dies*, goeinge the circuite of the churche' (Charles Wriothes-

ley, *A Chronicle of England . . . 1485 to 1559*, ed. William Douglas Hamilton, Camden Society, New Ser., xx, 1877, ii. 124, entry for 28 November 1554). The characterizing of the carol as processional song in the article 'Carol' in the fifth edition of *Grove's Dictionary of Music and Musicians* (ed. Eric Blom, London, 1954, ii. 84) is now undergoing modification and revision. The same article refers to British Museum MS. Egerton 3307 as the Windsor Manuscript, an unjustified designation. See Bibliography of Original Sources.

of owre ladye: Beryng ij candilstick*es* of syluer w*ith* the tapres on yt and a Sencer w*ith* a schyp.[1]

That carolling and religious processions were recognized in Scotland in 1558 as quite different things is well shown by two neighbouring passages in Sir Richard Maitland's poem 'Off the Quenis Maryage with the Dolphin of France'.

> All burrowis townis eu*e*rilk ma*n* ȝow prayis
> To mak bainfyris fairseis and clerk playis
> And throw ȝour rewis carrellis danss and sing
>
> .   .   .   .
>
> Preistis and clerkis and men of religioun
> with devote mynd gang in processioun[2]

It is puzzling that Robbins refers to a single clause of a letter written to the King by Archbishop Cranmer on 7 October 1544 which, if read throughout, shows plainly that English songs had *not* been used in processions before 1544. The 'songs' that Cranmer wants used in processions in English translations are the *Venite*, the *Te Deum*, and so on. 'As concerning the *Salve festa dies*, the Latin note, as I think, is sober and distinct enough; wherefore I have travailed to make the verses in English, and have put the Latin note unto the same. Nevertheless they that be cunning in singing can make a much more solemn note thereto. *I made them only for a proof, to see how English would do in song* [italics mine].'[3] None of the sacred selections referred to is a carol or anything like one, and Cranmer obviously disapproves of such polyphonic music as the important carol manuscripts preserve. One could hardly ask for stronger assurance, on higher authority, that the singing of English words in liturgical processions was unknown before this time. The proposed processional in English was never produced, and processions in church or churchyard were entirely abolished in 1547.[4]

Robbins does not recognize the one piece in the carol manuscript Eng. poet. e. 1 which is actually a processional hymn:

> Psallimus cantantes
> Domino nova cantica dantes.[5]

---

[1] Henry Littlehales, ed., *The Medieval Records of a London City Church* (*St. Mary at Hill*), *A.D. 1420–1559*, E.E.T.S., Or. Ser., Nos. 125, 128, 1904–5, pp. 378, 54, 16.

[2] [Sir] W. A. Craigie, ed., *The Maitland Folio Manuscript*, i, S.T.S., New Ser., No. 7, 1919, 28; ll. 19–21, 28–9.

[3] John Edmund Cox, ed., *Miscellaneous Writings and Letters of Thomas Cranmer*, The Parker Society (Cambridge, 1846), p. 412.

[4] F. E. Brightman and K. D. Mackenzie, 'The History of the Book of Common Prayer down to 1662', in W. K. Lowther Clarke and Charles Harris, eds., *Liturgy and Worship* (London, 1932), pp. 147–8. See also Edmund H. Fellowes, *English Cathedral Music from Edward VI to Edward VII*, revised by [Sir] J. A. Westrup (London, 1969), pp. 24–7.

[5] Printed Wright, *P.S.* xxiii. 60–1; with music, *E.B.M.* ii. 182.

Unlike all but one of the carols in the manuscript, it has its music written with it. But this single processional hymn is, as we should expect, in Latin. The burden and first strophe are printed at the beginning of an English song (which Robbins mistakenly calls a carol) by Richard Kele about 1550.[1] The English piece is not a translation of the Latin, but it follows its verse-form and its transfer of the phrase 'Amice Christi Johannes' from its liturgical association with St. John the Baptist to St. John the Evangelist, as in the carols No. 103 A b (which immediately precedes the Latin hymn in the manuscript) and No. 104 (from the same manuscript).

The one place in the ritual of the Church where it seems likely that carols in English may have been used is not in procession but at the conclusion of the Office during the Christmas season, where 'Benedicamus Domino—Deo gratias' is usually sung. Frank Ll. Harrison has pointed out that so-called 'Benedicamus-substitutes' were permitted at this one point and that certain carols, especially those which contain these Latin phrases, e.g. No. 426, the 'Agincourt' carol, and No. 39.1, would be suitable for this purpose. But it must be admitted that the carol manuscripts themselves contain no rubric which positively indicates such use.[2]

5. Non-Ritual Latin Poetry and the Carol

When we turn from the formal compositions included in Breviary and Missal to those medieval Latin lyrics, sacred and secular, which had no regular place in the order of service, we find many pieces which resemble the carol in metrical form as well as in subject and spirit. A number of these are to be found in the same manuscripts with collections of carols. Bodleian Library MS. Eng. poet. e. 1 opens with two Latin pieces, the first being a song to the Virgin with a 'nowell' burden:[3]

> Nowell, nowell, nowell, nowell,
> Myssus est ad virginem angelus Gabriell.
>
> Angelum misit suum Deus omnipotens,
> Ut unicum per filium ejus saluetur gens.
> 'Virgo, ave,' clamat ille, 'O Maria clemens,
> Concipies et paries, virgo semper manens.'
>   (etc.)

The second is a song on the convenience of ready money, written in a metrical form exactly corresponding to that most favoured by the English

---

[1] Reed, *Christmas Carols Printed in the Sixteenth Century* (Cambridge, Massachusetts, 1932), pp. 28–32.

[2] *Music in Medieval Britain*, pp. 416–18; *The Listener*, 27 Dec. 1956, p. 1086.
[3] Printed Wright, *P.S.* xxiii. 1.

carol (4a 4a 4a 4b 4B 4B). The first three stanzas show its form and manner:[1]

Semper vivit misere,
Qui non habet solvere.

Bonum vinum cum sapore
Bybit abbas cum priore;
Sed conventus de pejore
Semper solet bibere.

Bonum vinum in taberna,
Ubi vina sunt valarna,
Ubi nummus est pincerna,
Ibi prodest bibere.

Dum vadis ad bibendum
Te festina ad videndum
Quantum habes ad solvendum,
Antequam vis bibere.

Bodleian Library MS. Ashmole 1393, of the early fifteenth century, contains a Latin piece having the same Latin burden used by James Ryman with two English carols. It begins:

Ecce quod natura
Mutat sua iura,
Virgo parit pura
dei filium.

Ecce nouum gaudium,
Ecce nouum mirum,
Virgo parit filium,
Que non nouit virum:
Que non nouit virum,
Sed ut pirus pirum,
Gleba fert saphirum,
Dei filium.[2]

This is one of a large number of sacred Latin songs which are usually designated by the term *cantio* or *cantilena*. They are, strictly speaking, extra-liturgical, but they were produced under the auspices of the Church and were frequently introduced into services, particularly on feast days.

---

[1] *P.S.* xxiii. 2.

[2] f. 69^r. Printed *Early Bodleian Music*, ii. 64, burden and stanza 1. The same words are differently set in Bodleian Library MS. Arch. Selden B. 26, printed ibid., pp. 154–5, and in British Museum MS. Egerton 3307, f. 65^r. The piece is printed from all three manuscripts by John Stevens, *Mediaeval Carols*, Musica Britan- nica, iv (2nd edn., London, 1958), pp. 26, 32, 51. The words are also found with different music in *Piae Cantiones*, the famous book of *cantilenae* printed in Greifswald in 1582. See also Manfred F. Bukofzer, *Studies in Medieval and Renaissance Music* (New York, 1950), pp. 117, 152, 170.

The following Latin lines appear to have been borrowed by carols from such *cantilenae*:

Line	Carol No.	Text
In virginali gremio	82	*A.H.* xx, p. 47
Nascitur de (ex) virgine	58	*A.H.* ii, p. 163
Salve, sancta parens, } Omni labe carens }	200	*A.H.* xx, p. 209
Super omnes speciosa	202	*A.H.* xx, p. 154

Many of those *cantilenae* which have been collected in the *Analecta Hymnica* are provided with burdens of the type found in the carols, particularly those pieces dealing with the two favourite themes of the English religious carol, the Nativity and the praise of Mary. A fifteenth-century specimen from Germany shows how the *cantilenae* used the favourite carol-form of tail-rhyme stanza and burden linked to it by rhyme:

> Haec festa natalia
> Recolit ecclesia.
>
> Virgo parit filium
> Salvatorem omnium,
> Qui non animalium
>   Abhorret praesepia.
>
> Angelus haec loquitur,
> Pastoribus dicitur:
> De virgine nascitur
>   Rex gubernans omnia.[1]
>   (etc.)

Much the same form was in use at least two centuries earlier, as in the following:

> Hodie fit regressus
> ad patriam.
>
> Hodie splendor et lux
> Refulsit hominibus
> In tenebris sedentibus
>   Per gratiam.
>
> .   .   .   .
>
> Ergo nostra concio,
> Psallat cum tripudio
> Nato Dei filio.
>   Per gratiam.[2]

[1] *Analecta Hymnica*, xx. 123, burden and stanzas 1, 2.   [2] Ibid. 124, burden and stanzas 1, 7.

These are wholly Latin poems, and without question the work of educated churchmen. Whence do they derive their form that is so like that of English carol or French *chanson à danser*? There is no mark of the twin strophes of the prose here, and there is a burden, which the proses never have. There are still earlier Latin lyrics with burdens or something very like them. The ninth century offers us an 'Abecedarius' with a tone much like that of some moralizing English carols of six hundred years later. It begins thus in one version:

> Audax es, vir iuuenis,
> Dum feruet caro mobilis;
> Audenter agis, perperam
> Tua membra coinquinas.
>
> Adtende homo, quod pulvis es
> Et in pulverem reverteris.
>
> Brevis est tempus, iuvenis,
> Considera, quod moreris,
> Venitque dies ultimus
> Et perdes florem optimum.
>
> Adtende homo, quia de terra factus es
> Et in terra ponendus eris.
> (etc.)[1]

This 'Adtende homo' is a choral element, to be sure, but it resembles more a response in the service than a real burden. Also it is not invariable, but alternately appears in the two forms seen above. But another version, written down two centuries later in a Goliardic song-book,[2] presents a stanza-text almost identical with that quoted, and repeats the 'Adtende homo' in invariable form after every stanza, thus bringing it nearer to the burden of popular song. And if we turn to that other great collection of Goliardic verse, the *Carmina Burana*, we find burdens common enough.[3] The nature of the songs which contain them is sufficient evidence to show whence the Latin lyric learned to use a burden: the 90 classified in Schmeller's edition as 'Seria' include three pieces with burdens, the 193 'Amatoria, Potatoria, Lusoria', thirty-four.[4] The chorus-part of student-

[1] *Poetae Latini Aevi Carolini* (*Monumenta Germaniae Historica*, Berlin, 1923), iv. 495, stanzas 1, 2. Other pieces with similar repeated elements are on pp. 504, 507, 512, 515, 518, 524, 526, 559, etc.

[2] Cambridge University Library MS. Gg. 5. 35, printed Karl Breul, *The Cambridge Songs* (Cambridge, 1915), p. 66.

[3] The following pieces, in the edition by Carl Fischer (Zürich, 1974), have burdens: Nos. 3, 52, 56, 59, 63, 75, 80, 81, 82, 83, 84, 85, 86, 94, 95, 96, 109, 113, 115 a, 118, 130, 149, 152, 159, 179, 179 a, 180, 180 a, 181, 182, 182 a, 184, 185, 200, 204, 205, 217. The dramatic and prose pieces are not reckoned.

[4] The most famous of all Goliardic songs, 'Meum est propositum in taberna mori', is included with the English carols in British Museum MS. Sloane 2593, and the hardly inferior 'O potores exquisiti', is found both in the *Carmina Burana* and in British Museum MS. Egerton 3307.

song and *cantilena* is no development from alleluiatic sequence or processional hymn; it is modelled directly on the corresponding chorus-part of popular and secular songs.

Some of these burdens of the *Carmina Burana* are particularly interesting in that their words recognize the association with the dance of these Latin predecessors of the English carol. It is in the songs in praise of spring, the time when youths and maidens danced in the meadows, that the burden most consistently appears. Sometimes it is actually in the vernacular, as in the following piece, which reverses the arrangement of Latin and vulgar tongue common in the carols.

> Floret silva nobilis
> floribus et foliis.
> ubi est antiquus
> meus amicus?
> Hinc equitavit!
> eia! quis me amabit?

(Burden)   Floret silva undique,
                nah mine gesellen ist mir we.[1]

The dance is explicitly mentioned in the following macaronic piece:[2]

> Congaudentes ludite,
> choros simul ducite!
> iuvenes sunt lepidi,
> senes sunt decrepiti!

(Burden)   Audi bel' amia,
                mille modos Veneris!
                hahi zevaleria.
                    (etc.)

A similar invitation forms the burden of a song wholly in Latin:[3]

> Solis iubar nituit,
>   nuntians in mundum
> quod nobis emicuit
>   tempus letabundum.
> ver, quod nunc apparuit
>   dans solum fecundum,
> salutari meruit
>   per carmen iocundum.

(Burden)   Ergo nostra contio
                psallat cum tripudio
                dulci melodia!
                    (etc.)

[1] Ed. Fischer, No. 149.
[2] Ed. Fischer, No. 94, stanza 1 and burden.
[3] Ed. Fischer, No. 81, stanza 1 and burden.

It is significant that two lines of this burden form part of the sacred *cantilena*
of the thirteenth century quoted above.[1] The references in these *cantilenae* to
dancing as a proper means of expressing joy need not be attributed to imitation of classical poetry or of psalmody when it is recalled that dancing to the
accompaniment of song was one of the principal recreations of the people
whence the authors were recruited.[2] It was the festival folk-dance which
inspired such lines as the following:

> Manibus plaudite,
>   pedibus terite,
> Natus est parvulus,
>   ergo venite.

> Nova gaudia
> Et nova studia
> Et nova sint tripudia,
> Nam nova sunt solemnia,
> Novi regis praesentia . . .

> Sonet vox tripudii,
> *Gaudeamus socii*,
> Grata quies otii
>   In hoc florali gaudio,
>   Floris renovatio
>   Lusus est incitatio.[3]

The tendency in Goliardic verse to irreverent parody, of which so much
has been made, must not be allowed to obscure the probability of its having
acted as a transmitting medium for the influence operating in the other
direction, from vernacular folk-lyric to sacred Latin. Surely the authors of
the Nativity songs just quoted knew well the accent of amorous student
songs.

Even without any explanation we should recognize the imitation of vernacular dance-song in this Nativity piece from the 'Mosburg Gradual' of
1360:

> Verbum patris humanatur,
>   O, O,
> Dum puella salutatur,
>   O, O,
> Salutata fecundatur
>   Viri nescia.[4]

---

[1] p. cxi. Compare *Analecta Hymnica*, xx.
80, 88, 115.

[2] Compare the positive evidence for the
employment of dance-song as the musical basis
of Latin *cantilenae* provided by Bibliothèque
de Lille MS. 95 (facsimile in E. de Cousse-
maker, *Histoire de l'harmonie au moyen âge*,

Paris, 1852, plate xxvi), where a piece is headed:
'Cantilena de chorea super illam quae incipit
*Qui grieue ma cointise se iou lai ce me font
amouretes cau cuer ai*.'

[3] *Analecta Hymnica*, xx. 113, 63, 93.

[4] Ibid. 104–5.

The burden goes:

> Ey, Ey, Eya,
> Nova gaudia!

Explicit acknowledgement that some of his Latin *cantilenae* were written to the tunes and in the verse-form of secular and vernacular lyrics is made by the grammar master of the school at Saint-Denis who produced for the use of his scholars the twenty-seven pieces in Bibliothèque Nationale MS. 15131 of the late thirteenth century. Three of the songs have prefixed lines in French which identify the worldly songs from which the tunes and forms are borrowed. In one case we have the entire burden of the French song on the favourite subject of the nightingale:

> Joi te rossignol
> Chantez de sus i rain,
> Viar dinet namie
> De sus laure florie.

After the rubric 'Contra in Latino: Sancti Nicolai etc.' comes the burden of the Latin carol:

> Sancti Nicolai
>   vacemus titulis
> Cum summa laetitia
> Pangentes Alleluja.[1]

It is significant that the same Latin word *cantilena* is applied in many documents to both 'dissolute worldly songs', including those actually sung in the dance, and the festive religious songs in Latin which show similar form, for example the decree of a council at Avignon in 1209: 'amatoria carmina, vel cantilenae'; a thirteenth-century Franciscan *exemplum* from Ireland: 'in suis tripudiis, in suis fatuis cantilenis'; the life of Thomas Becket translated by Laurence Wade, monk of Christ Church, Canterbury, who matches the phrase of the Latin heading, 'cantilenas dissolutas sive ad lascivia[m] pertinentes', by the line 'Off al maner off karolles and songes dissolute'.[2]

These instances from the Continent (and there are others) are, of course, parallel to the case of the Red Book of Ossory, now in the Bishop's Palace at Kilkenny, in which are written sixty Latin lyrics, some, but not all, composed by the great fourteenth-century Franciscan Bishop of Ossory, Richard

[1] *Analecta Hymnica*, xxi. 82–3.
[2] Quoted by L. Gougaud, op. cit., p. 12; A. G. Little, ed., *Liber Exemplorum ad Usum Praedicantium*, British Society of Franciscan Studies, i (Aberdeen, 1908), p. 111; Corpus Christi College, Cambridge, MS. 298, f. 20ᵛ, text from manuscript.

de Ledrede.[1] The Latin memorandum at the foot of the first page of the songs must be cited once again here. In English translation it says:

> Be advised, reader, that the Bishop of Ossory has made these songs for the vicars of the cathedral church, for the priests, and for his clerks, to be sung on the important holidays and at celebrations in order that their throats and mouths, consecrated to God, may not be polluted by songs which are lewd, secular, and associated with revelry, and, since they are trained singers, let them provide themselves with suitable tunes according to what these sets of words require.

Before some sixteen of the Latin *cantilenae*, which are in many different verse-forms including several variations of the carol, are written scraps of varying length of English and French songs, obviously secular. It is plain that these are the incipits of the songs of which the tunes and verse-forms are being followed by the bishop. One which is twice used in this way is an English song of the nightingale:

> 'Do, do' nyghtyngale
> syng wel mury,
> 'Shal Y neure for thyn
> loue lenger karie.'

The burden of the Latin piece goes:

> Regem adoremus
> Superne curie;
> Matri iubilemus
> Regine glorie.

Most telling of all is the case which went unnoticed until a few years ago, a Latin *cantilena* to the Virgin which is marked 'mayde yn the moore lay'.[2] The exquisite fourteenth-century lyric which begins with this line is miraculously one of the only set of English vernacular songs of that date to be preserved, in Bodleian Library MS. Rawlinson D. 913 on an isolated half-leaf probably from the neighbourhood of Coggeshall, Essex. The English and Latin are alike in rhyme and verse-form, in this case a variation of the *rondel* which is found nowhere else in English and, as far as can be discovered, nowhere else in Latin. No clearer evidence of English secular song as the model followed by a writer of Latin *cantilenae* could be imagined. Richard 'of Leatherhead', like his clerks, was wholly English and a product of the same Franciscan friary at Canterbury that James Ryman was to inhabit a century later.

---

[1] Ed. Richard Leighton Greene, *The Lyrics of the Red Book of Ossory*, Medium Ævnm Monographs, New Ser., No. 5 (Oxford, 1974). Another edition by Edmund Colledge, O.S.A., attributes all the lyrics to Richard, ignores the appearance of some in other manuscripts, and has a questionable commentary on 'The Maid of the Moor' (*The Latin Poems of Richard Ledrede, O.F.M.*, Pontifical Institute of Mediaeval Studies, Studies and Texts, No. 30, Toronto, 1974).

[2] See Greene, op. cit., pp. x–xiii, 16, 32, 49.

Both carol and *cantilena* owe their form to the immemorial structure of the unlettered people's dance-song: burden, stanza, burden, often linked by rhyme. From the solemn hymn of the Office written by Ambrose and his successors, sung antiphonally by opposed and facing choirs (which are quite different things from a soloist and a chorus) and naturally without a burden but with a last stanza sung by all as a doxology, both carol and *cantilena* show a fundamental difference which must have made them variations in the life of monk or vicar-choral or choir-boy as welcome as the Christmas or saint's-day feast itself.

'It is important', in the words of F. J. E. Raby,

to remember one obvious thing. The peoples of Europe did not live without song, and for thousands of years they had had their songs of love and of death, their drinking-catches and their ballads. It is the continued flow of this stream of popular poetry, which has now perished as though it had not been, that must be taken into account in any attempt to obtain a reasonable view of the Latin lyric. The vernacular song was always there, whatever might happen to its learned counterpart.[1]

From this necessarily fragmentary review of some features of the Latin background of the English carol the ultimately popular character of the genre gains only confirmation. The qualities of form common to the carol and medieval Latin poetry are for the most part precisely those which derive from the poetry of the people and particularly from the dance-song. Where the service of the Church touches the carol it leaves only such effects as can be reconciled with the form already given by popular poetry, as the fate of 'Laetabundus' in English demonstrates. The hermit-saint, the musical theorist, the imitator of classical poetry—none of these sequestered religious could have given us the carol or its Latin counterpart, the *cantilena*. The Latin lyrics in lighter vein were valuable agents in transmitting the popular influence which shows itself in burdens and triply-rhymed stanzas, but they were not prime movers. Behind them, as behind the vernacular lyrics of Europe, is the song of the unlettered people, shaped by the physical conditions of its performance, the relentlessly regular periodicity of the dance, and the opposition of leader and chorus.

[1] *A History of Secular Latin Poetry in the Middle Ages*, 2nd edn. (Oxford, 1957), ii. 326–7. Interesting evidence of the indebtedness of both sophisticated vernacular lyric and Goliardic Latin verse to a common source in folk-song is discussed, with special reference to the *pastourelle*, in William Powell Jones, *The Pastourelle* (Cambridge, Massachusetts, 1931), chap. v.

CHAPTER IV

THE CAROL AS POPULAR SONG

THE phrase 'popular poetry' has often been used indiscriminately to describe two kinds of composition between which the line of demarcation, sharp enough in theory, is often difficult to draw in practice. The two categories are perhaps most clearly indicated in English by the respective labels 'popular by origin' and 'popular by destination', the former being applied to what is called in careful German usage *Volkspoesie*, the latter to *volkstümliche Poesie*. The term 'popular poetry' or 'popular song' is used here as equivalent to 'poetry popular by destination'; that is, it is applied to material the text of which is derived from written or printed sources, but which is designed to appeal to an audience including people of scant formal education and social refinement. The popular quality of such material is not dependent upon the circumstances of its composition; whether of unknown date and authorship, or preserved in the author's signed and dated holograph, it is popular if its appeal is to such an audience. The quantity of popular song is of course enormous; it includes the most varied subject-matter and metrical forms, and it is being added to every day.

The term 'folk-song', coined within the last century on the analogy of the German noun, is here used only in the sense in which it has been understood by the Folk-Song Society: to designate 'song and melody born of the people and used by the people as an expression of their emotions, and (as in the case of historical ballads) for lyrical narrative';[1] song, that is, which first makes its appearance in the oral tradition of a homogeneous community without 'book-learning'. Indigenous British folk-song not artificially 'revived' continues to disappear with the disappearance of these communities, and the versions which emigrated to North America and were transmitted for several generations are fading from their last homes in such isolated districts as the southern Appalachians in the United States. The conquest of these regions by radio and television and the greatly increased mobility of their population have been finishing it off in the years since World War II. Nevertheless, more traditional verse than was once supposed has been preserved in the game-songs and other rhymes and jingles of young children, as Iona and Peter Opie have shown in their fascinating work *The Lore and Language of School-children*.[2]

Some confusion, but no insuperable difficulty, has been created by the

---

[1] Frank Kidson and Mary Neal, *English Folk-Song and Dance* (Cambridge, 1915), p. 10.

[2] (Oxford, 1960).

very widespread use of the terms 'folk-song' and 'folk-singer' in the last few decades to designate a great range of performance and performers of almost any vocal music which is regarded as less sophisticated than the main repertory of the formal concert hall or even than the songs of the musical-comedy stage. 'Folk-songs' of this kind are of course the productions of known individual authors and composers and are as completely commercial in their purpose and means of dissemination as the 'popular' songs of the days of vaudeville and the early jazz bands. Through electronic recording and transmission even the most ephemeral of them reach millions of listeners, and they are closely woven into the daily lives and interests of most young people in western Europe and the Americas. It has even become quite usual for boys and girls in their teens to make public appearances as 'folk-singers', often playing their own accompaniment on a guitar or other stringed instrument. In the midst of this usually synthetic 'folk-music' there occasionally appear specimens of the older folk-song of simple and illiterate societies, adapted or appropriated with or without acknowledge-ment by commercial composers and performers. It is useless to indulge any pedantic regret over this situation, especially as the pseudo-primitive song often stirs an interest in the young listeners which is then transferred to genuine traditional folk-music. But careful definition of terms in a given context becomes more important than ever.

The only material which can be proved by positive external evidence to be English folk-song is that which has been taken down from the lips of singers who have learned it orally from other singers. The songs so collected possess certain characteristics of style, often more definite in the music than in the words, which enable one familiar with them to recognize as true folk-song similar material preserved in manuscript or printed sources whose exact provenance is not known. A considerable part of the matter collected in Child's canon of the ballads is admitted on this basis.

The only safe criterion, therefore, for use in an attempt to determine to what extent the medieval manuscript carol partakes of the nature of true folk-song is provided by the body of traditional material collected from the singers themselves by such recorders as the late Cecil Sharp and others. That much of this was current at the period when the carols were written down is not to be doubted. The unmistakably medieval legends embodied in ballads like 'Sir Hugh, or the Jew's Daughter'[1] which are still being sung show plainly the antiquity of such pieces. It is true that many genuine folk-songs show signs of more recent origin, such as references to particular voyages or wars which detain an absent lover, but the readiness with which oral tradition alters details to make them conform to the experience of a given group of singers renders it dangerous to deny the possibility of antiquity to many folk-songs which have a superficially modern aspect.

[1] Child, No. 155.

Hence it is not only permissible but pertinent to seek for points of similarity and difference between the carols of the fifteenth and sixteenth centuries and recently collected traditional song.

In a number of other pieces particular features are to be found which suggest the peculiarities of folk-song, but in no case has the entire poem a truly folk-character: the often-reprinted drinking-carol 'Bring us in good ale' is an example.[1] The stanzas are made up of a repeated formula together with a portion which is changed with each repetition, an old device used by very elementary folk-poetry:

> Bryng vs in no browne bred, fore that is mad of brane,
> Nore bryng vs in no whyt bred, fore therin is no game,
>> But bryng vs in good ale.

> Bryng vs in no befe, for ther is many bonys,
> But bryng vs in good ale, for that goth downe at onys,
>> And bryng vs in good ale.
>>> (etc.)[2]

A song built on this pattern cries aloud for improvisation, and new verses were doubtless added as it circulated.[3] But the words have a sophistication in their pretended delicacy as to diet which removes them from the class of real folk-poetry. It is also pertinent to note Sharp's observation on the absence of drinking-songs among the traditional pieces of England.[4] The device of repetition may well have been borrowed from current folk-song, but the piece itself was not. The same device of repetition is used, with even less change from stanza to stanza, in No. 25:

> Al the meryere is that place
>> The sunne of grace hym schynit in.

> The sunne of grace hym schynit in
>> In on day quan it was mor[we,]
> Quan our Lord God born was,
>> Withoute wem or sorwe.

> The sunne of grace hym schynit in
>> On a day quan it was pryme,
> Quan our Lord God born was,
>> So wel he knew his tyme.[5]

---

[1] No. 422.
[2] Version A, stanzas 1, 2. For repetition in folk-poetry see Gummere, *Beginnings*, pp. 205–11.
[3] A has four stanzas not in B, and B has two not in A.
[4] *English Folk-Song, Some Conclusions*, 3rd edn. (London, 1954), p. 98: 'Drinking songs, too, are scarcely ever to be found in the repertoire of the folk-singer. Incidental allusions to drink are common enough, but the thorough-going bacchanalian song . . . is unknown to the folk-singer—so far as my experience goes.'
[5] Burden, stanzas 1, 2.

This is not folk-song, of course, but the author may have learned his trick of a formula with much repetition and slow progression from such a piece as 'I haue XII oxen'[1] where only two words are changed with each new stanza. Simple repetition of a phrase at the beginning of successive stanzas also occurs in Nos. 12, 27, 54, 130, 132 A, and 230, but in each case it forms only a small part of the stanza and does not give the carol any particular likeness to folk-song. Nos. 423 and 430 are written more closely to a repetitive formula and suggest folk-song more strongly.

A related type of formula, characteristic of folk-narrative whether in prose or in verse, is that in which a number of persons (usually three) attempt the same action, or one person performs or experiences three successive phases of an action. It is frequent in the ballads, for example, at the beginning of 'The Cruel Brother':

> A gentleman cam oure the sea,
> *Fine flowers in the valley*
> And he has courted ladies three.
> *With the light green and the yellow*
>
> One o them was clad in red:
> He asked if she wad be his bride.
>
> One o them was clad in green:
> He asked if she wad be his queen.
>
> The last o them was clad in white:
> He asked if she wad be his heart's delight.[2]

This method of narration is used in an Epiphany carol in telling of the gifts of the Magi.[3] The text of the stanzas differs in the two extant versions, but the procedure is the same:

> Baltyzar was the ferste kyng;
> He browte gold to his offeryng
> For to presente that ryche Kyng
> And his moder Marie.
>
> Melchiar was the secunde kyng;
> He browte incens to his offering
> For to presente that ryche Kyng
> And his [moder Marie.]
>
> Jasper was the thred kyng;
> He browte myrre to his offeryng
> For to presente that ryche Kyng
> And his [moder Marie.][4]

[1] Balliol College, Oxford, MS. 354, f. 178ʳ; printed Dyboski, *Songs, Carols, and other Miscellaneous Poems*, p. 104.
[2] Child, No. 11 B, stanzas 1–4.
[3] No. 123.
[4] Version B, stanzas 8–10.

The presence of this formula in the carol is doubtless the effect of familiarity with narrative folk-song, but it does not appear with any great frequency in the carols generally and does not establish any one of them as a real folk-production.[1] It is used as a refrain in a folk-song preserved in several variants and beginning:

> My father left me an acre of land,
> *There goes this ivery.*
> My father left me an acre of land,
> *And a bunch of green holly and ivery.*[2]

Probably it is a similar refrain or burden that is affixed to a carol written on the back of a fifteenth-century indenture among the papers of the Corporation of Bridgwater.[3] Before the carol, which is a reworking of the prose 'Laetabundus', is written the line:

> Holy holy holy holy holy and yffy yffy;

after the carol:

> Holy holy and yfy yffy holy yffy Holi.

One of the clearest glimpses of a background of folk-custom and folk-song is given by the group of carols which treat of the holly and the ivy. In one wording or another 'holly and ivy' is a recurrent phrase in English folk-song, notably in the charming traditional piece which begins:

> The holly and the ivy,
> When they are both full grown,
> Of all the trees that are in the wood,
> The holly bears the crown.[4]

It is introduced more perfunctorily in the following doggerel sung by children as a *quête* song when begging for evergreens, apples, or pence:

> Holly and ivy,
> Mistletoe bough,
> Give me an apple,
> And I'll go now.
> Give me another
> For my little brother,
> And I'll go home,
> And tell father and mother.[5]

---

[1] The enumeration of the Five Joys of Mary in Nos. 231, 232 shows some influence of this formula. The Joys, in varying number, are the topic of many traditional songs, e.g. 'The Seven Joys of Mary' (*Journal of the Folk-Song Society*, v, 1918, 18, 'The Nine Joys of Mary' (ibid., p. 319),' The Ten Joys of Mary', Cecil J. Sharp, ed., *Folk Songs from Somerset*, 5th Ser., London, 1909, p. 66). The tradition of the Five Joys is, of course, originally learned and theological.

[2] *Journal of the Folk-Song Society*, ii (1906), 212; Child, No. 2 K, L.

[3] No. 14 a.

[4] Cecil J. Sharp, ed., *English Folk-Carols* (London, 1911), p. 18.

[5] *Folk-Lore*, xiv (1903), 177; reported as current about 1825.

It occurs in the begging conclusion of an otherwise lugubrious *quête* song
for St. John the Evangelist's Day in a mid-seventeenth-century collection:

> Now kindly for my pritty Song,
>   good Butler draw some beer,
> You know what Duties do belong
>   to him that sings so clear:
> Holly and Ivy, drink will drive me,
>   to the brown bowl of Perry,
> Apples and Ale, with a Christmas tale,
>   will make this Houshold merry.[1]

A number of carols, as many writers have noted, imply a traditional strife
between the holly and the ivy, which are connected respectively with men
and women. The most explicit statement of the opposition is in a little piece
with a refrain but no burden, which may be a real folk-song, perhaps a game-
song as the words suggest:

> Holvyr *and* Heyvy mad a gret party,
> Ho xuld haue the mays*tre*
>   In lond*es* qwer thei goo.

> Than spake Holuyr: 'I a*m* frece *and* jo[ly,]
> I wol haue the mays*tre*
>   In lond*es* qwer thei goo.'

> Than spake Heyvy: 'I *am* lowd *and* prowd,
> *And* I wyl haue the mays*tre*
>   In lond*es* qw*er* thei goo.'

> Than spak Holvyr, and set hy*m* downe on his kne:
> 'I prey the, je*n*tyl Heyvy, sey me no veleny,
>   In lond*es* qwer we goo.'[2]

Another holly-and-ivy piece, which is a true carol, is a good illustration
of the way in which folk-material might be utilized by the carol-writers.[3]
It is a song taunting Ivy with inferiority to Holly and with her exclusion
from the hall. In one version it has stanzas composed of two long lines with
a burden of the same form:

> Nay, Iuy, nay, hyt shal not be, iwys;
> Let Holy hafe the maystry, as the maner ys.

> Holy stond in the hall, fayre to behold;
> Iuy stond without the dore; she ys ful sore a-cold.

[1] Bodleian Library, Wood 110 (5), A₈ʳ ᵃⁿᵈ ᵛ; it reappears in a broadside of about 1815: *'Printed and Sold* by J. Marshall, Newcastle and Gateshead', Chetham Library, Manchester, Halliwell Collection, No. 920. Compare Carol No. 421.
[2] Bodleian Library MS. Eng. poet. e. 1, f. 30ʳ ᵃⁿᵈ ᵛ; text from manuscript.
[3] No. 136 A.

This version must be close to actual folk-song, somewhat touched up, perhaps, by the hand which recorded it. It strongly suggests a dramatic game during which it would be sung, and in which the feminine party of Ivy would be excluded from a company representing those in the 'hall' and would be grouped by itself 'without the door'.[1] The taunting tone of the burden is a familiar one in folk-song, as in the flyting.[2] The phrase 'as the maner ys' shows the feeling of the imperativeness of custom which is so marked a characteristic of the folk-mind; it suggests the lines preserved in a children's game-song recently in use:

> Go in and out the windows,
> As we have done before.

The identification of holly with the male and of ivy with the female is to be observed in a number of folk-customs from various parts of England. A communication to the *Gentleman's Magazine* in 1779, often cited in this connection, describes the burning at Shrovetide of two effigies known as the 'Holly-Boy' and the 'Ivy-Girl' by the girls and boys respectively of a village in east Kent.[3] This 'Ivy-Girl' has also been identified with the 'Harvest-May', the last sheaf of a harvest dressed as a girl and brought home on the last load by the women workers.[4] The sheaf is, of course, a very ancient symbol of woman and the fertility associated with her. Ivy appears openly as a fertility-charm in the Worcestershire and Herefordshire custom of giving a little of the ivy that has hung in the church to the ewes in the belief that this makes them tend to bear twin lambs.[5]

Holly and ivy are particularly connected with Christmas customs, being two of the evergreen plants principally used to deck houses at that season. There is a marked preference for holly for this purpose, ivy sometimes seeming to share the discredit attached to mistletoe because of heathen associations.[6] The sexual significance of the two plants is prominent in various

---

[1] Compare the 'scenarios' reconstructed for medieval French dance-songs by Joseph Bédier (*Revue des deux mondes*, pér. v, xxxi, 1906, 402–24) especially those in which one or more dancers are excluded from a group as 'vilain' or 'jalous', e.g.

> Vous qui amez, traiez en ça;
> En la, qui m'amez mie!

But it would seem that W. C. Hazlitt makes a doubtful conjecture when he writes that 'holly was used only to deck the inside of houses at Christmas . . .' (*Faiths and Folklore*, London, 1905, i. 318).

[2] Gummere (*Beginnings*, p. 307) calls this carol a flyting. There are no grounds for his

statement that 'it is holly for summer and ivy for winter'; the symbolism of holly and ivy is certainly sexual.

[3] xlix. 137. Holly and ivy also appear in February customs in the following begging-verse for Valentine's Day (G. F. Northall, ed., *English Folk-Rhymes*, London, 1892, p. 212):

> Holly and ivy tickle my toe,
> Give me red apples and let me go.

[4] Hazlitt, *Faiths and Folklore*, i. 319.
[5] *Notes and Queries*, 5th Ser., xi (1870), 206.
[6] T. F. Thiselton Dyer, *British Popular Customs* (London, 1911), p. 458; *Folk-Lore*, xxviii (1917), 421. According to *The Boke of Curtasye*

Christmas usages, including that of a strife between men and women.[1]
A seventeenth-century volume, *The Twelve Months*, alludes to it thus:
'Great is the contention of holly and ivy, whether master or dame wears the
breeches.'[2] Plainly related is the tradition reported from Oxfordshire that
a man must supply a maid with ivy, or she will steal his breeches.[3] Some kind
of contention between men and women in connection with the giving of
gifts at the New Year (which is still in the Yule season) is rather obscurely
hinted at in *Sir Gawain and the Green Knight*:

> And syþen riche forth runnen to reche hondeselle,
> 3e3ed 3eres-3iftes on hi3, 3elde hem bi hond,
> Debated busyly aboute þo giftes;
> Ladies la3ed ful loude, þo3 þay lost haden,
> And he þat wan watz not wrothe, þat may 3e wel trawe.[1]

It may be that the ladies are said to have lost, because the gifts were confined
to the men; a tradition reported from the East Riding of Yorkshire forbids
the receiving of gifts by women at Christmas.[4]

The exclusion of Ivy and her women from the hall in the carol has not
hitherto been satisfactorily explained by any of its commentators. The key
to it lies in the general disfavour with which folk-belief seems to have regarded
woman (and her symbolic plant) on Christmas Day itself. It takes this precise
form of exclusion in a number of customs behind which is the great importance attached to the omen of the 'first foot'. For a woman to be the first foot
on Christmas Day is generally considered unlucky; in a tradition reported
from three shires a woman is not permitted to enter a house at all on Christmas Day, but must sleep there the night before. In some instances the plant-
symbolism has been united with the custom of 'first-footing'. In Holderness

---

holly is to be placed in the hall during the season
when there is no fire:

> So longe squiers lyverés shalle hafe,
> Of grome of halle or ellis his knafe;
> But fyre shalle brenne in halle at mete,
> To *cena Domini* that men hase ete;
> Ther brow3t shalle be a holyn kene,
> That sett schalle be in erber grene,
> And that schalle be to Alhalawgh day,
> And oft be skyfted, as y the say.

Ed. James Orchard Halliwell (-Phillipps), 'The
Boke of Curtasye', *P.S.* iv (1841), 17, ll. 395–
402.

[1] The smooth variety of holly also appears
as a feminine symbol. 'Smooth holly, ivy, and
mistletoe hung behind shippon door before
noon on Christmas Day prevents cows mis-
carrying' (*Folk-Lore*, loc. cit.). Another belief

is that if smooth holly is brought first into
a house on Christmas Day the wife will rule
during the coming year, if rough holly, the
husband (loc. cit.; *Notes and Queries*, 11th Ser.,
vi, 1912, 486). The same alternative of smooth
holly instead of ivy was known to Gascoigne in
1576 (*Princely Pleasures at Kenilworth Castle*,
quoted by Hazlitt, loc. cit.): 'Mary, there are two
kinds of holly, that is to say he holly and she
holly. Nowe some will say that the she holly hath
no prickes, but thereof I entermeddle not.'

[2] By M. Stevenson; quoted by John Brand,
Popular Antiquities of Great Britain and Ireland
(London, 1841, i. 269).

[3] *Folk-Lore*, loc. cit.

[4] Ed. Tolkien and Gordon, ll. 66–70. The
editors' note on the passage says, 'how the
ladies might lose is not known'.

[5] *Folk-Lore*, xxviii (1917), 430.

on Christmas and New Year's mornings a sprig of holly would be laid outside the door to ensure that the first thing to enter should be a male.[1]

Margaret Dean-Smith has stated that 'the holly-and-ivy metaphor of the male and female principle . . . is rare in folk-song, despite its continuing prevalence in active Christmas custom'. She might be challenged for her further statement that 'the holly-and-ivy metaphor of masculine and feminine principle belongs to medieval literary conception, and seldom or never is found in this form in "folk-tradition"'.[2] It has strikingly survived to the present day in Somerset traditional song, as reported by R. L. Tongue. 'Green Ivy O', found at Taunton in 1906–7 and at Crewcombe in 1959, has a stanza for each of the four seasons, and the winter stanza may be thought to preserve a trace of the association of ivy with the Virgin Mary found in No. 138:

O the ivy O, she is Queen of old
And the holly he is red
Hang'n high on the farm and us wont come to no harm
Till the Chrissimass Days be told
O 'tis ivy O, green ivy O
O the ivy she is Queen of old.[3]

Even the birds mentioned in the carol are linked to old folk-beliefs. The owl is associated with ivy in many popular sayings, especially in the proverbial expression 'like an owl in an ivy-bush'. The owl as an object of derision and even of attack is also a well-known figure, as passages in *The Owl and the Nightingale* show. The owl is there twitted with her unpopularity as she sits in her ivy-bush:

Vorþi þu art loþ al fowel-cunne,
& alle heo þe dryueþ heonne,
& þe biscrycheþ & bigredeþ,
& wel narewe þe byledeþ:

Vor children, gromes, heme & hine,
Hi þencheþ alle of þine pine:
If hi mowe iseo þe sitte,
Stones hi doþ in heore slytte,
& þe totorneþ & toheneþ,
& þine fule bon toscheneþ.[4]

[1] *Notes and Queries*, 6th Ser., x (1884), 482. See also 7th Ser., x (1890), 5, 93, and [E.] Gutch, *Examples of Printed Folk-Lore Concerning the East Riding of Yorkshire*, County Folk-Lore, vi, Publications of the Folk-Lore Society, lxix (1912), 115.
The feminine associations of ivy occur also in Scottish folk-lore: 'Ivy was used as a protective for milk, milk products, and flocks. On the Quarter Days young girls used to pin three leaves of ivy into their night-shifts in order to dream of their future husbands' (F. Marian McNeill, *The Silver Bough*, i, Glasgow, 1957, p. 82).

[2] *Guide*, pp. 74, 57.

[3] *Somerset Folklore*, ed. K. M. Briggs, *County Folklore*, viii (1965), 208–10; see also Tongue, 'Two Somerset Carols', *Folk-Lore*, lxx (1959), 544–5.

[4] Ed. J. W. H. Atkins (Cambridge, 1922), Jesus text, ll. 65–8, 1115–20. Compare the seventeenth-century quotation, 'With that they all fell upon him, as an Oule in an ivie bush' (*Notes and Queries*, 9th Ser., ix (1902), 157).

An amusing example of the recurrence of the theme is found in Act II, Scene i of Nicholas Udall's *Roister Doister* (1566):

> *Dobinet Doughtie*: Then to our recorder, with toodleloodle poope,
>   As the howlet out of an yuie bushe should hoope.[1]

The B version of No. 136, committed to writing sixty or seventy years later than A, presents it in a smoother and more finished form, with stanzas composed of two couplets of long lines instead of one.[2] The presence of an additional couplet containing a formal simile ('But lyke a meyny of bullokkes', etc.) shows that an individual artist has laid his hand on the older material. The order of the stanzas has been changed, so that the likeness to a game-song is much obscured. If this interpretation is correct, the two versions of the piece illustrate a process of adaptation and reworking of folksong material which doubtless underlies other carols where the distinctive folk-characteristics of the original songs have been more completely eliminated by the work of the 'improver'.

Three other carols of the holly–ivy group show religious, semi-learned handling of the folk-theme. One, partisan to the holly, has a secular stanza-text, probably older than the 'Alleluia' burden and refrain.[3] Another takes the part of ivy, with a refrain from the Song of Songs.[4] Ivy is here taken to symbolize the Divine Spouse and the Virgin. The sanctification of ivy is done even more thoroughly by a truly medieval acrostic in a fifteenth-century carol written to counteract the prejudice against a plant which, as a symbol of womanhood like the Virgin, ought to be reverenced.[5] There is no folk-imagination here, only pedantry.

The more sophisticated and literary praise of ivy found in No. 139.1 is wholly secular and refers to the plant's remaining green in a severe winter and to its physical qualities as good medicine and as a preservative of masonry. No mention of mistletoe, which pagan associations kept out of all churches except York Minster, is found in any medieval carol. But ivy was used in England as a substitute for palm-branches in Palm Sunday processions and undoubtedly gained some additional sanctity thereby.[6] Both holly and ivy were among the plants most disliked and shunned by Scottish witches.[7]

The contrast between the typical manuscript carol and the type of folk-song on which it is ultimately dependent can be seen in a comparison of two pieces which take notice of the same great event, the Battle of Agincourt.

---

[1] Joseph Quincy Adams, ed., *Chief Pre-Shakespearean Dramas*, (Boston, 1924), p. 437, ll. 23–4. The same tradition survives into the seventeenth century in the broadside ballad 'The Turtle Dove' (William Chappell, ed., *The Roxburghe Ballads*, Hertford, 1874, ii. 595, ll. 89–96).

[2] No. 136 B.

[3] No. 137.

[4] No. 138.

[5] No. 139. Compare the connection of the Virgin with *holly* in the traditional piece referred to above, p. cxxii, and in the Cornish 'Sans Day Carol' (*Oxford Book of Carols*, No. 35).

[6] Theodor Erbe, ed., *Mirk's Festial*, i, E.E.T.S., Ex. Ser., No. xcvi, 1905, p. 115.

[7] F. Marian McNeill, op. cit. 82, 84.

One is a traditional song showing the true carol-structure, the 'Padstow May Song'. It is a dance-song for the May festival, divided into stanzas and burden. As preserved, it is in two parts, the 'Morning Song' and the 'Day Song'. One recorded text of the latter begins:

(Burden)   Awake, S. George, our English knight O!
          For Summer is a-come, and Winter is a-go.

(Stanza)   Where is S. George? and where is he, O?
          He's down in his long-boat upon the salt sea, O.

(Burden)   For to fetch Summer home, the Summer and May, O!
          The Summer is a-come, and Winter is a-go.

(Stanza)   Where are the French dogs, that made such boast, O?
          They shall eat the goosefeather, and we'll eat the roast, O![1]

The burden with its invocation of St. George, as sung before the first stanza, shows a connection with the widespread folk-drama of St. George which symbolizes the passing of winter and the resurrection of the fertilization-spirit, an observance having its roots far back in the customs of pagan Britain.[2] The age of the burden 'For Summer is a-come, and Winter is a-go' can only be guessed at; it may well be at least as old as whatever folk-song lies behind the thirteenth-century English words of the famous rota 'Sumer is i-cumen in'.[3] If the interpretation of H. Fleetwood Sheppard is correct, the stanzas quoted above refer to the first French expedition of Henry V, and the Battle of Agincourt, as do also the following stanzas from the associated 'Morning Song':

O where are the young men that here now should dance O?
Some they are in England and some they are in France O.

The young men of Padstow they might if they wold O,
Have builded a ship, and gilded her with gold O.[4]

The allusion to the 'gray goosefeather' presumably is in honour of the prowess of the English archers, and the prevalent belief that St. George

---

[1] Sabine Baring-Gould and H. Fleetwood Sheppard, eds., *A Garland of Country Song* (London, 1895), p. 94. When the song was heard by the present editor in 1932 the first stanza of the Morning Song (with St. George changed to King George in some of the younger mouths) was sung with the burden of the Day Song. The observance is described in A. K. Hamilton Jenkin, *Cornish Homes and Customs* (London, 1934), pp. 211–16; Claude Berry, *Cornwall* (London, 1949), pp. 178–85; *Devon and Cornwall Notes and Queries*, xii (1922), 145–52; perhaps a little too raptly by Violet Alford and Rodney Gallop, *The Traditional Dance* (London, 1935), pp. 142–6; and elsewhere. As is to be expected, the text of the songs varies considerably in different accounts. The whole ceremony has been exploited in recent years in radio and television broadcasts.

[2] On the St. George plays see Chambers, *The Mediaeval Stage*, i, chap. x, and *The English Folk-Play* (Oxford, 1933), pp. 170–4.

[3] This burden is also found in the 'Hal-an-Tow' song performed at Helston, Cornwall, on 8 May (Sabine Baring-Gould *et al.*, eds., *Songs of the West*, 6th edn., London, n.d., pp. 48–9). Stanzas on St. George and the goose feather occur as well. Compare the 'Furry Day Carol' (*Oxford Book of Carols*, No. 49).

[4] *A Garland of Country Song*, pp. 94–5.

fought for and with the English army at Agincourt may be responsible for
the incorporation of such stanzas into a song associated with a St. George
play.

Such a song, being made among the folk, naturally took no heed of the
prohibition attributed to King Henry by Holinshed: 'He would not suffer
any Dities to be made and sung by Minstrels, of his glorious victorie.' But
at least one song-writer disobeyed this injunction, and gave us the 'Agincourt
Carol', which begins:

> Deo gracias Anglia
> Redde pro victoria.
>
> Owre kynge went forth to Normandy
> With grace and myght of chyualry;
> Ther God for hym wrought mervelusly;
> Wherfore Englonde may calle and cry,
>   'Deo gracias.'[1]

The song cannot wholly have displeased the king, however, if it came to his
notice, for Holinshed adds: 'He would have the praise and thankes altogether
given to God.' This carol, accompanied in two manuscripts by a finished
musical setting, is obviously the work of a talented individual. But it is
probably the work of a talented individual who had heard folk-songs on
other campaigns if not on this same one; the spirit of the second stanza of
the 'Day Song' is echoed in the lines:[2]

> Than went oure kynge with alle his oste
> Thorwe Fraunce, for alle the Frenshe boste;
> He spared no drede of lest ne moste
> Tyl he come to Agincourt coste;
>   Deo gracias.

The character of the carols in manuscript as songs popular by destination
rather than as real folk-lyrics is further attested by the nature of the variations
which occur in different copies of the same piece. The distinctive mark of
the true folk-song is its perpetuation by an oral tradition which, operating
in a mostly unlettered community and hence released from control by written
copies, in the course of time works profound changes in the wording of any
song. The result is that of a piece so transmitted there will be almost as
many variants as singers or, in the case of communal pieces like the Padstow
song, compact groups of singers. This characteristic is well exemplified
in the numerous and wide variants of pieces in Child's ballad collection
which have been recorded since its publication. The variants of the carol-
texts, much as they often differ from each other, are not to be regarded as
products of the same method of transmission, as a little study of their relation-
ships will show.

[1] No. 426 a, burden and stanza 1.   [2] Stanza 3.

Of the 507 carols here collected 81 appear in more than one version. The most widely disseminated is one in honour of St. John the Evangelist, of which six copies are preserved, two of them in one manuscript.[1] The other pieces, grouped according to the number of extant texts, are as follows:

5 copies: No. 21.
4 copies: Nos. 23, 114, 125, 132, 149, 150, 157, 234, 239, 322, 468.1.
3 copies: Nos. 14, 27, 31, 36, 79, 86, 101, 117, 122, 151, 175, 187, 191, 232, 235, 337, 359, 370, 401, 402, 419.
2 copies: Nos. 7, 8, 12, 17, 18, 30, 35, 42, 81, 91, 95, 121.1, 123, 124, 131, 136, 145, 146, 148, 155, 161, 163, 172, 180, 185, 190, 230, 237, 238, 243, 331, 337, 338, 355, 356, 380, 386, 389, 395, 399, 402.1, 410, 413, 422, 424, 426, 433.1, 468.

Of about half of these carols the versions agree so closely as to show without question that they derive from written copies with no dependence on oral transmission and its consequent lapses of memory and perversions of meaning. The much-copied 'Amice Christi Johannes' belongs to this class.

The variations in the others give evidence in general of conscious activity on the part of individuals through whose hands they passed, rather than of uncontrolled oral tradition. That they were at times passed orally from one singer to another is certainly to be admitted, but only oral transmission within a limited group, intelligent and fully aware of the significance of the material, could have preserved such good texts. Almost unique external evidence for such a process is presented by the tradition of the Boar's Head Carol at Queen's College, Oxford.[2] Texts B and C b of this carol are given below: B as printed by Wynkyn de Worde in 1521, and C b as recorded in a letter written by a tutor of Queen's College in 1811.[3]

B	C b
Caput apri differo,	Caput Apri defero,
Reddens laudes Domino.	Reddens laudes Domino.

The bores heed in hande bring I,	The Boar's head in hand bear I,
With garlans gay and rosemary;	Bedeck'd with bays and rosemary;
I pray you all, synge merely,	And I pray you, my masters be merry,
Qui estis in conuiuio.	Quot estis in convivio.

The bores heed, I vnderstande,	The Boar's head, as I understand,
Is the chefe seruyce in this lande;	Is the rarest dish in all this land,
Loke, where euer it be fande,	Which thus bedeck'd with a gay garland
Seruite cum cantico.	Let us servire Cantico.

---

[1] No. 103; British Museum MS. Addit. 5665. Lydgate's No. 263 and the first stanza of No. 309 are excepted. Nos. 142 and 152, with their modern versions, are also excepted.

[2] No. 132.
[3] Quoted by T. F. Dibdin, ed., *Ames's Typographical Antiquities* (London, 1810–19), ii. 252.

Be gladde, lordes, bothe more and
    lasse,
  For this hath ordeyned our stewarde
To chere you all this Christmasse,
  The bores heed with mustarde.

Our Steward hath provided this
In honour of the King of Bliss;
Which on this day to be served is,
  In Reginensi Atrio.

The third stanza in the early version probably represents a corruption of a text which was originally in tail-rhyme like the other stanzas and after which the traditional Queen's College version is patterned.

A circumscribed tradition such as this, from which the irresponsibility of folk-singers is entirely absent, is what seems to lie behind most of the carol-variants. The generally excellent state of the Latin in different copies of macaronic carols shows that they had not been loosed into truly popular oral tradition, which would have lost no time in reducing passages in the unknown tongue to gibberish, or in replacing them by vernacular lines, probably irrelevant.

The prevailing points of difference between manuscript copies of the carols are substitution of one burden or refrain for another, as elsewhere discussed,[1] omissions and substitutions of stanzas, and changes in the order of stanzas. The frequency with which such omission and substitution occur in Middle English poetry of all types testifies to the liberties taken with manuscript material as well as the accidents which often befell it. Pieces intended for singing, like the carols, were doubtless intentionally shortened in some cases. On the other hand, to no form of poetry could verses be added more easily than to the carol. Although many of the carols are narrative after a fashion, as a rule they present no close sequence of events like that in a good narrative poem; there is seldom any logical link between stanza and stanza. They offer a constant invitation to versifiers to add, subtract, or transpose, and in the absence of a written copy it would be unusually easy to confuse the stanza-order. That faults of memory are responsible for some of the variations is shown by the fact that the first three or four stanzas of a carol are more usually preserved in the same order in variant versions than are later stanzas. Occasionally lapses from good sense are revealed by comparison with another version to be faults of the ear and not of the eye, but they are not many.

The method of transmission of these carol-texts is thus midway between the uncontrolled oral tradition of folk-song and the exclusively manuscript tradition of long and learned works. The repeated performance of a carol would involve its being committed to memory, and many people who never set pen to parchment doubtless learned some of these carols by word of mouth. But the same pieces, unlike folk-song, were also current in manuscript copies, against which singers who were not illiterate folk-singers could

---

[1] Below, pp. clxi–clxiv.

check their repertory. This is exactly the type of transmission usual in song which is popular by destination. The text of a modern 'pop' or 'country music' song lives out its not always brief existence under conditions which, on a larger scale, are much like those to which the carol-texts were subject. Great numbers of children and other half-educated people (no longer, however, technically a 'folk') learn it orally, and as sung by them it will show many minor variations of wording. But the wide circulation of authoritative copies in sheet music and phonograph records prevents any wide variation of the song itself like that which is inevitable in real oral tradition.[1] At the same time professional performers do not scruple to omit stanzas of the original text or to add new ones composed by or for themselves. The activity of some professional class, literate if not learned, is to be seen behind the English carol of the later Middle Ages and 'transition period'. Its more exact identification will be attempted in the following chapter.

There seem to be only two medieval manuscript carols which have survived to the twentieth century in outright oral tradition. One is the famous 'Corpus Christi', No. 322, discussed above, pp. lxx, lxxi. The other is No. 80, a carol which has become well known in its medieval text but with supplied music not found in the manuscript, British Museum, Harley 5396. The volume is a typical monastic miscellany, apparently owned in 1455 by someone in the Midlands, probably Northamptonshire, who used its blank spaces for commercial accounts. The Harley text begins:

> Christo paremus cantica:
> 'In excelsis gloria.'

> When Cryst was born of Mary fre
> In Bedlem, in that fayre cyte,
> Angellis songen with myrth and gle,
>   'In excelsis gloria.'

Shortly before 1909, Alice E. Gillington heard a folk-carol sung by a gipsy in the south of England and recorded it without recognizing its medieval source. Margaret Dean-Smith, in her admirable *Guide to English Folk Song Collections*, rightly calls the gipsy version a 'vulgarization'. It begins:

> Christ is born of maiden fair;
> Hark, the heralds in the air,
> Thus, adoring, descant there:—
>   'In Excelsis Gloria.'[2]

---

[1] An early and important recognition of the existence of manuscript texts in the midst of the process of oral transmission is that by H. M. Belden, 'Balladry in America', *The Journal of* *American Folk-Lore*, xxv (1912), 20.

[2] *Old Christmas Carols of the Southern Counties* (London, 1910), p. 15.

It is plain that there has been some influence here from modern evangelical hymnody: we recognize the herald angels of Wesley and Whitefield.

There are only three medieval manuscript carols which have been found in modern unlearned use. One appears most surprisingly in D'Urfey's *Pills to Purge Melancholy*, set to music 'by Mr. Tenoc'. Its text is in the medieval carol-form with an initial burden, though the burden is printed without separation from the stanzas. It begins:

> It is my Delight both Night and Day,
> To Praise the Women as much as I may;
>> Three things be glorious,
>> I'll tell you if I can,
> The Sun, an Angel, and a Woman.
>> (Burden repeated)[1]

This is clearly in direct descent from the doggerel in the carol-manuscript Bodl. Eng. poet. e. 1.[2] R. H. Robbins has rightly recognized the first two lines as a burden and listed the piece as a carol.[3] It appears to be derived from an even more primitive set of puzzle-verses in cipher, a 'Christmas game'.[4] The others, Nos. 142 and 152, occur in both the manuscript of an eighteenth-century collector in Cornwall and nineteenth-century print. See Notes and Bibliography of Original Sources.

All evidence combines to show, therefore, that the carol as a genre in written English is popular, that is, one degree removed from traditional folk-song, and yet lower in the scale of education and refinement than the courtly lyric or scholarly Latin poem. This does not imply that there are not considerable variations in the tone and style of the carols, marking what might be called 'degrees of popularity'. The miscellaneous character of the pieces brought together in a single manuscript is often striking, as in the volume just mentioned, Bodl. MS. Eng. poet. e. 1.

A piece like the following would appeal to the male half, at least, of the humblest audience which might be assembled in fifteenth-century England:

> Care away, away, away,
> Care away for euermore.

> All that I may swynk or swet,
> My wyfe it wyll both drynk and ete;
> And I sey ovght, she wyl me bete;
> Carfull ys my hart therfor.[5]

---

[1] Edn. of 1707, ii. 127; *repr.* John S. Farmer, *Merry Songs and Ballads Prior to the Year 1800* (privately printed, 1897), iv. 149–51.

[2] *Pr.* Wright, *P.S.* xxiii. 4–5.

[3] 'The Middle English Carol Corpus: Some Additions', *Modern Language Notes*, lxxiv

(1959), 200.

[4] Lucy Toulmin Smith, ed., *A Common-place Book of the Fifteenth Century* (London: privately printed, 1886), pp. 12–13; see Notes on No. 402.1.

[5] No. 406, burden and stanza 1.

The sentiment of another carol is such as the simplest man, if his heart be good, might be expected to understand and applaud:

> I pray yow all with hert and thovght,
> Amend me, and peyer me novght.
>
> Holy Wrytt sayth nothyng sother,
> That no man shuld apeyer other;
> Sythen I am [in] God thi broder,
> Amend me, and peyer m[e nought.]
>
> .   .   .   .
>
> If thou se I do gretly amys,
> And no man wott butt thou of this,
> Mak it not so yl as it is;
> Amend me, [and peyer me nought.][1]

But it would hardly be a group of peasants who would appreciate the abstract nouns and somewhat literary melancholy of such a complaint as this:

> For pencynesse and grett distresse
> I am full woo;
> Destitute frome all refute,
> Alone I goo.
> Whylome I present was with my soffreyne;
> Ignorawnt I was of dolowr and payne,
> For than I lyued
> Fro sorow depreued,
> Of plesure hauyng habundawnce and delice,
> But now, forsothe,
> Sore hytt me ruthe,
> Fortune contrarythe to my device.[2]

And the admonition

> Haue in mynd, in mynd, in mynd,
> Secuters be oft onekynd[3]

would presumably be of primary interest to those whose property was large enough to warrant their thinking about an executor.

A definite piece of testimony as to the class of person to whom the carols appealed is given by Balliol College, Oxford, MS. 354, which contains a large number of them. This manuscript is a commonplace book, once the property of Richard Hill, a London merchant who was sworn at Grocers' Hall on 10 November 1511.[4] This hardly justifies us, however, in labelling the carol 'bourgeois literature', for Hill was evidently a man of very catholic

---

[1] No. 337 b, burden and stanzas 1, 3.
[2] No. 439, burden and stanza 1.
[3] No. 382, burden.

[4] See the rather full family record printed from the manuscript by Dyboski, *Songs, Carols, and other Miscellaneous Poems*, pp. xiii–xv.

taste. It is evident, moreover, that he had access, direct or through intermediate copies, to a large body of carols which had earlier been current in
clerical, and specifically monastic, circles. The entries in the book include
such widely different pieces as a verse-treatment of the folk-tale of the Boy,
Stepmother, and Friar,[1] and two early poems of St. Thomas More.[2] There
are also a number of Latin verses and maxims.

It has often been said that carols were sung by 'minstrels'. Despite many unlearned and some learned statements to the contrary, it is necessary to say that
there is no record at all of the vocal performance of any of the English carols
by any professional entertainer of the kind to which the term 'minstrel' was
applied in the fourteenth, fifteenth, and early sixteenth centuries. It is surely
significant that the word 'minstrel' does not occur in the texts of the carols
themselves. The evidence that by 'minstrel' was then understood an instrumental musician playing for pay of one kind or another is simply overwhelming, as Ritson realized a century and a half ago in the midst of his annoyance
with Bishop Percy. A few significant references only will be quoted here. The
key verb is regularly 'play', not 'sing'.

When in 1324 in Cornhill a dealer in skins named Thomas de Lenne
was so angered at the music of a minstrel named Thomas Somer that he
struck him with a door-bar and pursued him to kill him, only to be
stabbed to death himself by the said Somer, it was playing and not singing that moved him to such violent criticism.[3]

Froissart records a musical incident when King Edward III was on
board ship before the Battle of Winchilsea. Sir John Chandos had brought
back from Germany a piece called a 'dance'. The King had his minstrels
play the accompaniment, but Chandos himself did the singing.[4]

In the mumming presented at Kennington for Richard II by the commons of London just before Candlemas of 1377 there was 'great noyse
of mynstralsye, trumpets, cornets and shawmes'. After dicing and gift-
giving, wine was brought, 'and they dronk with great joye, commanding
ye minstrels to play and ye trompets began to sound and other instruments to pipe, &c.'[5]

Nothing could be more explicit than the Black Book of Edward IV with
its prescriptions for the smallest details of the King's household establishment. The section beginning 'Mynstrelles, xiij,' is self-explanatory:

... whereof one is veriger that directeth them all in festiuall dayes to theyre stacions,
to blowinges and pipinges, to suche offices as must be warned to prepare for the
king and his houshold at metes and soupers, to be the more redy in all seruyces,

---

[1] Ibid., p. 120; see editor's note, p. xxvii.
[2] Ibid., pp. 72, 97.
[3] Edith Rickert, *Chaucer's World* (New York,
1948), pp. 17–18. It is plain, on the other hand,
that minstrels often provided instrumental

accompaniment to the song and dance of the
carole.
[4] Clair C. Olson, 'The Minstrels at the Court
of Edward III', *PMLA*, lvi (1941), 611–12.
[5] Chambers, *The Mediaeval Stage*, i. 394 n. 4.

and all thies sitting in the hall togyder, whereof sume vse trumpettes, sume shalmuse and small pipes.[1]

No reference whatever appears to singing by minstrels. The regular term for professional vocalists, those who sang in the Chapel Royal, for example, was 'singing men'.

During the coronation feast of Queen Elizabeth, wife of Henry VII, on 25 November 1487:

. . . as the high bourde was servid, the kings mynstrells played a song before the queene, . . . [followed by ceremonies of thanking and Garter's triple cries of *Largesse*]. Then played the queenes mynstrells, and after them the mynstrells of other estates.[2]

Hall's *Chronicle* for the reign of Henry VIII includes a number of passages which make clear the distinction between minstrels and singers. A good example is the account of the performance at 'the Conduit in Chepe', in the fourteenth year of the reign: '. . . then al the minstrels which were in the pagiant plaied & the angels sang.'[3]

Two matters of common sense may be mentioned in passing. Many of the instruments used by minstrels were of such a nature as to preclude any vocal performance by their players: bagpipes, trumpets, and other wind instruments. Only harpers, lute-players, and taborers could easily sing while playing, and such evidence as there is indicates that the harp was used to accompany narrative rather than lyric poetry.[4] A singer could accompany himself on a viol or other bowed instrument, but the manuscript illustrations do not suggest that it was a usual procedure.[5] The other point, rarely if ever remarked, is that in the usual arrangement of the medieval hall the musicians' or minstrels' gallery was located at the opposite end of the hall from the high table on floor or dais, and therefore at a distance quite suitable for instrumental music during dinner but ill-adapted to song in an age when the words counted for as much as the music and a singer needed to be near his audience.[6]

[1] A. R. Myers, ed., *The Household of Edward IV* (Manchester, 1959), p. 131.

[2] John Ives, *Coronacion of Queene Elizabeth*, p. 120, quoted by Arthur Taylor, *The Glory of Regality* (London, 1820), p. 278.

[3] (London, 1809, p. 640). A convenient and useful listing of the court minstrels whose names appear on official rolls of wages is given by Richard Rastall, 'The Minstrels of the English Royal Households 25 Edward I–1 Henry VIII: an Inventory', *Royal Musical Association Research Chronicle*, No. 4 (1964), 1–41. Not one is described as a singing man.

[4] 'In the Towneley play of the Prophets David refers to his 'mynstrelsy', i.e. his playing the harp with his 'fyngers ten', and it is clear that he is chanting narrative and not lyric, as he twice refers to his singing a 'fytt' (ed. George England and A. W. Pollard, E.E.T.S., Ex. Ser., No. lxxi, 1897, pp. 59–61.)

[5] John Stevens has pertinently pointed out that on 2 November 1495 two shillings were paid on behalf of the King 'To a woman that singeth with a fidell' ('Extracts from the Privy Purse Expenses of King Henry the Seventh . . .', Samuel Bentley, ed., *Excerpta Historica*, London, 1831, p. 105).

[6] See Glynne Wickham, *Early English Stages 1300 to 1660* (London, 1959), i. 222–3, 245.

The references in the works of Chaucer and in both the prose and verse romances likewise make it plain that 'minstrel' usually means 'instrumentalist' and 'minstrelsy' 'instrumental music'.[1]

The recorded names of minstrels, where they signify the skills or specialities of the bearers, show that they are instrumentalists; for example, John of Gaunt's minstrels 'Hankyn piper' and 'Jacobe Bumbepiper', both of whom received grants in 1380,[2] and the 'Menestrallis' who received rewards at the English court at Pentecost 1306, including 'Janin le Lutour', 'Gillotin Sautreour', 'Baudec le Tabourer', and others.[3]

Not merely documentary evidence, but also carvings in stone confirm this conclusion. For example, in Beverley, where there was a famous guild of minstrels, the well-known pillar which was their gift to St. Mary's Church shows four instrumentalists but no singers, and in the nave of the Minster itself the superb series of realistic sculptures in the north aisle represents all the figures in minstrels' dress in possession of instruments. The series includes one duo of vocalists, who, as if to make the point clear, wear choir vestments and hold a scroll on which are carved the words of their sacred song, 'Te deum laudamus'.

Even a cursory study of the use of the word 'minstrel' in Elizabethan times will show that a sharp and rather sudden derogatory change in its usual meaning and especially in its social and legal connotations took place around 1572. Its downgrading is well explained by Walter Woodfill in his *Musicians in English Society from Elizabeth to Charles I*.[4] It is well to be very cautious in drawing conclusions about medieval minstrels from post-Reformation allusions.

Too much has been made of the circumstance that all but a very little of the preserved music for the carols is sophisticated and polyphonic. The relatively late development of this music makes it certain that many if not most of the verbal texts of such settings were in existence before the writing of the preserved music and that they were sung to simple melodies now lost. Arguments that the carol-genre developed from such music rather than from popular and secular traditions are thus obviously invalid.[5] R. H. Robbins has not kept his studies clear of this fallacy.[6]

[1] Jeffrey Pulver states the matter clearly: 'The term "minstrelsy" would appear to have been applied exclusively to instrumental music' (*A Dictionary of Old English Music and Musical Instruments*, London, 1923, pp. 149–50).

[2] Eleanor C. Lodge and Robert Somerville, eds., *John of Gaunt's Register, 1379–1383*, Camden Society Publications, 3rd Ser., lvi, lvii, 1937, 113, 301.

[3] *Manners and Household Expenses of England* [etc.], Roxburghe Club, 1841, 141, from Exchequer Roll, reprinted by Chambers,

The Mediaeval Stage, ii. 234–8.

[4] Princeton Studies in History, ix (Princeton, 1953), pp. 57–8.

[5] 'Polyphonic music for soloists existed as early as the thirteenth century, but not until the mid-fifteenth did manuscripts call for—or even permit—choral singing' (Carolyn Wall, 'York Pageant XLVI and its Music', *Speculum*, xlvi, 1971, 694).

[6] 'Middle English Carols as Processional Hymns', *Stud. in Phil.* lvi (1959), 559–82.

The carol at its best found favour, no doubt, with all classes, 'both more and less', in its own favourite phrase. Undeniably the most successful specimens are those which keep the 'mean estate' which some of them praise, those which are neither vulgar nor stilted. The carols dealing specifically with Christmas festivities are the most satisfying, as they are the most numerous, because of this universality of appeal which reflects the traditional relaxation of social distinctions in the general winter rejoicing, a custom as old as the Saturnalia. Carols commanded a warm reception whether sung by the common people at 'Christmas dinners and brideales and in taverns and alehouses', or 'incontinently after the King's first course' at a palace feast, and, while some smack more of the tavern and others more of the court, most of them would not come amiss to the lips and ears of either company.

CHAPTER V

THE CAROL AND POPULAR RELIGION

1. *The Sanctification of Song and Dance*

THE ultimate origins of the carol are non-Christian. The direct progenitors of the ring-dances of nominally Christian France and England were the dances of the pagan spring and winter festivals. Some of these dances, to be sure, were thoroughly religious in purpose; often they were exercises of propitiation. Even the spring dances of women, with their accompanying licence of amorous song and conduct, probably expressed only a deeper element of worship of the deity of fertility so prominent in primitive religion.[1] But it is a long leap from such religion as this to the formalized, schematic Christianity of the medieval Church with its heavenly and earthly hierarchies, its elaborate ritual, and its enormous social, political, and intellectual activity. The difference, moreover, seemed much greater to the medieval churchman than it does to a modern historian of religions, for to the former all faiths save his own were but abominations and the snares of mankind's great Enemy.

Yet in the fourteenth and fifteenth centuries in England, the lyric form which grew out of the round dance, the carol, is particularly associated with the service of the Christian religion. Of the surviving specimens by far the greater number—about five out of every seven—treat of subject-matter which is either wholly religious or morally didactic in accord with Christian precepts. It will be helpful for the understanding of the carol texts themselves to reconstruct, as far as possible, the process, by no means an accidental one, which resulted in the widespread use for Christian purposes of a lyric form based on dance-song originally pagan.

The stubborn vitality shown by heathen customs among the people of European countries after their official acceptance of Christianity presented the medieval Church for centuries with a very real problem. As Bede bears witness, it was easier to break the idol-fanes of Britain than to eradicate customs of immemorial standing rooted in elementary human instincts. There were two ways in which the problem could be met, and both were used on many occasions and with varying success. One was direct proscription, the branding of a custom as sin to be punished on earth by the ecclesiastical authority and thereafter by God. The other, in the use of which the

---

[1] See the description of the phallic rites accompanying the Easter Week dance of the girls of a Scottish village in 1282, as reported in the *Chronicon de Lanercost* (Edinburgh, 1839), p. 109; also Chambers, *The Mediaeval Stage*, i. 160–72.

Church often showed herself wise and able, was assimilation, the identification of a pagan observance with some rite or practice of Christianity with which it might possess a common element. The merging of the Germanic Yule with the Christian Nativity season is an outstanding instance of this procedure.[1] Both these methods were frequently employed in the Middle Ages against the particular remnants of paganism which most concern the carol—the festival dance and the songs accompanying it.

The outright condemnation of popular song and dance was not particularly efficacious, to judge from the number of times that official pronouncements against the practice had to be repeated.[2] The following passage from the eighth-century *Dicta Abbatis Pirminii* is a typical early medieval expression of disapproval:

Bellationis et saltationis vel cantica turpia et luxuriosa velut sagitta diabolica fugite, nec ad ipsas ecclesias, nec in domibus vestris, nec in ullo alio loco facire non presumatis, quia hoc de paganorum consuetudine remansit.[3]

The conflict between the Church and these dances and songs was especially marked, not merely because the performances themselves were accompanied by wanton words and gestures, but also because of the people's habit of dancing on the eves of church festivals and in the hallowed precincts of the churchyard or even within the edifice itself. The clergy used hymns, psalms, and sermons in attempts to divert their attention, but the parishioners seem often to have preferred the more exciting pastime. Hence the exclusion of such dances from the neighbourhood of churches is specifically directed in a number of decrees. In the middle of the seventh century the Council of Chalon-sur-Saône ordained as follows:

Valde omnibus noscetur esse decretum ne per dedicationes basilicarum aut festivitates martyrum ad ipsa solemnia confluentes obscoena et turpia cantica, dum orare debent aut clericos psallentes audire, cum choris foemineis turpia quidem decantare videantur. Unde convenit ut sacerdotes loci illos a septa basilicarum vel porticus ipsarum basilicarum etiam et ab ipsis atriis vetare debeant et arcere.[4]

But 450 years later, in 1209, a council at Avignon found it necessary to repeat the prohibition,[5] and even in 1435 it was a matter of concern to the Council of Bâle that

Alii choreas et tripudia marium ac mulierum facientes homines ad spectacula et cachinnationes movent.[6]

---

[1] Chambers, *The Mediaeval Stage*, i, chap. xi.

[2] Twenty-two quotations from ecclesiastical denunciations of song and dance are given by L. Gougaud, O.S.B., 'La danse dans les églises', in *Revue d'histoire ecclésiastique*, xv (1914), 5–22, 229–45. See also Joseph Balogh, 'Tänze in Kirchen und auf Kirchhöfen', *Niederdeutsche Zeitschrift für Volkskunde*, Jahrgang 6, Heft 1 (1928), 1–14.

[3] Quoted, Gougaud, op. cit., p. 11.

[4] Quoted, Gougaud, loc. cit.

[5] Op. cit., p. 12; the decree was worded as follows: 'Statuimus ut in sanctorum vigiliis in ecclesiis historicae [histrionae], saltationes, obscoeni motus, seu choreae non fiant, nec dicantur amatoria carmina, vel cantilenae ibidem. . . .'

[6] Quoted Gougaud, op. cit., p. 13. For several

Concern on the part of church authorities over the sin of wanton dancing and singing was by no means roused only by the sports of lay folk. There are many records of disapproval and discipline directed at the clergy, both regular and secular, who indulged in such recreation. Three illustrations must stand for what could be a long anthology of such citations.

Statutes promulgated in 1338 by the Dean and Chapter of Wells alleged: 'Moreover [the Canons, in addition to hurrying through the psalms in church], are present personally, hunting, fowling and fishing; caring nothing for the clerical state; they take part in dances and masques and day and night prowl round the streets and lanes of the city leading a riotous existence, singing and shouting (*cum cantu et tumultu*). . . .' At Salisbury in 1418: 'Not only were the Canons and Vicars chatting in service times, but the Vicars were actually singing "balades and cantalenes in their Divine Services".'[1]

About 1400 Nicolas de Clamanges in his *De ruina et reparacione Ecclesie*, cap. 28, includes among prelates whose absence is more useful to the Church than their presence those who spend their sleepless nights 'in conviviis acuratissimis, in plausibus et choreis cum puellis et effeminatis'.[2]

Even nuns were known to succumb to the attractions of the convivial dance. Dame Isabel Benet of the Cistercian priory of Catesby in the diocese of Lincoln was a 'receiver' or purchasing agent of her convent and doubtless had marketing or other affairs to transact in Northampton, but, as with some modern business people, these did not consume all her time:

[In 1442] Also the said dame Isabel on Monday last did pass the night with the Austin friars at Northampton and did dance and play the lute with them in the same place until midnight, and on the night following she passed the night with the friars preachers at Northampton, luting and dancing in like manner.[3]

In some writing about the medieval lyric the assumption is made that secular songs, especially if not 'literary', were the property of lay people

medieval condemnations of the dance see also G. G. Coulton, *Five Centuries of Religion* (Cambridge, 1923–50), iii. 531–8; 71–3, 442–4.

The problem did not cease with the Middle Ages; witness the following item of news from France in *The Times* of 24 December 1931: 'Manifestations of the Christmas spirit appear to have begun in the Provinces earlier than usual this year. Several of the local clergy in the Morbihan district have been severely manhandled by their infuriated flock, while others have been treated to a choice programme of community catcalling. It appears that the clergy under the orders of their Bishop have been preaching a series of sermons on dancing in public-houses and its dangers, a practice of which the natives are excessively fond, and

public resentment or uneasiness at this condemnation of their idea of innocent amusement took this violent form. An innkeeper who obediently refused to allow any more dancing on his premises promptly had them wrecked.'

[1] Aelred Watkin, *Dean Cosyn and Wells Cathedral Miscellanea*, Somerset Record Society, lvi (1941), 23; Dora H. Robertson, *Sarum Close* (London, 1938), p. 9.

[2] Nicolas de Clamonges [Clemangiis], *Le Traité de la ruine de l'église*, ed. A. Coville (Paris, 1936), p. 135.

[3] A. Hamilton Thompson, ed., *Visitations of Religious Houses in the Diocese of Lincoln*, ii, part i, The Canterbury and York Society, Canterbury and York Series, xxiv (1919), 50.

alone. This can never have been the case. One must remember that every monk or nun or other professed religious was a boy or girl before joining the clergy, and no matter how edifying and scrupulous most reading and conversation may have become thereafter, the monk or nun had a memory filled with non-religious ditties learned in childhood, just as has every modern clergyman. Even if a boy became a 'little clergeon' at an early age, we may be sure that his repertory was not limited to what he learned on the form of the song-school or in the choir, as that of today's choir-boys most definitely is not. It is as dangerous an inference to assign the performance of non-religious songs to lay people alone as to assume that religious songs would not be sung at secular gatherings.

The modern reader of clerical denunciations of dance and song is likely to become sceptical of their validity. 'Surely', he says to himself, 'some carolling must have been quite innocent recreation. Are not these churchmen too free with their mention of the Devil as the patron of carollers?'

Without acquitting all the medieval clergy of narrow-mindedness or of hostility to the idea of young people enjoying themselves in their own way, we must yet recognize an aspect of the song-accompanied ring-dance which few, if any, previous writers on the carol have noticed. That is its supposed association with actual witchcraft. It is not necessary to commit oneself to any particular view of what history records as witchcraft to understand how this association would impair the moral standing of any and all caroles in a time and place of concern about witches' activities.

It is quite clear that the usual dance of the witches was the carole, in both its round and serpentine forms, or rather a perversion of it. An often reproduced title-page of 1639, that of *Robin Good-fellow, his mad prankes and merry iests*, printed by Thomas Cotes in London, shows a ring of men and women dancing in a circular track to the music of a piper, behind the large ithyphallic figure of Robin himself.[1] But the distinctive and damning feature of the witches' carole was that the dancers faced outwards instead of inwards and hence, by stepping to the left, moved widdershins or counter to the sun's motion, instead of sunwise as in all ordinary mortals' caroles.[2] This, like saying a sacred formula backwards, is a sure sign of black magic.

Carolling was often among the activities confessed by accused persons in the witchcraft persecutions of Scotland in the sixteenth and seventeenth centuries, when, as we shall see elsewhere, the carole was still very much alive. As in Kölbigk centuries before, the churchyard itself was a favoured venue. It is reported that in North Berwick in 1590 Barbara Napier joined the local covens at the church, 'where she danced endlong the kirkyard, and Gelie

---

[1] Margaret Alice Murray, *The God of the Witches* (London, 1956), plate 11.
[2] Often recorded; see Christina Hole, *Witch-craft in England* (London, 1945), p. 31; Margaret Alice Murray, *The Witch-cult in Western Europe* (Oxford, 1921), pp. 130–5.

Duncan played on a trump, John Fian masked led the ring, Agnes Sampson and her daughters and all the rest following the said Barbara to the number of seven score persons'. It is from the confession of Agnes that we get a rarity, the actual text of a couplet used as burden in such a dance:

[They] took handes on the land [after a voyage in sieves] and daunced this reill or short daunce, singing all with one voice.

> Commer, goe ye before, commer, goe ye.
> Gif ye will not goe before, commer let me.

Gelie or Geillis Duncan, the trumper, obligingly played this reel for the King, who summoned him 'in a wonderful admiration'.[1] It is striking that, like the song of the dancers of Kölbigk so long before, this burden refers to the action of the dance itself.

It was a special cause of concern that the people liked to hold their caroles, as did the young folk of Kölbigk, in the central and convenient flat space of the churchyard. Particular prohibitions of this practice are frequent. Ralph Baldock, Bishop of London, in April 1308 issued a strong rebuke to the people of Barking, who had held dances and wrestlings and lascivious sports in the cemetery and even in the parochial and conventual churches, to the scandal of the Church and to the peril of souls.[2]

In fifteenth-century England people were likewise dancing in church-yards, but it was apparently a breach of monastic discipline even to watch them. At Humberstone Abbey, Lincolnshire, in 1440, a brother named John Wrauby answered 'saucily and rebelliously' when the abbot 'took him to task for climbing up a gate to behold the pipe players and dancers [*ducentes choreas*] in the churchyard of the parish church'.[3] But almost a century after the Reformation the custom of such dancing was still alive in England, and Sir Thomas Overbury praises his Franklin for not objecting to it: 'He allowes of honest pastime, and thinkes not the bones of the dead brused any-thing, or the worse for it, though the Countrey Lasses daunce in the Church-yard after Even-Song.'[4]

The efforts of the Church to turn the customs of song and dance to pious ends without eliminating them entirely were rather more successful; they are certainly more interesting. It was a somewhat difficult matter to invest the dance with any degree of sanctity. There was a continuous tradition of dis-approval of the dance, running through the Middle Ages, which appears

---

[1] Robert Pitcairn, *Criminal Trials*, i, quoted by Murray, *The God of the Witches*, p. 107; ibid. i, quoted by Montague Summers, *The Geography of Witchcraft* (Evanston, Illinois, and New York, 1958), pp. 214–15.

[2] *Registrum Radulphi Baldock*, Canterbury and York Society, Canterbury and York Series,

vii (1911), 73–4.

[3] A. Hamilton Thompson, ed., *Visitations of Religious Houses in the Diocese of Lincoln*, ii, The Lincoln Record Society, xiv (1918), 140.

[4] *The Overburian Characters*, ed. W. J. Paylor, The Percy Reprints, xiii (Oxford, 1936), 78–9.

not only in official decrees but also in the discourses of preachers and in a number of their *exempla*. The Devil was reported to have shown his power over dancers on several occasions; a most interesting thirteenth-century *exemplum* from an Irish Franciscan collection records such an occurrence.[1] It tells how, in accordance with a folk custom, a group of Dacian women on the occasion of a birth made a straw doll,[2] which they carried in a dance, singing and making lewd gestures. To them suddenly appeared the Devil, responding to their song with such a loud voice that some of them fell dead. The preacher concludes by saying of his hearers:

Certe hic ludere possunt in suis tripudiis, in suis fatuis cantilenis; et absque dubio videre possunt hoc exemplo, quod ludi eorum non sunt eis nisi quedam ad mortem eternam preparacio.[3]

This diabolical taint which it preserved kept the dance from gaining any- thing like a real foothold in the service of the Church. There are many records of dancing in the church buildings themselves, and the custom has been continued into modern times in the cathedral of Seville, where the choir boys dance with castanets on certain feast-days.[4] The Dance of Death was actually performed on occasion, as in 1453 by the Franciscans at Besançon.[5] The dances of the people on fête days were sometimes admitted, and at other times the minor clergy themselves indulged in dancing and other revelry within the church doors, as during the Feast of Fools.[6] But the dance was at most tolerated; it was never actually encouraged by ecclesiastical authority and has almost always remained outside the official ritual.[7]

Occasionally a churchman recognized in a literary way that the associations of the dance need not be altogether unhallowed. Honorius of Autun in his *Gemma Animae* discusses the use of the dance as a means of worship by the ancients, its symbolic character with them, as representing the motion of the spheres, and the conversion of the dance by the faithful to the service of the true God. The dance of the Israelites after their deliverance from Pharaoh at the Red Sea, and the performance of David before the ark are cited. A por-

[1] A. G. Little, ed., *Liber Exemplorum ad Usum Praedicantium*, British Society of Fran- ciscan Studies, i (Aberdeen, 1908), 109–11. For a good example of a vernacular sermon against dancing see Böhme, *Geschichte des Tanzes*, i. 94–100. A well-selected garland of early denunciations can be found in Karl Voretzsch, *Introduction to the Study of Old French Literature*, tr. Francis M. Du Mont (New York, 1931), pp. 57–9.

[2] This doll is to be identified with the 'Har- vest-May' and 'Ivy-Girl' as symbolic of the female principle of fertility; see above, p. cxxiv.

[3] Little, op. cit., p. 111.

[4] The earliest date recorded for this famous dance is 1508. No early settings for it have been preserved; nineteenth-century music is now used (J. B. Trend, 'The Dance of the Seises at Seville', *Music and Letters*, ii, 1921, 10–28).

[5] Ibid., pp. 230–1.

[6] Chambers, *The Mediaeval Stage*, i. 326. For references to Easter ball-games in churches, particularly at Auxerre, see ibid., p. 128 n. 4, and Du Cange, *Glossarium*, s.v. 'Pelota (3)'.

[7] The chapter of Wells found it necessary about 1338 to prohibit dances and games within the cathedral and cloisters (Chambers, *The Mediaeval Stage*, i. 163 n. 1).

tion may be quoted as showing the likeness of the dance which Honorius had in mind to the carole:

Per *choreas* autem circuitionem voluerunt intelligi firmamenti revolutionem: per manuum complexionem, elementorum connexionem: per sonum cantantium, harmoniam planetarum resonantium: per corporis gesticulationem, signorum motionem: per plausum manuum vel pedum strepitum, tonitruorum crepitum.[1]

A more definitely Christian significance is given the dance in a sermon which is one of the most remarkable monuments of the medieval movement towards the moralization and allegorizing of casual and worldly acts and circumstances. It has sometimes been attributed to Stephen Langton, who was consecrated Archbishop of Canterbury in 1207, but it is more probably the work of a French author.[2] The sermon takes for its text one of the most popular of all medieval dance-songs, that of 'Bele Alis'.[3] After quoting this in full, the author explains his purpose:

Legimus quod de omni verbo ocioso reddituri sumus rationem in die iudicii, et ideo debemus errantes corrigere, errores reprimere, praua in bona exponere, vanitatem ad veritatem reducere.

He then points out the spiritual symbolism of the carole, not without a phrase of warning as to the originally worldly character of the dance:

Cum dico *Belle Aliz*, scitis quod tripudium primo propter vanitatem inuentum fuit; scilicet, in tripudio tria sunt necessaria, scilicet, vox sonora, nexus brachiorum, et strepitus pedum. Vt ergo possimus cum Domino tripudiare, hec tria in nobis habeamus: vocem sonoram, scilicet, predicationem lectam et gratam Deo et hominibus; nexus brachiorum, scilicet, geminam caritatem, scilicet, deleccionem Dei et Christi; strepitus pedum, s[cilicet], opera concordancia nostre praedicationi ad imitacionem Domini nostri Jhesu Christi qui primo cepit bona facere, et post ea docere.

By such ingenuity as this an attempt was made to divert into pious channels a popular interest which most churchmen agreed was inspired of the Evil One.

[1] Quoted Gougaud, op. cit., p. 17. The original is Lib. I, cap. cxxxix of the 'Gemma Animae', *Patrologia Latina*, clxxii, col. 587. One of the strongest and most frequently used medieval definitions of the dance, '*Chorea est Circulus cujus Centrum est Diabolus*', reappears as late as 1686 in Boston on the title-page of a tract possibly written by Increase Mather, where it is apparently restricted to 'mixt' dancing. The title of the tract is highly characteristic of its time and place: *An Arrow Against Profane and Promiscuous Dancing drawne out of the Quiver of the Scriptures, By the Ministers of Christ at Boston in New England* (Percy A. Scholes, *Music and Puritanism*, Lausanne thesis, Vevey [1934], p. 60).

[2] See A. Lecoy de la Marche, *La Chaire française au moyen âge*, 2nd edn. (Paris, 1886), pp. 91–3. The sermon is preserved in several manuscripts; the text here quoted is from the version in Trinity College, Cambridge, MS. B. 14. 39. It is collated with other texts of the sermon in Karl Reichl, *Religiöse Dichtung im englischen Hochmittelalter*, Münchner Universitäts-Schriften, Philosophische Fakultät, Texte und Untersuchung zur Englischen Philologie, Band i (München, 1973), pp. 379–88.

[3] The anonymous song, not the piece by Baude de la Quarière which begins 'Main se leva la bien faite Aelis'. Bele Alis has kept her place in French folk-song tradition into the twentieth century. See Patrice Corrault, *Formation de nos chansons folkloriques* (Paris, 1953–5), i. 151–5, 'Belle Aelis et sa postérité folklorique.' One version begins:

Je m'suis levé par un matin
Je suis entré dans mon jardin.

Secular song, whether associated with the dance or not, offered a far more promising field for the activities of the moralizing clergy. From the earliest period of Christianity vocal music had occupied an important place in divine worship, reaching its highest development in the Gregorian chant of the Mass. The hymns of the Office, as has been noted, were not far removed from the stanzaic form of popular song. Certainly there was nothing vicious in singing of itself. But the character of the pieces which were current among the people in the Middle Ages was often such as to cause grave concern to the guardians of their morals.

It is probably wise to accept with some reservations the adjectives applied by churchmen to the folk-song or popular song which they report as being sung at festivals. Merely frivolous or (as we should think) harmless love-lyrics were doubtless among the songs which were condemned as unprofitable or worse. But the repeated application of such terms as *obscoenus*,[1] *turpis*,[2] *luxuriosus*,[3] *indecens*,[4] *diabolicus*,[5] can hardly have been wholly unjustified. The erotic character of the May festival, so well expressed in the *Pervigilium Veneris*, survived in songs which celebrated freedom in love and heaped abuse upon husbands and faithfulness in marriage. The freedom from scruples common to the shepherdess-heroines of many Old French *pastourelles* might with some reason give alarm to a strict contemporary moralist, however tolerantly it behooves the literary historian to regard it.[6] From medieval Germany too are preserved a considerable number of *Schamperlieder* with erotic content which justifies their disrepute.[7] As collectors of folk-song know, oral tradition has preserved more than a few out of what must have been a great body of songs which by their frankness of expression would have offended pious ears, not to mention those songs which show positive immorality of sentiment.[8] The denunciations of the clergy, although touched with exaggeration, were not empty rhetoric. It is significant that in 1497 the word 'carol' could have a sinful connotation to Laurence Wade, the monk of Christ Church, Canterbury, who translated the life of Thomas Becket into English verse. In the section 'Qualiter euitabat cantilenas dissolutas siue ad lasciuia[m] pertinentes', Wade says of the prelate:

> And euer hys bord voyde (as the story doth ws shew)
> Off all maner off karolles and songes dissolute
> Sowndyng to luxury off harpe, pipe, and lute.[9]

[1] Decree of Council of Chalon-sur-Saône, quoted above, p. cxl.

[2] *Dicta Pirminii*, quoted above, p. cxl; 'Red Book of Ossory', f. 70, quoted in *Notes and Queries*, 1st Ser., ii (1850), 385.

[3] *Dicta Pirminii*, quoted above, p. cxl.

[4] Ordericus, lib. 12, p. 881, quoted Du Cange, *Glossarium*, s.v. 'Coraula'.

[5] St. Audoenus, lib. 2 *de Vita S. Eligii*, cap. 15, quoted Du Cange, *Glossarium*, s.v. 'Caraula'.

[6] Jeanroy, *Origines*, p. 21; William Powell Jones, *The Pastourelle*, chaps. i, ii.

[7] References to a number of these are given by Böhme, *Geschichte des Tanzes*, i. 236 n. 2.

[8] Cf. Sharp, *English Folk-Song*, pp. 102–3.

[9] Corpus Christi College, Cambridge, MS. 298, f. 20ᵛ.

Secular song was utilized in two ways by those intent on 'turning the depraved into the good'. The original wording of a song was occasionally taken and allegorized, or, much oftener, a worldly song was parodied or imitated in a religious one. The first process is well illustrated by the latter part of the sermon on 'Bele Alis' already quoted, which takes up the *chanson* line by line, explaining the spiritual significance of each phrase. 'Bele Alis', whose name is held to be composed of the privative *a* and Latin *lis*, hence meaning 'without strife', is identified with the Blessed Virgin; the five flowers which she plucks in the meadow are the flowers of charity, chastity, constancy, virginity, and humility; and so on. A similar sermon, possibly by the same author, declares the intention of 'spoiling the Egyptians to enrich the Hebrews' by turning light song to a good use. It is a *chanson* on the *mal mariée* theme which is here used as a text, beginning:

> Sur la rive de la mer,
> Fontenelle i sordeit cler.
> (etc.)

The river is shown to stand for the Virgin, the fountain for Christ, and so on through the poem. But it is to be remembered, says the preacher, that the song, taken literally, is vain and sinful.[1]

The thirteenth-century English sermon which embodies one of the earliest scraps of Middle English dance-song[2] proceeds in the same fashion. The couplet there taken as text is called one of many dance-songs 'þat litil ben wort', and, after invoking the same Scriptural authority as the sermon on 'Bele Alis',[3] the author brings forward a spiritual interpretation of the English lines:

> Atte wrastlinge my lemman i ches,
> and atte ston-kasting i him for-les.

A sentence or two will show the style:[4]

Wrastlinge is a manere of feite[n]ge; and sikirlike ne comid no man to his loue ne to his blisse, but he be god champiun & manlike feite agein hise 3 fomen: þo ben þe deuel of helle, his owene sinfule fles, and treȝe-cuuenant to werld . . . Bi þe 'ston' is vnderstondin þe harde herte of man and of womman, þat lat in Godis word atte ton ere & vt atte toþir. . . .

Sermons such as these had probably no more than a limited effect against the subversive tendencies of popular song, for it would be too much to expect the common man to work out a pious symbolism for every verse which was trolled. More widespread and more successful was the practice

---

[1] Lecoy de la Marche, op. cit., pp. 197–8. See also Thomas F. Crane, ed., *The Exempla of Jacques de Vitry*, Publications of the Folk-Lore Society, xxvi (London, 1890), No. cclxxiii.

[2] See above, pp. xlix, l.

[3] Matthew xii. 36.

[4] The entire sermon is printed by Max Förster, *Anglia* xlii (1918), 152–4.

of composing religious songs on the model of the secular pieces which it was hoped to displace. The religious carol, as represented in the texts here collected, is to be regarded as a product of this kind of activity. Some notice of its history will therefore be helpful to a study of the origins of the carol genre.

The influence of the popular lyric on the Latin *cantilena* has already been touched upon.[1] The singable lyrics attributed to Bishop Richard de Ledrede in the Red Book of Ossory (not the didactic poems which follow them and which are probably not of his authorship) are notable examples. The bishop, a fourteenth-century Franciscan, may have had to deal with conditions resembling those which led an English priest to forget himself during Mass. The story, as related in an Irish book of *exempla*, tells how the priest, having allowed to run in his mind the burden of a song sung the preceding night by a group of dancers outside the church, greeted the faithful not with the prescribed 'Dominus vobiscum', but with the words 'Swete leman dhin ore'.[2]

Evidence for the writing of vernacular religious lyrics on the pattern of love-songs is rather scarce in the British Isles before the emergence of the carol in fourteenth-century manuscripts.[3] On the Continent, however, it was an established practice as early as the thirteenth century.[4] About two hundred French *chansons pieuses* are preserved from this period, of which many are obvious imitations of *pastourelles* or other secular pieces. Among the most successful are those of Gauthier de Coincy, monk of Soissons, and author of the enormously popular *Miracles de Nostre Dame*. Some of these religious poems show the influence of the courtly school,[5] but others are nearer to the truly popular lyric in their form and manner. Such a piece as the following, in the form of a *ballette*, is plainly an imitation of popular song:[6]

> Ave Maria, j'aim tant.
>
> La beguine s'est levee
> de vesture bien paree:
> au moustier s'en est alee,
> Jhesu Crist va regretant.
>
> Ave Maria, j'aim tant.

---

[1] Above, pp. cxii–cxvi.

[2] Little, *Liber Exemplorum*, p. 111. The original source of the story is in the *Gemma Ecclesiastica*.

[3] There are striking examples in Carleton Brown, ed., *English Lyrics of the XIIIth Century* (Oxford, 1932), Nos. 54, stanza 1; 63, stanzas 1, 4; 90; 91.

[4] Amedée Gastoué, *Le Cantique populaire en France*, pp. 68–88. See also J. R. H. de Smidt, *Les Noëls et la tradition populaire* (Amsterdam,

1932), pp. 12–19.

[5] e.g. the religious poems of Thiebaut de Champagne.

[6] Printed by Karl Bartsch, 'Geistliche Umdichtung weltlicher Lieder', in *Zeitschrift für romanische Philologie*, viii (1884), 578, stanza 2. Bartsch points out a similar refrain in a *pastourelle* (ibid., p. 579). Jeanroy (*Origines*, p. 482) thinks the first lines here quoted are a parody of 'Aelis main s'est levée'.

In Germany the time of the Reformation brought the greatest activity in adapting popular song to religious purposes, Luther himself being the author of some of the best-known pieces.[1] But the method was well known to the two centuries preceding, as is shown by religious parodies preserved from the fourteenth century: A good example is a May-song written to a secular and popular melody.

Ich weiss mir einen meien
in diser heilgen zit,
Den meien, den ich meine,
der ewige fröide git:

Den meien, den ich meine,
daz ist der süsse gott,
der hie uff diser erden
leidt vil menigen spott.[2]

The fifteenth century, the time of greatest production of religious carols in England, was also marked in Germany by the writing of devotional songs in popular measures. Many of these closely resemble the carols in subjects and spirit, and occasionally in form. One such is the following 'Winacht lied' by Heinrich von Loufenberg, author of a large quantity of religious poetry in the vernacular:

In einem krippfly lag ein kind;
do stund ein esel vnd ein rind,
Do by wz ouch die maget clar,
maria, die dz kind gebar.

Jhesus der herre min,
der wz dz kindelein.[3]

These German songs were for the most part the work of professed religious men, like Heinrich, rather than of devout laymen like the courtly poets of the south of France who wrote *dansas d'Amors de Nostra Dona* and similar pious adaptations of polite love-songs. That songs written *for* the people by men in religious orders were actually taken up and sung *by* the people is shown by the reference in the *Limburg Chronicle* under the date of 1370 to a leprous monk of the Rhineland who is praised as the best maker of songs in the world. It records that 'was er sang, das sangen die Leute alle gern, und alle Meister pfiffen, und andere Spielleute führten den Gesang und das Gedicht'.[4]

But the greatest flowering of religious popular song took place in thirteenth-century Italy. Towards the end of the preceding century there had sprung up a popular zeal for devotional singing, fostered by the organization

[1] e.g. 'Von himel hoch da kom ich her' to the secular tune of 'Aus fremden Landen komm ich her' (Böhme, *Altdeutsches Liederbuch*, Leipzig, 1877, p. 623), and the more controversial 'Nun treiben wir den Papst heraus', to the tune of 'So treiben wir den Winter aus' (ibid., p. 740). Dance-tunes were especially favoured for such use. See John Schikowski, *Geschichte des Tanzes*, Berlin (1926), p. 53.

[2] Böhme, op. cit., p. 689, stanza 1.

[3] Philipp Wackernagel, ed., *Das deutsche Kirchenlied* (Leipzig, 1864, etc.), ii. 533, stanza 1 and burden. Other poems by Heinrich are printed, ibid., 528–611.

[4] Quoted by Böhme, *Altdeutsches Liederbuch*, p. xxii.

of musical fraternities calling themselves *laudesi*. These guilds were of the greatest service, not merely to religion, but to the cause of vernacular poetry as well; being composed of layfolk, they naturally preferred to sing in their own tongue rather than in the Latin of the church ritual.[1] The result was that in the thirteenth, fourteenth, and fifteenth centuries thousands of *laude* were composed and sung, varying widely in form and content, but alike in their popular character. Like the English carol, the Italian *lauda* occupies the middle ground between folk-song and learned lyric; it is the production of an individual author, but directed to an audience without special education or refinement, and patterned upon the songs with which such an audience would already be familiar. The *ballata* form remained a favourite with later writers of *laude* as with Jacopone da Todi.[2] A fourteenth-century *lauda* on the power of death illustrates the similarity in form, spirit, and subject-matter which exists in many cases between lyrics of this sort and the later English carol:

> Chi vuol lo mondo disprezzare
> sempre la Morte dee pensare.

> La Morte è fiera et dura e forte,
> rompe mura e passa porte,
> ell' è si comune sorte
> che verun ne può scampare.

> .   .   .   .   .

> Peccatori, or ritornate,
> li peccati abbandonate,
> della Morte ripensate,
> non vi trovi folleggiare.[3]

The burden, the dance-song stanza, the simplicity of language, and the didactic purpose are alike in both genres.

2. *The Franciscans and the Carol*[4]

The early history of the *lauda* is so closely associated with the beginnings of the Franciscan Order that it forms a natural introduction to a tradition

---

[1] Ippoliti, *Dalle Sequenze alle Laudi*, pp. 11–16.   [2] See above, pp. lx–lxiii.

[3] Eugenia Levi, ed., *Lirica italiana antica* (Florence, 1905), p. 40, *ripresa* and first and last stanzas. Compare carols Nos. 356, 368, 371, on similar themes.

[4] Now indispensable for any further study of the subject of this section is a learned and comprehensive work by David L. Jeffrey, *The Early English Lyric and Franciscan Spirituality* (Lincoln, Nebraska, 1975). It offers the best discussion in English of the Italian *lauda* (chap. 4, 'The Earliest Lyrics in Italy') in addition to its valuable historical and critical treatment of the Middle English religious lyrics, including the carols. The admiring reader of Professor Jeffrey's work will find it easy to forgive some occasional overstatement of the dominance of specifically Franciscan influence. His evidence is weighty and his presentation impressive. Since the work appeared while this edition was already in press, this general note must stand in place of a number of detailed footnote references.

of that religious body which is of particular interest for the history of the English carol. This is the tradition of vernacular religious song, begun by St. Francis himself and kept alive in his order even in those later days when the first flush of zeal had yielded to the laxness and corruption which made the Minorites the targets for so much satire and abuse. Subordinate yet complementary to the friars' principal mission of preaching, it has left its records in various times and places, some of which there will be occasion to notice here, and gives Franciscanism a claim to consideration as an important force in the shaping of the medieval lyric.[1]

Neither the great revival of popular religious fervour in thirteenth-century Italy nor the accompanying production of popular sacred poetry was literally initiated by Francis of Assisi, but the impetus which both received from the genius of the man himself and from the organizing of his followers into the Order of Friars Minor in 1209 was so great that their history is often begun with his conversion. It is not impertinent to note that the great mission of Francis was 'popular by destination' and not 'by origin'; he was prophet to the people and not of the people; he was no Italian Piers Plowman. Of gentle birth and having ample means, he turned from the life of a sophisticated young bachelor and soldier to a way of poverty and asceticism so extreme that it set him apart from those to whom he preached almost as much as his previous prosperity. His exhortation to his followers to become 'ioculatores Dei' has a more profound significance than is always attached to it: besides urging upon them the practice of religious song it recognizes the slightly spectacular quality inherent in many actions of the saint himself no less than in the more ludicrous practices of the literal-minded Brother Juniper. This mildly spectacular character of the friars' ways (still to be felt when one meets a sandalled Franciscan in the streets of a New World city) was one of the secrets of their mighty influence with the people of many lands who had become indifferent to the routine religion of the parish church.

Francis himself had the gift of composing songs out of the fullness of his heart, and his youthful acquaintance with the poetry of the worldly troubadours stood him in good stead. It was just after he had composed the beautiful 'Song of Brother Sun' that he gave his disciples the charge of sacred song. The *Speculum Perfectionis*[2] tells how he sent for Brother Pacifico, who was so talented that he had been called 'rex versuum' in the world, and desired him to mingle the singing of *laude* with his preaching. 'For', he said, 'what are the servants of God if not his minstrels who ought to stir and incite the hearts of men to spiritual joy?'

The greatest of the early Franciscan singers was Jacopone da Todi, whose

---

[1] Father Cuthbert, O.S.F.C., *The Romanticism of St. Francis* (London, 1915), p. 185: 'There can be little doubt that the singing of hymns in the vernacular owed its popularity, if not its origin, at least in Italy to the friars.'

[2] Ed. Paul Sabatier (Paris, 1898), cap. c.

laude have already been cited for their frequent use of dance-forms. Jacopone's poems are far finer than the ordinary popular lyric; they are often highly subjective, philosophical, contemplative, or concerned with specific incidents of the poet's material or spiritual life.[1] This did not keep them from being enthusiastically adopted and sung by companies of *laudesi*, many of which were connected with the Third Order of St. Francis.[2] They were widely imitated, and many *laude* have been attributed to Jacopone of which the true authors remain unknown.

The *laude* continued in favour throughout the fourteenth and fifteenth centuries, new ones constantly being composed and the old ones held in memory and passed from singer to singer. The models were still, as with Jacopone, the worldly and amorous songs of the people; their melodies were used and their words often closely parodied.[3] Continually circulating among the people, preaching that repentance which is so often the theme of the *laude*, threatening, amusing, teaching, and denouncing, were the friars, Dominicans among them, of course, though less prominent than the Minorites.[4] The theatrical methods of Fra Bernardino da Siena, who mingled with his preaching the telling of tales, the singing of songs, even the imitation of animals, show how the friars succeeded in bringing to the common people of Italy a religion freed from the chill of the cloister and the puzzle of Latin, a religion of which the *laude* were the lyrical expression.[5]

The tradition of religious song in the vernacular which uses verse-forms and music already familiar to the people persisted in the activities of the Franciscan order in other countries than Italy, notably France, Germany, Ireland, and England. The friars were explicit in their denunciation of the 'dishonest' songs and dances of the common folk and followed the Italians' example of replacing some of these songs with sacred parodies.[6]

---

[1] See the excellent biography by Evelyn Underhill, *Jacopone da Todi, Poet and Mystic, 1228–1306* (London, 1919).

[2] Ibid., p. 218.

[3] Philippe Monnier, *Le Quattrocento* (Paris, 1920), ii. 188.

[4] It is interesting to see the Franciscans taking a hand in the suppression of exactly the sort of festive dances that so disturbed the medieval church councils. The *Annales Minorum* record the efforts of two late fifteenth-century Minorites in this direction. Michael de Barga was a zealous preacher to shepherds and country folk. 'Tempore Bacchanalium per domos & plateas discurrens, puellas a choreis insanisque ludis revocabat, quosque comperiebat per ludicra et lubrica dies illos exigere, ad sobrietatem & severitatem retrahebat' (xiv. 230). Bernardinus Feltrensis was a similar reformer. 'Condemnavit quosdam ludos in-

honestos, & publica spectacula, ad quae nemo deinceps ausus est accedere' (ibid., 397). The anecdote which follows tells how a young man who persisted in leading the girls to dance in spite of the friar's warning died a miserable death for his sin.

[5] Monnier, op. cit., ii. 191–203.

[6] The English mendicant friar, probably a Franciscan, who composed in the late thirteenth century the collection of exempla known as *Speculum Laicorum* was severe in his condemnation of young women who danced the carole, saying that they broke divine, natural, and human laws, and referring to a girl whose punishment in hell was to whirl about in fire as retribution for the revolutions which she had been wont to make in ring-dances. (*Le Speculum Laicorum*, ed. J. Th. Welter, Thesaurus Exemplorum, fascicle v, Paris, 1914, capit. xxi, 'De choreatricibus et cantilenis', p. 32).

Jehan Tisserant, theologian and confessor to Queen Anne of Brittany, is the great exemplar in France. He is one of the earliest authors of *noëls*, if not actually the earliest. He is called by Gastoué 'le vrai fondateur du cantique populaire', and some of his songs, composed in the fifteenth century, have survived in use into recent times.[1] In fourteenth-century England the Anglo-Norman friar Nicholas Bozon, probably of the house at Nottingham, followed the practice of continental Franciscan preachers by including stanzaic verses in the vernacular in some of his sermons. A number of religious poems bearing his name are written in a manuscript formerly in the Phillipps Library at Cheltenham, now British Museum MS. Addit. 46919.[2] One of his compositions, at least, was sung at the beginning of his sermon in true early Franciscan fashion.[3]

Indeed it was not very long after the landing of the first Franciscan missionaries in England in 1224 that we find friar-poets who work precisely in the genre of the 'popular by destination'. Thomas of Hales wrote 'A Luue Ron' about 1275, sending it to a maiden in place of the love-song which she had requested.[4] Larger in amount and in some ways apparently nearer to the carol is the work of the English Franciscan William Herebert, who died in 1333. One of his poems, 'Make Ready for the Long Journey', a free translation of an Anglo-Norman piece by Bozon, has a three-line external refrain after each stanza, but an independent couplet at the beginning.[5] He also translated Latin hymns, antiphons, and other portions of the service and is hence an important figure in the development of preachers' use of vernacular verse, but he does not appear to imitate secular dance-songs, and the claims of R. H. Robbins for him as a 'developer' of the carol are exaggerated.[6]

Franciscan friars in Ireland in the early fourteenth century produced the famous Kildare collection of Anglo-Irish poems, of which the most significant for the history of the carol is the lullaby in long couplets with the

---

[1] *Le Cantique populaire*, p. 85; for a biography by Ubald d'Alençon, see *Études franciscaines*, vii (1902), 538–44, and on his works see M. Dominica Legge, *Anglo-Norman Literature and its Background* (Oxford, 1963), pp. 229–32.

[2] For a description of and extracts from this manuscript see Paul Meyer, 'Notice et extraits du MS. 8336 de la bibliothèque de Sir Thomas Phillipps à Cheltenham', *Romania*, xiii (1884), 497–541. See also B. Schofield, 'The Manuscript of a Fourteenth Century Oxford Franciscan', *British Museum Quarterly*, xvi (1951), 36–7.

[3] It is headed in the manuscript copy: 'S'ensuit le dicté en francois de [F]rere Jehan Tisserant . . . lequel il fait chanter à son sermon' (Gastoué, op. cit., p. 235).

[4] Carleton Brown, ed., *English Lyrics of the XIIIth Century* (Oxford, 1932), No. 43, pp. 68–74.

[5] Brown, *R. L. 14 C.*, pp. xiv, 15–29.

[6] A thorough and capable treatment of Herebert's translations is provided by Helmut Gneuss, 'William Hereberts Übersetzungen', *Anglia*, lxxviii (1960), 170–92. Gneuss is corrective of Robbins's 'Friar Herebert and the Carol', *Anglia*, lxxv (1957), 194–8, and shows that Herebert's verses have even less relation to the sung carol than was implied in the first edition of the present work. See also W. F. Schirmer, *Geschichte der englischen und amerikanischen Literatur*, 4th edn. (Tübingen, 1959), i. 121, and *Selection*, p. 14: 'Certainly very little of Herebert's verse is really singable.'

recurring phrase 'Lullay, lullay, little child', in the penultimate line of each stanza.[1] The first stanza runs:

> Lollai, lollai, litil child, whi wepistou so sore?
> Nedis mostou wepe, hit was iȝarkid þe ȝore
> Euer to lib in sorow and sich and mourne euere,
> As þin eldren did er þis, whil hi aliues were.
> Lollai, [lollai], litil child, child, lolai, lullow,
> In to uncuþ world icommen so ertow.

Friar John de Grimestone, the compiler in 1372 of National Library of Scotland, MS. Advocates 18.7.21, records a similar lullaby in which the little child is specifically the infant Jesus and also a carol which uses the same phrase in its burden, No. 155 a.

This volume contains a large number of English religious poems, among them several carols.[2] One of these uses as its burden the first line of the lullaby in the Kildare MS.; another, also a lullaby carol, reappears in shortened form in three later manuscripts.[3] The collection also includes a verse dialogue between Mary and her crucified Son which is without question the material whence were made the three versions of carol No. 157 by cutting the non-stanzaic poems into four-line stanzas and adding a burden.[4]

The interesting little piece which has for its burden the lines beginning 'Honnd by honnd we schulle ous take', one of the earliest English carols and the earliest 'Christmas carol' extant, was probably used by a friar in connection with his preaching.[5] It was written down before 1350 among some Franciscan sermon notes which also contain other rhyming lines in English.[6]

The name which most firmly connects English carol-writing with the Friars Minor is that of James Ryman, now known to have been of the friary at Canterbury, whose work has several times been mentioned. Ryman has fared rather badly at the hands of critics,[7] and there is perhaps little to attract the casual modern reader in the 166 pieces contained in the manuscript to which his name and the date 1492 are set.[8] But we should not be

---

[1] British Museum, MS. Harley 913; printed n part by W. Heuser, *Die Kildare-Gedichte*, Bonner Beiträge zur Anglistik, xiv (1904), 174.

[2] Nos. 149 a, 155 a, 271.

[3] Nos. 155 a, 149 a.

[4] Brown, op. cit., p. 85.

[5] No. 12; cf. Brown, op. cit., p. xii.

[6] Bodleian Library, MS. Bodley 26; see Brown, op. cit., p. 272. It is interesting that one marginal drawing in the early fourteenth century (in Queen Mary's Psalter, B.M. MS. Royal 2.B.VII) shows two nuns and two friars, one Franciscan and one Dominican, in a group,

and another shows a nun playing a psaltery and a Franciscan friar playing a gittern. A. G. Little suggests that the first drawing 'might serve as an illustration' to this burden, but the hands are crossed rather than held, and are connected by ribbons (*Franciscan History and Legend in English Medieval Art*, British Society of Franciscan Studies, xix, Manchester, 1937, p. 47). A good reproduction is included in David L. Jeffrey, op. cit., plate 8.

[7] e.g. Chambers, *Early English Lyrics*, p. 292.

[8] Cambridge University Library MS. Ee. 1. 12; printed by J. Zupitza in *Archiv für das*

too hasty in assuming that these pedestrian poems were equally uninteresting to the author's contemporaries. One of Ryman's carols, shortened but otherwise not much altered, appears in the little collection of fragments of carol-books printed by Richard Kele about 1550, which, being issued as articles of commerce and not missionary efforts, presumably include only songs of some popular appeal.[1]

At any rate, Ryman's body of verse, dull as much of it is, provides valuable testimony as to the methods which he and doubtless other carol-writers followed in producing songs of this type. His working over of the 'Laetabundus' prose is a good example.[2] Of the 166 pieces 119 are in carol-form. Ryman is thus responsible for a quarter of all the extant English carols of date earlier than 1550. He tried his hand at almost every device of style used in other carols and appears to have invented a few of his own. He used Latin freely, particularly in his burdens, and several times composed a series of carols in the same strain and using the same burden, either in identical form or with slight variations.[3] In a number of poems he used a stanza rhymed like rhyme-royal without a burden, while to others on similar themes and in the same stanza-form he added burdens, thereby adapting them for performance as carols.[4] Ryman is to be regarded as a conscientious, rather uninspired Franciscan, engaged in turning religious and profitable matter into vernacular songs in order to appeal to the people. His use of the carol-form is doubtless the result of observation of the popularity of the carol at the time he was writing, and there is every reason to believe that he meant his work to be more than a pious literary exercise—that he designed his poems to be sung by his preaching brothers and their audiences.

Ryman's carols are the latest before 1550 for which Franciscan authorship can be shown, but a purpose in all respects like that which prompted the friar-authors of medieval carol, *lauda*, or *noël*, led an Irish Franciscan of the seventeenth century to compose popular religious lyrics, some of them for Christmas, modelled on secular song. This friar, Luke Wadding, Bishop of Ferns and cousin of the famous compiler of the *Annales Minorum*, borrowed the melodies of such English and Irish songs as 'Fortune my foe' and 'I do not love cause thou art fair', for the verses of his *A Pious Garland*, which ran through five or six editions. The occasion of their composition was the same as that which stirred medieval religious men—the menace to

---

Studium der neueren Sprachen, lxxxix (1892), 167–338. The colophon containing Ryman's name does not specifically refer to thirty-nine of these poems, but, with the exception of a narrative song on the 'false fox' with a strong folk-flavour, they are identical in style with the others and are almost certainly Ryman's.

[1] No. 81 A. R. T. Davies is hardly justified in writing '. . . there is no evidence, for example, that the many verses of Friar Ryman were in the slightest acceptable to those for whom, presumably, this popularizer intended them' (*Medieval English Lyrics*, London, 1963, pp. 23–4). Davies wrongly states that there are 'several tunes' in the Ryman manuscript (p. 23 n. 1).   [2] See above, pp. c, ci.

[3] e.g. Nos. 207–11, 295–9.

[4] Compare, e.g., Nos. 258, 156 with their neighbours in the manuscript, printed by Zupitza, op. cit., pp. 262, 264–7.

the people's faith and morals of 'erotic and licentious' songs, which the pious numbers were designed to replace.[1]

Apart from this external evidence of the friars' activity in the realm of popular religious poetry, there are signs of strong Franciscan influence on the subject-matter and spirit of the carols. The tempering of the austerity of Christianity by the appeal to tender emotion and personal love for Christ, the invocation of pity for His sorrow in the cradle and suffering on the cross, which is particularly to be noted in the lullaby and crucifixion carols, are part of the legacy of Francis to the centuries which followed His ministry. An excellent expression of this religious attitude is to be found in the *Meditationes Vitae Christi*, attributed in the Middle Ages to the great Franciscan St. Bonaventure, but not actually from his hand, being addressed by a Friar Minor to a Poor Clare.[2] This work enjoyed an enormous vogue in England as in other countries, and an English version made in the early fifteenth century by Nicholas Love, a Carthusian prior, is extant in twenty-three manuscripts.[3] The emphasis which it lays upon the humanity of Christ, the suffering which He underwent, and the duty of the Christian to feel compassion for Him is strikingly similar to a corresponding emphasis in some of the carols.[4] The religion informing most of the sacred carols is in large measure a Franciscan Christianity.

In the ranks of the followers of St. Francis, therefore, the authors of many of the anonymous carols may conjecturally be placed. Unquestionably there were members of other religious orders who wrote carols; John Audelay, more gifted if less prolific as a carol-writer than Ryman, was a chaplain resident in an Augustinian house.[5] Audelay, however, was enough of a disciple of Francis to compose a carol in his honour,[6] and he was certainly touched by the Franciscan missionary spirit. The mendicant friars, and

---

[1] W. H. Grattan Flood, 'Noëls anglo-irlandais', in *Études franciscaines*, xxxviii (1926), 651–3. The article also notes another Irish Franciscan who wrote a similar piece, Archbishop MacCaghwell of Armagh.

[2] *The Catholic Encyclopedia* (New York, 1907), s.v. 'Bonaventure, Saint'.

[3] Ed. Lawrence F. Powell, *The Mirrour of the Blessed Lyf of Jesu Christ* (London, 1908): Love's version is an abridgement of the original. For a complete translation into Modern English see *Meditations on the Life of Christ*, trans. and ed. Isa Ragusa and Rosalie B. Green, Princeton Monographs in Art and Archaeology, xxxv (Princeton, 1961). On its popularity see Margaret Deanesly, 'Vernacular Books in England in the Fourteenth and Fifteenth Centuries', *Modern Language Review*, xv (1920), 353–8. Her suggestion of the Franciscan John de Caulibus of San Gemignano as the author

of the work has now been generally accepted (John Moorman, *A History of the Franciscan Order*, Oxford, 1968, p. 261).

[4] Compare, e.g., Nos. 157, 159, 160, 162, 163 with the chapter 'Of the passioun of our lorde Jesu criste' (Powell, op. cit., pp. 216 ff.) which begins: 'At the bygynnynge thou that desirest to haue sorwefull compassioun / thoruȝ feruent inward affeccioun / of the peynefull passioun of Jesu / thou moste in thy mynde depart in manere for the tyme the myȝt of the godhede fro the kyndely infirmyte of the manhede.'

Compare also the lullaby carols with such a passage as this (Powell, op. cit., p. 53): 'For as we mowen suppose he weped ofte sithes / as othere children done / to schewe the wrecchednesse of mankynde that he verrayly took.'

[5] See above, p. xxx.

[6] No. 310.

particularly the Minorites, were probably the most active group of carol-writers and carol-singers, the 'professional class' whose interest and activity propagated and preserved the texts of the carols.[1]

3. The 'Christmas Carol'

The two related aspects of the carol's history which have just been discussed, its character as religious imitation of secular song, and its intimate association with Franciscanism, have a definite bearing upon the specialization of the carol as a Christmas song. The form began to be associated with the Nativity season almost as soon as it appeared in English, and, as more and more carols were sung at that time, and the medieval round dance was left behind, the word 'carol' itself came to connote singing at Christmas rather than singing to a dance-measure. The large proportion of carols on the Nativity, the Epiphany, and the intervening feast days represents the response of the carol-writers to the challenge which the popular Christmas customs presented to their special veneration for the season. Christmastide, as the representative of the older pagan winter feast, was one of the chief occasions of popular rejoicing, and hence of those outbreaks of dance and song which so troubled the clergy.[2] It was on Christmas Eve that the famous carollers of Kölbigk disturbed the service with their revelry. And in England, where Christmas was decidedly the greatest popular feast, it was also a time when ribald songs were much in evidence. The concern of a good churchman at this situation is shown by a passage from the fifteenth-century compilation of Thomas Gascoigne:

Nativitas Domini nostri Jesu Xti. Ideo vos omnes, pro quorum salute Xtus venit, cavete et fugite in hoc sacro festo viciosa et turpia, et praecipue cantus inhonestos et turpes qui libidinem excitant et provocant, et memoriam turpibus imaginacionibus maculant, et laedunt, et ymagines imprimunt in mente, quas expellere difficillimum est.[3]

Gascoigne goes on to tell of his personal knowledge of a distinguished man who was unable to free his mind from the memory of a lewd song which he heard at Christmastime and died of the resulting melancholy.

Naturally enough, such songs were infrequently written down, but a few chance survivals indicate that there was plenty of scope for sanctifying activity in the Christmas song of the late Middle Ages. The morality play *Mankind*, preserved in the Macro MS. of about 1475, makes the enemies

---

[1] See above, p. cxxxii.
[2] See the long series of ecclesiastical prohibitions of pagan rejoicing at Christmas time cited in Chambers, *The Mediaeval Stage*, ii. 290–306.
[3] J. E. T. Rogers, ed., *Loci e Libro Veritatum* (Oxford, 1881), p. 144.

of Mankind join in a 'Crystemes songe' which Nought introduces with a couplet similar to many occurring in the carols:

> Now I prey all þe yemandry þat ys here
> To synge with ws with a mery chere:[1]

The song itself, while not erotic, is a triumph of coarseness. Nos. 460 and 461 in the present collection will surprise some readers by appearing in association with religious *Christmas carolles*. But Christmas was the time when such songs were most often heard, and this prevalence provides another good reason for the dominance of the Christmas theme among religious carols. Wycliffe complains that at Christmas men 'pleie a pagyn of þe deuyl, syngynge songis of lecherie, of batailis and of lesyngis', but he admits that 'ȝonge wymmen may sumtyme daunsen in mesure to haue recreacion and liȝtnesse, so þat þei haue þe more þouȝt on myrþe in heuene & drede more & loue more god þer-by, & synge honeste songis of cristis incarnacion, passion, resurexion & ascencion, & of þe ioies of oure ladi, & to dispise synne & preise vertue in alle here doynge'; a permission that includes a very fair summary of the principal themes of the religious carols.[2] It is to be noticed that in Wycliffe's time such songs are associated with the dance in a completely matter-of-fact way.

But the celebration of Christmas with godly song and rejoicing was a Franciscan tradition quite independent of the need for reform of popular customs. St. Francis himself took a particular interest in the feast of the Nativity and in devotion to Christ as the Babe of Bethlehem.[3] The long-accepted legend that he first instituted the custom of the Christmas crib at Grecia in 1223 testifies to this interest. Although recent investigation has shown that the crib was in occasional use in the eleventh century or earlier, Francis and his followers did help to make more popular this manner of honouring the Christ-Child.[4] The emphasis on the humility and poverty of the Divine Infant, which Nativity carol and *noël* so often exhibit, is characteristic of Franciscanism, which embraced humility and poverty as the highest of virtues. The ox and the ass, which appear so frequently in medieval Nativity poetry and art, owe their recognition in part to the love of dumb creatures which Francis preached and for which he is particularly remembered.[5]

---

[1] Mark Eccles, ed., *The Macro Plays*, E.E.T.S., No. 262, 1969, pp. 164–5. Compare the remark of the character 'Clargy' in Bale's *King Johan* (1536): 'Yea, god sped vs well, crystmes songes are mery tales' (ed. J. H. P. Pafford, The Malone Society Reprints, 1931, p. 27, l. 564).

[2] F. D. Matthew, ed., *The English Works of Wyclif Hitherto Unprinted*, E.E.T.S., Or. Ser., No. 74, 1880, p. 206; see also the citation from an Advent sermon in G. R. Owst, *Literature and Pulpit in Medieval England*, 2nd edn.

(Oxford, 1961), p. 484.

[3] See Clement A. Miles, *Christmas in Ritual and Tradition* (London, 1913), p. 36.

[4] L. Gougaud, 'La crèche de Noël avant Saint François d'Assise', in *Revue des sciences religieuses*, ii (1922), 26–34.

[5] Cf. *Speculum Perfectionis*, cap. cxiv: 'Quod [Franciscus] volebat suadere Imperatori ut faceret specialem legem quod in Nativitate Domini homines bene providerent avibus et bovi et asino et pauperibus.'

Two of the *laude* of Fra Jacopone da Todi celebrate the Nativity in the fashion of the later English carols, one of them ending with an exhortation to sing like that so often found in the English pieces:

> uomini iusti,—che sete endusti,
> venite a cantare . . .[1]

The particular devotion to the Virgin for which many Franciscans were noted was an additional reason for the attention given the Nativity by poets of the order.

The English religious carol, as preserved in manuscripts of the pre-Reformation period, far from being the spontaneous product of the popular joy at the Christmas season which sentimentalizing writers would like to make of it, is rather one weapon of the Church in her long struggle with the survivals of paganism and with the fondness of her people for unedifying entertainment. It stands removed from true folk-song by one more degree than does the carol genre as a whole; it is a pious imitation of secular popular song which is itself a development from folk-song.[2] That it was such a successful aid in the cause of religion, that the people accepted and sang the pious carol, even when written by so ungifted a poet as Ryman, speaks well for the close contact with the people and the showmanship of those who introduced it. These were qualities for which the friars were famous; without doubt more of their number than have left any written trace both composed and sang many carols like those here collected.

---

[1] *Le Laude*, ed. Ferri, No. lxiv; the other Nativity *lauda* is No. lxv.

[2] The procedure of supplying sacred words to fit secular and amorous tunes was vigorously continued in the broadsides and garlands of the seventeenth century. Two good examples appear in the pamphlet printed in London in 1661 (just after the Puritans' embargo on the Christmas carol had been lifted) by H. B. for Andrew Kemb of Southwark, *New Carolls for this merry time of Christmas*: 'A new Caroll of the birth of our blessed Saviour Jesus Christ. To the Tune of, Kisse and bid me welcome home', and 'A new Christmas Caroll for the bitter passion of our blessed Saviour. The Tune is, *The North-Country Lass*' (Bodleian Library, Wood 110 (4), A3^r and B3^r).

CHAPTER VI

THE BURDENS OF THE CAROLS

THE burden makes and marks the carol. The presence of an invariable line or group of lines which is to be sung before the first stanza and after all stanzas is the feature which distinguishes the carol from all other forms of Middle English lyric. Its originally choral character and its function in dance song have already been described. But the burdens of the English carols, like the *refrains* of the Old French *chansons*, have an intrinsic interest which is not wholly dependent on their importance for the structure of the pieces which they accompany. They are worth a brief examination for their own sakes, best made by isolating them to some extent from their associated stanza-texts.

Such an isolation is justified by the quasi-independent character of the burden of a carol, a trait which is not shared by the refrain, when there is one. The refrain, as defined in this essay, is a repeated element which forms part of a stanza, in the carols usually the last line. The burden, on the other hand, is a repeated element which does not form any part of a stanza, but stands wholly outside the individual stanza-pattern. The refrain is a member of the stanza; the burden is a member only of the carol as a whole. It is hardly necessary to say that in this work 'burden' is never used in its other and older sense of an under-song, words to be sung simultaneously with the stanza-text.

Both burden and refrain derive ultimately from choral repetition, and when a recurrent element of this sort has been incorporated into literary poetry, it is often difficult to say whether it is essentially interior or exterior to the stanza. Such is the case, for example, with the 'Cras amet qui nunquam amavit . . .' of the *Pervigilium Veneris* or with the *refrains* of many of the lyrics in Old French.[1] But in the English carol before 1550 there are few cases in which the character of a repeated line or lines can be in doubt. The usual arrangement in the manuscripts shows that the distinction was well recognized. The burden is almost invariably written at the head of the piece; in Balliol College, Oxford, MS. 354 it is sometimes marked 'fote'.[2] Its repetition after every stanza is usually assumed without written indication,

---

[1] Valuable observations on the origin and use of the refrain and its connection with songs which are performed by leader and chorus are made by C. M. [Sir Maurice] Bowra in *Primitive Song* (London, 1962), especially pp. 41–4.

[2] Not 'foot' in the sense of under-song, but equivalent to 'chorus' or 'burden' as here used; *O.E.D.*, s.v. 'Foot', 21 b. Compare Richard Huloet's *Dictionarie* (revised by John Higgins, London, 1572): 'Foote of a dittie, or verse, whiche is often repeted. Versus intercalaris. *Refrainctes de balades.*'

but not infrequently the first words and '&c.' will be found. A refrain, on the contrary, is ordinarily written in full with the stanza of which it forms a part. As most of the refrain-lines in carols occur as the *caudae* of tail-rhyme stanzas, they are often written to the right of the bracket enclosing the other lines of the stanza, in the customary way of treating the tail-rhyme form.[1]

It is plain that a burden is less closely tied to a given carol than is a refrain. Removal or damage of a refrain-line, in either oral or written transmission, is immediately obvious; the rhyme-pattern of the stanza is disturbed. Omission of the burden, while fundamentally more serious in that it changes the piece from a carol to an ordinary poem or song, yet may be superficially less noticeable, for no rhyme-pattern of a stanza is affected thereby. Conversely, it is fairly easy to make a carol of a song without a choral element by adding a burden to it. Neither is there any difficulty in substituting for one burden another of a rhythmic form which accommodates itself to the melody of a given piece.

Examination of the extant texts shows that such changes were actually made, although not with striking frequency. The transformation of a song without a burden into a carol is to be seen in No. 191. This charming and thoroughly artful little English–Latin poem is found in substantially the same form in two thirteenth-century manuscripts.[2] In the fifteenth century it reappears, made over into a carol, the last five lines of each original stanza being dropped and the burden 'Enixa est puerpera' prefixed.[3]

We may infer that the same thing has taken place with No. 123, of which the A-text has a burden and the B has not, and in No. 125, where A alone of the four texts has a burden. In the later A-text of No. 123 the redactor has substituted a Latin refrain, 'Deo Patri sit gloria', for the English lines of B ending in '. . . Marie', and has added a burden of the type which embodies the refrain:

> Alleluya, alleluia,
> Deo Patri sit gloria.

In the case of No. 125, the three texts without a burden probably represent the original form of the piece. The 'bob-and-wheel' stanza used is not frequent in carols, and the burden which appears in the Sloane MS. 2593

---

[1] e.g. No. 185 B, Bodleian Library MS. Arch. Selden B. 26, f. 10^v: facsimile in *Early Bodleian Music*, No. lii. In the later years of the carol's popularity the burden is occasionally marked *Quyre*, as in William Byrd's 'A Carol for Christmas Day' (1589) and the carol sung by 'Fowre Women bravelie apparelled' in *Promos and Cassandra*, part ii (1578), Act II, Scene ii, 'If pleasure be treasure '(Geoffrey Bullough, ed., *Narrative and Dramatic Sources of Shakespeare*, ii, London, 1967, 488–9). In the latter the solo part, the stanza, is divided line by line among the four singers, who unite in the burden.

[2] British Museum MS. Egerton 613, f. 2^r.; Trinity College, Cambridge, MS. B. 14. 39, f. 24^v.

[3] Bodleian Library MS. Ashmole 1393, f. 69^v. John Edwin Wells, *A Manual of the Writings in Middle English* (New Haven, 1926), p. 532, wrongly describes the piece as 'with music'; it is not so written.

seems ill fitted. It was probably added by someone who wished to make a carol out of what was already a very good song for the Epiphany.

The texts yield no plausible evidence for the loss of a burden from a carol without its replacement by another, except in No. 468 B. In No. 152 c stanzas from a carol alternate with stanzas from a Latin hymn. No. 79 B may be an instance, but it is possible that the third and fourth lines of the stanza were used as a burden rather than as a refrain.

The substitution of one burden for another occurs in a few cases which may be noted without any attempt to determine which burden is the earlier. No. 122 exhibits three different burdens in as many manuscripts:

> A.   Nowel, nowel, nowel.
>
> B.   Nowel, el, el, el,
>   Now is wel that euere was woo.
>
> C.   Conditor alme siderum,
>   Eterna lux credencium.

No. 35 appears in two versions with different burdens.

No. 157 presents an interesting case of a carol with different burdens in different versions. In B it begins as follows:

> (Burden)   'Mary modyr, cum and se:
>   Thi Son is naylyd on a tre.
>
> (Stanza 1)   'His body is wappyd all in wo,
>   Hand and fot; he may not go;
>   Thi Son, lady, that thou louyst soo,
>   Nakyd is naylyd vpon a tre.'

In C:

> (Burden)   Nowel, el, el, el, el, el, el, el,
>   el, el, el, el, el, el, el, el!
>
> (Stanza 1)   'Mary moder, cum and se:
>   Thi Sone is naylyd on a tre,
>   Hand and fot; he may not go;
>   His body is woundyn al in woo.'

In A:

> (Burden)   Gaudeamus synge we
>   In hoc sacro tempore;
>   Puer nobis natus est
>   Ex Maria virgine.
>
> (Stanza 1)   'Mary moder, come and se:
>   Thy Sone is nayled on a tre,
>   Hande and fote; he may not go;
>   His body is wrapped all in wo.'

These three versions represent the work of three different carol-writers bent on the same object, the turning into a carol of a sacred poem not in carol form. Their material was some text of the verse dialogue between Jesus and the Virgin which appears in Friar Johan de Grimestone's commonplace book,[1] a non-stanzaic piece in couplets, beginning:

> Maiden and moder, cum and se:
> Thi child is nailed to a tre,
> Hand and fot; he may nouth go;
> His bodi is wonden al in wo.

The individual whose work C represents simply added a 'noël' burden, the writer of A the more elaborate Latin–English lines. The author of B, however, took the first two lines of the poem to serve as a burden, and replaced them in the stanza with the weak and redundant third and fourth lines quoted above. It is to be noted that the three versions show different methods of breaking the original material up into stanzas: C is in four-line monorhyme stanzas (except stanza 1), B in regular four-line tail-rhyme stanzas, and A in similar tail-rhyme stanzas (except stanza 1).

Frequently one line of a couplet burden will differ in variants when the other line remains the same, or a line may be omitted or repeated in one version. The repetition or omission is probably due in many cases to the demands of the musical settings, remembered or understood by the scribes, but not written down. In No. 18, for example, the words of the burden:

> Nowel, nowel, nowel!
> To vs is born owr God Emanuel,

are to be sung once according to the music in Trinity College, Cambridge, MS. O. 3. 58, and twice according to that of Bodleian Library MS. Arch. Selden B. 26. When a line appears in the burden of one text of a carol and not in that of another, it is usually a conventional phrase like 'Now syng we all in fere', which is joined with 'Alma redemptoris mater' in the burden of No. 234 D, but is missing in A, B, and C.[2]

The greater part of those carols with burdens preserved in more than one version show none of these variations; in about two-thirds of the total number the burdens of the several texts are identical or vary only in a word or two.[3]

There are a number of burdens which are found attached to more than one carol. Repetitions of 'noël' and 'alleluia' to form a burden are found in

---

[1] No. 157 D.
[2] Cf. also Nos. 185, 237.
[3] In 45 of the 69: Nos. 7, 8, 17, 27, 30, 36, 42, 81, 91, 95, 114, 117, 124, 132, 136, 145, 150–2, 155, 161, 163, 172, 175, 180, 187, 190, 230, 232, 235, 238, 239, 331, 337, 338, 355, 356, 380, 386, 389, 395, 399, 410, 422, 426.

several pieces. Ryman's practice of using the same burden for several carols
has been noted. Other burdens which do double duty are the following:[1]

Man, be glad in halle and bour;
This tyme was born our Sauyour.   (Nos. 16, 27 A)

Nowel syng we now al and sum,
For Rex Pacificus is cum.   (Nos. 21 C, 29)

Lullay, lay, lay, lay,
My dere modyr, lullay.   (Nos. 142 a, 149 b)

Mary modyr, cum and se:
Thi Son is naylyd on a tre.   (Nos. 157 B, 158)

Synge we to this mery cumpane,
'Regina celi, letare.'   (Nos. 185 B, 186)

Inducas, inducas,
In temptationibus.   (Nos. 461, 461.1)

Single lines which are found in the burdens of two wholly different pieces
are the following:[2]

Timor mortis conturbat me.   (Nos. 369, 370)

Man, asay, asay, asay.   (Nos. 184, 359)

Amice Christi Johannes.   (Nos. 103, 104)

Care away, away, away.   (Nos. 406, 470)

Gramersy myn owyn purs.   (Nos. 390, 391)

Do well, and drede no man.   (Nos. 354, 387)

By far the most common form taken by the burdens of the carols is the
couplet. This predominance of the couplet burden may be regarded as a distinctive feature of the carol form, for in no other type of lyric with burden
or refrain is the couplet so common. The burden of a single line, so frequent
in medieval French lyrics and in traditional folk-song, is of exceptional
occurrence in the carols.[3] That it was not regarded as a good form by carol-
writers is shown by the number of cases in which a single line borrowed
from Latin hymnody is made into a couplet by the addition of a conventional
phrase.[4] Burdens of more than two lines are far more numerous, but still
form only about a fourth of the total number.[5] The ten-line burdens of

---

[1] In some cases with slight variations. Compare also Nos. 41 and 183.

[2] Omitting those lines which are only a series
of ejaculations like 'A, a, a, a', or set expressions
like 'Synge we, syng we'.

[3] Nos. 14 b and c, 30 B, 60.1, 93, 122 A,
149 d, 157 C, 191 A, 220–6, 234 A, B, and C,

236, 237 A, 243 b, 366. The division of burdens
into lines is a matter in which editors do not
always agree; some which I divide have been
printed elsewhere as one line.

[4] e.g. Nos. 21 A, B, D, 234 D.

[5] There are 115 in all, including those in
which the burden is a couplet repeated.

Nos. 263 a and 458 and the twice-repeated quatrain of No. 464 are the farthest removed of any from the simplicity of a burden adapted for dance-song.

Proper understanding of the burdens of carols is sometimes made more difficult for the reader by the irresponsibility of editors, not merely those of the time of Percy and Scott, but some of our own day as well. Reprinters, who rarely use the original manuscripts, omit burdens altogether, or remove them from their proper initial position, or fail to italicize them in accordance with the usage adopted for an edition.[1] It is very important that a commentator on a carol be sure of the reliability of his text before he undertakes to interpret the significance of the burden.

The linking of burden and stanza by rhyme, a practice common in French *chansons à danser* and in the Italian *ballata*, is frequent also in the carols. It is usually found in carols in tail-rhyme stanzas, the *caudae* rhyming with each other and with the couplet burden. Audelay uses a special device for the linking of stanza and burden, which is also found in a few carols other than his. This is the addition to the stanza of an invariable tag or phrase of a few words which rhymes with the burden and serves as a transitional element. Audelay's carol to St. Anne has such tags:

(Stanza 1)   Swete Saynt Anne, we the beseche,
           Thou pray fore vs to Oure Laday
      That heo wel be oure soulis leche
           That day when we schul dey;
      Herefore we say:

(Burden)   The moder of Mary, that merceful may,
    Pray fore vs both nyght and day.[2]

These are plainly survivals from the dance-song prototypes of the carol, where such tags served as cues to the chorus to join in the burden.

It would not be surprising to find that the carol, deriving its form ultimately from folk-song for the dance, and doubtless often sung to the melodies of secular dance-song, occasionally borrowed a burden entire from the same source. In the nature of things a burden of dance-song would have wider circulation and greater vitality than the stanza-text; the latter might be known only to the leader who sang the solo part, whereas the burden,

---

[1] An example is Gerald Bullett, whose anthology *The English Galaxy of Shorter Poems* (London, 1933) silently omits the burdens of Nos. 143, 173, 432, 445, and 463, and prints the burdens of Nos. 322 A and 422 A as if they were the first stanzas of these pieces. In his preface he says, '. . . on two or three occasions it has seemed to me legitimate and desirable to omit an otiose stanza' (p. ix). But he omits three, including the first, from No. 422

A. Fortunately there are few cases as disturbing as that of Francis Berry, who prints the famous 'Corpus Christi' (No. 322 A) without a burden and with an internal refrain in the stanzas (*Poets' Grammar*, London, 1958, p. 21). See R. L. Greene, 'The Burden and the Scottish Variant of the Corpus Christi Carol', *Medium Ævum*, xxxiii (1964), 58 n. 25.

[2] No. 311.

repeated after every stanza by the entire chorus, would inevitably be fixed
in the memories of many. Burdens, more than any other part of folk-song,
lay ready to the hand of the medieval song-writer who composed for the
people songs in the style of those they already knew.

The burden of No. 440, one of the earliest of all the carols here collected,
is regarded by critics generally as borrowed outright from folk-song.[1]
Whether any others are similarly taken over is less certain. The following are
the only ones which seem to the present writer to be possible survivors from
folk-song. Like 'Blow, northerne wynd', they are mostly associated with
love-songs:

> Hey now, now, now!   (No. 93)

> Com home agayne,
> Com home agayne,
> Min owine swet hart, com home agayne;
> Ye are gone astray
> Owt of youer way;
> There[fore] com h[o]me agayne.   (No. 270)

> Mery hyt ys in May mornyng,
> Mery wayys for to gone.   (No. 323)

> Care away, away, away,
> Care away for euermore.   (No. 406; compare No. 470.)

> Hey, howe!
> Sely men, God helpe yowe.   (No. 409)

> This day day dawes,
> This gentill day day dawes,
> This gentill day dawes,
> And I must home gone.
> This gentill day dawes,
> This day day dawes,
> This gentill day dawes,
> And we must home gone.   (No. 432)

> Who so lyst to loue,
> God send hym right good spede.   (No. 442)

> So well ys me begone,
> Troly, lole,
> So well ys me begone,
> Troly, loly.   (No. 446)

> Grene growith the holy,
> So doth the iue,
> Thow wynter blastys blow neuer so hye,
> Grene growth the holy.   (No. 448)

[1] See B. ten Brink, *Geschichte der englischen Litteratur*, i (Berlin, 1877), 382, and Notes on
No. 440.

[Nou] spri[nke]s the sprai;
Al for loue icche am so seek
   That slepen I ne mai.   (No. 450)

Rybbe ne rele ne spynne yc ne may
For joyghe that it ys holyday.   (No. 452)

Alas, ales, the wyle!
Thout Y on no gyle,
   So haue Y god chaunce.
Ala[s], ales, the wyle
   That euer Y cowde daunce!   (No. 453)

Were it vndo that is ydo,
   I wold be war.   (No. 455)

Wep no more for me, swet hart,
   Wepe no more for me;
As sharpe as a dart hathe perysht my hart
   That ye shod morne for me.   (No. 462)

Yow and I and Amyas,
   Amyas and yow and I,
To the grenewode must we go, alas!
   Yow and I, my lyff, and Amyas.   (No. 463)

Hey nony nony nony nony no,
Hey nony nony nony nony no!   (No. 463.1)

Vp, son and mery wether,
   Somer draweth nere.   (No. 469)

There are more than a few burdens, however, with wording which suggests imitation of folk-song, either direct or, in the case of religious carols, by imitation of secular popular song based on folk-song. One group of such burdens is made up of those composed in part of sounds of onomatopoeic or exclamatory value. A number are Latin, for example:[1]

   A, a, a, a,
   Nu[n]c gaudet ecclesia.

The same line is combined with English words in

   A, a, a, a,
   Yet I loue wherso I go,[2]

but usually in English burdens of this sort the exclamatory syllable is 'hey' or 'aye', as in

   Hey, hey, hey, hey!
   The borrys hede is armyd gay.[3]

---

[1] No. 114; similar burdens are those of Nos. 188, 232, 313, 429.
[2] No. 414.   [3] No. 135.

It occurs even with a carol having no suggestion of joviality:

> Hay, hay, hay, hay!
> Thynke on Whitson Monday.[1]

There can hardly be any doubt that the medieval Englishman often stamped his feet in a round dance in time with a 'hey, hey' of this sort. Similar use of the 'o' sound is less successful. 'Po, po, po, po,'[2] might go well enough, but there is artificiality in Ryman's

> O, O, O, O, O, O, O, O,
> O Deus sine termino.[3]

The imitation of the sounds of musical instruments in burdens is a kind of onomatopoeia more in evidence in French song than in English. Many a *chanson* uses a phrase like 'Don, don farilari don',[4] or 'Trairi deluriau, deluriau, delurièle',[5] and the sound of the drum is imitated in many a soldier song and even in the *noël*.[6] But the shepherd's pipe alone is represented in the burdens of the carols, and that only in one which begins with 'Tyrle, tyrlo'.[7]

Of a less elementary nature, but still closely related to the choral use of the burden in the dance, are those burdens which allude directly to the dancing group. Of these other lands have left far richer store than England, and those which do remain in English are principally to be found in traditional folk-song. There is but one example among the carols, the burden of No. 12:[8]

> Honnd by honnd we schulle ous take,
> And joye and blisse schulle we make,
> For the deuel of ele man haght forsake,
> And Godes Sone ys maked oure make.

These pious lines are plainly an imitation of the burden of some song for a round dance; the first two lines may be taken over unchanged from a secular piece.

There are a large number of burdens, however, which mention the singing group. These are mostly exhortations to sing and be merry, and, while they are probably not close imitations of folk-song, they do imply the communal performance of the carols which remained even after they were dissociated from actual dancing. In some it is merely the natural holiday spirit which is expressed, for example:

> Make we mery, bothe more and lasse,
> For now ys the tyme of Crystymas.[9]

---

[1] No. 425, on the execution of Archbishop Scrope.

[2] No. 134.

[3] No. 284; but see Note.

[4] Gérold, *Chansons populaires*, No. xxxvi.

[5] Julien Tiersot, *Histoire de la chanson popu-laire en France* (Paris, 1889), p. 153.

[6] 'Guillô, pran ton tamborin,' in de Smidt, *Les Noëls et la tradition populaire*, p. 223.

[7] No. 79 A.

[8] But compare No. 453.

[9] No. 11.

But more often, in keeping with the religious purpose of the carols, it is made plain that it is godly mirth which is to be enjoyed:

> Nowe lete vs syng and mery be,
> For Crist oure Kyng hathe made us fre.[1]

One such line is frequently combined with a Latin line to form a burden, thus:

> Now be we glad and not to sad,
> For verbum caro factum est.[2]

The burdens of the lullaby carols form a class by themselves. Their characteristic feature is a free use of the soothing onomatopoeia 'lullay'. This is, of course, in imitation of real folk-lullabies; a similar sound was used by those first-century nurses whom Persius reports as singing to their charges:

> Lálla lálla lálla, aút dormí aut lácte,[3]

and doubtless by many generations before them. The frequent appearance of such soothing sounds in a form of verse which has been so closely associated with social dance as the carol-burden may seem a little strange, even when it is recalled that a round dance about the Christmas crib has been a common feature of Continental celebrations.[4] The burden as a feature of lullabies has no doubt a long history of its own, quite independent of the dance. But the ultimate reason for its being is a need similar to that responsible for the dance-burden: the need for periodic repetition. The situation is neatly put by Tiersot in his discussion of the popular *berceuse*:

> Cette condition première [de la berceuse], c'est la régularité du rythme, la monotonie du dessin mélodique, dont le retour périodique et incessant . . . calme les nerfs et provoque le repos. Si déjà l'enfant parle, il faut en outre que les vers, par leur peu de signification, ne tiennent pas son attention en éveil: une série de syllabes formant des semblants de mots, . . . quelques paroles sans suite, des images très simples surtout, avec force diminutifs, et cela répété indéfiniment, . . . voilà ce qui convient à la berceuse.[5]

The burdens of the lullaby carols show just these qualities in greater or less degree, keeping a likeness to a real lullaby even when the matter of the stanzas is literary and religious dialogue, suggesting neither cradle nor dance. Even the song of the stricken mothers of the Innocents in the Coventry Plays has a burden with the proper monotony and slightness of idea:

> Lully, lulla, thow littell tine child,
> By, by, lully, lullay, thow littell tyne child,
> By, by, lully, lullay.[6]

---

[1] No. 55.   [2] No. 38.   *Ritual and Tradition*, p. 110.
[3] *Scholia*, iii. 16, in Frederic D. Allen, *Rem-*   [5] *Histoire de la chanson populaire en France*,
nants of Early Latin (Boston, 1908), p. 94.   p. 133.
[4] Especially in the *Kindelwiegen* of fifteenth-   [6] No. 112. Similar are Nos. 142 a, 143, 144,
century Germany. See Miles, *Christmas in*   146 A, 149, 153.

In a few pieces the subject of the stanza-text also intrudes into the burden, displacing the simple 'lulling' sounds, for example:

> Lullay, my chyld, and wepe no more,
> Slepe and be now styll;
> The Kyng of Blys thi Fader ys,
> As it was hys wyll.[1]

In one carol the opening formula of the *chanson d'aventure* type has been isolated and made into a burden.[2]

The many carols of prevailingly moral or sententious content are provided with burdens which reflect, or perhaps rather set, the tone of the entire piece, even as 'noël' strikes the note proper to a song of joy, or 'lullay' that for a slumber-song. No type of burden is better suited to these moralizing carols than one which states aptly the point of all its teaching, which embodies in an easily remembered couplet a sentiment which can appropriately be repeated after each stanza. Audelay recognized this, for example, when he wrote his defence of the established order with the heading 'Fac ad quod venisti'.[3] After the exposition of each stanza come, first the tag 'I say all gate:' and then the burden:

> Hit is the best, erele and late,
> Vche mon kepe his oune state.

Such a combination of sententious content and striking and compact expression constitutes the peculiar merit of the popular proverb, and it is not surprising to find that a number of carol-burdens embody expressions which served the Middle Ages as proverbs or bywords. One burden explicitly acknowledges the borrowing:

> An old sawe hath be fownd trewe:
> 'Cast not away thyn old for newe.'[4]

The currency of some of these apophthegms is attested by their preservation in other bits of contemporary writings. Two mildly cynical carols on the power of money have burdens embodying the line 'Gramercy my own purse'.[5] The same sentence appears as the refrain of a poem similar in sentiment but in the more literary eight-line refrain-stanza, printed with other proverbial and miscellaneous lore at the end of Wynkyn de Worde's 1496 edition of *The Boke of St. Albans*.[6] It is interesting to see the famous rallying-cry of

---

[1] No. 151 A. Similar are Nos. 145, 147.
[2] No. 150.
[3] No. 347.
[4] No. 346.

[5] Nos. 390, 391.
[6] Reprinted by Ritson, *Ancient Songs* (1877), p. 152.

John Ball's followers in the rebellion of 1381 doing duty, slightly adapted, as the burden of a quite uninflammatory carol on the narrative of the Fall:

> Now bething the, gentilman,
> How Adam dalf and Eue sp[an.][1]

Two other proverbs used as watchwords of the same insurrection appear in carol-burdens; they are written into the letter to the rebellious leaders of Essex which is well known for its allusion to the hero of *Piers Plowman*. The doggerel containing them is as follows:

> Iohan þe Mullere haþ ygrounde smal, smal, smal;
> þe Kynges sone of heuene schal paye for al.
> Be war or ye be wo;
> Knoweþ ȝour freend fro ȝour foo;
> Haueth ynow, and seith 'Hoo';
> And do wel and bettre, and fleth synne,
> And sekeþ pees, and hold ȝou þerinne;
> and so biddeþ Iohan Trewman and alle his felawes.[2]

The third line of the above begins the burden of a carol against pride:

> Man, be war er thou be wo:
> Think on pride, and let hym goo.[3]

The fifth occurs in the burden of a carol on the covetousness of men in high stations:

> Forsothe, I hold hym well and withowt woo
> That hath ynowgh and can say 'Whoo!'[4]

The second line of the burden of a carol of worldly counsel,

> Bewar, sqwyer, yeman, and page,
> For seruyse is non erytage,

had wide currency as a proverb.[5] It was apparently an established practice for a carol-writer to utilize as the burden of a piece some common moral or prudential saying suited to his purpose and at the same time accepted by the people to whom he addressed his song.[6] A few carols have burdens taken from similar maxims of the Latin Scriptures. That of No. 351, for example, is from Psalm lxii. 10:

> Diuisie si affluant,
> Nolite cor apponere.

---

[1] Thomas Walsingham describes Ball's preaching to an assembly at Blackheath on the text: 'Whan Adam dalfe and Eve span, who was than a Gentleman?' *Historia Brevis*, in William Camden, *Anglica, Normanica, Cambrica, a Veteribus Scripta* (Frankfurt, 1602), p. 275. The carol is No. 336.

[2] Kenneth Sisam, ed., *Fourteenth Century Verse and Prose* (Oxford, 1921), p. 161.
[3] No. 355; compare No. 325.
[4] No. 350.
[5] No. 381.
[6] On the importance of the proverb in medieval thought see J. Huizinga, *The Waning of the Middle Ages* (London, 1947), pp. 210–11.

Other carols which make use of recognizable proverbs in burden or stanza-text are Nos. 325, 338, 341, 344, 345, 348, 354, 374, 387, 389, 401 B, 407. It is noteworthy that the carols on the Nativity and other specifically religious subjects avoid inclusion of proverbs, even of those which are found in the Bible. The proverb is clearly felt by carol-writers to be a rhetorical form for use in moralizing rather than in rejoicing or worship. It is interesting that the folk-ballad, which so rarely includes moralizing, also maintains an almost complete taboo on proverbs. B. J. Whiting, in a thorough study, reckons as only 20 the actual proverbs to be found in nearly 2,100 variants of the 305 Child ballads, with only a trifling use of truly proverbial or 'sententious' remarks.[1] It is a circumstance which adds to the sharpness of demarcation between the genres of secular carol and narrative ballad.

The burden, in the carols here collected, is more than an irrelevant exclamatory chorus, such as it often is in folk-song, where its structural importance wholly overshadows its meaning. Like the carols themselves it is usually popular by destination rather than by origin; it may use folk-material, but seldom without adapting it to meet the requirements of a missionary purpose. Most of the burdens were probably written by the same hands that produced the associated stanza-texts, and so well do they sum up the matter of the stanzas that a classification of the carols by subjects could almost be made from examination of the burdens alone.

[1] 'Proverbial Material in the Popular Ballad', *The Journal of American Folk-Lore*, xlvii (1934), 22–44.

THE TEXTS

Emendation of the texts of the carols is as sparing as possible. The original spelling has been retained throughout, except that þ and ȝ have been transliterated into their modern equivalents and i and j are printed according to modern practice. Punctuation, capitalization, and division of words follow modern usage and have been supplied by the present editor. Manuscript abbreviations are expanded in italics, and words and letters supplied by the editor are enclosed in square brackets.

Erasures, scribal corrections, and minor palaeographical peculiarities are not recorded. Neither has it seemed worth while to record the errors in transcription, frequent in some texts, of previous editors. The record of previous publications in the Notes confines itself in general to unmodernized texts with some pretensions to scholarship.

The method of numbering the texts is patterned on that of Child's *English and Scottish Popular Ballads*. Each distinct carol is given a serial number. Variant versions of significant dissimilarity are indicated by suffixed capital letters and are printed in full. Versions consistently close to the text chosen as the best are represented by notes of those variant readings which affect the meaning, mere differences in spelling being ignored. In such cases the several texts are indicated by suffixed lower-case letters. The texts designated by A or a are those which are fullest, or, in cases of equal or nearly equal length, those which seem best in sense and style. Carols not in the first edition are designated by a number followed by a decimal, e.g. 418.1, 418.2. Variants now added to carols printed in the first edition are inserted in their appropriate places with added letters. See also the Preface to the Second Edition, p. vii.

THE CAROLS

1

British Museum. MS. Addit. 5665
XVI *cent.*

f. 19ᵛ

O radix Jesse, supplices
  Te nos inuocamus;
Veni vt nos liberes
  Que*m* iam exp*ec*tamus.
O radix Jesse, sup[pl]ices
  Te nos inuocamus;
Veni vt nos liberes,   [f. 20ʳ]
  Quem iam expectamus.

[1]

O of Jesse thow holy rote,
  That to thi pepill arte syker merke,
We calle to the; be thow our*e* bote,
  In the that we gronde all owre werke.

[2]

Thy laude ys exalted by lord*es*   [f. 19ᵛ]
  and kyng*es*;
No man to *pr*ayse the may suffice;
Off the spryngith vertu *and* all gode
  thyng*es*;
Come *and* delyuere vs fro owre malice.

[3]

Off the may no malice growe,
  That th*ou* thyselue arte pure godenesse;
In the be rotedde what we showe,
  And graunte ows blisse after owr*e* de -
  cesse.

MS. heading: In die natiuita*tis*.
stza. 2, l. 2. *written at the foot of the page, with
insertion indicated by carets.*

2

British Museum. MS. Addit. 5665
XVI *cent.*

f. 20ᵛ

O clauis Dauid inclita,
  Dans viam in portis,
O clauis Dauid inclita,
  Dans viam in portis,

B

Educ nos de carcere,
Educ nos de carcere
  Et de vmbra mortis.

[1]

O Dauid, thow nobell key,   [f. 21ᵛ]
  Cepter of the howse of Israell,
Thow opyn the gate *and* geff vs   [f. 22ʳ]
  way,
Thou open the gate and geff vs way,
  And saue vs fro owre fendys felle.

[2]

We be in *pr*ison; vn vs haue   [f. 21ᵛ]
  mynde,
And lose vs fro the bonde of synne,
For that th*ou* losest no man may bynde,
For that th*ou* losest no man may bynde,
  And th*at* th*ou* losest may no man
  bynde.

[3]

Lord, bowe thyn yer*e*; to the we calle;
  Delyuer*e* th*ou* vs fro wyckednesse,
And bryng vs to thy joyfull halle,
[And bryng vs to thy joyfull halle]
  Wher*e* eu*er* ys lyff wi*th*owten desstresse.

MS. heading: In die natiuita*tis*.
MS. marks burden: Chorus. Below it is: Smert.
A repetition of the burden is indicated by: O
  clauis vt supr*a*.
After stza. 2 is written: Troulouffe Jhon. *After
  stza. 3:* Smert Ric°.
The word Chorus *is written before the musical
  notation of the middle part which enters with
  stza. 1, l. 4.*

3

Cambridge University Library. MS. Ee.
  I. 12   By James Ryman (?), *c.* 1492

f. 58ᵛ

Farewele, Aduent; Cristemas is cu*m*;
Farewele fro vs both alle and sume.

[1]

With paciens thou hast vs fedde
And made vs go hungrie to bedde;
For lak of mete we were nyghe dedde;
  Farewele fro [vs both alle and sume.]

[2]

While thou haste be *with*in oure howse
We ete no puddyng*es* ne no sowce,
But stynking fisshe not worthe a lowce;
   Far*e*wele [fro vs both alle and sume.]

[3]

Ther*e* was no fresshe fisshe ferr*e* ne ner*e*;
Salt fisshe *and* samon was to dere,
And thus we haue had hevy chere;
   Far*e*wele [fro vs both alle and sume.]

[4]

Thou hast vs fedde w*ith* plaices thynne,
Nothing on them but bone and skynne;
Therfore our*e* loue thou shalt not wynne;
   Far*e*wele [fro vs both alle and sume.]

[5]

W*ith* muskill*es* gaping aftur*e* the mone
Thou hast vs fedde at nyght *and* none,
But ones a wyke, and that to sone;
   Far*e*wele [fro vs both alle and sume.]

[6]

Our*e* brede was browne, our*e* ale was
      thynne,
Our*e* brede was musty in the bynne,
Our*e* ale soure or we did begynne;
   Fare[wele fro vs both alle and sume.]

[7]

Thou art of grete ingratitude
Good mete fro vs for to exclude;   [f. 59ʳ
Thou art not kyende but verey reude;
   Far*e*wele [fro vs both alle and sume.]

[8]

Thou dwellest w*ith* vs ayenst oure wille,
And yet thou gevest vs not our*e* fille;
For lak of mete thou woldest vs spille;
   Far*e*wele [fro vs both alle and sume.]

[9]

Aboue alle thinge thou art a meane
To make oure chekes bothe bare *and* leane;
I wolde thou were at Boughton Bleane!
   Far*e*wele [fro vs both alle and sume.]

[10]

Come thou no more here nor in Kent,
For, yf thou doo, thou shallt be shent;
It is ynough to faste in Lent;
   Far*e*wele [fro vs bothe alle and sume.]

[11]

Thou maist not dwelle w*ith* none eastate;
Therfore w*ith* vs thou playest chekmate.
Go hens, or we will breke thy pate!
   Far*e*wele [fro vs both alle and sume.]

[12]

Thou maist not dwell w*ith* knyght nor
      squier;
For them thou maiste lye in the myre;
They loue not the nor Lent, thy sire;
   Far*e*wele [fro vs both alle and sume.]

[13]

Thou maist not dwell w*ith* labouring man,
For on thy fare no skille he can,
For he must ete both now *and* than;
   Fare[wele fro vs both alle and sume.]

[14]

Though thou shalt dwell w*ith* monke *and*
      frere,
Chanon *and* nonne ones euery yere,
Yet thou shuldest make vs better chere;
   Fare[wele fro vs both alle and sume.]

[15]

This tyme of Crist*es* feest natall
We will be mery, grete and small,
And thou shalt goo oute of this halle;
   Far*e*wele [fro vs both alle and sume.]

[16]

Aduent is gone; Cristemas is cume;
Be we mery now, alle *and* sume;
He is not wise that wille be dume
   In ortu Reg*is* omniu*m*.

stza. 1, l. 4. MS. far*e* wele fro &c.
stzas. 2–5, 9, 10, 12, l. 4. MS. far*e* wele &c.
stza. 6, l. 4. MS. fare wele &c.
stza. 7, 8, 15, l. 4. MS. fare wele &c.
stzas. 13, 14, l. 4. MS. far*e* &c.

4

Bodleian Library. Douce fragments   f. 48
                                  XVI *cent.*
f. 3ᵛ

   Farewell, Aduent, *and* haue good daye!
   Chrystmas is come; nowe go thy way.

[1]

Get the hence! What doest thou here?
Thou hast no loue of no beggere;
Thou makest vs fast with euyll chere,
    With 'Farewell, Aduent.'

[2]

Thou takest on the more tha*n* doth the
    Lent;
Thou dwellest so long that th*o*u art shent;
. . . .
      . . . . .

stza. 2, l. 2. Thou] Orig. Theu.

5

Bodleian Library. MS. Arch. Selden B. 26
                                    XV *cent*.
f. 8^r

    Go day, go day,
    My lord Syr*e* *C*ristemasse, go day!

[1]

Go day, Syr*e* *C*ristemas, o*u*r ky*n*g,
For eu*er*y ma*n*, both olde *and* yynge,
Ys glad *and* blithe of yo*ur* comynge;
    Go day!

[2]

Godys Sone so moche of myght
Fram heuen to erthe dov*n* is lyght
And borne ys of a mayde so bryght;
    Good day!

[3]

Heuen *and* erthe *and* also helle,
And alle th*a*t eu*er* in hem dwelle,
Of yo*ur* comynge they beth ful snelle;
    Good day!

[4]

Of yo*ur* comynge this clerkys fynde:
Ye come to saue al mankynde
And of her*e* balys hem vnbynde;
    Good day!

[5]

Alle ma*n*er of m*er*thes we wole make
And solas to our*e* hertys take,
My semely lorde, for youre sake;
    Good day!

Under the words of the refrain is written: Chorus.

6

British Museum. MS. Addit. 5665
                                    XVI *cent*.
f. 8^v

    'Nowell, nowell, nowell, nowell.'
    'Who ys there that syngith so,
        Nowell, nowell, nowell?'
    'I am here, Syre *C*rist*e*smasse.'
    'Wellcome, my lord S*er* *C*rist*e*smasse,
    Wellcome to vs all, bothe more   [f. 9^r
        and lasse,
        Com ner*e*, nowell.'

[1]

Di*e*vs wous garde, byewss*er*, tydyng*es*
    Y yow bryng:
A mayde hathe born a chylde full yong,
The weche causeth yew for to syng:
    Nowell, *nowell, nowell, nowell,   [*f. 9^v
    Nowell, nowell, nowell, nowell,
        Nowell, nowell.

[2]

Criste is now born of a pure   [f. 8^v
        mayde;
In an oxe stalle he ys layde;
Wher*e*for syng we all atte a brayde:
    Nowell, [nowell, nowell, nowell,
    Nowell, nowell, nowell, nowell,
        Nowell, nowell.]

[3]

Bev*v*ex bien par tutte la company,
Make gode chere *and* be ryght mery,
And syng wi*th* vs now joyfully:
    Nowell, [nowell, nowell, nowell,
    Nowell, nowell, nowell, nowell,
        Nowell, nowell.]

MS. heading: In die natiuitatis.

7

A. *Bodleian Library*. MS. Douce 302
                        By John Audelay, XV *cent*.
f. 28^r

    Welcu*m*, Yole, i*n* glod aray,
    In worchip of the holeday.

[1]

Welcu*m* be th*o*u, Heue*n* Kyng,   [f. 28^v
Welcu*m*, ibore i*n* hon mornyng,
Welcu*m* to the now wil we syng;
    Welcu*m*, Yole, for eu*er* *and* ay.

[2]

Welcum be thou, Mare myld,
Welcum be thou *and* thi child,
Welcum, fro the fynd thou vs schilde;
   Welcum, Yole, fore eu*er and* ay.

[3]

Welcum be ye, Steue*n and* Jone,
Welcum, child*er*n eu*er*echone,
Wellcum, Thomas, mart*er* allon;
   Welcum, Yole, for eu*er and* ay.

[4]

Welcum be thou, good New Yere,
Welcum, the xii days efere,
Welcum be ye all th*a*t bene here;
   Welcum, Yole, for eu*er and* ay.

[5]

Welcum be ye, lord *and* lady,
Welcum be ye, al this cu*m*pane;
Fore Yolis loue now makis mere!
   Welcum, Yole, fore eu*er and* ay.

MS. heading: In die natalis d*o*mini.

B. *British Museum.* MS. Sloane 2593
                        XV *cent.*
f. 32ʳ

   Wolcu*m*, Yol, thou mery ma*n*,
     In worchepe of this holy day.

[1]

Wolcum be thou, Heuene Kyng,
Wolcu*m*, born in on morweny*ng*,
Wolcu*m*, for ho*m* we xal syng:
   Wolcu*m*, Yol.

[2]

Wolcu*m* be ye, Stefne *and* Jon,
W[o]lcu*m*, Innoce*n*tes eu*er*ychon,
Wolcu*m*, Thomas, mart*er* on;
   Wolcu*m*, Yol.

[3]

Wolcu*m* be ye, good Newe Yer*e*,
Wolcu*m*, Twelthe Day bothe in fer*e*,
Wolcu*m*, seynt*es* lef *and* der*e*;
   Wolcu*m*, Yol.

[4]

Wolcu*m* be ye, Candylmesse,
Wolcu*m* be ye, Qwy*n* of Blys,
Wolcu*m* bothe to more *and* lesse;
   Wolcu*m*, Yol.

[5]

Wolcu*m* be ye th*a*t arn her*e*,
Wolcu*m* alle, *and* mak good cher*e*
Wolcu*m* alle a*n*other yer*e*;
   Wolcu*m*, Yol.

8

a. *Bodleian Library.* MS. Eng. poet. e. 1
                        XV *cent.*
f. 22ʳ

   Make we myrth
   For Crystes byrth,
     And syng we Yole tyl Ca*n*delmes.

[1]

The fyrst day of Yole haue we in my*n*d
How God was ma*n* born of owr kynd
For he the bond*es* wold onbynd
   Of all owr [syn]nes a*n*d wykednes.

[2]

The secund day we syng of   [f. 22ᵛ
   St[e]vene,
That stoned [was] *and* steyyd vp even
To God, that he saw stond i*n* hevyn,
   And crounned was for hys p*r*ovesse.

[3]

The iii day longeth to Se*n*t Joh*a*n,
Th*a*t was C*r*istys darlyng, derer non,
Whom he betok, whan he shuld gon,
   Hys moder der for hyr clennesse.

[4]

The iiii day of the chyldren yong
Th*a*t Herowd to deth had do wi*th* wrong,
And C*r*ist thei covd no*n* tell wi*th* tong
   But wi*th* the*r* blod bar hy*m* wytnesse.

[5]

The v day longeth to Se*n*t Thom*a*s,
Th*a*t as a strong pyller of bras
Held vp the Chyrch, *and* sclayn he was,
   For he stod wi*th* ryghtwessnesse.

[6]

The viii day tok Jhesu hys name,
That saved mankynd fro syn and shame,
And circumsysed was for no blame
　　But for ensample of meknesse.

[7]

The xii day offerd to hym kynges iii
Gold, myr, and cence, thes gyftes free,
For God, and man, and kyng was he:
　　Thus worschyppyd thei hys worthynes.

[8]

On the xl day cam Mary myld
Vnto the temple with hyr chyld
To shew hyr clen that neuer was fylyd,
　　And therwith endyth Crystmes.

stza. 5, l. 2. pyller] MS. pyr pyller. *The entire stanza is struck through in MS.*

b. *British Museum.* MS. Sloane 2593, ff. 33ᵛ, 34ʳ. XV cent.

stza. 1, l. 1. haue we] we han. l. 2. God was man born] man was born al of. l. 3. the bondes wold] wold the bondes. l. 4. [syn]nes] synne.
stza. 2, l. 2. stoned [was] and steyyd] stonyd was and fid. l. 3. To God, that he saw] with cryst ther he wold.
stza. 3. l. 1. iii] threde. l. 2. derer non] derest on. l. 3. Whom he betok] to hom he tok. l. 4. moder der] dere moder. hyr] his.
stza. 4, l. 1. iiii] forte. l. 2. with herowdes wretthe to deth were throng. l. 3. And] of. non] not. tell] speke. l. 4. hym] omits.
stza. 5, l. 1. v] fyfte. longeth to] halwyt. l. 2. That as a strong] ryth as strong as. l. 3. the chyrch] his kyrke. he] omits. l. 4. with] faste in.
stza. 6, l. 1. viii] eytende. l. 3. no] non. l. 4. ensample of] insaump [*MS. damaged*] and.
stza. 7, l. 2. and cence, thes] incens this. l. 3. was] is. l. 4. Thus worschyppyd thei] And thus thei worchepyd.
stza. 8, l. 1. On] omits. xl] forty. l. 3. shew] schewyn. l. 4. therwith] herewith.

9

Huntington Library. MS. HM. 147

f. 113ʳ
　　　　　　　　　　　　　　　　c. 1500

　　Welcum, welcum, welcum,
　　Christe, redemtor omneum.

[1]

Now ys cum owre Saueowre,
And now hathe Mare borne a flowre,
To all this wordill a grete soccowre,
　　Celi terreque Dominum.

[2]

Now be the Juys fallyn in fyghte
Of Seynt Stevyn, that nobull knyghte;
Because he sayde he saw a syghte,
　　Lapidauerunt Stephanum.

[3]

Seynt Johan, that was a martyr fre,
On Crystes lappe aslepe lay he;
Of hevyn he saw the preuete;
　　Aduocatur conviuio.

[4]

Erode, that was so full of syne,
Let sle the childryn of Israell kyn
Of too yere age and eke withyn
　　In Bethelem conuiuio.

[5]

Seynte Thomas, that was a marter good,
Ther came knyghtes bothe ferse and woode;
They steryde his brayne and schede his blode;
　　Sic passus est martyrrium.

[6]

Ther came three knyghtes with rache presens,
Offryde golde, myrre, frankeandsence;
Offryng with grete honnowre and reuerens,
　　Adorauerunt puerum.

stza. 5, l. 4. martyrrium] MS. martyerrium.

10

British Museum. MS. Addit. 14997

f. 44ᵛ　　　　　　　　　4 October 1500

　　Hay, ay, hay, ay,
　　Make we mere as we may.

[1]

Now ys Yole comyn with gentyll chere;
Of merthe and gomyn he has no pere;
In euery londe where he comys nere
　　Is merthe and gomyn, I dar wele say.

[2]

Now ys comyn a messyngere
Of yore lorde, Ser Nu Yere,
Byddes vs all be mere here
    And make as mere as we may.

[3]

Therefore euery mon that ys here   [f. 45ʳ]
Synge a caroll on hys manere;
Yf he con non we schall hym lere,
    So that we be mere allway.

[4]

Whosoeuer makes heve chere,
Were he neuer to me dere;
In a dyche I wolde he were,
    To dry hys clothys tyll hyt were day.

[5]

Mende the fyre, and make gud chere!
Fyll the cuppe, Ser Botelere!
Let euery mon drynke to hys fere!
    Thys endes my caroll with care away.

stza. 1, l. 1. MS. gentyll g chere.
At end: In die dominica prima post festum sancti
   Michaelis archangeli anno regis henrici
   septimi post conquestum anglie sextodecimo
   illa res erat scripta primo (in different hand).

11

Balliol College, Oxford. MS. 354
                     XVI *cent.*
f. 223ᵛ

    Make we mery, bothe more and lasse,
    For now ys the tyme of Crystymas.

[1]

Lett no man cum into this hall,
Grome, page, nor yet marshall,
But that sum sport he bryng withall,
    For now ys the tyme of Crystmas.

[2]

Yff that he say he can not syng,
Sum oder sport then lett hym bryng,
That yt may please at thys festyng,
    For now ys the tyme of Crystmas.

[3]

Yff he say he can nowght do,
Then for my loue aske hym no mo,
But to the stokkes then lett hym go,
    For now ys the tyme of Crystmas.

At end: Explicit.

12

a. *Bodleian Library.* MS. Bodley 26
                     c. 1350
f. 202ᵛ

    Honnd by honnd we schulle ous take,
    And joye and blisse schulle we make,
    For the deuel of ele man haght forsake,
    And Godes Sone ys maked oure make.

[1]

A child is boren amo[n]ges man,
And in that child was no wam;
That child ys God, that child is man,
And in that child oure life bygan.

[2]

Senful man, be blithe and glad:
For your mariage thy peys ys grad
    Wan Crist was boren;
Com to Crist; thy peis ys grad;
For the was hys blod ysched,
    That were forloren.

[3]

Senful man, be blithe and bold,
For euene ys bothe boght and sold,
    Euereche fote.
Com to Crist; thy peys ys told,
For the he yahf a hondrefo[l]d
    Hys lif to bote.

The repetition of the burden is indicated as
   follows: stza. 1. honnd by honnd thanne
   schulle ous take *et ceterum* quod *superius*
   dictum est. stza. 2. honnd by honnd thanne
   schulle ous take *and* joy *and* blisse schu[lle]
   we make &c. stza. 3. honnd by honnd *et*
   ceterum quod prius.
stza. 2, l. 2. your] MS. thour.
stza. 3, l. 5. he] MS. ye.

b. *University of London Library.* MS. 657,
   p. 287. XIV *cent.* (stza. 3).

stza. 3, l. 3. Euereche] for euery. l. 4. Thank
   thou hym, thi pay is told. l. 5. the] lytyl.
   yahf] yeuyth. l. 6. Hys] And. to] also to.

13

British Museum. MS. Addit. 5665
XVI *cent.*

f. 39ᵛ

Proface, welcom, wellcome.
This tyme ys born a chylde of grace,
That for vs mankynde hathe take,
   Proface.
This day is born a child of   [f. 40ʳ
   grace,
That for vs mankynde hathe take,
   Proface.

[1]

A kynges sone and an emperoure
Ys comyn oute of a maydynys toure,
With vs to dwelle with grete honowre,
   Proface.

[2]

This holy tyme of Cristesmesse   [f. 39ᵛ
All sorwe and synne we shulde relese
And caste away all heuynesse,
   Proface.

[3]

The gode lord of this place entere
Seith welcome to all that now apere
Vnto suche fare as ye fynde here,
   Proface.

[4]

Wellcome be this New Ere,
And loke ye all be of gode chere.
Oure Lorde God be at oure denere!
   Proface.

MS. heading: de natiuitate.
burden, ll. 3, 6, stza. 1, l. 3. vs] MS. vus.

14

a. *Bridgwater Corporation*. Muniments,
  123   XV *cent.*
dorse

Letabundus exultet fidelys chorus,
   Alleluia.

[1]

Now well may we myrthys make,
For Jhesu mankynd hath take
Of a mayden withoutyne make;
   Gaudeamus.

[2]

A kyng of kynges now forth ys browghth
Off a maydyne that synnyd nowghte,
Nether in ded nether in thowghhte,
   Res miranda.

[3]

An angell of counsell now ys bore
Off a mayde, as Y sayd before,
To saw all that was forlore,
   Sol de stella.

[4]

That sonne hath neuer downe-goyng,
And thys lyght no tyme lesyng;
Thys stere ys euermore scheyinyng,
   Semper clara.

[5]

Ryghht as the stere browghht forght a
   beme,
Oute of the wych commyghth a marvelose
   streme,
So dud that mayde withowtyn weme,
   Pari forma.

At head: MS. Holy holy holy holy holy and
   yffy yffy.
At end: MS. Holy holy and yfy yffy holy yffy
   Holi.
stza. 5, l. 4. Pari] MS. para.

b. *Bodleian Library*. MS. Arch. Selden B.
  26, f. 10ʳ. XV cent.

c. *British Museum*. MS. Addit. 5665,
  ff. 36ᵛ, 37ʳ. XVI *cent.* (burden and
  stanzas 1–3).

burden. b Alleluya. c Alleluya, alleluya.
stza. 1, l. 1. well] c omits.   l. 2. Jhesu] b c vs
  Jhesus. mankynd] b c manhode.   l. 3. b c
  Only for our synnes sake.   l. 4. b Alleluya,
  Alleluya. c de virgine Maria.
stza. 2, l. 1. A] c The.   l. 2 maydyne] b c
  maide.   l. 3. Nether . . . nether] c. Nere . . .
  nere.
stza. 3, l. 1. An] c The. now] b this day. c that
  day. ys] c was. bore] b c borne.   l. 2. c
  As prophesye sayde beforn. as] b omits.
  l. 3. To] b c For to. all] b c omit.
stza. 4, l. 2, And thys] b Nother his.
  l. 3. Thys] b The.
stza. 5, l. 1. browghht] b bryngeth.
  l. 2. Oute of the wych] b Of whom ther.
  l. 3. dud that] b. childede the. withowtyn]
  b withoute.
MS. heading: c de natiuitate.
b marks second Alleluia: Chorus.
c has Alleluya after stza. 1, l. 2 (not written in
  stzas. 2, 3) and after stzas. 2, 3, l. 4.

15

Bodleian Library. MS. Rawlinson C. 506
                                        XV *cent.*

f. 31ᵛ

> Now eue*ry* ma*n* at my request
> Be glad *and* me*ry* all in this fest.

[1]

This holy tym ou*re* Lord was born
To saue ma*n*kynd, th*a*t was forlorn,
As sayd p*r*ophet*es* her beforn,
    Therfor be glad all in this fest.

16

British Museum. MS. Sloane 2593
                                    XV *cent.*
f. 27ʳ

> Man, be glad i*n* halle *and* bo*ur*;
> This tyme was born o*ur* Sauyo*ur*.

[1]

In this tyme a chyld was born
To saue tho sowl*e* th*a*t wern forlorn,
For vs he werde garlond of thorn;
    Al it was for o*ur* hono*ur*.

[2]

The eytende day he was schorn   [f. 27ᵛ
To fulfylle the lawe th*a*t was beforn;
Of meknesse he blew his horn.
    .   .   .   .   .   .

[3]

On Good Fryday was don o*n* rode;
The Juwes spylty*n* his herte blode;
Mary his mod*er* be hy*m* stode.
    Ye be*n* o*ur* help *and* o*ur* soco*ur*.

[4]

On Esterne Day he ga*n* vp ryse
To techyn he*m* th*a*t wern o*n*wyse.
Jh*e*su, for yo*ur* wou*n*d*es* five,
    Ye be*n* o*ur* [help and our socour.]

[5]

On Halwy*n* Thursday he ga*n* vp steye
To his Fad*er* th*a*t sit on heye.
Jh*e*su, for yo*ur* curteysye,
    Ye be*n* [our help and our socour.]

[6]

On Qwytsu*n*day he ga*n* dou*n* sende
Wyt *and* wysda*m* vs to amende.
Jh*e*su, bryng vs to th*a*t ende
    Wi*th*outy*n* delay, *our* Sauyo*ur*.

stza. 2, l. 3. he] MS. be.
stza. 4, l. 4. MS. Ye be*n* o*ur* &c.
stza. 5, l. 4. MS. Ye be*n* &c.

17

a. *Corpus Christi College, Cambridge.* MS.
233   XV *cent.*
f. 95ᵛ

> Be merye, be merye,
>   I p*r*ay you eue*r*ychon.

[1]

A pryncypal poynth of charyte
It is so mery for to be,
    In hym th*a*t is but on.
    Be merye.

[2]

He th*a*t is but on in blys
To vs haue sent hys Son, iwys,
    To saue vs fro o*ur* fon.
    Be merie.

[3]

Mary, for you*re* Sonys sake,
Saue the*m* all th*a*t mery make
    And lengest holdyn vppon.
    Be mery.

[4]

For thei th*a*t make mery her*e*
And gladness, *and* in very goode cher,
    To blys tha*n* mote thei gon.
    Be mery.

b. *Trinity College, Cambridge.* MS. O. 3.
58, recto. XV *cent.* (burden and stanzas
1, 2, one stanza not in a, 3)

stza. 1, l. 2. so] *omits.*   for] *omits.*
stza. 2, l. 1. He] For he.   l. 2. haue] hath.
l. 4. *omits.*
After stza. 2 b *has the following stanza*:
    For of a maydy*n* a child was born
    To saue ma*n*kende, that was forlorn.
    Man, think theron.

stza. 3, l. 1. Mary] Now mary.   you*re*] thi.
l. 2. mery] merthe.   l. 3. holdyn vppon]
holdy on.   l. 4. *omits.*

18

a. *Trinity College, Cambridge.* MS. O. 3. 58
XV *cent.*

recto

Nowel, nowel, nowel!
To vs is born owr God Emanuel.

[1]

In Bedlem this berde of lyf
Is born of Marye, maydyn and wyf;
He is bothe God *and* man, I schryf;
   Nowel, nowel!
Thys *Pr*ince of Pees xal secyn al stryf
   And wone wyth vs *per*petuel.

[2]

This chyld xal bey vs wyth hys bloyd
And be naylyd vpon the royd;
Hys raunsum pasyth al erdly goyd;
   Nowel, nowel!
Allas, qwat wyth dar be so woyd
   To sle so je*n*tyl a jowel?

[3]

Be hys powste he his emprys
Schal take fro helle at hys vprys
And saue ma*nnen*de vpon this wys;
   Nowel, nowel!
Thus tellth vs the *pr*ophecys,
   That he is ky*n*g of heuen *and* helle.

[4]

This maydenys Sone to hys empere
Schal stey to heuene be his powere;
Hys Holy Gost vs alle xal lere;
   No[wel,] no[wel!]
Thei and the Fadyr in feere
   Schul re*n*gne o God, this leue I weel.

[5]

Pray we this chyld wyth good entent
In our deying he vs *pr*esent
Onto hys Fadyr omnypotent;
   Nowel, nowel!
The ferst tydyng of this testament
   Browth to vs Seynt Gabryel.

b. *Bodleian Library.* MS. Arch. Selden B.
26, f. 27ᵛ. XV *cent.* (burden and stzas.
1–3)

burden, l. 1. *omits one* Nowel, *repeats entire burden.*

stza. 1, l. 1. this berde] th*at* child.   l. 3. I
   schryf] take schrift.   l. 4. now.
l. 5. Thys] *omits.* secyn] sese.
stza. 2, l. 2. vpon the] on a.   l. 4. *omits.*
stza. 3, l. 1. he his emprys] this child shal ryse.
   l. 2. Fro helle he shal take his empryse.
   l. 3. vpon] in.   l. 4. *omits.*   l. 6. He*re*
be forne as they dyde tell.

19

Trinity College, Cambridge. MS. O. 3. 58
XV *cent.*

recto

Now may we syngyn as it is,
Quod puer natus est nobis.

[1]

This babe to vs that now is bore,
   Wundyrful werkys he hath iwrowt;
He wil not lese that was ilore,
   But baldly ayen it bowth.
      And thus it is,
      Forsothe, iwys,
   He askyth nouth but that is hys.

[2]

This chaffare louyd he rith weel:
   The prys was hey *and* bowth ful dere;
Qwo wold suffre and for vs feele
   As dede th*at* *pr*ince withowtyn pere?
      And th*us* it is,
      [Forsothe, iwys,
   He askyth nouth but that is hys.]

[3]

Hys raunsum for vs hath ipayd;
   Of resou*n* tha*n* we owyn to ben hys;
Be mercy askyd, and he be prayd,
   We may be rith kalange blys.
      And th*us* it is,
      [Forsothe, iwys,
   He askyth nouth but that is hys.]

[4]

To sum *pur*pos God made man:
   I leue weel to saluacyoun;
Qwat was his blood that fro hym ran
   But defe*n*s aye*n*s da*m*pnacyoun?
      And th*us* it is,
      [Forsothe, iwys,
   He askyth nouth but that is hys.]

[5]

Almythy God in Trynyte,
  Thy mercy we pray wyth hool herte:
Thy mercy may al woo make fle,
  And daungerous dreed fro vs do sterte.
    And thus it is,
    [Forsothe, iwys,
    He askyth nouth but that is hys.]
stza. 2, l. 4. withowtyn] MS. was owtyn.

20

Balliol College, Oxford. MS. 354
                            XVI *cent.*

f. 227ᵛ

  Now syng we right as it is,
  Quod puer natus est nobis.

[1]

This babe to vs now is born,
  Wonderfull werkes he hath wrowght:
He wold not lesse that was forlorn,
  But agayn he hath vs bowght.
    And thus it is,
    Forsoth, ywys,
    He asketh nothynge but that is his.

[2]

A dulfull deth to hym was mente
  Whan on the rode his body was spred,
And as a theff he was ther hente,
  And on a spere his liff was lede.
    And thus it is,
    Forsoth, ywis,
    He asketh nothynge but that is his.

[3]

'Man, why art thow vnkynd to me?
  What woldest thow I did for the more?
Geve me thy trew harte, I pray the;
  Yff thow be dampned it ruthe me sore.'
    And thus it is,
    Forsothe, ywis,
    He asketh nothyng but that is his.

[4]

'Man, I love the; whom loveste thowe?
  I pray the, torne to me agayn,
And thow shalt be as welcom nowe
  As he that never in syn was seyn.'
    And thus it is,
    Forsoth, ywys,
    He asketh nothynge but that is his.
MS. marks burden: fote.
stza. 1, l. 2. Wonderfull] MS. worderfull.
At end: Explicit.

21

A. *Balliol College, Oxford.* MS. 354
                                XVI *cent.*

f. 222ᵛ

  To blis God bryng vs all and sum,
  Christe redemptor omnium.

[1]

In Bedlem, in that fayer cyte,
A chyld was born of Owr Lady,
Lord and Prynce that he shuld be,
A solis ortus cardine.

[2]

Chyldren were slayn grett plente,
Jhesu, for the love of the;
Lett vs neuer dampned be.
Hostes Herodes ympie.

[3]

He was born of Owr Lady
Withowt wemmb of her body,
Godes Son that syttyth on hye,
Jhesu saluator seculi.

[4]

As the son shynyth thorow the glas,
So Jhesu in her body was;
To serue hym he geve vs grace,
O lux beata Trinitas.

[5]

Now ys born owr Lord Jhesus,
That mad mery all vs;
Be all mery in thys howse;
Exvltet celum lavdibus.
stz. 1, l. 4. solis] MS. solus. At end: Explicit.

B. *Bodleian Library.* MS. Eng. poet. e. 1
                                XV *cent.*

f. 35ᵛ

  To blys God bryng vs al and sum,
  Christe redemptor omnium.

[1]

In Bedlem, that fayer cyte,
Was born a chyld that was so fre,
Lord and Prince of hey degre,
Iam lucis orto sidere.

[2]

Jhesu, for the lowe of the
Chylder wer slayn grett plente
In Bedlem, that fayer cyte,
A solis ortus cardine.

[3]

As the sune schynyth in the glas,
So Jhesu of hys moder borne was;
Hym to serue God gyffe vs grace,
O lux beata Trinitas.

[4]

Now is he owr Lord Jhesus;
Thus hath he veryly vysyt vs;
Now to mak mery amo[n]g vs;
Exultet celum laudibus.

C. *Trinity College, Cambridge.* MS. O. 3. 58
XV *cent.*

recto

    Nowel syng we now al *and* sum,
    For Rex Pacificus is cum.

[1]

In Bedleem, in that fayr cete,
A child was born of a madyn fre
That xal a lord *and* prynce be,
A solis ortus cardine.

[2]

Childryn were slayn ful greth plente,
Jhesu, for the loue of the;
Qwerfore here sowlys sauyd be,
Hostis Herodes impie.

[3]

As sunne schynyth thorw the glas,
So Jhesu in his modyr was;
The to serue now graunth vs gras,
O lux beata Trinitas.

[4]

Now God is comyn to wurchepyn vs;
Now of Marye is born Jhesus;
Make we mery amongys vs;
Exultet celum laudibus.

stza. 1, l. 4. cardine] MS. cardine -e.

D. *Cambridge University Library.* MS. Ee.
1. 12   *c.* 1500.
f. 1ʳ

    Synge we now both all and sum:
    Christe redemtor omnium.

[1]

In Bethelem, that fayre cite,
Born was thys chylde so fayer *and* fre,
That Lorde *and* Kyng shal ever be,
A solis ortus cardine.

[2]

Ryght as the son shynyth on the glasse,
So Cryste Jesu in Owr Lady was;
Hym to sarue God sende vs grace,
O lux beata Trinitas.

[3]

Cheldren were slayne grete plente,
Jesu Crist, alle for the loue of the;
Lorde, helpe vs yf thy wyl it be.
Host*is* Herodes impie.

[4]

Now ys he boren of Owr Lady,
The Son of the Fader that sytthyt an hye;
For owr synnys cry we all mercy,
Jesu saluator seculi.

*At end in a later hand which has interlined
   several words in the carol itself:* Holy holy.
The burden is written again at the foot of the
   page with its melody: Synge we now all *and*
   sum, *Christe* redemtor omni*um*.

E. *British Museum.* MS. Addit. 31042
XV *cent.*

f. 94ᵛ

    Exultet celum laudibus.

[1]

In Bathelem, in that fare sete,
Jesus was borne of Mare fre ...

[2]

For he ys prens ...

burden, l. 1. Exultet] MS. Exultit
The burden is written again at the end: Exultet
   celum lawdibus.

22

Trinity College, Cambridge. MS. O. 3. 58
XV *cent.*

recto

    Now make we merthe al *and* sum,
    For Cristemesse now is icom,
       That hath no pere.
       Syng we alle in fere.
    Now joye *and* blysse,
    Thei xul not mysse
       That makyth good chere.

[1]

Now God Almythy doun hath sent
The Holy Gost to be present,
To lyth in Mary, maydyn verament,
That bar Goddys Sone with good entent.

[2]

Now Goddes Sone omnypotent,
In Mary mylde he hath hent
Flesch and blood, for he hath ment
Man to restore ayen to his rent.

[3]

To mylde Marye our hert be bent,
That blysful lady so be bent
To prey for vs we be not schent
To Jhesu Crist, here Sone so jent.

The repetition of the burden is indicated as
follows: stza. 2: that hath no pere. Syges &c.
stza. 3: that hath no pere &c.

23

A. *National Library of Scotland.* MS. Advocates 19. 3. 1   XV *cent.*
f. 59ʳ

    Jhesus, almyghty Kyng of Blys,
    Assumpsit carnem virginis.

[1]

As Holy Kyrke makys mynd,
    Intrauit ventris thalamum;
Fro heyuyn to erthe to saue monkynd
    Pater misit Filium.

[2]

Of Mary mylde Cryste wolde be borne,
    Sine virili semine,
To saue monkynd, that was forlorne
    Prime parentis crimine.

[3]

To Mare come a messenger,
    Ferens salutem homini;
Sche awnswerd hym with mylde chere,
    'Ecce ancilla Domini.'

[4]

'Mekely on the tho Holy Goste,
    Palacium intrans vteri;
Of al thyng meknes is moste
    In conspectu Altissimi.'

[5]

When he was borne that made all thyng,
    Pastor creator omnium,
Angelles thei began to syng,
    'Veni, redemptor gencium.'

[6]

Thre kynges come on goid Twelfth Day,
    Stella mycante preuia;
To seche that chylde thei toke tho wey,
    Portantes sibi munera.

[7]

A sterne forth ladde theis kynges all,
    Inquirentes Dominum;
Lyying in an asse stall,
    Invenerunt puerum.

[8]

For he was Kyng of Kynges heghe,
    Rex primus aurum optulit;
And allso Lorde and Kyng ful ryght,
    Secundus rex thus pertulit.

[9]

For he was God, mon, and Kyng   [f. 59ᵛ]
    Mirra mortem retulit;
He hus all to heuyn bryng
    Qui mortem cruce voluit.

stza. 6, l. 1. Twelfth] MS. xii.
stza. 8, l. 3. *The last three words are in a different
hand.*
At end: &c. Explicit.

B. *British Museum.* MS. Harley 275
                        XV *cent.*
f. 146ᵛ

    Joy we all now yn this feste,
    For verbum caro factum est.

[1]

Jhesus, almyghty Kyng of Blys,
    Assumpsit carnem virginis;
He was euer and euermore ys
    Consors paterni luminis.

[2]

All Holy Churche of hym makes mynd:
    Intrauit ventris thalamum;
From heven to erthe to saue mankynd
    Pater misit Filium.

[3]

To Mary came a messanger,
  Ferens sal*ute*m homini,
And she answered w*ith* myld cher*e*,
  'Ecce ancilla D*o*m*i*ni.'

[4]

'The myght of the Holy Goste,
  Palaci*um* intrans vteri;
Of all thyng mekenesse is moste
  In co*n*spectu Altissimi.'

[5]

When he was borne that made all thyng,
  Pastor creator o*mn*i*um*,   [f. 147^r]
Angellis then began to syng,
  'Veni, redemptor genci*um*.'

[6]

Thre kynges came the twelfth day,
  Stella nitente p*r*euia;
To seke the Kyng they toke the way,
  Baiulantes mun*er*a.

[7]

A sterre furth ledde the kyngis all
  Inquirentes Dominu*m*;
Lyggyng in an ox stall
  Inuener*un*t pu*er*um.

[8]

For he was Kyng of Kyng*es* ay,
  Prim*us* rex aur*um* optulit;
For he was God *and* Lord verray,
  Secu*n*dus rex thus p*er*tulit.

[9]

For he was man, the thyrd kyng
  Incensu*m* pulcr*um* tradidit;
He vs all to his blys brynge,
  Qui mori cruce voluit.

stza. 6, l. 1. twelfth] MS. xii.
stza. 8, l. 2. aur*um*] MS. aur*is*.

C. *British Museum*. MS. Egerton 3307
                               XV *cent.*

ff. 65^v, 66^r

  Almyghty Jh*es*u, Kyng of Blysse,
  Assumpsit carne*m* virginis;
  He was eu*er and* eu*er* ys
  Consors paterni luminis.

[1]

Holy Chyrch of hy*m* makyth mynd:
  I*n*trau*i*t v*entr*is thalamu*m*;
Fro heue*n* to erth to saue mankynd
  Pater mandau*i*t Filium.

[2]

To Mari co*m* a messenjer
  Fere*n*s salut*em* hominu*m*,
And sche answerd w*ith* myld steuen,
  'Ecce ancilla Domini.'

[3]

'Thorow the mygh*t* of the Holy Gost,
  Palacium int*ra*ns vteri,
Abou*n* al thyng meykness is best
  In conspectu Altissimi.'

[4]

Thre kynges apon the twelfth day, [f. 66^r]
  Stella micante p*r*euia,
To seyk O*ur* Lord thai toke the way,
  Baiulantes munera.

[5]

A ster beforn the kynges ay:
  P*r*imus rex auru*m* optulit;
He ys God *and* Lord v*er*ray:
  Secu*n*dus rex thus p*r*otulit.

[6]

He was namyd the thyrd kyng
  Incensu*m* pulcru*m qui* tradidit;
He vs al to blysse bryng
  Qui cruce mori voluit.

ll. 1, 2 of the burden and l. 2 of each stanza are
to be repeated as a chorus. ll. 1, 2 of the burden and l. 2 of stzas. 1–3 are written again
on f. 66^r.
stza. 4, l. 1. twelfth] MS. xii.

D. *Bodleian Library*. MS. Bodley 77
                               XV *cent.*

Binding Strips 1^v, 2^r

    trauit
fro heuene to herth

filium
    he was ev
    Consors pa

    To mary
    Ferens salu
    And sche a

Thorw the
Palacium in
boue all

Thre kyng
To seke our

A sterre bef
Inquirente

24

British Museum. MS. Sloane 2593
XV *cent.*

f. 4ᵛ

Eya, Jhesus hodie
Natus est de uirgine.

[1]

Blyssid be that mayde Mary;
Born he was of here body,
Godis Sone that syttit on hy,
Non ex uirili semine.

[2]

In a manjour of an as
Jhesu lay and lullyd was,
Harde peynis for to pas
Pro peccante homine.

[3]

Kynges comyn fro dyuerse londe
With grete yyftes in here honde;
In Bedlem the child they fonde,
Stella ducte lumine.

[4]

Man and chyld, bothe eld and ying,
Now in his blysful comyng
To that chyld mow we syng,
'Gloria tibi, Domine.'

[5]

Nowel, nowel, in this halle,
Make merye, I prey you alle;
Onto that chyld may we calle
Vllo sine crimine.

stza. 3, l. 1. dyuerse] MS. dyuesse.
stza. 4, l. 1. ying] MS. thing.

25

British Museum. MS. Sloane 2593
XV *cent.*

f. 11ᵛ

Al the meryere is that place
The sunne of grace hym schynit in.

[1]

The sunne of grace hym schynit in
In on day quan it was mor[we],
Quan our Lord God born was
Withoute wem or sorwe.

[2]

The sunne of grace hym schynit in
On a day quan it was pryme,
Quan our Lord God born was,
So wel he knew his tyme.

[3]

The sunne of grace hym schynit in
On a day quan it was non,
Quan our Lord God born was
And on the rode don.

[4]

The sunne of grace hym schynit in
On a day quan it was vndy[rn,]
Quan our Lord God born was
And to the herte stongyn.

26

British Museum. MS. Addit. 40166 (C 3)
XV *cent.*

f. 12ᵛ

O, O, O, O!
Exultet mundus gaudio.

[1]

All this worlde was ful of grace
When Goddes Son yborne was
Bytwyx an ox and an as,
Positus in presepio.

[2]

Withoute peyne other loure
Mary bare oure Sauyoure;
To hym we owth to do honoure,
Presulus in iubilo.

[3]

Mary was but thirteen [y]e[re]
When scho Goddes Son bere;
He ys a lorde without pere;
Gaude, mater, Filio.

[4]

Nere that chylde had be bore,   [f. 13ʳ
Mon and womon had be lore;
Angelis songon hym before,
Primo in seruicio.

[5]
He ys wordy to be a kyng
That of nowth hath made all thyng;
Fro heuen to vrthe, *with*oute lesyng,
   Scandens motu p*ro*pr*io*.

[6]
Mary moder, mayden of grace,
Quene of heuyn and solace,
Helpe vs to se God in the face,
   Quo sedet in solacio.

stza. 3, l. 1. thirteen] MS. xiii^tn. *The end of the
line is missing because of a small hole in the leaf.*

27

A. *British Museum.* MS. Sloane 2593
                              XV *cent.*
f. 24^r
  Ma*n*, be glad in halle *and* bo*ur*;
  This tyme was born o*ur* Sauyo*ur*.

[1]
In this tyme Cryst haght vs sent
His owy*n* Sone in p*re*sent
To dwelle *with* vs uerement,
   To ben o*ur* helpe *and* soco*ur*.

[2]
In this tyme ros a ster*re* cler
Ou*er* Bedlem, as bryght as fer,
In tokenyng th*at* he hadde no*n* per,
   Lord God, Kyng, *and* Emp*er*our.

[3]
In this tyme it is befalle:
He th*at* deyid for us alle,
Born he was in assis stalle
   Of Mary, th*at* swete flo*ur*.

[4]
In this tyme kemy*n* thre kyng*es*; [f. 24^v
He kemy*n* fro fer *with* ryche thing*es*
For to maky*n* her*e* offeryng*es*
   On her*e* knen *with* gret hono*ur*.

[5]
In this tyme prey we
To hy*m* th*at* deyid on the tre,
On vs haue m*er*cy *and* pete
   And bryng vs alle to his to*ur*.

B. *British Museum.* MS. Royal 20. A. I
                              XV *cent.*
f. 120^r
  Man*e*, be glad in halle and bowre;
  This time is bore our*e* Sauio*ur*.

[1]
Al on th*is* tyme God hath ows ysent
Hys ovne Sone on a present,
To dwelle wyt ous in verement,
   To be owre help *and* oure socoure.

[2]
Al on th*is* tyme hit ys byfalle:
He th*at* deyde for vs alle,
Ybore he was in a asse stalle,
   Al of Marie, th*at* swete flow*r*.

[3]
Al on th*is* tyme there were thre kynges;
Well rychellyche they browte offrenge
To presenty*n* wyt th*at* swete thenge
   T[h]at ys our*e* aldyr*e* Sauio*ur*.

[4]
Al on th*is* time a ster*re* wel bryt,
He mete wyth schep*er*deis on a nit;
He tewte hem the wey ful rit
   To scheche God owre Sauiowr*e*.

[5]
Al on th*is* time hit was a ster*re* wel cler*e*;
God made lyt wytowtow pyr*e*,
And God made goon and Kynge
   And Empe[rowre.]

stza. 5, l. 2. wytowtow] MS. wyt wytowtow.

C. *Balliol College, Oxford.* MS. 354.
                            XVI *cent.*
f. 220^r
  Make we mery in hall *and* bowr;
  Thys tyme was born owr Savyowr.

[1]
In this tyme God hath sent
Hys own Son to be p*re*sent,
To dwell *with* vs in verame*n*t,
   God, th*at* ys owr Savyowr.

[2]
In this tyme yt ys befall:
A child was born in an ox stall
And after he dyed for vs all,
   God, [that ys owr Savyowr.]

[3]

In this tyme an angell bryght
Mete iii shep*erdes* vpon a nyght;
He bade them go ano*n* ryght
    To God, th*a*t ys our Saviowr.

[4]

In thys tyme now p*r*ay we
To hym th*a*t dyed for vs on tre
On vs all to haue pytee,
    God, th*a*t ys owr Saviowr.

At end: Explicit.

28

British Museum. MS. Sloane 2593
                    XV *cent.*
f. 28ʳ

    Ma*n*, be merie as bryd on berie,
    And al thi car*e* let away.

[1]

This tyme is born a chyld ful good,
He th*a*t vs bowt vpon the rod;
He bond the deuyl, th*a*t is so wod,
    Til the drydful domysday.

[2]

Qua*n* the chyld of meche myght
Wold be born of Mary bryght,
A tokene he sente to kyng *and* knyght,
    A sterre th*a*t scho*n* both nyght *and* day.

[3]

The sterr*e* scon as bryght as fer
Ou*er* al the world bothe fer *and* ner,
In tokene he was wi*th*outy*n* per,
    And per*e*les he xal lasty*n* ay.

[4]

The eighth day he was circu*m*sise
For to fulfylle the p*r*ofecye[s];
The p*r*ofet*es* wi*th* word*es* wyse
    Hy*m* p*r*esent wi*th* ryche aray.

[5]

The twelfth day come ky*nges* thre
Out of the est wi*th* herte fre;
To worchepy*n* hym thei knelyd o*n* kne
    Wi*th* gold *and* myr *and* francincens.

stza. 3, l. 2. world] MS. wolrd.
stza. 4, l. 1. eighth] MS. viii.
stza. 5, l. 1. twelfth] MS. xii.

29

Bodleian Library. MS. Arch. Selden B. 26
                                XV *cent.*
f. 7ʳ

    Nowel syng we bothe al *and* som,
    Now Rex Pacificus ys ycome.

[1]

Exortu*m* est i*n* loue *and* lysse:
Now Cryst hys g*r*ac*e* he gan vs gysse,
And wi*th* hys body vs bought to blysse,
    Bothe all and sum.

[2]

De fructu ventris of Mary bryght:
Bothe God an[d] man in here alyght;
Owte of dysese he dyde vs dyght,
    Bothe alle *and* su*m*me.

[3]

Puer natus to vs was sent,
To blysse vs bought, fro bale vs blent,
And ellys to wo we hadde ywent,
    Bothe alle *and* su*m*me.

[4]

Lux fulgebit wi*th* loue *and* lyght,
In Mary mylde his pynon pyght,
In here toke kynde wi*th* manly myght,
    Bothe alle *and* su*m*me.

[5]

Gloria ti*bi* ay and blysse:
God vnto his grace he vs wysse,
The rent of heuen th*a*t we not mysse,
    Bothe alle *and* su*m*me.

30

A. *Bodleian Library*. MS. Arch. Selden
B. 26   XV *cent.*
f. 14ᵛ

    Nowel, nowel, nowel,
    Nowel, nowel, nowel!

[1]

Owt of yo*ur* slepe aryse *and* wake,
For God manky*n*d nowe hath ytake
Al of a maide wi*th*out eny make;
    Of al wome*n* she bereth the belle.
        Nowel!

[2]

And thorwe a maide faire *and* wys
Now man is made of ful g*re*te p*ri*s;
Now angelys knelen to ma*n*nys s*er*uys,
   And at this tyme al this byfel.
    [Nowel!]

[3]

Now man is bright*er* than the sonne;
Now man *in* heue*n* an hye shal wone;
Blessyd be God this game is bego*n*me,
   And his mod*er* emp*er*esse of helle.
    [Nowel!]

[4]

That eu*er* was thralle, now ys he fre;
Th*at* eu*er* was smalle, now grete is she;
Now shal God deme bothe the *and* me
   Vnto his blysse yf we do wel.
    Nowel!

[5]

Now man may to heuen wende;
Now heuen *and* erthe to hy*m* they bende;
He th*at* was foo now is our*e* frende;
   This is no nay th*at* Y yowe telle.
    Nowel!

[6]

Now, blessyd brother, gr*au*nte vs grace
A domesday to se thy face
And in thy courte to haue a place,
   Th*at* we mow there synge nowel.
    Nowel!

B. *Cambridge University Library*. MS. Ll.
  I. II   XV *cent.*
f. 32ʳ

   Nowell, nowell, nowell!

[1]

Out of y*our* slep*e* arise *and* wake,
For God mankynd now hath take
Al of a mayd w*ith*[out] make;
   Nowell!
   Of al women she berith the bell.

[2]

That er*e* was thrall nowe is made free;
That er*e* was small, nowe grete is he;
He shall deme bothe the and me
   Nowell!
   And kepe vs fromme the fynde of hell.

[3]

And thurghe that may both ware *and* wyse
Man is made of full grete pryse
To wynne the joye of paradyse
   Nowell!
   And be w*ith* Oure Ladye, emp*er*esse of
    hell.

31

a. *Bodleian Library*. MS. Arch. Selden
  B. 26   XV *cent.*
f. 15ʳ

   Make we joye nowe in this fest,
   In quo *Christus* nat*us* est.
    Eya!

[1]

A Patre vnigenit*us*
Thorw a maiden is com to vs.
Synge we to here and sey, 'Welcome!
Veni rede*m*ptor gencium.'

[2]

Agnoscat om*n*e seculu*m*:
A bryght sterre thre kynges [made] come
For to seke w*ith* here p*re*sens
Verbu*m* supernu*m* pr*o*diens.

[3]

A solis ortus cardine,
So myghty a lord was none as he,
For to oure kynde he hath yeue gryth,
Ada*m* par*en*s quod polluit.

[4]

Maria ventre concepit;
The Holy Gost was ay here with.
In Bedleem yborne he ys,
Consors pat*er*ni luminis.

[5]

O lux beata Trinitas!
He lay bytwene an oxe *and* asse.
Th*ou* moder *and* maiden fre,
Gloria tibi, D*omi*ne.

b. *Bodleian Library*. MS. Eng. poet. e. I, ff.
  32ᵛ, 33ʳ. XV *cent.*

c. *British Museum*. MS. Addit. 5665, ff. 28v, 29r. XVI *cent.* (burden and stzas. 1, 2).

burden, l. 1. nowe] b *omits.* Make we joye nowe] c Now make we joye. l. 3. b c *omit.* c *repeats entire burden.*
stza. 1, l. 2. c iii yong maydens cam till vs. Thorw] b to. l. 3. to here] b of hy*m.* c to hym.
stza. 2, l. 2. thre] b *omits.* c iii. b c *have* made. l. 3. seke] b take. l. 3, 4. c *substitutes* stza. 3, ll. 1, 2, *and adds:* Veni redemptor gencium.
stza. 3, l. 2. was] b c is. l. 3. For] b and. kynde] b lord. yeue] b *omits.* l. 4. b *omits.*
stza. 4, l. 3. In] b of hyr in. yborne] b now born.
stza. 5, l. 1. O lux] b Olme. l. 2. He] b Th*at. and*] b an a. l. 3. Thou] b By hys. *and*] b *omits.*
MS. heading: c de natiuitate.

32

Bodleian Library. MS. Arch. Selden B. 26
XV *cent.*

f. 23v

An heue*n*ly songe, Y der*e* wel say,
Is su*n*ge i*n* erthe to man this day.

[1]

This is the songe th*at* ye shul here:
God is come fra*m* his empere
And is made man w*ith* hye desire
This day.

[2]

He toke oure kynde al of a mayde;
By oxe *and* asse he was ylayde;
Nowe is fulfylled th*at* Scr*i*ptur*e* sayde
This day.

[3]

Ay Y wonder this in my mynde:
That he that alle may loose *and* bynde
Wolde be layde by beestis vnkynde
This day.

[4]

He is a lorde, and by nature
A maydnys breest he soke ful pure;
Heuen *and* erthe beth in his cure
This day.

33

Bodleian Library. MS. Arch. Selden B. 26
XV *cent.*

f. 28r

Laus, honor, *virtus*, gloria,
Et tibi decus, Maria.
Laus, honor, virtus, gloria,
Et tibi decus, Maria.

[1]

A songe to syng Y haue good ryght,
And myrth to make i*n* th*i*s pres*ens,*
For now ys borne a baro*n* of myght,
Mu*n*du*m* pugillo co*n*tinens.

[2]

This babe was borne on Youle nyght,
In Bedlehem of Oure Lady;
The name of hym is called ryght
Verbu*m* P*at*ris Altissimi.

[3]

That nowe is come pees for to make
Bytwene the Fader of Hevyn *and* vs;
And nowe for that childys sake
Exultet celu*m* laudib*us.*

[4]

Oure sy*n*ne to slee he toke the way
Into the worle fro heuyn riche blysse,
And therfore bothe nyght *and* day
Resultet t*er*ra gaudiis.

[5]

The childe fellyd alle the fendys pr*i*de
And w*ith* harde yren bonde hym i*n* cloos,
And w*ith* the blode of his dere syde
Soluit a pena misero[s.]

[6]

Nowe Jh*esu* Cryst, th*at* come so stylle
Into the wombe of Mary fre,
We pr*a*ye the, yyf hit be thy wylle,
Mane nobiscu*m,* Domine.

burden, l. 2. Maria] MS. mariia.

34

Bodleian Library. MS. Arch. Selden B. 26
XV *cent.*

f. 28v

Iblessid be th*at* Lord i*n* mageste
Qui nat*us* fuit hodie.

[1]

That Lord that lay in asse stalle
Cam to dye for vs alle,
To mak vs fre that erst were thralle,
   Qui natus fuit hodie.

[2]

Wel mowe we glad and mery bee,
Sith we were thralle and nowe be free;
The fende oure foo he made to flee
   Qui natus [fuit hodie.]

[3]

And, sith oure foo is fled fro vs,
We mowe wel synge and say ryght thus:
'Welcome he be, this Lorde Jesus
   Qui natus [fuit hodie.']

[4]

Nowe blessyd be this Lord benynge
That nolde his cruelle dethe resynge,
But for mankynde to dye endynge,
   Qui natus fuit hodie.

MS. heading (or signature): Childe.
*Stza. 1 is repeated in MS., apparently in error.
The repeated text varies as follows:* l. 1. That]
This.   l. 2. Cam] Come.   l. 4. Qui natus
&c.
stzas. 2, 3, l. 4. MS. Qui natus &c.

35

A. *Bodleian Library.* MS. Ashmole 1393
                     XV *cent.*
f. 69ᵛ

   Gloria tibi, Domine,
   Qui natus es de virgine.

[1]

A litil child ther is ibore,
Ysprong owt of Jesse more
To saue all vs that were forlore;
   Gloria tibi, Domine.

[2]

Jhesus, that is so full of might,
Ybore he was abowte mydnyght;
The angel song with all here myght,
   'Gloria tibi, Domine.'

[3]

Jhesus is that childis name;
Maide and modir is his dame;
And so owre sorow is turnyd to game.
   Gloria tibi, Domine.

[4]

Thre kynges ther cam with here presence
Of mirre and gold and frankencense,
As clerkes sing in here sequence.
   Gloria tibi, Domine.

[5]

Now sitte we down vpon owre knee
And pray that child that is so fre,
And with gode herte now sing we,
   'Gloria tibi, Domine.'

burden, l. 2. MS. marks: chorus.

B. *Balliol College, Oxford.* MS. 354
                     XVI *cent.*
f. 231ᵛ

   All this tyme this songe is best:
   'Verbum caro factum est.'

[1]

This nyght ther is a child born
That sprange owt of Jessis thorn,
We must synge and say therforn,
   'Verbum caro factum est.'

[2]

Jhesus is the childes name,
And Mary myld is his dame;
All owr sorow shall torn to game:
   Verbum caro factum est.

[3]

Hit fell vpon high mydnyght:
The sterres shon both fayre and bright;
The angelles song with all ther myght,
   'Verbum caro factum est.'

[4]

Now knele we down on owr kne,
And pray we to the Trynyte
Owr helpe, owr socowr for to be;
   Verbum caro factum est.

At end: Explicit.

36

a. *Cambridge University Library.* MS.
   Ii. 4. 11   XV *cent.*
f. 170ᵛ

   Puer nobis natus est
   De virgine Maria.

[1]

Lystenyt, lordyng*us* more and lees:
I bryng you tydyng of gladnes,
As Gab*ri*el beryt wytnes;
    Dica*m* vobis q*ui*a.

[2]

I bryng yow tydynges th*at* [ben] fwul
    gowde:
Now es borne a blyesful fowde
Th*at* bowt us alle upon the rode
    Sua morte pia.

[3]

For the t*r*espas of Ada*m*
Fro ys Fad*ur* Jh*e*su ho ca*m*;
Her*e* *in* herthe howre kende he na*m*
    Sua mente pia.

[4]

Mayde mod*ur*, swete v*i*rgine,
Was godnys may no ma*n* diuine,
Sche bar*e* a schild wyttowt pyne,
    Teste p*r*ofecia.

[5]

Mari mod*ur*, th*at* ys so fre,
Wyt herte mylde Y̆ p*r*ay to the
Fro [the] fend th*ou* kepe me
    Tua prece pia.

stza. 1, l. 2. tydyng] MS. tydynd.
stza. 4, l. 3. wyttowt] MS. wytt wot.

b. *British Museum*. MS. Harley 5396, f.
280ᵛ. XV *cent*. (burden and stzas. 1–4).

c. *Public Record Office*. Chancery Miscellanea, Bundle 34, File 1, No. 12, f. 1ʳ.
XV *cent*. (burden and stzas. 1–3, 5).

MS. heading (*in later hand*): b A Christmas
Caroll.
stza. 1, l. 1. Lystenyt, lordyng*us*] b Be glad
lordyng*es* bethe. c lordyngs be glad bothe.
l. 2. tydyng] b c tydyng*es*. gladnes] c grete
gladnesse. l. 3. beryt] b me beryth. c
berus. l. 4. c causa dico qu[ia].
stza. 2, l. 1. b c *have* ben. fwul] b c *omit*.
l. 2. Now es] b Mary hath. c to nyth was.
a blyesful] c his blessud.
stza. 3, l. 2. Fro ys Fad*ur* Jh*e*su] b For the fadyr
of heuyn. c Fro the fad*er* of. l. 3. b here
to myrth he us bygan. howre] c *omits*.
l. 4. b Teste p*r*osecia. c de v*i*rgine Maria.
stza. 4, l. 1. swete] b clene.
ll. 2–4. b Th*at* bare a child wi*th*outen syn
    Kepe vs all fre hell pyn,
    De virgine Maria.

---

stza. 5. c   Mare mod*er*, meke *and* mylde,
      Pray for vs al to the childe
      That he vs fro the fynde childe
      Tua p*r*ece pia.
Signature (?): b Wylyam northe of yorke.

37

Bodleian Library. MS. Eng. poet. e. 1
                        XV *cent*.
f. 18ᵛ

    Aye, aye, this is the day
    That we shall worshep eu*er* *and* aye.

[1]

A ferly thyng it is to mene,
    Th*at* a mayd a chyld haue borne
And syth was a mayden clene,
    As p*r*ophet*es* sayden herbeforne.
Iwys, it was a wonder thyng
Th*at* thowrow an aungell*es* gretyng
God wold lyght i*n* a mayden yyng,
    With aye,
    Aye, aye, I dar well say,
    Her maydenhed yede no[t] away.

[2]

Hys moder was a mayden myld,
    As Holy Kyrke wytnese *and* we;
Wi*th*ovten weme she bar a chyld,
    And so ded neu*er* no*n* but she.
A farly thyng it schuld befall,
But God hath all wome*n* thrall
In peynes to ber her chylderne all,
    With aye,
    Aye, aye, I dar wel say,
    She felt no*n* of th*at* aray.

[3]

Hys byrth was know that ylk nyghth
    In all the lond thorow *and* thorow;
Thedyr thei yedyn to se th*at* syghth,
    To Bethle*m*, th*at* fayer borow.
An angel bad th*at* thei shuld go: [f. 19ʳ
He seyd th*at* betwen*n*e beestys two
God*es* Sonne seker ye fynd so,
    With aye,
    Aye, aye, I dar well say,
    In a crybe thei found hy*m* th*er* he lay.

[4]

Thre kyng*es* ovght of Ynde lond,
    Thei cu*m* to seke th*at* ferly fode
Wi*th* rych p*r*esant*es* in th*er* hond;
    A sterre styffely afor he*m* yode.

A ferly thyng it was to se:
That sterre was mor than other thre;
Yt held the course to that contree,
    With aye,
  Aye, aye, I dar wel say,
Thei ded not mysse of redy way.

[5]

Whan thei with that lady mett,
  Thei fond hyr chyld vpon her kne;
Full curttesly thei her grett
  And present hym with yaftys thre.
As kyng thei yeffe hym gold so rede,
Myrre and sense to hys manhede;
Of hyr offryng thus we redde,
    With aye,
  Aye, aye, I dar well say,
The[i] worshepyd hyme on the twelfth
  day.

[6]

Mary moder, maydyn myld,
  To the we cry, to the we call:
Thou be owr socur and owr sheyld;
  Vs thou saue fro myschevys all.
Thou pray thi Sone, that Prynce   [f. 19ᵛ
  of Pees,
Of al owr synnes he vs relees
Ovght of this warld whane we shal cees,
    With aye,
  Aye, aye, so that we may
Wend with hym at domysday.

stza. 5, l. 10. twelfth] MS. xii.

38

Bodleian Library. MS. Eng. poet. e. 1
                   XV *cent.*
f. 19ᵛ

  Now be we glad and not to sad,
  For verbum caro factum est.

[1]

This may I preve withovghten lete:
Whan Gabriell Owr Lady grett,
On hys kne he hym sett
  So myldly:
'Thou shalt conseyve this sam day
  Saluatorem mundi.'

[2]

A sterre shoghne thorow Godes grace,
As Godes avne wyll yt was;

The shepperdes saw in that place
  Angelles two,
And hem among thei song a song:
  'Gloria in excelcis Deo.'

[3]

The chyld was born vpon Yole day
As prophettes to vs gan say;
Hys moder sang, 'Lullay, lullay,'
  Into the est;
Therfor mankynd withovghten end
  Syng, 'Verbum caro factum est.'

[4]

And then, be tokenyng of a starre,
iii kynges ther cam fro fare
And offeryd frankyngcens and myrre
  To Cryst so fre;
Than thei sayd with mery chere,
  'Mane nobiscum, Domine.'

[5]

Therfor pray we euerychone
To that barne that tym was born,
He saue vs all fro shame and schorne,
  In pes and rest,
And all mankynd withovghten end
  Syng, 'Verbum caro factum est.'

stza. 3, l. 1. vpon] MS. vpon I.

39

Bodleian Library. MS. Eng. poet. e. 1
                   XV *cent.*
f. 21ʳ

  Make we mery in this fest,
  For verbum caro factum est.

[1]

Godes Sonne, for the loue of mane
Flesshe and blode of Mary he nam,
As in the gospell seyth Sent Johan:
  Verbum caro factum est.

[2]

Of joy and myrth now mowgh we syng:
God with man is now dwellyng;
Holy Wrytt makyth now shewyng:
  Deus homo natus est.

[3]

God and man hath shewyd hys chyld
That hath vs bovght fro the develys wyld;
Hym to worshyp now be we myld;
  Congaudete m[ihi.]

[4]

This chyld*es* moder, eu*er*more
Maydy*n* she was, aft*er and* befor,
And so sayd the p*r*ophett in hys lore,
V*er*bo p*r*ophesye.

39.1

British Museum. MS. Egerton 3307
XV *cent.*

f. 51ᵛ

Nouo p*r*ofusi gaudio
Benedicamus Domino.

[1]

Omnes gentes plaudite,
Car nostre Sauey*our* est ne;
Ouer all blyssyd he be,
Rex alpha et O.

[2]

A solis ortus cardine,
Com le mound *est* long *et* le,
Al mankynd makith gle:
Ang*e*li canu*n*t Deo.

[3]

Enixa est puerpera
Que Seynt Espryt en engrossa;
Blyssyd be tym*e* th*a*t sche sayd, 'Ya'
Gabriele nuncio.

[4]

Ex illabata v*i*rgine
Est nascu le Roy de mageste;
The hyrd*es* hym se in low degre,
Iacent*em* in p*r*esepio.

[5]

Gl*or*ia tibi, D*omi*ne,
Fortim*e* de gr*a*ce *et* de pyte;
Of all thi goodness we thank the:
Benedicam*us* D*omi*no.

stza. 1, l. 4. O] MS. oo.
stza. 3, l. 4. nuncio] MS. nuncioo.
stza. 4, l. 3. degre] MS. do gre.

40

Bodleian Library. MS. Eng. poet. e. 1
XV *cent.*

f. 27²ᵛ

All th*a*t leue in Cristen lay,
Worschup eu*er*y Cristmes Day.

[1]

A ma*n* was the fyrst gylt,
And ther*for he was spylt;
The p*r*ofycy was neu*er* fulfylt
Thyl on the Cristmes Day.

[2]

The fyrst day th*a*t lely sprong,
J*hes*u Crist be us among;
Eu*er* we thowte it was to long
Thyl on the Cristmes Day.

[3]

It was dyrk, it was dym   [f. 28ʳ
For me*n* th*a*t leuyd in gret syn;
Lucyfer was vs al w*ith*in
Thyl on the Cristmes Day.

[4]

Ther was wepping, th*er* was woo,
For eu*er*y ma*n* to hel gan goo;
It was lityl mery thoo
Thyl on the Cristmes Day.

stza. 1, l. 3. fulfylt] MS. spylt.

41

Bodleian Library. MS. Eng. poet. e. 1
XV *cent.*

f. 29ʳ

Nowel, el, el, el, el!
I thank it a maydy*n* eu*er*y del.

[1]

The fyrst day wa*n* Crist was borne,
Ther sprong a ros owt of a thorne
To saue ma*n*kynd, th*a*t was forlorne;
I thanke it a maydy*n* eu*er*y dyll.

[2]

In an ox stall the chyld was fownd;
In por clothyng the chyld was wond;
He soferyd ma*n*y a dedly wond;
I thanke [it] a ma[y]d[yn] eu*er*y dy[ll.]

[3]

A garland of thornys on his hed was sett;
A scharp sper to his hart was smet;
The Jewys seydy*n*, 'Take the that!'
I tha[nke it] a may[dyn] eu*er*y dyl[l.]

[4]

The Juwys dedy*n* cryy*n* her   [f. 29ᵛ]
   p*er*lam*en*t
On the day of jugment;
They werry*n* aferd thei [s]huld he*m*
   sche[n]t;
   I thanke it a maydy*n* eu*er*y dyll.

[5]

Tho the peler he was bow[n]dyn;
Tho his hart a sper was stu*n*ggyn;
For us he sofered a dedly wondyn;
   I thanke it a maydy*n* eu*er*y dyll.

stzas. 2, 3, l. 4. *A tear in the MS. has obliterated
parts of these lines.*

42

a. *Bodleian Library.* MS. Eng. poet. e. 1
                        XV *cent.*

f. 53ʳ

O m*er*uelous *and* blessed natiuite
Off Godd*es* So*n*ne in diuinite.

[1]

Welcom*e* be thys blissed feest
   Off Jesu Christ in Trinite,
Th*a*t is reform*er* of owr reste,
   Lovyng peace *and* charite.

[2]

In tyme off peace thys chyld was borne,
   As it was shewed in p*r*ophecye,
To save mankynd, th*a*t was forlorn,
   For*e* Kyng off Peace he is trulye.

[3]

Born m*er*velously he was,   [f. 53ᵛ]
   Full off blysse *and* diuinite,
And she a mayd neu*er* the lesse,
   And so was neu*er* no*n*ne but she.

[4]

In his byrth holy was knytt
   God *and* man in his degre;
Mod*er* *and* mayd togeth*er* wer*e* sett
   Ferth in mans hart eu*er* to be.

[5]

Therfor*e* praye we to th*a*t Lord
   And to his mod*er*, mayden fre,
To mak vs wisse in wark *and* word
   To praysse *and* pleasse the Trinite.

---

b. *Huntington Library. Christmas carolles
newely Inprynted* (Richard Kele), pp.
[28, 29]. *c.* 1550. (burden and stzas. 1–3,
5).

burden, l. 1. m*er*uelous . . . blessed] *transposes.*
stza. 1, l. 2. Of goddes sonne in dyuynyte.   l. 4.
   Lovyng] Longe.
stza. 2, l. 2. it] *omits.*
stza. 3, l. 2. blysse] grace.   l. 3. mayd]
   mayden.
stza. 5, l. 1. we] *omits.*   l. 2. mod*er*, mayden]
   mother that mayden.   l. 3. wark *and*
   word] worde *and* ded.   l. 4. the Trinite]
   his deyte.
The repetition of the burden is indicated in b as
follows: stzas. 1–3: O blessed. &c.   stza. 4:
O maruelous. &c.
At end: Finis.

43

British Museum. MS. Lansdowne 379
                          XVI *cent.*

f. 38ʳ

Tydyng*es*, tydyng*es* that be trwe:
Sorowe ys paste, and joye dothe renwe.

[1]

Qwhereas Adam cawsed be synne
   Owre nature thus to be mortall,
A mayden Son dothe nowc bcgyn
   For to repayse vs from that fall,
     And th*a*t ys trwe:
   The name of hym ys Cryste Jh*e*su.

[2]

Sum of oure kynde hathe hadd suche grase
   That syn hys byrthe they dyd hym se,
Bothe Sonne and mother fase to fase
   In the chefe cyte calde Jure.
     And th*a*t ys trwe:
   Bothe kyng*es* and schepardes they yt
     knwe.

[3]

The p*r*ophett*es* th*er*of ware nothy*n*g dys-
     mayde,
   Of that tydyng*es* before th*a*t they hadde
     tolde,
For nowe yt ys fall ryghthe as they sayde:
   A clen mayde hathe born a kyng.
     And th*a*t ys trwe,
   For he ys born to ware the purpull hwe.

Above the burden is written: Jhesus.

44

Bodleian Library. MS. Eng. poet. e. 1
XV *cent.*

f. 52ᵛ

Blyssid be that lady bryght
That bare a chyld off great myght,
Withouten peyne, as it was right,
    Mayd mother Marye.

[1]

Goddys Sonne is borne;
    His moder is a maid,
Both after *and* beforne,
    As the prophycy said,
        With ay!
A wonder thyng it is to se,
How mayden *and* moder on may be;
Was there [neuer] nonne but she,
    Maid moder Marye.

[2]

The great Lord off Heaven
    Owr seruant is becom;
Thorow Gabriels stevyn
    Owre kynd haue benom,
        With ay!
A wonder thyng it is to se,
How lord *and* seruant on may be;
Was ther neuer nonne but he,
    Born off maid Marye.

[3]

Two sons togyther, they
    Owght to shyne bryght;
So did that fayer ladye
    Whan Jesu in her light,
        With ay!
A wo[n]der thyng is fall:
The Lord that bought fre *and* thrall
Is found in an assis stall
    By his moder Mary.

[4]

The sheperdes in her region,   [f. 53ʳ]
    Thei lokyd into heaven;
Thei se an angell commyng dovn,
    That said with myld steven,
        With ay!
'Joy be to God Almyght,
And pece in therth to man is dyte,'
For God was born on Chrismes nyght
    Off his moder Marye.

[5]

Thre kynges off great noblay,
    Whan that child was born,
To hym they tok the redy way
    And kneled hym beforn,
        With ay!
Thes iii kynges cam fro fare
Thorow ledyng off a stare
And offered hym gold, encence, *and* mure,
    And to hys modere Mary.

45

Balliol College, Oxford. MS. 354
XVI *cent.*

f. 178ʳ

Now let vs syng, both more *and* lesse,
Of Cristes commyng, 'Deo gracias.'

[1]

A virgyn pure,
This is full sure,
    Gabriell dide her grete,
And all her cure,
I am full sure,
Euer dyde endure.
    Deo gracias.

[2]

A babe was born
Erly by the morn
    And layd betwen the ox *and* the asse;
The child they knew
That was born new;
On hym thei blew.
    Deo gracias.

[3]

An angell full sone
Sang fro abone,
    'Gloria in excelsis.'
That lady alon
Myght mak no mone
For love of on.
    Deo gracias.

[4]

This babe vs bowght
Whan we were browght
    Into gret thowght *and* dredfull case;
Therfor we syng,
Both old *and* yonge,
Of Cristes commynge,
    'Deo gracias.'

At end: Explicit.

46

Balliol College, Oxford. MS. 354
XVI *cent.*
f. 221ʳ

Now syng we wyth joy and blys,
'Puer natus est nobys.'

[1]

Mary, flowr of flowers all,
Hath born a chyld *in* an ox stall
That Lorde *and* Prynce ys ou*er* vs all;
Pu*er* nat*us* es*t* nobis.

[2]

He was born on Owr*e* Lady
Withowt weme of her body,
Godys own Son truly;
Pu*er* nat*us* es*t* nobis.

[3]

By an apull of a tre
Bownd me*n* all made were we;
That child was born to make vs fre;
Pu*er* nat*us* es*t* nobis.

[4]

That chyld was don on the rode,
Wyth hys flesshe *and with* hys blod,
For owr helpe *and* for owr gud;
Pu*er* nat*us* es*t* nobis.

[5]

The thirde day he rose *and* to hevyn went;
Wytt *and* wysedom he vs sent
For to kepe his cu*m*aundment;
Pu*er* nat*us* es*t* nobis.

[6]

He shall cu*m* down at domysday
W*ith* blody wovnd*es*, I you say,
As he dyed on Gud Fryday;
Pu*er* nat*us* es*t* nobis.

[7]

Now pr*a*y we to that Hevy*n* Kyng
To send vs all his dere blessyng,
Shryft *and* hosyll at owr endyng;
Pu*er* nat*us* es*t* nobis.

stza. 5, l. 1. thirde] MS. iiiᵈᵉ.
At end: Explicit.

47

Balliol College, Oxford. MS. 354
XVI *cent.*
f. 227ʳ

Syng we with myrth, joye, *and* solas
In honowr of this Cristemas.

[1]

Glori*us* God had gret pyte
How longe mans sowle in payn shuld be;
He sent his Son to mak vs free,
    Which for man*us* sake
Off a maydyn pure
Agaynst nature
    Owr flesshe dide take.

[2]

In Bedlem owr Saviowr
Withowt fode in a manjowre
Was born (hit was his plesure)
    Best*es* amonge.
Angell*es* hevynly
Made armonye
    And joyffull songe.

[3]

The eighth day he was circonsisid,
Leste Moyses lawe shuld be dispised;
A name to hy*m* they haue devised:
    'Call hym Jh*es*us.'
For Gabryell
His moder dide tell
    That it should be thus.

[4]

A newe-made sterre, more large *and* clere
Than oth*er* sterres, than dide appere;
Fro Caldey the felosafers in fere
    Into Bedlem yt browght;
Ther it dide stond
Still till that they fonde
    Hym that they sowght.

[5]

The kyng*es* browght th*er* offrynge,
Gold th*at* betokneth a worthy kynge,
I[n]sens p*re*sthode, myr buryinge
    For his manhode.
The angell com,
Bade the*m* go home
    Not by Herode.

[6]

Trust i*n* God, ma*n*, *and* in no*n* other;
Mistrust hy*m* not; he is thy broth*er*;
Thow hast a mediatrix of his moder;
    Syke for thy synne;

Crye marcy;
He will not denye,
  Thy sowle to wynne.

MS. marks burden: fot*e*. The repetitions of the
  burden are indicated as follows: stzas. 1, 3,
  5, 6: syg.   stza. 2: syge.   stza. 4: syng we
  wi*th* myrth*e*.
stza. 3, l. 1. eighth] MS. viiith.   l. 6. did*e*]
  MS. dide did.
At end: Explicit.

48

Balliol College, Oxford. MS. 354
                           XVI *cent.*
f. 229^r
  Synge we all, for tyme it is:
  Mary hath born the flowre-de-lice.

[1]

For his love th*a*t bowght vs all dere,
Lystyn, lordyng*es* that ben here,
And I will tell you in fere
  Wherof com the flowr-de-lyce.

[2]

On Cristmas nyght whan it was cold,
Owr Lady lay amonge best*es* bolde,
And ther she bare Jh*es*u, Josepff tolde,
  And therof com the flowr-de-lice.

[3]

Off th*a*t berth witnesse Seynt Joh*a*n
That it was of myche renown;
Baptized he was in flom Jordan,
  And therof cam the flowr-de-lice.

[4]

On Good Fryday that child was slayn,
Betyn with skorges, *and* all to-flayn;
That day he suffred myche payn,
  And therof com the flowr-de-lice.

MS. marks burden: fote.
The repetition of the burden is indicated as
  follows: stza. 1: syng we.   stzas. 2, 3: syg.
  stza. 4: syg we.
At end: Explicit.

49

Balliol College, Oxford, MS. 354
                           XVI *cent.*
f. 221^v
  V*er*bu*m* P*at*ris hodie
  P*ro*cessit ex virgine.

[1]

The Son of the Fader of Hevyn Blys
Was born as thys day, I will not mys,
Man from thraldom to releve *and* lose;
  P*ro*cessit ex virgine.

[2]

He was born of a virgyn pure,
Not knowyng a ma*n*, as I you sure,
But all only by hevynly cure;
  P*ro*cessit ex virgine.

[3]

Gabryell the angell dyde grett
Mary knelyng in her closett;
Now ys fulfillyd th*a*t sayd the p*ro*fett:
  P*ro*cessit ex virgine.

[4]

Man, be glad, thou hast a cavse why
To thanke owr Lord God, th*a*t ys on hye:
For the to sofer *and* for to dye
  P*ro*cessit ex virgine.

stza. 3, l. 3. ys] MS ytt.
stza. 4, l. 1. glad] MS. ghad.
At end: Explicit.

50

Balliol College, Oxford. MS. 354
                           XVI *cent.*
f. 229^v
  I p*ra*y you, be mery *and* synge wi*th* me
  In worship of Cristys nativite.

[1]

Into this world this day dide com
Jh*es*u Criste, bothe God *and* man,
Lorde *and* s*er*uant in on p*er*son,
  Born of the blessid virgin Mary.

[2]

He th*a*t was riche wi*th*owt any nede
Appered i*n* this world i*n* right pore wede
To mak vs th*a*t were pore indede
  Riche withowt any nede trewly.

[3]

A stabill was his cha*m*bre; a crach was h*i*s
  bed;
He had not a pylow to lay vnder his hed;
Wi*th* maydyns mylk th*a*t babe was fedde;
  In pore clothis was lappid the Lord
    Almyghty.

[4]

A noble lesson here is vs tawght:
To set all worldly riches at nawght,
But pray we that we may be theder browght
    Wher riches ys everlastyngly.

MS. marks burden: fote.
The repetition of the burden is indicated as
    follows: stzas. 1, 2, 4: I pray.
At end: Explicit.

51

Balliol College, Oxford. MS. 354
                                    XVI *cent.*
f. 230ᵛ

    Wassaill, wassayll, wassaill, syng we
    In worshipe of Cristes natiuite.

[1]

Now joy be to the Trynyte,
    Fader, Son, *and* Holy Gost,
That on God is in Trynite,
    Fader of Hevyn, of myghtes most.

[2]

And joy to the virgyn pure
    That euer kepte her vndefiled,
Grundid in grace, in hart full sure,
    And bare a child as maydyn myld.

[3]

Bethelem *and* the sterre so shen,
    That shon iii kynges for to gide,
Bere witnesse of this maydyn clene;
    The kynges iii offred that tide.

[4]

And sheperdis hard, a[s] wretyn is,
    The joyffull songe that ther was songe:
'Glorya in excelsis!'
    With angelles voys it was owt ronge.

[5]

Now joy be to the blessidfull child,
    And joy be to his moder dere;
Joy we all of that maydyn myld,
    And joy haue they that mak good chere.

The repetition of the burden is indicated as
    follows: stza. 1: wassaill &c. stza. 2:
    wassayll. stzas. 3–5: wassaill.
At end: Explicit.

52

Balliol College, Oxford. MS. 354
                                    XVI *cent.*
f. 241ᵛ

    Now syng we, syng we,
    'Gloria tibi, Domine.'

[1]

Cryst kepe vs all, as he well can,
    A solis ortu[s] cardine,
For he ys both God *and* man
    Qui natus est de virgine.

[2]

As he ys Lord both day *and* nyght,
    Venter puelle baiulat;
So ys Mary moder of myght,
    Secreta que non noverat.

[3]

The holy brest of chastyte
    Verbo consepit Filium,
So browght before the Trinite
    Vt castytatis lyllyum.

[4]

Betwen an ox *and* an asse
    Enixa est puerpera;
In pore clothyng clothed he was
    [Q]ui regnat super ethera.

The repetition of the burden is indicated after
    each stanza by: syng we.
stza. 2, l. 2. Venter] MS. ventus.
stza. 4, l. 4. *The first letter has been destroyed by
    a tear in MS.*
At end: Explicit.

53

Cambridge University Library. MS. Ee.
    I. 12   By James Ryman, *c.* 1492
f. 43ʳ

    Ther is a chielde, a heuenly childe,
    Iborne this nyght of Marie myelde.

[1]

This chielde is, was, and ay shall be
One in Godhede, in persones thre.
    There is a childe, [a heuenly childe.]

[2]

This chielde is named Criste Jhesus
That nowe is borne for loue of vs.
    There is a chield, [a heuenly childe.]

[3]

Mortall nature this chielde hath take
Of oure thraldome vs free to make.
    There is a chield, [a heuenly childe.]

[4]

This chielde is God and man also,
Now borne to bringe vs out of wo.
    There is a chield, [a heuenly childe.]

[5]

His Fader is God of Heven Blis,
And virgyne Mary his moder is.
    There is a chield, [a heuenly childe.]

[6]

Fro heven to erthe this chielde come is
To suffre dethe for mannys mys.
    There is [a chield, a heuenly childe.]

[7]

On Good Friday vppon the roode
To save mankyende he shed his bloode.
    There is [a chield, a heuenly childe.]

[8]

This chielde was dede and in   [f. 43ᵛ]
        graue laye
And rose ayene on the thirde daye.
    There is [a chield, a heuenly childe.]

[9]

By his grete myght to blis he stide
And sittith on his Faders right side.
    There is [a chield, a heuenly childe.]

[10]

Whenne he shalle come and jugement
        make,
To blis with hym this chielde vs take.
    There [is a chield, a heuenly childe.]

stza. 1, l. 3. MS. There is a childe &c.
stzas. 2–5, l. 3. MS. There is a chield &c.
stzas. 6–9, l. 3. MS. There is &c.
stza. 10, l. 3. MS. There &c.

[1]

Mary so myelde and good of fame,
    By vertu of the Holy Goost,
Hath borne a chielde, Jhesus by name,
    To save mankyende, the whiche was lost.

[2]

Marie so myelde in hert *and* myende,
    As Gabriell to her behight,
Hath borne a chielde to save mankyende,
    The Son of God and King of Myght.

[3]

Marie so myelde, that quene of grace,
    Hath borne a chielde (Scripture seith
        soo)
To bringe mankyende out of that place
    Where is bothe peyne and endeles woo.

[4]

Mary so myelde in worde and thought
    Hath borne a chielde, Jhesus soo good,
The whiche ayene mankyende hath bought
    On the roode tree with his hert bloode.

[5]

Mary so myelde in dede and wille
    Hath borne a chielde that made alle
        thing,
To whom al thing obeyeth by skille
    As to theire prince, theire lorde   [f. 76ᵛ
        and king.

[6]

Mary so myelde, so pure and clene,
    Vnto hir chielde, that hath no pere,
By hir mekenes she is a meane
    That we shalle come to heven quere.

[7]

Mary so myelde, moder and may,
    Hath borne a chielde by hir mekenesse
That shall bringe vs at domesday
    Fro thraldom, peyn, woo, and distresse.

burden, l. 1. Mary] MS. Marry.

54

Cambridge University Library. MS. Ee.
    I. 12   By James Ryman, *c.* 1492
f. 76ʳ

    Mary so myelde of hert *and* myende
    Hath borne a child to save mankyende.

55

Cambridge University Library. MS. Ee.
    I. 12   By James Ryman, *c.* 1492
f. 85ᵛ

    Nowe lete vs syng and mery be,
    For Crist oure Kyng hathe made us fre.

[1]

Now for to syng I holde it best,
 And lete alle care and sorowe goo,
For Crist oure Kyng nowe in this fest
 Was born to bryng us owte of woo.

[2]

Thatte blessyd chyld tok flesshe *and* bloode,
 By vertu of the Holi Gost,
Of Mary myld, thatte meyde so goode,
 To saue mankynde, the whiche was lost.

[3]

When he was born of thatte myld [f. 86ʳ
  meyde,
 Thatt blessyd Lord and Heuen Kyng,
As long beforn prophetys hadde seyde,
 With on accorde angell*es* didde syng.

[4]

The angell*es* than seide, 'Joy mot be
 To God aboue in heuen blys,
And peas to man, for alle thatte he
 Hath offendid and done amys.'

[5]

The shepherd*es* than kepyng ther*e* folde
 Hurd fulle sweete songe and sawe grete
  light
When God and man, as prophet*es* told,
 Was mekely born vppon thatte nyght.

[6]

Syth man ys take ayen to grace
 And brought ayen to joye and blys,
Lete us alle make myrthe *and* solace,
 And lete us thanke our*e* Lorde of thys.

56

Cambridge University Library. MS. Ee.
I. 12 By James Ryman, *c.* 1492
f. 86ʳ

 Mirabile misterium:
 The Sone of God ys man becum;
 Mirabile.

[1]

The Faders Sone of Heuen Blys,
 Thatte is the lorde of every cost,
Of a pure meyde man becum ys
 To saue mankynd, the whiche was lost.
 Mirabile.

[2]

An angelle came to thatte meyde so fre
 And seide, 'Haile, Mary, fulle [f. 86ᵛ
  of grace;
The Lord of Alle now is with the
 In hert, in wombe, and euery place.'
 Mirabile.

[3]

He seide alsoo, withowten bost,
 Vnto thatt meyde, thatt angelle than,
'By vertu of the Holi Gost
 Thowe shalt conceyue both*e* God *and*
  man.'
 Mirabile.

[4]

And so withowten manys sede,
 By vertu of the Holy Gost,
Sche hath conceyuyd and born indede
 The Sone of God of myght*es* most.
 Mirabile.

[5]

The glasse is more pure and itte wasse
 Thorughe the which the sone did
  schyne;
So ys this meyde throughe whom did passe
 The Sone of God by grace dyuyne.
 Mirabile.

[6]

Aaron yerde, withowte moystowre,
 Thatte longe was sere, a flowr*e* hath*e*
  born;
So sche hath born our*e* Sauyowre
 To saue mankynde, thatt was forlorn.
 Mirabile.

[7]

A stone was kutte owte of an hylle
 Withowten helpe of manys honde;
A meyden pure in dede *and* wylle
 Hath born the lord of euery londe.
 Mirabile.

stza. 1, l. 5. MS. Mirabile &c.

57

British Museum. MS. Addit. 5665
        XVI *cent.*
f. 33ᵛ

 Tydyng*es* trew ther buthe come newe;
 Blessed be Jhesu.
 Tydyng*es* trew ther buthe come *new;
 Blessed be Jhesu.   [*f. 34ʳ

[1]

Tydynge*s* trew tolde ther ys trewe:
Jesu to be born of a mayde;
Now ys fulfilledde that prophesie sayde;
    Blessed be Jhesu.

[2]

Tydynge*s* trew an angell bryght   [f. 33ᵛ
Song, how ther ys sprong a lyghth
To all th*a*t leuen aryghth;
    Blessed be Jhesu.

MS. heading: de natiuitate.

58

British Museum. MS. Addit. 5665
                                XVI *cent.*
f. 34ᵛ

    Nascitur ex virgine,
    Sine virili semine.
    Nascitur ex virgine,
    Sine viri*li semine.   [*f. 35ʳ

[1]

A childe ys born of a mayde
    In redempcion of vs all;
Worshipe we both nyght *and* day,
    For vs was born in a oxe stall.

[2]

We buthe muche bou*n*de to God   [f. 34ᵛ
    Allmyght,
    That sende his Sone w*i*th gode entent
To be born of a mayde that ys bryght,
    That all mankynde shall noght [be] shent.

MS. heading: de natiuitate.
Signature: Smert.

59

British Museum. MS. Addit. 5665
                                XVI *cent.*
f. 52ᵛ

    Blessed mote th*o*u be, swete Jhesus,
        Qui hodie natus es nobis.
    Blessed mote th*o*u be, swete Jhesus,
        Qui hodie natus es *nobis.   [*f. 53ʳ

[1]

By thi burthe, th*o*u blessed Lord,
Ys made of variaunce now on acorde;
    Therfor we may shyng this:
Blessed mote th*o*u be, swete Jhesus,
Blessed mote th*o*u be, swete Jh[es]us,
    Qui hodie [natus es nobis.]

[2]

Vpon this heygh blessed day   [f. 52ᵛ
Jhesu in hys moder*es* armys lay;
    Wherefor to hym lete vs all say:
Blessed mote th*o*u be, swete Jhesus,
[Blessed mote thou be, swete Jhesus,
    Qui hodie natus es nobis.]

MS. heading: de natiuitate.
stza. 2, l. 3. vs] MS. v*us.*
Signature: Smert.

59.1

Yale University Library. Osborn Collection,
    Osborn Shelves a. 1.   XIV *cent.*
p. [306]

    Mayde and moder, glade thou be,
    For nou thou myst [th]y son ysee.

[1]

That ix moneythes [w]as enclus,
To brynge ous alle atte paradis.

[2]

Thou seken and mylkeyde ym wit your[e]
    brest,
To brynge ous to the joye that heuere salle
    leste.

[3]

Josep w[a]s a feble noursce,
Is so[ne] bytocke ocxe and asse.

The repetition of the burden is indicated as
    follows: stza. 1: Mayde and moder.   stza. 2:
    mayde and moder.   stza. 3: mari and Joceppe
    gla[d] ye3 be nou ye3 may youre son y seee.

60

Bodleian Library. Douce fragments f. 48
                                XVI *cent.*
f. 4ʳ

    In the honour of Christes byrth
    Syng we al with joye and myrthe.

[1]

In this tyme of Chrystmas,
Bytwyxte an oxe and an asse,
A mayden delyuered was
    Of Christ, her dere Son dere.

[2]

The husbande of Mary,   [f. 4ᵛ
[Saint] Joseph, stoode her by
And sayde he was ready
    To serue her if nede were.

[3]

When she her deare Sonne se,
She set him on her kne
And song, '"Hydder to me—"
    Cum basse thy mother, deare.'

[4]

On her lap she him layde,
And with her pappe he playde,
And euer sang the mayde,
    'Come basse thy mother, dere.'

[5]

With lyppes collyng,
His mouth ofte she dyd kysse
And sayd, 'Sweetehert myne,
    I pray you, make good chere.'

[6]

To this chylde let vs pray
That borne was on this day
Of Mary, the mylde may,
    To graunt vs all good chere.

At end: Finis.

60.1

*Cambridge University Library. MS. Addit.
7350, Box 2 By James Ryman, XV cent.*
f. 1ᵛ

    Te Deum laudamus &c.

[1]

Of Mary, a mayde withowt lesyng,
This day was borne a worthy kyng;
Therfor with joy now lett vs syng,
    'Te Deum [laudamus.']

[2]

Of Jessis rote ther sprang a flowr
That is moste swetist in odure;
Syng we to hym with great honour,
    'Te Deum [laudamus.']

[3]

On Christmas Day that child borne was,
Man to redeme for owr trespase;
Therfor syng we both more and lesse,
    'Te Deum [laudamus.']

[4]

On Good Fryday that childe wold dy
For owr trespace and owr folye;
Syng we to hym that sittith on hy,
    'Te Deum [laudamus.']

[5]

On the third day he rose fulle ryght
And harrowed hell by his great myght;
Sing we to hym bothe day and nyght,
    'Te Deum [laudamus.']

[6]

The gatis of heuyn they oponed abrode
By the vertu of that blyssid Lord;
Syng we to hym with one accord,
    'Te Deum [laudamus.']

[7]

Pray we all to that Lord of grace
That we may cume into that place
To syng with joy before his face,
    'Te Deum [laudamus.']

stza. 1, l. 4. MS. Te deum &cᵉᵗʳᵃ.
At end: Finis.
*Stza. 6 is written after stza. 2 in MS. with para-
    graph mark prefixed to indicate transposition,
    although there is no mark of insertion before
    stza. 7.*

61

*Cambridge University Library. MS. Ee.
1. 12   By James Ryman, c. 1492*
f. 44ʳ

    The Sone of God alone
    Hath made vs free echeone.

[1]

The Faders Sonne of Heven Blis
Of a pure [mayde] man bicome is
To forgeve man, that did amys,
    By his mekenes allone.

[2]

Bothe yonge and olde we were forlorn
For synne that Adam did beforne,
Till of a mayde this chielde was born
    To make vs fre alone.

[3]

Moder Mary and virgyne pure
Clothed hym with mortall vesture
And closed hym in her clausure
    Of chastite allone.

[4]

When he was thirti winter olde,
For xxx plates he was solde
To the Jewes wikked and bolde   [f. 44ᵛ
  By fals Judas alone.

[5]

Vpon his hede a crowne of thorne
The Jewes sette than with grete scorne,
And with scourges his flesshe they torne
  For our trespas alone.

[6]

The Jewes thanne of wikked moode
Nayled his bodye on the roode
Wheron he shed his precious bloode
  To make vs free alone.

[7]

He was dede and in his graue leyde
And rose ayene, as Scripture seide,
On the thirde day and to blis steyde,
  Both God and man alone.

[8]

Now beseche we this King of Grace
That we may haue a dwelling place
And euir to see his glorious face
  In heven blis echeone.

stza. 4, l. 1. thirti] MS. xxxᵗⁱ.
stza. 7, l. 3. thirde] MS. iiiᵈᵉ.

62

Cambridge University Library. MS. Ee.
  I. 12   By James Ryman, *c.* 1492
f. 45ᵛ

  The Sone of God is man become
  Pro salute fidelium.

[1]

The Sonne of God and King of Blis,
Whoos joye and blis shall neuir mys,
Of a pure mayde man become is
  Pro salute fidelium.

[2]

What tyme Adam, oure first parent,
Had geve consent to the serpent,
As man [to] die was his entent
  Pro salute fid[elium.]

[3]

Whenne he was xxx winter olde,
For xxx plates he was solde
By fals Judas to Jewes bolde
  Pro salute fidelium.

[4]

Vppon his hede a crowne of thorne
The Jewes sette thanne with gret scorne,
And with scourges his flesshe was torne
  Pro salute [fidelium.]

[5]

The Jewes than of wikked moode
Nayled his body on the roode
Wheron he shed his precious bloode
  Pro salute fid[elium.]

[6]

He was dede and in graue leyde,
And the thirde day, as Scripture seyde,
He rose ayene and to blis steyde
  Pro salute fid[elium.]

[7]

He toke with hym withoute delay   [f. 46ʳ
Moder Marie, wyfe and may,
The whiche incessantly doth pray
  Pro salute fidelium.

[8]

That Lorde and King by his grete myght
Cause vs to dwell in blisse so bright
That fro blis into Mary light
  Pro salute fid[elium.]

stza. 4, l. 4. MS. Pro salute &c.
stza. 6, l. 2. thirde] MS. iiiᵈᵉ.

63

Cambridge University Library. MS. Ee.
  I. 12   By James Ryman, *c.* 1492
f. 104ʳ

  The Sone of God in trone
  Hath take mankynd alone.

[1]

The Sone of God so full of myght
  Came downe fro heuen trone
And into Mary he dyd lyght
  To saue mankynde alone.

[2]

He that of nought a thyng wrought than
  (I take witnesse of Jhon)
Withowte syn he is made a man
  To saue [mankynde alone.]

[3]

As the sonne beame goith throughe the
    glasse
  And hurt to itt dothe none,
Throughe meyde Mary so did he passe
  To saue [mankynde alone.]

[4]

Bothe withowte peyn, woo, and dolowre,
  In flesshe, in felle, and bone,
Thatt meyde hath born oure Sauy[o]wre
  To saue [mankynde alone.]

[5]

For syn mankynd in helle was   [f. 104ᵛ
  cast,
  And confort it hadde none,
Till Crist Jhesus came atte the last
  To saue [mankynde alone.]

[6]

In derknes, peyn, dolowre, and woo
  Old faders made grete mone,
Callyng for Crist (Scripture seyeth soo)
  To [saue mankynde alone.]

[7]

Prophetes prechyd, as seyeth Scripture,
  In tyme full longe agone
Thatt Crist scholde come and take nature
  To [saue mankynde alone.]

[8]

Kutte of the hill withowte manys hond,
  Crist is the cornere stone,
Born of a meyde, I vnderstond,
  To [saue mankynde alone.]

stzas. 2–5, l. 4. MS. To saue cᵍ.
stzas. 6–8, l. 4. MS. To cᵍ.

64

Bodleian Library. Douce fragments f. 48
                        XVI *cent.*
f. 1ᵛ

  Come to Bethleem, and ye shal se:
  Puer natus est hodie.

[1]

A woman, a mayd in thought *and* deede,
  A fayrer with eyen myght no man see,
With her virgin paps her babe did fede;
  Puer natus est hodie.

[2]

The chyldes name is called Jesus;
  Gabryel sayde it shulde so be;
Joye we togyther, and syng we thus:
  'Puer natus est hodie.'

[3]

To make vs rych pore was he than,
  With mekenes and humylytie;
Doutles he is bothe God and man;
  Puer natus est hodie.

[4]

Kynges *and* prynces of this dyd here;
  Togyther they came a mayden to see
Lullyng her babe, her blessed Son dere;
  Puer natus est hodie.

[5]

N[o]w, blysful mayde th*a*t bare th*a*t byrthe,
  Pr[ay] thy Son that we may hym se;
.   .   .   .   .   .

Heading in original: A caroll of the byrth of
  Chryst.
*The first words of stza. 5, ll. 1, 2 are damaged by
small holes in the original. The continuation of
the carol is lost.*

65

Cambridge University Library. MS. Ee.
  I. 12   By James Ryman, *c.* 1492
f. 24ʳ

  Ecce quod natura
  Mutat sua iura:
  Virgo parit pura
    Dei Filium.

[1]

Bothe yonge and olde, take hede of this:
The cours of nature chaunged is;
  A mayde that neuir did amys
    Hath borne oure Sauyoure.

[2]

What tyme mankynde had done amys
And for his mys was put fro blis,
  A roose, a valent floure, iwis,
    Crist made springe of a thorne.

C

[3]

Criste hath made springe oute of   [f. 24ᵛ
    a thorne
A mayde that hym mekely hath borne,
Beyng bothe afture *and* beforne
    As pur*e* as lilly floure.

[4]

As a swete floure berith his odour*e*
This mayden myelde of grete honour*e*
Wi*th*outen maternall doloure
    Our*e* Sauyo*ur* hath borne.

[5]

Vpon a nyght an aungell bright
From blis downe light, saiyng full right,
'Thurgh Goddes myght a worthy wight
    Hath borne our*e* Savyoure.'

[6]

Than king*es* three fro ferr*e* cuntre
In her degre came for to se
This King so free of magestee
    That in Bedleme was borne.

66

Cambridge University Library. MS. Ee.
  1. 12   By James Ryman, *c.* 1492
f. 23ʳ

    Ecce q*uo*d natura
    Mutat sua iura:
    Virgo parit pura
        Dei Filiu*m*.

[1]

Beholde *and* see how that nature
Chaungith here lawe: a mayden pure
Shalle bere a chielde, (thus seith   [f. 23ᵛ
        Scripture)
    Jh*esus*, our*e* Sauyo*ur*.

[2]

Beholde, the flease of Gedeon
Wexed wete, that no dewe fel on;
Beholde, the yerde of Aaron
    Vnmoysted bare a floure.

[3]

The pr*o*phete Isay seith thus:
'A mayde shall bere a childe to vs
Whose name shall be called Jhesus,
    Our*e* helpe *and* o*ur* soco*ur*.

[4]

'A yerde shall goo oute of Jesse rote
Wherof a floure shall ascende full soote.'
This floure is Crist, our*e* helth *and* boote,
    This yerde, Mary, his bour*e*.

[5]

Seynt Mathew seith in the gospell,
'A mayde shall bere Emanuell,
That is to sey, God wi*th* vs to dwell,
    That louely paramo*ur*.'

[6]

Forsoth, to vs is borne a chielde;
A sonne is yeven to vs full myelde
Of virgyne Marie vndefielde
    To cease our*e* grete langour*e*.

[7]

This is the stone cutte of the hille,   [f. 24ʳ
Criste borne of Marie vs vntille
Wi*th*out synne in thought, dede, *and* wille
    To save vs fro dolo*ur*.

[8]

This chielde shall be the Prince of Peas,
Whose kingdome shall euir encrease,
Wherof the peas shall neuir ceas
    But encreace day and hour*e*.

[9]

Seint Anselme seith, 'So Criste did pas
Thurgh Marie myelde, as his wille was,
As the sonne beame goth thurgh the glas,
    That mayde full of honour*e*.'

67

Cambridge University Library. MS. Ee.
  1. 12   By James Ryman, *c.* 1492
f. 74ᵛ

    Right as the aungell tolde it is,
    That nowe is borne the King of Blis.

[1]

The pr*o*phesy fulfilled is
    Of the pr*o*phetes now alle *and* sume,
For why the Faders Sonne of Blis
    To save mankyende is man bicome.
        And why is this, but for our*e* mys,
        That now is borne the King of Blis?

[2]

His loue to vs was so feruent
That he came downe, that Lorde so
good,
Fro blisse into this vale present
And of Mary toke flesshe *and* blode.
And why was this, but for our*e* mys,
That now is borne the King of Blis?

[3]

And so our*e* nature he hath take   [f. 75ʳ
To his Godhede *wit*houten synne
And hath brought vs oute of that lake
Th*at* our*e* parent had brought vs in.
And why was this, but for our*e* mys,
That nowe is borne the King of Blis?

[4]

By vertu of the Holy Goost,
Into her*e* wombe that downe did light,
The Sonne of God of myght*es* moost
She hath brought furth, that mayden
bright.
And why was this, but for our*e* mys,
That nowe is borne the King of Blis?

[5]

As the sonne beame goth thurgh the glas,
And as a flour*e* berith his odoure,
So Crist of her conceyved was
And borne of her *wit*houte doloure.
And why was this, but for our*e* mys,
That now is borne the King of Blis?

[6]

Beholde *and* see the lowe destence
Of Criest, that is so high in trone,
To take nature for our*e* offence,
The whiche offence did neuir none.
And why was this, but for our*e* mys,
That now is borne the King of Blis?

[7]

When he was borne, that Lorde *and* King,
Oute of thraldome to bringe mankyende,
'Joye be to God,' aungell*es* did synge,
In Holy Scriptur*e* as we fyende.
And why was this, but for our*e* mys,
That now is borne the King of Blis?

[8]

Now beseche we this King of Grace
For to graunte vs a place in blis
And hym to se ther*e* face to face
There joye and peas shall neuir   [f. 75ᵛ
mysse.

And why is this, but for our*e* mys,
That nowe is borne the King of Blis?

68

British Museum. MS. Sloane 2593
XV *cent.*
f. 4ʳ
O flos de Jesse virgula,
Laus ti*bi* sit *et* glo*ri*a.

[1]

Ada*m* our fad*er* was in blis,
And for an appil of lytil prys
He loste the blysse of Paradys,
P*ro* sua sup*er*bia.

[2]

And alle th*at* euere of hy*m* cam
The ryth weye to helle nam,
Bothe Ysaac *and* Abrah*a*m,
Teste p*ro*fecia.

[3]

Tha*n* these p*ro*fet*es* p*re*chyd aforn
Th*at* a chyld xuld be born
To beye th*at* Ada*m* hadde forlorn
Sua morte p*ro*p*ri*a.

[4]

Moyses ferst in his lawe told
A chyld th*er* xuld be born so bold,
To beye ayyn th*at* Ada*m* sold
Sua nocte pessima.

[5]

Isaac, *wit*houte lesyng,
P*ro*feciid in his p*re*chyng
Of Jesse rote a flour xuld spryng,
De virgine purica.

[6]

Jeromy, th*at* was so yyng,
P*ro*fecyid of his comyng
Th*at* is veri Lord *and* Kyng,
Omni Patris gracia.

[7]

Ferth*er*emore, as I *y*ou telle,
Than p*ro*fecyid Danyelle;
Of hys comy*n*g he ga*n* spelle
Gentib*us* in Judea.

[8]

Qua*n* tyme cam of God Almyght
Th*a*t wolde brynge mankynde to ryght,
In a maydy*n* he ga*n* lyght
  Que vocat*ur* Maria.

[9]

Now is he born, th*a*t blysful chyld, [f. 4ᵛ
Of Mary mod*er*, mayde myld;
Fro the fynd he vs schyld,
  Qui creauit om*n*ia.

[10]

Prey we to hy*m* wit*h* al o*ur* mynde,
Th*a*t haght mad al ma*n*kynde,
He brynge vs alle to good ende
  In die nouissima.

69

Bodleian Library. MS. Arch. Selden B. 26
                                   XV *cent.*
f. 29ʳ

  Ueni, redemptor gencium;
  Ueni, redemptor genciu*m*.

[1]

This worle wo*n*dreth of al thy*n*ge
Howe a maide *con*ceyued a ky*n*ge;
To yeue vs al th*er*of shewy*n*ge,
  [V]eni, redemptor genciu*m*.

[2]

Whan Gabriel come wit*h* his gretynge
To Mary mod*er*, th*a*t swete thynge,
He gr*a*unted *and* saide wit*h* grete lykynge,
  'Veni, [redemptor gencium.']

[3]

Ambrose saide in his writynge
Cryst sholde be in a maide dwellynge,
To make sothe alle that syngynge:
  'Veni, [redemptor gencium.']

[4]

And Dauyd saide in his spellynge
That Truthe sholde be in erthe growynge,
To vs byer of alle thynge.
  Veni, [redemptor gencium.]

[5]

Cryst, ycrowned at oure begynny*n*ge,
Be wit*h* vs at oure endynge,
Vs to thy joye for to brynge;
  Veni, [redemptor gencium.]

stzas. 2–5, l. 4. MS. veni &c.

70

Cambridge University Library. MS. Ee.
1. 12   By James Ryman, *c.* 1492
f. 37ᵛ

  Now in this fest, this holy fest,
  Nunc puer nobis natus est,
  Nunc puer nobis natus est,
  Et puer nobis datus est.

[1]

Thus it is seide in *p*rophecye
(I take witnesse of Ysay):
'A mayde shall [bere] a chielde, truly,
Whose name shall be called   [f. 38ʳ
    Messy.'
  Now in this fest, [this holy fest.]

[2]

'He is oure Lorde,' seith Jheremy,
'And none like hym is ferr*e* ne nye;
In erthe he is seyn, verily,
Conu*er*saunt with people playnly.'
  Now in this fest, [this holy fest.]

[3]

This is the stone cut of the hille,
Crist borne of Mary vs vntille,
Wit*h*out synne in dede, thought, *and* wille,
The wille of God for to fulfille.
  Now in this [fest, this holy fest.]

[4]

'Alle king*es* vnto hym shall pray,
And alle people hym shall obay
And serue hym bothe by nyght *and* day.'
Thus seith Dauid, as ye rede may.
  Now in [this fest, this holy fest.]

[5]

'O Sonne of God,' Abacuc sayde,
'By whome al thing is wrought, now layde
In an oxe stalle, borne of a mayde,
And man become for mannys ayde.'
  Now [in this fest, this holy fest.]

[6]

Nowe preyse we alle this P*r*ince of Peas
Now borne our*e* bondes to   [f. 38ᵛ
    release
And alle our*e* care and woo to cease,
Our*e* joy *and* myrth for to increase.
  Now in [this fest, this holy fest.]

stzas. 1, 2, l. 5. MS. now in this fest &c.
stza. 3, l. 5. MS. now in this &c.
stzas. 4, 6, l. 5. MS. now in &c.
stza. 5, l. 5. MS. now &c.

71

Cambridge University Library. MS. Ee.
I. 12 By James Ryman, *c*. 1492
f. 41ᵛ

Bothe man *and* chielde, haue myende of
    this:
  How Godis Sonne of Blis
  Of Marie myelde man become is
    To deye for mannys mys.

[1]

A mayden myelde hath borne a chielde,
  A chielde of full grete price,
And is a moder vndefielde
  And quene of paradice.

[2]

The King of Blis his Fader is,
  And Jhesus is his name;
To bringe mankyende to heven   [f. 42ʳ
    blis
He hathe borne mannes blame.

[3]

He was and is and ay shall be
  (I take recorde of John)
Ay thre in personalite,
  In deite but oon.

[4]

And in a stalle this chielde was born,
  Bitwene bothe oxe and asse,
To save, for synne that was forlorn,
  Mankyende, as his wille wasse.

[5]

Whenne he was borne, that heuenly King,
  Of Mary, quene of blis,
Than 'Gloria,' aungel*les* did synge,
  'Deo in excelsis.'

[6]

The p*r*ophecy of Isay
  And p*r*ophetes alle *and* sume
Now ended is thus finally,
  For God is man become.

[7]

Nowe laude we God of heven blis
  With hert, w*ith* wille, and myende,
That of a mayde man bicom is
  To blis to bringe mankyende.

72

Cambridge University Library. MS. Ee.
I. 12 By James Ryman, *c*. 1492
f. 75ᵛ

A chielde is borne w*ith* vs to dwell,
  Nomen eius Emanuell.

[1]

'This is the stone kut of the hille,'
  Thus seith the p*r*ophete Daniell,
'Borne of a mayde in dede *and* wille,
  Nomen eius Emanuell.'
Scripture full welle to vs doth tell:
  Nomen eius Emanuell.

[2]

Thus seide the p*r*ophete Ysay
  Long tyme before, or it befell:
'A meyde shall bere a child, truly,
  Nomen eius Emanuell.'
Scripture full well to vs doth tell:
  Nomen eius Emanuell.

[3]

'He is our*e* Lorde,' seith Jeramye,
  'This chielde now borne w*ith* vs to dwell,
And non like hym is far*e* ne neye,
  Nomen eius Emanuell.'
Scriptur*e* full well to vs doth tell:
  Nomen eius Emanuell.

[4]

'The Sonne of God,' Abacuc seyde,
  'By whome al thing was made full well,
In an oxe stalle was porely leyde,
  Nomen eius Emanuell.'
Scriptur*e* full well to vs doth tell:
  Nomen eius Emanuell.

[5]

'Alle kinges vnto hym do pray,'
  Thus seith Dauid, as I you tell,
'And alle peoples hym shall obay,
  Nomen eius Emanuell.'
Scripture full well to vs doth   [f. 76ʳ
    tell:
  Nomen eius Emanuell.

[6]

Nowe lete vs pray, bothe alle *and* sume,
  To this aungell of alle counsell
To heuen blisse that we may cume,
  Nomen eius Emanuell.
Scriptur*e* full well to vs doth tell:
  Nomen eius Emanuell.

73

Bodleian Library. MS. Arch. Selden B. 26
                          XV *cent.*
f. 21ᵛ

   Alleluya, alleluya, alleluya,
   Alleluya, alleluya, alleluya.

[1]

A nywe werk is come on honde,
A nyw werk is com on honde
Thorw myght *and* gra*c*e of Godys sonde,
Thorw myght *and* gra*c*e of Godis   [f. 22ʳ
   sonde,
To saue the lost of eu*er*y londe,
   Alleluya, alleluya,
For now is fre th*at* erst was bonde;
   We mowe wel sy*n*ge all*elu*ia.

[2]

By Gabriel bygu*n*ne hit was:
Ryght as the su*n*ne shone thorwe the glas
Jh*es*u Cryst conceyued was,
   [Alleluya, alleluya,]
Of Mary moder, ful of grace;
   Nowe synge we here all*elu*ia.

[3]

Nowe is fulfylled the pr*o*phecie
Of Dauid and of Jeremie,
And also of Ysaie,
   [Alleluya, alleluya,]
Synge we therfore both loude *and* hye:
   Alleluya, alleluya.

[4]

Simeon on his armys ryght
Clypped Jh*es*u ful of myght
And sayde vnto th*at* barne so bryght,
   [Alleluya, alleluya,]
'Y see my Sauyo*ur* in syght,'
   And songe therwith alleluya.

[5]

Tho he saide, wi*th*oute lece,
'Lorde, th*o*u sette thy s*er*uant in pece,
For nowe Y haue th*at* Y eu*er* chece,
   [Alleluya, alleluya,]
Alle our*e* joyes to encrece
   Ther seyntes syngeth alleluya.'

[6]

Alleluya, this swete songe,
Oute of a grene branche hit spronge:

God sende vs the lyf th*at* lasteth longe!
   [Alleluya, alleluya,]
Nowe joye *and* blysse be hem amonge
   Th*at* thus cu*n*ne synge alleluya.

burden, l. 2, stza.1, ll. 2, 4, l. 6, *second* alleluya.
   MS. marks: Chorus.
Stzas. 2–6, ll. 1, 2 are to be repeated in singing,
   as written in stza. 1.
stza. 3, l. 3. Of] MS. Od.

74

Cambridge University Library. MS. Ee.
   1. 12   By James Ryman, *c.* 1492
f. 39ʳ

   The Sonne of God man bicome is
   Of virgyn Marie, quene of blis.

[1]

Oute of your*e* slepe arryse and   [f. 39ᵛ
   wake,
For God our*e* manhode now hath take,
Of our*e* synnes vs free to make,
   Of virgyn [Marie, quene of blis.]

[2]

To the sheperdes keping their*e* folde
That Crist was borne an aungell tolde,
And in Bethelem fynde hym they sholde
   Wi*th* virgyn [Marie, quene of blis.]

[3]

To Bethelem than they toke their*e* wey
And founde that chielde ther*e* where he ley,
In an oxe stalle in poore arraye,
   Wi*th* virgyn Mary, [quene of blis.]

[4]

Fro ferr*e* cuntree came king*es* three
To seke that King of Magestee,
The whiche was borne, to make vs free,
   Of v*ir*gyn [Mary, quene of blis.]

[5]

Gold, *and* myrre, and swete encense
Thise king*es* gave with gret reu*er*ence
To this King borne wi*th*out offence
   Of v*ir*gyn [Mary, quene of blis.]

[6]

Into Egipte Joseph fledde thoo,
Wi*th* the chielde and moder alsoo;
The aungell bade hym thidder   [f. 40ʳ
   goo
   Wi*th* virgyn [Mary, quene of blis.]

[7]

King Herode thanne chaunged his moode,
When Cristes birthe he vndrestoode,
The whiche hathe take bothe fleshe *and*
    blode
    Of virgyn [Mary, quene of blis.]

[8]

And in Betheleme in his grete fure
Children he slewe that were full pure,
For Cristes sake, that toke nature
    Of virgyn [Mary, quene of blis.]

[9]

Nowe beseche we that King of Grace
In blis that we may haue a place,
Therin to see his glorious face
    With virgyn [Mary, quene of blis.]

stzas. 1, 7, l. 4. MS. Of virgyn &c.
stzas. 2, 9, l. 4. MS. With virgyn &c.
stza. 3, l. 4. MS. With virgyn Mary &c.
stzas. 4, 5, 8, l. 4. MS. of virgyn &c.
stza. 6, l. 4. MS. With virgyn &c.

75

Cambridge University Library. MS. Ee.
    I. 12   By James Ryman, *c.* 1492
f. 33^r

    Angelus inquit pastoribus,
    'Nunc natus est Altissimus.'

[1]

Vpon a nyght an aungell bright
    Pastoribus apparuit,
And anone right thurgh God*des* myght
    Lux magna illis claruit.
        For loue of vs (Scripture seith thus)
        Nunc natus est Altissimus.

[2]

And of that light that was so bright
    Hii valde timuerunt;
A signe of blis to vs it is,
    Hec lux quam hii viderunt.
        For loue of vs (Scripture seith thus)
        Nunc natus est Altissimus.

[3]

'Drede ye nothing; grete joy I bringe,
    Quod erit omni populo;
For why to you Criste is borne   [f. 33^v
    nowe,
    Testante eu*a*ngelio.'
        For loue of vs (Scripture seith thus)
        Nunc natus est Altissimus.

[4]

'With good Joseph and Mary myelde
    Positum in presepio
Ye shall fynde that hevenly childe,
    Qui celi preest solio.'
        For loue of vs (Scripture seith thus)
        Nunc natus est Altissimus.

[5]

The aungell songe thoo w*ith* many moo,
    'Gloria in altissimis!
In erthe be peas to man also,
    Et gaudium sit angelis.'
        For loue of vs (Scripture seith thus)
        Nunc natus est Altissimus.

[6]

The shepeherdes ran to Bedleme than
    Et inuenerunt puerum,
The whiche is p*er*fecte God *and* man
    Atq*ue* Saluator omniu*m*.
        For loue of vs (Scripture seith thus)
        Nunc natus est Altissimus.

[7]

When in suche wise founde hym they had,
    Vt dictum est per angelum,   [f. 34^r
Ayene they came, beyng full glad,
    Magnificantes Dominum.
        For loue of vs (Scripture seith thus)
        Nunc natus est Altissimus.

[8]

Nowe lete vs singe w*ith* angelis,
    'Gloria in altissimis,'
That we may come vnto that blis
    Vbi partus est virginis.
        For loue of vs (Scriptur*e* seith thus)
        Nunc natus est Altissimus.

76

Cambridge University Library. MS. Ee.
    I. 12   By James Ryman, *c.* 1492
f. 34^r

    Gloria in altissimis,
    For nowe is borne the King of Blis.

[1]

Whenne Criste was borne, an aungell bright
To shepeherdes keping shepe that nyght
Came and seyde w*ith* heuenly light,
    'Now Crist is borne, [the King of Blis.']

[2]

They dred gretely of that same light
That shone so bright that tyme of nyght
Thurgh the vertu, the grace, *and* myght
  Of Godd*es* Son, [the King of Blis.]

[3]

The aungell seyde, 'Drede ye nothing;
Beholde, to you grete joye I bringe,   [f. 34ᵛ
And vnto alle that be lyving,
  For now is born the King of Blis.

[4]

'Go to Bedleme, and there ye shall
With Marie myelde in an oxe stall
Fynde an infante that men shull call
  The Son of God *and* King [of Blis.']

[5]

They went furth to Bethelem that stounde,
And, as he tolde, a childe they founde
In an oxe stalle in ragg*es* wounde,
  The Son [of God and King of Blis.]

[6]

The sheperdes tho went home ageyn,
Magnifiyng God, in certayne,
In alle that they had hard *and* seyne
  Of Godd*es* Sonne, [the King of Blis.]

[7]

On New Yeres Day (Scripture seith thus)
Circumcided for loue of vs,
The name tho was called Jhesus
  Of Godd*es* Sonne, [the King of Blis.]

[8]

On Twelfth Daye came king*es* three
With golde, encense, *and* myrre so free,
Vnto Bedlem to seke and see
  The Sonne of God *and* King of Blis.

stza. 1, l. 4. MS. now crist is borne &c.
stza. 2, l. 4. MS. Of godd*es* son &c.
stza. 4, l. 4. MS. the son of god *and* king &c.
stza. 5, l. 4. MS. the son &c.
stzas. 6, 7, l. 4. MS. of godd*es* sonne &c.
stza. 8, l. 1. Twelfth] MS. xiiᵗʰ.

77

Balliol College, Oxford, MS. 354
                      XVI *cent.*
f. 231ᵛ

  Man meve thy mynd, *and* joy this fest:
  Veryt*a*s de t*er*ra orta est.

[1]

As I cam by the way,
  I saw a sight semly to see:
Thre sheperdes rangyng in aray,
  Vpon the feld*e* kepynge ther fee.
  A sterre, they said, they dide espie
    Kastyng the bemes owt of the est,
  And angell*es* makyng melodye:
    'Veritas de t*er*ra orta e*st*.'

[2]

Vpon th*a*t sight they were agast,
  Sayinge thes word*es* as I say the:
'To Bedlem shortly lett vs hast,
  And ther we shall the trewthe see.'
The angell said vnto the*m* all iii
    To th*er* comfort or eu*er* he seste,
  'Co*n*solamini, *and* mery be;
    Veritas de terra orta est.

[3]

'Fro*m* hevyn owt of the highest see
  Rightwisnes hath taken the way,
W*ith* m*er*cy medled ple*n*tuowsly,
  And so co*n*seyved in a may.
  Miranda res this is, in fay,
    So seith the pr*o*phet in his gest;
  Now is he born, Scripture doth say:
    Veritas de t*er*ra orta est.'

[4]

Than passed the shep*er*des fro*m* th*a*t place
  And folowed by the sterres beme
Th*a*t was so bright affore th*er* face,
  Hit browght the*m* streight vnto Bethlem.
  So bright it shon over all the realme
    Tyll they ca*m* th*er* they wold not rest,
  To Jury *and* Jerusalem;
    Veritas de t*er*ra orta est.

At end: Explicit.

78

Balliol College, Oxford. MS. 354
                      XVI *cent.*
f. 224ʳ

  Can I not syng but hoy,
  Wha*n* the joly shep*er*d made so mych joy.

[1]

The shep*er*d vpon a hill he satt;
He had on hy*m* his tabard *and* his hat,
Hys tarbox, hys pype, *and* hys flagat;
Hys name was called Joly, Joly Wat,

For he was a gud herd*es* boy.
   V*ith* hoy!
For in hys pype he made so mych joy.

[2]

The shep*er*d vpon a hill was layd;
Hys doge to hys gyrdyll was tayd;
He had not slept but a lytill broyd
But 'Gloria *in* excelc*is*' was to hym sayd.
   V*ith* hoy!
For *in* his pipe he mad so myche joy.

[3]

The shep*er*d on a hill he stode;
Rownd abowt hy*m* his shepe they yode;
He put hys hond vnder hys hode;
He saw a star as rede as blod.
   V*ith* hoy!
For *in* his pipe he mad so myche joy.

[4]

'Now farwell Mall, *and* also Will;
For my love go ye all styll
Vnto I cu*m* agayn you till,
And eu*er*more, Will, ryng well thy bell.'
   V*ith* hoy!
For *in* his pipe he mad so mych joy.

[5]

'Now must I go th*er* Cryst was borne;
Farewell, I cu*m* agayn tomorn;
Dog, kepe well my shep fro the corn,
And warn well, warroke, whe*n* I blow my
      horn.'
   V*ith* hoy!
For *in* hys pype he made so mych joy.

[6]

The shep*er*d sayd ano*n* ryght,
'I will go se yon farly syght,
Wheras the angell syngith on hight,
And the star th*at* shynyth so bryght.'
   V*ith* hoy!
For *in* [his] pipe he mad so mych joy.

[7]

Whan Wat to Bedlem cu*m* was,
He swet; he had gon fast*er* tha*n* a pace.
He fownd Jh*es*u in a sympyll place
Betwen an ox *and* an asse.
   V*ith* hoy!
For *in* his pipe he mad so mych joy.

[8]

'Jh*es*u, I offer to the here my pype,
My skyrte, my tarbox, *and* my scrype;

Home to my felowes now will I skype,
And also loke vnto my shepe.'
   V*ith* hoy!
For in his pipe he mad so myche joy.

[9]

'Now, farewell, myne own   [f. 224ᵛ
      herd*es*ma*n* Wat.'
'Ye, for God, lady, even so I hat.
Lull well Jh*es*u in thy lape
And farewell, Joseph, wyth thy rownd
      cape.'
   V*ith* hoy!
For *in* hys pipe he mad so myche joy.

[10]

'Now may I well both hope *and* syng,
For I haue bene a Cryst*es* beryng.
Home to my felowes now wyll I flyng.
Cryst of hevy*n* to his blis vs bryng!'
   V*ith* hoy!
For *in* his pip*e* he mad so myche joy.

The repetition of the burden is indicated as
   follows: stza. 1: ca*n* I not sing but hay &c.
   stza. 2: ca*n* I not syng.   stzas. 3, 6–8: ca*n*
   I not sing but hoy &c.   stza. 4: ca*n* I not
   syng &c.   sta. 5: ca*n* I not sing &.   stza. 9:
   ca*n* I not sing.
Stzas. 6 and 7 are transposed in MS., the correc-
tion being indicated by the prefixed letters a
and b.
stza. 8, l. 2. MS. My scrype my tarbox *and* my
   skyrte.
At end: Explicit.

79

A a. *Bodleian Library.* MS. Eng. poet. e. 1
                              XV *cent.*
f. 60ʳ

   Tyrle, tyrlo,
   So merylye the shepp*er*des began to
      blowe.

[1]

Abowt the fyld thei pyped full right,
Even abowt the midd*es* off the nyght;
Adown frome heven thei saw cu*m* a lyght.
   Tyrle, tirlo.

[2]

Off angels th*er* came a co*m*pany
With mery song*es* *and* melody;
The shepp*er*des anno*nn*e gane the*m* aspy.
   Tyrle, tyrlo.

[3]

'Gloria in excelsis,' the angels song,
And said who peace was present among
To euery man that to the faith wold long.
    Tyrle, tyrlo.

[4]

The shepperdes hyed them to Bethleme
To se that blyssid sons beme,
And ther they found that glorious streme.
    Tyrle, tyrlo.

[5]

Now preye we to that mek chyld,
And to his mothere that is so myld,
The wich was neuer defylyd.
    Tyrle, tyrlo.

[6]

That we may cum vnto his blysse
Where joy shall neuer mysse;
Than may we syng in paradice,
    'Tyrle, tirlo.'

[7]

I pray yow all that be here
Fore to syng and mak good chere
In the worship off God thys yere.
    Tyrle, tirlo.

b. *Balliol College, Oxford. MS.* 354, f. 222^r.
XVI *cent.* (burden and stzas. 1–5).

burden, l. 1. Tyrly, tirlow, tirly, terlow.
stza. 1, l. 1. full] *omits.*   l. 2. So meryly the
   sheperdes began to blow.   l. 3. thei saw
   cum a lyght] that ys so hygh.
stza. 2, l. 1. Off] *omits.*   l. 3. gane them] that
   gan.
stza. 3, l. 2. who] that   l. 3. to] *omits.*   long]
   fong.
stza. 4, l. 2, sons] son.   l. 3. streme] leme.
At end: Explicit.

B. MS. destroyed. Text from Craig.
                     1534
[Burden lacking]

Song I

As I out rode this enderes night,
Of the thre joli sheppardes I saw a sight,
And all abowte there fold a star shone
    bright;
    They sange terli, terlow,
    So mereli the sheppards ther pipes can
    blow.

Song III

Doune from heaven, from heaven so hie,
Of angeles ther came a great companie
With mirthe and joy and great solem-
    nitye;
    The[y] sange terly, terlow,
    So mereli the sheppards ther pipes can
    blow.

The accompanying note in MS. reads: Theise
songes / belonge to / the Taylors *and* Shearemens Pagant. / The first and the laste the
shepheards singe / and the second or middle-
most [No. 112] the women singe.

80

British Museum. MS. Harley 5396
                       XV *cent.*
f. 273^v

    Christo paremus cantica:
    'In excelsis gloria.'

[1]

When Cryst was born of Mary fre
In Bedlem, in that fayre cyte,
Angellis songen with myrth and gle,
    'In excelsis gloria.'

[2]

Herdmen beheld thes angellis bryght,
[T]o hem apperyd with gret lyght
[A]nd seyd, 'Goddys Sone is born this
    nyght;
    In excelsis gloria.'

[3]

[A ky]ng ys comyn to saue kynde,
[In the] Scriptur as we fynde;
[Therfor]e this song haue we in mynde:
    'In excelsis gloria.'

[4]

[Then, L]ord, for thy gret grace,
[Grau]nt us in blys to se thy face,
[Wh]ere we may syng to the solas:
    'In excelsis gloria.'

MS. heading (*in later hand*): A Christmas
Caroll.
*The MS. is damaged at the margin. The first
letters of lines in the last three stanzas are
thereby destroyed.*

81

A. *Cambridge University Library.* MS.
Ee. 1. 12 By James Ryman, *c.* 1492
f. 38ᵛ

Be we mery now in this fest,
In quo Saluator natus est.

[1]

Now in Betheleme, that holy place,
To bringe man oute of woofull case,
Of virgyn Marie full of grace
  Saluator mundi natus est.

[2]

To the sheperdes keping theire folde
On Cristemas nyght an aungell tolde
That in Bethelem with bestes bolde
  Saluator [mundi natus est.]

[3]

They were compassed all aboute with light,
And they dredde of that heuenly sight.
'Drede not,' he seyde, that aungell bright,
  'Saluator [mundi natus est.]

[4]

'Beholde, to you grete joye I bringe:
This day of Mary, that good thinge,
In the citie of Dauid, that king,
  Saluator [mundi natus est.]

[5]

'And this infant there fynde ye   [f. 39ʳ
    shalle
In pore clothing in an oxe stalle.'
The aungelles tho lawded God alle;
  Saluator [mundi natus est.]

[6]

'Glorie to God,' the aungelles songe,
'And peas in erthe good men amonge;
To save mankyende, that had done wronge,
  Saluator [mundi natus est.']

[7]

They toke theire way with good entent,
And to Bethelem right sone they went,
To see and know what that worde ment:
  'Saluator [mundi natus est.']

[8]

They founde Joseph and Mary myelde,
Wyfe, moder, *and* mayde vndefielde,
And in a stalle they founde that childe.
  Saluator [mundi natus est.]

[9]

Now seke we alle with hert *and* myende
This yonge infant tille we hym fyende
That of a mayde to save mankyende
  De virgine nunc natus est.

stzas. 2–8, l. 4. MS. Saluator &c.

B. *Huntington Library. Christmas carolles
    newely Inprynted* (Richard Kele)
                                c. 1550
p. [25]

Be we mery in this feste,
In quo Saluator natus est.

[1]

In Betheleem, that noble place,
As by prophesy sayd it was,
Of the vyrgyn Mary full of grace
  Saluator mundi natus est.

[2]

On Chrystmas nyght an angel it tolde
To the shephardes kepyng theyr folde
That into Betheleem with bestes wolde:
  Saluator mundi natus est.

[3]

The shephardes were compassed ryght;
About them was a great lyght;
'Drede ye nought,' sayd the   [p. [26].
    aungell bryght,
  'Saluator mundi natus est.

[4]

'Beholde, to you we brynge great joy,
For why Jesus is borne this day
To vs of Mary, that mylde may;
  Saluator mundi natus est.

[5]

'And thus in fayth fynde it ye shall,
Lyenge porely in an oxe stall.'
The shephardes than lauded God all,
  Quia Saluator mundi natus est.

The repetition of the burden is indicated as
  follows: stzas. 1–3: Be we mery. &c.   stzas.
  4, 5: Be mery. &c.
At end: Finis.

82

Cambridge University Library. MS. Ee.
I. 12　　　By James Ryman, *c.* 1492

f. 34ᵛ

In terra pax hominibus,
Quia natus est Dominus.　　　　[f. 35ʳ]

[1]

To the shepeherdes keping theire folde
That Crist was borne an aungell tolde,
And in Betheleem fynde hym they sholde,
　Positum in presepio.

[2]

They went furth to Bethelem that stounde,
And, as he tolde, that chielde they founde
In an oxe stalle, in ragges wounde,
　Qui regnat sine termino.

[3]

The sheperdes tho went home agayn,
Magnifiyng God, in certayne,
In alle that they had hurde *and* sayne
　De Jhesu Dei Filio.

[4]

On New Yeres Day (Scripture seith thus)
Circumcided for loue of vs,
His name tho was callid Jhesus,
　Testante euangelio.

[5]

On Twelfth Day came kinges thre
With golde, encense, and myrre so free,
And founde that King of Majestee
　In virginali gremio.

[6]

When they came to Herode, that　[f. 35ᵛ]
　king,
He bade them goo axe inquiring
Where this childe was (*and* worde hym
　bringe)
　Qui celi preest solio.

[7]

Sleping an aungell bade them wake
And to Herod no waye to take;
Another way, no dought to make,
　Reuersi sunt cum gaudio.

stza. 5, l. 1. Twelfth] MS. xiiᵗʰ.

83

St. John's College, Cambridge. MS. S. 54
XV *cent.*

f. 1ʳ

Of X *and* M *and* other too:
Of I *and* E I syng allso.

[1]

X for Cristes hymselfe was dyth,
As clerkys redyn in story ryth,
Qwan X *and* M with word was lyth
　To saue us fro the fendes flyth.

[2]

M begynnyth a gloryos name:
Mary modyr, withowtyn fane;
Qwan X *and* M was borne in same,
　Ouerr goy begynnyth to spr[i]ng.

[3]

Of E I wyll syng yytte:
On Cristes crose that leter was sette;
Qwan X *and* E togethe*r* mette,　[f. 1ᵛ]
　M *and* E in herte was woo.

[4]

I begynnyth the name of Jon;
Quan X upon the rode was done,
M *and* I stod styll alone,
　And hys postyllys went hym fro.

[5]

Theis iiii leterys wor[ch]yppe we all,
For Crist was borne in ox stalle
To bryng us from the dewlys all
　With hys wondys rede *and* bloo.

stza. 1, l. 3. word] MS. wrod (?) *The* w *is not
clear.*　l. 4. fro] MS. for.
stza. 4, l. 4. went] MS. wnet.　fro] MS. foro.
stza. 5. *This stanza is struck through in MS., and
some words are barely legible.*

84

Cambridge University Library. MS. Ee.
I. 12　　　By James Ryman, *c.* 1492

f. 40ʳ

　To Criste singe we, singe we, singe we,
　In clennes and in charite.

[1]

Mankyende was shent and ay forlore
For synne that Adam did before
Till of Mary Jhesus was bore
　[In clennes and in charite.]

[2]

As a swete floure bereth his odour*e*,   [f. 40ᵛ
So hath she borne our*e* Sauyour*e*
To bringe mankyende out of dolour*e*
  In clennes [and in charite.]

[3]

As the sonne beame goth thurgh the glas,
Thurgh her body Jhesus did pas,
Taking nature, as his wille was,
  In cle*n*nes [and in charite.]

[4]

Prophecy seide longe tyme before
That of a mayde Criste sholde be bore
Mankyende to blis for to restore
  In clennes [and in charite.]

[5]

Fro heven to erthe Crist did enclyne
To bringe mankynde fro woo *and* pyne,
Whome preyse we now w*ith* lawde dyvyne
  In clennes [and in charite.]

[6]

Preyse we also Mary so myelde,
That bare this chielde, she vndefielde,
Fro mortalle dethe mankyende to shilde
  In clennez [and in charite.]

stza. 2, l. 4. MS. In clennes &c.
stza. 4, l. 4. MS. in clennes &c.
stza. 3, l. 4. MS. in cle*n*nes &c.
stza. 6, l. 4. MS. In clennez &c.

85

British Museum. MS. Addit. 5665
                     XVI cent.

f. 11ᵛ

  Man, be joyfull, *and* myrth th*o*u make,
  For Crist ys made man for thy sake.
  Man, be joyfull, *and* myrth th*o*u make,
  For Cr[i]st is *made man for   [*f. 12ʳ
    thy sake.

[1]

Man, be mery, I the rede,
  But bewhar what merthis th*o*u make.
Crist ys clothed yn thy wede,
  And he ys made man for thy sake.

[2]

He cam fro hys Fader sete   [f. 11ᵛ
  Into this worlde to be thy make;
Man, bewar how th*o*u hym trete,
  For he ys made man for thy sake.

[3]

Loke th*o*u mercy ewyr crye,
  Now and allway, rathe *and* late,
And he will sette the wonder hye,
  For he ys made man for thy sake.

MS. heading: In die natiuitatis.

86

A. *British Museum.* MS. Sloane 2593
                       XV *cent.*

f 9ᵛ

  All*e*l*ui*a, all*e*l*ui*a,
  All*e*l*ui*a, all*e*l*ui*a,
  All*e*l*ui*a, all*e*l*ui*a,
    Deo Pat*ri* sit gl*o*ria.

[1]

Saluator mu*n*di, D*o*mi*n*e,
Fad*er* of Heuene, blyssid th*o*u be;
Th*o*u gretyst a mayde w*ith* on 'Aue',
  Q*ue* vocat*ur* Maria.

[2]

Adesto nu*n*c p*ro*picius;
Th*o*u sendyst thi Sone, swete Jh*esu*s,
Ma*n* to become for loue of vs;
  Deo Pat*ri* sit gl*o*ria.

[3]

Ne mente*m* sompn*us* oprimat;   [f. 10ʳ
Betwyx a*n* ox *and* a*n* as
Cryst hymself, born he was
  De virgine Maria.

[4]

Te reformator sensuu*m*;
Bothe lytil *and* mekil *and* alle a[nd] su*m*,
Wolcum the tyme th*at* now is com:
  Deo Pat*ri* sit gl*o*ria.

[5]

Gl*o*ria tibi, D*o*mi*n*e,
Thre p*er*sonys in Trenyte;
Blyssid mot they alle be;
  Deo Pat*ri* sit gl*o*ria.

B. *Bodleian Library.* MS. Ashmole 189
                       XV *cent.*

f. 107ʳ

  Alleluya, alleluya,
  Deo Pat*ri* sit gl*o*ria.

[1]

Saluator mundi, Domine,
Fader of Heuene, yblessyd thou be;
Thou gretyst a mayde with one 'Aue';
    Alleluya, alleluya.

[2]

Adesto nunc propicius;
Thou sendyst thy Sonne, swete Jesus,
Man to becum for loue of vs;
    Alleluya Deo.

[3]

Te reformator sensuum;
Lytyll and mekell, all and some,
Make ye mery for hym that ys ycom;
    Alleluya Deo.

[4]

Gloria tibi, Domine,
Joy and blysse among vs be,
For att thys tyme borne ys he;
    [Alleluya Deo.]

stza. 2, l. 1. propicius] MS. propiciuus.
stza. 4, l. 2, and] MS. and and.

C. *Bodleian Library*. MS. Eng. poet. e. 1
                     XV cent.
f. 20ʳ

    Alleluia, alleluia,
    De virgine Maria.

[1]

Saluator mundi, Domine,
Fader of Hevyn, blessyd thou be,
And thi Son that commeth of the,
    De virgine Maria.

[2]

Adesto nunc propicius;
He sent hys Sonne, swet Jhesus,
A man becam for loue of vs,
    De virgine Maria.

[3]

Te reformator sensuum;
Lytyl and mekyll, mor and sum,
Worshyp that chyld that is cum
    De virgine Maria.

[4]

Gloria tibi, Domine,
Thre persons in Trinite;
Worshepe that chyld so fre,
    De virgine Maria.

87

British Museum. MS. Sloane 2593
                      XV cent.
f. 5ᵛ

    Jhesu, Jhesu, Jhesu, Jhesu,
    Saf vs alle thorw thi vertu.

[1]

Jhesu, as thou art our Sauyour,
That thou saue vs fro dolour;
Jhesu is myn peramour;
    Blyssid be thi name, Jhesu.

[2]

Jhesu was born of a may
Vpon Cristemesse Day;
Sche was may beforn and ay;
    Blyssid be thi name, Jhesu.

[3]

Thre kynges comen fro segent;
To Jhesu Cryst they browte present;
Lord God omnipotent,
    Saf us alle throw thi vertu.

[4]

Jhesu deyid and schad his blod
For al mankynde vpon the rod;
He graunt vs grace of happis good,
    I beseke the, swete Jhesu.

[5]

Jhesu, for thi moderes sake,
Kepe vs fro the fyndis blake,
Ayens hym that we mown wake,
    And saue vs alle throw thi vertu.

stza. 3, l. 1. comen] MS. comme. l. 3. omnipo-
tent] MS. ommipotent.

88

Cambridge University Library. MS. Ee.
    I. 12   By James Ryman, *c.* 1492
f. 37ʳ

    Nowe in this fest, thy holy fest,
    Saluator mundi natus est.

[1]

Auctor of helthe, Criste, haue in myende
That thou hast take fourme of mankyende,
Of a pure virgyn beyng borne
To save mankyende, that was forlorne.

[2]

O brightnes *and* light of the Fader of
  Myght,
O eternall hope of euery wight,
What prayers thy *seruantes* myelde to the
Thurgh alle this worlde doth yelde, thou
  see.

[3]

This *present* day berith witnesse clere,
Now come by compas of the yere,
That thou art come fro blis an hy,
The welthe of this worlde alone onely.

[4]

Heven and erthe, the see and al thing
That is theryn, joyeth lawding   [f. 37^v
The Fader of Blis, thyne auctor of birth,
W*ith* songe of melody and myrthe.

[5]

And we also, that w*ith* thy bloode
Be bought ageyn vpon the roode,
For the daye of thy natiuitie
A newe songe we do singe to the.

[6]

Glorie mote be, good Lorde, to the,
That arte borne of a virgyne free,
W*ith* the Fader and Holy Goost,
Both Three *and* One, of mygh*tes* moost.

89

British Museum. MS. Addit. 5665
XVI cent.

f. 17^v

  Haue m*er*cy of me, Kyng of Blisse,
  As muche as thy mercy ys.
  Haue m*er*cy of me, Kyng of Blisse,
  As much *as thy mercy ys.   [*f. 18^r

[1]

Of Mary Criste was bor*e*,
W*ith*owte wem of aney hore,
To saue vs that wer*e* forlor*e*,
  Kyng of all kyng*es*.

[2]

To v*s* he gaffe a sompell abowte   [f. 17^v
That we shulde noght be prowte,
For he was wrapped in a clawte,
  Kyng of all kyng*es*.

[3]

Pray we Jh*esu*, Heuen Kyng,
Allso after owre endyng,
To his blysse eu*er*lastyng,
  Kyng off all kyng*es*.

MS. heading: In die natiuitatis.
stza. 2, l. 1. vs] MS. v*us*.
Signature: Smert hared de Plymptr*e*.

90

St. John's College, Cambridge. MS. S. 54
XV cent.

f. 2^r

  Nowell, nowell, ell, ell:
  Iwys, yt ys a wu*n*der nowell.

[1]

Jh*esu* restyd in a may
xl wek*es* and a day;
Th*er*fore I may syng *and* say,
  'Nowell, ell, ell.'

[2]

At the fest of archit*ri*clyn
Crist t*ur*nyd wat*er* into wyn,
And th*er*fore xall this song be myn:
  'Nowell, ell, ell.'

[3]

Jh*esu*, asse th*ou* art Hewyn Kynge,
Grawnt v*s* all thi der*e* blyssynge,
Hosyll and schrift at our*e* endynge.
  Nowell, ell, ell.

stza. 3, l. 2. vs] MS. v*us*.   l. 3. schrift] MS.
schirft.

91

A. *British Museum.* MS. Addit. 5665
XVI cent.

f. 43^v

  Jhesu, fili virginis,
  Miserere nobis.
  Jhesu, fili virginis,
  Miserere *nobis.   [*f. 44^r

[1]

Jhesu, of a mayde th*ou* woldest be born,
To saue mankynde, that was forlorne,
  And all for owr*e* synnes.
  Miserere nobis.

[2]

Angelis ther were, mylde of   [f. 43ᵛ
     mode,
Song to th*a*t swete fode
  W*ith* joye and blisse.
  Miserere nobis.

[3]

n a cracche was th*a*t chylde layde;
othe oxe *and* asse w*ith* hym playde,
  W*ith* joye *and* blisse.
  Miserere nobis.

[4]

Then for v*s* he shadde his blode,
And allso he dyedde vn the rode,
  And for v*s*, ywysse.
  Miserere nobis.

[5]

And then to helle he toke the way,
To raunson h*e*m th*a*t ther*e* lay,
  W*ith* joy *and* blisse.
  Miserere nobis.

MS. heading: de natiuitate.
stza. 4, ll. 1, 3. v*s*] MS. v*us*.

B. *British Museum.* MS. Addit. 5665
                                        XVI *cent.*
f. 29ᵛ
  Jhesu, fili virginis,
  Miserere nobis.
  Jhesu, fili virgi*nis,   [*f. 30ʳ
  Miserere nobis.

[1]

Jhesu, of a mayde thow woldest be born,
To saue mankynde, th*a*t was forlorn,
  And all for owre mysse.
  Miserere nobis.

[2]

Born thow wher*e* of Mary free,   [f. 29ᵛ
And thow deidist vpon the rode tree
  For owre mysse.
  Miserere nobis.

MS. heading: de natiuitate.
stza. 1, l. 1. born] MS. bron.
Signature: Smert.

92

Cambridge University Library. MS. Ee.
1. 12   By James Ryman, *c.* 1492
f. 104ᵛ
  O rex noster Emanuel,
  Thou art welcu*m* with us to dwell.

[1]

Thou art solace in alle oure woo,
  And thou art oure confort as welle;
Therfore, goode Lorde, sith it is soo,
  Thou art welcum [with us to dwell.]

[2]

Thou hast take us alle fro our*e* foo,
  And thou hast brought us owte of helle;
Thou art oure Lorde; we haue no moo;
  Thou art welcum [with us to dwell.]

[3]

Thou were born of a meyden mylde
  Vppon a day, so itte befelle;
Therfore we sey, bothe man and childe,
  'Thou arte welcum with us to dwelle.'

stza. 1, l. 4. MS. Thou art welcum cᵒ.

93

Bodleian Library. MS. Eng. poet. e. 1
                                        XV *cent.*
f. 45ᵛ
  Hey now, now, now!

[1]

Swet Jh*e*s*u*s
Is cu*m* to vs,
  This good ty*m* of Crystmas;
Wherfor w*ith* prays
Syng we always,
  'Welcu*m*, owr Messyas.'

[2]

The God Almyght
And Kyng of Lyght,
  Whose powr is ou*er* all,
Gyue vs of gr*a*ce
For to purchas
  Hys realme celestyall.

[3]

Whe[r] hys au*n*gels
And archa*n*gels
  Do syng incessantly,

Hys p*r*incypates
And potestates
  Maketh gret armony.

[4]

The cherubyns   [f. 46ʳ
And seraphyns
  W*ith* th*er* tvnykes mery,
The trones al,
Most musycall,
  Syng the heuenly Kery.

[5]

The vertues clere
Ther tunes bere,
  Th*er* quere for to repaye,
Whose song to hold
Was manyfold
  Of domynacyons fayer.

[6]

W*ith* on acord
S*e*rue we th*a*t Lord
  W*ith* lavdes *and* orayson,
The wych hayth sent
By good assent
  To vs hys onely Sone.

[7]

Borne ful porly,
Redy to dey
  For to redeme vs all,
In the Jury
Of mayd Mary
  In a poore oxes stall.

[8]

He taught the sawes
Of Cryste*n* lawes
  To hys apostels twelue;
In flome Jordan
Of good Saynt Johan
  He was crystned hy*m*selue.

[9]

Hy*m*selfe ded preche   [f. 46ᵛ
And the folke tech
  The co*m*mavndm*e*ntes tene;
He went barfote,
Th*a*t swete herte rote,
  Exa*m*ple to al mene.

[10]

The lame *and* blynd,
Me*n* owt of mynd,
  And the demonyacle,

The deef *and* dombe,
Me*n* layd in tombe
  Wher hol by hys myracle.

[11]

The Jewes truly
Had g*r*ete enuy
  To se hys myght exp*r*esse;
Thei ded *con*spyre
By g*r*ete desyre
  To deth hy*m* for to dresse.

[12]

But by hys myght
Thei had no syght
  To know hys corpolence
Tyll vnwysse bold
Judas hy*m* sold
  For thyrty golde*n* pence.

[13]

Than thei hy*m* tost,
And at a post
  Thei bownd hy*m* lyk a thefe;
Thei ded hy*m* bete
W*ith* scorges g*r*ete
  To put hy*m* to reprefe.

[14]

Nakyd *and* bare
Hys flesch thei tare,
  And w*ith* a crowne of thorne
Thei ded hy*m* crowne
(The blod rane downe)
  And gaue hy*m* a rede *in* scorne.

[15]

W*ith* mokk*es and* mowes,   [f. 47ʳ
Buffetes *and* blowes,
  And oth*er* cursed thewes,
Thei gan to cry
Dyspytously,
  'Al hayle the Kyng of Jewes!'

[16]

W*ith* dredfull othes,
The wych hy*m* lothes,
  Thei cryd, 'Crucifige!'
To Caluary
Thei gane hy*m* hy;
  The crosse hymself bar he.

[17]

They hym naylyd
And yl flaylyd,
  Alas, th*at* innocent!
Lunges, blynd knyght,
W*ith* al hys myght
  W*ith* a spere hys hart rent.

[18]

Wat*ur and* blod
Fro hys hart yode,
  And yet th*at* blyssyd Sone
Prayd for thosse
Th*at* ware hys fose
  To get for them p*er*done.

[19]

Lo, what kyndnesse
I*n* owr dystresse
  Th*at* Lord ded schow vs than,
The deth to tak
Al for owr sake
  And bryng vs fro Satha*n*.

[20]

Owr Sauyour,   [f. 47ᵛ]
Our Creatur
  On the crosse deyed ther;
Of newe tourme*n*t
We do hy*m* rent
  Whan we hys me*m*bres swer.

[21]

Then let vs pr*ay*
Both nyght *and* day
  To hy*m* p*er* omn*i*a
Th*at* we may cu*m*
To hys kyn[g]dome
  In finis secula.

MS. heading: A song i*n* the tvne of / and I were
a mayd &c.
The burden is first written after stza. 1. The
repetition is indicated after each following
stanza save the last by: hey &c.

94

British Museum. MS. Lansdowne 379
                      c. 1500
f. 38ʳ

  Mirabilem misteriu*m*:
  The Son of God ys man becum.

[1]

A m*er*velus thyng I hafe musyd in my
  mynde:
  Howe th*at* Veritas spronge owghte of the
    grounde,
And Justicia for all mankynde,
  From heuen to erthe he cam adowne.

[2]

Than M*a*ria, that marcyfull maye,
  Seyng man was dampnde for hys tre[s]pas,
Hathe sent down Sapie*n*cia, the sothe to
  saye,
  Man to redeme and bryng to grase.

[3]

Celestyall cytezens, for vs th*at* yowe pr*ay*e
  To hym th*at* ys bothe Alpha and O,
That we maye be sauyd on dom*us*daye
  And browghte to th*at* blysse he bowghte
    vs to.

The repetition of the burden is indicated as
follows: stzas. 1, 2: Mirabilem misterium
&ce. stza. 3: Mirabile*m* misterium the son
of &ce.
stza. 3, l. 2. O] MS. oo.

95

a. *British Museum.* MS. Cotton Vespasian
  A. xxv   XVI *cent.*
f. 131ᵛ

  By reason of two *and* poore of one
  This tyme God *and* man was set at one.

[1]

God against nature thre wonders haith
  wrought:
  First of the vile earthe mad man w*i*thout
    man,
Then woman w*i*thout woman of man maid
  of nought,
  And so man w*i*thout man in woman than.
Thus, lo, God *and* man together begane,
  As two for to joine together in one,
  As at this good tyme to be sett at one;
    Thus God begane
    This world for to forme *and* to en-
      crease man.

[2]

Angell in heaven for offence was damned,
  And man also for beinge variable;
Whether shuld be saved was examyned,
  Man or yet angell; then God was greable

To answer for man, for man was not able,
  And said man had mocyon *and*
    angell had none,
Wherefore God *and* man shuld be
    seit at one.
  Thanke we him than
That thus did leaue angell *and* saved
  man.

[3]

The devill clamed man by bargan as this:
  For an appell, he said, man was bought
    and solde;
God aunswered *and* said the bargan was
    his:
  'Withe myne to be thyne how durst
    thoue be so bolde?
Man myne, syne thyne; wherfore thoue
    art now told
Thoue bought nought; then taike
    nought; thi bargan is [don;]
Wherfore God and man shal be set att
    one.'
  Nowe blessed be he,
For we that are bownde, loe, [f. 132ʳ
  nowe are maid free.

[4]

Betwene God *and* man th*er* was great
    distaunce,
For man said th*at* God shuld haue kept
    him vpryght,
And God said man maid all the variaunce,
  For th'apple to sett his com*m*aundement
    so light;
Wherfore, of his m*er*cye sparinge the
    ryght,
  He thought God and man shuld be
    set at one.
  Seing th*at* God *and* man was set at
    one,
    What kindnes was this,
To agree w*ith* man *and* the fault not his!

[5]

Withe man and woman th*er* was great
    traverse:
  Man said to the woma*n*, 'Woe myght
    th*o*u be!'
'Nay,' quod the woman, 'Why dost thoue
    reverse?
For womans entisinge woe be to the!
For God [made] man the heade and
    ruler of me.'

Thus God sawe man *and* woman were
    not at one;
  He thought in a woman to sett theime
    at one
    To our solace;
His m*er*cye he graunted for our trespace.

[6]

Of womanhede, lo, thre degres there be:
  Widowehede, wedlocke, and v*ir*ginnitie.
Widowehede clamed heauen; her title is
    this:
  By oppressions that mekelie suffrethe
    she,
A[nd] wedlocke by generac*i*on heauen
    hires shuld be,
And v*ir*gins clame by chastite alone.
  Then God thought a woman shoulde
    set them at one
    And cease th*er* strife,
For Marie was maden, widowe, and
    wife.

[7]

The ritche and the pore th*er*   [f. 132ᵛ
    title did reherse:
  The pore clamed heauen throughe his
    pacie*nt* havo*ur*;
He saide, 'Beati paup*er*es,' and further
    the v*er*se;
  The riche man by ritches thought hym
    in favo*ur*,
  For who was so ritche as was our
    Saviour?
  And againe who so pure as he was one
    In hey when he ley to set vs at one?
    Who grau*nt* vs peace
And at the last ende the great joyes
    endles.

burden, l. 1. *Above* poore *is written*: no.
stza. 3, l. 2. appell] MS. thappell.   l. 4.
thyne] MS. myne.   l. 6. *The last word is
covered by a binding strip.*
stza. 6, l. 5. *written in MS. after* l. 7.
At end: Finis.

b. *Tokyo, Toshiyuki Takamiya.* MS. Takamiya 6, f. 118ᵛ. *c.* 1531 (burden and
stzas. 1, 2).

MS. heading: A carolle.
burden, l. 1. two] ii.   l. 2. was] were.
stza. 1, l. 1. thre wonders] iii thyngys.
  l. 4. so] *omits.* l. 5. lo] *omits.* l. 6. two] ii.
  for] *omits.* l. 7. at this good] one this.
  l. 8. Thus] This. l. 9. for] *omits.* and]
  omits.
stza. 2, l. 1. Angell] Angellis. l. 2. man also]
  man. l. 3. shuld] these shulde. was] it
  was. l. 4. yet] *omits.* l. 9. did leaue
  lefte.

96

British Museum. MS. Addit. 5665
XVI *cent.*

f. 26ᵛ

> T[e Deum] laudamus,
> Te Dominum confitemur,
> Te et*er*num.

[1]

O blesse God in Trinite,   [f. 27ʳ
   Grete cause we haue to blesse thy name,
That now woldest sende downe fro the
   The Holy Gost to stynte our*e* blame.
     Te Deum laudamus.

[2]

Syng we to God, Fader eternall,   [f. 26ᵛ
   That luste to june w*ith* oure nature
The Sone of hym celestiall,
   Man to be borne oure saulis to cure:
     'Te Deum [laudamus.']

[3]

All te seynt*es* in heuen on hye,   [f. 27ʳ
   And all that buthe in erthe allso,
Geff laude *and* thangk*es* deuotelye
   To God abowe and syng hym to:
     'Te Deum [laudamus.']

MS. heading: de natiuitate d*om*ini.
The third line of the burden is marked: Faburdon.

97

Bodleian Library. MS. Douce 302
By John Audelay, XV *cent.*

f. 28ᵛ

> In reu*er*ens of oure Lord i*n* heue*n*,
> Worchip this mart*er*, swete Se*n*t Steue*n*.

[1]

Saynt Steue*n*, the first martere,
He ched his blod i*n* herth here;
Fore the loue of h*i*s Lord so dere
   He sofird payn *and* passion.

[2]

He was stonyd w*ith* stons ful cruelle,
And sofird h*i*s payn ful pasiently:
'Lord, of myn enmes th*o*u haue m*er*ce,
   Th*a*t wot not what thai done.'

[3]

He beheld i*n*to heue*n* on he
And se Jh*e*su stonde i*n* h*i*s majeste
And sayd, 'My soule, Lord, take to the,
   And foreyif myn enmys eu*er*echon.'

[4]

The*n*, whe*n* th*a*t word he had sayd,
God th*er*of was wel apayd;
His hede mekele to slep he layd;
   His sowle was takyn to heue*n* anon.

[5]

Swete Saynt Steue*n*, for vs th*o*u pr*a*y
To th*a*t Lord th*a*t best may,
Whan *our* soule schal wynd away,
   He grawnt *us* al remyssion.

MS. heading: In die s*an*c*t*i stephani.
stza. 1, l. 2. He] MS. h*i*t.

98

Trinity College, Cambridge. MS. O. 3. 58
XV *cent.*

recto

> Eya, martir Stephane,
> Prey for vs, we pr*e*y to the.

[1]

Of this mart*er* make we mende,
   Qui triu*m*phauit hodie
And to heuene blysse gan wende
   Dono celestis gracie.

[2]

Stonyd he was wyth stonys grete
   Feruor*e* gentis impie;
Than he say Cryst sitte in sete,
   Innixu*m* Patris dextere.

[3]

Thov pr*e*ydyst Cryst for thi*n* enmyse,
   O martir inuictissime;
Thou pr*e*y for vs that hye Justyse
   Vt nos purget a crimine.

At end: Amen.

99

British Museum. MS. Addit. 5665
XVI *cent.*

f. 22ᵛ

> Pray for vs that we saued be,
> Prothomartir Stephane.
> Pray for vs that we sauede be,
> Protho*martir Sthephane.   [*f. 23ʳ

[1]

In this vale off wrecchednesse
Yprewed was thy mekenesse;
Ther thow arte in joye and blisse,
  Circumfultus vndique.

[2]

With faith yarmed in feld to   [f. 22ᵛ]
  fyghth,
Sad thou stodest as Godys knygh[t],
Prechyng the pepill of Godes myghth,
  Manens plenus gratia.

[3]

Before the tyrand thou were broght;
Strokes off payne thou dredest noght;
God was with the in all thy thought,
  Spes eterne glorie.

[4]

With synfull wrecchys thou were   [f. 23ʳ]
  take;
Thy feyth thou woldest not forsake,
But rathere to dye for Godes sake,
  Circumfusio sanguine.

MS. headings: Stephen. Sancti Stephani.

100

Balliol College, Oxford. MS. 354
                       XVI *cent.*
f. 228ʳ

  Nowe syng we both all *and* sum,
  'Lapidauerunt Stephanum.'

[1]

Whan Seynt Stevyn was at Jeruzalem,
Godes lawes he loved to lerne,
That made the Jewes to cry so clere *and*
  clen,
  'Lapidaverunt Stephanum.'

[2]

The Jewes, that were both false *and* fell,
Agaynst Seynt Stephyn they were cruell;
Hym to sle they made gret yell
  Et lapidaverunt Stephanum.

[3]

They pullid hym withowt the town,
And than he mekely kneled down
While the Jewes crakkyd his crown,
  Quia lapidaverunt Stephanum.

[4]

Gret stones *and* bones at hym they caste;
Veynes *and* bones of hym they braste,
And they kylled hym at the laste,
  Quia lapidaverunt Stephanum.

[5]

Pray we all that now be here
Vnto Seynt Stephyn, that marter clere,
To save vs all from the fendes fere.
  Lapidaverunt Stephanum.

MS. marks burden: fote.
At end: Explicit.

101

A. *Huntington Library. Christmas carolles
newely Inprynted* (Richard Kele)
                           c. 1550
p. [33]
  To Saynt Steuen wyll we pray
  To pray for vs bothe nyght and day.

[1]

Of Saynt Steuen, Goddes knyght,
That preched the fayth day *and* nyght:
He tolde the Jewes, as it was ryght,
  That Chryst was borne of a may.

[2]

The Jewes sayd in grete scorne
That Christ was not of a mayde borne;
'Than,' sayd Steuen, 'ye are but lorne,
  And all that beleue in your lay.

[3]

'Now is spronge the welle of lyfe,
Of Mary, moder, mayde, and wyfe.'
Therfore the Jewes fell at stryfe,
  And with Steuen than dysputed they.

[4]

The wycked Jewes at the last,   [p. [34]]
Stones at Steuen they gan cast;
His hed and armes they all to-brast
  And made his body in foule aray.

[5]

Steuen, that was full mylde of mode,
Though he were all reed in blode,
In his prayers styll he stode,
  And cryeng to God thus he dyde say:

[6]

'Lorde God, for thy myghtfull grace,
Forgyue the Jewes theyr trespace,
And gyue theym grace to se thy face
    In the joye that lasteth aye.'

[7]

To heuen he loketh soone on hye,
To the Father and Sone truly,
And to the Holy Ghost he gan cry,
    'Receyue my soule, I the pray.'

[8]

God receyued his boone anone;
Downe came aungeles many one;
They toke his soule *and* to heuen dyd gone,
    To blyssednesse that lasteth ay.

[9]

To that blysse that is so goode,
Jhesu, that dyed vpon the roode,
Graunt vs for his precyous bloode [p. [35]
    Our saluacyon at domesday.

Heading in original: Of saynt Steuen.
stza. 5, l. 2. Though] Orig. Thought.
    l. 4. God] Orig. good.
At end: Finis.

B. *Huntington Library. Christmas carolles
    newely Inprynted* (Richard Kele)
                                    c. 1550
p. [42]

    Blessyd Stephan, we the praye,
    Pro nobis preces funde.

[1]

I shall you tell this ylke nyght
Of Saynt Stephan, Goddes knyght:
He tolde the Jewes that it was ryght
    That Cryst was borne of a mayde.

[2]

Then sayd the Jewes w*ith* grete scorne
That Goddes Sone myght not be borne;
Stephan sayd, 'Ye be forlorne,
    And all that byleueth on that lay.'

[3]

This Stepha*n*, wha*n* he was most p*er*fyte,
In Crystes lawe illumynate,
The Jewes hym toke with grete dyspyte
    Without the towne to lapidate.

[4]

The cursyd Jewes at the last,
Stones at Stephan they gan cast;
They bette hym and bounde hym fast
    And made his body in foule aray.

The repetition of the burden is indicated after
    each stanza by: Blessyd Stephan. &c.

C. *British Museum.* MS. Egerton 3307
                                    XV *cent.*
f. 54ᵛ

    The holy m*ar*ter Steue*n* we pray
    To be ou*r* soco*ur* both nyght and day.

[1]

I schal yow tell this ilk nyght
Of Seynt Steuen, God*es* knyght:
He told the Jewis th*at* it was ryght
    Th*at* C*ri*st was born of a may.

[2]

Than sayd the Jewis w*ith* grett scorn
Th*at* God Son myght not be born;
Steue*n* than sayd, 'Ye be forlorn,
    And all that leue*n* in that lay.'

[3]

Now ys sprong the wel of lyff
Of Mary, moder, madyn, and wyff;
Therfor the Jewis fel in stryff,
    Dysputy*ng* w*ith* Steue*n* aganys hys fay.

[4]

The cursyd Jewys at the last,
Stonys to Steuen thei gan cast;
Thei betyn hym and band hym fast
    And made hys body in fowle aray.

[5]

Into the feld thei led hym tho,
And than hym folowyd many a fo;
Thei greiuyd on hym and dyd hym wo;
    Hem though*t* thei had a nowbyll play.

[6]

The Jewys that wer bothe styff and strong,
Thei stonyd hym and dyd [hym] wrong—
Gret stonys abowte hym sprong—
    And sayd, 'Wee thi meyd schall pay.'

The text of the burden is repeated as chorus.
The burden is written again at the end: The
    holy martyr steue*n* we pr*ay*. To be our socou*r*
    bothe nyght and day.

102

Bodleian Library. MS. Douce 302
       By John Audelay, XV *cent.*
f. 28ᵛ

I pray youe, breder euerechon,
Worchip this postil, swete Saynt Jon.

[1]

Synt Jon is Cristis derlyng dere;
He lenyd on his brest at his sopere,
And ther he made hym wonderful chere
Tofore his postilis euerechon.

[2]

'Saynt Jon,' he said, 'my dere derlyng,
Take my moder into thi kepyng;
Heo is my joy, my hert swetyng;
    Loke thou leue not here anon.

[3]

'Jon, I pray the, make here good chere,
With al thi hert *and* thi pouere;
Loke ye to pert not in fere
    In wat cuntre that euer ye goon.

[4]

'I comawnd youe, my postilis alle,
When my moder doth on youe calle,
Anon on knyes that ye down falle,
    And do here worchip therwith anon.

[5]

'I pray youe al on my blessyng,
Kepe ye charete fore one thyng;
Thenke what I said in your waschyng,
    Knelyng tofore youe on a stone.

[6]

'Farewel now, I wynd away youe fro;
To Jerusalem I most goo
To be betrayd of my fo
    And sofir payn *and* passiown.'

[7]

'A, my Sun, my Heuen Kyng!'
Oure Lady therwith fell downe sonyng.
This was a dolful depertyng.
    Thai toke here vp with gret mon.

[8]

'A, my moder, my dere derlyng,
Let be thi wo *and* thi wepyng,
Fore I most do my Fader bidyng,
    Ellis redempcion were ther non.'

[9]

'Farewel, my fader, farewel, my childe.'
'Farewel, moder *and* maid mylde;
Fro the fynd I wil the childe
    And crowne the quene in heuen trone.'

[10]

Swete Saynt Jon, to the we pray,
Beseche that Lord that best may,
When our soulis schal wynd away,
    He grawnt vs al remyssion.

MS. heading: In die *Sancti* Johannis app*ostol*e
et Ewangeliste.
stza. 4, l. 3. knyes] MS. kynes.

103

A a. *Trinity College, Cambridge*. MS. O. 3.
58   XV *cent.*
recto

    Prey for vs the Prynce of Pees,
    Amice Cristi Johannes.

[1]

To the now, Cristes dere derlyng,
That were a maydyn bothe eld *and* yyng,
Myn herte is set to the to syng,
    Amice *Christ*i Johannes.

[2]

For thou were so clene a may,
The preuytes of heuene forsothe thou say
Qwan on Crystys brest thov lay,
    Amice *Christ*i Johannes.

[3]

Qwan Cryst beforn Pylat was browth,
Thov clene maydyn forsok hym nouth;
To deye wyth hym was al thy thowth,
    Amice *Christ*i Johannes.

[4]

Crystys moder was the betake,
A maydyn to ben a maydenys make;
Thov be oure helpe we be not forsake,
    Amice *Christ*i Johannes.

stza. 1, l. 2. *and* yyng] *written in left-hand margin, with insertion indicated by* a.

b. *Bodleian Library*. MS. Eng. poet. e. 1,
f. 40ʳ. XV *cent.*

c. *Balliol College, Oxford*. MS. 354, f. 222ʳ.
XVI *cent.*

d. *British Museum.* MS. Addit. 5665,
ff. 37ᵛ, 38ʳ. XVI *cent.*

e. *British Museum.* MS. Addit. 5665,
ff. 48ᵛ, 49ʳ. XVI *cent.* (burden and stzas.
1, 4).

MS. heading: d de Johanne. e de sancto
Johanne.
burden, l. 1. the] b d e thou. c to the.
l. 2. amice] b Amici (*so throughout*). d e
repeat entire burden.
stza. 1, l. 1. the now] c omits. Cristes dere
derlyng] d *words for one voice have* prince of
pes. dere] d *omits.* c e own. l. 2. That]
c d e The whyche. were] b c d was. a]
c d e *omit.* maydyn] b c e mayd. eld]
b c d e old. l. 3. Myn] c d e My. herte]
d e soule. to the] b for. c e a songe. d *omits.*
l. 4. Amice] b d Amici.
stza. 2. *The lines of this stanza appear in the
following different orders:* b c 1, 3, 2 4. d 3,
2, 1, 4.
l. 1. thou were] b c d he was. may] c mayd.
l. 2. preuytes] c prophettes. forsothe thou
say] b d ther he saye. c to hym sayd.
l. 3. Qwan] b c d *omit.* thov] b c d a slepe
he. lay] c layd.
stza. 3, l. 1. Qwan] d *omits.* l. 2. Thov] b
Hys. c thys. d The. maydyn] b c mayd.
l. 3. thy] b c d hys.
stza. 4, l. 1. the] b c d e hym. l. 2. A maydyn]
b e won mayd. c A mayd. a maydenys] b a
nodyrs. c a noder. d e a notherys.
l. 3. c pray we to hym that he vs not forsake.
d Troghffe theire helpe we shall not be forsake.
Thov be oure helpe] b To help that. e Be
they our helpe that.
At end: c Explicit.

B. *British Museum.* MS. Harley 4294
XV *cent.*
f. 81ᵛ

Prey we all to the Prynce of Pece,
Amice *Christi* Johannes.

[1]
I shall you tell of Crystes derlyng,
That was a mayd both old and yong;
My hert ys sett a song for to syng:
    Amice [Christi Johannes.]

[2]
Seynt Johan was so fayer a may,
[On] Crystes brest aslepe he layd;
[Hi]s pryvyteys of hevyn ther he sawe,
    Amice [Christi Johannes.]

[3]
Whan Cryst before Pylat was brought,
So clene a maydc forgat he nought;
For vs to dye was hys thought.
    Amice [Christi Johannes.]

[4]
Mary and Johan, by Cryst they stode;
Mary wept bothe water and blode
Whan she sawe her Sonne done on the
    roode.
    Amice [Christi Johannes.]

[5]
Mary, to Johan she was betake,
And for þe others make;
Prey we to Cryst we be nott forsake,
    Amice [Christi Johannes.]

*The MS. is damaged at the left-hand margin.
Some of the initial words of the lines have been
restored by a modern hand.*
stza. 2, l. 3. pryvyteys] MS. prytyteys.
stza. 5, l. 3. Prey] MS. prey y.

104
Bodleian Library. MS. Eng. poet. e. 1
XV *cent.*
f. 39ᵛ

To Almyghty God pray for pees,
Amice *Christi* Johannes.

[1]
O glorius Johan Euangelyste,
Best belouyd with Jhesu Cryst,
In cena Domini vpon hys bryst
    Eius vidisti archana.

[2]
Chosen thou art to Cryst Jhesu;
Thy mynd was neuer cast frome vertu;
The doctryne of God thou dydest renu
    Per eius vestigia.

[3]
Cryst on the rod in hys swet passyon
Toke the hys moder as to hyr sone;
For owr synnes gett grace and perdon
    Per tua sancta merita.

[4]
O most nobble of euangelystes all,
Grace to owr Maker for vs thou call,
And off swetenesse celestyall
    Prebe nobis pocula.

[5]

And aft*ur* the cowrs of mortalite
In heven w*ith* aungels for to be,
Sayyng 'Ozanna' to the T*r*inyte
Per seculoru*m* secula.

105

Balliol College, Oxford. MS. 354
XVI *cent.*
f. 228ᵛ

Pr*a*y for vs to the Trinite,
Joh*anne*s, *Christ*i care.

[1]

Thow dereste disciple of Jh*e*su Criste,
Most best belovid *and* best betriste,
Which at his last sop*er* did lye on his
    breste,
Sacra fluenta potare.

[2]

As he i*n* his passion to his dere moder
Toke the for her kep*er*, her son, *and* his
    broth*er*,
Pr*a*y th*a*t owr hart*es* may most of all other
Jh*e*su*m* semper amare.

[3]

And, as th*o*u the stronge veny*m*   [f. 229ʳ
    which ii me*n* had slayn
Drank w*ith*owt hurt *and* raysed the*m* agayn,
Pr*a*y th*a*t the veny*m* of syn may vs not payn,
Non poterit alligare.

[4]

As th*o*u ii men ther tresure dide restore,
Th*a*t had forsakyn *and* morned therfore,
Pr*a*y th*a*t we may fals riches forsak for
    eu*er*more,
Celis tesavrisare.

[5]

And pr*a*y th*a*t we may haue suche gr*a*ce
Here so to morne for owr trespas
Th*a*t we may stond siker beffore C*r*ist*e*s
    face,
Cu*m* venerit iudicare.

MS. marks burden: fote.
At end: Explicit.

106

*Huntington Library. Christmas carolles
    newely Inprynted* (Richard Kele) *c.* 1550
p. [35]

Pray for vs to God on hye,
Blyssed Saynt Johan and Our Lady.

[1]

O blessyd Johan the Euangelyst,
Ryght dere beloued of Jesu Cryst,
The preuyte of heue*n* in erthe thou wyst,
    As touchynge to the Trynyte.

[2]

That Prynce that is withouten pere,
To Johan he toke his mode[r] dere
All whyle she lyued in erthe here,
    That vyrgyns were, bothe he and she.

[3]

This noble Johan that we of rede
Informed vs of Chrystes dede
The whyle that he on erthe yede;
    In his gospell so fynde we.

[4]

Whan Chryst on crosse hanged   [p. [36]
    so hy,
He sayd vnto his moder Mary,
'Lo, there, thy sone standynge the by;
    And se thy moder, Johan,' sayd he.

[5]

Nowe pray we to this saynt echone
For vs to pray to God in trone,
Out of this lyfe whan we shall gone,
    To se hym in his mayeste.

Heading in original: Of saynt Joh*a*n.
At end: Finis.

107

*Huntington Library. Christmas carolles
    newely Inprynted* (Richard Kele) *c.* 1550
p. [5]

If thou be Johan, I tell it the
    Ryght with a good aduyce,
Thou may be glad Joh*a*n to be;
    It is a name of pryce.

[1]

The name of Johan wel prays I may
  It is full good, ywys;
'The grace of God' it is to say;
  It soundes nothyng amys.   [p. [6]
If thou be kyng in ryalte
  And of wyt full wyse,
Thou mayst be glad Johan to be;
  It is a name of pryce.

[2]

He is not worthy to hyght Johan,
  The oxe that is not whyght,
And thou art not worthy to hight Johan
  But grace be in the pyght.
If thou haue loue and charyte
  And voydest away all vyce,
Than art thou worthy Johan to be;
  It is a name of pryce.

[3]

Johan gaue baptyst vnto Chryst;
  Of grace was his prechyng;
And Saynt Johan Euangelyst
  Was Chrystes owne derlyng,
In penaunce and vyrgynyte
  He had full great delyce;
God graunt vs grace this Johan to be;
  It is a name of pryce.

[4]

If thou be cleped Nycolas,   [p. [7]
  Bothe in dede and fame,
Yet art thou Johan yf thou haue grace;
  It may well be thy name.
I tell the true the veryte,
  And so I haue done it, ywys:
Thou mayst be glad Johan to be;
  It is a name of pryce.

[5]

A comly wyght is now present;
  His name, ywys, is Johan;
Of his gret grace God hath sent
  To make vs merye eueruchone.
Be glad and mery in charyte,
  I pray you all lykewyse;
He is well worthy Johan to be;
  It is a name of price.

The repetition of the burden is indicated as
follows: stzas. 1–3: If thou be Johan. &c.
stzas. 4, 5: If thou be Johan. &c.
At end: Finis.

108

Bodleian Library. MS. Douce 302
                  By John Audelay, XV *cent.*
f. 28ᵛ

With al the reuer[en]s that we may
Worchip we Childermas Day.

[1]

Crist crid in cradil, 'Moder, ba ba!'
The childer of I[s]ral cridyn, 'Wa wa!'
Fore here merth hit was aga
  When Erod fersly cowth hem fray.

[2]

Al knaue childer with ii yere
Of age in Bedlem fere or nere,
Thai chedyn here blod with swerd and
    spere;
  Alas, ther was a rewful aray!

[3]

An hunderd and fourte thousand ther were;
Crist ham cristynd al in fere
In eor blod, and were martere,
  Al clene vergyns, hit is no nay:

[4]

The crisum childer to Crist con cry:
'We beth slayne fore gret enuy;
Lord, venge our blod fore thi mercy,
  And take our soulis to the, we pray.'

[5]

An heuenle voys answerd ayayn,
'Abyds a wyle, and sofer your payn;
Hent the nowmbir be eslayn
  Of your breder, as I you say.

[6]

'Fore ye han sofird marterdom   [f. 29ʳ
For Cristis sake, al and sum,
He wil youe crowne in his kyngdam,
  And folou the Lomb in joy for ay.'

MS. heading: In die sanctorum Innocencium.
stza. 6, l. 1. *This line is twice written, once as a
catch-line at the bottom of f.* 28ᵛ.

109

British Museum. MS. Addit. 5665
                        XVI *cent.*
f. 6ᵛ

Sonet laus per secula,
Innocentum gloria.
Sonet laus per secula,
Innocentum glori*a.   [*f. 7ʳ

[1]

Dic, Erodes impie,
  What awayleth thy cruellis
In ui[n]cules *pro* sanguine?
  Iputte in payne *with* grete dysstresse,
    Adiuuat te milicia?

[2]

Membra figi tenera   [f. 6ᵛ
  Thow gauest thy comowndement,
Matrum tenens viscera.
  Thy hope th*o*u lostte *and* thyn entent,
    Sternit dum milicia.

[3]

Reus nunc extinguere
  Infynyte *and* most of pyte,
Verens regnum perdere,
  In sorwe *and* woo thy see ys dyghtte;
    Vixit Dei milicia.

MS. heading: De innocentibus.
stza. 1, l. 3. ui[n]cules] MS. uiclues.

110

British Museum. MS. Addit. 5665
                              XVI *cent.*
f. 23ᵛ

  Psallite gaudentes,
  Infantum festa colentes.
  Psallite gaudentes,
  Infantu*m* festa colentes.

[1]

When God was born of Mary fre,   f. 24ʳ
Herode, the kyng of Galalee,
Was meued to malice by kyng*es* thre,
  Munera portantes,
  Munera portantes,
Regem natum venerantes.

[2]

Herode sende for men armed bryghth
To seke *and* sle [the] Kyng of Lyghth;
The blessed chylde drow fro Herod*es*
  myghth;

  .   .   .   .   .

  .   .   .   .   .

  Armati sunt perimentes.

MS. heading: de innocentibus.
stza. 2, l. 2. [the]] MS. &.   l. 4, 5, MS. *omits*
the repeated short line in this stanza.

111

British Museum. MS. Addit. 5665
                              XVI *cent.*
f. 24ᵛ

  Worcepe we this holy day,
  Th*a*t all Innocentis for vs pray.
  Worchepe we this holy day,
  That all Innocentis *for vs   *f. 25ʳ
  pray.

[1]

Herode, th*a*t was bothe wylde *and* wode,
Ful muche he shadde of Cristen blode,
To sle th*a*t chylde so meke of mode
  That Mary bare, th*a*t clene may.

[2]

Mary wi*th* Jh*e*su forthe yfrawght,   [f. 24ᵛ
As the angell hur towght,
To flee the londe till h*i*t wer*e* sowght;
  To Egyptte she toke hure way.

[3]

Herode sloo wi*th* pryde *and* synne
Thowsand*es* of ii yer*e and* wi*th*ynne;
The body of Criste he thoghft to wynne
  And to destrye the Cristen fay.

[4]

Now, Jh*e*su, th*a*t dyest for vs on   [f. 25ʳ
  the rode
And *c*ristendest Innocent*es* in hir blode,
By the p*r*ayer*e* of thy moder gode
  Bryng vs to blysse th*a*t lastith ay.

MS. heading: de innocentibus.
stza. 2, l. 4. Egyptte] MS. epytte.
stza. 4, l. 4. vs] MS. v*us*.

112

MS. destroyed. Text from Craig   1534

  Lully, lulla, *thow* littell tine child,
  By, by, lully, lullay, *thow* littell tyne child,
    By, by, lully, lullay!

[1]

O sisters too,
How may we do
  For to preserve this day
This pore yongling
For whom we do singe,
  By, by, lully, lullay?

[2]

Herod the king
In his raging,
  Chargid he hath this day
His men of might
In his owne sight
  All yonge children to slay.

[3]

That wo is me,
Pore child, for thee,
  And ever morne and may
For thi parting
Nether say nor singe,
  By, by, lully, lullay.

113

Bodleian Library. MS. Douce 302
              By John Audelay, XV *cent.*
f. 29ʳ

  I p*ra* you, sers, al i*n* fere,
  Worchip Seynt Thomas, thi*s* hole marter.

[1]

For on a Tewsday Thomes was borne,
And on a Tuysday he was p*re*st schorne,
And on a Tuysday his lyue was lorne,
  And sofyrd martyrda*m* wi*th* myld chere.

[2]

Fore Hole Cherche ryght al h*i*t was,
Ellis we had the*n* songyn 'Alas!'
And the child th*a*t vnborne was
  Schul haue boght his lyue ful dere.

[3]

Th*er* p*re*stis were thral he mad he*m* fre:
Th*a*t no clerke hongid schuld be
Bot eretyke or fore traytre,
  Yif one soche case fel th*er* were.

[4]

The[n] no child cristo*n* schuld be,
Ne clerke take ordere i*n* no degre,
Ne mayde mared i*n* no cu*n*tre
  Wi*th*out trebeut i*n* the kyng dangere.

[5]

Th*us* Hole Cherche he mad fre;
Fore fyfte poyntis he dyed treuly;
In heue*n* worchipt mot he be,
  And fad*er and* mod*er* hi*m* gete *and* bere.

MS. heading: de sancto Thome archie*piscop*o
  cantuarien*ci*.
stza. 4, l. 3. Ne] MS. the.

114

a. *British Museum.* MS. Sloane 2593
                              XV *cent.*
f. 23ᵛ

  A, a, a, a,
  Nu[n]c gaudet ecclesia.

[1]

Lestenytgh, lordyng*es*, bothe grete *and*
    smale;
I xal *yo*u telyn a wond*er* tale,
How Holy Cherche was brow[t] i*n* bale
  Cu*m* magna iniuria.

[2]

The greteste clerk of al this lond,
Of Cauntyrbery, ye vnd*er*stond,
Slawy*n* he was [with] wykkyd hond,
  Demonis pote*n*cia.

[3]

Knyt*es* kemyn fro Hendry Kyng,
Wykkyd me*n*, wi*th*oute lesyng;
Th*er* they dedy*n* a wond*er* thing,
  Feruentes insania.

[4]

They sowty*n* hy*m* al abowty*n*,
Wi*th*ine the paleys *and* wi*th*outy*n*;
Of Jh*es*u Cryst hadde they no*n* dowte
  In sua malicia.

[5]

They openyd her*e* mowthis wond*er* wyde;
To Thomeys they spoky*n* mekyl pryde:
'Here, treto*ur*, th*o*u xalt abyde,
  Ferens mort*is* tedia.'

[6]

Thomas answerid wi*th* mylde chere,
'If ye wil me slon in this maner*e*,   [f. 24ʳ
Let he*m* pasy*n*, alle tho arn her*e*,
  Sine co*n*tumilia.'

[7]

Beforn his aut*er* he knelyd adou*n*;
Th*er* they gu*n*ne to pary*n* his crown;
He sterdy*n* the braynys vp *and* dou*n*,
  Optans celi gaudia.

[8]

The turme*n*towr*es* abowty*n* sterte;
Wi*th* dedly wondys thei gu*n*ne hi*m* hurte;
Thomas deyid in Mod*er* Cherche,
  P*er*gens ad celestia.

[9]

Mod*er*, clerk, wedue, *and* wyf,
Worchepe ye Thomeys i*n* al your lyf
For lii poynt*es* he les his lyf,
    Contr*a* reg*is* consilia.

stza. 7, l. 1. aut*er*] MS. au*n*ter.

b. *Gonville & Caius College, Cambridge.*
MS. 383, pp. 68, 69. XV *cent.* (burden
and stzas. 1, 3, 2, 4–6, 8, 9).

c. *Public Record Office.* Chancery Miscellanea, Bundle 34, File 1, No. 12, f. 1ʳ ᵃⁿᵈ ᵛ.
XV *cent.*

d. *Balliol College, Oxford.* MS. 354, ff. 227ᵛ,
228ʳ. XVI *cent.* (burden and stzas. 1–5,
7).

burden. d marks: fote.
stza. 1, l. 1. Lestenytgh] b Herkenud. c Listenus.
    d lystyn. bothe] b c *omit.*   l. 2. xal] b
    wol. c d wil. telyn] b c d telle.
stza. 2, l. 1. greteste] b c chef. of al] d in.
    l. 2. Of] d Thom*as* of. ye] b yc. c d I.
    l. 3. Slawy*n* he was] b he was slay. b c d *have*
    with. wykkyd] c cursyd.   l. 4. Demonis]
    d Malor*um*.
stza. 3, l. 1. Knyt*es*] d The knyght*es*. kemy*n*]
    b wero*n* sent. c w*er* come*n*. d were sent.
    Hendry] b harry. c here. d harry the.
    ll. 2, 3. d *transposes*.   l. 3. Ther] d Th*at* day.
    dedy*n*] d dide. wond*er*] d wykid.   l. 4. d
    per Regis Imperia. Feruentes] b c Fre-
    me*ntes*. insania] c . . . ania.
stza. 4, ll. 1, 2. c *transposes*.   l. 1. sowty*n*] d
    sowght.   hy*m*] b d the byschop. c Tomas.
    l. 2. Wit*h*ine the paleys] b In hys paleys wyt
    in*n*e. c in the pales with i*n*. the] d his.
    paleys] d place.   l. 3. Cryst] c . . . ste.
    hadde they] b they haddon. d They had.
    l. 4. In] d per.   malicia] b superbia.
stza. 5, l. 1. b Wyt her mouth*us* they yenedon
    wyde. They] c hi. wonder] c *omits*. d
    wond*er*ly.   l. 2. b *And* seyde to hym wyt
    gret pr*ide*. c Thei sayden to Tomas wit gret
    pride. d *And* spake to hym wi*th* myche pryde.
    l. 3. Here, treto*ur*] b trayt*ur*. c Hoy trayt*ur*.
    d Traytor here.   xalt] b her*e* schal.   abyde]
    b abucge.   l. 4. Tedia] c ted. . . .
stza. 6, l. 1. Thomas] b he.   l. 2. ye wil me
    slon] b yc shal dye. c ye me slaie.
    l. 3. pasy*n*] b go.   alle tho arn] b th*at* ys. c
    th*at* byn.   l. 4. Sine] b absq*ue*.
stza. 7, l. 1. his] c d the.   adou*n*] c d dou*n*e.
    l. 2. Ther] c *omits*. d *And* than. gunne to] c
    began to. d *omits*. pary*n*] c pare. d pared.
    l. 3. He] c Thei. d *And*.   sterdy*n*] c turned,
    d stered.   brynys] c brayne.   *and*] d so.
    At end: d Explicit.
stza. 8, l. 1. The] b c *omit*.   sterte] b hy*m* gon
    st*er*te: c he*m* sterte.   l. 2. dedly] b
    wyckede. c sore.   thei] b hey.   gu*n*ne] b c
    omit.   l. 3. Thomas] b Th*er* he. c he.   in]

b on. Mod*er*] b c hys mod*ur*]   l. 4. b
Optans celi gaudia.
stza. 9, l. 1. Modir, clerk, wedue] b Clerk,
    mayde, wedewe. c Clerke, mayde*n*, *and*
    modir.   l. 2. Worchepe] b Werchepud. ye]
    b c *omit*.   *in* al you*r*] b in al her. c th*at* gaf vs.
    l. 3 for fyftene toke*n*us of gret strif] c Fore
    fiute i poyttes of . . . scef.

115

Bodleian Library. MS. Eng. poet. e. 1
                                                    XV *cent.*
f. 35ʳ

Pastor cesus i*n* gregys medio
Pace*m* emit cruorys p*re*cio.

[1]

As storys wryght *and* specyfy,
    Sent Thom*as*, thorow Godd*es* sond,
Beyng a byschop of Ca*n*turbery,
    Was martyrd for the ryght of Englond.

[2]

Hys mod*er* be blyssyd th*at* hym bar,
    And also hys fad*er* th*at* hym begatt,
For war we wel kep fro sorow *and* care
    Thorow the deth of the p*re*lat.

[3]

Thys holy mane of God was accept,
    For whatsoeu*er* th*at* he ded prayd,
Vs frome the dau*n*ger conser*u*yd *and* kepte
    Of the ra*n*son we xuld haue payd.

[4]

To *and* fyfty poynt*es* onresonabyll,
    *C*onsentyd of byschopp*es* many on,
Thou was no[th]yng therto agreabyll;
    Th*er*for thou suff*er*yd thi passyon.

[5]

Of knyt*es* cruell *and* also wykyd
    Th*ou* suff*er*yd thi deth wi*th* mylde mod;
Wherfor the Chyrch is gloryfyyd
    In the schedy[n]g of this blod.

[6]

To Cryst th*er*for lat vs p*re*y,   [f. 35ᵛ
    Th*at* for vs deyyd on the rood,
*C*onserue vs al both nyght *and* day
    Thorow the schedy*n*g of Thom*as* blood.

*The entire carol is defaced in MS. by a single
stroke through each line.*

115.1

British Museum. MS. Egerton 3307

         XV *cent.*

f. 62ᵛ

 Seynt Thom*a*s honou*r* w[e],
 Thorgh whos blod Holy Chyrch ys
 made fre.

[1]

Al Holy Chyrch was bot a thrall
Thorgh kyng *and* temperal lordys all,
To he was slane in Cristys hall
 And set all thing in vnite:
 Hys deth hath such auctorite.

[2]

The kyng exilyd hym owt of land
And toke hys good in hys hond,
Forbedy*ng* both fre and bond
 That no p*r*ayer for hy*m* schuld be:
 So fers he schewyd hys crewelte.

[3]

Al ben exilyd that to hym lang,
Wemen, chyldryn, old men among,
Yong babys th*a*t wepyd insted of song;
 Seynt Thomas said, 'Welcom ye be;
 Ilk lond is now you*r* awen contre.'

[4]

Sex yer he had pou*er*t and wo; [f. 63ʳ]
The seue*n*t yer hom he schuld go;
Su*m* hopyd of pes, sum dyd not so,
 Bot he was welcom to hys se,
 Derly desyryd of ilk degre.

[5]

The kyng bot lytyl whyl hy*m* sparyd:
Knyght*es* in chyrch hys crown of paryd;
Thus the corner-ston was swaryd
 Betwen clergy and temp*er*alte
 To knytt pes and vnite.

[6]

The corn ou*er*cast, the chaff lyght law:
The kyng in hys ost ys ou*er*thraw:
The tyler on ground hys brayn hath saw,
 As C*r*ist seyd hym at Pountane,
 'My chyrch w*ith* thi blod halowyd schal
  be.'

[7]

On Tewsday born, accusyd also,
On Tewsday exilid hys frend*es* fro,
Comfort of C*r*ist to dreyd no wo,

Clepyd hom, t*r*anslate was he—
Thus seuen Tewsdays worschypyd the
 see.

The burden and ll. 1 and 4 of each stanza are
to be repeated as chorus.

116

British Museum. MS. Addit. 5665

         XVI *cent.*

f. 41ᵛ

 Clangat tuba, martir Th[o]m[a,]
 Vt liberet sic Cristi vinea,
 Clangat tuba, martir Th[o]m[a,]
 Vt liberet sic *Christ*i vinea.

[1]

Oute of the chaffe was pured [f. 42ʳ]
 this corne,
And else the Cherch had ben forlorne;
To God*es* grange now where thow borne,
 O martir Th[oma,]
 O martir Th[o]m[a,]
 O martir Th[o]m[a.]

[2]

In London was bore this [f. 41ᵛ]
 martir sothely;
Of Caunterbury hadde he primacy,
To whom we syng deuotely:
 O martir Th[o]m[a,]
 O martir Thoma,
 O martir Thoma.

MS. heading: Sancto Th[ome]. *All the words
on f. 42ʳ and some of those on f. 41ᵛ are defaced
by a stroke through them. The name* Thoma
*has been partially erased in all but its last two
occurrences.*

117

a. *Bodleian Library.* MS. Douce 302

    By John Audelay (?), XV *cent.*

f. 29ʳ

 What tythyngis bryngst vs, messangere,
 Of C*r*istis borth this New Eris Day?

[1]

A babe is borne of hye natewre,
 A Prynce of Pese th*a*t eu*er* schal be;
Off heue*n and* erthe he hath the cewre;
 Hys lordchip is et*er*nete.
  Seche wond*er* tythyngis ye may here:
  Th*a*t God *and* mo*n* is hon in fere,
   Hou*r* syn had mad bot fyndis p*r*ay.

[2]

A semle selcouth h*i*t is to se:
The burd th*a*t had this barne iborne
This child co*n*seyuyd *i*n he degre
And maydyn is as was beforne.
    Seche wond*u*r tydyngus ye mow here:
    Th*a*t maydon *and* modur ys won yfere
    And lady ys of hye aray.

[3]

A wond*er* thyng is now befall:
    Th*a*t Lord th*a*t mad both se *and* su*n*,
Heue*n and* erth *and* angelis al,
    In monkynde ys now becu*m*me.
    Whatt tydy*n*gus bry*n*gu[st vs, messan-
        gere?]
    A faunt th*a*t is bot of on yere
    Eu*er* as ben *and* schal be ay.

[4]

These louele lade co*n* grete her chylde:
'Hayle, Su*n*, haile, Brod*er*, haile, Fad*er*
    dere!'
'Haile, doght*er*, haile, sust*er*, haile, mod*er*
    myld!'
This haylsyng was on coynt manere.
    Seche wo[n]d*er* tythyngis [ye may here:]
    This gretyng was of so he chere
    Th*a*t mans pyne h*i*t turnyd to play.

[5]

Th*a*t Lord th*a*t. al thyng mad of noght
    Is mo*n* becu*m* fore mo*n*s loue,
For w*i*th his blood he schul be boght
    From bale to blys th*a*t is aboue.
    Seche wond*er* tythyngis [ye may here:]
    Th*a*t Lord vs grawnt now o*u*r pray-
        oure,
    To twel *i*n heue*n* th*a*t we may.

MS. heading: In die circu[m]cicionis d*o*m*i*ni.
The repetition of the burden is indicated as
follows: stza. 3: What tythyngis bryngis
th*o*u vt sup*r*a.
burden, l. 1. After 1. What] MS. H what.
stza. 1. After l. 5. MS. *inserts* What tythyngis
bryngis the messangere.
stza. 3, l. 5. [vs messangere]] MS. vt sup*r*a. *The
line is written at the right of the stanza.*
stza. 4, l. 1. These] MS. iese.   l. 5. [ye may
here]] MS. vt sup*r*a.
stza. 5, l. 5 [ye may here]] MS. vt sup*r*a. *After*
l. 7. MS. Seche wond*er* tythyngis vt sup*r*a.

b. *Trinity College, Cambridge.* MS. O. 3.
58, recto. XV *cent.* (burden and stzas. 1,
3, 2, 4).

c. *Bodleian Library.* MS. Arch. Selden B.
26, ff. 15ᵛ, 16ʳ. XV *cent.* (burden and
stzas. 1, 2, 4, 3).

burden, l. 1. vs] b c th*o*u.   l. 2. New Eris]
b yolys. c yer*es.*
stza. 1, l. 1. 2. A] b The. c is.   th*a*t] c *and.*
After l. 5. c *inserts* (Chorus) what tydy*n*ges
vt sup*r*a.   l. 6. b That ma*n* is mad now
godd*es* pere. c that man is made now godys
fere.   l. 7. Hour] b qwom. c wha*m.*
stza. 2, l. 1. A] b That. semle] b semlyest.
selcouth] c syght. h*i*t is] b *omits.*
l. 2. The] b Th*i*s. had] b c hath. barne] b c
babe.   l. 3. This child co*n*seyuyd] b and
Lord *c*onceyuyd. c Conceyued a lord. i*n*]
b c of.   l. 4. *And*] b a. is] c *omits.* was]
c heo was.   l. 5. tydy*n*gus ye mow here]
b c &c.   l. 6. maydon] c maide. yfere]
b in fere.   l. 7. And lady ys] b. *And* sche
a lady. c and alwey lady. hye] b greth.
stza. 3, l. 2. Lord] b ky*n*g. mad both se] b c
formyd sterre.   l. 4. In] b c now i*n.* now
becu*m*me] b newe begu*n*ne. c by gu*n*ne.
l. 5. b Swich wu*n*der &c. c Suche &c.
l. 6. th*a*t] b *omits.* bot] b now. c not. on]
b c o.   l. 7. Eu*er* as ben] b That hath ben
eu*er*e. c Eu*er* hath ybe. be] b ben.
stza. 4, l. 1. These] b That. louele lade] b
louelyest. c maide. co*n*] b gan. c began to.
grete] c gretyn.   l. 2. c *And* saide sone
haile fad*er* dere.   l. 3. c he saide haile
moder haile maide mylde. doght*er*] b dowt*er*
he seyth.   l. 4. haylsyng] b heyly*n*g. c
gretynge. on] c *i*n.   l. 5. b Swich &c.
c Suche &c.   l. 6. This] b That. c here.
gretyng] b heyly*n*g. of so he chere] b of so
good ch*er*e. c in suche man*er*e.   l. 7. c hit
turned ma*n*nys peyne to play. h*i*t] b is.

118

British Museum. MS. Addit. 5665
                                          XVI *cent.*
f. 12ᵛ

    Make vs meri this New Yere,
    Thankyng God w*i*th hertely chere.
    Make vs mery thys New Yere
    Thankyng God *w*ith hertely   [*f. 13ʳ
        chere.

[1]

Gabriell, bryghth[er] then the sonne,
    Graci*u*sly grette that mayden fre;
Thorffe hir mekenesse *C*rist haue whe
    founde.
    Ecce ancilla D*o*mini.

[2]

Aue Maria, virgin bryght;   [f. 12ᵛ
    We joyeth of thy benignite;
The Holy Goste ys vn in lyght;
    Th*o*u hast conceyued thy Sone so fre.

[3]

Now ys that mayde gret with chylde,
  Hirselue alone also credebily;
Fro the fende she shall vs shylde;
  So sayeth bokys in hure story.

MS. heading: In die circumcisionis.
stza. 1, l. 3. whe founde] *written below the other
  words of the line.*   l. 4. Domini] MS.
  Domini ni.
stza. 2, l. 2. benignite] MS. virginite benignite.
  *The first word is apparently uncancelled through
  oversight.*
stza. 3, l. 3. Fro] MS. For.

119

*Huntington Library. Christmas carolles
newely Inprynted* (Richard Kele)
                                    c. 1550.

p. [23]

  To encrease our joy and blysse
  Christus natus est nobis.

[1]

Make we mery in hall and boure,
  And this gloryous lady honor we
That to vs hathe borne our   [p. [24]
    Sauyour,
  Homo sine semine.

[2]

For, as the sonne, that shyneth bryght,
  Perceth no glas that we may se,
So conceyued she Jesu full of myght
  Cum virginitatis honore.

[3]

Ysay prophecyed longe beforne
  How this Emanuel borne sholde be
To saue his people, that were forlorne,
  Dux exurget regere.

[4]

We were all in great dystresse
  Tyll this Lorde dyd make vs free,
Wherof this feste beryth wytnes;
  Uenit nos redimere.

[5]

A token of loue he fyrst now shewed,
  That he on vs wolde haue pytye,
Whan he for vs was crucyfed,
  Ut declaratur hodie.

[6]

Most gloryous lady, we the pray,   [p. [25]
  That bereth the crowne of chastyte,
Brynge vs to the blysse that lasteth aye,
  Feliciter congaudere.

Heading in original: De Circumcisione domini.
The repetition of the burden is indicated after
  stzas. 1, 2, 4–6 by: To encrease. &c.
At end: Finis.

120

Balliol College, Oxford. MS. 354
                                    XVI *cent.*
f. 223ᵛ

  What cher? Gud cher, gud cher, gud
      cher!
  Be mery and glad this gud New Yere.

[1]

'Lyft vp your hartes and be glad
In Crystes byrth,' the angell bad;
'Say eche to oder, yf any be sade,
  "What cher?"'

[2]

Now the Kyng of Hevyn his byrth hath
    take,
Joy and myrth we owght to make;
Say eche to oder for hys sake,
  'What cher?'

[3]

I tell you all with hart so fre,
Ryght welcum ye be to me;
Be glad and mery, for charite.
  What cher?

[4]

The gudman of this place in fere,
You to be mery he prayth you here,
And with gud hert he doth to you say,
  'What cher?'

At end: Explicit.

121

British Museum. MS. Addit. 40166 (C 3)
                                    XV *cent.*
f. 12ᵛ

  Who wot nowe that ys here
  Where he schall be anoder yere?

[1]

Anoder yere hit may betyde
This compeny to be full wyde,
And neuer onodyr here to abyde;
  Cryste may send now sych a yere.

[2]

Another yere hit may befall
The lest that is withyn this hall
To be more mastur then we all;
  Cryste [may send now sych a yere.]

[3]

This lordis that ben wonder grete,
They threton powre men for to bete;
Hyt lendith lytull in hur threte;
  Cryste may send sich a yere.

121.1

Magdalene College, Cambridge. MS. Pepys
2553 (Maitland Folio MS.), p. 18 (burden and stzas. 5–9).
                    By William Dunbar, 1570–86

Cambridge University Library. MS. Ll. 5.
10. (Reidpeth MS.) f. 1ʳ (stzas. 1–4, 10,
11, and *Responsio Regis*)   1622

  Schir, lat it never in toune be tald
  That I suld be ane Yowllis yald!

[1]

Now lufferis cummis with largess lowd,
Quhy sould not palfrayis thane be prowd
Quhen gillettis wil be schomd and schroud
  That ridden ar baith with lord *and* lawd?
  Ssir, lett it nevir in toun be tald
  [That I sould be ane Yuillis yald!]

[2]

Quhen I was young *and* into ply   [f. 1ᵛ
And wald cast gammaldis to the sky,
I had beine bocht in realmes by,
  Had I consentit to be sauld.
  Ssir, lett it nevir in toun be tauld
  [That I sould be ane Yuillis yald!]

[3]

With gentill horss quhen I wald knyp,
Thane is thair laid on me ane quhip;
To colleveris than man I skip,
  That scabbit ar, hes cruik *and* cald.
  Ssir, lett it nevir in toun be tald
  [That I sould be ane Yuillis yald!]

[4]

Thocht in the stall I be not clappit
As cursouris that in silk beine trappit,
With ane new houss I wald be happit
  Aganis this Crysthinmes for the cald.
  Ssir, lett it nevir in toun be tald
  That I sould be ane Yuillis yald!

[5]

Suppois I war ane ald yaid aver,   [p. 18
Schott furth our clewch to squische the
    cleuer,
And had the strenthis off all Strenever,
  I wald at Youll be housit and stald.
  Ssir, lat it neuer in toune be tald
  [That I suld be ane Yowllis yald!]

[6]

I am ane auld horss, as ye knaw,
That euer in duill dois drug and draw;
Gryt court horss puttis me fra the staw,
  To fang the fog be firthe and fald.
  Ssir, lat it neuer in toune be tald
  [That I suld be ane Yowllis yald!]

[7]

I heff run lang furth in the feild,
On pastouris that ar plane and peld;
I mycht be now tein in for eild,
  My bekis ar spruning he and bald.
  Ssir, lat it neuer in toun be tald
  [That I suld be ane Yowllis yald!]

[8]

My maine is turned into quhyt,
And thairoff ye heff all the wyt;
Quhen vthair hors hed brane to byt,
  I gat bot griss, grype giff I wald.
  Ssir, lat it neuer in towne be tald
  [That I suld be ane Yowllis yald!]

[9]

I was neuer dautit into stabell,
My lyff hes bein so miserabell,
My hyd to offer I am abell
  For evill schoud strae that I reiv wald.
  Ssir, lat it neuer in towne be tald
  [That I suld be ane Yowllis yald!]

[10]

And yett, suppois my thrift be thyne,   [f. 1ʳ
Gif that I die your aucht within,
Lat neuir the soutteris have my skin,
  With vglie gumes to be gnawin.
  Ssir, lat it neuir in toun be tald
  [That I sould be ane Yuillis yald!]

[11]

The court hes done my curage cuill
And maid me ane forriddin muill;
Yett, to weir trapp*ouris* at this Yuill
I wald be spurrit at everie spald.
S*s*ir, lett it nevir in toun be tald
[That I sould be ane Yuillis yald!]

Responsio Regis

Efter our wrettingis, thesaurer,
Tak in this gray horss, aul[d] Du*n*bar,
Quhilk in my aucht with sch*e*rvice trew
In lyart changeit is his hew.
Gar howss him now aganis this Yuill,
And busk him lyk ane bischopis muill,
For *with* my hand I haue indost
To pay quh*a*teuir his trapp*ouris* cost.

burden, l. 1. toune] MS. toume.
stza. 1, l. 2. palfrayis] MS. parfrayis.
   1.5. MS. S*s*ir &c.
stza. 5, l. 3. Strenever] MS. streneverne.
stzas. 6–8, l. 6. MS. &c.
stza. 9, l. 6. *This line is much faded, and not all
   the text can now be clearly read.*
After stza. 11. *Quod:* dumbar.   *Responsio*
MS. Respontio.

121.2

a. *National Library of Scotland.* MS. Advocates I. I. 6
                    By William Stewart, 1527
f. 95ᵛ

   Lerges, lerges, lerges ay:
   Lerges of this New Yeirday.

[1]

First, lerges, the King my cheife,
Quhilk come als quiet as a theif
And in my hand sled schillingis tway
To put his lergnes to preif
   For lerges of this New Yeirday.

[2]

Syne, lerges of my Lord Chancellar,
Quhen I to him ane ballat bare:
He sonyeit no*ch*t nor said me nay,
Bot gaif me quhill I wad had mair
   For lergenes [of this New Yeirday.]

[3]

Off Galloway the bischop new
Fur*ch*t of my hand ane ballat drew
And me deliuerit w*ith* delay

Ane fair haiknay but hyd or hew
   For [lergenes of this New Yeirday.]

[4]

Of [Halie] Croce the abbot ying,
I did to him ane ballat bring,
Bot or I past far him fray,
I gat na les nor deill a thing
   For [lerges of this New Yeirday.]

[5]

The Secretar bayth war and wyse   [f. 96ᵛ
Hecht me ane kast of his offyse,
And for to reid my bill alsway
He said for him that micht suffyse
   For lerges of this New Yeirday.

[6]

The Thesaur and Compttrollar,
Thay bad me cum I wait no*ch*t quhair,
And they suld gar, I wait no*ch*t quhay,
Gif me I wat no*ch*t quhat full fair
   For lerges [of this New Yeirday.]

[7]

Now lerges of my lordis all,
Bayth temporall and spirituall;
Myself sall euir sing and say
I haif thame found so liberall
   O[f] lerges [of this New Yeirday.]

[8]

Fowll fall this frost that is so fell;
It hes the wyt the trewth to tell;
Baith hand*is* and purs it bindis sway,
Thay may gife ne thing by thamesell
   For lerges [of this New Yeirday.]

[9]

Now lerges of my Lord Bothwell,
The quhilk in fredome dois excell;
He gaif to me ane cursour gray
Worth all this sort that I with mell
   For [lerges of this New Yeirday.]

[10]

Grit God releif M*a*rgaret our Quene,
For, and scho war as scho hes bene,
Scho wald be lerger of lufray
Than all the laif that I of mene
   For lerges of this new Yeirday.

stza 2, l. 5. MS. For lergenes &c.
stza. 3, l. 3. haiknay] MS. kaiknay.
stzas. 3, 4, 9, l. 5. MS. For &c.
stzas. 6, 8, l. 5. MS. For lerges &c.
stza. 7, l. 5. MS. o lerges &c.
At end: q stewart.

b. *Magdalene College, Cambridge.* MS.
Pepys 2553, pp. 220–1. XVI *cent.* (stzas.
2–4, 6–8).

MS. heading: Larges of This New Yeir Day
(in capitals).
stza. 2, l. 2. to him ane ballat] ane ballat till
   him.   l. 4 had] haue.
  stza. 3, l. 1. Galloway] the galloway.
  l. 2. Ane ballat of my bosome drew.
  l. 3. with] but.
stza. 4, l. 1. [Halie] Croce] halie crose.
  l. 2. I did to him] To him I did. l. 4. nor] na.
stza. 7, l. 2. stait] *omits.* euir] never.
  l. 5. [of]] For.
stza. 8, l. 1. is so fell] that evir it fell. l. 2. the
  trewth to] I bid nocht. l. 3. handis] hand.
  ll. 4, 5. Ye may gif na gude fra your sell
      For honour of this New yeir day.

At end: Finis.

122

A. *Bodleian Library.* MS. Douce 302
        By John Audelay (?), XV *cent.*
f. 31ʳ

Nowel, nowel, nowel.

[1]

Ther is a babe born of a may
  In saluacion of vs;
That he be heryd in this day,
  Vene, Creatore Spiritus.

[2]

In Bedlem, in that fayre plas,
  This blessid barne borne he was;
Him to serue God grawnt vs grace,
  Tu Trinetatis Vnitas.

[3]

The angelis to cheperdis songyn and sayd,
  'Pes in erth be mon vnto.'
Therwith thai were ful sore afrayd.
  'Glorea in exelsis Deo.'

[4]

The cheperdis hard that angel song;
  Thai heredon God in Trenete;
Moche merth was ham among.
  Iam lucis ortus sedere.

[5]

iii kyngis thai soght him herefore,
  Of dyuers lond and fere cuntre,
And askidyn were this barne was bore,
  Hostes Herodes impii.

[6]

He bed ham go seche this barne:
  'Anon this way to me he come,
That I may do hym worchip beforne,
  Deus creator omnium.'

[7]

The stere apered here face beforne,
  That gladid here hertes ful graciously,
Ouer that plase this babe was born,
  Jhesu saluotor seculi.

[8]

Thai knelid adowne with gret reuere[n]s:
  Gold, sens, and myr thai offerd him to;
He blessid ham ale that were present,
  Jhesu nostra redempcio.

[9]

The gold betokens he was a kyng,
  The sens a prest of dyngnete;
The myr betokynth his bereyng,
  Magne Deus potencie.

[10]

The angel hem warnyd in here slepyng
  At Erod the kyng thai schuld not cumme:
'That babe you bade on his blessyng,
  Christe redemptore omnium.'

[11]

Thai turnyd them another way
  Into kyngdom ful graciously;
Then thai begonon to syng and say,
  'Saluator mundy, Domine.'

MS. heading: In die epephanie &c.
stza. 6, l. 1. MS. *repeats* with bad *for* bed.

B. *British Museum.* MS. Sloane 2593
                      XV *cent.*
f. 27ᵛ

Nowel, el, el, el,
  Now is wel that euere was woo.

[1]

A babe is born al of a may
  In the sauasyoun of vs;
To hom we syngyn bothe nyght and day,
  'Veni, Creator Spiritus.'

[2]

At Bedlem, that blyssid p[l]as,
  The chyld of blysse, born he was;
Hym to serue Go[d] yeue vs gras,
  O lux beata Trinitas.

[3]

Th*er* come thre ky*nge*s out of the est
　To worchepe the Kyng th*a*t is so fre,
W*ith* gold *and* myrr*e and* francincens,
　A sol*is* ort*us* cardine.

[4]

The herd*es* herdyn an au*ngele* cry;　[f. 28ʳ
　A merye song the*n* su*ngy*n he:
'Qwy arn ye so sor*e* agast?
　Iam ort*us* sol*is* cardine.'

[5]

The au*ngele* comy*n* dou*n* w*ith* on cry;
　A fayr song the*n* su*ngy*n he
In the worchepe of th*a*t chyld:
　'Gloria tibi, D*omi*ne.'

stza. 3, l. 1. come] MS. cone.
stzas. 3, 4, l. 4. sol*is*] MS. sol*us*.

C. *Balliol College, Oxford.* MS. 354
　　　　　　　　　　　　　XVI *cent.*
f. 221ᵛ

　　Conditor alme sideru*m*
　　Ete*r*na lux crede*n*ciu*m*.

[1]

Ther ys a chyld borne of a may
　In saluaci*o*n of all vs;
That we shuld worship eu*er*y day
　W*ith* 'Veni, Creator Sp*iri*t*u*s.'

[2]

In Bedlem, in that holy place,
　Thys blessid child, born he was;
Hym to s*er*ue he geve vs gr*a*ce,
　W*ith* 'Trinitat*is* Vnitas.'

[3]

The shep*er*des hard th*a*t angels songe
　And worshypped God in Trynyte
Th*a*t so nygh was them amonge,
　Ia*m* luc*is* orto sidere.

[4]

Eche ma*n* began to cry *and* call
　To hym that syttyth on hye,
To hys blis to bryng them all,
　Jh*es*u saluator seculi.

burden, *after* l. 2. MS. &c.
At end: Explicit.

123

A. *Balliol College, Oxford.* MS. 354
　　　　　　　　　　　　　XVI *cent.*
f. 222ᵛ

　　Alleluya, al*le*l*u*ia,
　　Deo P*a*tri sit gloria.

[1]

Ther ys a blossu*m* sprong of a thorn
　To saue ma*n*kynd, th*a*t was forlorne,
As the p*ro*fett*es* sayd beforne;
　Deo P*a*tri sit gloria.

[2]

Th*er* sprong a well at Maris fote
　That torned all this world to bote;
Of her toke Jh*es*u flesshe *and* blod;
　Deo P*a*tri [sit gloria.]

[3]

From th*a*t well th*er* strake a strem
　Owt of Egypt into Bedlem;
God thorowgh his highnes t*ur*ned yt agayn;
　Deo [P*a*tri sit gloria.]

[4]

Th*er* was iii kyng*es* of dyu*er*s lond*es*;
　They thowght a thowght th*a*t was strong,
Hym to seke *and* thanke among;
　Deo [P*a*tri sit gloria.]

[5]

They ca*m* richely w*ith* th*er* p*re*sens,
　W*ith* gold, myre, *and* frankynsens,
As clerkys rede in th*er* sequens;
　Deo P*a*tri sit gloria.

[6]

The eldest kyng of them thre,
　He went formest, for he wold se
What domysma*n* th*a*t this shuld be;
　Deo P*a*tri sit gloria.

[7]

The medylmest kyng, vp he rose;
　He sawe a babe in armys close;
In medyll age he thowght he was;
　Deo P*a*tri [sit gloria.]

[8]

The yongest kyng, vp he stode;
　He made his offeryng rych *and* gud
To Jh*es*u Cryst, that shed his blod;
　Deo P*a*tri sit gloria.

[9]

Ther shon a star owt of hevyn bryght,
That men of erth shuld deme aright
That this was Jhesu full of myght;
    Deo Patri [sit gloria.]

stza. 5, l. 3. clerkys] MS. cherkys.
At end: Explicit.

B. *British Museum*. MS. Sloane 2593
                                    XV *cent.*

f. 12ʳ

    [Burden lacking]

[1]

Out of the blosme sprang a thorn
Quan God hymself wold be born;
He let vs neuere be forlorn,
    That born was of Marie.

[2]

Ther sprang a welle al at here   [f. 13ʳ
    fot
That al this word it t[u]rnyd to good
Quan Jhesu Cryst took fleych and blod
    Of his moder Marie.

[3]

Out of the welle sprang a strem
Fro patriarck to Jerusalem
Til Cryst hymself ayen it nem
    Of his moder [Marie.]

[4]

In wynter quan the frost hym fres,
A powre beddyng our Lord hym ches;
Betwyin an ox and an as
Godes Sone, born he was
    Of his [moder Marie.]

[5]

It was vpon the Twelwe Day
Ther come thre kynges in ryche aray
To seke Cryst ther he lay,
    And his [moder Marie.]

[6]

Thre kynges out of duye[r]s   [f. 12ᵛ
    londe
Swythe comyn with herte stronge,
The chyld to sekyn and vnderfonge
    That born was of Marie.

[7]

The sterre led hem a ryte way
To the chyld ther he lay;
He help vs bothe nyght and day
    That born was of Marie!

[8]

Baltyzar was the ferste kyng;   [f. 13ʳ
He browte gold to his offeryng
For to presente that ryche Kyng
    And his moder Marie.

[9]

Melchiar was the secunde kyng;
He browte incens to his offering
For to presente that ryche Kyng
    And his [moder Marie.]

[10]

Jasper was the thred kyng;
He browte myrre to his offeryng
For to presente that ryche Kyng
    And his [moder Marie.]

[11]

Ther they offerid here presens,   [f. 13ᵛ
With gold and myrre and francincens,
And clerkes redyn in here seqwens
    In Ephifunye.

[12]

Knel we down hym beforn,
And prey we to hym that now is born
[He] let vs neuer be forlorn,
    That born was of Marie.

Before stza. 1: dic ✠.
stza. 3, l. 4 [Marie]] MS. &c.
stzas. 4, 5, 9, 10, l. 4. [moder Marie]] MS. &c.
Stzas. 6, 7, *on f.* 12ᵛ *are marked for insertion in
    their appropriate place with* ✠.
stza. 9, l. 2. He MS. be.
stza. 12, l. 3. [He]] MS. &

124

A. *British Museum*. MS. Sloane 2593
                                    XV *cent.*

f. 14ʳ

    The sterre hym schon bothe nyght and
        day
    To lede thre kynges ther our Lord lay.

[1]

Jhesu was born in Bedlem Jude
Of mayde Mary, thus fynde we;
Out of the est come kynges thre
   With ryche presentes, as I yow say.

[2]

As they went forth in here pas,
The sterre schon al in here fas,
As bryght as gold within the glas,
   To Bedlem to ledyn hem the way.

[3]

Kyng Herowdes was most of pryse;
He seyde to tho thre kynges that wern so
   wyse,
'Go and sekit me yone child of pryse,
   And comit ageyn be me, I you pray.

[4]

'And I myself xal with yow wynde,
The chyld to worchepe, the child to fynde,
And worchepyn hym with all myn mynde,
   With al the onour that I may.'

[5]

Quan they kemyn into that plas
Ther Jhesu with his moder was,
They settyn hem doun and made solas,
   And euery kyng to other gan say.

[6]

Quan they haddyn offerid up here presens,
With gold and myrre and francincens,
As clerkes redyn in here sequens,
   He took it of hem and seyd not nay.

[7]

Quan they hadde offerid here offeryng
To Jhesu, that is Heuene Kyng,
Of an aungyl they hadd warnyng
   To wendyn hom be another way.

[8]

The aungyl cam fro Heuene   [f. 14ᵛ
   Kyng
And bad tho thre kynges ageyn hom wynd,
Therin to dwelle, therin to ben
   Til Kyng Herowdes endyng day.

[9]

Kyng Herowde wox wol ille
For tho thre kynges comyn hym not tille
For to fulfille his wykkyd wille,
   And to his knytes he gan say.

[10]

Kyng Herowdes wox wroth anon;
The chylderin of Israel he dede slon;
He wende Jhesu hadde ben the ton,
   And yyt he falyid of his pray.

[11]

Kyng Herowdes deyid and went to helle
For swete Jhesus, that we spelle;
God saf vs fro the peynis of helle
   And fro the wykkyd fyndes pray.

B. *Lord Harlech, National Library of Wales.*
   MS. Porkington 10   XV *cent.*
f. 198ᵛ

   The ster he schynythe bothe nyghte and
      day
   To lede iii kynges ther Jhesu lay.

[1]

Jhesu whas borne in Bedlem Jude   [f. 199ʳ
Alle off a mayden, so fyndythe whe;
Owte off the este com kynges iii
   Wythe ryche presente, as Y yow say.

[2]

The stuarde whas bolde off that contre
And bade Errod schollde com and see
Lyke as they wentyn alle y iii,
   Goyng furrthe yn ther jornay.

[3]

Furthe they wentyn, pas for pas,
And euer the ster schone on ther fase
Lyke as the son dothe throwe the glas,
   And ynto Bedleme they toke ther way.

[4]

When they com ynto the plas,
Jhesu wythe hys modyr whas;
They knelyd adowne and made solas,
   And euer[y] kyng tyll oder gan say.

[5]

When they had made vp hyr offeryng,
Gollde and myr and ryche thyng,
They lay adowne and toke restyng
   For alle a nyghte and alle a day.

[6]

As they lay in ther slepyng,   [f. 199ᵛ
Ther com a angell and browghte tydyng
And bade them wende nat by Errod the
   kyng
But bade them take another way.

[7]
Errod, off this he wyxyd full gryll,
That this iii kynges cam nat hym tylle
Alle to fullfyll hys false wylle,
    And tyll hys knyghteys he gan say.

[8]
Errod bade hys knyghtes anon
That they schollde into Bedlem gon
And sle the chyllderyn euerychon,
    And yet he faylyd off hys pray.

[9]
Angellys com to Owre Lady anon
And bade hyr into Egypte gone,
Theryne to dwelle, theryne to wonny,
    Yn tyme hyt wer Errodys endyng day.

[10]
Herrod dyyd and went to hell,
Theryn to wonny, theryne to dwell,
And yne the depyste pytte he fell,
    And ther he ys foreuer and ay.

The repetition of the burden is indicated after
each stanza by: The ster.
stza. 9, l. 3. dwelle, wonny] MS. *transposes.*
stza. 10, l. 1. hell] MS. dwell.

124.1

Canterbury Cathedral. MS. Add. 68
               XV *cent.*
f. 100ʳ

    The sterre shoon bothe nyght *and* day
    To lead thre kynges ther owr Lord lay.

[1]
Truthe it is ful sekyrly:
  Thre kynges ther were ful reuerent
That sowth Jhesu ryghth besyly
  Wyth holy deuociou*n and* good intent.

[2]
A ryghth fayer sterre to them dede peere,
  Ful orient in hys shynyng,
That browt hem forth alle i*n* feere
  To Jerusalem to here tydyng.

[3]
There thei askyd wit*h* on co*n*sent
  'Where is he that now born is
Kyng off J[e]wys verament?   [f. 100ᵛ
  Hym to seeke it is ow*er* blys.

[4]
'Just it is as trewloue knot—
  Hys sterre we seyn i*n* est ful brygth
Hym to wurschyp wyth all ower thowth
  Here we come*n* as it is rygth.'

[5]
Kyng Herrowdes wit*h* thys wex wode
  And dede seke up the propheceye;
He thout hym sone to swage hys bloode
  And yif it were trowth than he shuld dey.

[6]
Alle principalle prestys he dede present
  And scribys of the pepyl that thei wore
    there
Off Crystes berth to say here intent
  Ryghth as here bookes dede hem lere.

[7]
'Thow Bethlem i*n* Jewys lond
  In Jury princes thou art not leest;
For out [of] the a duke shal fond,
  Israel to rewyl my*n* pepyl best.'

[8]
Thus seyd the prophecye i*n* writyng swyr
  Off Jhesu Cryst off hom I syng:
That off Jewys he shuld haue cuyr
  And of Israel he shulde be kyng.

[9]
Trublyd than was, wit*h*outyn leese,
  Kyng Herrowdes thys heryng,
And al Jerusalem hym to pleese
  Ryght for hem grevyd swyche tydyng.

[10]
Than Herrowdes ful priuilyche   [f. 101ʳ
  The kyngges he clepyd that dilige*n*tly
The tyme off the sterre thei shuld hym teche,
  To hem that apperyd so propyrly.

[11]
Whan alle he here hartys wyst
  Sendyng hem forth he precepte:
'Dyligently goo atte yowr lyst
  And aske afftyr the chyld wit*h*outy*n* lette.

[12]
'But whan that chyeld ye haue cu*m* tylle,
  Comth ageyn, *and* tellyt me,
That I hym wurchyp may at wylle
  As it perteynith to my*n* degre.'

[13]

Thus he spake wol serpentyne
  With gret sorrow and mekyl smerte
Fore he than hopyd to see the tyme
  That he shuld stryke the chyld to herte.

[14]

Thus whan thei the kyng hade harde
  They yedyn here way, as it was beste;
'See the sterre', thei seey aftyrwarde,
  Ryghth hem precedyng in the este.

[15]

And whan the sterre thei had in syghte,
  Mery thei were and mad gret glee;
Lost thei nevir that ich lyght
  Tyl thei come ther thei wuld bee.

[16]

Into the howse than thei entryng
  Fond thei there that semely sygth,
The chyld Jhesus owre Hevyn Kyng
  With Mary hys modyr Owre Lady
  bryghth.

[17]

They fel prostrat with reuerence
  Vpon here knese semly to see
Gold, myere, and frankincens   [f. 101ᵛ]
  To hym offyrd ich off tho thre.

[18]

Whan thei here offryng thus had mad
  Answere in sleep receyvyd ful playn,
Al anoder way to hem fol glad
  But not to Herawdes turnyd thei agayn.

[19]

Thankyng God in Trinite,
  Wyth joy and myrth euerlastynge
Sone thei come hom to here cuntree:
  Thus was here pylgrimage brouth to
  ende.

[20]

Than wex Herrowdes in wroth ful grylle;
  He grugged, he gronyd, he cryed ful felle,
That the kynges come not hym tylle;
  Wherefore feel chyldyre dede he qwelle.

[21]

For in here dethe he put hys trost
  That Cryst shuld dey be gret resoun
Yif thei were slayn in euery coost,
  And specialy in Bethlem toun.

[22]

Butt yet he sped not off hys pray,
  Kyng Herrowdes that gryme syere,
But he to helle hath take hys way,
  Euere ther to dwelle in peynful fyer.

[23]

Innocentes by grace martyres yyng
  To hevyn were born with angelles brygth,
There to be cround of owr Heuenly Kyng—
  God bring vs alle to that ich lyghth.

[24]

Where we joy may with owr Kyng,
  With seyntes and angelles euerych one
The face off very God bothe Trine and
  One—
  I thank now God myn song is done.

Stza. 6 is written after stza. 9 in MS. The trans-
position is indicated by marginal A and B and
by that he inserted as a catchword after stza. 9.
burden, l. 2. lead] MS. laed
stza. 7, l. 1. Jewys] MS. Jwys.   l. 3. fond]
  MS. fongd.

125

A. *British Museum.* MS. Sloane 2593
                                     XV *cent.*
f. 17ʳ

  Reges de Saba venient;
  Aurum, tus, myrram offerent.
    Alleluia.

[1]

Now is the Twelthe Day icome;
The Fader and Sone togeder arn nome,
The Holy Gost, as they wern wone,
  In fere;
  God send vs good Newe Yere.

[2]

I wil you synge with al myn myght
Of a chyld so fayr in syght;
A maydyn hym bar this ender nyght,
  So stylle,
  As it was his wylle.

[3]

Thre kynges out of Galylie
Kemyn to Bedlem, that cete,
For to takyn into that se
  Be nyte;
  It was a ful fayr syte.

[4]

As they keme forght with here offeryng,
They mette with Herowdes, that mody
 kyng;
He askyd hem of here comyng
 That tyde,
And thus to hem he seyde:

[5]

'Fro qwens come ye, kynges thre?' [f. 17ᵛ]
'Out of the est, as thou mayst se,
To sekyn hym that euere xal be
 Throw ryte
Lord and Kyng of Myte.'

[6]

'Quan ye han at that Kyng ibe,
Comit ageyn this weye be me,
And tel me the sytes that [ye] han se;
 I praye,
Ye gon non other waye.'

[7]

Of Herowdys, that mody kyng,
He tokyn here leue of eld and yyng,
And for[th] they wente with here offeryng
 In syghte,
And ther they come be nyte.

[8]

Into Bedlem thei gunne pas; [f. 18ʳ]
The sterre gan schynyn in here fas
Brytter than euere schon sunne in glas
 In londe;
Jhesu with Mari thei fonde.

[9]

Quan they comyn into that plas [f. 17ᵛ]
Ther Jhesu with his moder was
Thei made offeryng with gret solas,
 Not ferre,
With gold, incens, and myrre.

[10]

As they wern homward iwent,
The Fader of Heuene an aungyl sent
To the thre kynges that made present
 Or daye,
And thus to hem gan saye:

[11]

'My Lord haght warnyd you of your fon,
Be Kyng Herowdes that ye not gon,
For, if ye don, he wil you slon

And traye;
Ye gon another waye.'

[12]

Quan they comyn hom to here [f. 18ʳ]
 cuntre,
Blythe and glad they wern alle thre
Of tho sytes that they had se
 Be nyte:
Jhesu and Mari bryte.

[13]

With tresoun to vs gan he sayn;
He trowid Jhesu to han slayn;
Into Egypt thei went ful playn
 Be syde;
Josep was here gyde.

[14]

Kyng Herowdes, he made his vow;
Gret plente of chylderin he slow;
He wende ther xuld a be Jhesu;
 I saye,
He falyid of his praye.

[15]

Herowdes was wod in ryalte;
He slow schylderin ryght gret plente
In Bedlem, that fayre cete,
 With stryf;
Ne left he non on lyf.

[16]

The chylderin of Israel cryid, 'Wa wa!'
The moderis of Bedlem cryid, 'Ba ba!'
Herowdes low and seyd, 'Aha!'
 That qwede,
'The Kyng of Juwys is dede.'

[17]

Almyty God in mageste, [f. 18ᵛ]
In on God personys thre,
Bryng vs to the blysse that is so fre
 In fere,
And send vs a good Newe Yere.

The burden is written again at the end: Reges
de Saba venient aurum tus mirra[m] offer . . .
(last letters obscured by binding).
Stza. 8 is written after stza. 13 in MS.

B a. *St. John's College, Cambridge*. MS. S.
54 XV *cent.*
f. 7ᵛ

 [Burden lacking.]

[1]

Now ys the Twelfth Day com,
Fadyr *and* Son togydyr wone;
The Holy Gost wi*th* hym is nowme
   Ifere;
   God send *vs* all a gud New Yer.

[2]

I xall yow syng thoro hys myghht
Of a chyld th*at* is so fayr of syghht;
A mayd hy*m* bare of C*ri*stynmes nyghht
   So styll,
   As yt was hys wyll.

[3]

iii kyng*es* th*er* cu*m* of Galely;   [f. 8ʳ
Thei cu*m* toward Bedlem Jude,
Hy*m* to sek *and* to se
   Be nyghht;
   Th*at* was a semly syghht.

[4]

As thei cu*m* wi*th* th*er* offryng,
The mete wi*th* Erawd, th*at* mody kyng;
He hasked he*m* of her cu*m*my[n]g
   Th*at* syd,
   And thus tyll he*m* he sayd:

[5]

'Fro qweth*ur* cu*m* ye, kyng*es* iii?'
'Owt of the est, as ye may se,
To sek hy*m* th*at* eu*er* xall be
   Of myghht
   Lord, Pr*i*nce, Kyng, *and* Knyght.'

[6]

'I pr*a*y yow, lord*es* all iii,
Qwa*n* ye haue th*at* chyld se,
Th*at* ye cu*m* ageyn be me
   And telythe
   Qwere th*at* fayr chyld dwellyth.'

[7]

'Kyng Herawd, we wyll not lete;
As th*ou* hast seyd yt xall be sete:
We cu*m* ageyn wi*th*owt lete
   And tell
   Qwer th*at* fayr chyld dwell.'

[8]

Qwan he had seyd hys lykyng,   [f. 8ᵛ
Syr Herawd, th*at* mody kyng,
And forth the went wi*th* th*er* offrynge
   Be nyghht,
   The stere gaue he*m* lyghht.

[9]

Be the stere th*at* schon so bryghht,
The iii kyng*es* tok wey full ryghht,
Be the hape of th*at* chyld so bryghht,
   Thoro gr*a*ce,
   To th*at* holy place.

[10]

Qwa*n* thei cu*m* to holy place
Th*er* Jh*es*u *and* hys mod*er* was,
Thei offryd to hy*m* wi*th* grete solace,
   In fer,
   Gold, encens, *and* myrre.

[11]

All thei wer both blythe *and* glade
Qwa*n* thei had her offryng mad,
As the Holy Gost he*m* bad,
   And dedyn
   Worschype God *and* yedyn.

[12]

Qwen the lordyng*es* wer went
The chyld an angell fro*m* hevyn sent
To the kyng*es* that mad pr*e*sent
   Or day,
   To tech he*m* the waye.

[13]

'My Lord warnyth yow euery-   [f. 9ʳ
   chone
Th*at* non of yow be Herowd gone,
For, yf ye don, ye xall he slone
   And stroy,
   And do yow mekyll noye.'

[14]

Thoro the myghht of God v*er*rey
The kyng*es* tokyn anod*ur* away;
Owt thei cu*m* or yt was day,
   Full ryghht;
   Home thei cu*m* that nyghht.

stza. 1, l. 1. Twelfth] MS. xii.   l. 5. vs] MS.
vus.
stza. 5, l. 5. Knyght] MS. knyghh.
stza. 7, l. 1. we] *MS. reading doubtful. There
are one or two illegible letters before and after
we.*

b. *Bodleian Library.* MS. Eng. poet. e. 1,
ff. 31ᵛ–32ᵛ. XV *cent.* (stzas. 1–6, 8, 10–14,
A 12, C 12).

stza. 1, l. 2. Fadyr *and* Son] The fadyr *and* the
son. wone] is won.   l. 3. wi*th*] his wyth.
is] *omits.*   l. 4. In fere.   l. 5. all a] *omits.*

stza. 2, l. 1. xall] wold. thoro hys] *and.* l. 2.
that is] *omits.* of] *in.* l. 3. mayd hym]
maydy*n.* of] on.
stza. 3, l. 1. ther] *omits.* of] fro. l. 2. Tho
bedle*m* that fayer sety. l. 3. for to ofer
and se. l. 5. That] it. semly] wol fayre.
stza. 4, l. 1. cu*m*] yedy*n.* l. 2. with] *omits.*
l. 4. syd] tym. l. 5. tyll] to. he sayd] gu*n*
say.
stza. 5, l. 1. Fro qwethu*r*] for wense. ye] ye
now. l. 3. To sek] for sekyng. hy*m*]
omits. l. 4. thowre ryth. l. 5. Prince]
omits.
stza. 6. Qwan ye haue at that chyld be,
    Cu*m* ageyn th*i*s wey be me
    And tell me as ye haue see;
        I prey,
      Go not anothyr wey.
stza. 8, ll. 1, 2. *transposes.* l. 1. Thei toke
her leue both held *and* yy*n*g. l. 2. Syr]
Of. l. 3. forth] for. went] yedy*n.*
stza. 10, l. 1. holy] that blysful. l. 2. Ther]
omits. and] with. l. 3. Thei] Ther thei.
to hy*m*] *omits.* l. 5. encens] sens.
stza. 11. b *has lines in the order* 2, 3, 1.
l. 1. All] The*n.* thei wer] wer th*e*i. blythe]
mery. l. 4. *And* lyth. l. 5. it was a
w[el] fayre syth.
stza. 12, l. 1. ano*n* as thei a wey we*n*t.
l. 2. The chyld] The fathyr of heun. from
hevyn] *omits.* l. 5. *And* this tyl he*m* he say.
stza. 13, l. 1. warnyth] warnyd. l. 2. non of
yow] ye not. l. 3. ye xall he] he wol yow.
l. 4. stroy] strow. l. 5. noye] woo.
stza. 14, ll. 1, 2. *transposes.* l. 1. God v*err*ey]
godd*es* lay. l. 2. The kyng*es* tokyn] Th*e*i
yedy*n* all. away] wey. l. 3. as the ang*e*l
tyl he*m* gan say. l. 4. fol tyth. l. 5. it
was a wol fayre syth.

For A 12 b *reads*

Qwan thei were cu*m* into hyr cu*n*tre,
Mery *and* glad then wer thei
For the syth that thei had se
    Be nyth,
For as th*e*i ca*m* be lyth.

For C 12 b *reads*

Prey we al w*i*th gud devocion
To that Lord of gret renown,
And of owre synnys we ask remyssion
    And grace,
I*n* heune to haue a place.

C. *British Museum.* MS. Harley 541
XV *cent.*

f. 214^r

[Burden lacking]

[1]

Now ys Crystemas ycu*m*,
Fadyr and Son togedyr in oon,
Holy Goste, as ye be oon,

In fer*e*-a;
God sende vs a good N[e]w Yer*e*-a.

[2]

I wolde yow synge, for and I myght,
Off a chylde ys fayre in syght;
Hys modyr hym bare thys yndyrs nyght,
    So styll-a,
And as yt was hys wyll-a.

[3]

The*re* ca*m* iii kyng*es* fro Galylee
Into Bethleem, that fayr*e* cytee,
To seke hym that eu*er* shulde be
    By ryght-a,
Lorde and Kynge and Knyght-a.

[4]

As they cam forth w*i*th there offrynge,
They met w*i*th the Herode, that mody
    kynge,
.   .   .   .   .
    Thys tyde-a,
And thys to them he sayde-a:

[5]

'Off wens be ye, yow kyng*es* iii?'
'Off the este, as ye may see,
To seke hym that eu*er* shulde be
    By ryght-a
Lorde and Kynge and Knyght-a.'

[6]

'Wen yow at thys chylde have be,
Cu*m* home ayeyne by me;
Tell me the syght*es* that yow have see;
    I p*r*ay yow,
    Go yow non odyr way-a.'

[7]

They toke her leve, both olde and yonge,
Off Herode, that mody kynge;
They went forth w*i*th there offrynge
    By lyghth-a,
    By the sterre that shoon so bryght-a.

[8]

Tyll they ca*m* into the place
There Jh*esu*s and hys modyr was;
Offryd they vp w*i*th grete solace
    In fer*e*-a
    Golde and sence and myrr*e*-a.

[9]

The Fadyr of Hevyn an awngyll down sent
To thyke iii Kynge*s* that made *p*resente,
.   .   .   .   .   .
    Thys tyde-a,
And thys to them he sayd-a:

[10]

'My Lorde have warnyd yow   [f 214ᵛ
    eu*er*ychone
By Herode Kynge yow go not home,
For, and yow do, he wyll yow slone
    And strye-a,
And hurte yow wondyrly-a.'

[11]

Forth then wente thys kynge*s* iii
Tyll they ca*m* home to ther*e* cuntre;
Glade and blyth they wer*e* all iii
Off the syght*es* that they had see,
    Bydene-a
The cu*m*pany was clene-a.

[12]

Knele we now her*e* adown;
P*r*ay we in good devocion
To the Kynge of grete renown
    Of g*r*ace-a
In hevyn to have a place-a.

stza. 2, l. 1. myght] MS. mygghht.
   l. 2. syght] MS. syghgght.   l. 3. nyght]
   MS. nyghght.
stza. 3, l. 4. ryght] MS. ryghght.   l. 5. Knyght]
   MS. knyghght.
stza. 5, l. 4. ryght] MS. ryghgght.   l. 5. Knyght]
   MS. knyghght.
stza. 6, l. 3, stza. 11, l. 5. syght*es*] MS. syghght*es*.
stza. 7, l. 4. lyghth] MS. lyghgth.   l. 5. bryght]
   MS. bryghght.
stza. 9, l. 2. To] MS. Thy To.

125.1

British Museum. MS. Egerton 3307
                       XV *cent.*
f. 55ᵛ
    Aue, rex angeloru*m*,
    Aue, rexq*ue* celor*um*,
    Aue, *p*rincepsq*ue* polorum.

[1]

Hayl, most myghty in thi werky*n*g,
Hail, th*o*u lord of all thing;
I offre the gold as to [f. 57ʳ] a kyng;
    Ave, rex angelorum.
The burden is to be repeated as chorus.

125.2

British Museum. MS. Egerton 3307
                       XV *cent.*
f. 58ᵛ
    Illuminare Jherusalem:
    The duke aperyth in Bedlem.

[1]

Hys signe ys a ster bryth
Th*at* shyneth ou*er* hym wyth lyght;
Yt ys nought come bott of hys myth:
    Illuminare Jerusalem.

[2]

Thys day iii kynge*s* made oblac*i*on;
He gyth to watyr s*a*nct*i*ficac*i*on;
His bapty*m* our renouacion:
    Illuminare Jerusalem.

[3]

The Holy Gost ou*er* hy*m* alyght;
The Faders vois was herd on hyght:
'This ys my Son; me plese hym ryght';
    Illuminare Jerusalem.

The burden is to be repeated as chorus (f. 59ʳ).
stza. 2, l. 3. His] MS. He.

126

Balliol College, Oxford. MS. 354
                       XVI *cent.*
f. 165ᵛ
    Be mery, all th*at* be p*re*sent:
    Om*n*es de Saba venient.

[1]

Owt of the est a sterre shon bright
For to shew thre kynge*s* light,
Which had ferre traveled by day *and* nyght
    To seke th*at* Lord th*at* all hath sent.

[2]

Therof hard Kyng Herode anon,
Th*at* iii kynge*s* shuld cu*m* thorow his regyon
To seke a child that pere had non,
    And after them sone he sent.

[3]

Kyng Herode cried to the*m* on hye,
'Ye go to seke a child truly;
Go forth *and* cu*m* agayn me by
    And tell me wher th*at* he is lent.'

[4]

Forth they went by the sterres leme
Till they com to mery Bethelem;
Ther they fond that swet barn-teme
    That sith for vs his blode hath spent.

[5]

Balthasar kneled first adown
And said, 'Hayll, Kyng most of renown!
And of all kynges thou berist the crown;
    Therfor with gold I the present.'

[6]

Melchior kneled down in that stede
And said, 'Hayll, Lord, in thy pryesthede!
Receyve ensence to thy manhede;
    I brynge it with a good entent.'

[7]

Jasper kneled down in that stede
And said, 'Hayll, Lord, in thy knyghthede!
I offer the myrre to thy Godhede,
    For thow art he that all hath sent.'

[8]

Now lordes and ladys in riche aray,
Lyfte vp your hartes vpon this day,
And ever to God lett vs pray,
    That on the rode was rent.

At end: Explicit.

127

Cambridge University Library. MS. Ee.
I. 12   By James Ryman, *c.* 1492
f. 51ᵛ

    Ortus est Sol Iusticie
    Ex illibata virgine.

[1]

Thre kinges on the Twelfth Daye,
    Stella micante preuia,
Vnto Betheleem they toke theire way,
    Tria ferentes munera.
        Hym worship we now borne so fre
        Ex illibata virgine.

[2]

They went alle thre that chielde to se,
    Sequentes lumen syderis,
And hym they founde in ragges wounde
    In sinu matris virginis.

Hym worship we now born so fre
Ex illibata virgine.

[3]

For he was King of Mageste
    Aurum sibi optulerunt;
For he was God and ay shal be,
    Thus deuote prebuerunt.
        Hym worship we now born so fre
        Ex illibata virgine.

[4]

For he was man, they gave hym than
    Mirram, que sibi placuit.
This infant shone in heven trone
    Qui in presepe iacuit.
        Hym worship we nowe borne   [f. 52ʳ
        so fre
        Ex illibata virgine.

[5]

Warned they were, these kinges thre,
    In sompnis per Altissimum
That they ayene no wyse shuld go
    Ad Herodem nequissimum.
        Hym worship we nowe borne so fre
        Ex illibata virgine.

[6]

Not by Herode, that wikked knyght,
    Sed per viam aliam
They be gone home ageyn full right
    Per Dei prouidenciam.
        Hym worship we now borne so fre
        Ex illibata virgine.

[7]

Joseph fledde thoo, Mary also,
    In Egiptum cum puero,
Where they abode till King Herode
    Migrauit ex hoc seculo.
        Hym worship we now born so fre
        Ex illibata virgine.

[8]

That heuenly King to blis vs bringe
    Quem genuit puerpera,
That was and is and shall not mys
    Per infinita secula.
        Hym worship we nowe borne   [f. 52ᵛ
        so fre
        Ex illibata virgine.

stza. 1, l. 1. Twelfth] MS. xiiᵗʰ.

128

Cambridge University Library. MS. Ee.
   I. 12   By James Ryman, *c.* 1492
f. 52ᵛ

    Beholde, to you gret joy I bring,
    For nowe is born Crist, Heuen King.

[1]

On Twelfthe Day came king*es* thre
W*ith* golde, encense, and myrre so fre
Vnto Bethelem to seke and see
    The Son of God, C*ri*st, Heuen King.

[2]

In her*e* way tho Herode, that kyng,
Bade them goo and axe inquiring
Wher*e* this chielde was, *and* worde hym
    bring,
    The Sonne [of God, Crist, Heuen King.]

[3]

They passed furth, and the sterre bright
Went before them *and* gave them light
Till they came where they had a sight
    Of Godd*es* Son, [Crist, Heuen King.]

[4]

Warned they were in their*e* slepe thoo
They shulde not go to Herode, their*e* foo;
Another way home they be goo
    By v*er*tu of C*ri*st, Heven King.

[5]

Into Egipte Joseph fledde thoo
W*ith* the chielde and moder alsoo;
The aungell bade hym thider goo
    W*ith* Mary *and* Crist, Heven King.

[6]

Herode, seyng he hadde a trayne,   [f. 53ʳ
Alle children of Israell hath slayne
For this chielde Crist, that is certayn
    The Son of God *and* Heven King.

stza. 1, l. 1. Twelfthe] MS. xiiᵗʰᵉ.
stza. 2, l. 4. MS. The sonne &c.
stza. 3, l. 4. MS. Of godd*es* son &c.

129

Cambridge University Library. MS. Ee.
   I. 12   By James Ryman, *c.* 1492
f. 53ʳ

    A sterre shone bright on Twelfthe Day
    Ouer that place where Jhesus lay.

[1]

On Twelfthe Day this sterre so clere
    Brought king*es* iii oute of the eest
Vnto that King that hath no pere,
    In Betheleem Jude, where he did rest.
    This sterre that day tho went away
    Fro that swete place where Jh*esu*s lay.

[2]

Bothe golde, encense, and swete myrre thoo,
    Alle thre they gave vnto that chielde,
The whiche is God *and* man alsoo
    Borne of a virgyne vndefielde.
    This sterre that day tho went away
    Fro that swete place where Jhesus lay.

[3]

For he was King of Mageste,
    They gave hym golde w*ith* grete reuer-
      ence;
For he was God in persones thre,
    Mekely to hym they gave encense.
    This sterre that day tho went away
    Fro that swete place where Jhesus lay.

[4]

For he was man, they gave hym than
    Mirre in token that he shulde   [f. 53ʳ
      dye
And be buried for synfull man
    And arise ayene and to blis stye.
    This sterre that day tho went away
    Fro that swete place wher*e* Jhesus lay.

[5]

Whenne their*e* offring alle thre had made
    To Crist, that King *and* Lorde of alle,
Right sone the sterre away did fade
    That brightly shone ouer that halle.
    This sterre that day tho went away
    Fro that swete place where Jhesus lay.

[6]

As they were goyng in their*e* way,
    They mette Herode, that mody king;
He bade them wite where that chield lay
    And come by hym and worde hym bring.
    This sterre that daye tho went away
    Fro that swete place wher*e* Jhesus lay.

[7]

King Herode fayne wolde them haue slayne,
    But they were warned on a nyght
They shulde not goo by hym agayne,
    By an aungell bothe faire *and* bright.

This sterre that day tho went away
Fro that swete place where Jhesus lay.

[8]

They were full glad, and, as he badde,
They be gone home another way,
And King Herode was wrothe *and* sadde
That he of them had lost his pray.
This sterre that day tho went away
Fro that swete place where Jhesus lay.

[9]

Into Egipte Joseph thoo fledde
With the moder *and* with the chielde,
Where they abode till he was dedde
And of his wille he was begiled.
This sterre that day tho went away
Fro that swete place where Jhesus lay.

[10]

Kyng Herode thanne in his grete   [f. 54r
     wreth,
Seyng of them his *pur*pose lorne,
Infan*tes* full yonge he put to deth
Thurgh alle Betheleem that tho were
     borne.
This sterre that daye tho went away
Fro that swete place where Jhesus lay.

[11]

Thanne, as the *pr*ophesie Ysay
Had *pr*ophesied long tyme before,
A voice was hurde in blisse an hye
Of grete weping *and* wayling sore.
This sterre that day tho went away
Fro that swete place where Jhesus lay.

[12]

Honoure to Criste, that now was borne,
As *pr*ophecy had saide before,
To save mankyende, that was forlorne,
And to his blisse for to restore.
This sterre that day tho went away
Fro that swete place where Jhesus lay.

burden, l. 1. Twelfthe] MS. xii.
stza. 1, l. 1. Twelfthe] MS. xii[the].

130

Cambridge University Library. MS. Ee.
     I. 12   By James Ryman, *c.* 1492
f. 58r

Of a mayden to vs borne is
The Sonne of God and King of Blis.

[1]

Nowe this tyme Rex Pacificus
Is man become for loue of vs,
And his name is called Jhesus,
     The Sonne of God *and* King of Blis.

[2]

On Twelfthe Daye came king*es* thre
W*ith* golde, encense, *and* myrre so fre
Vnto Betheleem to seke *and* see
     The Sonne of God *and* King of Blis.

[3]

On Twelfth Daye by grace dyvyne
Atte the fest of architriclyn
Crist turned water into wyne,
     The Sonne of God *and* King of Blis.

[4]

On Twelfthe Daye in Jordan floode
Of Jhon Baptist w*ith* a myelde moode
Criste was baptized, that Lorde so goode
     The Sonne of God *and* King of Blis.

[5]

Ouer his hed there stod a dove;
A voice was hurde in blis aboue:
'This is my chielde, the whiche I loue,
     The Sonne of God *and* King of Blisse.'

[6]

Bothe God *and* man, in our*e* nature
He sanctified the waters pure,
Of heuen blisse to make vs sure,
     The Sonne of God *and* King of Blisse.

stzas. 2, 4, l. 1. Twelfthe] MS. xii[the].
stza. 3, l. 1. Twelfth] MS. xii[th].

131

a. *British Museum.* MS. Addit. 5665
                              XVI *cent.*
f. 40v

Jhesus aute*m* hodie
Regressus est a Jordane.
Jhesus autem hodie
Regressus est a Jordane.

[1]

When Jh*e*sus C*ri*ste baptyzed was,   [f. 41r
The Holy Gost descended w*ith* grace;
The Fad*er* voys was herde in the place:
     'Hic est Filius meus; ipsum audite.'

[2]

There were thre persons and o   [f. 40ᵛ
    Lorde,
The Sone baptized with on acorde,
The Fader sayde this blessed worde:
    'Hic est Filius meus; [ipsum audite.']

[3]

Considere now, all Cristiante,
How the Fader sayde bycause of the
The grete mistery of the Trinite:
    'Hic est Filius meus; [ipsum audite.']

[4]

Now, Jhesu, as thou art bothe   [f. 41ʳ
    God and man,
And were baptized in flom Jordayn,
Atte oure last ende, we pray the, say than:
    'Hic est filius meus; [ipsum audite.']

MS. heading (repeated on f. 41ʳ): Epiphanie.
stza. 2, l. 1. o] MS. oo.   l. 4. [ipsum audite]]
    MS. cᵒ.
Signatures: f. 40ᵛ. Hyt ys gode to be gracius,
    sayde John Trouluffe. f. 41ʳ. Well Fare thyn
    herte, sayde Smert.

b. *Balliol College, Oxford.* MS. 354,
f. 178 ʳ ᵃⁿᵈ ᵛ. XVI cent.

burden, l. 2. egressus est de virgine.
ll. 3, 4. omits.
stza. 1, l. 2. with] by.   l. 3. the place] that
    place.
stzas. 1–4, l. 4. hic est filius meus dilectus ipsum
    audite.
stza. 2, l. 1. There] They. thre] iii.   and] in.
    l. 2. baptized] baptised was.
stza. 4, l. 2. were] was. in] at.
At end: Explicit.

132

A. *Balliol College, Oxford.* MS. 354
                         XVI cent.
f. 228ʳ

    Caput apri refero,
    Resonens laudes Domino.

[1]

The boris hed in hondes I brynge,
With garlondes gay and byrdes syngynge;
I pray you all, helpe me to synge,
    Qui estis in conviuio.

[2]

The boris hede, I vnderstond,
Ys cheff seruyce in all this londe;
Whersoever it may be fonde,
    Seruitur cum sinapio.

[3]

The boris hede, I dare well say,
Anon after the Twelfth Day
He taketh his leve and goth away,
    Exiuit tunc de patria.

MS. marks burden: fote.
stza. 3, l. 2. Twelfth] MS. xiiᵗʰ.

B. *Bodleian Library.* Rawlinson 4to. 598
  (10) (Wynkyn de Worde)   1521
verso

    Caput apri differo,
    Reddens laudes Domino.

[1]

The bores heed in hande bring I,
With garlans gay and rosemary;
I pray you all, synge merely,
    Qui estis in conuiuio.

[2]

The bores heed, I vnderstande,
Is the chefe seruyce in this lande;
Loke, where euer it be fande,
    Seruite cum cantico.

[3]

Be gladde, lordes, bothe more and lasse,
For this hath ordeyned our stewarde
To chere you all this Christmasse,
    The bores heed with mustarde.

Heading in original: A caroll bringyng in the
    bores heed.
burden, l. 2. laudes] Orig. laudens.
stza. 2, l. 2. chefe] Orig. thefe.
At end: Finis.
A MS. note at the head (XVI cent.) reads: a
    carrol to syng. The same hand has written after
    the Finis: Roger . . y . . e (surname illegible).

C a. *Queen's College, Oxford.* Traditional
    version   1921

    Caput apri defero,
    Reddens laudes Domino.

[1]

The Boar's head in hand bear I,
Bedeck'd with bays and rosemary.
And I pray you, masters, be merry,
  Quot estis in convivio.

[2]

The Boar's head, as I understand,
Is the bravest dish in all the land,
When thus bedeck'd with a gay garland.
  Let us servire cantico.

[3]

Our steward hath provided this,
In honour of the King of Bliss,
Which on this day to be served is,
  In Reginensi Atrio.

b. *Queen's College, Oxford.* Traditional version, 1811

stza. 1, l. 3. masters] my masters.
stza. 2, l. 2. bravest] rarest. the (2)] this.
  l. 3. When thus bedeck'd] Which thus bedeck'd.
The following readings are supplied from MS.
  notes in the Bodleian Library's copy of Dibdin's *Typographical Antiquities* (London,
  1812) 'from a MS. in the handwriting of T.
  Hearne, anno 1718':
stza. 1, l. 3. you] ye. be merry] merry be.
stza. 2, l. 2. rarest] bravest.
stza. 3, l. 1. hath] has.

133

British Museum. MS. Addit. 5665
                          XVI *cent.*
f. 7ᵛ

  Nowell, nowell, nowell, nowell,
  Tydyng*es* gode Y thyng[ke] to telle.
  Nowell, nowell, nowell, nowell,
  Tydyng*es* gode Y thyngke *to   [*f. 8ʳ
  telle.

[1]

The borys hede that we bryng here
Betokeneth a P*ri*nce withowte pere
Ys born this day to bye v*s* dere;
  Nowell, nowelle.

[2]

A bore ys a souerayn beste   [f. 7ᵛ
And acceptab[l]e in eu*er*y feste;
So mote thys Lord be to moste *and* leste;
  Nowell, [nowelle.]

[3]

This borys hede we bryng w*ith* song
In worchyp of hym that thus sprang
Of a virgine to redresse all wrong;
  Nowell, [nowelle.]

MS. heading: In die natiuitat*is.*
stza. 1, l. 3. vs] MS. v*us.*
Signature: Smert.

134

Bodleian Library. MS. Eng. poet. e. 1
                          XV *cent.*
f. 29ᵛ

  Po, po, po, po,
  Loue brane *and* so do mo.

[1]

At the begy*n*nyng of the mete
Of a borys hed ye schal hete,
And in the mustard ye xal wete,
  And ye xal syngyn or ye gon.

[2]

Wolcu*m* be ye th*at* ben here,
And ye xal haue ryth gud chere,
And also a ryth gud fare,
  And ye xal syngyn or ye gon.

[3]

Welcu*m* be ye eu*er*ychon,
For ye xal syngy*n* ryth anon;
Hey yow fast, th*at* ye had don,
  And ye xal syngyn or ye gon.

135

Lord Harlech, National Library of Wales.
  MS. Porkington 10   XV *cent.*
f. 202ʳ

  Hey, hey, hey, hey!
  The borrys hede is armyd gay.

[1]

The boris hede i*n* hond I bryng,
W*ith* garlond gay in porttoryng;
I pray yow all w*ith* me to synge, [f. 202ᵛ
  W*ith* hay!

[2]

Lordys, knyghtt*us* and skyers,
Persons, prystis, and wycars,
The boris hede ys the fur[s]t mes,
  W*ith* hay!

[3]

The boris hede, as I yow say,
He takis his leyfe *and* gothe his way
Son af*ter* the Tweylffyt Day,
    W*ith* hay!

[4]

The*n* co*m*mys i*n* the secund kowrs w*ith*
    mykyll pryd,
The crann*us and* the heyrro*n*us, the bytt*er*is
    by th*er* syde,
The p*er*trychys *and* the plowers, the wod-
    cok*us and* the snyt,
    W*ith* hay!

[5]

Larkys i*n* hoot schow, ladys for to pyk,
Good drynk th*er*to, lycyvs and fyn*n*,
Blwet of allmayn*n*, romnay and wyin,
    W*ith* hay!

[6]

Gud bred, alle, *and* wyin, da*re* I well say,
The boris hede w*ith* musterd armyd soo
    gay.

[7]

Furma*n*te to potdtage, w*ith* we*n*nissu*n* fyn*n*,
And the ho*m*buls of the dow, *and* all th*at*
    eu*er* co*m*mis in.

[8]

Cappons ibake, w*ith* the pesys of the roow,
Reysons of corrans, w*ith* odyre spysis moo.

stza. 1, l. 2. W*ith*] MS. W^tt (*so throughout*).
stza. 3, l. 3. Tweylffyt] MS. xii theylffyt.

136

A. *British Museum.* MS. Harley 5396
                                    XV *cent.*
f. 275^v

    Nay, Iuy, nay, hyt shal not be, iwys;
    Let Holy hafe the maystry, as the
        maner ys.

[1]

Holy stond in the hall, fayre to behold;
Iuy stond wit*h*out the dore; she ys ful sore
    a-cold.

[2]

Holy *and* hys mery men, they dawnsyn *and*
    they syng;
Iuy *and* hur maydenys, they wepyn *and*
    they wryng.

[3]

Ivy hath a kybe; she kaght yt w*ith* the colde;
So mot they all haf ae th*at* w*ith* Ivy hold.

[4]

Holy hat berys as rede as any rose;
The foster, the hunters kepe hem fro the
    doo[s].

[5]

Iuy hath berys as blake as any slo;
Ther com the oule *and* ete hym as she goo.

[6]

Holy hath byrdys, a ful fayre flok,
The nyghtyngale, the poppynguy, the
    gayntyl lauyrok.

[7]

Gode Iuy, what byrdys ast th*o*u?
Non but the howlat, th*at* kreye, 'How,
    how!'

MS. heading (*in later hand*): A Song on the Ivy
    and the Holly.
The repetition of the burden is indicated as
    follows: stza. 1: Nay Iuy.   stzas. 2, 6: Nay.
    stza. 3: Nay Iuy noy hyt.   stzas. 4, 5: Nay
    Iuy nay hyt.   stza. 7: Nay Iuy nay hyt
    shalnot.

B. *Balliol College, Oxford.* MS. 354
                                    XVI *cent.*
f. 251^r

    Nay, nay, Ive, it may not be, iwis,
    For Holy must haue the mastry, as the
        man*er* is.

[1]

Holy berith beris, beris rede ynowgh;
The thristilcok, the popy*n*gay dau*n*ce i*n*
    eu*er*y bow.
Welaway, sory Ivy, what fowles hast thow
But the sory howlet, th*at* syngith, 'How,
    how?'

[2]

Ivy berith beris as black as any slo;
Th*er* co*m*meth the wood*e*-colu*er and* fedith
    her of tho.
She liftith vp her tayll, *and* she cakk*es* or
    she go;
She wold not for [a] hundred poundes s*er*ue
    Holy soo.

[3]

Holy with his mery men, they   [f. 251ᵛ
  can daunce in hall;
Ivy and her jentyl women can not daunce
  at all,
But lyke a meyny of bullokkes in a waterfall,
Or on a whot somers day, whan they be mad
  all.

[4]

Holy and his mery men sytt in cheyres of
  gold;
Ivy and her jentyll women sytt withowt in
  fold,
With a payre of kybid helis cawght with
  cold;
So wold I that euery man had that with Yvy
  will hold.

The repetition of the burden is indicated as
  follows: stza. 1: na[y] (*MS. torn*).   stzas. 3,
  4: nay.
stza. 2, l. 1. slo] MS. sho.   l. 4. [a] hundred
  poundes] MS. C *libra*.
At end: Explicit.

137

Bodleian Library. MS. Eng. poet. e. 1
                           XV *cent.*
f. 53ᵛ
  Alleluia, alleluia,
  Alleluia, now syng we.

[1]

Her commys Holly, that is so gent;
To pleasse all men is his intent.
  Alleluia.

[2]

But, lord and lady off this hall,
Whosoeuer ageynst Holly call—
  Alleluia.

[3]

Whosoeuer ageynst Holly do crye,
In a lepe shall he hang full hye.
  Alleluia.

[4]

Whosoeuer ageynst Holly do   [f. 54ᵉ
  syng,
He maye wepe and handys wryng.
  Alleluia.

138

Bodleian Library. MS. Eng. poet. e. 1
                           XV *cent.*
f. 54ᵉ
  Ivy, chefe off treis it is;
  Veni, coronaberis.

[1]

The most worthye she is in towne—
  He that seyth other do amysse—
And worthy to bere the crowne;
  Veni, coronaberis.

[2]

Ivy is soft and mek off spech;
  Ageynst all bale she is blysse;
Well is he that may hyre rech;
  Veni, coronaberis.

[3]

Ivy is green with coloure bright;
  Of all treis best she is;
And that I preve well now be right:
  Veni, coronaberis.

[4]

Ivy beryth berys black;
  God graunt vs all his blysse,
Fore there shall we nothyng lack;
  Veni, coronaberis.

139

St. John's College, Cambridge. MS. S. 54
                           XV *cent.*
f. 12ᵉ
  Nowell, nowell, ell, ell!
  I pray yow, lystyn qwat I yow [tell.]

[1]

Ouer all gatis that I haff gon
  Amonge the grovys so fayer and grene,
So fayer a brownch than know I non
  As Ivy ys, and that I mene.

[2]

Ivy ys grene and wyl be grene
  Qweresoeuer a grow in stok or ston;
Therfore I red yow, so mut I chene,
  Ye love well Ivy eueryschon.

[3]

I xall yow tell a reson quy
  Ye xall low Ivy *and* thynk no chame:
The fyrst lett*er* begynn*y*th w*ith* I,
  And ryght yevyn so Jh*esus* name.

[4]

The secund lett*er* ys *an* V;
  I lykyn to a wurthy wyffe;
Mod*er* sche ys and maydy*n* trewe;
  Non but on I that eu*er* bar*e* lyffe.

[5]

The thyrd lett*er* is *an* E;
  I lykyn to Emanuell,
That is to sey, 'Cryst w*ith* vs be
  And eu*er*more for to dwell.'

[6]

As I lay in my*n* bed alone,   [f.12ᵛ
  A comely lady sent to me
And bebad me rede theis letterys euery-
    schon,
  And all the bett*er* xuld I be.

[7]

All how Holy be youre fon,
  And wile yow towch w*ith* tray *and* tene;
Mekenes of Ivy xall hym ou*er*gonne,
  And fayer [w]urdys eu*er* betwene.

[8]

Ou*er* all gatys that I have gone
  Among theis grouys fayer *and* grene,
I have be wery son anon;
  My botte sche was th*at* Ivy tre.

[9]

Thus Ivy full fay*er* I gan spelle;
  So fay*er* a brawnch know I non;
I p*ra*y yow tent qwat I yow tel,
  And love well Ivy eu*er*yschon.

burden, l. 2. *The last word is destroyed by a tear*
  in MS.
stza. 3, l. 2. *After* thynk *MS. has an incomplete*
  letter s.   l. 4. ryght] MS. ryghh.
stza. 4, l. 1. *an*] MS. &.
stza. 5, l. 1. *an*] MS. &.   l. 3. vs] MS. v*us*.
stza. 9, l. 1. Thus] MS. thus thus.

139.1

British Museum. MS. Egerton 3307
                XV *cent.*

f. 59ᵛ

  Ivy ys good *and* glad to se;
  Iuy is fair in hys degre.

[1]

Iuy is both fair *and* gren,
  In wynt*er* *and* in som*er* also,
And it is medecinable, I wen,
  Who knew the v*er*tus th*at* long th*er*to;
    Iuy,
  It is god *and* lusty
  And in hys kynd a wel god tre.

[2]

Iuy hathe v*er*tues full good,
  Namely spredy*ng* on the gr*ou*nd;
Whed*er* it be in town or wod,
  It helpyth the sor *and* makyth it sound;
    Iuy,
  In bok is fond ful sekerly
  Th*at* gren is gladsom [for] to se.

[3]

When other treyss most del fail,
  Than berith Iuy hys berys ful bold
In g*re*t stormys of snow *and* hail;
  It spar*es* for no wedyrs cold,
    Iuy,
  To bry*ng* furth fruit ful p*ro*perly
  To best *and* byrd ful g*re*t plente.

[4]

The farest byrd that flyth be skye   [f. 60ʳ
  For gladnesse of that lusty tree
Mygh*t* make hys nest in gren Iuy,
  To norrysch hys byrd*es* fayr and free,
    Iuy,
  Ther in ys couert wel p*ri*uy,
  To comforth hym that ther wyll bee.

[5]

Wher it takyth hold it kepyth fast
  And strenkyth it that is hym bye;
It kepyth wall from cost and wast,
  As men may se al day at hye;
    Iuy,
  I can tel no caus qwy
  Bot we must loue that gentyll tre.

The burden is to be repeated as chorus.
stza. 2, 3 are written again on f. 60ʳ.
stza. 2, l. 4. it] *from text on* f. 60ʳ.
stza. 3, l. 2. ful] Text on f. 60ʳ *omits.*

140

Bodleian Library. MS. Eng. poet. e. 1
                XV *cent.*

f. 38ʳ

  Reu*er*tere, reu*er*tere,
  The quene of blysse *and* of beaute.

[1]

Behold what lyfe th*at* we ryne ine,
Frayl to fale *and* eu*er* lyke to syne
Thorow owr enmys entysyng;
    Th*er*for we syng *and* cry to the:

[2]

Come hyder, Lady, fayryst flovre,
And kepe vs, Lady, from dolovre;
Defend vs, Lady, *and* be owr socovre,
    For we cease not to cal to the:

[3]

Torne owr lyfe, Lady, to Goddys luste,
Syne to fle *and* fleschly luste,
For aftur hy*m* *in* the we trust
    To kep vs frome adu*er*syte.

[4]

Thys holy day of Puryfycacyon   [f. 38ᵛ
To the te*m*ple th*ou* bare owr saluacyon,
Jh*e*su Cryst, thin own swet Sone,
    To whome th*er*for now syng we:

[5]

Farwell, Crystmas fayer *and* fre!
Farwell, Newers Day wi*th* the!
Farwell, the holy Epyphane!
    And to Mary now syng we:

MS. heading: Of the puryfyca*c*ion.
The repetition of the burden is indicated after
    each stanza by: reu*er*tere &c.
stza. 4, l. 2. saluacyon] MS. so saluacyon.

141

Balliol College, Oxford. MS. 354
                                   XVI *cent.*
f. 224ᵛ

    Now haue gud day, now haue gud day!
    I a*m* Crystmas, *and* now I go my way.

[1]

Here haue I dwellyd wi*th* mor*e* *and* lasse
From Halowtyde till Ca*n*dylmas,
And now must I fro*m* you hens passe;
    Now haue gud day!

[2]

I take my leve of kyng *and* knyght,
And erle, baron, *and* lady bryght;
To wild*er*nes I must me dyght;
    Now haue gud day!

[3]

And at the gud lord of this hall
I take my leve, *and* of gestes all;

Me thy*n*ke I her*e*, Lent doth call
    Now haue gud day!

[4]

And at eu*er*y worthy offycer,
M*er*chall, panter, *and* butler,
I take my leve as for this yer*e*;
    Now haue gud day!

[5]

Anoder yer*e* I trust I shall
Make mery in this hall,
Yf rest *and* pease i*n* Ynglond may fall;
    Now haue gud day!

[6]

But ofty*n*tymys I haue hard say
Th*at* he is loth to p*er*t away
Th*at* oftyn byddyth, 'Haue gud day!'
    Now haue gud day!

[7]

Now far*e* ye well, all i*n* fer*e*;
Now far*e* ye well for all this yer*e*;
Yet for my sake make ye gud cher;
    Now hau[e] gud day!

At end: Explicit.

142

A a. *St. John's College, Cambridge.* MS.
    S. 54   XV *cent.*
f. 6ᵛ

    'Lollay, lay, lay, lay,
    My der*e* modyr*e*, lullay.'
    'Lullay, my chyld.'

[1]

A chyld ys born, ewys,
Th*at* all this word xall blys;
Hys joy xall neu*er* myse,
    For Jh*e*su ys hys name.

[2]

On the good Yowe morne
The blyssfull chyld was borne,
To wer*e* a crown of thorne,
    [For Jhesu ys hys name.]

[3]

Of a mady*n* so good
He toke both fleche *and* blod;
For us he deyd upon the rode,
    [For Jhesu ys hys name.]

[4]

Of a medy*n* so trew
Hc toke both fleche *and* hewe;
For us he deyd on a tre,
   [For Jhesu ys hys name.]

[5]

On the Estern mo[r]n all blyth
He ros fro deth to lyue
To make us all blyth,
   [For Jhesu ys hys name.]

[6]

On the Good Fryday at no*n*   [f. 7^r
To the deth he was done;
For us he deyd on tre,
   [For Jhesu ys hys name.]

burden, *after* l. 2. MS. c°.
stzas. 2–6, l. 4. MS. vt su*pra*.
stza. 3, l. 2. both] MS. hoth.
stza. 5, l. 2. fro] MS. for.

b. *Westminster Abbey.* MS. 20, f. 20^r.
XV *cent.* (stzas. 1, 2, 6, 5, and one
stanza not in a. Stza. 1 is written continuously without brackets and is possibly
intended to be used as the burden).

stza. 1, l. 1. chyld] Babe.   l. 2. That all]
omits.   xall] to joy and.   l. 3. myse] fade
and misse.   l. 4. For] *And.*
stza. 2, l. 1. the good Yowe] *c*ristmasse day at.
   l. 2. The blyssfull] thys.   borne] i borne.
   l. 3. to saue vs all th*at* wer*e* for lorne.
   l. 4. *And* Jhes*u*s.
stza. 5, l. 1. On Estyr day so swythe.
   l. 3. blyth] bothe gladde *and* blythe.
   l. 4. *And* Jh.
stza. 6, l. 1. the] *omits.* at no*n*] so son*e*.
   l. 2. the] *omits.* done] i don*e*.   l. 3. Be
twyx all morne *and* none.   l. 4. *And* Jhesu.
b *has an additional stanza at the end as follows*:

   On the Holy Thursday
   To heven*e* he toke hys way,
   The*r* to abyde foreu*er* and day,
      And Jhes*u*s [is hys name.]

B a. *Bodleian Library.* Douce Addit. 137
                            1822
f. 23^r

[1]

On Christmas day in the morn,
Our Saviour he was born,
Whom the Jews did hold in scorn,
   Sweet Jesus is his name.

This babe was born I wish,
To be the King o[f] bliss,
Our Saviour as he is,
   Sweet Jesus is his name.

[2]

On New-years day so clear,
He Circumcised were,
To be the son of god most dear,
   Sweet Jesus is his name.

[3]

On the twelfth day as is expressed,
The Princes from the East,
Our Lord they did caress,
   Sweet Jesus is his name.

[4]

These Princes they did bring,
The free will offering,
Unto their heavenly king,
   Sweet Jesus is his name.

[5]

On Ash Wednesday we hear,
Our Saviour tempted were,
By Satan most severe,
   Sweet Jesus is his name.

[6]

On Good Friday so good,
They nailed him to the wood,
And spilt his precious blood,
   Sweet Jesus is his name.

[7]

On Easter Sunday so bright,
A glorious star gave light,
Our Saviour rose from death to life,
   Sweet Jesus is his name.

[8]

On Holy Thursday so clear,
Our Lady sat in her chair,
With her Lullaby so dear,
   Sweet Jesus is his name.

[9]

Six days out of seven,
Our Saviour to us was given,
And ascended up to Heaven,
   Sweet Jesus is his name.

   This Babe was born I wish,
   To be the king of bliss,
   Our Saviour as he is,
      Sweet Jesus is his name.

stza. 9, l. 3. ascended] Orig. asceuded.

b. *A Good Christmas Box, Containing a Choice Collection of Christmas Carols* (Dudley: G. Walters, 1847), pp. 96–8.

c. Frank Sidgwick, ed., *Popular Carols* (London: Chambers and Sidgwick, Ltd., 1908), pp. 29–31.

stza. 1, l. 3. b He was crown'd with a crown of thorns. c He was crowned with a crown of thorn.
chorus, l. 1. I wish] b (I wish). c I wis.
stza. 2, l. 3. To be] b c *omit*.
stza. 3, l. 1. On] b c *omit*. as] b c *omit*.
stza. 4, l. 2. The] b c A.   l. 3. their] b c our.
stza. 5, l. 2. b c Our Lord attempted were.
stza. 7, l. 1. so] c *omits*.   l. 3. death to life] b dead to life. c night.
stza. 8 b c On Holy Thursday we hear
　　　　Our Lord ascended were
　　　　Unto the heavenly choir:
　　　　Sweet Jesus is his name.
After stza. 8 b *and* c *have this stanza*:
　　　　On Whit Sunday so clear,
　　　　Our Lady sat in the chair,
　　　　A lull and a lull most dear:
　　　　Sweet Jesus is his name.
stza. 9, l. 1. seven] b c the seven.   l. 2. b c To us our Lord hath given.   l. 4. b And glorious for to reign.
Final chorus, l. 1. I wish] b (I wish). c I wis.

143

British Museum. MS. Sloane 2593
　　　　　　　　　　　　　　　　XV *cent.*
f. 32^r

　'Lullay, my*n* lykyng, my der*e* sone, my*n* swetyng,
　Lullay, my der*e* herte, my*n* owy*n* der*e* derlyng.'

[1]

I saw a fayr maydy*n* sytty*n and* synge;
Sche lullyd a lytyl chyld, a swete lordyng.

[2]

Th*at* eche Lord is th*at* th*at* made alle thinge;
Of alle lordis he is Lord, of all kyng*es* Kyng.

[3]

Th*er* was mekyl melody at th*at*　　[f. 32^v]
　chyld*es* berthe;
Alle tho wern in heuene blys, thei made mekyl m*er*th.

[4]

Au*n*gel*e* bryght, thei song th*at* nyght *and* seydy*n* to th*at* chyld,
'Blyssid be th*ou*, *and* so be sche th*at* is bothe mek *and* myld.'

[5]

Prey we now to th*at* chyld, *and* to his mod*er* dere,
Grawnt he*m* his blyssyng th*at* now makyn chere.

The repetition of the burden is indicated as follows: stza. 1: lull m*yn*.　stza. 2: lullay.

144

British Museum. MS. Addit. 5666
　　　　　　　　　　　　　　　　XV *cent.*
f. 4^v

　'Lullay, lullow, lully, lullay,
　Bewy, bewy, lully, lully,
　Bewy, lully, lullow, lully,
　Lullay, baw, baw, my barne,
　　Slepe softly now.'

[1]

I saw a swete se*m*ly syght,　　　[f. 5^r]
A blisful birde, a blossu*m* bright,
　Th*at* m*ur*nyn*g* made *and* mirth of ma*n*ge;
A maydin mod*er*, mek *and* myld,
In cr*e*dil kep a knaue child
　Th*at* softly slepe; scho sat *and* sa*n*ge.

The words of both burden and stanza are written twice in MS., once for each voice.

144.1

Stanbrook Abbey. MS. 3　　　XV *cent.*
f. 241^v

　Lullay, my fader, lullay, my brother,
　My*n* owyn dyre sone, lullay.

[1]

Ye ben my father by creacion;
My brother ye ben by natiuite;
Of Adam we coome bothe al *and* su*m*me;
　My owyn dyr*e* sone, lull*ay*.

[2]

Ye ben my fader that made me of nowght,
And w*ith* youre blode vs all dyre bowght;
I am you*re* moder; knowe ye me nowght?
　My owyn dyre sone, lullay.

[3]

Ye ben my fader *and* I youre chyld;
I am youre moder vndefyld;
Loke on youre moder that ys so myld;
   Myn owyn dyre sone, lullay.

[4]

Ye ben my fader eternally;
My sone ye ben, so most ye drey
For Adamys gylt—ye know wel why;
   Myn owyn [dyre sone, lullay.]

[5]

Ye ben my fader that [m]ay nowght dey;
With yow my sone thus schal I playe;
Youre payne myn herte perschyth in tweye;
   Myn owyn dyre sone, lullay.

stza. 3, l. 3. on] MS. in.
stza. 3, l. 1, stza. 5, l. 1. fader] MS. fadrer.
stza. 4, l. 4. MS. Myn owyn &c.
stza. 5, l. 1. *The first letter of* may *has been
destroyed by the burning of a hole in the leaf.
The burden appears to have been written at a time
different from that of the writing of the stanzas.*

145

a. *Bodleian Library.* MS. Eng. poet. e. 1
                               XV *cent.*

f. 34ʳ

  'Modyr, whyt os lyly flowr,
    Yowr lullyng lessyth my langovr.'

[1]

As I vp ros in a mornyng,
My thowth was on a mayd yyng
That song aslep with hyr lullyng
   Her swet Son, owr Sau[i]owr.

[2]

As sche hym held in hyr lape,
He toke hyr louely by the pape,
And therof swetly he toke a nappe,
   And sok hys fyll of the lycowr.

[3]

To hys modyr gen he seye,
'For this mylke me must deye;
It ys my kynd therwith to playe,
   My swet modyr, paramowr.'

[4]

The maydyn frely gen to syng,
And in hyr song she mad mornyng,
How he that is owr Hevyn Kyng
   Shuld shed hys b[lod] with gret delowr.

[5]

'Modyr, thi wepyng grevyth me sor;
But I wold dey, thou haddys be lor;
Do awey, modyr, *and* wep no mor;
   Thy lullyng l[es]syth my lango[wr.']

[6]

Swych mornyng as the maydyn   [f. 34ᵛ
   mad,
   I can not tell it in this howr;
Therfor be mery and glade,
   And make vs mery [for] owr Sav[i]owr.

stzas. 4, 5, l. 4. *A few letters have been destroyed
by a tear in MS.*
stza. 6, l. 4. [for]] *supplied from Wright. In the
present binding the word is not visible.*

b. *British Museum.* MS. Sloane 2593,
ff. 16ᵛ, 17ʳ. XV *cent.* (burden and stzas.
1–5).

stza. 1, l. 1. vp] me. a] on.   l. 3. That] che.
l. 4. swet] dere.
stza. 2, l. 1. held] tok al.   l. 2. hyr louely] that
maydyn.   l. 3. *And* tok therof a ryght god
nap.   l. 4. the] that.
stza. 3, l. 1. gen he] than he gan.   l. 4. para-
mowr] myn paramour.
stza. 4, l. 1. The maydyn] That mayde.   gen]
be gan.   l. 3. That here sone that is our
kynge.   l. 4. shed] schred.
stza. 5, l. 1. Modyr, thi wepyng] b Your wepyng
moder.   l. 2 thou haddys be] ye wern for.
l. 3. Do awey] dowey.   l. 4. Thy] Your.

146

A. *British Museum.* MS. Addit. 5465
                           XVI *cent.*

ff. 50ᵛ, 51ʳ

  'A, my dere, a, my dere Son,'
    Seyd Mary, 'A, my dere;
  A, my dere, a, my dere Son,'
    Seyd Mary, 'A, my dere;
  Kys thy moder, Jhesu,
  Kys thi moder, Jhesu,
    With a lawghyng chere.'

[1]

This endurs nyght   [ff. 51ᵛ, 52ʳ
I sawe a syght
   All in my slepe:
Mary, that may,
She sang lullay
   And sore did wepe.
To kepe she sought
Full fast aboute
   Her Son from colde;

Joseph seyd, 'Wiff,
My joy, my lyff,
  Say what ye wolde.'
'Nothyng, my spowse,
Is in this howse
  Vnto my pay;
My Son, a Kyng
That made all thyng,
  Lyth in hay.'

[2]

'My moder dere,   [ff. 52ᵛ, 53ʳ]
Amend your chere,
  And now be still;
Thus for to lye,
It is sothely
  My Fadirs will.
Derision,
Gret passion
  Infynytly, infynytely,
As it is fownd,
Many a wownd
  Suffyr shall I.
On Caluery,
That is so hye,
  Ther shall I be,
Man to restore,
Naylid full sore
  Vppon a tre.'

The repetition of the burden is indicated as
  follows: stza. 1: A my dere A my dere a my
  dere son vt supra.   stza. 2: A my dere A my
  dere a my dere son vt supra.

B. *British Museum.* MS. Harley 2380
                                   XV *cent.*
f. 70ᵛ

[Burden lacking]

[1]

This endres nyght,
About mydnyght,
  As I me lay for to sclepe,
I hard a may
Syng lullay;
  For powaret sor scow wrypt.
He sayd, 'Ba, bay;'
Sco sayd, 'Lullay,'
  The virgin fresch as ros in May.

[2]

Sar sco soght,
Bot fand sco nought

To hap hyre Son Jhesu fro cold;
Josef sayd, 'Belif,
Scuet wyfe,
  Tell me wat ye wald,
    Hartly I you pray.'
He sayd, 'Ba bay;'
Scho sayd, 'Lullay,'
  The virgin fresch as ros in May.

[3]

Scho sayd, 'Scuett spows,
Me thynk greuus
  [M]y child sud lig in hay,
S[ith] he is Kyng
And mayd al thyng,
  And now is powrest in aray.'
He sayd, 'Ba bay;'
Scho sayd, 'Lullay,'
  The virgin fresch as ros in May.

[4]

'Hire he is
That bers the prys
  In all thyng that he as wrowght;
To hap my barn
Som clas I yarn,
  Bot wat it I ne rowght,
    This Yoles Day.'
He sayd, 'Ba bay;'
Sco sayd, 'Lullay,'
  The virgin fresche as ros in May.

[5]

'Modere dere,
Amend youre chere,'
  Thus says hire Son Jhesu hir till;
'Al of I be
In poure degre,
  It is my Fadirs will.'
And said, 'Ba bay;'
Sco sayd, 'Lullay,'   [f. 71ʳ]
  The virgyn fresche as ros in May.

[6]

'A crown o thorn
For sawllis lorn
  Opon my hed me most ned were,
And till a tre
So nayled be,
  Thare payns thay wyl me dere.
    I mon asay.'
He sayd, 'Ba, bay;'
Scho sayd, 'Lullay,'
  The virgin fresch as ros in May.

[7]

'The trewght sal fal
Hout of the postill hall
　Vnto you, modere, alloon to duell;
Qwyll I call
Fro the fends thrall
　Adam out of hel
　　To joy verray.'
He sayd, 'Ba bay;'
Sco sayd, 'Lullay,'
　The virgin fresch as ros in May.

[8]

Sco sayd, 'Swett Son,
Wen sal this be
　That ye sal suffire al this w[o]?'
'Moder fre,
Al sal ye se
　At xxx ye[re] and thuo;
　　It is no nay.'
He sayd, 'Ba bay;'
Sco sayd, 'Lullay,'
　The virgin fresch as ros in May.

[9]

'Son, I yow ax,
Qwen sal you ris?'
.　.　.　.　.
'Moder, verray,
Apon the thyrd day
　That Judas has me said contray.'
He sayd, 'Ba bay;'
Sco sayd, 'Lullay,'
　The virgin fresch as ros in May.

[10]

'I sall vp steiien
That ye ma se,
　Apon my Fader ryght hand,
In blis to be,
And so sal ye,
　To were a croune garland
　　In blis for hay.'
He sayd, 'Ba bay;'
Sco sayd, 'Lullay,'
　The virgin fresch as [ros] in [May.]

[11]

'Syng me ere
My moder dere,
　Wet souet uois, I you pray;
Wep no mor,
Ye gref me fo[r]
　Your mour[n]ing this a way.
　　Sing ore say lullay.'

He sayd, 'Ba bay;'
Sco sayd, 'Lullay,'
　The virgin fresch as ros in M[ay.]

MS. heading (*in later hand*): an old songe.
stza. 1, l. 2. mydnyght] MS. mydayght.
stza. 5, l. 7. bay] MS. hay.　l. 9. fresche]
　MS. freschs.
stza. 9, l. 1. ax] MS. ix.

147

Bodleian Library. MS. Addit. A. 106
　　　　　　　　　　　　　XV *cent.*

f. 14ᵛ

　'Lullay, lullay, my lityl chyld,
　　Slepe and be now styll;
　If thou be a lytill chyld,
　　Yitt may thou haue thi wyll.'

[1]

'How suld I now, thou fayr may,
　Fall apon a slepe?
Better me thynke that I may
　Fall apon and wepe.
For he that mad both nyght and day,
　Cold, and also hette,
Now layd I am in a wispe of hay;
　I can noder go nor crepe.
Bot wel I wate, as well I may　　[f. 15ʳ
　Slepe and be now styll,
Suffre the paynes that I may,
　It is my Fader wyll.

[2]

'Seys thou noghte, thou fayr may,
　And heres thou noghte also
How Kynge Herod, that keyn knyght,
　And of his peres mo
That be abowte nyght and day
　My body for to slo,
Thai seke me both nyght and day
　A[n]t werke me mekyll wo?
Bot well I wate, as well I may
　Slepe and be now styll,
Suffre the paynes that I may,
　It is my Fader wyll.

[3]

'How suld I now, thou fayr may,
　How suld I now myrth make?
My songe is mad of "walaway,"
　For dred I begyn to whake,
For dred of that ilk day
　[Th]at I my deth sall take
And suffre the paynes that I may
　For synfull man sake.

For well I wate, as well I may
  Slepe *and* be now styll,
Suffre the paynes th*at* I may,
  It is my Fad*er* wyll.

[4]

'Bot yitt me thynk it well besett
  If ma*n* haue of me mynd,
And al my paynes well besett
  If ma*n* to me be kynd.
Thar is no deth [th]at sall me let,
  And I hym trew fynd,
On the rode for to sytt,
  My hand*es* for to bynd.
Bot well I wat, as well I may
  Slepe *and* be now styll,
Suffre the paynes th*at* I may,
  It is my Fad*er* wyll.'

148

A. *British Museum.* MS. Sloane 2593
                       XV *cent.*
f. 16ʳ

  A New Yer, a Newe Yer, a chyld was
    iborn,
  Vs for to sauy*n*, th*at* al was forlorn;
    So blyssid be the tyme.

[1]

The Fad*er* of Heuene his owy*n* Sone he sent
His kyngda*m* for to clemy*n*.
  So blyssid be the tyme.

[2]

Al in a clene maydy*n our* Lord was ilyght,
Vs for to sauy*n with* al his myght;
  So blyssid [be the tyme.]

[3]

Al of a clene maydy*n our* Lord was iborn,
Vs for to sauy*n*, th*at* al was forlorn;
  So blyssid [be the tyme.]

[4]

'Lullay, lullay, lytil chyld, my*n* owy*n* der*e*
  fode;
How xalt th*ou* sufferi*n* be naylid o*n* the
  rode?'
  So [blyssid be the tyme.]

[5]

'Lullay, lullay, lytil chyld, my*n* owy*n* der*e*
  smerte;
How xalt th*ou* sufferi*n* the scharp sper*e* to
  thi herte?'
  So [blyssid be the tyme.]

[6]

'Lullay, lullay, lytyl child; I sy*n*ge al for thi
  sake;
Many o*n* is the scharpe scho*ur* to thi body
  is schape.'
  So [blyssid be the tyme.]

[7]

'Lullay, lullay, lytyl child; fayr*e* happis the
  befalle;
How xal thou sufferi*n* to dry*n*ke ezyll *and*
  galle?'
  So [blyssid be the tyme.]

[8]

'Lullay, lullay, lytil chyld; I synge al beforn;
How xalt thou sufferi*n* the scharp garlong
  of thorn?'
  [So blyssid be the tyme.]

[9]

'Lullay, lullay, lytil chyld; qwy wepy th*ou*
  so sor*e*?
And art th*ou* bothi*n* God *and* ma*n*, qu*at*
  woldyst th*ou* be mor*e*?'
  So [blyssid be the tyme.]

[10]

Blyssid be the armys the chyld   [f. 16ᵛ
  bar abowte,
And also the tet*es* the chyld on sowkyd.
  So [blyssid be the tyme.]

[11]

Blyssid be the mod*er*, the chyld also,
With 'Benedicam*us* Do*m*ino.'
  So blyssid be the tyme.

stzas. 2, 3, l. 3. MS. so blyssid &c.

B. *St. John's College, Cambridge.* MS. S. 54
                       XV *cent.*
f. 11ʳ

  A Newyr, a Newyr, the chyld was borne;
  Fadyr of Hewy*n* hys owy*n* Son haue send
    His cy*n*[gdom] for to clemy*n*.

[1]

The chyld was bor*n*e this endyr nyth,
V*s* for to saue *with* all is myth.
  So blyssyd be [the] tyme.

[2]

The chyld was bor*n*e this end*es* day,
All of a clene mady*n*, as *you* tell may.
  So blyssyd [be the tyme.]

[3]

All of a cl[e]ne madyn *our* Lord was borne,
All for to wyn th*at* Adam had forlorn.
   [So blyssyd be the tyme.]

[4]

'Lullay, my letyll chyld, my own swete
     seynt;
[Man]y scharp schour*es* xall thi body hent.'
   [So blyssyd be the tyme.]

[5]

'Lullay, lay, letyll chyld, my   [f. 11ᵛ
   own suete foode;
How xuld I suffyr thi fayr*e* body for to be
   re*n*t on rode?'
   [So blyssyd be the tyme.]

[6]

'Lullay, lay, letyll chyld; we owth myrthys
   to make,
For many scharp schour*es* xall thi body
   schape.'
   [So blyssyd be the tyme.]

[7]

'Lullay, lay, letyll chyld, w[e] out to mak
   myrth,
And so out eu*ery* C*ri*sten ma*n* to worchyp
   thi byrth.'
   [So blyssyd be the tyme.]

[8]

Blyssyd be the mod*er* the chyld bar*e* about,
And so be the mod*er* the chyld gane soke.
   [So blyssyd be the tyme.]

[9]

Blysyd be the mod*er* the chyld cam to;
Benedicam*us* D*o*mi*n*o.
   So blyssyd be the tyme.

The repetition of the burden is indicated as
follows: stza. 1: a newyr. stza. 2: fad*er* of
hewe &c.
burden, l. 3, stza. 4, l. 2. *The letters supplied in
the text have been destroyed by a tear in the
MS.*
stza. 1, l. 2. V*s*] MS. v*us.*
stza. 2, l. 2. you] MS. y*ur.*
stza. 3, l. 1. madyn] MS. mad madyn.

149

a. *National Library of Scotland.* MS. Advocates 18. 7. 21   *c.* 1372
f. 3ᵛ

   'Lullay, lullay, la, lullay,
   Mi der*e* mod*er*, lullay.'

[1]

Als I lay vpon a nith,
   Alone i*n* my lo*n*ggi*n*g,
Me thouthe I sau a wo*n*der sith,
   A maide*n* child rokki*n*g.

[2]

The maide*n* wolde wi*th*oute*n* so*n*g
   Hir*e* child o slepe bri*n*gge;
The child thouthte sche de[d] hi*m* wrong
   And bad his mod*er* se*n*gge.

[3]

'Si*n*g nov, mod*er*,' seide th*at* child,
   'W*at* me sal befalle
Hereaft*er* wan I cu*m* to eld;
   So don modr*es* al!e.

[4]

'Ich a mod*er*, treuly,
   Th*at* kan hir*e* cr*e*del kepe
Is wone to lulle*n* louely
   And si*n*gge*n* hir*e* child o slepe.

[5]

'Suete mod*er*, fair *and* fre,
   Sithe*n* th*at* it is so,
I pr*e*ye the th*at* th*ou* lulle me
   And sing su*m*wat th*er*to.'

[6]

'Suete sone,' seyde sche,
   'Wer*o*ffe suld I si*n*gge?
Wist I neu*ere* yet mor*e* of the
   But Gabr*i*eles greti*n*gge.

[7]

'He gr*e*tte me godli o*n* is kne
   And seide, "Heil, Marie,
Ful of grace, God is wi*th* the;
   Ber*e*n th*ou* salt Messye."

[8]

'I wo*n*dr*e*de michil i*n* my thouth,   [f. 4ʳ
   For ma*n* wold I rith none,
"Mar*i*e," he seide, "dr*e*de the nouth;
   Lat God of heuene alone.

[9]

' "The Holi Gost sal don al this,"
   He seyde, wi*th*oute*n* wone,
Th*at* I sulde bere*n* ma*n*nis blis,
   The, my suete Sone.

[10]

'He seide, "Thou salt beren a king
  In Kinge Dauitis see;
In al Jacobs woniing
  Ther king suld he be."

[11]

'He seyde that Elizabeth,
  That baruine was before,
A child conceyued hath,
  "To me leue thou the more."

[12]

'I ansuerede blethely,
  For his word me paiyede,
"Lo, Godis seruant her am I;
  Be et as thou me seyde."

[13]

'Ther, als he seide, I the bare,
  On midwenter nith,
In maydened withouten kare,
  Be grace of God Almith.

[14]

'The sepperdis that wakkeden in the wolde
  Herden a wonder mirthe
Of angles ther, as thei tolde,
  In time of thi birthe.

[15]

'Suete Sone, sikirly,
  No more kan I say,
And, if I koude, fawen wold I
  To don al at thi pay.'

[16]

'Moder,' seide that suete thing,
  'To singen I sal the lere
Wat me fallet to suffring
  And don wil I am here.

[17]

'Wanne the seuene daighes ben don,
  Rith as Habraham wasce,
Kot sal I ben with a ston
  In a wol tendre place.

[18]

'Wanne the tuelue dayghes ben do,
  Be leding of a sterre
Thre kingges me sul seke tho
  With gold, ensens, and mirre.

[19]

'The fourti day, to fille the lawe,
  We solen to temple ifere;
Ther Simeon sal the sey a sawe
  That changen sal thi chere.

[20]

'Wan I am tuelue yer of elde,
  Joseph and thou, murningge,
Solen me finden, moder milde,
  In the temple techingge.

[21]

'Til I be thretti at the leste
  I sal neuere fro the sterue,
But ay, moder, ben at thin heste,
  Joseph and the to serue.

[22]

'Quan the thretti yer ben spent,
  I mot beginne to fille
Werfore I am hidre sent
  Thoru my Fadres wille.

[23]

'Jon Baptist, of merite most,
  Sal baptize me be name;
Than my Fader and the Holi Gost
  Solen witnessen wat I ame.

[24]

'I sal ben tempted of Satan,   [f. 4ᵛ
  That fawen is to fonde,
The same wise that was Adam,
  But I sal betre withstonde.

[25]

'Disciples I sal gadere
  And senden hem for to preche,
The lawes of my Fader
  In al this werld to teche.

[26]

'I sal ben so simple,
  And to men so conning,
That most partize of the puple
  Sal wiln maken me king.'

[27]

'Suete Sone,' than seyde sche,
  'No sorwe sulde me dere
Mitht I yet that day se
  A king that thou were.'

[28]

'Do wey, mod*er*,' seid th*a*t suete,
  'Th*e*rfor ka*m* I nouth,
But for to be*n* por*e and* bales bete
  Th*a*t ma*n* was i*n*ne brouth.

[29]

'Th*e*rfor*e* wan to *and* thretti yer be*n* do,
  And a litel more,
Mod*er*, th*o*u salt m*a*ke*n* michil mon
  And seen me deyghe sore.

[30]

'The sarpe swerd of Simeo*n*
  Perse sal thin h*e*rte;
For my car*e* of michil won
  Sor*e* the sale smerte.

[31]

'Sa*m*fuly for I sal deyghe,
  Ha*n*gende on the rode;
For ma*n*nis ra*n*soum sal I payghe
  My*n* owe*n* h*e*rte blode.'

[32]

'Allas, Sone,' seyde th*a*t may,
  'Sith*en* th*a*t it is so,
Worto sal I bide*n* th*a*t day
  To bere*n* the to this wo?'

[33]

'Mod*er*,' he seide, 'tak*e*t lithte,
  For liue*n* I sal ayeyne,
And i*n* thi ki*n*de thoru my mith,
  For elles I wrouthte i*n* weyne.

[34]

'To my Fad*er* I sal we*n*de
  I*n* myn ma*n*hed to heuene;
The H*o*li Gost I sal the se*n*de
  W*i*th hise sondes seuene.

[35]

'I sal the take*n*, wan time is,
  To me at the laste,
To be*n* w*i*th me, mod*er*, i*n* blis;
  Al this than haue I caste.

[36]

'Al this werld deme*n* I sal
  At the dom risingge;
Suete mod*er*, here is al
  Th*a*t I wile nou singge.'

[37]

S*e*rteynly this sithte I say,
  This so*n*g I h*e*rde singge,
Als I lay this Yolis Day,
  Alone i*n* my lo*n*ggingge.

The repetition of the burden is indicated after
  the last stanza by: Lullay.
The speakers in the dialogue are indicated by
  marginal notes prefixed to stanzas as follows:
  stza. 3. J.   stza. 6. Ma.   stza. 27. Ma.   stza.
  28. Jc.   stza. 32. Ma.   stza. 33. iu.
stza. 10, l. 2. Ki*n*g*e*] MS. ki*n*g*es*.
stza. 11, l. 1. Elizabeth] MS. elizabetgh.
  l. 3. hath] MS. hatgh.
stza. 14, l. 3. ther] MS. th*a*t.
stza. 15, l. 4. al at] MS. at al.
stza. 16, l. 1. *In right-hand margin* MS. th*u*s lo.
stza. 21, l. 4. *In right-hand margin* MS. n*o*ta.

b. *St. John's College, Cambridge.* MS. S. 54,
f. 4[r and v]. XV *cent.* (burden and stzas. 1–9).

c. *British Museum.* MS. Harley 2330, f.
120[r]. XV *cent.* (burden and stzas. 1–5).

d. *Cambridge University Library.* MS.
Addit. 5943, f. 169[r]. XV *cent.* (burden
and stza. 1).

burden, l. 1. b lullay lay lay lay. c lay lay lulay
  lay. d lolay lolay.   l. 2. d *omits.*
stza. 1, l. 1. lay] b me lay. c me went.   vpon a
  nith] b this endyres nyth. c this enderday.
  d on yole is nyght.   l. 2. Alone] b All on.
  in] b *omits.* c on.   longging] b loue lokyng.
  d lon . . .   l. 3. wond*er*] b semyly. c d wel
  fay*re*. sith] c may.   l. 4. maide*n*] b mayn.
  c louely. d may. child] b cradyll. d hir
  child. rokki*n*g] b kepyng.
stza. 2, l. 1. maide*n*] b modyr. c mayd. wolde]
  c went. wi*t*houten] c wi*t*howt.   l. 2. Hire
  child o slepe] b A slepe her*e* chyld to. c hir
  child on slepe to.   l. 3. thouthte] b hym
  thoghth.
stza. 3, l. 1. th*a*t] b c the   l. 2. me sal] b xall
  of me. c schal me.   l. 3. Hereaft*er*] c Aftur.
  to eld] b of age. c til eld.   l. 4. So don] b
  So chuld tho. c For so done.
stza. 4, l. 1. Ich a] b c For eu*er*y. truely] b c
  sekyrly.   l. 3. b Sche most syng lullay.
  l. 4. *And*] b To. singg*en*] b bryng. c bryng*eth*.
  o slepe] b on ssepe. c a slepe.
stza. 5, l. 1. fair *and* fre] b seyd he. c sayd the
  child.   l. 2. it] c *omits.*   l. 3. the] b c
  you. th*o*u lulle me] b ye roke me. c ye wold
  me roke.   l. 4. sing su*m*wat] b su*m* qwat
  sey.
stza. 6, l. 2. suld] b chyld xald.   l. 3. Wist]
  b wost. yet] b *omits.* of the] b be sothe.
  l. 4. But Gabrieles] b Than of a angyll.
stza. 7, l. 1. godli] b gladly. is] b *omits.*
  l. 2. *And*] b he. l. 4. b Thou xalte ber*e* m*er*cy.

stza. 8, l. 1. wo*n*drede michil] b wond*er* gretely.
l. 2. wold] b know.   rith] b *omits.*   l. 4. of
heuene] b all mythy.
stza. 9, l. 1. The] b Th*a*t.   don] b do.
l. 2. b Thow he be owt of won.   l. 3. Th*a*t I
sulde ber*en*] b and xall haue *er*.   l. 4. The, my
suete] b Goddys owne. *after stanza:* b deus.
The repetition of the burden is indicated as
follows: stza. 1: b lullay, c lull. d lolay.
stzas. 2, 3: b lullay, c lull.   stza. 4: c lulay.
stza. 5. c lullay.

150

A. *National Library of Scotland.* MS. Advocates 19. 3. 1   XV *cent.*

f. 210ᵛ

This endurs nyght
I see a syght,
    A sterne schone bryght as day,
And eu*er* ymong
A mede*n* song
Was, 'By by, lulley.'

[1]

This louely lady sete *and* song,
    And tyll hur chuld con say,
'My Son, my Lord, my Fadur der*e*,
    Why lyus th*ou* th*us* in hey?
    Myn one swete bryd,
    What art th*ou* kyd
        And know*us* the Lord of ey?
    Neu*er*thelesse
    I will not sesse
        To syng, "By, by, lulley."'

[2]

This chyld ontyll is modur spake,
    And thus me thowght he seyd:
'I am kend for Heuu*n* Kyng
    In cryb thowgh I be leyd.
    Angel*es* bryght
    Shall to me lyght,
        Ye wot ryght welle, in fey;
    Off this behest
    Gyffe me yowr*e* brest,
        And syng, "By, by, lolley."'

[3]

'My aune der*e* So*n*, to the I say
    Th*ou* art me lefe *and* dere;
How shuld I s*er*ue the to pey
    And plese on al maner*e*?
    All thi wyll
    I wyll fulfyll,

Th*ou* wottes ryght well in fey
    Neu*er*theleyse
    I wyll not sesse
        To syng, "By, by, lulley."'

[4]

'My der*e* moder*e*, whe*n* tyme it be,
    Ye take [me] vp on loft,
And sett me ryght apon yowr*e* kne,
    And hondul me full soft.
    In yowr*e* arme   [f. 211ʳ
    Ye hape me warme,
        Both be nyght *and* day;
    Gyff I wepe
    And will not slepe,
        To syng, "By, by, lulley."'

[5]

'My aune der*e* Son, sen it is th*us*,
    Th*a*t th*ou* art Lord of all,
Th*ou* shuld haue ordent the su*m* bydyng
    In su*m* kyng*us* halle.
    Me thenkus aryght
    A kyng or a knyght
        Shuld be in rych arey,
    And yett for this
    I woll not seysse
        To syng, "By *and* lulley."

[6]

'My aune der*e* Son, to the I say,
    Me thynk*us* it is no laye
Th*a*t kyng*us* shuld co*m* so fer to the,
    And th*ou* not to the*m* dray.
    Thow schw[l]n see
    The*n* kyng*us* iii
        Apon the Twelfe Day,
    And for th*a*t syght
    Ye may be lyght
        To syng, "By, by, lolley."

[7]

'May aune der*e* So*n*, sen it is th*us*,
    At all thyng is at thi wyll,
I pray the grant me a bone,
    Gyf it be ryght of skylle:
    Chyld or ma*n*
    Th*a*t will or can
        Be mery on this gud day;
    To heuu*n* blysse
    Grawnt hit vs,
        And syng, "By, by, lulley."'

The repetition of the burden is indicated as
follows: stzas. 1–4, 6, 7: This.   stza. 5. This
endurus nygh. After the burden is also written:
This. *Perhaps this is to indicate that the burden
is to be twice sung.*
stza. 2, l. 4. thowgh] MS. thowght.
stza. 4, l. 4. me] MS. me*n*.

B. *Bodleian Library.* MS. Eng. poet. e. 1
XV *cent.*

f. 17ᵛ

Thys endris nyghth
I saw a syghth,
 A stare as bryght as day,
And eue*r* among
A mayden song,
 'Lullay, by, by, lullay.'

[1]

Th*a*t lovely lady sat *and* song,
 And to hyr chyld sayd,
'My Sone, my Broder, my Fader der,
 Why lyest th*o*u thus i*n* haye?
 My swete byrd,
 Thus it ys betyde,
  Thow th*o*u be kyng veray,
 But neue*r*theles
 I wyll not ses
  To syng, "By, by, lullay."

[2]

The chyld than spak i*n* hys talkyng,
 And to hys moder sayd,
'I be ky*n*dde am*e* kyng,
 In crybbe thou I be layd.
 For aungell*es* bryght   [f. 18ʳ
 Done to me lyght,
  Th*o*u knowest it ys no nay;
 And of th*a*t syght
 Th*o*u mayst be lyght
  To syng, "By, by, lullay."'

[3]

'Now, swet Son, syn th*o*u art kyng,
 Why art th*o*u layd i*n* stall?
Why ne th*o*u ordende thi beddyng
 I*n* sum gret kyng*es* hall?
 Me thynkyth it is ryght
 Th*a*t kyng or knyght
  Shuld ly in good aray,
 And than among
 It were no wrong
  To syng, "By, by, lullay."'

[4]

'Mary moder, I a*m* thi chyld
 Thow I be layd in stall;
Lord*es* *and* duk*es* shal worsshyp me,
 And so shall kyng*es* all.
 Ye shall well se
 Th*a*t kyng*es* thre
  Shal come the Twelfth Day;
 For this behest
 Yefe me thi brest
  And syng, "By, by, lullay."'

[5]

'Now tell me, swet Son, I the p*r*ay,
 Thou art me leue *and* dere,
How shuld I kepe the to thi pay
 And mak the glad of chere?
 For all thi wyll
 I wold fullfyll,
  Th*o*u wotyste full well in fay,
 And for all th*i*s
 I wyll the kys
  And syng, "By, by, lullay."'

[6]

'My der mod*e*r, whan ty*m* it be,
 Thou take me vp on loft,
And set me vpon thi kne,
 And handyll me full soft,
 And [i]n thi arme
 Th*o*u hyl me warme,
  And kepe nyght *and* day;
 If I wepe
 And may not slepe,
  Than syng, "By, by, lullay."'

[7]

'Now, swet Son, syn it is so,
 Th*a*t all thyng is at thi wyll,
I p*r*ay the, grau*n*te me a bone,
 Yf it be both ryght *and* skyll:
 Th*a*t chyld or ma*n*   [f. 18ᵛ
 Th*a*t wyl or kan
  Be mery vpon my day,
 To blyse he*m* bryng,
 And I shal syng,
  "Lullay, by, by, lullay."'

stza. 4, l. 7. Twelfth] MS. xii.

C. *Balliol College, Oxford.* MS. 354
XVI *cent.*

f. 226ʳ

This enders nyght
I sawe a sight,
 A sterre as bryght as any day,
And euer amonge
A maydyn songe,
 'Lulley, by, by, lully, lulley.'

[1]

A lovely lady sat *and* sange,
 And to her Son thus gan she say:
'My Son, my Lord, my dere derlyng,
 Why ligg*us* thou thus in hay?
 Myn own dere Son,
 How art th*o*u cu*m*?

Art thou not God verey?
But neuerthelesse
I will not sees
   To syng, "By, by, lully, lulley."'

[2]

Than spake the child, that was so yong,
  And thus me thowght he said:
'I am knowen as Hevyn Kyng
  In cribbe thowgh I now be layd.
    Angelles bright
    To me shall light
    [Thou knowest it ys no nay;]
    And of that sight
    Ye may be light
      And syng, "By, by, lully, lulley."'

[3]

'Jhesu, my Son, Hevyn Kyng,   [f. 226ᵛ
  Why lyest thou thus in stall?
And why hast thou no riche beddyng
  In sum ryche kynges hall?
    Me thynkith by right
    The Lord of Myght
      Shuld lye in riche aray,
    But neuerthelesse
    I will not sese
      To synge, "By, by, lully, lulley."'

[4]

'Mary moder, quene of blis,
  Me thynkith it is no lawe
That I shuld go to the kynges
  And they shuld not to me drawe.
    But you shall see
    That kynges thre
      To me will cum on the Twelfth Day;
    For this beheste
    Geve me your brest,
      And syng, "By, by, lully, lulley."'

[5]

'Jhesu, my Son, I pray the say,
  As thou art to me dere,
How shall I serue the to thy pay
  And mak the right good chere?
    All thy will
    I wold fulfill,
      Thou knoweste it well, in fay;
    Both rokke the still
    And daunce the thertill,
      And synge, "By, by, lully, lulley."'

[6]

'Mary moder, I pray the,
  Take me vp on loft,
And in thyn arme thow lappe me warm
  And daunce me now full ofte.

   .   .   .   .   .
 .   .   .   .

    And yf I wepe
    And will not slepe,
      Than syng, "By, by, lully, lulley."'

[7]

'Jhesu, my Son, Hevyn Kyng,
  Yf it be thy will,
Graunt thow me myn askyng,
  As reason wold *and* skyll.
    Whatsoeuer they be
    That can *and* will be
      Mery on this day,
    To blis them brynge,
    And I shall syng,
      'Lulley, by, by, lully, lulley.'

MS. marks burden: fote. The repetition of the
burden is indicated after each stanza by:
This.
stza. 2, l. 7. *supplied from* B. ll. 8, 9. *written in
lower margin with carets to mark point of insertion.*
stza. 4, l. 7. Twelfth] MS. xiiᵗʰ.
At end: Explicit.

D. *British Museum.* MS. Royal Appendix
58   XVI *cent.*
f. 52ᵛ

Thys endere nyghth
I saw a syghth
  A sterre as bryghth as day,
And euer among
A maydyn song,
  'By, by, baby, lullay.'

[1]

Thys vyrgyn clere wythowtyn   [f. 53ʳ
  pere
  Vnto hur Son gan say,
'My Son, my Lorde, my Father dere,
  Why lyest thow in hay?
    Me thenke by ryght
    Thow kyng *and* knyght
      Shulde lye in ruche aray;
    Yet neuerthelesse
    I wyll nott cesse
      To syng, "By, by, lullay."'

[2]

Thys babe full bayne aunsweryd agayne,
And thus me thought he sayd:
'I am a kyng above all thyng,
Yn hay yff I be layd,
For ye shall see
That kyng*es* thre
Shall cum on Twelfe Day;
For thys behest
Geffe me [thy] *brest,   [*f. 53ᵛ
And sing, "By, baby, lullay."'

[3]

'My Son, I say, wythowttyn nay,
Thow art my derlyng der;
I shall the kepe whyle thow dost slepe
And make the goode chere;
And all thy whylle
I wyll fulfill,
Thow wotyst hyt well, yn fay;
Yet more then thys,
I wyll the kys
And syng, "By, baby, lullay."'

[4]

'My moder swete, when I haue slepe,
Then take me vp at last,
Vppon yo*ur* kne that [y]e sett me
And handell me full soft;
And yn yo*ur* arme
Lap me ryght *warme,   [*f. 54ʳ
And kepe me nyght *and* day,
And yff I wepe
And cannott slepe,
Syng, "By, baby, lullay."'

[5]

'My Son, my Lorde, my Father dere,
Syth all ys at thy wyll,
I pr*ay* the, Son, graunte me a bone,
Yff hyt be ryght *and* skylle:
That chylde or man
May or can
Be mery on thys day,
To blys them bryng,
And I shall syng,
"By, by, baby, lullay."'

[6]

'My mother shene, of heuyn quene,
Yo*ur* askyng shall I spede,
So that the myrth dysplease me nott
Yn [worde] *nor in dede.   [*f. 54ᵛ
Syng what ye wyll,
So that ye fullfyll

My ten co*m*maundement*es* ay;
Yow for to please
Let them nott sesse
To syng, "Baby, lullay."'

The burden is thrice written, once for each voice,
and is marked: Cor*us*.

stza. 2, l. 9, stza. 4, l. 3, stza. 6, l. 4. *The words*
supplied have been destroyed by a tear in MS.

151

A. *Bodleian Library*. MS. Eng. poet. e. 1
                                        XV *cent.*

f. 20ʳ

'Lullay, my chyld, *and* wepe no more,
Slepe *and* be now styll;
The Kyng of Blys thi Fader ys,
As it was hys wyll.'

[1]

This endrys nyght
I saw a syghth,
A mayd a cradyll kepe,
And eu*er* she song
And seyd among,
'Lullay, my chyld, *and* slepe.'

[2]

'I may not slep,
But I may wepe;
I a*m* so wobegone;
Slep I [w]old,
Butt I a*m* cold,
And clothys haue I none.'

[3]

Me thovght I hard
The chyld answard,
And to hys moder he said,   [f. 20ᵛ
'My moder der,
What do I her?
In crybbe why a*m* I layd?

[4]

'I was borne
And layd beforne
Bestys, both ox *and* asse;
Mi moder myld,
I a*m* thi chyld,
But he my Fader was.

[5]

'Adams gylt
This man*e* had spylt;

That syn grevyt me sore;
Ma*n*, for the
Her shal I be
   Thyrty wynt*er and* mor.

[6]

'Dole it is to se:
Her shall I be
   Hang vpon the rode,
Wit*h* baleis to-bete,
My wou*n*des to-wete,
   And yeffe my fleshe to bote.

[7]

'Her*e* shal I be
Hanged on a tre,
   And dye, as it is skyll;
Th*at* I haue bovght
Lesse wyll I novght:
   It is my Faders wyll.

[8]

'A spere so scharp
Shall perse my herte
   For dedys th*at* I haue done.
Fader of Grace,
Wher[to] th*o*u hase
   Forgetyn thi lytyll Son*n*e?

[9]

'Wit*h*ovtyn pety
Her shall aby
   And mak my fleshe al blo;   [f. 21ʳ
Ada*m*, iwys,
Th*at* deth it ys
   For the *and* many mo.'

B. *British Museum.* MS. Addit. 5666
                XV *cent.*
f. 2ᵛ

   'Lullay, my child, *and* wepe no more;
     Sclepe *and* be now styll;
   Kynge of Blis thi Fad*er* he es,
     And thus it es his wyll.'

[1]

This end*er* nithgt
I sauy ha sithgt,
   Ha may ha credill kepe,
Hande eu*er* schuy sang
Hande sayde inmang,
   'Lullay, my child, ande sle[pe.']

[2]

'I may nocht slepe;
I may bot wepe;

I ham so wobegony;
Slepe I wolde,
Bot me hes colde,
   Hande clothse hauf I nony.'

[3]

The chylde was swet,
Hande sor he wepe,
   Hande eu*er* me thoht he sayde,
'Moder dere,
Wat doy I here?
   In crache wy ham I layde?

[4]

'Adam gilt
Th*at* man has spilde,
   Th*at* syn rues me fole sor;
Man, for the
Here sal I be
   xxx yere ande mor.

[5]

'Dolles to dreye,
Ande I sale dye,
   Ande hyng I sale on the rode;
[My] w[oun]dys to wete,
My bals to bethe,
   Ande gif my fleches to blode.

[6]

'A spere so charpe   [f. 3ʳ
Sale thirll my hert
   For the dede that man has done;
Fadere ofe Blys,
Wartu th*o*u has
   Forsakin me thi Sone?'

*Part of the burden is twice written with the two
upper parts of the music on f. 2ʳ as follows:*
Lulay my childe ande wepe no mor.
Lullay my child ande wepe no mor slepe
   ande be now still.
*In an inverted position on the same leaf the first
two lines are again written, with two-part
music, over other faded and partly illegible
writing.*
burden, l. 3. Kyng*e*] MS. kyng*es.*
stza. 2, l. 5. colde] MS. clode.
stza. 4, l. 6. yere] MS. here.

C. *Cambridge University Library.* MS.
   Addit. 5943   XV *cent.*
f. 145ʳ

   'Lullay, lullay, thow lytil child,
     Slep *and* be wel stylle;
   The Kynge of Blys thy Fader is,
     As it was his wille.'

[1]

Thys other nyghth
Y say a syghth,
    A mayde a cradel kepe;
'Lullay,' sche songe
And seyde amonge,
    'Ly stille, my childe, and slepe.'

[2]

'How schold Y slepe?
Y ma not for wepe,
    So sore Y am bygone;
Slepe Y wolde;
Y may not for colde,
    And clothys hau Y none.

[3]

'For Adams gult
Mankunde is yspylde,
    And that me rewyth sore;
For Adam and Eue
Y schal leue
    Here thrytty wynter and more.'

stza. 1, l. 3. sche] MS. ye.
stza. 3, l. 2. yspylde] MS. ysplylde.

152

A a. *Balliol College, Oxford.* MS. 354
                                    XVI *cent.*

f. 225ᵛ

    Now synge we with angelis,
    'Gloria in excelcis.'

[1]

A babe is born to blis vs brynge;
I hard a mayd lulley and synge;
She said, 'Dere Son, leve thy wepyng;
    Thy Fader is the Kyng of Blis.

[2]

'Lulley,' she said, and songe also,
'Myn own dere Son, whi art thou wo?
Haue I not do as I shuld do?
    Thy grevance, tell me what it is.'

[3]

'Nay, dere moder, for the wepe I nowght,
But for the wo that shall be wrowght
To me or I mankynd haue bowght;
    Was neuer sorow lik it, ywis.'

[4]

'Pesse, dere Son, tell me not soo.
Thou art my child, I haue no moo;
Shuld I se men myn own Son sloo?
    Alas, my dere Son, what menys this?'

[5]

'My hondes, moder, that ye may see,
Shall be nayled vnto a tree;
My fete allso fast shall be;
    Men shall wepe that shall se this.'

[6]

'A, dere Son, hard is my happe,
To see my child that sokid my pappe,
His hondes, his fete, that I dide wrappe,
    Be so naylid, that neuer dide amysse.'

[7]

'A, dere moder, yet shall a spere
My hart in sonder all to-tere;
No wondre yf I carefull were
    And wepe full sore to thynk on this.'

[8]

'A, dere Son, shall I se this?
Thou art my child, and I thy moder, ywis.
Whan Gabryell called me "full of grace",
    He told me nothyng of this.'

[9]

'A, dere moder, thorow myn here
To thrust in thornes they will not spare;
Alas, moder, I am full of care
    That ye shall see this hevynes.'

[10]

'A, dere Son, leve thy wepyng;
Thou bryngyst my hart in gret mornyng;
A carefull songe now may I syng;
    This tydynges, hard to me it is.'

[11]

'A, pece, dere moder, I the pray,
And comforte me all that ye may,
And syng, "By by, lulley, lulley,"
    To put away all hevynes.'

MS. marks burden: fote.
The repetition of the burden is indicated as
    follows: stzas. 1, 11: now syg we. stza. 2:
    nowe syng. stzas. 3, 4, 6, 7, 9, 10: now.
    stza. 5: now syg.
At end: Explicit.

b. *Bodleian Library.* MS. Laud misc. 683, f. 105ᵛ. XV *cent.* (burden and stzas. 1–6).

c. *Lord Harlech, National Library of Wales.* MS. Porkington 10, ff. 201ʳ–202ʳ. XV *cent.* (stzas. 1, 3–8, 11, alternating with stanzas of Latin hymn, 'Christe qui lux es et dies').

MS. heading: b here begynneth a cristemasse song.
burden, l. 1. Now] b *omits.*
stza. 1, l. 1. babe] c baby. to blis vs] b our blysse to. c vs blys to.   l. 2. I hard a mayd] b a maide ther was dyd. c A mayddyn I hard. *and*] c *omits.*   l. 3. She said] c *omits.* leve] c now leyfe.
stza. 2, l. 1. said, *and* songe] b sange and saide. l. 3. as] b that.
stza. 3, l. 1. dere] b *omits.* the] b this. c yow. l. 2. the wo] c thingis.   l. 3. c Or that I have mankynd iboght. or] b *illegible.*
l. 4. neu*er* sorow lik it] b neu*er* no sorwe so lyk. c th*er* neu*er* payn lyke yt.
stza. 4, l. 1. Pesse] b a pees. tell] c say thou. l. 3. c Alas that I schwlde see this woo. l. 4. c Hyt w*er*e to me gret heyuenys. my dere Son] b dere child. menys] b menyth.
stza. 5, l. 1. My hond*es,* moder] b yis modre myn handis. may] b here. c now.
l. 2. Shall] b c they shal. vnto] b to. c one. l. 3. fast] b c fastened.   l. 4. Men] b that man. c. Full mony. shall se this] b seeth this. c hit schall see.
stza. 6, l. 1. A, dere Son] b allas dere child. c Alas dy*re* son. hard] c sowrov now. l. 2. child] b sone. sokid] b sook. c sokys. l. 3. c So rwthfully taky*n* ovt of my lape. his fete] b or feet. dide wrappe] b sholde lappe.   l. 4. c Hyt w*er* to me gret heyuenys. so naylid] b nailled so sore.
stza. 7, l. 1. A, dere] c Alsoo. yet] c th*er.* l. 2. hart i*n* souder] c tendu*re* hert.
l. 3. c The blud schall keuy*re* my body th*er.* l. 4. c Gret heyuenys yt schall be to see.
stza. 8. c 'A, dere Son, th*a*t is a heyvy cas; When Gabrell cnellyd before my face And sayd, "Heylle, lady, full of grace," He neu*er* told me noothing of this.'
stza. 11, ll. 1, 2. c 'Der*e* modyr*e*, peys, nowe I yow pray, And take noo sorrow for that I say. l. 3. *And*] c But. syng] c synge this song. lulley (2)] c *omits.*   l. 4. put] c dryfe.

B a. *Harvard College Library.* MS. HCL 25258.27.5*, 'Carol Book A'   1767 p. 8

[1]

There is a child born to our blessing shall bring:
I heard a maid 'lullo by lollo' to sing:

'Peace, my dear child, of thy weeping,
    For thou shall be our heavenly King.'
  Now sing we, *and* now sing we,
  'To the gloria O tibi, Domini.'

[2]

'O mother, O mother, your wishes are naught—
It is not for me such carols are wrought—
Such were never and nor no woman thought—
    To the gloria O tibi, Domini.'
  Now sing we, *and* [now sing we,
  'To the gloria O tibi, Domini.']

[3]

'O my dear Son, why sayest thou so?
Thou art my son; I have no more.
When Gabriel begate thee full of grace,
    Thou needest not tell me of this case.'
  Now sing we *and* [now sing we,
  'To the gloria O tibi, Domini.']

[4]

'O, they will thurs't, mother, my head from out my heart;
A crown of sharp thorns they will not spare;
And with sharp spears my heart they will tear;
    To the gloria O tibi, Domini.'
  Now sing we, *and* [now sing we,
  'To the gloria O tibi, Domini.']

[5]

'Come you here, mother, and you shall see,
My hands arc fast nailed to the root of a tree,
And my feet, mother, are fast   [p. 9 nailed thereby—
    A realice sight, mother, for you to see.'
  Now sing we, *and* [now sing we,
  'To the gloria O tibi, Domini.']

[6]

Now sing we, and now sing we,
'To the gloria O tibi, Domini.'
Now sing we both more or less,
    And welcome be this Merry Christmas.
  Now sing we, *and* now sing we,
  'To the gloria O tibi, Domini.'

At head: 3 Carrol.
Before stza. 2 the first line of stza. 4 has been written and erased.
stza. 4, l. 4. the] MS. yᵉ.
chorus 5, l. 1. and] MS. &&.

b. *Harvard College Library.* MS. HCL.
25258.27.5*, 'Carol Book B' 1777,
pp. 58, 59.
c. William Sandys, ed., *Christmas Carols,
Ancient and Modern* (London: Richard
Beckley, 1833), pp. 122, 123.
At head: b Carrol the XVIII.
stza. 1, l. 1. to our blessing shall bring] c. of
our blessed Virgin.   l. 2. lullo by lollo]
b Lullo by Lullo. c lullaby.   l. 4. shall]
b c shalt.
chorus 1, l. 2. O] c *omits.* tibi] b Tobi.
Domini] c Domine.
stza. 2, l. 1. naught] b c Nought.   l. 3. Such]
c Such carols.   and nor no] c nor no. c by.
l. 4. O] c *omits.* tibi] b Tobi. Domini] c
Domine.
choruses 2–4. c Now sing we, &c.
stza. 3, l. 2. more] c moe.   l. 3. begate] c
begot.   l. 4. case] b Cause.
stza. 4, l. 1. thurs't] c thrust.   from out my
heart] b c from my Hair.   l. 2. A crown of
sharp thorns] b A Crown of Thorns. c With
a crown of thorns.   will] b me will.
l. 3. they] b c *omit.*   l. 4. O] c *omits.*   tibi]
b Tobi.   Domini] c Domine.
stza. 5, l. 1. Come] c O come.   l. 2. are fast]
c and my feet,   to the root of a] c to the
rood.   l. 3. fast nailed] c fastned.   thereby]
b there.   l. 4. realice] b realous. c vile.
stza. 6. c *prints as if final chorus.*   l. 2. O] c
omits.   tibi] b Tobi.   Domini] c Domine.
l. 3. Now;] b c And now.   l. 4. Merry]
b *omits.*
chorus 6. c *omits.*   l. 1. and] b *omits.*
l. 2 tibi] b Tobi.

153

Balliol College, Oxford. MS. 354
                                        XVI *cent.*
f. 226ʳ

'Lulley, Jhesu, lulley, lulley.'
'Myn own dere moder, syng lulley.'

[1]

So blessid a sight it was to see,
How Mary rokked her Son so free;
So fayre she rokked *and* songe, 'By, by.'
'Myn own dere moder, syng lulley.'

[2]

'Myn own dere Son, why wepyst thou thus?
Ys not thy Fader Kyng of Blis?
Haue I not do that in me ys?
Your grevance, tell me what it is.'

[3]

'Therfor, moder, wepe I nowght,
But for the wo that shall be wrowght

To me, or I mankynd haue bowght;
Myn own dere moder, syng lulley.

[4]

'Moder, the tyme ye shall see
The sorowe shall brek your hart in three,
So fowle the Jewes shall fare with me;
Myn own dere moder, syng lulley.

[5]

'Whan I am nakid, they will me take
And fast bynd me to a stake
And bete me sore for manus sake
Myn own dere moder, syng lulley.

[6]

'Vpon the crose they shall me caste,
Honde *and* fote nayle me faste;
Yet gall shall be my drynk laste;
Thus shall my lyff passe away.

[7]

'A, dere moder, yet shall a spere
My hart in sonder all to-tere;
No wonder thowgh I carefull were;
Myn own dere moder, syng lulley.

[8]

'Nowe, dere moder, syng lulley,
And put away all hevynesse;
Into this world I toke the way;
Agayn to [heaven] I shall me dresse,
Ther joye is without end ay;
Myn own dere moder, syng lulley.'

MS. marks burden: fote.
The repetition of the burden is indicated after
each stanza by: lulley.
At end: Explicit.

154

Cambridge University Library. MS. Ee.
1. 12   By James Ryman, *c.* 1492
f. 102ᵛ

Mary hath borne alone
The Sonne of God in trone.

[1]

That meyden mylde here childe did kepe,
As moders doth echone,
Butt here dere Sonne full sore did wepe
For synfull man alone.

[2]

Sche rockyd hym and sunge, 'Lullay,'
  Butt euer he made grete mone;
'Dere Sonne,' she seyde, 'telle, I the pray,
  Why thou doist wepe alone.'

[3]

'Moder,' he seyde, 'I schall be sclayn,
  Thatt syn did neuer none,
And suffer dethe with woofull payn;
  Therfore I wepe alone.'

[4]

'Lullay,' she seyde, 'sclepe and be still,
  And lete be alle thy mone,
For alle thyng is atte thyn own will
  In heuen and erthe alone.'

[5]

'Modere,' he seyde, 'hou schulde I sclepe?
  Hou shulde I leve my mone?   [f. 103^r
I haue more cause to sobbe and wepe,
  Sith I shall die alone.'

[6]

'Dere Sonne,' she seyde, 'the Kyng of
    Blisse,
  Thatt is so highe in trone,
Knowith thatt thou diddist neuer amys—
  Why schuldist thou dy alone?'

[7]

'Modere,' he seyde, 'only of the
  I toke bothe flesshe and bone
To saue mankynde and make it fre
  With my hert bloode alone.'

[8]

'Dere Sonne,' she seyde, 'thou art equall
  To God, thatt ys in trone;
For man, therfore, thatt is so thrall,
  Why shuldist thou dye alone?'

[9]

'Moder,' he seyde, 'my Faders will
  And myn, they be butte one;
Therfore by skylle I most fulfill
  My Faders will alone.'

[10]

'Dere Sonne,' she seyde, 'sith thou hast
    take
  Of me bothe flesshe and bone,
Yff it may be, me notte forsake
  In care and woo alone.'

[11]

'For man I most the raunsome   [f. 103^v
    pay,
  The whiche to helle is gone,
Moder,' he seyde, 'on Goode Fryday,
  For he may notte alone.'

[12]

'Dere Sonne,' she seyde vnto hym thoo,
  'When thou fro me arte gone,
Then shalle I lyff in care and woo
  Withowte confort alone.'

[13]

'Moder,' he seyde, 'take thou no thought;
  For me make thou no mone;
When I haue bought that I haue wrought,
  Thou shalt not be alone.

[14]

'On the thirde day, I the behyght,
  After thatt I am gone,
I wyll aryse by my grete myght
  And confort the alone.'

stza. 13, l. 1. thought] MS. nought.
stza. 14, l. 1. thirde] MS. iii^{de}.

155

a. *National Library of Scotland.* MS. Advocates 18. 7. 21   *c.* 1372
f. 6^r

  Lullay, lullay, litel child,
    Qui wepest thou so sore?

[1]

Lullay, lullay, litel child,
Thou that were so sterne and wild
Nou art become meke and mild
  To sauen that was forlore.

[2]

But for my senne I wot it is
That Godis Sone suffret this;
Merci, Lord! I haue do mis;
  Iwis, I wile no more.

[3]

Ayenis my Fadris wille I ches
An appel with a reuful res;
Werfore myn hertage I les,
  And nou thou wepist therfore.

[4]

An appel I tok of a tre;
God it hadde forboden me;
Werfore I sulde dampned be,
    Yef thi weping ne wore.

[5]

Lullay, for wo, thou litel thing,
Thou litel barun, thou litel king;
Mankindde is cause of thi murning,
    That thou hast loued so yore.

[6]

For man, that thou hast ay loued so,
Yet saltu suffren peines mo,
In heued, in feet, in hondis to,
    And yet wepen wel more.

[7]

That peine vs make of senne fre;
That peine vs bringge, Jesu, to the;
That peine vs helpe ay to fle
    The wikkede fendes lore.

At end: Amen.

b. *British Museum*. MS. Harley 7358, f. 12ᵛ.
XV *cent.* (burden and stzas. 1, 2, 4, 3, 5, 6).

burden, l. 1. litel] thou lytel.   l. 2. wepest]
    wepys.
stza. 1, l. 1. *omits.* l. 3. Nou] Thou.   *After
    l. 3* b *has the following line*: Wyth the, marye,
    that wente with chyld.
stza. 2, l. 1. yc wot ywys for thus hyt ys.
    l. 4. I wile] Ihc nel.
stza. 3, ll. 1, 2. *transposes.*   l. 4. For al my
    wepyng so sore.
stza. 4, l. 1. Ich tock anappel of that tre.
    l. 2. That my fader forbyd hyt me.
    l. 3. I sulde dampned] y dampned schal y.
    l. 4. thi] my. ne wore] nere.
stza. 5, l. 3. murning] wepyng.   l. 4. That
    thou] Thou that. loued] y lyued.
stza. 6.   Yet thou schalt suffry paynys mo
            In herte, in fot, in hondes to;
            Ic wot, ywys, that ys also
                To sauy that were forlore.
The repetition of the burden is indicated as
follows: stza. 2: L.   stza. 5: Lollay lay.

156

Cambridge University Library. MS. Ee.
I. 12   By James Ryman, *c.* 1492
f. 69ᵛ

    O synfull man, beholde *and* se
    What thy Maker hath done for the.

[1]

'O my dere Sonne, why doest thou soo?
    Why doest thou suffre alle this payne?
Thou bringest my hert in care   [f. 70ʳ
    and woo,
Without offence to se the slayne,
To see the blede at euery vayne
    And to beholde thy louely syde
    With a sharpe spere wounded so
        wyde.

[2]

'To se thy hede crowned with thorne,
    The blode rennyng vppon thy face,
Thy flesshe also with scourges torne
Thus cruelly in euery place,
This is to me a woofull case,
    Sith that thou art myne owne dere
        chielde
    And I thy moder vndefiled.'

[3]

'My dere moder, wepe thou no more,
    And moorne no more, moder, for me,
For why it greveth me full sore
    In care *and* woo the for to see,
    Sith I haue take nature of the
        And am thy Sonne, as thou hast seide,
        Thou beyng bothe moder *and* meyde.

[4]

'This wofull payne now will I take
    And bitter dethe, moder, also,
Onely for synfull mannes sake,
    To bringe hym out of payne *and* woo
    And fro the fende, his mortall foo.
        Though that he be vnkyende to me,
        Yet will I die to make hym free.'

[5]

'Sith thou art King of Heven Blis
    And Lorde of Alle, dere Sonne, also,
Why shuldest thou die for mannes mys
    And suffre alle this payne *and* woo,
    Sith that he is thy mortall foo
        Thus with scourges for to scourge the
        And thus to nayle the on a tre?

[6]

'Myne owne dere Sonne, it greveth me
    For to beholde thy woundes smert, [f. 70ᵛ
To se the nayled on a tree,
    Thy blode bleding oute of thyn hert.
    Why doest thou bere mannes desert,
        Sith that to the he is vnkyende,
        And loue of hym thou cannest non
            fynde?'

[7]

'Scripture, moder, I must fulfille;
Wherefore I toke nature of the,
For why it is my Faders wille
That I shall die to make man fre.
It is the wille also of me
To suffre deth for mannes mys
And bringe hym to eternall blis.

[8]

'Sith man of me mercy doth craue,
And I am Lorde of Indulgence,
Of my pite I will hym save
And forgeve hym alle his offence.
With hym, truly, I will dispence
And pay his raunsom on the rode
With the treasoure of my hert blode.'

157

A. *Huntington Library. Christmas carolles
newely Inprynted* (Richard Kele) *c.* 1550

p. [31]

Gaudeamus synge we
In hoc sacro tempore;
    Puer nobis natus est
Ex Maria virgine.

[1]

'Mary moder, come and se:
Thy Sone is nayled on a tre,
Hande and fote; he may not go;
    His body is wrapped all in wo.

[2]

'Upon a tre nayled he is
To brynge vs all to heuen blyss
For Adam, that dyde amysse
    For an aple that was so fre.

[3]

'From his heed vnto his too
His skynne is torne, and flesshe also;
His body is bothe wanne and blo,
    And nayled he is on a tre.

[4]

'Thy louely Sone that thou hast borne
Is crowned with a crowne of thorne
To saue mankynde, that was but lorne,
    And brynge man but to his liberte.'

[5]

Whan Johan this tale began to tell,
Mary wolde no lenger dwell,

But went amonge the Jewes fell,
    Where she myght her Sone se.

[6]

'My swete Sone that arte me dere, [p. [32]
Why hangest thou on rode here?
Thy hede is wrythen all in a brere;
    Louely Sone, what may this be?'

[7]

'Moder, to Johan I the betake;
Johan, kepe this woman for my sake.
On rode I am, emendes to make
    For synfull man, as ye may se.

[8]

'This game of loue I must play
For mannes soule, it is no nay.
There is no man that goth by the way
    But on my body he may haue pyte.

[9]

'This payne that men haue me wrought,
For synfull soules I haue it bought;
Of all this smerte yet rewe I nought
    If man wolde be kynde to me.

[10]

'My blode coleth; my fleshe doth fall;
I am athryst; after drynke I call;
They gyue me eysyll menged with gall;
    A wors drinke may there none be.

[11]

'Fader, my soule to the I betake;
My body dyeth for mannes sake;
To hell I must withouten make [p. [33]
    Mankynde for to make fre.'

[12]

God, that deyed for vs all,
Borne of a mayde in an oxe stall,
Graunt vs his realme celestyall.
    Amen, amen, for charyte.

stza. 10, l. 4. none be] Orig. be none.
At end: Finis.

B. *Bodleian Library.* MS. Eng. poet. e. 1
                              XV *cent.*

f. 27² ʳ

    'Mary modyr, cum and se:
    Thi Son is naylyd on a tre.

[1]

'His body is wappyd all in wo,
Hand *and* fot; he may not go;
Thi Son, lady, th*a*t th*ou* louyst soo,
    Nakyd is naylyd vpon a tre.

[2]

'The blyssyd body th*a*t th*ou* hast born
To saue ma*n*kynd, th*a*t was forlorn,
His body, lady, is al to-torn,
    His hed w*ith* thornys, as ye may se.'

[3]

Wa*n* Joh*a*n th*i*s tal began to tell,
Mary wyld not le*n*ger dwell
Thyl sche ca*m* to th*a*t hyll
    Th*er* sche myth her owyn Son see.

[4]

'My swet Son, th*ou* art me der;
Qwy haue me*n* ha*n*g the her?
Thi hed is closyd wyth a brer;
    Qwy haue men soo doo to the?'

[5]

'Joh*a*n, th*i*s woma*n* I the betake;
Kep th*i*s woman for my sake;
On the rod I hy*n*g for ma*n*nys sake,
    For synful man, as th*ou* may se.

[6]

'This game *and* loue me must pley [f. 27² ᵛ
For synfull sowlis th*a*t ar to dey;
Ther ys no ma*n* th*a*t gothe be the wey
    Th*a*t on my peynis wyl lok *and* se.

[7]

'Fadyr, my sowle I the betake;
My body deth for ma*n*nys sake;
To hel I go w*ith*howtyn wake,
    Ma*n*nys sole to make fre.'

[8]

Prey we al to that blyssyd Son
That he vs help wa*n* we not mo*n*,
And bry*n*g us to blys th*a*t is abone.
    Ame*n*, ame*n*, ame*n*, for charite.

stza. 1. l. 4. tre] MS. trer.
stza. 5, l. 4. th*ou*] MS. the.

C. *British Museum.* MS. Sloane 2593
                                    XV *cent.*
f. 23ʳ

    Nowel, el, el, el, el, el, el, el,
        el, el, el, el, el, el, el, el!

[1]

'Mary mod*er*, cu*m* *and* se:
Thi Sone is naylyd o*n* a tre,
Hand *and* fot; he may not go;
His body is wou*n*dyn al in woo.

[2]

'Thi swete Sone th*a*t th*ou* hast born
To saue ma*n*kynde, th*a*t was forlorn,
His bed is wrethi*n* in a thorn;
His blysful body is all to-torn.'

[3]

Qu*a*n he this tale bega*n* to telle,
Mary wold no*n* leng*er* dwelle,
But hyid her*e* faste to th*a*t hylle
Th*er* Jh*e*su his blod bega*n* to spyll.

[4]

'My*n* swete Sone, th*a*t art me der*e*;
Qwy ha*n* men hangyd the her*e*?
Thi hed is wrethi*n* in a brer*e*;
My*n* louely Sone, qwer is thi*n* cher*e*?

[5]

'Thi*n* swete body th*a*t in me rest,
Thi*n* comely mowth th*a*t I haue kest!
Now on rode is mad thi nest;
Leue chyld, q*ua*t is me best?'

[6]

'Wo*m*man, to Jon I the betake;   [f. 23ᵛ
Jon, kyp this wo*m*man for my*n* sake.
For synful sowlys my deth I take;
On rode I ha*n*ge for manys sake.

[7]

'This game alone me muste play;
For sy*n*ful sowl*e* I deye today;
Th*er* is no*n* wyght th*a*t goth be the way
Of my*n* peynys ca*n* wel say.'

D. *National Library of Scotland.* MS.
    Advocates 18. 7. 21   *c.* 1372

f. 121ʳ

Jh*e*sus. Maide*n* *and* mod*er*, cu*m* *and* se:
    Thi child is nailed to a tr*e*,
    Ha*n*d *and* fot; he may nouth go;
    His bodi is wo*n*den al in wo.
    Al aboute*n* he is to-toren;
    His heued is wr*e*thi*n* w*ith* a thorn;
    His sides bothe*n* on blode be;
    W*ith* blod hes ble*n*t; he may nouth se.

Ma*ria*. Mi suete Sone, th*a*t art me der*e*,
Wat hast th*ou* do*n*? Q*ui* art th*ou* her*e*?
Thi suete bodi th*a*t i*n* me r*e*st,
Th*a*t loueli mouth th*a*t I haue kist!
Nou is on rode mad thi nest;
Mi der*e* child, q*ua*t is me best?

Jh*esus*. Jon, this wo*mma*n for my sake—
Wo*mma*n, to Jon I the betake.
Alone I am w*ithote*n make;
On rode I ha*n*ge for ma*n*nis sake.
This game*n* alone me must pleyghe
For ma*n*nis soule this det to deyghe.
Mi blod is sched; my fles is falle;
Me thristet sor*e*; for drink I calle;
Thei yeue*n* me eysil medlid w*ith* galle;
For ma*n*nis se*n*ne i*n* wo I walle.
Yef thei were*n* ke*n*de to loue*n* me outh,
Of al my peine me ne routh.
Fad*er*, my soule I the betake;
Mi bodi deyghet for ma*n*nis sake;
Se*n*ful soulcs i*n* hcllc lakc,
To he*m* I go, awey to take.
Ma*n*nis soule, th*ou* art my m*a*ke;
Loue me wel, I the nouth forsake,
And my mod*er* herteliche,
An th*ou* salt come*n* th*a*t blisse to
Th*er* my Fad*er* is for euer*m*o.

The names of the speakers are written in the right-
hand margin.
At end: Am*en*.

E. *British Museum.* MS. Addit. 31042
XV *cent.*
f. 94ᵛ
[No burden]

[1]

'Mare mod*er*, c*um* and se:
Thin awne der*e* chyld ys nalyd on tre,
Both fowt *and* hand; he may not go;
That blyssyd chyld ys lappyd in wo.

[2]

'That blyssyd chy'

158

Balliol College, Oxford, MS. 354 XVI *cent.*
f. 223ʳ

'Mary mod*er*, c*um and* se
Thy swet Son nayled on a tre.

[1]

'Thys blessyd babe th*a*t thou hast born,
Hys blessyd body ys all to-torne
To bye vs agayn, th*a*t were forlorne;
Hys hed ys crownyd w*ith* a thorn.'

[2]

'Crownyd, alas, w*ith* thorn or breer,
Or why shuld my Su*n* thus hang here?
To me thys ys a carefull chere.
Swet Son, thynke on thy moder dere.'

[3]

'Thes wykyd Jewes w*ith* ther falshed,
Vnder ther fete they ga*n* hy*m* tred;
They wovndyd hy*m* thorowgh hond *and*
hed;
They left hy*m* not till he was ded.'

[4]

'Alas, alas, now may I crye.
Why mygh[t] I not w*ith* my Son dye?
My hart ys replenyshed w*ith* petye,
Fulfylled w*ith* payn most pytuysly.'

[5]

'Mary moder, greve you not yll;
From hevyn he ca*m* this to fulfyll;
Becavse ma*n*kynd shuld not spill,
He toke hys deth w*ith* p*er*fitt gud will.'

The repetition of the burden is indicated after
each stanza by: Mari &c.
At end: Explicit.

159

Cambridge University Library. MS. Ee.
1. 12　　　　By James Ryman, *c.* 1492
f 77ʳ

Mary myelde made grete mone
For her dere Sonne alone.

[1]

When fals Judas her Son had solde
To the Jewes wikked and bolde,
As he before to hir had tolde,
She was wofull alone.

[2]

When he came to Cayphas and An
To be juged for synfull man,
In her hert she was woofull than
For hir der*e* Son alone.

[3]

When that she sawe his flessh to-torn,
And on his hede a crowne of thorn,   f. 77ᵛ
And how the Jewes hym did shorn,
    She was wofull alone.

[4]

When hir dere Son, Jhesus so goode,
Was nayled fast vppon the roode,
She sobbed and wept watre *and* bloode
    For hir der*e* Son alone.

[5]

Whenne hir dere Son on the thirde day
W*ith* hir did mete and thus did say:
'Hayle, holy moder, wyfe, and may!'
    She was joyfull [alone.]

160

Cambridge University Library. MS. Ee.
    1. 12   By James Ryman, *c.* 1492
f. 78ʳ

    Mary so myelde alone
    For her chielde made grete mone.

[1]

In p*r*ophesy thus it is saide,
The whiche no wyse may be denayde,
That Criest shulde be borne of a mayde
    To save mankyende alone.

[2]

Mielde Mary, thus this mayden hight;
Her Son Jhesus, so full of myght,
For to bringe vs ayene to light
    Died for vs alone.

[3]

Symeon seide the swerde shulde goo
Thurgh hir myelde herte of care *and* woo,
For her Son shuld dey, and no moo,
    To save mankyende alone.

[4]

This mayden wept watre and blode
To see her Son so myelde and goode
To suffre deth vpon the rode
    For synfull man alone.

[5]

Noo hert can thinke, noo tunge tell can
The peyne that this mayde suffred than
To se her Son, both God and man,
    To die for man alone.

[6]

As grevous payne to her, and woo,
It was to see her Sone die soo
As vnto hym, that died thoo
    To save mankyende alone.

stza. 5, l. 1. tell can] MS. can tell *with transposition indicated.*

161

a. *John Rylands Library, Manchester.* MS.
    Lat. 395   XV *cent.*
f. 120ʳ

    Sodenly afraide,
    Half wakyng, half slepyng,
    And gretly dismayde,
    A wooman sate weepyng.

[1]

With fauoure in hir face ferr passyng my
    reason,
And of hir sore weepyng this was the
    enchesone:
Hir Soon in hir lap lay, she seid, slayne
    by treason.
Yif wepyng myght ripe bee, it seemyd than
    in season.
    'Jhes*u*!' so she sobbid;
    So hir Soon was bobbid,
    And of his lif robbid,
    Saying thies word*es*, as I say thee:
    'Who ca*n*not wepe, come lerne at me.'

[2]

I said I cowd not wepe, I was so harde
    hartid.
Shee answerd me with wordys shortly th*at*
    smarted:
'Lo, nature shall move the; thou must be
    converted;
Thyne owne Fad*er* this nyght is deed,' lo,
    thus she thwarted,
    'So my Soon is bobbid,
    And of his lif robbid.'
    Forsooth than I sobbid,
    V*er*yfying the word*es* she seid to me:
    'Who ca*n*not wepe may lern at the.'

[3]

'Now breke, hert, I the pray; this cors lith
    so rulye,
So betyn, so wowndid, entreted so Jew-
    lye.

What wight may me behold *and* wepe nat?
  Noon truly,
To see my deed dere Soon lygh bleedyng,
  lo, this newlye.'
     Eu*er* stil she sobbid;
     So hir Soon was bobbid,
     And of his lif robbid,
Newyng the word*es*, as I say thee:
'Who ca*n*not wepe, co*m* lern at me.'

[4]

On me she caste hir ey, said,   [f. 120ᵛ
  'See, man, thy brothir!'
She kissid hym *and* said, 'Swete, am I not
  thy modir?'
In sownyng she fill there; it wolde be noon
  othir;
I not which more deedly, the toon or the
  tothir.
     Yit she revived *and* sobbid,
     So hir Soon was bobbid,
     And of his lif robbid.
'Who ca*n*not wepe,' this was the laye,
And wit*h* th*a*t word she vanysht away.

stza. 3, l. 5. Eu*er*] MS. Evu*er*.

b. *Trinity College, Cambridge.* MS. O. 9.
38, ff. 62ᵛ, 63ʳ. XV *cent.*

stza. 1, l. 3. lay] layd.   l. 5. Jh*esu*] Jh*esus*.
l. 9. at] of.
stza. 2, l. 2. with wordys shortly] schortly wi*th*
wordys.   l. 4. lo] *omits.*   l. 5. So] Jh*esus*
so.   l. 8. the] thys. she seid] seyng. me]
the.   l. 9. may] com. the] me.
stza. 3, l. 3. me] *omits.*   l. 4. lygh] *omits.*
l. 8. the] these.
stza. 4, l. 1. said] and seyd.   l. 3. In sownyng]
And swonyng. l. 6. So] how.   l. 8. was]
ys.   l. 9. word] wordys.
At end: Finis.

162

Balliol College, Oxford. MS. 354 XVI *cent.*
f. 230ʳ

  To see the maydyn wepe her So*n*nes
    passion,
  It entrid my hart full depe wi*th* gret
    co*m*passion.

[1]

Bowght *and* sold full t*r*aytorsly,
  And to a pylar bownde,
The Jewes bet hy*m* full pytuowsly
  And gave hym many a wownd*e*.

[2]

Full maydy*n*ly, full moderly,
  Whan she the crosse behelde,
The teris fro*m* her eyen fill;
  She said, 'Alas, my childe!'

[3]

Wi*th* sharpe thornes the fals Jewes
  Crownid his holy hede:
They naylid hy*m* fast to the crosse,
  For they wold haue hym dede.

[4]

Eysell *and* gall they gave hy*m* to drynk,
  And perc*y*d hym to the harte;
His blessid mod*er and* maydyn clene,
  She swowned for his smarte.

[5]

Now, Mary myld, p*r*ay for vs,
  And bryng vs to the blisse,
Th*a*t we may be in joy with th*e*,
  Wher th*a*t thy swet Son ys.

The repetition of the burden is indicated as
follows: stza. 1: to see the maydy*n* wepe &c.
stza. 2: to ssee the maydy*n* wepe &c. stza. 3:
to se the maydy*n* wepe &c. stza. 4: to see
the maydy*n* wepe. stza. 5: to se the maydy*n*
wepe her sonnes passio*n*.
At end: Explicit.

163

a. *Balliol College, Oxford.* MS. 354
                     XVI *cent.*
f. 230ʳ

  'O, my harte is woo,' Mary, she sayd so,
  'For to se my dere Son dye, *and* so*n*nes
    haue I no mo.

[1]

'Whan th*a*t my swete Son was thirti wynt*er*
    old,
Than the traytor Judas wexed very bold;
For thirti plat*es* of money his Mast*er* he
    had sold,
But whan I it wyst, Lord, my hart was
    cold!

[2]

'Vpon Shere Thursday tha*n* truly it was,
On my Sonnes deth th*a*t Judas did on
    passe;
Many wer*e* the fals Jewes th*a*t folowed hy*m*
    by t*r*ace,
And ther beffore the*m* all he kyssed my
    Sones face.

[3]

'My Son, beffore Pilat browght was he,
And Peter said iii tymes he knew hy*m* not,
   *per*de;
Pylat said vnto the Jewes, "What say ye?"
Tha*n* they cryed w*ith* on voys, "Crucy-
   fyge!"

[4]

'On Good Friday, at the mownt of Caluary,
My So*n* was don on the crosse, nayled w*ith*
   naylis iii;
Of all the fre*n*des th*a*t he had neu*er* on
   could he see
But jentill [John] the Evangelist, th*a*t still
   stode hy*m* by.

[5]

'Thowgh I were sorowfull, no ma*n* haue
   at yt wo*n*der,
For howge was the erthquak, horyble was
   the tho*n*der;
I loked on my swet Son on the crosse th*a*t
   I stode vnder;
Tha*n* cam Lunge*us* w*ith* a spere *and* clift
   his hart i*n* sond*er*.'

The repetition of the burden is indicated as
   follows: stzas. 1, 3: o my hart is woo &c.
   stza. 2: o my hart &c.   stza. 4: o my hart.
   stza. 5: o my.
stza. 1, ll. 1, 3. thirti] MS. xxx^{ti}.
At end: Explicit.

b. *Huntington Library. Christmas carolles
newely Inprynted* (Richard Kele),
pp. [14–16.] *c.* 1550.

b *prints the carol in short lines throughout, eight
to the stanza.*
burden, l. 1. she sayd] dyde say.   l. 2. *and*
sones haue I] Seyng I haue.
stza. 1, ll. 1, 3. thirti] xxx.   l. 2. wexed very]
He became wonders.   l. 3. he had] had
he.   l. 4. it wyst] wyst of that.
stza. 2, l. 1. Vpon] On.   tha*n* truly] Truely
than thus.   l. 2. on passe] compas.
l. 3. fals] *omits*.   l. 4. th*er*] *omits*.
stza. 3, l. 1. browght] Then brought.
l. 3. vnto] to.   What] Now what.   l. 4. Tha*n*]
omits.   wi*th*] all with.   Crucyfyge] Crucifige
Crucifige.
stza. 4, l. 2. don] *omits*.   nayled] And nayled.
iii] thre.   l. 4. [John]] Johan.   stode] dyde
stand.
stza. 5, l. 1. wer*e* sorowfull] sorowfull were.   at
yt] no.   l. 2. howge] how it.   erthquak]
erth quaked.   horyble] And horryble.
l. 3. on] vpon.   on (2)] *omits*.   I (2)] he.
l. 4. Tha*n*] *omits*.   cam Lunge*us*] Lungeus

came. sper*e*] long spere.   clift] claue.   i*n*
   sond*er*] asonder.
The repetition of the burden is indicated as
   follows: stzas. 1, 2: O my herte is wo.
   stzas. 3–5: O my hert is wo.
At end: Finis.

164

*Huntington Library. Christmas carolles
  newely Inprynted* (Richard Kele)
                          c. 1550
p. [17]

[Alo]ne, alone, alone, alone,
Sore I sygh, and all for one.

[1]

As I went this enders day,
Alone walkyng on my play,
I harde a lady syng and say,
   'Woo is me and all alone.'

[2]

To that place I drew me nere,
Of her songe somwhat to here.
There sat a lady with sory chere
   That sore dyd sygh and grone.

[3]

'Beholde my Sonne crowned w*ith* thorne,
And all his body rent and torne,
Put to deth with shame and skorne
   For mannes sake alone.'

[4]

Forsothe it was a wonderous syght
To se her chylde, how it was dyght
For to brynge mankynde to [lyght,] [p. [18]]
   To saue vs from our fone.

[5]

Sythe it wyll no better be,
Pray we to that chylde so free
That we may hym in heuyn se
   Whan we shall hens gone.

Heading in original: . . . our Lady and her
   sonne.
The repetition of the burden is indicated after
   stzas. 1–4 by: Alone alone. &c. The entire
   burden is printed again after stza. 5.
At end: Finis.
*The beginning of the burden and the end of
   stza. 4, l. 3 have been destroyed by a tear in the
   leaf.*

165

Deleted from this edition. See Note.

166

Balliol College, Oxford. MS. 354
 XVI *cent.*

f. 225^r

'Shall I, moder, shall I,
  Shall I do soo?
Shall I dye for mannys sake,
  And I never synned thereto?

[1]

'I was borun in a stall
  Betwen bestes two,
To this world browght in thrall,
  To leve in care and woo.

[2]

'Whan I was viii days elde,
  The lawe fulfilled I thoo,
Circumsised as a childe;
  Than began all my woo.

[3]

'Thowgh my Fader be a Kyng,
  Myselff I went hym froo
Into this world to suffre many a thyng—
  See, man, what thow haste do.

[4]

'Man, I am thy frend ay:
  Thyself art thy foo;
To my Fader lok thow pray,
  And leve thy synnes that thou hast do.

[5]

'The Jeves were so fell
  That to Judas could they goo;
They kyssed me, as I you tell;
  "Hayle, Kyng!" said they tho.

[6]

'They bond me to a pyler anon,
  Honde and fote both twoo;
They skorged me with skorges son;
  The blode ran my body froo.

[7]

'They clothed me in a mantell rede
  From the toppe to the too,
With a crown of thorn on my hede;
  With staves they bett it therto.

[8]

'They browght me into Cayfas hall,
  Ther he was bisshop thoo;
Fals witnes on me they gan call;
  Moder, what shall I doo?

[9]

'I toke the cros on my bak full still;
  To Caluary than muste I goo;
I sett it down vpon an hill
  With other crossis moo.

[10]

'They hangid me vp that tide,
  Hondes and fette they naylid also,
And a theff on euery side
  To lykyn my body too.

[11]

'With a spere both sharpe and kene
  They clave my hart in two;
Water and blode ther owt ran—
  See, man, what thou haste do!

[12]

'With a spere both sha[r]pe and hend
  They clave my harte in iii;
Than yeldyd I vp the gost and dyed,
  That here all men may see.'

[13]

God, that dyed on the rode
  And spred his armes in the este,
Send vs all his blessyng
  And send vs all good reste.

The repetition of the burden is indicated as
follows: stzas. 1, 13: shall I moder. stza. 2:
shall I moder. stzas. 3, 4, 5, 8, 9, 12: shall.
stzas. 6, 7, 10, 11: shall I.
At end: Explicit.

167

British Museum. MS. Royal 20. A. I
 XV *cent.*

f. 120^r

Jhesu, fore yowre manie,
  Yblessid mot yowre body be.

[1]

There was suim teme byfalle a cas
That al the wordel ylore was;
Therefore Jhesus a modire ches;
  Ybore he was of Owre Lady fre.

[2]

Jhesus amange the Jewes yede,
And of ys deth he hade gret drede,
And to his help we had gret nede
    Jhesus wist wel how hit chod be.

[3]

Judas wered of sypres bolde;   [f. 120ᵛ
To honde Pilatus Jhesus he solde;
On his ere it was ytolde
    How Jhesus sode ygiled be.

[4]

Judas wolde owre Lord haue custt;
Turmentowres stod him next,
Wat hi wold do wel Christ west:
    There y tok that child so fre.

[5]

To o pilere Jhesus hi bownde;
Hy tok here sciurges yn here hond;
Hy bet him there wyt mechill wronge;
    Hit was gret pete for to se.

[6]

The Jewes cride wundir lowde;
Hi naylede is body on the rode,
And is mod[er] by him stode;
The teris were of rede blode
    That che wep for here Sone so fre.

[7]

Longis nest wat he dede:
He chef that spere al in that tide;
He stonge God depe in is rit syde;
    The blode ran don enlonges that tre.

[8]

Enlonge the chaft that blod doun ran;
Longis wyt is hond he nam;
Wel st[i]llelyche Longis gan stonde;
He wypede is eyen wit ys hond;
    Anon myte the blynde knyght se.

[9]

Longis lokede wel an hy;
His sinnes there anon he sy;
'Lord,' he seyde, 'Y cry the mercy.'
    'Longis,' he sayde, 'foreyeue it be.'

[10]

At erthe hy browte that childe wel blythe;
He aros fro the det to the lyue;
To helle he wente wit ys wowndys fyue,
    That was gret pete fore to se.

stza. 2, l. 3, stza. 3, l. 3. his] MS. is his.
stza. 4, l. 3. Christ] MS. Christi.
stza. 10, l. 1. wel bly] *deleted in MS. A fourth
line is erased. Below it is written*: owre.

168

British Museum. MS. Sloane 2593
                        XV *cent.*
f. 22ʳ

    Synge we, synge we,
    'Gloria tibi, Domine.'

[1]

Man, if thou hast synnyd owth,
Chaunge redely thi thowth;
Thynk on hym that haght the bowth
    So dere vpon the rode tre.

[2]

Thynk, he cam for to ben born
To beyin ayen that was forlorn
Many a thousand yer beforn,
    Out of his owyn mageste.

[3]

Thynk, the Juwis quan hym tokyn,
Hese desipele hym forsokyn;
Alle the veynys on hym schokyn,
    For dowt of deth wold he not fle.

[4]

Thynk, the cros he dedyn hym bere;
Garlond of thorn he dedyn hym were,
False tretowres that they were,
    Til he kemyn ther he wolde be.

[5]

Thynk, he dedyn hym on the rode;
Thynk, it was al for our goode;
Thynk, the Juwys wyxin wode;
    On hym they haddy[n] non pete.

[6]

Thynk how sore he was bowndyn,   [f. 22ᵛ
Thynk, he sufferid harde woundys
Of the false helle howndys
    With schorge *and* spere *and* naylys thre.

[7]

Thynk, man, on the werste of alle:
He yeuyn hym drynkyn esyl *and* galle;
'Hely!' for peyne he gan to calle
    To his Fader in Trenite.

[8]

Thynk, ma*n*, wytt*er*ly;
Think, he bowt the bytt*er*ly;
Forsake thi sy*n*ne *and* to hy*m* cry
 That he haue m*er*cy vpon the.

stza. 2, l. 3. thousand] MS. m¹.

169

British Museum. MS. Sloane 2593
XV *cent.*

f. 28ʳ

 I may seyn to most *and* lest,
 'V*erbum* caro factu*m* est.'

[1]

Jh*esu* of his mod*er* was born;
For vs he werde garlond of thorn, [f. 28ᵛ
And ellys hadde we be*n* forlorn;
 He tok his deth for most *and* lest.

[2]

I xal y*ou* telle good skele qwy
Th*at* he was born of Mary:
For he deyid on Caluory;
 He tok [his deth for most and lest.]

[3]

He wrowt vs alle w*ith* his hond;
The fend*es* woldy*n* ado*n* vs wro*n*g;
He bowt vs ageyn w*ith* peynys strong;
 He tok his [deth for most and lest.]

[4]

A kerche thanne to hi*m* was fet;
A spe*re* to his herte was set;
Tha*n*n seyde the Juwy*s*, 'Haue th*ou* th*at*!'
 He [tok his deth for most and lest.]

[5]

The Juwis yeuy*n* hy*m* drynk esyl *and* galle
Qu*an* Jh*esu* aft*er* dry*n*k ga*n* calle;
God let vs neu*er* in sy*n*ne falle!
 He tok [his deth for most and lest.]

[6]

Prey we to th*at* Lord so fre,
For vs he deyid on a tre,
At domysday *our* helpe he be.
 He tok [his deth for most and lest.]

stzas. 2, 6, l. 4. MS. he tok &c.
stza. 3, l. 4. MS. he tok his &c.
stza. 4, l. 4. MS. he &c.

170

Bodleian Library. MS. Ashmole 1379
c. 1500

p. 32

 There blows a colde wynd todaye, to-
 daye,
 The wynd blows cold todaye;
 Cryst sufferyd h*is* passyon for manys sal-
 uacyon,
 To kype the cold wynd awaye.

[1]

Thys wynde be reso*n* ys callyd te*n*tacyon;
 Yt rauyghth both nyghth *and* daye.
Remember, ma*n*, how the Sauyor was slayne
 To kype the colde wyn[d]e awaye.

[2]

Pride and presumcyon *and* fals extorcyon,
 That meny ma*n* dothe betraye—
Ma*n*, cu*m* to co*n*trycyon *and* axe co*n*fessyon
 To kype the colde wynd awaye.

[3]

O Mary myld, for love of the chyld
 That dyed on Good Frydaye,
Be owr saluacyon frome mortall da*m*na-
 cyon,
 To kype the cold wynd awaye.

[4]

He was naylyd, h*is* blode was halyd, [p. 33
 Owre remyssyon for to by,
And for owr symnys all he dronke both
 eysell *and* gall,
 To kype the cold wynd awaye.

[5]

Slowthe, enuy, couyt*is*, *and* lechere
 Bl[e]we the cold wynd, as Y dare saye;
Agene suche pusyn he suffer[r]yd h*is* pays-
 scyon
 To kype the cold wynd awaye.

[6]

O ma*n*, remember the Lord so te*n*der
 Whyche dyed w*ith*owte denaye;
Hys hond*es* so smert laye next to h*is* hart
 To kepe the cold wynd awaye.

[7]

Now pr*ay* we all to the Kyng selestyall,
 That borne he was off mayde,
That we maye loue so w*ith* oth*er* mo,
 To kype the cold wynd awaye.

[8]

At the day of dome when we schall   [p. 34
    cum
Owr syn*n*s not for to denaye,
Mary, praye to the Sone th*a*t syghthy y*n*
    hys trone
To kype the cold wynd awaye.

[9]

At the last ynde, ma*n*, th*o*u schalt send
    And kype bothe nyghth and daye;
The most goodlyst tresyor ys Cryst the
    Sauyor
To kype the cold wynd awaye.

[10]

Here let vs ynde, *and* Cryst vs defend
    All be the nyghth *and* be daye,
And bryng vs to hys place where ys myrthe
    and solas
To kype the cold wynd awaye.

stza. 2, l. 3. co*n*trycyon] MS. co co*n*trycyon.
stza. 7, l. 3. maye] MS. maye maye.
stza. 9, l. 3. Cryst] MS. agenyst.
At end: finis.

171

Bodleian Library. Douce fragments f. 48
                                          XVI *cent.*
f. 2ᵛ

    Blow the wi*n*de styl, *and* blow nat so
        shyl;
    My blode, man, I shed for the al at wyl.
    Blowe the wi*n*de styl, *and* blowe nat so
        shyll;
    This paine to suffre is my Fathers wil.

[1]

Synfull man, thou art vnkynde
    To thy Maker th*a*t made the of nough[t;]
Thou shuld kepe *and* haue in mi*n*de
    Howe with my blode I the bought,
    To saue the from the paynes of hell,
    That w*it*h the fende th*o*u shulde nat
        dwell,
    Neyther rather to go.

[2]

To a piller bou*n*[d]e, both fote *and* hand,
Tyll al my senew[es a]brode dyd brast,
The Jues me bet w[hile] they coude stand,
    And, as they weryed, they dyd them rest

And arose agayne and scorged me so
    Tyll blode *and* fleshe wente the
        bones fro

                .   .   .   .

[3]

Wha*n* they me scorged sharpe *and* sure,
    They crowned me with a thorne,   [f. 3ʳ
A rede in my hande for a septure,
    And there they kneled me beforne.
    They sayde to me, 'Al hayle, my
        kynge!'
    For so was alway theyr sayenge,
    And mocked me so.

[4]

I bare the crosse, that was so longe,
    To Caluery, where my deth was dight.
My mother folowed with rufull songe;
    Seyng my trauel, she fel downe ryght.
    To se me in such payn ibrought
    For the syn, man, th*a*t thou hast
        wrought,
    She was full wo.

[5]

On the crosse they splayed me than,
    And all my body they drewe in brede
Tyl fleshe and blod thorow the skyn ran,
    My ha*n*des *and* fete with holes dyd blede.
    They went me fro with one assent,
    And made a knyght my herte to rent;
    Thus payned they me tho.   [f. 3ᵛ

[6]

They gaue me drynke th*a*t was nat fyne,
    The which was eysell myxte with gall;
They gaue it me instede of wyne,
    And I sayd than made an ende was al.
    Than went away my spirite to hell,
    To fetche the soules th*a*t there dyd
        dwel
    And in limbo lay.

The repetition of the burden is indicated as
    follows:
stzas. 1, 5: Blowe the wynde styl.
                This payne to suffre.
stzas. 2, 3, 6: Blowe the wynde styll.
                This payne to suffre.
stza. 4:   Blowe the wynde styll.
                This paynes to suffre.
stza. 2, ll. 1–3. *Several words are damaged by
    holes in the leaf.* l. 5. scorged] Orig.
    fcorged.
At end: Finis.

172

a. *Bodleian Library*. MS. Douce 302
By John Audelay, XV *cent.*
f. 31ᵛ

There is a floure spr[u]ng of a tre,
The rote therof is callid Jesse,
A floure of pryce;
Ther is non seche in paradise.

[1]

This flour is fayre *and* fresche of heue;
Hit fadis neuer bot euer is new;
The blisful branche this flour on grew
Was Mare myld, that bare Jhesu,
A flour of grace;
Ayayns al sorow hit is solas.

[2]

The sede herof was Godis sond,
That God himselue sew with his hond;
In Bedlem in that hole lond
[In] medis here herbere ther he hir fond;
This blisful floure
Sprang neuer bot in Maris boure.

[3]

When Gabreel this mayd met,
With 'Aue Maria' he here gret;
Betwene hem two this flour was set
And kept was, no mon schul wit,
Hent on a day,
In Bedlem hit con spred *and* spray.

[4]

When that floure began to spred
And his blossum to bede,
Ryche *and* pore of euere lede,
Thai maruelt hou this flour myght sprede,
Til kyngys iii
That blesful floure come to se.

[5]

Angelis ther cam out of here toure
To loke apon this freschele floure,
Houe fayre he was in his coloure,
And hou sote in his sauour,
And to behold
How soche a flour myght spryng in
golde.

[6]

Of lille, of rose of ryse,
Of prymrol *and* of flour-de-lyse,
Of al the flours at my deuyse,
That floure of Jesse yet bers the prys

As most of hele
To slake oure sorous eueredele.

[7]

I pray youe, flours of this cuntre,
Whereeuere ye go, wereeuer ye be,
Hold hup the flour of good Jesse
Fore your freschenes *and* youre beute
As fayrist of al,
And euer was *and* euer schal.

MS. heading: Alia cantalena de *sancta* maria.
The repetition of the burden is indicated after
stza. 7 by: Ther is a floure.
stza. 4, l. 2. his] MS. his his.   l. 5. kyngys]
MS. kyngnys.
stza. 6, l. 4. That] MS. Yet.

b. *Balliol College, Oxford*. MS. 354, f. 220ʳ,
XVI *cent,*

burden, l. 2. therof] of it.
stza. 1, l. 1. fayre *and* fresche] fresshe *and* fayer.
of] he.   l. 3. blisful branche this flour]
blessid stoke that yt.   l. 4. Was Mare
myld] ytt was mary.   l. 6. Ayayns al
sorow] of all flowers.
stza. 2, l. 1. hereof] of ytt.   l. 3. Bedlem in]
nazareth.   l. 4. and a maydyn yt fond.
l. 5. This blisful] A blessyd.   l. 6. Sprang]
yt sprynges.
stza. 3, l. 1. When] On knees.   this mayd met]
that maydyn gret.   l. 2. The holy gost
with her he mett.   l. 3. this] that.
l. 4. was, no mon schul wit] yt ys for yt was
dett.   ll. 5, 6.
        And kynges lede
        To bedlem ther yt began to spred.
stza. 4, l. 2. *And*] and *and*. blossum to bede]
blosomys for to woyde.   l. 4. Thai] *omits.*
this flour] that rose.   l. 5. kyngys iii] on
a day.   l. 6. herdmen cam that flowr to
asay.
stza. 5, l. 1. ther] *omits.*   l. 2. apon this
freschele] on that fayer.   l. 3. Houe fayre
he] hole yt was.   l. 4. and hole yt was in
his ardowr.   l. 5. *And*] *omits.*
l. 6. golde] mold.
stza. 6, l. 1. of (2)] whit *and.*   l. 2. prymrol]
prymrose.   l. 3. the] *omits.*   at] in.
l. 4. That] The.   yet] *omits.*   bers] beryth.
ll. 5, 6. For most of all
        to help owr sowles both gret *and*
        small.
stza. 7, ll. 1, 2.
        I praysse the flowr of gud Jesse
        Off all the flowers that euer shall be.
l. 3. Hold hup] vphold.   l. 4. and worship
it for ay bewte.   l. 5. As fayrist] for best.
l. 6. *And*] That.   and euer] or euer be.
At end: Explicit.

173

Trinity College, Cambridge. MS. O. 3. 58
                              XV *cent.*

recto

[T]her is [n]o rose of swych vertu
As is the rose that bare Jhesu.

[1]

Ther is no ro[se of] swych vertu
As is the rose that bar Jhesu;
    Alleluya.

[2]

For in this rose *con*teynyd was
Heuen *and* erthe i*n* lytyl space,
    Res miranda.

[3]

Be th*a*t rose we may weel see
Th*a*t he is God in personys thre,
    Pari forma.

[4]

The au*n*gelys su*n*gy*n* the sheperd*es* to:
'Gloria in excelcis Deo.'
    Gaudeam*us*.

[5]

[L]eue we all this wordly merthe,
And folwe we this joyful berthe;
    Tra*n*seam*us*.

burden, l. 1, stza. 1, l. 1, stza. 5, l. 1. *A few letters
have become illegible from damage by damp.*

[3]

As the sonne beame goth thurgh the glas,
Thurgh this roose that lilly did pas
To save mankynde, as his wille was,
    The whiche flo*ur* is [moost pure and
        bright.]

[4]

This roose so myelde, aye vndefielde,
Hath borne a childe for man so wilde,
By fraude begiled, from blis exiled,
    The whiche flo*ur* is moost pur*e and*
        bright.

[5]

This roose so good at the cros stode
W*i*th wofull moode when Crist, ou*re* foode,
Shed his hert bloode for man so woode,
    The which flo*ur* is moost pur*e and*
        bright.

[6]

This swete roose pray bothe nyght *and* day,
W*i*th*oute* denay, that we come maye
To blys for ay the redy waye,
    The which flo*ur* is moost pur*e* [and
        bright.]

stza. 3, l. 4. MS. The whiche flo*ur* is &c.
stza. 4, l. 4. The] MS. This.
stza. 6, l. 4. MS. The which flo*ur* is moost
pur*e* &c.
*A hand of cent. XVI has written in the left-hand
margin*: anthonys songe.

174

Cambridge University Library. MS. Ee.
    1. 12   By James Ryman, *c.* 1492
f. 24ᵛ

    A roose hath borne a lilly white,
    The whiche flo*ur* is moost pure *and*
        bright.

[1]

To this roose Aungell Gabriell
Seide, 'Thou shalt bere Emanuell,
Both God *and* man w*i*th vs to dwell,'
    The which flo*ur* is most pur*e and* bright.

[2]

This roose, the *pro*phete Ysaye   [f.25ʳ
Seyde, shulde conceyve *and* bere Messy
W*i*th*o*uten synne or velonye,
    The which flo*ur* is moost pur*e and* bright.

175

A. *Bodleian Library.* MS. Eng. poet. e. 1
                              XV *cent.*
f. 21ʳ

    Of a rose, a louely rose,
    Of a rose I syng a song.

[1]

Lyth *and* lystyn, both old *and* yyng,
How the rose begane to spryng;
A fayyrer rose to owr lekyng
    Sprong th*er* neu*er* i*n* kyng*es* lond.

[2]

v branchis of th*a*t rose th*er* ben,
The wyche ben both feyer *and* chene;
Of a maydyn, Mary, hevyn quene,
    Ovght of hyr bo[s]u*m* the branch sprong.

[3]

The [first] branch was of gret   [f. 21ᵛ]
  honou*r*:
Th*a*t blyssed Mary shuld ber the flour,
The*r* ca*m* an angell ovght hevyn toure
  To breke the devel*es* bond.

[4]

The secund branch was gret of myght,
Th*a*t sprong vpon Cr*i*stmes nyght;
The sterre shone *and* lemeghd bryght,
  Th*a*t ma*n* schuld se it both day *and*
  nyght.

[5]

The third branch gan spryng *and* spred;
iii kynges than to bra*n*ch gan led
Tho to Owr Lady in hur*e* chyldbed;
  Into Bethle*m* that bra*n*ch sprong ryght.

[6]

The fourth branch, it spro*n*g to hell,
The deuel*es* powr for to fell,
Th*a*t no sovle th*er*in shuld dwell,
  The bra*nn*ch so blessedfully sprong.

[7]

The fifth bra*n*ch, it was so swote,
Yt sprong to hevyn, both croppe *and* rote,
In eu*er*y ball to ben owr bott,
  So blessedly yt sprong.

stza. 2, l. 4. branch] MS. braich.
stza. 4, l. 4. nyght] MS. th nyght.
stza. 5, l. 1. third] MS. iii.   l. 3. chyldbed]
  MS. chyld bred.
stza. 6, l. 1. fourth] MS. iiii.
stza. 7, l. 1. fifth] MS. v.

B. *Balliol College, Oxford.* MS. **354**
                     XVI *cent.*
f. 220ᵛ

  Off a rose, a louely rose,
    And of a rose I syng a song.

[1]

Herkyn to me, both old *and* yonge,
How a rose began to sprynge;
A fayerer rose to my lykyng
  Sprong th*er* neu*er* in kyng*es* lond.

[2]

vi branches ar on th*a*t rose beme;
They be both bryght *and* shene;
The rose ys called Mary, hevy*n* quene,
  Of her bosu*m* a blossu*m* sprong.

[3]

The fyrst branch was of gret myght,
That spronge on Crystmas nyght;
The streme shon over Bedlem bryght,
  Th*a*t me*n* myght se, both brod *and* longe.

[4]

The seconde branch was of gret honowr,
Th*a*t was sent fro*m* hevyn towr;
Blessyd be th*a*t fayer flowr;
  Breke it shall the fend*es* bond*es*.

[5]

The thyrd branch wyde spred
Ther Mary lay in her bede;
The bryght strem iii kyng*es* lede
  To Bedlem, th*er* that bra*n*ch th*e*i fond.

[6]

The fourth branch sprong i*n*to hell,
The fend*es* bost for to fell;
Ther myght no sowle th*er*in dwell;
  Blessid be th*a*t tyme th*a*t bra*n*ch ga*n*
  spry*n*g.

[7]

The fifth branch was fayer in fote,
Th*a*t sprong to hevyn, tope *and* rote,
The*r* to dwell *and* be owr bote,
  And yet ys sene i*n* preestes hond*es*.

[8]

The sixth branch, by *and* by,
Yt ys the v joyes of myld Mary;
Now Cryst saue all this cu*m*pany
  And send vs gud lyff *and* long!

stza. 4, l. 1. seconde] MS. iiᵈᵉ.
stza. 6, l. 1. fourth] MS. iiiiᵗʰ.
stza. 7, l. 1. fifth] MS. vᵗʰ.
stza. 8, l. 1. sixth] MS. viᵗʰ.
At end: Explicit.

C. *British Museum.* MS. Sloane **2593.**
f. 6ᵛ.   XV *cent.*

  Of a rose, a louely rose,
    Of a rose is al my*n* song.

[1]

Lestenyt, lordyng*es*, bothe elde *and* yynge,
How this rose bega*n* to sprynge;
Swych a rose to my*n* lykynge
  In al this word ne knowe I no*n*.

[2]

The aungil cam fro heuene tour
To grete Marye with gret honour
And seyde che xuld bere the flour
  That xulde breke the fyndes bond.

[3]

The flour sprong in heye Bedlem,
That is bothe bryght and schen;
The rose is Mary, heuene qwyn;
  Out of here bosum the blosme sprong.

[4]

The ferste braunche is ful of myght,
That sprong on Crystemesse nyght;
The sterre schon ouer Bedlem bryght,
  That is bothe brod and long.

[5]

The secunde braunche sprong to   [f. 7ʳ
  helle
The fendys power doun to felle;
Therin myght non sowle dw[e]lle;
  Blyssid be the tyme the rose sprong.

[6]

The thredde branche is good and swote;
It sp[r]ang to heuene, crop and rote,
Therin to dwellyn and ben our bote;
  Euery day it schewit in prystes hond.

[7]

Pray we to here with gret honour,
Che that bar the blyssid flowr,
Che be our helpe and our socour
  And schy[l]d vs fro the fyndes bond.

stza. 4, l. 2. Crystemesse] MS. cyrstemesse.

176

Bodleian Library. MS. Arch. Selden B. 26
                                      XV *cent.*
f. 9ᵛ

  Off a rose synge we,
  Misterium mirabile.

[1]

This rose is railed on a rys;
He hath brought the Prince of Prys,
And in this tyme soth hit ys,
  Viri sine semine.

[2]

This rose is reed, of colour bryght,
Throw whom oure joye gan alyght
Vppon a Cristysmasse nyght,
  Claro Dauid germine.

[3]

Of this rose was Cryst ybore,
To saue mankynde, that was forlore,
And vs alle from synnes sore,
  Prophetarum carmine.

[4]

This rose, of flourys she is flour;
She ne wole fade for no shoure;
To synful men she sent socour,
  Mira plenitudine.

[5]

This rose is so faire of hywe;
In maide Mary, that is so trywe,
Yborne was Lorde of Vertue,
  Saluator sine crimine.

177

Bodleian Library. MS. Douce 302
                            By John Audelay, XV *cent.*
f. 30ʳ

  Heyle, of wymmen flour of all;
  Thou herst vs when we to the call.

[1]

Blessid mot thou be, thou berd so bryght,
Moder and maidon most of myght;
Thou art the ster of days lyght
  And kepust vs when we schul fall.

[2]

Of all berdis that euer was boren
Blessid mot thou be both euen and morn;
Throgh the were sauyd that were forelorne
  Mone on, beth gret and smale.

[3]

'Hayle' to the was swettle sayd
When Jhesu in the he was consayud,
And throgh the was the fende afrayd;
  Thou madist vs fre to make him thrall.

[4]

Hayle, chif chosun garbunkul ston;
Of the was borne both God and mon;
When synful mon he makis his mon,
  To him thou art treu as ston in wal.

[5]

Haile be thou, quene, emperes of hel;
Of al pete thou arte the wel;
We prayn the, dame and damesel,
  That thou bryng vs into thi hal.

MS. heading: *Et de sancta maria.*
stza. 5, l. 4. hal] MS. bal.

178

Balliol College, Oxford. MS. 354
XVI *cent.*

f. 177ᵛ

'Mater, ora Filium
Vt post hoc exilium
Nobis donet gaudium
Beatorum omnium.

[1]

'Fayre maydyn, who is this barn
That thou beriste in thyn arme?'
'Sir, it is a Kynges Son,
That in hevyn above doth wonne.

[2]

'Man to fader he hath non,
But hymself, God alone,
Of a maydyn he wold be born
To save mankynd, that was forlorn.

[3]

'Thre kynges browght hym presens,
Gold, myrre, and frankynsens,
To my Son, full of myght,
Kynge of Kynges and Lorde of Myght.'

[4]

'Fayre maydyn, pray for vs
Vnto thy Son, swet Jhesus,
That he will send vs of his grace
In hevyn on high to haue a place.'

The repetition of the burden is indicated after
each stanza by: Mater ora &c.
At end: Explicit.

179

Bodleian Library. MS. Arch. Selden B. 26
XV *cent.*

f. 14ʳ

Ave domina,
Celi regina.

[1]

Worshyp be the birth of the,
Quem portasti, Maria,
Both in boure and in cite;
Aue domina.

[2]

For thorwe oure synnes we were forlorne,
Infernali pena,
But nowe shal vs saue that thou hast borne;
Aue domina.

[3]

Almyghty Godys wyl hit was,
Felix fecundata,
That vppon the shal lyght his grace;
Aue domina.

[4]

Yblessyd be thou, maide mylde,
Que semper es amica
Bytwene mankynd and the Chylde;
Aue domina.

[5]

Lady, quene of paradyse,
Mater Dei electa,
Thou bare oure Lorde, that hye Justyse;
Aue domina.

[6]

With merthe and alle solempnite
Nato canunt omnia;
Thou berde of ble, welcome thou be;
Aue domina.

179.1

British Museum. MS. Egerton 3307
XV *cent.*

f. 67ʳ

Ave, plena gracia,
Dei mater Maria.

[1]

Hayle be thou, Mary most of honowr,
Thou bar Jhesu our Sauiour,
Maria,
Aue, plena gracia.

[2]

Hayle be thou, madyn, modir, and wyff,
Hayl be thou, stynter of our stryff,
Maria,
[Ave, plena gracia.]

[3]

Hayle be thou, qwen of paradysse,
Of al wemen thou berys prysse,
Maria,
[Ave, plena gracia.]

[4]

Thow pray for vs vnto thy Son,
In heuen blyss that we may won,
Maria,
Aue, p[lena] g[racia].

l. 1. of the burden and ll. 1 and 4 of each stanza
are to be repeated as chorus.
stza. 4, l. 4. g[racia]] MS. g. &c.

180

A. *Bodleian Library.* MS. Eng. poet. e. 1
XV *cent.*

f. 25^r

Of M, A, R, I,
  Syng I wyll a new song.

[1]

Of thes iiii letters purpose I,
Of M *and* A, R *and* I;
Thei betokyn mayd Mary;
  All owr joy of hyr it sprong.

[2]

Wi*th*ovghten wem of hyr body,
M *and* A, R *and* I,
Of hyr was borne a Kyng truly
  The Jewys dedyn to deth wi*th* wrong.

[3]

Vpon the movnte of Caluery,   [f. 25^v
  M and A, R and I,
Th*er* thei betyn hys bar body
  With schorg*es* th*at* war sharp *and* long.

[4]

Owr der Lady she stod hy*m* by,
M *and* A, R and I,
And wep[t] wat*er* ful bytt*er*ly
  And terys of blod eu*er* among.

stza. 4, l. 2. wep[t]] *A bit of paper is pasted over
the end of the word.*

B. *British Museum.* MS. Sloane 2593
XV *cent.*

f. 24^v

  M *and* A *and* R *and* I;
  Syngy*n* I wyl a newe song.

[1]

It wern fowre lett*er*ys of purposy,
M *and* A, R *and* I,
Tho wern lett*er*is of Mary,
  Of ho*m* al o*ur* joye sprong.

[2]

On the mownt of Caluory,
With M *and* A, R *and* I,
There he bety*n* his bryte body
  Wi*th* schorg*es* th*at* wern bothe scharp
    and long.

[3]

Our swete Lady stod hy*m* by,
With M *and* A *and* R *and* I;
Che wept wat*er* wi*th* her*e* ey,
  And alwey the blod folwyd among.

[4]

God, th*at* sit aboue the sky,
With M *and* A, R *and* I;
Saue now al this cu*m*pany,
  And send vs joye *and* blysse ammong.

181

Trinity College, Cambridge. MS. R. 4. 20
XV *cent.*

f. 169^v

  Honour be euer, wi*th*owtyn ende,
  To hym that fro the hevyn discende.

[1]

That was Jh*es*u oure Saueour,
  The oonly Son of God Myghty,
That beldyt in that bygly bowre
  Whiche is the wombe of mylde Mary.

[2]

Mylde that mayden may be cald,
  For wi*th* fylthe was she neuer fyled;
Full wele was hyr that had inwolde
  In hyr chief chawmbre suche a chylde.

[3]

She is the chief of chastyte,
  The conclaue and the clostre clene
Of hym that hyr humylite
  Commendyth amonge his sayntys be-
    dene.

[4]

Full worthy is she to co*m*mende
  For hir mekenes, as wytnes wele
That was the cause God Son descende
  For to be borne here for oure sele.

*The burden and stza. 1, ll. 1, 2, and part of 3 are
written again as a scribble by another hand on
f. 170^r.*

182

Bodleian Library. MS. Arch. Selden B. 26
XV *cent.*

f. 24^r.

  Hayl, Godys Sone i*n* T*r*inite,
  The secu*nd* in diuinite,
    Thy moder is a may.

[1]

Lo, Moises bush shynynge vnbrent,
The floures faire God there present;
Oure Lady with childe hit be ment
    As profetes saide in here lay.

[2]

This is Gedeonys wulle-felle,
On whom the dewe of heuen dyde dwelle;
The dewe of heuen on Mary fel
    Whan she conceyued Adonay.

[3]

Aronnys rodde, withoute licoure,
By merueyl bare bothe fruyte and floure;
So God and man, oure Sauyoure,
    A clene mayde hath borne this day.

[4]

This Jacobys sterre with shynynge leme
That Balaam sey in Balakkys reme
Figureth Mary, that in Bedleme
    Bare Jhesu and leyde in hay.

[5]

But God bewreyde by faire figure
His virginel progeniture.
Nowe Maryes Sone haue vs in cure,
    And graunte vs blys that lasteth ay.

183

Balliol College, Oxford. MS. 354
                                        XVI *cent.*
f. 177ᵛ

    Newell, newell, newell, newell!
    I thank a maydyn euery dele.

[1]

Vpon a lady fayre and bright
    So hartely I haue set my thowght,
In euery place, whereuer I light,
    On her I thynk and say right nowght.

[2]

She bare Jhesu full of pite,
    That all this world with his hond hath
        wrowght;
Soueraynly in mynd she is with me,
    For on her I thynk and say right nowght.

[3]

Trewe love, loke thou do me right,
    And send grace that I to blis be browght;
Mary moder, moste of myght,
    On the I thynk and say right nowght.

[4]

God, that was on the rode don,
    Grant that all men to blis be browght,
And to Mary I mak my mone,
    For on her I thynk and say right nowght.

The repetition of the burden is indicated as
follows: stzas. 1, 2: newell. stzas. 3, 4:
nowell.
At end: Explicit.

184

Bodleian Library. MS. Eng. poet. e. 1
                                        XV *cent.*
f. 33ʳ

    Man, asay, say, say;
    Make thi mone to Mary, that myld
        m[ay.]

[1]

Of all thi frendes sche is the flowr;
Sche wyll the bryng to thi honowr;
Mary to kall thou hast colowre;
    Assay, asay.

[2]

Sche bar Jhesu owr Sauyowr;
Of al myschyfe sche is socowr;
Mary is strowne in euery schowr;
    Asay, asay.

[3]

Sche is cundas, full of grace,   [f. 33ᵛ
That spryngyth and spredyth in euery
    place;
Mary to callyn gret ned thou has;
    Aasy, say.

[4]

Hyf thou be put in pouerte,
Or of thi frendes forsakyd thou be,
Mary his lady of gret pete;
    Asay, say.

[5]

Yyf thou be aferd of thi foly
Or of thi day wan thou xa[l]t dey
Mary his laydy of gret mercy;
    Asay, say.

[6]

So gracius and so gud sche is;
Sche bryng vs al into blys,
Ther Mary lady and qwen is;
    Asay, say.

burden, l. 2. *The last letters have been destroyed
by a tear in MS.*
stza. 6, l. 1. gracius] MS. graciuus.

185

A. *British Museum.* MS. Sloane 2593
XV *cent.*
f. 25ʳ

Synge we, synge we,
'Regina celi, letare.'

[1]

Holy maydyn, blyssid thou be;
Godes Sone is born of the;
The Fader of Heuene worchepe we.
Regina celi, letare.

[2]

Heyl, wyf, heyl, maydyn, heyl, brytgh of
ble!
Heyl, dowter, heyl, suster, heyl, ful of pete!
Heyl, chosyn to tho Personys Thre!
Regin[a celi, letare.]

[3]

Thou art empresse of heuene so fre,
Worthi maydyn in mageste.
Now worchepe we the Trenyte.
Regina [celi, letare.]

[4]

Lady so louely, so goodly to see,   [f. 25ᵛ
So buxsum in thi body to be,
Thou art his moder for humylite;
Regina celi, letare.

[5]

These ben curteys kynges of solumte;
They worchepyd thi Sone with vmylite,
Mylde Mary, thus rede we;
Regina [celi, letare.]

[6]

So gracius, so precyows in ryalte,
Thus jentyl, thus good, thus fynde we;
Ther is non swych in non cuntre;
Regina [celi, letare.]

[7]

And therfore knel we doun on our kne;
This blyssid berthe worchepe we;
This is a song of humylyte:
'Regina [celi, letare.']

stza. 3, l. 4. MS. Regina &c.

B. *Bodleian Library.* MS. Arch. Selden
B. 26   XV *cent.*
f. 10ᵛ

Synge we to this mery cumpane,
'Regina celi, letare.'

[1]

Holy maide, blessyd thou be;
Godys Sone is born of the,
The Fader of Heuen, thus lyue we;
Regina celi, letare.

[2]

Thow art emperesse of heuen fre;
Now art thou moder in mageste,
Yknytte in the blessed Trinite;
Regina celi, letare.

[3]

Hayl, wyf, hayl, maide, bryght of ble!
Hayl, doughter, hayl, suster, ful of pite!
Hayl, cosyn to the Persones Thre!
Regina celi, letare.

[4]

Lo, this curteys Kynge of degre
Wole be thy Sone with solempnite;
Mylde Mary, this ys thy fee;
Regina celi, letare.

[5]

Therfore knele we on oure kne,
Thy blysful berthe now worshype we
With this songe of melode:
'Regina celi, letare.'

186

British Museum. MS. Addit. 5665
XVI *cent.*
f. 4ᵛ

Syng we to this mery companey,
'Regina celi, letare.'
Syng we to this mery companey,
'Regina *celi, letare.'   [*f. 5ʳ

[1]

Benyng lady, blessed mote thow be,
That barest God in v[i]rginite;
Therfor syng we to the,
'Regina celi, letare,
Regina celi.'

[2]

O quene of heuen, that syttist in   [f. 4ᵛ
se,
O comfort of all captiuite,
Ryght causeth vs all to syng to the,
'Regina celi, letare,
[Regina celi.']

[3]

O blessed branche of hum[i]lite,
O causer of all felicete,
With joy and gladdenesse syng we to the,
'Regina celi, letare,
    [Regina celi.']
MS. heading: [D]e sancta maria.
stza. 2, l. 1. heuen] MS. hereuen.

187

A a. *Gonville & Caius College, Cambridge.*
    MS. 383   XV *cent.*
p. 68
    Virgo, rosa virginum,
    Tuum precare Filium.

[1]

Alle ye mouwen of joye synge;
Fro heuene ys come gode tythyng:
Mary mylde, that gode thyng,
    Iam concepit Filium.

[2]

Quene of heuene, wel the be!
Godes Sone ys boron of the
For te make vs alle fre
    Ab omni labe criminum.

[3]

Wanne that he of her bore was
In a crache wyt hey and gras,
And for houre synne diede on cros,
    Surexit die tercia.

[4]

Aftur hys ded, in hys vprysyng,
To heuene he toc hys vpstyyng;
Ther he dwellus, wytoute lesyng,
    Deus super omnia.

[5]

Marie, modur wytoute wemme,
Brytur than the sonne bem,
The has taken wyt hym
    Ad celi palacia.

[6]

Tho the we makun houre mone:
Pray for vs to thy Sone
That we mowen wyt hym wone
    In perhenni gloria.

b. *British Museum.* Printed Book C. 21.
    c. 12. XVI *cent.* (stzas. 2, 3. Initial
    burden lacking.)
stza. 2, l. 1. the] mote thou.   l. 2. Godes] for
    goddes.

stza. 3, l. 1. that] *omits.* her] hyre body.
    l. 2. crache wyt] crybbe of.   l. 3. *And* for
    houre synne] Sythen he.   on] vppon a.

B. *Balliol College, Oxford.* MS. 354
                                    XVI *cent.*
f. 249ᵛ
    Virgo, rosa virginum,
    Tuum precor Fillium.

[1]

Qvene of hevyn, blessyd mott thou be!
For Godes Son, born he was of the
For to make vs [alle] fre:
    Gloria tibi, Domine.

[2]

Jhesu, Godes Son, born he was
In a crybe with hay and gras,
And dyed for vs on the crose;
    Gloria tibi, Domine.

[3]

To Owr Lady make we owr mone,
That she may pray to her dere Son
That we may to his blis cum;
    Gloria tibi, Domine.

At end: Explicit.

188

British Museum. MS. Sloane 2593
                                    XV *cent.*
f. 8ᵛ
    A, a, a, a,
    Nu[n]c gaudet Maria.

[1]

Mary is a lady bryght;
Sche haght a Sone of meche myght;
Ouer al this word che is hyght
    Bona natalicia.

[2]

Mary is so fayr of face,
And here Sone so ful of grace;
In heuene he make us a place,
    Cum sua potencia.

[3]

Mary is so fayr and sote,
And here Sone so ful of bote,
Ouer al this word he is bote,
    Bona voluntaria.

[4]

Mary is bothe good *and* kynde;
Eu*ere* on vs che haght mende,
Th*at* the fend xal vs not sche*n*de,
Cu*m* sua malicia.

[5]

Mary is qwen of alle thinge,
And here Sone a louely Kynge.
God graunt vs alle good endynge!
Regnat Dei gr*a*cia.

*MS. transposes stzas. 2, 3, the correct order being
indicated by prefixed* a *and* b.

189

Cambridge University Library. MS. Ee.
  I. 12   By James Ryman, *c.* 1492
f. 13ᵛ

  Stella maris, micaris clare;
  Regina celi, letare.

[1]

Beholde and see, O lady free,
  Quem meruisti portare;
God *and* man is he; thus bileve we;
  Regina celi, letare.

[2]

King Assuere, thy Sonne so dere,
  Quem meruisti portare,
In blis so clere he hath no pere:
  Regina celi, letare.

[3]

Sith thy Sonne is the King of Blis,
  Quem meruisti portare,
With hym and his thou shalt not mys;
  Regina celi, letare.

[4]

That Lorde so good w*i*th soo   [f. 14ʳ
  myelde moode,
  Quem meruisti portare,
Vpon the roode shedde his hert bloode;
  Regina celi, [letare.]

[5]

O lady free, glad mayst thou be:
  Quem meruisti portare,
As he tolde the, aryse did he;
  Regina celi, letare.

[6]

By thy swete Childe so meke *and* myelde,
  Quem meruisti portare,

Man, that was wilde, is reconsiled;
  Regina celi, letare.

[7]

That Lorde, that wrought al thing of
  nought,
  Quem meruisti portare,
Mankynde hath bought *and* to blis brought;
  Regina [celi, letare.]

[8]

The heuenly quere that Lorde so dere,
  Quem meruisti portare,
With voices clere lawdith in fere;
  Regi*n*a celi, letar*e*.

[9]

That Lorde and King to blis vs bringe,
  Quem meruisti portare,
That we may synge w*i*th*out* ending,
  'Regi*n*a celi, letare.'

stza. 4, l. 4. MS. Regi*n*a celi &c.
stza. 7, l. 4. MS. Regina &c.

190

A. *Bodleian Library*. MS. Arch. Selden
  B. 26   XV *cent.*
f. 25ᵛ

  Nou*us* sol de virgine
  Reluxit nobis hodie.

[1]

Thow holy dought*er* of Syon,
  P*r*incesse of Hierusalem,
Today sp*r*ange of the alone
  The grayn of Jesse in Bethleem.

[2]

This day also the bryght sterre
  Th*at* Balam gan so to magnifye
Aroos of the to stynt o*ur* werre
  And in derknys vs to gye.

[3]

Thou ert also aboue echone
  A moder and a mayde trywe,
And the yerde eke of Aaron,
  Th*at* bare this day a burion nywe.

[4]

The orient lyght of Nazareth
  Th*ou* ert also, to stynt our*e* stryffe,
Th*at* broughtyst forth agaynys deth
  This day the sothfast Man of Lyffe.

[5]

Thow ert eke the flees of Gedeon,
  Ydewed *with* the Holi Goste,
The chaste temple of Salemon,
  Clere as c*ri*stal in eu*er*y coste.

[6]

Th*ou* ert eke the joye of Israel,
  To stynt all our*e* olde sorwe,
The gate the whyche Ezechiel
  Sawe alway clos, bothe eue *and* morwe.

[7]

And th*ou* ert eke the purpyl rose
  Th*at* whylom grewe in Jerico;
The Fadres wysdom to enclose,
  Th*ou* were the temple *and* to*ur* also.

B. *British Museum.* MS. Egerton 3307
                              XV *cent*

f. 53ʳ

  Nouus sol de virgine
  Reluxit nobis hodie.

[1]

The holy doghter of Syon,
  P*ri*nces of Jherusalem,
This day sp*ra*ng owt of the alon
  The g*ra*ne of Jesse in Bedlem.

[2]

This day also the brygh*t* ster
  That Balam gan to magnifi,
He ros of the to stynt o*ur* werr
  And in dirknes vs to gy.

[3]

Thow ert also abown ilkon
  A moder and a madyn trew,
And the yerd ek of Aaron
  Th*at* bar this day a burion newe.

[4]

The orie*n*t lyght of Nazareth
  Thow ert also, to stynt our stryff,
That broght forth agaynys deth
  This day the sothfast Man of Lyff.

[5]

Thow ert ek the fleys of Jedeon
  A-dewyd *with* the Holy Gost,
The chast tempyll of Salomon,
  Cler as c*ri*stal in e*v*ery cost.

[6]

Thow ert eke the joy of Israel
  To stynt all our old sorowe,
The gate whych Ezechiel
  Saw alway closse both eue*n* and morow.

[7]

And thow ert eke the purpyl rose
  That whylom grew in Jerico;
The Faders wysdom to enclos
  Th*ou* wer the te*m*pyl and tour also.

[8]

Now thow chast lylly flo*ur*
  Sp*ri*ggyng from the Jewis spyn,
Be our help and our soco*ur*
  Agaynis the venom serpentyn.

191

A. *Bodleian Library.* MS. Ashmole 1393
                                 XV *cent.*

f. 69ᵛ

  Enixa e*st* pu*er*pera.

[1]

A lady th*at* was so feyr*e and* bright,
  Velut mar*is* stella,
Browght forth Jh*esu*, full of might,
  Par*en*s *et* puella.

[2]

Lady, flo*ur* of all[e] thing,
  Rosa sine spina,
That barist Jh*esu*, Heuy*n* King,
  G*ra*c*i*a diu*in*a.

[3]

All this world was forlor*e*
  Eua p*e*ccatrice,
Til th*at* Jh*esu* was ybor*e*
  De te genitrice.

[4]

Of al wy*m*men th*ou* art beste,
  Felix fecu*n*data;
To al wery th*ou* art reste,
  Mat*er* honorata.

[5]

Wel I wote he is thi Sone,
  Ventre quem portasti;
The*n* wol g*ra*nt the thi bon*e*
  Infans que[m] lactasti.

[6]

Hou swete he is, hou meke he is,
  Ull*us* memorau[it];
In heuy*n* he is, *and* heuy*n* blis
  Nobis p*re*parauit.

[7]

Of all wy*m*men th*o*u berist the price,
  Mat*er* gr*a*ci*o*sa;
Grawnt vs all paradyce,
  Virgo gloriosa.

B a. *British Museum.* MS. Egerton 613
                         XIII *cent.*

[No burden]

[1]

Of on that is so fayr and bright,   f. 2^r
  Velud maris stella,
Brighter than the dayis light,
  Parens *et* puella,
Ic crie to the; thou se to me;
Leuedy, preye thi Sone for me,
  Tam pia,
That ic mote come to the,
  Maria.

[2]

Leuedi, flour of alle thing,
  Rosa s*i*ne spina,
Th*o*u bere Jh*e*su, Heuene King,
  Gr*a*ci*a* diuina.
Of alle th*o*u berst the pris,
  Leuedi, quene of parays
    Electa;
Mayde milde, moder es
    Effecta.

[3]

Of kare *con*sell thou ert best,
  Felix fecundata;
Of alle wery thou ert rest,
  Mater honorata.
Bisek him wiz milde mod
That for ous alle sad is blod
    I*n* cr*u*ce
That we moten komen til him
    In luce.

[4]

Al this world war forlore,
  Eua peccatrice,
Tyl our Lord was ybore
  De te genit*ri*ce.
With 'Aue' it went away

Thuster nyth, and comth the day
    Salutis;
The welle springet hut of the
    Uirtutis.

[5]

Wel he wot he is thi Sone,
  Uentre que*m* portasti;
He wyl nout werne the thi bone,
  P*ar*uu*m* que*m* lactasti.
So hende and so god he his,
He hauet brout ous to blis
    Su*per*ni,
That haues hidut the foule put
    Inferni.

*MS. has the stanzas in the order 1, 4, 2, 3, 5. The
correction is indicated by prefixed* a, b, *and* c.
stza. 4, l. 6. comth] MS. comgh.
At end: Explicit cant*us* iste.

b. *Trinity College, Cambridge.* MS. B. 14.
39, f. 24^v. XIII *cent.*

stza. 1, l. 1. Of on] For on.   l. 5. icrie the
  gr*a*ce of the.
stza. 2, l. 1. flour] best.   l. 5. the] that.
  l. 6. Leuedi] Heie.   of] in.   l. 8. Mayde]
  moder.   moder] a*n*t maidan.
stza. 3, l. 1. Of] I*n*   l. 3. Of] to.
  l. 5. Bisek] bi hold tou.   l. 8. That]
  bidde.   komen] come.   til] to.
stza. 4, l. 1. this] the.   war] it wes.   l. 2. Eua]
  Thoru eua.   l. 3. Tyl our Lord] toforn
  that jh*e*su.   l. 4. De] ex.   l. 5. With]
  Thorou.   it] e.   l. 6. Thuster] The thester.
stza. 5, l. 1. he wot] thou wost.   l. 3. wyl]
  nul.   l. 5. hende] god.   god] mild.
  l. 6. hauet brout ous to] bri*n*get us alle i*n* to
  is.   l. 8. That haues] he hauet.

c. *Bodleian Library.* MS. Rawlinson C. 510,
f. 232^r. XIII *cent.* (stza. 5, ll. 5–9 only.)

l. 6. to] into.   l. 5. That haues] and.

192

Cambridge University Library. MS. Ee.
I. 12   By James Ryman, *c.* 1492
f. 14^v

  O quene of grace, O Mary myelde,
  For vs thou pray vnto thy childe.

[1]

O closed gate of Ezechiel,
O plentevous mounte of Daniel,
  O Jesse yerde, O Mary myelde,
  For vs thou pray vnto thy childe.

[2]

O perfecte trone of Salamon,
O flore and flese of Gedeon,
  O moder of grace, O Mary myelde,
  For vs thou pray vnto thy childe.

[3]

O flamed bushe in alle stature
Of Moyses, of whome nature
  Jhesus hath take, O Mary mylde,
  For vs thou pray vnto thy childe,

[4]

O Aaron yerde moost of honoure,
O moder of oure Savioure,
  O gate of lyfe, O Marie myelde,
  For vs thou pray vnto thy childe.

[5]

O lanterne of eternall light,
By whome of Criste we haue a sight,
  O welle of grace, O Marie myelde,
  For vs thou pray vnto thy childe.

[6]

O spowse of Criste inmaculate,   [f. 15ʳ]
Assumpte to blisse and coronate,
  O quene of blis, O Marie myelde,
  For vs thou pray vnto thy childe.

[7]

Fulfilled is the prophesye,
For why thou hast brought furth Messy
  To save mankynde; O Mary myelde,
  For vs thou pray vnto thy childe.

[8]

Eternally that we may be
With thy swete Son Jhesus and the
  In heuyn blisse, O Mary myelde,
  For vs thou pray vnto thy childe.

[2]

O perfecte trone of Salamon,
O flore and flese of Gedeon,
O florent yerde of Aaron,
  Of thy conforte [lete vs not mys.]

[3]

O flamed busshe withoute leasure
Of Moyses, of whome nature   [f. 15ᵛ]
Jhesus Criste tooke, O virgyne pure,
  Of thy confort [lete vs not mys.]

[4]

O quene Hester moost meke of myende,
That were werthy of God to fynde
Mercy and grace for alle mankyende,
  Of thy [confort lete vs not mys.]

[5]

O stronge Judith, that Holoferne
Decapitate, that was so sterne,
Ayenst Sathan to feight vs lerne;
  Of thy confort [lete vs not mys.]

[6]

O lanterne of eternall light,
By whome of Criste we haue a sight,
'Fulle of alle grace' sith thy name hight,
  Of thy comfort [lete vs not mys.]

[7]

O spowse of Criste inmaculate,
Aboue alle aungelles sublimate,
In blis of thy Sonne coronate,
  Of thy conforte [lete vs not mys.]

[8]

O quene of blis perpetuall,
That we whiche be terrestriall
Maye come to blis celestiall,   [f. 16ʳ]
  Of thy conforte [lete vs not mys.]

stzas. 1, 2, 7, 8, l. 4. MS. Of thy conforte &c.
stzas. 3, 5, l. 4. MS. Of thy confort &c.
stza. 4, l. 4. MS. Of thy &c.

193

Cambridge University Library. MS. Ee.
  I. 12   By James Ryman, *c.* 1492
f. 15ʳ

  O virgyne Marie, quene of blis,
  Of thy conforte lete vs mys.

[1]

O closed gate of Ezechiell,
O plentevous mounte of Daniel,
O moder of Emanuel,
  Of thy conforte [lete vs not mys.]

194

Cambridge University Library. MS. Ee.
  I. 12   By James Ryman, *c.* 1492
f. 16ʳ

  Sancta virgo Maria,
  Dei genitrix pia.

[1]

Haile, perfecte trone of Salamon;
Haile, flore and flease of Gedeon;
Haile, ardent busshe of vision,
  Dei genitrix pia.

[2]

What tyme mankynde hath done amys
And for his mys was put fro blis,
By thy mekenes made free it is,
  Dei genitr*ix* pia.

[3]

As a swete floure berith his odoure,
So hast thou borne oure Sauyour*e*
To bringe mankynde oute of doloure,
  Dei genitrix pia.

[4]

Mankynde was shent and ay forlorne
For synne that Adam did beforne
Till Crist Jh*es*us of the was borne,
  Dei genitrix pia.

[5]

Hym that of hevyns not take myght be
With thy wombe thou haste   [f. 16ᵛ
  geve moost free,
Bothe God and man, thus beleue we,
  Dei genitrix [pia.]

[6]

The pr*o*phecy is done, no dowte.
A man thou hast geve all abowte
To whome heven and erth doth lowte,
  Dei genitrix pia.

[7]

O stronge Judith, O Hester meke,
That the serpentes hede of did streke,
At nede of the conforte we seke,
  Dei genitrix pia.

[8]

Moder and mayde in one persone
Was nevir none but thou allone;
Wherfore of the Crist made his trone,
  Dei genitrix pia.

[9]

As the sonne beame goth thurgh the glas,
Thurgh thy bodie so did he pas,
Taking nature, as his wille was,
  Dei genitrix [pia.]

[10]

In the is complete the prophecye
Of alle the pr*o*phetes, by and by,
That seide a mayde shulde bere Messye,
  Dei genitrix pia.

[11]

O lady free, O quene of blis,   [f. 17ʳ
Of thy conforte lete vs not mys,
For why thy name nowe called is
  Dei genitrix pia.

[12]

Lete thy mercy bothe springe *and* sprede;
Forsake vs not for oure mysdede,
But oute of drede to blis vs lede,
  Dei genitrix pia.

stzas. 5, 9, l. 4. MS. Dei genit*rix* &c.

195

Cambridge University Library. MS. Ee.
  1. 12   By James Ryman, *c.* 1492
f. 17ʳ

  To heuyn blis that we may come,
  O mater, ora Filium.

[1]

O quene of grace and of conforte,
Whose vertu we cannot reporte,
At nede to the sith we resorte,
  O m*ater*, ora Filiu*m*.

[2]

Moder and mayde in one persone
Was neuir none but thou alone;
Wherfore, goode lady, here our*e* mone:
  O mater, ora [Filium.]

[3]

Sith thou hast born in virginite
The secunde person in Trinite,
The Sonne of God in diuinite,
  O mater, ora Filium.

[4]

Sith of honoure thou arte so grete   [f. 17ᵛ
That next God in blis is thy sete,
Swete lady, thou vs not forgete;
  O mater, ora Filiu*m*.

[5]

Sith Criste of the mankyende wolde take
And the his moder so wolde make,
That he hath take thou not forsake;
  O mater, ora [Filium.]

[6]

Sith Criste by the hath made man free
W*ith* his hert bloode vpon a tree,
That for oure synne we lost not be,
  O mater, ora [Filium.]

stzas. 2, 5, 6, l. 4. MS. O mater ora &c.
*The following stanza, written after stza. 2, is
marked* vacat *in MS.*:
        For thy meke chaste virginite,
        As we rede in diuinitee,
        In the restyd the Trinite;
        O mater, ora Filiu*m*.

196

Cambridge University Library. MS. Ee.
I. 12   By James Ryman, *c.* 1492
f. 17ᵛ

O castitatis lilium,
Tuum precare Filium.

[1]

Sith thy Sonne is both God and man,
And by thy meane save vs he can,
That vs possede not fals Sathan,
    T[u]um *p*recare [Filium.]

[2]

Off thy swete Sonne sith thou mayst haue
W*it*hout delay what thou wilte crave,
That we come not into helle cave,
    Tuu*m* [precare Filium.]

[3]

Sith alle aungell*es* the doo obeye,   [f. 18ʳ
For loue of man, that in the leye,
So that we be not lost for aye,
    Tuu*m* *p*recare Filium.

[4]

Sith quene of blis thou arte electe,
By whome mankynde shulde be *p*rotecte,
Fro blis that we be not rejecte,
    Tuu*m* *p*recare Filium.

[5]

O blessed quene of paradise,
For oure trespas vs not despise,
But for vs in the lowest wyse
    Tuu*m* *p*recare Filium.

[6]

That oure offence forgeve may be,
And that we may, O lady free,
Dwelle w*it*h thy Sonne Jhe*s*us *and* the,
    Tuu*m* *p*recare Filium.
stza. 1, l. 4. MS. Tum *p*recare &c.
stza. 2, l. 4. MS. Tuu*m* &c.

197

Cambridge University Library. MS. Ee.
I. 12   By James Ryman, *c.* 1492
f. 18ʳ

O benigna, laude digna,
Tuo Nato nos consigna.

[1]

Sith Criste hath take both flesshe *and* blode
For thy clennes and thy myelde mode,

And bought mankynde vpon the rode,
    Tuo Nato [nos consigna.]

[2]

Sith euery man atte nede doth flee. [f. 18ᵛ
For helpe and comforte vnto the,
For synne that we ay lost not be,
    Tuo Nato nos [consigna.]

[3]

Sith by reason, by right and skille,
Thy Sonne thy wille ay woll fulfille,
That the fende ille mankynde not spille,
    Tuo Nato [nos consigna.]

[4]

Sith thou art quene of euery coost
And thy Sonne King of myghtes moost,
So that for synne we be not loost,
    Tuo Nato nos [consigna.]

[5]

Sith Crist thy Sonne hath take of the
Fourme of mankynde like as we be
To bringe vs fro captiuitee,
    Tuo Nato [nos consigna.]

[6]

Sith man to God by the is knytte
And aboue alle aungell*es* doth sitte,
That we come not into helle pitte,
    Tuo Nato [nos consigna.]
stzas. 1, 3, 5, 6, l. 4. MS. Tuo nato &c.
stzas. 2, 4, l. 4. MS. Tuo nato nos &c.

198

Cambridge University Library. MS. Ee.
I. 12   By James Ryman, *c.* 1492
f. 18ᵛ

O virgo su*m*me decora,
Pro nobis Cristum exora.

[1]

Sith of right thou mayst not forsake [f. 19ʳ
Mankyende, the whiche thy Sonne hath
    take,
Oure care *and* woo for to aslake
    Pro nobis [Cristum exora.]

[2]

Sith thou arte quene and thy Sonne King
Of blis that shalle haue noon endyng,
To that swete place vs alle to bring
    P*r*o nobis [Cristum exora.]

[3]

Of alle women sith thou art floure
And moder of oure Sauyoure,
To save and kepe vs froo doloure
    Pro nobis Christum [exora.]

[4]

Sith thou arte the lanterne of light
Shynyng aboue alle aungelles bright,
Of hym that we may haue a sight
    Pro nobis Christum [exora.]

[5]

Sith thou arte made emperesse of helle,
The payne wherof no tunge can telle,
That we for synne therin not dwelle
    Pro nobis Christum [exora.]

[6]

Sith oure trust is in the allone
Next God, that is bothe iii and One,
To here oure moone and graunte   [f. 19ᵛ
    oure boon
    Pro nobis Christum [exora.]

stza. 1, l. 4. MS. pro nobis &c.
stza. 2, l. 4. MS. pro nobis &c.
stzas. 3–6, l. 4. MS. pro nobis Christum &c.

199

Cambridge University Library. MS. Ee.
    I. 12   By James Ryman, *c.* 1492
f. 19ᵛ

    O clemens, O pia,
    O dulcis Maria.

[1]

O quene of mercy and of grace,
O oure comforte in euery case,
To whome we calle in euery place,
    O clemens, O pia.

[2]

O lady fre, O quene of blis,
Of thy conforte lete vs not mys,
For why thy name nowe called is
    O dulcis Maria.

[3]

O oure lodesterre bothe bright *and* clere,
O quene of blis havyng no pere,
O spowse of Criste moost swete *and* dere,
    O clemens, O pia.

[4]

Moder and mayde in one *p*ersone
Was neuir noon but thou allone;
Wherefor, good lady, here *oure* mone,
    O dulcis Maria.

[5]

O lanterne of eternall light,
Moost pure and clene, moost clere   [f. 20ʳ
    and bright,
Cause vs of Criste to haue a sight,
    O clemens, [O pia.]

[6]

O virgyne Mary, meke and myelde,
For vs thou pray vnto thy chielde
Fro blis that we be not exielde,
    O dulcis Maria.

[7]

O flos campi of swete odoure,
O Jesse yerde full of honoure,
O moder of oure Sauyoure,
    O clemens, O pia.

[8]

O virgyne pure, on vs thou rue,
And for oure synne vs not eschew,
But represent vs to Crist Jhesu,
    O dulcis Maria.

[9]

O floure of alle virginitie,
Replete with alle diuinitie,
O triclyne of the Trinitie,
    O clemens, O pia.

[10]

O welle of vertu and of grace,
Returne to vs thy louely face;
Forsake vs not for oure trespace,   [f. 20ᵛ
    O dulcis Maria.

[11]

O frag[r]ant roose, O lilly chaste,
O ardent busshe that did not wast,
Thyne eye of grace vpon vs cast,
    O clemens, O pia.

[12]

With louely chere pray thy Sonne dere,
King Assuere, in blis so clere,
That we in fere to hym may appere,
    O dulcis Maria.

stza. 5, l. 4. MS. O clemens &c.
stza. 8, l. 3. Crist Jhesu] MS. Jhesu Crist, *with
    transposition indicated.*

200

Cambridge University Library. MS. Ee.
I. 12   By James Ryman, *c.* 1492
f. 20ᵛ

Salue, sancta parens,
Omni labe carens.

[1]

O heuenly sterre so clere and bright,
In whome did light the Sonne of Right;
Wherefore we singe with alle oure myght,
'Salue, sancta parens.'

[2]

As the sonne beame goth thurgh the glas,
The Sonne of God thurgh the did pas,
Taking nature, as his wille was,
Omni labe carens.

[3]

Whenne Criste thy Sonne had   [f. 21ʳ
      suffred payne
And rose fro deth to lyfe agayne,
To the he seide, and not in vayne,
'Salue, [sancta parens.']

[4]

As grete peyne tho it was to the
Thyne owne dere Sonne in peyn to se
As vnto hym nayled on tree,
Omni labe carens.

[5]

But with alle joye thou were replete
Whenne thy dere Sonne with the did mete
And grete the with thies wordes swete:
'Salue, sancta [parens.']

[6]

No wonder was yf thou were gladde,
Seyng for whome thou haddest be sadde,
Thy Sonne, of whome alle joye is hadde,
Omni labe carens.

[7]

O moder of bothe God and man,
Aftur oure myght and as we can
We sey to the, as he seide than,
'Salue, sancta parens.'

[8]

Pray Criste that he vs not forsake,
That benignely of the hath take

Nature, mankynde fre for to make,
Omni labe carens.

stza. 3, l. 4. MS. Salue &c.
stza. 5, l. 4. MS. salue sancta &c.

200.1

University of Glasgow, Hunterian Museum.
      MS. 83   XV *cent.*
f. 21ʳ

Salue, sancta parens.

[1]

All heyle, Mary, and well thou be,
      Madyn and modere withoutyn offens;
For thy suffren virginite,
      Salue, sancta parens.

[2]

O curtasse qwheyn most comendable,
      O prynce pereles in pacience,
O virgyn victorius onvariable,
      Salue, sancta parens.

[3]

O consolatrix of contribulate,
      O suffren well of sapiens,
O mayden and moder immaculate,
      Salue, sancta parens.

[4]

O precious perele imperpetuell,
      O saffure off sadenesse sett in sentence,
O imparice both off hevyn and hell,
      Salue, sancta parens.

[5]

O well off grace celestiall,
      Brynge vs, lady, to thy presence;
Kepe vs well that we note fall,
      Salue, sancta parens.

The repetition of the burden is indicated after
      stza. 1 by: Salue sancta parens (with music
      of burden repeated) ut supra per figuram .2.
*Stza. 5 is written in a hand different from that of
      the first four stanzas.*

201

Cambridge University Library. MS. Ee.
I. 12   By James Ryman, *c.* 1492
f. 21ᵛ

Aue, regina celorum,
Flos et decus beatorum.

[1]

Haile, full of grace, Criste is with the;
Of alle women blessed thou be,
And blessed be the frute of the,
    Mater Regis angelorum.

[2]

Haile, swete moder of Crist Jhesu;
Haile, virgyne pure; on vs thou rue
And for oure synne vs not eschewe,
    O Maria, flos virginum.

[3]

Haile, flos campi of swete odoure;
Haile, moder of oure Sauyoure;
Haile, virginall floure of grete honoure,
    Velud rosa vel lilium.

[4]

Haile, lanterne of eternall light,
As the sonne beame as clere and bright;
Of Criste that we may haue a sight
    Funde preces ad Filium.

[5]

Haille, quene Hester with louely chere;
King Assuere, thy Sonne so dere,
Thy prayer clere pray thou to here
    Pro salute fidelium.

202

Cambridge University Library. MS. Ee.
    I. 12   By James Ryman, *c.* 1492
f. 22ʳ

    Gaude, mater gloriosa,
    Super omnes speciosa.

[1]

Haile, spowse of Criste oure Savioure;
Haile, lilly floure of swete odoure;
Haile, quene of blis of grete honoure,
    Super omnes speciosa.

[2]

Haile, vessell of all purite;
Haile, moder of humilite;
Haile, chaste floure of virginite,
    Super omnes speciosa.

[3]

Haile, Jesse roote full of vertue;
Haile, holy moder of Jhesu;
Haile, fragrant rose moost faire of hue,
    Super omnes speciosa.

[4]

Haile, lylly floure withouten thorne;
Haile, of whome Criste Jhesus was borne;
Haile, virgyne afture and beforne,
    Super omnes speciosa.

[5]

Haile, spowse of Criste louely and dere,
As the sonne beame as bright and clere;
Haile, oure conforte bothe ferre and nere,
    Super omnes speciosa.

[6]

O moder myelde, for vs thou pray, [f. 22ᵛ
Vnto thy childe that we come may
To heven blis, that lasteth aye,
    Super omnes speciosa.

stza. 4, l. 1. lylly] MS. llylly.

203

Cambridge University Library. MS. Ee.
    I. 12   By James Ryman, *c.* 1492
f. 25ʳ

    There sprunge a yerde of Jesse moore;
    There was neuer none suche   [f. 25ᵛ
        before,
    Ne non shal be:
    This yerde was Marie, virgyne fre.

[1]

As Aaron yerde withoute moistoure
Hath florisshed and borne a floure,
So hath she borne oure Savyoure
    Withouten touche of dishonoure
        Of mannes sede,
    For God his self in her did brede.

[2]

King Assuere was wrothe, iwis,
Whenne Quene Vasty had done amys,
And of her crowne priuat she is;
But, when Hester his yerde did kis,
        By hir mekenes
    She chaunged his moode into softnes.

[3]

King Assuere is God Almyght,
And Quene Vasty synag[ogu]e hight,
But, when Vasty had lost hir lyght,
Quene Hester thanne did shyne full bright,
        For she forth brought
    The Sonne of God, that alle hath
        wrought.

[4]
As Moyses yerde, that was so goode,
Turned the waters into bloode,
So did Mary moost myelde of   [f. 26ʳ
   moode
Vnder the cros, whereas she stoode
   Ful sore weping:
   Her teres ran with blode bleding.

[5]
She is that yerde that yevith vs light
Of Criste oure King to haue a sight;
She is redy bothe day and nyght
To yelde oure cause to God Almyght,
   To save oure sore,
   That quene of blis for euirmore.

[6]
Now beseche we that yerde so free
Mediatrix for vs to be
Vnto that King of Magestee,
In blis that we his face may see
   Withoute endyng
   Afture this fynalle departing.

stza. 3, l. 5. forth] MS. forsothe.

204

Cambridge University Library. MS. Ee.
  I. 12   By James Ryman, *c.* 1492
f. 78ʳ

  Stella celi, micaris clare;
  Regina celi, letare.

[1]
O quene of blisse, thy Son Jhesus,
  Quem meruisti portare,   [f. 78ᵛ
God *and* man is, we bileue thus;
  Regina celi, letare.

[2]
O lady free, the King of Grace,
  Quem meruisti portare,
Hath ordeyned the a joyfull place;
  Regina celi, letare.

[3]
O spowse moost bright, thy Son alone,
  Quem meruisti portare,
Thy place hath dight next to the trone;
  Regina celi, [letare.]

[4]
O moder dere of God and man,
  Quem meruisti portare,
Thou art more clere than tunge tell can;
  Regina celi, [letare.]

[5]
O moder myelde, thy Son so good,
  Quem meruisti portare,
For man so wielde died on the rode;
  Regina celi, letare.

[6]
O meke of myende, thy Son also,
  Quem meruisti portare,
Hath brought mankyende fro peyn *and*
  woo;
  Regina celi, letare.

[7]
O virgyn pure, as he behight
  Quem meruisti portare,
He rose full sure by his grete myght;
  Regina celi, letare.

[8]
O emperesse, that Emperoure
  Quem meruisti portare,
In oure distresse he is socoure;
  Regina celi, letare.

[9]
O heuenly sterre, the Prince of Peas,
  Quem meruisti portare,
Oure goostly werre by the doth seace;
  Regina celi, letare.

[10]
For vs thou pray Emanuell,
  Quem meruisti portare,
So that we may in heven dwell;
  Regina celi, letare.

stza. 3, l. 4. MS. Regina celi &c.
stza. 4, l. 4. MS. Regina celi &c.

205

Cambridge University Library. MS. Ee.
  I. 12   By James Ryman, *c.* 1492
f. 79ʳ

  O quene of pitee, moder of grace,
  In the high citee graunt vs a place.

[1]
O quene of pitee and of grace,
  O swete lady, to thy dere chielde,
That King, that Lorde of euery place,
  Pray thou for vs, thy seruauntes myelde,
That King, that Lorde of euery place,
  Fro blisse that we be not exiled [f. 79ᵛ
   For oure offence, trespas, and synne,
   But that swete place that we may
   wynne.

[2]

O princesse of eternall peace,
  O lady of aungelles moost bright,
Pray thy dere Sonne oure woo to seace
And bring vs fro derkenes to light,
  Of hym that we may haue a sight,
    That died for vs on the roode tree
    And shed his blode to make vs free.

[3]

O emperesse withouten pere,
  O queen also of heven blisse,
Of Criest Jhesu, thy Son so dere,
  What thou wilt aske thou shalt not mysse,
  For he is thyne, and thou art his.
    O swete lady, sith it is soo,
    Defende mankyende fro endeles woo.

[4]

O floure of alle virginitee,
  O moder of oure Savioure,
O chast bowre of the Trinitee,
  O virgyne pure moost of honoure,
  Be oure comfort, help, and socoure,
    And vttirly thou not forsake
    Mankynde, the which thy Son hath take.

[5]

O gate of lyfe, moder and wyfe,
  O hope and trust of synners alle,
In angwishe, woo, trouble, and stryfe
  For thy comfort we crie and calle,
  Bothe olde and yonge, both gret and
    small;
    Therfore oure help and comfort be,
    Sith oure trust is onely in the.

[6]

O louely spowse and peramoure
  Of Criest, that is bothe God and [f. 80ʳ
    man,
Thou hast born chielde without doloure,
  And so noon other woman can.
  Do thou thy cure, swete lady, than,
    Sith thou haast borne the Lord of Alle,
    So that mankyende be not made
      thralle.

[7]

O lantern of eternall light,
  O myrroure of humilitee,
In whom the Holy Goost did light
  Bicause of thy virginitee,
  Kepe mankyende fro captiuitee
    And fro that woofull place of helle,
    With the fowle fende that it not
      dwelle.

[8]

O heuenly sterre most bright and clere,
  Of alle sterres of hevyn so bright,
O swete lady, oure prayere here,
  And be oure guyde both day and nyght,
  That we may please that King of Myght
    So that we may come to that blis
    Wherof the joye eternall is.

206

Bodleian Library. MS. Eng. poet. e. 1
                                    XV *cent.*
f. 25ᵛ

  Salue, regina,
    Mater misericordie.

[1]

O blyssedfull berd, full of grace,
To all mankynd thou art solas,
Quene of hevyn in euery place,
    Salue.

[2]

To owr helth thou bar a chyld
And yet with syn wart neuer fylyd,
Mary moder, mek and myld,
    Salue.

[3]

Fro the fend thou vs defend,
And of syn thou vs ame[n]d;
Mary, thi mercy thou to vs send;
    Salue.

[4]

O worthy whyght, we worshep the,
Full of mercy and of pyte;
Wherfor we syng in ech degre,
    'Salue.'

[5]

And lat vs not fro the fale,
And therto we cry and also call,
Both yong and old, grett and small,
    'Salue.'

[6]

And bryng vs to thi Sonns blysse,
Wher that thi wonnyng is;
Of that we pray the that we not mys;
    Salue.

207

Cambridge University Library. MS. Ee.
I. 12   By James Ryman, *c.* 1492
f. 77ᵛ

Salue, regina glorie,
Mater m*isericord*ie.

[1]

Hayle, our*e* lod sterr*e* bothe bright *and*
    clere;
  Hayle, welle of grace and of pitee;
Hayle, spowse of Criest louely *and* dere,
  Mat*er* m*isericord*ie.

[2]

Hayle, flour*e* of alle virginitee;
  Hayle, full of grace, Criest is wi*th* the;
Hayle, temple of the Trinitee,
  Mater misericordie.

[3]

Hayle, quene of blisse, emp*er*esse of hell;
  Hayle, doughter Syon full of beautie;
Hayle, closed gate of Ezechiell,
  Mater m*isericord*ie.

[4]

O fragrant rose, O lilly chast,
  O violete of puritee,
Thyn ey of grace vpon vs cast,
  Mat*er* misericordie.

[5]

O quene of blisse, O virgyn pure,
  For confort we resorte to the;
On vs therfore do thou thy cure,
  Mater m*isericord*ie.

[6]

In tyme of nede, bothe grete and small,
  For subsidie we calle to the,
And by thy name thus we the call:
  'Mater m*isericord*ie.'

[7]

What tyme mankyende had done amys,
  By thy mekenesse it was made free
And brought ayene to heven blisse,
  Mater m*isericord*ie.

[8]

As the son beame goth thurgh the glas,
  The Son of God passed thurgh the,
Takyng nature, as his wille was,
  Mater m*isericord*ie.

[9]

Wi*th* the glorie of thy Son swete,
  O quene of blisse, O lady free,
Heven and erthe bothe be replete,   [f. 78ʳ
  Mater m*isericord*ie.   [f. 77ᵛ

[10]

Moder and mayde in one p*er*sone   [f. 78ʳ
  Was neuir noon, no noon shall be,
But thou alone, O heven trone,
  Mat*er* misericordie.

[11]

O lantern of eternall light,
  That gave them light that myght not see,
Cause vs of Criest to haue a sight,
  Mater m*isericord*ie.

[12]

O virgyne pure, O quene of blis,
  Cause vs to be in blisse wi*th* the,
Wher*of* the joye eter*n*all is,
  Mater m*isericord*ie.

208

Cambridge University Library. MS. Ee.
I. 12   By James Ryman, *c.* 1492
f. 87ᵛ

Salue, regina glorie,
Mater misericordie.

[1]

O Jesse yerde florigerat,
  The fruyte of lyff is sprunge of the,
The Prynce of Peas desiderat,
  M*ater* m*isericord*ie.

[2]

O quene of blisse celestiall,
  Childryn of Eve, we call to the
Here in this vale terrestriall,
  M*ater* m*isericord*ie.

[3]

When all mankynde for syn was lost,
  The Kyng of Grace was born of the
By vertu of the Holy Gost,
  M*ater* m*isericord*ie.

[4]

As the sonne beame goith t[h]rough the
    glasse,
  The Sonne of God passid throughe the,
And so bothe God and man he wasse,
  M*ater* m*isericord*ie.

[5]

Thatte Lord thatte in thy wombe did rest,
  The whiche hath made and   [f. 88ʳ
    create the,
Thou hast fedde with thy holy brest,
  M*ate*r m*isericord*ie.

[6]

Thatte Eve hath take awey fro us
  Thou yeldist with thi fruyte Jhesus;
Therfore thy name is callyd thus:
  'M*ate*r m*isericord*ie.'

[7]

The ierarchies with ordres nyne,
  For cause that Crist is born of the,
They honowre the with laude dyuyne,
  M*ate*r m*isericord*ie.

[8]

Besiche thatt Kyng of myght*es* most,
  The whiche hath take mankynd of the,
For oure syn thatte we be not lost,
  M*ate*r m*isericord*ie.

209

Cambridge University Library. MS. Ee.
  I. 12   By James Ryman, *c.* 1492
f. 88ʳ

  Salue, regina glorie,
  Mater misericordie.

[1]

O stronge Judith so full of myght,
  By thy vertu we be made fre,
For thou hast putte our*e* foo to flyght,
  M*ate*r m*isericord*ie.

[2]

O meke Hester*e* so fayr*e* of face,
  Kyng Assuere for loue of the
Hath take mankynd vnto his gr*ace*,
  M*ate*r m*isericord*ie.

[3]

O benigne meyde, moder*e* and wyff,
  Oure joye is wonne only by the; [f. 88ᵛ
Sothly thou art the gate of lyff,
  M*ate*r m*isericord*ie.

[4]

Whom alle this world, thatt ys so wyde,
  Myght not receyue, he lyght in the

And became man to be our gyde,
  M*ate*r m*isericord*ie.

[5]

We be most fre, that were most thrall,
  By thi mekenes, O lady fre;
Wherfore of right thus we the call:
  'M*ate*r m*isericord*ie.'

[6]

Sith thou hast born our*e* Sauyowr*e*,
  And alle oure trust is leyde in the,
Defend us ay fro all dolowr*e*,
  M*ate*r m*isericord*ie.

[7]

Lete notte the fende w*ith* all his fraude
  Make thrall thatt thy Sone hath made
    fre,
In blysse thatte we may gyff you laude,
  [Mater misericordie.]

[8]

Pray Crist, thy Sonne, that high Justyse,
  Thatte we may dwell w*ith* hym *and* the
In the sweete blysse of paradyse,
  [Mater misericordie.]

stzas. 7, 8, l. 4. MS. c⁹.

210

Cambridge University Library. MS. Ee.
  I. 12   By James Ryman, *c.* 1492
f. 88ᵛ

  Salue, regina glorie,
  Mater misericordie.

[1]

O fayr*e* Rachel semely in syght,
  Ther is no spotte of syn in the; [f. 89ʳ
Therfore of ryght thy name shall hight
  M*ate*r m*isericord*ie.

[2]

As Holy Writte thus concludith,
  For cause oure helthe is wone by the
Thou art bothe Ester and Judith,
  M*ate*r m*isericord*ie.

[3]

Holofernes, the fende, is hede
  With his owne swerde, O lady fre,
Thou hast smytte of and made hym dede,
  M*ate*r m*isericord*ie.

[4]

Aman alsoo, the fende, oure foo,
  Thou hast hangyd vppon a tre;
Thus thou hast brought mankynd *fro* woo,
  M*ater* m*isericord*ie.

[5]

O spowse of Crist so sweete and dere,
  Ther is no creature like the;
In heuen ne erthe thou hast no pere,
  M*ater* m*isericord*ie.

[6]

Alle creaturys dothe the honowre
  And doith obey, lady, to the,
For thou hast born oure Sauyowre,
  M*ater* m*isericord*ie.

[7]

Blessid thou be of wommen alle,
  For the sweete fruyte that came of the
Hath made us free, thatte ay wer*e* thralle,
  M*ater* m*isericord*ie.

[8]

Sith thou hast borne the Kyng of Gr*a*ce,
  And alle oure trust restith in   [f. 89ᵛ
    the,
In blysse cause us to haue a place,
  M*ater* m*isericord*ie.

211

Cambridge University Library. MS. Ee.
  I. 12   By James Ryman, *c*. 1492
f. 89ᵛ

  Salue, regina glorie,
  Mater misericordie.

[1]

Adam and Eve, thatte were vnywse,
  Were putte with ther*e* posterite
Fro the swete blysse of paradyse,
  M*ater* m*isericord*ie.

[2]

Butte thy swete Sone, Jhesus so good,
  To bryng us fro captiuite
Hath sufferd deth and shed his blood,
  Mater m*isericord*ie.

[3]

Jhesus, thy swete Sone, and no moo,
  Thatte Kyng of alle felicite,
Hath take us fro derknes and woo,
  Mater m*isericord*ie.

[4]

By vertu of his woundys wyde
  Thatt Lorde of alle humylyte
Hath ouercome the prynce of pryde,
  M*ater* m*isericord*ie.

[5]

Pray Crist thatte he us not forsake
  For our*e* syn and iniquite,
Butte into blysse thatt he us take,
  M*ater* m*isericord*ie.

212

Cambridge University Library. MS. Ee.
  I. 12   By James Ryman, *c*. 1492
f. 97ʳ

  Maria, mater gracie,
  Mater misericordie.

[1]

O prynces of eternall peas,
  O lady of all angel*les* bright,
Pray Crist our*e* bondage to releas
  And brynge us fro derknes to lyght,
  Of hym thatte we may haue a syght
    Thatt toke bothe flesshe *and* bloode of
      the,
    Mater misericordie.

[2]

O quene of pite and of grace,
  Pray thou for us, thy *seruantes* myld,
Thatte the dothe serue in euery   [f. 97ᵛ
    place,
  Fro blisse thatte we be nott exyled;
  Thoughe thatt we be wickyd *and* wyld,
    Yeitt we do hope and trust in the,
    Mater misericordie.

[3]

O emperesse withowten pere,
  With Crist reignyng above in blys,
For us pray to thy Sonne so dere
  Thatt we may reigne w*ith* hym *and* his,
  And of his joye neuer*e* to mys,
    But withowte ende theryn to be,
    Mater misericordie.

213

Huntington Library. Christmas carolles newely Inprynted (Richard Kele) *c.* 1550

p. [44]

Salue, regina, mater misericordie;
Uita, dulcedo, et spes nostra, salue.

[1]

O uery lyfe of swetnes and hope,
Of thy mercy sende vs a drope,
As thou bare Jesu, th*a*t our kynd dyd grop.

[2]

Unto our helth thou bare that chyld;
With spot of syn thou were neuer defyld,
Mary mother, bothe meke and myld.

[3]

We synners, lady, to the we crye
In this world to haue mercy;
We synge to the yet or we dye:

[4]

To the we call euer at our nede,
A frende specyall for all mannes nede,
Thou floure on felde of Adams sede.

[5]

Thy eyen of pyte from vs not hyde
Whyle we here in this world abyde;
Thou gouerne vs and be our guyde.

The repetition of the burden is indicated after stzas. 1–4 by: Salue regina mater m*isericordi*e. vita. &c.   burden, l. 1. misericordie] Orig. miseridordie.

214

Cambridge University Library. MS. Ee.
1. 12   By James Ryman, *c.* 1492

f. 9[r]

Vita, dulcedo, et spes
Nostra, Maria, tu es.

[1]

Perles prynces of euery place,
Of heuen, of erthe, of see, of sonde,
Moder of mercy and of grace,
Helpe thy seruauntys in euery londe.
Oure woo thou sese, our*e* joy increse;
Graunt us that pease that is endlese.

[2]

Pray thy Sone to vnbynde oure bonde
And brynge us owte of care and   [f. 9[v]
woo
And defende us with his right honde
And kepe us fro the fende, our*e* foo.
Our*e* woo th*o*u sease, [our*e* joy in-
crese;
Graunt us that pease that is endlese.]

[3]

Thoughe thatte Adam, our*e* first parent,
And Eve alsoo haue done offense,
Lete notte mankynde for ay be schent,
Sith thou art quene of indulgense.
Our*e* woo th*o*u sease, [our*e* joy increse;
Graunt us that pease that is endlese.]

[4]

Oure lyffe, our*e* sweetnes, our*e* truste alsoo,
Thou art only; therfore we calle
Only to the and to no moo,
Chyldryn of Eve, exyles most thralle.
Our*e* woo th*o*u sease, [our*e* joy increse;
Graunt us that pease that is endlese.]

[5]

Here in this vale of care and woo,
Sith thou art oure mediatrise,
Thyn eyen of mercy, of grace alsoo,
Turne thou to us in mercyfull wyse.
Our*e* woo thou sease, [our*e* joy increse;
Graunt us that pease that is endlese.]

[6]

O sweete Mary most meke and fre,
Thatt blessid fruyte of thy wombe,
Jhesus,
After thatte we departyd be
Fro thys exyle, schewe thou to us.
Our*e* woo thou sease, [our*e* joy increse;
Graunt us that pease that is endlese.]

[7]

O sweete lady, atte domysday
When the false schalle us accuse,
For us vnto thy Sone thou pray,
For syn thatte he us notte refuse.
Our*e* woo thou sease, [our*e* joy increse;
Graunt us that pease that is endlese.]

[8]

Lete notte the fende with alle his fraude
Brynge us to payn and endles   [f. 10[r]
woo,

Butte thatte to God we may gyff laude
In blysse with the and many moo,
Oure woo thou sease, [oure joy increse;
Graunt us that pease that is endlese.]

stzas. 2–4, l. 5. MS. Oure woo thou sease c°.
stza. 4, l. 4. Chyldryn] MS. C chyldryn.
stzas. 5–8, l. 5. MS. Oure woo thou sease c°.

215

Cambridge University Library. MS. Ee.
I. 12   By James Ryman, *c.* 1492

f. 96ʳ

Mekely we syng and seye to the,
'Maria, spes nostra, salue.'

[1]

Childryn of Eve, bothe grete and small,
Here in this vale of wrechidnesse
With grete wepyng to the we call
For helpe and grace in oure distresse,
And, as oure tunges can expresse,
Mekely we synge and seye to the,
'Maria, spes nostra, salue.'

[2]

Thou art, lady, and euer shalt be,
Quene of mercy, moder of grace;
Therfore atte nede, O lady fre,
Turne vnto us thi glorious face,
And confort us in euery case,
Syth we do syng and seye to the,
'Maria, spes nostra, salue.'

[3]

Thoughe itte be muche thatte we offende,
Yeit we be thyne for euermore;
Therfore thy grace to us extende,
Pure virgyn after and before,
For syn that we be notte forlore,
Syth we do sing and seye to the,
'Maria, spes nostra, salue.'

[4]

Thow doist habunde so in all wise
With goodness, grace, and all vertu,
So thatte oure laude cannott suffice
To the, sweete moder of Jhesu;
But yet oure prayers not   [f. 96ᵛ
eschewe,
Sith we do sing and seye to the,
'Maria, spes nostra, salue.'

[5]

Sweete and benigne mediatrise,
Thyn eyen of grace on us thou cast,
Sith thou art quene of paradise,
And lete not oure hope be in wast,
Butt schewe us thy Sonne atte the last,
Sith we do sing and seye to the,
'Maria, spes nostra, salue.'

[6]

O meke and mylde, full of pite,
For us pray to thatt Prince of Pease
Thatte we may cum to thatt cite
Wheroff the joye shall neuer sease
Butte multiplie and euer encrease,
Sith we do sing and seye to the,
'Maria, spes nostra, salue.'

burden. *The initial* M *serves for both lines.*
stza. 2, l. 4. vnto] MS. vnto vnto.

216

Cambridge University Library. MS. Ee
I. 12   By James Ryman, *c.* 1492

f. 96ᵛ

O regina clemencie,
O mater indulgencie.

[1]

O floure of all uirginite,
O moder of oure Sauyoure,
O chast boure of the Trinite,
Be oure confort, help, *and* socoure,
And defende us fro all doloure,
Atte nede to the sith we do fle,
O mater indulgencie.

[2]

O louely spowse and paramoure   [f. 97ʳ
Of Crist, thatte is bothe God and man,
Fro peyn of helle bittere and sowre
Pray hym kepe us, as he best can,
Thatt for oure sake hadde woundes wan
And with his bloode hath payede oure
fe,
O mater indulgencie.

[3]

O gate of liffe, moder and wyffe,
O hope and trust of synners all,
In care and woo, sorowe and stryffe,
Confort thou vs, bothe grete *and* small,
Mekely to the sith we do call
With hert and mynde, O lady fre,
O mater indulgencie.

217

Cambridge University Library. MS. Ee.
I. 12   By James Ryman, *c.* 1492
f. 102^r

O regina clemencie,
O mater indulgencie.

[1]

O Jesse yerde florigerat,
  The fruyte of liffe is sprunge of the,
The Prynce of Pes desiderat
  And Kyng of highe regalite.

[2]

O quene of blisse celestiall,
  Childryn of Eve, we calle to the
Here in this vale terrestriall,
  Bothe highe and lowe in our*e* degre.

[3]

Thatte Lorde thatte in thy wombe didde
    rest,
  The whiche hath made and creatt the,
Thou hast fedde with thy holy brest
  In all clennes and purite.

[4]

O meke Hester so fayr*e* of face,
  Kyng Assuere, for loue of the,
Hath take mankynde ayen to grace
  And fro all syn hath made it fre.

[5]

O benigne meyde, moder and wyffe,
  Oure joy is wonne only by the;
Sothly thou arte the gate of liffe
  The whiche Ezechiel didde se.

[6]

Pray thy sweete Sonne, that high   [f. 102^v
    Justise;
  Thatt we may dwell with hym and the
In the sweete blisse of paradyse,
  Wherof endyng never shall be.

At end: Ame*n*.

218

Cambridge University Library. MS. Ee.
I. 12   By James Ryman, *c.* 1492
f. 101^r

Regina celi, letare,
  With God and man alsoo,
Quem meruisti portare
  Withowten peyn and woo.

[1]

Regina celi, letare,
  For Crist, thy Sonne so dere,   [f. 101^v
Quem meruisti portare
  With gladde and joyfull chere,
Nunc te gaudet amplexare
  In blisse, thatt is so clere,
Et corona coronare
  As quene withowten pere.

[2]

Resurrexit, sicut dixit,
  Thy Sonne Jhesus so fre,
Quem gens seua crucifixit
  And naylde vppon a tre.
Mortem uicit et reuixit,
  And them with hym toke he
Quos amara mors afflixit,
  In blisse with hym to be.

[3]

O Maria, flos uirginum,
  Most fayre and sweete, iwys,
Velud rosa vel lilium
  Whoys blossome schalle not mys,
Funde preces ad Filium,
  Bothe God and man thatt ys,
Pro salute fidelium,
  Thatt he may graunt us blisse.

At end: Amen. Jhesu, fili Dauid, miserere nobis.

219

Cambridge University Library. MS. Ee.
I. 12   By James Ryman, *c.* 1492
f. 103^v

To the we make oure mone,
Moder of Crist, alone.

[1]

Sith thou hast born the Kyng of Gr*a*ce,
  Thatt sittith so highe in trone,
Therfore atte nede in euery case
  To the we make our mone.

[2]

Sith thou art quene of euery place,
  Thou maist graunt us oure bone;
Therfore, while we haue tyme *and* space,
  To the we make our [mone.]

[3]

Sith of mercy thou berist the mace,
  And so doth other*e* none,
Therfore before thy Sonnys face   [f. 104^r
  For us make thou thy mone.

[4]

Sith all oure trust is putte in the
    Next vnto God alone,
Therfore, moder of Crist so fre,
    At nede here thou our mone.

[5]

When we shall dye and yelde our gost
    And owte of this worlde gone,
Besiche thatte Lorde of myghtes most
    Mekely to here our mone.

[6]

When we shall stonde atte domysday
    Before thy Sonne echone,
Be oure confort then, we the pray
    Modere of Crist, alone.

220

Cambridge University Library. MS. Ee.
    I. 12   By James Ryman, *c*. 1492
f. 5ʳ

    Sancta Maria, ora pro nobis.

[1]

O moder mylde, mayde vndefylde,
Thatte we so wylde be notte begylde
    And euere exylde fro Crist and hys,
    Ora pro nobis.

[2]

O quene of grace most fayre of face,
Of alle solace ledyng the trace,
    Off the highe place thatte we nott mys,
    Ora [pro nobis.]

[3]

O lady fre off highe degre,
Thatte we may se thy Sone and the,
    And euer to be where alle joy ys,
    Ora pro nobis.

[4]

Thatte Crist us sende grace to amende
Oure tyme myspende or we hense wende,
    And atte oure ende to graunte us blys,
    Ora [pro nobis.]

stzas. 2, 4, l. 4. MS. Ora cᵒ.

221

Cambridge University Library. MS. Ee.
    I. 12   By James Ryman, *c*. 1492
f. 5ʳ

    Sancta Maria, ora pro nobis.

[1]

O uirgyn chast both furst and last,
That in tyme past by feith stedfast
    Conceued hast the Kyng off Blys,
    Ora pro nobis.

[2]

Oure wickydnesse we do confesse,
And oure excesse we do expresse;
    In oure distresse haue mynde of this,
    Et ora pro nobis.

[3]

O lady fre of high degre,   [f. 5ᵛ
That we may sc thy Sone and the,
    And euere to be where alle joye ys,
    Ora pro nobis.

222

Cambridge University Library. MS. Ee.
    I. 12   By James Ryman, *c*. 1492
f. 5ᵛ

    Sancta Maria, ora pro nobis.

[1]

O lylly flowre of swete odowre,
In whois chast bowre oure Sauyour
    With grete honowre conceyued is,
    Ora pro nobis.

[2]

O moder mylde, mayde vndefylde,
Thatte we so wylde be not exylde
    Fro thy swete chylde and fro all his,
    Ora pro nobis.

[3]

Thatte Crist us sende grace to amende
Oure tyme myspende or we hense wende,
    And atte oure ende to graunt us blys,
    [Ora pro nobis.]

223

Cambridge University Library. MS. Ee.
I. 12   By James Ryman, *c.* 1492
f. 5ᵛ

Sancta Maria, ora p*ro* nobis.

[1]

O spowsesse most dere, most bryght, most
    cler*e*,
In heuen quere hauyng no pere,
    To Assuere, the Kyng of Blys,
    Ora [pro nobis.]

[2]

O quene of grace most fayr*e* of face,
Of alle solas ledyng the trace,
    Of the highe place thatte we not mys,
    [Ora pro nobis.]

[3]

O highe prynces of blys endles,   [f. 6ʳ
To the Prynce of Pes for us thou pres;
    Vita et spes nostra cum sis,
    Ora p*ro* nobis.

224

Cambridge University Library. MS. Ee.
I. 12   By James Ryman, *c.* 1492
f. 6ʳ

Sancta Maria, ora pro nobis.

[1]

O tryclyn of the Trinite,
Replete with alle diuinite,
O flowre of alle uirginite,
    Ora pro nobis.

[2]

O blessid quene of heuen blys,
Wheroff the joye eternalle is,
Of the whiche blis thatte we not mys,
    Ora pro nobis.

[3]

O emperesse of helle alsoo,
Into thatte place thatt we not goo,
Where is derkenes and endles woo,
    Ora pro nob*i*s.

[4]

O spowsesse of Crist, oure Sauyowre,
The whiche restyd in thy chast bowre,
Thatte he kepe us fro alle dolowre,
    Ora p*ro* nob*i*s.

[5]

O sweete lady so meke and mylde,
Vnto Jhesu, thy blessid chylde,
Fro blysse thatt we be notte exylde,
    Ora pro nob*i*s.

[6]

Holy moder of Crist Jhesu,
Thatte is the Lorde of alle vertu,
Thatte he with grace may us renu,
    Ora p*ro* nobis.

[7]

Holy virgyn of virgyns alle,   [f. 6ᵛ
Thatt thy sweete Sone Jh*esus* may calle
Vs vnto hym, bothe grete and smalle,
    Ora pro nobis.

[8]

Thatte we, whiche be terrestrialle,
May leve this lyff so bestialle
And come to blysse celestialle,
    Ora pro nobis.

225

Cambridge University Library. MS. Ee.
I. 12   By James Ryman, *c.* 1492
f. 6ᵛ

Sancta Maria, ora pro nobis.

[1]

O spowsesse of Crist and paramo*ur*
Most of vertu, most of honowre,
O moder of oure Sauyowre,
    Ora pro nobis.

[2]

O emperesse of helle alsoo,
Where is bothe payn and endles woo,
Vnto thatte place thatt we not goo,
    Ora pro nobis.

[3]

O blessid quene of paradise,
Thatt Crist thy Sone, that high Justise,
Att his comyng us notte despise,
    Ora pro nobis.

[4]

O prynces of eternalle pese,
Thatt Crist oure care and woo may sese
And oure solas and joy inc018se,
    Ora pro nobis.

[5]

O pure uirgyn of uirgyns alle,
Thatte we may dwelle, both gret and
  smalle,
With Crist and the in heuen halle,
  Ora *pro* nobis.

226

Cambridge University Library. MS. Ee.
  I. 12   By James Ryman, *c.* 1492
f. 7ʳ

  Sancta Maria, ora pro nobis.

[1]

O meke Hester so mylde of mynde,
Thatte hast fownde grace for alle man-
  kynde,
Of God thatt we mercy may fynde,
  Ora *pro* nobis.

[2]

O stronge Judith, thatte of dydde smyght
The hede of Holoferne, thatte knyght,
Thatte we may putte the fende to flight,
  Ora *pro* nobis.

[3]

O closyd gate, throughe which alone
Jhesus didde passe, and othere none,
To Crist thy Sone sittyng in trone
  Ora *pro* nobis.

[4]

O Jesse yerde, the whiche didde flowre
And bare the fruyte of alle honowre,
That Criste defende us fro dolowre,
  Ora *pro* nobis.

[5]

To God, that is of myghtis most,
Fadere and Sone and Holi Gost,
So thatte for syn we be not lost,
  Ora *pro* nobis.

227

Cambridge University Library. MS. Ee.
  I. 12   By James Ryman, *c.* 1492
f. 7ʳ

  Cum sola sis spes hominum,
  Ora pro nobis Dominum.

[1]

O blessid mayde, moder and wyffe,
Graunter of pease, seaser of stryffe,
When we schalle die and ende *our* lyffe,
  Ora pro nobis Dominum.

[2]

The flesshe, the worlde, the fende alsoo,
Assawte us ay to worke us woo;
Into ther snare thatte we notte goo,
  Ora pro nobis Dominum.

[3]

O swete lady, thou be oure gyde   [f. 7ᵛ
By nyght and day atte euery tyde;
Into no syn that we notte sclyde,
  Ora pro no*bis* Dominum.

[4]

Of syn and vice thatte we may sease,
And in uertu ay to encrease,
And lede oure lyffe in goostly pease,
  Ora pro no*bis* Dominum.

[5]

Thatte we by grace so may procede
In wylle, in thought, in worde, and dede,
Thatte heuyn blysse may be our*e* mede,
  Ora pro no*bis* Dominum.

228

Cambridge University Library. MS. Ee.
  I. 12   By James Ryman, *c.* 1492
f. 7ᵛ

  O clemens, O pia,
  O dulcis Maria.

[1]

Sith thou hast born the Kyng of Grace,
The Lorde, the Prynce of euery place,
Be oure confort in euery case,
  O dul*cis* Maria.

[2]

Whatte thou wilte axe of thy swete Sone,
In heuen and erthe itte schalle be done;
For thy mekenes this hast thou wone,
  O dul*cis* Maria.

[3]

Therfore, sith thou art quene of blys,
In tyme of nede haue mynde of this:
Of thy conforte lete us notte mys,
  O dul*cis* Maria.

[4]

O dere suster, O mylde moder,   [f. 8^r]
Pray to thy Sone Crist, our*e* broder,
Sith thou mayst best of alle oder,
     O dulc*is* Maria.

[5]

Vppon mankynde do thou thy cure,
So thatte of blysse we may be sure
Wherof the joy schalle ay endure,
     O dulc*is* Maria.

229

Cambridge University Library. MS. Ee.
I. 12   By James Ryman, *c.* 1492
f. 8^v

     O mater summi Iudicis,
     Succurre nobis miseris.

[1]

O sweete lady, O uirgyn pure,
     O mater summi Iudicis,
On us mekely do thou thy cure;
     Succ*ur*re nob*is* mis*er*is.

[2]

Atte domysday, when we haue nede,   [f. 9^r]
     Tuis preclaris meritis
Then, we the pray, in worde and dede
     Succ*ur*re nob*is* mis*er*is.

[3]

Crist, thy sweete Sone, thoughe we offende,
     Qui lux est veri luminis,
Yet, sweete lady, atte our*e* last ende
     Succ*ur*re nob*is* mis*er*[is.]

[4]

Haue mynde, thou art the quene of blys
     Et mater expers criminis;
Haue mynde, lady, and thenke on this:
     Succ*ur*re nob*is* mis*er*is.

[5]

For oure trespas and oure offense
     Ne dampnemur cum impiis,
Sith thou art quene of indulgense,
     Succ*ur*re nob*is* mis*er*is.

stza. 3, l. 4. *The end of the line has been cut away
by the binder.*

230

a. *Balliol College, Oxford.* MS. 354
       By John Audelay (?), XVI *cent.*
f. 219^r

     'Aue Maria,' now say we so;
     Mayd *and* moder were neu*er* no mo.

[1]

Gaude Maria, Crist*es* moder,
     Mary myld, of the I mene;
Thou bare my Lord, thou bare my brod*er*,
     Thou bare a louly child *and* clene.
Thou stodyst full still w*ith*owt blyn
     Whan *in* thy ere that arand was done
     so;
Tho graci*us* God the lyght withyn,
     Gabrielis nu*n*cio.

[2]

Gaude Maria, yglent w*ith* gr*a*ce,
     Whan Jh*es*us thi Son on the was bore,
Full nygh thy brest thou ga*n* hym brace;
     He sowked, he sighhed, he wepte full
     sore.
Thou fedest the flowr th*a*t neu*er* shall
     fade
     Wyth maydons mylke *and* songe
     therto,
'Lulley, my swet, I bare the, babe,
     Cum pudoris lillio.'

[3]

Gaude Maria, thy myrth was away
     Whan Cryst on crose, thy Son, ga*n* die
Full dulfully on Gud Fryday,
     That many a moders son yt sye.
Hys blode vs browght fr*om* care and
     stryf;
     His watery wovnd*es* vs wisshe from
     wo;
The thyrd day, from dethe to lyff,
     Fulget resurreccio.

[4]

Gaude Maria, thou byrde so bryght,
     Bryghtter than blossu*m* th*a*t blowith on
     hill;
Joyfull thou wer*e* to se that sight
     Whan the appostles, so swet of will,
     All *and* su*m*, dide shryt full shryll
     Whan the fayrest of shape went you
     fro;
From erth to hevyn he styed full still,
     Motuq*ue* fertur pr*o*prio.

[5]

Gaude Maria, thou rose of ryse,
  Maydyn *and* moder both jentill *and* fre,
Prec*ius* prynces p*er*les of pris,
  Thy bowr ys next th*e* Trynyte.
Thy Son, as lawe askyth aright,
  In body *and* sowle the toke hym to;
Thou regned w*ith* hym, right as we fynd,
  In celi palacio.

[6]

Now, blessid byrde, we p*ray* the a bone:
  Before thy Son for vs thou fall,
And p*ray* hym, as he was on the rode done
  And for vs dranke asell *and* gall,
  That we may wone w*ith*yn th*at* wall
  Wher euer ys well w*ith*owt wo,
  And gravnt that gr*ace* vnto vs all
  In p*er*henni gaudio.

stza. 1, l. 8. Gabrielis] MS. Grabrielis.
At end: Explicit de qui*n*que gaudia.

b. *Bodleian Library.* MS. Douce 302,
ff. 31ᵛ, 30ʳ. XV *cent.* (burden and
stzas. 1–5).

MS. heading: Et alia de s*anct*a maria.
burden, l. 2. Mayd] mod*er.* moder] maydon.
  were] was. no] no*n*.
stza. 1, l. 2. myld, of the I mene] mod*er* of
  thyne*m*ne. l. 4. louly] cumle.
  l. 5. blyn] wene. l. 6. that] this. done
  so] doo. l. 7. Tho] whe*n*. *between* ll. 7
  and 8. aue maria vt sup*ra*.
stza. 2, l. 1. yglent] y gret. l. 2. on] of.
  l. 3. ga*n*] co*n*. l. 4. sowked] secud.
  sighhed] soukid. l. 5. the] th*at*.
stza. 3, l. 1. myrth] myght. l. 2. on crose,
  thy Son, ga*n*] thi son on cros co*n*.
  l. 5. browght] boght. l. 6. wisshe] was-
  chid. l. 7. thyrd] iii.
stza. 4, l. 2. blossu*m*] the blossu*m*. blowith]
  blomyth. hill] the hill. l. 3. Joyfull] Ful
  joyful. that sight] seche a syght. l. 4. Whan]
  And al. appostles] postilis. l. 5. Fore al
  and su*m* thai stod ful stil. l. 6. the] *omits*.
  went] he swond. l. 8. Motuq*ue*] motu.
stza. 5, l. 1. thou] th*at*. of] on. l. 2. Maydyn *and* moder] mod*er and* maid. both]
  omits. l. 3. prynces p*er*les] perrles p*ri*nces.
  pris] pes. l. 5. lawe askyth aright] loue
  al kno*n* of kynd. l. 6. In] Thi. the] he.
  l. 7. regned] restist. right] th*er*.

231

British Museum. MS. Sloane 2593
                    XV *cent.*
f. 9ʳ

  I may synge of a may,
    Of joyis fyve *and* m*er*this most.

[1]

The ferste joye, as I y*ou* telle:
With Mary met Seynt Gabrielle:
'Heyl, Mary, I grete the welle,
  W*ith* Fad*er and* Sone *and* Holy Gost.'

[2]

The secu*n*de joye, in good fay,
Was on Crystemesse Day;
Born he was of a may,
  W*ith* Fad*er* [*and* Sone *and* Holy Gost.]

[3]

The thredde joye, w*ith*outy*n* stryf:
Th*at* blysseful berthe was ful ryf
Qua*n* he ros fro ded to lyf,
  W*ith* Fad*er* [*and* Sone *and* Holy Gost.]

[4]

The forte joye, in good fay,   [f. 9ᵛ
Was vpon Halewy*n* Thursda[y]:
He stey to heuene in ryche aray,
  W*ith* Fad*er and* Sone *and* Holy Gost.

[5]

Th[e] fyfte joye, w*ith*outy*n* dene:
In heuene he crownyd his mod*er* clene;
Th*at* was wol in the eyr asene,
  W*ith* Fad*er* [*and* Sone *and* Holy Gost.]

stzas. 2, 3, 5, l. 4. MS. w*ith* fad*er* &c.
stza. 5, l. 3. in] MS. wil.

232

A. *St. John's College, Cambridge.* MS. S. 54
                              XV *cent.*
f. 2ʳ

  A, a, a, a,
  Gaudet cely d*omi*na.

[1]

Mary myld, for loue of the
Glad *and* blythe now may we be;
I yow telle, os ye may see,
  Tua qui*n*que gaudia.

[2]

The fyrst joy th*at* was sente the
Was qwan Gabryell gret the
And seyd, 'Mary, of chastite
  Effisier*is* gra*ui*da.'

[3]

The secund joy, it was full good:
Qwan Crist of the toke flesch *and* blode,
Withoutyn symne, with myld mode,
    Enixa est puerpera.

[4]

The third joy was of grette myth: [f. 2ᵛ
Qwan Crist was on the rode dyth,
Dede *and* beryd for oure ryth,
    Surrexit d[i]e tersia.

[5]

The fourth joy was on [a] day,
Qwan Crist to hewyn toke the way;
God *and* man, this is oure fay,
    Ascendit supra scidera.

[6]

The fifth joy in the gan lyth
Qwan thou were in hewyn with hym dyth;
All Holy Chyrche thou hast in myth,
    I[n] tua potencia.

stza. 2, l. 2. Gabryell] MS. grabryell.
stza. 3, l. 1. secund] MS. scecnd.   l. 3. mode]
MS. mede.
stza. 4, l. 1. third] MS. iii.   l. 3. ryth] MS.
ryyth.
stza. 5, l. 1. fourth] MS. iiii.   l. 3. fay] MS.
say.
stza. 6, l. 1. fifth] MS. v.

B. *Bodleian Library.* MS. Eng. poet. e. 1
                      XV *cent.*
f. 45ʳ
    A, a, a, a,
    Gaude celi domina.

[1]

Mary, for the loue of the
Glad *and* mery schal we be;
Whe schal syng vnto the
    Tua quinque gaudia.

[2]

The fyrste joy that came to the
Was whan the aungel greted the
And sayd, 'Mary, ful of charyte,
    Aue, plena gracia.'

[3]

The secund joye, that was ful good
Whan Goddes Son tok flesch *and* blood,
Withowt sorow *and* changyng of mood
    Enixa est puerpera.

[4]

The thyrd joy was ful of myght:
Whan Goddes Son on rood was pyght,
Deed *and* buryed *and* layd in syght,
    Surrexit die tercia.

[5]

The fourth joy was on Holy   [f. 45ᵛ
    Thursday,
Whan God to heven tok hys way;
God *and* man, withowten nay,
    Ascendit supra sydera.

[6]

The fyfth joy is for to come
At the dredful day of dome,
Whan he schal deme vs, al *and* some,
    Ad celi palacia.

[7]

Mary to serue God gyue vs grace,
And grete hyr with joys in euery place,
To cum afor hyr Sones face
    In seculorum secula.

MS. heading: Off the 5 joyes of owr lady.

C. *Balliol College, Oxford.* MS. 354
                           XVI *cent.*
f. 223ᵛ
    Ay, ay, ay, ay,
    Gaude celi domina.

[1]

Mary, for the loue of the
Blyth *and* glad may we be,
And I shall syng, as ye may se,
    Sua quinque gaudia.

[2]

The fyrst joy was sent to the
Whan Gabryell gretyd the
And sayd, 'Hayle, Mary, in chastite
    Efficiaris gravida.'

[3]

The second joy was full gud:
Whan Cryst toke both flesshe *and* blod,
Withowte syn talkyng of mode
    Inexsa est puerpera.

[4]

The thirde joy was of gret myght:
Whan Jh[es]u was on the rode dyght,
Dede *and* buryed in all menys syght,
    Surrexit die tercia.

[5]

The fourth joy was, with*out* [n]ay,
Whan Jh*es*u to hell toke the way,
And with hy*m* co*m* gret aray
   Ad celi palacia.

[6]

The fifth joy was on Holy Thursday:
Vnto hevyn he toke the way,
God *and* ma*n*, *and* so he ys for ay,
   Assendit sup*er* sidera.

stza. 4, l. 1. thirde] MS. iii^de.
stza. 5, l. 1. fourth] MS. iiii^th.
stza. 6, l. 1. fifth] MS. v^th.
At end: Explicit.

233

Balliol College, Oxford. MS. 354
                       XVI *cent.*
f. 228^v

  Gawde, for thy joyes five,
  Mary, moder, maydyn, *and* wyff.

[1]

Gaude, to whom Gabryell was sent,
  From Nazareth to Galalie,
And said that God O*m*nipotent
  Wold haue his Son be born of the.

[2]

Gaude: thow bare hy*m* with*owt* payn,
  And with payn thow saweste hy*m* dy on
    tre,
But gaude whan he rose agayn,
  For he appered firste to the.

[3]

Gaude: thow saweste hy*m* assende
  By his own strenth above the skye;
An hoste of angell*es* down he sent
  And assumpte thy sowle w*ith* thy bodye.

[4]

Gaude: thy dignyte ys gret,
  For next vnto the Trynyte
Above all seynt*es* is thy sete,
  And all joye is i*n* the sight of the.

[5]

Gaude, moder *and* maydyn pure,
  For thy joyes shall never cesse
(Therof thow art siker *and* sure)
  But ever florisshe *and* encrese.

MS. marks burden: fote.
stza. 3, l. 1. thow] MS. thowe thow.
At end: Explicit.

234

A. *Trinity College, Cambridge.* MS. O. 3. 58
                             XV *cent.*
recto
  Alma Redemptoris mater.

[1]

As I lay vpon a nyth,
My thowth was on a berde so brith
That men clepyn Marye ful of myth,
  Redemptor*is* mater.

[2]

[T]o here cam Gabryel wyth lyth
And seyd, 'Heyl be th*o*u, blysful wyth!
To ben clepyd now art th*o*u dyth
  Redemptoris mater.'

[3]

At that wurd that lady bryth
Anon conseyuyd God ful of myth;
Than men wyst weel that sche hyth
  Redemptoris mater.

[4]

[Q]wan Jh*es*u on the rode was pyth,
Mary was doolful of that syth
Til sche sey hym ryse vprith,
  Redemptoris mater.

[5]

Jhesu, that syttyst in heuene lyth,
Grau*n*t vs to comy*n* beforn thi sith
Wyth that berde that is so brith,
  Redemptoris mater.

burden, l. 1. Alma] MS. Alma a.

B. *Bodleian Library.* MS. Arch. Selden
  B. 26   XV *cent.*
f. 13^v
  Alma Redemptoris mater.

[1]

[A]s Y lay vpon a nyght,
My thought Y say a semly syght
Th*at* callid was Mary bright,
  Rede*m*ptor*is* mater.

[2]

Ther come Gabriel with lyght
And saide, 'Haile, thou swete wyght!
To be clepyd th*o*u art ydyght
  [Redemptoris mater.']

[3]

Ther she conceyved God Almyght,
That was in stalle with here al nyght,
And there men knewe what he hyght,
    Redemptoris mater.

[4]

Whan Jhesu was on the rode ypyght,
Mary was sory of that syght
Tyl that she say hym ryse vpryght,
    Redemptoris mater.

[5]

And after to heuen he toke his flyght,
Ther he is nowe in blysse bryght,
And with hym that swete wyght,
    Redemptoris mater.

The burden is again written in full after the
first stanza.

C. *British Museum.* MS. Sloane 2593
                                    XV *cent.*
f. 30ᵛ
    Alma Redemptoris mater.

[1]

As I lay vpon a nyght,
My thowt was on a mayde bryght
That men callyn Mary of myght,
    Redemptoris mater.

[2]

To here cam Gabriel so bryght
And seyde, 'Heyl, Mari, ful of myght!
To be cald thou art adyght
    Redemptoris [mater.']

[3]

After that word that mayde bryght
Anon conseyuyd God of Myght,
And therby wyst men that che hyght
    R[edemptoris mater.]

[4]

Ryght as the sunne schynit in glas,
So Jhesu in his moder was,
And therby wyt men that che was
    R[edemptoris mater.]

[5]

Now is born that babe of blys,
And qwen of heuene his moder is,
And therfore think me that che is
    R[edemptoris mater.]

[6]

After to heuene he tok his flyght,
And ther he sit with his Fader of Myght;
With hym is crownyd that lady bryght,
    Redemptoris mater.

stza. 4, l. 1. Ryght] MS. Rryght.

D. *Balliol College, Oxford.* MS. 354
                                    XVI *cent.*
f. 222ʳ
    Now syng we all in fere,
    'Alma Redemptoris mater.'

[1]

As I me lay on a nyght,
Me thowght I sawe a semly wyght
That clepid she was ryght
    Alma Redemptoris mater.'

[2]

To her com an angell with gret lyght
And sayd, 'Hayle be thou, blessid wyght!
To be cleped thou art right
    [Alma Redemptoris mater.']

[3]

At that word the maydyn bryght
Anon conceyved God Almyght;
Then knew Mary what she hyght:
    [Alma Redemptoris mater.]

[4]

Whan Jhesu on the rode was dyght,
Mary was sorofull of that syght
Tyll after she sawe hym ryse vpright,
    Alma Redemptoris mater.

stzas. 2, 3, l. 4. MS. vt supra.
At end: Explicit.

235

a. *Bodleian Library.* MS. Arch. Selden
        B. 26   XV *cent.*
f. 23ʳ
    Hayl, Mary, ful of grace,
        Moder in virginite.

[1]

The Holi Goste is to the sent
From the Fader Omnipotent;
Now is God withyn the went
    While the angel seide, 'Aue.'

[2]

Whan the angel 'Aue' byganne,
Flesh *and* blode togedre ranne;
Mary bare bothe God *and* manne
  Thorwe the v*er*tu of the dignite.

[3]

So seith the gospel of Syn Joh*a*n:
God *and* man is made al one
In flesch *and* blode, body *and* bone,
  O God in p*er*sonys thre.

[4]

And the p*r*ophete Jeremye
Telleth in his p*r*ophecie
That the Sone of Marie
  For vs deyde vppon a tre.

[5]

Moche joye was vs ygraunte
And in erthe pees yplaunte
Whan ybore was that faunte
  In the londe of Galile.

[6]

Mary, g*r*aunte vs of the blys
Ther*e*as thy Sonys wonynge ys;
Of th*a*t we haue ydone amys
  Pray for vs p*ur* charite.

*A later hand has drawn a crude sketch of a cock
opposite stza. 5 and has added the following
stanza at the end of the carol:*
  Hayl, blyssyd lade, qwych hays born
    God Son i*n* Tr*i*nite;
  I*n* the, laydy, he tuk hys plays
    Qwe*n* the angel sayd, 'Aue'.

b. *Trinity College, Cambridge, MS. O. 3.
58, recto. XV cent.*

c. *Huntington Library. Christmas carolles
newely Inprynted* (Richard Kele), p. [43],
c. 1550 (stzas. 2–6).

burden l. 1. Hayl, Mary, ful] b ...1...1(*MS.
  faded*).   l. 2. virginite] b virgyny—y—te—
  e—e.
stza. 1, l. 4. While the] b *MS. faded.*
stza. 2, l. 4. b Thorw v*er*tu *and* thowr dyngnyte.
  c Through the vertue of benygnyte.
stza. 3, l. 2. al] b but.   c bothe.   l. 3. blode,
  body] c breed/blode.   l. 4. O] c One.
stza. 4, l. 2. Telleth] b c Told.   l. 4. For vs
  deyde] b Schuld deye for vs.   c For vs sholde
  dye.   vppon a] b on rode.   c on.
stza. 5, l. 1. c He hath Joye to you graunted.
  was vs ygraunte] b to vs was graunth.
  l. 2. yplaunte] c hath plaunted.   l. 3. ybore]
  b th*a*t born.   c yborne.   that] b this.
  faunte] c faynted.

stza. 6, l. 1. of] b c *omit.*   l. 2. Ther*e*as] b
  Ther.   c where.   Sonys wonynge] c sone
  dwellynge.   l. 3. Of] c And of.   haue] b
  han.   l. 4. Pray] c Thou pray.   p*ur*] c for.
At end: b Amen. c Finis.

236

British Museum. MS. Sloane 2593
                                                  XV *cent.*
f. 28v

  Nowel, el, el, el, el, el, el, el,
    el, el, el, el, el, el, el, el!

[1]

'Nowel, el,' bothe eld *and* yyng,
'Nowel, el,' now mow we syng
In worchepe of o*ur* Heuene Kyng,
  Almyty God in Trinite.

[2]

Lestenyght, lordyng*es*, bothe leue *and* dere;
Lestenyt, ladyis, w*ith* glad cher*e*;
A song of m*er*the now mow ye her*e*,
  How Cryst o*ur* brother he wolde be.

[3]

An au*n*gyl fro hefne was se*n*t ful   [f. 29r
    snel;
His name is clepyd Gabriel;
His ardene he dede ful snel:
  He sat o*n* kne *and* seyde, 'Aue.'

[4]

And he seyde, 'Mary, ful of grace,
Heuene *and* erthe in eu*er*y place
W*ith* me, the tyme of lytyl space,
  Reco*n*silid it xuld be.'

[5]

Mary stod stylle as ony ston,
And to the au*n*gyl che seyde ano*n*,
'Tha*n* herd I neu*er*e of manys mon;
  Me think*it* wond*er* tho*u* seyst to me.'

[6]

The au*n*gyl answerd ano*n* ful wel,
'Mary, dryd the neu*er* a del;
Tho*u* xalt co*n*seyue a chyld ful wel;
  The Holy Gost xal schadue the.'

[7]

Mary, on bryst her*e* hand che leyd;
Stylle xe stod, *and* thus xe seyd:
'Lo, me her*e*, Godes owy*n* handmayd,
  W*ith* herte *and* wil *and* body fre.'

[8]

Mary mod*er*, mayde myld,
For the loue al of thi chyld,
Fro helle *p*et th*o*u vs schyld;
   'Ame*n*, ame*n*,' now sy*n*ge we.

237

A. *Bodleian Library.* MS. Eng. poet. e. 1
                              XV *cent.*

f. 26ʳ

   Regina celi, letare.

[1]

Gabriell, th*a*t angell bryght,
Bryght*er* than the sonne is lyght,
Fro hevyn to erth he [to]ok hys flyght;
   Letare.

[2]

In Nazareth, th*a*t gr[et] cete,
Befor a maydyn he knelyd on kne
And seyd, 'Mary, God is wi*th* the;
   Letare.

[3]

'Heyll, Mary, full of grace,
God is wi*th* the *and* eu*er* was;
He hath in the chosyn a place;
   Letare.'

[4]

Mari was afrayd of th*a*t syght,
Th*a*t ca*m* to her wi*th* so gret lyght;
Than seyd the angell, th*a*t was so bryght,
   'Letare.

[5]

'Be not agast of lest ne most;
In the is *con*seyuyd the Holy Gost,
To saue the sov*les* th*a*t war forlost;
   Letare.'

stza. 1, l. 3, stza. 2, l. 1. *The text is damaged by
small holes in MS.*

B. *Balliol College, Oxford.* MS. 354
                              XVI *cent.*

f. 221ᵛ

   Now syng we, syng we,
   'Regina celi, letare.'

[1]

Gabryell, that angell bryght,
Bryght*ter* than the son lyght,
From hevyn to erth he toke his flyght;
   Regina celi, letare.

[2]

In Nazareth, in that cyte,
Before Mary he fell on kne
And sayd, 'Mary, God ys wi*th* the;
   Regina celi, letare.

[3]

'Hayle be thou, Mary; of myt*es* most,
In the shall lyght the Holy Gost,
To saue the sowles th*a*t were lost;
   Regina celi, letare.'

[4]

Hayle be thou, Mary, maydy*n* shen;
Fro*m* the fend*es*, that be so kene,
Thou kepe *and* save vs all fro*m* tene;
   Regina celi, letare.

At end: Explicit.

238

A. *Balliol College, Oxford.* MS. 354
                              XVI *cent.*

f. 219ᵛ
   Nova, nova:
   'Aue' fitt ex 'Eva'.

[1]

Gabriell of hygh degre,
He cam down fro*m* the Trynyte
From Nazareth to Galalye,
   V*ith* nova.

[2]

He mete a maydyn in a place;
He kneled down before her face;
He sayd, 'Hayle, Mary, full of gr*a*ce.'
   V*ith* nova.

[3]

When the maydyn sawe all this,
She was sore abashed, ywys,
Lest that sh*e* had done amys;
   V*ith* nova.

[4]

Then sayd the angell, 'Dred not you;
Ye shall *con*ceyve in all vertu
A chyld whose name shall be Jh*es*u.'
   V*ith* nova.

[5]

Then sayd the mayd, 'How may this be,
God*es* Son to be born of me?
I know not of ma*n*ys carnalite.'
   V*ith* nova.

[6]

Then said the angell anon ryght,
'The Holy Gost ys on the plyght;
Ther ys nothyng vnpossible to God Al-
      myght.'
Vith nova.

[7]

Ther sayd the angell anon,
'Ytt ys not fully vi moneth agon
Syth Seynt Elizabeth conceyved Seynt Jo-
      han.'
Vith nova.

[8]

Then said the mayd anon a-hye,
'I am Godes own truly;
Ecce ancilla Domini.'
Vith nova.

At end: Explicit.

B. *Bodleian Library*. MS. Eng. poet. e. 1
f. 27¹ ʳ

   Noua, noua:
   'Ave' fit ex 'Eva'.

[1]

Gabryell of hyghe degree
Cam down from the Trenyte
To Nazareth in Galilee,
   With nova.

[2]

He fond the mayd al in hyr place;
He knelyd down befor hyr face
And seyd, 'Al heyl, full of grace.'
   With nova.

[3]

'Thou shalt conseyve and ber a chyld
Thov thou with syn wer neuer defylyd;
Thou hast fond grace, thou Mary myld.'
   With nova.

[4]

The byrd, abasshyd of all ble,
Answerd and seyd, 'How may this be?
Man thorow syn tovchyd neuer me.'
   With noua.

[5]

[The angell s]eyd onto that free,   [f. 27¹ ᵛ
['The Holy Gost sh]al lyght in the:
[God and] m[an in] on shal be.'
   With noua.

[6]

Syx [m]onthy[s i]s ner gon
Syn Elyz[abeth con]seyvd Johan;
She th[at was barre]n a babe haue borne.'
   With noua.

[7]

The ve[rgyn said] vnto the fere,
'Now hys we[ll be] don in me here,
And Godes mayd now se me here.'
   With noua.

*MS. is badly damaged. The restoration of the
text in stzas. 5, 6 follows Wright.*

C. *University of Glasgow, Hunterian
   Museum*. MS. 83   XV *cent*.
f. iii ᵛ

   Noua, noua, 'Aue' fit ex 'Eua'.

[1]

Gabriell off hye degre,
He cam down from Trinite,
From Nazareth to Galile,
   Noua.

[2]

'I met a madyn in a place;
I knelyd down afore hir face
And seyd, "Heile, Mary, ful of grace," '
   Noua.

[3]

When the maiden herd tell off this,
Sche was full sore abaschyd, iwis,
And wened that sche had don amysse,
   Noua.

[4]

Then seid the angell, 'Dred not thou,
For ye be conceyued with gret vertu,
Whoos name schal be called Jhesu.'
   Noua.

[5]

'It is not yit vi wekes agoon
Sen Elizabeth conceyved Johan,
As it was prophysed before.'
   Noua.

[6]

The[n] seid the mayden verely,
'I am youre seruaunt ryght truely:
Ecce ancilla Domini.'
   Noua.

*The burden is written again with the music.
The last seven lines are written in a hand different from that of the rest of the carol. This hand
has added at the end*: &c.

239

a. *Bodleian Library*. MS. Eng. poet. e. 1
XV *cent.*

f. 51ᵛ

'Nowell, nowell!'
This is the salutacion off the aungell
Gabriell.

[1]

Tydyng*es* trew th*er* be cu*m* new, sent frome
the T*r*inite
B*e* Gabriel to Nazaret, cite off Galile.
A clen*e* mayden *and* pure *v*irgyn, thorow
hyr*e* humilite,
Co*n*ceyvid the secu*n*d *per*son in diuinite.

[2]

Whan he fyrst p*r*esentid was before hyr*e*
fayer visag,
In the most demuer*e and* goodly wys he
ded to hyr*e* omag
And seid, 'Lady, frome heven so hy, th*at*
Lord*es* herytag
The wich off the born*e* wold be, I a*m* sent
on messag.

[3]

'Hayle, virgyn*e* celestiall, the mekest th*at*
eu*er* was;
Hayle, temple off deitie *and* myrrou*r* off all
grace;
Hayle, virgyn*e* puer, I the ensur*e*, wi*t*hin
full lyty[l] space
Th*o*u shalt receyu*e and* hy*m* conceyu*e* th*at*
shal bryng g*r*et solace.'

[4]

Sode*n*ly she, abashid truly, but not al thyng
dysmaid,
W*it*h mynd dyscret *and* mek spyryt to the
au*n*gel she said,
'By what man*er* shuld I chyld ber*e*, the
wich eu*er* a maid
Hau*e* lyvid chast al my lyf past *and* neu*er*
man*e* asaid?'

[5]

Than ageyn*e* to hire c*er*teyn answered the
au*n*gell,
'O lady der*e*, be off good cher*e*, *and* dred
the neu*er* a dell.
Th*o*u shalt *con*ceyu*e i*n thi body, mayden,
very God hy*m*self,
In whos byrth heven *and* erth shal joy,
callid Emanuell.

[6]

'Not [y]it,' he seid, 'vi monethys past, thi
cosyn Elyzabeth,
Th*at* was baren, *con*ceyvid Sent Joh*a*n; tru
it is th*at* I tell.
Syn she i*n* ag, why not in yought   [f. 52ʳ
mayst th*o*u *con*ceyu*e* as well,
If God wyl, whom*e* is possybyll to haue
don eu*er*y dell?'

[7]

Than*e* ageyn*e* to the aungell she answered
woman*n*ly,
'Whateu*er* my Lord co*m*maund me do I
wyll obey mekely.
Ecce, sum humilima ancilla D*o*mi*n*i;
Secu*n*du*m* verbu*m* tuu*m*,' she seid, 'fiat
mihi.'

stza. 4, l. 2. au*n*gel] MS. au*n*glel.

b. *Yale University Library*. MS. 365,
f. 79ᵛ. XV *cent.* (burden and stzas. 1, 2,
4–7).

c. *Balliol College, Oxford*. MS. 354, f. 229ᵛ.
XVI *cent.* (burden and stzas. 1–3, 7).

d. *Bodleian Library*. MS. Eng. poet. e. 1,
f. 41ᵛ. XV *cent.*, contemporary with a
(burden and stza. 1).

burden, l. 1. b Newell Newell N. N. c newell
newell newell newell. d Nowell nowell
nowell.   l. 2. salutacion] b song.   the (2)]
b c *omit*. aungell] c *omits*. c *marks burden
fote and indicates its repetition after each
stanza by*: newell.
stza. 1, l. 2. to] c *from*. cite] c to a Cite.
l. 3. *and*] b c a.   thorow] c by.   l. 4. Con-
ceyvid] c hath born. d hath *con*ceyuyd.
secund *per*son] c d *per*son second.   diuinite]
d deyte.
stza. 2, l. 1. he fyrst] c that he   l. 2. In] b
With.   the] b c *omit*.   he ded to hyr*e*] b to
hyr he ded.   l. 3. frome] b of.   l. 4. The
wich] c For he.   born*e*] c now born.
wold] b c wyll.   on] b of.   c on the.
stza. 3, l. 2. deitie] c the deite.   *and*] c hayll.
l. 3. full] c a.   l. 4. receyu*e*, conceyu*e*] c
transposes.
stza. 4, l. 1. she] b *omits*.   l. 2. mynd] b wynd
(*altered from* wynges).
stza. 5, l. 1. hir*e* c*er*teyn] b owre lady thus.
l. 3. *con*ceyue] b Rec . . . (*MS. faded*).
mayden] b mayd.   very God hy*m*self]
b godes very selle.   l. 4. heven] b bothe
heuyn.   callid] b *omits*.
stza. 6, l. 1. 'Not [y]it', he seid] b yt ys not yyt.
vi] b sex. Elyzabeth] b Elyzabell.   l. 2. Sent
Joh*a*n] b a chyld.   tru it] b trewthe.
tell] b the tell.   l. 3. Syn] b Sythe.   mayst
th*o*u] b ye may.

stza. 7, l. 1. ageyne to the aungell she] c bespak
the virgyn agayn *and*.   l. 2. Whateuer] b c
Watsoeuer. commaund] c comaundith.   do]
b to do.   c *omits*.   obey] b yt a bey.   mekely]
c trewly.   l. 4. verbum tuum] b tuum
verbum.   she said] b c *omit*.
At end: b *a nearly obliterated note*: The song of
a maydyn.   c Explicit.

240

Balliol College, Oxford. MS. 354
                                    XVI *cent.*
f. 219ᵛ

Now we shuld syng *and* say, 'Newell!'
Quia missus est angelus Gabriell.

[1]

From hevyn was sent an angell of light
Vnto a cyte that Nazareth hyght,
Vnto a mayd, a byrde so bryght
    And full of blis,
    Nomen Maria virginis.

[2]

The angell went furth, *and* nowght he sest;
Before that mayden he hym sone drest.
He sayd, 'All hayle! Thou art full blest
    And gracius,
    Quia tecum est Dominus.'

[3]

Whan Mary this hard, astoned was she
And thowght what thys gretyng myght be.
The angell her shewed of grace plente
    And gret solas,
    Et dixit, 'Maria, ne timeas.'

[4]

The angell sayd, 'Thou maydyn myld,
Thou shalt conceyve *and* bere a chyld;
Thy maydynhed shall neuer be defyled.
    Call hym Jhesus;
    Hic erat Altissimi Filius.'

[5]

Whan Mary, as bryght as crystall ston,
Thes wordes hard, answered anon
And asked how all this myght be done
    And sayd, 'How so,
    Quia virum non cognosco?'

[6]

The angell said, 'Thou maydyn still,
The Holy Gost shall the fulfill.'

The mayd answered with woyse so shryll
    And sayd mekely,
    'Ecce ancilla Domini.'

[7]

Sone after this this chyld was borne
In Bedleme in a wynters morne;
Now make we mery hym beforne
    And syng, 'Newell!'
    Quia missus est angelus Gabriell.

stza. 1, l. 3. byrde] MS. bryde.
At end: Explicit.

241

Balliol College, Oxford. MS. 354
                                    XVI *cent.*
f. 230ᵛ

What, hard ye not? The Kyng of Jheru-
    salem
Is now born in Bethelem.

[1]

I shall you tell a gret mervayll:
How an angell, for owr avayll,
Com to a mayd *and* said, 'All hayll!'

[2]

'All hayll!' he said, *and* 'full of grace,
God is with the now in this place;
A child thou shalt bere in lytill space.'

[3]

'A child?' she said, 'How may that be?
Ther had never no man knowlage of me.'
'The Holy Gost,' he said, 'shall light in the.

[4]

'And, as thou art, so shall thow be,'
The angell sayd, 'in virgynite,
Beffore *and* after in euery degree.'

[5]

The mayd answered the angell agayn:
'Yf God will that this be sayn,
The wordes be to me full fayn.'

[6]

Now will we all, in rejoysynge
That we haue hard this good tydyng,
To that child 'Te Deum' synge.

The repetition of the burden is indicated as
    follows: stza. 1: what hard ye not. stzas. 2,
    3, 5: what hard. stza. 4: what hard ye not
    &c. After stza. 6 it is replaced by: te deum
    laudamus.
At end: Explicit.

242

British Museum. MS. Sloane 2593
　　　　　　　　　　　　XV *cent.*
f. 10ʳ

Nowel, el, el, el, el, el, el, el, el, el, el, el!
Mary was gret with Gabriel.

[1]

Mary moder, meke and mylde,
Fro schame and synne that ye vs schyllde,
For gret on grownd ye gon with childe,
　Gabriele nuncio.

[2]

Mary moder, be not adred;
Jhesu is in your body bred,
And of your bryst he wil be fed
　Cum pudoris lilio.

[3]

Mary moder, the frewt of the
For vs was naylid on a tre;
In heuene is now his mageste;
　Fulget resurrecio.

[4]

Mary moder, the thredde day
Vp he ros, as I yow say;
To helle he tok the ryghte way;
　Motu fertur proprio.

[5]

Mary moder, after thin Sone
Vp thou steyist, with hym to wone;
The aungele wern glad quan thou were
　come
　In celi palacio.

243

a. *Cambridge University Library.* MS. Ee.
　I. 12　　　　By James Ryman, *c.* 1492
f. 11ʳ

Alma Redemptoris mater,
Quem de celis misit Pater.

[1]

The aungell seyde of high degree,
'Haile, full of grace, God is with the;
Of alle women blessed thou bee,
　Alma Redemptoris [mater.']

[2]

When she harde this, that mayden free,
In his worde sore affrayde was she
And thought what greting this myght be,
　Alma Redemptoris [mater.]

[3]

'Drede not, Marie,' to here seyde he;
'Thou haast founde grace, thou mayden
　free,
Of God, that is in persones three,
　Alma Redemptoris [mater.]

[4]

'Thou shalt conceyve and bere the same,
A Sonne of grete honoure and fame
Whome thou shalt calle Jhesus by name,
　Alma Redemptoris [mater.]

[5]

'This Sonne that shalle be borne of the,
That shall be of soo high degree,
The Sonne of God called shall be,
　Alma Redemptoris [mater.]

[6]

'And God shall geve hym Dauid see,
And in Jacobes howse reigne shall hee,
Of whoose kingdom none ende shall be,
　Alma Redemptoris [mater.']

[7]

Mary seide to the aungell than,
'How shall this be? Tell, yf thou can,
Sith I purpose to knowe no man,
　Alma Redemptoris [mater.']

[8]

The aungell seide, 'O lady free,　[f. 11ᵛ
The Holy Goost shalle light in thee,
Be whome Criste shalle conceyved be,
　Alma Redemptoris [mater.]

[9]

'Elizabeth, thy cosyn, loo,
In here age that bareyn did go,
Hath conceyved a childe also,
　Alma Redemptoris mater.'

[10]

To that aungell of high degree
'Goddes handemayde beholde,' seide she;
'As thou hast seide, be done to me,'
　Alma Redemptoris [mater.]

[11]

He toke his leve, that aungell bright,
Of here and went to blisse full right,
And she hath borne the King of Myght,
    Alma Redemptor*is* [mater.]

[12]

Glorious lady, quene of blisse,
Of thy comforte late vs not mysse,
Sith thy swete name now callid is
    Alma Redemptor*is* [mater.]

[13]

Lete thy mercy bothe springe *and* sprede;
Forsake vs not for oure mysdede,
But out of drede to blisse vs lede,
    Alma Redemptor*is* [mater.]

b. *Cambridge University Library*. MS. Ee.
1. 12, ff. 81ᵛ, 82ʳ. By James Ryman, *c.*
1492 (burden and stzas. 1–11).

burden, l. 2. *omits.*
stza. 1 (*and all following stanzas*), l. 4. R (*with
    mark of abbreviation*).
stza. 2, l. 2. In] Of.   affrayde] aferde.
stza. 5, l. 2. That] And.
stza. 6, l. 1.   And in the sete of megeste.
    l. 2. and in Jacobes howse] Of his fader*e* ay.
stza. 7, l. 1. Mary] Sche.   to] vnto.
    l. 3. p*ur*pose] entende.
stza. 9, ll. 2, 3. *transposes.*

244

Cambridge University Library. MS. Ee.
1. 12   By James Ryman, *c.* 1492

f. 11ᵛ

Inquit Marie Gabriell,
'Concipies Emanuel.'

[1]

The aungell seide of high degree,
'Haile, full of grace, Crist is w*ith* the;
Of alle women blessed thou be;
    Concipies Emanuel.'

[2]

This mayden marveyled in her   [f. 12ʳ
    thought
How and what wyse this shulde be wrought.
The aungell seyde, 'Mary, drede nought;
    Concipies [Emanuel.]

[3]

'Drede not,' he seide, 'thou mayden
    myelde;
Thou shalte conceyve and bere a childe,
And be a moder vndefielde,
    Cui nomen Emanuel.

[4]

'This childe that shalle be born of the
Shall be of grete and high degree
And Sonne of God callid shall be,
    Cui nomen Emanuel.

[5]

'And God shalle geve hym Dauid see,
And in Jacobes hows reigne shall he,
Of whose kingdome non ende shal be,
    Cui nomen Emanuel.'

[6]

To the aungelle this mayden free
Thanne seide, 'Telle me how this shal be,
Sith man shall be vnknow of me,
    Vt pariam Emanuel.'

[7]

'Drede not,' he seide, that aungell bright;
'The Holy Goost in the shalle light,
And thurgh vertu of God Almyght
    Concipies Emanuel.

[8]

'Elizabeth, thy cosyn, loo,
In her*e* age vi monethes agoo
Hath conceyved a childe alsoo:
    Concipies Emanuel.'

[9]

Magnifiyng God manyfolde,   [f. 12ᵛ
'Goddes handemayde,' she seyde, 'beholde;
To me be done as thou hast tolde,
    Vt pariam Emanuel.'

stza. 2, l. 4. MS. Concipies &c.

245

Cambridge University Library. MS. Ee.
1. 12   By James Ryman, *c.* 1492

f. 12ᵛ

Nowel, nowel, nowel, nowel,
Nowel, nowel, nowel, nowel!
Inquit Marie Gabriel,
'Concipies Emanuel.'

[1]

'Hayle, full of grace, Criste is with the,'
  To Mary seide aungel Gabriell;
'Of alle women blessed thou be;
  Concipies Emanuel.'

[2]

Whenne she hurde this, she dredde and
    thought
  What greting this was that he did telle.
The aungell seide, 'Mary, drede nought;
  Concipies Emanuel.

[3]

'Thou hast founde grace, thou mayden
    myelde,
  Before God, that in the dothe dwelle;
Thou shalt conceyve and bere a childe,
  Cui nomen Emanuel.

[4]

'He shall be grete and callid shall be
  The aungel of full grete counseill; [f. 13ʳ
In Dauid see aye reigne shalle he,
  Cui nomen Emanuel.'

[5]

'How shalle this be', this mayden thanne
  Seide, forsothe, vnto the aungelle,
'Sith I purpose to knowe no man,
  Vt pariam Emanuel?'

[6]

'The Holy Goost shalle light in the,
  And God shalle shadowe the eche dele;
The Sonne of God this childe shal be,
  Cui nomen Emanuel.

[7]

'Elizabeth, thy cosyn, loo,
  In here age, though it be mervell,
Hath conceyved a childe also:
  Concipies Emanuel.'

[8]

'Goddes handemayde beholde,' seide she
  To Gabriell, that archaungell;
'Thy worde in me fulfilled be,
  Vt pariam Emanuel.'

[9]

He toke his leve, that aungel bright,
  And went to blisse, therin to   [f. 13ᵛ
    dwelle,
And she hath borne the King of Myght,
  Cui nomen Emanuell.

[10]

Thus it was done, as I haue seide;
  As God it wolde, so it befelle:
Of Mary, wyfe, moder, and mayde,
  Nunc natus est Emanuel.

246

Cambridge University Library. MS. Ee.
I. 12   By James Ryman, *c.* 1492
f. 40ᵛ

  A meyden myelde a chielde hath bore,
  Mankyende to blis for to restore.

[1]

As longe before prophesy seyde,   [f. 41ʳ
  With vs to dwelle now Criste is come,
Borne of Mary, moder and meyde,
  To make vs free, bothe alle and sume.

[2]

As the sonne beame goth thurgh the glas,
  And as [a] floure berith his odoure,
So Criste Jhesus conceyved was
  And borne of her withoute doloure.

[3]

'Haille, full of grace, Criste is with the,'
  To her seide aungell Gabriell;
'Of alle women blessed thou be;
  Thou shalt conceyve Emanuell.'

[4]

This meyden myelde to hym seyde than,
  'How shall this be that thou doest telle,
Sith I purpose to know noo man,
  And shall conceyve Emanuell?'

[5]

'The Holy Goost shall light in the,
  And God shall shadew the eche dele
And worke right so that thou shalt be
  The moder of Emanuele.'

[6]

'The handemayde of oure Lorde beholde,'
  She aunswered hym, that mayden
    myelde;
'To me be done as thou hast   [f. 41ᵛ
    tolde:'
  And furthwithall she was with chielde.

[7]

And withoute maternall doloure
  She hathe borne Criste, that heuenly
    King.

That virginall floure moost of honoure,
  Out of thraldom mankyende to bringe.

[8]

Glorie mote be, good Lorde, to the,
  With the Fader and Holy Goost,
That art born of a virgyn free,
  Bothe God and man, of myghtes moost.

247

Cambridge University Library. MS. Ee.
  I. 12   By James Ryman, *c.* 1492
f. 67ᵛ

  In Criste Jhesu be we alle gladde,
  By whome oure joye endeles is hadde.

[1]

The high Fader of blisse aboue
  Hath sent his Sonne to take nature,
For his grete charite and loue,
  Of Marie myelde, that virgyne pure,
  And so on vs to do his cure
  And to bringe vs fro endeles woo
  And fro the feende, oure goostely foo.

[2]

Gabriell of so high degre
  Was sent fro God (Scripture seith soo)
To Nazareth of Galilee,
  And to Marie thus seide he thoo:
  'Haile, full of grace withouten woo,
  The Lorde God is dwelling with the;
  Of alle women blessed thou be.'

[3]

Whenne she hurd this, she was afrayde
  And thought what greting this myght be.
'Drede not, Marie,' the aungell seyde;
  'Thou hast founde grace, thou mayden
      free,
  Before one God in persones thre;
    Thou shalt conceyve and bere the
      same,
    The Sonne of God, Jhesus by name.

[4]

'He shalle be grete and called shall be
  The Sonne of the Highest of Alle,
And God shall geve hym Dauid see,
  And ay shall reigne in Jacobes halle,
  Whose high kingdome is eternall,
    For of heuen and erthe alsoo
    He is the Lorde; there is no moo.'

[5]

Marie seide to the aungell than,
  'Howe shall this be that thou   [f. 68ʳ
      doest hight,
Sith I purpose to know no man,
  And shall conceyve the King of Myght?'
  He aunswered her, that aungell bright,
    'The Holy Goost shall light in the,
    By whome Criest shall conceyved be.

[6]

'Elizabeth, thy cosyn, loo,
  In her olde age that bareyn went,
Hath conceyved a chielde alsoo
  By grace of God omnipotent;
  Wherefore, good lady, geve concent,
    For there shall be neuir a worde
    Inpossible vnto that Lorde.'

[7]

Magnifiyng God manyfolde,
  Vnto the aungell then seide she,
'The handemayde of oure Lorde beholde;
  As thou hast seyde, be done to me.'
  Thus conceyved this mayden free
    By her mekenes God and man thoo
    To bringe mankyende fro endeles woo.

[8]

This mayden myelde hath borne a chielde,
  As prophetes seide longe tyme before
To save mankyende, that was exielde,
  And to blisse it for to restore.
  Oure joye is wonne for euirmore,
    For Criste hath brought mankyende
      fro woo
    And fro the fende, oure mortall foo.

248

Cambridge University Library. MS. Ee.
  I. 12   By James Ryman, *c.* 1492
f. 68ʳ

  As Gabriell archaungell seyde,
  Now Criste is borne of a pure meyde.

[1]

That archaungell shynyng full bright
  Came vnto Marie, that myelde mayde,
Bringyng tydynges fro God Almyght,
  And vnto her mekely he sayde,
  'Haile, full of grace, be not afrayde;
    God is with the in euery place;
    Thou shalt conceyve the King of
      Grace.'

[2]

'Howe shalle this be,' this mayden [f. 68ᵛ
     than
Seyde to that archaungell so bright,
'Sith I purpose to knowe no man,
     And shall conceyve the Sonne of
          Myght?'
     'The Holy Goost in the shall light,
          And thurgh his working thou shalt be
          Moder of God in persones thre.'

[3]

'Ecce ancilla,' thenne seide she;
     'Beholde the handemayde of oure Lorde;
The wille of God be done in me
     In dede, in thought, in wille and worde.'
     And thus, as Scripture bereth recorde,
          Marie, that mayde moost of honoure,
          Hath borne Jhesus, oure Sauyoure.

[4]

The prophesy fulfilled is
     Of the prophetes nowe, alle and sume,
For why the Faders Sonne of Blis
     To save mankyende is man becume;
     To hym therfore be we not dume,
          But lete vs singe and make alle myrth
          In honoure nowe of his swete birth.

249

Cambridge University Library. MS. Ee.
     I. 12   By James Ryman, *c.* 1492
f. 77ʳ

     Mary hath borne alone
     The Sonne of God in trone.

[1]

Thus to her seide an aungell thoo:
'Haile, full of grace withouten woo,
Thou shalt conceyve and bere alsoo
     Both God and man alone.'

[2]

This mayden seide to the aungell,
'How shalle this be, to me thou tell,
A mayde sith I entende to dwell,
     Witnesse of God alone?'

[3]

The aungell saide, 'O mayden free,
The Holy Goost shall light in the,
And thurgh his workyng thou shalt be
     Moder of God alone.'

[4]

'Goddes handemayde beholde,' seide she;
'As thou hast seide, be done to me;
As oure Lorde wille, so moote it be;
     His wille be done alone.'

[5]

He toke his leve, that aungell bright,
Of hir and went to blisse full right,
And she hath born, as he behight,
     Both God and man alone.

250

Cambridge University Library. MS. Ee.
     I. 12   By James Ryman, *c.* 1492
f. 82ʳ

     'Heyle, Mary, meyden meke and mylde,
     Thou shalte conceyue and bere a chylde.'

[1]

An angelle, thatte was fayre and bryght,
Came to Mary with fulle grete lyght,
And vnto here he seyde fulle ryght,
     'Thou shalt conceyue and bere a chyld.'

[2]

When she hurde this, that blessid [f. 82ᵛ
     meyde,
Sore in here mynde she was afreyde
Of theys wordys thatte he hadde seyde:
     'Thou schalt conceyue and bere a chyld.'

[3]

'Drede notte,' he seide, thatt angelle bright;
'Thou hast founde grace in Goddys sight;
Withyn thy wombe by his grete myght
     Thou schalt conceyue and bere a chyld.'

[4]

She seide vnto the angell than,
'Hou shall this be? Telle, if thou can,
Sith I purpose to knowe no man,
     Thus to conceue and bere a chyld?'

[5]

He seyde, 'God, thatt is withowte ende,
The Holi Gost to the shall sende,
And, by grace thatt he shall extende,
     Thou shalt conceyue and bere a chyld.

[6]

'Thou shalte calle hym Jhesus by name,
A chyld of grete vertu and fame;
The Sonne of God shal be the same.
    Thou shalte conceyue and ber*e* a chyld.

[7]

'In the highe sete of mageste
Of his Fader*e* ay reigne shalle he,
Of whoys kyngdome none end   [f. 83ʳ
    shall be.
    Thou shalt conceyue and ber*e* a chylde.'

[8]

Sche answerde hym, thatt meyden fre,
'As thou hast seide, be done to me;
The wille of God fulfyllyd be,
    Thus to conceyue and ber*e* a chylde.'

[9]

He toke his leve, thatte angelle bright,
Of here and went to blysse full right,
And, by the grace of God Almyght,
    Sche conceyuyd and bore a chylde.

251

Cambridge University Library. MS. Ee.
I. 12   By James Ryman, *c.* 1492
f. 83ʳ

    Thys ys fulle tru; this ys fulle tru:
      Who can sey 'Nay' to thys?
    Mary ys modere of Jhesu,
      And God hys Fader*e* ys.

[1]

An angelle bright came downe w*ith* light,
    A message for to do
Vnto that meyde, and thus he seyde
    Fulle mekely here vnto:

[2]

'Haylle, Mary mylde, ay vndefylde,
    The Lorde God ys wyth the,
And his owne chylde so meke and mylde
    Of the nowe born wylle be.'

[3]

Also he seyde vnto thatte mayde,   [f. 83ᵛ
    Thatte was so meke and fre,
'Of women alle, bothe grete and smalle,
    Ay blessyd motte thou be.'

[4]

Off thatte tydyng thatt he dydde bryng
    This meyden meruelde sore,
Hou thatte hyghe Kyng thatt made al thyng
    Of here wombe wolde be bore.

[5]

Thatte angelle bright than seide full right,
    'Drede not, Mary so fre;
Thou hast founde grace befor*e* the face
    Of God in persons thre.

[6]

'In thy wombe thow shalt conceyue now
    A chylde and bere the same;
Of highe degre this childe shall be;
    Jhesus shalle be his name.

[7]

'The Lord of Alle to hym gyffe shalle
    A sete of mageste
Above in blysse, as right itte ys,
    Wheroff none ende shalle be.'

[8]

Sche answerd than, 'Telle, if thou can,
    Hou this dede shalle be wrought,
Sith I intende notte to offende
    With man in dede ne thought.'

[9]

'The Holi Gost, of myghtys most,   [f. 84ʳ
    Fro blysse shalle lyght in the,
By whoys vertu of Crist Jhesu
    The moder thou shalt be.

[10]

'Beholde alsoo, Elizabeth, loo,
    Thatte barayn long hath gon,
In here old age by highe suffrage
    Hath conceyuyd Saynt Jhon.

[11]

'Thatt Kyng and Lord th*at* w*ith* a worde
    Hath made al thyng of nought,
This dede in the now do shalle he
    Atte his wylle with a thought.'

[12]

'Beholde,' she seyde, 'God*des* handmeyde,'
    To hym, thatt maydyn mylde;
'Thy worde in me fulfyllyd be;'
    And soo she was with chylde.

[13]

Thatte angelle bright tho went full right
  Ayen to heuyn blys,
And, as he seyde, thatt blessyd meyde
  The modere of God ys.

252

Cambridge University Library. MS. Ee.
  I. 12   By James Ryman, *c.* 1492
f. 84ʳ

A meyden mylde hath born a chylde,
  Mankynde ayene to by;
Hys name Jhesus ys callyd thus
  And here name mylde Mary. [f. 84ᵛ

[1]

O man of molde, mekely beholde
  Hou God mankynd hath take,
As prophetis told many a folde,
  Of a meyde for thy sake.

[2]

An angelle bright came downe with light,
  True tydyngys for to telle;
He seyde full right, 'The Kyng of Myght
  In the truly wylle dwelle.'

[3]

Alsoo he seide vnto thatte meyde,
  'Thou shalte conceyue a chylde,
And thou shalt be, as I telle the,
  A meyden vndefylde.'

[4]

Of this thatt meyde was sore afreyde,
  Butte yett she dydde inclyne,
And so fulle sone this dede was done
  By Goddys grace dyuyne.

[5]

'Behold,' she seyde, 'Goddys handmeyde;
  Thy worde be done in me.'
And anon ryght by Goddys myght
  That tyme with chyld was she.

[6]

The Holi Gost, of myghtys most,   [f. 85ʳ
  Did make thatte meyde indede
To conceyue than bothe God *and* man
  Wythowten manys sede.

[7]

Bothe day and howre lete us honowre
  Mary, thatt meyden mylde,
Thatt nowe to us hath born Jhesus,
  And she neuere defylde.

253

Cambridge University Library. MS. Ee.
  I. 12   By James Ryman, *c.* 1492
f. 85ʳ

Mary so myld (Scripture seyeth thus)
Hath borne a chyld namyd Jhesus.

[1]

An angelle came vnto thatte mayde
  And knelyd downe vppon his kne,
And vnto here mekely he seyde,
  'Haille, fulle of grace, God ys with the.

[2]

'Of alle women blessid thou be;
  Thou shalt conceyue and bere alsoo
The Sone of God, O lady fre,
  Withowten peyn, dolowre, and woo.'

[3]

'Telle me,' she seyde, thatt meyden, than,
  'Hou I shalle conceyue and bere a chyld,
Syth I entende to knowe no man
  Butte ever to be clene, vndefyld.'

[4]

The angelle seyde, 'The Holi Gost   [f. 85ᵛ
  Fro blysse aboue shall lyght in the,
And Goddys Sone, of myghtes most,
  By his vertu conceyuyd shall be.'

[5]

'Ecce ancilla,' then seyde she
  And thankyd God many a fold;
'The wille of God fulfyllyd be
  In me, angelle, as thou hast told.'

[6]

And, as God wold, so itte was done:
  By here mekenes in virginite
Sche conceyued thatte tyme ful sone
  The Secunde Persone in Trinite.

254

Cambridge University Library. MS. Ee.
  I. 12   By James Ryman, *c.* 1492
f. 87ʳ

Mary so mylde, so meke, so fre,
Hath borne a chylde of hyghe degre,
And his name ys Jhesus.

[1]

An angelle seide to thatte meyde so fre,
'Hayle, fulle of grace, God is with the;
Of all women blessid thou be;
    Thou shalt conceyue Jhesus.'

[2]

When she hurde this, thatt blessid meyde,
Sore in here mynde she was afreyde
Of theys wordys thatte he hadde seyde:
    'Thou shalt conceyue Jhesus.'

[3]

'Drede not,' he seide, thatte angelle bryght;
'Thou hast founde grace in Goddys syght;
Withyn thy wombe by his grete myght
    Thou shalt conceyue Jhesus.'

[4]

Sche seide vnto thatte angelle than,
'Hou shalle this be? Telle, if thou can,
Sith I entende to knowe no man,
    And shalle conceyue Jhesus?'

[5]

He seide, 'God, thatt is withowte ende,
The Holi Gost to the shalle sende,
And, by gracc thattc hc shalle extende,
    Thou shalt conceyue Jhesus.

[6]

'Elyzabeth by highe suffrage
Hath conceyuyd in here old age
A chyld alsoo; withowte bondage
    Thou shalt conceyue Jhesus.'

[7]

Sche answerd hym, thatt meyde   [f. 87ᵛ]
  so fre,
'As thou hast seide, be done to me;
The wille of God fulfyllyd be,
    Thus to conceyue Jhesus.'

[8]

He toke his leue, thatt angell bryght,
Of here and went to blysse full ryght,
And forthwithall, as he behyght,
    Sche conceyuyd Jhesus.

stza. 6, l. 3. A] MS. Aa.

812715   G

255

Cambridge University Library. MS. Ee.
  I. 12   By James Ryman, *c.* 1492
f. 10ʳ
    I bryng tydyngys thatte be fulle tru:
    Who can sey 'Nay' to thys?
    Mary is moder of Jhesu,
      And God ys Fader ys.

[1]

An angelle came with fulle grete light
  And seyde, 'Haylle, fulle of grace,
The Lord of Alle by his grete myght
  In the hath take a place.'

[2]

And forthewithalle the Holi Gost
  Into here wombe dyd light,
And so thatte Lorde, of myghtys most,
  Was born of here by right.

[3]

Laude we thatte Lorde with hert and
  mynde,
  And loue we hym alsoo,
Thatte of a mayde hath take mankynde
  To bryng us owte of woo.

[4]

God bryng us alle vnto thatte blys
  Wheroff none ende schal be,
Where thatte maydyn and moder ys
  Wyth Crist, here Sone so fre.

256

*Huntington Library. Christmas carolles
  newely Inprynted* (Richard Kele)
                          c. 1550
p. [26]
    'Nowell, nowell, nowell, nowell!'
    This sayd the aungell Gabryell.

[1]

Lordes *and* ladyes all bydene,
  For your goodnes *and* honour
I wyll you synge all of a quene: [p. [27]]
  Of all women she is the floure.

[2]

Of Jesse there sprange a wyght,
  Isay sayd by prophesy,
Of whome shall com a man of myght;
  From dethe to lyfe he wyll vs bye.

[3]

There cam an aungell bryght of face,
    Flyenge from heuyn with full gret lyght,
And sayd, 'Hayle, Mary, full of grace,
    For thou shalt bere a man of myght.'

[4]

Astonyed was that lady free,
    And had meruayle of that gretynge;
'Aungell,' she sayd, 'how may that be,
    For neuer of man I had knowynge?'

[5]

'Drede the nothynge, Mary mylde;
    Thou art fulfylled with great vertew;
Thou shalt conceyue and bere a chylde
    That shall be named swete Jesu.'

[6]

She knelyd downe vpon her knee: [p. [28]
    'As thou haste sayd, so may it be.
With hert, thought, *and* mylde chere,
    Goddes handmayd I am here.'

[7]

Than began her wombe to sprynge;
    She went with chylde without man;
He that is Lorde ouer all thynge
    His flesshe *and* blode of her had than.

[8]

Of her was borne our Heuen Kynge,
    And she a mayden neuer the lesse;
Therfore be mery, *and* let vs synge
    For this new Lorde of Chrystmas.

Heading in original: A new caroll of our lady.
The repetition of the burden is indicated as
    follows: stzas. 1–7: Nowell. &c. stza. 8:
    Nowell Nowell. &c.
At end: Finis.

257

Cambridge University Library. MS. Ee.
    I. 12   By James Ryman, *c.* 1492
f. 26ʳ

    Vnto Marie he that loue hath,
    To here synge he, 'Magnificat.'

[1]

Thus seide Mary of grete honou*r*e:
    'My soule my Lord dothe magnifie,
And in my God and Sauyou*r*e
    My spirite rejoyseth verily.

[2]

'For he the mekenes hath beholde
    Of his handemayde, that Lorde   [f. 26ᵛ
        so good,
That I am blessed manyfolde
    All kynredes shall sey, of myelde moode.

[3]

'For he, that is so full of myght,
    So grete thing*es* to me hath done,
Holy his name is ay of right,
    By whome our*e* goostly helth is won.

[4]

'And in alle tho that hym doth drede
    (Truly thus seithe Holy Scripture)
His mercy doth bothe spring *and* sprede,
    And of heven they be fulle sure.

[5]

'Thys myghty Lorde of grete renowne
    By his swete Sonne the helthe hath
        wrought
Of meke people and hath put downe
    Prowde people onely with a thought.

[6]

'Tho that desireth that Lorde, our*e* helth,
    That King of Grace soo goode *and* swete,
Fro whome cometh alle goodenes *and*
        welth,
    With alle vertue they be replete.

[7]

'Of his grete mercy havyng   [f. 27ʳ
        myende,
    He toke nature in Ysraell
And became man to save mankynde,
    To oure faders as he did telle.'

[8]

Joye be to God in Trinitie,
    Fader and Sonne and Holi Goost,
That was *and* is *and* ay shall be
    Bothe iii *and* One, of myght*es* most.

258

Cambridge University Library. MS. Ee.
    I. 12   By James Ryman, *c.* 1492
f. 68ᵛ

    'Awake, Joseph, awake, awake,
    And to Marie thy way thou take.'

[1]

Josephe wolde haue fled fro that mayde,
  Not for noo synne ne for offence,
But to abyde he was affrayde
  In here so good *and* pure presence,
Extans virgo concipiens,
    The mysterie for cause he knew
    In her of so full grete vertue.

[2]

'With her,' he seide, 'why shulde I dwell?
  Than I of degre she is more,
And in vertue she doth excelle;
  I wille dep*er*te from her therefore.'
But God, that hath alle grace   [f. 69ʳ
    in store,
    Sent an aungell, that was full bright,
    Vnto Joseph vpon a nyght.

[3]

And vnto hym that aungell seide,
  'Drede not, Josephe, sonne of Dauid,
To take Marie thy wyfe, that mayde,
  For why the chielde that she goth w*ith*
Is Goddes Sonne; be not afrayde:
    Long time before Scriptur*e* hath sayde
    That a pure mayde shulde ber*e* a chield
    To save mankyende, that was exield.'

[4]

Joseph arose *and* went full right
  Vnto Marie, that mayden myelde,
And thurgh vertue of God Almyght
  He founde that mayden grete w*ith*
    chielde;
And yet she had hym not begielde,
    For why Jhesus, the Sonne of Right,
    Fro blis into her wombe did light.

[5]

Beholde how Eve, that woman wielde,
  Hath borne hir frute in care and woo,
But virgyne Marie, moder myelde,
  Hath borne her frute, but nothing soo,
  For she hath borne Criste *and* no moo
    For to defende vs fro the feende
    And geve vs blisse w*ith*oute*n* ende.

[6]

The frute of deth Eve gave to vs,
  But that pure mayde *and* moder dere
Gave vs the frute of lyfe, Jhesus;
  Wherfore next God she hath no per*e*

Aboue in blisse ne in erthe here,
For why her sete is next the trone
Of God, that is bothe iii and One.'

259

British Museum. MS. Addit. 5665
                                    XVI *cent.*
f. 10ʳ

  'Meruele noght, Josep, on Mary mylde;
  Forsake hyr not tho she be w*ith* childe.
  Maruell not, Josep, of Mare mylde;
  Forsake hir not tho she be w*ith* chylde.'

[1]

'I, Josep, wonder how hit may be,   [f. 10ᵛ
I, Josep, wond*er* how h*it* may be,
That Mary wex gret when Y and she
Euer haue leuyd in chastite;
Iff she be w*ith* chylde, hit *ys   [*f. 11ʳ
    not by me.'
  'Meruell not, Joseph;
  Merwell noght, Joseph.

[2]

'The Holy Gost w*ith* mercifull   [f. 10ᵛ
    disstens
In here hathe entryd w*ith*owte offens,
God and man conceyued by hys p*re*sens,
An[d] she virgyn pure w*ith*owte violens.
  Meruell no[t,] Joseph.'

[3]

'What the angell of God to me   [f. 11ʳ
    dothe say
I, Joseph, muste and will vmble obay,
Ellys p*ri*uely Y wolde haue stole away,
But now will Y s*er*ue her*e* tille th*at* Y day.'
  'M*er*uell not, Josep.'

[4]

'Josep, thow shalt her*e* mayde *and* moder
    fynde,
Here Sone Redemptor of all mankynde
Thy forefader*es* of paynes to vnbynde;
Therefor muse not this mater in thy
    mynde;
  Mer*u*ell not, [Joseph.']

burden, l. 2. tho] MS. they.   l. 4. tho] MS.
    thos.
stza. 1, l. 1. hit] *in margin in another hand for*
    this *deleted.*
stzas. 2–4, ll. 1, 5. *These lines are to be repeated*
    in singing, as written in stza. 1.
MS. heading: In die natiuitatis.

260

British Museum. MS. Addit. 20059

XV *cent.*

f. 6ᵛ

'M[er]vell nothyng, Joseph, that Mary
    be wi*th* child;
She hath conceyved *ver*e God *and* man
    and yet she undefiled.'

[1]

'Conceyved ma*n*, how may that be by
    reason broght abowte?'
'By gode reason above all reasons, hit may
    be withouten dowte;
For God made man aboue all reasons of
    slyme erthe most wyld;
Wherfore, Joseph, m*er*vell not thaghe Mary
    be withe chyld.

[2]

'Mary was bothe wyf *and* mother, *and* she
    a verrey mayde,
And conceyved God, our brother, as
    *p*rophett*es* before hade saide.
Sithe God made reason, why may not
    reason of his werk*es* be begyld?
Wherfore, Joseph, mervell not though
    Mary be *with* chyld.

[3]

'The erthe, ayer, sonne, *and* mone, fyre,
    wat*er, and* eue*ry* sterr
Is gode reason that above all reasons shuld
    passe o*ur* reasons ferr.
To reason wi*th* hym that made reason o*ur*
    reasons are but wyld;
Wherfore, Joseph, mervell not though
    Mary be wi*th* child.'

[4]

The hye *and* holy sacrament in verrey
    forme of bred   [f. 7ʳ
Is God and man, flesshe *and* blode, he that
    was quyck *and* ded.
Did reason this dede? Nay, nay; reason is
    ferr begylde;
His is gode reason above all reasons, Mary
    to be wi*th* child.

[5]

God, angell, soole, *and* devyll lett all clerks
    determyne;
By reason the be, but what the be reason
    cannot defyne.

Then s*er*ve the fyrst, *and* save the thrydde;
    the forte let be resyled,
And m*er*vell no more, but fast beleve Mary
    was maide wi*th* child.

The repetition of the burden is indicated as
follows: stza. 1: M*er*vell nothyng Joseph &c.
stzas. 2, 3: M*er*vell nothyng Joseph.
stzas. 4, 5: M*er*vell not Joseph.

261

Bodleian Library. MS. Eng. poet. e. 1

XV *cent.*

f. 47ᵛ

'Nowel, nowel, nowel,'
    Sy*n*g we wi*th* myrth;
Cryst is come wel,
    With vs to dewell,
    By hys most noble byrth.

[1]

Vnd*er* a tre
I*n* sportyng me,
    Alone by a wod syd,
I hard a mayd
Th*at* swetly sayd,
    'I a*m* wi*th* chyld this tyd.

[2]

'Gracyusly
Co*n*ceyuyd haue I
    The Son of God so swete;
Hys gra*c*yous wyll
I put me tyll,
    As mod*er* hy*m* to kepe.

[3]

'Both nyght *and* day
I wyl hy*m* pray
    And her hys lawes taught,
And eue*ry* dell
Hys trewe gospell
    I*n* hys apostles fraught.

[4]

'Thys goostly case   [f. 48ʳ
Dooth me embrace
    Wi*th*owt dyspyte or moke;
Wi*th* my derlyng
Lullay to syng
    And louely hy*m* to roke.

[5]

'Wi*th*owt dystresse
I*n* gr*et*e lyghtnesse
    I a*m* both nyght *and* day;

This heue*n*ly fod
I*n* hys chyldhod
   Schal dayly w*ith* me play.

[6]

'Soone must I syng
W*ith* rejoycyng,
   For the ty*m* is all ronne
Th*a*t I schal chyld,
All vndefyld,
   The Kyng of Hevens Sonne.'

MS. heading: A song vpon (now must I syng
&c.).
The repetition of the burden is indicated after
each stanza as follows: nowell &c.

262

Cambridge University Library. MS. Ee.
1. 12   By James Ryman, *c.* 1492
f. 22ᵛ

   Rarissima in deliciis,
   Iam ueni, coronaberis.

[1]

Come, my dere spowse and lady free;
   Come to thy Sonne in heven blis,
For why next me thy place shal be;
   Iam veni, coronaberis.

[2]

Come, my myelde dove, into thy cage,
   With joye and blis replete whiche is,
For why it is thyne heritage;
   Iam veni, coronab*e*ris.

[3]

Moost faire and swete, moost meke *and*
   myelde,
   Come to thy Sonne and King of Blis;
Moder *and* mayden vndefielde,
   Iam veni, [coronaberis.]

[4]

Thou art alle fayre, my spowse moost dere,
   And spotte of synne in the noon is;
Come fro Liban, to me appere;
   Iam veni, [coronaberis.]

[5]

Thy stature is assymylate   [f. 23ʳ
   To a palme tree and thy brist*e*s
To grapes, spowse inmaculate;
   Iam veni, coronaberis.

[6]

Off alle clennes I am the floure,
   The felde wherof thy pure soule is;
O virginall flour*e* moost of honour*e*,
   Iam veni, coronaberis.

[7]

Thy blessed body was my bowre;
   Wherefore my blis thou shallt not mys,
And alle seintes shalle the honoure;
   Iam veni, coronab*e*ris.

[8]

W*ith* thy brestes so pure and clene
   Thou haste me fedde; wherfore, iwis,
Of heven blis thou shalt be quene;
   Iam veni, coronab*e*ris.

stzas. 3, 4, l. 4. MS. iam veni &c.

263

a. *British Museum.* MS. Addit. 5465
   By John Lydgate (except burden)
                          XVI *cent.*
ff. 67ᵛ, 68ʳ

   'A, gentill Jhesu!'
   'Who is that that dothe me call?'
   'I a synner that offt doth fall.'
   'What woldist th*o*u haue?'
   'Mercy, Lord, of the I crave.'
   'Why, louyst th*o*u me?'
   'Ye, my maker I call the.'
   'Than leve thi syn, or I nyll the,
   And thynk on this lesson that now I
      teche the.'
   'A, I will, I will, gentyll Jhesu.'

[1]

'Vppon the cross nailid I   [ff. 68ᵛ, 69ʳ
   was for the,
Suffyrd deth to pay thi rawnsum;
Forsake thi syn, man, for the loue of me;
Be repentant; make playne *con*fession.
   To *con*trite hart*es* I do remission;
      Be not dispayryd, for I am not
         vengeable;
   Gayne gostly enmys thynk on my pas-
      sion;
      Whi art th*o*u froward syth I am mer-
         cyable?

[2]

'My blody wownd*es* downe   [ff. 69ᵛ, 70ʳ
   railyng be this tre,
Loke on them well, *and* haue *com*passion;
The crowne of thorne, the spere, the nailis
   thre,

Percide hand *and* fote of indignac*i*on,
My hert ryven for thi redempc*i*on.
  Lett now vs twayne in this thyng be
    tretable:
Loue for loue be just *con*uencion;
  Why art th*o*u froward sith I am mer-
    ciable?

[3]

'I hade on Pet*ur and* Mawd-   [ff. 70ᵛ, 71ʳ
  len pyte
For thi contrite of thy cont*ri*cion;
Saynt Tomas of Ind*es*, in crudelite
  He put his hand*es* depe in my syde
    adowne.
Role vp this mat*ur*; grave it in thi reson:
  Syth I am kynd, why art th*o*u vnstable;
My blode best t*ri*acle for thi t*ra*nsgression
Be th*o*u not froward syth I am m*er*ciable.

[4]

'Thynk agayne p*ri*de on my   [ff. 71ᵛ, 72ʳ
  humilitie;
Cum to scole; record well this lesson:
Gayne fals envy thynk on my charyte,
  My blode all spent by distillac*i*on.
  Whi did I this? To save the from p*ri*son.
  Afore thi hart hang this litell table,
Swett*ur* than bawme gayne gostly poy-
  son:
  Be th*o*u not affraide sith I am mer-
    ciable.'

[5]

Lord, on all synfull here   [ff. 72ᵛ, 73ʳ
  knelyng on kne,
Thy deth reme*m*bryng of humble afec-
  c*i*on,
O Jh*e*su, graunt of thi benignite
  That thi fyve wellis plentu*u*s of fusion,
  Callid thi fyve wond*es* by *com*putacion,
  May washe vs all from surfett*es* re-
    probable.
Now for thi moders meke mediacion,
  At hir request be to vs m*er*ciable.

The repetition of the burden is indicated after
each stanza by: A jentill Jhesu.
stza. 4, l. 5. save] *1st voice* have.
stza. 5, l. 7. moders] *erased in all parts, on f. 72ᵛ,*
replaced by justys *in a later hand.*
Signature: Sheryngam.

b. *Bodleian Library.* MS. Laud misc. 683,
ff. 14ᵛ–15ᵛ. XV *cent.*

c. *Bodleian Library.* MS. Laud misc. 598,
f. 50ʳ. XV *cent.*

d. *Bodleian Library.* MS. Rawl. poet. 32,
ff. 31ᵛ, 32ʳ. XV *cent.*

e. *Jesus College, Cambridge.* MS. 56,
ff. 70ᵛ–71ᵛ. XV *cent.*

f. *Cambridge University Library.* MS. Kk.
1. 6, ff. 196ᵛ, 197ʳ. XV *cent.*

g. *Cambridge University Library.* MS. Hh.
4. 12, f. 85ʳ ᵃⁿᵈ ᵛ. XV *cent.*

h. *British Museum.* MS. Harley 2255,
f. 111ʳ ᵃⁿᵈ ᵛ. XV *cent.*

i. *British Museum.* MS. Addit. 29729,
f. 131ʳ ᵃⁿᵈ ᵛ. XV *cent.* (stzas. 1–3, 5).

j. *British Museum.* MS. Cotton Caligula A.
ii, f. 134ᵛ. XV *cent.*

k. *Huntington Library.* MS. HM. 140
(formerly Phillipps 8299), f. 83ᵛ. XV *cent.*
(adds unique stanza).

l. *St. John's College, Oxford.* MS. 56,
f. 84ʳ (fragment). XV *cent.*

m. *British Museum.* MS. Harley 5396,
f. 294ʳ ᵃⁿᵈ ᵛ. XV *cent.*

n. *Bodleian Library.* MS. Hatton 73,
f. 4ʳ. XV *cent.* (stza. 5).

For all variant readings except those of m and n
see H. N. MacCracken, ed., *The Minor Poems
of John Lydgate,* pt. i (E.E.T.S., Ex. Ser.,
No. cvii, London, 1911), pp. 252–4.
MS. heading: m (*in later hand*) Our Lordys
Exhortacyon.
burden. *only in* a.
stza. 1, l. 3. man] m *omits.* l. 7. Gayne] m A
gayne.
stza. 2, l. 4. Percide] m Teyd. fote] m feet.
l. 6. now] m *omits.* l. 8. art thou] m artow.
stza. 3, l. 2. m For the gret constreynt of ther
contrycyon. l. 3. Saynt] m A Geyn
(*altered from* seyn). l. 4. hand*es*] m hand.
adowne] m down. l. 6. art th*o*u] m
artow.
stza. 4, l. 1. my] m myn. l. 5. from] m fro.
l. 6. Afore] m Aforn. l. 7. gayne] m gey
all. l. 8. affraide] m froward.
stza. 5, l. 1. kne] m n the*r* kne. l. 2. deth]
n passion. of] n with. l. 3. of] n them
of. ll. 4, 5. fyve] m v. l. 6. washe] m
washyn. all from] m fro all. surfett*es*
reprobable] m surfet*es* repreuable. n for-
fettys repugnable. l. 8. hir] n oure.
At end: m Explicit vnic*u*m librum.

264

British Museum. MS. Addit. 5465
XVI *cent.*
ff. 122ᵛ, 123ʳ

In a slumbir late as I was,
    I harde a voice lowde call *and* crye,
'Amende the, man, of thi trespace,
    And aske forgeveness or euyr thou
      dye.'
In a slumbir late as I was,
    I harde a voice lowde call *and* crye,
'Amende the, man, of thi trespace,
    And aske forgeveness or euyr thou
      dye.'

[1]

'Beholde,' he saide, 'my   [ff. 123ᵛ, 124ʳ
    creature,
Whome I did make so lyke vnto me,
What payns I sofferd, I the ensure,
    Where thou were thrall, to make the free.
    Vpon the cross *with* naylis thre
      Fast I was naylyd for thyne offence;
      Therfore remembir the or thou go
      hence.'

The repetition of the burden after the stanza is
indicated by: In a slumbir vt sup*ra*.

265

*Huntington Library. Christmas carolles
newely Inprynted* (Richard Kele)
c. 1550
p. [2]

Now synge we, as we were wont:
'Uexilla Regis prodeunt.'

[1]

The Ki*n*ges baner on felde is playd;
The cross*es* mistry ca*n* not be nayd,
To whom our Sauyour was betrayd,
    And for our sake,
    Thus sayth he:
    'I suffre for the;
    My deth I take.

[2]

'Behold my shankes; behold my knees;
Beholde my hed, armes, and thees;
Beholde, of me nothyng thou sees
    But sorowe and pyne;
    Thus was I spylt,
    Man, for thy gylte,
    And not for myne.

[3]

'Behold my body, how Jewes it donge
With knots of whipcord *and* scourges
    strong;
As stremes of a well the blode out spro*n*g
    On euery syde;
    The knottes were knyt,
    Ryght well made with wyt;
    They made woundes wyde.

[4]

'Man, th*o*u shalt now vnderstand, [p [3]
Of my head, bothe fote and hand,
Are four c and fyue thousand
    Woundes and syxty;
    Fyfty and vii
    Were tolde full euen
    Upon my body.

[5]

'Syth I for loue bought the so dere,
As thou may se thyself here,
I pray the with a ryght good chere,
    Loue me agayne,
    That it lykes me
    To suffre for the
    Now all this payne.

[6]

'Man, vnderstand now thou shall,
Insted of drynke they gaue me gall,
And eysell mengled therwithall,
    The Jewes fell;
    These paynes on me
    I suffred for the,
    To bryng the fro hell.

[7]

'Now, for thy lyfe thou hast   [p. [4]
    mysled,
Mercy to aske be thou not adred;
The lest drop of blode that I for the bled
    Myght clense the soone
    Of all the syn
    The worlde within,
    If thou haddest doone.

[8]

'I was more wrother with Judas
For he wold no mercy aske
Than I was for his trespas
    Whan he me solde;
    I was euer redy
    To graunt hym mercy,
    But he none wolde.

[9]

'Lo, how I hold my armes abrode,
The to receyue redy isprede!
For the great loue that I to the had
    Well may thou knowe
    Some loue agayne
    I wolde full fayne
        Thou woldest to me shewe.

[10]

'For loue I aske nothyng of the   [p. [5]
But stand fast in faythe, *and* syn thou fle,
And payne to lyue in honeste,
    Bothe nyght and day,
    And thou shalt haue blys
    That neuer shall mys,
        Withouten nay.'

[11]

Now, Jesu, for thy great goodnes,
That for man suffred great hardnes,
Saue vs fro the deuyls cruelnes,
    And to blys vs send,
    And graunt vs grace
    To se thy face
        Withouten ende.

The repetition of the burden is indicated as
follows: stzas. 1, 2: Now synge we. &c.
stzas. 3–10: Now syng we. &c. stza. 11:
Now. &c.
stza. 1, ll. 1, 2. *One initial* T *serves for both lines.*
At end: Finis.

266

St. John's College, Cambridge. MS. S. 54
                                        XV *cent.*
f. 9^r

    'Fadyr, my wyll yt is:
    Nolo mortem peccatoris.'

[1]

'Fadyr, I am thin owyn chyld
And born of Mary mek *and* myld;
    Fadyr, now my wyll yt is:
    Nolo mortem peccatoris.

[2]

'My hert is sore qwan I bethynk
And se mene trespas *and* in syn synk.
    For all that is done amyse
    Nolo mortem pec[catoris.]

[3]

'Thou falce fend, *with* all thi slent,
Y wyll no more mankynd be schent;
    Of hem thou getyst no ryght, ywys;
    [Nolo mortem peccatoris.']

[4]

Now mak we both joy *and* myrght
In worschyp of Cristys owyn byrtht.
    This is Goddes owyn word, ywys:
    ['Nolo mortem peccatoris.']

stza. 2, l. 4. MS. Nolo mortem &c.
stza. 3, l. 3. ryght] MS. ryghht.
stzas. 3, 4, l. 4. MS. vt supra.
stza. 4, l. 1. myrght] MS. myghht.

267

Cambridge University Library. MS. Ee.
    I. 12   By James Ryman, *c.* 1492
f. 47^r

    Hec sunt verba Saluatoris:
    'Nolo mortem peccatoris.'

[1]

'Haue myende for the how I was borne,
How with scourges my flesshe was torne,
And how I was crowned with thorne;
    Nolo mortem peccatoris.

[2]

'Haue myende also how lowe I light
Into a mayde so pure and bright,
Taking mercy, leving my myght;
    Nolo mortem peccatoris.

[3]

'Thinke how mekely I toke the felde,
Vpon my bak bering my shelde;
For payne ne dethe I wolde not yelde;
    Nolo mortem peccatoris.

[4]

'Lyft vp thy hert now, man, and see
What I haue done and doo for the;
Yf thou be lost, blame thou not me;
    Nolo mortem peccatoris.'

268

Cambridge University Library. MS. Ee.
    I. 12   By James Ryman, *c.* 1492
f. 47^v

    Thus seith Jhesus of Nazareth:
    'Of a synner I wille noo deth.'

[1]

Yf thou thy lyfe in synne haue ledde,
Amende the now; be not adredde,
For God his grace for the hath spredde;
    Of a synner he wille no deth.

[2]

Yf thou haue done as mekill ylle
As hert may thinke and dede fulfille,
Yf thou axe grace, thou shalt not spille;
    Of a synner he wil no deth.

[3]

Mary Magdalene did grete offence,
And yet with hir Crist did dispence
And gave her grace and indulgence;
    Of a synner he wille no deth.

[4]

She asked grace with hert contrite
And foryeuenes of hir delicte,
And he forgave here anone right;
    Of a synner he wille no deth.

[5]

Man, yf thou wilte thy synne forsake
And vnto Crist amendes make,
Thy soule to blis then wil he take;
    Of a synner he wille no deth.

269

Cambridge University Library. MS. Ee.
I. 12   By James Ryman, *c.* 1492

f. 47ᵛ

    Reuert, reuert, reuert, reuert;
    O synfull man, geve me thyn hert.

[1]

Haue myende howe I mankyende   [f. 48ʳ
    haue take
Of a pure mayde, man, for thy sake,
That were moost bonde moost fre to make;
    O synfull man, [geve me thyn hert.]

[2]

Haue myende, thou synfull creature,
I toke baptyme in thy nature
Fro filthe of synne to make the pure;
    O synfull man, geve [me thyn hert.]

[3]

Haue myende, man, how I toke the felde,
Vpon my bak bering my shelde;
For payne ne dethe I wolde not yelde;
    O synfull man, yeve me [thyn hert.]

[4]

Haue myende, I was put on the rode
And for thy sake shedde my hert blode.
Beholde my payne; beholde my moode;
    O synfull [man, yeve me thyn hert.]

[5]

Beholde me, hede, hande, foote, and side;
Beholde my woundes fyve so wyde;
Beholde the payne that I abyde;
    O synfull man, yeve me thyn hert.

[6]

Haue myende, man, how fast I was bounde
For thy sake to a pilloure rounde,
Scorged till my bloode fell to grounde;
    O synfull [man, yeve me thyn hert.]

[7]

Haue myende how I in fourme of bred
Haue left my flesshe and blode to wedde,
To make the quyk whenne thou art dedde;
    O synfull man, [yeve me thyn hert.]

[8]

Haue myende, man, how I haue   [f. 48ᵛ
    the wrought,
How with my bloode I haue the bought,
And how to blis I haue the brought;
    O synfull man, [yeve me thyn hert.]

[9]

O synfull man, beholde and see
What I haue done and do for the.
Yf thou wilte be in blis with me,
    O synfull man, yeve me thyn hert.

[10]

Bothe for my dethe and paynes smert,
That I suffred for thy desert,
I aske no more, man, but thyne hert;
    Reuert, reuert, reuert, reuert.

stzas. 1, 7, 8, l. 4. MS. O synfull man &c.
stza. 2, l. 4. MS. O synfull man geve &c.
stza. 3, l. 4. MS. O synfull man yeve me &c.
stza. 4, l. 4. MS. O synfull &c.
stza. 6, l. 4. MS. O synfull &c.

270

British Museum. MS. Royal 17. B. XLIII
                                          c. 1500
f. 184ʳ

    Com home agayne,
    Com home agayne,
  Min owine swet hart, com home agayne;
  Ye are gone astray
  Owt of youer way;
    There[fore] com h[o]me agayne.

[1]

Mankend I cale, wich lyith in frale;
  For loue I mad the fre;
To pay the det the prise was gret,
  From hell that I ranssomed the.

[2]

Mi blod so red for the was shed;
  The prise it ys not smale;
Remembre welle what I the tell,
  And com whan I the kale.

[3]

Mi prophetes all, they ded the cale;
  For loue I mad the free;

.   .   .   .   .   .
   .   .   .   .   .   .

[4]

And I miselfe *and* mi postels twelfe,
  To prech was all mi thovth
Mi Faders kyngedom both hole *and* sound,
  Which that I so derly bouth.

[5]

Therefore refreyne, *and* torne agayne,
  And leve thyne owene intent,
The which it is contrare, iwos,
  Onto mi commavndment.

[6]

Thow standest in dout *and* sekest about
  Where that thow mayst me se;
Idovles be set, mony for to gyt,
  Wich ys made of stone *and* tre. [f. 184ᵛ

[7]

I am no stoke, nor no payncted bloke,
  Nor mad by no mannes hand,
Bot I am he that shall los the
  From Satan the phinnes bonde.

stza. 1, l. 2. mad] MS. nad.
stza. 5, l. 1. Therefore] MS. there re fore.

271

National Library of Scotland. MS. Advocates 18. 7. 21   *c.* 1372
f. 124ᵛ

  Lu[u]eli ter of loueli eyghe,
    Qui dostu me so wo?
  Sorful ter of sorful eyghe,
    Thou brekst myn herte a-to.

[1]

Thou sikest sore;
Thi sorwe is more
  Than mannis muth may telle;
Thou singest of sorwe,
Manken to borwe
  Out of the pit of helle.

[2]

I prud *and* kene,
Thou meke an[d] clene
  Withouten wo or wile;
Thou art ded for me,
And I liue thoru the,
  So blissed be that wile.

[3]

Thi moder seet
Hou wo the beet,
  And therfore yerne sche yerte;
To hire thou speke,
Hire sorwe to sleke.
  Suet, suet wan, thin herte.

[4]

Thin herte is rent;
Thi bodi is bent
  Vpon the rode tre;
The weder is went;
The deuel is schent,
  Crist, thoru the mith of the.

The repetition of the burden is indicated after
each stanza by: Luueli (*underlined*).
stza. 3, l. 3. yerte] MS. yepte.

272

Bodleian Library. MS. Douce 302
             By John Audelay, XV *cent.*
f. 30ᵛ

  I haue a loue is Heuen Kyng;
  I loue his loue fore euermor

[1]

Fore loue is loue *and* eu*er* schal be,
  And loue has bene ore we were bore;
Fore loue he askys non oth*er* fe
  Bot loue ayayn; he kepis no more.
    I say herefore:

[2]

Trew loue is tresoure, trust is store
  To a loue to Godis plesyng,
Bot leude loue makis me*n* elore,
  To loue here lust *and* here lykyng.
    I say herefore:

[3]

In good loue th*er* is no syn;
  With*o*[u]t loue is heuenes;
Herefore to loue I nyl not bly[n,]
  To loue my God *and* hi*s* goodnes.
    I say herefore:

[4]

For he me louyd or I hi*m* knew,
  Th*er*for I loue hi*m* alth*er*best;
Ellis my loue I myght h*i*t rew;
  I loue wi*th* hi*m* to take my rest.
    I say herefore:

[5]

Of al loue*r*es that eu*er* was borne,
  H*i*s loue h*i*t passid eu*er*echon;
Nad he vs louy[d] we were forelorne;
  Wi*th*[out] is loue trew loue is non.
    I say herefore:

MS. heading: de amore dei *cetera.*

273

Balliol College, Oxford. MS. 354
                      XVI *cent.*
f. 223ʳ

  Into this world now ys cu*m*
  *Christ*e, redemptor o*mn*ium.

[1]

O worthy Lord *and* most of myght,
  Eterne Rex Altyssime,
The to honowr me thy*n*kyth ryght,
  I a*m* luc*is* orto sidere.

[2]

As thou art Lord of worthynes,
  Conditor alme sider*um,*
All vs to bryng owt of derknes,
  *Christ*e, rede*m*ptor om*n*ium.

[3]

Wi*th* bemys clere of righttuysnes
  Aurora lucis rutilat;
In joy th*er*of wi*th* all gladnes
  Uox clara, ecce, i*n*tonat.

[4]

Now glori*us* Lord *and* worthy Kyng,
  Jh*esu*, Saluator seculi,
Gra*n*t vs thy blis eu*er*lastyng,
  Su*mm*i lorgitor primii.

At end: Explicit.

274

St. John's College, Cambridge. MS. S. 54
                      XV *cent.*
f. 10ʳ

  Now Jh*esus*, rector a*n*ime,
  Ne cadem*us* sustine.

[1]

God, th*a*t all this word has wroghth
And wi*th* preci*us* blod hath both,
Of us sy*n*full me*n* haue thoute;
  Ne cadem*us* sustine.

[2]

Th*ou* arth Lord th*a*t mad all thyng,
For all gr*a*ce is i*n* thi geuyng;
Th*ou* saue us fro the fend*es* fowndyng,
  Defe[n]sor n*os*ter, Domi*n*e.

[3]

We haue iii e*n*mys qwer*e* th*a*t we we*n*de:
The werd, the flesch, *and* the fend*e*;
Th*ou* saue us fro hem, th*a*t we not
  sche[n]de;
  I*n*cidia*n*tes reprime.

[4]

I*n* all our*e* leue wyll [we] ar*e* her*e*
We haue but wo, tr*a*uyll, *and* car*e*,
Mete, dry[n]ke, *and* cloth—we haue no
  more
  Pro n*os*tro gr*a*ui op*er*e.

stza. 1, l. 1. word] MS. wrod.
stza. 2, l. 2. geuyng] MS. geuynyg.
stza. 3, l. 2. flesch] MS. fend*es*. fend*e*] MS.
  flesch.
stza. 4, l. 1. our*e*] MS. youre.

275

Cambridge University Library. MS. Ee.
I. 12   By James Ryman, *c.* 1492
f. 8ᵛ

Fili Marie uirginis,
Succurre nobis miseris.

[1]

O sweete Jhesu so meke and mylde,
    Fili Marie virginis,
Fro blysse thatt we be notte exylde,
    Succurre nobis [miseris.]

[2]

We scholde be lost for oure offense,
    Set tue matris meritis,
As thou art Lorde of Indulgense,
    Succurre nobis miseris.

[3]

Oure sowlys made to thi likenesse,
    Natura nostra fragilis;
Therfore in oure gostly sikenesse
    Succurre nobis miseris.

[4]

Vppon a tre thou madist us fre
    Effusione sanguinis;
Therfore alle we, Lorde, besiche the,
    Succurre nobis miseris.

[5]

Thoughe with the filthe we be infecte
    Primi parentis criminis,
Fro blysse thatte we be not rejecte,
    Succurre nobis miseris.

stza. 1, l. 4. MS. Succurre nobis c°.

276

Cambridge University Library. MS. Ee.
I. 12   By James Ryman, *c.* 1492
f. 46ᵛ

Of thy mercy lete vs not mys,
Fili Marie virginis.

[1]

O King of Grace and Indulgence,
By whome alle thyng hath existence,
Forsake not man for his offence,
    Fili Marie virginis.

[2]

Haue mercy, Lorde, haue mercy on me,
For thi mercyes that so grete be,
For why my soule dothe trust in the,
    Fili [Marie] virginis.

[3]

My prayere, Lorde, as swete encense,
Be directed to thy presence;
Forgeve my synne *and* negligence,
    Fili Marie virginis.

[4]

Thou shalt not, Lorde, despise, but know
A contrite hert and meked lowe;
Lorde, fro thy face thou me not throw,
    Fili Marie virginis.

[5]

With thy grace, Lorde, thou vs   [f. 47ʳ
    enspire,
Inflame vs with goostely desire,
And of thy loue burne vs with fire,
    Fili Marie virginis.

[6]

That we may come vnto that blis
Wherof the joye eternall is
Graunte vs, thou Prince of alle princes,
    Fili Marie virginis.

stza. 2, l. 4. MS. fili virginis &c.
In the lower margin of the page the burden is
    written again in a hand of late cent. XV or
    cent. XVI with notation of the melody: Of thy
    marci lete vs not mys: fili marie virginis.

277

British Museum. MS. Addit. 5665
                                    XVI *cent.*
f. 32ᵛ

Jhesu, Fili Dei,
Miserere me*i.   [*f. 33ʳ
Jhesu, Fili Dei,   [f. 32ᵛ
Miserere me*i.   [*f. 33ʳ

[1]

Glorius God in Trinite,
Well of man *and* pyte,
Thus cryed the woman of Canany:
    'Miserere mei;
    Miserere mei.'

[2]

Thou came fro heuen, fro thi fe,   [f. 32ᵛ
To this worlde, a man to be;
Therfor Y crye deuoteli,
  'Miserere mei;
  [Miserere mei.']

[3]

As thou haddest vn hir pyte,
So Y pray thou haue vn me;
Glorius God in Trinite,
  Miserere mei;
  [Miserere mei.]

MS. heading: de natiuitate.
Signatures: f. 32ᵛ Smert. f. 33ʳ Trouluffe.

278

*Huntington Library. Christmas carolles
newely Inprynted* (Richard Kele)
                  c. 1550

p. [47]

  Jesu Christe, Fili Dei viui, mise[rere
    no]bis,
    Alleluya.

[1]

Moost souerayn Lorde Chryst [Jesu,]
Born of a mayd that euer was true,
With grace and goodnesse thou vs endue
  That now singeth this:
  'Miserere nobis.'

[2]

Lorde of mercy by propre condycion,
That of mankynd made the redemption,
Graunt vs now this petycion
  That now syngeth this:
  'Miserere nobis.'

[3]

Jesu, preserue vs, and be our spede,
With grace to socour vs at our nede,
To do thy pleasure in worde and dede
  That now syngeth this:
  'Miserere nobis.'

[4]

Punysh not synners by thy myght,
But with mercy medled with ryght,
So that we may lyue in thy syght
  That now syngeth this:
  'Miserere nobis.'

[5]

[Now] God graunt vs repen-   [p. [48]
  taunce
[A]nd space for to do penaunce
And good lyfe to haue contynuance,
  That we may syng this:
  'Miserere nobis.'

The repetition of the burden is indicated as
  follows: stza. 1: Jesu christe fili dei viui.
  stzas. 2, 4: Jesu christe fili dei viui. &c.
  stza. 3: Jesu christe. &c.
At end: Finis.
*The text of the burden and of stanzas 1, 5 is
damaged by a tear in the leaf.*

279

Cambridge University Library. MS. Ee.
  1. 12   By James Ryman, *c.* 1492
f. 36ʳ

  O *Christe*, Rex gencium,
  O vita viuencium.

[1]

O orient light shynyng moost bright,
O Sonne of Right, adowne thou light,
And by thy myght now geve vs light,
  O *Christe*, Rex [gencium.]

[2]

O Savyoure moost of honoure,
Cum fro thy towre, cease oure   [f. 36ᵛ
  doloure,
Bothe day and houre waityng socoure,
  O vita viuencium.

[3]

O we in payne wolde, in certeyn,
Thou woldest refrayne, Lorde, *and* restreyn
Thyn hande ageyn of myght *and* meyn,
  O *Christe*, Rex gencium.

[4]

O Jesse rote moost swete and soote,
In ryende *and* rote moost full of boote,
To vs be bote, bounde hande *and* foote,
  O vita viuencium.

[5]

O Assuere, *Prince* wi*th*out pere,
Come fro thy spere, to vs draw nere;
Oure prayer here, O Lorde moost dere,
  O *Christe*, Rex gencium.

[6]

O corner*e* stone, that makist both one,
Here our*e* grete mone, and graunt *our*
          bone;
Cume downe anone, save vs echeone,
    O vita viue*n*ciu*m*.

[7]

O Prince of Peas, our*e* bonde release;
Our*e* woo thou cease, and graunt vs peas
In blis endeles, that shall not cease,
    O *Christ*e, Rex gencium.

[8]

O King of Myght and Sonne of   [f. 37ʳ
      Right,
O endeles light so clere and bright,
Of the a sight thou vs behight,
    O vita viue*n*ciu*m*.

stza. 1, l. 4. MS. O *Christ*e Rex &c.

279.1

British Museum. MS. Egerton 3307
                                   XV *cent.*
f. 55ʳ

        Qvi natus e*st* de virgine,
        Saluu*m* me fac, Domine.

[1]

Fader *and* Son and Holy Gost,
    Gret God in T*r*inite,
As th*o*u ert lord of myth most,
    Saluu*m* me fac, [Domine].

[2]

As th*o*u ert wysse *and* ryth wel wost
    This world ys bot a vanite,
When I schall dy *and* yeld my gost,
    Saluu*m* me f*a*c, [Domine].

[3]

Wher I slep, wher I wake,
    On lond or wat*er*, wer I be,
As th*o*u dyd dy for ma*n* sak,
    Saluu*m* me fac, [Domine].

*The text of the burden repeated as a chorus is
written at the end and marked*: Chorus.

280

Cambridge University Library. MS. Ee.
    1. 12   By James Ryman, *c.* 1492
f. 42ᵛ

    My herte is sette alone
    On God, bothe Thre and One.

[1]

I loue a louer that loueth me well,
    To alle mankyende whiche is socour*e*,
And his name Emanuell;
    Of alle louers he is the flour*e*.

[2]

His moder is a virgyne pure
    In worde, in dede, in wille, *and* thought,
Of whome he toke mortall nature
    To save mankyende, that had mys-
        wrought.

[3]

He was dede and beried in sight
    And rose ayene on the thirde daye
And steyed to blis by his grete myght,
    That was and is and shall be ay.

[4]

He is called King Assuere;
    Hester his moder callid is;
Crowned they be bothe ii in fere,
    He King, she quene, of heven blis.

[5]

Our*e* Lorde Jh*es*us of Nazareth,
    That for oure sake shed his hert bloode
And on the crosse did suffre deth,
    To vs mote be eternall foode.

stza. 3, l. 2. thirde] MS. iiiᵈᵉ.

281

Cambridge University Library. MS. Ee.
    1. 12   By James Ryman, *c.* 1492
f. 43ᵛ

    God, bothe iii and One,
    Is oure comforte alone.

[1]

Adam and Eve did geve concent
Vnto the feende, that vile serpent;
Wherfore mankyende to helle was sent
    W*i*thout comfort alone.

[2]

Whenne it therin long tyme hadde layne,
Crist, Goddes Sonne, came, in certayne,
To take nature and suffre payne
    To co*m*fort it alone.

[3]

As the sonne beame gothe thurgh the glas,
Thurgh virgyne Marie he did pas,
Taking nature, as his wille was,
  To save mankynde alone.

[4]

That Lorde so good vpon the   [f. 44ʳ]
  roode
Suffred vile dethe and shed his bloode,
Whoos flesshe and bloode is endeles foode
  To feithfull man alone.

[5]

Now beseche we that King of Grace
In blis for to graunte vs a place,
And hym to se there face to face,
  That is bothe iii and One.

282

Bodleian Library. MS. Eng. poet. e. 1
                        XV *cent.*

f. 31ʳ

  Off al the knottes that I se
  I prese the knot in Trinite.

[1]

An aungell fro heu[e]n gan lyth;
A greth a maydyn that was so bryth;
A treu knot ther was knyt
  Betwyn them both in Trinyte.

[2]

After this that fayyrly fod,
For hus he bled his hart blod
Qwan he was don on the rod;
  The knottes war knit with nales iii.

[3]

Wettnes of apostyll Johan:
He rose hup *and* wold gon;
The knot was knyt with marbyl ston
  Thorow the vertu of the Trinyte.

[4]

On Scher Thursday he steyd to heu[e]n;
Hys Fader hym blyssyd with myld steu[e]n,
For to fulfyl the deddes wyll,
  The knot was knit with persons iii.

[5]

God xal rysyn at domusday
Hys v knottes for to spray;
To al men he xal say,
  'Lo, man, what knot I knyt for the.'

283

Cambridge University Library. MS. Ee.
1. 12   By James Ryman, *c.* 1492

f. 44ᵛ

  Honoure to the alone,
  That art bothe iii and One.

[1]

O Lorde, by whome al thing is wrought,
And without whom is wrought right
  nought,
With hert, with myende, with   [f. 45ʳ]
  wille, and thought,
  Honour to the alone.

[2]

O, whiche haast made bothe day and
  nyght,
The firmament and sterres bright,
The sonne and mone to yeve vs light,
  Honour to the alone.

[3]

O, whiche hast take mortall nature
Of moder Marie, virgyne pure,
For to redeme eche creature,
  Honour to the alone.

[4]

O Fader without begynnyng,
O Sone of the Fader beyng,
O Holy Goost of bothe ii proceding,
  Honour to the alone.

[5]

O Fader, in whome alle strength is pight,
O Sone also, that Wisdome hight,
O Holy Goost, fro whome alle grace doth
  light,
  Honour to the alone.

[6]

O iii persones in one vnite,
Beyng but one God and one light,
One in substance, essens, *and* myght,
  Honour to the alone.

[7]

O Fader, O Sonne, O Holi Goost,
O iii *and* One, of myghtes moost,
Of lest and moost in euery coost
  Honour to the alone.

284

Cambridge University Library. MS. Ee.
  1. 12   By James Ryman, *c.* 1492
f. 50ʳ

  O, O, O, O, O, O, O, O,
  O Deus sine termino.

[1]

O Fader *with*oute begynnyng,
  O Sonne and Holi Goost also,
O iii and One *with*out ending,
  O De*us* sine termino.

[2]

O iii *per*sones in one vnyte,   [f. 50ᵛ
  Beyng but one God and no moo,
One in substaunce, essens, *and* myght,
  O De*us* sine termi*n*o.

[3]

O, whiche hast made bothe day *and* nyght,
  Heven *and* erthe rounde like an O,
By thy wisdome and endeles myght,
  O De*us* sine termi*n*o.

[4]

O, whiche of nought al thing hast wrought,
  O verbum in principio,
O, *with*out whom is wrought right nought,
  O De*us* sine termino.

[5]

O Prince of Peas, O Heven King,
  O fynall ender of our*e* woo,
O, whose kingdome hath non ending,
  O De*us* sine termino.

[6]

O maker of eche creature,
  O supplanter of oure foo,
O Sonne of Marie, virgyn pure,
  O De*us* sine termino.

[7]

We beseche the *with* alle oure myght,
  Or we depart this worlde fro,
Of forgevenes of our*e* delicte,
  O De*us* sine termino.

[8]

Criste graunte vs grace, that we come may
  To heven blisse, whenne we hens goo,
That deyed for vs on Good Friday
  Et regnat sine te*r*mino.

285

Cambridge University Library. MS. Ee.
  1. 12   By James Ryman, *c.* 1492
f. 59ʳ

  Te *P*atrem n*o*strum inuocamus,
  Te Deum verumq*ue* laudamus.

[1]

Thy creatures terrestriall,
  Te *P*atrem n*o*strum inuocamus,
With the high courte celestiall
  Te Deum verumq*ue* laudamus.

[2]

By daye and nyght, as it is right,   [f. 59ᵛ
  Te *P*atrem n*o*strum inuocamus,
With aungell*es* bright, *with* alle our*e*
    myght,
  Te Deum verumq*ue* laudamus.

[3]

O heuenly King, that aye shall reigne,
  Te *P*atrem n*o*str*u*m inuocamus,
With potestatis of myght *and* mayne
  Te Deum verumq*ue* laudamus.

[4]

By whome al thing, Lorde, did begynne,
  Te *P*atrem n*o*strum inuocamus,
With cherubyn and seraphyn
  Te Deum verum[que] laudamus.

[5]

O Lorde moost dere, that hast no pere,
  Te *P*atrem n*o*str*u*m inuocamus,
With the swete quere of apostles dere
  Te Deum verumq*ue* laudamus.

[6]

O endeles God and man so fre,
  Te *P*atrem n*o*strum inuocamus,
With thy *pro*phetes in their*e* degree
  Te Deum verumq*ue* laudamus.

[7]

O Prince, that put oure foo to flight,
  Te *P*atrem n*o*strum inuocamus,
With thy hoost of martres so bright
  Te Deum verumq*ue* laudamus.

[8]

Fader *and* Sonne *and* Holy Goost,
  Te *P*atrem n*o*strum inuocamus,
Bothe iii *and* One, of myght*es* moost,
  Te Deum verumq*ue* laudamus.

286

Cambridge University Library. MS. Ee.
I. 12   By James Ryman, *c.* 1492
f. 59ᵛ

Alpha et O quem vocamus,
Te Deum verum laudam*us*.

[1]

O God *and* man sempiternall,
That hast made vs free that wer*e* thrall,
Bothe grete *and* small, to the we calle,
Te Deum [verum laudamus.]

[2]

O our*e* Fader celestiall,
Our*e* foo *com*mitte so bestiall;
We, thy children terrestriall,   [f. 60ʳ
Te Deum verum [laudamus.]

[3]

To the, O Lorde so full of myght,
Aungell*es* alle of heuen so bright
Be assistent bothe day *and* nyght:
'Te Deum veru*m* [laudamus.']

[4]

The hevens also so bright *and* clere,
Moost specially the heuen empere,
Dothe laude the aye, O Lorde so dere:
'Te Deum [verum laudamus.']

[5]

The potestates vniversall
In thy high courte imp*er*iall
Geveth the honour*e* p*er*petuall:
'Te Deum verum [laudamus.']

[6]

Cherubyn *and* seraphyn wi*th* loue ardent
Euirmore crie wi*th* one assent,
'O Lorde God Sabaoth Omnipotent,
Te Deum [verum laudamus.']

[7]

Of the appostles the glorious quere,
O King *and* Prince *and* Lorde moost dere,
Geveth the laude *and* honoure in fere:
'Te Deum [verum laudamus.']

[8]

The p*r*ophetes alle in their*e* degree,
O endeles God in p*er*sones thre,
Thanke *and* preysing they geve to the:
'Te Deum [verum laudamus.']

[9]

O heuenly Prince moost glorious,
The tryumphe woone laborious,
Thy martirs singe victorius:
'Te Deum [verum laudamus.']

[10]

O endeles God, Fader of Light,
Alle Holy Churche, as it is right,
Lawde *and* preyse the bothe day *and* nyght:
'Te Deum [verum laudamus.']

[11]

Thy Sonne with the also, Jhesus,
Now man become for loue of vs,
We laude *and* honour*e*, seying thus:
'Te Deum [verum laudamus.']

[12]

The Holy Goost, that dothe procede
Of you both ii, as seith oure crede,
We laude *and* preyse in worde *and* dede,
Te Deum [verum laudamus.]

[13]

Bothe iii *and* One we knowleche the,
One in Godhede, in persones thre,
That euir were *and* ay shall be,
Te Deum [verum laudamus.]

[14]

O swete Jh*es*u, that on the roode
Hast redemed vs wi*th* thy hert bloode,
Wi*th* contrite hert *and* wi*th* myelde moode
Te Deum veru*m* [laudamus.]

burden, l. 2. verum] MS. verumque.
stzas. 1, 4, 6–13, l. 4. MS. Te deum &c.
stza. 2, l. 4. MS. Te deum verumq*ue* &c.
stzas. 3, 5, 14, l. 4. MS. Te deum veru*m* &c.

287

Cambridge University Library. MS. Ee.
I. 12   By James Ryman, *c.* 1492
f. 60ᵛ

Dulciter pangamus,
'Te Deum laudamus.'

[1]

O Fader of high majeste,
The Sonne and Holi Goost wi*th* the,
Bothe iii *and* One the knowlege we;
Te Deum [laudamus.]

[2]

O Sonne of God, Criste, Heuen King,
On his right side in blisse sitting,
Oure juge to be in tyme comyng,
    Te Deum [laudamus.]

[3]

O Holy Goost ay proceding
Of the Fader euirlasting
And of the Sonne withoute ending,
    Te Deum [laudamus.]

[4]

O iii persones in one vnite,
Beyng but one God and one light,
One in substaunce, essens, and myght,
    Te Deum [laudamus.]

[5]

Incessantly, Lorde, aungelles alle,
Apostles, potestates vniuersall,
Cherubyn, and seraphyn to the doth call,
    'Te Deum [laudamus.']

[6]

Fro day to day, Lorde, we blesse the,
And withoute ende thy name prayse we,
Of whose kingdome noon ende shall be;
    Te Deum [laudamus.]

stzas. 1–4, l. 4. MS. Te deum &c.
stzas. 5, 6, l. 4. MS. Te deum &c.

288

Cambridge University Library. MS. Ee.
    I. 12   By James Ryman, *c.* 1492
f. 60ᵛ

    Alpha et O quem vocamus,
    Te Deum verum laudamus.

[1]

Fader and Sonne and Holi Goost,
We knowledge the in euery coost,
Bothe iii and One, of myghtes moost,
    Te Deum verum [laudamus.]

[2]

Thre persones, one God, one light,
One in substaunce, essence, and myght,
By day and nyght, as it is right,
    Te Deum [verum laudamus.]

[3]

O high Fader, by whome al thing
Onely hathe take a begynnyng,
Of whose kingdome is none ending,
    Te Deum verum [laudamus.]

[4]

O Sonne of the Fader of Myght,
Onely bigote of hym by right,
As God of God and light of light,
    Te Deum verum [laudamus.]

[5]

O Holy Goost, that doost procede
Of the Fader and Sonne indede   [f. 61ʳ
Onely by loue (this is oure crede),
    Te Deum verum [laudamus.]

[6]

O endeles God, of myghtes moost,
That thou hast made lete not be lost,
Sith, thy seruauntis in euery cost,
    Te Deum [verum laudamus.]

stzas. 1, 5, l. 4. MS. Te deum verum &c.
stzas. 2, 6, l. 4. MS. Te deum &c.
stzas. 3, 4, l. 4. MS. Te deum verum &c.

289

Cambridge University Library. MS. Ee.
    I. 12   By James Ryman, *c.* 1492
f. 61ʳ

    Singe we alle this tyme thus:
    'Te Deum laudamus.'

[1]

The High Fader of blisse aboue
Sent his owne Sonne to oure behove,
Whome alle this worlde is bounde to love.
    Te Deum [laudamus.]

[2]

To become man he lothed nought
Of a pure mayde in dede and thought,
To make man fre, that he had wrought.
    Te Deum [laudamus.]

[3]

Whenne he was borne, that Lorde and
    King,
Oute of thraldome mankyende to bringe,
With one accorde aungelles did singe,
    'Te Deum [laudamus.']

[4]

Cherubyn *and* seraphyn w*ith* voices clere,
The appostles, the p*r*ophe*tes* and martirs in
    fere
Euirmore laudeth that Lorde so dere:
    'Te [Deum laudamus.']

[5]

The ierarchies w*ith* ordres nyne
To hym assiste and aye incline
And honou*r*e hym w*ith* laude diuine:
    'Te Deum [laudamus.']

[6]

Alle Holy Churche w*ith* melodie,
As it is right, dothe magnifie
His holy name and glorifie:
    'Te Deum laudam*us*.'

stzas. 1, 3, 5, l. 4. MS. Te deum &c.
stza. 2, l. 4. MS. Te deu*m* &c.
stza. 4, l. 4. MS. Te &c.

289.1

Cambridge University Library. MS. Addit.
    7350, Box 2   By James Ryman, XV *cent.*
f. 1ʳ

    Te Deum laudamus;
    Te D*ominum* confitemur.

[1]

The Father of heuyn from aboue
Hathe sent his Son to owr behoue,
Whom all erthe is bownde to loue;
    Te Deum laudam*us*.

[2]

Bothe heuyn *and* erthe in there degre,
Angell*es* w*ith* heuynly poteste,
With all ther myrth they syng to the:
    'Te Deum [laudamus.']

[3]

The cherubyns cry incessantly,
And the seraphyns w*ith* voyc*es* on hye,
Eu*er*more, 'Holy, holy, holy;
    Te Deum [laudamus.]

[4]

'O Lorde God Sabaoth so swete,
Heuyn *and* erthe bothe be replete
Withe thi powre in eu*er*y sete;
    Te Deu*m* [laudamus.']

[5]

Appostell*es*, p*r*ofet*tes*, *and* martirs bright,
Thi holy name praysyng both day *and*
    nyght,
To the thei syng, as it is right,
    'Te Deu*m* [laudamus.']

[6]

All holy churche w*ith* armony
Tunably sett dothe magnyfy
Thy holy name incessantly;
    Te Deu*m* [laudamus.]

[7]

Th[o]u arte the Father moste of myght;
Thy Son Jh*esus* truly he hight;
The Holy Gost shynyng full bright;
    Te Deu*m* [laudamus.]

[8]

Th[o]u arte the Son of great gladnes,
Thy Father Son by thy mekenes,
Vs to redeme to owre lyknes;
    Te Deu*m* [laudamus.]

[9]

For thi gift*es* many a fold,   [f. 1ᵛ
Benyng to thy s*er*uau*n*t*es* both yong *and*
    olde,
To syng to the we be beholde;
    Te Deu*m* [laudamus.]

[10]

Jh*esus* vs saue, owr comely Kyng,
From the fend*es* both olde *and* yong,
Et*er*nally that we may syng,
    'Te Deu*m* [laudamus.']

The repetition of the burden is indicated after
    stzas. 1, 2 by: &c.

290

Cambridge University Library. MS. Ee.
    1. 12   By James Ryman, *c.* 1492
f. 61ʳ

    Dulciter pangamus,
    'Te Deum laudamus.'

[1]

Of a mayde Criste did not forsake
Mankyende to take, man fre to make
And into blisse w*ith* hym to take.
    Te Deu*m* [laudamus.]

[2]

Alle erthily creatures that be
Mote laude *and* preyse that Lorde so fre
W*ith* hert *and* myende, to whom singe we,
'Te Deu*m* [laudamus.']

[3]

O *per*fecte God, O *per*fecte man,
That for vs hast take wound*es* wan,
W*ith* hert, wille, and thought, as   [f. 61ᵛ
    we can,
Te Deu*m* [laudamus.]

[4]

O shaper of heuen, erthe, se, *and* sonde,
O Lorde *and* Prince of euery londe,
That hast made vs fre, that wer*e* bonde,
Te Deum [laudamus.]

[5]

For thy grete gyftes manyfolde
Lent to *ser*uant*es* bothe yonge *and* olde,
The whiche thou hast create of molde,
Te Deu*m* [laudamus.]

[6]

O Criste, that thus hast take nature
Of myelde Marie, that virgyne pure,
Of heuen blis to make vs sure,
Te Deum [laudamus.]

[7]

O Fader, O Sonne, O Holi Goost,
O Thre *and* One, of myght*es* moost,
Thy myelde *ser*uant*es* in eu*er*y coost,
Te Deu*m* [laudamus.]

stzas. 1, 3, 4, 7, l. 4. MS. Te deu*m* &c.
stzas. 5, 6, l. 4. MS. Te deum &c.

291

Cambridge University Library. MS. Ee.
    I. 12   By James Ryman, *c.* 1492
f. 89ᵛ

    Dulciter pangamus,
    'Te Deum laudamus.'   [f. 90ʳ

[1]

O Fader of Eternall Blys,
    Qui semper es ingenitus,
Of whom alle grace *pro*cedyng ys,
    Te Deu*m* [laudamus.]

[2]

O Kyng of Nyght and lyght of lyght,
    Qui Patris extas Filius,
By day and nyght, as itte is ryght,
    Te Deu*m* [laudamus.]

[3]

O Crist, thatt art becum alsoo
    Marie primogenitus
To bryng us owte of payn *and* woo,
    Te Deu*m* [laudamus.]

[4]

Of the Fader*e* and Sone indede,
    O Amor, Sancte Spiritus,
Eternally thatte doist procede,
    Te Deu*m* [laudamus.]

[5]

Fader*e* and Sone and Holi Gost,
    Alpha et O quem credimus,
Bothe iii and i, of myght*es* most,
    Te Deu*m* [laudamus.]

stzas. 1–5, l. 4. MS. Te deu*m* c°.
stza. 5, l. 2. O] MS. OO.

292

Cambridge University Library. MS. Ee.
    I. 12   By James Ryman, *c.* 1492
f. 90ʳ

    Te Patrem rite uocamus;
    Te Deum Uite laudamus.

[1]

O endles God of Mageste,
    Te Patrem rite vocamus;   [f. 90ᵛ
Lord of alle thyng we knowlege the;
    Te Deu*m* Uite laudam*us*.

[2]

O Sone of God namyd Jhesus,
    Ad te sine lite clamamus,
That sheddist thi bloode for to ese us;
    Te Deu*m* Uite [laudamus.]

[3]

O Holy Gost, alsoo indede
    Te fontem uite pulsamus,
Of them bothe ii th*at* doist *pro*cede;
    Te Deu*m* Uite laudamus.

[4]

Fader*e* and Sone and Holi Gost,
　Vt tibi rite credamus,
Bothe iii and i, of mygh*tes* most,
　Te Deu*m* Uite lauda[m]*us.*

[5]

O Lorde and Kyng, to blysse us bryng,
　Deuote qui te oramus,
Withowte endyng thatte we may syng,
　'Te [Deum Uite laudamus.']

stza. 2, l. 4. MS. Te deu*m* uite c⁹.

293

Cambridge University Library. MS. Ee.
　I. 12　　　By James Ryman, *c.* 1492
f. 90ᵛ

　Syng we alle thys tyme th*us:*
　'Te Deum laudamus.'

[1]

Fader*e* of Blisse omnipotent,
　For thou hast made and create us,
Mekely therfore with on assent
　Te [Deum laudamus.]

[2]

The ierarchies of ordyrs nyne,
　They say, 'Sanct*us*, sanct*us*, sanct*us*';
Lorde of Vertu, with laude diuine
　Te [Deum laudamus.]

[3]

O Kyng of Myght and lyght of 　　[f. 91ʳ
　　lyght,
　Jhesu, that hast redemyd us,
By day and nyght, as it ys ryght,
　Te [Deum laudamus.]

[4]

Of the Fader*e* and Sone indede,
　O Holi Gost (Scripture seieth thus),
Eternally thou doist procede;
　Te [Deum laudamus.]

[5]

Fader*e* and Sone and Holi Gost,
　As Holy Chyrche so techith us,
Bothe iii and i, of mygh*tes* most,
　Te [Deum laudamus.]

294

Cambridge University Library. MS. Ee.
　I. 12　　　By James Ryman, *c.* 1492
f. 91ʳ

　Alpha et O quem vocamus,
　Te Deum verum laudamus.

[1]

O endles God of Majeste,
　Alpha et O quem vocamus,
Of whoys kyngdom none ende shall be,
　Te Deu*m* veru*m* laudamus.

[2]

O Sone of God, thatt Jhesus hight,
　Ad te pia mente clamamus,
For thou camyst downe to geue us light;
　Te Deu*m* veru*m* laudamus.

[3]

Fader and Sone *and* Holi Gost,
　Vt in fide maneamus,
Bothe iii and i, of mygh*tes* most,
　Te Deu*m* veru*m* laudamus.

[4]

By day and nyght, as it is ryght, 　　[f. 91ᵛ
　A laude tua non cessamus,
Butte with the tyght of alle our*e* myght
　Te [Deum verum laudamus.]

[5]

O Lorde and Kyng, to blysse us bryng,
　Te toto corde rogamus,
Withowte endying thatt we may syng,
　'Te [Deum verum laudamus.']

burden, l. 1, stza. 1, l. 2. O] MS. **oo.**
stza. 3, l. 1. and Sone] MS. *repeats.*
stza. 4, l. 4. MS. Te c⁹.

295

Cambridge University Library. MS. Ee.
　I. 12　　　By James Ryman, *c.* 1492
f. 91ᵛ

　Syng we alle thys tyme thus:
　'Te Deum laudamus.'

[1]

The Sonne of God, thatte all hath wrought,
To take nature he lothyd nought
Of a pure meyde in dede and thought;
　T[e Deum laudamus.]

[2]

This Lorde was born in an oxe stalle,
To make us fre, the which were thralle;
Therfore syng we, bothe sum and alle,
    'Te Deum [laudamus.']

[3]

The ierarchies with ordrys nyne
To hym assiste and ay inclyne;
Therfore syng we with laude dyuyne,
    'Te Deum [laudamus.']

[4]

This childe thatte nowe is born to us
Ys Goddes Sonne (Scripture seyeth thus),
And his name is callyd Jhesus;
    Te Deum [laudamus.]

[5]

Alle Holy Chirche with melodie,
As itte is right, dothe magnyfie
His holy name and glorifie:
    'Te Deum laudamus.'

stza. 2, l. 4. MS. Te deum cᵒ.
stzas. 3, 4, l. 4. MS. Te deum cᵒ.

296

Cambridge University Library. MS. Ee.
i. 12   By James Ryman, *c.* 1492

f. 92ʳ

Nowe syng we thys tyme thus:
'Te Deum laudamus.'

[1]

O endles God of Majeste,
On in Godhede, in persons thre,
Lorde of all thyng we knowlege the;
    Te Deum laudamus.

[2]

Angelles of heuen, that be so bryght,
And potestates so full of myght
Sey vnto the, as itt is ryght,
    'Te Deum laudamus.'

[3]

Cherubyn and seraphyn with loue ardent
Sey vnto the with on assent,
'Lorde of Vertu omnipotent,
    Te Deum laudamus.'

[4]

With endles voice they seye to the,
'Heuyn and erthe, Lorde, replete be
With glorie of thy majeste;
    Te Deum laudamus'.

[5]

The quere of the apostlys dere
Laudeth the ay with voicis clere,
And thus they sey with louely chere:
    'Te Deum laudamus.'

[6]

The number of the prophetes alsoo
Laudeth the ay with many moo,
Seying to the, 'Alpha et O,
    Te Deum laudamus.'

[7]

The hoste of martirs bright and clere
Laudeth the, Lorde, thatt hast no pere,
And thus they seye to the in fere:
    'Te Deum laudamus.'

[8]

Fadere and Sonne and Holi Gost,   [f. 92ᵛ
Bothe iii and i, of myghtes most,
We knowlege the in euery cost;
    Te Deum [laudamus.]

stza. 6, l. 3. O] MS. oo.
stza. 8, l. 4. MS. Te deum cᵒ.

297

Cambridge University Library. MS. Ee.
i. 12   By James Ryman, *c.* 1492

f. 92ᵛ

Syng we alle thys tyme thus:
'Te Deum laudamus.'

[1]

O swete Jhesu, we knowlege this:
Thatte thou art Kyng of Heuen Blis,
And endles God thy Fader is;
    Te Deum [laudamus.]

[2]

The Virgyns wombe thou hast not forsake,
Butte thou of itte mankynde hast take,
Man, thatte was bonde, fre for to make;
    T[e Deum laudamus.]

[3]
Deth ouercome and sette aside,
Thou hast openyd heuens full wide
To feithfull men thatt the abyde;
    Te Deum [laudamus.]

[4]
Thou sittist atte thi Faders right honde
Aboue in blisse, we vnderstonde,
The juge to be of euery londe;
    Te Deum [laudamus.]

[5]
Therfore helpe us, thou Lorde so goode,
Thatt hast bought us with thi hert bloode,
To whom we syng nowe with mylde
    moode,
    'Te [Deum laudamus.']

[6]
Make us, goode Lorde Jhesu most fre,
Withe endles joye rewardid to be
With thy saynctys in blysse with the;
    Te Deum [laudamus.]

[7]
Saue us, goode Lorde Jhesu, alsoo,
And defende us fro endles woo,   [f. 93ʳ
Into thi blisse thatte we may goo;
    Te Deum laudamus.

[8]
Goode Lorde, by day and eke by nyght
We laude and prayse the with oure myght
And blisse thy name, as itt is right;
    Te Deum [laudamus.]

[9]
Thatte itte may please the, Lord, we pray
For to kepe us fro syn this day,
In blisse thatte we may sing for ay,
    'Te Deum [laudamus.']

[10]
Thy mercy, Lorde, on us mot be,
Thatte with thy bloode hast made us fre,
Sith we do trust only in the;
    Te Deum [laudamus.]

stzas. 1, 3, 8–10, l. 4. MS. Te deum cᵒ.
stza. 2, l. 4. MS. Tᵉ.
stza. 5, l. 4. MS. Te cᵒ.
stza. 6, l. 4. MS. Te deum cᵒ.

298

Cambridge University Library. MS. Ee.
I. 12   By James Ryman, *c.* 1492
f. 93ʳ

    Synge we alle thys tyme thus:
    'Te Deum laudamus.'

[1]
O Fader of high majeste,
O Sonne and Holi Gost, all thre,
On God, on lyght, we knowlege the;
    Te Deum [laudamus.]

[2]
O Sonne of the Fader of Myght,
Ay procedyng of hym by right,
As God of God and lyght of lyght,
    Te Deum [laudamus.]

[3]
O Holi Gost, thatte doist procede
Of the Fadere and Sonne indede
Only by loue, as seyeth oure crede,
    Te Deum [laudamus.]

stzas. 1–3, l. 4. MS. Te Deum cᵒ.

299

Cambridge University Library. MS. Ee.
I. 12   By James Ryman, *c.* 1492
f. 93ʳ

    Nowe syng we thys tyme thus:
    'Te Deum laudamus.'   [f. 93ᵛ

[1]
The Sonne of God, oure Lorde Jhesus,
Ys man becum for loue of us;
Therfore syng we, and sey we thus:
    'Te Deum [laudamus.']

[2]
He hath bought us, thatt Lorde so goode,
And made us fre with his hert bloode;
Therfore syng we now with mylde moode,
    'Te Deum [laudamus.']

[3]
The Holi Gost he didde us sende
To dwelle with us ay withowte ende
And fro alle ille us to defende;
    Te Deum [laudamus.]

stza. 1, l. 4. MS. Te deum cᵒ.
stzas. 2, 3, l. 4. MS. Te deum cᵒ.

300

Cambridge   University   Library. MS. Ee.
I. 12   By James Ryman, *c.* 1492
f. 93ᵛ

Dulciter pangamus,
'Te Deum laudamus.'

[1]

The Faders Sonne of Heuen Blis
Of a pure meyde man becum ys
To saue mankynde, thatte did amys;
Te Deu*m* [laudamus.]

[2]

When he was born, thatt Lorde and Kyng,
Owte of thraldome mankynde to bryng,
With on accorde angelle*s* didde synge,
'T[e Deum laudamus.']

[3]

Cherybyn and seraphyn alsoo,
Tronis, potestat*es*, and many moo
Fulle sweetly sunge to that Lorde tho,
'Te Deu*m* [laudamus.']

stzas. 1, 3, l. 4. MS. Te deu*m* c⁹.

301

Cambridge   University   Library. MS. Ee.
I. 12   By James Ryman, *c.* 1492
f. 94ʳ

Dulciter pangamus,
'Te Deum laudamus.'

[1]

The Sonne of God hath take nature
Of mylde Mary, thatt uirgyn pure,
To saue mankynde (thus seith Scr*i*pture);
T[e Deum laudamus.]

[2]

When he was born, thatte Lorde and King,
Owte of thraldome mankynd to bring,
With on accorde angelle*s* didde sing,
'T[e Deum laudamus.']

[3]

O Lorde most dere, that hast no pere,
With the sweete quere of apostlys der*e*,
Bothe farre and nere w*ith* joyfull cher*e*
T[e Deum laudamus.]

[4]

The potestat*es* vniversall   [f. 94ᵛ
In thi highe court imperiall
Geuyth the honowr*e* perpetuall:
'T[e Deum laudamus.']

[5]

Cherubyn and seraphin w*ith* loue ardent
Euermore crie with on assent,
'O Lorde of Vertu omnipotent,
T[e Deum laudamus.']

[6]

O endles God in persons thre,
Thi prophet*es* alle in ther degre,
Laude and honowr*e* they geue to the:
'T[e Deum laudamus.']

[7]

O heuenly Prince most glorious,
The triumphe wonne laborious,
Thi martirs sing victorious,
'T[e Deum laudamus.']

[8]

With confessours, virgyns alsoo,
With heremit*es* and many moo,
For thou hast brought us owte of woo,
T[e Deum laudamus.]

302

Cambridge   University   Library. MS. Ee.
I. 12   By James Ryman, *c.* 1492
f. 93ᵛ

Te Patrem inuocamus;
Te Deumqu*e* laudamus.

[1]

To Crist Jhesu, thatte Lorde and Kyng,
Of whois kyngdome is none   [f. 94ʳ
     endyng,
With melody nowe lete us syng,
'T[e Deum laudamus.']

[2]

Thatt blessid Lorde didde not forsake
To his Godhede mankynde to take,
Man, thatte was bonde, most fre to make;
T[e Deum laudamus.]

[3]

The bitternes of dethe alsoo
Thatte Lorde hath take with peyn and woo,
To take us fro the fende, oure foo;
    T[e Deum laudamus.]

[4]

His sowle went downe tho into helle
And toke oute man, thatte there did dwelle,
Fro the fowle fende, thatt is so felle;
    T[e Deum laudamus.]

[5]

He rose ayen on the thirde day
For to schewe us the joyfull way
To heuen blisse, thatt lastith ay;
    T[e Deum laudamus.]

stza. 5, l. 1. thirde] MS. iii^{de}.

303

Cambridge University Library. MS. Ee.
    1. 12   By James Ryman, *c.* 1492
f. 94^v

    Te Deum laudamus;
        Te Dominum confitem*ur*.

[1]

Eternall God, Fader of Light,
Thatt madist al thyng by thi grete myght,
With worde and dede, as itte is right,
    T[e Deum laudamus.]

[2]

All thyn angell*es* in ther degre,
Heuens and all thatte in them be,
Incessantly they seye to the,
    'T[e Deum laudamus.']

[3]

Cherubyn and seraphyn w*ith* loue ardent
Sey vnto the with on assent,
'Lorde of Vertu omnipotent,
    T[e Deum laudamus.']

[4]

With endles voice they seye to the,   [f. 95^r
'Heuen and erthe, Lorde, replete be
With glory of thy mageste;
    T[e Deum laudamus.']

[5]

The quere of thy apostlys dere
Laudith the ay with louely chere,
And thus they seye w*ith* voicis clere:
    'T[e Deum laudamus.']

[6]

The number of thy prophet*es* alsoo
Geuyth the honowre w*ith* many moo,
And thus they seye: 'Alpha et O,
    T[e Deum laudamus.']

[7]

The hoste of martirs bright and clere
Laudith the ay, thatte hast no pere,
And thus they seye to the in fere:
    'T[e Deum laudamus.']

[8]

O highe Fader of Mageste,
Thy Sonne and Holi Gost with the,
On God, on Lorde, in p*er*sons thre,
    T[e Deum laudamus.]

[9]

O Sonne of the Fader of Myght,
Ay procedyng of hym by right,
As God of God and light of light
    T[e Deum laudamus.]

[10]

O Holi Gost, thatte doist procede
Off the Fader and Sonne indede
Only by loue, as seieth our*e* crede,
    T[e Deum laudamus.]

stza. 6, l. 3. O] MS. oo.

304

Cambridge University Library. MS. Ee.
    1. 12   By James Ryman, *c.* 1492
f. 95^v

With hert and mynd, w*ith* will and
        thought,
    Dulciter pangamus
To God most kynd, thatt all hath wrought,
    'Te Deum laudamus.'

[1]

O endles God, bothe iii and One,
    Fader and Sonne and Holi Gost,
Euer*e* sitting in heuen trone
    As Lord and King of myght*es* most,
    Therfore to the in euery cost
    Carmen istud modulamus
With contrite hert, withowten bost:
    'Te Deum verum laudamus.'

[2]

For thou art God omnipotent,
    The ordres ix of angel*les* bright
With on voice and with on assent
    Sey, 'S*anctus*, s*anctus*, s*anctus*,' to the of
        right;
    Therfore to the by day and nyght
        Carmen istud modulamus
    With all oure strenthe, with all *our*
        myght:
    'Te Deum verum laudamus.'

[3]

Thi creaturis celestiall,
    Thatte be in blisse with the so clere,
And we alsoo terrestriall
    Laude and preyse the bothe farre and
        nere,
    And vnto the, O Lord most dere,
        Carmen istud modulamus
    With melody and louely chere:
    'Te Deum verum laudamus.'

305

Cambridge University Library. MS. Ee.
    1. 12   By James Ryman, *c.* 1492
f. 8ʳ

    Pater de celis, De*us*,
        Miserere nobis.

[1]

O highe Fader of Heuen Blys,
Sith Crist thy Sone *our* broder is,
For his swete loue forgyff *our* mys,
    Et mis*er*ere nob*is*.

[2]

O Sone of God namyd Jhesus,
Sith with thy bloode th*o*u hast bought us,
Therfore to the we sey all thus:
    'Mis*er*ere nob*is*.'

[3]

O Holy Gost, thatt doist procede
Of the Fader and Sone indede,
Wyth thy vertu and grace us fede,
    Et mis*er*ere nob*is*.

[4]

O iii and i, of myghtys most,
Fader and Sone and Holy Gost,
As thou art Lorde of euery cost,
    Miserere nob*is*.

306

British Museum. MS. Addit. 5665
                                        XVI *cent.*
f. 46ᵛ

    To many a will haue Y go
    To fynde water to washe me fro woo.
    To maney a will haue Y go
    To fynde water to *washe me   [*f. 47ʳ
        fro woo.

[1]

I haue ysoghfte in many a syde
    To fynde wat*er* to washe me fro woo;
Yette cowde Y noght walke so wyde
    To fynde water to washe me so.

[2]

I haue herde speke off a wille;   [f. 46ᵛ
    Therof spryng[et]h stremes fele;
A man that thereof hadde his fille,
    Off his woo shulde come his wele.

[3]

That wille ys mercy, Y haue herde say,
    And shall be withowte ende;
Allmyghty God, to the we pray,
    Yeffe vs grace that wille to fynde.

MS. heading: ad placitum.

307

British Museum. MS. Addit. 5665
                                        XVI *cent.*
f. 51ᵛ

    For all Cristen saulys p*ra*y we:
    Requiem eternam dona eis, Domi[ne.]

[1]

O God, we p*ra*y to the in specyall   [f. 52ʳ
For all the saulis that sufferd payne infer-
        nall;
Now, Jh*es*u, for thi mercy graunt them
        lyffe et*er*nall,
    Et lux p*er*petua,
    Et lux p*er*petua luceat eis.

[2]

In aspeciall for the saulys th*a*t han   [f. 51ᵛ
        most nede,
    Abydyng in the paynes of derkenesse,
Weche han no socoure but almysdede:
    Et lux [perpetua,
    Et lux perpetua luceat eis.]

[3]

Now God, in heuen th*a*t art so hye,
   These saulys thou graunte joy *and* blysse,
For wham this day we syng *and* crye,
   'Et lux p*er*petua,
   [Et lux perpetua luceat eis.']

MS. heading: In fine natiuitat*is.*
burden, l. 2. Domi[ne]] MS. do domi.
stza. 2, l. 3. no] MS. no no.   l. 4. MS. Et
lux vt sup*ra*.

308

John Rylands Library, Manchester. MS.
  Lat. 395   XV *cent.*
f. 119ᵛ

  Peas, I hier a voyce saith, 'Man, thou
    shalt dye;
  Remembre the paynes of purgatorie.

[1]

'Why sittist thou so syngyng? Thenkyst
    thou nothyng
Th*a*t whoso best hoppith at laste shal haue
    the ryng?
Remembre thy Maker, and pray to that
    Kyng,
To that blisse that he bought the vnto the
    bryng.
    Thou schalt aby;
    This worlde defygh.

[2]

'I prove the by reason that thou art vn-
    kynde:
He that deid afore the is clene oute of thy
    mynde,
Thy frendis afore the; why art thou so
    blynde?
In p*ur*gatory paynyng there shalt thou
    them fynde.
    With doolefull cry,
    Thou shalt aby;
    This world defygh.

[3]

'Man, compasse in saying, in mynde every
    delle,
And pray for the soules so grete paynes
    fele,
In purgatory paynyng their sorowys to
    keele—
Thyself in no wors cas, and yit it is weele.
    This worlde defygh;
    Thou shalt abye.'

[4]

I haue herd this voice; wele Mary fulle
    of grace
Spekith it to me; ye, I will high me apaas
To the chirche me to amende; Lady, p*ra*y
    for space!
Lorde, leste I come to late! ye, alas, alas!
    I fere me I
    With doulfull cry
    I shall aby;
    This worlde defygh.

[5]

A, now am I thorugh th*a*t dey shall I
    thanne,
But yit, gentil neyghbore, tell me where or
    whan,
Or where shall I become? Why spekist
    thou not, man?
Is ther no creature that answere [f. 120ʳ
    me can?
    Now God me guy!
    I fere me I
    W*ith* dulfull cry
    I shal aby;
    This world defygh.

[6]

Than see I right wele ther is no way butt
    oon:
Now helpe me, deere Lady, Kateryn, and
    John,
Cristofer, *and* George, myne avowries
    echone;
Of the nombre dampned see that I be
    noone.
    Pray for me high;
    Now God me guy!
    I fere me I
    With dulfull cry
    I shall aby;
    This world defygh.

The repetition of the burden is indicated as
follows: stza. 1: pes I hier a voice. stza. 2:
peas. stza. 3: peas I hier a. stza. 4: pees.
stza. 6. peas I hier.

309

a. *Bodleian Library.* MS. Eng. poet. e. 1
                         XV *cent.*
f. 49ʳ

  Prey we to the T*ri*nyte
  And to al the holy co*m*pane
  For to bryng vs to the blys
  The wych shal neu*er* mysse.

[1]

Jhesus, for thi holy name
  And for thi beter passyon,
Saue vs frome syn and shame
And endeles damnacyon,
  And bryng vs to that blysse
  That neuere shal mysse.

[2]

O gloryusse Lady, quen of heuen,
  O mayden and O mothere bryght,
To thy Sonne with myld steven
Be owr gyde both day and nyght,
  That we may cum to that blysse
  The wych neuer shal mysse.

[3]

Gabryell and Raphaell,   [f. 49ᵛ]
  With cherapyn and seraphyn,
Archangell Mychaell,
  With all the orderes nyne,
  Bryng vs to that blysse
  The wych neuer shal mysse.

[4]

O ye holy patryarkys,
  Abraham, Ysaak, and many moo,
Ye were full blyssed in yowr werkes,
  With Johan the Baptyst also,
  For to bryng vs to that blysse
  The wych neuer shal mysse.

[5]

The holy apostoles of Cryst,
  Peture, Paule, and Bartylmewe,
With Thomas and Johan the Euangelyst,
  And Andrew, Jamys, and Matthewe,
  Bryng vs to that heuenly blysse
  The wych neuer shal mysse.

[6]

Pray for vs, ye seyntys bryght,
  Stevyn, Laurence, and Christofore,
And swete Georg, that noble knyght,
  With all the marters in the qwere,
  That we may cum to that   [f. 50ʳ]
    blysse
  The wych neuer shall mysse.

[7]

Blyssyd confessor, Sent Gregory,
  With Nycholas and Edward Kyng,
Sent Leonard and Antony,
  To yow we pray aboue all thyng
  To helpe vs to that blysse
  The wych neuer shal mysse.

[8]

O yow blyssed matrones,
  Anne and swet Sent Elsabeth,
With al the gloryus vyrgyns,
  Kateryne and noble Sent Margaret,
  Bryng vs to that heuenly blysse
  The wych neuer shal mysse.

[9]

All the company celestyall,
  The wych do syng so musycall,
To the Kyng Pryncypall
  Pray fore vs terrest[r]yall,
  That we may cum to that blysse
  The wych neuer shall mysse.

Stza. 1 only is also found in the following versions:

b. *Bodleian Library.* MS. Douce 54, f. 35ʳ.
XV *cent.*

c. *Bodleian Library.* MS. Rawlinson C.
48, f. 134ᵛ. XV *cent.*

d. *New College, Oxford.* MS. 310, f. 115ʳ.
XV *cent.*

e. *Bodleian Library.* MS. Gough Liturg.
7, f. 81ʳ. XV *cent.*

f. *British Museum.* MS. Arundel 285,
f. 178ʳ. XVI *cent.*

g. *British Museum.* MS. Harley 2445,
f. 136ʳ. XV *cent.*

h. *British Museum.* MS. Harley 2851,
f. 31ᵛ. XIV *cent.*

i. *British Museum.* MS. Addit. 27924
f. 221ʳ. XV *cent.*

j. 'Billyngs MS.', art. 3. XV *cent.*, ll. 1–4
only.

k. *Trinity College, Cambridge.* MS. O. 9.
38, f. 89ᵛ. XV *cent.*

stza. 1, l. 1. Jhesus] h O jhesu.   l. 2. for] d h i
omit.   l. 3. vs] d h i me.   l. 4. endeles]
b c from endles.   l. 5. vs] d h i me.   to] f
vnto.   that] b e g h i thi. c *omits.* d f the
l. 6. h for thi name. i *omits.*   That] b whych.
mysse] e f g haue ende swete Jhesu Amen.
h i *add:* swete jhesus lord amen (h *repeats*
jhesus). b *adds* (f. 35ᵛ): swete Jhesu amen.
d *adds:* amen. Thynk and thank god Quod
[*name erased*].

310

Bodleian Library. MS. Douce 302
                    By John Audelay, XV *cent.*
f. 32ʳ

  Saynt Frances, to the I say,
  Saue thi breder both nyght and day.

[1]

A hole confessoure thou were hone
And leuydist in contemplacion,
To thyng on Cristis passioun,
    That sofyrd deth on Good Fryday.

[2]

His passion was in the so feruent
That he aperd to thi present;
Vpon thi body he set his preynt,
    His v wondis, hit is no nay.

[3]

Vpon thi body thou hem bere
Affter that tyme ful iii ye[re;]
To al men syght thai did apere;
    No water myght wasche hem away.

[4]

Weder thou schuldist ete ore drenke,
On Cristis passion thou woldist thynke;
In v pertys wes thi pertyng
    Of his sustinans, sothe to say.

[5]

Crist he grawnt the specialy,
Fore on his passion thou hadist pete,
To feche thi breder out of purgatori,
    That lyin ther in rewful aray.

[6]

Thou thongis Crist of his swete sonde
And thoghtist to go to the Hole Londe;
Fore dred of deth thou woldist not wond
    To teche the pepil thi Cristyn fay.

[7]

Then Crist he knew well then entent
And turned the out of that talent
And bede the make thi testament
    And 'Come to me fore ens and ay.

[8]

'A, hole Frawnces, now I se
Fore my loue that thou woldist dye;
Thou schalt haue joy perpetual[e],
    Thou hast dyssired mone a day.'

[9]

His hole reule of relegiowne
To his breder he wrote anon
And prayd ham, fore Cristis passiowne,
    To kepe hit wel both nyght and day.

[10]

A sad ensampil here mow ye se,
On Cristis passioun to haue pete
And to leue in loue and charete;
    Then mere in hert be ye may.

[11]

His last prayer to Crist this was
Fore al that sustens this hole place:
'Gr[a]cious God, grawnt ham thi grace
    Tofore thi jugement at domysday.'

[12]

Pray we to Frawnses, that beth present,
To saue his breder and his couent,
That thai be neuer chamyd ne chent
    With wyckid man ne fyndis fray.

[13]

I pray youe, seris, pur charyte,
Redis this caral reuerently,
Fore I mad hit with wepyng eye,
    Your broder, Jon, the blynd Awdlay.

MS. heading: de sancto fransisco. The repetition of the burden is indicated after stza. 1 by:
Saynt frawnces to the I pray.
stza. 5, l. 3. out] MS. a out.

311

Bodleian Library. MS. Douce 302
                    By John Audelay, XV *cent*.
f. 31ʳ

    The moder of Mary, that merceful may,
    Pray fore vs both nyght and day.

[1]

Swete Saynt Anne, we the beseche,
    Thou pray fore vs to Oure Laday
That heo wel be oure soulis leche
    That day when we schul dey;
        Herefore we say:

[2]

Throgh the was gladid all this word
    When Mare of the borne was,
That bere that barne, that blissful Lord
    That grawntis vs al merce and grace;
        Herefore we say:

[3]

Baren thou were ful long before;
    Then God he se to thi mekenes,
That thou schuldist delyuer that was fore-
        lore,
    Mon soule, that lay in the fyndis distres;
        Herefore we say:

[4]

Fore Joachym, that hole housbond,
  Prayyd to God ful paciently
That he wold send his swete sond,
  Sum froyte betwene you two to be;
    Herefore we say:

[5]

Then God he grawntid graciously
  Betwene youe two a floure schul [f. 31ᵛ
    spryng;
The rote therof is clepid Jesse,
  That joye and blis to the word schal
    beryng;
    Herefore I say:

[6]

The blisful branche this floure on greue
  Out of Jesse, at my wettyng,
Was Mare myld, that bere Jhesu,
  Maydyn and moder to Heuen Kyng;
    Herefore I say:

[7]

Icallid Jhesus of Nazaret,
  God Sun of hi degre,
As here as mon that sofyrd deth
  And rynyd into Dauit dygnete;
    Herefore I say:

[8]

In Bedlem, in that blessid place,
  Mare myld this floure hath borne
Betwene an ox and an as,
  To saue his pepil, that was forelorne;
    Herefore I say:

[9]

Mater, ora Filium
  That he wyl affter this outlere
Nobis donet gaudium
  Sine fyne fore his merce.
    Herefore I say:

MS. heading: de sancta anna matre marie.
stza. 1, l. 1. Anne] MS. tanne.
stza. 5, l. 1. he] MS. hem.

311.1

British Museum. MS. Egerton 3307
                              XV *cent.*
f. 63ᵛ

  Enfors we vs with all our myght
  To loue Seynt Georg, Owr Lady knyght.

[1]

Worschip of vertu ys the mede
  And sewyth hym ay of ryght;
To worschip George than haue we ned,
  Whych is our souereyn Ladys knyght.

[2]

He kepyd the mad from dragons dred
  And fraid al France and put to fligh[t]
At Agyncourt, the crownecle ye red:
  The French hym se formest in fyght.

[3]

In hys vertu he wol vs led
  Agaynys the fend, the ful wyght,
And with hys banner vs ouersprede
  Yf we hym loue with all our myght.

312

British Museum. MS. Sloane 2593
                              XV *cent.*
f. 25ᵛ

  Synge we now, alle a[nd] sum,
  'Aue rex gentis Anglorum.'

[1]

A newe song I wil begynne
  Of Kyng Edmund, that was so fre,
How he deyid withoute synne,
  And bow[n]dyn his body was to a tre.

[2]

With arwys scharpe they gunne hym
    prykke;
  For non rewthe wold they lete;
As dropys of reyn they comyn thikke,
  And euery arwe with other gan mete.

[3]

And his hed also thei of smette;
  Among the breres thei it kest;
A wolf it kepte withoutyn lette;
  A blynd man fond it at the last.

[4]

Prey we to that worthi kyng,   [f. 26ʳ
  That sufferid ded this same day,
He saf vs, bothe eld and yyng,
  And scheld vs fro the fendes fray.

burden, l. 2. gentis] MS. gentes.

313

St. John's College, Cambridge. MS. S. 54
XV *cent.*
f. 3ʳ
  A, a, a, a,
  Salue Caterri[n]a!

[1]
Lystyn, lordyngys, qwatte I xall sey:
A grette marwell tell I may;
Of a louely medyn tell I may:
  Salue Caterri[n]a!

[2]
Of God[es] grace sche was full wys;
She was qweryd in hyrde wys
Of all dott[or]ys that were so wys;
  [Salue Caterina!]

[3]
W[u]nder marwelys be Godes grace:
Ther is no woman in this plase—
A woman is the [well] of grace;
  [Salue Caterina!]

[4]
Thorow the prayeur of Sent Cataryn
God send us a hows [to] twyl in,
That wordy lady and bryth and sch[e]ne;
  [Salue Caterina!]

[5]
Ther sche in fyre was done,   [f. 3ᵛ
Sche brent nere here nere bone;
Sche sted in hewen anone;
  [Salue Caterina!]

stza. 1, l. 1. lordyngys] MS. lordygnys.
  l. 2. marwell] MS. marmel.
stza. 5, l. 1. sche in] MS. in sche.
*Below this carol is written one line, apparently the
first of another carol begun but never finished:*
  Qwan crist was borne.

314

Bodleian Library. MS. Douce 302
            By John Audelay, XV *cent.*
f. 26ʳ
  Wenefrede, thou swete may,
  Thow pray for vs bothe nyght and day.

[1]
As thou were marter and mayd clene,
Therfor thou hadist turment and tene;
A princes loue thou myghtis haue bene,
  A lady of ryal aray.

[2]
Bot to that syn thou woldist noght sent;
To kepe the chast was thyn entent;
Therfore of Cradoc thou wast echent;
  Anon he thoght the to betray.

[3]
He was ful cursid and cruel,
And dred not God ne no parel,
Smot of thi hede; thou knelist ful stil;
  Hit ran into a dry valay.

[4]
Then Bewnou, thin unkul, with gret pete
Set thi hede to thi body;
Thou leuedust after merwesly
  xv yere, hit is no nay.

[5]
About thi nek hit was esene,
The stroke of the swerd, that was so kene,
A thred of perle as hit had bene;
  Hit besemyd the wel, sothle to say.

[6]
When Cradoc han don this cursid dede,
The erth him swoloud in that stede;
The foyre of hel hit was his mede,
  Therin to be fore euer and ay.

[7]
A wonderful wel ther sprong anon;
Seche on se neuer Cristyn mon;
Thi blod was sparpiled on euere stone;
  No water myght wasche hit away.

[8]
Ther ben mesis at that wel
That bene swete and sote of smel,
And yet ther is a more maruel:
  Heuenle bryddis in numerus aray.

[9]
Be the streme of that fayre wel
Ther went a myl-wele, as I you tel;
Hit bere down a child with gret parel;
  The wele stod stil, meght not away.

[10]
Then the moder cryd out and yeld,
'Alas, my child, he is spillid!'
Be the ladlis he him huld   [f. 26ᵛ
  And logh and mad gomun and play.

[11]

A mon, a grote downe he fell
Out of his hond into the well;
He se hit then al other wel,
  Thai myght not tak the grote away.

[12]

Also ther was a gret maruel:
Wyne was couchid in here chapel;
The wel stod styl, ran neuer a del;
  Hit trobild as hit had bene with clay.

[13]

Ther was no fuyre, treule to tele,
Myght hete the water of the wel,
To seth ne dyght no vetel,
  Wile that wyne in that chapil lay.

[14]

Then thai west wel afyne
Of Wynfryd hit was a syne;
Anon thai hurled out the wyne
  Into the stret on dele way.

[15]

Anon a merekel fel in that plas:
A mon of that wyne enpoysund was,
That was sauyd throgh Godis grace
  And Wynfryd, that hole may.

[16]

Anon this wel began to clere;
The streme ran forth as hit dede ere;
The plumys thai mad a hedus bere
  When thai began to play.

[17]

Fore ye chuld make no marchandyse
In Hole Cherche in no wyse;
God himselue he ded dispyse
  And drof hom forth in here aray.

[18]

Fore hit is a house of prayore,
Hold hile to Godis honour,
To worchip therin our Saueour
  With Mas, Matens, nyght and day.

[19]

Ther hath ben botynd mone a mon,
Blynd and crokid, that myght not gon,
Seke and sorouful mone hone,
  Ther at that wel there hur heed lay.

[20]

Then Wynfred anon chorun che was,
Echosun fore chefe to be abbas,
Fol of vertu and of grace,
  And seruyd God both nyght and day.

[21]

Then Bewnow toke his leue anon
And betoke here this tokyn:
'Ouer the se schal swem a stone
  To bryng vestementus, that ys noon nay.

[22]

'Yif that stone abyde with the,
Then wit wel that I schal dye;
God of my soule he haue mercy!
  Haue mynde on me the[n], I the pray.'

[23]

Then Wenfred heo knelid adowne
And toke mekele his benesoune;
This monke he toke his way anon
  Ouer the se to his abbay.

[24]

When that Bewnew he was dede,
The ston styl with here hit leuyd;
Then anon heo prayud
  He schul pas on his chornay.

[25]

Son after Wenefred heo dyid then
At Schrosbere men dedon here schryne;
Mone a merakil ther hath be syne
  Of dyuers pepul in fer cuntre.

[26]

Mone a merakil heo hath edo:
Prisonars feters ibroke a-two,
Blynd and crokid helid mone mo,
  That were in rewful aray.

[27]

Glad mai be al Schrosbere
To do reuerens to that lady;
Thai seche here grace and here mercy
  On pilgrymage ther euere Fryday.

[28]

Wynfrede, we the beseche
Now ryght with herfilly speche
That thou wilt be our soulis leche,
  The to serue, both plese and pay.

[29]

We prayn the, al that beth present,
Saue thyn abbay and thi couent,
That thai be neuer chamyd ne chent
  With wykkid mon ne fyndis pray.

[30]

I pray youe al, pur charyte,
Redis this carol reuerently,
Fore I hit mad with wepyng ye;
  Mi name hit is the blynd Awdlay.

The burden is written in red, by hand 'B' of MS.
stza. 15, l. 3. plumys] MS. pulmys.

315

British Museum. MS. Sloane 2593
                              XV *cent.*
f. 2ᵛ

  Alle maydenis, for Godes grace,
  Worchepe ye Seynt Nicolas.

[1]

Seynt Nicholas was of gret poste,
For he worchepid maydenis thre   [f. 3ʳ
That wer sent in fer cuntre,
  Common wommen for to be.

[2]

Here fader was man in powre aray;
Onto his dowteres he gan say,
'Dowterres, ye must away;
  No lenger kepe you I may.

[3]

'Dowteres, myn blyssing I you yeue,
For catel wil not with me thryue;
Ye must with yowre body leue;
  Your wordes ye must dryue.'

[4]

The eldest dowter swor be bred of qwete:
'I haue leuere beggyn myn mete
And getyn me good qwer I may gete
  Thann ledyn myn lyf in lecheri.'

[5]

The medil dowter seyde, so mote che the,
'I hadde leuere hangyd and drawyd be
With wylde hors to or thre
  Thann ledin my[n] lyf in lecher[i.']

[6]

The yongere lechery gan to spyse
And preyid Saynt Nicholas, as che was wise,

Saynt Nicholas, as he was wyse,
  'Help vs fro lech[e]r[i.']

[7]

Saynt Nicholas, at the townys ende,
Conseylid tho maydenis hom to wynde.
And throw Godes grace he xulde hem synde
  Husbondes thre good and hind[e.]

stzas. 5–7, l. 4. A few letters are illegible in MS.

316

British Museum. MS. Sloane 2593
                              XV *cent.*

f. 34ʳ

  Mak ye merie as ye may,
  And syng with me, I you pray.

[1]

In Patras, ther born he was,
The holy buschop Seynt Nycholas,
He wyst mekyl of Godes gras
  Throw vertu of the Trinite.

[2]

He reysyd thre klerkes fro deth to lyfue
That wern in salt put ful swythe
Betwyx a bochere and his wyfue
  And was hid in priuyte.

[3]

He maryid thre maydenys of myld mod;
He yaf hem gold to here fod;
He turnyd hem fro ille to good
  Throw vertu of the Trynyte.

[4]

Another he dede sekerly:
He sauyd a thef that was ful sly,
That stal a swyn out of his sty;
  His lyf thann sauyd he.

[5]

God graw[n]t vs grace here, eld and yyng,
Hym to serue at his plesyng;
To heuene blysse he vs bryng
  Throw vertu of the Trinit[e].

317

British Museum. MS. Sloane 2593
                              XV *cent.*

f. 21ᵛ

  Worchyp we, bothe more and lesce,
  Crystes body in furme of bred.

[1]

It is bred fro heuene ca*m*;
Fleych *and* blod of Mary it na*m*;
For the synnys of Ada*m*
  He sched h[i]s blod, th*a*t was so red.

[2]

'He th*a*t onworthi this bred ete,
The peyne of helle he xal gete,
My swete body awey to lete,
  And maky*n* his sowle to be*n* ded.'

[3]

He th*a*t this bred haght in mynde,
He xal leuy*n* wi*th*outy*n* ende;
This is bred to yeuy*n* a frende,
  Wi*th*outy*n* qwyt, wi*th*ine red.

[4]

On Schyre Thursday, al at the Messe,
To hese desipel*e* he seyde thisse:
'Etyght this bred; my*n* body it isse;
  Lok th*e*rof ye ha*n* no*n* dred.'

[5]

Aftyrward at her*e* sop*er*
He tok the wyn, th*a*t was so cler,   [f. 22ʳ
And blyssid it wi*th* mylde cher:
  'This is my*n* blod, th*a*t is so red.'

[6]

The Juwys wern bothe wylde *and* wode;
He putty*n* Jh*e*su vpon the rode,
For to spylly*n* his herte blode;
  For manys sy*n*ne he sufferid ded.

[7]

Jh*e*su, lynd vs this bred to ete,
And alle o*u*r sy*n*nys for to foryete,
And in heuene a place to gete
  Thɾow the v*er*tu of this bred.

318

Cambɾidge University Library. MS. Ee.
  I. 12   By James Ryman, *c.* 1492
f. 49ᵛ

  Ete ye this brede, ete ye this brede,
  And ete it so ye be not dede.

[1]

This brede geveth eternall lyfe,
Bothe vnto man, to chielde, *and* wyfe;
It yeldeth grace *and* bateth stryfe;
  Ete ye it so ye be not ded.

[2]

It semeth white, yet it is rede,   [f. 50ʳ
And it is quik and semeth dede,
For it is God in fourme of brede;
  Ete ye it so ye be not ded.

[3]

This blessed brede is aungell*es* foode,
Mannes also, perfecte and goode;
Therfore ete ye it wi*th* myelde moode;
  Ete ye it so ye be not dede.

[4]

This brede fro heven did descende,
Vs fro alle ille for to defende,
And to geve vs lyfe wi*th*oute ende;
  Ete ye it so ye [be not dede.]

[5]

In virgyne Mary this brede was bake
Whenne Criste of her manhoode did take,
Fre of alle synne mankyende to make;
  Ete ye it so ye be [not dede.]

[6]

Ete ye this brede wi*th*outen synne;
Eternall blis thanne shall ye wynne;
God graunte vs grace to dwell therin!
  Ete ye it so ye be not dede.

stza. 4, l. 4. MS. ete ye it so ye &c.
stza. 5, l. 4. MS. ete ye it so ye be &c.

319

Balliol College, Oxford. MS. 354
                                    XVI *cent.*
f. 223ʳ

  Mirabile misteriu*m*:
  In forme of bred ys God*es* Son.

[1]

Man, th*a*t in erth abydys here,
Thou mvst beleve wi*th*owten dure
In the sacrame*n*t of the auter
  Th*a*t God made hy*m*self at hys sop*er*.

[2]

Thowgh yt seme whit, yt ys rede;
Yt ys flesshe, yt semeyth bred;
Yt ys God in his ma*n*hed,
  As he hong vpon a tre.

[3]

Thys bred ys brokyn for you *and* me
Which p*ri*ste*s* co*n*secrate, as ye may se,
Which, flesshely ma*n* in Deite,
    Dyed for vs vpon a tre.

The repetition of the burden is indicated after
  each stanza by: Mirabile.
At end: Explicit.

320

British Museum. MS. Sloane 2593
                         XV cent.
f. 13ᵛ

    Of alle the spyc*es* th*at* I knowe,
      Blyssid be the qwete flo*ur.*

[1]

Qwete is bothe semely *and* sote;
Of alle spyc*es* th*at* is bote;
The v*er*tu spryng*it* out of the rote,
    So blyssid be the qw[e]te flo*ur.*

[2]

The secu*n*de vers I sey beforn:
Qwete is kyng of eu*er*y corn;
Jh*e*su hy*m*self for vs was born,
    So blyssid [be the qwete flour.]

[3]

The thredde vers, w*ith* God*es* gr*ace:*
Qw[e]te is good in eu*er*y place;
In qwete is port[r]eyid God*es* face,
    So [blyssid be the qwete flour.]

[4]

The forte vers, w*ith*oute stryf:
Of qwete is mad the bred of lyf,
Vs to receyuy*n* in clene lyf,
    So [blyssid be the qwete flour.]

[5]

The fyfte vers, w*ith*oute skorn:
Qwete is a spyce, a wol good o*n*;
Kyng th*at* is of eu*er*y corn,
    So [blyssid be the qwete flour.]

[6]

The sexte vers I xal you seye:
Jh*e*su Cryst, th*at* sit on heye,
He let vs neu*er* for hu*n*ger deye,
    So blyssid be the qwete flo*ur.*

stza. 2, l. 2. is] MS. is is.
stza. 3, l. 3. port[r]eyid] MS. porteyidid.
stzas. 3, 4, l. 4. MS. so &c.
stza. 4, l. 2. the] MS. the the.

321

Balliol College, Oxford. MS. 354
                           XVI cent.
f. 228ᵛ

    A blessid byrd, as I you say,
    Th*at* dyed *and* rose on Good Fryday.

[1]

On Cris*te*s day, I vnderstond,
An er*e* of whet of a mayd spronge,
Thirti wynter in erth to stond,
    To make vs bred all to his pay.

[2]

This corn was repyn *and* layd to grownd,
Full sore beten *and* faste bownd
Vnto a piler with cord*es* rownd;
    At his fyngers end*es* the blod ran owt
      th*at* day.

[3]

This corn was repyn w*ith* gret envye
Vpon the mownt of Caluary;
Tokyn he shewed on Shere Thursday:
    Mawndy he gaff to his dissiples ther.

[4]

Jh*e*su vpon his body the crosse bare;
Water *and* blode cam fro*m* hym ther;
This corn was skorged all in f[e]re
    Tyll it wexed blode rede.

[5]

A crown of thorn set on his hede,
And he was done on the rode
And betyn till his body was blody rede;
    Thus they bett Jh*e*su, owr det to pay.

MS. marks burden: fot*e.*
stza. 1, l. 3. Thirti] MS. xxxᵗⁱ.
At end: Explicit.

322

A. *Balliol College, Oxford.* MS. 354
                           XVI cent.
f. 165ᵛ

    Lulley, lulley; lully, lulley;
    The fawcon hath born my mak away.

[1]

He bare hy*m* vp, he bare hy*m* down;
He bare hy*m* into an orchard brown.

[2]

In th*at* orchard th*er* was an hall,
Th*at* was hangid w*ith* purpill *and* pall.

[3]

And in that hall ther was a bede;
Hit was hangid with gold so rede.

[4]

And yn that bed ther lythe a knyght,
His wowndes bledyng day and nyght.

[5]

By that bedes side ther kneleth a may,
And she wepeth both nyght and day.

[6]

And by that beddes side ther stondith a ston,
'Corpus Christi' wretyn theron.

The burden is written again in full after stza. 1.
The other repetitions of the burden are indicated as follows: stzas. 2–5: lully lulley.
stza. 6: lully lulley &c.
At end: Explicit.

B. Traditional version, North Stafford-
shire   XIX *cent.*
[No burden]

[1]

Over yonder's a park, which is newly begun,
    All bells in Paradise I heard them a-ring;
Which is silver on the outside, and gold
    within,
    And I love sweet Jesus above all things.

[2]

And in that park there stands a hall,
Which is covered all over with purple and
    pall.

[3]

And in that hall there stands a bed,
Which is hung all round with silk curtains
    so red.

[4]

And in that bed there lies a knight,
Whose wounds they do bleed by day and by
    night.

[5]

At that bed side there lies a stone,
Which is our blessed Virgin Mary then
    kneeling on.

[6]

At that bed's foot there lies a hound,
Which is licking the blood as it daily runs
    down.

[7]

At that bed's head there grows a thorn,
Which was never so blossomed since Christ
    was born.

C. Traditional version, Derbyshire
                                XIX *cent.*
[No burden]

[1]

Down in yon forest there stands a hall,
    The bells of Paradise I heard them ring,
It's covered all over with purple and pall,
    And I love my Lord Jesus above any-
    thing.

[2]

In that hall there stands a bed,
It's covered all over with scarlet so red.

[3]

At the bed-side there lies a stone,
Which the sweet Virgin Mary knelt upon.

[4]

Under that bed there runs a flood,
The one half runs water, the other runs
    blood.

[5]

At the bed's foot there grows a thorn,
Which ever blows blossom since he was
    born.

[6]

Over that bed the moon shines bright,
Denoting our Saviour was born this night.

D. Traditional version, Scotland
                                XIX *cent.*
[No burden]

The heron flew east, the heron flew west,
The heron flew to the fair forest;
She flew o'er streams and meadows green,
And a' to see what could be seen:
And when she saw the faithful pair,
Her breast grew sick, her head grew sair;
For there she saw a lovely bower,
Was a' clad o'er wi' lilly-flower;
And in the bower there was a bed
With silken sheets, and weel down spread:
And in the bed there lay a knight,
Whose wounds did bleed both day and
    night;

And by the bed there stood a stane,
And there was a set a leal maiden,
With silver needle and silken thread,
Stemming the wounds when they did bleed.

E. Traditional version, U.S.A.   1936
[No burden]

[1]

Down in yon forest be a hall,
  Sing May, Queen May, sing Mary.
It's coverlidded over with purple and pall,
  Sing all good men for the new-born baby.

[2]

Oh, in that hall is a pallet-bed,
Hit's stained with blood like cardinal red.

[3]

Oh at that pallet is a stone,
On which the virgin did atone.

[4]

Under that hall is a gushing flood,
From Christ's own side hit's water and
  blood.

[5]

Beside that bed a shrub-tree grows,
Since he was born, hit blooms and blows.

[6]

On that bed a young Lord sleeps,
His wounds are sick and see He weeps.

[7]

O hail yon hall where none can sin,
'Cause hit's gold outside and silver within.

323

Lord Harlech, National Library of Wales.
  MS. Porkington 10   XV *cent.*
f. 198ʳ

  Mery hyt ys in May mornyng,
    Mery wayys for to gone.

[1]

And by a chapell as Y came,
Mett Y wyhte Jh*e*su to chyrcheward gone,
Petur and Pawle, Thomas *and* Jhon,
  And hys desyplys eu*e*rychone.

[2]

Sente Thomas the bellys gane   [f. 198ᵛ
  ryng,
And Sent Collas the Mas gane syng;
Sente Jhon toke that swete offeryng,
  And by a chapell as Y came.

[3]

Owre Lorde offeryd whate he wollde,
A challes alle off ryche rede gollde,
Owre Lady the crowne off hyr mowlde;
  The son owte off hyr bosom schone.

[4]

Sent Jorge, that ys Owre Lady knyghte,
He tende the tapyrys fayre *and* bryte,
To myn yghe a semley syghte,
  And by a chapell as Y came.

The repetition of the burden is indicated after
each stanza by: Mery hyt ys.

324

Bodleian Library MS. Douce 302
         By John Audelay, XV *cent.*
f. 27ᵛ

  A, mon, yif th*o*u wold sauyd be,
  Foresake thi syn or h*i*t do the.

[1]

And loue thi God ou*er* al thyng,
  Thi neghbore as thiselfe, I say;
Let be y*our* hoth, y*our* false sweryng;
  In clannes kepe y*our* haleday.
    Leue ye me:

[2]

Thi fad*er*, thi mod*er* thou worchip ay;
  Scle no mo*n* fore wordle thyng;
Bacbyte no man nyght ne day,
  Fore this is Godis est *and* his bidyng.
    Leue ye me:

[3]

False witnes loke th*o*u no*n* bere;
  Dissayte ne theft loke th*o*u do no*n*;
Lechore th*o*u most foreswere;
  Here beth comawndmentis eu*e*rechon.
    Leue ye me:

[4]

Thagh th*o*u be kyng *and* were the croune,
  Mo*n*, haue mynd of thyn endyng;
The wele of Forteune wil tult the doune
  Whe*n* thou art cald to thi rekenyng.
    Leue thoue me:

[5]

Thou schalt acownt ful sekyrly
  Fore al the goodis that God the send,
Howe thou hast geton hom, in wat degre,
  How thou hast holdyn, hou thou hast
    spend.
    Leue ye me:

MS. heading: hic incipiunt decem precepta in
modum cantalene.

325

Bodleian Library. MS. Douce 302
                    By John Audelay, XV *cent.*
f. 27ᵛ

  In wele be ware ore thou be woo:
  Thenke wens thou come, wheder to goo.

[1]

Foresake thi pride and thyn enuy,
  Thou schalt fynd hit fore the best,
Couetyse, wrath, and lechory,
  Yif thou wilt set thi soule in rest.
    I say the so:

[2]

Glotery, slouth, al beth acurst;
  Thai ben the brondis in hel brenyng;
Beware betyme, or thou be lost:
  Thai bryng mon soule to euel endyng.
    I sai the so:

[3]

Ayayns pride take buxumnes;
  Ayayns wrath take charite;
Ayayns couetys take largenes;
  Ayayns enuy humelete.
    I sai the so:

[4]

Ayayns glotore take abstenens;
  Ayayns lechore take chastite;
Ayayns slouthe take besenes;
  Here is a gracious remede.   [f. 28ʳ
    I say the so:

[5]

Fore his loue that youe dere boght,
  Lerne this lesson, I youe pray;
Haue this in mynd; foreyete hit noght,
  Fore to heuen ther is non other way.
    I say the so:

MS. heading: de septem peccatis mortalibus.

326

Bodleian Library. MS. Douce 302
                    By John Audelay, XV *cent.*
f. 28ʳ

  Wele is him, and wele schal be,
  That doth the vii werkis of merce.

[1]

Fede the hungere; the thirste yif drenke;
  Clothe the nakid, as Y youe say;
Vesid the pore in prisun lyyng;
  Bere the ded; now I the pray.
    I cownsel the:

[2]

Herber the pore that goth be the way;
  Teche the vnwyse of thi conyng;
Do these dedis nyght and day;
  Thi soule to heuen hit wil the bryng.
    I cownsel the:

[3]

And euer haue pete on the pore,
  And pert with him that God the send;
Thou hast non other tresoure
  Ayayns the day of jugement.
    I cow[n]s[e]l the:

[4]

The pore schul be mad domusmen
  Apon the ryche at domysday;
Loo, se houe thai con onsware then,
  Fore al here reuerens, here ryal aray:
    I cownsel the:

[5]

'In hongyr, in thurst, in myschif well ay,
  After here almus ay waytyng,
Thay wold noght vs vesete nyght ne day—
  Thus wil thai playn ham to Heuen Kyng.
    I [co]w[nse]l the:

MS. heading: de septem opera misericor[die].
*MS. is so rubbed and faded in spots as to be
illegible. The last lines of stzas. 1–3 and 5 have
been partially erased.*

327

Bodleian Library. MS. Douce 302
                    By John Audelay, XV *cent.*
f. 28ʳ

  God hath yeuen, of myghtis most,
  The vii yiftis of the Hole Gost.

[1]

Mynd, resu*n*, *v*ertu, *and* grace,
Humelete, chast, *and* charete,
These vii yiftis God yeue*n* has
Be the *v*ertu of the Hole Gost to mo*n*
onle;
Ellis were we lost.

[2]

Mynd makis a mo*n* hi*m*selue to know,
And resu*n* him reulis i*n* his werkis all,
*And v*ertu makis h*i*s goodnes yknow,
And grace is grownd*e* of he*m* all;
Ellis were we lost.

[3]

Humelete p*r*ide he dothe downe falle;
Chast kepis the clene i*n* thi leuyng;
The*n* charete is chef of he*m* all;
Mo*n* soule to blis he dothe ho*m* breng;
Ellis were we lost.

[4]

Haue fay*t*he, hope, *and* charete;
These be the grownd of thi beleue;
Ellis sauyd th*ou* myght not be,
Thus Poule i*n* h*i*s pistil he doth p*r*eue;
Ellis were we lost.

[5]

Thi fay*t*he is thi beleue of Hole Cherche;
Onle i*n* hope God hath*e* hord*e*nt the,
Good workis th*a*t th*ou* schuld werche
And be rewardid i*n* heue*n* on hye;
Hellis were we lost.

[6]

The*n* charete, chef callid is he;
He cownselis vche mo*n* th*a*t is leuyng
To do as th*ou* woldist me[n] did be the,
And kepe Godis est *and* his bidyng;
Ellis were we lost.

MS. heading: de septem dona sp*iritu*s sancti.

328

Bodleian Library. MS. Douce 302
By John Audelay, XV *cent*.
f. 28ʳ

Thy v wittis loke th*a*t th*ou* wele spende,
And thonke th*a*t Lord th*a*t ha*m* the sende.

[1]

The furst h*i*t is thi heryng:
Loke th*ou* turne away thyne ere

Fro ydil wordis, vntrew talkyng;
The laus of God loke th*a*t th*ou* lere,
Lest th*ou* be chent.

[2]

The second h*i*t is thi seyng:
Thou hast fre choys *and* fre wil
To behold al wordle thyng,
The good to chese, to leue the ille,
Lest th*ou* be chent.

[3]

The third h*i*t is thi towchyng:
Worche no worke vnlawfully;
Gou*er*en thi fete i*n* thi walkyng
Toward heue*n*, *and* fle foly,
Lest th*ou* be chent.

[4]

The forth h*i*t is thi smellyng,
To sau*er* thi sustinans sote of smell;
Let resu*n* the rewle i*n* thyne etyng;
Beware, fore sorfet h*i*t may the spill,
Lest th*ou* bc chent.

[5]

The fifth h*i*t is thi tung tastyng
Thi mete, thi drynke, holsu*m and* clene,
Yif h*i*t be luste to thi lykyng,
The*n* mesuere h*i*t is a mary mene,
[Lest th*ou* be chent.]

MS. heading: de Quinque sensus.
stza. 2, l. 1. second] MS. ii.
stza. 3, l. 1. third] MS. iii.
stza. 4, l. 4. sorfet] MS. forfet.
stza. 5, l. 1. fifth] MS. v.

329

British Museum. MS. Sloane 2593
XV *cent*.
f. 4ᵛ

Gay, gay, gay, gay,
Think on drydful domisday.

[1]

Eu*er*y day th*ou* myght l*er*e
To helpe thiself qwil th*ou* art here;
Qu*an* th*ou* art ded *and* leyd on bere,
Cryst help thi sowle, for th*ou* ne may.

[2]

Thynk, ma*n*, on thi wytt*es* fyue;   [f. 5ʳ
Do su*m* good qwyl th*ou* art on lyve;
Go to cherche *and* do the schryve,
And bryng thi sowle in good aray.

[3]

Thynk, ma*n*, on thi synnys seuene;
Think how merie it is in heuene;
Prey to God w*ith* mylde stefne
    He be thi*n* help on domysday.

[4]

Loke th*at* th*ou* no*n* thing ster*e*
Ne no*n* fals wytnesse ber*e*;
Thynk how Cryst was stu*n*ge w*ith* spere
    Qu*an* he deyid on Good Fryday.

[5]

Lok th*at* th*ou* ne sle no*n* ma*n*
Ne do no*n* foly w*ith* no*n* womma*n*;
Thynk, the blod fro Jh*e*su ran
    Qu*an* he deyid, w*ith*outy*n* nay.

330

British Museum. MS. Addit. 5665
                                XVI *cent.*
f. 30ᵛ

    Spes mea in Deo est;
    Spes mea in Deo est.

[1]

When lordechype ys loste *and*   [f. 31ʳ
    lusti lekyng withall,
When felichepe fayleth, *and* frendechepe
    dothe falle,
Then can Y no comfort but cry *and* call,
    'Spes mea in Deo [est.']

[2]

When maystery ne mayntenaunce,   [f. 30ᵛ
    manhode ne myght,
When reson ne rechesse may rewell me
    aryght,
Then Y, w*ith* sorwe *and* care w*ith*in my
    herte plyght:
    'Spes mea [in Deo est.']

[3]

When age dothe growe, then grucche Y
    and grone;
When febelnesse fallith, then fawte Y sone;
Then can Y non other but cry *and* call
    anone,
    'Spes mea [in Deo est.']

MS. heading: ad placitum.
stza. 1, l. 4. MS. Spes mea in deo vt sup*ra*.

330.1

National Library of Scotland. MS. Advocates 1. 1. 6
                        By William Dunbar, 1568
f. 284ᵛ

    Now cu*m*is aige quhair yewth hes bene,
    And trew luve rysis fro the splene.

[1]

Now culit is Dame Venus brand,
Trew luvis fyre is ay kindilland,
And I begyn to vndirstand
    In feynit luve quhat foly bene.

[2]

Quhill Venus fyre be deid and cauld,
Trew luvis fyre nevir birnis bauld;
So as the ta lufe vaxis auld,
    The tothir dois incress moir kene.

[3]

No man hes curege for to wryte
Quhat plesans is in lufe p*er*fyte
That hes in fenyeit lufe delyt,
    Thair kyndnes is so co*n*trair clene.

[4]

Full weill is him that may imprent
Or onywayiss his hairt consent   [f. 285ʳ
To turne to trew luve his intent
    And still the quarrell to sustene.

[5]

I haif experie*n*ce by mysell:
In luvis court anis did I dwell;
Bot quhair I of a joy cowth tell
    I culd of truble tell fyftene.

[6]

Befoir quhair that I wes in dreid
Now haif I confort for to speid;
Quhair I had maugre to my meid
    I trest rewaird and tha*n*kis betuene.

[7]

Quhair lufe wes wont me to displeiss
Now find I into lufe grit eiss;
Quhair I had denger and diseiss
    My breist all confort dois co*n*tene.

[8]

Quhair I wes hurt w*ith* jelosy
And wald no luver wer bot I,
Now quhair I lufe wald all wy
    Als weill as I luvit, I wene.

[9]

Befoir quhair I durst no*ch*t for schame
My lufe discure nor tell hir name,
Now think I wirschep wer and fame
 To all the warld that it war sene.

[10]

Befoir no wicht I did co*m*plene,
So did hir denger me derene,
And now I sett no*ch*t by a bene
 Hir bewty nor hir twa fair ene.

[11]

I haif a luve farar of face,
Quhome in no denger may haif place,
Quhilk will me guerdoun gif and grace
 And m*er*cy ay quhe*n* I me mene.

[12]

Vnquyt I do no thing nor sane   [f. 285ᵛ]
Nor wairis a luvis tho*ch*t in vane;
I sal be als weill luvit agane;
 Thair may no jangler me prevene.

[13]

Ane lufe so fare, so gud, so sueit,
So riche, so rewthfull and discreit,
And for the kynd of ma*n* so meit
 Nevirmoir sal be nor yit hes bene.

[14]

Is none sa trew a luve as he
That for trew lufe of ws did de:
He suld be luffit agane, think me,
 That wald sa fane *our* luve obtene.

[15]

Is non but grace of God, I wiss,
That c*a*n in yewth considdir thiss:
This fals dissavand warld*is* bliss
 So gydis ma*n* in flo*ur*is grene.

At end: Finis q*uod* Dumbar.

The repetition of the burden is indicated as
 follows:
 stza. 1:
  Now cu*m*is aige quhair yewth hes bene
  and trew luve rysis fro the splene
 stzas. 2, 4:
  Now cu*m*is aige q*uh*air yewth hes bene
  and trew lufe rysis fro the splene
 stza. 3:
  Now cu*m*is aige &c.
  And trew lufe &c.
 stza. 5:
  Now cu*m*is aige &c.
  And trew lufe rysis &c.

stza. 6:
 Now cu*m*is aige &c.
 And trew &c.
stzas. 7, 8, 10, 13: Now &c.
                      And &c.
stza. 9:
 Now cu*m*is aige quhair yew*th* hes bene
 And trew lufe rysis fro the splene
stza. 11:
 Now cu*m*is aige q*uh*air yewth hes bene
 And trew lufe rysis fro the splene
stza. 12:
 Now cu*m*is aige q*uh*air yew*th* hes bene
 And trew luve rysis fro the splene
stza. 14:
 Now cu*m*is &c.
 And trew &c.
stza. 15:
 Now cu*m*is aige quhair yewth hes bene
 And trew luve rysis fro the splene
*In stza. 13 the first three lines are written in the
order 2, 1, 3. The correction is indicated by
prefixed numbers in MS.*

331

a. *Trinity College, Cambridge.* MS. O. 9. 38
                                   XV *cent.*
f. 69ᵛ

 Y concell yow, both more and lasse,
 Beware of swerynge by the Masse.

[1]

The Masse ys of suwch dygnyte
Nothynge to hyt comprysyd may be;
Ther ys p*re*sent yn the Trynyte
One God yn persons three.

[2]

The ierachy of angellys kynde,
All orders of seyntys ys had yn mynde,
Whych to forsake th*o*u art full blynde;
Leue thy swerynge; spyll not thy wynde.

[3]

Yn the Masse ys more mystery
Then droppys yn the see or sterrys yn the
  sckye,
Infenyte goodnys; Y tell the whye:
For God *and* man ys offeryd vpp truly.

[4]

Why sweryste th*o*u by the Masse, man soo
  woode,
Where ys thy helpe, thy lyuys foode,
Crystys body, hys precyowsse blode,
All thy saluacyon, nothyng but goode?

[5]

Man, swere no more, do aftyr my rede,
By the Masse, worde ne dede,
For, yf thow do, hell ys thy mede
Without endlys payne and euerlastynge
    drede.

[6]

Ordeynde to hym that swerith by the Masse
Ther ys fy[r]-lyght, woo, and euer 'alasse!'
Man, leue thy swerynge or thow passe,
And call on mercy for thy trespasse.

[7]

Then mercy cry, and call for grace,
Here on erth whyle thow haste space,
For, when erth hath coueryde thy face,
Then all that ys turnyd as hyt wasse.

b. *Balliol College, Oxford.* MS. 354, f.
230[r & v]. XVI *cent.* (stzas. 1–4, one stanza
not in a, 7).

stza. 1, l. 1. suwch] so high.   l. 2. Nothynge]
  That no thyng. comprysyd] comprehendid.
  l. 3. Ther] For ther.
stza. 2, l. 2. orders of] other. ys] *omits.*
  l. 3. Whych] The which. full] to.
  l. 4. spyll] and spill.
stza. 4, l. 1. thou] *omits.* man] thou man.
  l. 2. helpe] helth.
After stza. 4, b has the following stanza:
  Also thus seyth the prophete Zakarye,
  Witnesse beryng, as thou mayst see,
  And thus he seyth in his prophesye:
  That all swerers dampned shall be.
stza. 7, l. 2. on] in. l. 3. For] That. erth]
  the erth. l. 4. thy sowle in hevyn may
  haue a place.
The repetition of the burden is indicated as
  follows: stza. 1: I consaill you both more and
  lesse. stza. 2: I consaill you &c. stza. 3: I
  consayll you both more and lesse. stzas. 4,
  7, and unique stza.: I consaill.
At end: Explicit.

332

Bodleian Library. MS. Eng. poet. e. 1
                      XV *cent.*
f. 27[I v]

  Lefte owr hertes with good entent,
  And thanke [G]od, that al hath sent.

[I]

Man and wo[mm]an in euery place,
God hath yow sent vertu and grace;
Therfor spend wel owr space,
  And thanke God, that al hath sent.

[2]

If thou be a man herdy and strong,
With thi strenke do thou no wrong,
But lat reson rewll the among,
  And thank God, [that al hath sent.]

[3]

If thou haue wysdom at thi wyll,
Thorow thi wysdom do thou no yll;
Kep in thi hert both lovd and styll,
  And thank God, [that al hath sent.]

[4]

If thou be syk or elles pore,
God hymshelf may the socur,
With stedfast hert and thou hym honovr
  And thank God, [that al hath sent.]

[5]

What wo or tene the betyd,
God can help on euery syd;
Buxsumlych thou must abyd
  And thank God, [that al hath sent.]

burden, l. 2, stza. 1, l. 1. *The text is damaged by
  a small hole in the leaf.*
stzas. 2–5, l. 4. MS. *And thank god &c.*

333

Bodleian Library. MS. Ashmole 189
                      XV *cent.*
f. 104[r]

  Quid vltra debuit facere
  That Lorde that dyed for the and me?

[1]

Cryste made mane yn this maner of wyse:
Lyke vnto the Trynite he deyd the dewyse,
By resone, vertue, and orygynall justice,
And set the in the plesant place of paradyse.

[2]

He made the allso to be bothe lorde and
    kynge
Off erthe and off all creatures that beth
    theryn levyng,
Sonne, moone, and sterrys contynuall
    shynynge;
For thy sake fynallye he made all maner
    thynge.

[3]

Wyth thes grete gyftes thou cowdyst not be
    content,
Butt by grete presumpsione assentyst to the
    serpent

Bycause thou woldyst be lyke God omnipotent;
Thane all thy grete vertues, anone away
they wente.

[4]

Cryst thene beholdynge thy grete and
grewous fall,
Perseywynge the spoyled off thy gyftes
naturall,
Was anone meked with pyte paternall
The to make fre, that by synne was thrall.

[5]

The to redeme he founde sone remedye,
Vsynge humylite to thi pride clene con-
trarye,
For, whereas by pryde thou were fall
dedlye,
By hys humilite restored the full hylye.

[6]

For, whereas by pride thou were made dede,
With grete humylyte he toke one hyme
manhede,
Off a uyrgyne was ibore, the to restore
indede,
Off Jesseys lyne and off hys kynrede.

[7]

By frute of a tree thou felle to [f. 104ᵛ]
dampnacyone,
Thane beholde and see thy Makers
provysyone:
Howe by a tree restoreed thy saluacyone
One the crosse whene he suffred hys
passyone.

[8]

Thane were thou delyuerde fro the cap-
tyuyte,
And by feythe and baptyme restored the
agayne,
Remyttynge the blame of orygnall iniquite,
And the restored agayne to thy fre lyberte.

[8]

Sethe Cryste hathe the honoured thus by
his natyuyte,
Conueynge yne one persone thy nature with
the Deyte,
By merytes of hys passyone browght the to
felicite,
To this forseyde questyone an awnsuere
nowe geve we.

The repetition of the burden is indicated as
follows: stzas. 1–8: quid vltra. stza. 9: quid
vltra.
At end: Explicit.

334

Bodleian Library. MS. Eng. poet. e. 1
XV *cent.*
f. 24ᵛ

Why, why, what is this whi
But virtus verbi Domini?

[1]

Whan nothyng was but God alone,
The Fader, the Holy Gost, with the Son,
On was iii, *and* iii was On.
What is this why?
To frayn why I hold but foly;
It is non other sertenly
But virtus verbi D[omi]ni.

[2]

'Fiat' was a word ful bold,
That mad al thing as he wold,
Hevey[n] *and* erth *and* men of mold.
What is why?
To frayn why I hold but foly;
[It is non other sertenly
But virtus verbi Domini.]

[3]

The warld gan wax *and* multiply; [f. 25ʳ]
The planetes mad hem full besy
To rowll ychy thyng by *and* by.
What is why?
To frayne why I hold it but foly;
[It is non other sertenly
But virtus verbi Domini.]

[4]

The planetes wark nothyng in veyn,
But, as thei be ordent, so must thei reygne,
For the word of God wyl not ageyne.
What is why?
To frayne why I hold it but foly;
[It is non other sertenly
But virtus verbi Domini.]

[5]

Whan Bede had prechyd to the stonys dry,
The myght of God mad hem to cry,
'Amen!' Certys, this is no ly.
What is why?
To frayn why [I hold it but foly;
It is non other sertenly
But virtus verbi Domini.]

[6]

Herytyke*s* wonder of this thyng most:
How God is put i*n* the holy Host,
Her *and* at Rome *and* in eu*er*y cost.
   What is why?
To frayn why [I hold it but foly;
It is non other sertenly
But virtus verbi Domini.]

stzas. 2, 3, 4, ll. 6, 7. MS. &c.
stzas. 5, 6, ll. 5, 6, 7. MS. To frayn why &c.

335

Lord Harlech, National Library of Wales.
   MS. Porkington 10   XV *cent.*

f. 200ʳ

   Why, why, what ys this why?
   Hit ys no*n* nodyre sekur*e*ly
   But wert*us* wer*e*by D*o*m*i*ni.

[1]

Whan nothing whas but God alone,
The Fadyr*e*, the Holly Gost, *and* the Son*e*,
Who*n* ys iii, and iii ys Who*n*.

[2]

Heyuy*n and* erthe furst he wroght,
And odyr*e* creatu*r*s he made of noght,
All thing dyspossid lyk as he thowght.

[3]

Man, for an appull of lyttyll prys,
He lost the blys of paradys,
For he dessyryd for to be wys.

[4]

Tell me this resson yeve th*a*t th*o*u can:
How Goddys Son becam a man
Be lynnag of Dawyt and Nasson.

[5]

Marwell I have th*a*t pur*e* wyrgyn   [f. 200ᵛ
Myght co*n*sayfe Sappyens dewyne;
I trow hit passyt all wytt*us* thin.

[6]

The grettist Lord of sofferantte
Ys God himselfe in his humanyte;
For mankynd he dyid wppon a tre.

[7]

Ma*n*, th*o*u art but corrypptybull;
Tell me how hit may be possibull
That he schall lyue eu*er*, as sayth the
   Bybull.

[8]

Ma*n*, th*o*u art but infaynyt
To co*m*prehend nor to indyte
All this matters se in sennyt.

[9]

God hy*m*selfe byddyt vs by his se*n*ttens
To lo*v*fe owr*e* reson and owr*e* efydens
And to his wordys yef wholl credens.

The repetition of the burden is indicated after
   each stanza by: What.
stza. 9, l. 2. efydens] MS. eyfdens.

336

British Museum. MS. Sloane 2593
                                          XV *cent.*

f. 2ʳ

   Now bething the, gentilma*n*,
   How Ada*m* dalf *and* Eue sp[an.]

[1]

In the vale of Abraha*m*
Cryst hy*m*self he made Ada*m*,   [f. 2ᵛ
And of his rybbe a fayr wo*m*ma*n*,
   And thus this semly word began.

[2]

'Cu*m*, Adam, *and* th*o*u xalt se
The blysse of *p*aradis, th*a*t is so fre;
The*r*in stant an appil tre;
   Lef *and* frewt growit ther*o*n.

[3]

'Ada*m*, if th*o*u this appil ete,
Alle these joyis th*o*u xalt foryete
And the peynis of helle gete.'
   Thus God hy*m*self warnid Adam.

[4]

Qu*a*n God was fro Ada*m* gon,
Sone aft*er* ca*m* the fend ano*n*;
A fals treto*u*r he was on;
   He tok the tr*e and* krep ther*o*n.

[5]

'Qu*a*t eylyt the, Ada*m*? Art th*o*u wod?
Thi Lord haght tawt the lytil good.
He wolde not th*o*u vnderstod
   Of the wytt*es* th*a*t he can.

[6]

'Tak the appil of the tre
And ete ther*o*f, I bidde the,
And alle hese joyis th*o*u xalt se;
   Fro the he xal hedy*n* no*n*.'

[7]

Quan Adam hadde that appil ete,
Alle hese joyis wern foryete;
Non word more myght he speke;
     He stod as nakyd as a ston.

[8]

Thann cam an aungil with a swerd
And drof Adam into disert;
Ther was Adam sore aferd,
     For labour coude he werkyn non.

stza. 7, l. 1. appil] MS. appil t.

337

A a. *Bodleian Library.* MS. Arch. Selden
  B. 26   XV *cent.*
f. 5ʳ

     I pray yow all wyth o thowght,
     Amende me, and peyre me nowght.

[1]

Holy Wryt seyght, whech nothyng ys
     sother,
That no man shuld apeyre other;
Syth than in God Y am thy b[rothe]r,
     Amende me, and peyre me noughtgh.

[2]

This lore in the gospel eche man may se:
Yy[f th]y brothir trespace to the,
Betwene us two vpneme thow me;
     Amen[d me, and peyre me nought.]

[3]

Yyf thou se Y do gretly amys,
And no man wot but thou of this,
Make hit nought yit so euyl as yt is;
     Amend [me, and peyre me nought.]

[4]

Apeyr thou no man wyth thi word,
Nether in ernest nether in bord;
Let thi tong, that is thi sword,
     Amend euer and peyre nought.

[5]

God wyl thou schalt no man defame,
Ne apeyre no mannys name;
Ryght euen as thou woldist haue the same,
     A[mend me, and peyre me nought.]

[6]

Now to amend God yiue vs grace
Off repentaunce *and* very space
In hevyn to se his glorious face,
     Wher we schull amend *and* peyr nougth.

stza. 3, l. 4. MS. Amend &c.
stza. 5, l. 4. MS. A &c.
Stza. 4 is written to the right of stza. 5.
Signature: qd. J. D.

b. *Bodleian Library.* MS. Eng. poet. e. 1,
  f. 24ʳ ᵃⁿᵈ ᵛ. XV *cent.*

c. *British Museum.* MS. Addit. 5665,
  ff. 31ᵛ, 32ʳ. XVI *cent.* (burden and stzas.
  1–3).

MS. heading: c ad placitum.
burden. c *repeats, omitting second* me.   l. 1. I]
  c Y y.   o] b hert *and.*
stza. 1, l. 1. whech] b *omits.*   ys] b *omits.*
  l. 3. Syth than] b Sythen.   in God Y am]
  b I am ... (*MS. illegible*) God.   l. 4. me
  noughtgh] b m. ....
stza. 2, l. 1. lore] b *omits.*   l. 2. thy] c I thi.
  to] c *omits.*   l. 3. Betwene] c By twyxte.
  us] b yow.   vpneme thow me] b corectyd he
  be.   l. 4. b amend me &c.
stza. 3, l. 3. yit] b *omits.*   euyl] b yl.   l. 4. b
  amend me &c.
stza. 4, l. 1. thou] b *omits.*   l. 2. nether (2)] b
  ne.   l. 4. b amend me &c.
stza. 5, l. 1. God wyl] b Lok that.   schalt] b
  omits.   l. 2. name] b fame.   l. 3. cuen]
  b *omits.*   l. 4. amend me &c.
stza. 6, l. 3. In] b and in.   glorious] b *omits.*
  l. 4. we schull] b al thyng.

B. *British Museum.* MS. Egerton 3307
                                    XV *cent.*
f. 66ᵛ

     I pray yow all with on thoght,
     Amendith me, *and* pair me nogh[t].

[1]

Holy Wret seth—nothing ys sother—
That no man schuld apeir other:
Seth in God I am thi brother,
     Amendyth me, *and* payr me nogh*t*.

[2]

The lore in the gospell ilk man may se:
Yf thi brother trespas to the,
Betwen vs two snyb thou me;
     Amendyth me, *and* peyr me nogh*t*.

[3]

Yf thou se I do amysse,
And no man wot bo[t] thou of this,
Mak it noght so il as it ys;
    Amend me, and peyr me noght.

[4]

God byddes thou schalt no man defame,
No[r] apeyr no mans name,
Bot, euen as thou wold han the same,
    Amend me, and peyr me noght.

[5]

Apeyr thou no man with thi word,
Nother in ernest ne in bowrd;
Lat thi tong, that is thi sword,
    Amen euer and peyr noght.

[6]

Now to amend God gyf vs grace,
Of repentaunce and verre space,
In heuen ther to se hys face,
    Qwer we schall mend and peyr noght.

338

a. *Bodleian Library.* MS. Arch. Selden B.
  26   XV *cent.*
f. 29ᵛ

    Abyde, Y hope hit be the beste;
    Abyde, Y hope hit be the beste;
    Abyde, Y hope hit be the best,
        Sith hasty man lakked neuer woo.

[1]

A[byde, Y hope hit be the beste,
    Sith hasty man lakked neuer woo.]

[2]

Late euery man that wole haue reste
Euer ben avised what he wole doo.

[3]

Preue or ye take; thenke or ye feste;
    In wele be ware or ye be woo.

[4]

Vnder the busch ye shul tempeste
    Abyde tyl hit be ouer goo.

[5]

For longe tyme your hert shal breste;
    Abyde, Y consayl yow do soo.

*Stza. 1 is erased except for the initial, but the
music is left.*

b. *Trinity College, Cambridge.* MS. O. 3.
  58, recto. XV *cent.* (burden and stzas.
  1–3).

burden, l. 1. beste] beste-e-e.   l. 2. beste]
    beste-e.   l. 4. Sith] Syn.   lakked] wantyth.
    woo] woo-o-o.
stza. 1, l. 2. Sith] Syn.   lakked] wantyth.
    woo] woo-o-o.
stza. 2, l. 1. haue] han.   l. 2. wole] schal.
stza. 3, ll. 1, 2. or ye] er thou.
The repetition of the burden is indicated after
    stzas. 2, 3 by: Abyde I hope &c.

339

British Museum. MS. Sloane 2593
                                        XV *cent.*
f. 7ʳ

    Man, bewar, bewar, bewar,
    And kepe the that thou haue no car.

[1]

Thi tunge is mad of fleych and blod;
Euele to spekyn it is not good;
But Cryst, that deyid vpon the rood,
    So yyf vs grace our tunges to spare.

[2]

Thi lyppis arn withoute bon;
Spek non euyl of thi fon;
Man, I rede be Seynt Jon,
    Of euyl speche that thou be war.

[3]

Quan thou seyst thi euyl seying,
Be it of eld, be it of yyng,
Among many men thi speche may spri[n]g
    And make thin herte of blysse ful bare.

[4]

Therfore I telle the, be Seynt Austyn,
Ther xal non man of euele speche wyn
But sorwe and schame and meche syn
    And to his herte meche care.

[5]

Prey we to God and Seynt Margerete
That we mowun our tunges kepe,
Qwether we wake or slepe,
    And our body fro euele fare.

340

Bodleian Library. MS. Eng. poet. e. 1
XV *cent.*

f. 28ᵛ

A man that con his tong stere,
He ther not rek wer that he go.

[1]

Ittes knowyn in euery schyre
Wekyd tongges haue no per;
I wold thei wer brent in the fer
That warke men soo mykyl wo.

[2]

Ittes knowyn in euery lond
Wekyd tongges don gret wrong;
Thei make me to lyyn long
And also in myche car.

[3]

Yyf a man go in clotes gay,
Or elles in gud aray,
Wekyd tongges yet wyl say,
'Wer cam the by therto?'

[4]

Yyf a man go in cloys ill   [f. 20ʳ
And haue not the world at wyl,
Wekyd tongges thei wyll hym spyll
And sey, 'He ys a stake; lat hym goo.'

[5]

Now vs to amend God yeue vs grace,
Of repentens and of gud grace,
That we mut se hys glorius face;
Amen, amen, for charyte!

stza. 4, l. 4. sey] MS. seyd.

341

British Museum. MS. Sloane 2593
XV *cent.*

f. 30ʳ

Kep thi tunge, thi tunge, thi tunge;
Thi wykyd tunge werkit me w[o.]

[1]

Ther is non gres that growit on ground,
Satenas ne peny-round,
Wersse then is a wykkyd tunge
That spekit bethe euyl of frynd [and] fo.

[2]

Wykkyd tunge makit ofte stryf
Betwyxe a good man and his wyf;
Quan he xulde lede a merie lyf,
Here qwyte sydys waxin ful blo.

[3]

Wykkyd tunge makit ofte stauns,
Bethe in Engelond and in Frauns;
Many a man wyt spere and launs
Throw wykkyd tunge to ded is do.

[4]

Wykkyd tunge brekit bon,   [f. 30ᵛ
Thow the self haue non;
Of his frynd he makit his fon
In euery place qw[er] that he go.

[5]

Good men that stondyn and syttyn in this
      halle,
I prey you, bothe on and alle,
That wykkyd tunges fro you falle,
That ye mowun to hefne go.

342

Bodleian Library. MS. Eng. poet. e. 1
XV *cent.*

f. 50ᵛ

Off al the enmys that I can fynd
The tong is most enmy to mankynd.

[1]

With pety movyd, I am constreynyd
      To syng a song fore yowr comfort,
How that dyuers haue compleynyd
      Off tong ontru and ill report,
      Sayng thus withowt dysport:

[2]

Thys tong is instrument off dyscord,
      Causyng war and grett dystans
Betwyne the subjecte and the lord,
      The perfytt cause off euery grevans;
      Wherfore I syng withowt dysplesans:

[3]

Thow that prestes be neuer so pacient
      In towne, cite, or in cowrt ryall,
Thow the religyus be neuer so obedient,
      Yeit a ill tong wyll trobull them all;
      Wherfore this song reherse I shall:

[4]

Iff he th*a*t ill be anoth*er* do saye
  Hys pr*o*per*e* fawt*es* wold behold,
How oftym[m]is hym*e*self wer   [f. 51ʳ
    owt off the way,
  Sylens to hym*e* than shuld be gold,
  And wit*h* me to syng he wold be bold:

[5]

From*e* this tong, a venam*us* serpent,
  Defend vs, Fad*er*, to the we pray,
As th*o*u onto vs thi Son*e* hau*e* sent,
  Fore to be born*e* this pr*e*sent daye,
  Lesse th*a*t we syng *and* eu*er*more saye:

The repetition of the burden is indicated after
each stanza by: off all &c.
stza. 4, l. 3. oftym[m]is] *One minim is obliterated
by a spot.*

343

British Museum. MS. Harley 4294
                                    XV *cent.*
f. 81ᵛ

  He hath myn hart eu*er*y dele
  That can love true *and* kepe yt wele.

[1]

. . . . sit among*es* the knyght*es* all,
. . . e te counsell but ye be call,
[Her] *and* see, and sey not all;
  Whatsoeu*er* ye thynk, avyse ye wele.

[2]

In bower among*es* the byrd*es* bryght,
Spare thy tong, and spend thy syght;
. . . c . . t . . ace be nott to lyght;
  Whatsoeu*er* [ye thynk, avyse ye wele.]

[3]

An thou goo to the nale,
As m[er]i as a nyghtynghale,
Beware to whom*e* thou tell thy tale;
  Whatsoeu*er* [ye thynk, avyse ye wele.]

[4]

Lough neu*er* wit*h* no lowde crye;
N[or] rage nott for no velony;
. . . . . . frome rybawdry;
  [W]hatso[euer ye thynk, avyse ye wele.]

[5]

And thow goo vnto the wyne,
And thow thynk yt good and fyne,
Take thy leve whan*e* yt ys tyme;
  Whatsoeu*er* [ye thynk, avyse ye wele.]

[6]

Wit*h* thy tong thou mayst thyselfe spyll,
And wit*h* tonge thou mayst have all thy
    [wyll;]
Her and se, and kepe the styll;
  Whatsoeu*er* [ye thynk, avyse ye wele.]

stzas. 2, 3, 5, 6, l. 4. MS. what so eu*er* &c.
stza. 4, l. 4. MS. [W]hat so &c.
*MS. is badly faded at the left-hand margin.
After stza.* 6: and thow goo.

344

Bodleian Library. MS. Eng. poet. e. 1
                                    XV *cent.*
f. 22ʳ

  I hold hy*m* wyse *and* wel itaught
  Can bar an horn *and* blow it navght.

[1]

Blowyng was mad for gret game;
Of this blowyng cometh mekell grame;
Th*er*for I hold it for no schame
  To ber a horn *and* blow it nou[ght.]

[2]

Hornes ar mad both lovd *and* shyll;
Whan ty*m* ys, blow th*o*u thi fyll,
And, whan ned is, hold the styll,
  And ber a horne, *and* blow it novght.

[3]

Whatsoeu*er* be in thi thovght,
Her *and* se, *and* sey ryght novght;
Than schall me*n* sey th*o*u art wel tovght
  To bere [a horne and blow it nought.]

[4]

Of al the ryches vnder the son
Than was th*er* neu*er* bet*ur* wonne
Than is a tawght ma*n* for to konne,
  To ber [a horne *and* blow it nought.]

[5]

Whatsoeu*er* be in thi brest,
Stop thi movght wit*h* thi fyst,
And lok th*o*u thynk well of 'had-I-wyst,'
  And ber [a horne, *and* blow it nought.]

[6]

And when th*o*u syttyst at the ale,
And cryyst lyk an nyghttyngale,
Bewar to whom th*o*u tellist thi tale,
  But ber [a horne, *and* blow it nought.]

stzas. 3, 4, l. 4. [a horne and blow it nought.]]
  MS. &c.
stza. 5, l. 2. Stop] MS. *and* stop.
stzas. 5, 6, l. 4. [a horne, and blow it nought.]]
  MS. &c.

345

Balliol College, Oxford. MS. 354
                                    XVI *cent.*
f. 231ʳ

  He is wise, so most I goo,
  That can be mery *and* suffer woo.

[1]

Be mery *and* suffer, as I the vise,
Whereu*er* thow sytt or rise;
Be well ware whom thow dispise;
  Th*o*u shalt kysse who is thy foo.

[2]

Beware to whom th*o*u spek thy will,
For thy speche may greve the yll;
Here *and* see, *and* goo than still;
  But well is he th*a*t can do soo.

[3]

Many a ma*n* holdyth hy*m* so stowght
Whatsoeu*er* he thynk, he seyth it owt;
But if he loke well abowt,
  His tonge may be his most foo.

[4]

'Be mery' now is all my songe;
The Wise Ma*n* tawght both old *and* yonge:
'Who ca*n* suffer *and* hold his tonge,
  He may be mery *and* nothyng woo.'

[5]

Yff any man displese the owght,
Suffer w*ith* a mery thowght;
Let care away, *and* greve the nowght,
  And shake thy lappe, *and* lat it go.

The repetition of the burden is indicated after
  each stanza by: he is wise &c.
At end: Explicit.

346

Balliol College, Oxford. MS. 354
                                    XVI *cent.*
f. 231ʳ

  An old sawe hath be fownd trewe:
  'Cast not away thy*n* old for newe.'

[1]

An old-said sawe, 'Onknowen, onkyste,'
'Wher is lytyll love, th*er* is lytill tryste,'
And 'Ever bewar*e* of had-I-wyste.'
  And remembre this sawe, for it is new,
  Ell*es* must we drynk as we brewe.

[2]

The peple to plese, s*er*, it is payn,
P*er*aventure amonge twenti not twayn;
Hold me excused thowgh I be playn.
  This sawe is old; reme*m*bre it newe,
  Or ell*es* most we drynk as we brewe.

[3]

Another thynge, s*er*, m*er*ke we well:
'Two fac*es* in on hode, a fayre castell.'
He seyth hy*m*self he wil not medyll.
  Folk fayre lest seche in cowrt to shew,
  And ell*es* most we drynk as we brew.

[4]

Thyn old s*er*vant*es* here thus ar meved;
The tyme wyll cu*m* they must be releved:
Geve trust to the*m* th*a*t thow hast p*re*ved,
  And, if th*o*u do so, thow shalt not rewe,
  And ell*es* must th*o*u drynk as th*o*u
    doste brewe.

stza. 2, l. 2. twenti] MS. xxᵗⁱ.
At end: Explicit.

347

Bodleian Library. MS. Douce 302
                        By John Audelay, XV *cent.*
f. 29ᵛ

  Hit is the best, erele *and* late,
  Vche mo*n* kepe his oune state.

[1]

In wat ord*er* or what degre
  Hole Cherche hath bownd the to,
Kepe h*it* wele, I cownsel the;
  Dissire th*o*u neu*er* to go th*er*fro.
    I say allgate:

[2]

A hye worchip h*it* is to the
  To kepe thi state *and* thi good name,
Leud or lered, werehere h*it* be,
  Ellis God *and* mo*n* thay wol the blame.
    I say algate:

[3]

Fore iiii obisions now schul ye here
　That God hatis hile in his syght:
A harde prest, a proud frere,
　An hold mon lechoure, a couard knyght.
　　I say algate:

[4]

A prest schuld scheu vche mon mekenes
　And leue in loue and charite,
Throgh his grace and his goodnes
　Set al other in vnite.
　　I say algate:

[5]

A frere schuld loue all holenes,
　Prayers, penans, and pouert[e];
Relegious men, Crist hem ches
　To foresake pride and vayn glory.
　　I say algate:

[6]

An hold mon schuld kepe him chast
　And leue the synne of lechore;
Al wedid men schuld be stedfast
　And foresake the syn of avowtre.
　　I sai algate:

[7]

A knyght schuld feght ayayns falsnes,
　And schew his monhod and his myght,
And mayntene trouth and ryghtwysnes
　And Hole Cherche and wedowes ryght.
　　I say algate:

[8]

Here be al the foure astatis
　In Hole Cherche God hath ordent;
He bedis you kepe hem wel algate;
　Wos[o]euer hem chomys, he wyl be
　　schent.
　　I say algate:

MS. heading: Fac ad quod venisti.
The repetition of the burden is indicated after
　each stanza by: vt supra.

348

British Museum. MS. Addit. 5665
　　　　　　　　　　　　　XVI cent.
f. 14ᵛ

In euery state, in euery degre,
The mene ys the beste, as semeth me.
In euery state, in euery degre,
The *mene ys beste, as semeth [*f. 15ʳ
　me.

[1]

The hyere men clemmeth, the sorere ys the
　falle;
Banckes that lawe buthe sone ouerflowe;
The donder sownys perischeth castill ryall;
　The mene ys best, as semeth me.

[2]

Hill that buth hye sufferith many　[f. 14ᵛ
　showres;
A-law vpon the yerthe ys merey to be
Then in hey howsys other grete toures;
　The mene ys best, as semeth me.

[3]

Where the hegge ys lawest men doth ouer-
　skyppe;
To hew abow thy hedde, hit is but vanite,
Lest in thy yee ther falle a chyppe;
　The mene ys best, as semeth me.

MS. heading: ad placitum (repeated on f. 15ʳ).

349

Cambridge University Library. MS. Addit.
　　5943　　　　　　　　　　XV cent.
f. 145ᵛ

Lord, how scholde I roule me,
Of al men ipreysyd to be?

[1]

If Y halde the lowe asyse
And take aray of lytel pryse,
Then men wil say, 'He ys nowght wyse;
　He ys a fow; let hym be.'

[2]

And yyf I take the mene astate
And wyth non man maky debat,
Than men wil sey, erly and late,
　That I am worth no maner fe.

[3]

And yf Y take gryte aray,
Hors and hondes and clothes gay,
Than men wel say euery day
　That I passe my degre.

[4]

Then take thow hede of the oxe;
Go nowght to lowe for the foxe,
Nether to hey tyl thow be wox,
　For the kyte that wolde the sle.

[5]

Therfor loke that thow be scley:
For no thyng hew thow tow hey,
Last they falle don into thy ey,
  The spones that above the be.

stza. 4, l. 4. the] MS. they.

350

Balliol College, Oxford. MS. 354
                         XVI *cent.*
f. 226ᵛ

  Forsothe, I hold hy*m* well *and* wit*h*owt
    woo
  Th*a*t hath ynowgh *and* ca*n* say 'Whoo!'

[1]

I was wit*h* pope *and* cardynall,
And wit*h* bisshopis *and* prestes gret *and*
  small;
Yet was neu*er* no*n* of the*m* all
  That had ynowgh *and* cowld say 'Who!'

[2]

Now covitise begy*n*neth to wake,
And lechery ys to hym take
And seyth, 'His joy may not slake
  That hath ynowgh *and* ca*n* say "Who!"'

[3]

I was wit*h* empro*w*r, kyng, *and* knyght,
Wit*h* duke, erle, baro*n*, *and* lady brig*h*t;
Yet was no*n* of the*m* to my sight
  That had ynowgh *and* cowld say 'Who!'

[4]

Whan all thyng*es* fall away,
Tha*n* covetyse begyneth to play;
He is not here, I dare well say,
  That hath ynowgh *and* ca*n* say 'Who!'

The repetition of the burden is indicated as
  follows: stzas. 1, 2, 4: for soth I hold. stza. 3:
  for sothe I hold.
At end: Explicit.

351

Balliol College, Oxford. MS. 354
                         XVI *cent.*
f. 178ʳ

  Diuisie si affluant,
    Nolite cor apponere.

[1]

Yf God send the plentuowsly riches,
Tha*n* thank hartely wit*h* all meknes;

In thy mynd this p*r*overbe impresse:
  'Nolite cor appo*n*ere.'

[2]

And, while th*o*u hast it i*n* thy gou*er*nau*n*ce,
I co*n*saill the por*e* men to avau*n*ce,
Lest deth the apprese wit*h* his cruell lau*n*ce;
  Nolite cor appo*n*er*e*.

[3]

And thynk th*o*u must also p*er*te away
Fro*m* all thy riches; th*o*u mayst not say nay;
Th*er*fore the best th*a*t I ca*n* syng or say:
  Nolite cor appo*n*er*e*.

stza. 1, l. 4. Nolite] MS. Nolito.
At end: Explicit.

352

Cambridge University Library. MS. Ee. 1.
12   By James Ryman, *c.* 1492
f. 48ᵛ

  Hec sunt verba p*r*ophetica:
  'Amittes mundi prospera.'

[1]

O man, whiche art the erthe take froo,
Ayene into erthe thou shalt goo;
The Wyse Man in his lore seith soo:
  Amittes mundi [prospera.]

[2]

Bysshop or emp*er*ou*r*e though that thou be,
Kynge, prince, or duke of high degree,
Emp*er*esse or quene or lady free,
  Amittes mundi p*r*ospera.

[3]

Though of richesse thou haue thy wille,
Of mete and drinke having thy fille,
When dredefull dethe shall come the tille,
  Amittes mu*n*di [prospera.]

[4]

Job seith, 'Good Lorde, of me   [f. 49ʳ
  haue myende,
For why my lyfe is but a wyende;
To erth I shall ayene by kyende.'
  Amittes mundi p*r*ospera.

[5]

Thou shalt not, man, abyde here ay,
But as a floure shalt fade away;
Therfore to the I dare wele say,
  'Amittes mundi prospera.'

[6]

Criste graunt vs grace that we come may
To heven blis, that lasteth aye,
Where is no nyght, but ever day
  Et infinita prospera.

stza. 1, l. 4. MS. Amittes mundi &c.
stza. 3, l. 4. MS. Amittes mundi &c.

353

Cambridge University Library. MS. Ee. 1.
12   By James Ryman, *c.* 1492
f. 49ʳ

  Alle worldly welth passed me fro;
  Nunc in puluere dormio.

[1]

I hadde richesse, I had my helthe;
I had honoure and worldely welth;
Yet deth hath take me hens by stelthe;
  Nunc in puluere dormio.

[2]

Of alle solace I had my wille,
Of mete and drinke having my fille;
Yet dethe hathe smyt me with his bille;
  Nunc in puluere dormio.

[3]

I had beawte in hande and face;
I had comforte in euery case;
Yet, arested with dethys mace,
  Nunc in puluere dormio.

[4]

I hadde musyk, I hadde swete   [f. 49ᵛ
    songe,
And other game and myrthe amonge;
Yet dethe hathe felde me with his pronge;
  Nunc in puluere dormio.

[5]

I hadde konnyng, wisdome, and witte;
Manhoode and strengthe in me were knyt;
Yet dethe hath brought me to my pitte;
  Nunc in puluere dormio.

[6]

O man, which art erthe by thy kyende,
Whose lyfe is but a blast of wyende,
This dredefull worde bere in thy myende:
  'Nunc in puluere [dormio.']

[7]

While thou art here, man, wele the guyde,
For thou shalt not ay here abyde,
But thou shalt sei, man, at a tyde,
  'Nunc in [puluere dormio.']

[8]

Almyghty God graunte vs alle grace
Wele to expende oure tyme and space
Or that we come vnto that case:
  'Nunc in puluere dormio.'

stza. 6, l. 4. MS. nunc in puluere &c.
stza. 7, l. 4. MS. nunc in &c.

354

British Museum. MS. Addit. 5665
                            XVI *cent.*
f. 35ᵛ

  'Do well, and drede no man,'
  The best concell ys that Y can.
  'Do well, and drede no man,'
  The beste concell ys *that I can.
                            [*f. 36ʳ

[1]

Now to do well how shalt thou do?
  Herken to me, and Y shall the telle:
Jhesu with saule and mynde allso
  H[er]tely thou pray, then doiste thou
    well.

[2]

Euyn as thyselue with hole entent   [f. 35ᵛ
  To loue thy necghbore, as saith the
    gospell,
Thow hast by commaundement;
  Obserue thees too, then doist thou well.

MS. heading: ad placitum.

355

a. *British Museum.* MS. Sloane 2593
                            XV *cent.*
f. 9ʳ

  Man, be war er thou be wo:
  Think on pride, and let hym goo.

[1]

Pryde is out, and pride is inne,
And pride is rot of euery synne,
And pride will neuer blynne
  Til he haght browt a man in woo.

[2]

Lucyfer was au*n*gyl bryght
And conqwero*ur* of meche myght;
Throw his p*ri*de he les his lyght
And fil dou*n* into endeles woo.

[3]

Wenyst th*o*u, for thi gaye clothing
And for thin grete othis sweryng,
To be a lord or a kyng?
Lytil it xal avayle the too.

[4]

Qu*a*n thou xalt to cherche glyde,
Wermys xuln ete throw thi syde,
And lytil xal avayle thi p*ri*de
Or ony synnys th*a*t th*o*u hast doo.

[5]

Prey to Cryst, w*ith* blody syde
And othere wou*n*des grile *and* wyde,
Th*a*t he foryeue the thi pryde
And thi synnys th*a*t th*o*u hast doo.

b. *Balliol College, Oxford.* MS. 354, f.
249ᵛ. XVI *cent.* (burden and stzas. 1, 3, 2).

burden, l. 2. think] *And* thynk.
stza. 1, l. 2. rot] the begynyng.   l. 3. *And*] of.
wil neu*er* blynne] shall no ma*n* no thyng wyn.
l. 4. but sorow care *and* myche wo.
stza. 2, l. 1. au*n*gyl] an angell.   l. 2. *And*
conqwero*ur* of meche] covytow*r* of God*es*.
l. 3. Throw] . .w (*MS. torn*). les] lost.
lyght] sight.   l. 4. *And* fil] omits (lost by
tear *in MS.*).
stza. 3, l. 1. for] ma*n* for.   ll. 2, 3. transposes.
l. 2. *And*] or.   l. 3. a lord] an emprowr.
l. 4. Do a way ma*n* *and* thynk not so.
At end: Explicit.

356

a. *British Museum.* MS. Sloane 2593
XV *cent.*
f. 6ʳ

Synful ma*n*, for Godis sake,
I rede th*a*t th*o*u amendis make.

[1]

Thow th*o*u be kyng of to*ur* *and* town,
Thow th*o*u be kyng *and* were corou*n*,
I sette ryght not be thi renown
But if th*o*u wylt amendys make.

[2]

Th*a*t hast here is othere menys,   [f. 6ᵛ
And so it xal ben qu*a*n thou art hens;

Thi sowle xal abeye thi synnys
But if th*o*u wi[l]t ame*n*des make.

[3]

Thow th*o*u be bothe stef *and* strong,
And many a ma*n* th*o*u hast do wrong,
'Wellawey' xal be thi song
But [if thou wylt amendys make.]

[4]

Ma*n*, bewar, the weye is slede*r*;
Th*o*u xal slyde thou wost not qwed*er*;
Body *and* sowle xul go toged*er*
But [if thou wylt amendys make.]

[5]

[Man], ber not thi hed to heye
In pumpe *and* pride *and* velonye;
In helle th*o*u xalt be*n* hangyd hye
But if th*o*u wilt ame*n*des make.

stza. 4, l. 4. MS. but &c.
stza. 5, l. 4. if] MS. it.

b. *Bodleian Library.* MS. Eng. poet. e. 1,
ff. 30ᵛ, 31ʳ. XV *cent.* (burden and stzas.
1, 3, 5, 4).

burden, l. 1. Godis] cryst*es*.   l. 2. that] omits.
stza. 1, ll. 1, 2. transposes.   ll. 1, 2. be] byst.
l. 1. kyng] lord.   l. 2. corou*n*] the crowne.
l. 3. ryght] omits.   renown] gret renowne.
stza. 3, l. 1. 'Thow thou be] ma*n* thou art.
l. 2. *And*] omits.
stza. 4, l. 1. sleder] scheder.   l. 2. xal slyde]
mast scled*er*.   wost not] wonest.
l. 3. xul go] *and* all.
stza. 5, l. 1. [Man]] *MS. illegible.*   l. 2. In]
for.   velonye] lechery.   l. 3. In hel thi
sole xal sor aby.
The repetition of the burden is indicated as
follows: stza. 1: synful ma*n* for cryst*es* sake.
stzas. 3, 5, 4: vt sup*ra*.

357

British Museum. MS. Sloane 2593
XV *cent.*
f. 26ʳ

Ma*n*, be wys, *and* arys,
And thynk on lyf th*a*t leste*n*it ay.

[1]

Thynk, ma*n*, qwerof th*o*u art wrout;
Powre *and* nakyd th*o*u were hed*er* browt;
Thynk how Cryst thi sowle haght bowt,
And fond to se*r*uyn hy*m* to pay.

[2]

Thynk, man, on the dere yeres thre:
For hunger deyid gret plente,
Powre and ryche, bond and fre,
    Thei leyn dede in euery way.

[3]

Thynk, man, on the pestelens tweye:
In euery cuntre men gunne deye;
Deth left neyther for lowe ne heye,
    But lettyd hem of here pray.

[4]

Deth is wonder coueytous:
Quan he comit to a manys hous,
He takit the good man and his spows
    And bryngit hem in powre aray.

[5]

After cam a wyndes blast
That made many a man agast;
Stefue stepelys thei stodyn fast;
    The weyke fyllyn and blewyn away.

[6]

Many merueylis God haght sent
Of lytenyng and of thunder-dent;
At the Frere Camys haght it hent,
    At Lynne toun, it is non nay.

[7]

Lytenyng at Lynne dede gret harm
Of tolbothe and of Fryre Carm;   [f. 26ᵛ
Thei stondyn wol cole that stodyn wol
    warm;
    It made hem a wol sory fray.

[8]

Lok, man, how thou ledyst thi lyf,
And how thou spendyst thi wyttes v;
Go to cherche, and do the schryf,
    And bryng thi sowle in redy way.
stza. 5, l. 3. thei] MS. that.

358

Bodleian Library. MS. Eng. poet. e. 1
                                    XV *cent.*
f. 28ʳ

    Syng we to the Trinite,
    With 'Parce mihi, Domine.'

[1]

Game and ernest euer among,
    And among al othyr degre,
It is gud to thynk on my son[g],
    With 'Parce mihi, Domine.'

[2]

Qwan thou rysyst vpon thi rest,
    (I make this song for no vanite)
Make a cros vpon thi brest,
    With 'Parce mihi, Domine.'

[3]

Go thou to the chyrche, and her thi Mes,
    And ser[ue] God with humilite;
Aske foryeuenes of thi trespas,
    With 'Parce mihi, Domine.'

[4]

Qwan thou cumste home onto thi   [f. 28ᵛ
    tabyll,
    Thou art seruid with gret dignite;
Hold this song for no fabyll,
    With 'Parce mihi, Domine.'

[5]

Prey we bothe nyth and day
    The gret God in Trinite
Tho heu[e]ne God theche vs the way,
    With 'Parce mihi, Domine.'

stza. 2, ll. 2, 3. MS. *transposes.*

359

A a. *Balliol College, Oxford.* MS. 354
                                    XVI *cent.*
f. 220ᵛ

    Man, asay, asay, asay,
    And aske thou mercy whyle thou may.

[1]

Man, haue in mynd how herebeforn
For thy mysded thou wast forlorn;
To geve the mercy Cryst was born;
    Aske thou mercy whill thou may.

[2]

Yff thou thy lyff in syn hath lede,
Amend the now, and be not dred,
For Crystes mercy furth ys spred;
    [Aske thou mercy while thou may.]

[3]

Yff thy syn be never so yll,
Yett for no syn thou shalt spyll,
Amend the now yf that thou will;
    [Aske thou mercy while thou may.]

[4]

He that hath the hether browght,
He wold that thou mercy sowght;
Aske ytt, *and* he denyth ytt nowght;
    [Aske thou mercy while thou may.]

[5]

He that dyed on the rode
And shed for the his preci*us* blod,
He ys both mercyfull *and* gud;
    [Aske thou mercy while thou may.]

[6]

Mercy ys spred on the grownd,
Ther for to dwell a lytill stownd;
Lett vs seke till yt be fownd;
    [Aske thou mercy while thou may.]

[7]

Ytt for to fynd God geve vs grace
In this world while we haue space,
And after in hevyn to haue place;
    [Aske thou mercy while thou may.]

stzas. 2–7, l. 4. MS. vt sup*r*a.
At end: Explicit.

b. *Bodleian Library.* MS. Arch. Selden
B. 26, f 7ᵛ. XV *cent.* (burden and stzas.
1–3, 5, 4, 6).

burden, l. 1. Man] A man.   l. 2. thou (1)]
  omits.
stza. 1, l. 1. herebeforn] here by fore.
  l. 2. wast] where.   forlorn] fore lore.
  l. 3. To geve the] but mercy to yeue. Cryst
  was born] now C*r*iste ys bore.   l. 4. A say
  (*marked*: Chorus).
stza. 2, l. 1. Yff thou thy lyff in syn hath] In
  synne thy lyfe yf thou haue.   l. 2. the] hit.
  and] *omits.*   dred] a dradde.   l. 3. Crystes]
  he his.   ys] hath.   l. 4. A say.
stza. 3, l. 1. Yff] And they.   l. 2. Yett] *omits.*
  no] thy.   thou shalt] shalt thou not.
  l. 3. Amend the now] Nowe mercy to aske.
  th*a*t] *omits.*   l. 4. A say.
stza. 4, l. 1. hath the hether browght] the so
  dere hath bought.   l. 2. Mercy] *before* he.
  l. 3. Aske ytt, *and* he denyth] Yyf th*o*u seke
  he nyeth.   l. 4. A say.
stza. 5, l. 1. He] God.   on] vppon.
  l. 2. For thi mysdede he shadde his blode.
  l. 3. He ys both mercyfull] For his mercy ys
  ful.   l. 4. A say.
stza. 6, l. 2. for (1)] *omits.*   dwell] lest.   a lytill]
  for a.   l. 3. Lett vs] Ther fore thou hit.
  l. 4. A say.

B. *British Museum.* MS. Addit. 5665
                                    XVI *cent.*
f. 42ᵛ

    Man, asay,
    And axe mercy while th*o*u may.
    Man, asay, asay, asay,
    And axe mercy *while thow   [*f. 43ʳ
    may.

[1]

In synne yf th*o*u thi lyffe haue ledde,
Ame*n*de the, man, *and* be not adrad;
God for the his mercy hathe sprade;
    Asay, asay.

[2]

For thof thy synne be neuer*e* so [f. 42ᵛ
    ille,
Amende thysylue, man, yf that thou wille;
God will not that th*o*u spylle;
    Asay, [asay.]

[3]

For he that the so der*e* hathe boghfte,
Mercy he wolde that th*o*u soghfte;
Iff th*o*u h*i*t axske, he nayes h*i*t noghfte;
    Asay, [asay.]

[4]

Thy lyffe vn erthe her*e* thus th*o*u spende,
Prayng to Jh*e*su th*a*t th*o*u notte shende;
Then joy *and* blisse shall be thyn ende;
    Asay, [asay.]

MS. heading: ad placitum.

C. *Lincoln College, Oxford.* MS. Lat. 89
                                    XV *cent.*
f. 27ᵛ

    Ma*n*, assay, assay, assay,
    And aske mercy qwyls th*a*t th*o*u may.

[1]

Ma*n*, hafe mynd how herbefore
For thy mysdede th*o*u was forlore,
Bot mercy th[o]w cry for C*r*yst is bore;
    Assay, assay.

The repetition of the burden after the stanza is
indicated by: man asay vt sup*r*a.

360

Cambridge University Library. MS. Ee.
    1. 12   By James Ryman, *c.* 1492
f. 46ʳ

    Amende we vs while we haue space,
    For why nowe is the tyme of grace.

[1]

That holy clerke, Seint Augustyne,
Seith now is tyme for to inclyne
To vertue, and synne to resyne,
　　For why now is [the tyme of grace.]

[2]

Now, while we lyve, to do penaunce,
It is oure soules to avaunce
And into blisse for to enhaunce,
　　For why now is [the tyme of grace.]

[3]

Are we departe this worlde fro,
Oure soules we may save fro woo;
Whenne we be gone, we may not so,
　　For why now is [the tyme of grace.]

[4]

Do we so now, while we here be,
In worde and dede, that we may see
Almyghty God in mageste,
　　For why now [is the tyme of grace.]

[5]

In wille, in dede, in worde, *and* thought,
Axe we hym grace that vs hath　　[f. 46ᵛ]
　　bought,
Ayenst his wille that we haue wrought,
　　For why [now is the tyme of grace.]

[6]

Criste, that ay was, shall be, and is,
Graunte vs forgeuenes of oure mys
And graunte vs grace to dwell in blis,
　　For why now is the tyme of grace.

stzas. 1–3, l. 4. MS. For why now is &c.
stza. 4, l. 4. MS. For why now &c.
stza. 5, l. 4. MS. for why &c.

361

Balliol College, Oxford. MS. 354
　　　　　　　　　　　　　　　　XVI *cent.*
f. 221ʳ

　　Mary moder, I you pray
　　To be owr help at domysday.

[1]

Att domysday, whan we shall ryse
And cum before the hygh Justyce
And geve acownt for owr seruyce,
　　What helpyth than owr clothyng gay?

[2]

Whan we shall cum before hys dome,
What will vs helpe ther, all *and* some?

We shall stond as sory grome,
　　Yclad in a full pore aray.

[3]

That ylke day, withowt lesyng,
Many a man hys hondes shall wryng
And repent hym fore hys lywyng;
　　Then yt ys to late, as I yow say.

[4]

Therfor I rede, both day *and* nyght,
Make ye redy to God Almyght,
For in thys londe [n]ys kyng nor knyght
　　That wott whan he shall wend away.

[5]

That chyld that was born on Mary,
He glad all thys cumpany,
And for hys loue make we mery,
　　That for vs dyed on Gud Fryday.

At end: Explicit.

362

Bridgwater Corporation. Muniments, 123
　　　　　　　　　　　　　　　　XV *cent.*
recto

　　Hay, hay,
　　Take good hede wat youe say.

[1]

A domusday we schull ysee
Fadere *and* Sone in Trinite
With grete powere and magisti,
　　And angelys in grete aray.

[2]

An angele with a trumpat shall blow,
That all the worlde schall yt yknow;
They that beyne in yrth soo low,
　　They schull aryse all off the clay.

[3]

They that byne in [yrth] soo deppe,
They schull to thys trumpat take heed,
And aryse and full sorre wyppe
　　That euer they wer toyenst to fay.

[4]

God hymselffe Sune hyt ys
That schall [y]eue the dome, iwys,
And therfore avys hym that hath ido amys,
　　Fore there they schull rehersse here pay.

stza. 2, l. 1. An] MS. and.　　l. 3. yrth]
　　MS. yghrth.

363

British Museum. MS. Sloane 2593

XV cent.

f. 8ʳ

    Gay, gay, to be gay,
      I holde it but a vanite.

[1]

Yyng men that bern hem so gay,
They think not on domysday,
Quan they xul stonde in powre aray
    And for here dedes damnyd be.

[2]

God, that made se *and* sond,
With blody woundis he xal stond:
'Come ye, alle on my ryght hond,
    Ye chylderin that han seruyd me.'

[3]

To wykkyd men Jhesu xal say,
'Ye han led your lyf, bothe nyght *and* day,
Your sowle into a wykkyd way;
    Out of myn syte wynd ye!

[4]

'Quan I was nakyd, ye me not clad;
Quan I was hungry, ye me not fad;
Quan I was in prisoun *and* harde bestad,
    Ye wold not vysite me.

[5]

'Therfore myn chylderyn xuln han, iwys,
That ilke joye, that ilke blys,
That arte, haght ben, *and* alwey is
    Beforn myn angel[e] fayr *and* fre.'

364

*Huntington Library. Christmas carolles
newely Inprynted* (Richard Kele)

c. 1550

p. [48]

    A voyce from heuen to erth shall com:
    'Uenite ad iudicium.'

[1]

This voyce both sharp *and* also   [p. [45]]
    [shyll]
Shal be herd from heuen to h[ell;]
All mydle erthe it shall fulfyll:
    'Uenite ad iudicium.'

[2]

'Uenite' is a blyssed song
For them that for joye dooth longe
And shall forsake paynes strong:
    'Uenite ad iudicium.'

[3]

Glad in hert may they be
Whan Chryst sayeth, 'Uenite;
Ye blyssed chyldren, come to me,
    Into vitam eternam.

[4]

'Whan I hongred, ye gaue me meat;
Ye clothed me agaynst the heat;
In trouble ye dyde me not forgeat;
    Uenite ad iudicium.

[5]

'Ye socoured me at your doore
And for my sake gaue to the poore;
[The]rfore wyll I you socoore;   [p. [46]]
    Uenite ad iudicium.'

[6]

Sory in hert may they be
That hereth this heuy worde: 'Ite;
Ye cursed chyldren, go fro me,
    Into ignem eternum.

[7]

'Whan for nede that I dyde crye,
Confortlesse ye lete me dye;
Therfore now I you deny;
    Uenite ad iudicium.

[8]

'For by me ye set no store,
Ye shall abye ryght dere therfore
In hell with deuyls for euermore;
    Uenite ad iudicium.'

The repetition of the burden is indicated after
each stanza by: A voyce. &c.
stza. 4, l. 1. ye] Orig. ne.   l. 2. heat] Orig.
    weat.
stza. 1, ll. 1, 2, stza. 5, l. 3. *The original is torn.*
At end: Finis.

365

British Museum. MS. Sloane 2593

XV cent.

f. 3ʳ

    God, that alle mytes may,
    Helpe vs at our ending day.

[1]

This word, lordin*gg*es, I vn*d*erstonde,
May be lyknyd to an husbonde
Th*a*t tak*i*t a ferme into his honde,
  To yelde th*er*of serteyn pay.

[2]

Spende we neyth*er* speche ne   [f. 3ᵛ
    spylle,
Neyth*er* for good ne for ille;
We xuln yeuy*n* acou*n*t*es* grylle
  Befor*n* o*u*r Lord on domysdaye.

[3]

Leue lordyng*es*, bewar of this,
For ofty*n*tyme we don amys;
Th*er* is no*n* of vs, iwys,
  But th*a*t we trespasyn eu*er*y day.

[4]

This word, lordyng*es*, is but a farye;
It faryt ryght as a neysche weye,
Th*a*t now is wet *and* now is dreye,
  Forsothe, sertey*n*, as I y*o*u say.

[5]

Now is joye, *and* now is blys;
Now is balle *and* bitt*er*nesse;
Now it is, *and* now it nys;
  Thus pasyt this word away.

[6]

Now I hope, *and* now I synge;
Now I dau*n*ce, now I sprynge;
Now weyle, *and* now I wrynge;
  Now is wel, *and* now is way.

[7]

Now I hoppe, *and* now I dau*n*ce;
Now I p*r*ike, *and* now I prau*n*ce;
This day heyl, te morwe, p*er*chau*n*ce,
  We mown be ded *and* ley[d] in clay.

[8]

At domisday, qu*an* we xul ryse
And come befor*n* o*u*r heye Justyse
And yeuy*n* acou*n*t*es* of o*u*r seruise
And payin vp o*u*r laste pay—

[9]

Help vs, Mary, for th*a*n*n* is nede,
Help to excusyn o*u*r misdede,
As th*o*u art monewer*e* at o*u*r nede;
  Help vs tha*n*, *and* sey not nay.

366

St. John's College, Cambridge. MS. S. 54
                                    XV *cent.*
f. 10ᵛ

  Nowell.

[1]

This word is falce, I dar*e* wyll say,
And man xalt fade as dose hay,
For as a flo*u*r it fallys away;
  Tu*n*c no*n* ualebit corp*or*e.

[2]

Tell me sothe qwoso ca*n*ne:
Qwan he hys dede, qwat has he wan?
Qw[e]*r*e se ye ony rych dede ma*n*?
  Reuela mi*hi* hodie.

[3]

Thou plesyst hy*m* both nyth *and* day
And knele to s*er*ue hy*m* wyll to pay;
He may not hy*m* a good word say
  Cu*m* op*er*itur pulu*er*e.

[4]

Hys secutour*es*, wit*h*oute lete,
Yow he wyth cuces ow*er*sette;
Thei sey he ouyt so mykyll dette
  No*n* postest solui integ*r*e.

[5]

Qwan he is closyd i*n* hys gr*a*ue,
Tha*n* is he th*er* he may not craue;
As he haue done, so xall he haue:
  Oblitus pr*a*ue temp*or*e.

[6]

And th*er*for, ma*n*, or th*o*u hens wende,
Dele thi good w*i*t*h* thi honde,
And thynke wyll dede ma*n* haue no fro*n*d;
  Tu miser*er*is a*n*ime.

[7]

Lord, yyf us gr*a*ce so to do here   [f. 11ʳ
Th*a*t, qwan we are br*o*th on ber*e*,
Th*er* take our*e* sole, th*a*t th*o*u both der*e*,
  Pende[n]s alto arbore.

[8]

And gyfe us gr*a*ce so to spende
The god th*a*t th*o*u onto us se*n*de
Th*a*t we may sey at our*e* last end,
  'Laus summo regule.'

stza. 1, l. 1, stza. 3, l. 3. word] MS. wrod.
stza. 4, l. 2. wyth] MS. myth.
stza. 6, l. 4. miser*er*is] MS. miseret*is*.
stza. 7, l. 2. are] MS. l are.
stza. 8, l. 2. The] MS. Th*o*u.   l. 3. our*e*] MS.
  youre.

367

British Museum. MS. Addit. 5665
XVI cent.

f. 49ᵛ

O blessed Lord, full of pete,
Mane nobiscum, Domine.
O blessed Lord, full of pyte. [f. 50ʳ
Mane nobiscum, Domine.

[1]

This worlde ys but a vanite, [f. 49ᵛ
Subtile and fals and no surte; [f. 50ʳ
Wherefor we pray, for charite,
'Mane nobiscum, Domine.'

[2]

Extorcion hathe putte adowne [f. 49ᵛ
Owte of oure syghth ryght and resone;
Wherefor we pray vnte Sone,
'Mane nobiscum, Domine.'

[3]

What shull we do a domysday?
Ther shall we crye 'A, wellaway!'
But Oure Lady helpe vs to say,
'Mane nobiscum, Domine.'

[4]

O Lord, that arte in Trinite,
In joye and blisse and vnite,
Helpe vs of this mortalite;
Mane nobiscum, Domine.

MS. heading: Ad placitum.
The second couplet of the burden is written after
the first stanza on f. 50ʳ.

368

British Museum. MS. Sloane 2593
XV cent.

f. 7ᵛ

I drukke, I dare, so wil I may,
Quan I thynke on myn endyng day.

[1]

I am a chyld and born ful bare
And bare out of this word xal fare;
Yyt am I but wermys ware,
Thow I clothid go neuer so gay.

[2]

Thow I be of meche prys,
Fayr of face and holdyn wys,
Myn fleych xal fadyn as flour- [f. 8ʳ
de-lys
Quan I am ded and leyd in clay.

[3]

Quan I am ded and leyd in ston,
I xal rotyn, fleych and bon;
Fro myn fryndys I xal gon;
Cryst help myn sowle quan I ne may.

[4]

Quan I xal al my frendes forsake,
Cryst schyld me fro the fendes blake;
To Jhesu Cryst my sowle I betake;
He be our help on domysday.

stza. 1, l. 4. clothid] MS. clothis.
stza. 4, l. 1. forsake] MS. for fake.

369

Bodleian Library. MS. Douce 302
By John Audelay, XV cent.

f. 30ᵛ

Lade, helpe! Jhesu, merce!
Timor mortis conturbat me.

[1]

Dred of deth, sorow of syn
Trobils my hert ful greuysly;
My soule hit nyth with my lust then;
Passio Christi conforta me.

[2]

Fore blyndnes is a heue thyng,
And to be def therwith only,
To lese my lyght and my heryng;
Passio Christi conforta me.

[3]

And to lese my tast and my smellyng,
And to be seke in my body;
Here haue I lost al my lykyng;
Passio Christi conforta me.

[4]

Thus God he yeues and takys away,
And, as he wil, so mot hit be;
His name be blessid both nyght and daye;
Passio Christi conforta me.

[5]

Here is a cause of gret mornyng:
Of myselfe nothyng I se
Saue filth, vnclennes, vile stynkyng;
Passio Christi conforta me.

[6]

Into this word no more I broght,
No more I gete with me trewly,
Saue good ded, word, wil, and thoght;
Passio Christi conforta me.

[7]

The v wondis of Jhesu Crist,
    My midsyne now mot thai be,
The fyndis pouere downe to cast;
    Passio Christi conforta me.   [f. 32ʳ

[8]

As I lay seke in my langure,
    With sorow of hert and teere of ye,
This caral I made with gret doloure;
    Passio Christi conforta me.

[9]

Oft with these prayere I me blest:
    'In manus tuas, Domine;
Thou take my soule into thi rest;
    Passio Christi conforta me.'

[10]

Mare moder, merceful may,
    Fore the joys thou hadist, Lady,
To thi Sun fore me thou pray;
    Passio Christi conforta me.

[11]

Lerne this lesson of blynd Awdlay:
    When bale is hyest, then bot may be;
Yif thou be nyd nyght or day,
    Say, 'Passio Christi conforta me.'

MS. heading: Timor mortis conturbat me
c[etera].

370

a. *Bodleian Library.* MS. Eng. poet. e. 1
                                        XV *cent.*
f. 38ᵛ

    In what estate so euer I be,
    Timor mortis conturbat me.

[1]

As I went in a mery mornyng,
I hard a byrd bothe wep and syng;
Thys was the tenowr of her talkyng:
'Timor [mortis conturbat me.']

[2]

I asked that byrd what sche ment.
'I am a musket bothe fayer and gent;
For dred of deth I am al schent;
Timor [mortis conturbat me.]

[3]

'Whan I schal dey, I know no day;
What countre or place I cannot sey;
Wherfor this song syng I may:
"Timor [mortis conturbat me."]

[4]

'Jhesu Cryst, whane he schuld dey,
To hys Fader he gan sey;
"Fader," he seyd, "in Trinyte,
Timor [mortis conturbat me."]

[5]

'Al Crysten pepull, behold and se: [f. 39ʳ
This world is but a vanyte
And replet with necessyte;
Timor [mortis conturbat me.]

[6]

'Wak I or sclep, ete or drynke,
Whan I on my last end do thynk,
For grete fer my sowle do shrynke;
Timor [mortis conturbat me.']

[7]

God graunte vs grace hym for to serue,
And be at owr end whan we sterue,
And frome the fynd he vs preserue;
Timor [mortis conturbat me.]

stzas. 1–7, l. 4. MS. timor &c.

b. *Balliol College, Oxford.* MS. 354. f. 176ᵛ.
XVI *cent.* (burden and stzas. 1, 2, 4, 3).

c. *Huntington Library. Christmas carolles
newely Inprynted* (Richard Kele), p. [41].
c. 1550 (stza. 1, ll. 3, 4; stzas. 2–6).

burden, l. 1. estate so] b state that.
stza. 1, l. 1. went] b me walked.   a mery] b on.
stza. 2, l. 1. that] b this.   sche] b he.   l. 2. I]
    b he said I.   bothe] b c *omit.* fayer and]
    b *omits.*   l. 3. dred] c fere.   al] b nygh.
stza. 3, l. 1. I know] b know I.   ll. 2, 3.
    b *transposes.*   l. 2. What] b In what. c *omits.*
    countre . . . place] b *transposes.*   or] c nor.
    I cannot] b can I not.   l. 3. Wherfor]
    b Therfore.
stza. 4, l. 2. he gan] b lowd gan he. c gan he.
    sey] b c crye.
stza. 5, l. 3. And replet with] c For therin is but.
stza. 6, l. 1. I] c *omits.*   l. 3. do shrynke]
    c doth synke.
At end: b Explicit. c Finis.

371

Bodleian Library. MS. Eng. poet. e. 1
                                        XV *cent.*
f. 48ʳ

    Everemore, wheresoeuer I be,
    The dred off deth do troble me.

[1]

As I went me fore to solasse,
I hard a mane syght *and* sey, 'Alasse!
Off me now thus stond the casse:
  The dred off [deth do troble me.]

[2]

'I haue be lorde off towr *and* towne;
I sett not be my grett renowne,
For deth wyll pluck yt all downe;
  The dred off deth do tr*o*byll me.

[3]

'Whan I shal deye I ame not   [f. 48ᵛ
    suere,
In what cou*n*tre or *in* what howere;
Wherefore I sobbyng sey, to my power,
  "The dred off deth do troble me."

[4]

'Whan my sowle *and* my body dep*er*tyd
    shall be,
Off my jugme*n*t no man cane tell me,
Nor off my place wher th*a*t I shal be;
  Th*er*fore dred off deth do tr*o*ble me.

[5]

'Jh*e*su Cryst, whan th*a*t he shuld sofer hys
    passyon,
To hys Fader he seyd w*ith* gret deuocyon,
"Thys is the causse off my *in*tercessyon:
  The dred off deth do tr*o*ble me."

[6]

'Al Crysten pepul, be ye wysse *and* ware;
Thys world is butt a chery-fare,
Replett w*ith* sorow *and* fulfyllyd w*ith* car;
  Th*er*fore the dred off deth do tr*o*ble me.

[7]

'Wheth*er* th*a*t I be mery or good wyne
    drynk,
Whan th*a*t I do on my last daye thynk,
It mak my sowle *and* body to schrynke,
  Fore the dred off deth sore tr*o*ble me.'

[8]

Jh*e*su vs graunt hyme so to hon-   [f. 49ʳ
    owr
Thatt at owr end he may be owr socowr
And kepe vs fro the fend*es* powr,
  For than dred off deth shal not tr*o*ble
  me.

stza. 1, l. 4. MS. The dred off &c.
stza. 2, l. 3. pluck yt] MS. pluckyd.

372

Balliol College, Oxford. MS. 354
                                    XVI *cent.*
f. 229ʳ

  Alas, my hart will brek in thre;
  Terribilis mors co*n*turbat me.

[1]

Illa iuvent*us* that is so nyse
Me deduxit into vayn devise;
Infirm*us* su*m*; I may not rise;
  Terribilis mors co*n*turbat me.

[2]

Du*m* iuven*is* fui, lytill I dred,
Set se*m*per *in* sinne I ete my bred;
Iam duct*us* su*m* into my bed;
  Terribilis mors [conturbat me.]

[3]

Corpus migrat; *in* my sowle
Respicit demon, *in* his rowle;
Desiderat ip*se* to haue his tolle;
  Terribilis mors [conturbat me.]

[4]

*Christu*s se ip*su*m, whan he shuld dye,
Patri suo his ma*n*hode did crye,
'Respice me, P*ater*, that is so hye;
  Terribilis mors [conturbat me.']

[5]

Queso iam the Trynyte,
'Duc me fro*m* this vanyte
In celu*m*, ther is joy w*ith* the;
  Terribilis mors co*n*turbat me.'

MS. marks burden: fote.
stza. 1, l. 1. iuvent*us*] MS. iuvent*is*.
stza. 2, l. 1. iuven*is*] MS. iuvin*us*.   1. 2. sinne]
    MS. sinni.
At end: Explicit.

373

Balliol College, Oxford. MS. 354
                                    XVI *cent.*
f. 210ʳ

  To dy, to dy? What haue I
  Offendit, th*a*t deth is so hasty?

[1]

O marcyfull God, maker of all mankynd,
What menyth dethe in his mynd,
  And I so yonge of age?
Now deth is vnkynd,
For he seyth, 'Ma*n*, stop thy wynde':
  Th*us* he doth rage.

374

Balliol College, Oxford. MS. 354
XVI *cent.*
f. 210ʳ

So dye shall the*n*
All Cristyn men;
No ma*n* wottith his tyme ne when;
Wherfor thow may,
Yf th*o*u be hye,
Thynk no*n* oth*er* but th*o*u shalt dye.

[1]

In twenti yere of age, reme*m*bre we
eu*er*ychon
Th*a*t deth will not be strange to taste vs
by on *and* on;
W*i*th siknes grevows, which makith ma*n* to
grone,
Deth biddith, 'Beware: this day a ma*n*,
tomorrow non.'

[2]

In xl yere of age, wha*n* ma*n* is stowt *and*
stronge,
Trow ye th*a*t deth dare stryk hy*m* or do
hy*m* any wrong?
Yes, forsoth, w*i*th worldly deth he vill not
spar*e* among
And seyth, 'Ma*n*, beware; th*o*u shalt not
tary long.'

[3]

I[n] lx yere of age, the*n* tyme is cu*m* to
thynk
How he wil cu*m* to thi hows *and* sit on
the bynke,
Co*m*aundyng ma*n* to stowpe toward the
pitt*es* brynk;
Tha*n* farewell, world*es* joy, wha*n* deth shall
bid a ma*n* drynk.

[4]

The last age of ma*n*kynd is called de-
crepit*us*;
Wha*n* ma*n* lakkith reason, tha*n* deth
biddith hy*m* thus:
Owt of this world his lyf to pas w*i*th
mercy of Jhe*s*us;
Deth strykith w*i*th sword *and* seyth, 'Ma*n*,
it shal be thus.'

The repetition of the burden is indicated in the
margin at the left of each stanza by: ☩ so dy.
stza. 1, l. 1. twenti] MS. xxᵗⁱ.
At end: Explicit.

375

British Museum. MS. Addit. 5665
XVI *cent.*
f. 45ᵛ

The beste song, as hit semeth me:
'Peccantem me cotidie.'
The beste song, as semeth me:
'Peccante[m] me cotidie.'   [f. 46ʳ]

[1]

While Y was yong *and* hadde carage,
I wolde play w*i*th grome *and* page,
But, now Y am falle into age,
Timor mortis conturbat me.

[2]

Yowthe ys now fro me agon,   [f. 45ᵛ]
And age ys come me vpon;
Now shall Y say *and* pray anon:
'Parce michi, Domine.'

[3]

I pray God, Y can no more:
'Th*o*u boghfteste me w*i*th wond*es* sore;
To thy m*er*cy thow me restore;
Salu*u*m me fac, Domine.'

MS. heading: ad placitum.

376

*Huntington Library. Christmas carolles
newely Inprynted* (Richard Kele)
c. 1550
p. [7]

Be thou poore, or be thou ryche,
I rede, lyfte vp thyn eye,
And se in this we be all lyche:
Forsothe, all we shall dye.   [p. [8]]

[1]

Dethe began bycause of syn;
We syn bothe poore and ryche;
Therfore dethe wyll neuer blyn
To take vs all in lyche.
For our syn I rede we seche,
To heuen that we may hye,
For, be we neuer so fresh nor ryche,
Forsothe, we all shall dye.

[2]

Christ, that was bothe God and man,
He dyed for our gylt;
Nedes must we dye than,
With syn yf we be spylt.

We shall rote, bothe hert and mylt;
  'Mercy, Lorde!' we crye,
'It shal be, Lorde, ryght as thou wylt';
  Forsothe, all we shall dye.

[3]

How Chryst dyed for all our mys,
  I red, haue in thy thought;
To set thy mynde on wordly blys,
  For sothe, I holde it nought.
  For worldes blys Chryst he ne   [p. [9]
    rought;
  I rede the, it defy;
  Unto thy graue thou shalt be brought;
  Forsothe, we shall all dye.

[4]

If thou be pore, kepe the clene,
  And thank God of his sonde;
If thou be ryche, gyue and lende,
  Bothe to poore and bonde.
  Loke thou do thus with thy honde;
    Through Chryst to heuen thou shalt
    hye;
  Thou cannot long lyue in this londe;
  Forsothe, all we shall dye.

[5]

Though thou be ryche, I tell the before,
  Death wyll with the mete;
Of all thy goodes thou getest no more
  But a wyndyng shete.
  Therfore thy bales here thou bete;
    To God for mercy crye;
  Wepe for synnes with teares wete;
  Forsothe, all we shall dye.

[6]

Thou shalt dy thou wote note   [p. [10]
    whan,
  Nor thou wotest where;
To repent the tyme is now;
  This lesson I red the lere.
  How soone thou shalt be brought on
    bere
    It is not for the to try:
  Lete this lesson sound in thyn eare:
  Forsothe all we shall dye.

[7]

All we shall dye, and ryse agayne
  In one affynyte;
If we euyll dye, we go to payne;
  This is the veryte.
  If that we ryse in charyte,
    To blys than shall we stye;
  This is Gods equyte:
  Forsothe all we shall dye.

The repetition of the burden is indicated after
  each stanza by: Be thou poore. &c.
stza. 2, l. 7. as] Orig. us.
At end: Finis.

377

Trinity College, Cambridge. MS. R. 14. 26
                         XV *cent.*
f. 21ʳ

  Thynk we on *our* endy*ng*, I red,
    I red, I red;
  Thy*nk* we on *our* endy*ng*, I red, or we
    [gon.]

[1]

How schvld I bot I thogth on myn endy*ng*
    day?
For, qwhen th*at* I am ded *and* closyd i*n*
    clay,
Fre*n*dys I fynd bot a few, a few, be *my*
    fay,
Th*at* o*n*s on my lyf a god word wyll me
    saye.
  To K*ri*st I mak my mone;
  To K*ri*st [I mak my mone.]

[2]

Qwhyls I a*m* on lyf, fre*n*dys I fynd inowe
For to tak all my god *and* get th*at* thei
    mowe;
Thei t*ur*ne th*er* bak*es* opon me *and* mak
    me a mowe;
Thei dryf me to hethy*ng and* cal me Syr
    Hew.
  Swylk fre*n*dys kyp I [no*n*;]
  Swylk fre*n*dys kyp I no*n*.

[3]

Fre*n*d*es* I fynd inow th*at* stelys all bede*n*e;
Qwhoso wyll asay, su*m* schall be sene;
All *our* old eld this end i*n* tray *and* i*n* tene,
And all th*at* e*n*s swylk . . .
  Eu*er* be on *and* on;
  Eu*er* be on *and* on.

[4]

Of th*at* god th*at* God has se*n*d, th*er*of has
    thou no my*n*d;
Do su*m* god qwhyls· thou may, *and* th*at*
    schall tow fynd,
For, bot if th*ou* do, men th*at* ar vnkynd,
Thi sekt*ur*s wyll cu*m* aft*ur and* tak th*at*
    thei may fynd.
    Th*us* do thei ilkon;
    [Thus do thei ilkon.]

[5]

Bot a frend I fy*n*d th*a*t is tr*eue and* tr*e*st,
Mary, Godys mod*er*, as haue I god r*e*st;
Of all fr*e*nde*s* th*a*t I fy*n*d, hyr loue I best,
For warne sche war . . .
    Swyk on fynd I no*n*;
    [Swylk on fynd I non.]

The repetition of the burden is indicated as
follows: stza. 1: thy*n*k we on *our* endy*n*g I
red or we g. . . . stza. 2: Thy*n*k we o*n our*
endy*n*g &c. stza. 3: Thy*n*k we &c. stza. 4:
thyk we &c. stza. 5: Thy*n*k we &c.
stza. 1, l. 6. MS. to k*r*ist &c.

378

National Library of Scotland. MS. Advocates 19. 3. 1   XV *cent.*
f. 95ᵛ

    Man, in thi mynd loke thys be best:
    Quod omn*i*s caro fenum est.

[1]

As I me rode in a Mey morny*n*g,
    I loked abowte bothe est *and* west,
And at the last I hard a turtyll syng,
    'Q*uod* omn*i*s caro fenu*m* est.

[2]

'For sorwe,' sche says, 'I begynne to yell';
    Sche rentt of hur fedurs *and* bared hur
        brest;
Th*a*t caused hyr care I saw full wele:
    Quod omn*i*s [caro fenum est.]

[3]

'Sum tyme,' sche sayd, 'grettyst I was;
    In pryd *and* pofete now am I cast;
My bute ys fall me frome, alas!
    Quod o[mn]is caro [fenum est.]

[4]

'Sum tyme I went in purpull pall;   [f. 96ʳ
    In soro *and* care now ys my nest;
My fedurs so fast now fro me fall,
    Quod omn*i*s ca[ro fenum est.']

[5]

Thus I beheld thys t*u*rtull trew;
    For pete my hartt in sund*ur* brast,
For why this song to me was now:
    'Q*uod* o[mn]is caro fenu*m* est.'

[6]

To comford this byrd me thowth full long;
    Thoro byrkys *and* breris to hur I prest;

Wen sche me say sche told me this sung:
    'Q*uod* o[mn]is [caro fenum est.']

[7]

I askyd hyr whatt she had
    Th*a*t off hyr soro ryght noght sche sest;
To harken this the*n* sche me bad:
    'Q*uod* omn*i*s [caro fenum est.]

[8]

'Both pope, empror, card[in]all, kyng,
    Man *and* woman, byrd *and* best,
Thus sorofull thei scholl ones syng:
    "Q*uod* omn*i*s [caro fenum est."]

[9]

'As hey thei schall fayd *and* well away,
    And deth schall take yow to is nest;
Wherfor be resu*n* well prowue I may
    Q*uod* omn*i*s caro [fenum est.']

[10]

And thus this byrd partyd me fro
    And flew awey wher sche lykyd best,
Cryyng *and* syngyng w*i*th mekyll who,
    'Q*uod* omn*i*s [caro fenum est.']

[11]

Then I me awysyd *and* me bethowght
    In C*r*ist allwhey to tak my rest,
For all this whord aweylys noght,
    Quod omn*i*s caro [fenum est.]

burden, l. 1. mynd] MS. myad. loke] MS.
loket. l. 2. caro] MS. ca*n*en.
stzas. 1, 3, l. 4. caro] MS. carnm.
stza. 4, l. 3. so] MS. so so.
stza. 5, l. 4. caro] MS. carn*m*.
stza. 9, l. 1. fayd] MS. fa fayd.
stza. 10, ll. 1–3. *struck through in MS.*
stza. 11, l. 3. aweylys] MS. aaweylys.
    l. 4. caro] MS. carys.
At end: Explycit q*uod* John hawghton.

379

Trinity College, Cambridge. MS. O. 2. 53
                       XV *cent.*
f. 57ʳ

    When all ys don and all ys sayd,
    God must be known, seruyd, *and* obeid.

[1]

Yougth, luste, reches, or manhod—
Trustyth in any of thes, God forbed!
Though God sufferth, beware the rodde;
Who whyl be sure must ned*es* s*er*ue God.

[2]

For any sporte or price of appetyd
Furst serue God, then do whe ryght;
Let yougth folow yougth not worth a myte
.   .   .   .

[3]

In olld storys I haue herd tell
In excelent wytte he doth excell
That desyryth and inclynyth to sad coun-
    sell,
And whos that whyll not cannot doo well.

[4]

God many ways geuyth gyftes of grace;
Sum moo then sum manyfold hase.
Serue hym and thank hym wyll we haue
    space;
Yf whe doo not, he whyll torn hys face.

[5]

Remembre yourself, and be sure   [f. 57ᵛ
    of thys:
Whoo seruyth whell God cannot doo amys.
We cannot doo so mych as our deuty ys;
Then doo our best or we must, iwys.

[6]

Sythen thys ferre forthe, I wyl be playn:
God commaundyth that men certayn
Hys body and goodes shul not wast in vayn;
Mayhappe they lese most that hase most
    gayn.

[7]

What shal becume of thes perjuryd men
Whych whyll not spek for fere of when?
Without ye mend, full whell ye ken,
The deuyll in hell whyll mak your den.

[8]

A gentyll horse with a softe bytte
Woll torne on the ryght hond of hys owne
    wytt.
Yf they that shold doo woll not prove yt,
In them defaulte, in hym no wytt.

[9]

When God shuld be seruyd, some   [f. 58ʳ
    be att lawe;
Ytt prouyth ther aste nat worth a strawe:
Couetyse so swetly there bakes dothe clawe
That extorcyon whas neuer lesse awe.

[10]

Matere of a alpeny we be euer prollyng,
And euer we spek of pety pollyng;
The pore knaves haue mych enrollyng,
But the cobbes haue neuer comptrollyng.

[11]

Ther nedys to be no chyrche nowadays:
Euery cornyr ys a chyrche where carderes
    plays;
Hard att there elbowe the prestes euynsong
    says:
God is not content, seurly, with thes ways.

[12]

Thys makere as thys hymself doth clere:
Some he dothe se, and som he dothe here;
Ye se but few pore pepull appere;
Maters of a moneth is not sped in a yere.

The repetition of the burden is indicated as
    follows: stzas. 1, 2, 5, 6, 11: when all ys don.
    stzas. 3, 4, 7–10, 12: when all ys doon.
stza. 1, l. 2. God] MS. godes.
stza. 9, l. 1. God] MS. good.

380

a. *Trinity College, Cambridge.* MS. O.
7. 31   XV *cent.*
f. 202ᵛ

Be mery all with one accorde,
And be ye folowers of Crystes worde.

[1]

Then all your doyngs schold here in earthe
Present the facte of Crystis bearth:
His loging was simple; his liuing was
    beare;
His death was biter; we were hys care.

[2]

I wold our life now coulde be syche:
He was full poure, to make vs ryche,
Meke and lowly in all mens sight;
It was the candell which gaue vs lyght.

[3]

Bost not yourselfe ne your actes awans,
But one lament another chaunce,
For we be far from this degre,
For how we liue all men may see.

[4]

He shall his tounge from slander refrayne
Which will be pride no man disdayne;
So of all thinges I thinke it best
To liue and loue and be at rest.

[5]

All faire talke is not worth a strawe   [f. 203ʳ
Were love is not which fulfilith the laue;
Werefore in mittinge wher ye resorte
Belli no man with false reporte.

[6]

Care not to myche for worly pleasure,
Lest hereafter ye lose a better tresure,
For sorowe increseth, and enui is bold
When chereti is skantye and waxethe
     colde.

(Closing burden)

   Therfore be mery with one accorde,
   And be ye dores of Chrystes worde.

The repetition of the burden is indicated after
   stzas. 1–5 by: Be mery all.
burden, l. 2. folowers] MS. fouolors.
stza. 3, l. 3. far] MS. for.

b. *Trinity College, Cambridge.* MS. O. 7.
31, ff. 203ᵛ, 204ʳ. XV *cent.* (burden and
stzas. 1–3 and beginning of 4).

stza. 1, l. 1. doyngs] doyng.   l. 3. was (2)]
omits.
stza. 3, l. 1. awans] so vaunce.   l. 2. another]
anothers.   l. 3. far] farre farre.
stza. 4: he shall hys.
The repetition of the burden is indicated after
   each stanza by: be mery all. The closing
   burden is omitted.

381

British Museum. MS. Sloane 2593
                            XV *cent.*
f. 8ʳ

   Bewar, sqwyer, yeman, *and* page,
   For seruyse is non erytage.

[1]

If thou serue a lord of prys,   [f. 8ᵛ
Be not to boystous in thin seruys;
Damne not thin sowle in non wys,
   For seruyse is non erytage.

[2]

Wynteris wether *and* wommanys thowt
And lordis loue schaungit oft;
This is the sothe, if it be sowt,
   For seruyse [is non erytage.]

[3]

Now thou art gret; tomorwe xal I,
As lordys schaungyn here baly;
In thin welthe werk sekyrly,
   For [seruyse is non erytage.]

[4]

Than serue we God in alle wyse;
He xal vs quityn our servyse
And yeuyn vs yyftes most of pryse,
   Heuene to be our erytage.

stza. 2, l. 4. MS. for seruyse &c.
stza. 3, l. 4. MS. for &c.

382

Bodleian Library. MS. Eng. poet. e. 1
                            XV *cent.*
f. 13ʳ

   Haue in mynd, in mynd, in mynd,
   Secuters be oft onekynd.

[1]

Man, bewar, the way ys sleder;
Thy sowle sall go thou wottes not weder,
Body *and* sowle *and* al togeder;
   Lytyll joye ys son done.

[2]

Haue thi sowle in thi mynd;
The secators be ryght onkynd;
Mane, be thi own freynd;
   Lytyll joye ys son done.

[3]

In holy bok yt ys wreten
That sely sovle ys son forgeten,
And trev yt ys for to seken;
   [Lytyll joye ys son done.]

[4]

Her ys a song for me;
Syng another for the;
God send vs love *and* charite;
   [Lytyll joye ys son done.]

stzas. 3, 4, l. 4. MS. vt supra.

383

British Museum. MS. Sloane 2593
                                    XV *cent.*
f. 5ᵛ

  Now go gyle, gyle, gyle,
    Now go gile, gyle, go.

[1]

Gyle *and* gold togedere arn met;
Couetyse be hy*m* is set;
Now haght gyle leyd his net
  To gyle bothe frynd *and* fo.

[2]

The*r* is non man worght a schelle
But he cu*n* plete wi*th* wryt or bylle,
His neybow*r*es for to spylle
  And othe*r*e me*n* to werky*n* wo.

[3]

Coweytise in herte is lent;   [f. 6ʳ
Ryght *and* resou*n* awey is went;
Ma*n*, bewar th*o*u be not schent;
  Gyle wil thi herte slo.

[4]

Now haght gyle get hy*m* gre,
Bothe in town *and* in cete;
Gyle goth wi*th* gret mene,
  Wi*th* me*n* of lawe *and* othe*r*e mo.

[5]

Trewthe, heuene mot he wynne;
Gyle xal in helle brenne;
He th*a*t made al ma*n*kynde
  Amend he*m* th*a*t mys han do.

384

British Museum. MS. Sloane 2593
                                    XV *cent.*
f. 29ᵛ

  I may seyn, *and* so mown mo,
    Th*a*t in semenau*n*t goth gyle.

[1]

Semenau*n*t is a wond*er* thing:
It begylyt bothe knyght *and* kyng
And maki*t* maydenys of loue-longy*n*g;
  I warne y*o*u of th*a*t gyle.

[2]

Semeanau*n*t is a sly peynto*ur*;
It florchyt *and* fad*it* in many a flour
And maki*t* wo*m*men to lesy*n* he*r*e bryte
    colo*ur*
  Vpo*n* a lytil qwyle.

[3]

In semenau*n*t be thing*es* thre: [f. 30ʳ
Thowt, speche, *and* p*r*euyte,
And trewthe xuld the forte be;
  It is hens a thousand myle.

[4]

Trewthe is fer *and* sem*it* hynde;
Good *and* wykkyt it haght in mynde;
It faryt as a candel*e*-ende
  Th*a*t brenn*it* fro half a myle.

[5]

Many ma*n*, fayr*e* to me he spekyt,
And he wyste hy*m* wel bewreke;
He hadde we[l] leu*er*e my*n* hed to-breke
  Th*a*n*n* help me ou*er* a style.

[6]

God, th*a*t deyid vpo*n* the cros
(Ferst he deyid, *and* sythin he ros),
Haue m*er*cy *and* pete on vs:
  We leuy*n* he*r*e but a qwyle.

stza. 3, l. 4. thousand] MS. mˡ.

385

British Museum. MS. Sloane 2593
                                    XV *cent.*
f. 7ʳ

  God be wi*th* trewthe qw*er* he be;
  I wolde he wer*e* in th*is* cu*n*tre.

[1]

A ma*n* th*a*t xuld of trewthe telle,   [f. 7ᵛ
Wi*th* grete lordys he may not dwelle;
I[n] trewe story, as klerk*es* telle,
  Trewthe is put in low degr*e*.

[2]

In laydyis chau*m*ber*es* com*it* he not;
The*r* dar trewthe setty*n* no*n* fot;
Thow he wolde he may not
  Comy*n* among the heye mene.

[3]

With men of lawe he haght non spas;
They louyn trewthe in non plas;
Me thinkit they han a rewly grace
    That tre[w]the is put at swych degre.

[4]

In Holy Cherche he may not sytte;
Fro man to man they xuln hym flytte;
It rewit me sore in myn wytte;
    Of tre[w]the I haue gret pete.

[5]

Relygius, that xulde be good,
If trewthe cum ther, I holde hym wood;
They xuldyn hym rynde cote and hood
    And make hym bare for to fle.

[6]

A man that xulde of trewthe aspye,
He must sekyn esylye
In the bosum of Marye,
    For there he is forsothe.

stza. 5, l. 1. Relygius] MS. Relygiuus.

386

a. *Bodleian Library.* MS. Eng. poet. e. 1
                                        XV *cent.*
f. 60ᵛ

    God, that sytteth in Trinite,
    Amend this world, if thi will it be.

[1]

Vycyce be wyld and vertues lame,
And now be vicyce turned to game,
Therfore correccion is to blame
    And besyd his dignitie.

[2]

Pacyence hath taken a flyght,
And melady is out off syght;
Now euery boy will counterfett a knyght,
    Report hymself as good as he.

[3]

Princypally among euery state
In court men thynk ther is gret bate,
And peace he stondyth at the gate
    And morneth afture charite.

[4]

Envy is thyk and love thyne,
And specyally among owre kyne,
Fore love is without the dore and envy
    within,
And so kyndnesse away gane fle.

[5]

Fortewn is a mervelous chaunce,   [f. 61ʳ
And envy causyth gret distaunce
Both in Englond and in Fraunce;
    Exilyd is benyngnyte.

[6]

Now lett vs pray, both on and all,
And specyally vpon God call
To send love and peace among vs all,
    Among all men in Christente.

b. *Balliol College, Oxford.* MS. 354, f.
    227ʳ. XVI *cent.*

MS. marks burden: fote.   l. 2. it] *omits*
stza. 1, l. 2. now be vicyce] is is vice.   to] into.
    l. 4. And besyd] That so lesith.
stza. 2, l. 1. taken] tak.
stza. 3, l. 2. ther is] *omits.*   bate] debate.
    l. 3. *And*] For.   he] *omits.*
stza. 4, l. 1. thyne] ys thyn.   l. 2. kyne] eme
    Cristyn.   l. 3. the dore] *omits.*   within] ys
    within.
stza. 6, l. 3. peace] grace.   l. 4. Among] and
    amonge.
At end: Explicit.
The repetition of the burden is indicated as
follows: stza. 1: god that sittith in trinite &c.
stzas. 2–4: god that.   stzas. 5, 6: god that
sittith.

387

British Museum. MS. Addit. 5665
                                        XVI *cent.*
f. 50ᵛ

    The beste rede that I can:
    Do well, and drede no man.
    The best rede that Y can:
    Do well, and *drede no man.   [*f. 51ʳ

[1]

God sende vs pese and vnite
In Engelond, with prosperite,
And geffe vs grace to ouercome
All oure enemys and putte adowne,
    That we mow syng, as Y sayde than,
    'Do well, and d[r]ed no [man.']

[2]

Now pride *and* couetise allso, [f. 50ᵛ]
Adowne ye most, *and* many mo;
Adowne, bolsteris *and* peked shon,
For hit is derision.
    Therfor Y say as Y can,
    'Do well, *and* drede no man.'

[3]

Alas, this worlde kepith no se*r*tayne
Thorwfe fals lyuyng *and* mo*r*e no refrayne;
H*i*t is in wayne th*a*t Y complayne
Butte th*a*t oure Lorde *and* Souerayne
    Graunte v*s* grace th*a*t we mow say than,
    'Do well, *and* drede no man.'

[4]

Now to the, Lady, we do crye, [f. 51ʳ]
W*ith* thy swete Sone gra*n*de v*s* mercye,
And geffe v*s* p*er*fecte charite,
Grace, *and* loue w*ith* humilite,
    That we mow say, as Y began,
    'Do well, *and* drede no man.'

MS. heading: ad placitum.
burden, l. 4. man] MS. mam.
stza. 1, l. 6. [man]] MS. vt sup*r*a.
stza. 3, l. 5, stza. 4, ll. 2, 3. v*s*] MS. v*us*.

388

Bodleian Library. MS. Eng. poet. e. 1
                                    XV *cent.*

f. 16ᵛ

    In a blyssefull tyme th*a*t mane ys borne
    That may fynd frend to trust vpon.

[1]

Eu*er*y mane in hys degre [f. 17ʳ]
Cane say, yf he avysyd be,
Th*er* was more trust i*n* su*m* thre
    Than ys now in many [on.]

[2]

This warld ys now all changed new:
So many mene ben fou*n*d ontrew
Th*a*t in treuth lyven but few
    Feythfull to tryst vpon.

[3]

Su*m*ty*m* a ma*n* myght tryst anoth*er*
Better than now hys owne broder,
For thei ben fekyll as well as oth*er*,
    For few be trew to tryst vpon.

[4]

And if th*o*u tell a ma*n* thi hart,
To kepe it clos, as ys hys part,
vii yere aft*ur* it may the smart,
    For few be trew to tryst vpon.

[5]

A mans feyth ys now sett at novght;
Su*m*ty*m* th*er*by men sold *and* bovght;
Th*er*for I say thus in my thovght:
    Th*a*t few be trew to tryst vpon.

[6]

Yf th*o*u do be my cou*n*sayll,
Thynke well on the aft*ur*-tayll;
I warent the it wyll the avayll,
    For few be trew to tryst vpon.

[7]

So many men haue bene begylyd,
The fader ma[y] not tryst hys ovne chy[l]d;
I a*m* aferd trost ys exylyd,
    For few be trew to tryst vpon.

[8]

Yf th*o*u doo for a comonte [f. 17ᵛ]
All th*a*t now lyyth in the,
Skarsly shalt th*o*u thankyd be,
    For few be trew to tryst vpon.

[9]

Now no ma*n* kan know hys frend,
For doubelnese is so mekyll i*n* mynd;
Thus, in fayth, at the last yend,
    Few be trew to tryst vpon.

[10]

Whatsoeuer th*o*u thynk to do,
Beware to whom th*o*u speke*s* vnto,
For, I trow, whan al is do,
    Few be trew to tryst vpon.

[11]

Now, Jh*e*su, th*a*t art Heyvyn Kyng,
Thowrow thi moders prayyng
Thou send vs all a good endyng,
    For th*o*u art trew to tryst vpon.

389

a. *Bodleian Library.* MS. Eng. poet. e. 1
                                    XV *cent.*

f. 23ᵛ

    Man, be ware *and* wyse i*n*dede,
    And asay thi frend or th*o*u hast nede.

[1]

Vnder a forest that was so long
    As I me rod with mekyll dred,
I hard a berd syngyng a song:
    'Asay thi frend or thou hast ned.'

[2]

I therat stod and houed styll,
    And to a tre I teyd my sted,
And euer the byrd sang ful shyll,
    'Asay thi frend or thou hast ned.'

[3]

Me thovght it was a wonder noyse; [f. 24ʳ
    Alwey ner and ner I yed,
And euer she song with lovd voys,
    'Asay thi frynd or thou haue ned.'

[4]

I behyld that byrd full long;
    She bad me do as I the rede:
'Whether that thou do ryght or wrong,
    Asay thi frynd or thou haue ned.'

[5]

The byrd sat vpon a tre;
    With fethers gray than was hyr wed;
She seyd, 'And thou wylt do aftur me,
    Asay thi frend or thou haue ned.'

[6]

Of me I trow she was agast;
    She tok hyr flyghth in lengith and bred,
And thus she sang when she shan[g] last:
    'Asay thi frend or thou haue ned.'

[7]

Away full fast she gan hyr hyghe;
    God graunt vs well owr lyves to led,
For thus she sang w[he]n she gan flyghe:
    'Asay thi frynd or thou haue ned.'

stza. 1, l. 4. or] MS. or or.
stza. 5, l. 2. hyr] MS. hys.
stza. 6, l. 3. shan[g]] *The end of the word is damaged in MS.*
stza. 7, l. 3. w[he]n] *MS. rubbed.*

b. *Balliol College, Oxford.* MS. 354, f. 231ʳ ᵃⁿᵈ ᵛ. XVI *cent.* (burden and stzas. 1–3, 5, 4, 6).

burden, l. 2. thi] a.   hast] haue.
stza. 1, l. 1. Vnder] Thorow.   l. 2. me] *omits.*
    l. 4. thi] a   hast] haue.
stza. 2, l. 1. I therat] As I.   l. 3. And] *omits.*
    sang ful shyll] sat syngyng still.   l. 4. thi]
    a.   hast] haue.
stza. 3, l. 2. Alwey ner and ner.] *And* nere hond

the byrde.   l. 3. *And euer*] I wis.   lovd]
    a lowde.   l. 4. thi] a.
stza. 4, l. 1. that byrd full] her wonder.
    l. 2. She said do as I bide the in dede.
    l. 3. that] *omits.*   or] *and.*   l. 4. thi] a.
stza. 5, l. 1. vpon] high vpon.   l. 2. With] of.
    hys] her.   l. 3. *And* thou wylt do aftur
    me] do a[s] I bide the.   l. 4. thi] a.
stza. 6, l. 1. Of me I trow] I trow of me.
    l. 2. in lenghth and bred] away she yede.
    l. 3. And] *omits.*   sang] said.   l. 4. thi] a.
At end: Explicit.

390

British Museum. MS. Sloane 2593
                                    XV *cent.*
f. 6ʳ

Syng we alle, and sey we thus:
    'Gramersy myn owyn purs.'

[1]

Quan I haue in myn purs inow,
I may haue bothe hors and plow,
And also fryndis inow,
    Throw the vertu of myn purs.

[2]

Quan my purs gynnyght to slak,
And ther is nowt in my pak,
They wil seyn, 'Go, farwil, Jak;
    Thou xalt non more drynke with vs.'

[3]

Thus is al myn good ilorn
And myn purs al to-torn;
I may pley me with an horn
    In the stede al of myn purs.

[4]

Farwil, hors, and farwil, cow;
Farwil, carte, and farwil, plow;
As I pleyid me with a bow,
    I seyd, 'God! Quat is al this?'

391

St. John's College, Cambridge. MS. S. 54
                                    XV *cent.*
f. 3ᵛ

I may syng and sey, iwys,
    'Gremercy my owne [purse.']

[1]

In euery plas qwere that I wende
My purse is my owne frende;
Therfor gladly may I syng,
    'Gremercy my own purse.'

[2]

Qweresoeuer I goo in lond
My purse is redy at my hond;
Therfor this is a redy song:
 ['Gremercy my own purse.']

[3]

Qwereso I walke be the way
My purse xall help me allvay;
Therfor may I syng and say,
 ['Gremercy my own purse.']

[4]

If I be out in the cuntre,
And my purse be far fro me,
Than most I on beggyng fle,
 And far xall go and letyll xall haue.

[5]

And ye woll with fellechyp won,
Tay youre purse in yore bosom;
Than may I well my song vowyn:
 ['Gremercy my own purse.']

stzas. 2, 3, l. 4. MS. vt supra.

392

British Museum. MS. Sloane 2593
                                   XV *cent.*
f. 26ᵛ

 Go bet, Peny, go bet, go,
 For thou mat makyn bothe frynd and to.

[1]

Peny is an hardy knyght;
Peny is mekyl of myght;
Peny, of wrong he makyt ryght
 In euery cuntre qwer he goo.

[2]

Thow I haue a man islawe
And forfetyd the kynges lawe,
I xal fyndyn a man of lawe
 Wyl takyn myn peny and let me goo.

[3]

And if I haue to don fer or ner,
And Peny be myn massanger,
Thann am I non thing in dwer;
 My cause xal be wel idoo.

[4]

And if I haue pens bothe good and fyn,
Men wyl byddyn me to the wyn;
'That I haue xal be thi[n,']
 Sekyrly thei wil seyn so.

[5]

And quan I haue non in myn purs,
Peny bet ne peny wers,
Of me thei holdyn but lytil fors:
 'He was a man; let hym goo.'

393

British Museum. MS. Royal 17. B. XLVII
                                      XV *cent.*
f. 160ᵛ

 Money, money, now hay goode day!
  Money, where haste thow be?
 Money, money, thow goste away
  And wylt not byde wyth me.

[1]

Aboue all th[i]ng thow arte a kyng
 And rulyst the world ouer all;
Who lakythe the, all joy, parde,
 Wyll sone then frome hym fall.

[2]

In euery place thow makyste solas,
 Gret joye, sporte, and velfare;
When money ys gone, comforte ys none,
 But thowght, sorowe, and care.

[3]

In kynges corte, wher moncy dothe route,
 Yt makyth the galandes to jett,
And for to were gorgeouse ther gere,
 Ther cappes awry to sett.

[4]

In the heyweyes ther joly palfreys
 Yt makyght to lepe and praunce;
It maket justynges, pleys, dysguysynges,
 Ladys to synge and daunce.

[5]

For he that alway wantyth money
 Stondyth a mated chere,
Can neuer wel syng, lang daunce nor
  springe,
 Nor make no lusty chere.

[6]

At cardes and dyce yt bereth   [f. 161ʳ
  the pryce
 As kyng and emperoure;
At tables, tennes, and al othere games
 Money hathe euer the floure.

[7]

Wythe squyer and knyght and euery
  wygh[t]e
Money maketh men fayne
And causeth many in sume compeney
  Theyr felowes to dysdayne.

[8]

In marchandys who can deuyse
  So good a ware, I say?
At al tymys the best ware ys
  Euer redy money.

[9]

Money to i[n]cresse, marchandys neuer to
  cease
  Wyth many a sotell wyle,
Men say the[y] wolde for syluer and golde
  Ther owne faders begyle.

[10]

Women, I trowe, loue money also,
  To by them joly gere,
For that helpythe and of[t] causethe
  Women to loke full fayre.

[11]

In Westmynster Hall the criers   [f. 161ᵛ
  call;
  The sergeauntes plede apace;
Attorneys appere, now here, now ther,
  Renning in euery place.

[12]

Whatsoeuer he be, and yf that he
  Whante money to plede the lawe,
Do whate he cane, in ys mater than
  Shale proue not worthe a strawe.

[13]

I know yt not, but well I wotte
  I haue harde oftyntymys tell,
Prestes vse thys guyse, ther benefyce
  For moyeny to bey and sell.

[14]

Craftysmen, that in euery cite,
  They worke and neuer blynne;
Sum cutte, sume shaue, sume knoke, sum
  graue,
  Only money to wynne.

[15]

The plowman hymselfe doth dyge and delue
  In storme, snowe, frost, and rayne,
Money to get with laboure and swete,
  Yet small geynes and muche payne.

[16]

And sume for money lye by   [f. 162ʳ
  the wey
  Another mannes purse t[o] gett,
But they that long vse yt amonge
  Ben hangyd by the neke.

[17]

The beggers eke in euery strete
  Ly walowyng by the wey;
They begge, the[y] crye, of the[y] cume
  by,
  And all ys but for money.

[18]

In euery coste men loue yt moste,
  In Ynglonde, Spayne, and France,
For euery man lackyng yt than
  Is clene owte of countenaunce.

[19]

Of whate degre soeuer he be,
  Or werteouse conyng he haue,
And wante mone[y], yet men wyll sey
  That i heys but a knaue.

[20]

Where indede, so God me spede,
  Sey all men whate they cane,
Yt ys allwayes sene nowadayes
  That money makythe the man.

MS. heading: money money.
The repetition of the burden is indicated as
  follows: stzas. 1–9, 11, 12: money.   stzas. 10,
  13–20: money &c.
stza. 2, l. 1. place] MS. palce.
stza. 4, l. 1. the] MS. they.
stza. 7, l. 1. and (1)] MS. and &.
  l. 4. Theyr] MS. thery.
stza. 11, l. 1. Westmynster] MS. westmyaster.
stza. 12, l. 1. Whatesoeuer] MS. whate so euery.
  l. 4. proue] MS. not proue.
At end: finis.

393.1

Stanbrook Abbey. MS. 3
                                        XV *cent.*
f. iiiʳ

  Synge and blow, blow wel, blow;
    Synge wen so Y blo[w].

[1]

Jon Clerke of Toryton, I dar avow,
  He ys my lordys kynne,
For he hath ikepte the gryte sow
  With alle my lady swyne.

[2]

Y[e]tte therof ys no wonder:
Alle the towne ys my lorde vnder
And beth hys bounde blode;
What he commandeth, in good fay,
They dar nowght ones say nay
For the best balle in her hode.

[3]

Sythyn Jon ys but yong
And ys my lordys hyne,
Hyt ys no wonder thow he scour the gonge
And kepe my lordys swyne.

[4]

But by that hys berde be fulle grow
Adon to hys brest,
He wil loke to lye lowe
And sumwhat have hys rest.

[5]

And amonge alle my lordes blode
Hyt wil nowght passy[n] thre
That wil conne lesse goode
And cherle be ther than he.

[6]

And thow hys hert be nowght al ysett
To kepe the gryte bore,
He wil lerne euer lenger the bett
Ayenst he wexyt hore.

[7]

And therfor he schalle fare the bett,
Therof he schalle nowght fayle:
No man may hym benyme ne lett
The messe of the sow tayle.

The burden appears to have been written at a time
different from that of the writing of the stanzas.
burden, l. 1. *The MS. is stained at this point, but*
probably no further word had been written.

394

St. John's College, Cambridge. MS. S. 54
XV *cent.*
f. 7r

Pray we to Oure Lady dere
For here holy grace.

[1]

Sche saw theis women all bedene,
Both frow sorow and fro tene,
Madys and wyuys and weduys, I wene,
All be thei fayre in face.

[2]

Women be both good *and* hend,
Clen, curteys, cumly, *and* kend;
Yche a cu[m]pany is wele ame[n]de
Yf a woman be in a plase.

[3]

Of a woman com all oure blys;
Therfor I loue hem all, iwys;
Qwosoeuer seyth on hem amys,
Be God, he yawyd in hys face.

[4]

Were a man i[n] sore syynge,
A woman xall hym out bryng
And with a kys less hys morny[n]g
And sette hym in solace.

[5]

Thies men arne falce, fekyll in   [f. 7v
thoghth;
Women be wood that trow hem howt,
For well thie hote and hold it noth,
But spek i[n] here song.

[6]

Dere Lady, to thi Son thou pray
He synd theis women, os he wylle may,
Fro false men that downe hym tray,
That thei sene he[m] neuer in face.

burden, l. 1. Oure] MS. youre.
stza. 1, l. 2. fro (1)] MS. for.   l. 3. wene]
MS. weme.
stza. 4, l. 3. hys] MS. hyc.
stza. 6, l. 3. Fro] MS. for.
Above stza. 5 is written (in another hand): I what
maner mane.

395

a. *British Museum.* MS. Harley 7358
XV *cent.*
f. 8r

Wymmen beth bothe goude *and* truwe:
Wytnesse on Marie.

[1]

Wymmen beth bothe goud *and* schene,
On handes, fet, *and* face clene;
Wymmen may no beter bene:
Wytnesse on M[arie.]

[2]

Wymmen beth gentel on her tour;
A womman bar oure Sauyour;
Of al thys wor[ld] wymman ys flour:
W[ytnesse on Marie.]

[3]

Wyrchyp we wymma*n*ys face
Wer we seth hem on a place,
For wy*mm*a*n* ys the wyl of g*r*ace:
W[ytnesse on Marie.]

[4]

Loue a wo*mm*a*n* wi*th* herte tr*u*we:
He nel chongy for no newe;
Wymme*n* beth of wordes fewe:
W[ytnesse on Marie.]

[5]

Wymme*n* beth goud, wi*th*oute lesyng;
Fro sorwe *and* care hy wol vs bryng;
Wymma*n* ys flour of alle thyng:
W[ytnesse on Marie.]

stza. 2, l. 3. wymma*n*] MS. wymna*n*.
stza. 3, l. 1. wymma*n*ys] MS. wymna*n* ys.

b. *British Museum*. MS. Sloane 2593, f. 5^r.
XV *cent*. (burden and stzas. 1, 3–5).

burden, l. 1. beth] be.   l. 2. on] of.
stza. 1, l. 1. *omits*.   ll. 2, 3] ll. 1, 2.
l. 2. On] Of. fet] *and* body.   clene] arn
clene.   l. 3. may] mown.   *After* l. 3. In
eu*er*y place it is sene.   l. 4. on] of.
stza. 3, ll. 1, 2. It is knowy*n and* eu*er*e was
Th*er* a womma*n* is in plas.
l. 3. For] *omits*.   l. 4. wytnesse.
stza. 4, l. 1. Loue a wo*mm*a*n*] They louy*n* me*n*.
l. 2. nel] wyl not.   l. 3. beth] ben.
l. 4. wytnesse.
stza. 5, l. 1. beth goud] ben trewe.
ll. 2, 3. *transposes*.   l. 2. Fro sorwe *and*]
And out of.   hy wol] they mown.
l. 3. Wymma*n* ys flour of]wommen be trewe
in.   l. 4. on] of.

396

British Museum. MS. Harley 4294
XV *cent*.

f. 81^r

I am as lyght as any roe
To preyse wemen wher that I goo.

[1]

To onpreyse wemen yt were a shame,
For a woman was thy dame;
Our Blessyd Lady beryth the name
Of all women wher that they goo.

[2]

A woman ys a worthy thyng:
They do the washe and do the wrynge;

'Lullay, lullay,' she dothe the syng,
And yet she hath but care and woo.

[3]

A woman ys [a] worthy wyght;
She s*er*uyth a man both daye *and* nygh[t;]
Therto she puttytth all her myght,
And yet she hathe bot care and woo.

397

Bodleian Library. MS. Douce 302
By John Audelay, XV *cent*.

f. 30^r

For the loue of a maydo*n* fre
I haue me choso*n* to chastite.

[1]

Blessid mot be oure heue*n* quene,
Fore v*er*gyn *and* maydyn sheo was ful
cleene;
Soche anoth*er* was neu*er* yer sene
Th*at* so wel kept her virgynyte.

[2]

In word, in will, in dede, in thoght,
Here maydehood defowled sheo noght;
Th*er*fore the Lorde th*at* h*er*e hade wroght
Wolde be boron of hyr body.

[3]

Tofore alle maydenes to hyr he ches
Fore here clannes *and* here mekenes,
Fore mo*n* soule heo schuld reles
Eu*er* fro the fynd *and* his pouste.

[4]

Seynt Kateryn *and* Marget *and* Wynfred,
Th*at* louyd ful wel here maydhed,
The[i] sofird to smyte of here hede,
Fore defouled wold thai not be.

[5]

Th*er*fore thai be in heue*n* blis,
Where murth *and* melode eu*er* th*er* ys,
And soo shal all maydons, ywys,
That kepon heore worder *and* here degre.

[6]

Thai foloun O*ur* Lady wi*th* gret reu*er*ens
And don here s*er*uys i*n* here p*r*esens,
Fore ayayns the fynd thai made defense
Wi*th* the swerd of chastite.

MS. heading: de virg[i]nitate.

398

Bodleian Library. MS. Douce 302
               By John Audelay, XV *cent.*
f. 30^r

    I pray youe, maydys that here be,
    Kepe your state *and* your degre.

[1]

In word, in dede, in wyl, in thoght,
Your maydynhede defoule ye noght,
Lest to blame that ye ben broght
    And lese your state, your honeste.

[2]

An vndur marke Crist con you lene
To marc with; kepe hit clene;
Yif ye hit tame, hit wil be sene,
    Do ye neuer soo preuely.

[3]

Of that tresour men ben ful fayne,
And al here loue on youe thai lay[ne],
And mone a pene for hit thai pay[ne],
    Both seluer *and* gold, lond *and* fe.

[4]

Yif that tresoure ye don hit tame,
When hit is knowyn, ye wil haue chame;
Of[t] therfore ye berne gret blame,
    Neuer on be other ware wil be.

[5]

Nad that tresoure bene ewroght,
To blis we had not bene ebroght;
Hit faylis neuer ne fadis noght;
    Euer to mon hit is redy.

[6]

Yif ye kepyn wele that tresour,
Hit schal you bryng to hie honoure;
Thagh ye be fayre of freche coloure,
    Beute is noght without bonte.

[7]

Trewly nyer that tresoure were,
Of men ye schuld haue febul chere;
Avyse you whom ye lene hit here;
    Yif ye ben begild, that blame not me.

[8]

Fore other cownsel nedis youe non;
Then doth therafter euerechon,   [f. 30^v
Fore this tresoure has holpyn mone hone;
    Hit marys maydis vche cuntre.

MS. heading: Cantalena de virginibus.
stza. 3, ll. 2, 3. *MS. is damaged.*

399

a. Balliol College, Oxford. MS. 354
                              XVI *cent.*
f. 250^r

    Of all creatures women be best,
    Cuius contrarium verum est.

[1]

In euery place ye may well see
That women be trewe as tirtyll on tree,
Not lyberall in langage, but euer in secrete,
And gret joye amonge them ys for to be.

[2]

The stedfastnes of women will neuer be don,
So jentyll, so curtes they be euerychon,
Meke as a lambe, still as a stone;
Croked nor crabbed fynd ye none.

[3]

Men be more cumbers a thowsand fold,
And I mervayll how they dare be so bold
Agaynst women for to hold,
Seyng them so pascyent, softe, *and* cold.

[4]

For, tell a woman all your cownsayle,
And she can kepe it wonderly well;
She had lever go quyk to hell
Than to her neyghbowr she wold it tell.

[5]

For by women men be reconsiled;
For by women was neuer man begiled;
For they be of the condicion of curtes
    Gryzell;
For they be so meke *and* mylde.

[6]

Now say well by women, or elles be still,
For they neuer displesed man by ther will;
To be angry or wroth they can no skill,
For I dare say they thynk non yll.

[7]

Trow ye that women list to smater
Or agaynst ther husbondes for to clater?
Nay, they had leuer fast, bred *and* water,
Then for to dele in suche a mater.

[8]

Thowgh all the paciens in the world were
    drownd,
And non were lefte here on the grownd,
Agayn in a woman it myght be fownd,
Suche vertu in them dothe abownd.

[9]

To the tavern they will not goo,
Nor to the ale-hows neu*er* the moo,
For, God wot, th*er* hart*es* wold be woo
To spende ther husbond*es* money soo.

[10]

Yff here were a woma*n* or a mayd
That lyst for to go fresshely arayed,
Or with fyne kyrchers to go displayed,
Ye wold say, 'They be prowde'; it is yll
    said.

MS. marks burden: Fote.
stza. 9, l. 4. spende] MS. sspende.
The repetition of the burden is indicated after
each stanza by: Cui*us*.

b. *Bodleian Library.* MS. Eng. poet. e. 1,
ff. 55ᵛ, 56ʳ. XV *cent.*

stza. 2, l. 4. nor] ne.
stza. 4, l. 2. wonderly] wond*er.*
stza. 5, ll. 3, 4:
    Fore by women was neu*er* man betraied;
    Fore by women was neu*er* man bewreyed.
stza. 6, l. 3. can no] ca*n*not.
stza. 7, l. 1. wome*n*] they.   l. 2. for] *omits.*
    l. 4. dele] presse.
stza. 8, l. 3. a woma*n*] women.
stza. 9, l. 3. wold be] shulbe.
stza. 10, l. 3. kyrchers] kerchefs.   l. 4. yll]
    evil.

400

St. John's College, Cambridge. MS. S. 54
                                    XV *cent.*
f. 9ᵛ

    War yt, war yt, war yt wele:
    Weme*n* be as trew as stele.

[1]

Stel is gud, I sey no od*ur*;
So mown wemen be Kaymys brod*ur*;
Ylk on lere schrewdnes at od*ur*;
    Weme*n* be as trew as stele.

[2]

Stel is gud in eu*er*y knyf;
So kun th*es* women both flyt *and* stryfe;
Also thei cu*n* wele lye;
    Wome*n* [be as trew as stele.]

[3]

Stele is gud in eu*er*y nedyll;
So be th*es* women both falce *and* fekyll,

And of th*er* ars evyn ryght brytyll;
[Women be as trew as stele.]

[4]

Stele is both fayr *and* bryght;
So be th*es* women be candyllyght,
And som wyll both flyt *and* fyght;
[Women be as trew as stele.]

[5]

Stel is gud in lond *and* watyr;
So cun th*es* wome*n* both de*n and* flatyr,
And yyt for ned to play the faytur;
[Women be as trew as stele.]

stza. 2, l. 4. MS. wome*n* vt supra.
stzas. 3–5, l. 4. MS. vt sup*ra.*
stza. 4, l. 1. bryght] MS. bryghht.
    l. 2. candyllyght] MS. candyllyghht.
    l. 3. fyght] MS. fyghht.

401

A a. *Balliol College, Oxford.* MS. 354
                                    XVI *cent.*
f. 250ʳ

    Wome*n*, wome*n*, love of wome*n*
    Maketh bare pursis w*ith* su*m* me*n*.

[1]

Su*m* be mery, *and* su*m* be sade,
And su*m* be besy, *and* su*m* be bade;
Su*m* be wilde, by Seynt Chade;
    Yet all be not so,
For su*m* be lewed,
And su*m* be shrewed;
    Go, shrew, whersoeu*er* ye go.

[2]

Su*m* be wyse, *and* su*m* be fond*e*;
Su*m* be tame, I vnderstond;
Su*m* will take bred at a man*us* hond;
    Yet all be not so.
For su*m* be lewd*e*,
And su*m* be shrewed,
    Go, shrew, whersoeu*er* ye go.

[3]

Su*m* be wroth *and* ca*n*not tell   [f. 250ᵛ
    wherfore;
Su*m* be skornyng evermore,
And su*m* be tusked lyke a bore;
    Yet all be not so;
For su*m* be lewed,
And su*m* be shrewed;
    Go, shrewe, whersoeu*er* ye go.

[4]

Su*m* will be dronkyn as a mowse;
Su*m* be croked *and* will hurte a lowse;
Su*m* be fayre *and* good in a hows;
    Yet all be not so,
For su*m* be lewed,
And su*m* beo shrewed;
    Go, shrewe, whersoeu*er* ye go.

[5]

Su*m* be snowted like an ape;
Su*m* ca*n* nother play ne jape;
Su*m* of them be well shape;
    Yet all be not so,
For su*m* be lewed,
And su*m* be shrewed;
    Go, shrewe, whersoeu*er* ye go.

[6]

Su*m* can prate wi*th*owt hire;
Su*m* make bate in eu*er*y shire;
Su*m* ca*n* play chekmate w*ith* owr sire;
    Yct all they do not so,
For su*m* be lewed,
And su*m* be shrewed;
    Go, shrew, whersoeu*er* ye go.

MS. marks burden: fote.
At end: Explicit.

b. *Bodleian Library.* MS. Eng. poet. e. 1,
    ff. 56ʳ, 57ʳ. XV *cent.*

burden, l. 1. love of wome*n*] women women.
    l. 2. a song I syng even off women.
stza. 1, l. 2. besy] good.
stza. 3, l. 1. wroth] angry.
stza. 4, l. 3, stza. 5, l. 3, stza. 6, l. 2: Su*m*] *And*
    some.
stza. 6, ll. 2, 3. *transposes.*   l. 2. bate] debate.
    l. 4. they do] be.

B.*Lambeth Palace Library.* MS. Lambeth
    306   XV *cent.*

f. 135ʳ

    Women, women, loue of women
    Make bare purs w*ith* some men.

[1]

Some be nyse as a nonne hene,

.   .   .   .   .   .

.   .   .   .   .   .

    Yit al thei be nat soo;
Some be lewde,
Some all be schreude;
    Go, schrewes, wher thei goo.

[2]

Sum be nyse, and some be fonde,
And some be tame, Y vndirstond,
And some cane take brede of a manes
        hande;
    Yit all thei be nat soo;
[Some be lewde,
Some all be schreude;
    Go, schrewes, wher thei goo.]

[3]

Some cane prat withouten hire,   [f. 135ᵛ
And some make bate in eueri chire,
And some chekemate with oure sir*e*;
    Yit all they be nat so;
Some be lewde,
And sume be schreued,
    Go wher they goo.

[4]

Some be browne, and some be whit,
And some be tender as a tripe,
And some of theym be chiry-ripe;
    Yit all thei be not soo;
Sume be lewde,
And some be schreued,
    Go wher they goo.

[5]

Some of them be treue of love
Beneth the gerdell but nat above,
And in a hode a bone cane chove;
    Yit all thei do nat soo;
Some be lewde,
And some be schreud,
    Go where they goo.

[6]

Some cane whister, *and* some cane crie;
Some cane flater, and some cane lye,
And some cane sette the moke awrie;
    Yit all thei do nat soo;
Sume be lewde,
And sume be schreued,
    Go where thei goo.

[7]

He that made this songe full good
Came of the north and of the sothern blode,
And somewhat kyne to Robyn Hode;
    Yit all we be nat soo;
Some be lewde,
And some be schrewed,
    Go where they goo.

stza. 3, l. 1. prat] MS. part.
stza. 4, l. 2. a tripe] MS. attripe.

Stza. 7, ll. 5–7 are written again at the end (with
And *omitted and* chrwde *for* schrewed)
possibly to remedy the omission in stza. 2,
although there is no mark of insertion.
At end: Explicit.

402

a. *Bodleian Library*. MS. Eng. poet. e. 1
                                    XV *cent.*
f. 43ᵛ

Whane thes thyng*es* foloy*ng* be done to
    owr intent,
Than put wome*n* i*n* trust *and* con-
    fydent.

[1]

When nettuls i*n* wynt*er* bryng   [f. 44ʳ
    forth rosys red,
And al man*er* of thorn trys ber fygys
    naturally,
And ges ber p*er*les i*n* eu*er*y med,
And laurell ber cherys abu*n*da*n*tly,
And ok*es* ber dat*es* v*er*y plentuosly,
    And kysk*ys* gyfe of hony sup*er*flue*n*s,
    Than put wome*n* i*n* trust *and*
    fyde*n*s.

[2]

Whan box ber papur i*n* eu*er*y lond *and*
    towne,
And thystuls ber berys i*n* eu*er*y place,
And pyk*es* have naturally fethers i*n* th*er*
    crowne,
And bull*es* of the see syng a good bace,
And me*n* be the schyp*es* fyschys do
    trace,
    And i*n* wome*n* be fownd no i*n*cypye*n*s,
    Than put he*m* i*n* trust and co*n*fyde*n*s.

[3]

Whan whytyng*es* do walke forest*es* to chase
    hertys,
And heryng*es* th*er* hornnys i*n* forest*es*
    boldly blow,
And marmsatt*es* morn i*n* mor*es* *and* i*n*
    lakys,
    And gurnard*es* schot rok*es* owt of a
    crose-bow,
    And goslyng*es* hu*n*t, the wolfe to ou*er*-
    throw,
    And sprat*es* ber sperys i*n* armys of
    defe*n*s,
    Than put wome*n* i*n* trust *and* con-
    fyde*n*s.

[4]

Whan swyn be cony*n*g i*n* al   [f. 44ᵛ
    poy*n*tes of musyke,
And ass*es* be doct*ur*s of eu*er*y scye*n*s,
And katt*es* do hel me*n* be practysyng of
    fysyke,
And boserds to Scrypt*ur* gyfe ony
    crede*n*s,
And marcha*n*s by wi*th* horne i*n*sted of
    grot*es* *and* pe*n*s,
    And pyys be mad poet*es* for th*er*
    eloque[n]s,
    Than put wome*n* i*n* trust *and* con-
    fyde*n*s.

[5]

Whan spawrus byld chyrchys on a hyth,
    And wrenys cary sekk*es* onto the myll,
And curlews cary ty*m*ber, howsys to dyth,
    And semavs ber butt*er* to market to sell,
    And wodkok*es* wer wodk[n]yfys, cranis
    to kyll,
    And gren fynchys to goslyng*es* do
    obedye*n*s,
    Than put wome*n* i*n* trust *and* con-
    fyde*n*s.

[6]

Whan crowb*es* tak samon i*n* wod*es* *and*
    park*es*,
    And be tak wi*th* swyft*es* *and* snaylys,
And ca*m*mels i*n* the ayer tak swalows *and*
    lark*es*,
    And myse move movnta*n*s wi*th* wagyng
    of th*er* tayl*es*,
    And schypme*n* tak a ryd i*n*sted of sayll*es*,
    And whan wyfvys to th*er* husbo*n*des
    do no offe*n*s,
    Than put wome*n* i*n* trust *and* con-
    fyde*n*s.

[7]

Whan hantlop*es* sermovnt*es* eglys   [f. 45ʳ
    i*n* flyght,
    And swans be swyft*er* than hauk*es* of the
    tower,
And wremnys ses goshauk*es* be fors *and*
    myght,
    And musket*es* mak v*er*gese of crabb*es*
    sower,
    And schypp*es* seyl on dry lond sylt gyfe
    flower,
    And apes i*n* Westmynst*er* gyfe jug-
    me*n*t *and* sente[n]s,
    Than put wome*n* i*n* trust *and* con-
    fyde*n*s.

b. *Balliol College, Oxford.* MS. 354, f. 250ᵛ. XVI *cent.* (stzas. 1, 3, 5, 6).

c. *British Museum.* Printed Book I B. 55242. (Bartholomaeus Anglicus, *De Proprietatibus Rerum*, translated by Trevisa, printed by Wynkyn de Worde, 1495), ff. 00₅ᵛ, 00₆ʳ. XVI *cent.* hand (stzas. 1, 3, ll. 4–7, 5, 6, ll. 1, 2, defective).

MS. heading: b fravs fraude (*in another hand*).
stza. 1, l. 1. bryng forth] b bere. c bryngith forth.   l. 2. al maner of thorn trys] b thornys. c a thorne.   ber] c berith.   l. 3. ges] b bromes. c gressse.   ber] c berith.   perles] b c appylles.   l. 4. laurell] b lorelles. ber] c omits.   abundantly] b c in the (c his) croppis so hie.   l. 5. c omits.   very] b so. l. 6. kyskys] b lekes.   gyfe] c geven.   of] b c omit.   superfluens] b in ther superfluens. c in superfluens.   l. 7. b Than put in a woman your trust and confidens (*so in all other stanzas*). c Then put in women your trust and confidence.
stza. 3, l. 1. whytynges] b whityng.   do] b c omit.   forestes] b c in forestes.   to chase hertys] b c hartes for to chase.   l. 2. ther] b in perkys. c in parkes their.   in forestes] b c omit.   l. 3. b And flownders morehennes in fennes enbrace. c and marlynges moore hennys in moores doon vnbrase. l. 4. rokes] b rolyons. c rullions.   l. 5. goslynges] b gren gese.   hunt] b Ride in huntyng. c goo on huntyng.   l. 6. sprates] b c sperlynges.   ber] b Rone with. c beren. in armys of] b in harnes to. c and armour for. l. 7. b c as in stza. 1.
stza. 5, l. 1. spawrus] b c sparowys.   byld] c bylden.   on a hyth] b and stepulles hie. c and stepils on high.   l. 2. cary] c beren.   onto] b to.   l. 3. tymber, howsys to dyth] b clothes horsis for to drye.   to] c for to. l. 4. ber] b bryng. c bryngyn.   market] b the merket.   to (2)] c for to.   ll. 3–7 *partially torn away in* c.   l. 5. wodkokes] b woddowes.   cranis] b theves. c the crane for.   l. 6. gren fynchys] b griffons.   do] b c don.   l. 7. b as in stza. 1. c . . . women your trust and confidence.
stza. 6. (c *has only the ends of* ll. 1, 2). l. 1. crowbes] b Crabbis.   samon] b wodcokes. c . . . ecokkes.   wodes] b c forestes.   l. 2. be tak] b haris ben taken.   swyftes and] b swetnes of. c . . . esse of.   l. 3. in the ayer] b with ther here.   larkes] b perchis. l. 4. move movntans] b mowe Corn.   wagyng] b wafeyyng.   l. 5. b whan dukkes of the dunghill sek the blod of haylis.   l. 6. And] b omits.   wyfvys] b shrewed wyffes.   no] b non.   l. 7. b as in stza. 1.   At end: b Explicit quod Rc⁹ hill.
stza. 7 (ll. 1–3, *first two words of* l. 4 *cut off by binder in* c). l. 4. sower] c full sowre. l. 5. on] couer.   sylt] c and flyntes.   l. 6. apes] c

marmesettes.   in] c at gyfe]   c given· l. 7. c Then in women give trust and confidence.   At end: c and then in other thinges (*in another hand*).

402.1

Bodleian Library. MS. Eng. poet. e. 1
XV *cent.*
f. 13ʳ

Herfor and therfor and therfor I came,
And for to praysse this prety woman.

[1]

Ther wer iii wylly; 3 wyly ther wer:
A fox, a fryyr, and a woman.

[2]

Ther wer 3 angry; 3 angry ther wer:
A wasp, a wesyll, and a woman.

[3]

Ther wer 3 cheteryng; iii   [f. 13ᵛ] cheteryng ther wer:
A peye, a jaye, and a woman.

[4]

Ther wer 3 wold be betyn; 3 wold be betyn ther wer:
A myll, a stokefysche, and a woman.

stza. 1, l. 1. 3] MS. 3ᵗᵉ.

403

British Museum. MS. Sloane 2593
XV *cent.*
f. 9ᵛ

Man, bewar of thin wowyng,
For weddyng is the longe wo.

[1]

Loke er thin herte be set;
Lok thou wowe er thou be knet,
And, if thou se thou mow do bet,
Knet vp the heltre, and let here goo.

[2]

Wyuys be bothe stowte and bolde;
Her husbondes ayens hem durn not holde;
And, if he do, his herte is colde,
Howsoeuere the game go.

[3]

Wedowis be wol fals, iwys,
For [they] cun bothe halse and kys
Til onys purs pikyd is,
And they seyn, 'Go, boy, goo.'

[4]

Of madenys I wil seyn but lytil,
For they be bothe fals *and* fekyl,
And vnd*er* the tayl they ben ful tekyl;
  A twenty deuel*e* name, let hem goo!

404

Bodleian Library. MS. Eng. poet. e. 1
                                    XV *cent.*
f. 29ᵛ

  In soro *and* car he led hys lyfe
  Th*at* haue a schrow ontyll his wyfe.

[1]

Yyng me*n*, I red th*at* ye bewar   [f. 30ʳ
That ye cu*m* not in the snar,
For he is browt in meche car
  Th*at* haue a schrow onto his wyfe.

[2]

In a panter I am caute;
My fot his pennyd, I may not owt;
In sorow *and* car he his put
  Th*at* haue a schrow onto his wyf.

[3]

Wit*h* a qwene yyf th*at* th*o*u run,
Ano*n* it is told into the town;
Sorow he hath both vp *and* down
  Th*at* haue a schrow onto hys wyf.

405

British Museum. MS. Sloane 2593
                                    XV *cent.*
f. 24ᵛ

  How, hey! It is no*n* les:
  I dar not seyn qu*an* che seygh, 'Pes!'

[1]

Yyng me*n*, I warne y*o*u eu*er*ychon:
Elde wywys tak ye no*n*,
For I myself haue o*n* at hom;
  I dar not seyn qu*an* che seyght, 'Pes!'

[2]

Qu*an* I cu*m* fro the plow at non,   [f. 25ʳ
In a reuen dych my*n* mete is don;
I dar not asky*n* *our* dame a spon;
  I dar not [seyn quan che seyght, 'Pes!']

[3]

If I aske *our* dame bred,
Che takyt a staf *and* brek*i*t my*n* hed
And doth me renny*n* und*er* the led;
  I dar not [seyn quan che seyght, 'Pes!'

[4]

If I aske *our* dame fleych,
Che brek*i*t my*n* hed wit*h* a dych:
'Boy, th*o*u art not worght a reych!'
  I dar [not seyn quan che seyght, 'Pes!']

[5]

If I aske *our* dame chese,
'Boy,' che seyght, al at ese,
'Thou art not worght half a pese.'
  I dar not sey qu*an* che seyght, 'Pes!'

burden, l. 1. no*n*] *erased and almost illegible in
  MS.*
stzas. 2, 3, l. 4. MS. I dar not &c.
stza. 4, l. 4. MS. I dar &c.

406

Bodleian Library. MS. Eng. poet. e. 1
                                    XV *cent.*
f. 23ʳ

  Care away, away, away,
  Care away for eu*er*more.

[1]

All th*at* I may swy*n*k or swet,
My wyfe it wyll both drynk *and* ete;
And I sey ovght, she wyl me bete;
  Carfull ys my hart th*er*for.

[2]

If I sey ovght of hyr but good,
She loke on me as she war wod
And wyll me clovght abovght the hod;
  Carfull [ys my hart therfor.]

[3]

If she wyll to the gud ale ryd,
Me must trot all be hyr syd,
And whan she drynk I must abyd;
  Carfull [ys my hart therfor.]

[4]

If I say, 'It shal be thus,'
She sey, 'Thou lyyst, charl*l*, iwovs!
Wenest th*o*u to ou*er*come me thus?'
  Carfull [ys my hart therfor.]

[5]

Yf ony man haue svch a wyfe to [f. 23ᵛ
lede,
He shal know how 'iudicare' cam in the
Cred;
Of hys penans God do hym med!
Carfull [ys my hart therfor.]

stzas. 2–5, l. 4. MS. carfull &c.

407

Bodleian Library. MS. Eng. poet. e. 1
XV *cent*.
f. 42ᵛ

Nova, noua, sawe yow euer such?
The most mayster of the hows weryth no
brych.

[1]

Dayly in Englond meruels be fownd
And among maryd peple haue such
radicacyon,
Qwych to the vtermost expresse may no
thong,
Ne pene cane scribull the totall declara-
cyon,
For women vpon them tak such domy-
nacyon,
And upon themself thei tak so mych
That it causyth the mayster to abuse
a brych.

[2]

Syns that Eue was procreat owt of Adams
syde,
Cowd not such newels in this lond be
inuentyd:
The masculyn sex, with rygurnesse and
prid
With ther femals thei altercatt, therself
beyng schentyd,
And of ther owne self the corag is abatyd;
Wherfor it is not acordyng to syth to
mych,
Lest the most mayster may wer no
brych.

[3]

Yt is sene dayly both in borows and townys
Wheras the copuls han mad objurgacyon,
The gowd wyff ful humanly to hyr spowse
gaue gownys,
Wych [th]yng is oryginat of so gret pre-
sumpcyon

That often tymys the good man is fal in
a consumpcyon;
Wherfor, as I seyd, suffer not to mych
Lest the most mayster weryth no
brych.

[4]

Nat only in Englond, but of euery [f. 43ʳ
nacion,
The femynyng wyl presume men for to
gyd;
Yet God at the tym of Adams creacyon
Gaue man superiorite of them in euery
tyd;
But now in theys women is fyxyd such
pryd,
And upon themself wyl tak so mych
That it constreynyth the most mayster
to wer no brych.

[5]

But mayny women be ryght dylygent
And so demver ther husbondes aforne,
For of cryme or favt thei be innocent,
Butt falser than thei be wer neuer borne,
For wantenly ther husbondes thei wyl so
dorne
That owther thei wyl mak hym
nothyng rych
Or ellys the most mayster to wer no
brych.

[6]

An adamant stone it is not frangebyll
With nothyng but with mylke of a gett;
So a woman to refrayne it is not posybyll
With wordes, except with a staffe thou
hyr intrett;
For he that for a faut hys wyff wyl not
bett
Wherin sche offendyt hym very mych,
That gyder of hys hows must nedes
wer no brych.

[7]

A scald hed maye be coueryd and [f. 43ᵛ
not sene,
And many thynges mo may be sone
hyddyn,
But the hod of a—syr, ye wott what I
mene—
Wych with too hornys infeckyd was and
smyttyn,
By surgery to be helyd it is forbyddyn,
For thei haue such an yssue abow the
cheke
That it constereynyth the most master
to wer no bryke.

[8]

Wherfor, ye maryd men that with wyvys be
        acommoryd,
    Dysplease nott yowr wyuys whom that
        ye haue,
For, whan thei be angry or sumwhatt
        dysplesyd,
    Thei wyl gyffe a man a mark that he xal
        ber it to hys grafe;
    Whobeit, ther husbondes honeste to saue,
        Clokydly without thei obey very mych,
    And inwerdly the most mayster wer no
        brych.

[9]

Was not Adam, Hercules, *and* mythy
        Sampson,
    Dauyd the kyng, with other many mo,
Arystotyll, Vergyll, by a womans cauy-
        lacion,
    Browt to iniquyte *and* to mych woo?
    Wherfor, ye maryd men, ordur ye soo
        That with yowr wyfys yow stryfe not
        to mych,
    Lest the most mayster wer no brych.

stza. 8, l. 1. ye] MS. the.
stza. 9, l. 6. wyfys] MS. wyftys.

408

Balliol College, Oxford. MS. 354
                                    XVI *cent.*
f. 249ʳ

    'Alas,' sayd the gudman, 'this ys an hevy
        lyff!'
    And 'All ys well that endyth well,' said
        the gud wyff.

[1]

A lytyll tale I will you tell,
The very trowth, how it befell
And was trew as the gosspell
    Att the townys end.

[2]

Betwen the gudman *and* his make
A lytill stryf begon to wake;
The wyff was sumwhat shrew shake
    At the townys end.

[3]

He gafe a thyng ther hym lyst;
As son as his wyff yt wyst,
Vp she stode *and* bent her fyst
    At the townys end.

[4]

'Thou knave, thou churle,' gan she say,
'In the twente devyls way,
Who bade the geve my gud away
    At the townys end?

[5]

'Thou traytor, thou thef, thou mysgouerned
        man,
To love the furst when I began,
I wold thou had be hangyd than
    At the townys end.'

[6]

He lent her a strype two or iii;
'Owt! Alas!' then cryed she,
'I aske a vengaunce, thef, on the
    At the townys end.

[7]

'Thou stynkyng coward, so haue I grace,
Thou daryst not loke a man in the face;
Now lett them say I know the cace
    At the townys end.'

[8]

'What, dame? What hast thou but of me?
And I haue nothyng of the
But chydyng, brawlyng, evyll mvst thou
        the!
    At the townys end.'

[9]

The gudman myght no lengar forbere
But smote hys wyff on the ere
That she ouerthrew; then lay she ther
    At the townys end.

[10]

'Alas!' she sayd, 'I am but dede;
I trow the brayn be owt of my hed';
And yet ther was no blod shed
    At the townys end.

[11]

'Gett me a preest, that I were shryve,
For I wott well I shall not lyve,
For I shall dye or tomorow eve
    At the townys end.'

[12]

This tale must nedes trew be,
For he that sawe yt told yt me;
Aske ferder, *and* know shall ye,
    At the townys end.

[13]

Now euery man that ys alone,
That shuld be weddyd to such a on,
I cownsayl hym rather to haue non
    At the townys end.

[14]

Lest he be knokked abowt the pate;
Then to repent yt ys to late,
When on his cheke he ys chekmate
    A[t the townys end.]

stza. 4, l. 2. twente] MS. xx^te.
stza. 8, l. 3. brawlyng] MS. barwlyng.
stza. 14, l. 4. *A tear in MS. has destroyed most
    of the line.*
At end: Explici[t].

409

Bodleian Library. MS. Eng. poet. e. 1
                          XV *cent.*
f. 34^v

    Hey, howe!
    Sely men, God helpe yowe.

[1]

Thys indrys day befel a stryfe
Totwex an old man *and* hys wyfe;
Sche toke hym be the berd so plyght,
    With hey, how!

[2]

Sche toke hym be the berd so fast
Tyll bothe hys eyn on watyr gan brast,
. . . . . .
    With hey, how!

[3]

Howt at the dore as he can goo,
Met he with hys neybrys too:
'Neybyr, why wepyst soo?'
    With hey, ho[w!]

[4]

'In my hows ys swyche a smeke—
Goo ondyr, *and* ye schall wete.'
. . . . . .
    With hey, ho[w!]

stzas. 3, 4, l. 4. *The last letter is obscured by the
    binding.*

410

a. *Balliol College, Oxford.* MS. 354
                              XVI *cent.*
f. 241^r

    In villa, in villa,
    Quid vidistis in villa?

[1]

Many a man blamys his wyffe, perde,
Yet he ys more to blame than she;
Trow ye that any suche ther be
    In villa?

[2]

Ye, ye, hold your pease, for shame!
By Owr Lady, ye be to blame!
Wene you that womenys tonges be lame
    In villa?

[3]

Nay, God forbede, yt ys naturall
For them to be right lyberall,
Now I report me over all
    In villa.

[4]

On thyng, forsoth, I haue esspyed:
All women be not tong-tyed,
For, yf they be, they be bylyed
    In villa.

[5]

Yff owght be sayd to them sertayn,
Wene you thei will not answer agayn?
Yes, for euery word twayn,
    In villa.

[6]

Now in gud feyth, the soth to say,
They haue gret cavse from day to day,
For they may nother sport ne play
    In vi[lla.]

[7]

Ther husbondes controll them so streytly,
But yet no force for that hardely;
Ther skuse shall be made full craftyly
    In villa.

[8]

How say ye, women that husbondes haue?
Will not ye ther honowr saue
And call them lowsy stynkyng knave
    In villa?

[9]

Yes, so haue I hard tell or this,
Not fer owt of this cuntrey, ywys;
Of sum of them men shall not mys
    In villa.

[10]

God wot, gret cavse thei haue among,
But dowt ye not, ther hartes be strong,
For they may sofer no maner wrong
    In villa.

[11]

And, yff thei dyde, ther hartes wold brest;
Wherfor, in feyth, I hold yt best
Lett them alone, with evyll rest,
    In villa.

[12]

Ye husbondes all, with on asent,
Lett your wyffys haue ther yntent,
Or suerly ye will be shent
    In villa.

[13]

Ytt ys hard ayenst the strem to stryve:
For hym that cast hym for to thryve,
He mvst aske leve of hys wyff
    In v[illa.]

[14]

Or elles, by God and by the rode,
Be he never so wyld and wode,
Hys here shall grow thorow his hode
    In villa.

stza. 1, l. 2. he . . . she] MS. *transposes.*
stzas. 6, 13, l. 4. *The last few letters are obscured
    by a patch on MS.*
At end: Explicit.

b. *Bodleian Library.* MS. Eng. poet. e. 1,
    ff. 54ᵛ, 55ʳ. XV *cent.*

burden, l. 1. In villa.
stza. 1, l. 1. blamys] blame.
stza. 2, l. 3. you] ye.
stza. 3, l. 3. Now I] I now.
stza. 4, l. 1. On thyng, forsoth] Euery where.
    l. 3. For] *And.* be (1)] were.
stza. 5, l. 2. you] ye.   l. 3. for] by christ fore.
stza. 6, l. 3. ne] nor.
stza. 7, l. 1. streytly] secretly.   l. 3. Ther]
    Fore ther.   full] so.
stza. 8, l. 1. haue] haues.   l. 2. ye ther] yow
    owr. saue] saves.   l. 3. knaue] knaves.
stza. 9, l. 1. Yes] ye.
stza. 10, l. 1. thei haue] haue thei.
    l. 3. wrong] off wrong.

stza. 11, l. 2. feyth] soth.   l. 3. with evyll] in
    the devillis.
stza. 12, l. 3. suerly] by my trowth.
stza. 13. l. 2. hym (1)] he.   l. 3. leve of his
    wyff] off hys wiffe leve.
stza. 14, l. 2. and] ore.

411

Bodleian Library. MS. Douce 302
            By John Audelay, XV *cent.*
f. 30ᵛ

    Avyse youe, wemen, wom ye trust,
    And beware of 'had-I-wyst'.

[1]

Hit is ful heue chastite
    With mone maydyns now-o-day,
That louyn to haue gam and gle,
    That turnes to sorowe, sothly to say,
        All day thou sist.

[2]

Now yif a womon mared schal be,
    Anon heo schal be boght and solde,
Fore no loue of hert, truly,
    Bot fore couetyse of lond ore gold,
        Al day thou seest.

[3]

Bot thus Godis low and his wil wolde:
    Even of blod, of good, of ache,
Fore loue togeder thus come thai schuld,
    Fore this makis metle mareache,
        Ale day thou sees.

[4]

And the froyt that coms hom betwene,
    Hit schal haue grace to thryue and the
Ther other schal haue turment and tene
    Fore couetyse vnlaufully,
        All day thou seest.

[5]

Ther is no creatuere, as wretyn I fynd,
    Saue onele mon, that [doth] outtrache,
Bot chesyn hom makys of here oune kynd,
    And so thai makyn triu mareache,
        All day thou seest.

[6]

Bot now a lady wil take a page,
    Fore no loue, bot fleschele lust,
And so here blod is disperage;
    Thus lordus and lordchip al day ben lost,
        Al day thou seest.

[7]

Lordis *and* lorchip th*us* wastyn away
In Englond *in* mone a place,
Th*at* makis false ayrs, h*it* is no nay,
  And lese worchip, honowre, *and* grace,
    Al day th*ou* seest.

MS. heading: de matrimonio mulier*um*.
stza. 5, l. 3. chesyn] MS. thesyn.

412

Bodleian Library. MS. Douce 302
          By John Audelay, XV *cent.*
f. 29ᵛ

  And God wold gr*au*nt me my pr*ay*er,
  A child ayene I wold I were.

[1]

Fore pr*i*de *in* herte he hatis allone,
Worchip ne reu*er*ens kepis he non,
Ne he is wroth w*ith* no mon;
  In charete is al h*is* chere.

[2]

He wot neu*er* wat is envy;
He wol vche mo*n* fard wele hi*m* by;
He couetis noght vnlaufully,
  Fore chere-stons is his tresoure.

[3]

In hert he hatis lechori;   [f. 31ʳ
To here th*er*of he is sory;
He sleth the syn of glotere,
  Noth*er* etis ne drynkis bot for mystere.

[4]

Slouth he putis away algate
And wol be bese erle *and* late;
Al wyckidnes thus he doth hate,
  The vii dedle synus al *in* fere.

[5]

A gracious lyfe forsothe he has,
To God ne mo*n* doth no trespas,
And I in syn fal, alas,
  Eu*ere* day in the yere.

[6]

My joy, my myrth is fro me clene;
I turne to care, t*ur*ment *and* tene;
Ded I wold th*at* I had bene
  Whe*n* I was borne, *and* layd on bere.

[7]

Fore bet*ter* h*i*t were to be vnboren
The*n* fore my syn*us* to be forelorne,
Nere grace of God, th*at* is beforne,
  Almysdede *and* hole pr*ay*ere.

[8]

Now oth*er* cu*m*ford se I non
Bot schryue me clene w*ith* co*n*tricion
And make here trew satisfaccion
  And do my penans wyle Y am here.

MS. heading: Cantalena de puericia c[etera].

413

A. *Balliol College, Oxford.* MS. 354
                              XVI *cent.*
f. 252ʳ

  Hay, hay, by this day,
  What avayleth it me thowgh I say nay?

[1]

I wold fayn be a clarke,
But yet hit is a strange werke;
The byrchyn twygg*es* be so sharpe
Hit makith me haue a faynt harte;
  What avaylith it me thowgh I say nay?

[2]

On Mo*n*day *in* the mornyng whan I shall
    rise,
At vi of the clok, hyt is the gise,
To go to skole w*ith*owt avise,
I had lever go twenti myle twyse;
  What avaylith it me thowgh I say nay?

[3]

My master lokith as he were madde:
'Wher hast th*ou* be, thow sory ladde?'
'Milked dukk*es*, my moder badde.'
Hit was no m*er*vayle thow I were sadde;
  What vaylith it me thowgh I say nay?

[4]

My mast*er* pep*er*ed my ars w*ith* well good
    spede;
Hit was worse than fynkyll sede;
He wold not leve till it did blede;
Myche sorow haue he for his dede!
  What vayleth it me thowgh I say nay?

[5]

I wold my mast*er* were a watt,
And my boke a wyld catt,
And a brase of grehownd*es* in his toppe;
I wold be glade for to se that.
  What vaylith it me thowgh I say nay?

[6]

I wold my mast*er* were an hare,
And all his bok*es* hownd*es* were,
And I myself a joly hontere;
To blow my horn I wold not spare,
For if he were dede I wold not care.
     What vaylith me thowgh I say nay?

stza. 2, l. 4. twenti] MS. xx^ti.
At end: Explicit.

B. *Bodleian Library.* MS. Laud misc. 601
                              XV *cent.*

f. 115^v

     Hay y y y,
     Wat helpeyt me thow Y sey nay?

[1]

A Mu*n*day in the moreny[n]g va*n* Y vp rise,
At seue[n] a clo[k]ke at my deuise,
To scole Y must in eny wyse;
     Qu*oth* Y, 'Wat helpeyd me thow Y seyde
          nay?'

[2]

My mast*er* loke aboute . . .
He canat finde me in al the tyme, y, y;

.   .   .   .
     Wat hellpid me thou Y sey nay?

[3]

My mast[er] loke as he w*er*e made:
'Wer haste th*ou* be, th*ou* lityl [lade?']

.   .   .   .
.   .   .   .

stza. 1, l. 4. Y] MS. y y.

414

Bodleian Library. MS. Eng. poet. e. 1
                              XV *cent.*

f. 23^v

     A, a, a, a,
          Yet I loue wherso I go.

[1]

In all this warld [n]is a meryar lyfe
Than is a yong ma*n* with*o*vtyn a wyfe,
For he may lyven with*o*vghten stryfe
     In eu*er*y place wherso he go.

[2]

In eu*er*y place he is loved ou*er* all
Among maydyns gret *and* small,

In daunsyng, i*n* pypy*n*ge, *and* renn*y*ng at
     the ball,
     In eu*er*y [place wherso he go.]

[3]

Thei lat lyght be husbondme*n*
Whan thei at the ball rene;
Thei cast hyr loue to yong me*n*
     In eu*er*y [place wherso thei go.]

[4]

Than sey mayde*n*s, 'Farwell, Jacke,
Thi loue is pressyd al i*n* thi pake;
Th*ou* beryst thi loue behynd thi back
     In eu*er*y [place wherso thou go.']

stzas. 2–4 l. . . MS. In eu*er*y &c.

415

St. John's College, Cambridge. MS. S. 54
                              XV *cent.*

f. 9^v

     Ay, ay, be th*is* day,
     Y wyll mak mery qwyll Y may.

[1]

Qwyll mene haue her bornys full,
Th*er*of Y thynk my p*er*t to pull,
For, to car for the kyng*es* wolle,
     Yt war but selye, be my fay.

[2]

For, be yt werr*e*, or be yt pece.   [f. 10^r
For me may yt be neu*er* the les;
Lete he*m* sytte on the hye dese
     To s*er*ue he*m* in hys arey.

[3]

Me thynk th*is* word is wond*er* wery
And fadyth as the brymbyll bery;
Th*er*for Y wyll note but be mery;
     How long I xall [Y] cannot sey.

[4]

Syrs, *and* ye do aft*er* me,
Car ye not thow th*at* ye the;
Now Y red, do aftyr me,
     For Jak Rekles is my name.

416

British Museum. MS. Sloane 2593
                              XV *cent.*

f. 26^v

     We ben chapme*n* lyght of fote,
          The fowle weyis for to fle.

[1]

We bern abowty*n* no*n* catt*es* skynnys,
Pursis, p*er*lis, sylu*er* pynnis,
Smale wympel*e*[s] for ladyis   [f. 27ʳ]
    chy*n*nys;
    Da*m*sele, bey su*m* war*e* of me.

[2]

I haue a poket for the nonys;
Th*er*ine ben tweyne p*re*cyous stonys;
Da*m*sele, hadde ye asayid he*m* onys,
    Ye xuld the rath*er*e go*n* wi*th* me.

[3]

I haue a jelyf of God*es* sonde;
Wi*th*outy*n* fyt it can stonde;
It ca*n* smyty*n* *and* haght no*n* honde;
    Ryd yo*ur*self q*u*at it may be.

[4]

I haue a powd*er* for to selle;
Q*u*at it is ca*n* I not telle;
It mak*i*t maydenys wo*m*bys to swelle;
    Th*er*of I haue a quantyte.

417

British Museum. MS. Sloane 2593
                   XV *cent.*
f. 29ʳ

    P*re*negard, p*re*negard!
    Thus ber*e* I my*n* baselard.

[1]

Lesten*i*t, lordyng*es*, I y*o*u beseke:
Th*er* is no*n* ma*n* worght a leke,
Be he sturdy, be he meke,
    But he ber*e* a baselard.

[2]

My*n* baselard haght a schede of red
And a clene loket of led;
Me think*i*t I may ber*e* vp my*n*   [f. 29ᵛ
    he[d,]
    For I ber*e* my*n* baselard.

[3]

My baselard haght a wrethi*n* hafte;
Q*u*a*n* I a*m* ful of ale cawte,
It is gret dred of ma*n*slawtte,
    For the*n* I ber*e* [my*n* baselard.]

[4]

My baselard haght a sylu*er* schape;
Th*er*fore I may bothe gaspe *and* gape;
Me think*i*t I go lyk no*n* knape,
    For I ber*e* a baselard.

[5]

My baselard haght a trencher kene,
Fayr as rasou*r*, scharp *and* schene;
Eu*er*e me think*i*t I may be kene,
    For I ber*e* [my*n* baselard.]

[6]

As I yede vp in the strete,
Wi*th* a cartere I ga*n* mete;
'Felawe,' he seyde, 'so mot I the,
    Th*o*u xalt forgo thi baselard.'

[7]

The cartere his qwyppe bega*n* to take,
And al my*n* fleych bega*n* to qwake,
And I was lef for to ascape,
    And ther*e* I left my*n* baselard.

[8]

Qu*an* I ca*m* forght onto my*n* da*m*me,
My*n* hed was broky*n* to the pa*n*ne,
Che seyde I was a praty ma*n*ne,
    And wel cowde ber*e* my*n* basela[rd.]

stza. 3, l. 4. MS. for the*n* I ber*e* &c.
stza. 5, l. 4. MS. for I ber*e* &c.

418

Gonville & Caius College, Cambridge. MS.
    383   XV *cent.*
p. 41

    Hos is to hoth at hom,
    Ryd out; it wol agon.

[1]

Wan ic wente byyonde the see,
Ryche ma*n* for te bee,
Neu*er* the bet*ur* was me;
    Ic hadde leu*er* han be*n* at om.

[2]

Hammard wanne ic gan drawe,
Wyth a ryt hong*ur*y mawe,
A lytyl god ic was wel fawe;
    My fre*n*d*us* weru*n* my fulle fon.

[3]

A man th*at* nower nel abyde,
But sech contreys wyde,
Ofte tene schal hi*m* betyde;
    Myche yerne bryngeth lytel ho*m*.

[4]

A ma*n* th*at* nower nel groute,
But seche co*n*treys aboute,
Of his thrift he is i*n* doute;
    God ne schal he gete no*n*.

[5]

God, th*a*t is i*n* heuene cler,
And his swete mod*ur* derr*e*
And hys halwen al yfer*e*
    Yyf vs gr*a*ce wel to don.

Before burden (apparently the name of the air):
    alone y lyue alone.
The repetition of the burden is indicated after
stza. 5 by: wos is to.

418.1

Bodleian Library. MS. Rawlinson poet. 34
                                    XV *cent.*
f. 4ᵛ

    Huff a galaw*n*t vylabele—
    Thus syngyth galawnt*es* i*n* her*e* revele.

[1]

Galaw*n*t, pr*i*de thy father ys dede;
Thow hast hy*m* robbyd, as Y rede,
And clothyd the in galawnt*es* wede:
    Huff a galawntt.

[2]

Galawntt, w*it*h thy curtesy
Thow brekyst thy hose at kne,
And w*it*h a pacche th*o*u clowtyst aye:
    Huff a galawntt.

[3]

Thow th*a*t thow haue a stomag*er* the
        byforn*e*,
Thy schyrtte byhynd ys all to-torn*e*;
Ner*e* were thy pykyd schone th*o*u were
        forlorn*e*:
    Huff a galauntt.

[4]

Galaunt, yf th*o*u wylt haue thy hele,
Wrap thy bryst w*it*h clothys fele;
Than mayst th*o*u syng*e* vylabele:
    Huff a galauntt.

[5]

Butt galaunte bachelers ther be fele;
They*r*e gown*es* be sett w*it*h plytys fele;
To schortt yt ys theyr*e* kneys to hele:
    Huff a galauntt.

[6]

To galaunt to be yt ys noughtt,
For and hys purse were well ysought,
I hold hy*m* worse than nought:
    Huff a galauntt.

[7]

All abak he castys hys her*e*,
Fowr*e* enchys byn*e*th hy[s] *e*re—
I wold hys hed wer*e* off by the swer*e*:
    Huff a galauntt.

[8]

Theyr*e* hosyn of red, ful close thei be,
W*it*h a whytte bulwerk abowtt the kne;
A schrewd syghtt ytt ys to se:
    Huff a galawnt*t*.

[9]

Galaunt, by thy gyrdyl ther hangyth a
        purss;
Therin ys neyther peny ner crosse,
But three dysse and Cryst*es* curse:
    Huff a galaw[n]t*t*.

[10]

Galaunt, w*it*h thy daggar acrosse,
And thy hanggy*n*g pouche vpon thyn arse,
Thow art ful abyl to stele a horse:
    Huff a galauntt.

stza. 9, l. 3. three] MS. iij.
The burden is written again at the end:
    huff a galauntt vylabele
    Thus syngyth galaunt*es* in theyr*e* reuele
    w*it*h huff a Galauntt.

418.2

Bodleian Library. MS. Arch. Selden B. 26
                                    XV *cent.*
f. 19ʳ

    The m*er*the of alle this londe
    Maketh the gode husbonde
        W*it*h erynge of his plowe.

[1]

Iblessyd be C*ristes* sonde,
Th*a*t hath us sent i*n* honde
    Merthe *and* joye ynowe.

[2]

The plowe goth mony a gate,
Bothe erly *and* eke late,
    In wynt*er* in the clay.

[4]

Aboute barly and whete,
Th*a*t maketh men to swete,
    God spede the plowe al day!

[5]

Browne Morel *and* Gore
Drawen the plowe ful sore
  Al in the morwenynge.

[6]

Rewarde hem therfore
W*ith* a shefe or more
  Alle in the evenynge.

[7]

Whan men bygy*n*ne to sowe,
Ful wel her*e* corne they knowe
  In the mon*n*the of May.

[8]

Howe ev*er* Janyver blowe,
Whether hye or lowe,
  God spede the plowe allway!

[9]

Whan men bygy*n*neth to wede
The thystle fro the sede,
  In som*er* whan they may:

[10]

God lete hem wel to spede
And longe gode lyfe to lede,
  All th*at* for plowemen pray.

418.3

British Museum. MS. Royal 19. B. IV
                              XV *cent.*
f. 97ᵛ

  'Pax uobis,' quod the fox,
    'For I am comyn to toowne.'

[1]

It fell ageyns the next nyght
The fox yede to with all hys myghte,
Withoouten cole or candelight,
  Whan that he cam vnto the toowne.

[2]

Whan he cam all in the yarde,
Soore te geys wer ill aferde:
'I shall macke some of yowre berde
  Or that I goo from the toowne.'

[3]

Whan he cam all in the croofte,
There he stalkyd wundirfull soofte:

'For here haue I be frayed full ofte
  Whan that I haue come to toowne.'

[4]

He hente a goose all be the heye;
Faste the goos began to creye;
Oowte yede men as they myght heye
  And seyde, 'Fals fox, ley it doowne!'

[5]

'Nay', he saide, 'soo mot I the,
Sche shall goo vnto the wode with me;
Sche and I wnther a tre,
  Emonge the beryis browne.

[6]

'I haue a wyf, and sche lyeth seke;
Many smale whelppis sche haue to eke;
Many bonys they muste pike
  Will they ley adowne!'

419

A a. *Balliol College, Oxford.* MS. 354
                                    XVI *cent.*
f. 206ᵛ

  Hoow, gossip myne, gossip myn,
  Wha*n* will we go to the wyne?
  Good gossip*es* [myn.]

[1]

I shall you tell a full good sport,
How gossippis gader the*m* on a sort,
Ther seke bodyes to co*m*forte,
  Whan they mete
  I*n* lane or stret,
    God gossipis myn.

[2]

But I dare not, for th*er* dissplesau*n*s,
Tell of thes mat*er*s half the substance,
But yet su*m*what of th*er* gou*er*naunce
  As ferre as I dare,
  I will declare,
    Good gossipis myn.

[3]

'Good gossip myn, wher haue ye be?
Hit is so long sith I you see.
Wher is the best wyne? Tell you me.
  Can ye owght tell?'
  'Ye, full well,
    Good gossippis myn.

[4]

'I know a drawght of mery-go-down;
The beste it is in all this town;
But yet I wolde not for my gown
  My husbond wyste,
  Ye may me triste,
    Good gossippis myn.'

[5]

'Call forth owr gossippis by and by,
Elynore, Johan, and Margery,
Margret, Alis, and Cecely,
  For thei will cum,
  Both all and som,
    Good gossippis myn-a.

[6]

'And eche of them will sumwhat bryng,
Gose or pigge or capons wynge,
Pastes of pigynnes or sum other thyng,
  For we muste ete
  Sum maner mett,
    Good gossippis myn-a.'

[7]

'Go beffore by tweyn and tweyn,
Wisely, that ye be not seen,
For I mvste home and cum agayn
  To witt, ywis,
  Wher my husbond is,
    Good gossippis myn-a.

[8]

'A strype or ii God myght send   [f. 207ʳ
    me
Yf my husbond myght here see me.'
'She that is aferde, lett her flee,'
  Quod Alis than;
  'I dred no man,
    Good gossippis myn-a.

[9]

'Now be we in the tavern sett;
A drawght of the best lett hym fett,
To bryng owr husbondes owt of dett,
  For we will spend
  Till God more send,
    Good gossippis myn-a.'

[10]

Eche of them browght forth ther disshe;
Sum browght flesshe and sum fisshe;
Quod Margret meke now with a wisshe,
  'I wold Anne were here;
  She wold mak vs chere,
    Good gossippis myn-a.

[11]

'How say ye, gossippis, is this wyn good?'
'That is it,' quod Elynore, 'by the rode!
It chereth the hart and comforteth the blod;
  Such jonkers amonge
  Shall make vs leve long,
    Good gossippis [myn-a.']

[12]

Anne bade, 'Fill a pot of muscadell,
For of all wynes I love it well;
Swet wynes kepe my body in hele;
  Yf I had it nowght,
  I shuld tak thowght,
    Good gossippis myn-a.

[13]

'How loke ye, gossip, at the bordes end?
Not mery, gossip? God it amend!
All shall be well; els God defend!
  Be mery and glad,
  And sit not so sade,
    Good gossip myn-a.'

[14]

'Wold God I had don after your covnsell,
For my husband is so fell
He betith me lyke the devill of hell,
  And the more I crye,
  The lesse mercy,
    Good gossippis myn-a.'

[15]

Alis with a lowde voys spak than:
'Evis,' she said, 'littill good he can
That betith or strikith any woman,
  And specially his wyff,
  God geve hym short lyff,
    Good gossippis myn-a!'

[16]

Margret meke saide, 'So mot I thryve,
I know no man that is alyve
That gevith me ii strokes but he haue v!
  I am not afferd,
  Thowgh he haue a berde,
    Good gossippis myn-a.'

[17]

On cast down her shot and went away.
'Gossip,' quod Elynore, 'what dide she
    pay?
Not but a peny? Loo, therfor I say
  She shall no more
  Be of owr lore,
    Good gossippis myn-a.

[18]

'Suche gestes we may haue ynow,
That will not for ther shot alowe;
With whom com she? Gossip, with you?'
'Nay', quod Johan,
'I com aloon,
    Good gossippis myn-a.'

[19]

'Now rekyn owr shot, *and* go we hens.
What? Cummeth to eche of vs but iii
    pence?
Perde, this is but a small expens
    For suche a sorte,
    And all but sporte,
    Good gossipes myn-a.

[20]

'Torn down the stret wha*n* ye   [f. 207ᵛ
    cu*m* owt,
And we wil cumpas rownd abowt.'
'Gossip,' quod Anne, 'what nedith th*at*
    dowt?
    Your husbondes [be] pleased
    Wha*n* ye be eased,
    Good gossipes myn-a.

[21]

'Whatsoeu*er* any man thynk,
We co*m* for nowght but for good drynk;
Now lct vs go home *and* wynke,
    For it may be seen
    Wher we haue ben,
    Good gossippes myn-a.'

[22]

This is the thowght th*at* gossippis take:
Ons i*n* the wek mery will they make,
And all small drynk*es* thei will forsake,
    But wyne of the best
    Shall haue no rest,
    Good gossippes myn-a.

[23]

Su*m* be at the tav*er*n thrise i*n* the weke,
And so be su*m* eu*er*y day eke,
Or ell*es* th*ei* will gron *and* mak the*m* sek,
    For thy*n*gis vsed
    Will not be refused,
    God gossippes myn-a.

[24]

Who sey yow, women, is it not soo?
Yes, suerly, and th*at* ye wyll know;

And therfore lat vs drynk all a-row
    And off owr syngyng
    Mak a good endyng,
    [Gocd gossippis myn-a.]

[25]

Now fyll the cupe, *and* drynk to me,
And than shal we good felows be,
And off thys talkyng leve will we
    And speak then
    Good off women,
    [Good gossippis myn-a.]

burden, l. 1. *The end of the line is obscured by the binding.*
stza. 19, l. 2. pence] MS. d.
stza. 23, l. 1. thrise] MS. iii ˢᵉ.
Stzas. 24, 25, not in MS., are supplied from A b.
At end: Explicit.

b. *Bodleian Library.* MS. Eng. poet. e. 1, ff. 57ᵛ–59ᵛ. XV *cent.*

burden, l. 2. we] ye.   l. 3. *omits.*
stza. 1, l. 1. shall] wyll.   l. 3. to] for to.
    l. 5. lane] a lane.   l. 6. *omits in all stanzas.*
stza. 3, l. 4. ye] yow.   l. 5. Ye] *omits.*
stza. 4, l. 3. I wolde] wold I.   l. 4. wyste]
    it wyst.
stza. 5, l. 1. owr] yowr.
stza. 6, l. 2. or (1)] *omits.*
    ll. 4, 5. Fore a galon off wyn
                Thei will not wryng.
stza. 9, l. 1. the] *omits.*
stza. 11, l. 1. ye] yow.   l. 2. is it] it is.
    l. 3. chereth] cherisheth.   comforteth] com-
    fort.   l. 4. jonkers] jonckettes.
stza. 12, l. 1. bade] byd.   l. 4. it] off it.
    l. 5. thowght] gret thoug[ht].
stza. 13, l. 3. defend] it defend.
stza. 16, l. 3. gevith] gyve.   haue] shal haue.
    v] fyffe.   l. 5. he] I.   a] no.
stzas. 17, l. 1, away] her wey.   l. 4. no] be no.
    l. 5. Be] *omits.*
stza. 19, l. 2. Cummeth to] cost it.
stza. 20, l. 1. wha*n*] where.   l. 5. eased]
    reisyd.
stza. 22, l. 3. drynk*es*] drynk.   l. 5. haue] han.
stza. 23, l. 1. thrise] ons.   the (2)] a.

B. *British Museum.* MS. Cotton Titus A.
xxvi   XV *cent.*

    [Gode gosyp . . .]
·   ·   ·   ·   ·

[1]

'Go ye before be twayne and   [f. 161ʳ
    twayne,
Wysly, that ye be not isayne,
And I shall go home *and* com agayne,
    To witte what dothe owre syre.

[2]

'For yyff hit happ he dyd me se,
A strype or to God myght send me;
Yytte sche that is afer[d]e, lette her flee,
 For that is nowght be this fyre.'

[3]

That eueryche of hem browght ther dysche;
Sum browght fleshe, and som brought
 fyshe;
Quod Margery meke than with a wyise,
 'I wold that Frankelyne the harper were
  here.'

[4]

She hade notte so sone the word isayd,
But in come Frankelyn at a brayd;
'God saue youe, mastres,' he sayde;
 'I come to make youe some chere.'

[5]

Anon he began to draw owght his harpe;
Tho the gossyppes began to starte;
They callyd the tawyrner to fyll the quarte
And lette note for no coste.

[6]

Then seyd the gossyppes all in fere,
'Streke vp, harper, and make gode chere,
And wher that I goo, fere or nere,
 To owre hu[s]bondes make thou no
 [boste.']

[7]

'Nay, mastres, as motte I thee,
Ye schall newyr be wrayed for me;
I had leuer her dede to be
 As hereof to be knowe.'

[8]

They fylled the pottes by and by; [f. 161ᵛ
They lett not for no coste trully;
The harpyr stroke vpe merrely,
 That they myght onethe blowe.

[9]

They sette them downe; they myght no
 more;
Theyre legges they thought were passyng
 soore;
They prayd the harper, 'Kepe sum store,
 And lette vs drynke a bowght.'

[10]

'Heye the, tauernere, I praye the;
Go fyll the potteys lyghtyly,
And latte vs dry[n]ke by and by,
 And lette the cupe goo route.'

[11]

This ys the thowght that gossypus take:
Onys in the weke they wyll merey make,
And all smalle drynckys they wyll forsake,
 And drynke wyne of the best.

[12]

Some be at the tauerne onys in the weke,
And some be there euery day eke,
And ellse ther hartes will be sekke
 And gyffe her hosbondys ewyll reste.

[13]

When they had dronke and made them
 glad,
And they schuld rekyn, theyn they sad,
'Call the tauernere,' anone they bade,
 'That we were lyghtly hens.'

[14]

'I swere be God and by Seynt [f. 162ʳ
 Jayme,
I wold notte that oure syre at home
[Wiste] that we had this game,
 Notte for fourty pens.

[15]

'Gadyr the scote, and lette vs wend,
And lette vs goo home by Lurcas Ende,
For drede we mete note with owre frend
 Or that we come home.'

[16]

When they had there countes caste,
Eueryche of hem spend vi pence at the
 last;
'Alas,' cothe Seyscely, 'I am aggaste;
 We schall be schent eurychone.'

[17]

Fro the tauerne be they all goone,
And eueryche of hem schewythe her wys-
 dom,
And there sche tellythe her husband anone
 Shee had been at the chyrche.

[18]

Off her werke she takythe no kepe;
Sche must as for anowe goo sclepe,
And ells for aggeyr wyll sche wepe;
 She may no werkes wurche.

[19]

Off her slepe when sche dothe wake,
Faste in hey then gan sche arake,
And c[l]awthe her serwantes abowte the
 bake,
 Yff to here they outhe had sayd.

[20]

Off this proses I make an end
Becawse I wil haue wome*n* to be my frend;
Of there dewosyon they wold send
    A peny for to drynke at the end.

*Several leaves are missing from MS. immediately
   before this piece, which consequently lacks its
   burden and initial stanzas.*
The repetition of the burden is indicated as
   follows: stzas. 1, 2, 4, 9, 17, 20: gode gosyp.
   stza. 3: gode gosip. stzas. 5, 7, 8, 10–16, 18,
   19: good gosyp. stza. 6: god gossip.
*Stzas. 6 and 7 are transposed in MS., the correct
   order being indicated by a cross-mark.*
stza. 13, l. 3. the] MS. they.
stza. 16, l. **2.** pence] MS. ᵈ.
stza. 17, l. 4. chyrche] MS. chyrchee.
At end: Exsplycyt lytyll thanke.

C. *British Museum.* MS. Cotton Vitellius
   D. xii   XV *cent.*

f. 43ᵛ

[No burden]

[1]

Now shall youe her a tale fore youre dys-
   [port]
Howe gossypp*es* dyd gader in a sorte
Theyre syke bodyes to comefort
   And at the tauerne sone to mette,
     Go[od] go[syp;]
I dare notte for theyre dyssplcsans
Tell of this matter the substans
But su*m*what of her gou*er*nance:
   They wolde theyr lyppis wete,
     Good gosyp.

[2]

'Good gossyppe, where haue ye be?
Hit is long agoo sythe I youe ssee;
Where is thys beste wyne, now say ye?
   Cane thereof tell,
     Good gosyp?'
'I knowe a drawght of mery-goo-down*e*,
The best that is in all this towne,
[B]ut yit I wold nott for my gowne
   My husbonde wyst hit well,
     Gode gosy[p.']

[3]

'Call forthe youre g[os]sypp*es* by *and* by,
Katryn, Mawd, and Margerey,
Crystyan, Jone, *and* Sessely;
   They wull com*e* all in the sam*e*,
     'Good [gosyp.]

Eueryche of hym wyll sumwha[t bryng,]
Pygge, gosse, or capuns wyn[g,]
A pasti of pegenys, or su*m* [other thyng,]
   That we may make su*m* g[ame,
     Good gosyp.']

420

Balliol College, Oxford. MS. 354
                          XVI *cent.*

f. 251ᵛ

   Bon jowre, bon jowr*e* a vous!
   I am cu*m* vnto this hows
     V*ith* p*ar* la pompe, I say.

[1]

Is th*er* any good man here
Th*at* will make me any chere?
And if th*er* were, I wold cu*m* nere
   To wit what he wold say.
     A, will ye be wild?
     By Mary myld,
   .   .   .
   I trow yc will synge gay.

[2]

Be gladly, masters eu*er*ychon;
I am cu*m* myself alone
To appose you on by on;
   Let se who dare say nay.
     Sir what say ye?
     Syng on; lett vs see.
     Now will it be
   Thys or another day?

[3]

Loo, this is he th*at* will do the dede!
He te*m*pereth his mowth; th*er*fore take
                 hede.
Syng softe, I say, lest yowr nose blede,
   For hurt yowrself ye may;
     But, by God, th*at* me bowght,
     Your brest is so towght,
     Tyll ye haue well cowght,
   Ye may not th*er*wi*th* away.

[4]

Sir, what say ye wi*th* your face so lene?
Ye syng noth*er* good tenowre, treble, ne
                 mene.
Vtter not your voice withowt your brest be
                 clene,
   Hartely I you p*ra*y.
     I hold you excused;
     Ye shall be refused,
     For ye haue not be vsed
   To no good sport nor play.

[5]

Sir, what say ye with your fat face?
Me thynkith ye shuld bere a very good bace
To a pot of good ale or ipocras,
  Truly as I you say.
    Hold vp your hede;
    Ye loke lyke lede;
    Ye wast myche bred
  Euermore from day to day.

[6]

Now will ye see wher he stondith behynde?
Iwis, brother, ye be vnkynd;
Stond forth, and wast with me som wynd,
  For ye haue ben called a synger ay.
    Nay, be not ashamed;
    Ye shall not be blamed,
    For ye haue ben famed
  The worst in this contrey.

The repetition of the burden is indicated as
follows: stzas. 1, 2, 4: Bon Jowre. stza. 3:
bonjowr. stza. 5: Bon Joure. stza. 6: bon
Jowre.
At end: Explicit.

421

Balliol College, Oxford. MS. 354
                                          XVI *cent.*
f. 251ᵛ

  How, butler, how! Bevis a towt!
  Fill the boll, jentill butler, and let the cup
    rowght.

[1]

Jentill butler, bell amy,
Fyll the boll by the eye,
That we may drynk by and by;
  With how, butler, how! Bevis a towt!
  Fill the boll, butler, and let the cup
    rowght.

[2]

Here is mete for vs all,
Both for gret and for small;
I trow we must the butlar call;
  With how, butler, how! Bevis a towt!
  Fill the boll, butler, and lett the cupe
    rowght.

[3]

I am so dry I cannot spek;   [f. 252ʳ
I am nygh choked with my mete;
I trow the butler be aslepe;
  With how, butler, how! Bevis a towght!
  Fill the boll, butler, [and let the cup
    rowght.]

[4]

Butler, butler, fill the boll,
Or elles I beshrewe thy noll;
I trow we must the bell toll;
  With how, butler, how! Bevis a towght!
  Fill the boll, [butler, and let the cup
    rowght.]

[5]

Iff the butlers name be Water,
I wold he were a galow-claper,
But if he bryng vs drynk the rather;
  With how, butler, how! Bevis a towght!
  Fill [the boll, butler, and let the cup
    rowght.]

burden, l. 2. butler] MS. butlet.
stza. 3, l. 5. MS. Fill the boll butler &c.
stza. 4, l. 5. MS. Fill the boll &c.
stza. 5, l. 5. MS. Fill &c.
At end: Explicit.

422

A. *Bodleian Library.* MS. Eng. poet. e. 1
                                        XV *cent.*
f. 41ᵛ

  Bryng vs in good ale, and bryng vs in
    good ale;
  Fore owr blyssyd Lady sak, bryng vs in
    good ale.

[1]

Bryng vs in no browne bred, fore   [f. 42ʳ
  that is mad of brane,
Nore bryng vs in no whyt bred, fore therin
  is no game,
  But bryng vs in good ale.

[2]

Bryng vs in no befe, for ther is many bonys,
But bryng vs in good ale, for that goth
  downe at onys,
  And bryng vs in good ale.

[3]

Bryng vs in no bacon, for that is passyng
  fate,
But bryng vs in god ale, and gyfe vs inought
  of that,
  And bryng vs in good ale.

[4]

Bryng vs in no mutton, for that is often
  lene,
Nor bryng vs in no trypys, for thei be
  syldom clene,
  But bryng vs in good ale.

[5]

Bryng vs in no eggys, for ther ar many
    schell*es*,
But bryng vs in good ale, *and* gyfe vs
    noth[y]ng ellys,
    And bryng vs in good ale.

[6]

Bryng vs in no butter, for th*erin* ar many
    herys,
Nor bryng vs in no pygg*es* flesch, for th*at*
    wyl mak vs borys,
    But bryng vs in good ale.

[7]

Bryng vs in no podyng*es*, for th*erin* is al
    God*es* good,
Nor bryng vs in no veneson, for th*at* is not
    for owr blod,
    But bryng vs in good ale.

[8]

Bryng vs in no capons flesch, for th*at* is
    often der,
Nor bryng vs in no dok*es* flesch, for thei
    slober in the mer,
    But bryng vs in good ale.

*Stza. 1 is written last in MS. Its proper position
is indicated by a, the other stanzas being marked
b, c, etc.*

B. *British Museum.* MS. Harley 541
                           XV *cent.*
f. 214ᵛ

    Brynge vs home good ale, s*er*; brynge vs
        home good ale,
    And for owre dere Lady love, brynge vs
        home good ale.

[1]

Brynge home no beff, s*er*, for that ys full of
    bonys,
But brynge home good ale inowgh, for I
    love wyle th*at*,
    But [brynge vs home good ale.]

[2]

Brynge vs home no wetyn brede, for that ys
    full of braund,
Nothyr no ry brede, for th*at* ys of th*at*
    same,
    But [brynge vs home good ale.]

[3]

Bryng vs home no porke, s*er*, for th*at* ys
    very fat,
Nethyr no barly brede, for nethyr lovye I
    th*at*,
    But bryng vs home good ale.

[4]

Bryng vs home no muttun, s*er*, for th*at* ys
    togh and lene,
Nothyr no trypys, for they be seldyn clene,
    But bryng [vs home good ale.]

[5]

Bryng vs home no vele, s*er*, for th*at* wyll
    not dur*e*,
But bryng vs home good ale inogh to
    drynke by the fyr*e*,
    But [bryng vs home good ale.]

[6]

Bryng vs home no sydyr, nor no palde
    wyne,
For, and th*o*u do, thow shalt have Cryst*es*
    curse and myne,
    But [bryng vs home good ale.]

burden, l. 2. Lady] MS. lady lady.
stza. 1, l. 3. MS. but c.
stzas. 1, 2, 5, 6, l. 3. MS. but &c.
stza. 4, l. 1. muttun] MS. mwttun.   l. 3. MS.
    but bryng &c.

423

Bodleian Library. MS. Eng. poet. e. 1
                          XV *cent.*
f. 52ʳ

    Doll thi ale, doll; doll thi ale, dole;
    Ale mak many a man*e* to haue a doty
        poll.

[1]

Ale mak many a man*e* to styk at a brere,
Ale mak many a man*e* to ly in the myer*e*,
And ale mak many a man*e* to slep by the
    fyer*e*;
    W*ith* doll.

[2]

Ale mak many a man*e* to sto*m*byl at a ston*e*,
Ale mak many a man*e* to go dro*n*ken home,
And ale mak many a man*e* to brek hys ton*e*;
    W*ith* doll.

[3]

Ale mak many a man*e* to draw hys knyfe,
Ale mak many a man*e* to mak gret stryfe,
And ale mak many a man*e* to bet hys wyf;
With dole.

[4]

Ale mak many a man*e* to wet hys chek*es*,
Ale mak many a man*e* to ly *in* the stret*es*,
And ale mak many a man*e* to wet hys shet*es*;
With dole.

[5]

Ale mak many a man*e* to sto*m*byll at the
　　blokk*es*,
Ale mak many a man*e* to mak his hed hau*e*
　　knokk*es*,
And ale mak many a man*e* to syt *in* the
　　stokk*es*;
With dol.

[6]

Ale mak many a mane to ryn*e*　　　[f. 52ᵛ
　　ou*er* the falows,
Ale mak many a mane to swer*e* by God *and*
　　Al-Halows,
And ale mak many a man*e* to hang vpon the
　　galows;
With dol.

424

A. *Balliol College, Oxford.* MS. 354
　　　　　　　　　　　　　　XVI *cent.*

f. 177ᵛ

　　As I walked by a forest side,
　　I met wi*th* a foster; he bad me abide.

[1]

At a place wher he me sett　　　[f. 178ʳ
He bad me, what tyme an hart I met,
That I shuld lett slyppe *and* say, 'Go bett!'
　　Wi*th* 'Hay, go bet! Hay, go bett! Hay,
　　go bett! How!'
　　We shall haue game *and* sport ynow.

[2]

I had not stond ther but a while,
Ye, not the mou*n*tenau*n*ce of a myle,
But a gret hart ca*m* re*n*nyng wi*th*owt any
　　gile;
　　Wi*th* 'Th*er* he goth! Th*er* he goth! th*er*
　　he gothe! How!'
　　We shall haue game *and* sport ynow.

[3]

I had no sonner my hownd*es* lat goo
But the hart was overthrowe;
Than eu*er*y man began to blowe;
　　With 'Tro-ro-ro! Tro-ro-ro! Tro-ro-ro!
　　Trow!'
　　We shall haue game *and* sport ynow.

At end: Explicit.

B. *Bodleian Library.* Rawlinson 4to. 598
　　(10) (Wynkyn de Worde)　　　　1521

recto

　　As I came by a grene forest syde,
　　I met with a forster th*a*t badde me abyde;
　　　With 'Hey, go bet! Hey, go bet! Hey,
　　　go [bet!] Howe!'
　　We shall haue sport and game ynowe.

[1]

Underneth a tre I dyde me set,
And with a grete hert anone I met;
I badde let slyppe and sayd, 'Hey, go bet!'
　　With 'Hey, go bet! Hey, go bet! [Hey go
　　bet!] Howe!'
　　We shall haue sport and game ynowe.

[2]

I had not stande there but a whyle,
Not the mountenaunce of a myle;
There came a grete hert without gyle:
　　'There he gothe! There he gothe! [There
　　he gothe! How!']
　　We shall haue sporte and game ynowe.

[3]

Talbot my hou*n*de, with a mery taste,
All about the grene wode he gan cast;
I toke my horne and blewe him a blast;
⎧[a] With 'Tro-ro-ro-ro! Tro-ro-ro-ro!
⎪　　[Tro-ro-ro-ro! Ro!']
⎨[b] With 'Hey, go bet! Hey, go bet! [Hey,
⎪　　go bet! How!']
⎪[c] 'There he gothe! There he goth!
⎩　　[There he goth! How!']
　　We shall haue sport and game ynowe.

Heading in original: A caroll of huntynge.
stza. 2, l. 4. [There he gothe! How!]] Orig. &c.
stza. 3, l. 4 [b]. [Hey, go bet! How!]] Orig. &c.
l. 4 [c]. [There he goth! How!]] Orig. &c.
The three different texts of stza. 3, l. 4 were
apparently to be sung simultaneously by three
different voices.
At end: Finis.

424.1

County Archives Office, Maidstone, Kent.
K. A. O. U 182 Z1 XV *cent.*

verso

Man of mightt, that al hed ydyght
 An knowys heuery wronge,
Into de blysse dow ws wysse,
 Dow spedys yn owre songe.

[1]

Det peruynkkle hed ykowmbyrght owre
 town,
 Tyl vs het ybent hys boghe;
We han be wendyt yn gret tresoun—
 That is rigt wel yknowe.
The brere het ybrowt de wed adown
 An layd hys leyghuys loywe;
Kyng of Blysse de brere de vysse,
 An al his rotys stronge.

[2]

The leuis of de brere bryght
 Byt ysclydyn owt of his sclym,
To hele here sores det byght of might,
 An we plokyt hym yn tyme.
God grette that brere semyly of syght
 That peruynkle han naut lyme;
Kynk of Blysse de brere de vysse,
 An al hys rote[s] stronge.

[3]

That bryghte brere schel sprede an sper·
 ynge,
 That ys greffit wyt grace,
An fet wher [   ] lyke [   ]
 Maye perwynk [   ] hys face.
Pernk' schel have wel heuyle endyng,
 An al hys rotes to rasse;
Kyng of Blysse de brere de wysse,
 An al hys rotes stronge.

[4]

Dang we God [de] halle hes ysent
 Of al dys wordes [w]ele,
An denk wre lyf ys ws but ylent—
 How l[ong] canne we naut telle;
Do we so we be naut yschent
 Wele we haue sp[a]ce to duelle;
Kyng of Blysse de brere de wysse,
 An al hys rotes stronge.

*The empty square brackets indicate completely
illegible passages in MS.*
stza. 1, l. 1. Det] MS. Set. l. 8. rotys] MS.
retys.
stza. 2, l. 1. brere] MS. breres.

812715 K

425

Trinity College, Cambridge. MS. R. 4. 20
 XV *cent.*

f. 171ʳ

Hay, hay, hay, hay!
Thynke on Whitson Monday.

[1]

The Bysshop Scrope, that was so wyse,
Nowe is he dede, and lowe he lyse;
To hevyns blys yhit may he ryse
 Thurghe helpe of Marie, that mylde
 may.

[2]

When he was broght vnto the hyll,
He held hym both mylde and styll;
He toke his deth with full gode wyll,
 As I haue herde full trewe men say.

[3]

He that shulde his dethe be,
He kneled down vppon his kne:
'Lord, your deth, forgytte it me,
 Full hertly here to yowe I pray.'

[4]

'Here I wyll the commende
Thou gyff me fyve strokys with thy hende,
And than my wayes thou latt me wende
 To hevyns blys, that lastys ay.'

The repetition of the burden is indicated after
 each stanza by: hay.
At end (*in another and later hand*): per me
 thomam henry persone.

426

a. *Bodleian Library.* MS. Arch. Selden
 B. 26 XV *cent.*

f. 17ᵛ

Deo gracias Anglia
Redde pro victoria.

[1]

Owre kynge went forth to Normandy
With grace and myght of chyualry;
Ther God for hym wrought mervelusly;
Wherfore Englonde may calle and cry,
 'Deo gracias.'

[2]

He sette a sege, the sothe for to [f. 18ʳ
    say,
To Harflu tovne with ryal aray;
That tovne he wan and made a fray
That Fraunce shal rywe tyl domesday;
  Deo gracias.

[3]

Than went oure kynge with alle his oste
Thorwe Fraunce, for alle the Frenshe
    boste;
He spared no drede of lest ne moste
Tyl he come to Agincourt coste;
  Deo gracias.

[4]

Than, forsoth, that knyght comely,
In Agincourt feld he faught manly;
Thorw grace of God most myghty
He had bothe the felde and the victory;
  Deo gracias.

[5]

There dukys and erlys, lorde and barone
Were take and slayne, and that wel sone,
And summe were ladde into Lundone
With joye and merthe and grete renone;
  Deo gracias.

[6]

Now gracious God he saue oure kynge,
His peple, and alle his wel-wyllynge;
Yef hym gode lyfe and gode endynge,
That we with merth mowe sauely synge,
  'Deo gracias.'
The burden is again written in full after stza. 1
  and marked: chorus.
*Stza. 3 is written after stza. 6 in MS. It is
marked a, and stza. 4 is marked b.*

b. *Trinity College, Cambridge.* MS. O. 3.
58, recto. XV *cent.* (burden and stzas. 1,
2, 4–6).
stza. 2, l. 1. the sothe for] for sothe.
stza. 3, l. 1. Than went hym forth owr kyng
  comely.   l. 3. myghty] meruelowsly.
  l. 4. the . . . the] *omits.*
stza. 5, l. 1. dukys and erlys, lorde] lordys eerlys.
  l. 2. take and slayne] slayn and takyn. wel]
  ful.   l. 3. ladde] browth.   l. 4. merthe]
  blysse.   l. 5. D. g.
stza. 6, l. 1. Now gracious] Almythy. saue]
  kepe.   l. 3. And yeue hem grace withoutyn
  endyng.   l. 4. That we with merth mowe]
  Than may we calle and.
The burden is again written in full after stza. 1.

427

British Museum. MS. Addit. 31042
                           XV *cent.*

f. 110ᵛ

  The Rose es the fayreste flour of alle
    That euermore wasse or euermore schall,
      The Rose of Ryse;
    Off alle thies flourres the Rose berys
    pryce.

[1]

The Rose it es the fairest flour;
The Rose es swetteste of odoure;
The Rose, in care it es comforthetour;
The Rose, in sekenes it es saluoure,
  The Rose so bryghte;
In medcyns it es moste of myghte.

[2]

Witnesse thies clerkes that bene wysse:
The Rose es the flour moste holdyn in
  prysse;
Therfore me thynke the Flour-de-Lyse
Scholde wirchipe the Rose of Ryse
  And bene his thralle,
  And so scholde other floures alle.

[3]

Many a knyghte with spere and launce
Folowede that Rose to his plesance;
When the Rose bytyde a chaunce,
Than fadide alle the floures of Fraunce
  And chaungyde hewe
  In plesance of the Rose so trewe.
MS. heading: A Carolle for Crystynmesse.

428

Bodleian Library. MS. Douce 302
        By John Audelay, XV *cent.*
f. 29ʳ

  A, Perles Pryns, to the we pray:
  Saue our kyng both nyght and day.

[1]

Fore he is ful yong, tender of age,
Semele to se, o bold corage,
Louele and lofte of his lenage,
  Both perles prince and kyng veray.

[2]

His gracious granseres and his grawndame,
His fader and moder, of kyngis thay came;
Was neuer a worthier prynce of name
  So exelent in al our day.

[3]

His fader, fore loue of Mayd Kateryn
In Fraunce he wroght turment and tene;
His loue hee sayd hit schuld not ben
    And send him ballis him with to play.

[4]

Then was he wyse in wars withall
And taght Franchemen to plai at the ball;
With tenes-hold he ferd ham hall;
    To castelles and setis thei floyn away.

[5]

To Harflete a sege he layd anon
And cast a bal vnto the towne;
The Frenchemen swere be se and sun
    Hit was the fynd that mad that fray.

[6]

Anon thai toke ham to cownsele;
Oure gracious kyng thai wold asayle;
At Agyncowrt, at that patayle,
    The floure of Frawnce he fel that day.

[7]

The Kyng of Frawns then was   f. 29ᵛ
    agast,
Mesagers to him send in hast,
Fore wele he west hit was bot wast
    Hem to witstond in hone way.

[8]

And prayd hym to sese of his outrage
And take Kateryn to mareage;
Al Frawnce to him schuld do homage
    And croune him kyng afftyr his day.

[9]

Of Frawnce he mad him anon regent
And wedid Kateren in his present;
Into Englond anon he went
    And cround our quene in ryal aray.

[10]

Of Queen Kateryn our kyng was borne
To saue our ryght that was forelorne
Oure faders in Frawns had won before;
    Thai han hit hold mone a day.

[11]

Thus was his fader a conqueroure
And wan his moder with gret onoure;
Now may the kyng bere the floure
    Of kyngis and kyngdams in vche cuntre.

[12]

On him schal fal the prophece
That hath ben sayd of Kyng Herre:
The hole cros wyn or he dye
    That Crist habud on Good Fryday.

[13]

Al wo and werres he schal acese
And set all reams in rest and pese
And turne to Cristyndam al hethynes;
    Now grawnt him hit so be may.

[14]

Pray we that Lord is lord of all
To saue our kyng, his reme ryal,
And let neuer myschip vppon him fall
    Ne false traytoure him to betray.

[15]

I pray youe, seris, of your gentre,
Syng this carol reuerently,
Fore hit is made of Kyng Herre;
    Gret ned fore him we han to pray.

[16]

Yif he fare wele, wele schul we be,
Or ellis we may be ful sore;
Fore him schal wepe mone an e;
    Thus prophecis the blynd Awdlay.

MS. heading: de rege nostro henrico sexto.
burden, l. 1. Pryns] MS. peryns.
stza. 2, l. 2. moder] MS. moderis.
stza. 13, l. 2. all] MS. all al.

429

Lambeth Palace Library. MS. Lambeth 306
                                            1461–4
f. 136ʳ

    A, a, a,
    Edwardeus Dai gracia.

[1]

Sithe God hathe chose the to be his knyt
And posseside the in thi right,
Thoue hime honour with al thi myght,
    Edwardes, Dai gracia.

[2]

Oute of the stoke that longe lay dede
God hathe causede the to sprynge and
    sprede
And of al Englond to be the hede,
    Edwardes, Dei gracia.

[3]

Sithe God hathe yeuen the thorough his
     myghte
Owte of that stoke birede in sight
The floure to springe *and* rosse so white,
     Edwardes, Dai gracia.

[4]

Thoue yeve hem lawde and praisinge,
Thove vergyne knight of whom we synge,
Vndeffiled sithe thy begynyng,
     Edwardes, Dai gracia.

[5]

God save thy contenewaunce
And so to prospere to his plesance
That eu*er* thyne astate thou mowte en-
     hau*m*nce,
     Edwardes, Dai gracia.

[6]

Rex Anglie *et* Francia, Y say,
Hit is thine owne; why saist th*ou* nay?
And so is Spayne, that faire contrey,
     Edwardes, Dai gracia.

[7]

Fy on slowtfull contenewaunce
Where conquest is a noble plesance
And regesterd in olde reme*m*berance,
     Edwardes, Day gracia!

[8]

Wherfor, prince and kyng moste myghti,
Remember the, subdeue of thi regaly,
Of Englonde, Fraunce, *and* Spayn trewely,
     Edwardes, Dai gracia.

stza. 2, l. 1. lay dede] MS. lade day.
stza. 5, l. 2. prospere] MS. prospede.
At end: Explicit.

430

British Museum. MS. Addit. 19046
                                   c. 1470
f. 74^r

     Nowell, nowell, nowell, nowell!
     And Cryst saue mery Y[n]glon[d] *and*
         sped yt well!

[1]

Tyll home sull Wylekyn, th*i*s joly ge*n*tyl
     schepe,
All to houre combely Kyng Hary th*i*s cnat
     ys knyt;
     Th*er*fore let vs all syng nowel.

[2]

Tyll home sull Wylekyn, th*i*s joly ge*n*tyl
     mast,
All to my Lorde Prynce, th*a*t neu*er* was
     caste;
     Th*er*fore let vs all syng nowel.

[3]

Tyll home sull Wylekyn, th*i*s joly ge*n*tyl
     nore,
All to my Lorde Chaberlayne, th*a*t neu*er*
     was for-sore;
     Th*er*fore let vs all syng nowell.

[4]

Tyll home sull Wylekyn, th*i*s joly ge*n*tyll
     sayle,
All to my Lorde Fueryn, th*a*t neu*er* dyd
     fayle;
     Th*er*fore let vs all syng nowell.

The burden is written at the end in MS.,
followed by: fy amen q*uo*d Jonys.
The repetition of the burden is indicated as
follows: stza. 1: nowell. stza. 2: nowel.
stza. 3: Nowel.

431

Trinity College, Dublin. MS. D. 4. 18 (432)
                                   c. 1461
f. 70^v

     Now is the Rose of Rone growen to a gret
         honoure;
     Therfore syng we eu*er*ychone, 'Iblessid
         be that floure.'

[1]

I warne you eu*er*ychone, for [ye] shuld
     vnderstonde,
Ther*e* sprange a Rose in Rone *and* sprad
     into Englonde,
He that moued oure mone thorough the
     gr*a*ce of Godd*es* sonde;
That Rose stonte alone the chef flo*ur* of this
     londe.
     Iblessid be the tyme that eu*er* God sprad
         that floure.

[2]

Blessid be th*a*t Rose ryall, that is so fressh
     of hewe;
Almighty Jh*es*u blesse that soule th*a*t the
     sede sewe,
And blessid be the gardeyn th*er* the Rose
     grewe;

Cristes blessyng haue thei all that to that
  Rose be trewe,
  And blessid be the tyme that euer God
    sprad that floure.

[3]

Betwix Cristmas and Candelmas,   [f. 72ᵉ
  a litel before the Lent,
All the lordes of the northe, thei wrought
  by oon assent;
For to stroy the sowthe cuntre thei did all
  hur entent;
Had not the Rose of Rone be, al Englond
  had be shent.
  Iblessid be the tyme that euer God sprad
    that floure.

[4]

Upon a Shrof Tuesday, on a grene leede,
Betwyx Sandricche and Saynt Albons many
  man gan blede.
On an As Wedynsday we levid in mykel
  drede;
Than cam the Rose of Rone downe and
  halp vs at oure nede.
  Blessid be the tyme that euer God sprad
    that floure.

[5]

The northen men made hir bost whan thei
  had done that dede:
'We wol dwelle in the southe cuntrey and
  take al that we nede;
These wifes and hur doughters, oure purpose shul thei spede.'
Than seid the Rose of Rone, 'Nay, that
  werk shal I forbede.'
  Blessid be the tyme that euer God sprad
    that floure.

[6]

For to saue al Englond the Rose did his
  entent,
With Calys and with loue Londone, with
  Essex and with Kent,
And al the south of Englond vnto the watyr
  of Trent,
And, whan he saw the tyme best, the Rose
  from London went.
  Blessid be the tyme that euer God sprad
    that floure.

[7]

The wey into the northe cuntre the Rose
  ful fast he sought;
With hym went the Ragged Staf, that
  many man dere bought;

So than did the White Lyon; ful worthely
  he wrought;
Almighti Jhesu blesse his soule that tho
  armes ought!
  And blessid be the tyme that euer God
    sprad that floure.

[8]

The Fysshe Hoke cam into the felde with
  ful egre mode;
So did the Cornyssh Chowghe and brought
  forthe all hir brode;
Ther was the Blak Ragged Staf, that is
  bothe trewe and goode;
The Brideld Horse, the Watyr Bouge by the
  Horse stode.
  Blessid be the tyme that euer   [f. 72ᵛ
    God spred that floure.

[9]

The Grehound and the Hertes Hede, thei
  quyt hem wele that day;
So did the Harow of Caunterbury and
  Clynton with his Kay;
The White Ship of Brystow, he feryd not
  that fray;
The Blak Ram of Couentre, he said not ons
  nay.
  Blessid be the tyme that euer God spred
    that floure.

[10]

The Fawcon and the Fetherlok was ther
  that tyde;
The Blak Bulle also, hymself he wold not
  hyde;
The Dolfyn cam fro Walys, iii Carpis be
  his syde;
The prowde Libert of Salesbury, he gapid
  his gomes wide.
  Blessid be the tyme that euer God spred
    that floure.

[11]

The Wolf cam fro Worce[s]tre; ful sore he
  thought to byte;
The Dragon cam from Glowcestre; he bent
  his tayle to smyte;
The Griffen cam fro Leycestre, fleying in
  as tyte;
The George cam fro Notyngham, with
  spere for to fyte.
  Blessid be the tyme that euer God spred
    that floure.

[12]

The Boris Hede fro Wyndesover with
  tusshes sharp and kene,
The Estrich Feder was in the felde, that
  many men myght sene;
The Wild Kat fro Norhamptone with hur
  brode nose—
Ther was many a fayre pynone wayting
  vpon the Rose.
    Blessid be the tyme that euer God spred
    that floure.

[13]

The northen party made hem strong with
  spere and with sheld;
On Palme Sonday affter the none thei met
  vs in the feld;
Within an owre thei were right fayne to fle
  and eke to yeld;
xxvii thousand the Rose kyld in the feld.
    Blessid be the tyme that euer God spred
    that floure.

[14]

The Rose wan the victorye, the feld, and
  also the chace;
Now may the housbond in the south dwell
  in his owne place,
His wif and eke his faire doughtre [f. 71ʳ
  and al the goode he has;
Soche menys hath the Rose made by vertu
  and by grace.
    Blessid be the tyme that euer God sprad
    that floure.

[15]

The Rose cam to loue Londone, ful ryally
  rydyng;
ii erchbisshops of Englond thei crovned the
  Rose kyng.
Almighti Jhesu save the Rose and geue hym
  his blessyng,
And al the reme of Englond joy of his
  crownyng,
    That we may blesse the tyme that euer
    God sprad the floure.

At end: Amen pur charite.

431.1

Trinity College, Dublin. MS. E. 5. 10
  (516)   1458
f. 30ʳ
    Stere welle the good shype;
    God be our gyde.

[1]

Our shyp is launched from the grounde,
Blessed be God, both saue and sownde;
Our maryners han the shypmen founde,
    By there taklynge will abyde.

[2]

This noble shyp made of good tree:
Our souerayne lord, Kyng Harry;
God gyde hym from aduersyte
    Where that he go or ryde.

[3]

The shyp was charged with a mast:
Crased it was; it m[a]y not last;
Now hath he one that wol not brest;
    The old is leyde on syde.

[4]

Thys fayre mast is [a] myghty yeard
Of whom fals shrewes be afere[d];
Hys name of ryght is Prince Edward;
    Long myht he with vs abyde.

[5]

The ship hath closed hym a lyght
To kepe her course in wey of ryght,
A fyre cressant that berneth bryght,
    With fawte was neuer spyed.

[6]

Thys good lyght that is so clere
Call Y the Duke of Exceter,
Whos name in trouthe shyned clere;
    Hys worshyp spryngeth wyde.

[7]

Thys shyp hath a sterne full good,
Hem to gyde in ebbe and flood
Ageyne the wawes bothe wild and wode
    That rynneth on euery syde.

[8]

The sterne that on this shype is sette
Ys the Duke Somerset;
For ragged rokkes he woll not lette
    To sterre in ebbe and eke in tyde.

[9]

Ther is a sayle yeard full good and sure,
To the shyp a grete treseur;
For all stormes it woll endure;
    It is trusty atte nede.

[10]

Now the sayle yeard Y woll rehersse:
The Erle of Penbroke, curtys and [f. 30ᵛ
    ferce;

Acros the mast he hyeth travers,
  The good shyp for to lede.

[11]

The mast hath a well good stay,
With shrowthes sure, Y dare wel say,
In humble wyse hym to obey
  Yf he to them hath nede.

[12]

The Duke of Bokyngham, thys stay is he;
Thys shrowdes be sure in thare degre,
Devenshyre and Grey and Becheham the
    free,
  And Scales with them in tyde.

[13]

The shyp hath a well good sayle
Of fyne canvas that woll not fayle,
With bonet three for to travayle,
  That mekell beth of pryde.

[14]

This good sayle, Y onderstond:
The Erle of Northumberland,
Ros, Clyfford, and Egremond,
  The trouthe is not to hyde.

[15]

Ther is a toppe the mast on hyght,
The shyp to defende in all hys ryght
With his fomen when he schall fyght;
  They dare hym not abyde.

[16]

The Erle of Shrovesbury the toppes name;
He kepeth the shyp from harme and
    blame;
The Erle of Wylchyre one of the same
  That kepeth the shyp from drede.

[17]

Thys good shype hath ankers thre;
Of bether mettel the[re] may non be,
To strenthe the shyp be londe and se
  When he woll stop hys tyde.

[18]

The fu[r]st anker hole and sounde,
He is named the Lord Bea[u]monde;
Willyers and Ryveres trouthe yn them
    found;
  In worshyp they hem gyde.

[19]

Now help, Saynt George, Oure Lady
    knyght,
And be oure lodes sterre day and nyght,

To strengthe oure kyng and Englond ryght
  And fell oure fomenns pryde.

[20]

Now is oure shype dressed in hys   [f. 31ʳ
    kynde,
With hys taklyng befor and behynde;
Whos loue it not, God make hym blynde,
  In peynes to abyde.

MS. heading: De naui vel puppe anno domini
  mlccccº lviijº littera dominicalis g
stza. 19, l. 2. lodes] MS. lordes.

432

British Museum. MS. Addit. 5465
                                    XVI *cent.*
ff. 108ᵛ, 109ʳ

  This day day dawes,
  This gentill day day dawes,
  This gentill day dawes,
    And I must home gone.
  This gentill day dawes,
  This day day dawes,
  This gentill day dawes,
    And we must home gone.

[1]

In a gloryus garden grene   [ff. 109ᵛ, 110ʳ
Sawe I syttyng a comly quene
Among the flouris that fressh byn.
She gadird a floure and set betwene;
  The lyly-whighte rose me thought I
    sawe,
  The lyly-whighte rose me thought I
    sawe,
    And euer she sang:

[2]

In that garden be flouris of [ff. 110ᵛ, 111ʳ
    hewe:
The gelofir gent, that she well knewe;
The floure-de-luce she did on rewe,
And said, 'The white rose is most trewe
  This garden to rule be ryghtwis lawe.'
  The lyly-whighte rose me thought I
    sawe,
    And euyr she sang:

The repetition of the burden is indicated after
  each stanza by: this day day dawes this day
  day dawes this gentill day day dawes vt
  supra.
burden, l. 1. day (1)] *3rd voice* gentill.
  l.2. day (2)] *2nd and 3rd voices omit.*
Signature (ff. 108ᵛ, 109ʳ): P.

433

British Museum. MS. Addit. 5465
XVI *cent.*
ff. 40ᵛ, 41ʳ

'I loue, I loue, *and* whom loue ye?'
'I loue a floure of fressh beaute.'
'I loue another as well as ye.'
  'Than shal be provid here anon
  Yff we iii can agre in on.'

[1]

'I loue a flour of swete odour.'
'Magerome gentyll or lavendour,
Columbyne goldis of swete flavour?'
  'Nay, nay, let be;
  Is non of them that lykyth me.

[2]

'Ther is a floure where so he   [ff. 41ᵛ, 42ʳ
  be,
And shall not yet be namyed for me;
Prymeros, violet, or fressh daysy,
  He pass them all in his degre;
  That best lykyth me.

[3]

'On that I loue most en-   [ff. 42ᵛ, 43ʳ
  terly.'
'Gelofyr gentyll or rosemary,
Camamyll, borage, or savery?'
  'Nay, certenly;
  Here is not he that plesyth me.

[4]

'I chese a floure fresshist of   [ff. 43ᵛ, 44ʳ
  face.'
'What is his name that thou chosen has?
The rose, I suppose? Thyn hart vnbrace!'
  'That same is he,
  In hart so fre, that best lykyth me.

    Now haue I louyd, *and* whom loue
      ye?'
    'I loue a floure of fressh beaute.'
    'I loue anothyr as well as ye.'
      'Than shal be provid here anon
      Yff we iii can agre in oon.'

[5]

'The rose it is a ryall floure.'   [ff. 44ᵛ, 45ʳ
'The red or the white? Shewe his colour!'
'Both be full swete *and* of lyke savoure;
  All on they be;
  That day to se it lykyth well me.'

[6]

'I loue the rose, both red   [ff. 45ᵛ, 46ʳ
  and white.'
'Is that your pure perfite appetite?'
'To here talke of them is my delite.
  Joyed may we be
  Oure prince to se, *and* rosys thre.'

    'Nowe haue we louyd, *and* loue will we
    This fayre fressh floure full of beaute;
    Most worthy it is, as thynkyth me.
      Than may be provid here anon
      That we iii be agrede in oon.'

The repetition of the burden in its first form is
indicated after stza. 1 by the first four lines
and: vt supra. It is written again in full after
stzas. 2, 3. The burden as written after stza. 4
is repeated in full after stza. 5.
stza. 3, l. 5. plesyth me] *3rd voice* best lykyth
me.
Signature: (f 41ᵛ) Syr Thomas Phelyppis.

433.1

a. *British Museum.* MS. Cotton Julius
  B. xii   1488
f. 50ᵛ

  England, now rejoysse, for joyous may
    thou bee
  To see thy king so flowring in dignytie.

[1]

O moost noble king, thy fame doth spring
  and sprede,
Henry the Seventh, our souueraigne in
  yche region;
Al Englande hath cause thy grace to loue
  and drede,
  Seing ambassates seche for protecc[i]on,
  For aide, helpe, socour, whiche lieth in
    thyn elecc[i]on.
England, now rejoysse, for joyous may
  thou bee
To see thy kyng so flowring in dignitie.

[2]

This realme a season stode in great jeopar-
  die
  When that noble prince disceased, King
    Edwarde,
Whiche in his dayes gate honour ful noblye;
  Aftur his disceasse nygh hand al was
    marred:
  Eche region this londe dispised, myschief
    when they harde;
Wherfor now rejoyse, for joyouse may thou
  bee
To se thy king so flowring in dignytie.

[3]

Fraunce, Spayne, Scotlande, and Bretayne,
Flawnders also,
 Thre of theym present keping thy noble
 feste
Of Seynt George in Wyndesor, ambassat*es*
 co*m*myng moo,
 Yche of theym in hono*ur*, bothe the mor
 and the leste,
 Seching thy g*ra*ce to haue thy noble
 beheste;
Wherfor now rejoysse, for joyous may thou
 bee
To see thy king so flouring in dignitie.

[4]

O knyghtly order, clothed in robes w*ith*
 Garter,
 The quenes g*ra*ce, thy moder, in the
 same,
The nobles of thy realme riche in aray aft*ur*,
 Lord*es*, knyght*es*, and ladies vnto thy
 great fame;
 Now shall all ambassat*es* knowe thy noble
 name;
By thy fest royall now joyous may thou bee
To see thy king so flowring in dignitie.

[5]

Here this day Sent George, the [f. 51*r*
 pat*ro*ne of this place,
 Honowred w*ith* the Gart*er*, chief of
 chevalrye,
Chaplayns, Chapell singing, p*ro*cessions
 keping space,
 W*ith* archebisshops and bisshops besene
 noble,
 Much people p*re*sent to see thee, King
 Henry;
Wherfor now, Seint George, all we pray to
 thee
To kepe our souu*er*ayne in his dignytie.

stza. 1, l. 2. Seventh] MS. vij.

b. Elias Ashmole, *The Institution, Laws &*
Ceremonies of the Most Noble Order of the
Garter (London, 1672), pp. 594, 595
'from MS. penes Arth. Com. Anglesey,
fol. 169'

burden] *omits.*
stza. 1, l. 1. moost] famous Noble. 1. 4. ambassat*es*] Embassadores. 1. 6. may] mayest.
 l. 7. flowring] floreshe.
stza. 2, l. 6. now] *omits.* may] mayst.
 l. 7. flowring] floresh. dignytie] high dig-
netye.

stza. 3, l. 3. ambassat*es*] Ambassadors. moo]
 more. l. 5. leste] lesse.
l. 5. beheste] begeste. l. 6. for] and.
may] maiste. l. 7. flouring] florishing.
stza. 4, l. 2. grace] grace and. moder] Mother
 clothed. l. 4. ambassat*es*] Embassadors.
 l. 6. may] mayest. l. 7. flowring] florish-
 inge.
stza. 5, l. 1. the] *omits.* l. 3. Chapell] *omits.*
 p*ro*cessions] processyon. space] the same.

434

British Museum. MS Addit. 5465
 XVI *cent.*
ff. 104*v*, 105*r*

 From stormy wyndis *and* grevous wethir,
 Good Lord, preserve the Estrige Fether.
 From stormy wyndis *and* grevous wethir,
 Good Lord, p*re*serue the Estrige Fethir.

[1]

O blessed Lord of heuyn [ff. 105*v*, 106*r*
 celestiall,
 Which formyd hast of thi most speciall
 g*ra*ce
Arthur oure prynce to vs here terrestriall,
 In honour to rayne, Lord, g*ra*unt hym
 tyme *and* space,
 Which of aliaunce
 Oure p*ri*nce of plesaunce
 Be inerytaunce
 Of Ynglond *and* Fraunce
 Ryght eyre for to be;
 Wherfore now syng we:

[2]

Wherfore, good Lord, syth [ff. 106*v*, 107*r*
 of thi creacion,
 Is this noble p*ri*nce of riall lynage,
In eu*er*y case be his p*re*seruacion,
 W*ith* joy to rejose his dew enerytaunce,
 His ryght to optayne,
 In honour to rayne,
 This eyre of Brytayne,
 Of Castell *and* Spayne
 Ryght eyre for to be;
 Wherefore now syng we:

[3]

Now, good Lady among [ff. 107*v*, 108*r*
 thi saynt*es* all,
 Pray to thi Son, the secund in T*ri*nite,
For this yong p*ri*nce, which is *and* daily shal
 Be thi s*er*vaunt w*ith* all his hart so fre.

O celestiall
Modir maternall,
Emprise infernall,
To the we crye *and* call,
    His savegard to be;
Wherefore now syng we:

The repetition of the burden is indicated as
  follows: stza. 1: From stormy wyndis (*2nd
  voice* From stormy wyndis *and* grevous vt
  supra.) stza. 2: From stormy wynd*es* vt
  supra (*1st voice* wyndis). stza. 3: From
  stormy wyndis vt supra.
stza. 3, l. 4. Be] *2nd voice repeats.*   l. 9. *3rd
  voice* ryght ayre for to be.
Signature (f. 104ᵛ): Edmund Turges.

435

British Museum. MS. Addit. 5665
                                XVI *cent.*
f. 44ᵛ
    Jhesu, for thy mercy endelesse,
    Saue thy pepill, and sende vs pesse.
    Jhesu, for thy mercy endelesse,
    Saue thy pepill, and sende vs   [f. 45ʳ
    pesse.

[1]

Jh*es*u, for thy wond*es* fyff,
    Saue fro shedyng C*r*istayn blode;
Sese all grete trobil of malice *and* stryffe,
    And of our*e* n*e*ighbor*es* sende vs tydyng*es*
        gode,
        Blessed Jh*es*u,
        Blessed Jhesu.

MS. heading: ad placitum.
The repetition of the burden is indicated by:
  Jh*es*u for thi vt sup*ra*.
stza. 1, l. 4. vs] MS. v*us.*

436

British Museum. MS. Addit. 5465
                                XVI *cent.*
ff. 115ᵛ, 116ʳ
    Enforce yo*ur*selfe as Goddis knyght
    To strenkyth yo*ur* comyns in ther ryght.
    Enforce yo*ur*selfe as Goddis knyght
    To strenkyth yowr comyns in ther ryght.

[1]

Souerayne Lorde, in erth   [ff. 116ᵛ, 117ʳ
    most excellent,
    Whom God hath chose oure gyde to be,
W*i*th gyfft*es* grete *and* euydent
    Of marshiall power *and* also hye dygnite,

Sith it is so, now let yo*ur* labour be
    Enforcyng yo*ur*selfe w*i*th all yo*ur*
        myght
    To strenkyth yo*ur* comyns in ther
    ryght.

[2]

God hath gyff you of his   [ff. 117ᵛ, 118ʳ
    goodness
Wisdome w*i*th strenkyth *and* soueraynte
All mysdone thyng*es* to redress,
    And specially hurtis of thi co*m*mynalte,
    Which crye *and* call vnto yo*ur* majeste.
    In yo*ur* p*er*son all ther hope is pyght
    To haue recouer of ther vnryght.

The repetition of the burden is indicated after
  stza. 2 by: Enforce yo*ur*selfe (*1st voice*
  Enforce yo*ur*. *2nd voice* Enforce vt sup*ra*).
Signature (f. 115ᵛ): Edmund Turges.

437

Deleted from this edition. See Note.

438

College of Arms. MS. I. 7   1548
f. 37ᵛ

    Syng 'vp', hart, syng 'vp', hart, an[d]
        syng no more 'do[w]ne',
    But joy in King Edward, th*a*t wereth the
        crowne.

[1]

Sur, songe in tyme past hath ben 'dow*n*e-a-
    downe,'
And longe yt hath lasted in towre and
    towne:
To very moche myter 'down' hath ben
    added,
But 'vp' is more sweter to make our hart*es*
    gladded.

[2]

King Edward vp spring from puerilitee
And toward*es* vs bryngeth joy and tran-
    quilitee.
O*ur* hart may be lyght and mery chere;
He shall be of soche might that all the
    worlde may him fare.

[3]

His father, late our soverainge, both day
    and also howre,
That in yoy he might raigne lyke a prynce
    of high powre,

By say and land hath provided for him eke,
That never kinge of Englande had ever the
leke.

[4]

He hath gotten allreddy Boullen, that godly
towne,
And byddeth syng spedly 'vp' an[d]
'downe'.
When he waxeth wight and to manhod doth
springe,
He shall be streight of iiii realmes the kinge.

[5]

Ye childrine of England, for the honor of
the same,
Take bow and shafte in hond; larne
shewtag to frame,
That yow another day may so do your partes
That to serve your kinge as well with
handes as with hartes.

[6]

Ye children that is towardes, syng 'vp' and
'downe',
And never play the cowardes to him that
werith the crowne,
But allway doo your cure his pleasure to
fulfyll;
The[n] shall yow kepe right shure the
honour of England styll.

MS. heading: A ballet of the kinges Majestie.
The repetition of the burden is indicated after
each stanza by: Syng vp hart &c.
stza. 1, l. 4. gladded] MS. gladden.
stza. 5, l. 4. serve] MS. sevre.

439

Bodleian Library, MS. Eng. poet. e. 1
XV *cent.*
f. 14ʳ

For pencynesse *and* grett distresse
  I am full woo;
Destitute frome al refute,
  Alone I goo.

[1]

Whylome I present was with my soffreyne;
Ignorawnt I was of dolowr and payne,
  For than I lyued
  Fro sorow depreued,
Of plesure hauyng habundawnce and
  delice,
  But now, forsothe,
  Sore hytt me ruthe,
Fortune contrarythe to my device.

[2]

Whane Fortune flatery ay de-   [f. 14ᵛ]
  seveabyll
My hert en[t]ycyed by prosyrs delectabyll,
  I thowght in mynd
  I schuld ay fynd
The whele of Fortunat fyxyd fast,
  Nott for no chawnce
  To make delyawnce
Whyle my terme of lyff had past.

[3]

Butt now prosyrs glorius be myxyd with
  gall,
Whyche bytter ys and tedius ouer all,
  Venumus os poyson,
  To me full naysom,
And from her palyse ryall
  Ful cruelly
  And onavysedly
Sche heth soferyd me to fall.

[4]

And into gret dole and mysery,
Devoyd of all felyce[te,]
  With her avtrage
  Me puttyng to damnag,
  With hert contrystant thyse wordes I sey:
  'For pencynesse
  And hyre distresse
Fad doth my yoye and wannych awey.'

[5]

For, by her rygurus and crabyd   [f. 15ʳ
  violence,
Preuentyd me sche hath of my pretence,
  Constreynyng me to fulfyll
  That repugnant is to my wyll,
For, theras I neuer entendyd to be abcent,
  Distawnce of place,
  My herd myschavnce and case,
Vtterly hath alteryd my purpose and
  entent.

[6]

Schuld I not morne and in hert be sad,
Whan slydery tym, wych neuer abydyng
  had,
  Schuld do me payn
  By Fortuns dissayn,
And al memory on me tak away,
  That the dyseys
  The hert on thynkys
Wher syght ys novt, ferwel thowght, and
  haue gud day!

[7]

Thus my enmye mortale doyth de*ter*my*ne*,
W*ith* dystawnce of place, *and* curre*nt* ty*me*
  Me wyl co*n*fownd,
    And neu*er* to red[o]wnd,
But me co*n*sume *and* vtt*er*ly wast,
    And of al resort
    Of joy *and* co*m*fort
Desolate me make *and* in penurye me
  cast.

[8]

Whome nature excelle*n*tly hath   [f. 15^v]
  avawncyd,
And heuynly grace gyft*es* most *and* syngu-
  larly hath e*n*ha[wncyd,]
    In bewte, in sagacite,
    In facu*n*d spech *and* i*n* benyngnyte,
  In behauyowr gudly, me vmbyll in
    spyryt,
    And sondry w*er*tuse
    Wych canot dyscuse,
Frome hy*m* am I sewrd be Fortuns despit.

The repetition of the burden is indicated as
follows: stza. 1: for pi*n*cy. . . . stza. 2: For
pe*n*cyness. stza. 3: For pi*n*cynesse. stzas.
4–6: For pe*n*cynesse. stza. 7: For pi*n*c . . .
(*MS. torn*).
stza. 5, l. 7. My herd] MS. hyherd.
stza. 7, l. 3. co*n*fownd] MS. co*n*sownd.

440

British Museum. MS. Harley 2253
                              XIV *cent.*
f. 72^v

  Blow, northerne wynd,
    Sent thou me my suetyng;
  Blow, northerne wynd,
    Blou, blou, blou!

[1]

Ichot a burde in boure bryht
That fully semly is on syht,
Menskful maiden of myht,
  Feir ant fre to fonde;
In al this wurhliche won
A burde of blod *and* of bon
Neuer yete Y nuste non
  Lussomore in londe.

[2]

With lokkes lefliche *and* longe,
With frount *and* face feir to fonde,
With murthes monie mote heo monge,
  That brid so breme in boure,

With lossom eye, grete ant gode,
With browen blysfol vnder hode,
He th*at* reste hi*m* on the rode
  Th*at* leflich lyf honoure!

[3]

Hire lure lumes liht
Ase a launterne a-nyht,
Hire bleo blykyeth so bryht,
  So feyr heo is ant fyn;
A suetly suyre heo hath to holde,
With armes, shuldre, ase mon wolde,
Ant fyngres feyre for te folde;
  God wolde hue were myn!

[4]

Middel heo hath menskful smal,
Hire loueliche chere as c*r*istal,
Theghes, legges, fet, ant al
  Ywraht wes of the beste;
A lussum ledy lasteles
Th*at* sweting is *and* euer wes;
A betere burde neuer nes
  Yheryed with the heste.

[5]

Heo is dereworthe in day,
G*r*aciouse, stout, ant gay,
Gentil, jolyf so the jay,
  Worhliche when heo waketh,
Maiden murgest of mouth;
Bi est, bi west, by north, *and* south,
Th*er* nis fi[th]ele ne crouth
  Th*at* such murthes maketh.

[6]

Heo is coral of godnesse;
Heo is rubie of ryhtfulnesse;
Heo is c*r*istal of clannesse
  Ant baner of bealte;
Heo is lilie of largesse;
Heo is paruenke of prouesse;
Heo is salsecle of suetnesse
  Ant ledy of lealte.

[7]

To Loue, th*at* leflich is in londe,
Y tolde hi*m*, as ych vnderstonde,
Hou this hende hath hent in honde
  On huerte th*at* myn wes,
Ant hire knyhtes me han so soht,
Sykyng, Sorewyng, *and* Thoht,
Tho thre me han in bale broht
  Ayeyn the poer of Pees.

[8]

To Loue Y putte pleyntes mo: [f. 73^r]
Hou Sykyng me hath siwed so
Ant eke Thoht me thrat to slo
   With maistry, yef he myhte,
Ant Serewe sore in balful bende,
That he wolde for this hende
Me lede to my lyues ende,
   Vnlahfulliche in lyhte.

[9]

Hire Loue me lustnede vch word
Ant beh him to me ouer bord
Ant bed me hente that hord
   Of myne huerte hele:
'Ant bisecheth that swete ant swote,
Er then thou falle as fen of fote,
That heo with the wolle of bote
   Dereworthliche dele.'

[10]

For hire loue Y carke ant care;
For hire loue Y droupne ant dare;
For hire loue my blisse is bare,
   Ant al ich waxe won;
For hire loue in slep Y slake;
For hire loue al nyht ich wake;
For hire loue mournyng Y make
   More then eny mon.

The repetition of the burden is indicated as
follows: stza. 1: blow &c.   stza. 2: Blou &c.

441

Gonville & Caius College, Cambridge.
  MS. 383   *XV cent.*
p. 210

   Thei Y synge and murthus make,
     It is not Y wolde.

[1]

Myn owne dere ladi fair and fre,
Y pray [y]ow in herte ye ruwen on me,
For al my lykyng is on the
   Wan Y on yow beholde.

[2]

Were we to togadere beyne,
Thou myst me lysse of my peyne;
Y am agast; it wol not geyne;
   Myn herte falluth colde.

[3]

Myself Y wol myn arnde bede;
The betur Y hope for te spede;
Non so wel may do myn nede—
   A womman so me tolde.

The repetition of the burden is indicated as
follows: stza. 1: Thei y etc. stza. 2: Thei y
synge &c. stza. 3: Thei y &c.
The name of the air is written at the head: le bon
l. don. *It is followed by one stave of a crudely
written melody.*

441.1

Lincoln College, Oxford. MS. 100
                        XV cent.
f. 2^v

   My dere an dese that so fayr ys,
     Of lufe gentyl and fre,
   I kan not ly, withowtyn lese,
     My lady lele best lyks me.

[1]

I saw neuer joy lyk to that sight
   Os my fayre lady schen;
Her brows thay er both brant and bright,
   With ii gray lawhyng een.

[2]

Here syds er lang, chapyn of ryght,
   That semle er to se;
Be Crist, and yt wer in my myght,
   Scho suld my treuluf be.

[3]

Scho suld be my hertes qwen
   That is so fayr and sqwete;
Alas, scho dos me tray and teen:
   I may noght with her met.

The repetition of the burden is indicated after
stza. 3 by: My der on des &c.
stza. 3, l. 1. qwen] MS. sqwen.

442

Cambridge   University   Library. MS.
  Ff. 1. 6   *XV cent.*
f. 136^v

   Who so lyst to loue,
     God send hym right good spede.

[1]

Some tyme Y loued, as ye may see;
A goodlyer ther myght none be,
Here womanhode in all degre,
   Full well she quytt my mede.

[2]

Vnto the tyme, vpon a day,
To sone ther fill a gret affray;
She badde me walke forth on my way;
   On me she gaff none hede.

[3]

I askid the cause why and wherfor
She displeside was with me so sore;
She wold nat tell, but kepe in store;
    Pardy, it was no nede.

[4]

For if Y hadde hure displeased
In worde or dede or hire greued,
Than, if she hadde be sore meved,
    She hadde cause indede.

[5]

But well Y wote Y hadde nat done
Hure to displese, but in grete mone
She hath me left and ys agone;
    For sorwe my herte doth blede.

[6]

Some tyme she wold to me complayne
Yff she had felt dysease or payne;
Now fele Y nought but grete disdayne;
    Allas, what is youre rede?

[7]

Shall Y leue of and let hure go? [f 137ʳ
Nay, nere the rathere will Y do so;
Yet, though vnkyndnesse do me wo,
    Hure will Y loue and drede.

[8]

Some hope that when she knoweth the case,
Y trust to God that withyne short spase
She will me take agayne to grace;
    Than haue Y well abydde.

[9]

And for trew louers shall Y pray
That ther ladyes fro day to day
May them rewarde so that they may
    With joy there lyues lede.

The repetition of the burden is indicated as
follows: stzas. 2, 5: wo so lyst &c. stzas. 3, 4,
6–9: wo so list &c.
At end: Amen pur Charyte.

443

Canterbury Cathedral. Christ Church
Letters, Vol. II, No. 173   *c.* 1500

'I pray yow, cum kyss me,
My lytle pretty Mopse,
I pray yow, com kyss me.'

[1]

'Alas, good man, most yow be kyst?
Ye shall not now, ye may me trust;
Wherefore go where as ye best lust,
    For, iwyss, ye shall not kyss me.'

[2]

'Iwyss, swet hart, yff that ye
Had askyd a gretur thyng of me,
So onkynd to yow I wold not haue be;
    Where[fore,] I pray yow, com kyss me.'

[3]

'I thynke very well that ye ar kynd
Whereas ye lowe and set yore mynd,
But all yore wordes be but as wynd,
    Wherefore nowe ye shall not kyss me.'

[4]

'I do but talke, ye may me trust,
But ye take everythyng at the worst.'
'Wherefore I say, as I sayd furst,
    Iwyss, ye shall not kyss me.'

[5]

'I pray yow, let me kyss yow.
Iff that I shall not kyss yow,
Let me loke, let me kyss yore karchos
    nocke;
I pray yow, let me kyss yowe.'

[6]

'All so I say as I furst haue sayd,
And ye wyll not therewith be dysmayd;
Yet wyth that onsar ye shall be payd:
    Iwyss, ye shall not kyss me.'

[7]

'Now I se well that kyssys ar dere,
And, yff I shold labur all the hole yere,
I thynke I shold be neuer the nere;
    Wherefore, I pray yow, cum kyss me.'

[8]

'Neuer the nere, ye may be shewre,
For ye shall not so sone bry[n]g me yn vre
To consent vnto yore nyse plesure,
    Nor, iwyss, ye shall not kyss me.'

[9]

'I pray yow, com and kyss me,
My lytle prety Mopse,
And yff that ye wyll not kyss me,
    I pray yow, let me kyss yow.'

[10]

'Well, for a kyss I wyll not styck,
So that ye wyll do nothyng but lyck,
But, and ye begyn on m[e] for to pryck,
    Iwyss, ye shall not kyss me.'

[11]

'Now I se well that ye ar kynd;
Wherefore [ye] shall cum know my mynd,
And euer yore ow[ne] ye shall me fynd
    At all tymys redy to kyss yow.'

stza. 11, l. 2. cum] *reading uncertain; MS. is
very faint.* l. 3. ow[ne]] *MS. rubbed, last
part of word illegible.*
At end: Finis quod wulstane p . . . sone.

444

Canterbury Cathedral. Christ Church
Letters, Vol. II, No. 174   *c.* 1500

For [wele or w]oo I wyll not fle
To love that hart that lovyth me.

[1]

That hart my hart hath in suche grace
    That of too hartes one hart make we;
That hart hath brought my hart in case
    To loue that hart that lovyth me.

[2]

For one the lyke vnto that hart
    Never was nor ys nor never shall be,
Nor never lyke cavse set this apart
    To love that hart that lovyth me.

[3]

Whyche cause gyveth cause to me *and*
    myne
To serve that hart of suferente,
And styll to syng this later lyne:
    To love that hart [that lovyth me.]

[4]

Whatever I say, whatever I syng,
    Whatever I do, that hart shall se
That I shall serue with hart lovyng
    That lovyng hart [that lovyth me.]

[5]

Thys knot thus knyt who shall vntwyne,
    Syns we that knyt yt do agre
To lose nor slyp, but both enclyne
    To love that hart [that lovyth me?]

[6]

Farwell, of hartes that hart most fyne,
    Farwell, dere hart, hartly to the,
And kepe this hart of myne for thyne
    As hart for hart for lovyng me.

burden, l. 1. *MS. is torn.*
stza. 2, l. 1. vnto] MS. wnto.
stzas. 3–5, l. 4. [that lovyth me]] MS. &c.

445

British Museum. MS. Harley 7578
                                      XVI *cent.*

f. 85ʳ

My lady is a prety on,
A prety, prety, prety on,
My lady is a prety on
    As *ever I saw.   [*f. 85ᵛ

[1]

She is gentyll *and* also wysse;
Of all other she berith the price
    That ever I saw.

[2]

To here hir syng, to se her dance!
She wyll the best herselfe avance
    That euer I saw.

[3]

To se her fyngers that be so small!
In my consail she passeth all
    That ever I [saw.]

[4]

Nature in her hath wonderly   [f. 86ʳ
    wroght;
Crist neuer sych another bowght
    That euer I sawe.

[5]

I have sene many that have bewty;
Yet is ther non lyk to my lady
    That euer I saw.

[6]

Therfor I dare this boldly say:
[I] shall have the best *and* farest may
    That ever *I saw.   [*f. 86ᵛ

The repetition of the burden is indicated as
follows: stzas. 1, 5: my lady is.   stza. 2: my
lady.   stzas. 3, 4: my.   stza. 6: my lady is
a prety on a prety prety prety on.

446

British Museum. MS. Sloane 1584
                                        XV *cent.*
f. 45ᵛ

So well ys me begone,
  Troly, lole,
So well ys me begone,
  Troly, loly.

[1]

Off *ser*uyng men I wyll begyne,
  Troly, loley,
For they goo mynyon trym,
  Troly, loley.

[2]

Off mett *and* drynk *and* feyr clothyng,
  Troly, loley,
By dere God, I want none,
  Troly, loley.

[3]

His bonet is of fyne scarlett,
  Troly, loley,
W*ith* here as black as geitt,
  Troly, lolye.

[4]

His dublett ys of fyne satyne,
  Troly, lolye,
Hys shertt well mayd *and* tryme,
  Troly, lolye.

[5]

His coytt itt is so tryme *and* rownde,
  Troly, lolye,
His kysse is worth a hundred pounde,
  Troly, loly.

[6]

His hoysse [is] of London black,
  Troly, lolye,
In hyme ther ys no lack,
  Troly, lolye.

[7]

His face yt ys so lyk a ma*n*,
  Troly, lolye,
Who can*e* butt love hyme tha*n*?
  Troly, lolye.

[8]

Whersoeu*er* he bee, he hath my hert,
  Troly, loly,
And shall to deth depart,
  Troly, lolye.

stza. 3, l. 4. Troly] MS. Torly.
stza. 5, l. 3. hundred pounde] MS. C¹.
The burden is written again at the end:
  So well ys me begon*e* troly loly
  S[o] well ys me begone Troly lolye.

446.1

British Museum. MS. Addit. 5665
                                        XVI *cent.*
ff. 38ᵛ, 39ʳ

How shall Y plece a creature uncerteyne?

[1]

Your light greuans shall not me co*n*strayn*e*
To avoyde y*our* custu*m*abyll disdayn*e*;
That ye loth Y love—wrappe th*at* yn your
  trayne!
How shold Y [plece a creature uncer-
  teyne?]

[2]

Yo*ur* on-syttyng spech puttyth   [f. 38ᵛ
  me to payn*e*,
Wit*h*owt cause, God knowyth; Y do not
  fayn*e*.
With hert Y wyll you plece *and* your love
  attayn*e*:
How sholde Y plece a creature oncertayn*e*?

[3]

Whe*n* Y fynde you stedfast *and* c*er*tayn*e*,
Y am right glad, tristy*n*g h*it* woll remayne;
But light credens turnyth yo*ur* love agayn*e*;
How shold Y plece a c*r*eature oncertayne?

[4]

An olde seyde saw: hasty men   [f. 39ʳ
  sone slayn*e*;
Love me lytell and longe; hot love doth not
  reyne;
Speke or ye smyte; barke or ye byte; holde
  yowre ho*n*d*es* twayn*e*:
How shold Y plece a creature oncertayn*e*?

stza. 1, l. 4. MS. How shold Y vt su*pra*.
stza. 3, l. 2. remayne] MS. remanyne.

447

British Museum. Book K. 1. e. 1
                                        1530
F₁ᵛ

  Joly felowe, joly,
  Joly felowe, joly,
  Yf thou haue but lytyll mony,
  Spend it not i*n* foly,

But spe*n*d yt on a prety we*n*che,
And she shal help the at a pi*n*che;
 Hey, joly felow, jo*ly, joly, [*F₂ʳ
 Hey, joly felow, joly,
  Hey, joly.

[1]

A prety we*n*che may be plesur;
In dalyance she may endure,
Yf she be trym, proper, *and* pure. [F₂ᵛ

[2]

Lytell mony doth gret com*fort [*F₃ʳ
Spende on the mynyon sort
Delytyng in honest dysport.

The repetition of the burden is indicated as
 follows: stza. 1: Joly felow joly joly: vt supra.
 stza. 2: Joly felow joly: vt supra.
stza. 2, l. 3. dysport] orig. dysporst.
At end: Finis.

448

British Museum. MS. Addit. 31922
  By King Henry VIII, XVI *cent.*
f. 37ᵛ
 Grene growith the holy,
 So doth the iue,
 Thow wynt*er* blastys blow neu*er* so hye,
 Grene growth the holy.

[1]

As the holy grouth grene [f. 38ʳ
 And neu*er* chaungyth hew,
So I am, euer hath bene,
 Vnto my lady trew.

[2]

A[s] the holy grouth grene
 With iue all alone
When flowerys cannot be sene,
 And grenewode leuys be gone.

[3]

Now vnto my lady
 Pro*m*yse to her I make,
Frome all other only
 To her I me betake.

[4]

Adew, myne owne lady,
 Adew, my specyall,
Who hath my hart trewly,
 Be suere, *and* eu*er* shall.

MS. heading: The. kyng. H. viii.
The burden is written three times, once for
 each voice.
The repetition of the burden is indicated as
 follows: stza. 1: grene growth. &c. stzas. 2–4:
 vt sup*r*a.
burden, l. 1. growith] *2nd voice* growth. *3rd
 voice* grouth. l. 2. iue] *2nd voice* Iuye.
 l. 3. blastys] *2nd voice* blas*tes*.
 l. 4. growth] *2nd, 3rd voices* grouth.

448.1

British Museum. MS. Addit. 31922
         XVI *cent.*
f. 104ᵛ
 Whill*es* lyue or breth is in my brest,
 My sou*e*rayne lord I shall loue best.

[1]

My sou*e*rayne lorde for my poure [f. 105ʳ
  sake
vi coursys at the ryng dyd make,
Of which iiii tymes he dyd it take;
 Wherfor my hart I hym beqwest,
 And of all other for to loue best
  My sou*e*rayne lorde.

[2]

My soverayne lorde of pusant pure
As the chefteyne of a waryowere,
W*ith* spere and swerd at the barryoure
 As hardy w*ith* the hardyest,
 He pro*u*ith hymselfe, that I sey best,
  My sou*e*rayne lorde.

[3]

My sou*e*rayne lorde in eu*er*y thyng
Aboue all other as a kyng,
In that he doth no co*m*paryng,
 But of a trewth he worthyest
 To haue the prayse of all the best,
  My sou*e*rayne lorde.

[4]

My sou*e*rayne lorde when that I mete,
His cherfull contena*n*ce doth replete
My hart w*ith* jo[i]e, that I behete
 Next God but he, and eu*er* prest
 W*ith* hart and body to loue best
  My sou*e*rane lorde.

[5]

So many v*er*tuse geuyn of grace
Ther is none one lyue th*at* hace;

Beholde his fauo*ur* and his face,
    His p*er*sonage most godlyest:
A vengeance on them th*at* loueth nott
    best
        My soue*r*ayne lorde!

[6]

The soue*r*ayne Lorde that is of all
My soue*r*ayne lorde saue principall!
He hath my hart and eu*er* shall;
    Of God I ask for hym request,
    Off all gode fortu[n]es to send hym best,
        My soue*r*ayne lorde.

stza. 3, l. 4. worthyest] MS. worthyest is.
Signature: W. cornyshe.

449

British Museum. MS. Royal Appendix 58
                                    XVI *cent.*
f. 6ʳ

    Why soo vnkende, alas?
    Why soo vnkende to me?
    Soo to be kende to me.

[1]

Syne the tyme I knew yow fyrst
You were my joy and my trust.

[2]

Erly *and* late I am ryght fayne
You*r*e love *and* favou*r* to attayne.

[3]

Ys ther no grace ne remedy,
But euer to morne eternally?

[4]

Off my po*ur* seruys ye may be sure
As long as lyff dothe last *and* dure.

[5]

Hope dothe to me consolac*i*on,
Els sholde I reu in dysperac[i]on.

[6]

Ye haue my hart; ye haue my love;
Gode sende me youre*s*, that syttyth above.

The burden is repeated in full after stanza 1.
    The other repetitions are indicated as follows:
    stza. 2: why soo vnkend &c.   stzas. 3, 4:
    why soo vnkende &c.   stza. 5: why soo
    vnkend.   stza. 6: why.
burden, l. 3. *written only after stza. 1.*
stza. 2, l. 2. You*r*e] MS. youere.
stza. 4, l. 2. dure] MS. dur*er*e.

450

Lincoln's Inn. MS. Hale 135
                                    XIV *cent.*
f. 135ᵛ

    [Nou] spri[nke]s the sprai;
    Al for loue icche am so seek
        That slepen I ne mai.

[1]

Als I me rode this endre dai
    O mi [pleyinge,]
S[ei]h I hwar a litel mai
    Bigan to singge:
'The clot him clingge!
Wai es him i louue-l[on]gi[n]ge
    Sal libben ai.'

[2]

Son icche herde that mirie note,
    Thider I drogh;
I fonde hire [in] an herber swot
    Vnder a bogh
    With joie inogh.
Son I asked, 'Thou mirie mai,
    Hwi sinkes tou ai?'

[3]

Than answerde that maiden swote
    Midde wordes fewe:
'Mi lemman me haues bihot
    Of louue trewe.
He chaunges anewe;
Yiif I mai, it shal him rewe
    Bi this dai.'

The repetition of the burden is indicated as
    follows: stza. 1: Nou sp*r*inkes &c.   stza. 2:
    Nou sp*r*inkes the sprai &c.   stza. 3: Now
    s[p]*r*i[n]k . . . (*the line is partly concealed by
    the binding*).
stza. 1, l. 1. MS. this endre dai als i me rode.
l. 5. clingge] MS. clingges.
stza. 3, l. 6. Yiif] MS. thiif.
*MS. is much rubbed and worn at the beginning
    of the text.*

450.1

Public Record Office. Exchequer Miscellany
    22/1/1   *c.* 1530
dorse

    Alone, I lyue alone,
    And sore I syghe for one.

[1]

No wondre thow I murnyng make
For grevous syghys th*at* myne hert doth take,
And all ys for my lady sake.

[2]

She th*a*t is causer of my woo,
I m*er*well that she wyll do so,
Sithe I loue hir *and* no moo.

[3]

Thys am I brought into lou*er*s dawnce;
I wot neu*er* how to fle the chawnce;
Wherefore I lywe yn great penaunce.

[4]

My mynde ys so yt is content
W*ith* hir dayly to be p*re*sent,
And yet my s*er*uis ys there myssespente.

[5]

Trow ye that I wold be glade
To seke a thynge th*a*t wyll not be hade?
Saw I neu*er* man*e* so sore bestad.

[6]

Onis me to lowe yff she began,
No man w*ith* tong nore pen tell can
The joy in me th*a*t wold be than.

[7]

Now p*ra*y we hym th*a*t may p*ur*chase
To send ws bett*er* tyme *and* space
That Y may stond all in hir g*ra*ce.

The words of the burden and stza. 1 are
written 3 times, once for each voice.
The repetition of the burden is indicated as
follows: stzas. 2, 3, 7: alone. stzas. 4, 5:
alone &c.
stza. 2, l. 3. great] MS. gretat.

451

Cambridge University Library. MS. Addit.
5943 XV *cent.*
f. 178ᵛ

Wolde God that hyt wer*e* so
As I cowde wysshe bytuyxt vs too!

[1]

The man that I loued altherbest
In al thys contre, est other west,
To me he ys a strange gest;
What wonder est thow I be woo?

[2]

When me were leuest that he schold duelle,
He wold noght sey onys far*e*welle;
He wold noght sey ones far*e*well
Wen tyme was come that he most go.

[3]

In places ofte when I hym mete,
I dar noght speke, but forth I go;
W*ith* herte *and* eyes I hym grete;
So trywe of loue I know no mo.

[4]

As he ys myn hert loue,
My dyrward dyre, iblessed he be;
I swer*e* by God, that ys aboue,
Non hath my loue but only he.

[5]

I am icomfortyd in euery side;
The colures wexeth both fres and newe;
When he ys come *and* wyl abyde,
I wott ful wel that he ys trywe.

[6]

I loue hym trywely *and* no mo;
Wolde God that he hyt knywe!
And euer I hope hyt schal be so;
Then schal I chaunge for no new.

stza. 6, l. 2. hyt knywe] wer*e* trywe *interlined.*
*Another hand has interlined feminine pronouns
as follows:*
stza. 1, l. 1. The man] sche.　　l. 3. he] sche.
stza. 2, ll. 1, 2, 3, 4. he] sche.
stza. 3, ll. 1, 3. hym] hyre.
stza. 4, ll. 1, 2, 4. he] sche.
stza. 5, ll. 3, 4. he] sche.
stza. 6, l. 1. hym] hyre.　　l. 2. he] sche.

452

Gonville & Caius College, Cambridge. MS.
383 XV *cent.*
p. 41

Rybbe ne rele ne spynne yc ne may
For joyghe th*a*t it ys holyday.

[1]

Al this day ic ha*n* sou[ght;]
Spyndul ne werue ne vond Y nought;
To myche blisse ic am brout
Ayen this hyghe [ho]lyda[y].

[2]

Al vnswope ys owr*e* vlech,
And owr*e* fyre ys vnbech;
Oure ruschen be*n* vnrepe yech
Ayen this hy halyday.

[3]

Yc moste feschu*n* worton in;
Predele my kerchef vnd*ur* my khyn;
Leue Jakke, lend me a pyn
    To *p*redele me this holiday.

[4]

Now yt draweth to the non*e*,
And al my cherr*us* be*n* vndon*e*;
Y moste a lyte solas mye schon*e*
    To make he*m* dowge this holiday.

[5]

Y moste mylkyn i*n* this payl;
Outh me bred al this schayl;
Yut is the dow vnd*ur* my nayl
    As ic knad this holyday.

[6]

Jakke wol brynge me onward i*n* my wey,
Wyth me desyre for te pleyghe;
Of my dame sta*n*t me no*n* eyghe
    An neu*er* a god haliday.

[7]

Jacke wol pay for my scoth
A Sonday atte the ale-schoch;
Jacke wol sowse wel my wroch
    Eu*er*y god halida[y.]

[8]

Sone he wolle take me be the hond,
And he wolle legge me on the lond,
Th*at* al my buttock*us* be*n* of son[d,]
    Opon this hye holyday.

[9]

In he pult, *and* out he drow,
And eu*er* yc lay on hy*m* y-low:
'By God*us* deth, th*o*u dest me wow
    Vpon this hey holyday!'

[10]

Sone my wo*m*be began te swelle
A[s] greth as a belle;
Durst Y nat my dame telle
    Wat me betydde this holyday.

The repetition of the burden is indicated as
  follows: stza. 1: Rybbe &c.   stzas. 2-10: R.
stza. 1, ll. 1, 4. *A few letters have been destroyed
  by a tear in MS.*
stza. 2, ll. 2, 3. MS. *transposes. The correction is
  indicated by the letters* a *and* b.
stza. 8, l. 2. me] MS. me*n*.
stza. 10, l. 3. Durst] MS. drurst.

453

Gonville & Caius College, Cambridge MS.
  383.   XV *cent.*
p. 41

    Alas, ales, the wyle!
    Thout Y on no gyle,
      So haue Y god chau*n*ce.
    Ala[s,] ales, the wyle
      That eu*er* Y cowde dau*n*ce!

[1]

Ladd Y the dau*n*ce a Myssom*ur* Day;
Y made smale t*r*ipp*us*, soth for to say.
Jak, our*e* haly-wat*ur* cle[r]k, co*m* be the way,
And he lokede me vpon; he thout th*at* he
      was gay.
    Thout yc on ne gyle.

[2]

Jak, our*e* haly-wat*ur* clerk, the yong*e*
    strippely*n*g,
For the chesou*n* of me he com to the ryng,
And he t*r*ippede on my to *and* made a
    twynkely*n*g;
Eu*er* he ca*m* n*er*; he spar*et* for no thyng*e*.
    Thout Y on [no gyle.]

[3]

Jak, ic wot, p*r*eyede i*n* my fayr*e* face;
He thout me ful werly, so haue Y god gr*a*ce;
As we t*ur*ndu*n* owr*e* dau*nc*[e] i*n* a narw
    place,
Jak bed me the mouth; a cussyng*e* th*er* was.
    Thout Y on no g[yle.]

[4]

Jak tho began to rowne i*n* my*n* ere:
'Loke th*at* thou be p*r*iuey, *and* gr*a*unte th*at*
    thou the ber*e*;
A peyr*e* wyth glouus ic ha to thy*n* wer*e*.'
'G*r*amercy, Jacke!' th*at* was my*n* answer*e*.
    Thout*e* yc [on no gyle.]

[5]

Sone aft*ur* eue*n*song Jak me mette:
'Com ho*m* aft*ur* thy glou*us* th*at* yc the
    byhette.'
Wan ic to his cha*m*bre co*m*, dou*n* he me
    sette;
From hy*m* mytte Y nat go wa*n* [we] wer*e*
    mette.
    Thout Y [on no gyle.]

[6]

Schet*us and* chalon*us*, ic wot, a wer*e*
    yspredde;
Forsothe tho Jak *and* yc wente*n* to bedde;
He p*r*ikede, *and* he p*r*ansede; nolde he
    neu*er* lynne;
Yt was the murgust nyt th*at* eu*er* Y cam
    ynne.
    Thout Y [on no gyle.]

[7]

Wan Jak had do*n*, tho he ro*n*g the bell;
Al nyght th*er* he made me to dwelle;
Of y t*r*ewe we hadd*un* yser*u*ed the reaggeth
    deuel of helle;
Of othur smale burdus kep Y nout to telle.
    Thout Y [on no gyle.]

[8]

The oth*er* day at p*r*ime Y com ho*m*, as ic
    wene;
Meth Y my dame, coppud *and* kene:
'Sey, th*ou* stro*n*ge str*u*mpeth, war*e* hastu
    bene?
Thy t*r*ippy*n*g *and* thy dau*n*cy*n*g, wel it wol
    be sene.'
    Thout Y [on no gyle.]

[9]

Eu*er* bi on *and* by on my damme reched
    me clot;
Eu*er* Y ber it p*r*iuey wyle th*at* Y mouth,
Tyl my gurdul aros, my wombe wax out;
Euel yspu*n*ne yern, eu*er* it wole out.
    Thout Y on no gyle.

Only the last two lines of the burden are written
    at the head of the piece in MS.: Allas alas
    the wyle th*at* eu*er* y coude dau*n*ce. The entire
    burden is written after stza. 1.

454

St. John's College, Cambridge. MS. S. 54
                                    XV *cent.*
f. 2ᵛ

    A, der*e* God, qwat I am fayn,
        For I am madyn now gane.

[1]

Th*i*s enth*er* day I mete a clerke,
And he was wylly i*n* hys werke;
He p*r*ayd me w*ith* hy*m* to herke,
    And hys cownsell all for to le[r]ne.

[2]

I trow he cowd of g*r*amery;
I xall now a good [s]kyll wy:
For qwat I hade siccu[r]ly,
    To warne hys wyll had I no may.

[3]

Qwan he and me browt un *us* the schete,
Of all hys wyll I hy*m* lete;
Now wyll not my gyrdyll met;
    A, der*e* God, quat xal I say?

[4]

I xall sey to ma*n and* page   [f. 3ʳ
Th*at* I haue bene of pylgrymage;
Now wyll I not lete for no q[w]age
    W*ith* me a clerk for to pley.

stza. 3, l. 4. xal I] MS. I xal.

455

Gonville & Caius College, Cambridge.
    MS. 383   XV *cent.*
p. 210

    Wer*e* it vndo th*at* is ydo,
        I wold be war.

[1]

Y louede a child of this cuntr*e*,
And so Y wende he had do me;
Now myself the sothe Y see,
    Th*at* he is far.

[2]

He seyde to me he wolde be trewe
And chau*n*ge me for no*n*e oth*ur* newe;
Now Y sykke *and* am pale of hewe,
    For he is far.

[3]

He seide his saw*us* he wolde fulfulle;
Th*er*fore Y lat hi*m* haue al his wille;
Now Y sykke *and* mou*r*ne stille,
    For he is far*e*.

The repetition of the burden is indicated as
    follows: stza. 1: wer*e* it undo th*at* is ido &c.
    stzas. 2, 3: wer*e* it undo &c.
The air is indicated by the following line written
    before the burden: bryd on brer*e* y tell yt to
    non*e* oth*ur* y ne dar. *After stza.* 1 *is written*
    and deleted: brid on the brer*e* &c.

456

Cambridge University Library. MS. Ff. 5.
48   XV *cent.*
f. 114ᵛ

   I haue forsworne hit whil I life,
      To wake the well-ey.

[1]

The last tyme I the wel woke,
Se*r* John caght me wi*th* a croke;
He made me to swere be bel *and* boke
   I shuld not tell[-ey.]

[2]

Yet he did me a wel wors turne:
He leyde my hed agayn the burne;
He gafe my maydenhed a spurne
   And rofe my bell[-ey.]

[3]

Sir John came to oure hows to play
Fro euensong tyme til light of the day;
We made as mery as flowres i*n* May;
   I was begyled-ay.

[4]

Sir John he came to ou*r* hows;
He made hit wond*ur* copious;
He seyd that I was gracious
   To beyre a childe-ey.

[5]

I go wi*th* childe, wel I wot;
I schrew the fad*ur* th*at* hit gate,
Wi*th*outen he fynde hit mylke *and* pap
   A long while-ey.

*Below the carol in the same hand is the signa-
ture* (?): bryan hyf my name iet.

456.1

Huntington Library. MS. EL. 1160
                     c. 1500
f. 11ᵛ

   Hey, noyney!
   I wyll loue our Se*r* John *and* I loue eny.

[1]

O Lord, so swett Se*r* John dothe kys
   At eu*er*y tyme when he wolde pley;
Off hymselfe so plesant he ys,
   I haue no powre to say hym nay.

[2]

Se*r* John loue[s] me, *and* I loue hym:
   The more I loue hym the more I maye;
He says, 'Swett hart, cu*m* kys me trym';
   I haue no powre to say hym nay.

[3]

Se*r* John to me is p*r*oferyng
   For hys pleasure ryght well to pay,
And in my box he putt*es* hys offryng;
   [I haue no powre to say hym nay.]

[4]

Se*r* John ys taken in my mouse-trappe;
   Fayne wold I haue hem bothe nyght
     [a]nd day;
He gropith so nyslye abought my lape,
   I haue no po[w]re to sa[y hym nay.]

[5]

Se*r* John geuyth me reluys ryng*es*
   With praty plesure for to assay,
Furres off the fynest wi*th* othyr thynges
   [I haue no powre to say hym nay.]

*The burden is written thus by a different hand in
the margin of f. 73ᵛ:* hey troly loly hey troly
loly I must loue our sur John *and* I loue eny
o lord.
stza. 2, l. 1. is] MS. In.
stza. 5, l. 1. reluys] MS. relyus.

457

British Museum. MS. Sloane 2593
                         XV *cent.*
f. 34ʳ

   'Kyrie, so kyrie,'
   Janky*n* syngyt merie,
      Wi*th* 'aleyson.'

[1]

As I went on Yol Day in owr*e* p*r*osessyon,
Knew I joly Ja*n*ky*n* be his mery ton.
[Kyrieleyson.]

[2]

Janky*n* bega*n* the Offys o*n* the   [f. 34ᵛ
     Yol Day,
And yyt me thynkyt it dos me good, so
     merie gan he say,
'Kyrieleyson.'

[3]

Janky*n* red the Pystyl ful fayr*e and* ful wel,
And yyt me thinkyt it dos me good, as eu*er*e
   haue I sel.
[Kyrieleyson.]

[4]

Jankyn at the Sanctus crakit a merie note,
And yyt me thinkyt it dos me good: I payid
for his cote.
[Kyrieleyson.]

[5]

Jankyn crakit notes, an hunderid on a knot,
And yyt he hakkyt hem smallere than
wortes to the pot.
K[yrieleyson.]

[6]

Jankyn at the Angnus beryt the pax-brede;
He twynkelid, but sayd nowt, *and* on myn
fot he trede.
[Kyrieleyson.]

[7]

Benedicamus Domino: Cryst fro schame me
schylde;
Deo *gracias* th*erto*: alas, I go with chylde!
K[yrieleyson.]

stza. 7, l. 2. chylde] MS. schylde.

458

British Museum. MS. Royal Appendix 58
XVI *cent.*
f. 6ᵛ

Kytt hathe lost hur key, hur key,
   Goode Kytt hath lost hure key;
She ys soo sory for the cause
   She wottes nott what to say
She ys soo sory fore the cause
   She wott not what to say, to say,
      Goode Kytt, good Kytt,
She ys soo sory for the cause,
She wot not [what] to say, to say,
      Good Kytt.

[1]

Kytt she wept; I axyde why soo   [f. 7ʳ
   That she made all thys mone;
She sayde, 'Alas, I am soo woo;
   My key ys lost and gone.'

[2]

Kyt she wept *and* cryede one hye
   And fore hure key dyd axe;
She beheyght to Seynt Sythe a key
   And offryde to hym a key of wexe.

[3]

'Kyt, why dyd ye losse youre key?
   Foresothe, ye were to blame;

Now euery man to yow wyll say
   Kyt Losse-Key ys youere name.'

[4]

Kyt she wept *and* cryed, 'Alas!'
   Hur key she cowde not fynde;
In fayth, I trow yn bouerr she was
   With sum that were not kende.

[5]

'Now farewell, Kytt, I can no more;
   I wot not what to say,
But I shall pray to Gode therefore
   That yow may fynde your key.'

The repetition of the burden is indicated as
follows stza. 1: kytt has lost hure key vt
supra. stzas. 2, 3: kyt hathe lost hur key &c.
stza. 4: kyt hath lost hur keye &c. stza. 5:
kyt hath lost hure key.

459

*Huntington Library. Here Folowythe dyuers
Balettys and dyties solacyous deuysed by
Master Skelton Laureat* (Richard Pynson)
By John Skelton, XVI *cent.*
f. 1ᵛ

With lullay, lullay, lyke a chylde,
Thou slepyst to long; thou art begylde.

[1]

'My darlyng dere, my daysy floure,
   Let me,' quod he, 'ly in your lap.'
'Ly styll,' quod she, 'my paramoure;
   Ly styll hardely, *and* take a nap.'
Hys hed was heuy, such was his hap,
   All drowsy, dremyng, dround in slepe,
   That of hys loue he toke no kepe.

[2]

With 'ba, ba, ba,' *and* 'bas, bas, bas,'
   She cheryshed hym, both cheke and
      chyn,
That he wyst neuer where he was;
   He had forgoten all dedely syn.
He wantyd wyt her loue to wyn;
   He trusted her payment *and* lost all
      hys pray;
   She left hym slepyng and stale away.

[3]

The ryuers rowth, the waters wan;
   She sparyd not to wete her fete;
She wadyd ouer; she found a man
   That halsyd her hartely and kyst her
      swete.

Thus after her cold she cought a hete.
  'My lefe,' she sayd, 'rowtyth in hys
    bed;
  Iwys, he hath an heuy hed.'

[4]

What dremyst thou, drunchard, drousy
    pate?   [f. 2^r
Thy lust *and* lykyng is from the gone.
Thou blynkerd blowboll, thou wakyst to
    late;
  Behold, thou lyeste, luggard, alone.
  Well may thou sygh, well may thou
    grone,
    To dele wyth her so cowardly;
  Iwys, powle hachet, she bleryd thyne I.

*Stzas. 1–3 are on 1^v of an unsigned gathering at
the beginning of the volume, stza. 4 on 2^r.*
The repetition of the burden is indicated as
follows: stza. 1: with hey lullay. &c.
stzas. 2, 3: wyth hey lullay. &c.
At end: Qd skelton Laureate.

460

*Huntington Library. Christmas carolles
newely Inprynted* (Richard Kele)
                        c. 1550
p. [18]

  Synge dyllum, dyllum, dyllum, dyllum!
    I can tell you, and I wyll,
    Of my ladyes water-myll.

[1]

It was a mayde of brenten ars;
She rode to myll vpon a horse;
Yet was she mayden neuer the worse.

[2]

Layde she was vpon a sacke;
'Stryke softe,' she sayd, 'hurt not my backe,
And spare not; let the myll clacke.'

[3]

Iwys, the myller was full nyce;   [p. [19]
His mylstones hanged bothe by a vyce
And wolde be walkynge at a tryce.

[4]

This mayd to myll ofte dyd resorte
And of her game made no reporte,
But to her it was full great conforte.

The repetition of the burden is indicated as
follows: stza. 1: Synge dyllum. &c. stzas. 2,
3: Syng dyllum. &c. stza. 4: Synge dyllum &c.
At end: Finis.

460.1

Cambridge University Library. MS. Addit.
  7350, Box 2   *c.* 1500
f. 2^r

  Podyng*es* at nyght *and* podyng*es* at none;
  Were nat for podyng*es* the world wer*e*
    clene done.

[1]

'I pray yow, maydens eu*er*ychone,
Tell me wherfore ye make so grete mone;
Yf ye haue nede podyng*es* to bye,
Cu*m*me hether to me, for I haue plentye.

[2]

'Will ye haue of the podyng*es* that lye on
    the shelf?'
'Nay, I will haue a podyng that will stand
    by hy*m*self;
Therfor I pray yow hartely,
Lett me haue hym, for that will I bye.'

[3]

'Will ye haue of the podyng*es* cu*m* out of
    the panne?'
'No, I will haue a podyng that grows out of
    a man,
For he may helpe me at my nede;
Therfor I pray yow now lett me spede.'

[4]

'How sey ye, mayd*es*, will ye eny more?
Speke now betyme, for I haue lytyll store;
Yett I haue one su*m*tyme, I dare say,
A handfull *and* half besid*es* the assey.'

[5]

'What is the price?' seyd thelder mayde;
She spake firste, for she hadd asseyd;
Fourtie pens she gaue hy*m* in hande
And seyd she wold haue hy*m* to lerne hy*m*
    stand.

[6]

Then spake the yonger mayd*es* eu*er*ychone:
'Happie th*o*u arte, for now th[o]u haste one,
But, *and* we lyve another yere, as plese God
    we may,
We will haue eche of us one whatsoeu*er* we
    pay.'

At end: Finis qu*od* E (*followed by what appears
to be a cipher cancelled*).

461

Huntington Library. Christmas carolles newely Inprynted (Richard Kele)

c. 1550

p. [19]

Inducas, inducas,
In temptationibus.

[1]

The nunne walked on her prayer;
Inducas, [inducas,]
Ther cam a frere and met with her
In temptation[i]bus.

[2]

This nunne began to fall aslepe;
Inducas, [inducas,]
The frere knelyd downe at her fete
In temptationibus.

[3]

This fryer began the nunne to   [p. [20]]
grope;
Inducas, [inducas,]
It was a morsell for the Pope,
In temptationibus.

[4]

The frere *and* the nunne, whan they had
done,
Inducas, [inducas,]
Eche to theyr cloyster dyd they gone
Sine temptationibus.

The burden is repeated in full after each stanza.
stza. 1, l. 2. Orig. Inducas. &c.   l. 4. Orig.
In temptationbus. &c.
At end: Finis.

461.1

*Cambridge University Library. MS. Addit.
7350, Box 2   XVI cent.*

f. 2ʳ

Inducas, inducas,
In temptacionibus.

[1]

Ther was a frier of order gray,
Inducas,
Which loued a nunne full meny a day
In temptacionibus.

[2]

This fryer was lusty, proper, and yong,
Inducas,
He offerd the nunne to lerne her syng
In temptacionibus.

[3]

O the re me fa the frier her tawght,
Inducas,
Sol la, this nunne he kyst full oft
In temptacionibus.

[4]

By proper chaunt and segnory,
Inducas,
This nunne he groped with flattery
In temptacionibus.

[5]

The fryers first lesson was 'Veni ad me,'
Inducas,
'*Et* ponam tollum meum ad te,'
In temptacionibus.

[6]

The frier sang all by bemoll,
Inducas,
Of the nunne he begate a cristenyd sowle
In temptacionibus.

[7]

The nunne was taught to syng depe,
Inducas,
'Lapides expungnauerunt me,'
In temptacionibus.

[8]

Thus the fryer lyke a prety man,
Inducas,
Ofte rokkyd the nunnys quoniam
In temptacionibus.

At end: Finis short *and* swete.
stza. 7, l. 1. taught] MS. taughght.

462

British Museum. MS. Harley 1317

c. 1500

f. 94ᵛ

Wep no more for me, swet hart,
Wepe no more for me;
As scharpe as a dart hathe perysht my
hart
That ye shod morne for me.

[1]

Apon a mornyng of May,
In the mornyng grey,
  I walkyd plesantly
To a garden gren,
So freshe besen
  That joy hyt was to se.

[2]

Ther walkyd I
Al soburly,
  Musyng myselffe alon,
Tyll sodenly
I blenkyd myn y
  Wher I spyyd won.

[3]

Whych in gret payn,
Me thowt sarteyn,
  Hyt semyd that he was;
Hys gown al blake
Apon hys bake,
  Lyke lede hys colore was.

463

British Museum. MS. Addit. 31922
                              XVI *cent.*
ff. 45ᵛ, 46ʳ

  Yow and I and Amyas,
    Amyas and yow and I,
  To the grenewode must we go, alas!
    Yow and I, my lyff, and Amyas.

[1]

The knyght knokett at the   [f. 46ʳ
  castell gate;
The lady meruelyd who was therat.

[2]

To call the porter he wold not blyn;
The lady said he shuld not com in.

[3]

The portres was a lady bryght;
Strangenes that lady hyght.

[4]

She asked hym what was his name;
He said, 'Desyre, your man, madame.'

[5]

She said, 'Desyre, what do ye here?'
He said, 'Madame, as your prisoner.'

[6]

He was cownselled to breffe a byll
And shew my lady hys oune wyll.

[7]

Kyndnes said she wold yt bere,
And Pyte said she wold be ther.

[8]

Thus how thay dyd we cannott say—
We left them ther *and* went ower way.

The words of the burden are written three
  times, once for each voice.
The repetition of the burden is indicated as
  follows: stzas. 1, 2 you *and* I *and* amyas vt
  sup*ra*. stzas. 3–8: you a*nd* I vt sup*ra*.
burden, l. 3. we] *2nd voice* I.
Signature: Cornysh.

463.1

British Museum. MS. Addit. 31922
                              XVI *cent.*
f. 36ʳ

  Hey nony nony nony nony no,
  Hey nony nony nony nony no!

[1]

This other day
I hard a may
  Ryght peteusly co*m*playne:
She sayd allway
Wit*h*owt denay
  Her hart was full of payne.

[2]

She said, alas,
Wit*h*owt trespas
  Her dere hart was vntrew:
'In eu*er*y place
I wot he hace
  Forsake me for a new.

[3]

'Seth he vntrew
Hath chosen a new
  And thynk*es wit*h her to rest,
And will not rew,
And I, so trew;
  Wherfore my hart will brest.

[4]

'And now I may
In no man*er* a way
  Optayne that I do sew;
So eu*er and* ay,
Wit*h*owt denay,
  Myne owne swet hart, adew.

[5]

'Adew, derlyng,
Adew, swettyng,
    Adew, all my welfare;
Adew, all thyng
To God *per*teynyng,
    Cryst kepe yow frome care.

[6]

'Adew, full swete,
Adew, ryght mete
    To be a ladys pere';
With terys wete
And yes replete
    She said, 'Adew, my dere.'

[7]

'Adew, farewell,
Adew, la bell,
    Adew, bothe frend and foo;
I can nott tell
Wher I shall dwell,
    My hart it greuyth me so.'

[8]

She had nott said
But at a brayde
    Her dere hart was full nere
And saide, 'Goode mayde,
Be not dismayd,
    My love, my derly*ng* dere.'

[9]

In armys he hent
That lady gent;
    In uoydyng care *and* mone
That day thay spent
To ther intent
    In wyldernes alone.

stza. 5, l. 6. frome] MS. forme.
stza. 9, l. 4. That] MS. they.
stza. 2, l. 1. She] MS. Sshe.

464

British Museum. MS. Addit. 5465
                                          XVI *cent*.
ff. 111ᵛ, 112ʳ

    Smale pathis to the grenewode,
    Will I loue *and* shall I loue,
    Will I loue *and* shall I loue
        No mo maydyns but one.

Smale pathis to the grenewode,
Will I loue and shall I loue,
Will I loue *and* shall I loue
    No mo maydyns but one.
Smale pathis to the grenewod,
Will I loue *and* shall I loue,
Will I loue *and* shall I loue
    No mo maydyns but one.

[1]

Loue is naturall to eu*er*y   [ff. 112ᵛ, 113ʳ
    wyght,
    Indyfferent to eu*er*y creature,
Chaungyng his course, now hevy, now
    lyght,
    As fortune fallyth, I yow ensure;
        So rennyth the chaunge from one to one.
    Smale pathis to the grenewode,
    Will I loue *and* shall I loue,
    Will I loue *and* shall I loue
        No mo maydyns but one.

[2]

One is good, but mo were   [ff. 113ᵛ, 114ʳ
    bettyr
    Aff*ter* my reason *and* jugeme*nt*,
Consideryng dyu*er*s fayrer *and* fetter,
    Plesaunt, buxum, *and* eu*er* obedient,
        Tyll sum of them begyn to grone.
    Smale pathis to the grenewode,
    Will I loue *and* shall I loue,
    Will I loue *and* shall I loue
        No mo maydyns but one.

[3]

But I will do as I saide   [ff. 114ᵛ, 115ʳ
    furst,
    So it is best, as thynkyth me,
To put in one my faithful trust,
    Foreu*er* yff she will trew be,
        And loue her only whereeu*er* she gone.
    Smale pathis to the grenewode,
    Will I loue *and* shall I loue,
    Will I loue *and* shall I loue
        No mo maydyns but one.

The repetition of the burden is indicated as
follows: stza. 1: Smale pathis to the grene
wode. (*1st voice adds* vt supra). stza. 2: vt
supra (*1st voice* Smale pathis). stza. 3:
Smale pathis to the grene wode vt supra.
stza. 1, l. 5. chaunge] *1st voice* chaunce.

465

Deleted from this edition. See Note.

466

British Museum. MS. Addit. 31922
XVI *cent.*

ff. 69ᵛ, 70ʳ

I am a joly foster,
I am a joly foster,
  And haue ben many a day,
  And foster will I be styll,
  For shote ryght well I may,
  For shot ryght well I may.

[1]

Wherfor shuld I hang vp my   [ff. 70ᵛ, 71ʳ
  bow vpon the grenwod bough?
I cane bend *and* draw a bow and shot well
  enough.

[2]

Wherfor shuld I hang vp myne   [f. 71ʳ
  arrow vpon the grenwode lynde?
I haue streng[t]h to mak it fle *and* kyll
  bothe hart *and* hynd.

[3]

Wherfor shuld I hang vp my horne vpon
  the grenwod tre?
I can blow the deth of a dere as well as any
  th*at* eu*er* I see.

[4]

Wherfor shuld I tye vp my hownd vnto the
  grenwod spray?
I can luge and make a sute as well as any in
  May.

The words of the burden and stza. 1 are written
three times, once for each voice.
The repetition of the burden is indicated as
follows: stza. 1: I am a Joly foster.
stzas. 2–4: I am.
stza. 1, l. 1. bough] *3rd voice* bought.
  l. 2. enough] *2nd voice* enowght.   *3rd voice*
enought.

466.1

a. *British Museum.* MS. Addit. 31922
XVI *cent.*

f. 39ᵛ

Blow thi horne, hunt*er*, and blow thi
  horne on hye!
Ther ys a do in yond*er* wode; in faith,
  she woll not dy:
  Now blow thi horne, hunt*er*, and blow
  thi horne, joly hunt*er*!

[1]

Sore this dere strykyn ys,   [f. 40ʳ
  And yet she bled*es* no whytt;

She lat so fayre, I cowde nott mys;
  Lord, I was glad of it!

[2]

As I stod under a bank,
  The dere shoffe on the mede;
I stroke her so that downe she sanke,
  But yet she was not dede.

[3]

There she gothe! Se ye nott
  How she gothe ouer the playne?
And yf ye lust to haue a shott,
  I warrant her barrayne.

[4]

He to go, and I to go,
  But he ran fast afore;
I bad hym shott and strik the do,
  For I myght shott no more.

[5]

To the couert bothe thay went,
  For I fownd wher she lay;
An arrow in her hanch she hent;
  For faynte she myght nott bray.

[6]

I was wery of the game;
  I went to tauern to drynk;
Now the construccyon of the same—
  What do yow meane or thynk?

[7]

Here I leue and mak an end
  Now of this hunt*ers* lore;
I thynk his bow ys well vnbent,
  Hys bolt may fle no more.

stza. 4, l. 4. more] MS. mere.
Signature (in different hand): W Cornysh.

b. *British Museum.* MS. Royal Appendix
58, f. 5ᵛ. XVI *cent.* (Burden only).
l. 1. and] cu*m*.   l. 2. Ther ys a do in yond*er*
wode] In yonder wode there lyeth a doo
l. 3. Now] cu*m*.   and] cu*m*.

467

British Museum. MS. Addit. 17492
By Sir Thomas Wyatt, 1530

f. 78ᵛ

Grudge on who liste, this ys my lott:
Nothing to want if it ware not.

[1]

My yeris be yong, even as ye see;
All thing*es* thereto doth well agre;

Yn feithe, in face, in eche degre,
No thing doth want, as semith me,
   If yt ware not.

[2]

Some men dothe saye that frindes be skace,
But I have founde, as in this cace,
A frinde wiche gyvith to no man place
But makis me happiest that euer was,
   Yf [yt ware not.]

[3]

A hart I have, besidis all this,
That hathe my herte, and I have his.
If he dothe will, yt is my blis,
And when we mete no lak th[e]re is,
   Yf [yt ware not.]

[4]

Yf he can finde that can me please,
A thinckes he dois his owne hertes ease,
And likewise I coulde well apease
The chefest cause of his misease,
   Yf [yt ware not.]

[5]

A master eke God hath me sente
To hom my will is hollye lente
To serue and love for that intente
That bothe we might be well contente,
   Yf [yt ware not.]

[6]

And here an ende: yt dothe suffise
To speke fewe wordes among the wise;
Yet take this note before your eyes:
My mirth shulde doble ons or twise,
   Yf yt ware not.

The burden is written again in full after stza. 2:
  Groudge on who list this is my lot no thing
  to want if yt ware not. The repetition after
  other stanzas is indicated as follows: stza. 4:
  Groudge on &c. no thing to want &c.
  stza. 6: Groudge on who liste &c.
stzas. 2–4, l. 5. MS. yf &c.
stza. 5, l. 5, MS. yf c.

468

A. *British Museum.* MS. Addit. 17492
      By Sir Thomas Wyatt, XVI *cent.*
f. 20r

  As power and wytt wyll me assyst,
  My wyll shall wyll evyn as ye lyst.

[1]

For as ye lyst my wyll ys bent
In euerythyng to be content,

To serve in love tyll lyff be spent
And to reward my love thus ment,
   Evyn as ye lyst.

[2]

To fayn or fable ys not my mynd,
Nor to refuce suche as I fynd,
But, as a lambe of humble kynd
Or byrd in cage, to be assynd,
   [Evyn as ye lyst.]

[3]

When all the flokk ys cum and gone,
Myn eye and hart agreythe in one,
Hathe chosyn yow only alone
To be my joy or elles my mone,
   [Evyn as ye lyst.]

[4]

Joy yf pytty apere in place,
Mone yf dysdayn do shew hys face;
Yet crave I not as in thys case
But as ye lede to follow the trace,
   [Evyn as ye lyst.]

[5]

Sum in wordes muche love can fayn,
And sum for wordes gyve wordes agayn;
Thus wordes for wordes in wordes remayn,
And yet at last wordes do optayn,
   [Evyn as ye lyst.]

[6]

To crave in wordes I wyll eschew,
And love in dede I wyll ensew;
Yt ys my mynd bothe hole and trew,
And for my trewthe I pray you rew,
   [Evyn as ye lyst.]

[7]

Dere hart, I bydd your hart farewell
With better hart than tong can tell;
Yet take thys tale as trew as gospell:
Ye may my lyff save or expell,
   [Evyn as ye lyst.]

stzas. 2–7, l. 5. MS. &c.
At end: fynys.

B. *British Museum.* MS. Addit. 18752
      By Sir Thomas Wyatt, XVI *cent.*
[Burden lacking]

[1]

Evyn as you lyst my wyll ys bent   [f. 89v
Yn everythynge to be content,
To serue yn loue tyll lyf be spent
And to reward my loue yncontynent,
   Even as you lyst.

[2]

To fayn or fabele ys not my mynd,
Nor to refuse suche as I fynd,
But, even as a lambe humbull *and* kynd
Or*e* byrd yn cage, to be assynd,
    Even as yo*u* lyst.

[3]

When all the folke ys co*m and* gon,
My joye *and* hart agreeth yn one,
And hath ychosen yo*u* only alone
To be my joye or ells my mon,
    Even as you lyst.

[4]

Yf pyte appeyr yn his plas,
Or yf dysdayn shew his fas,
Yet craue I nothyng yn this cas
But as yo*u* lyst to folow the tras,
    Even as yo*u* lyst.

[5]

Some yn word*es* movche loue   [f. 90ʳ
    doth fayne,
And some for wordes gyue word*es* agayne;
Thys word*es* for word*es* yn word*es* remayn,
And yet at last word*es* dow obtayne,
    Even as ye list.

[6]

To craue yn wordes I woll eschewe,
And loue yn ded I woll ensue
Wythe the, my hole hart faythfull *and* trew,
And of my trewth I pray yo*u* rew,
    Eve*n* as yo*u* lyst.

[7]

Der hart, I bed yo*u* now fawrwell
Wi*t*h as good hart as tong ca*n* tell;
Thys tall take trew as the gospell:
My lyfe yo*u* may both saue *and* spylle,
    Even as yo*u* lyst.

At end: fynys.

468.1

A. *University of Pennsylvania Library.*
MS. Latin 35
    By Sir Thomas Wyatt (?), XVI *cent.*
f. [iii]ʳ

I ham as I ham, *and* so will I be;
But howe I ham none knowithe truly.

[1]

I lede my lyff indifferently;
I meane nothinke but honeste;

Though folkes jugge diversly,
Yet I ham as I ham *and* so will I be.

[2]

Sum there be that dothe mystrowe:
Su*m* of pleasure *and* su*m* of woo;
Yet for all that nothinke they knowe,
For I ham as I ham whereue*r* I goo.

[3]

Sum ther be that dothe delyght
To jugge folkes for envy *and* spythe;
But whether they juge wronge or ryght,
I ham as I ham *and* soo will I wryght.

['envoy']

    Adew sewte syster neve[r] . . .
        Dep*a*rtinge is a payne;
    But myrthe renewithe . . .
        When louyers meate agen.

stza. 1, l. 1. indifferently] MS. in in differently.
l. 3. Though] MS. Thought.
stza. 3, l. 1. Sum] MS. Sun (with contraction
π over n).

B. *British Museum.* MS. Addit. 17492
    By Sir Thomas Wyatt (?), XVI *cent.*
f. 85ʳ

[No burden]

[1]

I am as I am, and so will I be,
But how that I am none knowth trulie;
Be yt evill, be yt well, be I bonde, be I fre,
I am as I am, and so will I be.

[2]

I lede my lif indifferentely;
I meane no thing but honestelie,
And thoughe folkis judge full dyverslye,
I am as I am, and so will I dye.

[3]

I do not rejoyse nor yet co*m*plaine;
Bothe mirthe and sadnes I doo refraine
Ande vse the meane sens folk*is* woll fayne;
Yet I am as I am, be it plesure or payne.

[4]

Dyvers do judge as theye doo troo,
Some of plesure and some of woo;
Yet for all that no thyng theye knoo
But [I] am as I am wheresoever I goo.

[5]

But sins judgers do thus dekaye,
Let everye man his judgement saye;
I will yt take yn sporte and playe,
For I am as I am, whosoever saye naye.

[6]

Woso judgith well, wele God him sende;
Woso judgith evill, God theim amende;
To judge the best therefore intende,
For I am as I am, *and* so will I ende.

[7]

Yet some there be that take delyght
To judge folk*is* thought for envye *and*
    spight,
But whyther theye jud[g]e me wrong or
    right,
I am as I am, and so do I wryght.

[8]

Praying you all that this doo rede
To truste yt as you doo y*our* crede,
And not to think I chaunge my wede,
For I am as I am, howe ever I spede.

[9]

But how that is I leve to you;
Judge as ye list, false or true;
Ye kno no more then afore ye knewe;
Yet I am as I am, whatever ensue.

[10]

And fro*m* this minde I will not flee,
But to you all that misjudge me
I do proteste, as ye maye see,
That I am as I am, and so will I bee.
At end: *finis.*

C. *Trinity College, Dublin.* MS. D. 2.
    7 [160]
        By Sir Thomas Wyatt (?), XVI *cent.*
f. 107^r
[No burden]

[1]

I doo not rejoyse nor yet complayne;
Both myrth and sadnes I doo refrayne
And vse the mene sens folkys wyll fayne;
Yet I am as I am, be hit plesure or payne.

[2]

Men doo judge as the[y] doo trow,
Sum of pleasure *and* sum of woo;
Yet for all that nothing the[y] know,
But I am as I am whersoeu*er* I goo.

[3]

But sens that judggers take that way,
Let eu*ery* man his judgement say;

I wyll hit take in sport and play;
Yet I am as I am, woosoeu*er* say nay.

[4]

Who judggis well, God well them send;
Whoo judgith yll, God them amend;
To juge the best therfore intend,
For I am as I am, and soo wyll I end.

[5]

Yet sum ther be that take delyght
To judge folkes thowght by outward sight;
But whether the[y] judge wrong or right,
I am as I am, and soo doo I wright.

[6]

I pray ye all that this doo rede
To trust hit as ye doo y*our* cred,
And thynck not that I wyll change my
    wede,
For I am as I am howsoeu*er* I spede.

[7]

But how that ys I leue to you:
Judge as ye lyst, false or trew;
Ye know no more then afore ye knew,
But I am as I am, whatsoeu*er* insew.

[8]

And frome this mynd I wyll not flye;
But to all them that mysejudge me
I do protest, as ye doo se,
That I am as I am, and soo wyll I dy.
MS. heading: F.

D. *National Library of Scotland.* MS.
    Advocates 1. 1. 6
        By Sir Thomas Wyatt (?), XVI *cent.*
f. 250^r
[No burden]

[1]

I am as I am, and so will I be,
Bot how that I am nane knawis trewlie;
Be it evill, be it weill, be I bund, be I fre,
I am as I am, and so will I be.

[2]

I leid my lyfe indifferently;   [f. 250^v
I mene na thing bot honesty;
And, tho men juge dyuersly,
I am as I am, and so will I be.

[3]

I do not rew nor yit complane;
Baith mirth and sadnes I do refrane
And vse the folk*is* that ca*n* not fane;
I am as I am, be it plesou*r* or pane.

[4]

Diuerss do juge as thay trow,
Sum of plesour *and* sum of wo;
Yit for all that nothing thay knaw:
I am as I am quhairevir I go.

[5]

Bot sen that jugeris do tak that wey,
Lat every ma*n* his judgeme*n*t say;
I will it tak in sport and pley,
For I am as I am, quhaevir sa nay.

[6]

Quha jugeis weill, weill God him send;
Quha jugeis evill, God thame amend;
To juge the best th*air*foir intend:
I am as I am, and so will I end.

[7]

Yit sum thair be that tak*is* delyt
To juge folk*is* thot for inwy *and* spyt;
Bot quhiddir thay juge me wra*n*g or ryt,
I am as I am, and so will I wryt.

[8]

Praying yow all that this dois reid
To trest it as ye do your creid,
And not to think that I chenge my weid:
I am as I am, howevir I speid.

[9]

Bot how that is I leif to yow:
Juge as ye list, owdir fals or trew;
Ye knaw no moir tha*n* afoir ye knew;
I am as I am, quhatevir eschew.

[10]

And frome this mynd I will not fle;
Bot to yow all that misjugeis me
I do protest, as ye may se,
That I am as I am, and so will I be.
stza. 2, l. 3. tho] MS. tho^t.
At end: Finis.

469

Cambridge University Library. MS. Ff. 1. 6
XV *cent.*

f. 139^v
 Vp, son and mery wether,
  Som*er* draw*eth* nere.

[1]

Somtyme Y louid, so do Y yut,
In stedfast wyse and not to flit,
But in dang*er* my loue was knyt,
 A pitous thyng to hir*e*.

[2]

For when Y offrid my s*er*uice,
I to obbey in humble wyse
As fer ferth as Y coude deuise,
 In contyna*u*nce and cher*e*.

[3]

Grete payne for nought Y dude endur,
Al for that wyckid creatur*e*;
He and no mo, Y you ensur,
 Ou*er*threw al my mat*er*.

[4]

But now, Y thancke [God] of hys sond,
I am escapid from his band
And fre to pas by se and land
 And sur*e* fro yer*e* to yer*e*.

[5]

Now may Y ete, drynke, and play,
Walke vp and doune fro day to day,
And herkyn what this loue*r*s say,
 And laugh at ther*e* man*er*.

[6]

When Y shal slepe Y haue good rest;
Somtyme Y had not altherbest,
But, ar that Y cam to this fest,
 Y bought h*it* al to der*e*.

[7]

Al that affray ys clene agoo;
Not only that, but many mo,
And, sith Y am ascapid so,
 I thencke to hold me her*e*.

[8]

But al the crue that suffren smert,
I wold thay sped lyke y*ur*e desert,
That thay myght synge w*ith* mery hert
 This song w*ith* vs in fer*e*.
stza. 6, l. 3. cam] MS. can.
At end: desor mais.

470

Gonville & Caius College, Cambridge.
MS. 383 XV *cent.*
p. 68
 Care away, away, away,
  M*ur*nyn*g*e away!
 Y am forsake, anoth*er* ys take;
  No mor*e* mu*r*ne yc may.

[1]

I am sory for her sake;
 Yc may wel ete *and* drynke;
Wa*n*ne yc sclepe yc may not wake,
 So muche on her*e* yc thenke.

[2]

I am brout in suche a bale
And brout in suche a pyne,
Wa*n*ne yc ryse vp of my bed,
Me liste wel to dyne.

[3]

I am brout in suche a pyne,
Ybrout in suche a bale,
Wa*n*ne yc haue rythe god wyne,
Me liste drynke no*n* ale.

470.1

British Museum. Printed Book, MK. 8. k. 8
By John Rastell (?), XVI *cent.*

recto

[Care awey, a]wey, awey,
Mornyng awey;
I am forsake, another ys take,
No lenger morne I may.

[1]

Now she that I
Louyd trewly
Beryth a full fayre face;
Hath chosen her
A new louer;
God send her euyll grace.
Syth she ys gone
Remedy none
There ys that I can sey;
Wherfore I synge,
'Away mornynge,
All thought *and* care awey.'

[2]

I woyd her
In goode maner;
Grete loue tyll her I had;
This fayre woma*n*
She letyd tha*n*
As though she had be glade.
But at the last
She pleyd a cast
And grauntyd vnto me
In wynd *and* wedder
To were a fether;
Hyt wyll no better be.

[3]

At our meti*n*ge
And last partynge
She gaue me a p*r*oude skorne,
And saeyd that I
Was a semely
Persone to were an horne;
Wherfore I sey

In ernyst *and* play
To mach with such a make
A thousand fold
Yet rather I wold
The deuyll had her take.

[4]

I haue her lost
For all my cost,
Yet for all that I trowe
I haue p*er*chau*n*ce
A fayre ryddau*n*ce
And am quyt of a shrew.
I say no more,
I can no more,
The mone ys at the full:
That all his lyfe
Hath a shrewde wyfe,
He hath a crowe to pull.

stza. 3, l. 1. our] Orig. your.

471

Balliol College, Oxford. MS. 354
XVI *cent.*

f. 241ᵛ

Hay, hey, hey, hey!
I will haue the whetston and I may.

[1]

I sawe a doge sethyng sowse
And an ape thechyng an howse
And a podyng etyng a mowse;
I will haue the whetston *and* I may.

[2]

I sawe an vrchyn shape *and* sewe
And anoder bake *and* brewe,
Scowre the pot*tes* as th*ei* we*re* new;
I will haue the whetston *and* I may.

[3]

I sawe a codefysshe corn sowe
And a worm a whystyll blowe
And a pye tredyng a crow;
I will haue the whetston *and* I may.

[4]

I sawe a stokfysshe drawyng a harow
And anoder dryveyng a barow
And a saltfysshe shotyng an arow;
I will haue the whetston *and* I may.

[5]

I saw a bore burdeyns bynd
And a froge clewens wynd
And a tode mvstard grynd;
I will haue the whetston *and* I may.

[6]

I sawe a sowe bere kyrchers to wasshe;
The second sowe had an hege to plasshe;
The thirde sow went to the barn to
    throsshe;
    I will haue the whetston *and* I may.

[7]

I saw an ege etyng a pye;
Geve me drynke, my mowth ys drye;
Ytt ys not long syth I made a lye;
    I will haue the whetston *and* I may.
stza. 6, l. 3. thirde] MS. iii^{de}.
At end: Explicit.

472

British Museum. MS. Cotton Vespasian
A. xxv   XVI *cent.*
f. 126^v

Newes, newes, newes, newes!
Ye never herd so many newes!

[1]

A . . . . . upon a strawe,
    Cudlyng of my cowe;
Ther came to me Jake Dawe

  .   .   .   .   .

[2]

Our dame mylked the mares talle;
    The cate was lykyng the potte;
Our mayd came out wyt a flayle
And layd her vnder fat.

[3]

In ther came our next neyghbur,
    Frome whens I cannot tell,
But ther begane a hard scouer;
    'Have yow any musterd to sell?'

[4]

A cowe had stolyn a calfe away
    And put her in a sake;
Forsoth, I sel no puddynges today;
    'Maysters, what doo youe lake?'

[5]

Robyne ys gone to Hu[n]tyngton
    To bye our gose a flayle;
Lyke Spip, my yongest son,
    Was huntyng of a snalle.

[6]

Our mayd John was her tomorowe;
    I wote not where she forwend*e*;
Our cate lyet syke and takyte gret sorowe;

  .   .   .   .   .   .

*MS. is badly written, and part of the first line is
illegible.*
The repetition of the burden is indicated after
    stzas. 1–5 by: newes newes.
stza. 4, l. 1. calfe] MS. clafe.
stza. 6, l. 2. forwend*e*] MS. forweme.

473

*Huntington Library. Christmas carolles
newely Inprynted* (Richard Kele)
                               c. 1550
p. [20]

My harte of golde as true as stele,
    As I me lened to a bough,
In fayth, but yf ye loue me well,
    Lorde, so Robyn lough!

[1]

My lady went to Caunterbury,
    The Saynt to be her bothe;
She met with Cate of Malmes-   [p. [21]]
    bery;
    Why wepyst thou in an apple rote?

[2]

Nyne myle to Mychelmas,
    Our dame began to brew;
Mychell set his mare to gras;
    Lorde, so fast it snew!

[3]

For you, loue, I brake my glasse;
    Your gowne is furred with blew;
The deuyll is dede, for there I was;
    Iwys, it is full trew.

[4]

And yf ye slepe, the cocke wyll crow;
    True hart, thynke what I say;
Jacke Napes wyll make a mow,
    Loke who dare say hym nay.

[5]

I pray you, haue me now in mynde;
    I tell you of the mater:
He blew his horne agaynst the wynde;
    The crow gothe to the water.

[6]

Yet I tell you mekyll more: [p. [22]]
    The cat lyeth in the cradell;
I pray you, kepe true hart in store,
    A peny for a ladell.

[7]

I swere by Saynt Katheryn of Kent,
  The gose gothe to the grene;
All our dogges tayle is brent;
  It is not as I wene.

[8]

'Tyrlery lorpyn,' the lauerocke songe;
  So meryly pypes the sparow;
The cow brake lose; the rope ran home;
  Syr, God gyue yow good morow.

The repetition of the burden is indicated as
  follows: stzas. 1, 3–8: My hart. &c. stza. 2:
  My harte. &c.
burden, l. 3. me] Orig. my.
stza. 1, l. 4. wepyst] Orig. shepyst.
At end: Finis.

473.1

British Museum. Printed Book C. 39. b. 17.
*A new interlude and a mery of the Nature
of the iiij. elementes.*
             By John Rastell, *c.* 1517
[E$_8$^{r}]

Downe downe downe &c.

[1]

Robyn Hode in Barnysdale stode
And lent hym tyl a mapyll thystyll;
Than cam Our Lady *and* swete Saynt
    Andrewe;
Slepyst thou, wakyst thou, Geffrey Coke?

[2]

A hundred wynter the water was depe;
I can not tell you how brode;
He toke a gose nek in his hande,
And ouer the water he went.

[3]

He start vp to a thystell top
And cut hym downe a holyn clobe;
He stroke the wren betwene the hornys,
That fyre sprange out of the pygg*es* tayle.

[4]

Jak boy, is thy bowe i-broke?
Or hath any ma*n* done the wrygguldy
    wrage?

He plukkyd muskyllys out of a wyllowe
And put them into his sachell.

[5]

Wylkyn was an archer good
And well coude handell a spade;
He toke his bend bowe in his hand
And sat hym downe by the fyre.

[6]

He toke with hym sixty bowes and ten,
A pese of befe, another of baken;
Of all the byrdes in mery Englond,
So merely pypys the mery botell.

stza. 2, l. 1. hundred] Orig. .C.
stza. 6, l. 1. sixty] Orig. .lx.

474

*Huntington Library. Christmas carolles
newely Inprynted* (Richard Kele)
                        c. 1550
p. [22]

  Gebit, gebit, gebit, gebit,
  Lux fulgebit hodie.

[1]

Ipse mocat me;
An aple is no pere tree
  In ciuitate Dauid.   [p. [23]]

[2]

Notum fecit Dominus:
By the byll one knoweth a gose
  In ciuitate Dauid.

[3]

Aparuit Esau:
A red gowne is not blew
  In ciuitate Dauid.

[4]

Uerbum caro factum est;
A shepe is a peryllous beste
  In ciuitate Dauid.

The repetition of the burden is indicated as
  follows: stzas. 1–3: Gebit. &c. stza. 4:
  Gebit. gebit. &c.
At end: Finis.

FRAGMENTS OF TEXTS PROBABLY IN CAROL FORM

i

Bodleian Library. Douce fragments f. 48
XVI *cent.*

. . . . . .

[1]

Whan Alleluya is alofte,   [f. 4ʳ]
I go gay and syt softe,
And than I am mery ofte
   As any byrde on brere.

[2]

Whan Laus Tibi cometh to towne,
Than me behoueth to knele downe
And euer to be in orisowne,
   As it were a frere.

[3]

Soone at Easter commeth Alleluya,
With butter, chese, and a tansay;
It is nothynge to my pay
   That he taryeth away so longe.

[4]

Myght I byde Shere Thursday,
Laus Tibi shall go away,
[A]nd I haue wepte that I may,
   Though he neuer come vs amonge.

At End: Finis.
Repr., E. Flügel, *Anglia*, xii (1889), 588, *N.L.*,
  p. 124 (as if part of No. 4); *facs.* Reed, p. 15.
Although imperfect at the beginning, so that
  no burden is preserved, this complaint of Lent
  is probably a true carol. It belongs to the same
  class of 'personified season' carols as Nos. 3,
  4, 141. Compare the *balade* to Lent by
  Deschamps (ed. G. Raynaud, *Œuvres complètes*, Paris, 1878–1903, x. xxvii).
stza. 1, l. 1. i.e. except during the time from
  Septuagesima to Easter, during which
  'Alleluia' is not said in the liturgy.
stza. 2, l. 1. i.e. in Lent, when 'Laus tibi
  Domine' replaces 'Alleluia' in the services.
stza. 3, l. 2. *tansay*: a pudding, omelet, or cake
  flavoured with the herb tansy, a dish prepared and eaten at Easter time.

ii

Gonville & Caius College, Cambridge.
MS. 383   XV *cent.*
p. 210
Now this Yol, &c.

[1]

Mari mulde hath boren a chylde,
  Crist lyth in cradul bonde;
He put his mouth to syk *and* couth
  To bringe vs out of bonde.

[2]

A douti knyt ys fallon in fit:
  Seynt Steuene be his name;
With stocus of stonus thei bursten his
    bonus—
  The Jewus were to blame.

[3]

Seynt Jon kepte wile Crist slepte
  On rode for all man . . .
Mari, the flour, was of myche onour,
  Scheld us from scl . . .

[4]

The childron [of Israel] cried, 'Wa, wa!'
  Her wondus smertus sore;
Crist in cradul seide, 'Ba, ba!
  Man synne . . .'

[5]

. . . s werkus, prestus *and* clercus,
  He tawt hem to wyrche;
.   . . . . . for trewthe
  For lawus of Holi Cherche.

[6]

The seue[n]the . . .
  [Cri]st his blod gan blede;
Tak hit in mynde . . .

. . . . . .

The repetition of the burden is indicated after
  stza. 1 by: this yo. . . .
stza. 1, l. 3. syk] MS. syb.

The defects in stzas. 4, 5, 6 are the result of wear and the loss of the lower left-hand corner of the leaf.

The carol is written at the bottom of a page which has been much worn and torn, with consequent damage to the text. The original carol doubtless had other stanzas, or at least one for the Epiphany, but no more were written in this MS., probably from lack of space.

The neglecting to write the burden in full at least once is most unusual and implies that it was so well known that only the first words were necessary.

stza. 4. Compare No. 108, stza. 1, ll. 1, 2 and No. 125 A, stza. 16, ll. 1, 2.

stza. 5. On St. Thomas of Canterbury.

stza. 6. On the Circumcision.

iii

St. John's College, Cambridge. MS. S 54
XV *cent.*

The borys hed haue we in broght;   [f. 1ʳ
Lok ye be mery in hert *and* thoght!
And he th*a*t all th*i*s world has wrowt
    Saue yow *and* eke me!

l. 1. broght] MS. broghht.   l. 2. thoght]
MS. thoghht.

Pr. James & Macaulay, p. 68. They note (p. 86):
'This is presumably the last stanza of a piece which was written mainly on the first leaf.'

iv

St. John's College, Cambridge. MS. S. 54
XV *cent.*

    . . . d wasche ye,   [f. 13ᵛ
And goo to met i*n* honest[e.]

[1]

. . . . ye xall ete
. . . . blys be yo*ur* mete
. . . er ye be.

[2]

. . . . fest bega*n*ne
. . . . e both God *and* ma*n*
. . . washe.

[3]

. . . . xii day
. . . . is no nay
. . . . . .

[4]

. . . . the blod
. . . . yo*u* good
. . . [thin]ke on me.

[5]

Qwan ye haue was[hed] . .   [f. 14ʳ
My pascho[n] . . . . .
    Th*a*t I suffyrd . .

[6]

Loke [n]ot the . . . .
To sytte at . . . . .
    I*n* hewne . . . . .

[7]

So to w . . . . . .
Th*a*t we m . . . . .
    Ame*n* . . . . .

Pr. James & Macaulay, p. 85.

The repetition of the burden is indicated after stzas. 2, 3 by: vt sup*r*a, after stza. 4 by: vt sup.

stza. 5, l. 3. suffyrd] MS. surffyd

The outer edge of the leaf is damaged, both r. and v.

v

British Museum. MS. Sloane 2593
XV *cent.*

[1]

. . . .
    . . . . . .
. . . .
'Th*o*u wost wol lytyl ho is thi foo. [f. 2ʳ

[2]

'Ma*n*, loke th*o*u haue this gys,
    Quatsu*m*eu*er*e thou xalt doo:
Of thi speche the wil avys;
    Thou wost wol lytil ho is thi foo.

[3]

'Ma*n*, rewle thi tu*n*ge in swych a gys
    Th*a*t no*n* mysspeche come the froo,
For tha*n* thou dost as the wys;
    Thou wost wol lytil ho is thi foo.

[4]

'Idil speche I rede th*o*u spys:
    Lok to hom th*o*u seyst thi wil too;
Qwethe*r* th*o*u stonde, walke, or ryde,
    Thou wost wol lytil ho is thi foo.'

[5]

The bryd seyde on his devys,
    'Th*o*u mytyst telle su*m* ma*n* thi woo;
He wol it we*re* dublyd thryis:
    Thou wost wol lytil ho is thi foo.'

[6]

'If thou wy[l]t beryn awey the prys,
  Lestene this song, *and* synge thertoo:
"Of thi speche the wil avys;
  Thou wost wol lytil ho is thin foo."'

The portion of this piece which is preserved
begins with the last line of a stanza on what
was formerly f. 49 of the original volume.
It is impossible to say certainly how many
stanzas are lost or whether the piece had a
burden. It appears to be a *chanson d'aventure*
of the type in which a bird is the speaker
encountered by the narrator. *Pr.* Wright,
Wart. Club, p. 1; B. Fehr, *Archiv*, cix
(1902), 41. Both treat the first line as a burden, in spite of the index mark in the MS. to
connect the line with a preceding stanza.

vi

St. John's College, Cambridge. MS. S. 54
                                   XV *cent.*

Women ben good for lo[ve]   [f. 13ʳ
  . . . . that sit above.

[1]

In evyn ther sitte a lady;
Off all women sche   .   .   .
Women to loue yt y .   .   .

[2]

Women to loue y   .   .   .   .
To loue women   .   .   .   .
Women to loue   .   .   .

[3]

Women xall in   .   .   .   .
Day nye nyth   .   .   .   .
Womenys cump [any] .   .

[4]

Iwys, I hold   .   .   .   .
That of no w   .   .   .   .
Women to good .   .   .

[5]

Women ben goo[d] .   .   .
Women to vus   .   .   .   .
Women to lo[ve]   .   .   .

Pr. James & Macaulay, p. 85.

vii

Cambridge University Library. MS. Addit.
  5943   XV *cent.*
    Of alle thynges that   [last fly-leaf, ʳ
      God .   .   .

[1]

Wymmen ben fayre for t   .   .   .
Wommen ben fayre in   .   .   .
Wommen were ymad of   .   .   .

[2]

Ho so wol yse God on h   .   .   .
Whirschepe he wymmen   .   .   .
For they ben myri &c.

[3]

Of a womman God wa .   .   .   .
Al we schulle be glad   .   .   .   .
And he boughte vs, that w   .   .

[4]

A womman was ybore   .   .   .
Al the world he for so   .   .   .
Sche bare a chylde that   .   .   .

*The text has been damaged by the cutting-down
of the right-hand edge of an originally larger
leaf. To the left of the text are two roughly
drawn heads in profile, one with a mitre. At
the foot of the page are a few lines of scribbles,
one line blotted out.*

viii

British Museum. MS. Addit. 5666
                                   XV *cent.*

    I have loued so many a day,   [f. 3ᵛ
    Ligtly spedde, bot better I may.

[1]

This ender day wen me was wo,
Naghtgale to meue me to,
  Vnder a bugh ther I lay.

Music for one voice. *Pr.*, with music, Ritson,
  Ancient Songs (1877), p. xlvi.
This fragment appears to be the burden and
part of the first stanza of a carol using the
chanson d'aventure formula, probably on an
amorous theme.

ix

Cambridge University Library. MS. Addit.
  2764 (1) C   XV *cent.*

recto

[1]

Of Mary de .   .   .   .
With all this noo   .   .
Ke yt the byr   .   .   .

[burden]

  Farewell lo   .   .   .

[2]

The kyng of he . . .
As here n . . .
And my k . . .
Of the byrth . . .
Greet *and* fin . . .

[burden]

Farewell lo. . .

The fragment is part of a roll of carols, formerly loose as f. 219 of MS. Ii. 5. 18. There is music for two voices. On the verso of this fragment is written a part of a legal document in Latin prose concerning an Abbot John.
B.-R. *Supp.* *2636.5.

X

Bodleian Library. MS. Bodley 77 (Summary Catalogue No. 2265). Strips removed from binding   XV *cent.*

These fragments of texts with part-music appear on parchment used in binding a volume containing five Latin musical treatises. The MS. is of Hereford provenance and reached the Bodleian Library in the first decade of cent. XVI. The strips were kindly brought to my attention by R. W. Hunt of the Bodleian, who had already recognized the two strips here numbered 1 and 2 as belonging to a version of Carol No. 23. The collection consists of twelve strips varying in width from ¾ in. to 1 in. and having variously lengths of 3⅜ in., 4¾ in., and 8 in. All are written in the same hand. The scraps of text are presented here in the hope that other correspondences with them may be found.

Strips 1ᵛ and 2ʳ Carol No. 23 D.

Strip 1ʳ	cristus the prophc	2ᵛ	be Qu is ebore and n
Strip 3ʳ (Latin)	proles	3ᵛ	[Fragments of two initials in red]
Strip 4ʳ (Latin)	occessit proces tus	4ᵛ (Latin)	ni ea namque cel yla suum natu celi ecce sur sole pene partum aste penti strator sol re lendor p
		(English)/	with good [? separate piece]
Strip 5ʳ (Latin)	qu te Ang Mons Virg vt v sic il cebum [?] In obs In stab Claro f [ ] st	5ᵛ (Latin)	ne i n ci sis In

The Latin *cantilena* in carol-form from which Strips 4 and 5 were cut appears to be a version of No. 67 in John Stevens, *Mediaeval Carols*, Musica Britannica, iv, from B.M. MS. Egerton 3307, f. 67ᵛ. It has as its burden: 'Verbum patris hodie / Processit ex virgine', and as its first line: 'Salve, festa dies, partus virginalis'.

Strip 6ʳ	Thi	6ᵛ	Corus (in red)
	As		tus
	No		
	He		
	That		
	No		
	Wh		

Strip 7ʳ	s kyng	7ᵛ	e m*er* Ey
	clerkys		ge
	w may		
	may wel		
	of nought		
	w lete vs		
	an we go		
	t to heue		
	e m*er*y and		

This fragment is apparently from an English carol of the Nativity season, perhaps similar to No. 14. It cannot be identified as an actual variant of any carol in this collection.

Strip 8ʳ (Latin)	enit	8ᵛ (Latin)	ex vir
	storibus i		sit ex
	ci lantib*us*		irgina
	pura lux		
	n leditur		
	ditur post		
	intima i		
	scitur illu		
	onitur te		
	omne [?] sp		
(English?)	her tis	[?separate piece.]	

This fragment may be a part of the text of Stevens's No. 67, which appears on Strip 5.

Strip 9ʳ	e That h	9ᵛ (Latin)	Que*m*
	auit de		I. de s*ancto* [in red]
	glory		a N
	pre		ci
			uia

Strip 10ʳ	eco ron	10ᵛ (Latin)	monauit
	It was so		Johanne e
	gud [?] so		Pes [?]e be
			ascitur cia

Strips 9 and 10, which are contiguous, appear to contain fragments of an unidentified English and Latin macaronic carol on St. John the Evangelist.

Strip 11ʳ	sta 3 [in red]	11ᵛ	us ho
	patre		we
			Seynt ste

The text on 11ᵛ is obviously from a piece on St. Stephen.

| Strip 12ʳ (Latin) | odie | 12ᵛ | That holy |
| | die | | |

Strip 12 may be from the same composition as Strip 11.

The presence in these strips of fragments of two pieces found in the important carol-manuscript B.M. Egerton 3307 suggests that the lost MS. from which the strips were cut may have had other correspondences with Egerton.

BIBLIOGRAPHY OF ORIGINAL SOURCES

A. MANUSCRIPT

COTTON JULIUS B. XII

Paper, $11 \times 7\frac{3}{4}$ in., ff. 316 (some leaves misplaced). Cent. XVI.

Written in several hands, the main body of the MS. in one hand, that of the carol, No. 433.1 a.

A printed copy of Leland's *Collectanea*, pp. 185–257, is bound as pp. 8–66 of the volume.

Principal contents: Historical and genealogical miscellanea, including genealogies of families who came into England with William the Conqueror, accounts of feasts and ceremonies, and copies of legal and official documents, fifty-nine items in all.

COTTON TITUS A. XXVI

Paper, $8\frac{3}{4} \times 6$ in., ff. 293. Centt. XVI, XVII.

The volume is composed of several different MSS. bound together. Five leaves have been cut out between ff. 25 and 26.

Written in several hands. The carol is in the same hand as the religious poetry preceding it and *Ypotis* following it. The same hand appears again on ff. 145–207.

Principal contents: Hymns and songs, French and Italian, some with music. An illustrated Italian treatise on naval architecture. A Latin herbal, alphabetically arranged. A treatise, *De Pulsibus*. English material: A life of St. Alexis, in verse; *Merita Missae*, in verse; Lydgate's *Fifteen Joys of Our Lady*; Carol No. 419 B, imperfect at beginning; *Ypotis*; Lives of SS. Mary Magdalene and Catherine; *The Seven Sleepers*; *St. Julian the Harbourer*.

The MS. is apparently from Chester or its neighbourhood (see Notes on No. 419). A draft of a letter from a schoolboy to his parents on ff. 179^r, 180^r gives the names of John and James Stryttell [Strethull] of Mobberly, near Knutsford, Cheshire. There was a manor called Strethull, and a family of the name is recorded from Mobberly in the seventeenth and eighteenth centuries (George Ormerod, *The History of the County Palatine and City of Chester*, 2nd edn., revised Thomas Helsly, London, 1882, i. 418, 468). On f. 144 is a note of ownership in the name of Richard Redhood, and on f. 266^r another in the names of Sir Christopher Septvans alias Harflete, Thomas Septvans alias Harflete, and their father, rector of Wingham and Ash in Kent, and there are statutes of ordination of the secular college of Wingham.

COTTON VESPASIAN A. XXV

Paper and parchment, $8\frac{1}{4} \times 6\frac{1}{8}$ in., ff. 205. Centt. XV, XVI.

Parts of several MSS. bound together, written in several hands. Carol No. 472 is written on one of two parchment leaves (ff. 125, 126) which did not originally belong with the other material. It is in a hand of cent. XVI (early), which appears only on these two leaves. It has also written:

f. 125ʳ 'per me Wyllum Covsien' and a short bit of verse: 'After droght commythe rayne.'

f. 125ᵛ Scribbles with names 'thomas a beltton' and 'Rychard cartar'.

f. 126ᵛ 'thomas bewelto, thomas bewelton, thomas barton of appelton [Yorks.] that hit hys a myll in appelton feld wytnis that hur[?]th.'

On f. 126ʳ in another hand is the beginning of an indenture dated 12 February in the reign of Philip and Mary, but without a year.

The other English poems in the MS., including several labelled as carols, were written after 1550. Of these, No. 95 a is included in the present volume, as version b shows it to have been composed before this date. It is in the same hand as the English carols and songs which precede and follow it. The dates recorded here and there are from 1573 to 1578.

Principal contents: Carols Nos. 95 a, 472. Other English songs and verses. Miscellaneous material in English and Latin, principally theological.

On f. 180ᵛ is the name 'William Asheton'.

On f. 205ʳ is written in a hand of cent. xvii: 'This is master Jac his booke' and 'R. Boutant'. Later owners were Henry Savill and Sir John Anstis.

For other description of the volume see [K.] Böddeker, 'Englische Lieder und Balladen aus dem 16. Jahrhundert', in *Jahrbuch für romanische und englische Sprache und Literatur*, Neue Folge, ii (1875), 82–5.

The song, not in carol form, beginning 'A bonne, God wot', connects this MS. with South Yorkshire by its unusual extended reference to the generous hospitality of 'Mr. Wortley', i.e. Sir Thomas Wortley, who built a hunting lodge in Wharncliffe Chase, near Sheffield, in 1510:

> Mr. Wortley,
> I dar well say,
> I tell you as I thinke,
> Would not, I say,
> Byd hus this day,
> But that we shuld have drink.
>
> His men so tall,
> Walkes up his hall,
> With many a comly dishe . . .

(f. 168ᵛ, stza. 2, ll. 7–12; stza. 3, ll. 1–3; *pr.* Thomas Wright, 'Festive Songs', *P.S.* xxiii. 18–19)

According to Hunter's *South Yorks*, ii. 31, quoted in *V.C.H. Yorks.*, i. 523, Sir Thomas 'was knight of the body to four successive kings' and died in 1514. Hunter quotes from the 'family journal':

'he had such delite in huntinge, that he did build in the middest in his forest of Wharncliffe a house or lodge, at which house he did lye at, for the most part of the grease tyme; and the worshipfull of the country did ther resorte unto him, beinge ther with his pastime and good cheere; many tymes he would go into the forest of the peeke and set up ther his tent with gret provision of viteles, having in his company many worshipfull persons with his own familie, and would remain ther vii weeks or more, hunting and makinge other worthy pastimes unto his companye.'

COTTON VITELLIUS D. XII

Paper, 7½ × 5 in. A single leaf, separated from the MS. to which it once belonged, written in one hand. Cent. xv.

Contents: Carol No. 419 C.

On recto the concluding page of a copy of *The Siege of Rhodes*, in the same hand as the carol-analogue.

See the description and analysis by Rossell Hope Robbins, who first noticed this text, 'Good Gossips Reunited', *The British Museum Quarterly*, xxvii (1963), 12–14.

EGERTON 613

Vellum, $8\frac{1}{2} \times 5\frac{1}{2}$ in., ff. 74, the last from another volume. Centt. XIII, XIV, XV. Some leaves are damaged.

Written in several hands, with some initials in red and green. The carol variant is in a hand (cent. XIII) different from those of the other items.

Principal contents: Carol No. 191 B a. Norman-French material: A letter on the sufferings of Christ; The Pseudo-Gospel of Nicodemus; Account of the finding of the Cross by St. Helena; *The Exaltation of the Cross*; The *Bestiary* of Guillaume de Normandie, with pen-drawings; *Poema Morale*. Other English poems: A song of the Passion: 'Somer is comen and winter gon'; An orison to the Virgin: 'Blessed beo thu lauedi'; A song on the love of the Virgin: 'Litel uotit eniman'; *Poema Morale* (two copies).

EGERTON 3307

Vellum, $11\frac{1}{2} \times 8\frac{3}{4}$ in., ff. 88. (*c.* 1450.) Imperfect at beginning. Written in several hands, all the carols in one hand, which has also written the Latin *cantilenae*.

Contents: Portions of the Mass and processional music, chiefly for Holy Week. The processional hymn *Salve festa dies* with a strophe to St. George. A motet in honour of St. Dunstan. A Goliardic drinking song found also in *Carmina Burana*. English carols and Latin *cantilenae*, all with polyphonic musical settings by anonymous composers. The liturgical part of the MS. is completely divided from the carols and *cantilenae*. This very important MS. has a close relationship to Bodl. MS. Arch. Selden B. 26, with which it has six correspondences too close for much intermediate transmission; there are also correspondences with several other carol MSS. See Appendix, No. x.

Carols Nos. 23 C, 39.1, 101 C, 115.1, 125.1, 125.2, 139.1, 179.1, 190 B, 279.1, 311.1, 337 B.

The provenance of the MS. has been much discussed. The immediate provenance was not revealed by the dealer who sold it to the British Museum. Schofield's attribution to the college of St. George's, Windsor (which he confuses with the Chapel Royal of the King's household), is open to many serious objections. The present editor has set forth at some length the case for Meaux Abbey (Cistercian) near Beverley, Yorks., at that time a house of luxury and culture, with one of the largest libraries in England, a fine organ, and a reputation for good living and rather too free hospitality to women guests. Compare the popular jingle on the monastic houses of Holderness:

> If you go to Nun Keling, you shall find your body filling,
> Of whig or of whay,
> But go to Swine, and come betime,
> Or else you go empty away.
> But the Abbot of Meaux doth keep a good house
> By night and by day.

(G. F. Northall, *English Folk-Rhymes*, London, 1892, p. 90). Under Henry VI the Chapel Royal (as well as the chapel and college at Windsor) was languishing in contrast. John Burell, one of the identified composers of the Old Hall MS. and a gentleman of the Chapel Royal, became a corrodian at Meaux. This attribution was accepted by the late Manfred Bukofzer. Stevens expresses doubt, but offers no alternative beyond Windsor.

Frank Ll. Harrison rejects the suggestion of Meaux 'for liturgical reasons', holding that the service-pieces of the Sarum rite would not have been permitted in a Cistercian monastery where 'the uniformity of its texts and music was rigorously imposed'. But Meaux cheerfully ignored other Cistercian regulations against luxury, the presence of women, and church decoration. (For the practice of Fountains and other Cistercian houses see H. K. Andrews and Thurston Dart, 'Fourteenth-Century Polyphony in a Fountains Abbey MS Book', *Music and Letters*, xxxix, 1958, 2–3, and Denis Stevens 'The Second Fountains Fragment: A Postscript', ibid., p. 153.) Harrison's statement, that 'the presence of carols suggests that the collection was written for a collegiate church or household chapel' is surprising in view of the definitely monastic origin of many MSS. containing carols. Margaret Bent (see quotation below), whose opinion must command great respect, has doubts about the association with Meaux, but has not declared for another specific place of origin (private communication).

It can no longer be alleged that sophisticated polyphonic music of the kind found in this MS. was unknown or rare in Yorkshire. As Carolyn Wall has pointed out in her study of the music in a York mystery play, 'It is also clear that the music of Yorkshire was not behind that of London in polyphonic sophistication and stylistic inventiveness' ('York Pageant XLVI and its Music', *Speculum*, xlvi, 1971, 693). It is also pertinent to quote the important study 'The Old Hall Manuscript' by the scholars now engaged in re-editing this dominating collection of fifteenth-century English music:

> 'A third important centre is in Yorkshire. This county had a long and flourishing musical tradition, both in its monasteries and collegiate churches, to which song schools were often attached. Features establishing a link between OH [now B.M. MS. Addit. 57950] and Yorkshire are as follows: a) the presence of Burell at Meaux Abbey and as precentor of York, b) the association of Walter Cooke, perhaps the composer, with York, c) the obvious strong link with the Fountains repertory. In addition the two Agnus settings, Nos. 133 & 141, use a chant which is common to the York and Roman Use but which is omitted from most Sarum books' (Andrew Hughes and Margaret Bent, *Musica Disciplina*, xxi, 1967, 121).

Accomplished choirs of singing-men and boys were found in many monasteries, not merely in London, Westminster, and Windsor. See Edmund H. Fellowes, *English Cathedral Music from Edward VI to Edward VII* (London, 1941), p. 6.

Although some commentators have doubted that the dialect of the English carols is compatible with the location of Meaux Abbey, these doubts are unwarranted. The language of fifteenth-century Holderness was essentially Midland with some Northern forms. The carols in this MS. taken together exhibit much the same proportion of Northern characteristics as No. 377, which is from a MS. known to come from the neighbourhood of Beverley. It must be remembered (in addition to the fluidity of dialectal lines in the fifteenth century) that Meaux was north of Midland territory only by the width of the Humber, which was a thoroughfare rather than a barrier. But court singers would be certain to eschew and probably ridicule 'ilk' and three lines rhyming 'law / overthraw / saw' (No. 115.1).

For full descriptions of the MS. and discussions of provenance see Bertram Schofield, 'A Newly Discovered 15th-Century Manuscript of the Chapel Royal—Part I', *Musical Quarterly*, xxxii (1946), 509–36; Manfred F. Bukofzer, '[idem]—Part II', ibid. xxxiii (1947), 38–51, and *Studies in Medieval and Renaissance Music* (N.Y., 1950), pp. 113–75; Richard L. Greene, 'Two Medieval Musical Manuscripts: Egerton 3307 and Some University of Chicago Fragments', *J.A.M.S.* vii (1954), 1–34; Stevens, *Med. Carols*, p. 125; Frank Ll. Harrison, *Music in Medieval Britain* (London, 1958), p. 275. Further detailed description and analysis of the musical aspects of the MS. together with an edition of the liturgical first part appear in Gwynn S. McPeek and Robert White Linker, *The British Museum Manuscript Egerton* 3307 (London, 1963). McPeek is reluctant to abandon the assignment of provenance to Windsor, but his linguistic argument is not convincing, and it should be clear that, if a court connection is to be made, the Chapel Royal is a much more likely choice. Two examples may suffice. McPeek writes: 'The third person singular feminine pronoun is always the Midland *sche*, never the Northern *ha*.' But Bodl. MS. Digby 77, certainly written at Meaux, has *sche* (f. 148ᵛ). In No. 115.1, stza. 3, l. 5 he misreads the Northern form *Ilk* as *Ill*.

In two places an amateurish scribe (or two) has added a cross patonce and the 'words' or mottoes 'Mieulx en de cy' and 'En de cy mieulx'. These must be regarded as marks of ownership, but not necessarily as indications of the place of writing. Though the motto has not been found elsewhere (after much laborious search), puns in such use were ubiquitous, and 'Meaux' was pronounced then as now, exactly like 'mieulx', i.e. 'mews'. The coat of arms of Meaux contained a cross patonce, a charge by no means common, and a cross of this particular form will rarely, if ever, be found as a marginal notation for performance or other directions. There are correspondences in texts with Bodleian Library MS. Eng. poet. e. 1, probably from Beverley, and with National Library of Scotland MS. Advocates 19. 3. 1, certainly from the north-east. If another occurrence of the motto is eventually found, that may settle the matter, perhaps in favour of a yet unsuggested religious house or individual owner.

HARLEY 275

Paper (except ff. 1*, 2*, 159, 160 vellum), 8½ × 5½ in., ff. 162. Cent. xv.

Written in several hands. The carol is in a hand (of the latter part of the century) different from those of the other items.

Contents: Religious prose treatises as follows: Richard Rolle's *Emendatio Vitae* and *Incendium Amoris*; St. Bernard's *Meditationes*; Innocent III's *De Contemptu Mundi* (imperfect); Rolle's *Lectiones de Servicio Mortuorum* (*Job*); *Liber Elucidarius*, attributed to Anselm; Origen's *De Cantico Canticorum*; *Speculum Humane Salvacionis*; 'Si Ecclesiastica Sententia in aliquibus debeat exerceri'. Carol No. 23 B. 'Tractatus de Supersticione, Incantacione, seu Divinacione.' 'De Penitencia Ade et Eve.' Two medical recipes.

The volume is apparently from Essex. A letter on f. 148ᵛ, dated 1451, from Thomas Kemp, Bishop of London, to Sir Thomas Davell (Davall) concerns the marriage of William Stratton and Johanna Clerk in the parish church of Dunmow.

HARLEY 541. Collectanea, principally by Sir Simonds D'Ewes.

Paper, 8¼ × 6 in., ff. 229. Centt. xv, xvi, xvii.

Written in several hands. The two carols are in the same hand, which wrote nothing else in the volume.

Principal contents: Carols Nos. 125 C, 422 B. A collection of Welsh proverbs translated into Latin by John Davies. A prayer by Paul D'Ewes. A life of St. Catherine. John More's journal of the House of Commons. The Mass defended against a book of errors, A.D. 1606. Two diplomatic documents, in French. A religious tract. Part of a masque for the entertainment of Queen Elizabeth. Alexander King's Latin oration at Edinburgh. Michael Lok's notes on Russia. A description of Holland. A poem on the family of Stanley. Poems of cent. xv: 'The Lytylle Childrenes Lytill Boke'; The lines 'Wit hath wonder', etc.; A love-song; Lydgate's *Dietary*; Dialogue between Nurture and Kind; *The A B C of Aristotle* (2 copies). A prayer to the Virgin. Lists with a few notes (by John Stow) of officials, churches, gates, halls, and trades of London. Lists of English lords, knights, bishops, and mayors.

HARLEY 1317

Paper, $11\frac{1}{4} \times 8\frac{1}{4}$ in., ff. i+101. Centt. xv (second half), xvi (first half). Owing to a mistake in numbering, there are two ff. 94. The second is designated as f. 94*.

Written principally in one hand. Two others have added scribbles and household accounts towards the end. The carol is the only item written in a fourth hand.

Contents: An abridgement of the laws of England, in Latin and French. Carol No. 462. Letter from one John Stevenson to his brother. Index to the laws above. Letter of Henry VIII to one William Eliot, in Latin. Household accounts. Among the scribbles on f. 94ᵛ are two snatches of songs: 'And I were mayden', 'loley to syng and sey as here'.

The following names appear: 'homffrey dymmok' (variously spelled), 'John taylbotte', 'Edwarde torpyn', 'frances torpin'. These names connect the MS. with Gloucestershire in cent. xvi. John Talbot held prebends of Nassingham, Ailesbury, and Clifton; John Stevenson was a prebendary of Lichfield in 1557; Francis Turpin was a prebendary of Westminster in 1542.

HARLEY 2253

Parchment, $11\frac{1}{2} \times 7\frac{3}{8}$ in., ff. 142. Cent. xiv (*c.* 1330–40).

Written principally in one hand, that of the scribe who also wrote part of British Museum MS. Royal 12 C. xii. The carol is in the same hand as all the other English poetry. Another hand, of cent. xiii (late), wrote the Anglo-Norman pieces of the first forty-two leaves.

The MS. is a miscellany of English, French, and Latin prose and poetry, compiled in Herefordshire or its neighbourhood in the west Midlands. Thomas Wright's suggestion of Leominster Priory, a cell of St. Mary's Abbey, Reading, as a precise point of origin is now regarded as not established. This one MS. is of overwhelming importance in the records of English lyric poetry of the earlier cent. xiv. It has been the object of deservedly detailed and expert study, notably by G. L. Brook, the editor of *The Harley Lyrics* (Manchester, 1948) and by N. R. Ker, editor of the superb *Facsimile of British Museum MS. Harley* 2253, E.E.T.S., Or. Ser., No. 255, 1965. Ker's complete catalogue of the contents is now authoritative. Older landmarks in the scholarship devoted to the MS. are H. Wanley and others, *Catalogus Librorum Manuscriptorum Bibliothecae Harleianae* (London, 1808), and K. Böddeker, ed., *Altenglische Dichtungen des MS. Harl.* 2253 (Berlin, 1878).

Principal contents: Anglo-Norman religious pieces in prose and verse; a life of St. Ethelbert, in Latin; English and French lyric poems, religious and secular, including Carol No. 440; a French treatise on pilgrimages; the verse-romance *King Horn*; French and Latin religious and devotional prose pieces; Latin account of the martyrdom of St. Wistan.

HARLEY 2330

Parchment, $5\frac{3}{4} \times 4$ in., ff. ii+122. Cent. xv.

Written in two hands, the carol in one, the remainder of the volume in another, with initials in red and blue. The carol is preceded by two blank leaves.

Contents: English translations of St. Augustine's *Contra Julianum* and *Tractatus de Creatione Primi Hominis*. Carol No. 149 c.

On f. 17ʳ (inverted) is: 'Elizabeth Vincent'; on f. 45ʳ (inverted): 'Robert Vincent his Booke' both of cent. xvi.

HARLEY 2380

Paper and parchment, $8\frac{1}{4} \times 5\frac{1}{2}$ in., ff. 79. Cent. xv.

The margins are damaged throughout. ff. 78, 79 are small fragments.

Written principally in two hands, the bulk of the medical material in one, the carol and other English poetry in the other.

Principal contents: A collection of medical recipes, with a table of contents prefixed. Carol No. 146 B. Other English poems, including: 'This is Gods aun complaynt'; 'Thurght a forest als I went' ('The Bird with Four Feathers'); 'The blyssed barn in Betlem born' (a miracle of the Virgin, imperfect).

HARLEY 4294

Paper, except f. 82 parchment, $11\frac{3}{4} \times 7\frac{3}{8}$ in., ff. 82. Cent. xv (second half), xvi (first half).

Written in two hands, the first, of cent. xv, extending throughout the *Dialogues*. The carols are in the second hand, of cent. xvi (early), which has also written the other verses and the medical recipes. On the parchment last leaf are some merchants' accounts in still another hand, some scribbles, among them 'Henry by the grace of god kynge', and 'Ambrose' several times repeated.

Contents: Translation in English verse of the *Dialogues of Sydrac and Boctus* (imperfect at beginning), cent. xv, with marginal notes in a hand of cent. xviii. Didactic verses, signed Ricardus Spery, *beg*. '[Wo] worth your hartes so planted in pryde' B.–R. 4216. Two medical recipes, one for the sweating sickness, the other 'The quenys preseruatyfe'. Carols Nos. 103 B, 343, 396.

Accounts on f. 82ʳ connect the MS. with Bromley, apparently Bromley in Kent since going to London is casually recorded.

HARLEY 5396

Parchment and paper, $8\frac{1}{2} \times 5$ in., ff. 311. Centt. xii, xv.

Three MSS. bound as one. Written in several hands. All the English poems, including the carols, are in one hand (cent. xv), the same which wrote the accounts.

Principal contents: Latin sermons, collected by John Felton of Oxford, fellow of Magdalen College and Professor of Theology. Holkot's (?) treatise *Convertimini*. An antidotary, arranged alphabetically (imperfect at beginning). English poems: Carols Nos. 36 b (signed Wylyam northe of yorke), 80, 136 A; A hymn at the Elevation of the Host; A hymn to the Virgin; A tale against wedlock-breaking; 'Our Lady's Song of the Child That Sucked Her Breast'; *The Ten Commandments*; *A Pennyworth of Wit* (imperfect); *Good Rule Is Out of Remembrance*; *Turn Up Her Halter and Let Her Go*; *Our Lord's Exhortation*; *The Bysom Leads the Blind*; *How the Wise Man Taught His Son*; The 'Long Charter of Christ' (A-text); *The Tournament of Tottenham*; *Alas, That Any Kind Man Wants Good*; *A Tale of King Henry II* (imperfect).

Accounts, apparently of a Midlands merchant, for such articles as red wine, vinegar, wool, wax, 'cloth of Rone', sheepskins, a horse, dated 'the xxxiiii of kyng henry the VI' (1455). Among the places named in the accounts are Woolaston and Weston (Glos.), Coventry, London, Henbury (Glos., or perhaps Hanbury in Staffs. or Worcs.), Northampton, Barton (which one is not indicated), Kingsthorp (Northants.), Uppingham (Rutl.).

On f. 285ʳ is: 'Iste liber pertinet Ricardo Taylour.' On f. 282ᵛ, in the hand of the carols is the phrase: 'end betwene thoms dyer *and* wel belovyd'.

HARLEY 7358

Paper, $5\frac{7}{8} \times 4\frac{1}{2}$ in., ff. 25. Cent. XIV (second half).

Written throughout, including the carols, in one hand.

Contents: Miscellanea, principally theological, including a drawing of a crucifix labelled 'Crux fidelis' and another of a hand. A Latin treatise on the Cross and the woods of which it was made. A Latin treatise on the Sacraments. Latin liturgical notes, those referring to the Virgin and St. Thomas of Canterbury crossed out. A prayer to St. Apollonia as the healer of toothache. Carol No. 395 a. A list of saints' days. *De annis embolismalibus* in Latin verse. Carol No. 155 b.

From East Lulworth, Dorset (not East Walworth as stated in the first edition of this work, p. 328), a small village on the coast six miles west of Corfe Castle. The MS. contains the form of a will dated from there in 1374. The colophon gives the name of the scribe as 'Sperhauckus de est lolleworth', i.e. John Sperhauck, rector of 'Chaluedonharyng', i.e. Chaldon Herring or East Chaldon, near East Lulworth (*Papal Letters*, ix. 5, under date of 1438). The MS. may have been derived from material in Bindon Abbey (Cistercian), from the ruins of which Lulworth Castle was later built by the Howards, Earls of Suffolk. On f. 10ᵛ is 'Edwardus Willem willem'.

HARLEY 7578

Parchment and paper, leaves of varying sizes, ff. 129. Centt. XV, XVI, XVII.

The volume is made up of parts of several MSS. now bound together. The section containing the carol (No. 445) is a part-book of songs of cent. XVI, $5\frac{3}{4} \times 7\frac{3}{4}$ in. It is written in several hands, the carol being in the same hand as the songs before and after it.

On f. 117ᵛ is the name 'Thomas Awdcoron' (repeated as 'Adcorne') in a hand of cent. XVI, and the following note: '17 February, 1717–18, This Book given to Humfrey Wanley, by James Mickleton of Grayes Inne, Esq: containing a Collection of old Songs, &c. used within and without the Bishoprick of Durham.' On f. 83ʳ is a note to the same effect in the hand of Joseph Ritson.

For a list of the contents of the entire volume see *Catalogus Librorum Manuscriptorum Bibliothecae Harleianae* (London, 1808); for a list of the other English songs see A. Hughes-Hughes, *Catalogue of Manuscript Music in the British Museum* (London, 1908).

The song-section of the MS. is notable for containing the full text of the fascinating and still somewhat puzzling festival dance-song from Durham which begins 'Alone walking' (f. 106) in which are embedded the charming lines with the refrain [? burden] 'The baylly berith the bell away / the lylle the rose the rose I lay', which have been subjected to some fanciful and uninformed criticism. The important articles which are indispensable to students of MS. and poem are B. Colgrave and C. E. Wright, 'An Elizabethan Poem About Durham', *The Durham University Journal*, xxxii (1940), 161–8, and Madeleine Hope Dodds, 'Some Notes on "An Elizabethan Poem About Durham"', ibid. xxxiii (1940), 65–7.

LANSDOWNE 379

Paper, $7\frac{5}{8} \times 5\frac{1}{4}$ in., ff. 86. Centt. XVI (first half), XVII. Some leaves are much damaged and mended. ff. 23ʳ–35ᵛ are printed.

Written by several hands. The carols are in the hand which wrote ff. 9ʳ–22ᵛ, the prescriptions, and the continuation of the printed item.

Principal contents: Oratio D. *Johannis Damasceni*, in Greek and Latin verse (cent. XVII). English sermons on the Eucharist, for Easter, and for All Saints. A copy of Bishop

William Lyndewode's *Constitutiones Provinciales* printed by Wynkyn de Worde, imperfect at beginning and at end, the deficiency at the end supplied in MS. Carols Nos. 43, 94. Prescriptions for the stone, toothache, etc. Notes on the temperaments of the body and the four elements. Notes on chronology. English prayers (imperfect) by a member of the Charterhouse, London.

On f. 1^r is the note: 'I bought this Book out of the Library of Sir Joseph Jekyl It was formerly Lord Somers. / James West / February 173$\frac{8}{9}$'.

ROYAL 17. B. XLIII

Vellum, 7$\frac{7}{8}$ × 5$\frac{1}{2}$ in., ff. 187. Cent. xv.

Written in four different hands. The carol is in a hand (*c.* 1500) different from those of the rest of the volume, except for some scribbles on ff. 183^v, 184^r, among them the unhelpful name 'Joh*a*n' thrice repeated. There is no evidence of provenance.

Contents: Mandeville's *Travels* in the defective English version. The romance *Sir Gowghter*. *St. Patrick's Purgatory*. The above are in a hand of cent. xv (first half). *The Vision of Tundale*, written A.D. 1451 (imperfect at beginning). Carol No. 270.

ROYAL 17. B. XLVII

Paper (except ff. i, ii, 1, 52, 53 vellum). 8$\frac{1}{4}$ × 5$\frac{3}{8}$ in., ff. ii+175. Cent. xv (middle).

Written in several hands. The carol is in the same hand of cent. xv (late) as the following small items: ff. 88^v, 89^r. Three medical prescriptions. f. 113^r. Two English quatrains *beg.*: a. 'O Lord of hevyn *and* kyng of might' B.-R. 2490; b. 'Shall I go to her agayn'. ff. 114^r, 119^r. Legal notes.

Principal contents: A commonplace book of forms for legal documents and letters in Latin, French, and English. Lydgate's *Dietary*. *Prudence* (one stanza of Burgh's *Cato Major*). Carol No. 393.

On vellum scraps are the names of owners: 'magister Leye' (possibly of the family of Leigh of Herriard in Hampshire) (cent. xv); William Challner and Thomas Cheke (cent. xvi).

ROYAL 19. B. IV

Vellum, 12 × 8$\frac{1}{2}$ in., ff. 98. Cent. xv (second half).

Contents: *Les Diz mouraulx des philosoffes*, a French translation by Guillaume de Thignonville of the *Dicta Moralia*; *Le Liure delarguement que font ensemble pourete et richece*, poem in French by Jean Bruyant, notary of Paris. In an English hand of about 1500 on the verso of the penultimate leaf, Carol No. 418.3. On f. 98^r, in another hand of cent. xv, are seven lines of French verse beginning: 'Puisque je suis a mesnage' and scribbles in several hands. On f. 3^r there is a miniature of a philosopher reading.

ROYAL 20. A. I

Vellum, 8$\frac{5}{8}$ × 6 in., ff. iv+122. Cent. xv (first half).

Written in three hands. The two carols are in different hands, and the *Travels* in a third.

Contents: Mandeville's *Travels*, in French, written by Jean de Bourgogne of Liège. Carols Nos. 27 B, 167.

The hand of No. 167 has added a colophon to the *Travels*. The hand of No. 27 B has written on f. 121^v a confused scrap (of a lullaby carol?): 'Werede ye fede *and* ye chelleth fynde In fayth wyth owtenne a baby y buffed y billed y loffid y lapped y led in clos.' On f. 122^r another hand has written three lines of an English hymn to the Virgin: 'amonge al merthes manny / we chol senge of o lady / In al this wordil nis svch a siht.'

ROYAL Appendix 58

Paper, $5\frac{7}{8} \times 7\frac{7}{8}$ in., ff. 60. Cent. XVI (first quarter).

Written in several hands, with musical settings throughout. Of the carols Nos. 449, 458 are in the same hand, No. 150 D in another. Both hands have written other pieces as well. There are also music for a Mass and instrumental music for lute and virginals. John Stevens (*Music and Poetry in the Early Tudor Court*, London, 1961, pp. 129–32) discusses this 'complex and puzzling manuscript'.

Contents: Carols Nos. 150 D, 449, 458, 466.1 b. Other English songs (some imperfect) by Cornish, Parker, Cooper, Drake, and anonymous composers.

The words of the entire MS. are printed by E. Flügel, 'Liedersammlungen', etc., *Anglia*, xii (1889), 256–72.

SLOANE 1584

Paper and vellum, $5\frac{3}{8} \times 3\frac{3}{8}$ in., ff. 96. Cent. XV.

Written principally in one hand, that of John Gysborn, Premonstratensian Canon of Coverham, Yorks. Another hand has written the history of confession, and still others have added a few medical recipes. The carol is in Gysborn's hand, but not the other English song.

Principal contents: Theological material, including instructions for deacons and sub-deacons, questions to be asked in confession, prayers, etc. Medical recipes. Carol No. 446. A sermon for Easter. Directions for making colours, enamelling, etc. A history of confession. English love-song: 'Greuus ys my sorowe'.

On f. 12^r is written: Scriptum per me Johannes Gysborn Canonicus de Couerham.

On f. 26^v is a drawing of Christ's wounds, on ff. 27^r–28^r alphabets of initials, on f. 28^v a conventional design, and on f. 83^v a drawing of a gaily dressed man dancing.

SLOANE 2593

Paper (except part of f. 12 parchment), $5\frac{7}{8} \times 4\frac{3}{8}$ in., ff. 37. Cent. XV (first half).

The MS. is a part of a larger volume, of which the rest is not known to exist. A previous numbering shows the present f. 2 to have been formerly f. 49 of a volume. The first remaining piece in the MS. is imperfect at the beginning. There is no music. All the songs and carols are in one hand (A). At the end are minor items in three other hands as follows (all cent. XV): B. Notes on ff. 35^v and 36^v. C. Medical recipes on f. 36^v. D. Scribbles on f. 37^v.

Contents: Carols Nos. 7 B, 8 b, 16, 24, 25, 27 A, 28, 68, 86 A, 87, 114 a, 122 B, 123 B, 124 A, 125 A, 143, 145 b, 148 A, 157 C, 168, 169, 175 C, 180 B, 185 A, 188, 231, 234 C, 236, 242, 312, 315–17, 320, 329, 336, 339, 341, 355 a, 356 a, 357, 363, 365, 368, 381, 383–5, 390, 392, 395 b, 403, 405, 416, 417, 457, App., No. v. Other English songs. Three Latin songs: the famous 'Meum est propositum in taberna mori', a rondeau, 'Procedenti puero' also found in a MS. from Tours of about 1148 (Victor Luzarche, ed., *Office de Pâques ou de la Résurrection* [etc.], Tours, 1856, pp. 64–6, and in *Anal. Hym.* xx. 90, No. 93), and a *cantilena*, 'Non pudescit corpore', in praise of St. Thomas of Canterbury, which is undefaced and therefore shows that the MS. did not continue in use in a secular house.

This important MS. is from Bury St. Edmunds, almost certainly from the great Benedictine monastery there. It contains the only preserved English carol in honour of St. Edmund (No. 312, on which see Notes). It also offers the only two known English carols in honour of St. Nicholas (Nos. 314, 315). The boy-bishop who was rewarded at Bury, e.g. in 1418, 1429, and 1537, was there known as 'the bishop of St. Nicholas'

(*Reports of the Historical Manuscripts Commission*, xiv, Appendix, part viii, pp. 124–5, 'Seven Sacrist rolls of the abbey'). There was an altar dedicated to St. Nicholas in the monastery church. For an account of the very unusual guild of the Translation of St. Nicholas (the 'Dussegild') see M. D. Lobel, *The Borough of Bury St. Edmund's* (Oxford, 1935), p. 73 n. 1. The whole MS. is written in a specifically East Anglian form of language. The memorandum on f. 36ᵛ reads: 'Johannes bardel debet istum librum the qweche bardel is of . . . dwellyd . . . In In.' The omissions are tantalizing, but Bardel (Bradel, Bardwell) is a Suffolk name found in and near Bury and infrequent elsewhere. Bardwell is a parish near Ixworth. The name is borne by one of the 'knights of St. Edmund' mentioned in the *Chronicle* of Jocelin de Brakelond (ed. H. E. Butler, London, 1949, p. 121). The owner of this MS. may be the same monk of Bury who is one of two named in inscriptions in Bodl. MS. Holkham Misc. 37: f. 197ᵛ 'Liber dompni Johannis Berdwell [the surname incompletely erased] monachi sancti E.'; f. 198ʳ 'Eadmundo sancto pertinet iste liber.' The other monk whose name is in the book is John Wulfspett.

The entire MS. is printed by Thomas Wright, *Songs and Carols, Publications of the Warton Club*, iv (London, 1856). Many of the pieces are again printed by B. Fehr, 'Die Lieder der Hs. Sloane 2593', in *Archiv*, cix (1902), 33–70, with general observations on the collection.

ADDIT. 5465. 'The Fayrfax MS.'

Vellum (paper interleaved where parts of original are missing and ff. i, ii, 1), 11½×8 in., ff. ii+124. Cent. xvi (first quarter).

Leaves are missing after ff. 9ᵛ, 10ᵛ, 11ᵛ, 19ᵛ.

Written throughout in a single hand, with initials in red and blue. All the pieces have musical settings.

Contents: Carols Nos. 146 A, 263 a, 264, 432–4, 436, 464. Other English songs, sacred and secular, many with composers' names: Cornish, Fayrfax, Davy, Banastir, Newark, Sheryngham, Tutor (Tudor), Turges, Browne, Sir Thomas Philipps (List from Stevens, *M. & P.*, p. 151).

This volume was owned by Dr. Robert Fayrfax (d. 1529), a Gentleman of the Chapel Royal and an organist. His arms are on the title-page. Later owners were Charles Fairfax, Ralph Thoresby of Leeds, and John White of Newgate Street, London.

For further description and for verbal texts of the contents see John Stevens, *Music and Poetry in the Early Tudor Court* (London, 1961), pp. 351–85, also critical comment *passim*. B. Fehr prints most of the texts: 'Die Lieder des Fairfax MS.', *Archiv*, cvi (1901), 48–70. Some are printed by Joseph Ritson, *Ancient Songs* (London, 1790, 1829, 1877), and by E. Flügel, *Neuenglisches Lesebuch*, i (Halle, 1895). Dom A. Hughes has written 'An Introduction to Fayrfax', *Musica Disciplina*, vi (1952), 83. The entire MS. is edited by John Stevens, *Early Tudor Songs and Carols*, Musica Britannica, xxxvi (London, 1975).

ADDIT. 5665. 'Ritson's MS.'

Paper and vellum, 10×7 in., ff. 1+149. Cent. xvi (first quarter).

The volume is well written, with some initials in red and blue. All the texts are provided with musical settings. In some cases the words of a piece for a second voice are written in red, now badly faded. There are eight different hands in the volume, according to a MS. memorandum affixed at the end. All the carols are in the second of these hands, which begins on f. 4ᵛ and writes ff. 4ᵛ–38ʳ, 39ᵛ–47ʳ, 48ᵛ–53ʳ, 54ᵛ, 55ʳ, 56ᵛ–59ʳ.

Contents: Carols Nos. 1, 2, 6, 13, 14 c, 31 c, 57–9, 85, 89, 91 A and B, 96, 99, 103 A d and e, 109–11, 116, 118, 131 a, 133, 186, 259, 277, 306, 307, 330, 337 c, 348, 354, 359 B, 367, 375, 387, 435, 446.1. Other English songs, sacred and secular. Latin masses and motets. A French song, 'Votre trey dowce regaunt plesaunt'. Though some of the Latin pieces derive from the Sarum Processional, the MS. as a whole is not made up of processional music.

John Stevens lists the composers named as follows: 'Richard Smert; John Trouluffe; John Cornish; Henry Petyr; Sir Thomas Packe; Sir William Hawte, *miles*; Edmund Sturges (Turges?); T. B. (B. T.?); J. Norman; W. P.; and, by implication, Henry VIII ['Passetyme with good cumpanye', two versions]'. (*Music and Poetry in the Early Tudor Court*, London, 1961, p. 338.)

'Deeds and receipts in the MS. are as follows: (i) receipt to the rector of Langtre, south-west of Torrington, near the west coast of Devon; (ii) banns for the church of Bycklegh, a few miles north of Exeter; (iii) power of attorney from the master of a chapel in East Tilbury, Essex, but dated at Pyworthy in Devon (just east of Bude, Cornwall). All three are dated *c.* 1510' (loc. cit.). Smert was rector of Plymtree, near Exeter, from 1435 to 1477 (ibid., p. 5). The volume may have been connected with Exeter Cathedral. It was presented to the British Museum by Joseph Ritson in 1795.

Most of the English pieces are printed as plain texts by B. Fehr, 'Die Lieder der Hs. Add. 5665', *Archiv*, cvi (1901), 262–85. Others are printed by Joseph Ritson, *Ancient Songs* (London, 1790, 1829, 1877), E. Flügel, *Neuenglisches Lesebuch* I, (Halle, 1895), and John Stafford Smith, *Musica Antiqua* (London, [1812]). John Stevens (op. cit.) prints some of the English verbal texts, and his work is indispensable for its description and discussion of the collection. It is supplemented by his edition of twenty pieces with their music in *Early Tudor Songs and Carols*, Musica Britannica, xxxvi (London, 1975). An unpublished Yale doctoral dissertation is devoted to the MS.: Catharine K. Miller, *A Fifteenth Century Record of English Choir Repertory*, B.M. Add. MS. 5665 (1948), which I have consulted by permission. It is largely superseded by Stevens and by Frank Ll. Harrison, *Music in Medieval Britain* (London, 1958).

ADDIT. 5666

Paper (except f. i parchment), $5\frac{1}{4} \times 3\frac{3}{4}$ in., ff. 22. Cent. xv (first half).

Written in three hands, the songs, carols, and prose tract in one, the accounts in another, and notes on ff. 5^v, 7, 8^r in a third.

Contents: A fragment of a lullaby, much faded. Carol No. 151 B. Song, 'Now has Mary born' (imperfect). Carol, App., No. viii. Carol No. 144. Treatise of Latin grammar, in Latin prose. Expense accounts of John White, dated 12 Henry IV (1411). White's name also appears on ff. 7^v, 8^r, and in the following notes: f. 6^v 'Robertus Brouuham *et* Johannes White sunt ssemper Boni *et* omnibus temporibus ut dicit Thomas krim et semper erunt'; f. 7^r 'Robertus brouuham precepit Johanni White vt diceret: Johanni pepir q[u]od veniret tali die. Johannes White vt dicit brouuham.'

On f. 18^r is drawn a device of a tree and a pierced heart with the motto: 'pur vere amur je su mort' and 'Fuit homo'. On f. 22^v are three lines of French love-verse.

The note written on f. 1^v of the volume is certainly erroneous. It states that the volume is in the hand of Friar John Brackley of Norwich, the friend and adviser of the Paston family. None of the hands, however, is that of Brackley as represented in his preserved holograph letters (British Museum MS. Addit. 34888).

ADDIT. 14997

Paper, $5\frac{3}{4} \times 4\frac{3}{4}$ in. (some leaves of other sizes), ff. 115. Centt. xv, xvi (first half). The volume is imperfect at the beginning, and the margins of many leaves are damaged and repaired.

Written by several hands. The carol is in the same hand as some of the Welsh poems, the charms and medical recipes, and the schoolboy's song.

Contents: Poems in Welsh by a large number of different bards. Charms and medical recipes, in Latin and English. Two stanzas, in English, begging another drink for the singer, not in the hand of the carol. Carol No. 10, with date of 1500. A schoolboy's macaronic end-of-term song.

The MS. is obviously of Welsh origin and was in Welsh ownership until its presentation to the British Museum in 1844 by the Cymmrodorion Society.

ADDIT. 17492. 'The Devonshire MS.'

Paper, $9\frac{1}{16} \times 6$ in., ff. 121. Cent. XVI (first half). ff. 1, 93, 94, 96 are fragments, f. 96 an older vellum fragment. There are numerous blank leaves not numbered. ff. 3, 119, 120, 123 (in recent revised foliation) are fragments of an original end-leaf or end-leaves, and ff. 121, 122 are fragments of a MS. of cent. XV used in the binding.

Written in several hands. Raymond Southall (*The Courtly Maker*, New York, 1964, pp. 172–3) distinguishes a minimum of twenty-three, of which he designates three as 'major', those of Mary Shelton, Mary Fitzroy, and Margaret Douglas. His attributions are recorded in detail on his p. 173. A. K. Foxwell (*A Study of Sir Thomas Wyatt's Poems*, London, 1911, Appendix A) assigns f. 57 to Lord Darnley, ff. 44ᵛ–47ᵛ to Thomas Howard, and f. 67ᵛ to Anne Boleyn. If these attributions are correct, Carol No. 468 A is in the hand of Mary Fitzroy, and Nos. 467 and 468.1 B are in that of Mary Douglas.

Principal contents: Carols Nos. 467, 468 A, 468.1 B. Poems by Sir Thomas Wyatt (some with the initials 'T. V.') and others of the court circle. A few earlier pieces by Chaucer, Hoccleve, and Sir Richard Roos. Some attributions are still uncertain in spite of much recent discussion of the MS.

The volume appears to have belonged at one time to Mary Shelton. It came into the library of the Duke of Devonshire (hence its informal name), from whom it was borrowed by G. F. Nott for use in editing Wyatt's works. It was acquired from Nott's estate by the British Museum in 1848.

For description and history of the MS. see, in addition to the works by Foxwell and Southall, Kenneth Muir and Patricia Thomson, eds., *Collected Poems of Sir Thomas Wyatt* (Liverpool, 1969), pp. xiii–xv, with detailed list of poems, and for minute textual analysis see H. A. Mason, *Editing Wyatt* (Cambridge, 1972), pp. 13–21.

ADDIT. 18752

Vellum and paper, $8\frac{1}{4} \times 5\frac{3}{4}$ in., ff. 216. Centt. XIV, XV, XVI.

Written in several hands. The carol is in a hand that has written some of the other poems.

Principal contents: Carol No. 468 B. Other English poetry (cent. XVI). Latin treatises on astrology, medicine, etc. *Secretum Philosophorum* (imperfect). Several herbals. Copies of two letters, one addressed to Robert Oxtone, Archdeacon of Coventry (1408). The order of guests at the Queen's table at the coronation banquet of Catherine of Valois, wife of Henry V (1421). Lists of courses at banquets, one given to the King by Sir John Cornewelle.

The following names appear in the MS.: John Gryntter of Hawkchurch (Dorset), Margaret Chechester.

ADDIT. 19046

Paper, $8\frac{1}{2} \times 5\frac{7}{8}$ in., ff. 132. Cent. XV.

Written by several hands. The one carol is in the hand which wrote the English glosses in the margins of ff. 65^r–73^r, and the scribbles on f. 82^v. The name of John Jones of Carmarthen is signed to several of the pieces.

Principal contents: Carol No. 430. Proverbs, in Latin distichs. 'Liber parvi doctrinalis de parabilis philosophie'. Latin verses on synonyms (imperfect). Latin and English rules of grammar. 'De regimine vocum'. Latin verses giving the names of familiar objects. Lydgate's *Stans Puer ad Mensam.*

On f. 73^v is the note in a hand of cent. xv: 'Thomas stanlye est possessor huius libri testis est Robertus cavtu*m*.' A later hand has apparently attempted to cancel the word 'huius' and replace it by 'nullius'.

ADDIT. 20059

Vellum, 5⅝ × 3½ in., ff. 101. Centt. XIII, XV.

Written in several hands. The carol is in a hand different from that of several other religious poems on ff. 98^v–101^r: it is written transversely on ff. 6^v, 7^r.

Among the earlier items in the MS., not related to the carol, is an account in Latin of the appearance of the B.V.M. to St. Thomas of Canterbury. In its first line the name and archiepiscopal style of St. Thomas have been cancelled.

Carol No. 260 is among the material copied from this MS. by Joseph Hunter in 1826 into a volume marked 'Antiquities of Common Life, Poetry, etc. etc., Begun at Bath about 1820'. It was printed from this MS., B.M. Addit. 24542, in the first edition of this work. Its presence in the original MS. was noted by Beatrice N. Geary in her Oxford thesis.

ADDIT. 31042

Paper (except ff. 1, 2, 182, 183 vellum), 10⅝ × 7½ in., ff. 183. Cent. xv (middle).

Written principally by one hand, that of Robert Thornton, scribe of the 'Thornton MS.', Lincoln Cathedral A. 5. 2. Carol No. 427 is in his hand but appears to have been written at a different time from the poems which precede and follow it. The two leaves directly following the incomplete text of the carol have been torn out. The four flyleaves are from a breviary of cent. xv.

Principal contents: A fragment of the *Cursor Mundi.* Carols Nos. 21 E, 157 E, in a later hand, not Thornton's. *The Northern Passion. The Destruction of Jerusalem. The Siege of Melayne.* The romance *Sir Ottuel.* Lydgate's *Dietary.* A song: 'The werlde es tournede up so downe'. *The Quatrefoil of Love.* Prayer in verse: 'Haile, holy spyritt'. Lydgate's *The Virtue of the Mass.* Carol No. 427. The story of the Three Kings, in verse, imperfect at beginning.

Thornton was of Ryedale, near Helmsley, Yorks., and the language of the MS. is accordingly northern. See the New Paleographical Society, *Facsimiles of Ancient Manuscripts* (London, 1913–30), 2nd Ser., ii, plate 45. A note on f. 49^r (cent. xv late) reads: 'John Nettleton's boke'. The name is also on f. 139^v. According to M. Y. Offord, 'This is presumably the John Nettleton of Hutton Cranswick in the East Riding of Yorkshire, whose name occurs in a list, thought to have been compiled in about 1565, of owners of medieval manuscripts' (*The Parlement of the Thre Ages*, E.E.T.S., Or. Ser., No. 243, 1959, p. xii). Sir Israel Gollancz and Magdalene M. Weale (*The Quatrefoil of Love*, E.E.T.S., Or. Ser., No. 195, 1935, p. viii) date the hand as cent. xvi (middle). See also Karl Brunner, *Archiv*, cxxxii (1914), 316–27.

For a full discussion of the two fragmentary variants, Nos. 21 E, 157 E, and a useful list of still other descriptions of the MS., see the article by the scholar who first noticed the carol-texts, Karen Hodder, 'Two Unpublished Middle English Carol-Fragments', *Archiv*, ccv (1969), 378–83.

ADDIT. 31922. 'Henry VIII's MS.'

Vellum, 12 × 8¼ in., ff. 129. Cent. xvi (first quarter).

The volume has musical settings throughout and some initials in blue, red, and gold. It is well written in four different hands as follows: A. ff. 3ᵛ–21ʳ, 26ʳ; B. ff. 21ᵛ–25ᵛ, 27ʳ–124ʳ; C. ff. 124ʳ–128ʳ; D. f. 90ʳ. Hand D. has written only the music for an instrumental piece.

Contents: Carols Nos. 437, 448, 448.1, 463, 466, 466.1. Secular songs, mostly in English, but a few in French and Flemish. The composers include King Henry VIII, Cornish, Cooper, Farthyng, Fayrfax, Kemp, Rysbye, Daggere, Dunstable, Pygott, Floyd. Arrangers of songs not in English include Agricola, Hayne van Ghyseghem, Barbireau, and others. Forty-nine pieces of instrumental music. The tenor parts of four songs occur in British Museum MS. Royal Appendix 58.

All earlier descriptions of the MS. are made obsolete by John Stevens, *Music and Poetry in the Early Tudor Court* (London, 1961), and *Music at the Court of Henry VIII*, Musica Britannica, xviii (London, 1958). The former contains the verbal texts, the latter the edited music of the entire MS.

These earlier descriptions include the following, recorded here for convenient reference:

William Chappell, 'Some Account of an Unpublished Collection of Songs and Ballads by King Henry VIII and his Contemporaries', *Archaeologia*, xli (1867), 371–86 (with four facsimiles). Also in *Popular Music of the Olden Time*, revised by H. G. Wooldridge (London, 1893; *repr.* N.Y., 1961), 39–46.

E. Flügel, 'Liedersammlungen', etc., *Anglia*, xii (1889), 226–56, with printing of all verbal texts.

H. B. Briggs, *A Collection of Songs and Madrigals of the 15th Century*, Plainsong and Mediaeval Music Society (London, 1891), p. xvi.

[Sir] E. K. Chambers and Frank Sidgwick, *Early English Lyrics* (London, 1907), p. 300.

Lady Mary Trefusis, *Songs, Ballads, and Instrumental Pieces Composed by King Henry the Eighth*, Roxburghe Club (Oxford, 1912).

Among former owners of the volume were the family of Sir Charles Montolieu Lamb, Bt., the 11th Earl of Eglinton, and Stephen Fuller, M.D. The British Museum acquired it in 1882.

On f. 129ᵛ are scribbled in a hand of cent. xvi: 'Ser John leed in the parishe of Benynden' and 'vynsent Wydderden ys an onest man so sayeth Nycolas Benden cuius est contrarium verum est'; also the names of Sir John Berde [of Benenden], Davey Jones, and Jane Reve.

Stevens endorses the suggestion of Chappell that the MS. travelled from the Court to the parish of Benenden, Kent, because of the residence there of Sir Henry Guilford, Controller of the Household. Stevens suggests that Guilford may have commissioned the writing of the fine volume. He is recorded as producing and acting in court entertainments.

ADDIT. 40166 (C3). Cent. xv. A fragment of two leaves, one much decayed, containing an English poem on signs of the Judgement (six days only, instead of the usual fifteen), rules of Latin syntax with English marginalia. Carols Nos. 26, 121, both in the same hand.

From Hailes Abbey, Gloucestershire (Cistercian); see Note on No. 121.

LONDON: UNIVERSITY OF LONDON LIBRARY

657. (Formerly Helmingham Hall LJ. i. 7; sold at Sotheby's, 14 June 1965)

Paper (except six vellum fly-leaves), $11\frac{1}{2} \times 8$ in., ff. vi+181. Cent. XIV. Some leaves have a corner cut out.

Written in several hands, the carol-stanza in the hand of the sermon in which it occurs and the sermon preceding it.

Contents: Theological material in Latin prose, including: *Convertimini* with index; *De Fide Catholica*, with English verses interspersed; a short tract on whether a parish priest should celebrate several masses in one day; *De Decem Preceptis*; *Sermones*, in one Carol No. 12 b.

On f. 11^r in a hand of cent. XV is a receipt from a *capellanus*, William Hautboys, to another, John Everard.

On f. 181^v in a hand of cent. XV is a note of ownership by Robert Sevyer, parish priest of Blakeney, Norfolk.

For full description see N. R. Ker, *Medieval Manuscripts in British Libraries*, i, *London* (Oxford, 1969), pp. 374–6. Ker points out that a John Everard 'became rector of Aylmerton, near Cromer, in 1494'. The MS. is also described in G. Helmstedt, ed., *Speculum Christiani*, E.E.T.S., Or. Ser., No. 182, 1933, pp. cviii–cxii.

LONDON: COLLEGE OF ARMS

I. 7. Records of Coronations and Other Ceremonies

Paper, $16 \times 11\frac{1}{2}$ in., ff. i+92. Centt. XVI, XVII, XVIII. ff. 1, 92 are fragments.

Written in several hands. The carol is in the hand which wrote the rest of the account of the coronation of Edward VI.

Principal contents: *Forma Coronationis Regum et Reginarum*. An account in English of the funeral of Queen Elizabeth, wife of Henry VII. An account of the coronation of Henry VIII. A Proclamation by Edward VI. A description of the procession through the City to Westminster on the occasion of the coronation of Edward VI, including: A song (not a carol) at the conduit in Cheapside. Carol No. 438. An account of the funeral of the Earl of Oxford. An account of the funeral of the Bishop of Westminster, A.D. 1500. An account of the coronation of Queen Mary. An account of the coronation of Charles I as King of Scotland at Holyrood, A.D. 1633. An account of the coronation of Queen Anne, A.D. 1702.

A note on f. 1^r reads: 'A booke of the forme of coronation *and* buriall of diuers estates belongyng to thomas hawlay rex Clarenseuex. gyuen to Clarenceu . . . by wyll . . .'

LONDON: LAMBETH PALACE

LAMBETH 306

Paper, $11\frac{5}{8} \times 8$ in., ff. 204. Centt. XV, XVI.

Written in several hands, ff. 46^v to 71^v being in that of John Stow, the antiquary. The carols are in a hand of cent. XV (second half). A printed prose life of St. Winifred is bound with the MS.

Principal contents: The *Brut*. Historical notes by Stow. *Libeaus Desconus*. *The Trental of St. Gregory*. A life of St. Eustace. Hymns to the Virgin. Lydgate's *Horse, Goose, and Sheep*. A poem on 'the letters that shall save England'. Carols Nos. 401 B, 429. Other courtly and religious poems. A list of the retinue of Edward III at Calais. *The Stations of Rome*. Directions for keeping hawks. The 'proper terms' for game. The tale of the knight who married a widow's daughter. A decree of the City of London, concerning St. Peter's, Cornhill. Verses on the purchase of land. *The Battle of Brantown*.

Many medical recipes written *passim*, some on the same leaves as the two carols.

LONDON: PUBLIC RECORD OFFICE

CHANCERY MISCELLANEA, Bundle 34, File 1, No. 12

Paper, $5\frac{5}{8} \times 4$ in., ff. 2. *c.* 1400.

Written in one hand. Much faded and stained, in parts illegible.

Contents: Carol No. 36 c. Carol No. 114 c. Latin verses on the Epiphany. Macaronic English and Latin verses on pride, *beg.*: 'Pryde pryde wo thou be ma*ter* vic*iorum*' (B.–R. 2774) which occur also in a MS. of the Marquess of Ormonde, Kilkenny Castle, Ireland.

There is no indication of the provenance of this fragment. Conceivably the two leaves were removed from a volume because of their containing the carol on St. Thomas of Canterbury.

EXCHEQUER MISCELLANEA, 22/1/1

Paper, $17\frac{1}{4} \times 11\frac{3}{4}$ in., a single leaf, damaged at the margins. Centt. XV, XVI.

Contents: recto. A draft of an inquisition, dated 21 June 1457, into a riot in Gloucestershire. verso. Carol No. 450.1, written about 1530, by an Exchequer clerk, though in an ordinary cursive hand, not a law-hand.

For a description and a facsimile see John Saltmarsh, 'Two Medieval Love-Songs Set to Music', *The Antiquaries Journal*, xv (1935), 12–15.

LONDON: LINCOLN'S INN

HALE 135

Vellum, $13\frac{5}{8} \times 8\frac{3}{4}$ in., ff. 135. Centt. XIII (late), XIV (early).

Written in one hand, except for the fly-leaves, ff. 1, 135, 136. The carol is in a hand, different from that of the body of the book, which has written several memoranda concerning swans dated 1302–5. There are scribbles in hands of various dates on ff. 1, 137ʳ.

Contents: The *De legibus Angliae* of Henry de Bracton with prefixed table of contents. Carol No. 450. Memoranda on the swans of Alan de Thornton, to whom the volume belonged in the time of Edward I. 'He appears to have resided in Lincolnshire, and was probably a relation of Gilbert de Thornton, who was chief justice of the king's bench in the 18th. . . . The motto, in a recent hand on the first page [f. 5ʳ], περι παντος την 'Ελευθεριαν [*sic*], seems to mark it as having once belonged to Selden' (Joseph Hunter, *A Catalogue of the Manuscripts in the Library of the Honourable Society of Lincoln's Inn*, in *Three Catalogues*, London, 1838, p. 340).

For a fuller description see N. R. Ker, *Medieval Manuscripts in British Libraries*, i, London (Oxford, 1969), pp. 132–3. Ker identifies Alan de Thornton as employed by the abbot of Ramsey.

LONDON: WESTMINSTER ABBEY

20

Vellum and paper, $6\frac{7}{8} \times 5\frac{1}{8}$ in., ff. 38. Centt. XIV, XV.

Written in several hands. The carol is in a hand different from those of the other items.

Contents: The *Tractatus de Sphaera* of Johannes de Sacro Bosco. An arithmetical treatise. Carol No. 142 A b. An astronomical diagram. A treatise on grammar. Verses on grammar.

On f. 38ᵛ are written the name John Foster, the date 1489, and on a scroll the 'word' or motto 'audaces fortuna iuvat'. On an endpaper is the name Thomas Moyle. There are many John Fosters, and this one has not been identified. The 'word' or motto is attributed to the family of Forster in England by Jh. de Champeaux, *Devises, cris de guerre, légendes—dictons* (Dijon, 1890), p. 105. Though this 'word' is used by many modern armigerous families, it has not been found associated with any individual or institution in cent. XV. The provenance of the MS. remains unknown.

OXFORD: BODLEIAN LIBRARY

ARCH. SELDEN B. 26 (Summary Catalogue No. 3340)

Parchment and paper, 10¼ × 7⅛ in. Centt. VIII, XV, XVII.

The volume comprises five unrelated MSS. Only Part I contains any carols. A few leaves of Part I are stained.

Part I (cent. XV, middle). A collection of English and Latin songs and carols, with well-written music in black and red. The initials are in blue and red and some of the refrain-lines in red. This part of the MS. is reproduced in facsimile in *Early Bodleian Music*, i (London, 1901), with transcriptions ibid. ii. 74–180.

Contents: Carols Nos. 5, 14 b, 18 b, 29, 30, 31 a, 32–4, 69, 73, 117 c, 176, 179, 182, 185 B, 190, 234 B, 235 a, 337 a, 338 a, 359 A b, 418.2, 426 a. Other two- and three-part songs and antiphons in Latin, French, and English.

There are ten different hands in the MS. To the list given by Padelford in *Anglia*, xxxvi (1912), 81, should be added a hand [J] which attached an additional stanza on f. 23ʳ. All the carols except No. 337 a and the accompanied words of Nos. 18 b, 29, 33, 34, are in hand 'F' of Padelford's list. Padelford's dating of 1570–5 is an obvious error.

This very important MS. must be from Worcester. The stanza added to No. 235 a is accompanied by a crude drawing of a cock from the same pen. A cock, in the later cent. XV, was the very widely known and frequently depicted rebus or badge of John Alcock, successively Bishop of Rochester, Worcester, and Ely, joint Lord Chancellor of England, Master of the Rolls, founder of Jesus College, Cambridge, and of the grammar school at Hull. Alcock was notoriously fond of applying his rebus wherever possible, and it is, of course, the principal charge and crest of the arms of Jesus College. It could hardly indicate anyone else. The carelessly written stanza has the northern spelling to be expected of Alcock, a native of Beverley and educated there. No document in Alcock's own hand, surprisingly, appears to be extant, but there is a specimen of his signature as Bishop of Worcester on a bond dated 22 June 1483 (Public Record Office, Ancient Deeds A 9322). This could be from the same hand as the stanza, but cannot be judged certainly so. The whole MS. of carols is earlier than Alcock's episcopate (1476–86); we may conjecture that it came into his possession and that he added to the carol, probably from memory, another stanza known to him.

The MS. has a very high proportion of carols and Latin songs to the Virgin, and it may well have been connected with the boys' choir of the Chapel of the Blessed Mary in the nave. In 1478 Alcock endowed this chapel with £100 for masses and antiphons and responds for his own soul and those of his parents and benefactors (Ivor Atkins, *The Early Occupants of the Office of Organist and Master of the Choristers of . . . Worcester*, Worcestershire Historical Society, 1918, pp. 2–8).

The language of the texts is appropriate to Worcester, as is the speed-the-plough carol No. 418.2, on which see the Note. Worcester was a house where there was much carolling; see Introduction, p. xl. The language may be compared with that of B.M. MS. Addit. 37787, edited by Nita S. Baugh as *A Worcestershire Miscellany* (Philadelphia, 1956).

A specially interesting entry in the Journal of Prior More may indicate that MSS. like this were added to when new and desirable carols were sung by visitors. Among the Christmas expenses for 1518 are 16*d*. 'rewarded to syngars of carralls at cristmas day at ny3th', and, according to two successive entries, 6*s*. 8*d*. 'payd to Richard skryvenar for wrytyng at 4*d*., 4*d*., 2*d*., 1*d*., 4*d*., 2*d*., 2*d*.', 'rewarded for carralls'. This is a large payment, possibly at overtime rates, to a scribe, who would not usually be working on Christmas Day. We know from other entries that this Richard was capable of writing not only the Journal itself but 'ij queres of a masseboke' for which he was paid 4*s*. He must have written a good deal on this Christmas (ed. Ethel S. Fegan, Worcestershire Historical Society, 1914, pp. 76, 80, 82).

The word 'Childe' written at the top of f. 28ᵛ in a hand different from that of the carol below (No. 34) has been taken to be that of the composer, and Frank Ll. Harrison has suggested that it may refer to William Child, assistant master at Eton in 1446 to 1449, later a Fellow of New College, Oxford, and rector of West Lydford, Somerset, who died in 1487 (*Music in Medieval Britain*, London, 1958, pp. 420, 456). Since composers' names in general are not given by this MS., it is more probably a note of ownership. The Childe family were important tenants of Worcester Priory, and in the early cent. XVI Prior William More entrusted much business to Richard Childe and gave him many rewards (Fegan, op. cit., *passim*).

The MS. has a special connection with B.M. MS. Egerton 3307, having six pieces in common with it. The music in some of these is so similar as to rule out the possibility of oral transmission or even many intervening MSS. If Egerton 3307 is correctly assigned to Meaux Abbey or its neighbourhood, Alcock, revisiting Hull and his native Beverley, may have been an agent of the transmission. One carol found in both MSS. (No. 337) is marked in the Selden MS. with the initials J. D. These may refer to the great composer John Dunstable, as the music is in a style used by him, but there is no further evidence. As a canon and prebendary of Hereford Dunstable could easily have had contact with Worcester.

ASHMOLE 189 (Summary Catalogue No. 6777)

Paper, 8½ × 5⅞ in., ff. 219. Cent. XV. The volume consists of four MSS. bound together.

Written in several hands. The carols are in the same hand as the other religious poems and as the Golden Table and the astronomical pieces. According to a Latin couplet written in cipher on f. 70ᵛ this scribe was Richard Wraxall, abbot of Athelney Abbey, Somerset (Benedictine), in 1517 and 1518. The treatise on thunder is in another later hand, that of Richard Coscumb (or Robert Coscob), prior in 1534 of Muchelney Abbey, Somerset (Benedictine), who owned the MS.

Principal contents: Part I. 'The boke of Astronomy and of phylosophy.' On f. 69ᵛ in an early sixteenth-century hand is: 'Be hyt knowyuth son to All men that y Gylbart Banystur hafe receyd of wyllum Buttelar.' This may possibly be the composer Gilbert Banastir.

Part II. *The Table of Pythagoras*. Astronomical treatises. A treatise of the significance of thunder according to the time heard. English songs and carols: Carols Nos. 86 B, 333; 'Regem regum a mayde hath borne' (English translation of the 'Laetabundus' prose; Introduction, p. ci); 'Fadyr and sone and holy gost'; 'Fadyr and sone and holy gost', with refrain, 'Parce mihi domine'; 'Swete lady now ye wys'; 'Thys yonder nyghth y sawe a syghte'; 'Omnipotentem semper adorant Operacyons hevenly and yerthly all' (macaronic, English and Latin); 'Thou synfulle man of resone'; 'Wette ye alle that bene here' ('The Short Charter of Christ'); *The Fifteen O's of Christ.*

Part III. A German MS. in Latin and German, containing astrological and medical pieces, including the *Thesaurus Pauperum.*

Part IV. Fragments of miscellaneous astronomical and physiognomical material, and the list of 'proper terms' for beasts and birds.

For fuller description see W. H. Black, *Catalogue of the Manuscripts Bequeathed . . . by Elias Ashmole, Esq.* (Oxford, 1845). There is a convenient and clear note about the provenance and the two named monastic officers in Brown, *R.L. 15 C.*, p. 295.

ASHMOLE 1379 (Summary Catalogue No. 4666)

Paper, $5\frac{1}{8} \times 6\frac{1}{4}$ in., pp. 38. *c.* 1500.

Written in two hands. The carol is in a hand different from that of the other material.

Contents: A prose treatise of the medicinal properties of rosemary, in English. A poem on the same subject, in English (imperfect). Carol No. 170.

The provenance is not apparent. In the same hand as the carol is written on p. 3: 'Robertus Hyckys hujus libri possessor. Robert Hyckys ys the ower of thys boke'. A bit of account-roll pasted on the last leaf is dated 1519–20 and bears the names of John Colcootte and Roger Deyer.

ASHMOLE 1393 (Summary Catalogue No. 7589)

Paper and vellum, $5\frac{3}{4} \times 3\frac{7}{8}$ in. (Part V; there are slight variations of size in other parts), ff. 70. Cent. xv. The margins of some leaves are damaged.

The volume comprises parts of five different MSS., bound together and written in several hands. The carols and the medical material in Part V are in the same hand.

Principal contents: I. Alchemical, magical, and medical formulas. II. Recipes for dyeing and alchemical formulas. III. A religious tract, 'What thynges disposethe a man rightly to life'. IV. Latin devotional verses. A revelation of St. Thomas of Canterbury. V. Medical treatises. Astronomical notes. The song, 'Loue wolle I wit*h*oute eny variance', with music. A Latin *cantilena*, 'Ecce quod natura' (see Introduction, p. cx). Carols Nos. 35 A, 191 A.

See also W. H. Black, *Catalogue of the Manuscripts Bequeathed . . . by Elias Ashmole, Esq.* (Oxford, 1845), and for the English songs and carols, *Early Bodleian Music* (London, 1901), ii. 61–5 (*facs.*, ibid. i, No. xxviii).

BODLEY 26 (Summary Catalogue No. 1871). Religious Homilies, etc.

Vellum, $5\frac{7}{8} \times 4$ in., ff. ii+208. ff. 112–123 are missing. Centt. XIII, XIV.

Parts of ten different MSS. bound together. Written in several hands. The carol is in the same hand as sermons and notes which precede it.

Principal contents: Latin sermons and religious treatises on the Gospel of Luke, for Palm Sunday, on St. Thomas of Canterbury, St. Agatha, Habakkuk, etc. Latin treatises on St. John the Evangelist, St. Stephen, St. Laurence. Latin sermons and sermon notes by a Franciscan, with bits of English verse interspersed. Carol No. 12 a (in notes on the locks on the heart of a sinner, and their keys). Astrological and other fragments. The treatise on arithmetic of Johannes de Sacro Bosco, in Latin. A treatise of physiognomy, in Latin. An astrological chart.

Formerly owned by Thomas Twyne, who gave it to the Bodleian in 1612. For fuller Description see Madan, *Summary Catalogue* (ii, pt. 1, 91). Its earlier provenance is not known, but stanza 3 of the carol is also found in the former Helmingham Hall MS. LJ. 1.7 from Norfolk (now University of London MS. 657).

DOUCE 302 (Summary Catalogue No. 21876). The Poems of John Audelay

Parchment, 10¾ × 7⅞ in., ff. ii + 36 (the first and last paper fly-leaves). Cent. xv (first half). The MS. is imperfect at the beginning, and there are gaps in the text after f. 7ᵛ and f. 19ᵛ. In parts the writing is faded and rubbed.

Written in double columns, in three hands, as follows: A. ff. 1ʳ–34ᵛ (col. 1); B. f. 35ʳ, and corrections throughout; C. f. 34ᵛ (col. 2).

Contents: Poems by John Audelay: Carols Nos. 7 A, 97, 102, 108, 113, 117 a, 122 A, 172 a, 177, 230 b, 272, 310, 311, 314, 324–8, 347, 369, 397, 398, 411, 412, 428. Other English poems (the numbers are those assigned in Whiting's edition): 1. Instruction in Christian living (imperfect); 2. Counsels to those in religious orders; 3. Of nine virtues (imperfect); 4. 'De effusione sanguinis Christi'; 5. 'Quomodo Jhesus fuit reprobatus a Judeis'; 6. De psalterio passionis'; 7. 'De septem verbis Jhesu Christi pendentis in cruce'; 8. 'De salutacione corporis Jhesu Christi'; 9. 'De meritis misse; quomodo debemus audire missam'; 10. 'Quomodo Dominus Jhesus Christus apparuit Sancto Gregorio in tale effugie'; 11. 'De visitacione infirmorum et consolacione miserorum'; 12. A call to repentance; 13. 'De passione Domini nostri Jhesu Christi et de horis canonicis'; 14. 'Hore canonice passionis Jhesu Christ[i]'; 15. 'De epistola Domini nostri Jhesu Christi de die Dominica'; 16. 'Narracio quo Michel duxit Paulum ad infernum'; 17. An appeal of God to men; 18. Audelay's 'Counsel of Conscience'; 19. 'Salutaciones beate Marie virginis'; 20. 'Alia oracio de sancta Maria virgine'; 21. 'Hec salutacio composuit Angelus Gabrielus'; 22. 'Psalmus de Magnificat'; 23. 'Salutacio Sancte Brigitte virginis'; 25. 'Salutacio Sancte Wenefrede virginis'; 26. A salutation to St. Anne; 27. A salutation on the Vernicle; 53. On the Paternoster; 54. 'De tribus regibus mortuis'; 55. 'Sapiencia huius mundi stulticia est apud Deum'. A religious treatise in prose, on the allegory of a bed as the type of the soul prepared for Christ. The Latin poem *Cur Mundus Militat sub Vana Gloria*.

Audelay was a chaplain resident in the Augustinian monastery of Haughmond, Shropshire. On f. 35 is the following erased note (transcribed by N. R. Ker): 'The owner of thys boke who lyst to demawnd / Ihon Barkre hyt ys a chanon of Launde [Augustinian priory of St. John Baptist, Launde, Leicestershire] / gyvyn to hym hyt was, with a gud mynd / Be on Wyatt a mynstral both curtess and [kynd].' A second erased note on the same page records ownership by 'Wm Vyott a mynstrall yn Coventre.' This is the only note of ownership by a minstrel in all the carol MSS.—and the minstrel gives the volume to a religious.

For a full description of the MS. see Ella Keats Whiting, ed., *The Poems of John Audelay*, E.E.T.S., Or. Ser., No. 184, 1931, pp. vii–xi. Whiting prints all the contents of the MS. except the last two items listed.

ENG. POET. e. 1 (Summary Catalogue No. 29734)

Paper, 4⅜ × 6 in., ff. 65 (numbered in error to 64, two successive leaves being marked 27), of which ff. 11–62 belong to the MS. proper, the remainder to the modern binding. Cent. xv (second half). The margins of a good many leaves are mended, and the writing is rather faded in some places. Written in two hands, as follows: A. ff. 11ʳ–50ʳ; B. ff. 50ᵛ–61ʳ, part of ff. 41ᵛ, 42ʳ, two deleted lines on f. 34ᵛ.

There is music on ff. 40ᵛ, 41ᵛ (full settings), and on f. 50ᵛ (for the burden of a carol only).

On f. 13ᵛ is a diagram, apparently of a maze.

Contents: Carols Nos. 8 a, 21 B, 31 b, 37–41, 42 a, 44, 79 A a, 86 C, 93, 103 A b, 104, 115, 125 B b, 134, 137, 138, 140, 145 a, 150 B, 151 A, 157 B, 175 A, 180 A, 184, 206, 232 B, 237 A, 238 B, 239 a and d, 261, 282, 309 a, 332, 334, 337 b, 340, 342, 344, 356 b, 358, 370 a, 371, 382, 386 a, 388, 389 a, 399 b, 401 A b, 402 a, 402.1, 404, 406, 407,

409, 410 b, 414, 419 A b, 422 A, 423, 439. Songs not in carol form: Latin songs: 'Angelum misit suum Deus omnipotens'; 'Bonum vinum cum sapore'; 'Et virgine natus, Christe, es sine macula'; 'Psallimus cantantes'. English songs: 'Now ys wele and all thyng aryght'; 'Wold God that men myght sene'; 'Tydynges I bryng yow for to tell'; 'Man, be war, or thou knyte the fast'; 'Man upon mold, whatsoever thou be'; 'Holvyr and Heyvy mad a gret party' (see Introduction, p. cxxiii); 'The best tre if ye tak entent' (macaronic English and Latin). Recipe: 'A good medycyn for sor eyen'.

A nineteenth-century transcript of this collection is in the British Museum, MS. Addit. 25478.

The entire MS. is printed by Thomas Wright, *Songs and Carols, Percy Society Publications,* xxiii (London, 1847). (Note: Chambers and Sidgwick's charge of mis-citation by 'Flügel, Fehr, and others', in *Early English Lyrics,* p. 306, is itself an error.)

Formerly owned by Joseph Mayer, before him by Thomas Wright (who lost it). The few scribbles of cent. XVI on f. 62ᵛ give no clue to earlier ownership. It was acquired by the Bodleian in 1857. There is no external evidence that it was made 'presumably for the use of a professed minstrel' (Madan, *Summary Catalogue,* v. 679).

It is highly probable that this excellent and varied collection of carols comes from Beverley Minster, Yorkshire. A special devotion to St. John the Evangelist is indicated by its being the only MS. to offer two distinct English carols to this saint (Nos. 103 A b, 104) and by its including the Latin processional hymn, not elsewhere found complete, in honour of St. John, 'Psallimus cantantes', marked 'Cantus' and provided with the only full musical setting in the MS. The first strophe of this hymn, followed by English strophes in the same form, is found in Richard Kele's *Christmas carolles newely Inprynted* of about 1550. In the region of the dialect of the MS., East Midland with some northern forms, there was no other religious house of importance dedicated to St. John the Evangelist. The generous selection of convivial poetry and especially the satire on abbots and monks in the Goliardic 'Bonum vinum cum sapore' accord well with the life of the prosperous and by no means ascetic secular canons of the college at Beverley. No other MS. except Balliol 354 has correspondences with so many of the known carol MSS. This indicates a place of much intercourse with other houses, and Beverley in the fifteenth century was a place of great importance, high in the favour of Henry V, on a main route to the north, and eleventh in size among all English cities.

The fact that the carol to St. Thomas of Canterbury in this MS. (No. 115) and the St. Thomas stanza of No. 103 A b are defaced indicates that the book was in an institution continuing through the Reformation, such as Beverley Minster, rather than in a monastery. It is worth noting that the carol to St. Thomas in Egerton 3307 (No. 115.1) is not defaced.

One reading of the MS. as a whole will serve to correct Rosemary Woolf's unhappy comment: 'A comparison of the carol with the lyric, however, throws into relief the learned and unpopular character of a substantial group of them, particularly those in the Ryman Manuscript and MS. Eng. poet. e. 1' (*The English Religious Lyric in the Middle Ages,* Oxford, 1968, p. 383 n. 3).

LAUD MISC. 601 (Summary Catalogue No. 1491)

Parchment, 12½×8¾ in., ff. 116. Centt. XIV, XV.

The body of the MS. is written in one hand; there are several other hands in numerous scribbles on the fly-leaves, one of which has written the incomplete carol-text.

Principal contents: Richard Rolle's *Prick of Conscience.* Carol No. 413 B.

On f. 116ᵛ are several staves of crudely written music and a mark of ownership obliterated by ink. On f. 116ʳ is written the name John Morgan, not in the hand of the carol.

LAUD MISC. 683 (Summary Catalogue No. 798)

Vellum, 7¾ × 5½ in., ff. i+151. Centt. xv, xvii. One leaf has been torn out between ff. 107, 108. ff. 59, 60 have been torn and neatly stitched.

Written in two hands, Lydgate's poetry and the carols in one (cent. xv), the two prose treatises in the other (cent. xvii). A few other hands have added notes and scribbles.

Contents: Poems by John Lydgate, including Carol No. 263 b. Carol No. 152 A b. An anonymous treatise on military musters, imperfect at beginning. 'A discourse of John Yonge, gentleman, for a Bancke of money to be established for the releef of the common necessitie', with a dedicatory letter to Queen Elizabeth I prefixed.

On f. 107ʳ are a few accounts. On f. 105ʳ is written (cent. xv): 'thys boke ys mastres Coles boke.' On f. 108ʳ is: 'John Coker is my name'; on f. 151ʳ (inverted) 'John Coker is the tru oner of this booke 1630 in march'. Below it in another hand is some doggerel abusive of John Coker, dated 1632. On f. 151ᵛ in another hand is: 'Joh*ann*es yonge mih*i*.' On f. 149ᵛ is: 'Johannes Stephanus' (defaced). The name John Stevens is written *passim* with notes in the same hand. On f. iᵛ is written the name of Archbishop Laud with the date 1639.

RAWLINSON C. 506 (Summary Catalogue No. 15353)

Paper, 5⅞ × 4⅜ in., ff. 304. Cent. xv (first half). Thirty leaves of the original volume are missing; ff. 1–5, 304 are smaller leaves from a thirteenth-century service-book.

Written in several hands.

Principal contents: A medical treatise by Peter of Salerno. Miscellaneous charms. Verses on blood-letting. A table of dates for Easter. Carol No. 15, in the same hand as the preceding material. A treatise of urines. A lunar calendar. A treatise of diseases of the head and stomach. The gynaecological *Practica* ascribed to Trotula. The *Surgery* of Rogerus Venetius. A medical lexicon. A translation of Lanfranc's *Antidotarium*. A lexicon of herbs. Directions for choosing horses, for fishing, for hawking, for dyeing.

Former owners were Thomas Hearne, the antiquary, and Henry Dingley (1547).

A hand of cent. xv (late) has written on f. 303ᵛ: 'Ego Humfridus Harrison, capellan*us*, sana m[ente] condo testa*mentum* meu*m* in hunc modo. In p*r*imis.'

RAWLINSON POET. 34 (Summary Catalogue No. 14528)

Paper, 11¾ × 8½ in., ff. iii+23. Cent. xv.

Written in several hands. Carol No. 418.1 is in the hand which has written other items, including *Disputacio inter Clericum et Philomenam*, Lydgate's *Passion of St. Erasmus*, *The Passion of St. Katherine*, a poem: 'ix poyntes of gret vertu', the romance of *Sir Degare*. The hand appears to be that of John Bigge.

A second hand has written a *Life of St. Margaret*, and a third has written an acrostic poem to the Virgin, *beg.*: 'Away feynt lufe full of varyaunce'.

ADDIT. A. 106 (Summary Catalogue No. 29003). Medical and Scientific Treatises, with Religious Poems

Paper (except vellum fly-leaves, ff. 1–3, 286–7, 8 × 5½ in., ff. 295. Cent. xv (second half), except fly-leaves, cent. xiii.

The volume is made up of six MSS. bound together.

Written in several hands, as follows: A. ff. 1–3, 286–7; B. ff. 4ʳ–195ᵛ, 221ʳ–230ᵛ; C. ff. 198ʳ–219ᵛ; D. ff. 232ᵛ–266ʳ; E. f. 266ᵛ; F. ff. 267–276ᵛ. A few other hands have added brief scribbles or single recipes.

Principal contents: Two English translations of the treatise on the plague by John of Burgundy. *The Quatrefoil of Love*, in 13-line stanzas. Cato's *Distichs*, in English. Three herbals. An English translation of a treatise of precious stones. A poem on lucky and unlucky days. A treatise on the medicinal properties of water. Many medical recipes. Carol No. 147, in hand B.

Among the scribes' names are 'Charke Plenus amoris / Totum nomen habes Johannem si superaddes', 'Edmundus Chader'.

Formerly owned by Col. J. Sidney North. Earlier owners were John Pryste (f. 196ᵛ) and possibly Harry Fonston (f. 277ᵛ).

For fuller description see Madan, *Summary Catalogue* (v. 540).

See W. D. Macray, *Annals of the Bodleian Library* (2nd edn., Oxford, 1890), p. 21 n., on the frequency of the name Plenus-Amoris in MS. colophons.

OXFORD: BALLIOL COLLEGE

354. The Commonplace Book of Richard Hill, citizen and grocer of London: 'A Boke of dyueris tales and balettes and dyueris Reconynges etc.'

Paper, $11\frac{1}{2} \times 4\frac{1}{2}$ in., ff. 256. Cent. XVI (first half).

Entries appear to have been made in the volume over a period of some thirty years, 1536 being the latest date definitely assignable.

Some leaves are slightly wormed, and the margins of many have been damaged and mended. The lower half of one quire has been cut off.

Most of the volume, including all the carols, is written in one hand, that of Richard Hill, the owner and compiler, which varies in entries of different dates. There is no basis for the attribution by Coxe of the writing to one John Hyde. The memoranda on f. 17ʳ beginning 'The birth of children of me Richard Hill', are in this hand, as is the 'Explicit quod Hill' at the end of some pieces. For biographical information on the compiler see W. P. Hills, 'Richard Hill of Hillend', etc. *N. & Q.* clxxvii (1939), 452–6.

On f. xviᵛ is 'John Hylles boke', probably referring to a son of Richard. On f. clxxviiiᵛ (cent. XVI) is 'Iste liber pertinet John Stokes'. Stokes has not been identified.

The leaves of the volume are not correctly numbered throughout. There are errors in both original and modern numbering. In the latter f. 249 follows f. 241, though there is no gap at this point. All references in this edition are to the existing modern numbering.

Principal contents: *The Seven Sages of Rome*. Selected tales from Gower's *Confessio Amantis*. 'Jack, His Stepdame, and the Friar'. Sir Thomas More's *Fortune*. *The Siege of Rouen* by John Page. *The Trental of St. Gregory*. Lydgate's *Stans Puer ad Mensam*. The courtesy-book 'Little John'. *The Boke of Curtasie* in English and French. Lydgate's *The Myrrour of Mankynd*. Dunbar's 'London, thou art the flower of cities all'. *The Nutbrown Mayde*. Miscellaneous short religious and secular poems. Collectanea of useful information, medical prescriptions, household recipes, topographical information, puzzles, and riddles. Carols Nos. 11, 20, 21 A, 27 C, 35 B, 45–52, 77, 78, 79 A b, 100, 103 A c, 105, 114 d, 120, 122 C, 123 A, 126, 131 b, 132 A, 136 B, 141, 150 C, 152 A a, 153, 158, 162, 163 a, 166, 172 b, 175 B, 178, 183, 187 B, 230 a, 232 C, 233, 234 D, 237 B, 238 A, 239 c, 240, 241, 273, 319, 321, 322 A, 331 b, 345, 346, 350, 351, 355 b, 359 A a, 361, 370 b, 372–4, 386 b, 389 b, 399 a, 401 A a, 402 b, 408, 410 a, 413, 419 A a, 420, 421, 424 A, 471.

For complete description of the MS. and full list of contents see Roman Dyboski, *Songs, Carols, and other Miscellaneous Poems*, E.E.T.S., Ex. Ser., No. ci, 1907, pp. xiii–lix, and E. Flügel, 'Liedersammlungen des xvi. Jahrhunderts', *Anglia*, xxvi (1903), 94–105.

Further details and some corrections are given by [Sir] Roger A. B. Mynors, *Catalogue of the Manuscripts of Balliol College, Oxford* (Oxford, 1963).

Dyboski and Flügel print a large proportion of the contents of the MS.

Some of the earlier MSS. from which Hill copied carols and other articles may have been commodities of his trade. C. H. Talbot remarks: '. . . it was not merely the stationers who dealt in books and book materials, but bankers, merchants, and even grocers' ('The Universities and the Mediaeval Library', in Francis Wormald and C. E. Wright, eds., *The English Library before* 1700, London, 1958, p. 73). See also E. A. Savage, *Old English Libraries* (London, 1912), p. 207.

OXFORD: LINCOLN COLLEGE
LAT. 89

Paper, 12 × 9⅛ in. (over binding), ff. 32. Cent. xv.

ff. 27–31 are from another MS. not now identified. These leaves contain a *Kyrie Eleison* with music, a trope 'Rex virginum', some fragments of Latin text with music, and Carol No. 359 C.

The main body of the MS. contains a copy of the *Melos Contemplativorum* of Richard Rolle of Hampole, imperfect at beginning and end (chapters 4–56 only).

LAT. 100

Parchment, 9 × 6 in., ff. 93. Cent. xii.

Contents: Vegetius, *De Re Militari*. Sextus Julius Frontinus, *Strategematicon Rei Militaris*. Eutropius, *Breviarium Historiae Romanae*. Carol No. 441.1, in hand of cent. xv. On f. 3ʳ Latin verses *beg.*: 'His sua Willelmus detrivit tempora libris'.

The MS. was given to the library of Lincoln College by Robert Flemmyng.

CAMBRIDGE: UNIVERSITY LIBRARY
Ee. 1. 12

Parchment, 7⅞ × 5½ in., ff. 110. Cent. xv (1490–1500). Three leaves are cut out between ff. 108, 109.

Written in three hands as follows: A. ff. 1ʳ–2ᵛ, one line on f. 46ᵛ; B. ff. 3ʳ–10ʳ, 81ᵛ–105ᵛ; C. ff. 11ʳ–80ᵛ (possibly Ryman's own hand). Another hand (cent. xvi) has added a few corrections to f. 1ʳ and has written a burden on f. 110ʳ. Other scribbles are on ff. 109ᵛ, 110ᵛ. On f. 81ʳ is some crude musical notation without words, and on ff. 105ʳ, 107ʳ are a few lines of writing erased to illegibility. R. T. Davies erroneously writes: 'There are several tunes in this MS.' (*Medieval English Lyrics*, London, 1963, p. 23 n. 1). Ryman's authorship is established by a colophon on f. 80ʳ: 'Explicit liber ympnorum et canticorum quem composuit Frater Iacobus Ryman ordinis Minorum ad laudem omnipotentis dei et sanctissime matris eius marie omniumque sanctorum anno domini millesimo CCCCᵐᵒ LXXXXIIᵒ.' The first C and the L in the date have been erased.

Contents: English songs and translations of hymns by James Ryman, a Franciscan. Carols Nos. 3, 21 D. Carols by James Ryman: Nos. 53–6, 61–3, 65–7, 70–2, 74–6, 81 A, 82, 84, 88, 92, 127–30, 154, 156, 159, 160, 174, 189, 192–205, 207–12, 214–29, 243 a and b, 244–55, 257, 258, 262, 267–9, 275, 276, 279–81, 283–305, 318, 352, 353, 360.

The contents of the entire MS., except for ff. 1, 2, 110, are printed by I. Zupitza in *Archiv*, lxxxix (1892), 167–338.

Ff. 1. 6. The Findern Anthology

Paper, 8¼ × 5⅞ in., ff. 159. Cent. xv (second half). Many leaves have been removed and replaced by blank leaves in the modern binding.

Written by many different hands. The two carols are in different hands. No. 442 is the only piece in its hand. No. 469 is in the same hand as a poem beginning 'Alas what planet was y born vndir' and signed 'Crocit dytyn'.

Contents: English, principally poetry, including: Carols Nos. 442, 469. Chaucer's *Complaint unto Pity*, *Parliament of Fowls*, *Complaint to his Purse*, *Anelida and Arcite*, *Complaint of Venus*, *Truth*. Several tales from Gower's *Confessio Amantis*. Hoccleve's *Litera Cupidinis*. The romance *Syr Degrevaunt*. Burgh's *Cato Major*. Various short poems. *The Chronicles of Saints and Kings of England*.

Among the scribes who have signed their work are 'lewestou*n*', 'nicholaus plenus amoris', 'Clanvowe', 'W. Caluerly'.

There is an inventory of clothes at Findern (Derbyshire) and on f. 59ᵛ a note: 'A rekenyng betw[e]ne John wylsu*n and* mest*er* tynderne. *The* furst tyme that I went into lestershyre wi*th* richard lathbery. I spent iiid.' etc.

At the end of *Syr Degrevaunt* are the names 'Elisabet Koton' and 'Elisabet Frauncys'.

This MS. is of particular value in that it gives evidence of the textual interest of well-to-do women in secular and courtly poetry when removed as far from London as Derbyshire. For a complete listing of the contents and much detailed bibliographical and biographical information see R. H. Robbins, 'The Findern Anthology', *PMLA*, lxix (1954), 610–42. Robbins prints a number of the short poems in this article and in his *Secular Lyrics*.

Ff. 5. 48

Paper, 8 × 5½ in., ff. 135 (f. 1 missing). Cent. xv (second half).

Written in two hands, ff. 79ʳ–92ᵛ in one, the remainder of the volume, including the carol, in the other.

Principal Contents: Myrc's *Instructions for Parish Priests* (imperfect at beginning). *The ABC of Aristotle*. *The Northern Passion*. *Signs of Death*. Remedies for the Seven Deadly Sins. A tale in verse of an incestuous daughter. A tale of King Edward and the shepherd. Dialogue between a nightingale and a clerk. A verse *fabliau* of a basin. *The Tournament of Tottenham*. The tale of the adulterous Squire of Falmouth. Two lamentations of the Virgin. A prayer of the Five Joys of the Virgin. *St. Michael and the Annunciation*, from the *South-English Legendary*. Part of *The Southern Passion*. 'The mourning of a hare'. Weather prophecies. Carol No. 456. Verses on provisions for a feast. *Robin Hood and the Monk* (Child, No. 119).

The colophon to *The Northern Passion* is in the name of Gilbertus Pylkynton.

Ii. 4. 11

Vellum, 9⅜ × 6⅝ in., ff. 170. Centt. xiv, xv.

Written principally in one hand (cent. xiv), with coloured initials. The list of Latin words is in another hand and the table of names in a third. The carol, which is surrounded by scribbles, is the only item in a fourth hand (cent. xv, first half).

Contents: *Liber Etymologiarum*. A few Latin hexameters. A list of Latin words. A table of etymologies of Biblical names. Carol No. 36 a.

Ll. 1. 11

Parchment, $8\frac{5}{8} \times 6\frac{3}{8}$ in., a single leaf, damaged at lower right-hand corner. Cent. xv. Now f. 32, bound with miscellaneous unrelated MSS.

Contents: Carol No. 30 B. Accounts on verso.

Ll. 5. 10. 'The Reidpeth MS.'

Paper, $11\frac{3}{8} \times 7\frac{1}{2}$ in., ff. ii+67. Some leaves are missing. A.D. 1622.

Written in one hand, that of John Reidpeth, with colophon on f. 1ʳ: 'a me ioan*ne* reidpeth septimo decembris . . . ffinis m . . .,

Contents: Scottish poems, principally those of William Dunbar, selectively transcribed from the 'Maitland Folio MS.', Magdalene College, Cambridge, Pepys 2553, some eighty-five pieces in all. The transcript has many errors, and the spelling of the Maitland MS. is often changed. Carol No. 121.1 by William Dunbar, stzas. 1–4, 10, 11 and the 'Responsio regis' being preserved in this transcript though lost from the Maitland Folio.

Directly under Reidpeth's colophon on f. 1ʳ with date of 1623 is written this note of other ownership: 'Ex libris christopheri cokburne ffinis amen'. The MS. eventually came into the large and famous library of John Moore, bishop successively of Norwich and of Ely. After his death in 1714 this collection of 20,000 books and 1,790 MSS. was bought by King George I and presented to Cambridge University.

For further description and a full list of contents see [Sir] W. A. Craigie, ed., *The Maitland Folio Manuscript*, ii, S.T.S., New Ser., No. 20 (1927), 7–10.

ADDIT. 5943

Paper (except six fly-leaves parchment), $8\frac{1}{2} \times 5\frac{3}{4}$ in., ff. vi+179. Cent. xv (first quarter). ff. 1, 8 are mostly, ff. 155–9 completely, torn out.

Written principally in one hand (A). The carols, memoranda, and accounts are in several other hands as follows (all of cent. xv): B. f. 145ʳ, Carol No. 151 C; C. f. 145ᵛ, Carol No. 349; D. ff. 161ʳ–169ʳ, French, Latin, and English songs with music; E. f. 169ʳ, Carol No 149 d; F. f. 170ʳ, Prayers, f. 170ᵛ, English erotic folk-songs, f. 172ᵛ, English poem, 'Ecce ancilla domini', f. 178ᵛ, Carol No. 451, ff. 179ʳ–180ᵛ, Accounts; G. The hand of the owner, Johannes ——, in other memoranda; H. Building accounts on f. iiiʳ; I. Book-hand on fly-leaves, ff. iiᵛ, iv. A few other hands are represented by short scribbles.

Principal contents: Latin sermons for various Sundays and feast-days throughout the year, the first imperfect at the beginning. Latin poem, 'Urbanus'. Latin tracts on religious subjects, confession, the Holy Spirit, Articles of Faith, etc. Richard Rolle's *Emendatio Vitae* and *Melos Contemplativorum*. Reckonings of eclipses of the sun and moon from 1415 to 1462, with diagrams. Carols Nos. 149 d, 151 C, 349, 451, App., No. vii. Other English, French, and Latin songs. Latin theological material on fly-leaves (cent. xiv). Various accounts and memoranda. On f. iiiᵛ a quaint note: 'Muncy, tumpha, myfmaffe-mofe'.

A Latin note on f. penult.ᵛ records that the book is the property of John —— (the surname is thoroughly erased), now (10 December 1418) a Carthusian monk at the Priory of Hinton, Somerset, to whom it has been given by Thomas Turke, formerly perpetual vicar of 'Biere' (Beer, Somerset).

Some of the accounts record receipt, apparently by an archdeacon, of sums from various west-country vicars, including those of Horton, Staunton, Sheepwick, Hungerford. Other names written in the MS. are 'hennyng*is* harpe*r*' and 'wy*m*undus'. A modern hand on f. ii has written 'Hh. Price 1800', and another has (wrongly) noted 'Hendon'. The MS. was formerly owned by Lord Howard de Walden.

The songs from this MS. are printed by L. S. M[ayer], *Music Cantelenas Songs Etc. from an Early Fifteenth Century Manuscript*. (London, privately printed, 1906).

ADDIT. 7350, Box 2

Paper, $7\frac{3}{4} \times 5\frac{5}{8}$ in., a fragment of two leaves, now cut in two horizontally at the middle. Cent. XV (late), XVI.

Written in three hands, Carols Nos. 60.1, 289.1 in the first, No. 461.1 in the second, No. 460.1 in the third. No. 460.1 has been half-heartedly cancelled by lightly drawn crossed lines.

For detailed description of the fragment, discovered by Peter Dronke among miscellaneous papers of Henry Bradshaw, see Rossell Hope Robbins, 'The Bradshaw Carols', *PMLA*, lxxxi (1966), 308–10.

CAMBRIDGE: CORPUS CHRISTI COLLEGE

233

Paper, $8\frac{3}{8} \times 5\frac{1}{2}$ in., ff. 182. Cent. XV (second half).

Written throughout, except for the carol, in one hand, that of the owner, 'Hampshyre'. Some initials are decorated with pen-work; on f. 85ᵛ is a sketch of a bagpiper. The carol is in another hand of *c.* 1500.

Principal contents: Latin grammatical treatises with illustrative verses and occasional English passages. *Liber Facetiae. Proverbia Alani de Insulis. Ecloga Theoduli.* Carol No. 17 a.

'Constat Hampshyre' is written *passim*.

On f. 70ᵛ is: 'Expl. Ethroclita quod Hampshyre [t]este T. Bowes et Brudenell et Howtyng et Trew'. 'Lychefelde' and 'Gvndys' also appear, and on f. 26ᵛ is: 'Coplay'.

The owner was probably the William Hampshire who was admitted to King's College, Cambridge, from Eton in 1479. The other names are probably those of university contemporaries. A William Bowes proceeded to King's from Eton in the same year, a John Gundys the next year. There were several Lichfields at Cambridge in cent. XV, though none are recorded at the same dates as Hampshire.

Sir Robert Brudenell, born in 1461 and later a Chief Justice, was at Cambridge in Hampshire's time. See J. and J. A. Venn, *Alumni Cantabrigienses* (Cambridge, 1922).

CAMBRIDGE: GONVILLE AND CAIUS COLLEGE

383

Paper, $8\frac{7}{8} \times 5\frac{7}{8}$ in., ff. 108. Cent. XV (middle). The edges are badly worn, and a few leaves are torn. The numbering is by pages.

Written principally in two hands as follows: A. pp. 1–70, 101–216; B. pp. 71–100. All the carols are in hand A, probably that of the owner, Wymundus London.

The MS. is a trilingual student's exercise and commonplace book, with forms of letters in French and Latin. There are many memoranda and much penmanship practice. The carols are written in odd spaces in the same fashion as other notes and memoranda. Two of the English carols appear with a French carol between them (see Introduction, pp. xxxv–xxxvi). Other contents include: Latin grammatical notes and verses. A note from Sidonius' *De Natura Rerum* on the names of animals. Much miscellaneous and some confused material, including Latin grammatical exercises. Latin treatises on passages of Scripture used in the liturgy. The statute 'Quia emptores terrarum'. Accounts in French. Instructions for keeping accounts, with specimens. An English verse-riddle. Carols Nos. 114 b, 187 A, 418, 441, 452, 453, 455, 470, App., No. ii.

The MS. is from Oxfordshire and very probably the work of an Oxford student. Among the places mentioned in memoranda of various kinds are 'Tadmerton a la ostel de Joh. Tayrel' [Tadmarton, Oxon, four miles south-west of Banbury, a manor of Abingdon Abbey]; 'couentre'; 'Lyd3erd Trego3' [Lydiard Tregoze, Wilts.]; 'Hanlee' [Henley]; 'Beckley in com. oxonn.'; 'Wyttely' [Wheatley, Oxon, cited as domicile of Robert 'Walteper', i.e. of Waterperry, Oxon]; 'Myddynhall est bonus puer' [i.e. surname from Mildenhall, near Marlborough, Wilts.]; 'Wynchecomb' [Glos., near Cheltenham]; 'Ooxsenfoord' as domicile of Johan Ware. It is quite possible that this Wymundus London was the 'London' and 'w London' whose name occurs regularly in the bursary books of Magdalen College, Oxford, in 1484–5. This London was a chorister, promoted demy in 1485, and would be an appropriate person to have noted down secular and quite unacademic songs which obviously refer to the countryside of Oxfordshire (A. B. Emden, *A Bibliographical Register of the University of Oxford to A.D. 1500*, Oxford, 1958, ii. 1158).

A copy of a letter in French on p. 45 reads: 'le porteur de cestes est seneschel de nostre hostiel et est appellee Sir Walter trimenel'.

CAMBRIDGE: MAGDALENE COLLEGE

PEPYS 2553. 'The Maitland Folio Manuscript'

Paper, $10\frac{1}{2} \times 4\frac{3}{4}$ in. (mounted), ff. ii+183. *c.* 1570–1.

Written principally in one hand, with short entries by nine others.

Contents: A very important collection of early Scottish poetry of centt. xv and xvi, including poems by William Dunbar, Gavin Douglas, Sir Richard Maitland, Schaw, Clappertoun, Arbuthnot, Lord Thirlstane, Alexander Montgomerie, G. H., King James VI, and twenty-nine anonymous pieces.

Carol No. 121.1 by William Dunbar (burden and stzas. 5–9); stzas. 1–4, 10, 11 and the 'Responsio regis' were in a gathering of the original MS. which has been lost.

Some eighty-five pieces from the MS., including most of those by Dunbar, were copied by John Reidpeth, in 1622, into what is now Cambridge University Library MS. Ll. 5. 10, 'The Reidpeth Manuscript'. This transcript preserves the text of eight pages later lost from the Maitland Folio, including part of Carol No. 121.1.

The MS. remained in the Maitland family, headed by the Earls, and finally the Duke, of Lauderdale, until given by the latter to Samuel Pepys, who died in 1703. Pepys bequeathed the MS. to Magdalene College, Cambridge, by the will which established the Pepysian Library.

For a fuller description of the MS. and texts of its contents see [Sir] W. A. Craigie, ed., *The Maitland Folio Manuscript*, 2 vols., S.T.S., New Ser., Nos. 7 (1919) and 20 (1927).

CAMBRIDGE: ST. JOHN'S COLLEGE

S. 54 (259)

Paper, $5\frac{3}{4} \times 4\frac{1}{8}$ in., ff. 14. Cent. xv (second half). The MS. is incomplete at the beginning and end, the two outer leaves of the quire having been lost. ff. 13, 14 are mere fragments, and the other leaves are worn and torn. It is enclosed in a contemporary vellum wallet-like wrapper, and is of unusual interest as a pocket-book of carols in its original form.

Written in four hands as follows: A. f. 1 (one stanza), f. 2ʳ (in part), ff. 3ᵛ–4ᵛ, 7ᵛ–10ʳ, 12ʳ–14ᵛ; B. f. 1 (remainder), ff. 2ʳ–3ᵛ, 4ᵛ–7ᵛ, 10ʳ–11ᵛ; C. f. 3ʳ (one stanza); D. f. 6ᵛ (burden, not distinguished by James and Macaulay).

Contents: Carols Nos. 83, 90, 125 B a, 139, 142 A a, 148 B, 149 b, 232 A, 266, 274, 313, 366, 391, 394, 400, 415, 454, App., Nos. iii, iv, vi. English song on the Epiphany (no burden): 'Qwan crist was borne in bedlem'.

On the inside of the cover is written: 'puer natus hodie syt we down on owr kne' (scrap of a carol; cf. No. 35 A, stza. 5). 'Fuit homo miserens et deus.'

There is no mark of ownership. The MS. is certainly from East Anglia, but cannot be placed more exactly. It has obvious similarities and correspondences with B.M. Sloane 2593 and Bodl. Eng. poet. e. 1. It was given to the library of the College by Thomas Baker, the antiquary, who was a fellow and resident until his death in 1740.

The entire MS. is described and printed by M. R. James and G. C. Macaulay in *M.L.R.* viii (1913), 68–87.

CAMBRIDGE: TRINITY COLLEGE
B. 14. 39

Vellum, 7⅜ × 5⅜ in., ff. 87. Cent. XIII. Bound in one volume with MS. B. 14. 40.

Written in several hands. The carol-source is in the same hand as the ballad *Judas* and much of the other English poetry, but in a different hand from that of the sermon on 'Bele alis'. The dialect is that of the South-west Midland region.

Principal contents: De Ordine Creaturarum. Miscellaneous Latin verse, mostly religious. Latin prayers and notes. A sermon on 'Bele alis matyn se leua' (see Introduction, p. cxlv). French poetry. including a legend of St. Nicholas and tales from the Gospels. *The Proverbs of Alfred*. English religious poetry, including: A life of St. Margaret; Carol No. 191 B b; the ballad *Judas*; 'Wolle ye iheren of Twelte Day'; *Debate between the Body and the Soul*.

For an exhaustive description of the MS. see Karl Reichl, *Religiöse Dichtung im englischen Hochmittelalter*, Münchener Universitäts-Schriften Philosophische Fakultät, Texte und Untersuchung zur Englischen Philologie, Band i (München, 1973), with full edition of the contents. Reichl distinguishes twelve hands.

O. 2. 53

Paper, 8¼ × 5¼ in., ff. 74. Centt. XV, XVI. f. 74 is a fragment.

A commonplace book, written in several hands. The carol is the only item in its hand (*c.* 1500).

Principal contents: Carol No. 379. Miscellaneous Latin verses. Medical recipes. Short English religious and political verses. A record of the birth of Prince Edward in 1470. Forms of indentures, etc., mentioning Bromley, Orpington, and Wimbledon. Note of the birth of 'robard ramston', 17 Henry VIII. A 'moralized' version of 'Come over the burn, Bessy' (cent. XVI). Ecclesiastical and theological extracts in English and Latin. Instructions for setting a harp, by J. Stowell.

A note on f. 72ᵛ mentions the following places: Worth Stratton, Cricklade (both in north-eastern Wiltshire), Sevenhampton, Barnsted Manor, and Grimsby.

For full list of contents see M. R. James, *The Western Manuscripts in the Library of Trinity College, Cambridge*, iii (Cambridge, 1902).

O. 3. 58

Vellum roll, 6 ft. 8 in. × 7 in., in three sections laced together. Cent. xv (first half). In parts faded and injured by damp. The roll format is unique among English carol-MSS.

All the carols are in one hand, with music. The staves and some notes are in red and the initials in red and blue.

Contents: recto, Carols Nos. 17 b, 18 a, 19, 21 C, 22, 98, 103 A a, 117 b, 173, 234 A, 235 b, 338 b, 426 b. At the head are two lines in red, now almost entirely illegible. Part of the second line gives 'Chris*t*i . . . m . . . matr*i*s eius . . . *s*anctorum'.

verso (in another and later hand). Latin masses: 'De Sancta Trenitate; De Angelis; Officium Corporis Christi; De Sancta Cruce' (incomplete).

The MS. was presented to the Library in 1838 by H. O. Roe.

All the carols are printed by J. A. Fuller Maitland and W. S. Rockstro, *English Carols of the Fifteenth Century* (London, [1891]).

O. 7. 31

Paper, 5¾ × 3⅞ in., ff. 206. Centt. xv, xvi. The first twenty-one leaves have been scorched. The carol is in a different hand from that of the breviary (*c.* 1500).

Contents: Breviary (Sarum, imperfect at beginning): Proprium de Tempore; Commune Sanctorum; Proprium Sanctorum; Special offices for the Virgin, SS. John Evangelist, Martin, and Benedict. Carol No. 380 a and b. Two medical recipes. Scribbled notes which mention the birth of a prince, and deaths of 'abbot Tony', 'abbot Westfyld', 'abbot cha*m*pyo*n*', also 'blacheth fylde', 'elect*us* ad breconia*m*'.

On the basis of liturgical evidence N. R. Ker has assigned this MS. to the Benedictine abbey of St. Martin at Battle, Sussex, which had a cell at Brecon (*Medieval Libraries of Great Britain*, London, 1941, p. 5).

O. 9. 38

Paper, 11¾ × 4¼ in., ff. 95. Centt. xv, xvi. The edges are much worn, and some leaves are badly damaged.

Written for the most part in one hand of *c.* 1450. The carols are in this hand. There are short entries in six later hands.

The volume is a commonplace book. It has the size and shape of a commercial account-book, resembling in its format as well as the diversity of its contents Balliol College, Oxford, MS. 354. It was written at Glastonbury Abbey, presumably by one of the monks, but the name of this scribe and owner does not appear.

The MS. is the subject of an exemplary and exhaustive study, a 'descriptive index' by A. G. Rigg, *A Glastonbury Miscellany of the Fifteenth Century*, Oxford English Monographs (London, 1968). The same scholar has made a complete edition of the contents in an unpublished D.Phil. thesis at Oxford.

Principal contents (in English and Latin): *Apocalypsis Goliae. De Poena Coniugii. De Virtute Clavium. De Musica et Organis. Contentio inter Aquam et Vinum. Satyricum in Abbates. De Civitatibus Anglicis.* The Paris Pageant for Henry VI (1431). English poems on gardening and hawking. English didactic poems: 'Revertere'; 'Who sayth soth he schall be schent': 'Parce mihi Domine' ('The Bird with Four Feathers'); 'And ever more thanke God of all'; 'Hyre and se and say not all'; Lydgate's 'As ryghth as a rams horne': 'Beware the blynd etyth meny a flye'; 'What ever thowe saye avyse the well'. *De Symonia et Avaricia.* 'De Cantu "Alma Redemptoris Mater" ' ('The Boy of Toledo'). *Narratio de Duobus Militibus.* Latin epitaph on Joseph of Arimathea. Latin poem on the two St. Josephs. *Estas et Hiems. Praedicatio Goliae. De Ingratitudine,* 'editus a fratre Stephano

Deuerell monacho Glaston'. *Tryvytlam de Laude Universitatis Oxonie*. Latin poem on the friars with 'O-and-I' refrain. *De Petro de Gauestone* (Latin parodies). Satirical *Descriptio Northfolchiae*. Carols Nos. 161 b, 309 k, 331 a. Copies of letters, one from Nicholas, Abbot of Glastonbury, concerning a council of 1433. *Historiae de Santa Cruce, de Pilato, de Juda Iscariota*. Many miscellaneous short notes and verses in Latin and English.

R. 4. 20

Vellum, 10 × 7¼ in., ff. 172. Cent. xv. f. 172 is a fragment.

Written principally in one hand of the first half of cent. xv. The two carols and other verses are in another hand of the second half of the century. Various other hands are represented by scribbles and in the love-letter.

Principal contents: Mandeville's *Travels* in English. One complete and several partial copies of an English love-letter (cent. xvi). Lydgate's *Siege of Thebes*. English poems: Carols Nos. 181, 425; 'A gentyll fortune'; 'I have nowe sett myn herte so hye'; Advice in verse from a father to sons and a mother to daughters; 'O tonge so often herebyfore'; 'Hayll, mary' (fragment).

Among the names written here and there in the MS. are: Danyell Dunstayn, Parnell Wilford, 'Sire Thomas Potter, preste', Rowland Kenston, John Hyde, William Kelyng. The coat of arms in the decoration on f. 1ʳ has not been identified, but is obviously a mark of ownership; M. R. James gives the blazon as '"apparently" party per fess *arg.* and *sa.* with a lion rampant counterchanged' (*The Western Manuscripts in the Library of Trinity College, Cambridge*, ii (Cambridge, 1900), 147.

The MS. was presented to the College in 1663 by a fellow, Dr. Crane.

R. 14. 26

Paper and vellum, 5¾ × 4¼ in., ff. 150. Cent. xv (first half). A number of leaves have been cut out.

Written for the most part in one hand. The carol is in a different hand.

Principal contents: Miscellaneous Latin notes and verses. Latin questions on music. Carol No. 377. Latin sermon on the *Ave Maria*. Various Latin logical treatises. Latin sermons in the form of logical discourses. Latin treatise on music. St. Thomas Aquinas's *De Ente et Essentia*. Various accounts with the date 1617.

The MS. is from Yorkshire. Two of the logical treatises are signed 'Pynchebeke'. On f. 1ᵛ in a hand of cent. xv (late) is a copy of a bond given by 'Thomas Pierson de houeden in Com. Ebor. Clericus' to John Palmer. On f. 2ʳ is the name Alan Stele, and on f. 11ʳ in a hand of *c*. 1500 is: 'This booke bylong*es* to the good wyfe Sanderson at Beurelay Dwellyng*e* in Weddynsday merkyt &c. *per* me Joha*n*nem Aulaby.'

The MS. was given to the library by John Wilson.

CANTERBURY: CATHEDRAL LIBRARY

CHRIST CHURCH LETTERS, vol. II, No. 173

Paper, one leaf, 11¾ × 4¼ in. Cent. xvi (first half). Stained and faded, with several holes at the bottom which render the text imperfect.

Contents: Carol No. 443.

CHRIST CHURCH LETTERS, vol. II, No. 174

Paper, one leaf, 8½ × 6 in. Cent. xvi (first half). Stained and with a small tear at the top which damages the text of the first line.

Contents: Carol No. 444.

The above two MSS. formerly bore the press marks S. B. b. 34 and b. 185, under which they are described in the *Reports of the Historical Manuscripts Commission*, v, Appendix, p. 458. They are now pasted into a modern volume.

ADD. 68 (formerly Z. 8. 33)

Vellum, 5½ × 3¾ in., ff. iv+101. Cent. xv (second half).

Written in one hand. An uncorroborated note of cent. XVIII on f. 1ʳ reads: 'This manuscript was writ by William Brewyn Chantry Priest at Saint Thomas Shrine in Christ-Church in *Canterbury*. Anº. 1477. No. 32.' On f. 1ᵛ under a scrap of accounts remaining after the leaf has been cut off at the top, in a hand of cent. XVI, is 'Allex Cooke'.

Principal contents: An account in Latin, attributed to William Brewyn, of the seven principal churches of Rome, with some attention to other churches; description of relics; legends of saints; a guide to pilgrimages to the Holy Land.

English pieces in verse: 'Thow holy moder of God Almygth' B.-R. *Supp.* 3675; 'Joy thou virgyn as it is ry3th' B.-R. *Supp.* 1808; 'Joy thou Mary with virgyn flower' B.-R. *Supp.* 1807; Carol No. 124.1; 'The prince of prests to hym gan say' (on the martyrdom of St. Stephen, imperfect at beginning) B.-R. 3448.8.

The volume was bought from a London bookseller by the Dean and Chapter of Canterbury. It is known to have been in the library of Sir Henry Ingilby, of Ripley Castle, Yorks. Many of the MSS. of this library have been assigned to Fountains Abbey and Bridlington Priory, and the dialect of the English pieces is consonant with an origin in the south of Yorkshire rather than Canterbury.

The MS. is described and the Latin contents translated by C. Eveleigh Woodruff, *A XVth Century Guide-book to the Principal Churches of Rome Compiled c. 1470 by William Brewyn* (London, 1933). I have followed Woodruff in his account of the contents of this MS.

MANCHESTER: JOHN RYLANDS LIBRARY

LAT. 395 (formerly 18932)

Vellum and paper, 8⅛ × 5½ in., ff. ii+146. Cent. xv.

Written principally in two hands. The carols are in the same hand as the other English verse.

Principal contents: Richard Rolle of Hampole's *Postillae super Canticum Canticorum, Incendium Amoris, De Amore Dei*. Extracts from St. Bonaventure and others. *De Sancta Katerina. Meditaciones Passionis Christi*. English verses: 'Man with good aduertisement'. Carols Nos. 161 a, 308. 'VI Vertuous Questions and thanswers'. *De Vitis Patrum*. St. Augustine's *De Laude Psalmorum. De Ieiunio*. Miscellaneous Latin verses. *Legenda Sancti Sampsonis Archiepiscopi*. Printed *Propositio Clarissimi Oratoris Magistri Johannis Russell . . . ad . . . Karolum ducem Burgundie . . .* etc. (Caxton, *c.* 1476). *Autores Biblie*.

On f. 117ᵛ is: 'quod W. Ebsham'; on f. 119ᵛ 'quod Stevens E.'

The MS. was formerly in the library of Earl Spencer at Althorp.

Previous owners were the 5th Duke of Marlborough, Robert Triphook, and the Reverend John Brand, the antiquarian. See Henry Guppy, ed., *Propositio Johannis Russell*. The John Rylands Facsimiles, i (Manchester and London, 1909).

BRIDGWATER, SOMERSET: TOWN HALL

BRIDGWATER CORPORATION MUNIMENTS, 123

Parchment, a single strip, 10⅛ × 3⅜ in. Cent. xv.

Contents: A Latin indenture, dated 8 August 1471, between one Master Maurice, prebendary of the prebendal church of Llangoullo, in the diocese of St. Davids, and Sir Hugh,
perpetual vicar of that church, and one Thomas ap Rees ap Davyd of that parish,
conveying to the latter two parties the said church for five years at a rent of twenty
shillings per annum. Scribbles in the hand of the carols: 'hay hay w . . .' / 'a and . . .'
dorse. Carols Nos. 14 a, 362.

The carols are in a hand different from that of the indenture, but of about the same date.

The fragment is described in the *Reports of the Historical Manuscripts Commission*, iii,
Appendix, pp. 316–17.

CALLOW END, WORCESTER: STANBROOK ABBEY

3

Vellum, 9⅞ × 6⅝ in., ff. iv + 242. (An earlier fly-leaf, f. 1, is missing.) Centt. xiv, xv.

Written in several hands; the two carols, though separated by the main body of the MS.,
appear to have been written by the same hand but at different times. This hand, though
identified by N. R. Ker as that of John Morton, once owner of the MS., appears to me
to differ significantly.

Principal contents: Carol No. 393.1. A collection of homilies by Haymo on the gospels for
Sundays through the year and for some feast days and the common of saints (*Pat.
Lat.* cxviii). A treatise on original sin by the Augustinian friar Egidius. A list of relics
in the church of St. James at Compostella and a list of indulgences granted there, signed
'Walterum Sluter'. Copies of two letters, one from Dame Elizabeth de Botreaux to John
Stafford, Bishop of Bath and Wells, the other apparently from John Chaundler, Bishop
of Salisbury, to Henry Chichele, Archbishop of Canterbury. Carol No. 144.1.

The MS. has notes of ownership (cent. xv) written by John Morton, rector of Berwick
St. John, Wilts. (d. *c.* 1441), who bought it for 10*s.* from William Okele and Robert
Wylkyns, executors of the will of John Stone, preceding rector of St. John (d. 1420).

The volume has the bookplate of Ambrose Lisle Phillipps of Garendon (d. 1878). The
date and circumstances of its acquisition by Stanbrook Abbey are not known.

A fuller description, to which these notes are indebted, is given by N. R. Ker, 'Middle
English Verses and a Latin Letter in a Manuscript at Stanbrook Abbey', *Medium
Ævum*, xxxiv (1965), 230–3.

MAIDSTONE, KENT: KENT ARCHIVES OFFICE

K. A. O. U 182 Z1

A single leaf, paper, 10⅝ × 3⅞ in. Cent. xv.

Much damaged at the margins, rubbed and faded, in a few places completely illegible.

Contents: Carol No. 424.1. Below, in a later hand, a Latin memorandum.
    On the verso a rental for the district of Ashford, Kent.

The fragment is described by M. B. Parkes in Felix Hull, *Guide to the Kent County Archives
Office* (Maidstone, 1958), p. 230. Dr. Hull and his staff have been generous with expert
help in the use of this far from legible MS.

EDINBURGH: NATIONAL LIBRARY OF SCOTLAND

ADVOCATES 1. 1. 6. 'The Bannatyne MS.'

Paper, 12 × 7 in. (original leaves), 16⅜ × 10½ in. (mounted), bound in two volumes, ff. (vol. i) 191, (vol. ii) 206. Completed A.D. 1568.

Written mostly in one hand, that of the compiler, George Bannatyne, with a few entries in several later hands.

Contents: The most important extant collection of early Scottish poetry, including pieces by William Dunbar, Robert Henryson, Gavin Douglas, King James I, Walter Kennedy, Sir David Lyndsay, and others, with some anonymous pieces and some English poems by Chaucer, Lydgate, and Hoccleve, some 430 in all.

Carols Nos. 121.2 by William Stewart, 330.1 by William Dunbar, 468.1 D by Sir Thomas Wyatt [?] (transposed into Scots). Another poem elsewhere attributed to Wyatt, similarly transposed, is ascribed in the MS. to Alexander Scott: 'Lo quhat it is to lufe'.

George Bannatyne, born in 1545, was a merchant and moneylender of Edinburgh. He claims to have transcribed the contents of the MS. in three months during an epidemic of plague, but the collection of the materials and the planning of the huge anthology must have required a longer period.

The MS. remained in the possession of Bannatyne's descendants until it was given by his great-grandson, William Foulis of Woodhall, to William Carmichael of Skirling, whose son, the fourth Earl of Hyndford, presented it to the Advocates Library in 1772.

The standard edition of the MS. is that by W. Tod Ritchie, *The Bannatyne Manuscript Written in Tyme of Pest 1568*, 4 vols., S.T.S., 3rd Ser., No. 5 (1933); New Ser., Nos. 22, 23 (1928), 26 (1930). Vol. i of this work contains a detailed description of the MS. and an account of its history, including various documents concerned with the volume and its compiler.

ADVOCATES 18. 7. 21

Vellum, 6⅞ × 4⅝ in., ff. i + 166. Cent. XIV (second half). The margins of the leaves in the latter half are damaged.

Written throughout in one hand, that of the compiler, John de Grimestone, a Franciscan.

Principal contents: A preacher's commonplace book, alphabetically arranged, of Latin theological materials, with much verse in English and Latin interspersed. The verse contents are systematically analysed and indexed in Edward Wilson, *A Descriptive Index of the English Lyrics in John of Grimestone's Preaching Book*, Medium Ævum Monographs, New Ser., No. ii (Oxford, 1973), a work now indispensable to users of the MS.

Carols No. 149 a, 155 a, 157 D, 271.

Wilson, referring to unpublished research of A. McIntosh, localizes the dialect of the English writing in south-west Norfolk and cites the suggestion of Eilert Ekwall that the compiler takes his name from Grimston near King's Lynn, Norfolk (pp. xiv, xvi).

On f. 9ᵛ is: 'Orate pro anima fratris Johannis de Grimistone qui scripsit istum librum cum magna solicitudine Anno domini 1372. Aue maria pro anima sua pro amore dei'.

Other names in memoranda are: Nicolas de Roma, Robert Coldon, Thomas Holder, Walter Hankke or Haukke. Later unidentified names which appear are: William Broin [c. 1500], James Stuart 1699, William Young 1702. See Wilson, op. cit., pp. xiii–xvi. The volume was probably acquired by the Advocates Library between 1800 and 1825.

ADVOCATES 19. 3. 1

Paper, 8¼ × 5½ in., ff. 216. Cent. XV (second half).

Written principally in one hand, that of John Hawghton. Some short items are in various other hands. Carols Nos. 23 A, 378 are written by Hawghton, No. 150 A by another hand, in which are also the prognostics from thunder.

Principal contents: Carols Nos. 23 A, 150 A, 378. Other English religious poetry: Bks. V–VII of Lydgate's *Life of Our Lady*; *The Trental of St. Gregory*; Lydgate's *Stans Puer ad Mensam*. A prose life of St. Katherine. The romances *Sir Gowther* and *Sir Ysumbras*. The tale of *Sir Amadas*. English poems on 'marvels' and deceit. Prognostics from thunder on different dates. 'Proper terms' for game, etc. Medical and alchemical recipes. Accounts, one of 'gorgye Hopkyns [u]nto xx pond of god boldurs'. Latin hymn with music (one part): 'Deus creator omnium'.

The MS. is from Lincolnshire or its neighbourhood, but the identification of the scribe as John Hawton or Howton of Bardney Abbey, made in *Selection*, p. 183, should be regarded as possible rather than established. (Mr. N. R. Ker has kindly and expertly advised caution on this point.)

An account of expenses on f. 173ᵛ begins: 'M[emorandum] þat þes bene þe parcell þat I hawfe spend þe ferst when I went to gybbysmere' [Gibsmere, near Southwell, the country seat of the bishops of Lincoln ('my lord harsbechope' in the account)]. Other places mentioned in the MS. are 'Stapylforthe' [Stapleford, Lincs.] and Somerton Castle at Boothby, Lincs. Other names in the MS. are 'gorge sawton', 'Rychard harysun', 'Roger restun', 'Mychaell shrybroke' (owner of the book). Other scribes' names occurring are 'John Allwod', 'heeg', 'hyheg'.

GLASGOW: UNIVERSITY OF GLASGOW, HUNTERIAN MUSEUM

83 (T. 3. 21)

Vellum and paper, $11\frac{3}{8} \times 8\frac{5}{8}$ in., ff. 148. Cent. xv. Some sixteen leaves are missing.

Written principally in two hands. The carols are in two different hands.

Contents: John of Trevisa, *Fructus Temporum*, translation of Ralph Higden, *Polychronicon*. Carols Nos. 200.1, 238 C. English song with music for one voice: 'Nowe well *and* nowe woo', in the hand of the first four stanzas of No. 200.1. A list of monarchs of the world.

There are various scribbles and names of owners of the MS. or other persons: 'John Parker', 'John B. Samsone', 'Thys ys meyster wyllam Bromwells boke whoeuer stelythe this Boke shall be hangyd on hoke as he as Ima[n]', 'Samson erdyswycke [Erdesicke]', 'Sampsone Walkedey', 'Johan chyldyrys', 'marget chyldyrys', 'francis ades', 'hary omondis off irone key in london'.

Bound in cent. xvii for Henry, Prince of Wales, with his insignia.

For fuller description see John Young and P. Henderson Aitken, *A Catalogue of the Manuscripts in the Library of the Hunterian Museum in the University of Glasgow* (Glasgow, 1908).

DUBLIN: TRINITY COLLEGE

D. 2. 7 (160). The Blage Manuscript

Paper, $12\frac{3}{4} \times 7\frac{1}{2}$ in., ff. 186, now bound in three volumes. Centt. xv, xvi.

Contents: Middle English poems: *Peter Idle's Instructions to his Son* (imperfect); A lament of the Virgin: 'Who cannot weep come learn at me'.

Poems by Sir Thomas Wyatt and others, compiled by Wyatt's friend Sir George Blage (1512–1551) and including Carol No. 468.1 C and two poems by Blage himself. For a complete list of these poems see Kenneth Muir and Patricia Thomson, eds., *Collected Poems of Sir Thomas Wyatt* (Liverpool, 1969), pp. xii, xiii.

A partial index of first lines shows that some poems once in the MS. are now missing.

The MS. was in Archbishop Ussher's library, acquired by Trinity College in 1666. For a description and history see Kenneth Muir, 'An Unrecorded Wyatt Manuscript', *The Times Literary Supplement*, 20 May 1960, p. 328, and especially the Introduction to his edition, *Unpublished Poems* [by] *Sir Thomas Wyatt and his Circle*, English Reprints Series No. 18 (Liverpool, 1961).

D. 4. 18 (432)

Vellum and paper, $7\frac{5}{8} \times 5$ in., ff. 155. Centt. XIII, XV. The volume is made up of two unrelated MSS. bound together.

Written in several hands. The carol is in the same hand as the other political songs.

Principal contents: Part I (cent. XIII). French religious poetry, one piece with music. Two dialogues of St. Gregory. An All-Saints sermon by St. Edmund of Canterbury. A Latin hymn: 'Summe summi tu patris unice'. A life of St. Eustace in French verse. Ecclesiastical edicts, in Latin, with glosses.

Part II (cent. XV, imperfect at beginning). English: Dialogue in verse between Palamon, Arcite, and Emylye; *King Robert of Sicily*; The 'Seven Scoles'; *King Palaan*; *A Miracle of Our Lady*; 'A story of an onhappy boye'; *A Lament of Our Lady*; Verses on the Battle of Northampton; Verses on Yorkist policy; An acrostic poem on 'Warwyk'; Carol No. 431; Verses on the Yorkist lords; A list of Christian, and another of English, kings; The 'Dublin' play of *Abraham and Isaac*; A list of mayors and bailiffs of Northampton; A table of dates of Easter (imperfect); A tract by Richard Rolle of Hampole: 'Tary not for to turne the to God'. Theological miscellanea in Latin. Fictitious coats of arms of the Twelve Peers of France.

See Sir F. Madden, 'Political Poems', etc., *Archaeologia*, xxix (1842), 330–47, where the carol and three other poems are printed.

There is a brief description of the MS. by R. Brotanek, 'Abraham und Isaak', *Anglia*, xxi (1898), 21–2.

The first section of the volume appears to have been at the Benedictine priory of Belvoir, Lincolnshire, a cell of St. Albans (N. R. Ker, *Medieval Libraries of Great Britain*, London, 1941, p. 6).

E. 5. 10 (516)

Parchment and paper, $8\frac{1}{4} \times 5\frac{5}{8}$ in., ff. 223. Centt. XV, XVI. Written in several hands.

Principal contents: Prophetic and historical miscellanea in English and Latin. A prophecy of the Prior of Bridlington. 'Convertimini' (English verses). 'A devout salutation of *Ave regina celorum*' signed 'Benett'. Selections from the Fathers, in English. *Stans Puer ad Mensam*. Verses and genealogical notes on English kings. A prophecy in Latin verse written by 'Master Reginald' in 1210. Historical notes. Carol No. 431.1. '*Mirabilia Anglie.*' 'Libellus de bellis compilatus per magistrum Johannem de liniano anno domini m° ccc° xiv.' Macaronic verses: 'Syngyn y wolde but alas'. Verse prophecy in English: 'When þe dede arysen (The Cock in the North)'. English verses: 'In the monyth of may'. Prose treatise: *Nemo*. 'Articuli sancti Thome Cantuariensis episcopi' (summarized in notes on No. 114 a). List of noble and gentle casualties at Tewkesbury.

On f. 72ʳ in hand of cent. XVI: 'To his welbelovyd freind William danbie Georgij Nevile militis dominus danby de latimer'. On f. 'Cxxxxlj'[!]: 'Robert bordvne'.

The MS. appears to have come from Yorkshire.

SAN MARINO, CALIFORNIA: HENRY E. HUNTINGTON
LIBRARY AND ART GALLERY

EL. 1160

Paper, 9×6 in., ff. 132. *c.* 1500.

Contents: Two legal treatises in 'law French' by Sir Thomas Littleton, 'The Old Tenures' and the 'Treatise on Tenures' or 'Tenores Novells', written throughout in one hand. Many short miscellaneous entries in a number of different hands of centt. XVI and XVII. These include: Carol No. 456.1; two imperfect versions of the lyric by Sir Thomas Wyatt 'I muste go walk the woodes so wyld' found in the Blage MS. (Trinity College, Dublin, D. 2. 7); other fragments of English verse; legal memoranda containing many personal names mostly connected with place-names of Northamptonshire and contiguous counties, and the name of John Bullocke of the Inner Temple.

The MS. came to the Huntington Library in 1917 with other MSS. from the Bridgewater Library, formerly the property of the Earls of Ellesmere.

This brief description is condensed and adapted from that prepared for the Huntington Library by H. C. Schulz.

HM. 147

Vellum, 10⅝×7¾ in., ff. 114. Cent. xv.

Written in two hands, the body of the MS. in one of *c.* 1450, in another of *c.* 1500 the carol and a note on the front fly-leaf describing the bounds of the 'chace of cramborne', Cranborn Chase, which lies in Dorsetshire, Hampshire, and Wiltshire, and extends on the north as far as Salisbury.

Contents: Prose translation of the *Somme le Roi* of Laurentius Gallus. Carol No. 9.

The initials 'T. M.' are stamped on the sides of the sixteenth-century binding, but are not a certain indication of ownership, as the sides may have been previously used on another book. On the recto of the last leaf (now pasted to the cover as an endpaper) is written in a hand of cent. XVI (early) the name 'I. Touk [or Tonk]'.

The above information on this MS., which I have seen since the preparation of the first edition of this work, was kindly supplied to me by Godfrey Davies, of the Huntington Library. See H. C. Schulz, 'A Christmas Carol', in *Huntington Library Bulletin*, No. 6 (Cambridge, Massachusetts, 1934), 'Notes', pp. 165–6.

NEW HAVEN, CONNECTICUT: YALE UNIVERSITY, BEINECKE
RARE BOOK AND MANUSCRIPT LIBRARY

365. The Book of Brome

Paper, 8×5½ in., ff. 81. Cent. xv (second half).

Written in three hands. The carol is in the same hand as the other poems in the volume.

Principal contents: *Rules for Conduct*, in verse. Ciphers and puzzles. *On Casting Dice*, in verse. *The Catechism of Adrian and Epotys*. The 'Brome' mystery play of *Abraham and Isaac*. *The Fifteen Signs of Doomsday*. Accounts of Robert Melton of Stuston, apparently a steward of the Cornwallis family. A prescription for jaundice. *Owain Miles. The Life of St. Margaret* in verse (imperfect). 'Felson Book' or accounts of payment for commonrights at Stuston, the parish adjacent to Brome. Roll of taxes and church duties. Various legal forms, in Latin and English. Articles of inquiry at courts baron and leet. A list of prayers to be said. Carol No. 239 b. Directions for a trental. A fragment of Lydgate's *Seven Wise Counsels*.

The MS. was probably the property of the Cornwallis family of Brome Manor, Suffolk, where it was found by its first editor, Lucy Toulmin Smith, in the early 1880s. It then belonged to Sir Edward Kerrison. After many years out of use it was located by the present editor in the possession of Sir Edward's niece, the late Hon. Mrs. R. Douglas Hamilton, at Oakley House near Brome. It then passed successively to her nephew, Major E. M. Hovell, and to his cousin, Mr. Denis Hill-Wood, who deposited it on loan in the Ipswich and East Suffolk Record Office, Ipswich. Its location had once again become unknown to scholars, and it was again located, this time by Mr. D. Charman, at the instance of Professor Norman Davis. It was bought from Mr. Hill-Wood by Yale University in 1966 and is now in the collection of the Beinecke Rare Book and Manuscript Library.

For fuller description and an edition of the entire contents see Lucy Toulmin Smith, *A Common-place Book of the Fifteenth Century* (London, privately printed, 1886) and the more modern account by Norman Davis, *Non-Cycle Plays and Fragments*, E.E.T.S., Supplementary Texts, 1, 1970, pp. lviii–lxiii. Another description is that by Thomas E. Marston, *Yale University Library Gazette*, xli (1967), 141–5. A bit of its history is recorded by the present editor, ibid. xlii (1967), 107–8. For some further description and a facsimile of one page see Stanley J. Kahrl, 'The Brome Hall Commonplace Book', *Theatre Notebook*, xxii (1968), 157–61.

OSBORN SHELVES a. 1

Vellum, $5\frac{3}{8} \times 3\frac{1}{2}$ in., ff. ii+157. Cent. XIV.

Contents: One page of a musical exercise, cut down from a larger size.

A calendar, with one coloured pen-drawing for each month. To the entry for 23 September, 'tecle virg*inis*', a later cursive hand has added: 'coron*ate* de assumpcione s*a*nctie [sic] marie', i.e. the feast of St. Thecla of Iconium, crowned as virgin and martyr. The rest of the note refers to the 'Second Assumption' of the Virgin Mary, celebrated in some places on 23 September. On the page for December the entry for the day of St. Thomas of Canterbury has been erased, indicating English ownership in cent. XVI if not origin. Latin psalter with illuminated initials. The first 'Beatus' page is missing, and the first verse of the psalm has been added to the next page in a hand of cent. XVI. In a cursive hand on the last leaf, cut down like the first, but before it was written, after two lines of unconnected Latin, a quatrain: 'Ergo n*ost*ra concio sallat dei filio sallat sine vicio benedicamus d*omi*no.' In another hand in modified carol-form, a song in honour of the Virgin, in French, beginning: 'Une bone chanson ay trouve', somewhat similar to the French carol in Gonville and Caius College, Cambridge, MS. 383, p. 210. See Introduction, p. xxxv. In the same hand on the verso, Carol No. 59.1. See also *Report of the Tenth Congress of the International Musicological Society* (Ljubljana, Yugoslavia, 1970), p. 305.

The MS. was purchased in 1965 by James M. Osborn from Lawrence Witten of New Haven.

CAMBRIDGE, MASSACHUSETTS: HARVARD COLLEGE LIBRARY

HCL 25258. 27. 5*

Paper. 1767–77.

Three manuscript collections of 'Christmas carols', mostly traditional and not known from sources earlier than 1550. The pamphlets, now bound together, are carefully written, without music and with some attempt at imitation of illumination in medieval style. On f. 1r of the bound volume is the following note by Davies Gilbert, the editor of

Some Ancient Christmas Carols, with the Tunes to which they were formerly sung in the West of England (London, 1822): 'The three Carol Books bound up in this Volume were procured for me by Mr Paynter of Boskenna from Persons in the Deanery of Burian. I received them from Mr. George John in Octr. 1824—& they were bound together in the course of that year—D. G.' Boskenna is a village in south-west Cornwall near St. Buryan. On the deanery of Buryan, abolished in 1864, see Charles Henderson, *Essays in Cornish History* (Oxford, 1935), pp. 93–107.

The books are designated as A, B, and C. Gilbert has provided an alphabetical index of first lines for all three books in one table which also records the occurrences of the songs in his printed collection and indicates those for which music is given in either MSS. or printed edition. The care with which the MSS. are written shows that they were regarded as possessions of some value. The colophons of Book B tell that it was not written by its owner. On p. 4 is inscribed: 'JOHN WEBB his Carrol Book 1777', on p. 19 'JOHN WEBB'S CARROL BOOK October 19th 1777', and on p. 91 'JOHN WEBB. HIS BOOK Written by JOHN THOMAS JUNR of St. Just Octobeʳ. 31ˢᵗ 1777'. There are naïve illuminations in water-colour and a coloured title-page with a head of Christ. Book A is less pretentiously decorated with ruling and pen-work and is dated 1767. See R. L. Greene, 'The Traditional Survival of Two Medieval Carols', *E.L.H.* vii (1940), 223–38, from which the paragraph above is reproduced.

Carols No. 152 B a and b appear in Books A and B respectively, without music or any indication of a customary or borrowed air.

PHILADELPHIA, PENNSYLVANIA: UNIVERSITY OF PENNSYLVANIA LIBRARY

LAT. 35

Vellum, 8⅝ × 6⅜ in., ff. 186. Centt. XV, XVI.

Written principally in one hand of cent. XV. The hand of the carol differs from this hand and from two others which have written a note and an index of incipits of sermons at the end of the volume.

Contents: Fifty-eight Latin sermons by John Felton, vicar of St. Mary Magdalene, Oxford. Carol No. 468.1 A.

There is no certain evidence of the provenance of the MS. or of the identity of the scribe of the carol. The MS. was written in England, and an Oxford origin seems probable. Before being given to the University of Pennsylvania Library it was owned by James P. R. Lyell, whose bookplate it bears and who purchased it from Bernard Quaritch of London on 11 June 1952. The first notice of the carol (without attribution to Wyatt) was published by John Morford, 'A Middle English Lyric in Manuscript', *The Library Chronicle of the Friends of the University of Pennsylvania Library*, xxv (1959), 80–3.

PRIVATELY OWNED MSS.

BROGYNTYN, OSWESTRY: LORD HARLECH; ON DEPOSIT IN ABERYSTWYTH: NATIONAL LIBRARY OF WALES

PORKINGTON 10

Parchment and paper, 5½ × 4¼ in., ff. 211. Cent. XV (third quarter).

Written in several hands.

Principal contents: An astrological treatise, calendar, etc., 1462–81. An anatomical figure of a man and medical information. Weather-lore. The romance *Gawain and the Carle of Carlisle*. A treatise on grafting and horticulture. A treatise on book-illumination. A moral English verse dialogue with a bird. English poetry: A song in which the wives at the ale complain of their husbands; 'Lord how shall I me complayne' ('When I sleep I may not wake'); a verse-translation of the *Visio Fulberti*; the 'Hours of Man's Life'; *Earth upon Earth*; 'How the Virgin Came to the Devil', and tales of SS. Martin and Anthony from the *Northern Homily Collection*; *The Knyght and his Wyfe*; a song to the Virgin; *The Life of St. Katherine*; *The Good Wife's Counsel to her Daughter*; 'Ever say well or hold thee still'; 'Do for thi selfe wyle thou art here'; *The Friar and the Boy* ('Jack, his Stepdame, and the Friar'); *The Siege of Jerusalem*; Carols Nos. 124 B, 135, 152 A c, 323, 335; 'Mercy Passeth Righteousness'; *The Complaint of a Hare*.

The volume is written in the language of the West Midlands and has apparently been in Wales during part of its existence. There are a number of Welsh names in scribbles, among them 'Griffyth Owen of the County of Carnarvon'. On f. 52ᵛ the name 'H. Hattun' written on a scroll may be that of a compiler.

The MS. has been in the possession of the family of Ormsby-Gore for more than a century and was kept at Brogyntyn (formerly Porkington) before its deposit at Aberystwyth. The provenance has not been more closely determined. A very full account of the MS. is given by Auvo Kurvinen in *Neuphilologische Mitteilungen*, liv (1953), 33–67.

TOKYO, JAPAN: TOSHIYUKI TAKAMIYA

TAKAMIYA 6

(Formerly Helmingham Hall LJ. 1. 10)

Vellum, 12¼ × 8 in., ff. 119. Centt. xv, xvi. Some leaves have been cut out wholly or in part.

Written in two hands, the *Chronicle* in one (cent. xv), the carol and the other poem in the second (cent. xvi, first half).

Contents: Hardyng's *Chronicle of England* (to Edward IV). English poem: 'A lamentable complaynt of *our* saviour . . . kyng eternall, to sinfull mane his brother naturall'. Carol No. 95 b.

The hand of the carol has written on f. 119ᵛ notes of some executions in 1531, and, at another time, notes of similar events in 1534.

On f. 115ᵛ is written in another hand: 'This is John Ravells boke have wittnes Robard Crafft and Tomas Winay, Robard Chamberlyn and other more'.

In the binding is a strip from accounts of cent. xiv relating to Waltham and Essex.

The MS., formerly owned by Lord Tollemache, was sold for him at Sotheby's in 1969 and was owned for short periods by Hofmann and Freeman of Sevenoaks, Kent, and Bernard Quaritch, Ltd. of London, before its acquisition by the present owner.

B. PRINTED

LONDON: BRITISH MUSEUM

PRINTED BOOK C. 21. c. 12

Printed by Wynkyn de Worde. Imperfect at beginning.

Cocke Lorelles bote, unique copy, n.d. [?1518].

Carol No. 187 A b is written on the recto of a blank leaf at end, C₄ʳ. It is written partly in a book hand, which then changes to a cursive hand. Above the carol-variant the same hand has written: 'John boll ouse thys boke gode make hym a goode man amen amen In the name of gode amen In the yere of oure lorde M . . .' Below this is written and lightly cancelled: 'O [?] god gretest in degre In whom begynnyng non may be many godhed persons thre'.

On C_2^v are the names Robarte and Robarte Ihaxssne [Jackson].

PRINTED BOOK C. 39. b. 17

A new interlude and a mery of the nature of the iiij elements, *declarynge many proper poynts of phylosophy naturall, and of dyvers straunge effects & causes,* etc.

Imperfect, wanting sig. D and all after E, $6\frac{1}{2} \times 3\frac{7}{8}$ in., printed by John Rastell, date uncertain, but probably *c.* 1520.

Contents: The interlude, with Carol No. 473.1 on [E_{viii}^r].

The bibliographical history of the unique volume is discussed by A. Hyatt King, 'Rastell Reunited', *Essays in Honour of Victor Scholderer*, ed. D. E. Rhodes (Frankfurt, 1970) and 'The Significance of John Rastell in Early Music Printing', *The Library*, 5th Ser., xxvi (1971), 197–214.

PRINTED BOOK K. 1. e. 1. *The Book of XX Songes*

The bass part of a set of printed song books, with the title leaf of the triplex part.

$7\frac{1}{8} \times 5\frac{1}{2}$ in., ff. 53.

On f. 1^v is a list of contents headed: 'In this boke ar conteynyd .xx. songes .ix. of .iiii. partes / and .xi. of thre partes.' Colophon dated 10 October 1530.

On title-page is: ¶ Bassus.

In a binding at Westminster Abbey there have been found the title leaf of the medius part-book and a leaf with the colophon of an unidentified printer: 'Imprynted in London at the signe of the black mores . . .'. Before this discovery the printing had been attributed to Wynkyn de Worde. It is 'the earliest English book of printed songs in mensural notation' (Stevens, *M. & P.*, p. 467).

The songs are set to music by Cornish, Pygot, Ashwell, Fayrfax, Cowper, Gwynneth, Jones, Tauernar, and in four cases without a composer's name. No. 447 (anonymous) is the only piece the music of which indicates that it was sung in the carol-fashion.

For a description of the volume see Rudolf Imelmann in *Shakespeare-Jahrbuch*, xxxix (1903), 123–5. On the leaves from the medius part and for modern complete description see H. M. Nixon, 'The Book of XX Songs', *The British Museum Quarterly*, xvi (1951), 33–6, with facsimile.

The songs are printed without music by E. Flügel in *Anglia*, xii (1889), 589 ff.; by Imelmann, op. cit., 125–37. Facsimiles of five pages are printed by Edward Bliss Reed, *Christmas Carols Printed in the Sixteenth Century* (Cambridge, Massachusetts, 1932), pp. 4–8.

PRINTED BOOK MK. 8. k. 8

A single leaf, $12 \times 7\frac{1}{2}$ in., printed by John Rastell, with his device, *c.* 1525.

Contents: recto. Carol No. 470.1.

The broadside has been used as a paste-down in some book of either Westminster Abbey or Westminster School. On the verso are written eighteen lines of scribbles, some cancelled. These yield the names of John Grace, Richard Empson, Thomas Whetamsted, and Thomas Phyllyp, identified as monks of Westminster.

The leaf, acquired by the British Museum in 1904 from Ludwig Rosenthal Antiquariat of Munich, is authoritatively described and discussed by A. Hyatt King, 'The Significance of John Rastell in Early Music Printing', *The Library*, 5th Ser., xxvi (1971), 197–214 (with facsimile).

OXFORD: BODLEIAN LIBRARY

DOUCE ADDIT. 137

A scrapbook containing eighty-five broadside carol-sheets from provincial presses, principally at Birmingham and York. Many of the sheets are so printed that they can be cut apart for separate sale. The printers represented are W. Wright, T. Bloomer, Watson, and Daniel Wrighton of Birmingham, and C. Croshaw and M. W. Carrall of York. Some sheets are dated from 1822 to 1827 by manuscript notes.

Carol No. 142 B a is found in two identical copies, the one at f. 23ʳ dated 1822 by a manuscript note. The sheet is a single-carol broadside in two columns, with two woodcuts, one representing a woman, a boy, and a girl, the other a man and a boy. It has no imprint, but it was presumably issued by T. Bloomer, 53 Edgbaston-street, Birmingham, as it is placed in a long series of Bloomer's productions.

For an account of other broadsides from Bloomer's press in the collection see R. L. Greene, 'The Traditional Survival of Two Medieval Carols', *E.L.H.* vii (1940), 230–1.

DOUCE FRAGMENTS f. 48

Four leaves, paper, $5\frac{1}{4} \times 3\frac{3}{8}$ in., printed by William Copland [?] *c.* 1550. Somewhat damaged, with holes and rubbed spots.

The fragment is without colophon or signature. It is part of a volume the rest of which is not known to be extant in any copy. The two parts of the fragment (ff. 1, 4, and ff. 2, 3) are not consecutive.

Contents: f. 1ʳ. Title-page: Christmas ca|rolles newely Imprinted. [In the middle a woodcut of the Nativity within a decorative border. Above it a capital C, below it three ornaments.]

　f. 1ᵛ Carol No. 64 (incomplete).

　f. 2ʳ 'Quid ultra debuit facere?', imperfect at the beginning, three stanzas only. Whether it had a burden in this text or not cannot be known. In the other known text, Bodl. MS. Rawlinson C. 86, f. 65ʳ (cent. xv) (*pr.* Sandison, *Chanson d'Aventure*, p. 110) there is no burden. The MS. version has fourteen stanzas, of which those here printed are Nos. 2, 3, 4.

　ff. 2ᵛ–3ᵛ Carol No. 171.

　f. 3ᵛ Carol No. 4 (imperfect at end).

　f. 4ʳ Song of Advent, probably a carol, imperfect at beginning, App., No. i.

The fact that these last two items both contain abuse of Advent has led to the assumption that they are parts of the same piece, e.g. by E. Flügel, *Anglia*, xii (1889), 588. The difference in stanza form shows that this is not the case, not to mention the improbability of one carol's being long enough to fill the two or more pages which must have intervened in the original volume.

　f. 4ʳ and ᵛ Carol No. 60.

The fragment is reproduced in facsimile by E. B. Reed, *Christmas Carols Printed in the Sixteenth Century*, pp. 9–16.

RAWLINSON 4to. 598 (10)

A single leaf, paper, 5×4 in., damaged and mended at both edges and with a mended tear in the middle. Printed by Wynkyn de Worde in 1521.

This fragment is obviously the last leaf of a carol-book printed for sale. It is the earliest printed item in the bibliography of English carols. See T. F. Dibdin, ed., *Ames's Typographical Antiquities* (London, 1810–19), ii. 250–2, 394.

Contents: recto. Carol No. 424 B.

verso. Carol No. 132 B and the following colophon: Thus endeth the Christmasse carol = |les / newely enprinted at Londo*n* / in the | fletestrete at the sygne of the sonne by | wynkyn de worde. The yere of our lor = |de. M. D. xxi.

The verso of the fragment is reproduced in facsimile by E. B. Reed, *Christmas Carols Printed in the Sixteenth Century*, p. 3.

SAN MARINO, CALIFORNIA: HENRY E. HUNTINGTON LIBRARY AND ART GALLERY

Christmas carolles newely Inprynted.

A collection of one complete pamphlet printed by Richard Kele and parts of five others not certainly printed by him.

The title-page of the complete pamphlet reads: ¶ Christmas ca = |rolles newely Inprynted. [Woodcut of the Crucifixion with two woodcut floral side-ornaments.] ¶ Inprynted at London in the Powl = |try by Rychard Kele, dwellyng at the | longe shop vnder saynt Myldre = |des chyrche.

The entire collection is reproduced in facsimile by Edward Bliss Reed, *Christmas Carols Printed in the Sixteenth Century* (Cambridge, Massachusetts, 1932).

The bibliographical information given in Reed's Introduction, pp. xl–lxiv, is incomplete. In the following analysis of the items bound together the page numbers in brackets assigned by Reed are used for convenience of reference.

1. [1]–[16] *Christmas carolles newely Inprynted*, properly speaking a complete pamphlet of eight leaves.
2. [17]–[30] Second pamphlet lacking A$_i$, its title therefore unknown.
3. [31]–[40] Third pamphlet, originally of six [?] leaves, lacking A$_i$, its title therefore unknown.
4. [41], [42] Fourth pamphlet, one leaf only, unsigned.
5. [43], [44] Fifth pamphlet, one leaf only, signed A$_{iii}$.
6. [45]–[48] Sixth pamphlet, folded in reverse in this binding, unsigned. This may be the second half of an eight-leaf pamphlet like Bodl. Douce fragments f. 48, also unsigned.

The carols are found in the items listed as follows:

1. Nos. 265, 107, 376, 163 b.
2. Nos. 164, 460, 461, 473, 474, 119, 81 B, 256, 42 b.
3. Nos. 157 A, 101 A, 106.
4. Nos. 370 c, 101 B.
5. Nos. 235 c, 213.
6. Nos. 278, 364.

Two pieces not in regular carol-form are included: 'Psallemus cantantes' and *A caroll oj the Innocentes*: 'Marke this songe for it is trewe'.

Reed did not understand the simple misfolding of the sixth pamphlet in the present binding, and called the correct order of leaves 'barely possible' (p. xlv). Items 1 and 6 are in the same type and are both presumably from Kele's shop. Item 2 is in a different type and hence cannot certainly be said to be of Kele's printing. Item 3 is in the same type as 2. Items 4 and 5 are in the same type as 2 and 3 and may have been originally in one gathering, not certainly printed by Kele. Though the detailed bibliographical information in Reed's Introduction, pp. xl–lxiv, must be used with caution, his biographical account of Kele and his summary of the known history of the bound leaves are valuable.

Here Folowythe dyuers Balettys and dyties solacyous deuysyd by Master Skelton Laureat.
$6\frac{15}{16} \times 5$ in., pp. 8, printed by Richard Pynson, *c.* 1520.

The title-page reads: HEre Folowythe dyuers | Balettys and dyties sola= | cyous deuysyd by Master Skel = |ton Laureat. Below is a woodcut of the poet, crowned with a wreath and reading in a lectern, with the legend: Arboris omne ge|nus viridi conce= | dite lauro.

Contents: Carol No. 459. Other poems by Skelton: 'The auncient acquaintance madam betwen vs twayn'; 'Knolege Aquayntance resort fauour with grace'; 'Cuncta licet cecidisse putas discrimina rerum'; 'Go pytyous hart rasyd with dedly wo'.

NOTE

Descriptions of the MSS. containing Nos. 263 c, d, e, f, g, h, i, j, k, l, n, and 309 b, c, d, e, f, g, h, i, j, versions which are not in carol-form, are omitted from this bibliography. The MSS. of No. 263 k (Huntington Library, MS. HM. 140 formerly Phillips 8299) and No. 309 j (the 'Billyngs MS.') I have not seen. The latter MS. was formerly in the collection of William Bateman at Lomberdale House, Derbyshire, and has not been traced since its sale in 1893. See Hilda M. R. Murray, *Erthe upon Erthe* (E.E.T.S., Or. Ser., No. 141, London, 1911), p. 35.

The MS. of Nos. 79 B, 112 was destroyed by fire at Birmingham in 1879.

No. 402 c is a casual MS. entry in one copy of an unrelated printed book, as is No. 187 A b.

NOTES

1. O Radix Jesse

Music for two and three voices. *Pr.* Fehr, p. 268; with music, Stevens, *Med. Carols*, p. 77. B.–R. 2533.

The source of this carol is the third Advent Antiphon (*Br. Sar.* i, col. clv): 'O radix Jesse qui stas in signum populorum, super quem continebunt reges os suum, quem gentes deprecabuntur: veni ad liberandum nos, jam noli tardare.' The antiphon is based on Isaiah xi. 1.

2. O Clavis David

Music for two and three voices. *Pr.* Fehr, p. 268; with music, Stevens, *Med. Carols*, p. 78. B.–R. 2409.

The source of this carol (a companion piece to No. 1) is the fourth Advent Antiphon (*Br. Sar.* i, col. clv): 'O clavis David, et sceptrum domus Israel, qui aperis et nemo claudit, claudis et nemo aperit: veni et educ vinctum de domo carceris, sedentem in tenebris et umbra mortis.' The antiphon is based on Isaiah xxii. 22.

stza. 2, l. 5. This line is obviously the result of an error in copying, the scribe having been confused by the repetition of the previous line. The correct reading was probably something like 'And that thou byndest may no man twynne'.

3. Farewell to Advent

Pr. Zupitza, 238, notes, xcv, 274; A. G. Little, *Archaeologia Cantiana*, liv (1942), 2; Greene, *Selection*, p. 53; Sisam, p. 504; Davies, p. 231; Oliver, p. 76 (in part); R. M. Filmer, *A Chronicle of Kent 1250–1760* (London, n.d.), p. 28. B.–R. 4197.

It is hard to believe that this carol is the original composition of Ryman, in view of the more patient piety of the rest of his pieces. The single stanza on the same theme on f. 74ᵛ of the MS. is more characteristic of him, and was undoubtedly suggested by stza. 12 of this carol (*pr.* Zupitza, 272):

> Prince, duke *and* erle, lord, knyght, *and* squier,
> With alle other in youre degree,
> Caste oute Aduent into the myer*e*,
> For he *with* vs to long hath be,
> And welcome we that King so fre
> That now was borne for loue of vs
> Of mayde Mary, named Jhesus.

The personification of Advent as a periodic visitor is parallel to that of Christmas in Nos. 5, 6, 141, and of the New Year in No. 10. A similar personification of Lent is indicated by stza. 12, l. 3, with which compare No. 4, stza. 2, l. 1, and No. 141, stza. 3, l. 3. It is probable that Advent was sometimes actually impersonated as we know Christmas and Lent to have been. In a procession in Norwich in January 1448 appeared 'Lenten cladde in white with redde herrings skinnes and his hors trapped with oyster shelles after him in token yᵗ sadnesse and abstinence of merth shulde followe and an holy tyme' (E. L. Guilford, *Select Extracts Illustrating Sports & Pastimes in the Middle Ages*, London, 1920, p. 52).

E. F. Jacob cites this carol in connection with a discussion of the importance of regular supplies of fish, specifically to the monks of Ryman's own town ('Chichele and Canterbury', R. W. Hunt *et al.*, eds., *Studies in Medieval History Presented to Frederick Maurice Powicke*, Oxford, 1948, p. 396).

stza. 2, l. 2. *sowce*: pickled pork.

stza. 5, l. 1. Compare a line in the song of complaint against Lent, 'Wo worthe the, Lenttone, that ever thowe wast wrought' (Thomas Wright, ed., *Songs and Ballads*, London, 1860, No. v, p. 14):

> Muskyls ly gapyng agenste the newe mone.

stza. 9, l. 3. The mention of Boughton Blean, the hamlet best known through Chaucer's *Canon's Yeoman's Prologue*, l. 3, is a sign that the carol comes from Canterbury, whether of Ryman's original authorship or not. In 1384 there was a good-sized chapel and hospital for lepers and infirm persons at Boughton-under-Blean which would have been an appropriate haven for such a meagre figure as Advent (*V.C.H. Kent*, London, 1926, ii. 208). With stza. 10, l. 1 compare the proverbial phrase of emphasis 'neither in Kent nor Christendom' which Grose (*A Provincial Glossary*, London, 1787) lists as local to Kent. It appears, however, in Spenser's *Shepherd's Calendar* (Sept., l. 153) and elsewhere. See V. S. Lean, *Collectanea* (Bristol, 1902), i. 107.

4. Farewell to Advent

Repr. Flügel, *Anglia*, xii (1889), 588, *N.L.*, p. 124 (as if one piece with App., No. i, the fragment on the next page of the original); *facs.* Reed, p. 14. B.-R. *Supp.* 905.5.
burden, l. 1. Compare the burden of No. 141 and notes on that carol.

5. Good Day, Sir Christmas!

Music for two voices. *Pr.* Padelford, p. 89; C. & S., p. 233; Davies, p. 214; Silverstein, p. 113; with music, *E.B.M.* ii. 107, *facs.* No. xlvii; Terry, p. 39; Stevens, *Med. Carols*, p. 12; Robbins, *Christmas Carols*, p. 16. B.-R. 1004.
See notes on No. 6.
stza. 3, l. 3. *snelle*: keen, lively, here with the connotation of gladness.

6. A Welcome to Christmas

Music for two and three voices. *Pr.* Fehr, p. 266; Sandys, *Carols*, p. 17, Sandys, *Christmastide*, p. 224; Wright, *P.S.* iv, 'Christmas Carols', 51; Ritson, *Ancient Songs* (1790), p. 128, (1829), ii. 17, (1877), p. 161; A. H. Bullen, *Carols and Poems* (London, 1885), half-title, verso; Joshua Sylvester, pseud., *A Garland of Christmas Carols, Ancient and Modern* (London, 1861), p. 165; John Julian, *A Dictionary of Hymnology*, 2nd edn. (London, 1925), p. 209; with music, *Mus. Ant.*, p. 26; *Oxford Book of Carols*, Music Edn., p. 40; Terry, p. 57; Stevens, *Med. Carols*, p. 67; Robbins, *Christmas Carols*, p. 9. B.-R. 681.

The personification of Christmas in this carol, as in No. 5, is one of the most frequent features of popular celebrations, occurring in many centuries and many lands. It persists to the present day in 'Father Christmas'. This figure has been especially prominent in mummers' plays. With the greeting in this carol compare his speech as presenter of such a play:

> Here comes I, Father Christmas, welcome or welcome not,
> I hope Old Father Christmas will never be forgot.
>
> (Chambers, *M.S.* i. 216)

See also the similar personification of Yule in the burden of No. 7 and notes on No. 3.
The dramatic character of the carol is obvious. It may have been actually used in a ceremony of admitting to the hall a singer representing Sir Christmas. In the present setting of the burden, however, the challenge and welcome are in three parts, the words of Sir Christmas in two. The long 'nowel' refrain is unusual and is probably an addition by the composer of this setting.
stza. 1, l. 1. *byewsser: beau sire*. This French phrase of greeting is likewise used in an English context by Pilate in the Towneley play of the Talents, l. 409: 'Dew vows [garde] mon senyours!' (ed. George England and A. W. Pollard, E.E.T.S., Ex. Ser., No. lxxi, 1897, 292).
stza. 2, l. 3. *atte a brayde*: in a quick movement, suddenly.

7. A Welcome to Yule

A. *Pr.* C. & S., *M.L.R.* v. 483; Whiting, p. 186; Greene, *Selection*, p. 55; Sandys, *Christmastide*, p. 218.
B. *Pr.* Wright, *Wart. Club*, p. 93, *P.S.* iv, 'Christmas Carols', 4; Ritson, *Ancient Songs* (1790), p. 81, (1829), i. 140; (1877), p. 120; Sandys, *Carols*, p. 3; C. & S., p. 232; Edmondstoune Duncan, *The Story of the Carol* (London, 1911), p. 63. B.-R. 3877.

The alternative ways of regarding the Christmas season as composed of the twelve days to Epiphany or of the forty to the Purification are illustrated by the two versions. Audelay's welcome is to 'the xii days efere'; in the anonymous B the line is to 'Twelfthe Day' as one of the series of feasts, and a stanza not in A extends the welcome to Candlemas. Both traditions flourish in popular custom, some communities of England removing Christmas greenery, for instance, after Twelfth Night, others leaving it until Candlemas. Compare Nos. 8, 141. The inclusion of Candlemas, an occasion on which the Virgin is the centre of attention, naturally leads to her being 'welcomed' in that connection and to the omission of stza. 2 of A.

Audelay's original authorship of the carol is doubtful. Probably his version was made with more or less revision from a prototype which took the form of B under other hands.

Erik Routley (*The English Carol*, London, 1958, p. 74) errs by associating this carol with 'John Awdelay (*fl.* 1559–1577), stationer and printer'.

8. The Christmas Feasts

a. *Pr.* Wright, *P.S.* xxiii. 24; Reed, pp. xxx–xxxi; Greene, *Selection*, p. 56; Davies, p. 167.
b. *Pr.* Wright, *Wart. Club*, p. 98, *P.S.* iv, 'Christmas Carols', 17.
B.–R. 3343.

The device of devoting one stanza each to the important days of the Christmas season, as used here and in No. 9 and App., No. ii, is probably educational as well as rhetorical in intention. Compare the last stanza of a late fifteenth-century *noël* by Jehan Tisserant (Bibliothèque Nationale, MS. français 2368, f. 14ʳ):

> Par douze jours fut nouel aco*m*ply,
> Par douze vers sera mon chant finy,
> Par cha*s*cun jour j'en ay fait vng coupplet.

A similar device survives in traditional English folk-song, but without the ecclesiastical application, in the well-known cumulative piece, 'The Twelve Days of Christmas' (W. H. Husk, *Songs of the Nativity*, London, [1868], p. 182). In their comment on the modern song, first found in a children's book of about 1780, *Mirth without Mischief*, Iona and Peter Opie (*The Oxford Dictionary of Nursery Rhymes*, Oxford, 1952, pp. 122–3) suggest that it may be 'an irreligious travesty' of a carol like this one. But the carol is not cumulative; its stanzas are too long for cumulative use, and it does not notice some of the twelve days.

9. The Christmas Feasts

Pr. H. C. Schulz, *Huntington Library Bulletin*, No. 6 (Cambridge, Mass., 1934), 'Notes', p. 166; Brown, *R.L. 15 C.*, p. 122. B.–R. 2334.
burden, l. 2, stza. 2, l. 4. See tables in Introduction, pp. lxxxvi, civ.
stza. 2, l. 1. This is probably meant to be taken metaphorically in the spiritual sense, but compare App., No. ii, stza. 2, l. 1.
stza. 6, l. 1. *knyghtes*. The substitution for 'kings' may be merely a copyist's error.

10. Christmas Mirth

Pr. K. Hammerle, *Archiv*, clxvi (1923), 204; Robbins, *Secular Lyrics*, p. 3; Greene, *Selection*, p. 57; Sisam, p. 513; Silverstein, p. 117. B.–R. 2343.

On the implied context of this carol see Introduction, p. xli, and the 'messenger' burden of No. 117. The macaronic complaint of a schoolboy, 'On days when I am callit to þe scole' (*pr.* K. Hammerle, *Archiv*, clxvi. 203), immediately precedes this carol in the MS. and is in the same hand, a circumstance which strengthens the probability that the carol relates to a scholastic celebration and is not the utterance of a professional 'minstrel' as suggested in the notes in the first edition p. 355. See notes on No. 413.

'A Plea for Another Drink' (*pr.* Robbins, *Secular Lyrics*, p. 5, notes pp. 228–9) is in a different hand and is probably not directly related to this carol. Its very interesting use in English of a Welsh lyric form is well explained by Robbins, but it seems to be more suitable to the visitation of a known neighbour by an amateur singer than to use by a 'minstrel'.

It is unusual to find the same rhymes used in all stanzas of a carol, as here. Compare Nos. 22, 234. burden. This was still in circulation in 1553. It is sung in the interlude *Respublica*, v. viii:

> haye, haie, haie, haie,
> I wilbe merie while I maie.

([Sir] W. W. Greg, ed., E.E.T.S., Or. Ser., No. 226, 1952, 57)

stza. 5, l. 4. The last words of the carol, 'care away', are of frequent occurrence in the refrains or burdens of popular song. See notes on No. 470. The phrase also appears in an old jingle from Nottinghamshire on Care Sunday or Passion Sunday, the second before Easter:

> Care Sunday, care away,
> Palm Sunday and Easter Day.

(P. H. Ditchfield, *Old English Customs Extant at the Present Time*, London, 1901, pp. 69–70) The meaning of 'Care' as applied to the Sunday is uncertain.

The expression was current as an indication of cheerful social song in the seventeenth century. *Lachrymae Londinienses* (1626) warns the reader:'If you expect in these ensuing Lines any scarce credible or feigned matters of wonderment, made in some Tauerne or on some Ale-bench, to tickle your Eares and help you to sing Care-away, you will be deceiued' (*Plague Pamphlets of Thomas Dekker*, ed. F. P. Wilson, Oxford, 1925, p. 245, quoted by Louis B. Wright, *Middle-Class Culture in Elizabethan England*, Chapel Hill, N.C., 1935, p. 447). The phrase, written as one word, is thought worthy of a gloss in the *Promptorium Parvulorum*: 'sorwles: *Tristicia procul*' (ed. A. L. Mayhew, E.E.T.S., Ex. Ser., No. cii, 1908, col. 70).

Further testimony to the custom of calling upon each guest at a feast for a song is found in the amusing apology for declining this contribution made by the fifteenth-century verses beginning 'If i synge ȝe wyl me lakke' (Robbins, *Secular Lyrics*, No. 4, p. 4. See also R. L. Greene, 'If I Sing, Tie Up Your Cows', *N. & Q.* ccix, 1964, 88–9.)

11. Christmas Sports

Pr. Dyboski, p. 15; Flügel, *N.L.*, p. 123, *Fest.*, p. 69; 'Lieder.', p. 241; Pollard, p. 86; C. & S., p. 234; Norman Hepple, *Lyrical Forms in English* (Cambridge, 1911), p. 19 (burden omitted); Frost, p. 261; Robbins, *Secular Lyrics*, p. 3; Greene, *Selection*, p. 58; Sisam, p. 527; Oliver, p. 110; Davies, p. 277. B.–R. 1866.

The carol is written as if to be sung by a master of festivities or 'Lord of Misrule' with power to 'punish'. The obligation of each person present to contribute to the general entertainment is characteristic of many English holiday customs. Compare No. 10.

stza. 1, l. 2. The marshal of a medieval hall had the duty, among others, of seating the guests at any feast. A groom served under a marshal, building the fires and performing other practical tasks in the hall. See F. J. Furnivall, ed., *The Babees Book* (E.E.T.S., Or. Ser., No. 32, 1868) for *The Book of Curtasye*, Bk. III, ll. 379–422, which deal with the marshal.

stza. 3, l. 3. *stokkes.* R. J. Schoeck rightly calls attention to the use of actual stocks at the order of a Lord of Misrule at Christmas (review of Robbins, *Secular Lyrics*, *Anglia*, lxxi, 1953, 356). See Chambers, *M.S.* i. 408–9 for instances at Oxford colleges.

12. Of the Nativity

a. *Pr.* Brown, *R.L. 14 C.*, p. 110; [Sir] E. K. Chambers, *English Literature at the Close of the Middle Ages*, The Oxford History of English Literature (Oxford, 1945), p. 80; A. Obertello, *Liriche religiose inglesi del secolo quattordicesimo* (Milan, 1947), p. 104 (with Italian translation); Kaiser, *Med. Engl.*, p. 290; Greene, *Selection*, p. 59; Sisam, p. 183.

b. Collated in first edition.

B.–R. 29.

This piece, which occurs in some Franciscan sermon notes, is the earliest Nativity carol yet discovered. See Brown's notes, *R.L. 14 C.*, pp. xii, 272, and Introduction, pp. cliv, clxviii.

The discrepancy in the metre between the first stanza and the other two might be accounted for by regarding the piece as made up of two originally different sets of verses. The third stanza, at least, must have circulated without a burden, as it so appears in b, where it is also quoted in a Latin homily, without any indication that it is there regarded as part of a carol or song.

It is equally possible that the short third and sixth lines were omitted in error from the first stanza, perhaps through confusion with the four-line form of the burden. For the first stanza to be sung to the same melody as the other two, such lines would, of course, be indispensable.

Margit Sahlin (*Étude sur la carole médiévale*, p. 58) says of this carol that it is 'certainement un de ces *noëls* ou *lullaby carols* (*kindelwiegenlieder*) que l'on chantait en dansant autour d'un berceau arrangé sur l'autel ou autre part dans l'église, comme il était d'usage en bien des endroits'. There is no evidence for so positive a statement. But even if the piece were used for a dance around such a Christmas crib the derivation of the burden from secular dance-song is still probable. R. H. Robbins (*Stud. in Phil.*, lvi, 1959, 576) oddly attempts to make Dr. Sahlin's suggestion inconsistent with such a dance-song origin. As a matter of fact, the text in MS. Bodley 26 immediately follows a reference to the wedding feast of the Lamb in Revelation xix. 9: '... et hic est cena de qua in apocalipsi "beati qui ad cena[m] agni vocati sunt", ad quam cenam specialiter vocat deus 3ª hominum genera sicut alibi etc.' Quotation of the carol seems to have been suggested to the preaching friar by the mention, not of any church service, but of the revelry at a feast, the known setting of many later carols. Note l. 6, 'For your marriage', which is hardly intelligible in the carol without the sermon-context. The subject of rejoicing rather than of the Nativity scene itself is further emphasized by the note written beside and below the third stanza: 'Secundum primus thema tristicia vestra convertetur in gaudium Joh. 16. Verba ista sunt Christi ad discipulos ...' (John xvi. 20). See Homer G. Pfander, *The Popular Sermon of the Medieval Friar in England* (N.Y., 1937), pp. 45–6.

stza. 1, l. 2. *wam*: spot, stain.

stza. 2, l. 2. *peys ys grad*: peace is proclaimed.

13. Of the Nativity

Music for two and three voices. *Pr.* Fehr, p. 274; Sandys, *Carols*, p. 14; Wright, *P.S.* iv, 'Christmas Carols', 53; with music, Stevens, *Med. Carols*, p. 96; Robbins, *Christmas Carols*, p. 82. B.–R. 3587 (under 'This day ys borne a chylde of grace'); B.–R. *Supp.* 54.5.

Like No. 120 this is a welcome expressed by a singer on behalf of a host.

burden, l. 1. *Proface*: 'a formula of welcome or good wishes at a dinner or other meal', O.E.D. Fr. *bon prou vous fasse*, may it do you good.

stza. 1, l. 2. *toure*: in allusion to the 'tower of ivory' as a type of the Virgin's body.

14. Of the Nativity

a. *Pr. Reports of the Historical Manuscripts Commission*, iii, Appendix, p. 316; T. Bruce Dilks, *Pilgrims in Old Bridgwater* (Bridgwater, 1927), p. 35; Greene, *Selection*, p. 60.

b. Music for two and three voices. *Pr.* Padelford, p. 91; with music, *E.B.M.* ii. 109, *facs.* No. li; Terry, p. 2; Stevens, *Med. Carols*, p. 14; Robbins, *Christmas Carols*, p. 20.

c. Music for two and three voices. *Pr.* Fehr, p. 273; with music, Stevens, *Med. Carols*, p. 94. B.–R. 2377.

The burden of a is taken from the famous 'Laetabundus' Nativity prose. See Introduction, pp. xcviii–civ. In the other versions the burden is reduced to 'Alleluia'. The holly-and-ivy phrase attached to a in the MS. is probably an indication of the tune of a popular carol intended for use with the religious piece. It need not have been a holly-and-ivy carol in its full content, for preserved folk-song gives us examples of the words used in other contexts. For instance, a nineteenth-century Irish version of the 'Hunting of the Wren' sung on St. Stephen's Day by young men *en quête* contains the lines:

> Sing holly, sing ivy—sing ivy, sing holly,
> A drop just to drink, it would drown melancholy.

The singers carried a holly-bush decorated with ribbons and wrens (T. Crofton Croker, *Researches in the South of Ireland*, London, 1824, p. 232). More than a hundred years later the song was recorded in Vermont with a stanza recalling the association of birds with the two trees:

> Between the holly and ivy tree
> Were all the birds come singing to me,
> Sing holly, sing ivy,
> To keep next Christmas, it will be holly [*sic*].

(Helen Hartness Flanders and Marguerite Olney, *Ballads Migrant in New England*, N.Y., 1953, p. 58)

The sophisticated settings of the other two versions probably replaced simpler and more popular tunes in the case of this carol as of others.

15. Of the Nativity

Pr. W. D. Macray, *Catalogi Manuscriptorum Bibliothecae Bodleianae, Part. V, Fasc. II* (Oxford, 1878), p. 266. B.–R. 3609.

The burden and one stanza of this carol are written at the top of the page in the MS., the rest being left blank. Several leaves immediately following have been torn out, and others are blank. Apparently the writer began to use a vacant part of the volume for a collection of carols and soon thought better of it.

16. Of the Nativity and Life of Christ

Pr. Wright, *Wart. Club*, p. 78, *P.S.* iv, 'Christmas Carols', 12. B.–R. 1574.

The burden is the same as that of No. 27 A and B.

stza. 1. Lines rhyming 'born' and 'forlorn' and usually with similar content are so frequent in the carols as to constitute the favourite cliché of the carol genre. They occur in Nos. 20, 41, 61, 68, 71, 91, 101, 123, 129, 142, 148, 157, 158, 168, 169, 176, 177, 178, 179, 194, 311, and 359. It is noticeable that the phrasing occurs only in stanzas, never in a burden.

stza. 2, l. 1. *schorn*: circumcised.

17. Be Merry in the Nativity

a. *Pr.* F. A. Patterson, 'Shakspere and the Medieval Lyric', B. Matthews and A. H. Thorndike, eds., *Shaksperian Studies* (New York, 1916), p. 444.

b. Music for two voices. *Pr.*, with music, Fuller Maitland, p. 11; Terry, p. 48; Stevens, *Med. Carols*, p. 4; Robbins, *Christmas Carols*, p. 30.

B.–R. 88.

stza. 3, l. 3. *holdyn vppon*: continue.

18. Of the Nativity

a. Music for two voices. *Pr.* Padelford, p. 110; Brown, *R.L. 15 C.*, p. 111; with music, Terry, p. 42; Stevens, *Med. Carols*, p. 2.

b. Music for two and three voices. *Pr.* Padelford, p. 110; with music, *E.B.M.* ii. 155, *facs.* No. lxxxvi; Terry, p. 36; Stevens, *Med. Carols*, p. 27.

B.–R. 1473.

stza. 1, l. 3. *I schryf* (b *take schrift*): I confess (with connotation of ascribing praise, *O.E.D.*, s.v. 'Shrive', 4.b).

stza. 3, l. 1. *powste*: power. *emprys*: adventure, undertaking.

stza. 4, l. 5. The MS. is faded almost into illegibility at the beginning of the line. Terry's emendation, 'For lo the Son', is impossible.

stza. 5, ll. 5, 6. i.e. in the Annunciation.

19. Of the Nativity

Music for two voices. *Pr.* Dyboski, p. 177; with music, Fuller Maitland, p. 9; Terry, p. 46; Stevens, *Med. Carols*, p. 4. B.–R. 3574 (with No. 20).

The burden and stza. 1 also appear as burden and stza. 1 of No. 20.

20. Of the Nativity and Passion

Pr. Dyboski, p. 30; Flügel, *Fest.*, p. 76, 'Lieder.', p. 254; C. & S., p. 116. B.–R. 3574 (with No. 19).

The burden and stza. 1 also appear as burden and stza. 1 of No. 19. The refrain is the same throughout both carols.

stzas. 3, 4. Compare Nos. 268, 269.

stza. 3, l. 2. Compare No. 333.

stza. 4, l. 2. See note on No. 269, burden.

21. Of the Nativity

A. Dyboski, p. 12; Flügel, *Fest.*, p. 67, 'Lieder.', p. 239; Greene, *Selection*, p. 61.
B. *Pr.* Wright, *P.S.* xxiii. 52.
C. Music for two voices. *Pr.* C. & S., p. 138; with music, Fuller Maitland, p. 13; Terry, p. 49; Stevens, *Med. Carols*, p. 5.
D. Music for one voice (burden only). *Pr.* first edition; with music, Stevens, *Med. Carols*, p. 111 (burden only).
B.-R. 1471.
E. *Pr.* Karen Hodder, *Archiv*, ccv (1969), 378; *facs.*, ibid. 380.
Not in B.-R.
For the sources of the Latin lines see table in Introduction, pp. lxxxvi, lxxxvii.

A. stza. 4, ll. 1, 2. Compare No. 234 C, stza. 4, ll. 1, 2. Of all the figures of speech which the Middle Ages applied to the Virgin Mary none is more prominent in the carols than the simile which likens the action of the Holy Spirit in causing her to conceive to the sun's shining on a glass, which it penetrates without injuring. It is, of course, echoed and re-echoed in theological writings, so that it is idle to point to a particular passage as a 'source' for any particular carol. The most authoritative use of the figure and the one which probably reached the most readers is that of St. Augustine, which is incorporated in the sixth Lectio for Matins on the Third Sunday in Advent (*Br. Sar.* i, col. cvi): 'Solis radius specular penetrat, et soliditatem ejus insensibili subtilitate pertransit: . . . ad ingressum et egressum ejus specular integrum perseverat. Specular ergo non rumpit radius solis: integritatem virginis ingressus aut egressus numquid vitiare poterat deitatis?' The figure also appears in Nos. 56, 63, 66, 67, 73, 84, 174, 194, 200, 207, 208, 246, 281.

D. stza. 1, l. 3. This line, suggestive of a formula on the gifts at Epiphany to follow, may result from a recollection of some such lines as those in No. 127, stzas. 3, 4, and No. 129, stzas. 3, 4, both by James Ryman. There is a tenuous possible connection in the occurrence of D on f. 1 of Ryman's MS., though not in the same hand as the other carols.

E. stza. 2, l. 1. This unfinished line obviously comes, probably by memory only, from a formula on the significance of the gifts at the Epiphany.

22. Of the Nativity

Music for two voices. *Pr.*, with music, Fuller Maitland, p. 17; Terry, p. 50; Stevens, *Med. Carols*, p. 7; Robbins, *Christmas Carols*, p. 22. B.-R. 2315.
The carol keeps the same rhyme throughout the stanzas. Compare Nos. 10, 234.
stza. 2, l. 4. *rent*: in the sense of 'inheritance'.

23. Of the Nativity

A. *Pr.* W. B. D. D. Turnbull, *The Visions of Tundale* (Edinburgh, 1843), p. 139; K. Breul, *Englische Studien*, xiv (1890), p. 402; C. & S. p. 134; Brown, *R.L. 15 C.*, p. 123: Davies, p. 218.
B. *Pr.* J. Williams, *N. & Q.*, 2nd Ser., ix (1860), 439.
C. Music for two and three voices. *Pr.* Greene, *Selection*, p. 62; with music, Stevens, *Med. Carols*, p. 52.
D. (fragment) Music for two and three voices. *Previously unpublished.*
B.-R. 340.
The burden proper to C is probably only the first two of the four lines found in the MS. and here printed, as the music calls for only two lines and the chorus-repeats of the burden do not include more. M. F. Bukofzer has established the rule for the texts of polyphonic carols that no words not in the initial burden are introduced into the chorus-repeats. The scribe of the Egerton MS. probably had in mind or in hand a version with different music or with none which did include the second pair of lines. There may well be influence from No. 31, which is the only other carol to use the line 'Consors paterni luminis' from a hymn for Matins on the Tuesday after the Octave of Epiphany (*Hym. S.*, p. 47) and which has as the first line of its burden a line very much like the first line of B. For a fuller discussion of the relations of the three texts see R. L. Greene, review of Stevens, *Med. Carols*, *J.A.M.S.* vii (1954)), 80–2.

Text C, though inferior to the other two, probably represents the earliest form of the carol. The recovery of this text invalidates Brown's statement that 'the arrangement in Harley seems to be correct' (p. 320). The burden of B is a commonplace, apparently substituted when the earlier burden was made into, or mistaken for, a first stanza. The finding of the Egerton text confirms the note in the first edition of this work that A represents the original arrangement (p. 357). A has four stanzas (2, 5, 7, 8), B three (1, 5, 7) which are not in C.

Except for the hymn-line already mentioned and the phrase 'Ecce ancilla Domini', the Latin lines appear not to be borrowed but to have been composed with the English lines to make a true macaronic poem.

stza. 6, l. 1. This odd line undoubtedly results from a misreading of the 'For he was man' that appears in stza. 9, l. 1 of B. Note also 'For he was man' in stza. 4, l. 1 of Ryman's No. 127. The following Latin line has been adjusted here by the insertion of 'qui'. The 'incensum' of both texts should, of course, be 'myrrham'. ll. 2, 3. There seems to be a definite echo of this passage in stza. 5 of the priest Sir Richard Shanne's 'Christmas Caroll' (1611):

> To seeke that babe they tooke the waie,
> They had good speede in theyr Jurney,
> > Stella micanta par via.
> > > (*pr.* Hyder E. Rollins, *PMLA*, xxxviii, 1923, 141)

See also note on No. 127, stza. 1, ll. 1, 2.

24. Of the Nativity

Pr. Wright, *Wart. Club*, p. 9, *P.S.* iv, 'Christmas Carols', 5; B. Fehr, *Archiv*, cvii (1901), 48; Sandys, *Carols*, p. 6; John Julian, *A Dictionary of Hymnology*, 2nd edn. (London, 1925), p. 208. B.-R. 527.

25. Of the Nativity

Pr. Wright, *Wart. Club*, p. 34; B. Fehr, *Archiv*, cix (1902), 51; Sitwell, *Atlantic Book*, p. 11; Sisam, p. 436. B.-R. 3472.

The highly repetitive character of this carol, so like that of traditional game-songs, indicates that its author was imitating closely the methods of folk-song. This is emphasized by the occurrence of the carol in the MS. among other pieces which are not carols, but which use the same device of repetition and are even more obviously affected by folk-song, e.g. 'I haue a yong suster', which precedes the carol, and 'I haue an newe gardyn', which follows it. Compare also Nos. 27, 54.

There is no reason to suppose, with Stephen Manning, that 'two singers might have alternated singing the stanzas.' His statement that 'the thought in the first two stanzas practically repeats itself, as it does in the last two' is quite unintelligible (*Wisdom and Number*, Lincoln, Nebraska, 1962, p. 24).

The allusions to the canonical hours may have been suggested by the traditional correspondence of the events of the Passion to the several hours, but they do not conform. The Sarum *De Horis Canonicis Hymnus* (*Br. Sar.* iii, cxxxi), for instance, has Sext as the hour for the fixing to the cross and None as the time of the piercing.

stza. 1, l. 4. *wem*: stain.

26. Of the Nativity

Pr. first edition. B.-R. 226.

stza. 1, l. 4. Probably from Luke ii. 16.

stza. 2, l. 1. *loure*: look of pain.

stza. 3, ll. 1, 2. Mary's age at the time of her marriage was set at fourteen by one medieval tradition, in accordance with the Pseudo-Gospel of Matthew, viii. 1. The Book of James, however, sets it at twelve (viii. 2, 3), and Lydgate's *Life of Our Lady* (Cambridge University Library, MS. Mm. 6. 5, stza. 215) fixes her age at the Nativity at sixteen.

stza. 4, l. 1. *Nere*: were it not that. Compare No. 398, stza. 6, l. 1.

27. Of the Nativity

A. *Pr* Wright, *Wart. Club*, p. 68, *P.S.* iv, 'Christmas Carols', 11; Dyboski, p. 170.
B. *Pr.* first edition.

C. *Pr.* Dyboski, p. 7; Flügel, *Fest.*, p. 61, 'Lieder.', p. 231; Frost, p. 262.
B.–R. 1575.
The repetition of the opening formula in each stanza is probably in this, as in other carols, an imitation of folk-song style.
A. stza. 5, l. 4. *tour*: i.e. heaven.
B. stza. 3, ll. 2, 3. There may be an echo of these lines in the priest Sir Richard Shanne's 'Christmas Carroll', 'Come, love we god of might is most' (1611), stza. 3, ll. 1, 2:

> The hirde men come with theyr offring,
> ffor to present *that* pretie thinge.
>   (*pr.* Hyder E. Rollins, *PMLA*, xxxviii, 1923, 141)

B. stza. 5. The failure of the sense at the end of B is paralleled by a sudden change for the worse in the writing. The hand is the same as that of the other stanzas, but the scribe is evidently less master of himself.

28. Of the Nativity

Pr. Wright, *Wart. Club*, p. 80, *P.S.* iv, 'Christmas Carols', 14; Greene, *Selection*, p. 63. B.–R. 3643.
stza. 4, ll. 3, 4. This wholly unhistorical reference to the presence of the prophets at the Circumcision is probably the result of the writer's acquaintance with some form of dramatic service or procession of the prophets in which they appeared in appropriate costumes. See Karl Young, *The Drama of the Medieval Church* (Oxford, 1933), chap. xxi. As Young points out (ii. 153–4), this observance took place in some churches, notably Tours and Rouen, on the Feast of the Circumcision. The author of the carol has apparently taken somewhat literally the symbolic marshalling of the prophets which is based ultimately on the famous pseudo-Augustinian sermon *Contra Judaeos, Paganos, et Arianos.*

29. Of the Nativity

Music for two voices. *Pr.* Padelford, p. 87; with music, *E.B.M.* ii. 104, *facs.* No. xlv; Terry p. 32; *O.B.C.*, Music Edn., p. 128; J. Copley, *Seven English Songs and Carols of the Fifteenth Century*, Leeds School of English Language Texts and Monographs, No. 6 (Leeds, 1940), p. 16; Stevens, *Med. Carols*, p. 11; Robbins, *Christmas Carols*, p. 32; Noah Greenberg, *An English Song Book* (Garden City, New York, 1961), p. 68. B.–R. 753.
The unusual palindromic arrangement of the rhymes should be noted: stza. 1 rhymes with stza. 5, stza. 2 rhymes with stza. 4, and stza. 3 stands alone.
The Latin phrases at the beginnings of the stanzas are from the Christmas services. Compare No. 474.
stza. 4, l. 2. *his pynon pyght*: set up his pennon.

30. Of the Nativity

A. Music for three voices. *Pr.* Padelford, p. 96; C. & S., p. 115; Greene, *Selection*, p. 64; Davies, p. 195; Oliver, p. 115; Gray, *Themes and Images*, p. 96, *Lyrics*, p. 7; with music, *E.B.M.* ii. 124; *facs.* No. lx; Terry, p. 34; Stevens, *Med. Carols*, p. 18; Robbins, *Christmas Carols*, p. 18; *facs.* F. Blume, *Die Musik in Geschichte und Gegenwart* (Kessel and Basel, 1952), ii. 857–8.
B. Music for two voices. *Pr.*, with music, Stevens, *Med. Carols*, p. 114.
B.–R. 2733.
Douglas Gray gives a brief and sound critical commentary on this carol and points out its indebtedness to Romans xiii. [12], used as an Epistle in Advent (*Themes and Images*, pp. 96–8).
stza. 1, ll. 1, 2. These lines occur with slight variation in No. 74, stza. 1, ll. 1, 2, by James Ryman.
l. 4. *bereth the belle.* This common phrase denoting excellence is variously explained. Grose (*A Classical Dictionary of the Vulgar Tongue*, ed. E. Partridge, London, 1931, p. 32) calls it an allusion to the custom of putting a bell on the harness of the lead-horse of a team. Gomme (*The Gentleman's Magazine Library*, London, 1886, ii. 90) and others think it refers to the giving of a bell as the prize for country races. *O.E.D.* suggests that it may be from 'bell-wether'. The sense of carrying off a prize (literal or metaphorical) for excellence is clearly its meaning in the much admired refrain, 'The bailey beareth the bell away', where the North Bailey at Durham is being praised. See the

important text and exposition of the much misinterpreted poem (from the same MS. as Carol No. 445), B. Colgrave and C. E. Wright, 'An Elizabethan Poem About Durham', *The Durham University Journal*, xxxii (1940), 161–8, and Madeleine Hope Dodds, 'Some Notes on "An Elizabethan Poem About Durham" ', ibid. xxxiii (1940), 65–7.

31. Of the Nativity

a. Music for two voices. *Pr.* Padelford, p. 97; Greene, *Selection*, p. 65; with music, *E.B.M.* i. 122, *facs.* No. lx; Terry, p. 28; *O.B.C.*, Music Edn., p. 46; Stevens, *Med. Carols*, p. 19; Robbins, *Christmas Carols*, p. 28.

b. *Pr.* Wright, *P.S.* xxiii. 48; Padelford, p. 98.

c. Music for two and three voices. *Pr.* Wright, *P.S.* iv, 'Christmas Carols', 57; Fehr, p. 270; Padelford, p. 98; with music, Stevens, *Med. Carols*, p. 85; Robbins, *Christmas Carols*, p. 25. B.-R. 18.

For the sources of the Latin lines see table in Introduction, pp. lxxxvi–lxxxviii. The arrangement of the Latin as first and fourth lines of couplet-rhymed stanzas is unique in the carols.

32. Of the Nativity

Music for two voices. *Pr.* Padelford, p. 108; with music, *E.B.M.* ii. 146, *facs.* No. lxxviii; Terry, p. 4; Stevens, *Med. Carols*, p. 23. B.-R. 3619.

33. Of the Nativity

Music for two and three voices. *Pr.* Padelford, p. 112; Oliver, p. 30; with music, *E.B.M.* ii. 157, *facs.* No. lxxxvii; Stevens, *Med. Carols*, p. 28; Robbins, *Christmas Carols*, p. 42. B.-R. 93.

The Latin lines are better assimilated to the English context than those in many macaronic carols, particularly those in the tail-rhyme stanza. For sources see table in Introduction, pp. lxxxvi–lxxxviii.

stza. 6, ll. 1, 2. Barbara C. Raw points to these lines as one of the rare examples in English lyrics of the idea of silence at the conception of Christ, which is the theme of the much praised 'I Sing of a Mayden' ('As Dew in Aprille', *M.L.R.* lv, 1960, 413).

34. Of the Nativity

Music for two voices. *Pr.* Padelford, p. 112; Brown, *R.L. 15 C.*, p. 118; with music, *E.B.M.* ii. 158, *facs.* No. lxxxviii; Stevens, *Med. Carols*, p. 29; Robbins, *Christmas Carols*, p. 34. B.-R. 3283.

The name 'Childe' is written above the music in the MS. It has been taken to be the name of a composer, but it may equally well be a mark of ownership. See the description of the MS. in the Bibliography of Original Sources, p. 315.

35. Of the Navitity

A. *Pr. E.B.M.* ii. 65; C. & S., p. 132.

B. *Pr.* Dyboski, p. 49; Flügel, *Fest.*, p. 82, 'Lieder.', p. 268; Pollard, p. 95. B.-R. 63, 3635.

A. stza. 1, l. 2. *more*: root. Compare *Sir Beves*, ll. 70, 71 (cited *O.E.D.*, s.v. 'More', *sb.*[1]):

> A ffeyrer child was nevure none bore,
> Sithe god spronge of Jesses more.

'Thorn', the reading of B, is probably due to the necessity of a rhyme with the form 'born'.

A. stza. 4. This appears as stza. 5 of No. 123 A (B, stza. 11) and as stza. 6 of No. 124 A, where it is more appropriate. The sequence referred to is probably that for the Mass on Epiphany, of which ll. 9, 10 run (*Sar. Miss.*, p. 465):

> Huic magi munera deferunt preclara aurum simul thus et myrram.
> Thure deum predicant. auro regem magnum. hominem mortalem myrra.

B. burden, l. 2, and refrain. John i. 14.

36. Of the Nativity

a. *Pr. Rel. Ant.* i. 203.
b. *Pr.* Wright, *P.S.* iv, 'Christmas Carols', 33; C. & S., p. 118.
c. Collated in first edition.
B.–R. 463.
burden, l. 1. From the Office of the Mass for Christmas Day (*Sar. Miss.*, p. 29): 'Puer natus est nobis et filius datus est nobis . . .' l. 2. This phrase is of frequent occurrence, but it had especial prominence as the refrain of a favourite *cantilena* of the eleventh century, 'In hoc anno circulo'. In a translation of the song into a Southern French dialect the Latin phrase was retained (G. Thurau, *Der Refrain in der französischen Chanson*, Berlin, 1901, p. 278).

37. Of the Nativity

Pr. Wright, *P.S.* xxiii. 15; Sisam, p. 469. B.–R. 34.
The end of the stanza, with the short refrain-line 'With aye' and the couplet of one repeated and one varied line, shows influence of the bob-and-wheel stanza of narrative verse.
stza. 3, l. 6. See note on No. 72, stza. 4, ll. 1–3.
stza. 5, l. 6. Both myrrh and incense are here related to Christ's manhood. The incense is traditionally the sign of His Godhead. See note on No. 47, stza. 5, l. 3.

38. Of the Nativity

Pr. Wright, *P.S.* xxiii. 17. B.–R. 3630.
burden, l. 2. John i. 14.
stza. 1, l. 1. *lete*: opposition.
stza. 3, l. 4. Mary's singing 'into the est' is an unusual detail of the Nativity scene. It may be in anticipation of the coming of the Magi, or because of the Star, or simply because of Mary's own association with that direction, as in her correspondence to the closed gate of Ezekiel's vision, which was the eastern gate.

39. Of the Nativity

Pr. Wright, *P.S.* xxiii. 21. B.–R. 997.
burden, l. 2. John i. 14.
stza. 4, l. 3. *prophett*: Isaiah is the one in mind.

39.1. Of the Nativity

Music for two voices; *pr.* Greene, *Selection*, p. 68; with music, Stevens, *Med. Carols*, p. 36. B.–R. *Supp.* 2674. 5.
This carol is unique in being trilingually macaronic throughout and in having less than a quarter of its words in English. With the exception of the single word 'noël', which had become thoroughly naturalized, French words and phrases are extremely rare in the carols. Fewer than a dozen carols contain any French at all, and such expressions as are used are of the simplest kind. See Introduction, p. xxxvi.
stza. 1, l. 1. Psalm xlvii. 1. This phrase begins a set of macaronic couplets calling for drink in the carol-manuscript B.M. Sloane 2593, ff. 10ᵛ, 11ʳ.:

> Omnes gentes plaudite;
> I saw myny bryddis setyn on a tre.

stza. 2, l. 2. *le*: wide.
stza. 5, l. 2. *Fortime*: Most strong or very strong.

40. Of the Nativity

A. *Pr.* Wright, *P.S.* xxiii. 39; C. & S., p. 117.
B. *Previously unpublished.*
B.–R. 76.
burden, l. 1. *lay*: religion, belief, from OF. *lei* in sense of 'religious law'.

stza. 1, l. 1. *gylt*. The context demands the sense of 'guilty person', but *O.E.D.* does not record this meaning of the word.

41. Of the Nativity

Pr. Wright, *P.S.* xxiii. 42; C. & S., p. 140. B.–R. 3344.
The burden also appears as the burden of No. 183.
stzas. 3–5. The author badly confuses the events of the Passion, the wounding with a spear being transferred from the Crucifixion to the mockery and flagellation.

42. Of the Nativity

a. *Pr.* Wright, *P.S.* xxiii. 83.
b. *Repr. facs.* Reed, p. 46.
B.–R. 3876.
stza. 1, l. 3. *reformer of owr reste*: improver of our spiritual peace.

43. Of the Nativity

Pr. C. & S., p. 133; Brown, *R.L. 15 C.*, p. 119. B.–R. 4065 (lists a second MS. in error, corrected in B.–R. *Supp.*).
burden, l. 1. Compare No. 255, burden, l. 1. Compare the exclamatory use of 'tidings' in a stage direction of the play 'King Herod' in *Ludus Coventriae* (ed. K. S. Block, E.E.T.S., Ex. Ser., No. cxx, 1922, p. 273: 'here xal A massanger com in-to þe place rennyng and criyng Tydyngys.'
stza. 2, l. 4. *Jure*: Jewry, Judea. Bethlehem is meant; the line may have read originally 'of Jure'.
stza. 3, ll. 1, 2. With this conception of the prophets as aware of and rejoicing in the Nativity compare No. 28, stza. 4, ll. 3, 4, and note thereon.

44. Of the Nativity

Pr. Wright, *P.S.* xxiii. 82; C. & S., p. 136; Davies, p. 222. B.–R. 998.
The unusual stanza-form of this carol shows definite influence from the bob-and-wheel stanza of narrative verse.
stza. 3, l. 1. *Two sons togyther*. This figure probably results from the combination in the writer's mind of the 'sol de stella' of the 'Laetabundus' prose and the favourite 'sun through glass' simile for Mary's conception of Jesus.
stza. 5, l. 1. *noblay*: nobility.

45. Of the Nativity

Pr. Dyboski, p. 3; Flügel, *N.L.*, p. 117, *Fest.*, p. 55, 'Lieder.', p. 195. B.–R. 103.
stza. 2, ll. 4, 5. The acknowledgement of Christ's majesty by the ox and the ass is told in the Pseudo-Gospel of Matthew, xiv. l. 6. A particularly attractive passage on this derivative detail of the animals' care for the infant is found in Nicholas Love's *The Mirrour of the Blessed Life of Jesu Christ* in its chapter on the Nativity:

And anone the Oxe and the Asse/ knelynge doun/ leyden her mowthes on the cracche/ brethynge at hir neses upon the child/ as they knewen by resoun that in that colde tyme the childe so sympely hiled had nede to be hatte in that manere (quoted by Elizabeth Zeeman, 'Nicholas Love—A Fifteenth-century Translator', *R.E.S.*, New Ser., vi, 1955, 119).

stza. 3, l. 2. *abone*: above. ll. 4, 5. i.e. the Virgin alone among women escaped the pangs of childbirth, as recorded in Pseudo-Matthew, xiii. Other carols which mention this circumstance are Nos. 25, 26, 37, 65, 67, 233, 246.

46. Of the Nativity

Pr. Dyboski, p. 8; Flügel, *N.L.*, p. 116, *Fest.*, p. 63, 'Lieder.', p. 234; Frost, p. 266. B.–R. 2097.
burden, l. 2. See note on No. 36, burden, l. 1.
stza. 7. Compare No. 90, stza. 3.

47. Of the Nativity

Pr. Dyboski, p. 29; Flügel, *Fest.*, p. 74, 'Lieder.', p. 253. B.–R. 916.

stza. 4, l. 3. *Caldey*: Chaldea. *felosafers*: the Magi, more commonly called kings, as in stza. 5.

stza. 5, l. 3. Priesthood is the less usual of the two meanings variously assigned to the gift of incense, the other being Christ's Godhead. This interpretation is orthodox and recognized, however; compare the Response after the sixth Lectio in Matins for Epiphany (*Br. Sar.* i, col. cccxxiv):

> In auro ut ostendatur regis potentia:
> in thure sacerdotem magnum considera.
> Et in mirra Dominicam sepulturam.

The doctrine of Christ's priesthood concerns itself with the sacrificial aspect of His life and death and would be a natural reference for a writer who wished to emphasize, as in this carol, the human qualities of the Saviour.

Compare also *Cursor Mundi* (Trinity text), ll. 11497–9 (ed. R. Morris, E.E.T.S., Or. Ser., Nos. 57 etc., 1874–93):

> Melchior coom alþer neest
> And kud he was boþe god & prest
> Wiþ sense bifore him he felle,

and a late fifteenth-century *noël* by Jehan Tisserant (Bibliothèque Nationale, MS. français 2368, f. 45ᵛ):

> L'or demonstre qu'il est roy,
> L'encens qu'il est le grant prestre.

48. Of the Nativity

Pr. Dyboski, p. 37; Flügel, *Fest.*, p. 77, 'Lieder.', p. 260; C. & S., p. 139; Brougham, p. 8. B.–R. 825.

The fleur-de-lis or lily is a frequent symbol for Christ. Compare 'Maiden Mary and her Fleur-de-Lys' from the Vernon MS. (*pr.* Brown, *R.L. 14 C.*, p. 181), where the plant is likened to Mary, the blossom to Christ. As here, each stanza ends with the word 'fleur-de-lys'.

49. Of the Nativity

Pr. Dyboski, p. 9; Flügel, *Fest.*, p. 64, 'Lieder.', p. 235. B.–R. 3473.

burden. See table in Introduction, pp. lxxxvii, lxxxviii. The same Latin couplet appears as the burden of a Latin Nativity song in Bibliothèque de l'Arsenal MS. 3653, f. 9ᵛ (cent. xv, late), also as the burden of the Latin *cantilena* beginning 'Salve, festa dies, partus virginalis', in B.M. MS. Egerton 3307, f. 67ᵛ, *pr.* Stevens, *Med. Carols*, No. 67, pp. 54–5.

stza. 2, l. 3. *cure*: care.

stza. 3, l. 2. *knelyng in her closett*. The Annunciation is variously represented in medieval art as taking place in a garden or within doors. See note on No. 172, stza. 2, l. 4. Albertus Magnus claimed to settle the matter in his *Liber de Laudibus Gloriosissime Dei Genitricis Marie*, etc. (Basle, 1475), cap. lxiii: '*Si ostio clauso venit et si ad solam et in qua positione fuit*', etc. 'Ad primum respondemus per beatum Bernardum qui dicit: ingressus ad eam puto in secretarium pudici cubiculi vbi illa forsan clauso super se ostio orabat patrem suum in abscondito[.] solent angeli astare orantibus. . . . [Dicit Bernardus etiam:] Beatissimam autem virginem in aduentu eius inclinatis genibus et eleuatis puris manibus erectis in celum oculis . . . deuotissimas preces cum lacrimis fudisse.' The writer of this carol follows him.

50. Of the Nativity

Pr. Dyboski, p. 38; Flügel, *Fest.*, p. 78, 'Lieder.', p. 260; Pollard, p. 92. B.–R. 1601.

stza. 3, l. 1. *crach*: crib.

51. Of the Nativity

Pr. Dyboski, p. 45; Flügel, *Fest.*, p. 80, 'Lieder.', p. 265; Frost, p. 259; Greene, *Selection*, p. 66. B.–R. 2346.

The use of 'wassail' in religious carols is so rare in comparison with its occurrence in traditional folk-song for Christmas that one suspects that its pagan associations were still felt strongly enough to cause disapproval. 'Yule', on the other hand, is freely used.

52. Of the Nativity

Pr. Dyboski, p. 49; Flügel, *Fest.*, p. 82, 'Lieder.', p. 271; Pollard, p. 96. B.–R. 608.
For the sources of the Latin lines see table in Introduction, pp. lxxxvi–lxxxviii.

53. Of the Nativity

Pr. Zupitza, 210, notes, xciv, 395–6. B.–R. 3585.

54. Of the Nativity

Pr. Zupitza, 275, notes, xcvi, 167–8. B.–R. 2122.
The use of a repetitive formula at the beginning of the stanza is like that of No. 25, on which see note.
stza. 6, l. 3. *meane*: intermediary, intercessor.

55. Of the Nativity

Pr. Zupitza, 292, notes, xcvi, 316–17. B.–R. 2310.
Stza. 4 is Ryman's own paraphrase of the 'Gloria in Excelsis'.

56. The Mystery of the Incarnation

Pr. Zupitza, 293, notes, xcvi, 317–19. B.–R. 3334.
burden. Compare the burdens of Nos. 94, 176, 319.
stza. 5, l. 1. The statement that the glass is not only unharmed but 'more pure' is an unusual strengthening of the hackneyed figure. 'And' is for 'than', according to *O.E.D.* 'an erroneous expansion of northern dial. *an, en*'.

57. Of the Nativity

Music for two and three voices. *Pr.* Fehr, p. 272; with music, Stevens, *Med. Carols*, p. 91; Robbins, *Christmas Carols*, p. 39. B.–R. 3737.
The rhyme fails in stza. 1, l. 1. The whole line is possibly corrupt.
burden, ll. 1, 3. Compare No. 239, stza. 1, l. 1.

58. Of the Nativity

Music for two and three voices, by Richard Smert. *Pr.* Fehr, p. 272; with music, Stevens, *Med. Carols*, p. 92. B.–R. 31.

59. Of the Nativity

Music for two and three voices, by Richard Smert. *Pr.* Fehr, p. 278; with music, Stevens, *Med. Carols*, p. 109; Robbins, *Christmas Carols*, p. 36. B.–R. 581.

59.1. Of the Nativity

Previously unpublished. Not in B.–R. or *Supp.*
This rather crude and amateurishly written carol is probably among the earliest in the collection. It may have been written down before 1400. It has been written on a fly-leaf of a neat but not costly psalter with calendar. See *Report of the Tenth Congress of the International Musicological Society* (Ljubljana, Yugoslavia, 1970), p. 305.
stza. 3. This stanza phrases quite dryly the popular tradition of Joseph as ineffectual at the actual birth: 'He entrusted his son to ox and ass.'

60. Of the Nativity

Repr. Flügel, *Anglia*, xii (1889) 588, *N.L.*, p. 125; *facs.* Reed, p. 15. B.–R. *Supp.* 1575.5.

60.1. Of the Nativity

Pr. R. H. Robbins, *PMLA*, lxxxi (1966), 309. B.–R. *Supp.* 2635. 5.

There can be no doubt of Ryman's authorship of this carol, as asserted by Robbins, who points to parallels in Nos. 53, 61, 62, 91 (p. 308 n. 6). It joins the group of Nativity carols which relate a summary, usually scanty, of the life and death of Christ. The burden and refrain link it to Ryman's group of carols on the *Te Deum* (Nos. 285–304).

stza. 1, l. 1. *lesyng*: lying.

61. Of the Nativity

Pr. Zupitza, 212, notes, xciv, 397–9. B.–R. 3332.

stza. 4, ll. 1, 2. Compare No. 163, stza. 1.

62. Of the Nativity

Pr. Zupitza, 214, notes, xciv, 401–2. B.–R. 3467.

63. Of the Nativity

Pr. Zupitza, 324, notes, xcvii, 141. B.–R. 3470.

For the use of 'alone' compare Nos. 154, 159, 160, 249, 281.

stza. 6, l. 2. *Old faders*: the patriarchs awaiting their release from limbo.

64. 'A Caroll of the Byrth of Chryst'

Repr. Flügel, *Anglia*, xii (1889), 588; *facs.* Reed, p. 10. B.–R. 107.

The text is incomplete, as the page following in the preserved fragment contains part of another piece. It is probable, however, that only two lines are lost, for what remains of stza. 5 is in a conventional formula for final stanzas.

65. Of the Nativity

Pr. Zupitza, 186, notes, xciii, 390–3. B.–R. 546.

The burden is that of a Latin song with music in Bodleian Library MSS. Ashmole 1393 and Arch. Selden B. 26, *pr.* *E.B.M.* ii. 63, 154. See Introduction, p. cx. The first stanza of this carol is a paraphrase of the Latin.

stza. 2, l. 3. *valent*: vigorous, flourishing. *O.E.D.* gives this as the only citation.

66. Of the Nativity

Pr. Zupitza, 185, notes, xciii, 383–90; Greene, *Selection*, p. 67. B.–R. 488.

The burden is the same as that of No. 65, on which see note.

stza. 3. Isaiah vii. 14.

stza. 5. Matthew i. 23.

stza. 9. Ryman is well informed in associating this figure with St. Anselm, even though the passage may not be found in an acknowledged work. R. W. Southern calls it 'a simile much used in the school of Anselm' and quotes this exchange from B.M. MS. Royal 8. A. IV (cent. xv):

> Heretici obiectio in Ancelmum:
>
> Nunquam natura mutare solet sua iura,
> Ut virgo pareret quin virginitate careret.
>
> Responsio Ancelmi:
>
> Radio solari nequit vitrum violari
> nec vitrum sole nec virgo puerpera prole.

('St. Anselm and His English Pupils', *Mediaeval and Renaissance Studies*, i, 1943, 10)

Dr. R. W. Hunt kindly pointed out this vindication of Ryman's learning.

67. Of the Nativity

Pr. Zupitza, 272, notes, xcvi, 165–6. B.–R. 3450.

stza. 3, l. 3. *lake*: dungeon, underground prison.

stza. 5, ll. 3, 4. See note on No. 45, stza. 3, ll. 4, 5.

stza. 6, l. 1. *destence*: sense of rank, here implying condescension.

68. Of the Nativity

Pr. Wright, *Wart. Club*, p. 7; B. Fehr, *Archiv*, cix (1902), 43. B.–R. 118.

stza. 1, ll. 2, 3. With 'man' for 'Adam' these lines appear as stza. 3, ll. 1, 2, of No. 335.

stza. 2, l. 3. The patriarchs are particularly mentioned because of the teaching that they had to abide in hell or limbo until the coming of Christ.

stza. 4, l. 1. Moses is properly enough called a prophet (Deuteronomy xxxiv. 10–12) but did not expressly foretell the Nativity as here stated.

stza. 5, l. 1. *Isaac*: an obvious blunder for Isaiah.

stza. 6, l. 1. Jeremiah began his prophetic career at an early age. He was not, however, so explicitly a Messianic prophet as the carol states. See Jeremiah xxxi. 15–22.

stza. 7, l. 2. Daniel is counted as a particular prophet of the Messiah by virtue of his 'prophecy of the seventy weeks' (Daniel ix. 24–7).   l. 3. *spelle*: speak.

69. Of the Nativity

Music for two and three voices. *Pr.* Padelford, p. 113; with music, *E.B.M.* ii. 160, *facs.* No. lxxxix; Stevens, *Med. Carols*, p. 30. B.–R. 3659.

burden. See table in Introduction, p. lxxxviii.

stza. 3. This statement would, of course, be justified by many passages in the works of St. Ambrose, or indeed of almost any other theological writer, but capp. v–xiii of his *De Institutione Virginis Liber Unus* may be instanced (*Pat. Lat.* xvi, cols. 327–39).

stza. 4, ll. 1–3. Psalm lxxxv. 11: 'Veritas de terra orta est.'   l. 1. *spellynge*: speaking.

70. Of the Nativity

Pr. Zupitza, 203, notes, xciv, 200–2. B.–R. 3724.

stza. 1, l. 3. Isaiah vii. 14.

stza. 2, ll. 1, 2. Jeremiah x. 6.

stza. 3, l. 1. See notes on No. 72.

stza. 4. Psalms cxxxviii. 4, cxlviii. 11.

stza 5. Daniel ii. 34.

71. Of the Nativity

Pr. Zupitza, 209, notes, xcv, 391–2. B.–R. 67.

stza. 3, l. 2. Ryman's reference is probably to John xiv.

72. The Prophecies Fulfilled

Pr. Zupitza, 274, notes, xcvi, 166–7. B.–R. 3620.

stza. 1, ll. 1, 2. Daniel ii. 34.

stza. 2, ll. 1–3. Isaiah vii. 14.

stza. 3, l. 1. Jeremiah x. 6.

stza. 4, ll. 1–3. On the interesting history of the supposed prophecy by Habakkuk that Christ should be born in the presence of an ox and an ass see John Williams, in *N. & Q.*, 2nd Ser., x (1860), 456, in answer to a query on the opening lines of the Christmas song in B.M. MS. Cotton Vespasian A. xxv, f. 138ʳ (*pr.* Wright, *P.S.* iv, 'Christmas Carols', 36):

> As said the prophet Abacuc,
> Betwixt too bestes shulde lye our buk.

It appears in a *Tractus* in the Good Friday service: 'In medio duorum animalium innotesceris.' It is based on a passage in Habakkuk iii. 2 which rests on a mistranslation of the Hebrew text found only in the Septuagint and older Latin translations. The Pseudo-Gospel of Matthew xiv applies it to the Nativity.

stza. 5, ll. 1–3. Psalm cxxxviii. 4, cxlviii. 11.

73. Of the Nativity

Music for two and three voices. *Pr.* Padelford, p. 106; with music, *E.B.M.* ii. 140, *facs.* Nos. lxxiv, lxxv; Stevens, *Med. Carols*, p. 22. B.–R. 81.

stza. 3, l. 2. David is included among the prophets by virtue of the 'Messianic' psalms. On Jeremiah see note on No. 68, stza. 6, l. 1.   l. 3. Isaiah vii. 14.

stzas. 4, 5. The Presentation in the Temple, Luke ii. 22–38.

stza. 5, l. 1. *lece*: falsehood.

stza. 6, l. 2. *grene branche*: the Virgin. The figure here is the same as in Hoccleve's poem 'A Lamentacioun of the Grene Tree Complaynyng of the Losyng of hire Appil' translated from the *Pèlerinage de la vie humaine* (ed. F. J. Furnivall, E.E.T.S., Ex. Ser., No. lxxii, 1897, p. xxxvii). Mary is the green tree, the cross the dry tree, Jesus the fruit of one hanged on the other. The figure has obvious relations to the 'rose of ryse' and 'Aaron's rod'.

74. Of the Nativity

Pr. Zupitza, 206, notes, xciv, 203–5. B.–R. 2734.

stza. 1, ll. 1, 2. These lines occur with slight variation in No. 30, stza. 1, ll. 1, 2.

75. Of the Shepherds

Pr. Zupitza, 197, notes, xciv, 188–90; Davies, p. 229. B.–R. 3837.

This is one of the most successful macaronic carols, continuous sense being kept in alternate English and Latin. The Latin lines are not mere borrowings from the Gospel, although Ryman follows closely the account in Luke ii. 8–20. See Introduction, p. lxxxii.

76. Of the Shepherds

Pr. Zupitza, 199, notes, xciv, 190–3. B.–R. 3930.

stza. 5, l. 1. *stounde*: hour, time.

77. Of the Shepherds

Pr. Dyboski, p. 48; Flügel, *Fest.*, p. 81, 'Lieder.', p. 267, Pollard, p. 94. B.–R. 343.

This carol uses the *chanson d'aventure* opening and is one of the comparatively rare instances of the ballade stanza being adapted to the carol form by the addition of a burden.

burden, l. 2. Psalm lxxxv. 11, used as an Antiphon in Matins on Christmas Day (*Br. Sar.* i, col. clxxvii).

stza. 1, l. 4. *fee*: beasts, flock.

stza. 2, l. 2. This appears as stza. 1, l. 8 of No. 161.   l. 7. Isaiah xl. 1, in the second Lectio for Matins on Christmas Day (*Br. Sar.* i, col. clxxiv): 'Consolamini, consolamini, popule meus, dicit Deus vester.'

stza. 3, l. 1: *see*: seat.   l. 3. *medled*: mingled.   l. 5. *Miranda res*: from the 'Laetabundus' prose; see Introduction, p. xcviii.   l. 6. *gest*: tale.

78. Jolly Wat the Shepherd

Pr. Dyboski, p. 16; Flügel, *N.L.*, p. 117, *Fest.*, p. 76, 'Lieder.', p. 243; Pollard, p. 87; C. & S., p. 127; A. S. Cook, *A Literary Middle English Reader* (Boston, 1915), p. 468; Frost, p. 270; Lord David Cecil, *The Oxford Book of Christian Verse* (Oxford, 1940), p. 2; Frank Kermode, *English Pastoral Poetry* (London, 1952), p. 50; Greene, *Selection*, p. 69; Sisam, p. 526; Silverstein, p. 115; Gray, *Themes and Images*, p. 116, *Lyrics*, p. 9. B.–R. 3460.

The carol of Wat is justly famous for its gaiety and realism. Its similarity in conception and tone to the shepherd scenes in the mystery plays is striking. The occurrence of the Northern word 'warroke' and the payment of twopence to actors playing 'Joly Wat and Malkyn' at York in 1447 suggest that the original home of the carol may have been Yorkshire (Lucy Toulmin Smith, ed.,

York Plays, Oxford, 1885, p. xxxviii). The offering of homely gifts to the infant Jesus is paralleled as well in various French *noëls*, e.g. J. R. H. de Smidt, *Les Noëls et la tradition populaire* (Amsterdam, 1932), Nos. 9A, 10, 19A. Acquaintance with mystery plays is probably responsible for the introduction of the incident in this carol and in a well-known *noël* by Jehan Tisserant in Bibliothèque Nationale MS. français 2368, f. 67^r (stza. 7):

> Je luy donnay vng vray don,
>> Nau, nau,
> Mon billart *et* ma pellote,
> Et Guillot mon compagnon,
>> Nau, nau,
> Sa trude et sa marote.

The wish to provide an analogy to the gifts of the Magi is doubtless the ultimate reason for the use of the incident.

stza. 1, l. 1. This line seems to have survived as the first line of a round in Ravenscroft's *Pammelia* (1609); see note on No. 79, burden, l. 1.　l. 3. *flagat*: flask.　l. 6. The 'vith' of this line in all stanzas has been printed by many editors as 'vt'. But a 'v' for 'w' is not to be wondered at. Compare Alfred Williams, *Folk-Songs of the Upper Thames* (London, 1923), Introduction, p. 19: 'Many old singers invariably said *chorius* for chorus, and substituted *v* for *w*, saying *ven* and *Villiam* for when and William.'

stza. 2, l. 3. *broyd*: brayd, short time.

stza. 4, l. 1. Mall appears to be a favourite ewe (compare Chaucer's *Nun's Priest's Tale*, l. 11); Will, the bell-wether.

stza. 5, l. 4. *warroke*: warroch (Sc.). a stunted or puny child, here apparently applied by Wat to his helper. See John Jamieson, *An Etymological Dictionary of the Scottish Language* (Paisley, 1879–82), s.v. 'Warroch'.

stza. 8, l. 2. The rhyme demands the transposition of 'scrype' and 'skyrte' instead of the MS. reading.

stza. 9, l. 4. *cape*: cope, cloak. This line has attracted some attention because of its bit of visual detail. It may be a reminiscence of the costume given Joseph in a mystery play, as suggested by W. J. Phillips (*Carols: Their Origin, Music, and Connection with Mystery Plays*, London, [1921], p. 108), hardly, as Esmé Wingfield-Stratford thinks, a reference to his 'round hat' or halo in a church window (*The History of British Civilization*, London, 1930, pp. 350–1). Douglas Gray aptly refers to the phrase from the alliterative *Morte Arthure*: '"a renke in a rounde cloke", i.e. one with no train or skirts' (*N. & Q.* ccviii, 1963, 431).

The first stanza appears to have one line too many, l. 5. The form of the stanza is really more satisfactory with this 'extra' line, and it may be wondered whether in singing it may have been inserted in all the stanzas.

79. Of the Shepherds

A a. *Pr.* Wright, *P.S.* xxiii. 95; Flügel, 'Lieder.', p. 237; Greene, *Selection*, p. 71; Silverstein, p. 115; Gray, *Lyrics*, p. 8.

b. *Pr.* Dyboski, p. 11; Flügel, *N.L.*, p. 117, 'Lieder.', p. 237, *Fest.*, p. 66; Mary G. Segar and Emmeline Paxton, *Some Minor Poems of the Middle Ages* (London, 1917), p. 9; Sitwell, *Atlantic Book*, p. 12; Frost, p. 269.

B. Music for three voices. *Pr.* Hardin Craig, *Two Coventry Corpus Christi Plays* (E.E.T.S., Ex. Ser., No. lxxxvii, 1902), 31, 32; Thomas Sharp, *A Dissertation on the Pageants or Dramatic Mysteries* (Coventry, 1825), pp. 113, 114; Pollard, pp. 272, 273; Frank Kermode, *English Pastoral Poetry* (London, 1952), p. 50; with music, Sharp, op. cit., pp. 115, 118; John C. Cutts, *Renaissance News*, x (1957), 5–7. See also R. L. Greene, ibid. 142.

Combined texts. C. & S., p. 126; Brougham, p. 6. B.-R. 112.

The two stanzas used in the 'Taylors and Shearemens Pagant' are marked as different songs because of their use in different parts of the play. As there sung, with the burden ending the stanza, their character as parts of a carol is somewhat obscured. The date of B is given by the following note (Craig, loc. cit.): 'Tys matter / nevly correcte be Robart Croo / the xiiijth dey of marche / fenysschid in the yere of owre Lorde God / M CCCC & xxxiiij^{te}. / then beyng mayre mastur Palmar / also mastris of the seyd fellyschipp Hev Corbett / Randull Pynkard and / John Baggely.'

burden, l. 1. *Tyrle, tyrlo*: A regular onomatopoeic phrase for the sound of a pipe. It should not be listed among 'terms of abuse' and those 'whose meaning had better be left undefined' as is done by Maurice Evans (*English Poetry in the Sixteenth Century*, London, 1955, p. 52), even though Skelton uses it in two different vulgar senses in 'Colin Clout' and in 'The Tunning of Elinour Rumming' (*The Complete Poems of John Skelton Laureate*, ed. Philip Henderson, 3rd edn., London, 1959, pp. 278, 120). In the latter poem it is used jovially for the ale-drinker's eructation:

> Sit we down a row,
> And drink till we blow,
> And pipe 'Tirly Tirlow!'

A. stza. 1, l. 1. *right*: properly, in due order.
A. stza. 3, l. 3. *long*: adhere.
A. stza. 4, l. 3. *streme*: beam of light.

Compare the round or canon in Thomas Ravenscroft's *Pammelia* (1609):

> Jolly shepherd and upon a hill as he sate,
> So loud he blew his little horn, and kept right well his gate.
>
> Early in a morning,
> Late in an evening,
> And ever blew this little boy, so merrily piping:
>
> Tere liter lo.

> (E. H. Fellowes, ed., *English Madrigal Verse*, 3rd edn., revised Frederick W. Sternfeld and David Greer, Oxford, 1967, p. 201)

These editors cite the even closer parallel from *The Maid's Metamorphosis* (1600), in which Mopse sings:

> Terlitelo, terlitelo, terlitelee, terlo,
> So merrily this shepherd's boy
> His horn that he can blow,
> Early in a morning, late, late, in an evening,
> And ever sat this little boy
> So merrily piping.

> (Ibid., pp. 704–5)

There is hardly need for research to prove that shepherds and pipes are certainly associated, but V. A. Kolve offers interesting comments based on study of the drama: 'We may begin by noting that in the Middle Ages shepherds were traditionally thought of as musicians. As late as 1555 it was customary for shepherds to provide music at Beverley . . .' (*The Play Called Corpus Christi*, Stanford, California, 1966, p. 170).

This carol and its companion piece in the Coventry plays, No. 112, are the only vernacular songs in the medieval English drama of which both words and music are still extant (Nan Cooke Carpenter, 'Music in English Mystery Plays', in John H. Long, ed., *Music in English Renaissance Drama*, Lexington, Kentucky, 1968, p. 27).

80. Of the Nativity

Pr. Wright, *P.S.* iv, 'Christmas Carols', 32; C. & S., p. 130; Sandys, *Carols*, p. 2; Albert S. Cook, *A Literary Middle English Reader* (Boston, 1915), p. 464, Bullen, p. 6.

B.–R. 3932.

A survival into the present century of some of the phrasing of the first three stanzas and the refrain of this carol is presented as a 'Surrey Carol' by Alice E. Gillington, *Old Christmas Carols of the Southern Counties* (London, 1910), No. 10, p. 15. In her preface she intimates that the pieces which she has 'collected and edited' have come to her from gipsies in southern England, but she does not comment on this particular song, to which she assigns the first line as title: 'Christ Is Born of Maiden Fair'. She prints the three stanzas as follows:

> Christ is born of maiden fair;
> Hark, the heralds in the air,
> Thus, adoring, descant there:—
> 'In Excelsis Gloria!'

> Shepherds saw those angels bright
> Carolling in glorious light:—
> 'God, His Son, is born tonight!
>   'In Excelsis Gloria!'
>
> Christ is come to save mankind,
> As in Holy Page we find;
> Therefore this song bear in mind
>   'In Excelsis Gloria!'

The music published with the piece consists of a melody with piano accompaniment.

A modernized version of the text in MS. Harley 5396, with music credited to H. S. Irons, appears in Charles L. Hutchins, ed., *Carols Old and Carols New* (Boston, 1916), No. 96, p. 88. Hutchins also prints the Gillington text, with differing music credited to H. J. Gauntlett (ibid., No. 339, p. 293). Margaret Dean-Smith calls the Gillington text one 'with only slight modification' of the MS. version (*Guide*, p. 58). Users of the whole Gillington collection should consult her expert description (*Guide*, p. 35). See also Introduction, p. cxxxii.

stza. 3, l. 1. *kynde*: 'mankind' rather than 'nature'.
stza. 4, l. 1. There is no more reason for restoring the first word as 'Then' than as 'Jhesu' or something else, but I follow Chambers and Sidgwick.

81. Of the Shepherds

A. *Pr.* Zupitza, 204, notes, xciv, 202–3; Greene, *Selection*, p. 72.
B. *Repr.* Bliss, p. 56; Wright, *P.S.* iv, 'Christmas Carols', p. 58; Sandys, *Carols*, p. 20; W. H. Husk, ed., *Songs of the Nativity* (London, 1868), p. 54; *facs.* Reed, p. 43. B.–R. 2332.

82. Of the Shepherds and the Kings

Pr. Zupitza, 200, notes, xciv, 193–4. B.–R. 3775.
stza. 2, l. 1. *stounde*: hour, time.   l. 4. Zupitza gives as source Daniel, *Thes. Hym.* i. 334:

> Hic iacet in presepio
> Qui regnat sine termino.

83. Of the Nativity and Passion

Pr. James & Macaulay, p. 69; R. L. Greene, *Bodleian Quarterly Record*, vii (1932), 40. B.–R. 4241.

Other carols which use letters in similar fashion are Nos. 139, 180. The letters forming the theme of this carol are the same (except for E) as those in a fourteenth-century poem on the Passion which also uses the 'O-and-I' refrain-element found elsewhere in Middle English poetry. The poem, which appears with others at the end of a volume of Wycliffe's sermons, may possibly be the actual source of this carol (Bodleian Library MS. Don. c. 13, f. 165ᵛ, *pr.* Beatrice D. Brown, *Bodleian Quarterly Record*, vii, 1932, 2). Stza. 2, ll. 5, 6, and stza. 4 are the parts of the poem which show the greatest likeness to the carol (text from MS.):

> With an O. and an I.: þis is of lettres foure,
> X. and M., I. *and* C, þat we gon firste honoure.
>
> X. for Crist, Goddis Son, was sett, þat duleful ded gon die,
> M. for Mary, þe chekes wett, when he hingkid sa hie,
> I. for Jon, þe teres lett for dole þat Crist gon die,
> C. for cros, þer þai mett; þir foure fandit to flie.
> With an O. *and* an I: M. *and* I. made mane
> When X. was nailid apon C. betwix þaim twa alane.

The E of the carol is almost certainly an error for C. See Greene, loc. cit.
stza. 1, l. 4. *flyth*: strife, attack.

What seems to be a scrap of a quotation from this poem is written as a marginal note opposite Lydgate's *Siege of Thebes* in Trinity College, Cambridge, MS. R. 4. 20, f. 114ʳ:

> M and I made gret mone wh . . .

This MS. contains two carols, Nos. 181 and 425. The words as written may be the beginning of a riddle, for they appear in No. [55] of the riddle-book of the Holme family of Chester in about 1640 (B.M. MS. Harley 1960, f. 6^v, *pr.* Frederick Tupper, Jr., *PMLA*, xviii, 1903, 226):

Q. M & I mad[e] grat mone w^n + (C) upon + (C) was left alone
A. Mary & john mourned w^n christ was one the crose.

The seventeenth-century collection *The Booke of Mery Riddles* gives it thus (Tupper, p. 259):

A thousand and one (M and I) made great moan,
When a hundred (C) upon a hundred (C) was left alone.

84. Of the Nativity

Pr. Zupitza, 297, notes, xciv, 205–6. B.–R. 2087.

85. Of the Nativity

Music for two and three voices. *Pr.* Fehr, p. 267; Wright, *P.S.* iv, 'Christmas Carols', 55; with music, Stevens, *Med. Carols*, p. 69. B.–R. 2044.

This carol gives direct expression in stza. 1 to the attitude implied in many others: rejoice, but be careful that your mirth is hallowed, or at least innocent. Compare No. 150 D, stza. 6, ll. 3, 4.

86. Of the Nativity

A. *Pr.* Wright, *Wart. Club*, p. 28; B. Fehr, *Archiv*, cix (1902), 49.
B. *Pr.* Brown, *R.L. 15 C.*, p. 117; Oliver, p. 20.
C. *Pr.* Wright, *P.S.* xxiii. 18; Stevens, *M. & P.*, p. 51.
B.–R. 3070.

The initial lines of the stanzas are from the hymn 'Salvator mundi, Domine'. See table in Introduction, pp. lxxxvii–lxxxviii.

The burdens and refrains of A and B are better suited to the matter of the carol than those of C, which are apparently due to a reviser with a more particular devotion to Mary. The occurrence of the 'De virgine Maria' refrain in stza. 3 of A (compare the 'Que vocatur Maria' of stza. 1) may mean that a version like C was already current at the time that A was written down.

A. stza. 3, ll. 2, 3. A commonplace phrase found in several carols. These two lines appear almost verbatim in the Coventry Shearmen and Taylor's Pageant:

Be-twyxt an ox and an as
Jesus, this kyng, borne he was.

(Hardin Craig, ed., *Two Coventry Corpus Christi Plays*, E.E.T.S.,
Ex. Ser., No. lxxxvii, 1902, 16, ll. 461–2)

87. To Christ

Pr. Wright, *Wart. Club*, p. 12, *P.S.* iv, 'Christmas Carols', 6. B.–R. 1662.
stza. 3, l. 1. *segent*: [?] throne, OF. *sege*.

88. To Christ on His Nativity

Pr. Zupitza, 203, notes, xciv, 199–200. B.–R. 449.

Ryman has here put into the carol-form his translation of the hymn 'Christe, redemptor omnium' (*pr.* Zupitza, 194), omitting the first two stanzas and replacing the Latin lines from the hymn by English text. The translation is reasonably close. The hymn, for Christmas Day, is found in several versions, e.g. *Anal. Hym.* ii. 36, li. 49. The latter seems to have been Ryman's original.

89. Of the Nativity

Music for two and three voices, by Richard Smert. *Pr.* Wright, *P.S.* iv, 'Christmas Carols', 55; Fehr, p. 268; with music, *The Oxford History of Music*, 2nd edn. (Oxford, 1932), ii. 340; Stevens, *Med. Carols*, p. 75. B.–R. 2636.

stza. 1, l. 2. *hore*: uncleanness.
stza. 2, l. 1. *sompell*: example.   l. 3. *clawte*: clout, rag.

90. Of Christ

Pr. James & Macaulay, p. 69. B.-R. 1744.

stza. 2, l. 1. *architriclyn*: Lat. *architriclinus*, the friend of the bridegroom and ruler of the marriage-feast (John ii. 9).

stza. 3. Compare No. 46, stza. 7.   l. 3. *Hosyll*: housel, the Eucharist.

91. Of the Nativity

A. Music for two and three voices. *Pr.* Wright, *P.S.* iv, 'Christmas Carols', 54; Sandys, *Carols*, p. 15; Fehr, p. 271; John Julian, *A Dictionary of Hymnology*, 2nd edn. (London, 1925), p. 209 (omits stza. 1); with music, Stevens, *Med. Carols*, p. 101.

B. Music for two and three voices, by Richard Smert. *Pr.* Fehr, p. 275; with music, Stevens, *Med. Carols*, p. 86.

B.-R. 1738.

The two versions of this piece preserved with different musical settings in the same MS. provide a definite instance of a carol's being altered to suit the purpose of an artistic and individual writer or composer, with no question of change in oral tradition. Compare also No. 103 A d and e.

A. stza. 2, l. 2. *fode*: child.

A. stza. 3, l. 1. *cracche*: crib.

A. stza. 5, l. 2. *hem*: i.e. the patriarchs released by the Harrowing of Hell.

B. stza. 1, l. 3. *mysse*: sin.

92. To Christ on His Nativity

Pr. Zupitza, 325, notes, xcvii, 141–2. B.-R. 3667.

93. Of the Nativity and Passion

Pr. Wright, *P.S.* xxiii. 69; Greene, *Selection*, p. 74; Davies, p. 241. B.-R. 3235.

The heading of the piece in the MS. indicates that this is a carol written to the tune of a secular song, probably the lament of an abandoned girl.

The incomplete piece printed by Stevens, *M. & P.*, pp. 418–19, from B.M. MS. Addit. 31922, ff. 106ᵛ–107, has a setting which the words of this carol would fit. It begins:

> And I war a maydyn,
>   As many one ys,
> For all the golde in England
>   I wold not do amysse.

In the form 'Hey now now' this burden appears as the only other words written for each of two rounds in the same MS., ff. 21ᵛ and 25ᵛ, by Kempe and Faredyng respectively (Stevens, *M. & P.*, pp. 390, 391).

stzas. 3–5. All the nine orders of angelic beings are specifically named, although not in traditional order of rank.

stza. 4, l. 3. *tvnykes*: tunicles, choir vestments.   l. 6. *Kery: Kyrie eleison*.

stza. 8, l. 4. *flome*: river.

stza. 9, l. 5. *herte rote*: a term of endearment.

stza. 12, l. 3. *corpolence*: bodily substance. *O.E.D.* records this use only from 1625.   l. 4. *vn-mysse*: unwise.   l. 6. *thyrty golden pence*. The substitution of gold coins for the silver of the Biblical account is a feature of the legend which identifies the money taken by Judas with the coins for which Joseph was sold, which were later held by the Queen of Sheba, and which were given to Jesus by Melchior. Mary lost the coins, according to the legend, and they were found by a shepherd, who placed them in the Temple. See C. Horstmann, ed., *The Three Kings of Cologne*, E.E.T.S., Or. Ser., No. 85, 1886, 94–100, 248–51.

stza. 16, l. 3. *Crucifige*: Mark xv. 13, 14; Luke xxiii. 21; John xix. 15.

stza. 17, l. 4. *Lunges*. See notes on No. 167, stzas. 7, 8.

stza. 20, l. 6. *hys membres*: 'by' is to be understood.

94. Of the Incarnation

Pr. Brown, *R.L. 15 C.*, p. 109. B.-R. 78.
burden, l. 1. Compare the burdens of Nos. 56, 176, 319.
stza. 1, l. 2. Psalm lxxxv. 11: 'Veritas de terra orta est'.   l. 3. Ibid. 10: '. . . iustitia et pax osculatae sunt'.
stza. 2, l. 3. Wisdom ix. 10: 'Mitte illam [sapientiam] de caelis sanctis tuis'. God is there addressed, of course, not Mary.
stza. 3, l. 1. *Celestyall cytezens*: the saints.

95. Of the Incarnation

a. *Pr.* Wright, *P.S.* iv, 'Christmas Carols', 41; [K.] Böddeker, *Jahrbuch für romanische und englische Sprache und Literatur*, Neue Folge, ii (1875), 98.
b. *Pr.* F. J. Furnivall, *N. & Q.*, 7th Ser., viii (1889), 484; Brown, *R.L. 15 C.*, p. 185. B.-R. 933.
This carol is of the argumentative theological type like Nos. 260, 333, and uses the longer line favoured for that sort of composition. The a-version was written down about 1573, but is included in this collection as b shows the carol to have been composed not later than about 1530. It is probably not of much earlier date.
Compare the long poem, intended for Easter, in Bodl. MS. Digby 102, f. 109ᵛ, with the title 'God and man ben made atte on' and beginning 'Glade in god, this solempne fest' (*pr.* J. Kail, *Twenty-Six Political and other Poems*, E.E.T.S., Or. Ser., No. 124, 1904, 46), and the 'De arte lacrimandi', stza. 5, l. 8 (see note on No. 161). Heinrich Corsdress points to a source for stza. 1 in St. Anselm's *Cur Deus Homo*, ii. 8 and quotes the pertinent passage:

> quatuor modis potest deus facere hominem: videlicet aut de viro et de femina, sicut assiduus usus monstrat; aut nec de viro nec de femina, sicut creavit Adam; aut de viro sine femina, sicut fecit Evam; aut de femina sine viro, quod nondum fecit. Ut igitur hunc quoque modum probet suae subjacere potestati, et ad hoc ipsum opus dilatum esse, nihil convenientius, quam ut de femina sine viro assumat illum hominem (Christum) (*Die Motive der mittelenglischen geistlichen Lyrik . . ., und ihr Verhältnis zur lateinischen Hymnologie des Mittelalters*, [Diss. Münster], Weimar, 1913, p. 6).

stza. 2, l. 6. *mocyon*: motive.
stza. 5, l. 1. *traverse*: dispute, controvery.
stza. 6, l. 5. *generacion*: child-bearing.
stza. 7, l. 3. *and further the verse*: Matthew v. 3, 'Beati pauperes spiritu, quoniam ipsorum est regnum caelorum.' The 'spiritu' is rather lost sight of in the present application.

96. A Te Deum for the Nativity

Music for two voices. *Pr.* Wright, *P.S.* iv, 'Christmas Carols', 56; Fehr, p. 270; with music, Catharine K. Miller, *Renaissance News*, iii (1950), 62; Stevens, *Med. Carols*, p. 83. B.-R. 2388.
The last phrase of the burden is marked 'Faburdon'.
stza. 2, l. 2. *luste*: was pleased.

97. Of St. Stephen

Pr. C. & S., *M.L.R.* v. 483; Whiting, p. 187. B.-R. 3057.
stzas. 2, 3. Acts vii. 55–60.
stza. 4, l. 2. *apayd*: pleased, satisfied.

98. Of St. Stephen

Music for two voices. *Pr.*, with music, Fuller Maitland, p. 23; Terry, p. 54; Stevens, *Med. Carols*, p. 9. B.-R. 2665.
stza. 1, l. 1. *mende*: mind, remembrance.
stza. 3, l. 3. Compare No. 179, stza. 5, l. 3, No. 209, stza. 8, l. 1, and No. 361, stza. 1, l. 2.

99. Of St. Stephen

Music for two and three voices. *Pr.* Fehr, p. 269; with music, Stevens, *Med. Carols*, p. 80. B.–R. 1578.

stza. 3, l. 1. *the tyrand*. Actually Stephen was brought before the council of the synagogue (Acts vi. 12). The author of the carol is referring to Pilate; see the apocryphal Revelation of Stephen (M. R. James, ed., *The Apocryphal New Testament*, Oxford, 1924, pp. 565–8).

stza. 4, l. 1. *With synfull wrecchys*: i.e. by the Jews.

100. Of St. Stephen

Pr. Dyboski, p. 32; Flügel, *N.L.*, p. 113, 'Lieder.', p. 256. B.–R. 4012.

stza. 1, l. 2. *lerne*: teach.   l. 3. *clen*: (?) clear in tone. The line probably had only 'clen' originally, 'clere' being added to make the meaning plain. *O.E.D.* gives an example of 'clen' in this sense only from about 1100.

stza. 3, ll. 2, 3. The phrasing has probably been influenced by carols about St. Thomas of Canterbury; compare No. 114, stza. 7.

stza. 5, l. 3. *the fendes fere*: fear of the fiend.

101. Of St. Stephen

A. *Repr. facs.* Reed, p. 51.

B. *Repr. facs.* Reed, p. 60.

C. Music for two voices. *Pr.* Greene, *Selection*, p. 78; with music, Stevens, *Med. Carols*, p. 39.

B.–R. *Supp.* 2652. 5, 1363. 5.

Reed unaccountably fails to note that the two versions are essentially the same carol. B is incomplete at the end and is followed in the present binding by a leaf with the incomplete No. 370 c. It was not originally in the same carol-book as A.

The occurrence of this carol in two differing texts in the printed carol-books of Richard Kele is a highly interesting sign of the popularity with a later secular public of fifteenth-century carols of monastic circulation. Stzas. 1, 2, and 4 of B are verbally very close to the text of C, probably too close to be the result of completely oral transmission. B even has 'ylke' in its first line for the 'ilk' of C, in a place where, as Stevens remarks, the music seems to require a final *e*.

It would not be surprising to find C in use at Meaux Abbey, for Stephen was a favourite saint of the Cistercian order, which had Stephen Harding as its founder (Nita Scudder Baugh, ed., *A Worcestershire Miscellany*, Philadelphia, 1956, p. 25 n. 1).

stza. 2, l. 4. *lay*: religion.

A. stza. 8, l. 1. *boone*: prayer.

C. stza. 3, l. 4. *fay*: faith, here Stephen's active teaching, appears to be illogically placed and indeed redundant.   l. 2. *greiuyd on*: caused physical pain to.

C. stza. 6, l. 4. *meyd*: meed, reward; 'we'll pay you off.'

102. Of St. John the Evangelist

Pr. C. & S., *M.L.R.* v. 484; Whiting, p. 188, B.–R. 2929.

stza. 1. John xiii. 23.

stza. 5, ll. 3, 4. John xiii. 14–17.

103. Of St. John the Evangelist

A a. Music for two voices. *Pr.* Davies, p. 157; with music, Fuller Maitland, p. 25; Terry, p. 55; Stevens, *Med. Carols*, p. 10.

b. *Pr.* Wright, *P.S.* xxiii. 60; Greene, *Selection*, p. 79.

c. *Pr.* Dyboski, p. 11; Flügel, 'Lieder.', p. 237.

d. Music for two and three voices. *Pr.* Fehr, p. 273; Dyboski, p. 172; with music, Stevens, *Med. Carols*, p. 95.

e. Music for two and three voices. Collated Fehr, p. 273; *pr.*, with music, Stevens, *Med. Carols*, p. 105.

B. *Pr.* first edition.

B.–R. 3776.

This carol is found in more different texts (as a carol) than any other. B differs from the A-texts in being written in the third person as a narrative and not addressed directly to St. John. The change from the more usual version has been thoroughly made, in the burden as well as in the stanzas.

burden, l. 2. See table in Introduction, p. xcvii.

A. stza. 2, l. 2. *preuytes*: secrets.

A. stza. 4, l. 2. This is a commonplace found in most accounts of the life of St. John. Compare, for example, that in *The South English Legendary*, ed. Charlotte D'Evelyn and Anna J. Mill, ii, E.E.T.S., No. 236, 1956, 595, ll. 34-6:

> And for þer nas noþer of ham.þat clene maide nas
> Clene maide to wardi oþer.riȝt it was to do
> þeruore inis swete warde.oure Louerd hure tok two

104. To St. John the Evangelist

Pr. Wright, *P.S.* xxiii. 59. B.-R. 2443.

burden, l. 1. This is perhaps altered from the form of No. 103 to make it a topical plea. Compare the prayers for peace in Nos. 387, 435.

stza. 1, l. 3. *In cena Domini*: from the Response to the third Lectio in Matins for St. John's Day (*Br. Sar.* i, col. ccxviii): 'Iste est Johannes qui supra pectus Domini in cena recubuit.'

stza. 3, ll. 1, 2. John xix. 26-7.

105. To St. John the Evangelist

Pr. Dyboski, p. 35; Flügel, 'Lieder.', p. 258. B.-R. 3669.

The episode alluded to in stza. 3 frequently appears in hymns and antiphons to St. John and is told in the third and fourth Lectiones in Matins for St. John's Day (*Br. Sar.* i, cols. ccxvii, ccxix). The miracle is recorded in various apocryphal writings. According to the version in the Acts of John, Aristodemus, the chief priest, challenges John to prove the truth of his God by drinking poison. After two condemned men have drunk of the poison and have immediately succumbed, John, having prayed, drains the cup and is unharmed. For the further conviction of Aristodemus he restores to life the two poisoned criminals. The conversion of priest and people follows (M. R. James, ed., *The Apocryphal New Testament*, Oxford, 1924, pp. 262-4). The episode told in stza. 4 is also from the Acts of John (ibid., pp. 257-62). After the philosopher Craton had persuaded two wealthy brothers to invest their entire inheritances in two jewels and to break these in pieces as a sign of the contempt of riches, John rebuked him. At Craton's challenge John prayed and caused the broken gems to be restored. Craton and his followers were converted by the miracle, and the two brothers sold the gems for the relief of the poor. Repenting of their bargain, they were miraculously given their wealth again, in the form of gold rods and pebbles, but, after hearing John tell the story of Lazarus and witnessing the restoration to life of the youth Stacteus, they were reconverted to poverty, and the treasure returned to wood and stone. William O. Wehrle (*The Macaronic Hymn Tradition in Medieval English Literature*, Washington, D.C., 1933, p. 81) overlooks this story and attempts to explain the stanza as referring metaphorically to the miracle of the poison.

burden, l. 2, stza. 1, l. 4. See table in Introduction, p. xcvii. The prose from which the line is taken is in honour of St. John the Baptist.

106. Of St. John the Evangelist

Repr. facs. Reed, p. 53; B.-R. *Supp.* 2392. 5.

stza. 1, l. 3. *preuyte*: secret.

stza. 2, l. 2. *toke*: betook, entrusted.

stza. 3, l. 3. *yede*: went.

107. The Good Name of John

Repr. facs. Reed, p. 23. B.-R. *Supp.* 3438. 8.

stza. 1, l. 3. The 'meaning' of the name John is frequently mentioned in medieval hymns and theological writings, e.g. St. Isidore, *Etymologiae*, lib. vii, cap. ix (*Pat. Lat.* lxxxii, col. 288):

'*Joannes*, quodam vaticinio ex merito nomen accepit; interpretatur enim *in quo est gratia*, vel *Domini gratia*. Amplius enim eum caeteris apostolis dilexit Jesus.'

stza. 2, ll. 1, 2. I am not able to document this allusion closely, although the symbolism of innocence is plain. It does not occur in orthodox writings on St. John; it may have reference to some popular tradition now lost. The white ox may stand specifically for the virginity of St. John Evangelist, the 'clean maid', as the two completely white bulls out of a herd of 150 in Sir Gawain's dream in the 'aunceyant chapell' are interpreted by the hermit Nacien as standing for Sir Galahad and Sir Percivale, 'maydyns and clene withoute spotte' in contrast to the other knights of the Round Table' (*The Works of Sir Thomas Malory*, ed. Eugène Vinaver, 2nd edn., Oxford, 1967, ii. 942–6).

Somewhat more remote is Lydgate's reference to the white cattle of Falerii which were valued as sacrifices (Ovid, *Amores*, III. xiii. 3, 4, 13, 14):

> And in Falisio, as hym liste to wrighte,
> Is a welle that causeth eke of newe
> When thei drinken oxen to be whighte
> And sodenly for to change her hewe.
> What merveile tha*n* thoue the welle trewe,
> The welle of helth and of life eterne,
> The Lorde of al so as Y can discerne?
>
> (Cambridge University Library, MS. Mm. 6. 5, *The Life of Our Lady*, stza. 116)

l. 4. *But*: unless.   *pyght*: set.

stza. 3, l. 1. *baptyst*: baptism.

stza. 5. The reference may be to someone representing either the Baptist or the Evangelist at a celebration. There may be an allusion to a custom somewhat like that reported from Marseilles and involving an ox not specified as white. E. Louis Backman, citing Bérenger-Féraud's *Réminiscences populaires de la Provence*, notes:

> In the Corpus Christi procession in Marseilles, until the middle of the nineteenth century, . . . there was a fat ox in the middle of the procession; it was decorated with flowers and was ridden by a small boy dressed as John the Baptist. The ox and rider were surrounded by a group of children dressed as Hercules. Bérenger-Féraud thinks that the ox is a kind of memento of Celtic customs, according to which oxen were sacrificed on certain days to certain gods, the names of which 'are long since forgotten' (*Religious Dances in the Christian Church and in Popular Medicine*, trans. E. Classen, London, 1952, p. 116).

There is an association of the ox with St. John the Evangelist in a thirteenth-century observance of his day by priests in Paris. 'The encyclopaedias of Diderot and d'Alembert mention that at the festival of the sub-deacons on St. Stephen's Day the Song of the Ass or the Song of the Fools was sung, but at the priests' festival of St. John they sang "*la prose du bœuf*" (the song of the ox)' (op. cit., pp. 63–4. See also Chambers, *M.S.* i. 336, n. 1).

The well-attested custom at the Abbey of Bury St. Edmunds of elaborate fertility rites for women which involved a white bull is a suggestive analogue, but there is no preserved record of a connection with either St. John. There is a full report of the ceremony in Edmund Gillingwater, *An Historical and Descriptive Account of St. Edmund's Bury* ([Bury St. Edmunds], 1804); see also Dugdale's *Monasticon Anglicanum* (1821), iii. 133.

108. Of the Innocents

Pr. C. & S., *M.L.R.* v. 485; Whiting, p. 189; Greene, *Selection*, p. 79. B.–R. 601.

stza. 1, ll. 1, 2. These lines appear in App., No. ii, stza. 4. Compare No. 125 A, stza. 16, ll. 1, 2. l. 3. *aga*: gone, away.   l. 4. *cowth hem fray*: did kill them.

stza. 2, l. 1. The tradition was that Herod was called to Rome directly after his interview with the Magi and was a year on the road each way. Hence, when he returned, he ordered the killing of all male children of two years and under. Compare Myrc's *Festial* (Part I, ed. T. Erbe, E.E.T.S., Ex. Ser., No. xcvi, 1905, 36).

stza. 3, l. 1. Audelay's figure of 140,000 as the number slain is not quite the customary one. The number was generally put in the Middle Ages at 144,000, in defiance of all historical possibility, by identifying the Innocents with the white-clad host of Revelation xiv. 3. Compare the Towneley play of Herod the Great, ll. 487–9 (ed. G. England and A. W. Pollard, E.E.T.S., Ex. Ser., No. lxxi, 1897, 180):

> A hundreth thowsand, I watt / and fourty ar slayn,
> And four thowsand; ther-at / me aght to be fayn;
> Sich a morder on a flat / shall neuer be agayn.

l. 3. *eor*: their.

stza. 4, l. 1. *crisum*: in their chrisom-cloths or baptismal robes, innocent children (usually applied to those a month old or less).

stza. 5, l. 3. *Hent*: until.

stza. 6, l. 4. Revelation xiv. 4.

109. Of the Innocents

Music for two and three voices, *Pr.* Fehr, p. 265; with music, Stevens, *Med. Carols*, p. 65. B.–R. 680.

The carol is addressed to Herod in the same manner as the hymn 'Hostis Herodes impie'.

stza. 2, l. 1. Perhaps from a prose of the Innocents (*Sar. Miss.*, p. 464, strophe 14): 'Castra militum dux iniquus aggregat ferrum figit in membra tenera.'

stza. 3, l. 4. Thy throne is put in sorrow and woe.

110. Of the Innocents

Music for two and three voices. *Pr.* Fehr, p. 269; with music, Stevens, *Med. Carols*, p. 81. B.–R. 3950.

111. Of the Innocents

Music for two and three voices. *Pr.* Fehr, p. 269; Sandys, *Carols*, p. 18; with music, Stevens, *Med. Carols*, p. 82. B.–R. 1212.

stza. 1, l. 1. *wylde and wode*. The tradition of Herod as a raging tyrant, reflected in such phrases as this, was fostered by its dramatic value for mystery plays.

112. The Mothers of the Innocents

Music for three voices. *Pr.* Hardin Craig, *Two Coventry Corpus Christi Plays* (E.E.T.S., Ex. Ser., No. lxxxviii, 1902), 32; Davies, p. 292; Thomas Sharp, *A Dissertation on the Pageants or Dramatic Mysteries* (Coventry, 1825), p. 114, Pollard, p. 272; Elizabeth Posten, *The Penguin Book of Christmas Carols* (Harmondsworth, 1965), pp. 64–5; Gray, *Themes and Images*, p. 119, *Lyrics*, p. 14; with music, Sharp, pp. 116–17; *Oxford Book of Carols*, Music Edn., p. 44; Robbins, *Christmas Carols*, p. 74, etc. B.–R. *Supp.* 2251. 8.

This carol, like No. 79 B, on which see note, is one of the few which are known to have been sung in the performance of a mystery play. Unlike the song of the shepherds, it may have been written expressly for use in the shearmen and tailors' play. Its dramatic value is certainly greater. The use of a lullaby burden in this particular context may seem curious; it must carry the colloquial sense of farewell to one who is or has been loved. Compare notes on Nos. 322, 459. The similarity of the stanza-form to that of other lullaby carols makes it seem likely that the piece was written to the tune and with the burden of an already existing lullaby carol.

stza. 3, l. 3. *may*. The emendation from *say* was originally made by G. L. Kittredge.

113. Of St. Thomas of Canterbury

Pr. C. & S., *M.L.R.* v. 486; Whiting, p. 190. B.–R. 838.

The importance of Tuesdays in the life of St. Thomas is dwelt on in both prose and poetical treatments of his life, e.g. Herbert de Boseham's *Vita Sancti Thomae* (ed. J. C. Robertson, Rolls Series, London, 1877), lib. iv, cap. 3, the life in *The Early South-English Legendary* (ed. C. Horstmann, E.E.T.S., Or. Ser., No. 87, 1887, 177), ll. 2458–75, and most strikingly in a fifteenth-century English hymn beginning 'Gaude, lux Londoniarum' (*Anal. Hym.* xxix. 89). Each of the seven stanzas of the hymn describes an important Tuesday in Thomas's life, his birth, his summons by the King, his exile, the revelation of his future martyrdom, his official recognition as a martyr

Audelay seems to be alone in ascribing his being 'shorn priest' to a Tuesday as well. He was actually ordained a priest on Saturday, 2 June 1162.

Audelay, as is natural for one so solicitous of the rights of the clerical orders, exaggerates somewhat the services of Thomas to the Church, and his exposition of the points at issue is hardly the historical one.

Stza. 3 reflects the major crux of the 'criminous clerks' in the controversy of Thomas with the King, Becket maintaining that clergy accused of robbery, murder, felony, etc., should be tried only in ecclesiastical courts, and only for a second offence be delivered to the King's justice. Stza. 4 seems to be a misinterpretation of the King's policy of appropriating the revenues of vacant ecclesiastical offices.

stza. 2, ll. 3, 4. These are an interesting parallel to the better-known lines of the ballad *The Hunting of the Cheviot* (Child, No. 162).

stza. 4, l. 4. *dangere*: power, jurisdiction, with a special application to a debt or obligation.

stza. 5, l. 2. See note on No. 114, stza. 9, l. 3.   l. 4. The sense of the line seems to be: 'May the father and mother who got and bore him be honoured in heaven.' Compare No. 115, stza. 2, ll. 1, 2.

114. Of St. Thomas of Canterbury

a. *Pr.* Wright, *Wart. Club*, p. 66; T. Wright, *Songs and Carols* (London, 1836), No. xi; Greene, *Selection*, p. 82; Tydeman, p. 51.

b. *Pr.* K. Brunner, *Anglia*, lxi (1937), 151; Brown, *R.L. 15 C.*, p. 189.

c. Collated in first edition.

d. *Pr.* Dyboski, p. 31; Flügel, *N.L.*, p. 113, 'Lieder.', p. 255, Mary G. Segar and Emmeline Paxton, *Some Minor Poems of the Middle Ages* (London, 1917), p. 19. B.-R. 1892.

The account of Becket's murder given in this carol follows fairly closely the historical facts as recorded in the early prose lives of the saint, e.g. Herbert de Boseham's *Vita Sancti Thomae* (ed. J. C. Robertson, Rolls Series, London, 1877), lib. vi.

stza. 4, l. 2. *paleys*: the Archbishop's Palace at Canterbury, whence Becket fled to the Cathedral. Compare Herbert de Boseham, lib. vi, cap. 1.

stza. 5, ll. 3, 4. The calling of the Archbishop 'traitor' by the knights is recorded in various lives, together with his denial of its justice.

stza. 6. This characteristically unselfish thought of Becket's for his household and servants is noted in several lives, e.g. Herbert de Boseham, lib. vi, cap. 4.

stza. 7, l. 1. *auter*: The altar in the NW. transept of Canterbury Cathedral. See Paul A. Brown, *The Development of the Legend of Thomas Becket* (Philadelphia, 1930), pp. 117–20.   ll. 1–3. These gruesome details are authentic. As Carleton Brown points out (p. 331), this stanza, as also in c, is out of strict chronological order. The stanza is lacking in b, while in d the next stanza is lacking. Brown makes unnecessary difficulty over 'Optans celi gaudia', which obviously modifies the 'he' of stza. 7, l. 1, not the plural pronoun referring to the murderers.

stza. 9, l. 3. *poyntes.* The references to 'points' in this and other carols of St. Thomas (Nos. 113, 115) have puzzled previous editors (e.g. Wright and Whiting). In a and No. 115 their number is fifty-two; in c and No. 113 it is fifty; b has 'fyftene tokenus'.

The correct explanation is provided by an exposition in Middle English in T.C.D. MS. E. 5. 10, f. 122^r and ^{v} (XV cent.), headed 'Articuli sancti Thome Cantuariensis episcopi', and beginning:

> Ye schulle vnderstond how that kynge harre þe secunde at his peralament at Northehampton made a blanke charter and commandyd all the lordes of the lande to pute to theyre Seales. The glorious ma[r]ter saynt Th[omas] was bode to put to his seale and he sayde nay telle that he harde þe pointes that schulde be wrytyn in the sayde Charter. The fyrst po[yn]t was this that þer schulde no prest ne clerke monke chanon ne frere no more reuerence then another seculer mon schulde haue.

The paragraph marks and the 'also's' that follow indicate a list of fourteen points which may very briefly be summarized as follows:

2. No abbot, 'prior, 'person vicary', or parish priest should ask duties or tithes.

3. A fee of 20s. to the king from any commoner putting his child to school.

4. Fees to the king from those taking minor and priest's orders.

5. Fees for burial in consecrated ground.
6. Duties to the king and lord when a husband predeceases his wife.
7. Fee to the king from any couple married in church.
8. Fee to the king for a child's christening.
9. Fee to the king for a mother's purification.
10. Fee to the king for confirmation by a bishop.
11. Death by hanging for a father and burning for a mother in the case of murder or negligence in the death of a child under the age of seven.
12. Offenders against temporal law taking sanctuary in a church to be sought out, a man hanged, and a woman burnt, and the church to require reconsecration.
13. Commoners to eat white bread, pullet, capon, pig, goose, veal, or mutton only on four days in the year.
14. No commoner spending less than ten pounds a year to wear any coloured cloth.

The list concludes: 'thise poyntys with other mo were the poyntes that saynt Thomas of Caunterbury suffred martyrdom for.'

A curious survival of the tradition of fifty-two points as late as 1532 is found in the petition to Cromwell of William Umpton, one of the grooms of the King's Hall, who had been a prisoner in the Tower for fourteen months, 'loaded with irons'. According to poor Umpton, 'a pardoner of St. Thomas's hospital at Woodstock said that St. Thomas of Canterbury died for 52 points concerning the commonwealth; "which 52 your said orator denied, one excepted for the clergy, and that the said 52 points were a dance called Robin Hood [apparently equivalent to frivolous nonsense]." Then the pardoner asked him if he would compare Robin Hood with St. Thomas before my lord of Lincoln; on which he fortuned to ask the same pardoner why St. Thomas was a saint rather than Robin Hood? For this he was accused of heresy . . .' (James Gairdner, ed., *Letters and Papers . . . of the Reign of Henry VIII*, London, 1880, v. 551). Umpton was ahead of his time, and his petition was fruitless.

There is another reference to 'points' in Garnier de Pont Sainte Maxence's *La Vie de Saint Thomas le Martyr* (ed. C. Hippeau, Paris, 1859), pp. 83–4, which tells how Thomas conferred with the Pope, spreading before him the MS. of the Constitutions of Clarendon. To William of Pavia's objections to his arguments Thomas answered 'mot à mot . . . ad chescun point solu'. These disposed of, Thomas

> Reveneit à ses poinz, cum se fust Salemons;
> Diseit sa cause avant, od mult beles resons,
> Bién ad duré entr'els demi-jor la tençons;
> Car cil li ert par tot point à point as gernons.

The number of the 'points' is not mentioned.

115. Of St. Thomas of Canterbury

Pr. Wright, *P.S.* xxiii. 51. B.–R. 405.
The defacing of this carol and of No. 116 in the MSS. is interesting evidence of the lengths to which the dishonouring of St. Thomas was carried at the Reformation. In this case it was done to a MS. about half a century old.
burden. See table in Introduction, p. civ.
stza. 3, ll. 3, 4. The reference is to the revenues from vacant benefices which King Henry wished to assume. Compare No. 113, stza. 4.
stza. 4, l. 1. See note on No. 114, stza. 9, l. 3.

115.1. Of St. Thomas of Canterbury

Music for two and three voices. *Pr.* Greene, *Selection*, p. 80, *J.A.M.S.* vii (1954), 7; with music, Stevens, *Med. Carols*, p. 48. B.–R. *Supp.* 187.5.
This carol on St. Thomas, like No. 114 in all its four MSS. and Audelay's No. 113, has been spared the defacement prescribed by Henry VIII in 1538 for all memorials of the saint. But the text of No. 115 has been cancelled, and in No. 116 the name 'Thoma' has been erased.
The narrative in this carol follows the accepted accounts, but it is more explicitly biased against the King than any of the other carols about Becket.

stzas. 2, 3. Compare Lectio ii at First Nocturn of Matins on St. Thomas's Day (*Br. Sar.* i, col. ccxlix):

Confiscantur interim in Anglia omnes archiepiscopi redditus, vastantur praedia, possessiones diripiuntur: et excogitato novo supplicii genere, tota simul proscribitur Thomae cognatio. Omnes etiam amici ejus, vel familiares, vel quicunque eum quocumque titulo contingebant, sine delectu conditionis aut fortunae, dignitatis aut ordinis, aetatis aut sexus, pariter relegantur. Nam et senes et decrepiti, vagientes in cunis, et mulieres in puerperio decubantes, in exilium acti sunt.

stza. 4. Compare Lectio iii at Second Nocturn (*Br. Sar.* i, col. ccli):

Suscipitur itaque a clero et populo cum gaudio inaestimabili illachrimantibus omnibus et dicentibus, Benedictus qui venit in nomine Domini. Sed post dies paucos iterum damnis et injuriis supra modum et numerum affectus est . . .

stza. 5. Compare Lectio iii at First Nocturn (*Br. Sar.* i, col. ccl):

Sex igitur annis exulans, continuis variis et innumeris afflictus injuriis, et quasi lapis vivus in structuram caelestis edificii multimodis tunsionibus atque pressuris conquadratus: quo magis impulsus est ut caderet, eo firmius et immobilius stare probatus est.

stza. 6, l. 1. Compare Response at Vespers on the eve of St. Thomas (*Br. Sar.* i, col. ccxlv):

Jacet granum oppressum palea,

and the lines from the following Versicle and Prose:

Cadit custos vitis in vinea:
dux in castris, cultor in area.

Fit pastoris caede sanguinea.
Pavimenta Christi marmorea
Sacro madent cruore rubea,

as well as Lectio v at Second Nocturn (col. ccliii):

Sic itaque granum frumenti oppressit palea, sic vineae custos in vinea, dux in castris, in caulis pastor, cultor in area caesus est. . . .

ll. 4, 5. These lines suggest an acquaintance with the twelfth-century Anglo-Norman poem *La Vie de Thomas Becket par Beneit* (or a derivative of it), ll. 967, 970–2 (ed. Börje Schlyter, Études Romanes de Lund, iv, Lund, 1941):

La voiz [of Christ] dist . . .
'Kar en tun sanc est glorifiee
Tute seynte Iglise e honuree
Sanz lunge atente.'

stza. 7. See note on No. 113. The 'seven' of this carol shows acquaintance with the tradition of the Tuesdays, though this stanza mentions only six.

An association with Meaux Abbey is more than possible for this carol, for the *Chronicle* of the abbey devotes a remarkable amount of space to a record of the career of St. Thomas, some sixteen pages in the modern edition, and the catalogue of the abbey library lists three copies of the *Passio Sancti Thomae*. It should be remembered that Thomas had been a prebendary of Beverley, next door to Meaux, which had a special devotion to him. Thomas's strong opponent, Roger, Archbishop of York, was a well-hated enemy of Meaux, from which the monks believed that he stole some land.

116. Of St. Thomas of Canterbury

Music for two and three voices. *Pr.* Fehr, p. 275; with music, Stevens, *Med. Carols*, p. 98. B.-R. 2731.

On the figures of the 'good grain' (ultimately derived from the parable of the sower) and of the 'vineyard' see notes on No. 115.1.

burden. See table in Introduction, p. xcvii.

117. Of the Nativity and New Year

a. *Pr.* C. & S., *M.L.R.* v. 487; Whiting, p. 191; Greene, *Selection*, p. 83; Sisam, p. 386.

b. Music for two voices. *Pr.*, with music, Fuller Maitland, p. 21; Terry, p. 52; Stevens, *Med. Carols*, p. 8; Robbins, *Christmas Carols*, p. 78.

c. Music for two voices. *Pr.* Padelford, p. 90; with music, *E.B.M.* i. 125, *facs.* Nos. lxii, lxiii; Terry, p. 8; *O.B.C.*, Music Edn., p. 84; Stevens, *Med. Carols*, p. 20.

B.-R. 21.

It would seem that the original conception of the author was that the entire stanza should be sung by a soloist, representing the messenger, and the burden with its query by a chorus in regular carol-fashion. The two settings preserved, however, are for two parts throughout, and in c the last four lines of the stanza are marked as a chorus. Stevens's note on the partial repetition of the burden which is marked *Chorus* supersedes both the note on this point in the first edition of this work and that in *O.B.C.*, Music Edn., p. 51. J. Copley has discussed the musical settings in detail and objects to the *O.B.C.* interpretation, but is probably in error in asserting that Audelay intends a repetition of only the first line of the burden in a (*N. & Q.* cciv, 1959, 387-9).

The spirited rhythm is so much superior to Audelay's usual metres that his original authorship must be regarded as doubtful.

The version in the T.C.C. MS. roll has 'yolys' in l. 2 of the burden in place of Audelay's 'New Eris' and the 'yeres' of the Selden MS. The New Year's burden (prefixed in spite of the Nativity content of the stanzas) is particularly interesting in the light of the probability of the Selden manuscript's Worcester provenance, as it appears from Prior William More's journal that carols were sung in hall there on New Year's Day as well as on Christmas and other days of the Nativity season. Both carols and some kind of observance involving 'messengers' at the annual feast for civic officials appear together in the journal's entry for Epiphany 1519 (Ethel S. Fegan, ed., *Journal of Prior William More*, Worcestershire Historical Society, 1914, p. 77):

Item in rewards for the bryngyng of yere giffs 4*s.* 8*d.* 8*d.*
Item in rewards to pleyers children when ye balys with ther company dyned with me . . . 12*d.*
Item to syngers of carralls 20*d.* Item rewarded to iiij pleyers a pon ye Epiphani Day belonging to sir Edward beltenop 3*s.* 4*d.* Item in rewards to serten persons beyng messyngers 5*s.* 8*d.*

stza. 1, l. 3. *cewre*: cure, spiritual care.
stza, 2, l. 1. *semle selcouth*: seemly wonder or marvel.   l. 2. *burd*: maiden.
stza. 4, l. 4. *haylsyng*: embracing, salutation.   *coynt*: quaint (with connotation of daintiness or prettiness).

118. Of the Annunciation and New Year

Music for two and three voices. *Pr.* Fehr, p. 267; with music, Stevens, *Med. Carols*, p. 70. B.-R. 887.

The affixing of the New Year's burden and the marking of the carol as for the Feast of the Circumcision are quite arbitrary. Whatever 'occasional' quality it has is definitely more suitable to a time before the Nativity (stza. 3). The piece provides a good warning against the notion that a medieval 'Christmas carol' can be distinguished by its subject-matter.

119. Of the Circumcision

Repr. Bliss, p. 54; *facs.* Reed, p. 41. B.-R. *Supp.* 2039. 5.

stza. 1, l. 1. *hall and boure*: the two principal divisions of the medieval English dwelling, hence, as here, 'all through the house'. Compare Chaucer, *Nun's Priest's Tale*, l. 12.

stza. 5, l. 1. The 'token of love' is the shedding of Christ's blood at His circumcision as the type and promise of that blood He was to shed later on the cross.

120. What Cheer?

Pr. Dyboski, p. 15; Flügel, *N.L.*, p. 123, *Fest.*, p. 69, 'Lieder.', p. 242; Frost, p. 261; Greene, *Selection*, p. 84; Davies, p. 288. B.-R. 1873.

The last stanza suggests that the carol was designed for use by a singer welcoming a company on behalf of their host. Compare No. 13, stza. 3. The 'What cher?' refrain is admirably effective when conceived as sung by the soloist of the verses. It is at once the cue to the assembly to join in the burden and a challenge which is pointedly repeated and answered by them in the words of the hearty burden.

The failure of the rhyme in the last stanza is not unparalleled in the carols. Holthausen's suggestion of 'lere' (*Anglia*, xvii, 1895, 444) is possible.

121. Of the New Year

Pr. Robbins, *Hist. Poems*, p. 62; Greene, *Selection*, p. 85; Oliver, p. 34. B.–R. 320.

This carol is obviously designed to be sung at a social gathering, probably a dinner, but it contrasts sharply in tone with the other New Year carols. It is more similar in theme and tone to the anonymous Christmas song of 1555–60 with refrain but no burden in the Maitland Folio Manuscript (No. lxxiv, pp. 211–12, *pr.* [Sir] W. A. Craigie, i, S.T.S., New Ser., No. 7, 1919, 238–9):

> In honour of this christinmes
> Now everie man suld him address
> To sing and dance and mak gud cheir
> wait nane how lang he levis heir

(Five stanzas in all; the fourth line is the refrain.)

The burden is even more closely paralleled by a convivial song of the mid-eighteenth century (*The Thrush. A Collection of the Most Celebrated English and Scotch Songs*, London, 1749, Song 45, pp. 33–4, stza. 1):

> He that will not merry, merry be
> With a gen'rous Bowl and a Toast,
> May he in Bridewell be shut up,
> And fast bound to a Post.
> Let him be merry, merry there,
> And we'll be merry, merry here,
> For who can know where we shall go
> To be merry another Year?

The last four lines are repeated as a refrain in the three following stanzas.

Robbins (*Hist. Poems*, p. 278) suggests an approximate date of 1445, at the end of the Hundred Years' War, saying, 'The return of soldiers and the formation of private armies, the continued famine conditions (e.g. 1438, 1439, 1445), and the economic turbulence of servants seeking better jobs all point to such a date.' He gives it the title 'The Day Will Dawn'.

The theme of mutability is common enough in carols, e.g. Nos. 381, 382, 386, 388, and the hope of reunion expressed in No. 141, stza. 5, is somewhat wistful. But it may be that Robbins's title and comment and the note in the first edition of this work, '. . . the democratic spirit of the last stanza is something different from the ordinary pious depreciation of worldly greatness', imply a wider political significance than the carol actually has. The fragment of MS. in which its only copy is preserved is shown by the presence (on the same page as the carol) of a carefully, if crudely, drawn coat of arms (Argent, a lion rampant gules with a cross above it within a bordure sable bezantée) to have come from the Cistercian abbey of Hailes in Gloucestershire, which bore these arms of its founder and great benefactor, Richard, Earl of Cornwall (the crozier for difference is not laid across the lion here). Since the carol appears to come from a period when Hailes was undergoing hardship and impoverishment, from which it was to be rescued by the restoration of pilgrimages to its treasured relic of the Holy Blood, it should perhaps be regarded as a reflection of the discontent of a particular abbey, which in the preceding century had had to summon the King's aid 'against persons who threatened and assaulted their men and servants and carried away their goods' (William Page, *V.C.H.*, *Gloucester*, London, 1907, ii. 97), rather than a general proletarian protest.

121.1. The Petition of the Gray Horse, Auld Dunbar

Pr. [John Pinkerton,] *Ancient Scotish Poems Never Before in Print*, i (London and Edinburgh, 1786), 112 (in part); David Laing, *The Poems of William Dunbar*, i (Edinburgh, 1834), 149, *repr. Blackwood's Magazine*, xxxviii (1835), 304; James Paterson, *The Works of William Dunbar* (Edinburgh, 1863), p. 282; John Small, *The Poems of William Dunbar*, ii, S.T.S., 1893, 215;

George Eyre-Todd, *Mediaeval Scottish Poetry* (London and Edinburgh, n.d.), p. 208; Julius Schipper, *The Poems of William Dunbar* (Vienna, 1894), p. 274; W. Mackay Mackenzie, *The Poems of William Dunbar* (Edinburgh, 1932), p. 46; M. M. Gray, *Scottish Poetry from Barbour to James VI* (London, 1935), p. 162 (in part); Hugh MacDiarmid, *Selected Poems of William Dunbar* (Glasgow, 1955), p. 36; James Kinsley, *William Dunbar, Poems* (Oxford, 1958), p. 94; John MacQueen and Tom Scott, *The Oxford Book of Scottish Verse* (Oxford, 1966), p. 115; etc. B.-R. *Supp.* 2349.5.

Of the various 'petition' poems of Dunbar, this, the only one in carol-form, is one of the best, if not the very best, and can stand comparison with Chaucer's *Complaint to His Purse*. The comparison of the undervalued poet to the aged, cruelly neglected animal is forcefully maintained, but lightened with gleams of humour. The stanzas are printed here in the order of Small's S.T.S. edition, which seems justified by internal evidence. Beginning with a location in time, as with 'Now', is characteristic of Dunbar. The carol cannot be exactly dated, but its emphasis on age and length of service would indicate a time not much earlier than 1510, and the appeal would seem more appropriate before the increase of his pension in that year from £20 to £80.

The actual authorship of the *Responsio Regis* is uncertain. Schipper was sure that it was written by the King himself. But it seems to be completely in Dunbar's own style and it may (as I think, it should) be regarded as the poet's suggestion of what a proper answer to his petition would be.

burden, l. 2. *Yuillis yald*: The key phrase of the whole carol to which are anchored all the details of the sustained metaphor of the ageing poet as the worn-out horse. A *yald* or *yaud* (related to 'jade') is a horse enfeebled with age; a *Yuillis yald* is a person exposed to scorn for having gained no new garment to wear at Christmas time. Kinsley (p. 135) states that the phrase 'survived until recently in Aberdeenshire as *eelshard*'. Kinsley also refers to the Treasurer's Accounts of the Scottish king which show that at New Year's time in both 1505–6 and 1506–7 Dunbar was given a money payment in compensation for the gown which had not been bestowed at Christmas.

stza. 1, l. 1. Now that lovers (of the King) come (at New Year) with loud cries of 'Largess!' l. 2. *palfrayis*: palfreys, light saddle-horses.   l. 3. When mares will be adorned and dressed. l. 4. That are ridden by both lord and vulgar (person).

stza. 2, l. 1. *into ply*: in good condition.   l. 2. *cast gammaldis*: cut capers (gambols), frisk. l. 3. I could have been bought in neighbouring kingdoms.

stza. 3, l. 1. *knyp*: nip, feed.   l. 3. *colleveris*: colliers' horses.   l. 4. That are scabby, are lame and cold.

stza. 4, l. 2. *cursouris*: coursers, war-horses.   l. 3. *hous*: housing, horse-cloth.   *happit*: covered.

stza. 5, l. 1. *aver*: cart-horse.   l. 2. Thrust forth from our gorge to crop the clover.   l. 3. The reference has not been fully explained, but it may refer to the 'strength' or healing virtue of Loch na Naire in Strathnaver, Sutherlandshire. See *Folklore, Myths and Legends of Britain* (London, 1973), p. 451.

stza. 6, l. 2. *duill*: sorrow.   *drug*: pull hard.   l. 3. Large horses of the court keep me from the straw fodder.   l. 4. To take the moss or coarse grass remaining in winter by the clearing in the woods and the sheep-fold.

stza. 7, l. 2. *plane and peld*: flat and bare.   l. 3. *tein in for eild*: taken in because of my age. l. 4. My teeth are projecting high and boldly, i.e. the old horse is long in the tooth.

stza. 8, l. 2. And you have all the blame for it.   l. 4. I got only grass (instead of bran), if I would take it.

stza. 9, l. 1. *dautit*: petted, fondled.   l. 4. For badly cleaned [?] straw that I would seize. *Schoud* has not been certainly explained.

stza. 10, l. 1. *thrift be thyne*: living be poor.   l. 2. If I die within your ownership.   l. 3. *soutteris*: shoemakers.   l. 4. To be gnawed with ugly gums (the shoemaker chewing the leather to make it pliable).

stza. 11, l. 1. *done my curage cuill*: caused my courage to cool.   l. 2. *forriddin*: overworked. l. 3. *trappouris*: trappings.   l. 4. I would be spurred in every limb.

Responsio Regis, l. 3. *aucht*: ownership.   l. 4. *lyart*: grey.   l. 5. *Gar howss him*: cause him to be given a housing.   l. 6. *busk*: adorn, deck.   l. 7. *indost*: endorsed, guaranteed.

121.2. Largess of This New Year Day

a. *Pr.* Allan Ramsay, *The Ever Green* (Edinburgh, 1724), ii. 38; [Lord Hailes], *Ancient Scottish Poems* (Edinburgh, 1770), p. 190; J. Sibbald, *Chronicle of Scottish Poetry from the Thirteenth*

Century to the Union of the Crowns (Edinburgh, 1802), ii. 40; James Barclay Murdoch, *The Banna-tyne Manuscript*, part ii ([Glasgow], The Hunterian Club, 1875), p. 274; W. Tod Ritchie, *The Bannatyne Manuscript*, ii, S.T.S., New Ser., No. 22, 1928, 254.

b. *Pr.* [Sir] W. A. Craigie, *The Maitland Folio Manuscript*, i, S.T.S., New Ser., No. 7, 1919, 248.

The heading of b might be interpreted as a one-line burden, but it is more probably intended only as a title. Craigie prints two lines which are deleted in the MS. at the end of the preceding piece:

> Precelland prince þat hes na peir
> I ferlie in this first new ȝeir
> ffinis.

His note designating these lines as 'properly the beginning of the next piece' is erroneous. The couplet must be a false start, abandoned as not belonging to this text, even though it does seem to be part of a stanza addressed to a sovereign, as is the first stanza of a. The 'Finis' can only be a scribal error.

The lack of the burden in b may reflect a decline in fashion of the full carol-form. The omission of the stanzas concerning the King, the Secretary, Lord Bothwell, and Queen Margaret probably results from a changed situation at court which makes them no longer topical.

Although the colophon of the carol gives only the surname 'Stewart', the authorship may be confidently assigned to William Stewart, the translator into verse of Hector Boece's history of Scotland as *The Buik of the Croniclis of Scotland* (ed. William B. Turnbull, Rolls Series, London, 1858). He may also be assumed to be the author of two other pieces in the Bannatyne MS., 'Schir sen of men ar diuerss sortis', which immediately follows this carol and has the colophon 'Finis of Stewart to þe kingis Grace', and 'Precellend prince havand prerogatyue' (ff. 88ᵛ, 89ʳ), which has the colophon 'Finis q stewart', with 'w' interlined before the surname. In the latter the King is addressed as one of 'so tendir aige'. The poem 'This hindir nycht by the hour of nyne', which immediately precedes it in the Bannatyne MS., has there no colophon, but the text in the Maitland Folio MS. has the colophon 'Quod williame stewart to þe king' (pp. 353-5). The problems of attribution of poems to William and to Stewart of Lorne are tabulated in the notes of Douglas Hamer to ll. 44-6 of Sir David Lindsay's 'The Testament of the Papyngo' (*The Works of Sir David Lindsay of the Mount 1490-1555*, iii, S.T.S., 3rd Ser., No. 6, 1935, 76). The lines read:

> And Stewarte, quhilk disyrith one staitly style,
> Full Ornate werkis daylie dois compyle.
>
> Stewart of Lorne wyll carpe rycht curiouslie.
>
> (op. cit., i, S.T.S., 3rd Ser., No. 1, 1931, 57)

Sibbald's designation of Stewart of Lorne as the author of the carol because of this mention of his 'carping' has no other evidence to support it.

What little is known of William Stewart's life is set forth in Turnbull's preface to his edition of the *Croniclis* (pp. vii-xiv) and in Hamer's notes. He was probably born about 1481. He appears in the Register of the University of St. Andrews as Determinant in 1499 and as Licentiate in 1501. The accounts of the Lord High Treasurer for the years 1526-7 and 1529-30 list valuable grants of cloth at Yule and pensions of twenty and forty pounds respectively. These gifts hardly justify such complaints of niggardly treatment as are made in this highly satirical carol.

The solicitation of New Year's gifts here recounted is obviously localized at Stirling Castle and more particularly at the Chapel Royal establishment. See Charles Rogers, *History of the Chapel Royal of Scotland* (Edinburgh, 1882). The cry of 'largess' by a herald or other officer when a distribution of money or gifts in kind was to take place at a ceremonial feast was still in use in both England and Scotland in the sixteenth century. The works of Dunbar give ample testimony to the importance of New Year's Day as a time for substantial gifts from royal and noble personages.

stza. 1, l. 1. King James V, having reached his majority at the age of fourteen, was chief of the Stewart clan, to which the poet belonged. The measure of his liberality is represented as being a furtive bestowal of two shillings. But the King was under the close control of the Earl of Angus and probably had little cash of his own in hand.

stza. 2, l. 1. *my Lord Chancellar*: the Earl of Angus, estranged husband of Margaret the Queen Dowager.   l. 2. *ballat*: here a general term for any short poem or song.   l. 3. *sonyeit*: excused himself.   l. 4. i.e. I should have liked to have more than he gave me.

stza. 3, l. 1. Henry Wemyss became Bishop of Galloway in 1526, and the adjective 'new' determines Sibbald's dating of the carol at the next New Year. The see of Galloway had been united with the Chapel Royal in 1504, so that the bishop was also head of the Chapel and constantly at court in Stirling. Wemyss was an illegitimate son of James IV, perhaps by a mother whose family name he used. l. 3. The sense and idiom suggest emendation to 'but', the reading of b. l. 4. *haiknay but hyd or hew*: literally a middle-sized horse without hide or colour. It must have a slang figurative meaning—possibly 'nothing at all'.

stza. 4, l. 1. The young Abbot of Halie Croce or Holyrood was William Douglas, brother of the Earl of Angus, about thirty-two years old in 1527. l. 4. I got no less than nothing.

stza. 5, l. 1. *Secretar*: Sir Thomas Erskine of Brechin, a member of a wealthy family.

stza. 6, l. 1. *Thesaur*: The Lord High Treasurer, Sir Archibald Douglas of Kinspindie. *Compttrollar*: James Colvill of Ochiltree, later of Easter Wemyss.

stza. 9, l. 1. *Lord Bothwell*: Patrick Hepburn, third Earl of Bothwell, whose mother was a Stewart, the daughter of the Earl of Buchan. Sibbald notes: 'This may account for his favour to a Stewart, and the consequent eulogy.' l. 2. *fredome*: generosity. l. 4. *with mell*: have to do with.

stza. 10, l. 1. *Margaret our Quene*: The Queen Dowager, widow of James IV and sister to Henry VIII, in 1527 married to the Earl of Angus but estranged and seeking a divorce, hence not at court. The poet says that if she were still Queen, she would be 'lerger of lufray', more generous in friendship than the others. l. 4. *the laif*: the rest. *of mene*: mention.

122. Of the Epiphany

A. *Pr.* C. & S., *M.L.R.* vi. 70; Whiting, p. 198; Kaiser, *Anth.*, p. 442, *Med. Engl.*, p. 295 (in part).

B. *Pr.* Wright, *Wart. Club*, p. 79, *P.S.* iv, 'Christmas Carols', 13; Dyboski, p. 171; Sandys, *Christmastide*, p. 226.

C. *Pr.* Dyboski, p. 10; Flügel, *Fest.*, p. 65, 'Lieder.', p. 236.

B.–R. 3526, 20.

For the sources of the Latin lines see table in Introduction, pp. lxxxvi–lxxxviii.

A. stza. 9, l. 2. *prest*: See note on No. 47, stza. 5, l. 3.

123. Of the Epiphany

A. *Pr.* Dyboski, p. 12; Flügel, *Fest.*, p. 67, 'Lieder.', p. 239; Greene, *Selection*, p. 86.

B. *Pr.* Wright, *Wart. Club*, p. 36; B. Fehr, *Archiv*, cix (1902), 52; Brown, *R.L. 15 C.*, p. 126.

B.–R. 3527, 2730.

The lack of the burden in B is possibly accidental, as the MS. has been disturbed at this point. A parchment leaf, the only one in the volume, now comes before f. 23ʳ. Before stza. 1 appears: dic. + This is perhaps the revising scribe's indication of an 'Alleluia' burden.

A. stza. 1, l. 1. The figure of the blossom from the thorn (carelessly reversed in B) is a slight variation of the 'Rod of Jesse' and 'Root of Jesse' symbolism. Compare *Cursor Mundi*, Fairfax text, ll. 9269–72 (ed. R. Morris, E.E.T.S., Or. Ser., No. 57, etc.)

> Iesse he [Isaiah] saide of his roting
> certanly a wande sulde spring
> out of þat wande a flour suld brest
> atte sulde bringe vs alle to rest.

No. 35 B begins:

> This nyght ther is a child born
> That sprange owt of Jessis thorn.

A. stza. 2, l. 1. *well*. See note on No. 306. The use of a well as a figure of Christ here is related to a legend told of the Nativity in Myrc's *Festial* (part i, ed. T. Erbe, E.E.T.S., Ex. Ser., No. xcvi, 1905, 26):

> Yn tokenyng of þys þyng, þat same day Cryst was borne yn Bedeleem, a well yn Rome of watyr turned ynto oyle and ran soo all þat day, schewyng þat þe well of grace and of mercy was borne þat day þat schuld ȝeue grace and mercy to all þat wold come to hym þerfor.

The well of mercy as a figure applied to Christ appears in a hymn rom the Thornton MS. (*pr.* Patterson, p. 131), but it is more often associated with Mary, as in Chaucer's *Prioress's Tale*, l. 204, and Nos. 199, 207. A well as the type of the divine mercy appears in No. 306 and in the Sloane MS., f. 32ᵛ, where 'lauacra pura gurgitis selestis angnus attigit peccata' is translated (Wright, *Wart. Club*, p. 96):

> The welle haght waschyn vs fro wo,
> The lomb of heuene is comyn vs to.

A. stza. 3, l. 1. *strake*: flowed.   l. 2. Whatever the reason for the different readings, the symbolism is valid in both versions. In A the birth of Christ is connected with the previous long captivity of Israel in Egypt. In B the allusion is to Christ's descent from the ancient line of Israel.

A. stza 5 (B. stza. 11). This appears as stza. 4 of No. 35, on which see note, and as stza. 6 of No. 124 A. The sequence referred to is probably that for the Mass on Epiphany, of which ll. 9, 10 run (*Sar. Miss.*, p. 465):

> Huic magi munera deferunt preclara aurum simul thus et myrram.
> Thure deum predicant. auro regem magnum. hominem mortalem myrra.

It appears to have been something of a *passe-partout* stanza. It has a recognizable survival in various versions of the favourite traditional carol 'The First Nowell', e.g. *O.B.C.*, No. 27, stza. 6:

> Then entered in those wise men three,
> Fell reverently upon their knee,
> And offered there in his presence
> Both gold and myrrh and frankincense.

A. stzas. 6–8 (B. stzas. 8–10). See Introduction, p. cxxi.

124. Of the Epiphany

A. *Pr.* Wright, *Wart. Club*, p. 40; B. Fehr, *Archiv*, cix (1902), 54.
B. *Pr.* Brown, *R.L. 15 C.*, p. 124.
B.–R. 1785.
burden. This unique property of the Star in the East, which is not mentioned in the gospel story, is included in the account of the Star's 'wonderfull governaunce' in a sermon in B.M. MS. Royal 18. B. XXIII, f. 130ʳ; 'Also, other steres, sawynge the sonne, clerely lyththens only by ny3the. But this stere shyned wondir clerely by day qwhils the sonne shyned, and also by ny3the' (G. R. Owst, *Literature and Pulpit in Medieval England*, Cambridge, 1933, p. 506).
A. stza. 2 (B. stza. 3), l. 3. The 'sun through glass' of B is, of course, the familiar figure for the conception of Christ, here given another application. The 'gold within the glass' of A has no such obvious source. The author may have been thinking of the sheen of the gold and glass of a reliquary, pyx, or other piece of ecclesiastical jewellery. Compare No. 125 A, stza. 8.
A. stza. 6. Compare Nos. 35, stza. 4, 123 A, stza. 5. The absence of the stanza in B suggests that it has been borrowed from one of these other carols.
B. stza. 7, l. 1. *gryll*: angry.
B. stza. 9, l. 3. *wonny*: remain.   l. 4. *Yn tyme*: until.

124.1. Of the Epiphany

Pr. C. Eveleigh Woodruff, *A XVth Century Guide-book to the Principal Churches of Rome Compiled c. 1470 by William Brewyn* (London, 1933), p. 81. B.-R. *Supp.* 3810.3.
stza. 2, l. 3. *in feere*: together.
stza. 3, l. 3. *verament*: truly.
stza. 5, l. 3. *swage hys bloode*: cool his anger.
stza. 7, ll. 1, 2. Matthew ii. 6.
stza. 11, l. 2. *precepte*: commanded.
stza. 15, l. 3. *ich*: same.
stza. 20, l. 1. *grylle*: fierce.
stza. 24, l. 4. An engaging (and unique) acknowledgement that the carol is a long one.

125. Of the Epiphany

A. *Pr.* Wright, *Wart. Club*, p. 49; B. Fehr, *Archiv*, cix (1902), 56; Greene, *Selection*, p. 87.
B a. *Pr.* James & Macaulay, p. 77.
   b. *Pr.* Wright, *P.S.* xxiii. 46.
B.–R. 2339.
   C. *Pr.* Wright, *P.S.* iv, 'Christmas Carols', p. 23; Sandys, *Christmastide*, p. 220; J. P. Edmond,
N. & Q., 6th Ser., vi, (1882), 506, from text in Lumley's *Bibliographical Advertiser* (1841); B.
Fehr, *Archiv*, cvii (1901), 55; Bullen, p. 250; Rickert, p. 10. B.–R. 2333.
   This long narrative of the Epiphany appears in only one of the four preserved texts as a true
carol with a burden. In that case the burden is not well adapted metrically to the stanza—text C,
however, begins without a heading at the top of a page of MS., and, as the preceding page in the
present binding is in a different hand and contains unrelated matter, it is possible that a page with
a burden has been lost. The probability is that the original form of the piece was that of a song
without a burden, particularly as the 'bob-and-wheel' type of stanza is not frequently combined
with a burden. Compare No. 123.
   A. burden. See table in Introduction, pp. lxxxvi, lxxxviii.
   A. stza. 8. See No. 124 A, stza. 2, and note thereon.
   A. stza. 16, ll. 1, 2. Compare App., No. ii, stza. 4, and No. 108, stza. 1, ll. 1, 2.
   C. stza. 11, l. 5. *Bydene-a*: together.

125.1. Of the Epiphany

Music for three voices. *Pr.* Greene, *Selection*, p. 90; with music, Stevens, *Med. Carols*, p. 40.
B.–R. *Supp.* 1070.5.
   This carol of only one stanza is obviously the beginning of a longer one, not preserved, on the
Epiphany with at least two more stanzas for the other Magi and their gifts. The burden may have
been suggested by the

              Ave, regina celorum,
              Mater Regis angelorum

of the Antiphon of the Virgin which so begins (*Horae Eboracenses*, Publications of the Surtees
Society, cxxxii, 1920, p. 29).

125.2. Of the Epiphany

Music for two and three voices. *Pr.* Greene, *Selection*, p. 90; with music, Stevens, *Med. Carols*,
p. 43. B.–R. *Supp.* 1320.5.
   This carol follows the tradition that the baptism of Christ took place on the anniversary of the
Epiphany. See notes on Nos. 130, 131.
   burden, l. 2. *duke*: sovereign prince.
   stza. 2, l. 3. The 'He' of the MS. must be a scribal error for 'His'.
   stza. 3. Matthew iii. 16–17; Mark i. 10–11; Luke iii. 22.

126. Of the Epiphany

Pr. Dyboski, p. 1; Flügel, *N.L.*, p. 122, 'Lieder.', p. 176; Frost, p. 258. B.–R. 2732.
   burden, l. 2. From a Versicle in Vespers for the Eve of Epiphany, etc. (*Br. Sar.* i, col. cccxix).
   stza. 4, l. 1. *leme*: light.   l. 3. *barn-teme*: offspring.
   stza. 7, l. 3. The myrrh is conventionally the sign of Christ's mortality; here it has apparently
been transferred to His Godhead, as the incense is assigned to His priesthood and manhood.
   stza. 8, l. 1. The suggestion of an aristocratic audience is to be noted. It is not necessarily to be
taken literally; it may allude to a Twelfth Night assembly in its character of the court of a King
or Lord of Misrule.

127. Of the Epiphany

Pr. Zupitza, 224, notes, xciv, 419–20, *Alt- und mittelenglisches Uebungsbuch*, 8th edn. (Vienna
and Leipzig, 1907), p. 191. B.–R. 3710.

This is an accomplished macaronic piece on the same plan as No. 75.

stza. 1, l. 2. Compare No. 23 A, stza. 6, ll. 1, 2. L. 2 appears as 'Stella micanta *par via*' in stza. 5 of 'A Christmas Carroll maid by Sir Richard Shanne priest' of the Roman Catholic Shann family of Methley, Yorkshire, written down in 1611 in B.M. MS. Addit. 38599, f. 135ᵛ, *pr.* Hyder E. Rollins, *PMLA*, xxxviii (1923), 141. Four stanzas are printed with music in *O.B.C.*, Music Edn., No. 10. The editors comment: '. . . this has the characteristics of a fifteenth-century carol, and the tune is in a style contemporary with the words'.

128. Of the Epiphany

Pr. Zupitza, 225, notes, xciv, 420. B.–R. 2690.

129. Of the Epiphany

Pr. Zupitza, 226, notes, xcv, 259–61. B.–R. 2691.

stza. 11, ll. 1–4. *Ysay.* This is in error for Jeremiah. The reference is to Matthew ii. 18 and Jeremiah xxxi. 15: 'Vox in excelso audita est lamentationis, luctus, et fletus Rachel plorantis filios suos, et nolentis consolari super eis, quia non sunt.'

130. Of the Epiphany

Pr. Zupitza, 236, notes, xcv, 272. B.–R. 2367.

This carol, like No. 131, is based on the tradition which early grew up in the Church that the visit of the Magi, the baptism of Christ in Jordan, and the miracle of Cana all took place on the same day of the year. It is so stated in Myrc's *Festial* (part i, ed. T. Erbe, E.E.T.S., Ex. Ser., No. xcvi, 1905, p. 48):

The þretten day aftyr his burþe, he was schewet by offryng of þre kynges; and þat same day, ix and xxᵗⁱ wyntyr and xiii dayes aftyr, he was folowet yn þe watyr of flem Iordan. And þat same day, twelmo[n]þe aftyr, he turnet watyr ynto wyne at þe weddyng yn þe Cane of Galyle.

Compare the Antiphon to the Magnificat in the Second Vespers of Epiphany in the modern Roman Breviary.

The miracle at Cana was probably so dated because of association of the water involved in it with the baptismal water of Jordan. The baptism of Christ was even more dominant in early celebration of the Epiphany than the visit of the Magi, and in the first centuries of the Western Church baptisms were usually performed on that date.

stza. 3, l. 2. *architriclyn.* See note on No. 90, stza. 2, l. 1.

stza. 5. Matthew iii. 17; Mark i. 10, 11; Luke iii. 22.

131. Of Christ's Baptism

a. Music for two and three voices, by John Trouluffe and Richard Smert. *Pr.* Fehr, p. 274; with music, Stevens, *Med. Carols*, p. 97.

b. *Pr.* Dyboski, p. 4; Flügel, *Fest.*, p. 55, 'Lieder.', p. 196.

B.–R. 3975.

a. burden. Luke iv. 1 (used as Gospel in the Third Nocturn on Epiphany): 'Jesus autem plenus Spiritu Sancto regressus est a Jordane.'

b. burden. The substitution of 'Egressus est de virgine' is probably the result of some one's wish to make the carol more appropriate to Christmas Day itself. If may, however, represent a reminiscence of the venerable tradition that Christ's baptism took place on the anniversary of His birth rather than on that of the visit of the Magi.

stza. 1. Response 7 in the third Nocturn on Epiphany (*Br. Sar.* i, col. cccxxvi): 'Hodie in Jordane baptizato Domino aperti sunt caeli: et sicut columba super eum Spiritus mansit, et vox Patris intonuit, Hic est Filius meus dilectus in quo michi complacui.'

132–5. The Boar's Head Carols

The number of extant carols on the theme of the boar's head may seem surprisingly small in view of the amount that has been written about the custom. The picturesqueness of the observance, its survival at Queen's College, Oxford, now much imitated elsewhere, and the excellence of the traditional tune of No. 132 have combined to give these carols a prominence out of proportion to their number.

Nos. 134 and 135 are merely convivial; Nos. 132 and 133, particularly the latter, show the artificial Christianizing of the custom.

The emphasis on the place of the boar's head as the first course of a meal and on mustard as its accompaniment reflects definite points of medieval etiquette. See the fourteenth- and fifteenth-century bills-of-fare in Thomas Austin, ed., *Two Fifteenth-Century Cookery-Books* (E.E.T.S., Or. Ser., No. 91, 1888), pp. 67–9, and the directions for a 'dynere of flesche' in F. J. Furnivall, ed., *The Babees Book* (E.E.T.S., Or. Ser., No. 32, 1868), p. 164: 'Furst set forthe mustard & brawne of boore þe wild swyne.' Compare the *al fresco* luncheon of the shepherds in the *Towneley Plays*, ed. G. England and A. W. Pollard (E.E.T.S., Ex. Ser., No. lxxi, 1897), p. 107:

> 'lay furth of oure store,
> lo here! browne of a bore.'
> 'Set mustard afore,
> oure mete now begyns,'

and a boar's head song of 1607 (*pr.* Wright, *P.S.* iv, 'Christmas Carols', p. 63):

> Lett this boares-head and mustard
> Stand for pigg, goose and custard,
> And so you are welcome all.

The loss of the first leaf of St. John's College, Cambridge, MS. S. 54 has left only the last stanza of a boar's head piece which was probably a carol (App., No. iii).

The song in Bodl. MS. Eng. poet. e. 1 (*pr.* Wright, *P.S.* xxiii. 25) which tells how the singer has killed an attacking boar recalls the traditional account of the origin of the Queen's College custom, although the weapon in the song is a sword and not a choking volume of Aristotle. In stza. 2 of the song the hearers are told: 'Take yow bred and musterd therto.'

132. A Carol Bringing In the Boar's Head

A. *Pr.* Dyboski, p. 33; Flügel, *N.L.*, p. 123, *Fest.*, p. 77, 'Lieder.', p. 257; C. & S., p. 235; *Babees Book*, p. 398; Pollard, p. 92; Greene, *Selection*, p. 91; Sisam, p. 532; Davies, p. 278.

B. *Repr.* Ritson, *Ancient Songs* (1790), p. 125, (1820), ii. 16, (1877), p. 159; J. Cundall, *A Booke of Christmas Carols* (London, 1846), p. [9]; J. Ames, *Typographical Antiquities*, ed. T. F. Dibdin (London, 1810–19), ii. 251; Joshua Sylvester, *pseud.*, *A Garland of Christmas Carols, Ancient and Modern* (London, 1861), p. 155; E. Flügel, *Anglia*, xii (1889), 587, *N.L.*, p. 123; Bullen, p. 170; Mary G. Segar and Emmeline Paxton, *Some Minor Poems of the Middle Ages* (London, 1917), p. 14; etc.

C. *Pr.*, with music, J. R. Magrath, *The Queen's College* (Oxford, 1921), ii. 240–1; etc. See Introduction, pp. cxxx–cxxxi.

B.–R. 3313.

A is probably earlier than B and later than No. 135, on which see Note. The last stanza marks the ceremonial serving of the boar's head as a custom confined to the Christmas season. The 'byrdes syngynge' of stza. 1, l. 2 may mean an actual garnishing of the charger with captive live birds, a procedure not too elaborate for a Tudor feast.

Stza. 3 of B, which changes the metre and has hackneyed commonplaces for ll. 1 and 3, may be patched up from an imperfect recollection of the stanza which appears as the third of C. If this is the case, the stanza had probably a Latin fourth line differing from that of C, which adapts it to the Queen's College hall.

It is more likely that the college adopted a well-known carol from popular circulation than that a carol originating in the college gained currency of the kind indicated by No. 135 and Hill's and Wynkyn de Worde's recordings. Magdalen College, Oxford, had a boar's head as Christmas decoration in 1488–9, though there is no record of a procession (William Dunn Macray, *A Register of the Members of St. Mary Magdalen College, Oxford*, New Ser., i, London, 1894, p. 21).

Some of the special pride of place enjoyed by the boar's head at dinner on Christmas Day was probably due to the fact that in the time of Edward II the open season for boar ran from Christmas to Candlemas (James Edmund Harting, *British Animals Extinct Within Historic Times*, Boston, 1880, p. 80). There is a modern parallel in the importance attached by some people to having grouse on the dinner table on the twelfth of August. According to F. Marian McNeill, the boar's head, like all pork, was shunned in Scotland and totally banned from court when James I, who observed the taboo, succeeded Elizabeth I. The turkey was brought in from the New World just in time to become the festal meat for Christmas (*The Silver Bough, iii, A Calendar of Scottish National Festivals Hallowe'en to Yule*, Glasgow, 1961, p. 69). The wild boar became extinct in England in the seventeenth century, but the exact date is not established (Harting, op. cit., p. 100).

133. A Boar's Head Carol

Music for two and three voices. *Pr.* Wright, *P.S.* iv, 'Christmas Carols', p. 50; Flügel, *N.L.*, p. 124; Ritson, *Ancient Songs* (1790), p. 127, (1829), ii. 16, (1877), p. 160; Sandys, *Carols*, p. 16; Sandys, *Christmastide*, p. 223; R. T. Hampson, *Medii Aevi Kalendarium* (London, 1841), i. 95; Greene, *Selection*, p. 91; with music, *Mus. Ant.*, p. 22; Stevens, *Med. Carols*, p. 66; Robbins, *Christmas Carols*, p. 13. B.-R. 3315.

The boar's head as a symbol of Christ occurs only in this carol, as far as I am aware. In the better known No. 132 it is said to be served in Christ's honour, but it is not explained symbolically, as here. See also App., No. iii.

134. A Boar's Head Carol

Pr. Wright, *P.S.* xxiii. 42; Robbins, *Secular Lyrics*, p. 48. B.-R. 436.

burden, l. 1. Not, as it might seem, merely a repetitive nonsense phrase, but the sound used to call pigs, like the modern 'Pig, pig, pig!' or 'Soo-ee!' and hence a suitable burden with which to greet a boar's head and brawn. Compare the play *Misogonus* (?1577), Act III, Scene i. Codrus enters, calling two hens and his lost sow in what has not hitherto been recognized as a carol:

> Po, po, po,
> Come Jacke, come Jacke,
> Heave slowe, heave slowe

how now my mosters did none of yow see my sondid sowe
thers nere a one in our end oth towne Ime sure hath worse happe.
when I sett hir out to mast would I had out hir to my pesse mowe.
This lucke in dede both bullchinge [bull-calf] and sowe gone all at a clappe.
[Three stanzas in all]
(R. Warwick Bond, ed., *Early Plays from the Italian*, Oxford, 1911, p. 221, stzas. 1, 2)

This is a hog-call from the Yorkshire dialect which Codrus speaks, hence appropriate to a feasting carol from Beverley. In the MS. the burden is written as one line, and the last four words have been added by a different hand.　　l. 2. 'I' or 'We' is to be understood at the beginning. *brane*: brawn, boar's flesh.

stza. 3. It is implied that guests will be called on to sing after this, the first, course. Compare the carol reported as sung after the King's first course, Introduction, p. xxix.

135. A Boar's Head Carol

Pr. Wright, *P.S.* iv, 'Christmas Carols', 3; *Rel. Ant.* ii. 30; Sandys, *Christmastide*, p. 230; F. J. Furnivall, *The Babees Book*, p. 264; Robbins, *Secular Lyrics*, p. 49; Silverstein, p. 145. B.-R. 3314.

All the stanzas are written in the MS. as belonging to one piece. The original carol, however, plainly ended with stza. 3, which records the departure of the boar's head after Twelfth Day. The stanzas in a different metre which follow, with their incidental mention of the boar's head, must have been taken from another piece, to a different tune. The first part has a common source with No. 132 A, stzas. 1 and 3 being substantially the same except for the refrain. As they appear in this carol, without Latin or religious allusion, they are probably nearer to the ultimate original than the more artistic version of No. 132, which was written down about half a century later.

The second part is a mere versifying of a medieval bill-of-fare. Recipes for some of the dishes mentioned are referred to by Furnivall, op. cit.

The note contributed by Chappell to Furnivall, loc. cit., calling the burden an accompaniment or undersong and not a chorus between stanzas is not justified in view of the usual carol practice and the absence of music for this piece.

stza. 4, l. 2. *bytteris*: bitterns.　　l. 3. *snyt*: snipe.

stza. 5, l. 1. *schow*. Furnivall suggests *sewe*, stew.   l. 3. *Blwet of allmaynn*: 'brouet of almayne or 'breuet de almond', a dish of crushed almonds done up with milk.   *romnay*: a sweet Greek wine, much drunk in the fifteenth century.

stza. 7, l. 1. *Furmante to potdtage*: frumenty as a pottage, a favourite dish made of wheat and milk.   l. 2. *hombuls of the dow*: umbles or numbles of the doe, i.e. certain of the entrails of the deer used as food. This is an earlier use of the form with the *h* than any recorded by *O.E.D.*

stza. 8, l. 1. *roow*: roe, deer.

136. Holly Against Ivy

A. *Pr.* Ritson, *Ancient Songs* (1790), p. 74, (1829), i. 132, (1877), p. 114; Sandys, *Carols*, p. 1; Joshua Sylvester, *pseud.*, *A Garland of Christmas Carols, Ancient and Modern* (London, 1861), p. 144; C. Russell, *N. & Q.*, 12th Ser., vi (1920), 22; E. Arber, *The Dunbar Anthology* (London, 1901), p. 145; Dyboski, p. 189; Greene, *Selection*, p. 92; Sisam, p. 451; Davies, p. 175; etc.

B. *Pr.* Dyboski, p. 116; Flügel, *Fest.*, p. 83, 'Lieder.', p. 279; C. & S., p. 239; Greene, *Selection*, p. 93; Davies, p. 280.

B.–R. 1226.

On the background of folk-lore see Introduction, pp. cxxii–cxxvii.

The highly imaginative commentary of E. Stredder in *N. & Q.*, 8th Ser., ix (1896), 4, has received no support.

Version A, from a Midland MS. of the mid-fifteenth century, unquestionably derives from an older text than does Richard Hill's Version B, and it gives the clearer suggestion of a carol which was used in some sort of game between men and women. Version B, with its four-line stanzas which use some of A's couplets in a different order, is definitely more self-conscious and literary. Its 'chairs of gold', its long simile of a herd of bullocks used to characterize the clumsiness of any dancing done by women, and its long treatment of the wood-pigeon, still among the most despised of English birds, and its insult to ivy all impress the hearer as belonging to a sophisticated and on the whole less successful reworking of a simple original. Nevertheless it is B that gives the only suggestion of a direct connection with the very popular traditional song 'The Holly and the Ivy', most texts of which begin one or more stanzas with 'The holly bears a berry'. Apparently this one phrase at least has survived from the Middle Ages to appear in a piece of which Margaret Dean-Smith insists on the modernity (*Guide*, p. 74): 'Although now so well-known, the text of "The Holly and the Ivy", with the possible exception of the Cornish version given in [*J.F.S.S.* viii (1931), 113–15], (cp. "Cherry, holly and ivy" in the same number [pp. 111–12]) appears to derive from a single source, a Birmingham broadside published by Wadsworth, according to Husk "about one-and-a-half centuries since", i.e. c. 1710.' But it was probably not written in a Birmingham printing-office.

A. stza. 4, l. 1. See B. J. W., *Proverbs*, R 199.

A. stza. 5, l. 1. See ibid., S 385.

A. stza. 6, l. 2. *poppynguy*. Rather than to the parrot, as usual, the word must refer here to an English bird, probably the sometimes disliked green woodpecker, although *O.E.D.* first records such use from 1612. Walter de la Mare has a well-informed note confirming this meaning:

'Poppynguy' may perhaps be the jay, but it would be pleasanter company for the lark, if here it means the green woodpecker. He drills out his holes in the small hours of the morning, his slender barb-tipped tongue busy with what stirs therein. He drums for his lady-love and yaffles or laughs out glassy and clear, in the sunny green tops of the woods (*Come Hither*, new edn., London, 1928, p. 650).

A. stza. 7, l. 2 (B. stza. 1, l. 4). The association of the owl with ivy is traditional over many centuries, and the expression 'like an owl in an ivy-bush' is proverbial. See, for example, William George Smith, *The Oxford Dictionary of English Proverbs* (Oxford, 1935), p. 44. The expression sometimes refers to the enmity of the smaller birds towards the owl and their concerted attacks on it. In *The Owl and the Nightingale* human attack is also described (ll. 65–8, 1115–20). Compare a simile from the seventeenth century, 'With that they all fell upon him, as an Oule in an ivie bush' (*N. & Q.*, 9th Ser., ix, 1902, 157).

J. Payne Collier's ballad, 'Full mournfully hootes Madge Howlet, / Under the ivy bushe', is apparently one of his fabrications made to fit entries in the Stationers' Register and has no evidential value (*Twenty-five Old Ballads and Songs*, London, 1869, p. 32).

137. In Praise of Holly

Pr. Wright, *P.S.* xxiii. 84; C. & S., p. 238; F. A. Patterson, B. Matthews, and A. H. Thorndike, *Shaksperian Studies* (New York, 1916), p. 444; Robbins, *Secular Lyrics*, p. 46. B.-R. 1195.
See Introduction, p. cxxvii.
stza. 3, l. 2. *lepe*: basket. The reference is to a punishment or forfeit. Compare the New Year's custom of Cumberland and Westmorland reported in the *Gentleman's Magazine* in 1791 (lxi, part ii, 1169): '. . . the *Faex Populi* assemble together, carrying *stangs* [poles] and baskets. Any inhabitant, stranger, or whoever joins not this ruffian tribe in sacrificing to their favourite Saint-day, if unfortunate enough to be met by any of the band, is immediately mounted across the stang (if a woman, she is basketed), and carried, shoulder height, to the nearest public house, where the payment of six pence immediately liberates the prisoner.'
The feminine form of the punishment is obviously the appropriate one for a detractor of Holly. C. & S. rather ruthlessly gloss 'lepe' as 'noose'.
Hoisting in a basket as a punishment for male defaulters on bets at a cockfight is reported from eighteenth-century England by the visitor Z. C. von Uffenbach (Rosamond Bayne-Powell, *Travellers in Eighteenth-Century England*, London, 1951, p. 86).

138. In Praise of Ivy

Pr. Wright, *P.S.* xxiii. 85; C. & S., p. 236; Robbins, *Secular Lyrics*, p. 46; Greene, *Selection*, p. 93; Sisam, p. 480; Davies, p. 228. B.-R. 3438.
See Introduction, p. cxxvii.
burden, l. 2. See note on No. 262, burden, l. 2.

139. In Praise of Ivy

Pr. James & Macaulay, p. 83. B.-R. 2735.
Compare other carols on the virtues of letters, Nos. 83, 180.
stza. 4, l. 1. *V*: pronounced, of course, as 'U'.
stza. 6, l. 2. Is the comely lady meant to be the Virgin herself? At any rate she conforms to the tradition of the female sponsorship of Ivy, and the stanza makes of the carol a *chanson d'aventure*.
stza. 7, l. 2. *tray*: deceit.   ll. 3, 4. Compare No. 138, stza. 2, l. 1. James and Macaulay's reading of 'burdys' may have been due to a recollection of No. 136.

139.1. In Praise of Ivy

Music for two and three voices. *Pr.* Greene, *Selection*, p. 94; with music, Stevens, *Med. Carols*, p. 44. B.-R. *Supp.* 1651.5.
The association of ivy with Christmas is not made explicit in this interesting carol, but from its inclusion in the series of carols in this MS. we can safely assume that it was meant for use in the Nativity season. It differs from the other holly–ivy carols in that it sings the praise of the plant itself, making no symbolic application.
stza. 2, l. 2. Here the reference seems to be to ground ivy (*Nepeta hederacea*); in the next stanza it shifts to climbing ivy (*Hedera helix*).   l. 4. There are many medieval prescriptions for the use of ivy in medicine, e.g. *Liber de Diversis Medicinis* in the Thornton MS. (Lincoln Cathedral A. 5. 2), mid-fifteenth century, from the North Riding of Yorkshire and written by the scribe of No. 91 (ed. Margaret Sinclair Ogden, E.E.T.S., Or. Ser., No. 207, 1938, p. 17): 'An oþer [for toothache]. Tak yven and salte & stampe to-gedir & mak a playster & laye to þe cheke, for þat hales wale'; and *An Herbal* [1525, printed by Richard Banckes of London] (ed. Sanford V. Larkey and Thomas Pyles, N.Y., 1941, p. 27): 'The virtue thereof is, if it be sodden in wine till it be thick, and then lay it all hot to a botch, it shall break it.' An infusion of ivy is often recommended for sore eyes. A long list of its medical uses is given by Hermann Fischer, *Mittelalterliche Pflanzenkunde* (Munich, 1929), p. 211.   ll. 5, 6. The phrase 'In bok' suggests that the author of the carol may have known the widely circulated *Blason des Couleurs*, written between 1435 and 1458 by Sicille, Herald of King Alphonse V of Aragon (ed. Hippolyte Cocheris, Paris, 1860). Compare 'De la Couleur Verde et de ses Livrees' (p. 83): 'La couleur verde est délectable à la veue et luy donne grant plaisir, et traict les yeulx à la regarder et les reconforte, et pare quant ils sont grevez.'

stza. 3, l. 3. The reference to 'gret stormys of snaw and hail' rather strongly suggests a North-of-England origin for the carol.

The fairest bird, otherwise unspecified, cannot be the owl traditionally associated with ivy. This is another mark of originality in this carol; it may even be a reply to the taunt directed toward Ivy in No. 136.

stza. 5, l. 3. Widely differing opinions have long been held as to the effect of a growth of ivy on masonry. The *Encyclopaedia Britannica* (14th edn., s.v. 'Ivy') holds with the author of the carol: '. . . a fair growth of ivy on sound walls that afford no entrance beyond the superficial attachment of the claspers is, without any exception whatever, beneficial. It promotes dryness and warmth, reduces to a minimum the corrosive action of the atmosphere, and is altogether as conservative as it is beautiful.' But many caretakers believe the opposite.   l. 4. *at hye*: Stevens glosses 'at eye', i.e. at first sight or plainly. This makes good sense, of course, but for the possibility of a reference to the lost hamlet of Hythe in Holderness see R. L. Greene, *J.A.M.S.* vii (1954), 24–5. 'Eye' and 'Hythe' as place-names were more or less interchangeable, and a famous confusion of Eye in Suffolk and Hythe in Kent once resulted. The hamlet of Hythe was still well enough remembered in the eighteenth century to be given a special note on a map of Holderness.

140. Of the Purification

Pr. Wright, *P.S.* xxiii. 56; Greene, *Selection*, p. 95. B.–R. 503.

This is a farewell to the Christmas season which emphasizes, not the festal aspect of Candlemas like No. 38, but its religious meaning, in which the Virgin is, of course, the central figure. It is unusual in praying for 'purification' of the individual soul, through Mary's help, and in not confining itself to the historic incident of her own ritual appearance in the Temple (Luke ii. 22–4).

The 'revertere' of the burden is probably from Canticles vi. 12: 'Revertere, revertere, Sulamitis; revertere, revertere, ut intueamur te,' rather than Isaiah xliv. 22: '. . . revertere ad me, quoniam redemi te.' Compare the burden of *Carmina Burana* (ed. Carl Fischer, Zürich and Munich, 1974), No. 181:

> Revertere, revertere
> iam, ut 'intueamur' te.

141. Farewell to Christmas

Pr. Dyboski, p. 18; Flügel, *N.L.*, p. 126, *Fest.*, p. 72, 'Lieder.', p. 245; Pollard, p. 89; Frost, p. 328; Greene, *Selection*, p. 96; Sisam, p. 531. B.–R. 1198.

Like No. 140 this carol puts 'the end of Christmas' at Candlemas rather than at Twelfth Day. See note on No. 7. Less usual in popular tradition is the notion of stza. 1, l. 2 that Christmas begins as early as 'Hallowtide', i.e. the first of November.

The personification of Christmas is parallel to that in Nos. 5, 6, 7, 8, to which this piece forms an interesting complement. The refrain and burden are like an echo of No. 5. The whole carol implies some sort of dramatic presentation with the impersonation of Christmas by a singer. An aristocratic or at least a well-to-do gathering is the audience to which it is expressly directed.

A closely similar conception of a farewell to Christmas is the basis of the delightful seventeenth-century song for Candlemas beginning:

> Christmas hath made an end,
> Welladay, welladay.
> (Norman Ault, ed., *Seventeenth Century Lyrics*, London, 1928, p. 324)

In this song Lent is also personified as in Nos. 3, 4.

stza. 2, ll. 1, 2. Compare No. 350, stza. 3, ll. 1, 2.

stza. 4, l. 2. *Merchall*. See note on No. 11, stza. 1, l. 2.   *panter*: pantryman.

stza. 6. Compare Gower, *Confessio Amantis*, Bk. iv, ll. 2814–15:

> Bot he seith often, 'Have good day',
> That loth is forto take his leve.

142. Of the Nativity

A a. *Pr.* James & Macaulay, p. 76; Greene, *Selection*, p. 97.

b. *Pr.* J. A. Robinson and M. R. James, *The Manuscripts of Westminster Abbey* (Cambridge, 1909), p. 76; R. L. Greene, *E.L.H.* vii (1940), 225.

B a. *Repr.* R. L. Greene, *E.L.H.* vii (1940), 228.
b, c. Collated loc. cit.
B.–R. 30.

The 'lollay' burden of this carol is written in a hand different from that of the stanzas in a space presumably left for it at the top of the page. The piece is not a regular lullaby carol, but is related to the type through its presenting a narrative of the life of Christ such as is given at much greater length in No. 149 a, a carol which has as its burden the first two lines of this burden. It seems likely that A b represents the earlier form, using as burden what is in A a the first stanza. Significantly these four lines are not bracketed in the MS. as the following stanzas are. The change is of the same type as that found in No. 157.

For a fuller discussion and collation of texts see Greene, op. cit., pp. 225–31.

Another traditional piece with an obvious relation to 'Sweet Jesus' is 'All in the Morning', which Margaret Dean-Smith (*Guide*, p. 47) treats as a version of this carol. It is found in Sandys, *Carols*, pp. 117–18, with title 'Upon Christmas Day', and in R. Vaughan Williams, *Eight Traditional English Carols* (London, 1919), p. 4, as derived from W. H. Shawcross, *A Garland of the Old Castleton Christmas Carols* (Castleton, 1904), pp. 10–12. Shawcross's text begins as follows:

> It was on Christmas Day,
> And all in the morning,
> [repeated as l. 2 of all stanzas]
> Our Saviour was Born,
> And our Heavenly King;
>
> And was not this a joyful thing,
> And sweet JESUS they call'd Him by Name.
> [repeated as refrain after each of next four stanzas]

'A General Carrol for any time' in the pamphlet *New Christmas Carrols* (*c.* 1642) uses as a stanza-refrain: 'Good Lord was not this a joyful [*stza. 4*, sorrowful; *stza. 5* woful] thing? / Sweet *Jesus* is his name.' (Bodl. Wood 110 (5), B3ᵛ).

143. Of the Virgin and Child

Pr. Wright, *Wart. Club*, p. 94; B. Fehr, *Archiv*, cvii (1901), 49; C. & S., p. 131; G. Bullett, *The English Galaxy of Shorter Poems* (London, 1947), p. 7; Greene, *Selection*, p. 98; Davies, p. 166; Gray, *Lyrics*, p. 12; etc. B.–R. 1351.

The metre of this, the masterpiece of the lullaby carols, makes the same effective use of the 'rest' as does 'I sing of a maiden'. One is inclined to attribute it to the same unknown author.

144. The Virgin's Lullaby

Music for two voices. *Pr.*, with music, Ritson, *Ancient Songs* (1790), p. xxxviii, (1829), i. liv, (1877), p. xlvii; Stevens, *Med. Carols*, p. 1; M. F. Bukofzer, *J.A.M.S.* vii (1954), 74; Robbins, *Christmas Carols*, p. 70. B.–R. 1352.

There is no satisfactory reason for attributing the authorship of the carol to Friar John Brackley, the friend of the Pastons. See Bibliography of Original Sources.

The burden is not marked for division into lines, and the arrangement here made is an arbitrary one. The carol is probably incomplete.

stza. 1, l. 2. *birde*: maiden.   l. 3. *of mange*: among, meanwhile. 'that mornig made and' is written in Cambridge University Library MS. Ii. 4. 11 at the side of the text of No. 36 a and in the hand of that carol. It may indicate that the scribe of No. 36 a knew this piece.

144.1. The Virgin to Her Child

Pr. N. R. Ker, *Medium Ævum*, xxxiv (1965), 233.

This lullaby carol, recently brought to notice by N. R. Ker, develops the theme of Mary's child as both her father and her brother with considerable charm and with a lyric unity not always found in carols of its type. Both burden and stanzas keep to the structure of a monologue in simple and direct style. John Morton, owner of the MS., may possibly have been the author of the carol, but I must doubt this identification, since the hand in which it is written differs, in my judgement, from the undoubted hand of Morton in a memorandum on a preceding page and another on the same page with the carol.

stza. 1, l. 2. The failure of the rhyme suggests a defect of memory in oral transmission.

stza. 4, l. 2. *drey*: endure. l. 3. *perschyth*: tears.

145. Of the Virgin and Child

a. *Pr.* Wright, *P.S.* xxiii. 50; Sitwell, *Atlantic Book*, p. 7.
b. *Pr.* Wright, *Wart. Club*, p. 48.
Composite text. *Pr.* C. & S., p. 141.
B.–R. 361.
burden, l. 1. See B. J. W., *Proverbs*, L 285.

stza. 1, l. 2. This is a slight variation from the usual *chanson d'aventure* opening in the carols in which the singer says definitely that he saw or heard the incident described. An earlier reading 'Me thought I saw', etc. may be conjectured.

stza. 5, l. 2. *thou haddys be lor*. One wonders what any reader has ever made of Dame Edith Sitwell's glossing: 'thou hadst by the law'.

146. Of the Virgin and Child

A. Music for three voices. *Pr.* Fehr, p. 60; Sandys, *Carols*, p. 11; C. & S., p. 157; Sitwell, *Atlantic Book*, p. 17; Stevens, *M. & P.*, p. 366; with music, *Madrigals by English Composers of the Close of the Fifteenth Century* (Plainsong and Mediaeval Music Society, London, 1893), No. 5; Stevens, *Early Tudor Songs*, p. 78.
B. *Pr.* Brown, *R.L. 15 C.*, p. 4.
B.–R. 3597.

The two preserved versions of this carol, while differing widely in details and sharing some features with others of the lullaby-dialogue group, are yet recognisable as deriving from a common original. The grouping into longer stanzas is probably the result of adapting words of a musically simpler carol to the longer melody of a more sophisticated setting.

The poverty of the Holy Family and lack of clothing for the infant Jesus are used picturesquely in various Middle English accounts of the Nativity which aim at arousing pity after the fashion of the *Meditationes Vitae Christi*. Compare the Nativity Legend from British Museum MS. Egerton 1993, ll. 585–8 (*pr.* C. Horstmann, *Altenglische Legenden*, Paderborn, 1875, p. 91):

> Heo nedde whar inne oure lorde winde, þo he was ibore,
> Bote in feble cloutes and olde. and somme to tore,
> þer inne oure ledi him wond. and bond him wiþ aliste,
> And leide him on awisp of hei; þer was apore giste.

See also the poem in National Library of Scotland MS. Advocates 18. 7. 21 and British Museum MS. Harley 7322 (*pr.* Brown, *R.L. 14 C.*, p. 91) on the Christ Child's sufferings from cold.

The language and spelling of B show that it was written down in the North. The simile of the refrain in B appears also in Lydgate's *Life of Our Lady* (Cambridge University Library MS. Mm. 6. 5, stza. 54) and in 'A Song of Love to the Blessed Virgin' in the Vernon MS., ll. 95–6 (*pr.* Brown, *R.L. 14 C.*, p. 178):

> Heo is of colour and beute
> As fresch as is þe Rose In May.

It is applied to the Virgin's tears of blood in the 'De arte lacrimandi', stza. 71, ll. 5, 6 (see note on No. 161). Compare Chaucer, *Legend of Good Women*, l. 613. With 'flower' or 'flowers' in place of 'rose' the image persists in the sixteenth century, e.g. in Lewis Wager's play of *The Life and Repentaunce of Marie Magdalene* (*c.* 1560): 'Freshe and flourishyng as the floures in May', and in the morality *The World and the Child* (1522): 'I am as fresshe as flourys in maye', both cited by B. J. Whiting, *Proverbs in the Earlier English Drama*, Harvard Studies in Comparative Literature, xiv (Cambridge, Massachusetts, 1938), p. 313.

A. stza. 1, l. 15. *pay*: liking.
B. stza. 1, l. 6. *powaret*: poverty.
B. stza. 2, l. 3. *hap*: wrap.

B. stza. 4, l. 5. *clas*: clothes. *yarn*: yearn (for), desire. l. 6. *Bot wat*: but. *rowght*: reached, obtained.

B. stza. 6, l. 6. *dere*: injure.

B. stza. 7, ll. 1–3. The meaning is somewhat obscure. It may be: 'It shall fall to the truest out of all the apostles (i.e. John) to dwell with you.' ll. 4–6. Adam will be rescued with the other patriarchs by Christ's harrowing of hell.

B. stza. 9, ll. 5, 6. Christ will rise on the third day after His betrayal. The author apparently regards the betrayal as belonging to the same day as the Crucifixion.

147. The Christ Child to His Mother

Pr. Brown, *R.L. 15 C.*, p. 3; Silverstein, p. 107; Tydeman, p. 48. B.–R. 1264.

The burden represents Mary as speaking, the stanzas Jesus. The carol appears to be of Northern origin.

stza. 3, l. 4. *whake*: quake.

stza. 4, ll. 1, 3. *besett*: employed, expended.

Brown (p. 293) points out the similarity of this piece to the long carol No. 149 a.

148. Of the Virgin and Child

A. *Pr.* Wright, *Wart. Club*, p. 46, *P.S.* iv, 'Christmas Carols', 8; Brougham, p. 5 (in part); Brown, *R.L. 15 C.*, p. 120; R. S. Thomas, *The Penguin Book of Religious Verse* (Harmondsworth, 1963), p. 43 (in part).

B. *Pr.* James & Macaulay, p. 83.

B.–R. 3329.

The changed rhythm in the stanzas beginning with 'Lullay' in both A and B suggests that the carol is made from two earlier pieces. The burden as found in A is better as regards both language and sense than in B. The burden of B has been made by incorporating a part of the first stanza with the initial line of the original burden. Compare Nos. 23, 142, 157.

A. stza. 6, l. 2. *schour*: assault.

A. stza. 9, l. 1. This line appears as the burden of No. 155, on which see note.

149. Of the Virgin and Child

a. *Pr.* Brown, *R.L. 14 C.*, p. 70; Davies, p. 112; A. Obertello, *Liriche religiose inglesi del secolo quattordicesimo* (Milan, 1947), p. 110 (with Italian translation); Sarah Appleton Weber, *Theology and Poetry in the Middle English Lyric* (Columbus, Ohio, 1969), pp. 61–8.

b. *Pr.* James & Macaulay, p. 72.

c. *Pr.* Sandison, p. 103.

d. Music for one voice. *Pr.*, with music, Mayer, sheet i; Stevens, *Med. Carols*, p. 110; Robbins, *Christmas Carols*, p. 73.

B.–R. 352.

The long Northern version a of this carol, which is in the earliest MS., is probably the original from which the other texts are abridged. The MSS. of b and d give no indication that their scribes had any idea of writing more, but c was apparently not finished by its writer. Miss Sandison's note (loc. cit.) describes the MS. accurately: 'Sufficient space is left at the foot of the page for at least one strophe; this part of the page is badly rubbed, as if a few more lines, including another *lull* in the margin, have been erased.'

Mrs. Weber alleges 'ballad-like characteristics' for this carol (p. 244). She says further that 'It is difficult to believe that the refrain [burden] would be repeated after each of the 37 stanzas' and makes an unsupported suggestion of the repetition of the burden after groups of five stanzas. The length of the carol need not surprise anyone; compare the thirty stanzas of Audelay's carol to St. Winifred (No. 314).

In the post-medieval period 'Christmas carols' which seem over-long to an impatient modern are not unknown. 'All ye who are to mirth inclined' had twenty-three verses in 1631, and *The Decree* or 'Let Christians all with one accord rejoice' (1847) had twenty-three (Erik Routley, *The English Carol*, London, 1958, p. 128). George Borrow refers to the *carvals* in the Isle of Man as being of 'enormous length' (ibid., p. 219).

stza. 9, l. 2. *wone*: delay. Mrs. Weber attempts to make 'withouten wone' mean 'without custom or 'outside the law of women; that is, without pain' (pp. 75, 243–4). This is an obvious syntactical impossibility, as the phrase precedes the introductory 'that' of the clause which she would take to include it. She wrongly attributes this gloss to Carleton Brown, who does not offer it in this place.

stza. 19, stza. 30, ll. 1, 2. Luke ii. 34–5: '. . . Ecce positus est hic in ruinam, et in resurrectionem multorum in Israel, et in signum cui contradicetur: et tuam ipsius animam pertransibit gladius, ut revelentur ex multis cordibus cogitationes.'

stza. 21, l. 2. *sterue*: (?) die. Emendation to 'suerue' (as in Brown) improves the sense.

stza. 24, l. 2. *fawen*: eager. *fonde*: tempt, prove.

stza. 28, l. 3. *bales bete*: relieve miseries.

150. Of the Virgin and Child

A. *Pr. Rel. Ant.* ii. 76; Dyboski, p. 175; A. Brandl and O. Zippel, *Middle English Literature*, 2nd edn. (New York, 1949), p. 114; Greene, *Selection*, p. 99.

B. *Pr.* Wright, *P.S.* xxiii. 12; C. & S., p. 121; John Julian, *A Dictionary of Hymnology*, 2nd edn. (London, 1925), p. 209; F. E. Budd, *A Book of Lullabies 1300–1900* (London, 1930), p. 34; Sisam, p. 466.

C. *Pr.* Dyboski, p. 25; Flügel, *N.L.*, p. 120, 'Lieder.', 250; Lord David Cecil, *The Oxford Book of Christian Verse* (Oxford, 1940), p. 5 (omits burden).

D. Music for three voices. *Pr.* Flügel, *N.L.*, p. 119, *Anglia*, xii (1889), 270; Mary G. Segal and Emmeline Paxton, *Some Minor Poems of the Middle Ages* (London, 1917), p. 44; with music, Terry, p. 60; music of D with text of B, *O.B.C.*, Music Edn., p. 82.

Flügel divides the stanzas wrongly, apparently misunderstanding the nature of the burden.

B.–R. 3627.

Stephen Manning, in an explication of B, attempts to connect this carol with the Annunciation rather than the Nativity: 'Mary thus fulfills her role as mother, as Jesus requested, but only to intercede for her spiritual children who celebrate her day ("Lady Day", March 25, the feast of the Annunciation)' (*Wisdom and Number*, Lincoln, Nebraska, 1962, p. 50). But in A the reading is 'this gud day', in C 'this day', in D 'thys day', and the Epiphany is clearly meant. The further suggestion: 'In perhaps typical feminine fashion, she makes fulfilling her request the condition for lulling her Son . . .' is not the only over-ingenious interpretation which Manning offers in this work.

A. stza. 3, l. 3. *to pey*: acceptably.

A. stza. 4, l. 6. *hape*: wrap.

A. stza. 6, l. 4. *dray*: draw, go.   l. 5. *schwln*: shalt.

A. stza. 7, l. 4. *skylle*: reason, judgement.

D. stza. 2, l. 1. *bayne*: willing.

D. stza. 6, ll. 3, 4. See note on No. 85.

B. The last line of the burden in this version reappears in a lullaby carol in the *chanson d'aventure* formula written by William Forrest at some time between 1561 and 1572 and preserved in B.M. MS. Harley 1703, ff. 88ᵛ–89ᵛ (*pr.* Rudolph Kapp, *Heilige und Heiligenlegenden in England*, Halle/Saale, 1934, i. 303–4). The whole piece is a striking survival of the medieval convention of the type, including internal rhyme as found in Version D. The burden and first stanza are as follows:

> All this night longe: eueramonge:
> a voyce, eare ye were daye,
> I harde, that ronge: and thus it songe
> Lulla by bye: lullay.

> Att doore I lookde yn: where I fownde a gynne,
> and there: I dyd beehoulde
> A goodlye mayden: with lyllye whyte skinne,
> her hare: yallowe as goulde:
> who with cheere benigne: most sweetly dyd singe,
> lulla by: by lulla:

(Kapp prints J for I.)

It is quite possible that all versions of the carol derive at least the burden from a secular *chanson d'aventure* which itself appears (perhaps only in part) in the same MS. as D, f. 10ᵛ:

> Thys yonders nyght
> I herd a wyght
> most heuyly complayne
> And ever a mong
> thys was hys song
> Alas I dye for payne
> Alas I dye for payne.

(E. Flügel, *Anglia*, xii, 1889, 265. The MS. reading in the third line of 'heuynly' for 'heuvyly' may be a significant scribal slip.)

151. Of the Virgin and Child

A. *Pr.* Wright, *P.S.* xxiii. 19; C. & S., p. 119; A. S. Cook, *A Literary Middle English Reader* (Boston, 1915), p. 466; Sisam, p. 472.

B. Music for two and three voices. *Pr.*, with music, Ritson, *Ancient Songs* (1877), xlviii (in part); Stevens, *Med. Carols*, p. 110 (burden only); Robbins, *Christmas Carols*, p. 72 (burden only).

C. *Pr.* Mayer, sheet x.

B.–R. 3596.

A. stza. 8, ll. 4–6. Matthew xxvii. 46; Mark xv. 34.

B. stza. 5, l. 1. *Dolles to dreye*: pains to endure.   l. 5. *bals to bethe*: miseries to relieve.

152. A Dialogue of the Virgin and Child

A a. *Pr.* Dyboski, p. 21; Flügel, *Fest.*, p. 73, 'Lieder.', p. 247; Pollard, p. 90; R. L. Greene, *E.L.H.* vii (1940), 232; Greene, *Selection*, p. 101.

b. *Pr.* H. N. MacCracken, *Modern Language Notes*, xxiv (1909), 225 (with collation of A a).

c. *Pr.* Brown, *R.L. 15 C.*, p. 1; Davies, p. 197.

B a. *Pr.* R. L. Greene, *E.L.H.* vii (1940), 235.

b. Collated ibid. 236.

c. *Pr.* Joshua Sylvester, *pseud.*, *A Garland of Christmas Carols, Ancient and Modern* (London, 1861), p. 41.

B.–R. 22.

Stza. 7, ll. 1–3 of this lullaby dialogue which predicts the sufferings of Christ in His Passion are found as stza. 7, ll. 1–3 of No. 153, a similar dialogue.

In A c there is no burden, and the stanzas (omitting the second and tenth) appear in alternation with stanzas of the Latin hymn 'Christe qui lux es et dies'. There is no relation between the texts, no indication is given of how, if at all, the resulting piece is to be sung. This is the only instance in and the carols of such an arrangement.

Two of the traditional texts of the carol come from 1767 and 1777. They are found in two carefully prepared MS. books of carols then in use in Cornwall which were written for one John Webb in the neighbourhood of Boskenna. For a fuller description see Richard L. Greene, *E.L.H.* vii (1940), 234–6. In these survivals there is no initial burden but a chorus after each stanza only.

According to Sandys, the version in his book is also from Cornwall (p. cxxvi).

The version of B c printed by Joshua Sylvester (pseudonym of John Camden Hotten) cannot be regarded as coming from an original or differing source. Hotten gives no reference for his text, and it is in all probability that of Sandys, with the following minor variants:

stza. 3, l. 3. bespoke *for* begot.

stza. 4, l. 2. me will *for* will me.

stza. 5, l. 2. feet *for* my feet.   fastened *for* fastned.

That carols of the Passion were used in the fifteenth century, as in modern folk-singing, to celebrate the Nativity season is shown by the heading of the Laud misc. version: 'here begynneth a cristemasse song'. The device of having the infant Jesus recount in the future tense the details of His crucifixion has survived into modern times in French folk-song, e.g. 'Complainte de la Passion' in Lucien Decombe, ed., *Chansons populaires recueillies dans le Département d'Ille-et-Vilaine*

(Rennes, 1884), pp. 242–3. Two stanzas of this piece, which was used as a *quête* song, somewhat resemble stanzas of the carol:

> Avant qu'il soit vendredi nuit,
>   Vous voirez mon corps pendre;
> Et vous voirez mes bras tendus,
> Tant qu'ils pourront s'étendre.

> Vous voirez mon chef couronné
>   D'un couronn' d'épin' blanche;
> Vous voirez mon côté percé
> De trois grands coups de lance.

153. Of the Virgin and Child

Pr. Dyboski, p. 23; Flügel, *N.L.*, p. 119, 'Lieder.', p. 249; Frost, p. 267. B.–R. 3161.

There are two variations from the regular rhyme-scheme in this carol. Stza. 2, l. 4, which repeats the end-word of the preceding line, is probably due to a blunder in copying. The last stanza has six lines, cross-rhymed, with a final couplet. It may be borrowed wholly or in part from another piece on the same subject.

154. A Dialogue of the Virgin and Child

Pr. Zupitza, 321, notes, xcvii, 139–40; Sisam, p. 507. B.–R. 3284.

The use of 'alone' as a single refrain-word in each stanza of this carol is effective and well managed. Compare Nos. 63, 159, 160, 249, 281.

155. A Lullaby for the Christ Child

a. *Pr.* Brown, *R.L. 14 C.*, p. 80; Lord David Cecil, *The Oxford Book of Christian Verse* (Oxford, 1940), p. 17 (omits burden); A. Obertello, *Liriche religiose inglesi del secolo quattordicesimo* (Milan, 1947), p. 118 (with Italian translation and *facs.*); Greene, *Selection*, p. 103; Gray, *Lyrics*, p. 13.

b. *Pr.* W. Heuser, *Die Kildare-Gedichte* (Bonner Beiträge zur Anglistik, xvi, Bonn, 1904), p. 211. B.–R. 2024.

Heuser prints the carol in a form that is not justified by the MS. and that obscures the true structure. He takes the burden to be an integral part of each stanza and prints it as the first two lines of each. The bracketing of the stanzas in the MS. shows that the regular carol-form was intended by the writer.

This carol is unique among the lullabies in being addressed to the infant Christ by the author as spokesman for sinful mankind. Its burden is taken from the melancholy lullaby found among the Kildare poems (British Museum MS. Harley 913, f. 32ʳ, *pr.* Brown, *R.L. 14 C.*, p. 35) of the earlier part of the same century, or from a common source. It also appears as stza. 9, l. 1 of No. 148 A. See Introduction, pp. cliii–cliv, and F. E. Budd, *A Book of Lullabies: 1300–1900* (London, 1930), pp. 2, 3. The carol, although in the shorter line and tail-rhyme stanza, shares with the earlier Franciscan lullaby its fine austerity of spirit mingled with real tenderness.

The fanciful commentary of Lewis J. Owen and Nancy H. Owen (*Middle English Poetry: An Anthology*, Indianapolis, 1971, pp. 356–8), which purports to find number symbolism in the seven stanzas made up of various fours and threes, would be more convincing if the b-text also had seven stanzas instead of six.

156. A Dialogue of the Virgin and Child

Pr. Zupitza, 263, notes, xcv, 403–5. B.–R. 2530.

157. Of the Passion

A. *Repr.* Bliss, p. 49; *facs.* Reed, p. 49.

B. *Pr.* Wright, *P.S.* xxiii. 38; C. & S., p. 146; Lord David Cecil, *The Oxford Book of Christian Verse* (Oxford, 1940), p. 41; Greene, *Selection*, p. 104.

C. *Pr.* Wright, *Wart. Club*, p. 65, *P.S.* iv, 'Christmas Carols', p. 10; Reed, p. 82.

D. *Pr.* Brown, *R.L. 14 C.*, p. 85.

B.–R. 1219, 2111, 2036.

E. *Pr.* Karen Hodder, *Archiv*, ccv (1969), 378; *facs.* ibid. 380.

Not in B.–R.

On the structure of the different versions of this carol see Introduction, pp. clxii–clxiii.

A, C. stza. 1, l. 4 (B, l. 1, D, E, l. 4). Compare ll. 310–11 of the Digby play 'The Burial of Christ' (ed. F. J. Furnivall, E.E.T.S., Ex. Ser., No. lxx, London, 1896, 181–2):

> From the Crowne of the hede vnto the too,
> This blessit body was wrappit all in woo,

and the poem on the Passion from C.U. Lib. MS. Dd. 11. 89, ll. 59–60 (*pr.* R. H. Bowers, *Three Middle English Religious Poems*, University of Florida Monographs, Humanities, No. 12, Gainesville, 1963, p. 34):

> Hys swete body was wrappid alle in wo,
> Wyth blode & bytter wondus sore.

E. This fragment, written closely after the fragmentary 21 E, resembles D in lacking a burden. It is extensively annotated by Hodder, loc. cit. It indicates that this carol of Kele's was related to a version set down in Yorkshire.

A. stza. 3, l. 3. *blo*: pale.

B. stza. 1, l. 1. *wappyd*: wrapped; but see *O.E.D.*, s.v. 'Wap', v^1. 1. b.

B. stza. 7, l. 3. *wake*: (?) track, trace. 'Not found before the 16th c., but possibly much older', *O.E.D.*

B. stza. 8, l. 2. *wan we not mon*: when we may not (help ourselves).

D. l. 8. *blent*: blinded.

D. l. 24. *walle*: boil (figurative).

D. l. 26. *me ne routh*: I should not reck.

D. l. 29. *lake*: dungeon.

158. The Sorrowing Mary

Pr. Dyboski, p. 13; Flügel, *N.L.*, p. 112, 'Lieder.', p. 240; Reed, p. 84. B.–R. 3575.

The burden is almost identical with that of No. 157 B, and stza. 1 is a rearrangement of stza. 2 of No. 157 C.

The carol is a dialogue between Mary and St. John the Evangelist, who speak alternate stanzas, although St. John is not named. See Hermann Thien, *Über die englischen Marienklagen* (Kiel, 1906), p. 46.

159. The Sorrowing Mary

Pr. Zupitza, 277, notes, xcvi, 169–70. B.–R. 3944.

This is a conventional presentation of the *planctus Mariae* theme. It is not listed by G. C. Taylor, 'The English "Planctus Mariae"', *Modern Philology*, iv (1907), 605–37.

For the use of the word 'alone' compare Nos. 63, 154, 160, 249, 281.

stza. 2, l. 1. *An*: Annas, the father-in-law of Caiaphas, the High Priest, who was a former holder of that office and still retained influence.

stza. 4, l. 3. *watre and bloode*. See note on No. 180 A, stza. 4, l. 4.

160. The Sorrowing Mary

Pr. Zupitza, 280, notes, xcvi, 172. B.–R. 1524.

For the use of the word 'alone' compare Nos. 63, 154, 159, 249, 281.

stza. 3, ll. 1, 2. See note on No. 149, stzas. 19, 30.

stza. 4, l. 1. See note on No. 180 A, stza. 4, l. 4.

161. Who Cannot Weep, Come Learn at Me

a. *Pr.* [Sir] Egerton Brydges, *Censura Literaria* (London, 1905–9), x. 186; Brown, *R.L. 15 C.*, p. 17; Sisam, p. 486; Silverstein, p. 102; Gray, *Lyrics*, p. 21.

b. *Pr.* F. J. Furnivall, *Hymns to the Virgin and Christ* (E.E.T.S., Or. Ser., No. 24, London, 1867), 126; C. & S., p. 144.

B.–R. 4189.

The carol is a *planctus Mariae*, No. xvii in the list of Taylor, op. cit. The refrain also appears as the refrain of some stanzas of the 'De arte lacrimandi' (*pr.* from British Museum MS. Harley 2274 by R. M. Garrett, *Anglia*, xxxii, 1909, 270–94).

stza. 1, l. 2. *enchesone*: occasion, cause.   l. 6. *bobbid*: buffeted. But the word has a special meaning here; it indicates that the tormentors of Christ played 'the bobbid game' with him, i.e. Hot Cockles, in which the buffeted player must guess who smites him from behind. See G. R. Owst, *Literature and Pulpit in Medieval England* (Cambridge, 1933), pp. 510–11, and Rosemary Woolf, *The English Mystery Plays* (Berkeley, California, 1972), pp. 254–5.

stza. 2, l. 4. *thwarted*: opposed (in speech), retorted.

stza. 3, l. 1. *rulye*: pitiably.

stza. 4, l. 8. *laye*: strain, purport. *O.E.D.* first records from 1529.

162. Of the Passion

Pr. Dyboski, p. 41; Flügel, 'Lieder.', p. 263; Mary G. Segar and Emmeline Paxton, *Some Minor Poems of the Middle Ages* (London, 1917), p. 48. B.–R. 548.

The burden appears as the first stanza of a poem on the Hours of the Passion in Cambridge University Library MS. Ee. 1. 12, f. 1ᵛ (preceding Ryman's works):

> I hard a maydyn wepe
> For here Sonnys passyon;
> Yt enterd into my hart full deipe
> Wyth grete contricion.

At the foot of the page the stanza is again written with a crudely noted melody. The last few words have been cut off by a binder. The rest of the poem is not verbally related to this carol.

163. The Sorrowing Mary

a. *Pr.* Dyboski, p. 40; Flügel, 'Lieder.', p. 262; C. & S., p. 142; Sitwell, *Atlantic Book*, p. 18, *Planet and Glow-worm* (London, 1944), p. 75; Sisam, p. 533.

b. *Repr.* Bliss, p. 51; *facs.* Reed, p. 32.

B.–R. 4023.

See Thien, *Über die englischen Marienklagen*, p. 19. The piece is No. xviii in the list of Taylor, op. cit.

The second line of the burden is one of the few phrases of the MS. carols which are found in recognizable form in recorded traditional folk-song. In a Shropshire version of the folk-song 'The Seven Virgins' Mary says:

> While I do see my own son die
> When sons I have no more?
>
> (*Journal of the Folk-Song Society*, v, 1918, 22, stza. 7)

An almost identical phrasing in a Manx version is recorded ibid. vii (1924), 283.

stza. 2, l. 1. *Shere Thursday*: Maundy Thursday.

stza. 3, l. 4. *Crucyfyge*: Mark xv. 13, 14; Luke xxiii. 21; John xix. 15.

stza. 5, l. 2. Matthew xxvii. 54. The 'how it was the erth quaked' of b is an easy mistake in written transmission, less likely in oral. It is an indication that the Kele text was taken from a MS. copy rather than from oral tradition, unless it be a mere printer's-error.

164. Of Our Lady and Her Son

Repr. facs. Reed, p. 35; B.–R. *Snpp.* 377.5.

This carol is a true *planctus Mariae*. It was first published after the appearance of the works of Thien and Taylor.

burden, l. 1. Compare the burden and *chanson d'aventure* opening of the song in B.M. MS. Addit. 5465, f. 49ʳ (*pr.* B. Fehr, *Archiv*, cvi, 1901, 59; with music, Stevens, *Early Tudor Songs*, p. 76):

> Alone, alone, alone, alone,
> Alone, alone, alone.
> Here sytt alone, alas, alone.
>
> As I me walkyd this endurs day, etc.

165. Of the Passion

Deleted from this edition. As Stevens points out, *M. & P.*, p. 374, the music is not that of a true carol.

166. Christ's Account of His Passion

Pr. Dyboski, p. 19; Flügel, *N.L.*, p. 121, 'Lieder.', p. 246. B.–R. 1383.

The stanzas of this carol form a more or less conventional address of Christ to sinful man, but the burden is addressed to the Virgin and is cast in the future tense. It seems probable that the burden was borrowed from a piece of the 'cradle-prophecy' type like No. 151. Stza. 8, l. 4, which is similarly out of its proper context, may be an intrusion from the same source.

Stzas. 11 and 12 use the repetitive device of folk-song.

167. Of the Passion

Pr. first edition. B.–R. 3550.

burden, l. 1. *manie*: meinie, followers, i.e. Christians.

stza. 3, l. 1. 'Judas wore (cloth) of Cyprus bold.' Perhaps the last word should be 'gold', as 'Cyprus' was often applied to cloth of gold or to fine fabric with which gold was used for ornament. See *O.E.D.*, s.v. 'Cypress'³.   l. 2. *To honde*: Into the hands of.

stza. 6, l. 4. See note on No. 180, stza. 4, l. 4.

stza. 7, l. 1. *Longis*: Longinus, the legendary name of the Roman soldier who pierced the side of Christ with his spear (John xix. 34).

stza. 8. The legend tells how Longinus was cured of a disease of the eyes by a drop of the holy blood and was converted.

168. Think on Christ's Passion

Pr. Wright, *Wart. Club*, p. 61; B. Fehr, *Archiv*, cix (1902), 62. B.–R. 2061.

stza. 2, l. 1. Compare No. 357 for similar use of the imperative at the beginning of stanzas.

stza. 7, l. 3. *Hely*: i.e. 'Eloi', Mark xv. 34, Matthew xxvii. 46: 'Et hora nona exclamavit Jesus voce magna dicens, "Eloi, Eloi, lamma sabacthani?"'

169. Of the Passion

Pr. Wright, *Wart. Club*, p. 81; B. Fehr, *Archiv*, cix (1902), 67. B.–R. 1739.

stza. 2, l. 1. *skele*: reason.

stza. 4, l. 1. *kerche*: handkerchief.

170. The Cold Wind

Pr. Greene, *Selection*, p. 105. B.–R. 3525 (indexed by first line of burden).

Even if no parallel were preserved, the burden of this carol would suggest that it is a sacred parody of a secular song in general circulation. That it should be so regarded is made practically certain by the presence in *A Compendious Book of Godly and Spiritual Songs* (1567), among other 'moralized' pieces, of one which is obviously based on the same prototype:

> The wind blawis cauld, furius & bauld,
> This lang and mony day:
> But Christis mercy, we man all die,
> Or keip the cauld wind away.

> This wind sa keine, that I of meine,
> It is the ryte of auld,
> Our Faith is inclusit, and plainlie abusit,
> This wind hes blawin to cauld.

(Burden and stza. 1, ed. A. F. Mitchell, S.T.S., No. 39, 1897, 189–92)

The same image, again associated with the Passion, appears in the burden of No. 171. Bertrand H. Bronson discusses at some length the likeness of the central image of this carol to that which begins the ballad *The Unquiet Grave* (Child, No. 78). See *The Traditional Tunes of the Child Ballads*, ii (Princeton, 1963), 234.

The tradition of a cold wind on Calvary probably derives from John xviii. 18: 'And the servants and officers stood there, who had made a fire of coals; for it was cold: . . .' It is used in the poem on the Passion in C.U. Lib. MS. Dd. 11. 89, ll. 217–20 (*pr.* R. H. Bowers, *Three Middle English Religious Poems*, University of Florida Monographs, Humanities, No. 12, Gainesville, 1963, pp. 38–9):

> The bitternesse of that colde wynd
> Asayled His body on euery syde
> And hosliche [hostilely] on Hym blew byfore & byhynd
> And scharpliche a serchid His woundus wyde.

The passage continues with the figure of Christ as a shepherd sheltering His flock from the winds.

Bowers refers to the 'Privity of the Passion' in Carl Horstmann, ed., *Yorkshire Writers* (London, 1895–6), i. 203: 'for, as þe gospell sais, þe wedire was colde.'

171. Christ Tells of His Passion

Repr. facs. Reed, p. 12. B.–R. 3112.

With the burden compare that of No. 170, with l. 4 the refrains of No. 147. The method of abbreviating the burden between stanzas is unusual.

stza. 5, l. 1. *splayed*: spread.

stza. 6, l. 4. *made an ende was al*: John xix. 30: 'Consummatum est.'

172. Mary and Her Flower

a. *Pr.* C. & S., *M.L.R.* vi. 73; C. & S., p. 110; Whiting, p. 202; [Loyd Haberly], *Alia Cantalena de Sancta Maria* (Long Crendon, Bucks., 1926); Sitwell, *Atlantic Book*, p. 8; Sisam, p. 388.

b. *Pr.* Dyboski, p. 6; Flügel, *N.L.*, p. 115, *Fest.*, p. 60, 'Lieder.', p. 230. B.–R. 3603.

Audelay's version is the better of the two and seems to be the earlier. b substitutes clichés in stza. 6, ll. 5, 6, and stza. 7, ll. 1, 2, where Audelay's final stanza has a complete and pretty conception.

J. Copley notes the identity in metre between version a of this carol and No. 203 by Ryman and No. 427 ('John Audelay's Carols and Music', *English Studies*, xxxix, 1958, 210–11). There is no evidence that they were sung to the same setting.

burden, l. 2. The likening of the lineage of the Virgin to a tree with Jesse for root is familiar in ecclesiastical art, as in the 'Jesse windows'. The ultimate source is Isaiah xi. Compare No. 311, stza. 5, l. 3.

stza. 1, ll. 3, 4. Audelay uses these lines again in No. 311, stza. 6.

stza. 2, l. 4. See note on No. 49, stza. 3, l. 2. In spite of the 'ingressus' of Luke i. 28, medieval pictorial art often shows the Annunciation as taking place out of doors or in a garden (in allusion to the 'hortus clausus' of Canticles iv. 12).

stza. 3, l. 5. *Hent*: until.

stza. 4, l. 2. *bede*: form a bead or bud.   l. 3. *lede*: nation.

stza. 5, l. 6. Dame Edith Sitwell glosses 'golde' as 'mould', apparently misinterpreting the textual note on b. Although she prints Audelay's version, she labels the carol 'anonymous'.

stza. 6, l. 1. *of ryse*: on branch, or bush.   l. 2. Compare *Meditations on the Life and Passion of Christ* (ed. C. D'Evelyn, E.E.T.S., Or. Ser., No. 158, 1921, 3, ll. 95–8):

> Thow, clene mayde wiþoute viole,
> Art likned to þe premerole.
> Whan floures weron welked and al y-gone,
> Lyk prymerole þou sprang alone.

l. 5. *hele*: health, healing virtue.

173. Mary, the Rose

Music for two voices. *Pr.* C. & S., p. 105; M. G. Segar, *A Mediaeval Anthology* (London, 1915), p. 65; Greene, *Selection*, p. 107; Sisam, p. 408; Oliver, p. 82; Gray, *Themes and Images*, p. 88,

Lyrics, p. 12; etc.; with music, Fuller Maitland, p. 27; Terry, p. 56; John Stevens, *There Is No Rose of Such Virtue*, Fayrfax Series, No. 16 (London, 1951); Stevens, *Med. Carols*, p. 10. B.–R. 3536.

The last lines of this carol are taken from the demistrophes of the 'Laetabundus' prose. See Introduction, pp. xcviii–xcix. It is unusual in its employment of the same words for burden and first stanza.

In its frequent use of the rose as a symbol of the Virgin the Church applied to her the words of Ecclesiasticus xxiv. 18: 'Quasi palma exaltata sum in Cades, et quasi plantatio rosae in Jericho.'

Douglas Gray praises the style of this carol 'for its economy and clarity' and offers a brief and sensible analysis of the text (*Themes and Images*, pp. 88–9).

174. Mary, the Rose

Pr. Zupitza, 187, notes, xciii, 393–5. B.–R. 3779.

stza. 3, l. 2. The use of the lily as the symbol of Christ may be influenced by the frequent inclusion of that flower in pictorial representations of the Annunciation, where it is primarily the sign of Mary's purity. For the fleur-de-lis as symbol of Christ see also No. 48 and note thereon.

stza. 5, l. 2. *foode*: spiritual food.

175. Mary, the Rose-Bush

A. *Pr.* Wright, *P.S.* xxiii. 21; Greene, *Selection*, p. 108; Oliver, p. 120.

B. *Pr.* Dyboski, p. 7; Flügel, *N.L.*, p. 116, *Fest.*, p. 62; 'Lieder.', p. 232; Pollard, p. 85.

C. *Pr.* T. Wright, *Songs and Carols* (London, 1836), No. v; Wright, *Wart. Club*, p. 16; C. & S., p. 103; Dyboski, p. 170; J. C. Stobart, *The Chaucer Epoch*, The Epochs of English Literature, i (London, [1906]), p. 16; Sir A. Quiller-Couch, *The Oxford Book of English Verse* (Oxford, 1939), p. 12; Lord David Cecil, *The Oxford Book of Christian Verse* (Oxford, 1940), p. 30; Sitwell, *Atlantic Book*, p. 6; Sisam, p. 429.

B.–R. 1914, 1893.

The five 'branches' represent the Five Joys of the Virgin. A is plainly the nearest to the original of the three texts. C has lost two stanzas, and the symbolism is consequently less clear. B, on the other hand, adds a sixth 'branch' in its last stanza as the sign of all the Joys collectively.

A. stza. 4, l. 3. *lemeghd*: gleamed.

A. stza. 5, l. 2. *to*: the.

A. stza. 7, l. 3. *ball*: bale, sorrow.   *bott*: boot, help.

B. stza. 7, l. 2. *tope* (C. stza. 6 *crop*) *and rote*: entirely, completely.   . 4. *in preestes hondes*: i.e. as the Host, when it is shown by the priest in the Mass.

176. Mary, the Rose

Music for two voices. *Pr.* Padelford, p. 90; with music, *E.B.M.* ii. 108, *facs.* No. l; Terry, p. 10; Stevens, *Med. Carols*, p. 13; Robbins, *Christmas Carols*, p. 68. B.–R. 3638.

burden, l. 2. Compare burdens of Nos. 56, 94, 319.

stza. 1, l. 1. *railed on a rys*: set or arrayed on a bush.

stza. 4, l. 2. *shoure*: attack.

177. To the Virgin

Pr. C. & S., *M.L.R.* vi. 75; Whiting, p. 205. B.–R. 536.

stza. 1, l. 1. *berd so bryght*: a stock epithet for Mary, borrowed from secular romance.

stza. 5, l. 2. See note on No. 306.   l. 4. *hal*. The emendation seems to be necessary; 'hall' for heaven is frequent in ME. Whiting retains 'bal' and glosses 'world, sphere', a sense not recorded by *O.E.D.* as applied to heaven.

178. To the Virgin

Pr. Dyboski, p. 2; Flügel, *N.L.*, p. 111, *Fest.*, p. 53, 'Lieder.', p. 189; Pollard, p. 83. B.–R. 755.

The Latin burden appears in partial translation as the last stanza of Audelay's carol to St. Anne, No. 311. L. 1 of the burden appears in burden, l. 2, and refrain of Ryman's No. 195. It is taken from a votive antiphon found in a Sarum Gradual, Bodl. MS. Rawl. liturg. d. 3, f. 71ʳ (Frank Ll. Harrison, *Music in Medieval Britain*, London, 1958, p. 295). This antiphon had a special use at Lincoln from 1380 on: the choristers gathered at the site of Bishop Bokingham's tomb and together with prayers and a psalm sang a votive antiphon, *Mater ora filium* being prescribed for two seasons, from the Purification to Easter and from Trinity to Christmas. 'The gathering of the singers at an altar, before an image or in some other designated place was the regular manner of singing the evening votive antiphon from the mid-fourteenth century to the Reformation' (ibid., pp. 82–3).

The salutations 'Fayre maydyn,' and 'Sir,' and the dramatic dialogue form show imitation of the *pastourelle* type of secular poetry with its encounter and dialogue between knight or clerk and maiden.

179. To the Virgin

Music for two voices. *Pr.* Padelford, p. 95; with music, *E.B.M.* ii. 121; *facs.* No. lix; Terry, p. 26; Stevens, *Med. Carols*, p. 17. B.-R. 4229.

stza. 1, l. 1. *birth*: the one born, child.

stza. 5, l. 3. *Justyse*. Compare No. 98, stza. 3, l. 3, No. 209, stza. 8, l. 1, and No. 361, stza. 1, l. 2.

stza. 6, l. 3. *berde of ble*: maiden of (fair) visage.

179.1. To the Virgin

Music for two voices. *Pr.* Greene, *Selection*, p. 109; with music, Stevens, *Med. Carols*, p. 54. B.R. *Supp.* 1030.5.

stza. 2, l. 2. *stynter of our stryff*. Compare No. 227, stza. 1, l. 2: 'Graunter of peace, seaser of stryffe'.

stza. 3, ll. 1, 2. Compare the thirteenth-century poem 'Of on that is so fair and bright', No. 191 B a, stza. 2, ll. 5, 6:

> Of alle thou berst the pris,
> Leuedi, quene of parays,

and the carol derived from it, No. 191 A, stza. 7, l. 1.

180. Of Mary and the Letters of Her Name

A. *Pr.* Wright, *P.S.* xxiii. 31; Greene, *Selection*, p. 109; Sisam, p. 479; Davies, p. 163.
B. *Pr.* Wright, *Wart. Club*, p. 69; B. Fehr, *Archiv*, cix (1902), 64.
B.-R. 1650.

For the use of initial letters in other carols, see Nos. 83, 139. The rhetorical device of using the letters of Mary's name in an acrostic survives at least into seventeenth-century verse in her honour.

A rather laboured acrostic poem in praise of Mary, which includes 'I for Ivy' (compare No. 139), is somewhat doubtfully attributed to Ben Jonson. It is prefixed to Antony Stafford's *The Femall Glory*, and is entitled 'The Ghyrlond of the blessed Virgin Marie'. It also sets M for myrtle, A for almond, R for rose, and E for eglantine. The fifth stanza explicates thus:

> The fourth is humble *Ivy*, intersert,
> But lowlie laid, as on the earth asleep,
> Preserved, in her antique bed of *vert*,
> No faith's more firme, or flat, than where't doth creep.

([*Works*,] ed. C. H. Herford and Percy and Evelyn Simpson, Oxford, 1947, viii. 412–13). See Louis Martz, *The Poetry of Meditation* (New Haven, 1954), p. 223 n. 2.

An elaborately alliterative medieval example occurs in the speech of the angel in the Play of Mary in the Temple, *Ludus Coventriae*, ed. K. S. Block, E.E.T.S., Ex. Ser., No. cxx, 1922, 80, ll. 244–51:

> In ȝour name Maria. ffyve letterys we han
> M. Mayde most mercyfull and mekest in mende
> A. Auerte of þe Anguysch þat Adam began
> R. Regina of regyon Reyneng with-owtyn ende
> I. Innocent be Influens of Jesses kende
> A. Aduocat most Autentyk ȝour Antecer Anna
> hefne and helle here kneys down bende
> Whan þis holy name of ȝow is seyd Maria.

In the Play of the Parliament of Heaven in the same cycle an acrostic seems to be intended by the four capital letters in l. 196 (ibid., p. 103):

> The name of þe mayde ffre
> Is Mary þat xal Al Restore.

Compare the acrostic on Ivy in No. 139.

stza. 1, l. 1. The reading of B is obviously the result of misunderstanding, probably oral. 'Purposy' is not elsewhere recorded by O.E.D. It is possible that it is here used with the sense of 'purport, importance'.

A. stza. 4, l. 4. *terys of blod.* Mary's weeping of blood is a detail which frequently occurs in ME. accounts of the Passion, e.g. in Nos. 159, 160, and in *The Northern Passion*, Additional text, ll. 1747–50:

> Oure lady herde thies wordis swete
> and teris of blode scho gane downe lete
> all was hir face by rowne with blode
> whene scho by helde Ihesu one the rode.
> (ed. Frances A. Foster, E.E.T.S., Or. Ser., No. 145, 1913, i. 204.)

The Harleian text has (l. 1750): 'þat water and blude both scho gret.' The tradition is probably due to a wish to provide a parallel to the water and blood which flowed from the side of Christ (John xix. 34).

Compare also William Nassyngton (?), 'St. Mary's Lamentation on the Passion of Christ', C. Horstmann, ed., *Yorkshire Writers* (London, 1896), ii. 275, ll. 53–60.

181. Of Christ and His Mother

Pr. Brown, *R.L. 15 C.*, p. 110. B.–R. 3297.
stza. 1, l. 3. *beldyt*: took his abode.   *bygly*: habitable, pleasant.
stza. 2, l. 3. *inwolde*: enveloped.
stza. 3, l. 2. *conclaue*: inner chamber.   l. 4. *bedene*: together.
stza. 4, l. 4. *sele*: prosperity, good fortune.

182. Of the Virgin

Music for two voices. *Pr.* Padelford, p. 108; with music, *E.B.M.* ii. 147, *facs.* No. lxxix; Stevens, *Med. Carols*, p. 24. B.–R. 1931.

This, like some of Ryman's carols of the Virgin, is a mere catalogue of the familiar 'types'.
stza. 1, l. 4. *lay*: teaching.
stza. 2, l. 4. *Adonay*. The Old Testament Hebrew name for the Deity which is substituted in reading for the Ineffable Name, Yahve. Compare Exodus vi. 3, Judith xvi. 16, where it appears in the Vulgate.

183. Of the Virgin

Pr. Dyboski, p. 2; Flügel, *N.L.*, p. 126, *Fest.*, p. 54, 'Lieder.', p. 190. B.–R. 3835.
The burden also appears as that of No. 41.
The refrain of the stanzas has the air of having been taken over from an amorous lyric. Stza. 3, l. 1 has the same ring.
stza. 1, l. 2. This line occurs with identical wording in 'I hafe set my hert so hye' from Bodl. MS. Douce 381, where it is applied to Christ (*pr.* Brown, *R.L. 14 C.*, p. 229, l. 6), and in 'A Song of Love to the Blessed Virgin' from the Vernon MS. (*pr.* ibid., p. 178, l. 9).

184. Of the Virgin

Pr. Wright, *P.S.* xxiii. 49. B.–R. 2618.
burden, l. 1. *asay*: try, i.e. apply yourself to seek help from Mary. Compare the burden of No. 359.
stza. 1, l. 3. *colowre*: reason.
stza. 2, l. 3. *strowne in every schowr*: strewn (i.e. present) in every distress.
stza. 3, l. 1. *cundas*: kind, gentle.

185. To the Virgin

A. *Pr.* Wright, *Wart. Club*, p. 71; B. Fehr, *Archiv*, cix (1902), 64; Padelford, p. 92.

B. Music for two voices. *Pr.* Padelford, p. 91; with music, *E.B.M.* ii. 110, *facs.* No. lii; Terry, p. 24; Stevens, *Med. Carols*, p. 14.

B.–R. 1230.

A. stza. 2 (B. stza. 3), l. 1. *brytgh of ble*: fair of countenance.   l. 3. A. *chosyn*, B. *cosyn*: A gives the better reading, but B is acceptable, 'cousin' meaning merely 'next of kin'. See *O.E.D.* s.v. 'Cousin', 1b.

A. stza. 4, l. 2. *buxsum*: submissive.

186. To the Virgin

Music for two and three voices. *Pr.* Fehr, p. 265; Padelford, p. 92; Brougham, p. 11 (stanzas in order 2, 3, 1); with music, *Mus. Ant.*, p. 21 (in part); Stevens, *Med. Carols*, p. 62; Robbins, *Christmas Carols*, p. 56. B.–R. 507.

stza. 2, l. 1. *se*: throne.

187. To the Virgin

A a. *Pr.* K. Brunner, *Anglia*, lxi (1937), 150; Brown, *R.L. 15 C.*, p. 33.

b. *Previously unpublished.*

B. *Pr.* Dyboski, p. 49; Flügel, 'Lieder.', p. 274.

B.–R. 236.

B appears to be a later abridgement of A. The substitution of the refrain 'Gloria tibi, Domine' for the Latin fourth lines destroys the rhyme with the burden and generally weakens the effectiveness of the piece.

A. stza. 3, l. 2. *crache*: crib.

188. Of the Virgin

Pr. Wright, *Wart. Club*, p. 23; B. Fehr, *Archiv*, cix (1902), 48; C. & S., p. 108. B.–R. 2103.

stza. 3, l. 2. *bote*: goodness   l. 3. *bote*: help.

189. To the Virgin

Pr. Zupitza, 172, notes, xciii, 299–307. B.–R. 489.

stza. 2, l. 1. The explicit use of Ahasuerus as a type of Christ is much less frequent than that of Esther as a type of the Virgin.

190. To the Virgin

A. Music for two voices. *Pr.* Padelford, p. 109; Rickert, p. 17; with music, *E.B.M.* ii. 151, *facs.* No. lxxxii.

B. Music for two voices. *Pr.* Greene, *Selection*, p. 110; with music, Stevens, *Med. Carols*, p. 36.

B.–R. 3674.

stza. 2, l. 2. Balaam prophesies 'Orietur Stella ex Jacob' (Numbers xxiv. 17). This carol ignores Balaam's disrepute in the New Testament (2 Peter ii. 16; Jude 11; Revelation ii. 14).

stza. 3, l. 4. *burion*: burgeon, bud.

stza. 4, l. 1. *orient lyght*. Compare No. 279, stza. 1, where Ryman applies this figure to Christ.

stza. 7, ll. 1, 2. The familiar figure of a rose for the Virgin is here specialized as the flower also called Rose of the Virgin, Rose of the World, and Rose of Sharon, the last title also frequently applied to Christ.

stza. 8, ll. 1, 2. The 'Jewis spyn' is a thorn here standing for the whole stalk of the Old Testament genealogy of Christ. Probably by confusion rather than in an intentionally bold mixed metaphor, the 'lily-flower' is here made to spring from a thorn. In some folk-legend the Annunciation is located at a thorn-tree rather than in Mary's 'bower'.

191. To the Virgin

A. *Pr. E.B.M.* ii. 65, *facs.* No. xxviii; Brown, *R.L. 15 C.*, p. 34.

B a. *Pr.* R. Morris, *An Old English Miscellany* (E.E.T.S., Or. Ser., No. 49, London, 1872), p. 194; *Rel. Ant.* i. 89; E. Mätzner, *Altenglische Sprachproben* (Berlin, 1867), i. 53; J. C. Stobart,

The Chaucer Epoch (London, [1906]), p. 15 (in part); C. & S., p. 92; Patterson, p. 96; A. S. Cook, *A Literary Middle English Reader* (Boston, 1915), p. 457; Carleton Brown, *English Lyrics of the XIIIth Century* (Oxford, 1932), p. 26; William O. Wehrle, *The Macaronic Hymn Tradition in Medieval English Literature* (Washington, D.C., 1933), p. 30; Sir Arthur Quiller-Couch, *The Oxford Book of English Verse* (Oxford, [1939]), p. 11 (in part); Bruce Dickins and Richard M. Wilson, *Early Middle English Texts* (Cambridge, 1951), p. 125; Kaiser, *Med. Engl.*, p. 286; Oliver, p. 92; Davies, p. 53; Silverstein, p. 22; Sisam, p. 19; James J. Wilhelm, *Medieval Song* (N.Y., 1971), p. 349; Gray, *Lyrics*, p. 5; etc.

b. *Pr.* Carleton Brown, op. cit., p. 24; collated with B a, C. & S., p. 346.

A, B a, B b. *Pr.* Karl Reichl, *Religiöse Dichtung im englischen Hochmittelalter*, Münchener Universitäts-Schriften, Philosophische Fakultät, Texte und Untersuchung zur Englischen Philologie, Band i (München, 1973), pp. 293–5.

B.–R. 61, 2645.

c. *Pr.* R. W. Hunt, 'The Collection of a Monk of Bardney: A Dismembered Rawlinson Manuscript', *Mediaeval and Renaissance Studies*, v (1961), 54. This text is not listed in B.–R.

The leaf containing these last five lines of the poem, all that remains of the B c version, is a fragment and was presumably preceded by a copy of the earlier lines, now lost. The close similarity to B a and b of what remains suggests that there were probably no significant variants in the lost portion.

The process of turning an already existing poem in another form into a carol, seen here as in No. 157, is probably responsible for a number of other carols of which the older originals have not been preserved. For another poem to Mary in the same stanza-form as B see C. & S., p. 89, Patterson, p. 148.

A. burden. See table in Introduction, p. lxxxvi.

B. stza. 3, l. 1. *consell*: counsellor.

B. stza. 4, l. 6. *Thuster*: dark.

B. stza. 5, l. 3. *werne*: deny. *bone*: request.   l. 8. *put*: pit.

192. To the Virgin

Pr. Zupitza, 173, notes, xciii, 307–13. B.–R. 2404.

stza. 1, l. 1. Ezekiel xliv. 1–3.   l. 2. Daniel ii. 34–5.

stza. 2, l. 1. 3 Kings x. 18–20.   l. 2. Judges vi. 37–40.

stza. 3, ll. 1, 2. Exodus iii. 2.

stza. 4, l. 1. Numbers xvii.

193. To the Virgin

Pr. Zupitza, 174, notes, xciii, 313–17. B.–R. 2405.

stza. 2, l. 1. 3. *florent*: blossoming. Not recorded before 1542 in *O.E.D.*

stza. 3, l. 1. *leasure*. Zupitza notes: 'leasure, das durch Vermittelung des Französischen vom lat. *laesura* [hurting, injuring] kommen muss, finde ich weder in englischen noch in französischen Wörterbüchern.' It is possibly Ryman's coinage for 'leasing', lying, the phrase being the familiar one for emphasis.

stza. 5, l. 2. *Decapitate*. Not recorded before 1610 in *O.E.D.* Zupitza notes: 'bei Skeat erst aus Cotgrave belegt.'

194. To the Virgin

Pr. Zupitza, 175, notes, xciii, 317–26. B.–R. 1074.

stza. 6, l. 3. *lowte*: bow down.

stza. 7, l. 2. *serpentes*: i.e. of Holofernes as the type of Satan.

195. To the Virgin

Pr. Zupitza, 176, notes, xciii, 326–8. B.–R. 2543.

burden, l. 2. See notes on No. 178, burden, and on No. 311, stza. 9.

196. To the Virgin

Pr. Zupitza, 177, notes, xciii, 328–30. B.-R. 3152.
burden, l. 1. 'Castitatis lilium' begins strophe 6 of a Sarum prose to the Virgin (*Sar. Miss.*, p. 494).

197. To the Virgin

Pr. Zupitza, 178, notes, xciii, 330–3. B.-R. 3123.
stza. 3, l. 1. *skille*: sense of the proper or fitting.
stza. 4, l. 1. *coost*: region, part of the world.

198. To the Virgin

Pr. Zupitza, 179, notes, xciii, 334–8. B.-R. 3136.
burden. Zupitza notes: Daniel, *Thes. Hym.* ii. 319:

> Vale, o valde decora,
> Et pro nobis Christum exora.

199. To the Virgin

Pr. Zupitza, 180, notes, xciii, 369–74. B.-R. 2544.
stza. 7, l. 1. *flos campi*: Canticles. ii. 1: 'Ego flos campi et lilium convallium.'
stza. 9, l. 3. *triclyne*: Lat. *triclinium*, a couch for reclining at meals. *O.E.D.* gives this as the only citation for figurative use in English.

200. To the Virgin

Pr. Zupitza, 181, notes, xciii, 374–7. B.-R. 2460.
burden, l. 1. From the Office of the Mass of the Virgin from the Purification to Septuagesima (*Sar. Miss.*, p. 389).

200.1. To the Virgin

Music for one voice. *Pr.* R. H. Robbins, *Modern Language Notes*, lviii (1943), 41; with music, Stevens, *Med. Carols*, p. 111. B.-R. 182.
stza. 1, l. 3, stza. 3, l. 2. *suffren*: sovereign.
stza. 3, l. 1. *consolatrix*: feminine consoler; *contribulate*: those greatly troubled (neither word in *Middle English Dictionary*).
stza. 4, l. 1. *perele*: pearl, *imperpetuell*: eternal (with intensive prefix, not in *Middle English Dictionary*; l. 2 *sadenesse*: earnestness, seriousness. *sentence*: truth, especially of doctrine, spiritual meaning deeper than an obvious meaning. The word may be studied at length in D. W. Robertson, Jr., *A Preface to Chaucer* (Princeton, 1962), especially pp. 314–16.

201. To the Virgin

Pr. Zupitza, 182, notes, xciii, 378–9. B.-R. 1042.

202. To the Virgin

Pr. Zupitza, 183, notes, xciii, 379–80. B.-R. 1080.

203. Of the Virgin

Pr. Zupitza, 188, notes xciii, 395–8. B.-R. 328.
See note on No. 172.
stza. 2, ll. 1, 2. Esther i. 12.   l. 3. *priuat*: deprived.   ll. 4–6. Esther v. 2.
stza. 4, ll. 1, 2. The first plague of Egypt, Exodus vii. 20.   ll. 3–6. See note on No. 180 A, stza. 4, l. 4.

204. To the Virgin

Pr. Zupitza, 280, notes xcvi, 173. B.–R. 2542.

The next poem after this in Ryman's MS., 'O emperesse, the emperoure' (*pr.* Zupitza, 282), uses the same stanza-form and the same refrain but has no burden.

205. To the Virgin

Pr. Zupitza, 283, notes, xcvi, 175–7. B.–R. 2545.

This carol is followed in the MS. by the colophon which names Ryman as the author (f. 80ʳ):

'Explicit liber ympnor*um* et canticor*um* quem composuit Frater Iacobus Ryman ordinis Minor*um* ad laudem om*n*ipotentis dei et s*an*ctissime matris eius marie om*n*iumq*ue* s*an*ctorum anno do*m*ini mill*e*simo CCCC^mo LXXXXII°.'

The first C and the L in the date have been erased.

206. To the Virgin

Pr. Wright, *P.S.* xxiii. 32. B.–R. 2400.

burden. See table in Introduction, p. cv.

stza. 4, l. 1. *whyght*: wight, creature.   l. 3. *in ech degre*: in each station of life.

207. To the Virgin

Pr. Zupitza, 278, notes, xcvi, 170–2. B.–R. 1072.

stza. 6, l. 2. *subsidie*: help.

208. To the Virgin

Pr. Zupitza, 295, notes, xcvi, 320–21. B.–R. 2466.

stza. 1, l. 1. *florigerat*: flower-bearing. Not in *O.E.D.*   l. 3. *desiderat*: desired. *O.E.D.* does not record as adjective before 1640.

stza. 7, l. 1. *ierarchies*: the three hierarchies comprising the nine orders of angels according to the formulation commonly attributed to Dionysius the Areopagite.

209. To the Virgin

Pr. Zupitza, 297, notes, xcvi, 321–2. B.–R. 2559.

stza. 8, l. 1. *that high Justyse.* Compare No. 98, stza. 3, l. 3, No. 179, stza. 5, l. 3, and No. 361, stza. 1, l. 2.

210. To the Virgin

Pr. Zupitza, 298, notes, xcvi, 322–3. B.–R. 2426.

stza. 3, l. 1. *Holofernes*: Judith xiii. 8–10.

stza. 4, l. 1. *Aman*: Esther vii. 10.

211. To the Virgin

Pr. Zupitza, 299, notes, xcvi, 323–4. B.–R. 116.

212. To the Virgin

Pr. Zupitza, 312, notes, xcvii, 134. B.–R. 2540.

213. To the Virgin

Repr. facs. Reed, p. 62. B.–R. *Supp.* 2577.3.

The carol is incomplete at the end. It is a free paraphrase of the antiphon 'Salve regina, mater misericordiae'. See Introduction, p. cv, and Reed's note, p. 89. It does not, however, resemble the antiphon in form. The burden is made from the first two lines of the antiphon.

stza. 1, l. 3. *kynd*: nature.   *grop*: take, assume, with the further connotation of understanding.

stza. 4, l. 3. *floure on felde*: the 'flos campi' of Canticles ii. 1.

214. To the Virgin

Pr. Zupitza, 335, notes, xcvii, 149–50. B.–R. 2745.

215. To the Virgin

Pr. Zupitza, 311, notes, xcvii, 132–3. B.–R. 597.

216. To the Virgin

Pr. Zupitza, 312, notes, xcvii, 133. B.–R. 2435.

217. To the Virgin

Pr. Zupitza, 320, notes, xcvii, 138–9. B.–R. 2467.
This carol is composed of verses which appear in Nos. 208, 209, with the refrain-lines replaced by lines of English text.
stza. 1, l. 1. *florigerat*, l. 3. *desiderat*: see notes on No. 208.

218. To the Virgin

Pr. Zupitza, 319, notes, xcvii, 137–8. B.–R. 2801.
For the sources of the Latin lines see table in Introduction, p. cv.

219. To the Virgin

Pr. Zupitza, 323, notes, xcvii, 140. B.–R. 3148.
stza. 2, l. 2. *bone*: request.
stza. 3, l. 1. *mace*: sceptre.

220. To the Virgin

Pr. Zupitza, 327, notes, xcvii, 143–4. B.–R. 2527.
The internal rhymes of this and the two following carols are unusual in this stanza-form and show Ryman's interest in metrical experiment.

221. To the Virgin

Pr. Zupitza, 328, notes, xcvii, 144. B.–R. 2578.

222. To the Virgin

Pr. Zupitza, 328, notes, xcvii, 144. B.–R. 2480.

223. To the Virgin

Pr. Zupitza, 328, notes, xcvii, 144. B.–R. 2554.

224. To the Virgin

Pr. Zupitza, 329, notes, xcvii, 145. B.–R. 2575.
stza. 1, l. 1. See note on No. 199, stza. 9, l. 3.

225. To the Virgin

Pr. Zupitza, 330, notes, xcvii, 145–6. B.-R. 2555.

226. To the Virgin

Pr. Zupitza, 331, notes, xcvii, 146–7. B.–R. 2508.

227. To the Virgin

Pr. Zupitza, 331, notes, xcvii, 147. B.–R. 2396.

228. To the Virgin

Pr. Zupitza, 332, notes, xcvii, 147–8. B.–R. 3149.

229. To the Virgin

Pr. Zupitza, 334, notes, xcvii, 149. B.–R. 2563.

230. Of the Five Joys of Mary

a. *Pr.* Dyboski, p. 65; Flügel, *Fest.*, p. 56; 'Lieder.', p. 226; Pollard, p. 84.
b. *Pr.* C. & S., *M.L.R.* vi. 74; Whiting, p. 203.
B.–R. 895.

The carol is based on a hymn of the Five Joys, 'Gaude virgo, Mater Christi' (*Horae Eboracenses*, Publications of the Surtees Society, cxxxii, Durham, 1920, 63). It is not a translation, however.

Audelay's original authorship must be regarded as doubtful. It is noticeable that this is the only carol in his MS. to use this verse-form.

All the preserved MS. carols in Middle English use the orthodox number of five for the Joys. Seven and twelve and ten are found in traditional folk-songs on the theme collected in modern times, none of which is a direct survival of the texts here selected. According to the note of William H. Husk to his song 'The Twelve Good Joys of Mary', 'The extension of the Seven joys to Twelve is confined to the northern parts of the country, being only found in broadsides printed at Newcastle late in the last, or early in the present century' (*Songs of the Nativity*, London, 1868, p. 87). *O.B.C.*, Music Edn., in its note to its No. 70, 'Joys Seven', misleadingly refers to 'the Seven Joys of the Sloane MS.'.

Lydgate's poems of the Fifteen Joys and of the Fifteen Joys and Sorrows, the first 'translated out of Frenshe into Englisshe', are formal and literary, with little relation to traditions of the carol (MacCracken, part i, Nos. 50, 51).

a. stza. 1, l. 5. *withowt blyn*: without fail. **b.** *mene*: doubt.
a. stza. 2, l. 1. *yglent*: made radiant.
b. stza. 1, l. 2. *emne*. Whiting (p. 254) glosses as 'equal', adding, 'The reading is not very satisfactory from the point of view either of meaning or of rhyme.' Chambers and Sidgwick (*M.L.R.* vi, 1911, 83) had suggested 'ene', lamb. The later MS. of a, which gives the better reading 'of the I mene', doubtless represents the correct version. The 'thynemne' of Audelay's MS. is probably a scribal blunder which escaped the corrector's eye.

231. Of the Five Joys of Mary

Pr. Wright, *Wart. Club*, p. 26; Sandys, *Carols*, p. 58; B. Fehr, *Archiv*, cix (1902), 48; E. Duncan, *The Story of the Carol* (London, 1911), p. 166. B.–R. 3347.

stza. 3, l. 2. *ryf*: famous, renowned.
stza. 5, l. 1. *dene*: disdain, reproach.

The joys or 'blessings' of Mary, in varying number, survive into modern times as a theme in songs on broadsides and in oral tradition. See, for example, *O.B.C.*, Music Edn., No. 70, 'Joys Seven', with useful note. The interesting American version which begins 'The first blessing Mary had was five and one', printed by George P. Jackson, *Down-East Spirituals and Others* (N.Y., 1939), p. 62, can hardly be called 'a Virginia version' of this particular carol, in spite of Evelyn K. Wells's comment (*The Ballad Tree*, N.Y., 1950, p. 200). Another American version, recorded in Vermont from oral tradition, lists twelve joys, using this formula:

> The first joy that Mary had, it was the joy of one
> To see her son Jesus, a well belov-ed son.
> A well-belov-ed son, good man,
> And a blessed man was He.
> Father Son and Holy One
> And Christ eternally.

> The next joy that Mary had, it was the joy of two
> To see her son Jesus go through the world, go through, *etc.*

> (Helen Hartness Flanders, *et al.*, *The New Green Mountain Songster*, New Haven, 1939, pp. 185–7)

Mrs. Flanders regards this folk-song as a modern version, but it can hardly be called a direct survival. Her note gives references to still other carols of the joys.

232. Of the Five Joys of Mary

A. *Pr.* James & Macaulay, p. 70.
B. *Pr.* Wright, *P.S.* xxiii. 68; Greene, *Selection*, p. 111.
C. *Pr.* Dyboski, p. 15; Flügel, 'Lieder.', p. 242.
B.–R. 2098.
stza. 3, l. 4. See table in Introduction, p. lxxxvi.
A. stza. 4, l. 2. *dyth* (B. *pyght*, C. *dyght*): fastened.

233. Of the Five Joys of Mary

Pr. Dyboski, p. 33; Flügel, 'Lieder.', p. 257.
B.–R. 898.

234. Of the Virgin

A. Music for two voices. *Pr.* Padelford, p. 95; C. & S., p. 106; Brown, *R.L. 15 C.*, p. 108; with music, Fuller Maitland, p. 7; Terry, p. 44; Stevens, *Med. Carols*, p. 3.
B. Music for two and three voices. *Pr.* Padelford, p. 93; Dyboski, p. 172; with music, *E.B.M.* ii. 119, *facs.* No. lviii; Stevens, *Med. Carols*, p. 16.
C. *Pr.* Wright, *Wart. Club*, p. 88; B. Fehr, *Archiv*, cix (1902), 68; Padelford, p. 94; Dyboski, p. 172.
D. *Pr.* Dyboski, p. 12; Flügel, 'Lieder.', p. 238; Padelford, p. 93.
B.–R. 354.
An unusual feature of this carol is the use of the same rhyme throughout. Compare Nos. 10, 22. C. stzas. 4 and 5, which do not conform, are probably borrowed from another piece.
burden. See Introduction, p. cv.
A. stza. 1, ll. 1, 2. Compare the opening of No. 149.
A. stza. 4, l. 1. *pyth* (B. *ypyght*, D. *dyght*): fastened.
C. stza. 4, ll. 1, 2. Compare No. 21 A, stza. 4, ll. 1, 2.

235. To the Virgin

a. Music for two and three voices. *Pr.* Padelford, p. 107; Brown, *R.L. 15 C.*, p. 110; Greene, *Selection*, p. 112; with music, *E.B.M.* ii. 144, *facs.* No. lxxvii; Terry, p. 22.
b. Music for two and three voices. *Pr.*, with music, Fuller Maitland, p. 3; Terry, p. 40; Stevens, *Med. Carols*, p. 2; Robbins, *Christmas Carols*, p. 60.
c. *Repr. facs.* Reed, p. 61.
B.–R. 3385.
stza. 2, l. 4. None of the three variants is quite satisfactory. The original reading may have been 'Trinite'.
stza. 3, l. 1. John i. 14, x. 30.
stza. 4. There is nothing in the book of Jeremiah to justify such a definite statement. The author is relying on Jeremiah's general reputation as a prophet.
a. stza. 5, l. 2. *yplaunte*: planted.   l. 3. *faunte*: infant.

236. Of the Annunciation

Pr. Wright, *Wart. Club*, p. 83; *P.S.* iv, 'Christmas Carols', 15. B.–R. 2384.
The occurrence of the 'Listen' formula in stza. 2, l. 1, and the words of stza. 1 suggest that the latter may once have formed the burden and that the 'Nowel, el' burden is a later addition.
stza. 3, l. 1. *snel*: quickly.
stza. 5, l. 1. See B. J. W., *Proverbs*, S 772.   l. 3. *manys mon*: carnal intercourse. Compare Trevisa's *Higden*, vi. 29 (quoted by *O.E.D.* s.v. 'Mone' *sb*[1]): 'He was i-bore of þe mayde Marie by vertu of God wiþ oute mannys mone (L[at]. *non humano semine*).'

237. Of the Annunciation

A. *Pr.* Wright, *P.S.* xxiii. 33.
B. *Pr.* Dyboski, p. 10; Flügel, *Fest.*, p. 65, 'Lieder.', p. 236.
B.–R. 890
burden. See Introduction, p. cv.

238. Of the Annunciation

A. *Pr.* Dyboski, p. 5; Flügel, *Fest.*, p. 58, 'Lieder.', p. 229; Frost, p. 264; with music from C, Noah Greenberg, *An English Songbook* (Garden City, N.Y., 1961), p. 66.
B. *Pr.* Wright, *P.S.* xxiii. 36.
C. Music for one voice. *Pr.* R. H. Robbins, *Modern Language Notes*, lviii (1943), 40; with music, Stevens, *Med. Carols*, p. 111; Robbins, *Christmas Carols*, p. 64.
B.–R. 889.
burden, l. 2. This is one of the plays on words most beloved of medieval theologians. It occurs in many hymns and prose writings. See Introduction, pp. lxxxiv, lxxxv.
A. stza. 8, l. 1. *a–hye*: aloud.
B. stza. 4, l. 1. *of all ble*: in all her countenance.
B. stza. 5, l. 1. *that free*: that noble one.
B. stza. 7, l. 1. *fere*: companion (Gabriel).

239. Of the Annunciation

a. Music for one voice. *Pr.* Wright, *P.S.* xxiii. 79; Greene, *Selection*, p. 113; collated with c, Dyboski, p. 177; with music, William Chappell, *Old English Popular Music*, revised H. E. Wooldridge (London, 1893), p. 30; Terry, p. 30; *E.B.M.* ii. 183; Stevens, *Med. Carols*, p. 110; Robbins, *Christmas Carols*, p. 62.
b. *Pr.* Lucy Toulmin Smith, *A Common-place Book of the Fifteenth Century* (London, privately printed, 1886), p. 122; collated with c, Dyboski, p. 177.
c. *Pr.* Dyboski, p. 39; Flügel, *Fest.*, p. 78, 'Lieder.', p. 261; Pollard, p. 93.
d. Music for one voice. *Pr.*, with music, Wright, *P.S.* xxiii. 62.
B.–R. 3736.
stza. 7, ll. 3, 4. Expanded and partially transposed from the words of Luke i. 38.

240. Of the Annunciation

Pr. Dyboski, p. 4; Flügel, *N.L.*, p. 114, *Fest.*, p. 57, 'Lieder.', p. 228; Mary G. Segar and Emmeline Paxton, *Some Minor Poems of the Middle Ages* (London, 1917), p. 11; Frost, p. 263.
B.–R. 878.
Except for the last line, the Latin tags of this carol are taken from the narrative in Luke i with minor adaptations.
burden, l. 2. Luke i. 26.
stza. 2, l. 1. *sest*: ceased.

241. Of the Annunciation

Pr. Dyboski, p. 44; Flügel, *Fest.*, p. 79, 'Lieder.', p. 264. B.–R. 1363.
The three-line stanza without *cauda* is unusual. The introduction of 'Te Deum laudamus' in place of the abbreviated burden after the last stanza may indicate that another phrase, omitted in writing, was used with the other stanzas.

242. Of the Annunciation and Other Joys of Mary

Pr. Wright, *Wart. Club*, p. 29, *P.S.*, iv, 'Christmas Carols', 7; Sandys, *Carols*, p. 7; Greene, *Selection*, p. 114. B.–R. 2113.
For the source of the Latin lines see note on No. 230.
burden, l. 1. Compare No. 236, burden.

243. Of the Annunciation

a. *Pr.* Zupitza, 167, notes, xciii, 281–94.
b. *Pr.* Zupitza, 286, notes xcvi, 311.
B.–R. 3304.
The two almost identical versions of this carol are not variants in the usual sense; they represent two workings of the same material by the same author. Both are close to No. 244.
a. burden. See Introduction, pp. cv, cvi.
stza. 6, l. 1. *see*: throne.

244. Of the Annunciation

Pr. Zupitza, 169, notes, xciii, 294–6. B.–R. 3303.
stza. 5, l. 1. *see*: throne.

245. Of the Annunciation

Pr. Zupitza, 170, notes, xciii, 297–9. B.–R. 1043.
stza. 4, l. 3. *see*: throne.

246. Of the Annunciation

Pr. Zupitza, 208, notes, xciv, 389–91. B.–R. 398.

247. Of the Annunciation

Pr. Zupitza, 258, notes, xcv, 396–8. B.–R. 3378.
The form of this carol and of No. 248 is less popular and more literary than those most used by Ryman. The lines are four-stress, but the rhyme-scheme is that of rhyme royal.
stza. 4, l. 3. *see*: throne.

248. Of the Annunciation

Pr. Zupitza, 260, notes, xcv, 398–9. B.–R. 3267.
stza. 1, l. 6. This agrees verbally with the Englished *Ave Maria* of Myrc's *Instructions to Parish Priests* (ed. E. Peacock, E.E.T.S., Or. Ser., No. 31, 1868), ll. 422–3:

> Hayle be þow, mary fulle of grace,
> God ys wyþ þe in euery place.

249. Of the Annunciation

Pr. Zupitza, 277, notes, xcvi, 169. B.–R. 3726.
On the use of 'alone' in this carol compare Nos. 63, 154, 159, 160, 281.

250. Of the Annunciation

Pr. Zupitza, 288, notes, xcvi, 311–13. B.–R. 283.

251. Of the Annunciation

Pr. Zupitza, 289, notes, xcvi, 313–14. B.–R. 278.

252. Of the Annunciation

Pr. Zupitza, 291, notes, xcvi, 314–15. B.–R. 2501.

253. Of the Annunciation

Pr. Zupitza, 292, notes, xcvi, 316. B.–R. 279.

254. Of the Annunciation

Pr. Zupitza, 294, notes, xcvi, 319–20. B.–R. 282.

stza. 6, l. 3. *bondage*: Zupitza's suggestion of 'Wochenbett' will hardly do. Either 'subjection to the will of a man' or 'bondage of sin' may be Ryman's meaning.

255. Of the Annunciation

Pr. Zupitza, 336, notes, xcvii, 151. B.–R. 280.

burden, l. 1. Compare the burden of No. 43.

256. Of the Annunciation

Repr. Bliss, p. 57; Sandys, *Carols*, p. 21; *facs.* Reed, p. 44. B.–R. *Supp.* 1984.5.

Although it is headed by its printer 'A new caroll of our lady', the style of this piece points to a date of composition nearer 1500 than 1550 or thereabouts, the time of its appearance in print.

stza. 1, l. 1. *bydene*: together.

stza. 6. The apparent deviation from the usual cross-rhyme here may be due to an accidental transposition of ll. 2, 3.

257. The Magnificat

Pr. Zupitza, 189, notes, xciv, 161–6. B.–R. 3725.

The carol is a paraphrase of the Magnificat of Mary, Luke i. 46–55.

258. The Trouble of Joseph

Pr. Zupitza, 260, notes, xcv, 399–401. B.–R. 1802.

This carol gives an unusual interpretation of Joseph's resolution to flee from Mary, one more to his credit than the customary one, based on Matthew i. 18–23 and the Book of James xiii–xvi, which is implied in No. 259, stza. 3.

259. The Trouble of Joseph

Music for two and three voices. *Pr.* Sandys, *Carols*, p. 13; Fehr, p. 266; Wright, *P.S.* iv, 'Christmas Carols', 52; John Julian, *A Dictionary of Hymnology*, 2nd edn. (London, 1925), p. 209 (omits burden); Greene, *Selection*, p. 115; with music, *Mus. Ant.*, p. 24; Stevens, *Med. Carols*, p. 68. B.–R. 1322.

The carol is cast in the form of a dialogue between Joseph and the informing angel. Stza. 3 alludes to his previous resolution to desert Mary, presumably on the grounds of her guilt.

burden. Compare burden of No. 260, which is not, however, a carol of the trouble of Joseph, but a pedantic theological discussion of 'reason'.

stza. 1. Compare Myrc's *Festial*, 'De Anunciacione Dominica' (part i, ed. T. Erbe, E.E.T.S., Ex. Ser., No. xcvi, 1905, 107): 'But when Ioseph se hur gret wyth chyld, he meruelt gretly how þat myght be.'

stza. 2, l. 1. *disstens*: condescension.

260. Mary's Virginity Explained

Pr. Brown, *R.L. 15 C.*, p. 184. B.–R. 651.

This carol was printed in the first edition of this work from a nineteenth-century transcript by Joseph Hunter. The pedantic play on the word 'reason' resembles Audelay's reiteration of 'love' in No. 272. There may be an echo of the controversy which grew up around Bishop Reginald Pecock, who was called to account by the Council of Westminster in 1457 for having given too much importance to the element of reason in his well-intended *Repressor* of about 1449. Pecock recanted, and to him are ascribed the lines 'Witt hath wunder that reson ne tell can', etc., on the same theme as this carol (B.–R. 4181).

In spite of the burden and refrain addressed to Joseph the carol is not primarily on the story of his incredulity or 'trouble' like Nos. 258, 259, but is a theological argument addressed to doubting man.

stza. 5, l. 3. *resyled*: withdrawn from consideration.

261. Of the Virgin's Motherhood

Pr. Wright, *P.S.* xxiii. 73; Greene, *Selection*, p. 116; Davies, p. 236; Silverstein, p. 114. B.–R. 3822.

This interesting carol presents a clear case of religious imitation of secular lyric. The prototype is a song of the genre in which a betrayed maiden laments her pregnancy, a theme represented in Nos. 452–7, and common in medieval French lyrics as well. The blessed state of the Virgin and her rejoicing would have the effect of a striking contrast to hearers familiar with the type of song parodied. The first stanza may have come without much change from such a piece.

The heading in the MS. names the air for which the carol is designed. It is not otherwise known.

stza. 5, l. 4. *fod*: child.

262. To the Virgin

Pr. Zupitza, 184, notes, xciii, 380–3. B.–R. 641.

The entire carol is based on Canticles iv and vii. The Virgin is identified with the loved one of the Song of Songs in accordance with frequent medieval practice. Compare F. J. Furnivall, ed., *Hymns to the Virgin and Christ* (E.E.T.S., Or. Ser., No. 24, 1867), 1, and Carol No. 138.

burden, l. 2. Canticles iv. 8.

stza. 2, l. 1. *myelde dove*: Canticles ii. 10, v. 2.

stza. 4. Canticles iv. 7, 8: 'Tota pulchra es, amica mea, et macula non est in te. Veni de Libano', etc.

stza. 5. Canticles vii. 7: 'Statura tua assimilata est palmae et ubera tua botris.'

263. Our Lord's Exhortation

a. Music for four voices by Sheryngham. *Pr.* Fehr, p. 63; Stevens, *M. & P.*, p. 371; with music, John Stafford Smith, *A Collection of Ancient Songs* (London, [1779]), p. 34; Stevens, *Early Tudor Songs*, p. 98.

b. *Pr.* MacCracken, part i, p. 252.

c, d, e, f, g, h, i, j, k, l. Collated with b, loc. cit.

g. *Pr.* F. J. Furnivall, *Political, Religious, and Love Poems* (E.E.T.S., Or. Ser., No. 15, 1866), 141.

m, n. Collated with a in first edition.

B.–R. 3845.

The burden which makes a carol of Lydgate's well-known poem of Christ's appeal to man was doubtless added to the stanzas at the instance of the composer of the music of a. Little is known of Sheryngham, not even his Christian name. He is also the composer of 'My wofull hart' in the same MS. (f. 9ᵛ). The note of R. Eitner (*Biographisch-bibliographisches Quellen-Lexikon der Musiker und Musikgelehrten*, Leipzig, 1903, ix. 157) is not very helpful.

Stevens (*M. & P.*, p. 372) notes: 'The only indication that the burden was repeated in full after each verse is one *ut supra* (verse 4, Voice II, f. 72); it may not always have been so repeated. The verses are strophic.'

stza. 2, l. 1. *railyng*: gushing.   l. 6. *tretable*: reasonable.   l. 7. *conuencion*: agreement, covenant.

stza. 3, ll. 3, 4. John xx. 27.   l. 3. *crudelite*: cruelty.   l. 7. *triacle*: syrup, medicine.

stza. 4, l. 6. *table*: tablet, i.e. as an amulet.

stza. 5, l. 4. *fusion*: pouring out.

264. The Call of Christ

Pr. B. Fehr, *Archiv*, cvi (1901), 70; Stevens, *M. & P.*, p. 385; with music, Stevens, *Early Tudor Songs*, p. 151. B.–R. 1457 (indexed by first line of burden); B.–R. *Supp.* 490.5.

This carol, the last item in its MS., is possibly incomplete. Its brevity is unusual in the type of religious lyric to which it belongs, the direct appeal of Christ in the name of His sufferings.

The opening *chanson d'aventure* formula is here put into the burden, as in No. 150.

265. Christ to Sinful Man

Repr. Bliss, p. 48; A. Dyce, *The Poetical Works of John Skelton* (London, 1843), i. 144; Philip Henderson, *The Complete Poems of John Skelton Laureate*, 3rd edn. (London, 1959), p. 16; etc.; *facs.* Reed, p. 20. B.-R. 3404; *Supp.* 1119.

See Reed's note (p. 71), which properly denies the long-standing attribution of this carol to Skelton. Reed follows Friedrich Brie, *Englische Studien*, xxxvii (1907), 25–6. He also points out the source of stzas. 2, 3, 5, 7–10 in a poem of about 1500 in the Makculloch MS. (*pr.* as two pieces by George Stevenson, *Pieces from the Makculloch and the Gray MSS. together with The Chepman and Myllar Prints*, S.T.S., No. 65, Edinburgh, 1918, 33–6). Reed prints the stanzas used in the carol (op. cit., pp. 72–3).

See also Introduction, pp. xc, xci. George C. Taylor ('The Relation of the English Corpus Christi Play to the Middle English Religious Lyric', *Modern Philology*, v, 1907, 26–7) cites parallels between this carol and the Towneley Play of the Resurrection (ll. 314 ff.).

stza. 1, l. 1. *playd*: displayed.

stza. 2, l. 2. *thees*: thighs.

stza. 3, l. 1. *donge*: beat.

stza. 4. This is hardly to be understood as meaning '405,060 on head, foot, and hand, 57 on body', as Dyce's punctuation suggests. The early medieval tradition set the number of Christ's wounds at 5,466. A practice arose in the fourteenth century of reciting fifteen Paternosters each day in memory of the Sacred Wounds, the total for a year thus being 5,475. This figure is found in some verses in British Museum MS. Addit. 37049, f. 24ʳ (cent. xv):

> The nowmer of Jhesu Cristes wowndes
> Ar fyve thowsande foure hondreth sexty *and* fyftene,
> The whilk *in* his body war felt *and* sene.

This points to the 'fyfty' of the present stanza as a corruption of 'fyftene' and the 'vii' as an intruder. Compare note on No. 114, stza. 9, l. 3. As it here reads the stanza gives the total of 5,517, for which I know of no precedent.

Still another number, 5,461, is given as the sum total of the wounds in the rubric to a prayer earning an indulgence of Pope Benedict XII in a book of Hours of the B.V.M. of the fifteenth and sixteenth centuries, Sir John Soane's Museum in London, MS. 7 (N. R. Ker, *Medieval Manuscripts in British Libraries, i, London*, Oxford, 1969, 292).

Another computation, of 4,600, appears in 'Mary's Lamentation to St. Bernard on the Passion', l. 605 (*pr.* Carl Horstmann, *Yorkshire Writers*, London, 1896, ii. 281). In the poem on the Passion in C.U. Lib. MS. Dd. 11. 89, ll. 93–4, the number has been inflated to nine thousand (*pr.* R. H. Bowers, *Three Middle English Religious Poems*, University of Florida Monographs, Humanities, No. 12, Gainesville, 1963, p. 35 and p. 59 n.).

A. Brandl, reviewing Reed's edition, points out that the language of this carol shows a northern origin, whereas all the other carols printed by Kele are in the London dialect (*Archiv*, clxv, 1934, 248).

266. Christ's Intercession for Sinners

Pr. James & Macaulay, p. 79; Greene, *Selection*, p. 118.
B.-R. 782.

The first stanza of this carol, modified, appears as the first stanza of a poem without a burden and with twenty-three six-line stanzas, each ending with the refrain-line 'Nolo mortem peccatoris'. It describes Christ's sufferings in an address to God the Father and turns at the end to an appeal to sinful man of the usual type. It is signed by John Redford, the author of the morality play *Wit and Science*, and is included among other poems at the end of that play in B.M. MS. 15233 (*pr.* J. O. Halliwell-[Phillipps], *The Moral Play of Wit and Science*, Shakespeare Society Publications, xxxvii, London, 1848, pp. 68–73). It is written in two hands, one of which wrote the text of the play and the other of which wrote other poems, including the songs for the play. Redford was Master of the Choristers of St. Paul's Cathedral in 1535. The whole length of his tenure is uncertain.

James G. McManaway has discovered in the Folger Shakespeare Library, Washington, D.C., MS. Loseley 58 a transcript of Redford's poem, with slight verbal variations and the transposition of two stanzas, in the hand of Sir William More (1520–1600) and bearing the endorsement 'two dyttyes geven me by my .L. mountegou', i.e. Anthony Browne, first Viscount Montagu (1526–92). According to Mr. McManaway's dating by watermark the transcript must have been made between 1589 and 1592.

The first and second stanzas of this poem form the text of a six-part motet composed by Thomas Morley (1557–c. 1603), organist of St. Paul's and Gentleman of the Chapel Royal, in B.M. MSS. Addit. 29372–7, with the title *Tristitiae Remedium* and the date 1616. Prefixed to the text is the burden in the form in which it appears in Ryman's No. 267 (text from Cantus part):

> Nolo mortem peccatoris [*bis*]
> Haec sunt verba Salvatoris,

but with the lines transposed.

burden, l. 2. From Ezekiel xxxiii. 11: 'Dic ad eos, vivo ego, dicit Dominus Deus. Nolo mortem impii, sed ut convertatur impius a via sua, et vivat.' The same phrase occurs in translation in the burden of No. 268, by Ryman:

> Thus seith Jhesus of Nazareth:
> Of a synner I wille noo deth.

Stza. 4 shows that the carol was definitely intended for use at Christmas.

267. Christ to Sinful Man

Pr. Zupitza, 217, notes, xciv, 406. B.–R. 1124.
burden, l. 2. Ezekiel xxxiii. 11. Compare the burdens of Nos. 266, 268.

268. Christ to Sinful Man

Pr. Zupitza, 217, notes, xciv, 407. B.–R. 1434.
The burden of this piece is a free translation of that of No. 267.
stza. 2, l. 3. *spille*: be lost.
stza. 3, l. 2. *dispence*: deal mercifully.

269. Christ to Sinful Man

Pr. Zupitza, 218, notes, xvic, 407–10; Silverstein, p. 117; B.–R. 1125.
The source of the burden is given by Zupitza as Isaiah xliv. 22: '. . . revertere ad me, quoniam redemi te.' The 'revertere' burden of No. 140, on the other hand, because of its connection with Mary, seems more probably to have been suggested by Canticles vi. 12: 'Revertere, revertere, Sulamitis; revertere, revertere, ut intueamur te.' See note on No. 140. Compare also the fifteenth-century *chanson d'aventure* on the text 'Revertere', which ends all stanzas except the first with that word (*pr.* F. J. Furnivall, *Hymns to the Virgin and Christ*, E.E.T.S., Or. Ser., No. 24, 1867, 91).
stza. 7, l. 2. *to wedde*: as a pledge.

270. Christ's Call to Mankind

Pr. Greene, *Selection*, p. 118; Davies, p. 256; Silverstein, p. 119. B.–R. 2086.
This is a significant example of the use of a secular and amorous burden with stanzas written for a religious purpose. The carol was undoubtedly designed to be sung to a well-known secular tune. It is a parallel to the better-known cases of the religious imitation of the popular sixteenth-century song 'Come o'er the burn, Bessie' (*Madrigals by English Composers of the Close of the Fifteenth Century*, Plainsong and Mediaeval Music Society, London, 1890, No. 2) and of the like-wise popular 'The hunt is up' (J. P. Collier, ed., *Extracts from the Registers of the Stationers' Company*, London, 1848, i. 129–30). Compare also the 'New Notborune Mayd vpon the Passion of Cryste' (E. F. Rimbault, *P.S.* vi, 'Poetical Tracts', London, 1842, p. 33), and the examples in *A Compendious Book of Godly and Spiritual Songs*, S.T.S., No. 39, 1897 (*The Gude and Godlie Ballatis*), 'With huntis vp', pp. 174–7, 'Iohne, cum kis me now', pp. 158–61, and others.

The burden seems to be definitely related to the lines which begin the address of Christ to man in Victoria and Albert Museum MS. Dyce 45 (*c.* 1560), ff. 21ᵛ, 22ʳ. The lines of this song are bracketed as if in three-line stanzas, but the rhyme shows that there must earlier have been a six-line grouping. The song begins:

> Swete harte, be trwe,
> Chaunge for [no] newe,
> Come home to me agene;
> I shall full swetely
> Take the to mercye
> And delyver the owte of payne.

After the address of Christ these rather pedantic lines of explanation occur, supporting the probability that the piece is sacred parody of a secular love song:

> Thys lover trwe
> Whoo wolde renewe
> Mans soule to vertuose lyfe
> Ys Chryste Jesu
> Wythe hys vertu,
> Mans soule to be hys wyfe.

If not the same secular song, then two which are closely similar in sentiment and verse-form must lie behind the carol and the song in the Dyce MS. The MS. also contains a text of the moralized 'Grievous is my sorrow', another version of which is in the *Gude and Godlie Ballatis*. The secular original is in B.M. MS. Sloane 1584, which contains No. 446.

The phrasing of the burden appears again in an attractive fragment which is not in this metre but may nevertheless have been intended as a carol. It has been cancelled in the MS. B.M. Royal Appendix 58, f. 8ᵛ. B.-R. *Supp.* 3413.3.

> The lytell prety nyghhtyngale
> Among the leuys grenne
>
> Y wold I were I wold I were with hyr all nyghth
> But yet ye wot no what I meanes
> Then swet hart cum home swet hart cum home agayn
> For fallynge of the snow
> For & your host wyth heysso a hoo
> Ye may not cum home cum home
>
> The lytell prety nyghtyngale
> Amonge the leuys grene y wold I were

Text (normalized) from Flügel, 'Lieder.', p. 262.

stza. 6, l. 3. The 'idols' are probably the images displayed at shrines where contributions are made. The use of the word here in such a sense is earlier than any instance recorded by *O.E.D.* The author of the carol had Wycliffite or Lollard leanings. Silverstein denies the presence of 'someone's iconoclastic prejudice' and sees the poem as 'producing a startling dramatic effect of shifting focus' (p. 119). This denial is hardly tenable in view of such lines as these against the Lollards:

> Thes Lollardes that lothen ymages most
> With mannes handes made and wrouȝt,
> And pilgrimages to be souȝt;
> Thei seien hit is but mawmentrie.
> He that this lose first up brouȝt,
> Had gret lust in lollardie.
>
> He wer ful lewde that wold byleve
> In figure mad of stok or ston,
> Yut fourme shulde we none repreve,
> Nether of Marie ne of Jon,

> Petre, Poule, ne other none
> Canonised by clergie;
> Than the seyntes everychone
> Be litel holde to lollardie.

(Thomas Wright, ed., *Political Poems and Songs*, Rolls Series, London, 1859–61, ii, 246)
For the opposing view of 'stocke or stone,/ Gaily painted' see 'The Complaint of the Ploughman' (ibid. i. 331).

271. To Christ

Pr. Brown, *R.L. 14 C.*, p. 87; Davies, p. 111; Sisam, p. 198; Silverstein, p. 62. B.–R. 3691.
The curious burden of this piece is addressed to the tear shed by Christ over man's waywardness. The stanzas are addressed to Christ.
stza. 3, l. 3. *yerte*: cried out. This emendation was suggested by Brown.
stza. 4. This appears as stza. 4 of 'Christ's Gift to Man' in Hunterian Museum MS. V. 8. 15, *pr.* Brown, op. cit., p. 113, but belongs originally to this carol, as Brown points out (p. 267).   l. 4. 'The weather is changed.' The Hunterian MS. reading gives better sense: 'Wrong is went.'

272. Of the Love of God

Pr. C. & S., *M.L.R.* vi. 79; Whiting, p. 210; Sisam, p. 390. B.–R. 831.
Audelay plays on the word 'love' in this carol to the extent of using it (or a derivative) at least once in every line except the refrain-lines. Compare No. 444.
stza. 3, l. 3. *blyn*: cease.
stza. 4, l. 2. *altherbest*: best of all.

273. To Christ

Pr. Dyboski, p. 14; Flügel, *Fest.*, p. 68, 'Lieder.', p. 241. B.–R. 2586.
On the sources of the Latin lines see table in Introduction, pp. lxxxvi–lxxxviii.

274. To Christ

Pr. James & Macaulay, p. 81. B.–R. 972.
stza. 2, l. 3. *fendes fowndyng*: confounding by the fiend.
stza. 3, l. 1. *wende*: go.

275. To Christ

Pr. Zupitza, 333, notes, xcvii, 148–9. B.–R. 2561.

276. To Christ

Pr. Zupitza, 216, notes, xciv, 404–6; burden only, with music, Stevens, *Med. Carols*, p. 111. B.–R. 2476.
stza. 4, ll. 1, 2. Psalm li. 17: '. . . cor contritum et humiliatum, Deus, non despicies.'   l. 2. *meked lowe*: made meek.

277. To Christ

Music for two and three voices. *Pr.* Fehr, p. 272; Patterson, p. 71; with music, Stevens, *Med. Carols*, p. 90. B.–R. 918.
Patterson points out the likeness of this piece to No. vii of 'The .xv. oos in englysshe': 'O Blessyd Jesu, well of endless pyte', etc. (W. Maskell, *Monumenta Ritualia Ecclesiae Anglicanae*, 2nd edn., London, 1882, iii. 278).
burden. See note on No. 278, burden, l. 2.
stza. 1. Matthew xv. 22–8.   l. 2. *man*: obviously a corrupt reading, defective in both metre and sense. The original reading may have been 'mercy'.
stza. 2, l. 1. *fe*: property, estate. Patterson, reading 'se', glosses as 'sea'. I see no reason for his assumption (p. 170) that these lines are supposed to be spoken by the woman rather than by the poet in his own person.

278. To Christ

Repr. facs. Reed, p. 65. B.–R. *Supp.* 2217.5.

burden, l. 1. This is made from two phrases of the Canon of the Mass, 'Domine Jesu Christe, Fili Dei vivi', the prayer before the Host (*Br. Sar.* ii, col. 497), and the 'miserere nobis' of the Agnus. Compare the burden of No. 277.

stza. 4, l. 2. *medled*: mingled.

279. To Christ

Pr. Zupitza, 202, notes, xciv, 196–9. B.–R. 2534.

The internal rhymes are like those in Nos. 220–3, also by Ryman. The phrases of the burden appear as well in two short scraps of verse by Ryman (*pr.* Zupitza, 338).

stza. 1, l. 1. Compare No. 190, stza. 4, l. 1, where the figure is applied to the Virgin.

stza. 4, l. 2. *ryende*: rind, bark.

stza. 6, l. 1. *cornere stone*: Matthew xxi. 42, Luke xx. 17, where it is quoted by Christ from Psalm cxviii. 22: 'Lapidem quem reprobaverunt aedificantes hic factus est in caput anguli.'

279.1. To the Trinity

Music for two and three voices. *Pr.* Greene, *Selection*, p. 120; with music, Stevens, *Med. Carols*, p. 40. B.–R. *Supp.* 772.5.

burden, l. 1. Also used as burden, l. 2 of No. 35 A; in the third-person form as in this carol used as stza. 1, l. 4 of No. 52.

burden, l. 2; stzas. 1–3, l. 4. From the Versicle following the 'Timor Mortis' Response in the *Officium Mortuorum* (*Br. Sar.* ii, col. 278): 'Deus in nomine tuo salvum me fac Domine, et in veritate tua libera me.' It is used as the last line of No. 375. It also appears as the refrain of a prayer in quatrains in Bodl. MS. Ashmole 189, f. 105ʳ (*pr.* Brown, *R.L. 15 C.*, p. 85).

stza. 1, ll. 1, 2. The formula of the Trinity is a ready-composed four-measure line and is naturally a commonplace, as in No. 288 and others of Ryman's carols to the Trinity. 'Of myght(es) most' is almost inevitable as a rhyme, and Ryman so uses it in Nos. 288, 290, 293, 304, and with 'As Lord and King' in No. 305. There does not appear to be any question here of direct connection with any of Ryman's compositions.

stza. 2, l. 2. This commonplace appears as l. 18 of No. 370 a and as l. 2 of No. 367.   l. 3. *most*: knowest.

stza. 3, l. 1. *Wher*: whether.   l. 2. *wer*: wherever.

280. To Christ

Pr. Zupitza, 210, notes, xciv, 392–4. B.–R. 1328.

stza. 1, l. 1. Compare Audelay's carol No. 272.

281. Of Christ

Pr. Zupitza, 211, notes, xciv, 396–8. B.–R. 115.

For the use of 'alone' compare Nos. 63, 154, 159, 160, 249.

282. The Knot of the Trinity

Pr. Wright, *P.S.* xxiii. 45; K. Breul, *Englische Studien*, xiv (1890), 404. B.–R. 281.

Throughout the carol the word 'knot' probably carries the implication of Christ's perfect love, a 'knot' like that of which Usk makes so much in *The Testament of Love*: 'But for-as-moche as every herte that hath caught ful love is tyed with queynt knittinges, thou shalt understande that love and thilke foresayd blisse toforn declared in thise provinges, shal hote the knot in the hert.' (W. W. Skeat, *Chaucerian amd Other Pieces*, Oxford, 1897, p. 61). See Claes Schaar, 'Usk's "knot in the hert" ', *English Studies*, xxxvii (1956), 260–1. It also appears in the last line of the version of 'Ecce, ancilla domini' in MS. Advocates 19.3.1 (*pr.* K. Breul, 'Zwei mittelenglische Christmas Carols', *Englische Studien*, xiv, 1890, 402).

A close parallel to the use of the figure in this carol occurs in Gabriel's Annunciation speech in the Shearmen and Tailors' Pageant, ll. 92–5 (ed. H. Craig, *Two Coventry Corpus Christi Plays*, E.E.T.S., Ex. Ser. lxxxvii, 1902, 4):

> Now blessid be the tyme sett
> That thou wast borne in thy degre!
> For now ys the knott surely knytt
> And God conseyvide in Trenete.

stza. 1, l. 2. *A greth*: he greeted.
stza. 2, l. 1. *fayyrly fod*: fair child, Christ.
stza. 3, l. 1. *Johan*. The account of the Resurrection in John xx.   l. 2. *He*: Christ.   l. 3. *marbyl ston*: the stone which was rolled away from the sepulchre.
stza. 4, l. 3. *wyll*. An obvious corruption. The rhyme-word was probably 'seven'.
stza. 5, l. 2. *knottes*. Here the knots stand for the five wounds which Christ will show at the Judgement.   *spray*: splay, display.

283. To the Trinity

Pr. Zupitza, 213, notes, xciv, 399–401. B.–R. 2485.
stza. 5, l. 1. *pight*: lodged.

284. To the Trinity

Pr. Zupitza, 222, notes, xciv, 415–17. Frances M. Comper, *Spiritual Songs from English MSS.* (London, [1936]), p. 178; Greene, *Selection*, p. 120.
B.–R. 2432.
This carol shows Ryman at his most characteristic as a mannered and repetitious versifier. Nevertheless it has appealed to a modern composer, Thomas Canning, who has set it to music, together with Nos. 270 and 359 a in 'An Offering of Carols and Rounds' first performed in 1958.
Stza. 3, l. 2 gives one clue to the mystic meaning of this carol, as does the refrain-line with its allusion to the infinity of God, of which the circle, O, is the symbol. The O's of the Advent Antiphons may have been in the author's mind as well.
stza. 6, l. 2. *supplanter*: overthrower.

285. To the Trinity

Pr. Zupitza, 240, notes, xcv, 276–7. B.–R. 3728.
This carol is a free paraphrase of the *Te Deum*, ll. 2–9.

286. To the Trinity

Pr. Zupitza, 241, notes, xcv, 277–80. B.–R. 2448.
Stzas. 3–12 of this carol form a free paraphrase of the *Te Deum*, ll. 3–14.
stza. 2, l. 2. *committe*: consign, as to prison, confine.
stza. 4, l. 2. *empere*: empyrean, the highest and fiery heaven.

287. To the Trinity

Pr. Zupitza, 243, notes, xcv, 280–1. B.–R. 2431.
This carol paraphrases part of the *Te Deum* as follows: stza. 2 is based on l. 18, stza. 5 on ll. 3, 4, stza. 6 on l. 24.

288. To the Trinity

Pr. Zupitza, 244, notes, xcv, 281–2. B.–R. 781.

289. To the Trinity

Pr. Zupitza, 245, notes, xcv, 282–4. B.–R. 3379.
Part of this carol is based on the *Te Deum* as follows: stza. 2 on l. 16, stza. 4 on ll. 4, 7–9, stza. 5 on l. 3, stza. 6 on l. 10.

289.1. To the Trinity

Pr. R. H. Robbins, *PMLA*, lxxxi (1966), 309. B.–R. *Supp.* 3328.5 (the reference to B.–R. 2168 is erroneous).

Though unattributed in the MS. fragment, this carol is certainly by Ryman and is obviously another in his series of exercises on the *Te Deum*. Stza. 1 is almost identical with stza. 1 of No. 289. Stza. 9 is a variant of stza. 5 of No. 290. Robbins sums up the situation in his introductory note (p. 308): 'Altogether . . . seven of the ten quatrains . . . show verbal resemblances to at least ten of Ryman's other "Te deum" carols . . .' The list may be found in Robbins's Note 4.

290. To the Trinity

Pr. Zupitza, 246, notes, xcv, 284–5. B.–R. 2603.

291. To the Trinity

Pr. Zupitza, 299, notes, xcvi, 324. B.–R. 2429.

292. To the Trinity

Pr. Zupitza, 300, notes, xcvi, 324–5. B.–R. 2419.

293. To the Trinity

Pr. Zupitza, 301, notes, xcvi, 325. B.–R. 785.
Stza. 2 is based on the *Te Deum*, ll. 3, 5.
stza. 2, l. 1. See note on No. 208, stza. 7, l. 1.

294. To the Trinity

Pr. Zupitza, 301, notes, xcvi, 325–6. B.–R. 2417.
stza. 4, l. 3. *tyght*: action, behaviour. Not recorded after 1330 in *O.E.D.*

295. Of Christ

Pr. Zupitza, 302, notes, xcvi, 326. B.–R. 3471.
Stza. 5 is based on the *Te Deum*, l. 10.
stza. 3, l. 1. See note on No. 208, stza. 7, l. 1.

296. To the Trinity

Pr. Zupitza, 303, notes, xcvi, 326–7. B.–R. 2418.
Part of this carol is a paraphrase of the *Te Deum* as follows: stzas. 3, 4 of ll. 4, 6, stzas. 5, 6, 7 of ll. 7, 8, 9.
stza. 2, l. 2. *potestates*: powers.

297. To Christ

Pr. Zupitza, 304, notes, xcvi, 327–8. B.–R. 2562.
This carol is a paraphrase of ll. 14–29 of the *Te Deum*.

298. To the Trinity

Pr. Zupitza, 305, notes, xcvi, 328–9. B.–R. 2430.

299. Of Christ

Pr. Zupitza, 306, notes, xcvi, 329. B.–R. 3469.

300. Of Christ

Pr. Zupitza, 306, notes, xcvi, 329–30. B.–R. 3333.
stza. 3, l. 2. *Tronis, potestates*: thrones and powers, the names of two of the orders of angels.

301. Of Christ

Pr. Zupitza, 307, notes, xcvii, 129–30. B.–R. 3468.
This carol is based on the *Te Deum* as follows: stza. 3 on l. 7, stza. 4 on l. 3, stza. 5 on l. 4, stza. 6 on l. 8, stza. 7 on l. 9.

302. Of Christ

Pr. Zupitza, 307, notes, xcvi, 330. B.–R. 3751.
Stzas. 2, 3 of this carol are based on the *Te Deum*, ll. 16, 17.

303. To the Trinity

Pe. Zupitza, 308, notes, xcvii, 130–1. B.–R. 731.
This carol is a free paraphrase of the *Te Deum*, ll. 1–13.

304. To the Trinity

Pr. Zupitza, 310, notes, xcvii, 131–2. B.–R. 2416.
Zupitza mistakenly prints with this piece the first line of the *Te Deum* and the first line of No. 297, which were written at the bottom of f. 95^r, apparently in error, and abandoned as a false start.
Stza. 2 is based on the *Te Deum*, ll. 3–5.

305. To the Trinity

Pr. Zupitza, 333, notes, xcvii, 148. B.–R. 2462.

306. The Well of Mercy

Music for two and three voices. *Pr.* Flügel, *N.L.*, p. 113; with music, Stevens, *Med. Carols*, p. 104. B.–R. 1315.
The figure of a well as the type of the Divine mercy is a frequent one in Middle English religious poetry. See note on No. 123 A, stza. 2, l. 1. It appears in 'The Castle of Love' in the Vernon MS. (ed. C. Horstmann, E.E.T.S., Or. Ser., No. 98, 1892, 373, 376). It is sometimes applied directly to Christ, as in a hymn from the Thornton MS. (*pr.* Patterson, p. 131), but oftener to the Virgin, as in Chaucer's *Prioress's Tale*, l. 204. Compare Nos. 123, 199, 207, 395. It was one of the metaphors most likely to appeal to the mind of the people, coinciding as it did with the widespread interest and belief in holy wells and their virtues. Compare 'Do mercy to fore thi jugement', ll. 41–2 (*pr.* Patterson, p. 87):

> let neuer the deuelle with sorow depraue
> That waschen was in holy welle.

stza. 2, l. 2. *fele*: many.

307. A Prayer for the Dead

Music for two and three voices. *Pr.* Fehr, p. 278; with music, Stevens, *Med. Carols*, p. 108. B.–R. 2453.
burden, l. 2, stzas. 1–3, ll. 4, 5. From the Office of the Mass for the Dead (*Sar. Miss.*, p. 431, also in Ordinary of the Mass, ibid., p. 219).

308. Of Purgatory

Pr. [Sir] Egerton Brydges, *Censura Literaria* (London, 1805–9), viii. 401; Brown, *R.L. 15 C.*, p. 254. B.–R. 4163.
The cumulative pattern of short lines at the ends of the stanzas was probably imitated from folk-song, in which it still survives. The same musical phrase was probably meant to be used for each of the added short lines when the carol was sung. The style of the whole carol is somewhat elliptical.
stza. 1, l. 2. *haue the ryng*: win the prize for dancing. Brown cites British Museum MS. Addit.

37049, f. 85ᵛ: 'Who so hops þe best sal hafe þe ryng' (p. 342). Compare 'The Lamentatyon of Edward, late Duke of Buckyngham' in Bodl. MS. Rawlinson C. 813, ll. 43–6:

My souerreigne lorde, Henry þe viijth, þat ryall Kyng,
louyd me & trustyd me & butt to well,
yet my vnkynde harte euer hopped for the ryng,
trustyng þat fortune wolde haue turned her whell.

(*pr.* F. M. Padelford, *Anglia*, xxxi, 1908, 365)

Compare also the proverb found in John Heywood's *A Dialogue Containing Proverbs* (*John Heywood's Works and Miscellaneous Short Poems*, ed. Burton A. Milligan, Illinois Studies in Language and Literature, Urbana, xli. 23):

Where wooers hoppe in an out, long time may bryng
Him that hoppeth best, at last to haue the ryng.

See also B. J. W., *Proverbs*, R 139.   l. 5. *aby*: atone, make amends.
stza. 3, l. 1. *compasse*: consider, ponder.   *delle*: bit.   *keele*: cool.
stza. 4, l. 1. *wele*: well, the common figure of Mary as the well of grace.
stza. 5, l. 1. *thorugh*: certain.   l. 5. *guy*: guide.
stza. 6, l. 3. *avowries*: patron saints.

309. A Litany

a. *Pr.* Wright, *P.S.* xxiii. 76; Patterson, p. 68. B.–R. 1704.

b, c, d, e, f, g, h, i. Readings collated in first edition of this work and repeated here. B.–R. *Supp.* under 1703 lists additional MSS. containing stza. 1.

Patterson (p. 169) points out that the carol is based on the Litany of the York Use. This would be natural if its place of origin was Beverley Minster.

The first stanza is adapted from the rhymed prayer to the Holy Name of Jesus widely current in the fourteenth and fifteenth centuries. The resulting piece is the only one of its sort, and the content seems at first glance rather unsuitable for a carol. Actually the repetitive nature of the carol-form with its burden would make the words quite effective in performance, especially if a soloist sang the stanzas and an assembly the burden. See Introduction, p. xxvii.

The collation of nine texts of this prayer is here reproduced from the first edition as illustrative of its popularity and wide dissemination. The prose commentary following b in Bodl. MS. Douce 54 is discussed at length by John C. Hirsh ('A Fifteenth-Century Commentary on "Ihesu for Thy Holy Name"', *N. & Q.* ccxv, 1970, 44–5). Douglas Gray describes 'an old piece of wood', the remains of a version of this prayer cut on the end of a pew in the church at Warkworth, near Banbury (*N. & Q.* ccxii, 1967, 131–2). The prayer is found in oral tradition debased to a local and personal jingle referring to Sir Ralph Ashton, a severe vice-constable of Ashton-under-Lyme in the fifteenth century:

Sweet Jesu, for thy mercy's sake
And for thy bitter passion,
Oh save me from a burning stake,
And from Sir Ralph of Assheton.

(G. F. Northall, *English Folk-Rhymes*, London, 1892, p. 33)

310. To St. Francis of Assisi

Pr. C. & S., *M.L.R.* vi. 81; Whiting, p. 212; Greene, *Selection*, p. 122. B.–R. 44.

stza. 1. St. Francis had a particular devotion to the Passion of Christ, as recorded in the *Vita Prima S. Francisci Confessoris, Auctore Thoma de Celano*, lib. i, cap. x (*Acta Sanctorum*, Oct., tom. ii, Paris, 1866, p. 706): 'Recordabatur assidua meditatione verborum eius [Christi] et sagacissima consideratione ipsius opera recolebat: praecipue incarnationis humilitas et caritas passionis ita eius memoriam occupabant, ut vix valeret aliud cogitare.'

stza. 3, ll. 1, 2. Actually St. Francis received the stigmata only two years before his death.

stza. 4. Apparently Audelay means that St. Francis divided his food in five parts in memory of Christ's five wounds. I have not seen this elsewhere recorded of the saint. The *Appendix Inedita ad Vitam Primam Auctoribus Tribus ipsius Sancti Sociis* (*Acta Sanctorum*, Oct., tom. ii, p. 727) says: 'non solum autem affligebat se in lacrymis, sed etiam abstinentia cibi et potus ob memoriam Dominicae passionis.'

stza. 6. St. Francis set out in 1212 on a mission to the heathen in Palestine, but his ship was wrecked, and he was forced to return. In 1219 he actually went to the Near East and attempted the conversion of some Mohammedans, but soon returned to Italy.

l. 1. *thongis*: thankedst.   *sonde*: gift.   l. 3. *wond*: shrink.

stza. 7, l. 2. *talent*: purpose.   l. 3. *testament*: the Testament of St. Francis containing his last instructions to his brethren, dictated by him shortly before his death.

stza. 9. The first Rule was given out by St. Francis and orally approved by Pope Innocent III in 1210, not, as the carol implies, later than the Testament. The latter enjoins obedience to the Rule as it had been revised in the saint's lifetime.

Whatever Audelay's own status in the religious hierarchy may have been, he was no enemy of the friars as such, but only of those who gave way to avarice or other sins, as passages in his works make plain (Whiting, No. 2, ll. 470–545). He expresses admiration for the founders of the orders in the same poem (ll. 430–1):

> þe furst founders of the freres *and* of the iiij oordyrs
> weron iiij be[rn]es i-blest of oure Saueour, I say.

The 'breder' of the burden is probably meant to designate not only the friars of Francis's own order but his 'brothers' in the wider sense of all Christians.

311. To St. Anne

Pr. C. & S., *M.L.R.* vi. 71; Whiting, p. 200. B.–R. 3244.

It is possible that this carol was intended for use at a feast of St. Anne (26 July) as well as at Christmas. See E. Roscoe Parker, *The Middle English Stanzaic Versions of the Life of Saint Anne* (E.E.T.S., Or. Ser., No. 174, 1928), p. x. The fashion of devotion to St. Anne and the formation of guilds in her honour was growing rapidly in England at the time this carol was written down, her day having been made a feast of obligation in 1382. The diocese of Hereford, which included southern Shropshire, though not Haughmond itself, was particularly zealous in this devotion. See M. V. Ronan, *S. Anne, Her Cult and Her Shrines* (London, 1927), pp. 78–9, 84.

Audelay's account of the saint's life follows the accepted narrative as it appears in the Book of James or Protevangelium, and in the first part of the Pseudo-Gospel of Matthew based thereon.

stza. 6, ll. 1, 3. These lines are also used by Audelay as stza. 1, ll. 3, 4 of No. 172 a.   l. 2. *at my wettyng*: to my knowledge.

stza. 7. This appears with slight variation as ll. 33–6 of an Annunciation song, 'Ecce ancilla Domini', found in two fifteenth-century MSS. (*pr.* K. Breul, *Englische Studien*, xiv, 1890, 401).

stza. 9. This stanza is a partial translation of the Latin lines which form the burden of No. 178. l. 2. *outlere*: exile.

Compare also the burden of No. 195.

311.1. Of St. George

Music for two voices. *Pr.* B. Schofield, *Musical Quarterly*, xxxii (1946), 513; J. Copley, *N. & Q.* cciii (1958), 239; Greene, *Selection*, p. 124; Davies, p. 185; with music, Stevens, p. 49. B.–R. *Supp.* 4229.5.

The widespread national devotion to St. George prevents assigning this carol on internal evidence to any particular locality. There are references to him in Nos. 308, 309 a, 323, 431.1, and 433.1.

The carol appears to have been suggested by a non-liturgical rhyming prayer, the Commemoration of St. George widely circulated in the Prymer or Hours of the Blessed Virgin Mary (*Horae Eboracenses*, Publications of the Surtees Society, No. cxxxii, 1920, 131–2; also in Sarum). It was well known on the Continent, and is edited from five MSS. (two of English origin) in *Anal. Hym.* xv. 206, and from another in xxxiii. 84. The York version begins:

> Georgie martyr inclite,
> te decet laus et gloria.

Stza. 2, l. 1 on the maid and the dragon can hardly be referred to any specific source; it may be noted that it corresponds to the lines at about the same point in the York prayer, ll. 4–8:

per quem puella regia
existens in tristicia,
coram dracone pessimo
te rogamus [rogans in *Anal. Hym.*] corde intimo
saluata est . . .

Stza. 3 seems to echo the Respond to the Versicle immediately following: '. . . ita eiusdem intercessione hostes nostros visibiles et invisibiles, ne nocere nobis valeant, precedere digneris.'

burden, l. 2. The most hackneyed epithet of St. George. It appears in No. 323, as well as in 'Speed Our King on His Journey [to France, 1430]', Brown, *R.L. 15 C.*, p. 196. It is the key line of a charm for a hag-ridden horse dated 1571 (George Lyman Kittredge, *Witchcraft in Old and New England*, Cambridge, Massachusetts, 1929, p. 220):

In nomine patris, &c.
Saint George our Ladyes Knight,
He walked day so did he night,
Untill he hir found,
He hir beate and he hir bounde
Till truely hir trouth she him plyght
That she would not come within the night,
There as Saint George our Ladys Knight,
Named was three tymes, Saint George.

A variant of the same charm is recorded as a remedy for the nightmare (supposed to be caused by the Incubus) in Reginald Scot's *The Discoverie of Witchcraft* (1584), ed. Brinsley Nicholson (London, 1886), p. 68.

stza. 1, l. 1. Honour is the reward of virtue (Davies).   l. 2. *seweth*: follows.

stza. 2, ll. 3, 4. The reference is to the famous apparition of St. George reported to have been seen above the field of Agincourt; 'the crownecle ye red' indicates that the carol must have been written at some interval of time after the battle and suggests that it is the product of a monastic house, the sort of place where a chronicle would be kept and read. Compare the expression of Lydgate in his poem to St. Edmund, l. 77 (MacCracken, part i, p. 126): 'Slain at Geynesboruh, þe cronycle who lyst se'. It is rather remarkable that no reference to St. George appears in the Agincourt Carol itself (No. 426).

312. Of St. Edmund

Pr. Wright, *Wart. Club*, p. 73; T. Wright, *Songs and Carols* (London, 1836), No. xiii; Ritson, *Ancient Songs* (1790), p. 84, (1829), i. 143, (1877), p. 123; *The Suffolk Garland* (Ipswich, 1818), p. 351; Greene, *Selection*, p. 124. B.–R. 80.

This is the only extant English carol in honour of the patron saint of Bury St. Edmunds. It makes use of the most picturesque part of his legend. He was captured by the Danes at Hoxne in Suffolk in 870 and offered terms which his religious convictions would not allow him to accept. After his refusal the Danes beat him with cudgels and tied him to a tree for further scourging. He was then shot at until covered with arrows and finally beheaded. The head, thrown into the undergrowth of Heglesdune Forest, was discovered in the keeping of a wolf. I do not find the 'blind man' elsewhere recorded, some accounts giving the credit to a watchful native Christian, others to a miraculous pillar of light. The wolf, according to the legend, followed the head to the grave.

See J. B. Mackinlay, O.S.B., *Saint Edmund, King and Martyr* (London and Leamington, 1893), pp. 131, 141–4.

burden, l. 2. The first line of the antiphon for St. Edmund's Day (20 November), I Vespers (*Br. Sar.* iii, col. 1073). It was, of course, an antiphon specially valued at Bury. When Henry VI made his memorable visit to the abbey on Christmas Eve of 1433, he dismounted at the abbey gate and was escorted by a solemn procession to the high altar, this antiphon being sung the while (Craven Ord, 'Account of the Entertainment of King Henry the Sixth at the Abbey of Bury St.

Edmunds', *Archaeologia*, xv, 1806, 67). Lydgate's poem 'To St. Edmund' implies constant use of the antiphon at Bury, saying of the town and monastery (MacCracken, part i, p. 127, ll. 95–6):

> Aue rex gentis shal ech day be ther song
> Callyng to þe for helpe in ther most neede.

On two early fourteenth-century motets based on this antiphon and thought to be from Bury see Bukofzer, chap. i, and Frank Ll. Harrison, *Music in Medieval Britain* (London, 1958), p. 146.

stza. 2, l. 2. *lete*: stop.   l. 3. See B. J. W., *Proverbs*, R 12.

stza. 4, l. 4. *fray*: attack.

313. Of St. Catherine of Alexandria

Pr. James & Macaulay, p. 71. B.–R. 1900.

stza. 2. Catherine, martyred about 313, was famous for her learning and wisdom as well as for her Christian devotion. The 'doctors' who 'queried' her were fifty learned heathen philosophers set by the emperor Maximinus to dispute with, and, if possible, convert her. The maiden converted the doctors instead, as well as another fifty who took their places.

stza. 3. This stanza is obviously corrupt.   l. 3. This seems to belong to some such carol as No. 395. Compare stza. 3 of that piece.

stza. 4, l. 2. *twyl*: dwell.

stza. 5. There appears to be confusion here between Catherine's fate and that of the doctors whom she converted. The latter were burnt by the emperor, but their bodies were found with not a hair consumed. Catherine herself, according to the legend, was first put on the spiked wheel, and, after this had been miraculously destroyed, was beheaded and her body borne by angels to Mount Sinai, where it yet remains.

314. Of St. Winifred

Pr. Whiting, p. 171. B.–R. 413.

The occurrence of this piece before the verse 'I pray yow, syrus', etc., as well as its unusual length, has led to its being omitted from previous discussions of Audelay's group of carols, in spite of its final stanza. G. H. Gerould (*Saints' Legends*, Boston, 1916, p. 256) calls it '*St. Wenefred*, which the author curiously termed a "carol"'. The use of 'Redis' instead of 'Singis' in the last stanza might be taken to show recognition by Audelay that he was in this case writing a literary narrative instead of a lyric to be sung. But the word is similarly used in No. 310, and the rhyming of the fourth line of each stanza with the burden leaves no doubt that the piece is intended as a true carol. Compare the carol of forty stanzas to St. Catherine by William Forrest, A.D. 1561 (*pr.* Rudolf Kapp, *Heilige und Heiligenlegenden in England. Studien zum 16. und 17. Jahrhundert*, i, Halle, 1934, pp. 294–6). Probably J. Copley has this piece in mind, though he uses the plural, when he writes that some of Audelay's carols 'are not too suitable for musical performance', some because they 'have far too many stanzas' ('John Audelay's Carols and Music', *English Studies*, xxxix, 1958, 211). The fact that the burden was added by a different hand and in red has probably led readers of the MS. to regard it as a title. Audelay's other poem in honour of St. Winifred, which is not a carol, follows this piece in the MS. (*pr.* Whiting, p. 175).

Audelay's life of St. Winifred is probably based on tradition local to Shrewsbury rather than on a particular written source. It does not follow either of the two principal medieval accounts of the saint, that in British Museum MSS. Cotton Claudius A. v and Lansdowne 436, and that by Robert, Prior of Shrewsbury (both *pr. Acta Sanctorum*, Nov., tom. i, pp. 702 ff.). Details in Audelay's narrative which are lacking in both are the miracles of the boy on the mill-wheel, the dropped groat, the wine in the chapel, and the stone as a sign of St. Beuno's death. In the account of the stone's acting as ferry to Winifred's gift of a vestment Audelay agrees with the Cotton MS. life rather than with that of Robert, in which the vestment floats in a wrapping of cloth miraculously kept dry.

That the mill-wheel incident was a local tradition is rendered more probable by the fact that it was reported with slight change and circumstantial detail as happening in the seventeenth century. 'On the fourth of *April*, One thousand six hundred and sixty six, about five of Clock in the Afternoon,' one Hugh Williams, a boy of eight, fell into the mill-wheel at Holywell and was carried around by it, but was unharmed by St. Winifred's grace, although the clearance was only two inches and he of full size for his age (William Fleetwood, *The Life and Miracles of St. Wenefrede*, 2nd edn., London, 1713, p. 104).

Whiting's note (p. 247) properly points out that Myrc's account is unrelated, but she ignores the Cotton MS. life and says, 'No manuscript of Robert of Shrewsbury has been found'.

stza. 2, l. 3. *Cradoc*: or Caradoc, the king's son who attempted an attack on Winifred's chastity while her parents were at church, pursued her from the house, and finally beheaded her.

stza. 3, l. 4. *dry valay*. Compare the life by Robert, Bodl. MS. Laud misc. 114, f. 145ʳ: 'Locus uero ubi sanguis illius effusus est primitus sicca uallis dicebatur.'

stza. 4, l. 1. *Bewnou*: St. Beuno, who was preaching in the church where Winifred's parents were at the time.

stza. 7, l. 3. *sparpiled*: scattered.

stza. 8, l. 1. *mesis*: mosses.

stza. 10, l. 3. *ladlis*: the float-boards or paddles of the mill-wheel.

stza. 14, l. 1. *afyne*: finally.

stza. 16, l. 3. *plumys*: pumps. *bere*: noise.

stzas. 17, 18. Mark xi. 15–17.

stza. 25, l. 1. 'Son after' is not to be taken with l. 2. The translation to Shrewsbury occurred in 1138, five hundred years after the saint's death.

stza. 26, l. 2. A particular instance is given in the Cotton MS. life of a man in chains for many years, from whose hands they fell after he had washed in the well, but Audelay speaks of it as happening at Shrewsbury.

stza. 27, ll. 1, 2. There may be a reference here to the natural gratification of Shrewsbury people at the order of 1391 for the feast of St. Winifred to be observed throughout the province of Canterbury.

stza. 28, l. 2. *herfilly*: heartful, sincere.

stza. 29, l. 4. *fyndis pray*. This phrase is common enough in religious poetry to render unnecessary Whiting's emendation to 'fray'. Compare No. 117 a, stza. 1, l. 7.

315. Of St. Nicholas

Pr. Wright, *Wart. Club*, p. 4; T. Wright, *Songs and Carols* (London, 1836), No. ii. B.–R. 3034.

The burden alludes to St. Nicholas's special character as patron saint of maidens. The story which follows, that of the three daughters of a decayed gentleman of Patara, is one of those most frequently told of the saint's life. The spirited speeches of the daughters were doubtless put into the carol for the sake of their moral effect on the hearers. The last two lines hastily summarize the solution of the difficulty. Nicholas filled three bags with gold on three successive nights and slipped them through the window of the maidens' house, thus providing them with the needed dowries.

stza. 1, l. 1. *poste*: power. Compare the Life of St. Nicholas in *The Early South-English Legendary* (ed. C. Horstmann, E.E.T.S., Or. Ser., No. 87, 1887, 245), l. 173: 'For-to wurthschipien þane guode man: þat is of so gret pouste.'

316. Of St. Nicholas

Pr. Wright, *Wart. Club*, p. 99; T. Wright, *Songs and Carols* (London, 1836), No. xix; Greene, *Selection*, p. 125. B.–R. 1522.

stza. 1, l. 1. *Patras*: Patara in Lycia.

stza. 2. The legend of St. Nicholas and the three young clerks or children rescued from the brine-vat is familiar from medieval art. Charles Cahier suggests (*Caractéristiques des saints dans l'art populaire*, Paris, 1867, i. 304) that it may be a popular corruption through misinterpretation of pictures or carvings of the more plausible story of the three officers condemned to death by Constantine and saved by Nicholas's intervention. The small tower in which these three were represented could easily be mistaken for a tub.

stza. 3. See note on No. 315.

stza. 4. The saving of a pig-stealer is plainly related to the character of St. Nicholas as the unofficial patron saint of thieves, but I have not met with the incident in any written life of the bishop. Possibly it results from a misunderstanding of some pictorial or sculptured representation of Nicholas with a swine-shaped devil. Compare Karl Meisen, *Nikolauskult und Nikolausbrauch im Abenlande* (Düsseldorf, 1931), p. 434: 'Ist aber der Begleiter des Nikolaus im Volksbrauche auf diese Weise als Teufelsfigur erkannt . . .'

317. Of the Eucharist

Pr. Wright, *Wart. Club*, p. 60; B. Fehr, *Archiv*, cix (1902), 63; Brown, *R.L. 15 C.*, p. 180. B.–R. 1627.

burden, l. 2. The phrasing is after that of the vernacular prayers at the elevation of the Host, e.g. Myrc's *Instructions to Parish Priests* (ed. E. Peacock, E.E.T.S., Or. Ser., No. 31, 1868), ll. 290–1:

> Ihesu, lord, welcome þow be
> In forme of bred as I þe se.

Shorter versions are listed in B.–R., Nos. 1729, 1734. Compare also 'A preyer at þe leuacioun' in the Vernon MS. (ed. C. Horstmann, *The Minor Poems of the Vernon MS.*, part i, E.E.T.S., Or. Ser., No. 98, 1892, 24, ll. 1–3):

> Welcome, Lord, In fourme of Bred!
> In þe is boþe lyf and Ded,
> Ihesus is þi nome.

stza. 1, l. 1. John vi. 58: 'Hic est panis qui de caelo descendit.'
stza. 2. As elsewhere in the carols, the person is changed without express indication.   l. 2. 1 Corinthians xi. 29: 'Qui enim manducat et bibit indigne, iudicium sibi manducat et bibit . . .'
l. 3. *lete*: abandon, leave.
stza. 4, l. 1. *Messe*: i.e. the Last Supper.

318. Of the Eucharist

Pr. Zupitza, 221, notes, xciv, 413–15; Greene, *Selection*, p. 126. B.–R. 3583.

burden, l. 2. John vi. 50: 'Hic est panis de caelo descendens, ut si quis ex ipso manducaverit, non moriatur.' Compare John vi. 58.

stza. 2. R. H. Robbins has pointed out the circulation as a separate verse of what is essentially this stanza. Of the three versions which he records the nearest to this stanza is that in Durham Cathedral MS. V. i. 12, f. 65ʳ:

> Hit semeth whiȝth and hit is reed:
> Hit is quyk and semeþ deed:
> Hit is flessh and semeth breed:
> And verey God in His Godhead.

('Popular Prayers in Middle English Verse', *Modern Philology*, xxxvi, 1939, 344)

See note on No. 319, stza. 2.

319. Of the Eucharist

Pr. Dyboski, p. 14. B.–R. 2076.
burden, l. 2. Compare the burdens of Nos. 56, 94, 176.
stza. 1, l. 2. *dure*: dere, offence, hurt.
stza. 2. See note on No. 318, stza. 2, of which this is a variant.

320. In Praise of Wheat

Pr. Wright, *Wart. Club*, p. 38; B. Fehr, *Archiv*, cix (1902), 53. B.–R. 3920.
Wheat is here praised as the material of the Host. Compare Nos. 317–19, 321, also *The Southern Passion* (ed. Beatrice D. Brown, E.E.T.S., Or. Ser., No. 169, 1927), ll. 189–90:

> ffor oure lord him likneþ to whete: and to oþer corn non,
> þerffore [we] makeþ his swete body: of þe whete-corn al-on.

There is a touch of folk-song in the enumeration of the 'verses'.
stza. 1, l. 2. *bote*: (the best) remedy.
stza. 3, l. 3. *Godes face*: perhaps an allusion to the design imprinted on the wafer of the Host.
stza. 6, l. 3. This line appears to carry a reminiscence of the 'dear years' of 1345–7, which are mentioned in No. 357 from the same MS.

321. Christ, the Ear of Wheat

Pr. Dyboski, p. 34; Flügel, *N.L.*, p. 112, 'Lieder.', p. 258; Greene, *Selection*, p. 127. B.–R. 2681.

A longer treatment of the allegory of this carol is found in the Vernon *Proprium Sanctorum* as a homily on John xii. 24–6: '. . . nisi granum frumenti cadens in terram mortuum fuerit, ipsum solum manet,' etc. (ed. C. Horstmann, *Archiv*, lxxxi, 1888, 83). The same symbolism is also applied to St. Thomas of Canterbury (ibid., p. 102); compare No. 116, stza. 1.

burden, l. 1. *byrd*: youth.

stza. 3, l. 4. *Mawndy*: the new commandment (*mandatum novum*) which Jesus gave His disciples at the Last Supper, John xiii. 34.

322. The Corpus Christi Carol

A. *Pr.* Dyboski, p. 103; Flügel, *N.L.*, p. 142, *Anglia*, xxvi (1903), 175; C. & S., p. 148; Annie G. Gilchrist, *J.F.S.S.* iv (1910), 53; Rickert, p. 193; Albert S. Cook, *A Literary Middle English Reader* (Boston, 1915), p. 440; [Sir] W. W. Greg, *R.E.S.* xiii (1937), 88; Charles Williams, *New Book of English Verse* (N.Y., 1936), p. 112; Mary G. Segar, *A Mediaeval Anthology* (London, 1915), p. 35; [Sir] E. K. Chambers, *English Literature at the Close of the Middle Ages* (Oxford, 1945), p. 111; MacEdward Leach, *The Ballad Book* (N.Y., 1955), p. 692; David Daiches, *A Critical History of English Literature* (London, 1960), 80 (omits burden); R. L. Greene, *Medium Ævum*, xxix (1960), 10, *Selection*, p. 128; John Speirs, *Medieval English Poetry: The Non-Chaucerian Tradition* (London, 1957), p. 76; Davies, p. 272; David C. Fowler, *A Literary History of the Popular Ballad* (Durham, North Carolina, 1968), p. 58; Oliver, p. 108; Douglas Gray, *Themes and Images*, p. 164; Sisam, p. 524; Tydeman, p. 53; Grigson, p. 308; etc. B.–R. 1132.

B. *Pr.* ε.τ.κ., *N. & Q.*, 3rd Ser., ii (1862), 103; Annie G. Gilchrist, *J.F.S.S.* iv (1910), 53; Rickert, p. 194; Leach, loc. cit.; R. L. Greene, *Medium Ævum*, xxix (1960), 11; *Selection*, p. 128; *O.B.C.*, p. 222; Grigson, p. 308; with music, *O.B.C.*, Music Edn., p. 402.

C. *Pr. O.B.C.* (London, 1928), p. 81; R. L. Greene, *Medium Ævum*, xxix (1960), 11, *Selection*, p. 129; with music, R. Vaughan Williams, *Eight Traditional English Carols* (London, [1919]), p. 14; *O.B.C.*, Music Edn., p. 134.

D. *Pr.* James Hogg, *The Mountain Bard* (Edinburgh, 1807), p. 13 n.; Edith C. Batho, *The Ettrick Shepherd* (Cambridge, 1927), p. 31; R. L. Greene, *Medium Ævum*, xxix (1960), 11, *Selection*, p. 130; Grigson, p. 309.

E. *Pr.*, with music, A[nne] G. G[ilchrist], *Journal of the English Folk Dance and Song Society*, iv (1942), 122; Douglas Brice, *The Folk-Carol of England* (London, 1967), p. 72.

See Introduction, pp. lxx–lxxi.

This hauntingly beautiful carol has been subjected to more praise and more critical discussion than any other in this collection. George Kane points to it as the only surviving carol which 'can be called completely successful' (*Middle English Literature*, London, 1952, pp. 174–5). This is an unfairly harsh judgement on the others. But the survival in centuries of oral tradition of changed but recognizable versions of this piece, or, more probably, of an earlier folk-song from which it has been adapted, attests its power.

The first sustained attempts at commentary on versions A, B, and C are those of Annie G. Gilchrist and others in the *Journal of the Folk-Song Society* (iv, 1910, 52–66). The texts are there printed with the recorded music of B and C. Edith C. Batho was the first scholar to associate with them the Scottish version D printed by James Hogg from his mother's recitation in *The Mountain Bard*, published at Edinburgh in 1807 ('The Life of Christ in the Ballads', *Essays and Studies by Members of the English Association*, ix, 1924, 93, and *The Ettrick Shepherd*, Cambridge, 1927, pp. 30–2).

Version E was learned from the singing of Amos Curtis of Brasstown, North Carolina, by Evelyn K. Wells, and recorded from her singing by R. Vaughan Williams as recently as 1936.

Later research has seemed to me to invalidate most of Miss Gilchrist's explication of A in terms of the Grail legend and Glastonbury tradition, and I omit the summary of her theory which appeared in the first edition of this work. Sir Edmund Chambers makes a cogent criticism: 'It has been suggested that the original carol was in some way connected with the Grail. This is rather a wild conjecture, since a Grail poem ought surely to have a Grail vessel in it, and there is none' (*English Literature at the Close of the Middle Ages*, Oxford, 1945, p. 112). Nor do I find satisfying

Miss Batho's alternative suggestion of a poem on the Entombment. But the Wounded Knight may nevertheless stand for Christ, as she suggests; see below in this note.

There are no other carols which are even faintly Arthurian, but there are a number which are politically topical. The grounds for accepting 'Corpus Christi' as a partisan allegorical piece on King Henry VIII's desertion of Catherine of Aragon for Anne Boleyn are discussed at some length by the present editor: 'The Meaning of the Corpus Christi Carol', *Medium Ævum*, xxix (1960), 10–21, and 'The Burden and the Scottish Variant of the Corpus Christi Carol', ibid. xxxiii (1964), 53–60.

It may be proper to quote here a key paragraph from the article first mentioned (p. 13):

> My suggestion now is that the 'Corpus Christi' version of the carol is a song, quite possibly adapted from a song already current in oral tradition (whether or not Eucharistic or related to the Grail legend)[,] which refers specifically to the displacement of Queen Catherine of Aragon by Anne Boleyn in the affections of King Henry VIII. It would then necessarily date from the time of Catherine's rural exile at the More, Buckden Palace, and Kimbolton Castle. In fact, when closer attention than any yet given is applied to the material in the Balliol manuscript, the commonplace book of Richard Hill, grocer, it is hard to see how in the London of the date of its writing such an interpretation can be avoided.

The handwriting and location of the carol in the volume, as well as its omission from the table of contents, show that it was written down at a later time than all the other carols except No. 126 (see Note 30 of the article).

It is highly significant that the burden with its 'fawcon' is not found in the versions other than 'Corpus Christi'. The widely exhibited and universally known heraldic *badge* (not coat of arms) of Anne Boleyn was a white falcon, crowned, with sceptre and roses on a root. Verses written for her coronation repeatedly allude to it, as do the 'prophecy' beginning 'A ffawkyn downe shall fall' and the ballad 'Anne Boleyn's Fortune', which calls her 'a fawcon fayre of fflyghte'. The sculptured badge can be seen today in Hampton Court Palace and King's College Chapel, Cambridge. The use of heraldic badges in medieval political poetry is surely too well known to need much illustration, but reference may be made to Carols Nos. 431–4 in this collection. An anonymous article in *The Times Literary Supplement* accepts the 'unmistakable allusion' of the burden (20 January 1961, p. 47).

The imagery of the stanzas finds its best commentary, in my opinion, in the account of Queen Catherine's banishment given in Nicholas Harpsfield's highly partisan *Treatise on the Pretended Divorce between Henry VIII. and Catharine of Aragon*. Two important passages must be quoted:

> Before she departed at Kimbolton, she had lyen two years at Bugden, passing her solitary life in much prayer, great alms, and abstinence. And when she was not this way occupied, then was she and her gentlewomen working with their own hands something wrought in needlework costly and artificially, which she intended to the honour of God to bestow upon some churches. There was in the said house of Bugden a chamber with a window that had a prospect into the chapel, out of the which she might hear divine service. In this chamber she enclosed herself sequestered from all other company a great part of the day and night, and upon her knees used to pray at the said window leaning upon the stones of the same. There was some of her gentlewomen which did curiously mark and observe all her doings, who reported that oftentimes they found the said stones so wet after her departure as though it had rained upon them. It was credibly thought that in the time of her prayer she removed the cushions that ordinarily lay in the same window, and that the said stones were imbrued with the tears of her devout eyes.

> Then was there nothing so common and frequent and so tossed in every man's mouth, in all talks and at all tables, in all taverns, alehouses, and barbers' shops, yea, and in pulpits too, as was this matter, some well liking and allowing the divorce, some others most highly detesting the same.   (Ed. Nicholas Pocock, Camden Society, London, 1878, pp. 199–200, 177)

It is well to remember, as some commentators do not, that 'orchard brown' most probably means a dark garden, not necessarily of the colour brown. In C, D, and E there is a 'forest', in B a 'park', both of which are terms applied to royal country property, not necessarily wooded. The wounded knight may very well stand for Christ, as in some other interpretations. Harpsfield writes of Catherine as in her death taking Christ for her mate. That the body of Christ suffers a freshening of its wounds from blasphemy, even casual oaths, is a widespread medieval conception, and King

Henry, in the view of Catherine's supporters, was grievously wounding that body. 'Corpus Christi', the body of Christ, is a recognized term for the Church as well as for the Eucharist, and its appearance in this context is entirely appropriate.

The same article suggests, more tentatively, that the hound, which appears only in version B from late oral tradition, may be a recollection of the gruesome anecdote circulated after King Henry's death of the mysterious dog which lapped the blood leaking from the royal coffin, as the dogs in Scripture did with King Ahab's blood (Harpsfield, pp. 202–4). The missing links here are obvious. But no other even partially satisfactory explanation has been offered. I do not accept the 'Mithraic' reading given by G. R. S. Mead (*J.F.S.S.*, iv, 1910, 65).

The second article mentioned calls attention to the significant use by James Hogg of version D as a song well known in Scotland which refers to the notorious adultery of King James IV with Madam Grey. It becomes the central feature of a long episode in Hogg's prose tale 'The Bridal of Polmood', strikingly parallel to the crisis in the English royal marriage. This important piece of evidence is not dealt with even by Douglas Gray, the most scholarly of those critics who have questioned the political application of 'Corpus Christi' (*Themes and Images*, pp. 164–7). Gray unfortunately seems to accept the notion that the phrase 'purple and pall' has an ecclesiastical significance. But no point about the poem is more obvious than the thoroughly established usage of the cliché 'purple and pall' as definitely indicating a royal and secular, not a churchly, setting. He also seems to accept the idea of the stone as an altar-stone. An altar-stone would not be 'standing', nor would any virgin or Queen Catherine dream of kneeling on one.

Other recent commentary may be recognized as eccentric or fanciful. Stephen Manning would have the 'refrain' [burden] spoken by either Mary or Ecclesia, and for him the 'mak' is 'obviously' Christ (*Wisdom and Number*, Lincoln, Nebraska, 1962, pp. 115–18). The impressionistic comments of Francis Berry (*Poets' Grammar*, London, 1958, chap. ii, part 3, and appendix 1) and John Speirs (*Medieval English Poetry: The Non-Chaucerian Tradition*, London, 1957, pp. 76–80) are not helpful. The treatment of the carol by the Reverend Douglas Brice, who dates A in the fourteenth century, does not improve matters (*The Folk-Carol of England*, London, 1967, pp. 70–7). The Reverend Erik Routley contributes the phrase 'multiple mythology' to the discussion, but for the most part echoes the Grail theory (*The English Carol*, London, 1958, pp. 61–4).

Version E from oral tradition in the Appalachian country of the United States has even less coherence than the two nineteenth-century versions from England. It is nearer to C than to B, but its internal refrain differs from that common to those two texts. It has undergone still more influence from the 'Christmas carol' of folk-tradition in the second line of the refrain. The occurrence of 'Queen' in the first line may be only a parallel to the substitution of King George for St. George in folk-song and folk-play, but it is just possible that it is a wan survival of the connection with Queen Catherine.

The bed in E is not a stately catafalque but the simple pallet of the rural Southerners' experience. It derives its red from the blood of the wounds rather than from gold or silk, though the wounds of the 'young Lord' are not mentioned until stza. 6. The stone is the same kneeling-place for prayer as in B and C. The 'flood' of C, not found in A or B, a magnification of the tradition of the flow of water and blood from Christ's riven side, is probably a result of influence from comparatively late evangelical hymnody as exemplified in Cowper's masterpiece, with its rhyming lines: 'There is a fountain filled with blood. . . . And sinners plunged beneath that flood.' The thorn is here a 'shrub-tree'. I am now doubtful of the often-alleged direct connection with the famous Glastonbury thorn. It is more probable that this feature has strayed into the modern versions of the carol from some such source as the widely disseminated ballad *The Elfin Knight* (Child, No. 2). In the variants of this ballad it is consistently a thorn that does *not* blossom, as it is in B. A very recent American version of the ballad, collected in New York State in 1965 uses it thus:

> You must dry it under an old buck-thorn
> Every rose grows merry in time
> That never has blossomed since Adam was born
> And then you will be a true lover of mine.
> (Bertrand H. Bronson, *The Traditional Tunes of the Child Ballads*, iv,
> Princeton, 1972, 440, stza. 2, ll. 5–8)

In E it is the 'young Lord', not the virgin, who weeps, and the silver and gold are more logically applied to the hall than to the park as they are in B.

There is similarity between the rhetorical formula of the carol and that of such sequential game-songs as 'The Key of the Kingdom' (cited by Speirs from Walter de la Mare's anthology *Come Hither*, London, 1928, p. 3), but no direct relationship to any recorded song of the type has been proved. It is equally doubtful that there is any close connection between 'Corpus Christi' and the ballad *The Three Ravens* (Child, No. 26) and its cognate *The Twa Corbies*, in spite of knight, hawk, and lady (faithful or faithless). The doubt must be cast alike on Bronson's suggestion of the ballad as the source of the carol (op. cit. i. 308) and David C. Fowler's counter-suggestion of the carol as the source of the ballad (*A Literary History of the Popular Ballad*, Durham, North Carolina, 1968, pp. 63–4).

With regret I must note my disagreement with my old teacher, Gordon Hall Gerould, when in a rightly influential work he declares: 'Again, the very lovely *Over Yonder's a Park* or *Corpus Christi* is truly a ballad, for it pictures an intensely dramatic situation and does so altogether in the manner of the *genre*' (*The Ballad of Tradition*, Oxford, 1932, p. 33). None of the texts as we have them is really narrative: the situation is dramatic, but it is also static, and the lack of a progression of events keeps these texts from qualifying as ballads under Gerould's own fundamental definition: '. . . the ballad is a folk-song that tells a story' (op. cit., p. 3). They gradually reveal the details of an impressive picture, but it is after all a still picture, and it attains to a high degree an atmosphere of timelessness.

A. burden. The MS. gives no warrant for regarding this initial and external burden as an internal refrain of the ballad-type like the refrains of B, C, and E. Both Edith C. Batho (*Essays and Studies*, ix, 1924, 93–4), and Francis Berry (*Essays in Criticism*, v, 1955, 299–314, and *Poets' Grammar*, London, 1958, pp. 20–35) make this mistake. The 'lully' of the first line has been generally misinterpreted even by Sir Edmund Chambers (loc. cit.), as having its primary meaning of a sound for soothing an infant. But just at the time of this burden this word with its companion 'by by' was in well-established use as slang or colloquial language for the lamenting song of a rejected lover. A telling instance is Skelton's Carol No. 459; another is No. 396. An especially good illustration is found in the poem, possibly by Wyatt, which begins:

> Ffarewell all my welfare,
>   My shue is trode awry;
> Now may I karke and care
>   To syng *lullay by by*.
> (Kenneth Muir, ed., *Collected Poems of Sir Thomas Wyatt*, London, 1949, p. 97)

The attempts of some critics to make the falcon stand for death are unconvincing. Stephen Manning writes, '. . . the falcon is probably death' (op. cit., p. 15). John Speirs refers to 'the catastrophe of the "faucon"—the fiend or death perhaps—snatching up and carrying off one's mate' (op. cit., p. 76). David C. Fowler states, 'The second line of the refrain [burden] . . . is a chivalric metaphor referring to the death on the cross, and as such it beautifully balances the lullaby refrain preceding it' (op. cit., p. 59). Lewis J. and Nancy H. Owen remark, 'The falcon, as bird of prey, is, of course, an appropriate symbol of death, and the aimless wanderings—"he bare him up, he bare him down"—properly suggest the mysterious journey which death requires.' They add, '. . . the falcon, a royal bird as well as a bird of prey, can also become God . . .' (*Middle English Poetry: An Anthology*, Indianapolis, [1971], p. 355). Both Fowler and the Owens misunderstand the satirical force of the first line of the burden. No instance of a falcon's standing for death in Middle English literature is known to me.

John Stevens correctly points to a similarity of feeling and of some images between this carol and the *lai* of *Yonec*, in which there are a castle and a wounded knight, the *ami* who has previously visited the imprisoned heroine in the form of a great bird (*Medieval Romance*, London, 1973, pp. 113–14). But it is worth noting that in the *lai* the bird is equated not with death but with a lover.

The speculation here summarized is in strong contrast to the plain fact that the heraldic falcon was ubiquitously and constantly associated with the unpopular Anne Boleyn. To criticize her other than obliquely was highly dangerous. The modern reader, probably indifferent to heraldry altogether, may find it hard to realize the strength of the image. Yet it is certain that, as I have previously written, 'To an English hearer in 1533 "The fawcon hath born my mak away" would immediately suggest the winning away of the King by Anne Boleyn.' It would have been as hard for Richard Hill or any other Londoner to avoid that association as it would have been for a subject of

Edward VIII in December 1936 to avoid an immediate topical application of the well-worn phrase 'the woman I love'. An alert lady in Oxford (simultaneously with the present editor) noted the parallel of the carol with the topical parody of a long-known religious song which is recorded by Iona and Peter Opie in their superb book *The Lore and Language of Schoolchildren* (Oxford, 1960, p. 6):

A notorious instance of the transmission of scurrilous verses occurred in 1936 at the time of the Abdication. The word-of-mouth rhymes which then gained currency were of a kind which could not possibly, at that time, have been printed, broadcast, or even repeated in the music halls. One verse, in particular, made up one can only wonder by whom,

> Hark the Herald Angels sing,
> Mrs. Simpson's pinched our king,

was on juvenile lips not only in London, but as far away as Chichester in the south, and Liverpool and Oldham in the north.

'There is every reason', as is said in the article 'The Burden and the Scottish Version', 'to recognize Richard Hill's version as a song of a virtuous queen, famous for prayer and tears, whose royal mate has been taken from her by a lady known to all England as the white falcon.'

A. stza. 1, l. 1. *He.* The use of the masculine pronoun need cause no difficulty. The actual hunting falcon is the female bird, but the heraldic falcon granted as a badge to Anne Boleyn is masculine, as in the crest authorized for Shakespeare's father and in modern blazons. Anne had been given the masculine title of Marquis of Pembroke, not Marchioness, as is sometimes erroneously said.   l. 2. *He bare hym.* This means simply that the falcon went to the 'orchard'; it is a reflexive construction with the same meaning as the 'flew' of version D. The objection of Douglas Gray results from his apparently taking 'hym' as having 'mak' for its antecedent and is of no force: 'As it stands, the link which is present in the Hill version between the burden and the first stanza is awkward—why should the king carried off by Anne be brought into the orchard of Buckden to see the weeping queen?' (op. cit., p. 165). The poem does not say that the King is deposited anywhere, only that he has been stolen or won and that the falcon went up and down and to the orchard. There is no awkwardness. Davies similarly misreads the passage (p. 364), as I have done myself in previous comment. The first two lines of version D give the clue.

A. stza. 2, l. 1. *hall.* This indicates a secular building; it is not a synonym for 'church'.   l. 2. *purpill and pall.* As mentioned above, this stock phrase is regularly applied to hangings or clothing indicative of secular royalty or nobility. It cannot refer here to liturgical colours; red or black would be called for in church decoration at Passion time. The context prevents the taking of 'pall' to mean a covering for a bier or altar or, as the Owens gloss it, 'white linen cloth to cover the chalice' (op. cit., p. 16).

A. stza. 5, l. 1. *may*: maiden. It is quite reasonable for this word to be applied to Queen Catherine in a song favourable to her, since she steadfastly maintained as a central point in the whole controversy that her marriage to the immature and sickly Prince Arthur had not been consummated. Henry's own claim that Catherine had never been *his* lawful wife should not be forgotten. In Shakespeare's *Henry VIII* Catherine makes a very significant dying request:

> When I am dead, good wench,
> Let me be us'd with honour: strew me over
> With maiden flowers, that all the world may know
> I was a chaste wife to my grave.

> (IV. ii. 168–71)

C. stza. 6. This stanza, like the internal refrain of E, has the look of a comparatively late addition to the inherited text, designed to make the song especially appropriate for Christmas after that season had attained its near-monopoly of carolling. The moon shining bright is an image familiar in folk-song of the Nativity but not in medieval carols, where the more orthodox star rules the heavens. The internal refrain of B and C is likewise on a Christmas theme incongruous with the body of the piece: it probably comes from some version of the folk-song which is worked into the late sixteenth-century part-song 'All Sons of Adam'. A popular Scottish version has the lines, 'Our Lord harpit, our Lady sang / and all the bells of heav'n they rang / on Christsonday at morn' (Kenneth Elliott and Helena Mennie Shire, eds., *Music of Scotland 1500–1700*, Musica Britannica, xv, London, 1957, p. 153).

323. Of the Mass

Pr. Sandison, p. 102; Brown, *R.L. 15 C.*, p. 183; [Sir] E. K. Chambers, *English Literature at the Close of the Middle Ages*, Oxford History of English Literature, ii, part 2 (Oxford, 1945), p. 111; Greene, *Selection*, p. 130; Oliver, p. 119; Sisam, p. 423; Tydeman, p. 52; Grigson, p. 313. B.–R. 298.

This *chanson d'aventure*, with its unusual religious imagery and its characteristic style, quite unlike that of most religious carols, has a good claim to be considered as true folk-song, that is, a piece originating outside learned clerical society and passed on by oral transmission. The burden is certainly a borrowing from a secular May song, possibly by the borrowing of a tune, though there is no music in the MS. The occurrence of stza. 1, l. 1 as the fourth line of the second and fourth stanzas tempts to the idea that perhaps it should be shifted to that position in the first stanza, but, if this is done, the result is unsatisfactory.

The only other occurrence in poetry known to me of the conception of Christ as officiating priest is in a version of the ballad *The Famous Flower of Serving-Men* (Child, No. 106) collected as recently as 1942 from Mrs. Belle Richards of Colebrook, New Hampshire, by Marguerite Olney and published in Helen Hartness Flanders and Marguerite Olney, eds., *Ballads Migrant in New England*, p. 125:

> 'Twas all alone I dug his grave
> And all alone in it him I laid,
> *While Christ was priest and I was clerk*
> *I laid my love in the clay-cold earth.*

Mrs. Flanders remarks (loc. cit.): 'I have looked through many regional collections as well as the monumental work of Professor Francis James Child and of Cecil Sharp but have not discovered the especial grief of this passage.' The special magic of the passage is found in this carol, and the likeness of the image confirms the editor's judgement that it comes from the reservoir of unlearned tradition.

A curious though slight similarity occurs in a folk charm for the grippe from Leinstrand, Trondheim, Norway, used by Lisbet Nypen in 1670 (R. H. Robbins, ed., *The Encyclopedia of Witchcraft and Demonology*, N.Y., 1959, pp. 363–4):

> Christ walked to the church with a book in his hand. Came the Virgin Mary herself walking. 'Why are you so pale, my blessed son?' 'I have caught a powerful grippe [? *greb*]'. 'I cure you of powerful grippe—cough grippe, intestinal grippe, back grippe, chest grippe—from flesh and bone, to beach and stone, in the name of the Father, Son, and Holy Ghost.'

Douglas Gray in a private letter has suggested that this carol may have in its background the tradition of 'Christ as Priest and victim (*idem sacerdos, idem victima* &c.) of the Perpetual Sacrifice' and also 'the recollection of Christ's "Eucharistic" action of breaking the bread &c.'. In a review of *Selection* he also refers to 'St. Paul's remark that Jesus was made a high priest for ever after the order of Melchis[e]dec' (*N. & Q.* ccviii, 1963, 431). See also Gray's reference to the so-called 'Friday spell' (*Themes and Images*, p. 164).

stza. 1, l. 2. *wyhte*: wight, strong, mighty. Brown glosses as preposition 'with'. It might be for 'white'; compare 'pale' above.   l. 3. *Jhon*: the Evangelist.

stza. 2, l. 2. *Collas*. Sandison, following Madan, conjectures 'Nicholas', which seems probable.

stza. 3, l. 3. *mowlde*: top of the head.

stza. 4, l. 1. *knyghte*. Misread by Sandison as 'brighte'. See notes on No. 311.1.

324. Of the Ten Commandments

Pr. C. & S., *M.L.R.* v. 479; Whiting, p. 181. B.–R. 304.

Audelay takes some liberties with the Commandments as they were prescribed to be taught by the Synod of Lambeth (1281). In stza. 1, l. 2, he introduces Christ's injunction from Matthew xix. 19: 'Diliges proximum tuum sicut teipsum.' Compare stza. 3, ll. 1, 2 of 'Keep Well Christ's Commandments' (*pr.* Brown, *R.L. 14 C.*, p. 148):

> And let þi neiȝhebor, frend and fo,
> Riht frely of þi frendschupe fele.

He also omits the Ninth and Tenth Commandments against covetousness and adds one of his own against backbiting.

burden, l. 2. A proverbial exhortation. Compare Chaucer, *Physician's Tale*, l. 286, *Parson's Tale*, § 2.

stza. 4, l. 1. Compare No. 356, stza. 1, ll. 1, 2.   l. 3. *tult*: tilt, throw.

325. Of the Seven Deadly Sins

Pr. C. & S., *M.L.R.* v. 480; Whiting, p. 182. B.–R. 858.

burden, l. 1. A frequently quoted medieval proverb. It is made the text, in the form 'Man, be warre er the be woo', of a long poem in Bodl. MS. Digby 102, f. 112ʳ (*pr.* J. Kail, *Twenty-six Political and other Poems*, i, E.E.T.S., Or. Ser., No. 124, 1904, 60), which has as refrain: 'Eche man be war er hym be wo.' Compare 'Great Cato', Bk. IV, l. 565 (*pr.* F. J. Furnivall, *The Minor Poems of the Vernon MS.*, part ii, E.E.T.S., Or. Ser., No. 117, 1901, 602): 'In þi weolþe þou thenk of wo', and No. 338, stza. 3, l. 2.

stza. 3. Audelay's prescription of definite remedies for the Sins is in the manner of systematic medieval treatments of the subject, of which Chaucer's *Parson's Tale* is the best known. l. 1. *buxumnes*: obedience.   l. 3. *largenes*: generosity.

326. Of the Seven Works of Mercy

Pr. C. & S., *M.L.R.* v. 480; Whiting, p. 183. B.–R. 792.

Audelay is again somewhat original in his tabulation of the Seven Works, and deviates slightly from the list formulated by the Synod of Lambeth. He seems to have in mind the seven 'corporal' works, but of these he omits to mention the ransoming of the captive and the visiting of the sick. The injunction to 'teach the unwise' he takes over from the list of 'spiritual' works. In the long poem of his own which seems to have served him as a quarry of carol-material (Whiting, No. 1, ll. 173–8) his list is the same. The carol is evidently a recasting and expansion of this passage.

Two poems on the subject from MS. Lambeth 491, f. 295ʳ and ᵛ (*pr.* K. D. Bülbring, *Archiv*, lxxxvi, 1891, 388–90) follow the orthodox lists of corporal and spiritual works respectively.

stzas. 3–5. Audelay has taken these stanzas with some changes from another of his own longer poems (Whiting, No. 17, ll. 197–200, 213–20). The reference is to Matthew xxv. 31–40.

327. Of the Seven Gifts of the Holy Ghost

Pr. C. & S., *M.L.R.* v. 482; Whiting, p. 185. B.–R. 2173.

Audelay's formulation of the Seven Gifts differs from that of other literature on the subject. The traditional gifts are those enumerated in Isaiah xi. 2, 3: 'Et requiescet super eum spiritus Domini: spiritus sapientiae et intellectus, spiritus consilii et fortitudinis, spiritus scientiae et pietatis; et replebit eum spiritus timoris Domini.' These appear in a Vernon MS. lyric (*pr.* C. Horstmann, *The Minor Poems of the Vernon MS.*, part i, E.E.T.S., Or. Ser., No. 98, 1892, 34). Audelay's 'mind' can be identified with 'intellectus' and 'resun' with 'consilium', but the others he has taken from the Cardinal Virtues.

burden. Compare ll. 1–3 of the Vernon MS. lyric:

> God þat art of mihtes most,
> þe seuen ʒiftus of þe holigost
> I preye þat þou ʒiue me.

stzas. 4–6. These are based on St. Paul's teaching in 1 Corinthians xiii. Audelay may have been led to include these virtues by the fact that 'faith' and 'charity' are reckoned among the gifts of the so-called 'second class' or *charismata*, which have the authority of this and other passages of St. Paul's writings. He has certainly confused his theology.

328. Of the Five Wits

Pr. C. & S., *M.L.R.* v. 481; Whiting, p. 184. B.–R. 3346.

Audelay's carol is cast in the imperative like the poem on the 'fyve Inwyttys' from MS. Lambeth 491, f. 295ʳ (*pr.* K. D. Bülbring, *Archiv*, lxxxvi, 1891, 388), but there is no further resemblance. Compare also the 'orysoun for sauynge of þe fyue wyttes' from the Vernon MS. (*pr.* C. Horstmann, op. cit., p. 35).

stza. 5, l. 3. *luste*: pleasure.   l. 4. This line is a popular proverb. Compare Draxe's *Treasurie of Ancient Adagies* (1616, *repr.* M. Förster, *Anglia*, xlii, 1918, 395): 'Measure is a merrie meane', and see B. J. W., *Proverbs*, M 454.

329. A Call to Righteous Living

Pr. Wright, *Wart. Club*, p. 10; B. Fehr, *Archiv*, cix (1902), 44; C. & S., p. 180; Davies, p. 156. B.–R. 739.

The note in the first edition of this work, taking the word 'gay' in its usual sense of 'merry, thoughtless', refers to the 'obvious incongruity between the two lines of the burden' and suggests that the first line may be borrowed from some secular song. The syllable 'gay' (sometimes spelled *gué*) is common in the refrain of French songs, e.g.:

> Gay, gay, gay, la rira dondaine,
> Gay, gay, gay, la rira dondé.

> (G. Thurau, *Der Refrain in der französischen Chanson*, Litterarhistorische
> Forschungen, xxiii, Berlin, 1901, p. 27)

The burden should be compared with that of No. 363.

But a special meaning for the key word 'gay', hitherto unsuspected, has been convincingly suggested by Siegfried Wenzel (*Neuphilologische Mitteilungen*, lxxvii, 1976, 85–91). It is surprising that he does not refer as well to No. 363, which is separated from this piece by only three leaves in the same MS., for his significant discovery concerns a source which may well be common to both carols.

Wenzel points to a Latin exemplum extant in several versions and probably at least a century older than the preserved texts of the two carols. It is a lurid account of the terrifying end of an unrepentant malefactor named Gay (Gayus), whose damnation is attested by a dance (*chorea*) of demons around the death-bed. In their taunts the devils repeat his name in a fashion which strongly suggests the burdens of both carols. In a fifteenth-century MS. of the *Distincciones* of John Bromyard (Bodl. MS. Bodley 859) the chorus howls 'Gay, Gay, tu morieris', in alternation with the soloist's one-line 'stanzas': 'Gay, Gay, tu ponderaberis', 'Gay, Gay, tu dampnaberis'. In another version (Jesus College, Cambridge, MS. 13) a second 'stanza' is inserted: 'Gay, Gay, tu iudicaberis'.

The same exemplum occurs in a much condensed form in *Fasciculus Morum* (Bodl. MS. Rawlinson C. 670). A more interesting version is found in Worcester Cathedral MS. F. 126, where the antiphonal carol-like song of the devils is translated into English verse for the hearers of the sermon:

> Gay, Gay, þou ert yhent,
> Gay, þou schalt deyn.
> Gay, Gay, þou ert iblent,
> Gay, þou [schalt deyn].
> Gay, þou ert ydempnit,
> Gay, þou schalt deye.

In this version the dying man is a 'medieval playboy', not an officer or a judge as in the others and has taken the name 'gay Gay'. There can be little doubt that this exemplum was known to the author or authors of both No. 329 and No. 363. Davies's suggestion that 'gay' is to be read as a common noun (p. 335) may be disregarded.

stza. 2, l. 1, stza. 3, l. 1. Compare No. 357, stzas. 1–3.

stza. 4, l. 1. *non thing stere*: burn or offer incense to nothing. The allusion is to the Commandment. This is a later use of 'stere' than any recorded by *O.E.D.*

330. My Hope Is in God

Music for two and three voices. *Pr.* Fehr, p. 271; with music, Stevens, *Med. Carols*, p. 87. B.–R. 3988.

The words of this piece are notable for their extensive use of alliteration. They are probably older than the MS. and the musical setting, as is the case with some of the other carols in the volume.

stza. 2, l. 3. *plyght*: folded, enclosed.

stza. 3, l. 1. *grucche*: complain.   l. 2. *fawte*: am in want.

330.1. Of Love Earthly and Divine

Pr. [Lord Hailes], *Ancient Scottish Poems* (Edinburgh, 1770), p. 100; J. Sibbald, *Chronicle of Scottish Poetry from the Thirteenth Century to the Union of the Crowns* (Edinburgh, 1802), ii. 20 David Laing, *The Poems of William Dunbar*, i (Edinburgh, 1834), 221; James Paterson, *The Works of William Dunbar* (Edinburgh, 1863), p. 303; John Small, *The Poems of William Dunbar*, ii, S.T.S., 1893, 179; Julius Schipper, *The Poems of William Dunbar* (Vienna, 1894), p. 351; James Barclay Murdoch, *The Bannatyne Manuscript*, iii (Glasgow, 1896), 826; W. Tod Ritchie, *The Bannatyne Manuscript*, iv, S.T.S. New Ser., 1930, 91; W. Mackay Mackenzie, *The Poems of William Dunbar* (Edinburgh, 1932), p. 101; James Kinsley, *William Dunbar, Poems* (Oxford, 1958), p. 68 (in part); etc. B.–R. *Supp.* 2306.5.

This carol is generally taken to be the expression of the personal experience and feelings of the ageing Dunbar. It is a straightforward and eloquent statement of the greater worth of the spiritual love which replaces the sexual desire of youth. Utley correctly points out that it should have been included in the first edition of this collection (p. 209).

burden, l. 2. *splene*: the spleen regarded as the seat of the affections, equivalent to modern 'heart'. Schipper (p. 94) compares with this line *The Thrissil and the Rois*, l. 12: 'a lark sang fro the splene'.

stza. 1, l. 2. *feynit*: false, lacking true worth.

stza. 2, l. 3. *the ta*: the one.

stza. 3, l. 1. *curege*: spirit, poetic ability.   l. 4. *kyndnes*: essential nature.

stza. 6, l. 3. *maugre to my meid*: ill-will for my reward.   l. 4. I count on reward and thanks from time to time.

stza. 9, l. 2. *discure*: disclose.

stza. 10, ll. 1, 2. Formerly I complained to no one, so much did her aloofness disturb me.

stza. 11, l. 3. *guerdon*: reward.   l. 4. *mene*: complain, ask pity.

stza. 12, l. 1. *Vnquyt*: unrewarded.   *sane*: say.   l. 2. *wairis*: spend.   l. 4. *jangler*: chatterer, gossip.   *prevene*: forestall.

stza. 13, l. 3. *kynd*: nature.

stza. 14, l. 1. *he*: i.e. Christ.   l. 4. *fane*: eagerly.

stza. 15, l. 1. *but*: without.   l. 4. *flouris grene*: the flower of youth.

331. Against Swearing by the Mass

a. *Pr.* in first edition.

b. *Pr.* Dyboski, p. 42; Flügel, 'Lieder.', p. 263.

B.–R. 3424.

stza. 1, l. 2. *comprysyd*: compared, brought together in one category. For 'comprehended' in this sense, as in b, *O.E.D.* gives only a modern citation.

stza. 2, l. 1. *ierachy*: the hierarchy of the nine orders of angels.

332. Be Thankful and Patient

Pr. Wright, *P.S.* xxiii. 37. B.–R. 2041.

stza. 3, l. 1. See B. J. W., *Proverbs*, W 385.

stza. 5, l. 3. *Buxsumlych*: obediently.

333. A Remonstrance with Man

Pr. Brown, *R.L. 15 C.*, p. 162. B.–R. 610.

This carol, like No. 260, suffers from its argumentative tone and pedestrian versification. With it compare the long poem, on the same theme and with l. 2 of the burden as its refrain, in Bodl. MS. Rawlinson C. 86, f. 65ʳ (*pr.* Sandison, p. 110; also found in part in the printed Douce fragments f. 48, f. 2ʳ, *repr. facs.* Reed, p. 11).

burden, l. 1. Compare National Library of Scotland MS. Advocates 18. 7. 21, f. 125ʳ (*pr.* Brown, *R.L. 14 C.*, p. 88):

> Mi folk, nou ansuere me
> an sey wat is my gilth;
> wat miht i mor ha don for þe
> þat i ne haue fulfilth?

See also K. Böddeker, ed., *Altenglische Dichtungen* (Berlin, 1878), p. 231, ll. 9, 10.
stza. 2, l. 3. Compare ll. 49–50 of the Rawlinson C. 86 lyric:

> I made þe sonne with sterres of heven
> The mone also with bryght shynyng.

334. Of the Power of God's Word

Pr. Wright, *P.S.* xxiii. 30; Sisam, p. 478. B.–R. 4000.

The burden and first stanza of this carol appear as well in No. 335, which, however, lacks the long refrain attached to each stanza.

stza. 1, l. 5. *frayn*: ask.

stza. 2, l. 1. *Fiat*: Genesis i. 3.

stzas. 3, 4. This is the unique reference to astrology in the carols. The author is careful to make explicit the subordination of the planets' influence to God's power over them.

stza. 3, l. 3. *rowll*: roll, move.

stza. 5. This refers to one of two miracles recorded in the *Venerabilis Bedae Vita Anonymo Auctore* (*Pat. Lat.* xc, cols. 53–4): 'Primo, quia cum ex nimia senectute oculis caligasset, et discipulo duce ad lapidum congeriem pervenisset, discipulus ei suadere coepit quod magnus esset ibi populus congregatus qui summa affectione et silentio ipsius praedicationem exspectabant. Cumque sanctus ferventi spiritu elegantissimum sermonem fecisset, et conclusisset *Per omnia saecula saeculorum*, lapides responderunt: *Amen, Venerabilis Presbyter.*'

335. Of the Power of God's Word

Pr. Brown, *R.L. 15 C.*, p. 187. B.–R. 4001.

The burden and first stanza of this carol are the same as those of No. 334, except for the added second line of the burden and the omission of the long refrain from the stanza. There are no other parallels between the two beyond the similarity of general theme.

stza. 3, ll. 1, 2. With reference to Adam instead of man these lines appear as stza. 1, ll. 2, 3 of No. 68.

stza. 4, l. 3. *Nasson*: Naasson, the son of Aminadab, Luke iii. 32–3.

stza. 8, l. 1. *infaynyt*: the sense requires rather the opposite, 'finite'.   l. 3. *se*: so.

336. Of Adam's Sin

Pr. Wright, *Wart. Club*, p. 2; T. Wright, *Songs and Carols* (London, 1936), No. i; Sisam, p. 426. B.–R. 1568.

On the burden see Introduction, pp. clxx–clxxi. Among other occurrences of the proverb in one form or another may be noted the beginning of a lyric in C.U. Lib. MS. Dd. 5. 64. III, f. 35ᵛ (*pr.* Brown, *R.L. 14 C.*, p. 96):

> When adam delf & eue span, spir, if þou wil spede,
> Whare was þan þe pride of man þat now merres his mede,

and the fourteenth-century Latin couplet in British Museum MS. Harley 3362, f. 7ʳ:

> Cum vanga quadam tellurem foderit Adam,
> Et Eva nens fuerat, quis generosus erat?

This is called the 'parent phrase' by G. F. Northall (*English Folk-Rhymes*, London, 1892, p. 100): it is rather a rendering of the popular proverb with which it also appears in the collection of proverbs in Balliol College, Oxford, MS. 354 (*pr.* Dyboski, p. 131). It had a currency in Germany as well; see *N. & Q.*, 4th Ser., v (1870), 610, ix (1872), 415.

stza. 1, l. 1. *vale of Abraham*: the vale of Hebron, the second home of Abraham. Owing to a mistranslation in the Vulgate it was regarded as the burial-place of Adam and hence as the Garden of Eden. See *The Catholic Encyclopedia* (N.Y., 1910), s.v. 'Hebron', and compare *Cursor Mundi* (Trinity text), ll. 1415–16 (ed. R. Morris, E.E.T.S., Or. Ser., No. 57, etc., 1874, 1893, 89):

> Grauen he was bi Seth þon
> in þe vale of Ebron.

stza. 7, l. 4. The author makes the eating of the apple the cause of Adam's nakedness rather than of his being aproned! The omission of Eve's part in the temptation is striking. See B. J. W., *Proverbs*, S 776.

stza. 8, l. 4. i.e. he knew no trade by which to make a living.

337. Amend Me and Pair Me Not

A a. Music for two voices. *Pr.* Padelford, p. 86; with music, *E.B.M.* ii. 87, *facs.* No. xli.

b. *Pr.* Wright, *P.S.* xxiii. 29; Brown, *R.L. 15 C.*, p. 278.

c. Music for two and three voices. *Pr.* Fehr, p. 271; with music, Stevens, *Med. Carols*, p. 88.

B. Music for two voices. *Pr.* Greene, *Selection*, p. 131; Sisam, p. 416; with music, Stevens *Med. Carols*, p. 53. B.–R. 1234.

The music of A a is annotated with the initials 'J. D.' They may possibly refer to the famous John Dunstable as the real or reputed composer, but there is no supporting evidence.

burden, l. 2. *peyre*: impair, make worse.

stzas. 2, 3, 5. The same teaching, with some verbal parallels, appears in the unpublished treatise (? by one Lacy) 'How þat a man sall knowen þe *per*elles þat longeth to schrifte' in St. John's College, Oxford, MS. 94, f. 149ʳ (text from MS.):

> Than if þat þou knowe a þinge openly,
> > helpith to amende it preuyly.
> Sclaund*ur* no man be enuye, ne openly,
> > bot helputh to amende it charitabully.
>
> .   .   .
>
> Bot if þat þou wolt amende þi broþer be way of charite,
> þan take him bi twynne hym and te,
> And þan speke to him charitabelly *and* with mekenes,
> for to amende his liifinge to uertu *and* to goodnes.

stza. 2, ll. 2, 3. Luke xvii. 3: '. . . si peccaverit in te frater tuus, increpa illum . . .' The speaker of the carol is here the 'brother'; the reading of B, 'snyb' or 'rebuke', is more true to the Scripture than the 'vpneme' or 'uphold' of A a or the 'corectyd he be' of A b.

stza. 4, l. 2. (B. stza. 5, l. 2). *bord*: jest.

338. Against Haste

a. Music for one, two, and three voices. *Pr.*, with music, Fuller Maitland, p. 19; Stevens, *Med. Carols*, p. 8.

b. Music for one, two, and three voices. *Pr.* Padelford, p. 114; C. & S., p. 189; with music, *E.B.M.* ii. 161, *facs.* No. xc; Stevens, *Med. Carols*, p. 31.

B.–R. 111.

The carol is almost entirely put together from proverbs.

burden, l. 4. See B. J. W., *Proverbs*, M 97.

stza. 3, ll. 1, 2. See B. J. W., *Proverbs*, P 429, T 204, W 45. *feste*: confirm or seal a bargain. l. 2. See note on No. 325, burden, l. 1.

stza. 4. This is one of the *Proverbs of Hendyng*: 'Under boske shal men weder abide' (*Rel. Ant.* i. 113).

stza. 5, l. 1. i.e. if a hasty decision miscarries.

339. Against Evil Speech

Pr. Wright, *Wart. Club*, p. 18; *Rel. Ant.* ii. 165. B.–R. 3733.

stza. 2, l. 1. Compare No. 341, stza. 4, ll. 1, 2, and note thereon.

340. Against Wicked Tongues

Pr. Wright, *P.S.* xxiii. 41; J. E. Masters, *Rymes of the Minstrels* (Shaftesbury, 1927), p. 12. B.–R. 1633.

burden, l. 2. He need not fear wherever he goes.

stzas. 3, 4. Compare No. 349.

stza. 4, l. 4. *stake*: a dull, slow fellow. Compare the proverbial uses listed by *O.E.D.* s.v. 'stake', e.g. Gower, *Confessio Amantis*, Bk. VI, ll. 190–2:

> . . . I fro hire go
> Ne mai, bot as it were a stake,
> I stonde avisement to take.

E.D.D. lists it as having the meaning 'a silly person' in Cumberland and in Westmorland in 1778.

341. Against a Wicked Tongue

Pr. Wright, *Wart. Club*, p. 87; *Rel. Ant.* ii. 167; C. & S., p. 191; Greene, *Selection*, p. 132; Sisam, p. 444. B.-R. 3537.

stza. 1, l. 2. *Satenas*: The Satin-flower, also called Penny-flower. See *Leaves from Gerard's Herball*, ed. Marcus Woodward (Boston, 1931), p. 256. *peny-round*: the ground pennywort; ibid., p. 120: 'Navelwoort, or Penniwoort of the Wall: There is a kinde of Navelwoort that groweth in watery places, which is called of the husbandman Sheeps bane, because it killeth sheepe that do eat thereof: it is not much unlike the precedent [the non-poisonous variety of the wall] but the round edges of the leaves are not so even as the other; and this creepeth upon the ground, and the other upon the stone walls.'

stza. 2, l. 4. *blo*: livid.

stza. 3, l. 1. *stauns*: dissension.

stza. 4, ll. 1, 2. An ancient and widespread proverb of ultimately Biblical origin (Proverbs xxv. 15, or Ecclesiasticus xxviii. 17. See Archer Taylor, *The Proverb*, Cambridge, Massachusetts, 1931, p. 58). It occurs among the *Proverbs of Alfred*, ll. 460–1 (ed. Helen P. South, New York, 1931, p. 121). For a long list of its occurrences see Max Förster, 'Kleinere mittelenglische Texte', in *Anglia*, xlii (1918), 200 n. 7, and 'Frühmittelenglische Sprichwörter', in *Englische Studien*, xxxi (1902), 6. See also B. J. W., *Proverbs*, T 384.

stza. 5, l. 1. Note the suggestion of the varying degrees of the audience.

342. The Mischief of the Tongue

Music for one voice (burden only). *Pr.* Wright, *P.S.* xxiii. 78; burden only, with music, Stevens, *Med. Carols*, p. 111. B.-R. 4198 (erroneous duplicate entry 2612).

The last line of each stanza forms a kind of link between the sense of the stanza and that of the burden, which is to be repeated at that point.

stza. 3, ll. 3, 4. These lines mark the author as a religious person annoyed by the circulation of slanders against his order.

stza. 5, l. 1. Compare Psalm cxl. 3: 'Acuerunt linguas suas sicut serpentis . . .'

343. Of Discreet Behaviour

Pr. Rel. Ant. i. 252. B.-R. *50; *Supp.* *3119.5.

stza. 2, l. 1. *byrdes*: ladies.

stza. 3, l. 1. *nale*: ale. The first three lines of this stanza occur also as stza. 6, ll. 1–3 of No. 344.

l. 2. See B. J. W., *Proverbs*, N 110.

344. Against Blowing One's Own Horn

Pr. Wright, *P.S.* xxiii. 23; C. & S., p. 192; J. E. Masters, *Rymes of the Minstrels* (Shaftesbury, 1927), p. 8; Sisam, p. 474. B.-R. 543.

burden. Apperson (*English Proverbs and Proverbial Phrases*, London, 1929, p. 310) cites this as the earliest instance of the familiar metaphor for boasting. The couplet appears in almost identical form in a short passage of moral advice in St. George's Chapel, Windsor, MS. E. I. I., f. 95ᵛ (*pr.* M. R. James, 'The Manuscripts of St. George's Chapel, Windsor', *The Library*, 4th Ser., xiii, 1932, 74):

> he is wise and wele tawght
> that can bere an horne *and* blow it not.

See also B.-R. 432 and *Supp.* 1137.5. Richard Edwards uses it in the form 'I can weare a horne & blow it not' in the play *Damon and Pithias* (1563-4), Tudor Facsimile Texts (1908), sig. F$_{iii}$^{v} (ed. B. J. Whiting, p. 350). See also B. J. W., *Proverbs*, H 488.

  stza. 1, l. 2. *grame*: harm.

  stza. 2, l. 1. *shyll*: shrill.

  stza. 3, l. 2. Compare No. 345, stza. 2, l. 3, and note thereon.

  stza. 5, l. 3. See B. J. W., *Proverbs*, H 9.

  stza. 6. The first three lines also occur as ll. 1-3 of No. 343, stza. 3.

345. Suffer and Be Merry

  Pr. Dyboski, p. 46; Flügel, *N.L.*, p. 141; 'Lieder.', p. 265; Greene, *Selection*, p. 133. B.-R. 470.

There is an unpublished fifteenth-century poem on this same theme in Nat. Lib. W. MS. Peniarth 395, f. 345^r (B.-R. 4121), with the refrain 'thenke on this word: "suffren I mot"'. It begins:

> Who so kon suffre *and* hald hym styll,
> I trow he schall fynde hit for the best.

  burden, l. 1. *so most I goo*: so may I (be able to) walk.

  stza. 1, l. 1. Adapted from *The Proverbs of Wysdom* (ed. Zupitza, *Archiv*, xc, 1898, 243-8, l. 105): 'Be þou mery, þow þou be hard betid.'

  stza. 2, l. 3. Compare No. 344, stza. 3, l. 2. The line is an adaptation of one of *The Proverbs of Wysdom* (Zupitza, op. cit., l. 99): 'Hyre and se, and be styll.' In the version from Bodleian Library MS. Bodley 9 it is 'Here, and se, and sey not'. As 'Hyre, and se, and sey not all!' it forms the refrain of a *chanson d'aventure* in Trinity College, Cambridge, MS. O. 9. 38, f. 26^v (*pr.* Sandison, p. 121). A Scottish version uses rhyme: 'The fairest thing that may befall to heir and sie and tell [say *interlined*] not all' (M. L. Anderson, ed., *The James Carmichaell Collection of Proverbs in Scots*, Edinburgh, 1957, p. 105). See also B. J. W., *Proverbs*, H 264.

  stza. 3, l. 4. See B. J. W., *Proverbs*, T 376.

  stza. 4, l. 2. *The Wise Man*: the author of *The Proverbs of Wysdom* or *The Wise Man's Proverbs*.

  stza. 5, l. 4. *lappe*: flap of the gown.

346. Against Changing Servants

  Pr. Dyboski, p. 47; Flügel, 'Lieder.', p. 266. B.-R. 294.

  burden, l. 2. See B. J. W., *Proverbs*, N 97, O 27.

  stza. 1, l. 1. See B. J. W., *Proverbs*, U 5.   l. 2. See B. J. W., *Proverbs*, L 559.   l. 3. An often-repeated proverb. See notes on No. 411, burden, and B. J. W., *Proverbs*, H 9.

  stza. 2, l. 1. See B. J. W., *Proverbs*, P 133.

  stza. 3, l. 7. Compare the description of the character Dissimulation in Skelton's 'The Bouge of Court', l. 428: 'Then in his hood I saw there faces twain' (*The Complete Poems of John Skelton Laureate*, ed. Philip Henderson, 3rd edn., London, 1959, p. 50). In the same author's *Magnificence* the character Cloaked Collusion says of himself: 'Two faces in a hode covertly I bere' (ibid., p. 187). For other occurrences see note by H. E. Rollins in his edition of *The Paradise of Dainty Devices* (Cambridge, Massachusetts, 1927), p. 197.

347. Of the Estates of Men

  Pr. C. & S., *M.L.R.* vi. 68; Whiting, p. 195; Kaiser, *Anth.*, p. 442, *Med. Engl.*, p. 295; Davies, p. 171. B.-R. 1588.

This carol is a striking expression of Audelay's faith in the existing order of society. Compare his attitude in No. 411, stanzas 6, 7. The verses on the 'four estates' are in the same spirit as those in 'A Series of Triads' (*pr.* Brown, *R.L. 15 C.*, No. 177). In that poem the 'three points of mischief' are poor men proud, a rich man a thief, an old man a lecher, only the last of which Audelay includes. The three estates of the poem are the usual ones of the priest, the knight, and the labourer. Audelay's introduction of the friars as an estate is less surprising than his seeming to regard old men as constituting one by themselves. He may have had in his mind some current formula like that of the five evil things mentioned in a thirteenth-century rhyme (B.M. MS. Cotton Cleopatra C. vi, ff. 21ᵛ, 22ʳ, *pr. Rel. Ant.* ii. 15):

King conseilles
Bissop loreles
Wumman schameles
Hold-man lechur
Jong-man trichur
Off alle mine live
Ne sau I worse five.

Audelay's division of society into four estates seems to be of his own devising. Ruth Mohl (*The Three Estates in Medieval and Renaissance Literature*, New York, 1962, pp. 47, 80, 204–5, 220–1, 318) records several instances of classifications into four estates, but none of these agrees with Audelay's, which she does not mention.

stza. 1, l. 5. *allgate*: at any rate.
stza. 2, l. 3. *Leud or lered*: ignorant or learned.
stza. 3, l. 1. *obisions*: abuses.
stza. 8, l. 4. *chomys*: shames.

348. Of the Mean Estate

Music for two and three voices. *Pr.* Fehr, p. 267; with music, Stevens, *Med. Carols*, p. 72. B.-R. 3382.

burden, l. 2. A proverb, recorded by T. Draxe, *Bibliotheca Scholastica* (London, 1633), p. 124 (ed. M. Förster, *Anglia*, xlii, 1918, 395). See also B. J. W., *Proverbs*, M 446.

stza. 1, l. 1. A widely current proverb, recorded in *Bibliotheca Scholastica*, p. 7: 'The higher I climbe the greater is my fall.' It is made into a couplet in the sixteenth-century Harington MS. at Arundel Castle, f. 28ʳ:

His fall is nye
that Clymes to hie.

(*pr.* Ruth Hughey, *The Arundel Harington Manuscript of Tudor Poetry*, Columbus, Ohio, 1960), i. 99. It is put into the mouth of Lucifer in the Macro play of *Wisdom* (l. 444): 'Who clymyt hye, hys fall gret ys', and Esther applies it to Haman in the play *Godly Queen Hester* (l. 1175), noted by B. J. Whiting, *Proverbs in the Earlier English Drama* (Cambridge, Massachusetts, 1938), pp. 75, 44. l. 3. *donder sownys*: thunder-sounds. This line and stza. 2, l. 1 suggest that the author may have known Horace's lines on the same theme (*Odes*, II. x. 9–12):

saepius ventis agitatur ingens
pinus et celsae graviore casu
decidunt turres feriuntque summos
fulgura montes.

stza. 2, l. 1. See B. J. W., *Proverbs*, H 385.
stza. 3, l. 1. See B. J. W., *Proverbs*, H 322.   ll. 2, 3. Another proverb, appearing among those in Balliol College, Oxford, MS. 354, f. 200ᵛ (*pr.* Dyboski, p. 132): 'He that heweth to hye, þe chippis will fall in his eye', and in 'Proverbs of Good Counsel' in British Museum MS. Harley 2252, f. 3ʳ (*pr.* F. J. Furnivall, *Queene Elizabethes Achademy* [etc.], E.E.T.S., Ex. Ser., No. viii, 1869, 68, l. 21): 'over þⁱ hed loke thowe never hewe'. J. A. Ray (*A Collection of English Proverbs*, Cambridge, 1678, p. 154) gives it as 'Looke not too hie lest a chip fall into thine eye', and adds that 'Hew' is the Scottish version. Apperson (*English Proverbs and Proverbial Phrases*, London, 1929, p. 300) records it from as early as 1300. Compare No. 349, stza. 5, and see B. J. W., *Proverbs*, H 221.

349. Of Discreet Conduct

Pr. Mayer, sheet b; Brown, *R.L. 15 C.*, p. 285; Greene, *Selection*, p. 134; Sisam, p. 374. B.-R. 1415.

It seems clear that either this carol or, more probably, a common source, was known to Dunbar when he wrote his verses beginning 'How sowld I rewill me, or quhat wyiss' with refrain 'Lord God, how sall I governe me?' (*The Poems of William Dunbar*, ed. John Small, ii, S.T.S., 1893, 95–7). The thesis of Dunbar's ten stanzas is the same: no matter what posture or style of life I adopt, detractors will give it an unfavourable interpretation. The Scots poem concludes:

> To do the best my mynd salbe,
> Latt every man say quwat he will.
> The gratious God mot governe me.

350. Against Greed and Covetousness

Pr. Dyboski, p. 26; Flügel, *N.L.*, p. 141, 'Lieder.', p. 252. B.–R. 1386.

burden, l. 2. See Introduction, p. clxxi. Compare the lines on the wise man in B.M. MS. Harley 116, f. 170ᵛ (for three shorter versions see B.–R. 1139):

> He ys wyse that can be ware er he be wo;
> He ys wyse that can do well and say also;
> He ys wyse that can ber yeue betwene frend and foo;
> He ys wyse that hath inoghth and can say 'Hoo';
> He ys wyse that [hath] on wyffe and wol no moo.

stza. 3, ll. 1, 2. Compare No. 141, stza. 2, ll. 1, 2.

351. Against Pride

Pr. Dyboski, p. 3; Flügel, 'Lieder.', p. 195. B.–R. 1412.
burden. Taken verbatim from Psalm lxii. 10.
stza. 2, l. 3. *apprese*: oppress, attack.

352. Against Love of Riches

Pr. Zupitza, 219, notes, xciv, 410–12. B.–R. 2506.

stza. 1, ll. 1, 2. Ecclesiastes iii. 20: 'Et omnia pergunt ad unum locum: de terra facta sunt et in terram pariter revertuntur.'　　l. 3. *The Wyse Man*: Solomon, the reputed author of Ecclesiastes.
stza. 4, l. 1. Job vii. 7: 'Memento quia ventus est vita mea', etc.

353. Of the Vanity of Riches

Pr. Zupitza, 220, notes, xciv, 412–13. B.–R. 1298.

burden, l. 2. Job vii. 21: '. . . ecce nunc in pulvere dormiam . . .' Skelton uses 'nunc in pulvere dormio' in the refrain of his poem 'On the Death of the Noble Prince, King Edward the Fourth' (*The Complete Poems of John Skelton Laureate*, ed. Philip Henderson, 3rd edn., London, 1959, p. 1).
stza. 2, l. 3. *bille*: weapon, halberd.

354. Do Well, and Dread No Man

Music for two and three voices. *Pr.* Fehr, p. 272; with music, Stevens, *Med. Carols*, p. 93. B.–R. 2370.

Compare the couplet in 'Proverbs of Good Counsel' in B.M. MS. Harley 2252 (*pr.* F. J. Furnivall, *Queene Elizabethes Achademy*, E.E.T.S., Ex. Ser., No. viii, 1869, p. 68):

> The beste wysdom þat I can,
> ys to doe well, & drede no man.

Compare No. 387, burden, and the line 'Do weill & dout no man', from a seventeenth-century proverb collection in Erskine Beveridge, ed., *Fergusson's Scottish Proverbs* (S.T.S., New Ser., No. 15, Edinburgh, 1924), 29.
stza. 2, l. 4. *thees too*: the two commandments given by Christ, Matthew xxii. 37–40.

355. Against Pride

a. *Pr.* Wright, *Wart. Club*, p. 24; *Rel. Ant.* ii. 166; C. & S., p. 183.
b. *Pr.* Dyboski, p. 50; Flügel, 'Lieder.', p. 274.
B.-R. 2771.
burden, l. 1. See B. J. W., *Proverbs*, W 45.
stza. 1, l. 2. This proverbial expression is found twice in Henry Medwall's play *Nature* (late fifteenth century), spoken unwittingly by Sensuality to Pride: 'Ye be radix viciorum. Rote of all vertew', and knowingly by Meekness: 'The rote of all syn / ys Pryde ye know well' (sigs. C$_{iii}$ [v], H$_{iv}$ [v], *Tudor Facsimile Texts*, London, 1908, cited by B. J. Whiting. *Proverbs in the Earlier English Drama*, Harvard Studies in Comparative Literature, xiv, Cambridge, Massachusetts, 1938, pp. 79, 80). See also B. J. W., *Proverbs*, P 389

356. Make Amends

a. *Pr.* Wright, *Wart. Club*, p. 15; B. Fehr, *Archiv*, cix (1902), 45; C. & S., p. 186.
b. *Pr.* Wright, *P.S.* xxiii. 44.
B.-R. 3707.
Compare the *chanson d'aventure* with the refrain 'amendes make' in the Vernon MS., f. 411^v (*pr.* Brown, *R.L. 14 C.*, p. 198), especially ll. 57-60:

> ȝif þou be kyng and croune bere,
> And al þis world be at þi wil,
> ȝit schaltou be pore as þou was ere,
> And þat þou knowest bi puire skil.

stza. 1, ll. 1-3. Compare No. 324, stza. 4, l. 1, No. 371, stza. 2, ll. 1, 2.
stza. 2, l. 3. *abeye*: atone for.
stza. 4. This occurs as stza. 1 of No. 382. l. 1. *sleder*: slippery.

357. Of the Tokens of God's Displeasure

Pr. Wright, *Wart. Club*, p. 73; Greene, *Selection*, p. 135. B.-R. 3566.
The 'dear years', the 'two pestilences', and the 'wind's blast' referred to in this carol set the date of its composition as not long after 1362, when these events would have been fresh enough in people's minds to make the allusions effective. The two plagues would be the great epidemics of 1348-9 and 1361-2, during the latter of which occurred the violent windstorm of 15 January 1362, mentioned by various chroniclers and in *Piers Plowman*. See Skeat's note on C. Passus VI, ll. 115, 117 (*The Vision of William concerning Piers the Plowman*, Oxford, 1886).

The special reference to damage by lightning at Lynn makes it fairly certain that the carol was written by someone in East Anglia and possibly in Lynn itself. I have been able to find no record of this particular destruction of the tolbooth and the Carmelite friary either in published histories of the town or by inquiry of local antiquarians. The later history of the Carmelite steeple implies that it had been built a hundred years before 1362. Its fall on a calm day, 9 April 1631, is well attested, and Charles Parkin (*An Essay towards a Topographical History of the County of Norfolk*, London, 1808, viii. 523) says that at that time it had 'continued upwards of 360 years'.

The tone of stza. 7, ll. 3, 4, does not suggest that the author was himself one of the afflicted community. He might have belonged to one of the several rival orders with houses in Lynn, and one is tempted to suggest the Franciscans, whose steeple not only 'stood fast' in the tempest of 1362 but rises over King's Lynn to the present day.

The calamity would have been well known in Bury St. Edmunds, of course, and the carol may have originated there. It would have had considerable local application in the mid-fifteenth century, as the western tower of the abbey fell in 1430, and nine years later a violent storm did much damage.

With this carol compare the verses on the later visitations of 1382 (*pr.* Brown, *R.L. 14 C.*, p. 186) especially ll. 57-62:

> þe Rysing of þe comuynes in londe,
> þe Pestilens, and þe eorþe-quake—
> þeose þreo þinges, I vnderstonde,
> Beo-tokenes þe grete vengaunce & wrake
> þat schulde falle for synnes sake,
> As þis Clerkes conne de-clare.

stza. 1. Compare the first stanza of the fifteenth-century poem with 'O-and-I' refrain in C.U. Lib. MS. Gg. 1. 32, f. 3ʳ (*pr.* Brown, *R.L. 15 C.*, p. 256; text from MS.):

> Thynk, man, qware off thou art wrought, th*at* art so wlonk *in* wede;
> Thynk hou th*o*u art hedyr brought, *and* of thyn end take hede;
> Thynk hou der*e* God has the bought, w*ith* blysful blode to blede;
> Thynk, for his gyle was it noght, bot, ma*n*, for thi mysdede.

Compare also No. 329, stzas. 2, 3.

358. Of Religious Duties

Pr. Wright, *P.S.* xxiii. 40. B.–R. 893.

burden, l. 2. 'Parce mihi, Domine' occurs as the refrain of the widely current 'Bird with Four Feathers' (B.–R. 561, 3714) and in a prayer to the Trinity in Bodl. MS. Ashmole 189, f. 105ᵛ. Its source is Job vii. 16, whence it is incorporated in the Matins of the Office of the Dead, Lectio 1 (*Br. Sar.* ii, col. 273).

stza. 5, l. 3. To heaven God teach us the way.

359. Of Divine Mercy

A a. *Pr.* Dyboski, p. 8; Flügel, 'Lieder.', p. 233; Padelford, p. 87.

b. Music for two voices. *Pr.* Padelford, p. 87; with music, *E.B.M.* ii. 106, *facs.* No. xlvi; Terry, p. 38; Stevens, *Med. Carols*, p. 12.

B. Music for two and three voices. *Pr.* Fehr, p. 275; Dyboski, p. 171; with music, Stevens, *Med. Carols*, p. 100.

C. *Previously unpublished.*

B.–R. 2053.

burden, l. 1. *asay*: try, i.e. apply yourself to seek mercy. Compare the burden of No. 184.

A. stza. 3, l. 2. (**B.** stza. 2, l. 3) *spyll*: be lost.

A. stza. 6, l. 2. *stownd*: time.

360. Let Us Amend

Pr. Zupitza, 215, notes, xciv, 402–4. B.–R. 3272.

stza. 1, l. 1. *Seint Augustyne.* Zupitza suggests several passages from Augustine's works which Ryman may have had in mind (*Pat. Lat.* xxxvii, cols. 284, 357; xxxviii, cols. 131, 150). A more likely source is the *Enarratio in Psalmum C, vers. 1* (*Pat. Lat.* xxxvi, col. 1282): '. . . forte invenimus modo tempus esse misericordiae, futurum autem tempus judicii. Quomodo est primo tempus misericordiae? . . . Misericordiae tempus est, nondum judicii.' Ryman's 'for why' may be a reminiscence of the 'Quomodo'.

361. Of Doomsday

Pr. Dyboski, p. 9; Flügel, 'Lieder.', p. 234. B.–R. 425.

stza. 1, ll. 1–3 occur as stza. 8, ll. 1–3 of No. 365.

stza. 1, l. 2. *hygh Justyce*: Christ. Compare No. 98, stza. 3, l. 3, No. 179, stza. 5, l. 3, and No. 209, stza. 8, l. 1; also Chaucer, *An ABC*, l. 37: 'Whan we shule come bifore the hye justyse', and l. 200 of 'An ABC Poem on the Passion of Christe': 'Be-forn ih*e*su, þat hey Iustyce' (F. J. Furnivall, ed. *Political, Religious, and Love Poems*, E.E.T.S., Or. Ser., No. 15, 1866, 277).

stza. 4, l. 1. *rede*: advise.

stza. 5. This points to the use of the carol at Christmas gatherings.

362. Of Doomsday

Pr. Reports of the Historical Manuscripts Commission, iii, Appendix, 316. B.–R. 17.

stza. 3, l. 4. *toyenst to fay*: hostile to the faith.

stza. 4, l. 4. *rehersse here pay*: reckon up their reward.

363. Of the Last Judgement

Pr. Wright, *Wart. Club*, p. 21; B. Fehr, *Archiv*, cix (1902), 47. B.–R. 4281.

The whole carol is based on Matthew xxv. 31–6, 41–4. The burden is probably an adaptation of one from a secular song. Compare the burden of No. 329 and Siegfried Wenzel's important note thereon.

364. Of the Last Judgement

Repr. facs. Reed, pp. 66, 63. B.–R. *Supp.* 3645.8.

This carol, like No. 363, is based on Matthew xxv.

Reed (p. xlv) took the burden to be an 'explanatory refrain' to a woodcut marking the end of a volume and suggested that the burden of this piece was on a lost leaf preceding p. [45]. But the leaves containing his pp. [45–6] and [47–8] are folded the wrong way in the present binding. See R. L. Greene, review of Reed in *Modern Language Notes*, xlviii (1933), 133 and Bibliography of Original Sources.

Song No. [82] in John Hall's *The Court of Virtue* (1565) has for its title: '*A voyce from heaven to you shall come,* / Venite ad iudicium', and as the refrain-line of each of its thirteen stanzas: 'venite ad iudicium' (ed. Russell A. Fraser, New Brunswick, N.J., 1961, pp. 178–81). This work, intended as an antidote to *The Court of Venus* and Tottel's *Songs and Sonnets*, contains many pious songs to be sung to current secular and sacred tunes. Some are actual sacred parodies of secular songs, e.g. of Wyatt's well-known 'Blame not my lute' (No. 75).

stza. 1, l. 1. *shyll*: shrill.

stza. 8, l. 2. *abye*: atone.

365. Of the Vanity of the World

Pr. Wright, *Wart. Club*, p. 5; B. Fehr, *Archiv*, cix (1902), 42; C. & S., p. 181. B.–R. 3658.

This carol appears to have been assembled from verses on two different but related subjects. Stzas. 1–3 and 8, 9 deal with man's accountability for his actions, whereas stzas. 4–7 are on the familiar theme of the mutability of worldly fortune. The fact that one stanza also appears in another carol points to the piece's being a composite one.

stza. 1, ll. 1–3. The author has Matthew xiii. 24–30 in mind, but he has confused the simile as found there. The world is to be likened to the farm and man in general to the husbandman.

stza. 2. Matthew xii. 36: 'Dico autem vobis, quoniam omne verbum otiosum quod locuti fuerint homines, reddent rationem de eo in die iudicii.' l. 1. *spylle*: waste. l. 3. *grylle*: severe, exact.

stza. 4, l. 1. *farye*: tumult, scene of disorder. The earliest citation in *O.E.D.* is from 1500. See B. J. W., *Proverbs*, W 664. l. 2. *neysche*: nesh, soft, i.e. muddy.

stza. 6, l. 3. *wrynge*: suffer.

stza. 7, ll. 3, 4. See B. J. W., *Proverbs*, T 351.

stza. 8, ll. 1–3. These occur as stza. 1, ll. 1–3 of No. 361. l. 4. *pay*: payment, accounting.

stza. 9, l. 3. *monewere*: moneyer, i.e. the treasurer of grace, continuing the figure of the preceding stanza.

366. Of the Vanity of the World

Pr. James & Macaulay, p. 82; Greene, *Selection*, p. 136. B.–R. 3654.

stza. 1, ll. 2, 3. James i. 10, 11: '. . . sicut flos foeni transibit: Exortus est enim sol cum ardore, et arefecit foenum, et flos eius decidit, et decor vultus eius deperiit.'

stza. 2, l. 3. There is a reference here to the proverb 'There was never a poor wooer nor a rich dead man'; see B. J. W., *Proverbs*, M 323.

stza. 4, l. 2. *wyth cuces owersette*: put off with excuses. Executors have a bad name in medieval literature; compare the burden and stza. 2 of No. 382. The frequent interest of the religious orders in obtaining legacies and the resulting conflicts and litigations may have had something to do with the prejudice. Audelay mentions the unreliability of executors; see Whiting, No. 2, l. 89, No. 11, ll. 99, 345–7.

stza. 6, l. 2. Compare the abuse of executors and the tales of their falsity in *Handlyng Synne*, ll. 6293–508 and 6257–62, especially ll. 6293–9 (ed. F. J. Furnivall, E.E.T.S., Or. Ser., No. 119, 1901):

> ʒe ryche men, before ʒow se,
> þe whyles ʒe are yn ʒoure pouste;
> On ʒoure soules, y rede ʒow þenke;
> y warne ʒow of ʒoure eyres blenke;
> Ne haueþ no trust of ʒoure sokoure,
> Nat of ʒoure owne executoure;
> ʒyueþ ʒeself with ʒoure hondys.

In the same vein are the lines in one of the pieces not in carol-form in Bodl. MS. Eng. poet. e. 1 (Wright, *P.S.* xxiii. 34):

> What thou doest with thyn hond, that shalt thou fynd.
> Wyves be rekeles, chyldren be onkynd,
> Exceecuturs be covetys and hold that thei fynd.

There is a long disquisition, with *narraciones*, on executors good and bad in *Peter Idley's Instructions to His Son*, Book ii, ll. 1618–2002 (ed. Charlotte D'Evelyn, Boston, 1935, pp. 185–91).

367. Of the Vanity of the World

Music for two and four voices. *Pr.* Fehr, p. 277; with music, Stevens, *Med. Carols*, p. 106. B.–R. 3652.

burden, l. 2. For source see table in Introduction, p. lxxxvii. A lyric in the Vernon MS. uses the same phrase as refrain (*pr.* F. J. Furnivall, *The Minor Poems of the Vernon MS.*, part ii, E.E.T.S., Or. Ser., No. 117, 1901, 733).

stza. 1, l. 1. This also occurs as stza. 5, l. 2 of No. 370. It is used as the second line of the burden of a carol by John Thorne in B.M. MS. 15233 (another version in Bodl. MS. Rawlinson poet. 185). The poem appears as No. 56 in *The Paradise of Dainty Devices* (ed. H. E. Rollins, Cambridge, Massachusetts, 1927), attributed to 'Master Thorn'. The couplet is there printed as if a title and not a burden; Rollins refers to it as a 'sub-title' in the Rawlinson 185 version. See his note (pp. 225–6) and his *Old English Ballads 1553–1625* (Cambridge, 1920), pp. 265–9.

368. Of the Fear of Death

Pr. Wright, *Wart. Club*, p. 20; B. Fehr, *Archiv*, cix (1902), 46; C. & S., p. 184. B.–R. 1268.

burden, l. 1. *drukke*: droop, cower.   *dare*: tremble with fear.

stza. 1, l. 1. Job i. 21: '. . . nudus egressus sum de utero matris, et nudus revertar illuc . . .' Compare the hymn 'De Miseria Hominis', stza. 2 (*Anal. Hym.* xxi. 93):

> Nudus ingrederis,
> Nudus egrederis,
> Egressus cum pavore.

369–72

The 'Timor Mortis' Carols

The phrase which forms the text for these carols is from the Response to the seventh Lectio in the third Nocturn of Matins in the *Officium Mortuorum* (*Br. Sar.* ii, col. 278): 'Peccantem me quotidie et non poenitentem timor mortis conturbat me. Quia in inferno nulla est redemptio miserere mei Deus et salva me.' See Patterson, pp. 180–83, and R. L. Greene, *M.L.R.* xxviii (1933), 235–8.

Compare with these carols Lydgate's 'Timor Mortis Conturbat Me' (*pr.* MacCracken, part ii, p. 828). Of all poems with this refrain William Dunbar's 'Lament for the Makaris' is unrivalled in melancholy power. If a burden were added, it could be used as a carol (*The Poems of William Dunbar*, ed. W. Mackay Mackenzie, London, 1950, 20–3). It appears that Dunbar took from the carol genre the theme and verse form of this superb poem, though the preserved text does not include a burden. The surviving carols on this theme do not use the *ubi sunt* formula to call a roll of the great and good as Dunbar does, but concentrate on the meaning for the individual of the dread of his own death.

A useful background for this group of carols is presented by Rosemary Woolf in chapter ix of *The English Religious Lyric in the Middle Ages* (Oxford, 1968). It is surprising to find her showing such lack of understanding as appears in the statements in her Appendix D on the carol. Here she calls 'unsuitable for the Christmas season' pieces which are 'unfitted by tone, as, for instance, the warnings of death or the Last Judgement' and adds the astonishing sentence: 'It is difficult to imagine any season of the year in which the singing of fear-inspiring carols would be appropriate, since presumably in the penitential seasons of Lent and Advent carol singing would not be appropriate at all' (ibid., pp. 384–5, 388).

369. Of the Fear of Death

Pr. C. & S., *M.L.R.* vi. 80; Whiting, p. 211; Sisam, p. 391; Davies, p. 170; Silverstein, p. 105. B.–R. 693.

This is one of the most personal of all the carols, and its directness and apparent sincerity, as well as its tale of personal affliction, set it apart from the more conventional laments on the 'Timor mortis' theme.

stza. 1, l. 3. *nyth*: is hostile to.   l. 4. This line is taken from the rhymed prayer 'Anima Christi sanctifica me' (Daniel, *Thes. Hym.* i. 345), as noted by Whiting. This was not, strictly speaking, a hymn in Audelay's time. Audelay uses it as well in his poem on the Psalter of the Passion (Whiting, No. 6, l. 9).

stza. 8, ll. 1, 3. Audelay approximates these lines in his poetical 'colophon' (Whiting, No. 18, ll. 482, 484).

stza. 9, l. 2. Luke xxiii. 46: 'Et clamans voce magna Jesus ait: Pater, in manus tuas commendo spiritum meum . . .'

stza. 11, l. 2. An old and widely current proverb equivalent to 'darkest before dawn', recorded by Draxe, *Bibliotheca Scholastica* (London, 1633, p. 91): 'When bale is highest, boot is next.' It appears in *The Owl and the Nightingale*, ll. 687–8; see note in the edition of J. W. H. Atkins (Cambridge, 1922, p. 59).   l. 3. *nyd*: annoyed, troubled.

370. Of the Fear of Death

a. *Pr.* Wright, *P.S.* xxiii. 57; Flügel, 'Lieder.', p. 192; Patterson, p. 102; Kaiser, *Med. Engl.*, p. 290; Greene, *Selection*, p. 137; James J. Wilhelm, *Medieval Song* (N.Y., 1971), p. 363.

b. *Pr.* Dyboski, p. 3; Flügel, 'Lieder.', p. 191; C. & S., p. 150; Mary G. Segar and Emmeline Paxton, *Some Minor Poems of the Middle Ages* (London, 1917), p. 41; Sisam, p. 525.

c. *Repr. facs.* Reed, p. 59. B.–R. 375.

Other carols which make use of the convention of a talking bird are Nos. 378 and 389.

A couplet like that of the burden appears to have been a commonplace at the time of the carol. At Witney the tomb of Richard Wayman and his wives bore the inscription (*c.* 1500):

> Man in what state that ever thou be
> Timor Mortis should trouble thee,
> For when thou least wenyst,
> Veniet te Mors superare.
>
> (F. G. Brabant, *Oxfordshire*, London, 1919, p. 257)

Douglas Gray records three other occurrences of the burden in epitaphs, on the Acworth brass at Luton and the brass of William Busby at Great Tew, Oxon. (both 1513), and on the tomb of William Lawnder, priest, at Northleach, Glos. (1530) ('In What Estate So Ever I Be . . .', *N. & Q.* ccv, 1960, 403–4).

stza. 2, l. 2. Medieval hawking etiquette designated the musket, a small sparrow-hawk, as the bird appropriate to the use of a 'holy-water clerk'.

stza. 3, ll. 1, 2. Compare the poem on the 'Timor mortis' theme in MS. Longleat 29, f. 145ᵛ, † a. 7, ll. 1–4 (*pr.* R. L. Greene, *M.L.R.* xxviii, 1933, 236):

> þer is no þyng þat ever God made
> More certeyn to us þan oure deþe is,
> But more uncerteyne þyng none is yhadd
> þan þe ourre off deþe to us, ywysse.

stza. 4, ll. 3, 4. These words are not recorded in the canonical Scriptures as said by Jesus.

stza. 5, l. 2. This appears as the refrain of No. 279.1 and stza. 1, l. 1 of No. 367. It is, of course, a commonplace. It is still doing service in the burden of a mid-sixteenth-century carol in Bodl. MS. Rawlinson poet. 185, ff. 4ᵛ–5ᵛ (*pr.* Hyder E. Rollins, *Old English Ballads 1553–1625*, Cambridge, 1920, pp. 265–9):

> O mortall man, behold and see,
> This world is but a vanetie.

The carol is also found in B.M. MS. Addit. 15233, signed 'Mr. Thorne', and in *The Paradise of Dainty Devices* (1576) (ed. H. E. Rollins, Cambridge, Massachusetts, 1927, p. 54). l. 3. *necessyte*: hardship.

371. Of the Fear of Death

Pr. Wright, *P.S.* xxiii. 74; Flügel, 'Lieder.', p. 193; Patterson, p. 100. B.–R. 376.

The substance of this carol is very similar to that of No. 370, but the use of a man instead of a bird as the speaker makes this piece the more effective.

stza. 2. Compare No. 356, stza. 1.

stza. 6, l. 2. *chery-fare*: the fair held in the cherry-orchards, often a gay and frivolous occasion. 'Formerly a frequent symbol of the shortness of life and the fleeting nature of its pleasures', *O.E.D.* Compare Audelay's long didactic poem beginning 'God haþ grauntyd grace', ll. 280–1 (Whiting, No. 2):

> Fore al þe worchyp of þis word hit wyl wype sone away;
> Hit falls and fadys forþ, so doþ a chere fayre,

and *Speculum Misericordie* from the 'Delamere' MS., l. 72:

> This worlde is but a cherie feyre.
>
> (*pr.* R. H. Robbins, *PMLA*, liv, 1939, 942)

See also B. J. W., *Proverbs*, W 664.

372. Of the Fear of Death

Pr. Dyboski, p. 36; Flügel, 'Lieder.', p. 259; Patterson, p. 103; C. & S., p. 149; Davies, p. 279. B.–R. 1444.

Patterson's note (p. 181) that this is a partial translation, part of the line being left in the Latin and the other part put into English, lacks supporting evidence, especially in view of the procedures followed in other macaronic carols. He refers to Chambers (C. & S., p. 286): '. . . the tags of Latin which indicate a habit of translating the couplets of a caudated poem, while leaving the *caudae* themselves in the original.' But see Introduction, pp. lxxxi–lxxxiv. An attempt to make a rhymed 'partial translation' of a Latin piece in units of half-lines, as here, will prove illuminating.

stza. 3, l. 2 *rowle*: roll, list of sinners. For a picturesque instance of a demon with a roll see Audelay's 'De meritis misse', ll. 291–305 (Whiting, No. 9). Those who talk after the priest begins the Mass are threatened thus in 'A Treatise of the Manner and Mede of the Mass' from the Vernon MS:

> þe foule fend . so fel is
> He writ ʒor wordes . I-wis
> On A Rolle . euerichon.
> (ll. 287–9, T. F. Simmons, ed., *The Lay Folks Mass Book*,
> E.E.T.S., Or. Ser., No. 71, 1879, 136)

There may be a conscious reference to Titivillus, the demon who records such offences, or it may refer to the story in 'Jacob's Well' which M. D. Anderson reports as the subject of grotesque church sculpture: '[A misericord at Ely] refers to the story told in the sermon manual "Jacob's Well", of how a devil was seen writing down all the idle talk he overheard in church and having to draw out the scroll with his teeth, because it was all too short for his purpose.'

Titivillus appears in Brown, *R.L. 15 C.*, No. 179 and elsewhere, but the demon in this carol is probably Satan himself, as in the verse legend of SS. Augustine and Gregory in B.M. MS. Harley 3954 (*pr. Rel. Ant.* i. 59).

stza. 4. See note on No. 370, stza. 4, ll. 3, 4.

373. Of Death

Pr. Dyboski, p. 92; Flügel, 'Lieder.', p. 223; Silverstein, p. 122. B.-R. 2511.

I believe that previous editors have been mistaken in their interpretation of the relation of this piece and No. 374, which directly follows it in the MS. See notes on that carol. There were probably more stanzas than one in this carol originally.

374. Of Death and the Ages of Man

Pr. Dyboski, p. 93; Flügel, 'Lieder.', p. 224. B.-R. 1587.

stza. 1, l. 4. A proverb, occurring with others in the MS. containing the carol, f. 191ᵛ (*pr.* Dyboski, p. 129). It also appears as the title of a pamphlet in 1644: *To day a man, To morrow none, or Sir Walter Rawleighs Farewell to his Lady, &c.* (*repr.* E. W. Ashbee, London, 1872). See B. J. W., *Proverbs*, T 351.

Dyboski appears uncertain whether this carol and No. 373 are to be regarded as one piece or two. He prints both under one number but with a supplied title before stza. 1 of this piece. The marking of the burden in the MS. with a cross, which, together with 'so dy', is repeated in the margin opposite each stanza, makes it fairly plain that the division here made is the one intended by the scribe.

375. Of Repentance in Age

Music for two and three voices. *Pr.* Fehr, p. 276; Patterson, p. 100; with music, Stevens, *Med. Carols*, p. 103. B.-R. 4077.

burden, l. 2. See note on Nos. 369-72.

stza. 2, l. 4. See note on No. 358, burden, l. 2.

stza. 3, l. 4. From the Versicle following the 'Timor mortis' Response (*Br. Sar.* ii, col. 278): 'Deus in nomine tuo salvum me fac Domine, et in veritate tua libera me.'

376. We All Must Die

Repr. facs. Reed, p. 25. B.-R. *Supp.* 672. 4.

burden, l. 2. *rede*: advise.   l. 3. *lyche*: alike.

stza. 1, l. 3. *blyn*: hesitate.

stza. 2, l. 5. *mylt*: spleen.

stza. 3, l. 1. *mys*: sin.   l. 5. *rought*: cared.

stza. 4, l. 2. *sonde*: gift.   l. 5. Compare No. 366, stza. 6, l. 2, and note thereon.

stza. 5, l. 5. *bales*: woes. *bete*: help.

stza. 6, ll. 1, 2. See note on No. 370, stza. 3.   l. 4. *red the lere*: advise thee to learn.

377. Put No Trust in Earthly Friends

Pr. in first edition. B.-R. 1263.

burden, l. 1. *red*: advise.

stza. 2, l. 4. *hethyng*: scoffing, derision.

stza. 3, l. 1. *bedene*: together.   l. 3. *tray*: affliction.

378. All Flesh Is Grass

Pr. in first edition. B.-R. 358.

Nos. 370, 389 are other carols in the form of *chansons d'aventure* which make use of the 'talking bird' convention.

burden, l. 2. Isaiah xl. 6. Compare 1 Peter i. 24. The scribe seems to have been uncertain of the cases of 'caro'.

stza. 5, ll. 1, 2. This couplet is approximated in the burden of a piece in the late sixteenth-century 'ballad' Bodl. MS. Rawlinson poet. 185, f. 4ᵛ: 'A pretie dittie and a pithe intituled O mortall man' (see also No. 370, stza. 5, l. 2):

> O mortall man behold and see,
> This world is but a vanetie.

379. An Exhortation to God's Service

Pr. in first edition. B.-R. 4285.

stza. 1, l. 2. *Trustyth*: (imperative).

stza. 2, l. 3. See B. J. W., *Proverbs*, M 611.

stza. 8, ll. 1, 2. See B. J. W., *Proverbs*, H 506.

stza. 9, l. 2. *aste*: haste.   l. 4. *awe*: held in awe.

stza. 10, l. 1. *prollyng*: prowling, cheating.   l. 2. *pollyng*: extortion.   l. 3. *enrollyng*: i.e. in the court records.   l. 4. *cobbes*: important men.   *comptrollyng*: calling to account.

stza. 11, l. 2. *carderes*: card-players. *O.E.D.* records first from *c.* 1530.

380. Follow Christ's Word

a. *Pr.* in first edition.
b. Collated in first edition. B.-R. 3515.

381. Service Is No Heritage

Pr. Wright, *Wart. Club*, p. 22; B. Fehr, *Archiv*, cix (1902), 47; C. & S., p. 185; Greene, *Selection*, p. 138; Sisam, p. 431; Davies, p. 154. B.-R. 1433.

The second line of the burden of this carol is one of the commonest and longest-lived of medieval proverbs. On its origin see *N. & Q.*, 1st Ser., viii (1853), 586–7, in connection with its occurrence in Scott's novels. Swift quotes it in 'Mrs. Frances Harris's Petition', l. 41, and 'Directions to Servants', chap. x. It is the refrain of a *chanson d'aventure* in Bodl. MS. Rawlinson poet. 36, f. 2^r (*pr.* Sandison, p. 119), and it is used by Hoccleve in *The Regiment of Princes*, l. 841. It appears reversed in the 'Consail and Teiching at the Vys Man Gaif His Sone', ll. 371–2 (*pr.* J. R. Lumby, *Ratis Raving*, E.E.T.S., Or. Ser., No. 43, 1870, 100):

> Be weill wyllyt in thin office,
> For heritage is na seruice.

Shakespeare puts it in the mouth of the Clown in *All's Well That Ends Well*, Act I, Scene iii. See also B. J. W., *Proverbs*, S 169.

burden, l. 1. Compare l. 46 of the *chanson d'aventure*: 'Of gret gentelye yeman and page.'

stza. 1, l. 1. *prys*: worth.

stza. 2. The triad in this proverb appears in a Scottish version of the early seventeenth century: 'Winters nicht and womans thocht and lords purpose changes oft' (M. L. Anderson, ed., *The James Carmichaell Collection of Proverbs in Scots*, Edinburgh, 1957, p. 109). See also B. J. W., *Proverbs*, W 374.

stza. 3, l. 2. *baly*: jurisdiction, authority.

382. Little Joy Is Soon Done

Pr. Wright, *P.S.* xxiii. 4. B.-R. 2050.

burden. See note on No. 366, stza. 4, l. 2.

stza. 1. This occurs as stza. 4 of No. 356.   l. 1. *sleder*: slippery.   l. 4. See B. J. W., *Proverbs*, J. 62.

stza. 3, l. 1. *holy bok*. The nearest analogue to this sentiment in Scripture is Psalm xxxi. 12: 'Oblivioni datus sum, tamquam mortuus a corde.' The carol-writer probably uses the phrase merely for emphasis.   l. 3. *seken*: try, test.

stza. 4. This implies a custom of singing in turn like that shown in Nos. 10, 11.

383. Of Covetous Guile

Pr. Wright, *Wart. Club*, p. 13; B. Fehr, *Archiv*, cix (1902), 49. B.-R. 1020.

burden, stza. 5, l. 1. Compare the following lines in B.M. MS. Royal 17. B. XVII (*pr.* C. Horstmann, *Yorkshire Writers*, London, 1896, ii. 65):

> Now gos gyle in euer-ilk flok,
> And treuthe is sperrid vndre a lok.

The imperative phrase also occurs in *Piers Plowman*, B. Passus XVIII, ll. 354–5:

> And I [Christ], in lyknesse of a leode. that lorde am of heuene,
> Graciousliche thi *gyle* haue quytte. go *gyle* ageine *gyle*!
> (Quoted by Elizabeth Salter, *Piers Plowman: An Introduction*, Oxford, 1962, p. 40)

stza, 2. l. 2. *plete*: plead, go to law.
stza. 3, l. 1. *lent*: lighted, arrived.
stza. 4, l. 1. *gre*: favour, good will.

384. Of Seeming

Pr. Wright, *Wart. Club*, p. 86; *Rel. Ant.* ii. 166; C. & S., p. 190. B.–R. 3085.
stza. 5. See B. J. W., *Proverbs*, M 196.
stza. 4, l. 1. *hynde*: at hand, near.
stza. 5, l. 2. *bewreke*: avenged.
stza. 6, l. 2. *sythin*: afterwards.

385. Of Truth's Banishment

Pr. Wright, *Wart. Club*, p. 19; *Rel. Ant.* ii. 165; C. & S., p. 187; Robbins, *Hist. Poems*, p. 146; Greene, *Selection*, p. 139; Sisam, p. 430. B.–R. 72.
stza. 2, l. 4. *heye mene*: fine company.
stza. 3, l. 3. *rewly*: sorry.
stza. 4, l. 2. *flytte*: shift, pass on.
stza. 5, l. 3. *rynde*: rend, tear.
stza. 6, l. 2. *esylye*: calmly, quietly.

386. Of the Flourishing of Vice

a. *Pr.* Wright, *P.S.* xxiii. 96.
b. *Pr.* Dyboski, p. 27; Flügel, 'Lieder.', p. 252.
B.–R. 3852.
a. stza. 2, l. 2. *melady*: melody, apparently in the sense of concord or harmony, in spite of the mixed figure which results.   l. 3. Apparently a stock complaint. It appears later (1515–20) in a speech by the character Counterfeit Countenance in Skelton's *Magnificence*: 'A knave will counterfeit now a knight' (*The Complete Poems of John Skelton Laureate*, ed. Philip Henderson, 3rd edn., London, 1959, p. 178).
a. stza. 3, l. 2. *bate*: debate, discord.
a. stza. 5, l. 2. *distaunce*: dissension.
b. stza, 4, l. 2. *eme Cristyn*: 'even-Christians', fellow Christians.

387. Do Well, and Dread No Man

Music for two and three voices. *Pr.* Fehr, p. 277; with music, Stevens, *Med. Carols*, p. 107. B.–R. 962.
burden, l. 1. *rede*: counsel.   *can*: know.   l. 2. A proverb. Compare No. 354, burden, and note thereon. The burden is made from a proverbial couplet which appears among the 'Proverbs of Good Counsel' in B.M. MS. Harley 2252, f. 3ʳ:

> The beste wysdom þat I Can,
> ys to doe well, & drede no man.
> (*pr.* F. J. Furnivall, *Queene Elizabethes Achademy*,
> E.E.T.S., Ex. Ser., No. viii, 1869, 68, ll. 9–10)

The entry at B.–R. 432 lists as another text of this collection a piece in St. George's Chapel, Windsor, MS. E. I. I., f. 95ᵛ, which is actually a different composition.
stza. 2, l. 3. *bolsteris*: padded shoulders, one of the fashions to which moralists took exception.

Compare the speech of a demon in the *Towneley Plays*, xxx, ll. 287–90 (ed. G. England and A. W. Pollard, E.E.T.S., Ex. Ser., No. lxxi, 1897, 376):

> yit a poynte of the new gett / to tell will I not blyn,
> Of prankyd gownes & shulders vp set / mos & flokkys sewyd wyth in;
> To vse sich gise thai will not let / thai say it is no syn,
> Bot on sich pilus I me set / and clap thaym cheke and chyn.

peked shon: perhaps the most notorious of extreme fashions in medieval men's costume. Compare Myrc's *Instructions to Parish Priests*, ll. 41 ff. and 1031–3 (ed. E. Peacock, E.E.T.S., Or. Ser., No. 31, revised, 1902):

> [questions to be asked in confession]
> Hast þou ben prowde of any gyse
> Of any þynge þat þou dedust vse,
> Of party hosen, of pyked schone?

These long toes were finally forbidden by statute under Edward IV in 1465. See John Stow, *Survey of London* (London, 1912), p. 314. The carol must therefore have been written at about that time, some fifty years before the date of the MS. in which it is found.

stza. 3, l. 2. *refrayne*: restraint. *O.E.D.* records only from 1560.

388. Trusty Friends Are Rare

Pr. Wright, *P.S.* xxiii. 10. B.–R. 743.
stza. 6, l. 2. *aftur-tayll*: the reckoning or accounting that follows.
stza. 8, l. 1. *comonte*: community.

389. Try Your Friend Before You Need Him

a. *Pr.* Wright, *P.S.* xxiii. 28; C. & S., p. 193; Greene, *Selection*, p. 140.
b. *Pr.* Dyboski, p. 47; Flügel, 'Lieder.', p. 267; Sisam, p. 534.
B.–R. 3820.
For the convention of the talking bird in a *chanson d'aventure* carol compare Nos. 370, 378.

burden, l. 2. One of the *Wise Man's Proverbs* (l. 14, *pr.* F. J. Furnivall, *Englische Studien*, xxiii, 1897, 442). It is among those in Balliol College, Oxford, MS. 354, f. 200ᵛ (*pr.* Dyboski, p. 132). In Draxe's *Bibliotheca Scholastica* (London, 1633, p. 74) it appears as 'Trie thy friend before that thou hast need of him'. It is worked into a ballad stanza in *A lytell geste of Robyn Hode*:

> God that was of a mayden borne
> Leve vs well to spede
> For it is good to assay a frende
> Or that a man have nede.
>
> (Child, No. 117, fytte ii, stza. 112)

See also B. J. W., *Proverbs*, F 625.
stza. 2, l. 1. *houed*: waited.   l. 3. *shyll*: shrilly.

390. Gramercy Mine Own Purse

Pr. Wright, *Wart. Club*, p. 14; T. Wright, *Songs and Carols* (London, 1836), No. iv; Sisam, p. 428. B.–R. 3959.

burden, l. 2. This proverbial phrase is also used in the burden of No. 391 on the same theme. A poem with the refrain 'Ever, Gramercy, myn owne purse' is in Wynkyn de Worde's edition of *The Boke of St. Albans, repr.* Ritson, *Ancient Songs* (1790), p. 89, (1829), ii. 6, (1877), p. 152. Mayor John Shillingford of Exeter echoes the phrase in describing his merry mood in a letter to his 'Fellows' from London, 2 November 1447:

… therfor y take right noght by and sey sadly *si recte vivas, &c.* and am right mery and fare right well, ever thankyng God and myn awne purse. And y liyng on my bedde atte writyng of this right yerly, myryly syngyng a myry song, and that ys this, Come no more at oure hous, come, come, come. Y woll not dye nor for sorowe ne for anger, but be myry and fare right well, while y have mony; … (Stuart A. Moore, ed., *Letters and Papers of John Shillingford, Mayor of Exeter 1447–50*, Camden Society, London, 1871, p. 16).

Unfortunately he gives us no more of the song; what he quotes sounds like a carol-burden. See B. J. W., *Proverbs*, P 442.

John A. Yunck refers to an interesting parallel to the burden and refrain of this carol and No. 391: '. . . a fifteenth-century Welsh *cywydd* by Sion Cent, whose stanzas end with the identical refrain: "Fy mhwrs, gormersi am hyn." ' He has published further comment on 'penny-poems' in 'Dan Denarius: the Almighty Penny and the Fifteenth Century Poets', *American Journal of Economics and Sociology*, xx (1961), 207–22, and *The Lineage of Lady Meed*, University of Notre Dame Publications in Mediaeval Studies, xvii (Notre Dame, Indiana, 1963), 309.

stza. 2, l. 3. Tauno F. Mustanoja cites this carol as an instance of the use of the proper name 'Jack' to designate 'an ordinary man'. It is used to imply low social status in the sixteenth-century proverb: 'Jacke would be a gentleman if he could speake Frenche' ('The Suggestive Use of Christian Names in Middle English Poetry', Jerome Mandel and Bruce A. Rosenberg, eds., *Medieval Literature and Folklore Studies: Essays in Honor of Francis Lee Utley*, New Brunswick, N.J., 1970, p. 60).

Stza. 3, l. 2, stza. 4, l. 3 with their horn and bow more probably indicate that Jack has taken to hunting the deer than that he has become a 'vagabond musician', as suggested in the note in the first edition of this work.

391. Gramercy Mine Own Purse

Pr. James & Macaulay, p. 72. B.–R. 1484

burden, l. 2. See note on No. 390, burden, l. 2.

stza. 1, l. 2. This 'saying' also occurs in *The Castle of Perseverance*, ll. 2520–1, where it is spoken by the character Avaricia:

> & þou schalt fynde soth to sey
> þi purs schal be þi best fremde [*sic*]
>
> (David Bevington, ed., *The Macro Plays*, The Folger Facsimiles, i,
> New York and Washington, D.C., 1972, p. 105)

It is noted by B. J. Whiting, *Proverbs in the Earlier English Drama*, Harvard Studies in Comparative Literature, Cambridge, Massachusetts, 1938, p. 71.

stza. 5, l. 3. *vowyn*: affirm, declare.

392. Sir Penny

Pr. Wright, *Wart. Club*, p. 75; T. Wright, *The Latin Poems Commonly Attributed to Walter Mapes* (London, 1841), p. 361; Ritson, *Ancient Songs* (1790), p. 76, (1829) i. 134, (1877), 116; W. C. Hazlitt, *Remains of the Early Popular Poetry of England* (London, 1864–66), iv. 359; E. Arber, *The Dunbar Anthology* (London, 1901), p. 79; Robbins, *Secular Lyrics*, p. 50; Kaiser, *Anth.*, p. 317, *Med. Engl.*, p. 550; Sisam, p. 441; etc. B.–R. 2747.

The personification of 'Penny' is met with in a number of medieval vernacular and Latin compositions. Compare especially the Latin 'Gospel of Money' (*pr.* Paul Lehmann, *Parodistische Texte*, Munich, 1923, pp. 7–12), the 'Penny-Catechism' (ibid., pp. 15–16), the thirteenth-century 'Versus de Nummo' (*pr.* Wright, *Latin Poems*, p. 355), the English 'Sir Peni' (ibid., p. 359), and the similar poem in *Rel. Ant.* ii. 108. There is also an anonymous sixteenth-century Scottish poem of 'Sir Penny' (*pr.* [Sir] W. A. Craigie, *The Maitland Folio Manuscript*, i, S.T.S., New Ser., No. 7, 1919, 399).

burden, l. 1. Compare the rhyme scribbled in Gonville & Caius College, Cambridge, MS. 261, f. 234ʳ (cent. xiv):

> Spende and God schal sende;
> Spare and ermore care.
> Non peni, non ware;
> Non catel, non care,
> Go, peni, go.

Compare the speech of 'The Cornysh dawe' in *The Parliament of Byrdes*, which includes more proverbs, ll. 148–9:

> For here is nought els with friende nor foe,
> But go bet peny go bet go.
>
> (W. C. Hazlitt, *Remains*, iii. 174)

Compare also the burden of No. 424.

stza. 3, l. 3. *dwer*: doubt.

stzas. 4, 5. Compare No. 390, stzas. 1, 2.

393. Money, Money

Pr. J. O. Halliwell[-Phillipps], *Nugae Poeticae* (London, 1844), p. 46; Robbins, *Hist. Poems*, p. 134. B.-R. 113.

See notes on Nos. 390–2.

stza. 3, l. 2. *jett*: strut, swagger.

stza. 4, ll. 1, 2. Compare the still current proverb: 'Money makes the mare go.' See B. J. W., *Proverbs*, M 627.   l. 3. *dysguysynges*: allegorical entertainments, the forerunners of the Tudor masques.

stza. 5, l. 2. *a mated chere*: with the air of one checkmated or baffled.

stza. 6, l. 3. *tables*: backgammon.

stza. 8. See B. J. W., *Proverbs*, M 632.

stza. 20, l. 4. See B. J. W., *Proverbs*, M 628.

393.1. Against John Clerke of Torrington

Pr. N. R. Ker, *Medium Ævum*, xxxiv (1965), 231.

This carol is of extraordinary interest as the unique extant example of a satirical attack on a named but obscure person in a named locality. It is, in fact, an English flyting, as aggressive and abusive as some of the specimens in Middle Scots. In spite of earnest effort by the present editor, including a personal visit to Great Torrington, North Devon, and consultation with well-informed local antiquarians, no identification of John Clerke, kinsman of 'my lord', yet swineherd and cleaner of the privy, has so far been made. Nor can the author of this harsh personal attack be named. If the piece was composed some little time before the writing of the text in this MS., 'my lord' could be John Holland, half-brother of King Richard II and successively Earl of Huntingdon and Duke of Exeter, who held the barony of Torrington before he was beheaded in 1400 for rebelling against Henry IV. See J. J. Alexander and W. R. Hooper, *The History of Great Torrington in the County of Devon* (Sutton, [1948]), chap. v. But the satire would lose point with the lapse of time.

Neither the Borough of Great Torrington nor the parish church of St. Michael and All Angels possesses any records of the fifteenth or earlier centuries, and there are no monuments of that time in church or churchyard. Both the Reverend P. G. Harrison, vicar of the church, and Mr. S. J. Parkes, former town clerk of Great Torrington, gave the editor all possible assistance.

Even without the personal identifications the carol is of great value as an undoubted example of the use of the genre in a local, topical, and completely secular way. This character of the piece is obvious, although the author, like the scribe, may have been a cleric. There is no sign of derivation from liturgy or theology, nor is there any suggestion of secular parody of an existing religious song. A comparison with another recently noticed carol of local and satirical interest, No. 424.1 from Ashford, Kent, suggests that we have in these two casually written isolated pieces survivors of a possibly great number of non-religious and topical carols in at least partly oral circulation.

As with No. 144.1, which is written in the same hand, I am doubtful of the authorship of John Morton, in view of the difference between the hand of this carol and that of Morton's undoubted memoranda. See Note on No. 144.1. There is no record of Morton's having lived in Torrington.

The account of N. R. Ker errs in saying that the carol is not divided into stanzas in the MS. The stanzas are both bracketed and separated by spaces. The irregularity of stza. 2 appears to be recognized, but mistakenly interpreted, by the scribe in his bracketing of the first two lines by themselves.

stza. 3, l. 2. *hyne*: rustic servant.   l. 3. *scour the gonge*: clean the privy.

394. In Praise of Women

Pr. James & Macaulay, p. 76. B.-R. 3098.

The reaction of the honour paid to Mary on the earlier medieval attitude of disapproval of women is well shown in this piece. A sense of antagonism between the sexes is present, however, as in some other carols, for the praise of women involves depreciation of men.

stza. 1, l. 1. *saw*: save.   *bedene*: together.

stza. 2, l. 1. *hend*: smart, pretty.

395. In Praise of Women

a. *Pr.* Wright, *Wart. Club*, p. 106; C. & S., p. 198; Mary G. Segar, *A Mediaeval Anthology* (London, 1915), p. 108; Greene, *Selection*, p. 142.

b. *Pr.* Wright, *Wart. Club*, p. 11; T. Wright, *Songs and Carols* (London, 1836), No. iii; F. J. Furnivall and J. W. Hales, *The Percy Folio Manuscript* (London, 1867–8), iii. 545.

B.–R. 4219.

The excellence of the Virgin Mary is emphasized in this piece, as in No. 394, as justification for an admiration for women in general. Unlike many of the carols to the Virgin, it praises her less as the recipient of a special supernatural sanctity than as the embodiment of all the good qualities to be found in her earthly sisters. The claim of stza. 4, l. 3 is unusual even in poems devoted to the praise of women, and here it is rested on the tradition of Mary's reticence. This was fostered by the fact that Scripture records her speaking on only four occasions, the Annunciation, the Visitation, the finding of Jesus in the Temple, and the Marriage at Cana.

Compare the long poem in similar strain printed from the Auchinleck MS. by E. Kölbing, *Englische Studien*, vii (1884), 103; see also F. Holthausen, *Archiv*, cviii (1902), 290 and cx (1903), 102, and the poem with refrain 'Of wimmen comeþ þis worldes welle', printed from the Vernon MS. by Brown, *R.L. 14 C.*, pp. 174–7 as well as Dunbar's 'In Prays of Woman', especially l. 2: 'Off erthly thingis nane may bettir be' (*The Poems of William Dunbar*, ed. W. Mackay Mackenzie, London, 1960, p. 83).

stza. 2, l. 1. *on her tour*: in their degree or order.

stza. 4, l. 2. See B. J. W., *Proverbs*, N 97.

396. In Praise of Women

Pr. Rel. Ant. i. 275; C. & S., p. 197; Robbins, *Secular Lyrics*, p. 31; Kaiser, *Anth.*, p. 297, *Med. Engl.*, p. 470; Sisam, p. 521; Grigson, p. 207; Davies, p. 283. B.–R. 3782.

burden, l. 1. Compare 'Deo Gracias' in the Vernon MS., f. 407ᵛ, ll. 9–10 (*pr.* Brown, *R.L. 14 C.*, p. 138):

> þou₃ I beo riche of gold so red,
> And liht to renne as is a Ro.

The expression is apparently a stereotyped comparison, and there is no need to indulge, with Utley, any 'suspicion about the poet's thorough sincerity' or to find that 'The first line of the burden suggests the wild and unreasonable thoughts of youth' (p. 272). The roe appears twice in proverbial comparisons in the Child ballads, according to B. J. Whiting's survey. The Earl of Erroll is 'as bold' (Child, No. 231 A) and 'Rodingham' is 'as swift' (Child, No. 59 B). See Introduction, p. clxxii and Whiting's 'Proverbial Material in the Popular Ballad', *The Journal of American Folk-Lore*, xlvii (1934), 30, also B. J. W., *Proverbs*, R 168.

stza. 2, ll. 2, 3. *the*: dative of the pronoun 'thou', *pace* Utley. L. 190 of Lydgate's 'A Mumming at Hertford' (*pr.* MacCracken, part ii, p. 680) may be an echo of this carol:

> Whoo can hem wasshe. who can hem wring alsoo?

Utley (pp. 271–2) discusses the line at some length and finds support for the figurative meaning of 'wash' and 'wring' in Lydgate. But he hardly makes a valid case for interpreting the whole carol as satire on women rather than praise.

The next lines seem to mark a turn in the thought, rather than a continuation:

> Wryng hem, yee, wryng, so als God vs speed,
> Til þat some tyme we make hir nases bleed.

There is no sense in which women 'wash' their husbands.

It is well to remember that there were women in audiences where carols were sung and that there is no reason to deny them an innings.

stza. 3, l. 1. This recalls the line 'A woman is a wonder thyng', in 'The Clerk and the Nightingale, I', l. 29 (*pr.* Robbins, *Secular Lyrics*, p. 173).

397. Of Virginity

Pr. C. & S., *M.L.R.* vi 76; Whiting, p. 206. B.–R. 535.

stza. 3. l. 4. *pouste*: power.

stza. 4, l. 1. In connection with Audelay's choice of these three names from among the virgin saints it is perhaps significant to note that St. Catherine and St. Margaret are the two female saints among the sculptures still preserved at the entrance to the chapter house at Haughmond. St. Winifred's name would of course be ever ready to a Shropshire pen. All three were beheaded after refusal to yield their virginity. See Nos. 313, 314.

398. The Treasure of Virginity

Pr. C. & S., *M.L.R.* vi. 77; Whiting, p. 207. B.-R. 1595.
stza. 2, l. 1. *vndur*: secret.   l. 3. *tame*: injure.
stza. 3, l. 4. *fe*: property.
stza. 5, ll. 1, 2. i.e. had it not been for the virginity of Mary.   l. 3. Compare No. 172, stza. 1, l. 2, and No. 230, stza. 2, l. 5.
stza. 7, l. 1. *nyer*: were it not that. The emendation suggested by Whiting (p. 254), following Professor R. J. Menner, of 'nyed', meaning 'approach with lustful purpose', is unnecessary. An exactly similar use of 'nere' occurs in No. 26, stza. 4, l. 1.   l. 3. *lene*: let have.
stza. 8. Audelay's praise of the worldly value of chastity is consonant with his prudential attitude throughout. Compare his No. 411.

399. Women Are Excellent—or the Contrary

a. *Pr.* Dyboski, p. 112; Flügel, 'Lieder.', p. 275; J. E. Masters, *Rymes of the Minstrels* (Shaftesbury, 1927), p. 28; Robbins, *Secular Lyrics*, p. 35; Greene, *Selection*, p. 143; Davies, p. 221 (in part).
b. *Pr.* Wright, *P.S.* xxiii. 88; Kaiser, *Anth.*, p. 311, *Med. Engl.*, p. 478.
B.-R. 1485.
The regular return of the contradicting or 'destroying' burden makes the carol-form a good one for the employment of this particular type of humour. One can see the possibilities of mirth raised by its performance before women who might not at first understand the Latin of the burden. Chaucer's Chantecler and his translation of *Mulier est hominis confusio* come inevitably to mind. Among others Lydgate uses a similar device in his poem with the refrain 'So as þe crabbe goþ forwarde' (MacCracken, part ii, p. 465). For a long discussion of this piece see Utley, p. 165.
burden, l. 2. Utley (p. 256) points out the use of this phrase at the end of *The Scholehouse* by Edward Gosynhill [?].
The spirit of the satire is similar to that of a poem on the virtues of women which reverses its meaning with a change of punctuation. A short version appears in the Harington MS. at Arundel Castle, f. 107ᵛ):

> All women have vertues noble & excellent
> Whoe can prove that: they do offende
> Daylye: they serve god withe good intent
> Seldome: they displease theyr husbands to their lives ende
> Alwayes: to please them they doe intende
> Never: in them a man shall finde shrewdnes
> Commonly: suche qualityes have women more or lesse

(Ruth Hughey, ed., *The Arundel Harington Manuscript of Tudor Poetry*, Columbus, Ohio, 1960, i. 185; for a long note on other versions see ibid. ii. 208–10)

Compare the use of the same Latin tag in the scribbled insult on f. 129ᵛ. of the courtly song-book B.M. MS. Addit. 31922: 'vynsent Wydderden ys an onest man so sayeth Nycolas Benden Cuius est contrarium verum est.' A variant of the same phrase used to emphasize the truth of a statement appears as the second line of the burden of one of the late sixteenth-century carols in Corpus Christi College, Cambridge, MS. 168, a piece deploring the increase in sheep-farming:

> The blacke shepe is a perylous beast;
> *Cuius contrarium falsum est.*
>   (*pr.* James Goodwin, 'Six Ballads with Burdens', *P.S.* xiii. 4)

stza. 1, l. 2. A familiar and trite comparison.

stza. 2, l. 4, stza. 4. Compare *Peter Idley's Instructions to His Son*, Book II, ll. 1049–55:

> Jangelyng in churche among hem is not vsed,
> To telle of her housbandrye al the wooke before;
> And also hir housbandis shall not be accused,
> How croked and crabbed they be euermore.
> All suche thyngis, loo! they can kepe in store:
> They be as cloos and couert as the horn of Gabriell
> That will not be herde but from heuene to hell.
>
> (ed. Charlotte D'Evelyn, Boston, 1935, p. 125)

stza. 3, l. 1. *cumbers*: cumbrous, troublesome.

stza. 4. In the midst of the generalized and diffuse praise of women in Lydgate's *Reson and Sensuallyte* there is a close parallel to this stanza at the end of the section on the 'Maiden's Fifth Pawn' (ll. 6364–71):

> And what ye lyst to ha secre,
> Tel yt a woman boldely,
> And thow maist truste feythfully
> Thow shalt never here yt more,
> Thogh at hir herte yt sitte sore,
> Lever she had, for any peyne,
> Ewene for to breste a-tweyne
> Than a counsayll to discure.

There may even be a reference to the burden of this carol in the marginal note opposite l. 6368: 'Cui*us* cont*r*ariu*m* es*t* veru*m* (ed. Ernst Sieper, i, E.E.T.S., Ex. Ser., No. lxxxiv, 1901, 167).

stza. 5, l. 3. *Gryzell*: a form with final *d* was doubtless used by the original author of a.

stza. 8. The love of women for the ale-house and the conversation there is one of the most frequent objects of derision among their satirical critics. Compare No. 419 for a more sympathetic view of this recreation.

400. Women Compared to Steel

Pr. James & Macaulay, p. 80. B.–R. 3214.

burden, l. 1. *war*: take heed of.   l. 2. 'As true as steel' was already proverbial in the Middle Ages. See B. J. W., *Proverbs*, S 709.

stza. 1, l. 2. *Kaymys*: Cain's. The line appears to be a condemnation of women which likens them to 'Cain's brothers' in the same derogatory sense in which the term was applied to the friars by their enemies.   l. 3. *schrewdnes*: mischief, wickedness.

stza. 2, l. 2. *flyt*: quarrel. *stryfe*: strive.

stza. 5, l. 2. *den*: deign, condescend.   l. 3. *faytur*: begging impostor, cheat.

401. Of the Different Sorts of Women

A a. *Pr.* Dyboski, p. 113; Flügel, 'Lieder.', p. 276.

b. *Pr.* Wright, *P.S.* xxiii. 89; J. E. Masters, *Rymes of the Minstrels* (Shaftesbury, 1927), p. 30; collated with A a and B, Dyboski, p. 189.

B. *Pr. Rel. Ant.* i. 248, Wright, *P.S.* xxiii. 103; F. J. Furnivall, *The Wright's Chaste Wife* (E.E.T.S., Or. Ser., No. 12, 2nd edn., London, 1869), 23.

Composite text. C. & S., p. 214.

B.–R. 3171.

The two widely differing versions of this carol probably represent the activities of at least two different authors, writing to the same air and according to an easy and suggestive formula.

burden. Compare a hitherto unpublished scribble in Huntington Library MS. 501, f. vi [152ʳ], written in a fifteenth-century hand different from that of the religious poem published from this MS. as No. 57 in Brown, *R.L. 15 C.*:

> wyne Dice & wemen makyt empty porss
> with some men.

A. stza. 1, l. 5. Compare P. L. Heyworth, ed., *Jack Upland, Friar Daw's Reply, and Upland's Rejoinder*, Oxford English Monographs, (London, 1968), p. 74, l. 42: 'For su*m*me be*n* lewid, su*m*me be*n* shrewid, su*mm*e falsly supposid.' Heyworth's note (p. 140) calls the rhyming phrase 'a formula with a very wide currency in the fifteenth century' and suggests this carol as the cause of its popularity. 'Lewd' probably means 'stupid' and 'shrewd', 'unscrupulous', as used by John Paston the First, writing to Margaret Paston: '. . . outher ye gader shrewdly or ellis ye spend lewdly' (Norman Davis, ed., *Paston Letters*, Oxford, 1958, p. 40).

A. stza. 4, l. 1. A proverbial comparison. See Chaucer, *Knight's Tale*, l. 403, *Wife of Bath's Prologue*, l. 246. See also B. J. W., *Proverbs*, M 731.

B. burden. Halliwell-Phillipps mistakenly prints this as part of the first stanza. Its true character is indicated in the MS. by brackets. The first stanza has lost two lines.

B. stza. 1, l. 1. See B. J. W., *Proverbs*, N 182.

B. stza. 2, l. 3. Compare Wyatt's 'They fle from me that sometyme did me seke', ll. 5, 6:

> That sometyme they put theimself in daunger
> To take bred at my hand, and now they raunge.
> (*Collected Poems of Sir Thomas Wyatt*, ed. Kenneth Muir, London, 1963, p. 28

B. stza. 3 (A. stza. 6), l. 2. *bate*: strife. l. 3. *chekemate with*: i.e. be a match for.

B. stza. 4, l. 2. *tender as a tripe*: the proverbial simile for toughness ironically reversed. It is obscured by Halliwell-Phillipps, who reads 'accripe'. See B. J. W., *Proverbs*, T 481. l. 3. *chiryripe*: i.e. rosy and luscious.

B. stza. 5, ll. 1, 2. Compare the couplet from 'The Characteristics of Counties' in British Museum MS. Harley 7371, *pr. Rel. Ant.* i. 269 (and from another source, ibid. ii. 43):

> Northampton, full of love
> Beneath the girdel, and not above.

B. stza. 5, l. 3. A proverbial allusion to cuckolding; compare No. 407, stza. 7, ll. 3–6, and Lydgate's 'The Pain and Sorrow of Evil Marriage', ll. 78–80 (*pr.* MacCracken, part ii, p. 459).

B. stza. 6, l. 3. *moke*: (?) muck, dust. The meaning of the line is obscure.

B. stza. 7. The author knows the wisdom of anonymity in the case of a piece like this one. Authorship by Robin Hood is apparently a proverbial figure used to indicate what is unworthy of credence. Tyndale uses it in 'The Obedience of a Christian Man' to emphasize his scorn of Origen: 'Yea, verily, Aristotle, and Plato, and even very Robinhood, is to be believed in such a point, that so greatly maintaineth our holy father's authority and all his disguisings' (*The Works of the English and Scottish Reformers*, ed. T. Cloutt (Thomas Russell, pseud.), London, 1828, ii. 254).

402. When To Trust Women

a. *Pr.* Wright, *P.S.* xxiii. 66; H. Macaulay Fitzgibbon, *Early English and Scottish Poetry* (London, 1888), p. 200; Denys K. Roberts, *Straw in the Hair* (London, 1953), p. 149 (in part); Silverstein, p. 151; Tydeman, p. 58.

b. *Pr.* Dyboski, p. 114; Davies, p. 223.

c. *Pr.* R. M. Garrett, *Anglia*, xxxii (1909), 358. B.-R. 3999.

The burden was written by the same hand as the rest of the carol, but at a different time. This probably indicates the adaptation to carol music of a song not originally written as a carol, a probability which is strengthened by the absence of burdens in b and c.

The particular absurdities used to elaborate the misogynic theme in stzas. 3–6, especially those of animals engaged in human pursuits, show the work of the same kind of imagination which produced similar grotesqueries in other medieval arts, notably sculpture and drawing. They especially bring to mind the curious animals which appear in the margins of the famous Bodleian MS. of the *Romance of Alexander* (MS. Bodley 264, *pr. facs.*, M. R. James, Oxford, 1933). For a similar use of absurdities to mean 'never' compare the poem in the same MS., f. 16ʳ ᵃⁿᵈ ᵛ, 'Wold God that men myght sene', stza. 4, ll. 1–3:

> Whan brome wyll appeles bere
> And hemlocke hony in feere,
> Than sek rest in lond.
> (*pr.* Wright, *P.S.* xxiii. 9–10)

An interesting Scottish analogue appears anonymously in the Bannatyne MS. (1568). It begins, 'I ʒeid the gait wes nevir gane', and concludes:

> The mowss grat þat the cat wes deid
> That all hir kin mycht rew
> Quhen all thir tailis are trew in deid
> All wemen will be trew.

(W. Tod Ritchie, ed., *The Bannatyne Manuscript*, iii, S.T.S., New Ser., No. 23, 1928, 67)

The rhetorical device of a list of impossibilities as a way of saying 'never' persists into modern times in folk-song. An interesting parallel to this carol is the piece recorded by Alfred Williams from the singing of Charles Tanner of Brampton:

> When roses grow on thistle tops,
>   And brimstone's took for sugar candy,
> And women can't eat sugar sops,
>   Oh, then my love and I'll be married.
>
> When a cobbler works without an awl,
>   And London into York is carried,
> When smoke won't rise, nor water fall,
>   Oh, then my love and I'll be married.

(*Folk-Songs of the Upper Thames*, London, 1923, p. 200, stzas. 1, 3)

stza. 1, 1. See B. J. W., *Proverbs*, N 94.   l. 2. See ibid., T 223, and Matthew vii. 16, Luke vi. 44. l. 6. *kyskys*: kecks, a term applied to a number of hollow-stalked umbelliferous plants, here probably teazles.

stza. 2, l. 4. *bulles of the see*: seals.   l. 6. *incypyens*: foolishness.

stza. 3, l. 3. *marmsattes*: small monkeys of any sort.   l. 4. *gurnardes*: gurnets, a species of fish.

stza 4, l. 1. See B. J. W., *Proverbs*, S 972.   l. 4. *boserds*: buzzards.

stza. 5, l. 1. *spawyns*: spawns.   l. 4. *semavs*: sea-mews.   l. 5. *wodknyfys*: knives for cutting up game.

stza. 6, l. 1. *crowbes*: corbies, ravens.   l. 5. *ryd*: road or bridle-path.

stza. 7, l. 4. *musketes*: male sparrow-hawks.   *vergese*: verjuice, sour fruit juice used in cooking and medicine.   l. 5. *sylt*: shall.   l. 6. *Westmynster*: i.e. Westminster Hall, where courts were held.

b, c. stza. 1, l. 4. *croppis*: tops of trees.

c. stza. 3, l. 3. *marlynges*: merlings, an alternative name for whitings.

b, c. stza. 3, l. 6. *sperlynges*: smelts.

b. stza. 5, l. 6. *griffons*: griffon-vultures.

b. stza. 6, l. 5. *the blod of haylis*: the alleged blood of Christ, preserved as a relic at Hailes Abbey, to which it was given in 1270 by the founder, Richard, Earl of Cornwall.

402.1. A Set of Threes

Pr. Wright, *P.S.* xxiii. 4; J. E. Masters, *Rymes of the Minstrels* (Shaftesbury, 1927), p. 20; F. M. Padelford, *The Cambridge History of English Literature* (Cambridge, 1927), ii. 437; Silverstein, p. 153. B.-R. 3552.

The rather rudimentary carol which has been made out of an antifeminist formula probably taken from oral tradition does not appear very singable to a modern reader, but its surroundings in the MS. and the definite burden show clearly that it was regarded as a song. The occurrence of the same form of the jest, definitely as a carol with initial burden, in Thomas d'Urfey's *Pills to Purge Melancholy* shows that it survived for two centuries at least as a piece to be sung (*Songs Compleat, Pleasant and Divertive*, London, 1719, iv. 127-9, with music by 'Mr. TENOE'). The burden in this version is ironic, as in the fifteenth-century carol:

> It is my Delight both Night and Day,
> To Praise the Women as much as I may.

The closest correspondence is between stza. 2 of the older carol and stza. 5 of the later one:

> Three things will be Angry,
> I'll tell you if I can,
> A Wasp, A Weasel, and a Woman.

Stza. 3 of the older carol is quite similar to stza. 7 of the later one:

> Three things will be a Chattering
> I'll tell you if I can,
> A Pye, a Popinjay, and a Woman.

Stza. 4 of the older carol has the same triad as stza. 9 of the later one, which reads:

> Three things must be Beaten,
> I'll tell you if I can,
> A Stock-fish, a Mill-stone, and a Woman.

The friar of stza. 1 has naturally failed to survive, and the fox surprisingly appears coupled with an ape in the last of the three initial stanzas, which are favourable to women:

> Three things there be Loving,
> I'll tell you if I can,
> An Ape, an old Fox, and a Woman.

There must have been a failure either of memory or of transcription at some point. One suspects that the reading should have been 'Lowring' as below.

A medieval version of the jest has been made into a set of five puzzles using a rather transparent cipher on f. 1ᵛ of the fifteenth-century Brome MS., now Yale University, Beinecke Rare Book and Manuscript Library, MS. 365. It does not deserve the dignity of a variant of this carol, and is obviously not meant to be sung (B.–R. *Supp.* 3256.3). The puzzles are given here with the solution provided by the first editor of the MS.:

Take iij claterars.
B p k f.	A pie.
B k b k.	A iai (jay).
B x p m b n.	A woman.

Take iij lowrars.
B b p f.	A ape.
B p w l f.	A owle.
B x p m b n.	A woman.

Take iij schrewys.
B x b s p f.	A waspe.
B x f s k l l.	A wesill.
B x p m b n.	A woman.

Take iij angry.
B f f r k f r.	A frier.
B f f p x.	A fox.
B x p m b n.	A woman.

Ther be iiij thyngs take gret betyng.
B s t p k f k s c h.	A stockfisch.
B m k l s t p n.	A milston.
B f f f d k ɪ b f d.	A fedirbed.
B x o p m b n.	A wooman.

(Lucy Toulmin Smith, ed., *A Common-place Book of the Fifteenth Century*, London, privately printed, 1886, pp. 12–13 and *facs.*) In the rubric of the last group a 'iij' has been altered to 'iiij' by the insertion of a minim in black. The editor notes on 'stockfish': 'A kind of fish dried for keeping, especially in the north. It was so hard that it required much beating and soaking in water, to render it eatable . . .'

The reading 'myll' of the older carol is probably better than the 'millstone' of the later one and of the puzzle below, since the reference would seem to be to the beater which keeps the grain flowing in the hopper rather than to the stone. Compare No. 460, stza. 2, l. 1, 'let the myll clacke', and Chaucer, *The Reeve's Tale*, l. 119: 'How that the hopur wagges til and fra'.

403. Against Hasty Wedding

Pr. Wright, *Wart. Club*, p. 27; B. Fehr, *Archiv*, cix (1902), 49; Robbins, *Secular Lyrics*, p. 37; Silverstein, p. 130. B.–R. 1938.

With the burden compare the *Towneley Plays*, xiii, ll. 91–3 (ed. G. England and A. W. Pollard, E.E.T.S., Ex. Ser., No. lxxi, 1897, 119):

> Bot yong men of wowyng / for god that you boght,
> Be well war of wedyng / and thynk in youre thoght,
> 'had I wyst' is a thyng / it seruys of noght.

burden, l. 2. Utley (pp. 179–80) notes that this line occurs in 'A Dispitison bitwene a God Man and the Deuel', Carl Horstmann, ed., *The Minor Poems of the Vernon Manuscript*, i, E.E.T.S., Or. Ser., No. 98, 1892, 345.

stza. 1, l. 2. *knet*: tied, married.   l. 4. i.e. cast off the old love. The phrase is borrowed from hawking. Compare the song in British Museum MS. Harley 5396, f. 293ᵛ (*pr. Rel. Ant.* i. 75), with the refrain: 'Turne up hur halter and let hur go.' See also B. J. W., *Proverbs*, H 49.

stza. 2, l. 4. See B. J. W., *Proverbs*, G 22.

stza. 4, l. 3. A similar phrase for sexual excitability occurs in *Piers Plowman*, A. Passus III, l. 126: 'Heo is tikel of hire tayl.' See B. J. W., *Proverbs*, T 8.

404. Beware of a Shrewish Wife

Pr. Wright, *P.S.* xxiii. 43; C. & S., p. 209; J. E. Masters, *Rymes of the Minstrels* (Shaftesbury, 1927), p. 23. B.–R. 4278.

This carol shows influence from the *Golias de Coniuge non Ducenda*, perhaps through Lydgate's English translation, 'The Pain and Sorrow of Evil Marriage', in Bodl. MS. Digby 181, f. 7ʳ (*pr.* T. Wright, *The Latin Poems Commonly Attributed to Walter Mapes*, London, 1841, p. 295). Compare especially the last couplet (p. 299):

> Wherefore, yonge men, to eschewe sorowe and care
> Withdrawe your foot or ye fall in the snare.

Note also the following (p. 298) from a spurious stanza (MacCracken, part ii, p. 460):

> It is trewe, I tell you, yonge men everychone,
> Women be varyable and loue many wordes and stryfe;
> Who can not appease them lyghtly or anone,
> Shall haue care and sorowe al his lyfe.

The Latin version appears in some of the MSS. with the *Confessio Goliae*, from which is taken the famous drinking song 'Meum est propositum', included in the MS. of this carol.

A piece similar to this in sentiment and style was probably the basis for a three-voice canon in the unison in Ravenscroft's *Pammelia* (1609), No. xxix:

> What hap had I to marry a shrow
> for she hath give me many a blow,
> and how to please her alacke I doe not know.
>
> From morne to even her tongue neere lies,
> Sometimes she braules, sometimes she cries,
> Yet I can scarse keepe her tallants from my eyes.
>
> If I go abroad, and late come in,
> Sir knaue (saith she) where haue you beene
> And doe I well or ill, she claps me on the skin.

stzas. 2, 3. The plight of the husband in these two stanzas is very like that of Hobbe the Reeve in Lydgate's *A Mumming at Hertford*:

> Whane he komeþe home ful wery frome þe ploughe,
> With hungry stomake deed and paale of cheere,
> In hope to fynde redy his dynier;
> þanne sitteþe Beautryce bolling at þe nale.

> And cely Robyn, yif he speke a worde,
> Beautryce of him dooþe so lytel rekke,
> þat with hir distaff she hitteþe him in þe nekke.
>
> (MacCracken, part ii, 676, ll. 34–7, 50–2)

stza. 2, l. 1. *panter*: fowler's snare.
stza. 3, l. 1. *qwene*: quean, light wench.

405. A Young and Hen-Pecked Husband's Complaint

Pr. Wright, *Wart. Club*, p. 70; T. Wright, *Songs and Carols* (London, 1836), No. xii; C. & S., p. 207; Robbins, *Secular Lyrics*, p. 38; Kaiser, *Anth.*, p. 309, *Med. Engl.*, p. 475; Greene, *Selection*, p. 144; Sisam, p. 440; Oliver, p. 78; Tydeman, p. 57. B.-R. 4279.

Similar realistic treatment of the theme of this carol survives in modern folk-song, e.g. 'Single Men's Warning', collected by Cecil Sharp from Tom Sprachlan at Hambridge in 1903 (James Reeves, *The Idiom of the People*, London, 1958, pp. 199–200, stza. 5):

> When dinner time come to home I repair
> And a hundred to one if I find my wife there
> She's gossipin' about with the child upon her knee
> And the turk of a sign of a dinner for me.

stza. 1, ll. 1, 2. The marriage of young men to older women was much commoner in the Middle Ages than in modern times. The frequency of early widowhood and the great importance of marriage in relation to matters of property were contributing causes. The classic instance is, of course, the matrimonial history of Chaucer's Wife of Bath.

stza. 4, l. 3. See B. J. W., *Proverbs*, R 250.

406. A Hen-pecked Husband's Complaint

Pr. Wright, *P.S.* xxiii. 26; C. & S., p. 208; J. E. Masters, *Rymes of the Minstrels* (Shaftesbury, 1927), p. 9; Charles Williams, *The New Book of English Verse* (New York, 1936), p. 109; W. H. Auden, *The Oxford Book of Light Verse* (Oxford, 1938), p. 63; Sisam, p. 475. B.-R. 210.

The burden, in sense the reverse of appropriate, was doubtless taken from another song, or common to several. Compare that of No. 470. In the play *Misogonous* (? 1577), II. ii, there occurs a long four-part song 'to the tune of hartes ease' which begins:

> Singe care away, with sport & playe,
> pastime is all our pleasure
> (R. Warwick Bond, ed., *Early Plays from the Italian*, Oxford, 1911, p. 197, ll. 69–70).

See also note on No. 10, stza. 5, l. 4.

The locution is discussed at length by F. L. Utley, 'How Judicare Came in the Creed', *Mediaeval Studies*, viii (1946), 303–9. The carol is treated as No. 20 in *The Crooked Rib*.

407. Of the Tyranny of Women

Pr. Wright, *P.S.* xxiii. 64; J. E. Masters, *Rymes of the Minstrels* (Shaftesbury, 1927), p. 14. B.-R. 667.

Apperson (*English Proverbs and Proverbial Phrases*, p. 66) cites this carol as the earliest instance of the use of the phrase 'to wear the breeches' in the sense of 'to dominate the household'. It appears in Shakespeare's *2 Henry VI*, I. iii, ll. 147–8.

On the whole medieval and later tradition of the 'struggle for the breeches' see John Grand-Carteret, *La Femme en Culotte* (Paris, *c.* 1900), chap. i, 'La dispute pour la culotte à travers les âges', with an illustration from a misericord at Rouen Cathedral. See also B. J. W., *Proverbs*, M 406.

It has persisted through the centuries; compare 'Will the Weaver' in Alfred Williams, ed., *Folk-Songs of the Upper Thames*, London, 1923, p. 106, ll. 3, 4.

stza. 1, l. 2. *radicacyon*: rooting.   l. 3. *thong*: acknowledgement.

stza. 2, l. 2. *newels*: news, Fr. *nouvelles*.   l. 6. *syth to mych*: say too much.

stza. 3, l. 2. *objurgacyon*: chiding. *O.E.D.* records from 1550.

stza. 6, ll. 1, 2. A bit of lore ultimately derived from Pliny, *Naturalis Historia*, lib. xxxvii, cap. xv: '. . . hircino rumpitur sanguine.'

stza. 7, l. 1. *scald*: scabbed. See B. J. W., *Proverbs*, H 229.

408. Strife in the House

Pr. Dyboski, p. 110; Flügel, 'Lieder.', p. 271. B.–R. 65.

stza. 1, l. 3. See B. J. W., *Proverbs*, G 399.

stza. 2, l. 3. *shrew shake*: '? cured of shrewishness', *O.E.D.* 'Shrewishly inclined' (Dyboski) fits the context better.

stza. 8, l. 3. *the*: thrive.

stza. 9, l. 3. *ouerthrew*: fell over.

409. The Old Man Worsted

Pr. Wright, *P.S.* xxiii. 51; J. E. Masters, *Rymes of the Minstrels* (Shaftesbury, 1927), p. 27; Sisam, p. 481. B.–R. 3593.

burden, l. 1. This exclamation, repeated as refrain, is found in other songs and seems to have a connotation of complaint. Compare the bird-allegory lyric in B.M. MS. Addit. 5665, f. 146ᵛ, 'Hay how the mavys / on a brere' (*pr.* Fehr, pp. 264–5), and the variants in No. 405 (How, hey!), No. 413 A (Hay, hay), and No. 425 (Hay, hay, hay, hay!).

stza. 1, l. 3. *plyght*: twisted, tangled.

stza. 4. The old man's choice of excuse contains an implicit allusion to a well-known and appropriate proverb, used by Innocent III in the form: 'Tria sunt quae non sinunt hominem in domo permanere: fumus, stillicidium, et mala uxor.' See Archer Taylor, *The Proverb* (Cambridge, Massachusetts, 1931), pp. 40, 50, 58, 160–4, and B. J. W., *Proverbs*, T 187.

410. Women Will Have Their Word

a. *Pr.* Dyboski, p. 109; Flügel, 'Lieder.', p. 269.

b. *Pr.* Wright, *P.S.* xxiii. 86; J. E. Masters, *Rymes of the Minstrels* (Shaftesbury, 1927), p. 24. B.–R. 2090.

The burden is possibly a parody of the famous Easter Prose, 'Victimae paschali laudes', strophe 4 (*Sar. Miss.*, p. 468):

> Dic nobis maria quid vidistis in via.

An English burden perhaps suggested by this one is found in a satirical piece on the clergy of the late sixteenth century in Victoria and Albert Museum MS. Dyce 43, f. 22ʳ:

> In towne-a, in towne-a,
> God wolde hyt were layde down-a.

Utley (pp. 187–8) would interpret the stanzas as a dialogue 'in need of a series of quotation marks'. But when it is remembered that the burden, sung as a chorus after each stanza, is a question which in effect is given another answer by the soloist of the stanzas, the need for postulating two speakers is not established. Utley misreads 'lyberall' in stza. 3: '. . . women are right liberal and speak only to defend themselves.' Here, as in No. 399, stza. 1, l. 3, it means talkative, indiscreet in speech, and is not a word of praise. In view of the context of material prosperity set by stza. 13 there is probably no implication of cuckoldry, such as Utley suggests, in the proverb of stza. 14.

stza. 1, ll. 1, 2. These two lines, with the pronouns of the second reversed, are spoken by 'Ancilla' in Henry Medwall's *Fulgens and Lucres* (repr. facs., N.Y., 1921, sig. c₅ᵛ):

> Many a man blamyth his wyf parde
> And she is more to blame than he.

stza. 5, l. 3. Compare Lydgate's 'A Mumming at Hertford', ll. 63–4 (pr. MacCracken, part ii, p. 677).

stza. 13, l. 1. A proverb of wide currency. See B. J. W., *Proverbs*, S 830. It is one of the very few proverbial phrases which B. J. Whiting's survey finds in popular ballads (Child, Nos. 83 F, 112 D). See Introduction, p. clxxii and Whiting's 'Proverbial Material in the Popular Ballads', *The Journal of American Folk-Lore*, xlvii (1934), 36. ll. 2, 3. See B. J. W., *Proverbs* ,L 164.

stza. 14, l. 3. i.e. he shall go in rags. See B. J. W., *Proverbs*, H 22.

411. Of the Decadence of Marriage

Pr. C. & S., *M.L.R.* vi. 78; Whiting, p. 208. B.–R. 1630.

This carol, with the exception of the burden and first stanza, is taken bodily from another poem by Audelay which is in long stanzas (Whiting, No. 1, ll. 78–103). Except for a few insignificant verbal changes, the only alteration necessary was to omit the short lines joining the quatrains of the long stanzas and to replace them by the tag 'All day thou sist'.

burden, l. 2. One of the most frequently quoted English proverbs. For a long list of its occurrences see notes by H. E. Rollins in his editions of *The Paradise of Dainty Devices* (Cambridge, Massachusetts, 1927), p. 182, and *A Handful of Pleasant Delights* (Cambridge, Massachusetts, 1924), p. 104. It is made into a couplet with the same rhyme-word as in this burden in B.M. MS. Harley 2252, f. 3ʳ, ll. 56–7 (*pr.* F. J. Furnivall, *Queene Elizabethes Achademy*, E.E.T.S., Ex. Ser. No. viii, 1869, 69–70):

> Beware, my son, ever of 'had-I-wyste';
> hard ys to know whom on may tryst[e].

See also B. J. W., *Proverbs*, H 9.

stza. 1, l. 3. *gam and gle*: sport and mirth.

stza. 3, l. 2. 'The parties to a match should be equal in birth, in wealth, and in age!'

stza. 5, l. 3. *chesyn*. Whiting's emendation.

stza. 6. Audelay's attack may here be directed against the putting into practice of the theorics ot courtly love. He is a strong believer in social distinctions. Compare No. 347.

stza. 7. Fashionable adultery not only is a disgrace to the upper classes but also creates unrightful heirs to places and wealth.

412. A Carol of Childhood

Pr. C. & S., *M.L.R.* vi. 69; Whiting, p. 197. B.–R. 840.

The attitude of reverence for childhood expressed by Audelay in this carol is unusual in the Middle Ages and has been deservedly praised. Nevertheless, the expression of it is rather stiff and conventional with its systematic introduction of the Deadly Sins and is more probably inspired by the words of Jesus (Matthew xviii. 3, Mark x. 15, Luke xviii. 17) than by sympathetic association with real children. With the pleasant touch of the cherry-stones in stza. 2, l. 4, compare Lydgate's condemnation of his youthful self for the same play ('Testament', ll. 646–8, *pr.* MacCracken, part i, p. 353):

> My wyttes fyve in wast I did alle vse,
> Redier cheristones for to telle
> Than gon to chirche, or here the sacryng belle.

stza. 1, l. 2. i.e. he assumes no worldly dignity.

stza. 3, l. 4. *mystere*: bodily need.

stza. 4, l. 1. *algate*: at any rate.

413. The Schoolboy's Complaint

A. *Pr.* F. J. Furnivall, *The Babees Book* (E.E.T.S., Or. Ser., No. 32, 1868), p. 403; Flügel, 'Lieder.', p. 283; B. White, *The Vulgaria of John Stanbridge* [etc.], (E.E.T.S., Or. Ser., No. 187, 1932), p. xii; H. S. Bennett, *England from Chaucer to Caxton* (London, 1928), p. 45; Kaiser, *Med. Engl.*, p. 559 (omits burden); Greene, *Selection*, p. 145; Sisam, p. 544; Davies, p. 289

B. *Previously unpublished.*

B.–R. 1399.

The contents of this carol, as well as the fairly frequent occurrence of carol-texts in MSS.

containing school notes, e.g. Gonville & Caius College, Cambridge, 383, Corpus Christi College, Cambridge, 233, and B.M. Cotton Titus A. xxvi, suggest that schoolboys, as well as monks and friars, were recorders and transmitters of carols.

Compare the even more rebellious monologue of a much-beaten schoolboy from Lincoln Cathedral MS. 132, f. 100ʳ, in which it is inserted between the school texts of the *Accentuarius* and *Dictionarius* (*pr*. Robbins, *Secular Lyrics*, p. 105):

> Wenest þu, huscher, with þi coyntyse,
> Iche day beten us on þis wyse,
> As þu wer lord of toun?

and the reminiscence of a sad old man in 'The Day of Life—Night Comes Soon!', ll. 33–6 (*pr*. Brown, *R.L. 15 C.*, pp. 230–3):

> At vnder-day to skole I was I-sete,
> To lerne good as chyldern dothe,
> But when my master woold me bete,
> I wold hym cowrs & wax folle rowthe.

See also Sydney H. Nicholson, *Quires and Places Where They Sing* (London, 1942), p. 25.

The 'Lamentation of Boys Learning Prick-Song' quoted in the note to this carol in *Selection* is confidently declared by Sydney Race to be not by John Redford, Choirmaster of St. Paul's, but one of the forgeries of John Payne Collier ('The Moral Play of Wit and Science', *N. & Q.* cxcviii, 1953, 392).

A. stza. 1, l. 3. The schoolboy is not exaggerating. Compare 'The anatomy or particular description of a byrchen broome or besome' (an adaptation of a popular ballad), in John Hall, *The Court of Virtue* (1565), ed. Russell A. Fraser (New Brunswick, New Jersey, 1961), p. 266, ll. 18–25:

> A byrchen besome that ye a broome calle,
> Is made of a wyth, a staffe, and twygs smalle:
> By whych all folke of eche age and estate,
> May gouerned be, yf nourture they hate,
> As fyrst the smalle twygges do serue a good shyft,
> The buttockes of boyes to hoyse vp or lyft.
> From which it is sometymes nedefull to draw,
> Abundance of bloud to kepe them in awe.

A. stza. 2, l. 2. *vi of the clok*. The usual time for children to rise. If our scholar had been at Eton at about this time, he would have kept even earlier hours. See G. G. Coulton, *Social Life in Britain from the Conquest to the Reformation* (Cambridge, 1918), p. 81. The later hour in B would have been quite exceptional.   l. 3. *avise*: consideration, i.e. argument.

A. stza. 3, l. 3. *Milked dukkes*. A saucy answer equivalent to 'None of your business'. Compare *E.D.D.*, s.v. 'Duck sb¹ 2. Phr. (3): [West Yorkshire]. . . . This curious answer is made to an inquisitive person: "What is to' doin?" "Mucking ducks wi' an elsin [Cleansing ducks with a shoemaker's awl]." ' In Skelton's *Magnificence* the character Counterfeit Collusion exclaims, in derision of wives who ape new and courtly fashions: 'What, Margery Milk Duck, marmoset!' (*The Complete Poems of John Skelton Laureate*, ed. Philip Henderson, 3rd edn., London, 1959, p. 179).

A. stza. 4, l. 2. *fynkyll sede*: fennel seed; the beating was sharper than fennel sauce.   l. 3. That chastisement as vigorous as this was not unusual is amusingly shown by the *vulgaria* from Magdalen College School, Oxford, in B.M. MS. Arundel 249 (*pr*. William Nelson, *A Fifteenth Century School Book*, Oxford, 1956, pp. 13–14):

> 'I wyll make youe an example by a cosyn of myne that [was sent] to his absey [ABC's] hereby at the next-dore. and if he come wepynge after his maister hath charede [driven] away the flees from his skynne, anone his mother loketh onn his buttockys yf the stryppys be a-sen. And the stryppys appere, she wepyth and waileth and fareth as she were made. then she complayneth of the cruelte of techers . . .' Such pampering, says the author, brings to a bad end, even to hanging or beheading!

A. stza. 5, l. 1. *watt*: hare.   l. 3. *toppe*: top of the book.

The very fragmentary text of B is probably a jotting from an imperfect memory of a heard text rather than a copy from a written one.

414. The Wandering Bachelor

Pr. Wright, *P.S.* xxiii. 27; C. & S., p. 210; J. E. Masters, *Rymes of the Minstrels* (Shaftesbury, 1927), p. 7; H. S. Bennett, *England from Chaucer to Caxton* (London, 1928), p. 31; Robbins, *Secular Lyrics*, p. 6; Sisam, p. 477. B.–R. 1468.

stza. 2, l. 3. *rennyng at the ball*: probably stool-ball, as that was the principal ball-game in which maidens joined with men and which involved running. See F. W. Hackwood, *Old English Sports* (London, 1907), p. 141.

stza. 3, l. 1. *lat lyght be*: think little of.

stza. 4. The bachelor of the carol is apparently a chapman or pedlar, or it may be a cheery friar; compare No. 416.

415. The Carol of Jack Reckless

Pr. James & Macaulay, p. 80. B.–R. 4078.

stza. 1, l. 1. *bornys*: barns.   l. 2. i.e. he will help himself to what he needs.   l. 3. *wolle*: will.

stza. 2, l. 3. *hem*: i.e. other men.   *hye dese*: the high dais, the regular seat of the lord and his guests. Jack will have nothing to do with that class of persons.

stza. 4, l. 2. *the*: thrive.   l. 3. *red*: advise.

416. A Pedlar's Carol

Pr. Wright, *Wart. Club*, p. 76; T. Wright, *Songs and Carols* (London, 1836), No. xvi; Robbins, *Secular Lyrics*, p. 6; Tydeman, p. 64; Oliver, p. 106; B.–R. 3864.

burden, l. 2. The wretched condition of nearly all roads in the Middle Ages was notorious. To be 'light of foot' and without a heavy pack was a great advantage.

stza. 1. The rogue of this song contrasts his 'wares' with those of the ordinary pedlar, or possibly of the wandering friar. Compare Chaucer's Friar with his tippet 'farsed ful of knyves', and Wycliffe's account of friars in his tract 'On the Leaven of the Pharisees' (F. D. Matthew, ed., *The English Works of Wyclif hitherto Unprinted*, E.E.T.S., Or. Ser., No. 74, 1880, 12):

ʒif þei becomen pedderis berynge knyues, pursis, pynnys and girdlis and spices and sylk and precious pellure and forrouris for wymmen, and þerto smale gentil hondis, to gete loue of them and to haue many grete ʒiftis for litil good ore nouʒt; þei coueiten euyle here neiʒeboris goodis.

See also the song against the friars printed by Thomas Wright (*Political Poems and Songs*, Rolls Series, London, 1859, i. 264):

> For thai have noght to lyve by,
>   thai wandren here and there,
> And dele with dyvers marcerye,
>   right as thai pedlers were.
>
> Thai dele with purses, pynnes, and knyves,
> With gyrdles, gloves, for wenches and wyves;
> Bot ever bacward the husband thryves
>   Ther thai are haunted tille.

The same theme was utilized in Elizabethan times by the eccentric Thomas Whythorne, who wrote in his own appalling system of spelling a ballad 'vpon an old grownd [tune] (on þe which I had seen the lyk mad befor)':

> Der was A frier men kald Robard
>   sing busk vnder þe brier
> And all þat euer he met hee mard
>   it waz A venʒeans frier.
>
> Hee war no bre[e]ch hiz gear grew wyld
>   sing busk vnter þe brier
> þe maidz and wyvz hee gat with chyld
>   it waz A freutful frier

> Hee gav þem lases, needlz and pinz
> sing busk vnder þe brier
> which giftz of women much loov winz
> it was A pleazing frier
>
> (stzas. 1, 5, 6; James M. Osborn, ed., *The Autobiography of Thomas Whythorne*,
> Oxford, 1961, pp. 125–6)

stza. 2, l. 4. *rathere*: sooner.

stza. 3, l. 1. *jelyf*: jelly; here slang for penis, rather than the suggestion in *O.E.D.*: 'perh[aps] in imitation of jolif, archaic form of jolly.' Compare the seventeenth-century piece 'A Man's Yard', Bodl. MS. Rawlinson poet. 216, f. 94ᵛ, stza. 2, l. 4: 'That ne're had feet, and yet can stand' (*pr.* John S. Farmer, *Merry Songs and Ballads, repr.* N.Y., 1964, i. 10). *sonde*: gift. l. 4. *Ryd*: guess.

stza. 4, l. 1. A 'powder' of directly contrary effect was offered by a mountebank in a carol or antimasque in *Gesta Grayorum*, part ii:

> This powder doth preserve from fate.
> This cures the maleficiate;
> Lost maidenhead this doth restore,
> And make them virgins as before.
>
> (John Nichols, *The Progresses and Public Processions of Queen Elizabeth*,
> new edn., London, 1823, iii. 332)

417. The Braggart and His Baselard

Pr. Wright, *Wart. Club*, p. 84; T. Wright, *Songs and Carols* (London, 1836), No. xvii; F. W. Fairholt, *P.S.* xxvii, 'Satirical Songs and Poems on Costume', 50; C. & S., p. 243; Sisam, p. 442. B.–R. 1896.

Though the speaker in this carol is apparently a young layman, the baselard, or long dagger worn at the girdle, constituted a disciplinary problem at the college of Higham Ferrers, according to a report made to Bishop William Alnwick during his visitation of July 1442: 'Also he says that certain chaplains of the college wear long baslards beneath their gowns, for what purpose he knows not, and that they haunt the public taverns, to wit, Calvertone and Munde; and the master is slack in correcting these matters. The chaplains appeared and make denial' (A. Hamilton Thompson, ed., *Visitations of Religious Houses in the Diocese of Lincoln*, ii, The Lincoln Record Society, xiv, 1918, 137, Latin text facing).

burden, l. 1. *Prenegard*: the warning of a provoked and armed man.

stza. 1, l. 2. *leke*: a common term of contempt. See B. J. W., *Proverbs*, L 185.

stza. 2, l. 1. *schede*: sheath.   l. 2. *loket*: a plate or band on the sheath.

stza. 3, l. 1. *wrethin*: decorated with scroll-work.

stza. 4, l. 1. *schape*: cross-bar or guard.   l. 2. *gaspe and gape*: yawn as a sign of nonchalance. l. 3. *knape*: knave, rascal.

stza. 5, l. 1. *trencher*: blade.

stza. 8, l. 2. *panne*: brain-pan.

418. Fare Far and Have Little

Pr. Greene, *Selection*, p. 146. B.–R. 3971.

The note written before the burden of this carol to indicate the air of another piece to which it is to be sung is especially interesting, as we have two other songs which begin with the same words: 'alone y lyve alone'. Both are in later MSS. One is No. 450.1. The preservation of the second line of its burden confirms that the burden of this carol should be accented thus:

> Hos ís to hóth at hóm,
> Ryd oút; it wól agón.

The other occurrence is in B.M. MS. Addit. 31922, f. 22ʳ (*pr.*, with music, Stevens, *Henry VIII*, p. 17). The verbal text is the same.

All three of the preserved songs seem to have derived from a popular prototype: this carol with its good advice against vagabondage and its pious conclusion, and the two much more courtly love-songs, one with part-music and the other in a collection of part-songs.

The same burden appears with a short *chanson d'aventure* of the Passion in Richard Kele's print (No. 164):

> [Alo]ne, alone, alone, alone,
> Sore I sygh, and all for one.

It is apparent that in England as well as in France and other countries sophisticated poets and composers of secular as well as sacred pieces drew freely on texts in more general circulation for the starting-points of their compositions. See Stevens, *M. & P.*, pp. 40–8, 390.

burden, l. 1. *Hos*: whoso, whoever.

stza. 2, l. 3. *fawe*: fain, glad.

stza. 3, l. 4. *Myche yerne*: very swift, active: 'a fast rolling stone'. See B. J. W., *Proverbs*, L 400.

stza. 4, l. 1. *groute*: root or dig up the earth, i.e. work on the land.

stza. 5, l. 3. *halwen*: saints.

418.1. Huff! A Gallant!

Pr. F. J. Furnivall, *Academy*, 1269 (29 August 1896), p. 146; Robbins, *Hist. Poems*, p. 138. B.-R. 892.

The type of strutting and boastful dandy satirized in this carol appears both in other poems and songs and in late medieval drama. A long macaronic poem found in several MSS. and beginning 'Syng I wolde, but alas! *descendunt prospera grata*' has a line which reads 'Huf a galaunt the atowch, *unguentum stillat amoris*' (*pr.* F. W. Fairholt, 'Satirical Songs and Poems on Costume', *P.S.* xxvii, 1849, p. 47, l. 89; for other versions see B.-R. 3113). An acrostic poem on the Deadly Sins shows another gallant (*pr.* Hazlitt, *Remains*, iii. 131 and elsewhere; see B.-R. 1874 for another occurrence). A lively character named Curiosity proclaims himself a gallant in the Digby play of Mary Magdalene; his entrance speech announces:

> Hof, hof, hof, a frysch new galavnt,
> ware of thryst, ley þat a-doune!
> (ed. F. J. Furnivall, E.E.T.S., Ex. Ser., No. lxx, 1896, 73)

A conspicuous parallel to this carol is found in the character Sensual Appetite in John Rastell's interlude *The Nature of the Four Elements*, who sings:

> Make rome syrs and let vs be mery
> with huffa galand synge tyrll on the bery,
> And let the wyde worlde wynde.
> Synge fryska Ioly with hey troly loly,
> For I se well it is but a foly
> For to haue a sad mind.
> (ed. John S. Farmer, The Tudor Facsimile Texts, London, 1908, sig. B₂ᵛ)

burden, l. 1. *Huff*: In addition to the instances just cited, this exclamation occurs in similar use by the character Riot in *The Interlude of Youth*: 'Huffa! huffa! who calleth after me?' (W. C. Hazlitt, *A Selection of Old Plays*, London, 1874, ii. 13) and as applied to a woman in the poem 'The Pryde and Abuse of Women':

> Huffa! goldylocx, joly lusty goldylocx;
> A wantontricker is come to towne.
> (Hazlitt, *Remains*, iv. 239, ll. 117–18)

l. 2. *vylabele*: willable, to be desired. It does not fit the context very well; a corruption of some other text may be suspected.

stza. 3, l. 1. *stomager*: at this period a man's waistcoat.   l. 3. *pyked schone*: see note on No. 387, stza. 2, l. 3, and Robbins's note (*Hist. Poems*), p. 323, on the prohibition of these long 'pikes' by law in 1465. The poem in B.M. MS. Harley 372 beginning 'Ye prowd galonttes hertlesse' has as the first two lines of its second stanza:

> With youre longe peked schone,
> Therfor your thrifte is almost don.
> (Thomas Wright, ed., *Political Poems and Songs*, Rolls Series, London, 1859–61, ii. 251)

stza. 4, l. 1. *haue thy hele*: keep thy health.   l. 2. *fele*: many.

stza. 5, ll. 2, 3. Compare 'Ye prowd galonttes hertlesse', stza. 4, l. 3: 'Leve your schort stiffid dowbelettes and your pleytid gownys.'

stza. 7, l. 3. *swere*: neck.

stza. 8, l. 2. *bulwerk*: padding above or at the knees, perhaps in imitation of military dress. See *Middle English Dictionary*, s.v. 'bulwerk', n. 2. Furnivall's suggestion of 'ruff' (Robbins, loc. cit.) will not do.

stza. 9, l. 2. *crosse*: Any English coin marked on one face with a cross. l. 3. *Crystes curse*: slang for emptiness of purse. Compare 'Crystofer catchepoll [a petty bailiff] a crystes course gaderer' in *Cock Lorell's Bote* (ed. E. F. Rimbault, *P.S.* vi, 1843, 4, l. 20), and the poem against pride cited by Robbins (loc. cit.): 'He putth hys hand in hys powrs cum nichyll intus fuerat/ He ffownd non þer saw godeys cowrs hoc non sibi deerat' (B.-R. 2774); also Hoccleve, *De Regimine Principum*, ll. 655–6: 'The feende, men seyne, may hoppe in a pouche/ whan that no crosse therein may appeare.'

stza. 10, l. 2. A purse hanging outside the clothes was regarded as foppish.

418.2. Speed the Plough

Music for two and three voices. *Pr.* Padelford, p. 104; C. & S., p. 241; [Sir] E. K. Chambers, *English Literature at the Close of the Middle Ages* (Oxford, 1945), p. 95; Robbins, *Hist. Poems*, p. 97; Greene, *Selection*, p. 147; Sisam, p. 382; with music, Stevens, *Med. Carols*, p. 112; *E.B.M.* ii. 132, *facs*. No. lxix. B.-R. *Supp.* 1405.5.

This delightful carol, omitted from the first edition of this work, has been properly recognized as belonging to the genre by Stevens (*Med. Carols*, 1st edn., 1952, p. 124) on 'the balance of the evidence', of which the stanza-marks prefixed to each group of three lines are the strongest (see also review of *Med. Carols* by M. F. Bukofzer, *J.A.M.S.*, vii, 1954, 64). The pairing of successive three-line stanzas by the rhyme of their final lines shows that the lyric was not first written as a carol but was adapted to the form from a song in six-line stanzas, a common medieval metre. There is no way of telling whether this adaptation was made by the composer of the music in this MS. or by some predecessor. The manner of its performance is unusual: the burden is sung in two parts, its last line repeated in three, and the stanza sung first in two parts and repeated in three.

As Stevens has pointed out, the carol is very probably intended for use on Plough Monday, the first Monday after the Epiphany. Plough Monday celebrations and feasts are recorded into modern times from many parts of England, frequent features being the drawing through the village streets of a decorated plough by the young men, with singing, dancing, and *quête*. This carol, of course, is intended for more sophisticated performance, probably by choir-boys. It would be highly appropriate to Worcester Priory, which had a number of agricultural manors and much business with plough-land, ploughmen, and oxen. See, for example, Sidney Graves Hamilton, ed., *Compotus Rolls of the Priory of Worcester of the XIVth and XVth Centuries*, Worcestershire Historical Society, 1910, *passim*.

The ploughman figures, sometimes perfunctorily, in many songs from modern oral tradition, for example, a version of *The Jolly Ploughboy* (Aldingbourne, Sussex, *c*. 1850–60) which was used as a Christmas carol and begins with Cain and Abel (Annie G. Gilchrist, *J.F.S.S.* viii, 1931, 136). For other traditional songs see *Guide*: (The) Pretty/Simple Plough-Boy, p. 99; (The) Painful/Faithful Plough, p. 98; (The) Oxen Ploughing, loc. cit.; (The) Lark in The Morn, p. 83.

stza. 2, l. 3. *in the clay*. This would be appropriate to a carol from Worcestershire, where much of the soil in about half the county is a heavy clay (*V.C.H.*, *Worcester*, London, 1906, ii. 310–12).

stza. 3, l. 3. '(God) speed the plough' is, of course, a widely used expression and toast through the centuries. It it is on the wall of many an inn today as a decorated motto or combined with a pictorial figure in a print. Robbins (p. 301) refers to the Middle English poem in twelve stanzas in B.M. MS. Lansdowne 762, f. 5ʳ (*pr.* W. W. Skeat, *Pierce the Ploughmans Crede*, E.E.T.S., Or. Ser., No. 30, 1867, 69–72), to a play 'God spede the Plough', acted in 1593 and 1594, and to a book of the same title entered in the Stationers' Register in 1601.

stza. 4, l. 1. *Browne Morel* and *Gore*. 'Browne' and 'Morel' (dark-coloured) seem to be the names of the plough-oxen. 'Gore' has presented difficulty to previous editors. Neither Stevens's 'dark-coloured' nor Robbins's suggestion of 'gray' meets the case. It is more likely that it is a dialect word for 'goad' and that the meaning is either 'Brown, Morel, and the goad' or alternatively, with 'Brown' as an adjective, 'Brown Morel and Gore', the second ox being named for the goad. 'Gored stick' with the meaning 'cattle goad' is found in a recent version of an American folk-song (Alan Lomax, ed., *The Folk Songs of North America*, Garden City, N.Y., 1960, p. 111). In any event there can be only two proper names:

> Thre oxen in plowgh may neuer wel drawe,
> Noþer be craft, ryȝt, ne lawe
> ('The Boke of Curtasye', bk. ii, ll. 287–8, *The Babees Book*, p. 307)

'Morel' appears more often as the name of a horse, e.g. in the sixteenth-century 'A merry Ieste of a Shrewde and curste Wyfe lapped in Morelles skin' (*pr.* Hazlitt, *Remains*, iv. 180–226), where 'morel' means 'black'.

Nevertheless, it seems certain that oxen rather than horses are the animals of this carol. 'Oxen rather than horses dragged the plough: they were more manageable and cheaper and when they were past service they provided meat' (Paul Murray Kendall, *The Yorkist Age: Daily Life During the Wars of the Roses*, N.Y., 1962, p. 197). Extremely interesting details about the use of oxen and horses with the medieval plough are given by Rowland E. Prothero, *English Farming, Past and Present* (London, 1912), pp. 12–13.

In the chorus of a ploughboy's song in modern oral tradition, 'known throughout Devon and Cornwall at the beginning of the 19th century', the names of oxen are introduced in much the same fashion as in the carol:

> With my Hump-a-long! Jump-a-long!
> Here drives my lad along!
> Pretty, Sparkle, Berry,
> Good-luck, Speedwell, Cherry!
> We are the lads that can follow the plough.
> (S. Baring-Gould, H. Fleetwood Sheppard, and F. W. Bussell, eds., *Songs of the West*,
> 5th edn., ed. Cecil J. Sharp, London, [1913], pp. 16–17)

A parallel from French folk-song is quoted in the notes, p. 17.

stza. 5. The injunction to reward the oxen with sheaves is figurative and apparently equivalent to saying, 'Treat them like the human labourers', the men's bonus at harvest-time being reckoned in sheaves. This was the case as early as 1182 at Ripple, Worcs., where it was established that 'those who bind sheaves at reaping shall have a sheaf each; those who stack the corn likewise' (translated from Latin original, Marjory Hollings, ed., *The Red Book of Worcester*, Worcestershire Historical Society, 1934, p. 169). In Aberdeenshire this reward is no ordinary sheaf, but the last one of the reaping, ceremoniously and reverently cut and gathered and kept in the truss till Christmas morning, when it is given to one or more of the horses or cattle (Mrs. Macleod Banks, ed., *British Calendar Customs, Scotland*, i, Publications of the Folk-Lore Society, London, 1937, 63).

There must have been many songs of the plough of true folk-origin in actual work, like spinning and milking songs, for the medieval ploughman would sing at his work for a practical reason, as would the milkmaid or the American cowboy. The thirteenth-century *Fleta* tells us:

> The Plough-driver's art consisteth herein, that he drive the yoked oxen evenly, neither smiting nor pricking nor grieving them. Such should not be melancholy or wrathful, but cheerful, jocund and full of song, that by their melody and song the oxen may in a manner rejoice in their labour (G. G. Coulton, *Social Life in Britain from the Conquest to the Reformation*, Cambridge, 1919, p. 166).

It is conceivable that a carol on this theme may be the result of a learned clerical composer's interest in an air heard in the fields. At least it has been reported that the 'tone or tune with which the driving of oxen is accompanied is mentioned by agricultural writers as resembling the chanting of a cathedral service' (Moore, *History of Devonshire*, i. 426 n., quoted by the editor of *Report and Transactions of the Devonshire Association*, xxxvii, 1905, 116).

stza. 7, l. 3. See B. J. W., *Proverbs*, G 239.

418.3. The Fox and the Goose

Pr. R. H. Bowers, *Journal of English and Germanic Philology*, li (1952), 393; Robbins, *Secular Lyrics*, p. 43; George Perkins, *Journal of American Folklore*, lxxiv (1961), 235; Sisam, p. 511. B.–R. 1622.

That this piece is in carol-form was first recognized by R. H. Robbins ('The Burden in Carols', *Modern Language Notes*, lvii, 1942, 22).

George Perkins has made an exhaustive and valuable study of the widely disseminated English and American folk-song which recounts a similar exploit by a fox and has some verbal and metrical likeness to the medieval carol ('A Medieval Carol Survival: "The Fox and the Goose"', *Journal of American Folklore*, lxxiv, 1961, 235-44; see also his later article, ibid. lxxvii, 1964, 263-5). It is clear that there are elements in the modern song which must derive from the fifteenth century or earlier; perhaps even a common ancestor can be postulated for this carol-text and the very popular modern folk-song. But the many texts of the latter collected and analysed by Perkins are hardly to be regarded as variants close enough to be collated at large in this edition. The initial burden is not found in any modern text. The frequency of 'town' or a word rhyming with it as the final word of stanzas is significant. Noticeable also is the rhyme-pattern of stza. 2: 'yard, feared, beard', which is found in the text quoted by Perkins from Sabine Baring-Gould's *Songs of the West* (revised edn., London, [1906]):

> At last he came to a farmer's yard,
> Where ducks and geese were all afear'd,
> 'The best of you shall grease my beard,
> Before I leave the Town O!'

But the rhyme 'yerde, ferde' occurs in the song not in carol-form found in James Ryman's MS. and printed by Robbins, *Secular Lyrics*, p. 44, with the title 'The False Fox'), as does the rhyme of 'neck' with a form of 'quack' (here delightfully 'wheccumquek'). We are obviously seeing outcroppings of an underlying layer of stanzaic popular poems on the central theme of a farmyard foray by a fox.

It is interesting, if nothing more, that the French lines written on the page following this carol in the MS. use a trapped Reynard as a metaphor in a brief satire on marriage:

> Puisque je suis a mesnage,
> Je my tendray sagement.
> Je soulloye estre sauuage;
> Je suis priue maintenant.
> Aucunes gens vont disant
> Que Regnart es attrape
> Puisque je suis marie.
>
> (Sir George F. Warner and Julius P. Gilson, *Catalogue of Western Manuscripts in the Old Royal and King's Collections*, ii, London, 1921)

stza. 2, l. 3. I shall overcome some of you.
stza. 4, l. 1. *all be the heye*: in a twinkling (Robbins).
stza. 6, l. 2. *to eke*: besides.   l. 4. *Will*: while.

419. The Gossips' Meeting

A a. *Pr.* Dyboski, p. 106; Flügel, *N.L.*, p. 149, 'Lieder.', p. 208; A. S. Cook, *A Literary Middle English Reader* (Boston, 1915), p. 372; Greene, *Selection*, p. 148; Sisam, p. 537;.

  b. *Pr.* Wright, *P.S.* xxiii. 91; H. Macaulay Fitzgibbon, *Early English and Scottish Poetry* (London, 1888), p. 226; H. S. Bennett, *England from Chaucer to Caxton* (London, 1928), p. 134 (in part); G. G. Coulton, *Life in the Middle Ages* (Cambridge, 1954), iii. 141; Kaiser, *Med. Engl.*, p. 479 (in part); M. Pollet, *John Skelton*, Études anglaises, No. 9 (Paris, 1962), p. 251; J. E. Masters, *The Gossips* (Shaftesbury, 1926). B.-R. 1362.

  B. *Pr.* Ritson, *Ancient Songs* (1790), p. 77, (1829), i. 136, (1877), p. 117; Dyboski, p. 187; Wright, *P.S.* xxiii. 104; Edward Arber, *The Dunbar Anthology* (London, 1901), p. 108; Flügel, 'Lieder.', p. 213 (in part). B.-R. *32; *Supp.* 2358.5.

  C. *Pr.* R. H. Robbins, *British Museum Quarterly*, xxvii (1963), 12.

Robbins's valuable discovery of C provides a text of the initial stanzas which are missing from B because of the defect in the MS. Several leaves are missing immediately before f. 161ʳ, at the top of which the remaining text begins. The abbreviated form, 'gode gosyp', as written at the side of each stanza, is all that remains of the burden. The MS. spaces the version as comprising three stanzas of ten lines each without a burden. He thinks it 'probably the original version'.

Some such piece as this was doubtless the model for 'The Good Gossippes songe' in the Chester play of the Deluge (ed. H. Deimling, E.E.T.S., Ex. Ser., No. lxii, 1893, 57). This is the more probable as the MS. is connected with Mobberly, Cheshire, not far from Chester. Stanza 15 of this version contains a local allusion, not identified:

> Gadyr the scote, and lette us wend,
> And lette us goo home by Lurcas Ende.

One may conjecture a temporary place-name of 'Lucas End' from the dwelling in Watergate Street of Henry Lucas, 'hopper', who in 1542 was among the sixteen important tenants summoned to stand the special Christmas watch. Watergate Street was one of the places where disreputable ale-rooms were to be found in cellars. A hopper must have been a dealer in hops, introduced only in 1524, regarded as an adulterant by Noah's wife in the Chester play, and forbidden by statute later in the same reign. Chester was notorious as the only city permitting females between fourteen and forty to keep ale-houses, a practice eventually prohibited because of the resulting 'great slander and dishonest report' (Rupert H. Morris, *Chester in the Plantagenet and Tudor Reigns*, [Chester, 1895], pp. 236, 248, 314, 425, 431).

A song in Pepys's collection of ballads (Magdalene College, Cambridge, Pepysian Library, i. 436–7) tells of 'Fowre wittie Gossips' whose meeting to drink wine parallels much of the action of this carol.

Utley (pp. 152–3, 241–3) calls the carol the closest parallel to Skelton's *The Tunning of Eleanor Rummyng*, which he says may have some verbal echoes. Both poems use the theme of the gathering of 'gossips' at an alehouse, and there are some points of likeness in details, though not in verse-form. H. L. R. Edwards points to the similarities in *Skelton: The Life and Times of a Tudor Poet* (London, 1949), p. 117. Maurice Pollet overemphasizes the connection in calling the carol 'une source inédite du poème' and printing as his second appendix the text of A b from Wright with 'parallels' from *Eleanor Rumming* (op. cit., pp. 131, 251–4). The only significant verbal parallel is the use of the names Elinour, Joan, Margery, Alice, and Cicely, which can hardly be thought a coincidence. Pollet ignores texts A a, B, and of course C. Utley also cites similarities in the prose *The gospelles of dystaues* in the Huntington Library (not reprinted), 'Leve, lystynes to me' in National Library of Wales, MS. Porkington 10 (*pr.* F. J. Furnivall, *Jyl of Breyntford's Testament*, London, 1871, p. 27), the play of *Tom Tyler* (*c.* 1558, known from the 'second impression' of a century later), and Dunbar's 'The Ballad of Kynd Kittok' (W. M. Mackenzie, ed., *The Poems of William Dunbar*, London, 1960, p. 169). The last-named is rather remote.

The theme is used again, without verbal parallels to the carol, in the long and dull poem *'Tis Merrie When Gossips Meete* (London, 1602, *repr.* Hunterian Club Publications, No. 30, Glasgow, n.d.). In this piece the harper's proffered services are refused. The theme of discussion of the gossips' husbands is ironically expanded and systematized in the nineteenth tale of *Merie Tales of the Mad Men of Gotham* (1630) by 'A. B. of Phisike Doctour' (ed. Stanley J. Kahrl, The Renaissance English Text Society, Evanston, Illinois, 1965, pp. 17–18).

In B 'Frankelyne the harper' comes in and plays for the gossips' dancing. Utley thinks that this suggests the use of the carol by minstrels, hardly a necessary inference. The last stanza solicits payment for the song, but it does not imply any instrumental accompaniment such as a minstrel would give; it could well be spoken by an amateur like one of the craftsmen-players. The change in the rhyme-scheme suggests that this conclusion is not an organic part of the carol. The colophon perhaps indicates a lack of success with the appeal: 'Exsplycyte lytyll thanke'.

Nan Cooke Carpenter remarks that the song of the gossips in the Chester play 'is a unique inter-polation [of secular music in the plays]. Here for the first time in any play, as far as we know, is a vernacular song used for specifically dramatic purposes' ('Music in the English Mystery Plays', *Music in English Renaissance Drama*, ed. John H. Long, Lexington, Kentucky, 1968, p. 16).

stza. 1, ll. 4, 5. There seems to be a definite echo of these lines in the seventeenth-century broad-side ballad 'Cuckold's Haven':

> When these good Gossips meet
> In Alley, Lane, or Street,
> (Poore men, we doe not see't!
> with Wine and Sugar sweet,
> They arme themselues, and then, beside,
> their husbands must be hornify'd.

(The Second Part, ll. 73–8, *repr. Roxburghe Ballads*, i, London, 1873, 205)

A. stza. 4, l. 1. *mery-go-down*: strong ale.
A b. stza. 6, l. 5. *wryng*: suffer.
A. stza. 9, ll. 4, 5. See B. J. W., *Proverbs*, G 261.
A. stza. 11, l. 4. *jonkers*: junkets, merrymakings.
A. stza. 12, l. 1. *muscadell*: muscatel, the strong wine of muscat grapes.
A. stza. 16, ll. 4, 5. Compare Chaucer's *Nun's Priest's Tale*, l. 100: 'Have ye no mannes herte, and han a berd?'
A. stza. 17, l. 1. *shot*: reckoning.
A. stza. 23, ll. 4, 5. See B. J. W., *Proverbs*, T 182.
B. stza. 4, l. 2. *at a brayd*: with a quick movement, suddenly.
B. stza. 8, l. 4. *onethe*: scarcely.

420. A Singer's Greeting

Pr. Dyboski, p. 117; Flügel, 'Lieder.', p. 280; Robbins, *Secular Lyrics*, p. 1; Sisam, p. 540. B.-R. 1609.

This carol, like Nos. 10, 11, shows the visiting vocalist not merely as a performer but as an organizer of the company for general song. The stanzas addressed to the different members of the audience are such as a professional entertainer could count on to be appropriate to figures likely to be found in almost any gathering. The modern variety artist knows the same trick.

burden, l. 3. *par la pompe*: i.e. with ceremony or celebration.
stza. 2, l. 3. *appose*: examine, interrogate like a schoolmaster.
stza. 3, l. 2. *tempereth his mowth*: 'tunes up'.   l. 6. *towght*: taut, congested.
stza. 5, l. 3. *ipocras*: the famous 'lusty' sweet wine.

421. Fill the Bowl, Butler

Pr. Dyboski, p. 118; Flügel, 'Lieder.', p. 282; C. & S., p. 227; Robbins, *Secular Lyrics*, p. 10; H. A. Mason, *Humanism and Poetry in the Early Tudor Period* (London, 1959), p. 151; Greene, *Selection*, p. 153; Sisam, p. 542; Davies, p. 276; Silverstein, p. 147. B.-R. 903.

burden, l. 1. *Bevis a towt*: *buvez à tous*.   l. 2. *rowght*: go round.

stza. 1, l. 1. Compare the refrain of the cumulative drinking song reprinted from *Deuteromelia* (1609) by E. G. Rimbault, *A Little Book of Songs and Ballads* (London, 1851), p. 120: 'Sing, gentle butler, *balla moy*'.   l. 3. *by and by*: at once.

stza. 4. The same mode of petition to the butler is found in the well-known traditional 'Gloucestershire Wassail' (*O.B.C.*, 1928, No. 31). Stanza 7 reads:

> Come, butler, come fill us a bowl of the best,
> Then we hope that your soul in heaven may rest;
> But if you do draw us a bowl of the small,
> Then down shall go butler, bowl and all.

A similar stanza was found in Vermont in 1940 attached to the traditional song of hunting the wren on St. Stephen's Day:

> If you will fill it with the small,
> It will not answer my boys at all;
> But if you fill it of the best,
> I hope it's in heaven your soul may rest.
>
> (Helen Hartness Flanders and Marguerite Olney, *Ballads Migrant in New England*,
> N.Y., 1953, p. 59)

l. 2. *noll*: head.
stza. 5, l. 1. A good pun, as 'Walter' was so pronounced.   l. 2. *galow-claper*: gallows-bird, by reference to the swinging motion of a suspended body.   l. 3. *rather*: sooner.

422. Bring Us In Good Ale

A. *Pr.* Wright, *P.S.* xxiii. 63; W. Chappell, *Popular Music of the Olden Time* (London, [1853]), i. 43; F. J. Furnivall, *The Babees Book* (E.E.T.S., Or. Ser., No. 32, 1868), p. 363; W. Sandys, *P.S.* xxiii, 'Festive Songs', p. 16; Eliza Gutch, *Notes on the Months* (London, 1866), p. 418;

T. Wright, *Gentleman's Magazine*, New Ser., xvii (1864), 597; F. W. Hackwood, *Inns, Ales, and Drinking Customs of Old England* (New York, n.d.), p. 328; *E.B.M.* ii. 184; C. & S., p. 222; J. E. Masters, *Rymes of the Minstrels* (Shaftesbury, 1927), p. 21; G. Bullett, *The English Galaxy of Shorter Poems* (London, 1947), p. 20 (omits stzas. 1, 7, 8); Robbins, *Secular Lyrics*, p. 9; Kaiser, *Anth.*, p. 311, *Med. Engl.*, p. 478; Greene, *Selection*, p. 154; Oliver, p. 104; Sisam, p. 482; Davies, p. 217; Silverstein, p. 146.

B. *Pr.* Ritson, *Ancient Songs* (1790), p. xxxiv, (1829), i. xlix; Polecarp Chener, *N. & Q.*, 2nd Ser., x (1860), 471; Wright, *P.S.* xxiii. 102.

B.-R. 549.

A is preceded in the MS. by a pleasantly simple modal melody, under the notes of which are written the burden and first stanza of No. 53. This is followed by the gloss: 'Thys is the tewyn for the song foloyng yf so be that ye wyll haue a nother tewyn it may be at yowr plesur for I haue set all the song.' This has been taken to indicate that 'Bring Us in Good Ale' was to be sung to the tune given, but the melody neither fits the stanza of the drinking-song nor suggests a convivial air. A difference in the ink with which 'Bring Us in Good Ale' begins (see facsimile in *E.B.M.*, No. c) shows that some kind of break occurred just at that point in the writing of the manuscript. The words of No. 239 a are given in full ten leaves farther on, in accordance with an annotation written by another hand ('fo 10') directly after the words 'the song foloyng'. Apparently they should have followed the music directly but through mistake were entered elsewhere, and the space left vacant was filled with the words of the drinking-song, which undoubtedly had a very good tune of its own but was never meant to be sung to the 'Nowell, nowell,' melody. The note on this question in *O.B.C.* (1928, p. 43) is misleading and gives as the source of the tune B.M. MS. Sloane 2593, which has no music.

A. stzas. 1, 2. There is an obvious echo of the substance of these lines in the dialogue and song of Nicholas Udall's *Roister Doister* (about 1552), Act I, Scene iii, ll. 304–7:

> M[argerie] Mumbl[ecrust]. And swéete malte maketh ioly good ale for the nones.
> Tib Talk [apace]. Whiche will slide downe the lane without any bones.
> Cantet. Olde browne bread crustes must have much good mumblyng,
> But good ale downe your throte hath good easie tumbling.

(ed. G. Scheurweghs, Materials for the Study of the Old English Drama, xvi, Louvain, 1939, 12)

A. stza. 1, l. 1. Concerning the bread for the household of King Edward IV it is said in the regulations for the Office of Bakehouse: 'But for the more party than hit ys to brown and therefore now of long tyme continued hit hath be put into a more certayntie, and not to bult hit to sore vppon the gurgeonez [coarse refuse] of branne' (A. R. Myers, ed., *The Household of Edward IV: The Black Book and the Ordinance of 1478*, Manchester, 1959, p. 166). The bran thus sifted out was to be carefully accounted for and delivered to the 'avener', the official in charge of the feed for the horses.

A. stzas. 2, 5. Compare the 'Proverbial Rhyme' quoted by John Ray (*A Collection of English Proverbs*, Cambridge, 1678, p. 293):

> He that buys land buys many stones,
> He that buys flesh buys many bones,
> He that buys eggs buys many shells,
> But he that buys good Ale buys nothing else.

A. stza. 7, l. 1. *al Godes good*. This is an East Anglian term for barm or yeast, which housewives sometimes came to a monastic kitchen to obtain, as at Mettingham College, Suffolk, where they managed to get some of the ale as well (A. Jessopp, ed., *Visitations of the Diocese of Norwich*, A.D. 1492–1532, Camden Society, 1888, p. 46). But barm is an unlikely constituent for puddings, though Walter de la Mare glosses the phrase as 'yeast' (*Come Hither*, new edn., London, 1928, p. 69). The meaning here is probably 'God knows what', close to *O.E.D.* 2: 'Applied to what is considered to be without human owner, and therefore open to be appropriated by any one.' There is no culinary or other reason for Robbins's unattractive emendation to 'gotes blod' (pp. 10, 232).

A. stza. 8, l. 2. *mer*: mere, pond.

B. stza. 5, l. 1. *dure*: keep.

B. stza. 6, l. 1. *palde*: flat, stale.

The formula of this carol is one that would make improvisation of further stanzas inevitable among singers of any spirit at all. There is little external evidence for the custom of improvising verses in carols, but it must have occurred very often, and must sometimes have been inspired in a group, whatever one thinks about communal authorship in narrative ballads. Alumni of collegiate singing bouts will need no convincing.

423. Of the Effects of Ale

Pr. Wright, *P.S.* xxiii. 81; W. Sandys, ibid., 'Festive Songs', p. 17; F. W. Hackwood, *Inns, Ales, and Drinking Customs of Old England* (New York, n.d.), p. 327; C. & S., p. 224; J. E. Masters, *Rymes of the Minstrels* (Shaftesbury, 1927), p. 22; D. K. Roberts, *Straw in the Hair* (London, 1953), p. 47; Greene, *Selection*, p. 155; Sisam, p. 483. B.-R. 163.

The vigorous disapproval expressed in this carol of the nearly universal English beverage is surprising, especially in view of the convivial associations of carol-singing. It marks the piece as certainly the work of a moralizing religious, probably, to judge from its realistic observation of drunkenness in humble life, a friar.'

The above note on this carol in the first edition of this work has roused some dissent, particularly from John Speirs (*Medieval English Poetry: The Non-Chaucerian Tradition*, London, 1957, p. 88), who calls it 'unbelievable' and accuses the editor of 'apparently having missed the kind of humour the song expresses'. He adds, 'The rollicking rhythm alone should have saved Greene.' Utley (p. 165) remarks: 'But surely "Doll [*warm, mull*] thy ale" is a burden which destroys the sting of serious charges in the stanzas proper, which go to the extreme length of threatening the ale-drinker with the gallows.' On the other hand Arthur K. Moore (*The Secular Lyric in Middle English*, Lexington, Kentucky, 1951, p. 171) accepts the piece as 'a prohibitionist carol', though he calls the burden 'lively'.

The editor may have helped to suggest these comments by glossing 'doll' as 'warm, mull', citing *Promptorium Parvulorum*: 'Dollyn, as alle or oder lyke: Tabefacio', a meaning which does imply some conflict between burden and stanzas. It should rather be glossed as 'weaken; cause or permit to become flat or "dead"', as in *Catholicon Anglicum*, p. 103: 'Dollyd as wyne or ale; *Defunctus, vapidus; vapiditas, vappa,* dollyng [B.M. MS. Addit. 15562]' Note also *Babees Book*, part ii, p. 79: '*dowld,* dead, flat (Yorkshire), Halliwell'; not '*dollyd,* sum what hotte, *tepefactus.* Prompt.' The contradiction then disappears.

There is every reason to believe that the carol is the work of a religious, though we may give up the friar, for it appears in a MS. probably from a college of canons. That it was written down in the MS. at a different time from other carols is shown by the difference in ink and appearance of the hand in comparison with the matter preceding and following, so that it may well have had a different source from that of 'Bring us in good ale'. There is no arguing about a sense of humour, but other medieval literature gives no warrant for assuming that all warnings against drunkenness are ironic or that the misadventures mentioned here are to be regarded as mirth-provoking, singly or in a cumulative list. Chaucer's Pardoner speaks some serious words about drunkenness although under an ale-stake with tankard in hand (*Pardoner's Tale*, ll. 87–126). In the Chester play of Christ's Descent into Hell some MSS. give a humorous addition to the scene in which Secundus Demon cries to 'mulier', the ale-wife:

> welckome, dere ladye, I shall thee wedd!
> for many a heavye and droncken head,
> cavse of thy ale, were broughte to bed,
> farre worse then anye beaste.

> (ed. J. Matthews, E.E.T.S., Ex. Ser., No. cxv, 1916, 331)

The situation is humorous, but the words are not ironic. For an abundance of warning against the effects of ale in sermons rather than songs see G. R. Owst, *Literature and Pulpit in Medieval England* (Oxford, 1961), pp. 425–41. Owst comments: '. . . from the beginnings of Mendicant oratory, as in patristic literature, the follies of the inebriate, both ludicrous and tragical, were held up to audiences in all their grim reality—to audiences, moreover, that we happen to know were often all too ready, like Chaucer's Friar, to laugh and "gale" at the wrong moment' (p. 426). A bit from a sermon in B.M. MS. Addit. 41321, f. 97ᵛ, is a good counterpart to l. 2 of this carol: 'And ofte as thei goth homward toward hire beddes, thei drencheth hemself in dichis bi the weie'

(p. 429). Or note the translated mnemonic verses in B.M. MS. Lansdowne 762, f. 99ʳ (*pr. Rel. Ant.* i. 288):

> Who that drynketh wele, mych is he the gladder;
> Who that drynketh to moch, more is he the madder;
> Whan he goth to his bed, his slepe is the sadder;
> At morowe whan he waketh, his brayne is the bradder;
> Whan he loketh in his purce, his sorowe is the sadder.

Any reader who thinks the rhythm 'rollicking' is advised to recite aloud first No. 422 and then this carol and compare the effects.

burden, l. 2. *doty poll*: stupid head, *O.E.D.* does not record this use, but gives 'doddy poll', as transferred to the possessor of the head.

stza. 1, l. 1. *styk at a brere*: probably figurative and proverbial rather than literal: to get into trouble. Compare the *Vulgaria* of Robert Whittinton, printed by Wynkyn de Worde, 1520 (ed. Beatrice White, E.E.T.S., Or. Ser., No. 187, 1932), 98, ll. 14–16:

> Thou art a sure spere at nede. that leues a man stykkinge in the breres.
> Fidus es / vbi opus est: hominem malis impeditum deficies.

stza. 5, l. 1. *blokkes*: stones or other obstructions, 'stumbling blocks'.

stza. 6, l. 1. *falows*: ploughed land. Compare the proverb using the three rhyme-words of this stanza in Chaucer, *Wife of Bath's Prologue*, ll. 655–8, and the variant of it in *Rel. Ant.* i. 233.

424. A Carol of Hunting

A. *Pr.* Dyboski, p. 103; Flügel, 'Lieder.', p. 194; F. M. Padelford, *Early Sixteenth Century Lyrics* (Boston, 1907), p. 138; Sisam, p. 526. B.–R. 418.

B. *Repr.* Joseph Haslewood, *The Book containing the Treatises of Hawking; Hunting . . . printed at Westminster by Wynkyn de Worde* [etc.] (London, [1811]), p. 58; Flügel, loc. cit., *Anglia*, xii (1889), 587, *N.L.*, p. 151; Padelford, op. cit., p. 75; C. & S., p. 245; etc.

It is difficult to be certain of the exact arrangement of stanza and burden intended in B because of the abbreviated manner of its printing. The buyers of the little book would be expected to know the music.

A. stza. 1, l. 3. *Go bett*: go better, a cry of encouragement. Compare Chaucer, *Legend of Good Women*, l. 1213, and No. 392, burden.   l. 4. *How*: not a meaningless syllable, but a prescribed cry to hounds. Marcelle Thiébaux cites William Twiti's *Craft of Venery*: 'ʒe shalle sey thus "howʒe, venes y, moun amy"' and the *Master of Game*: 'He shalle say þus to hem here, How amy, how amy' (*The Stag of Love*, Ithaca, N.Y., 1974, p. 206, n. 59).

A. stza. 2, l. 2. *mountenaunce*: extent.   *myle*: i.e. time enough to go a mile.   l. 3. *withowt any gile*: i.e. 'I speak truly', an emphatic phrase.

stza. 3, l. 4. A cry of alarm as well as one of success, imitative of one of the code of hunting-horn signals. Compare John Bale's *King Johan* (1536), l. 1378 '(offstage): Sedicyon. Alaru*m* Alaru*m*, tro ro ro ro ro, tro ro ro ro ro, tro ro ro ro ro' (ed. John Henry Pyle Pafford, The Malone Society Reprints, 1931, p. 65).

424.1. The Briar and the Periwinkle

Previously unpublished.

This carol is unique among those extant in being both politically partisan and definitely localized in a provincial village. It is written on the verso of a scrap of late fifteenth-century rent-roll of Ashford, Kent. In its local connection it resembles No. 393.1 from Great Torrington, North Devon, more than any other carol in this collection, even though it does not name its village as does that satirical piece. It is the only preserved carol which exhibits its peculiar features of dialect. The language is presumably that of mid-Kent, though in its use of 'd' for 'th' it resembles some of the letters written for Margaret Paston by at least one of her amanuenses (e.g. Letter 126 in Norman Davis, ed., *Paston Letters and Papers of the Fifteenth Century*, part i, Oxford, 1971, p. 218).

The use of flowers as symbols or badges in political verse of this period is common enough (e.g. Nos. 427, 431, 433). The writer of this carol is a strong partisan of the 'briar', which here must be a rose-briar rather than a bramble. Its reference in an Ashford context seems almost certainly to be to Sir John Fogge of the manor of Repton, the most conspicuous parishioner of Ashford and a man of national prominence, knighted on 27 June 1461, just before the coronation of Edward IV (William A. Shaw, *The Knights of England*, London, 1906, ii. 13). By Edward he was made Treasurer of the Household and a Privy Councillor, and, in conjunction with Sir John Scott, also served as Chamberlain to Edward, Prince of Wales (Edward V). He married as his second wife Alice Hawte, a first cousin of the queen Elizabeth Woodville. During this reign he founded a short-lived college in Ashford and paid for an extensive restoration and improvements in Ashford parish church. On the accession of Richard III he declined the overtures of the new monarch, and was deprived of all his honours and lands, which were bestowed on one William Malyverer. But Henry VII promptly restored the properties, including the principal manor of Repton, to Fogge, and he once again flourished as an important and influential citizen of Kent until his death in 1490.

Sir John's handsome tomb in Ashford church, though stripped of much of its original splendour, still exhibits a brass inscription-plate of unusual design with a circular border of entwined roses on long stems. Equally significant were the sculptured effigies now for ever gone. They are described in a paper by A. J. Pearman ('Ashford Church', *Archaeologia Cantiana*, xxviii, 1909, pp. lxxxiii–lxxxiv):

> These [ornaments] consisted of brass effigies of himself and his two wives, Alice Crioll and Alice Haute. 'He was attired in rich plate armour and decorated with the Yorkist collar of suns and roses, with the white lion of March attached. His head reclined on his helmet adorned with mantlings and crest. At his feet sat an Italian greyhound. On either hand lay his two wives. Their mantles were fastened with roses, at the feet of each crouched a dog with knotted leading strings. On the south side of the tomb . . . were three shields of arms, Crioll, Haute, and Valoignes impaling Fogge. On the north side the center ornament was an angel supporting an inscription-plate within an endless circle, formed of rose sapling sticks firmly bound together, perhaps to represent the stability of family unity, the vitality of which is indicated by four small sprouts of rose branches with leaves and blossoms. Four large bosses of the united Roses proclaimed a Yorkist's acquiescence in the peaceful conclusion of intestine commotions.'

There are two small designs of roses below the inscription. Canon Pearman gives a translation of the long Latin inscription, not necessary to quote here, but part of the inscription around the margin of the tomb-slab is significant: 'Edwardi quarti regis specialis Amator, semper Catholicus, Populi vulgaris amicus . . .'.

It seems impossible to doubt that the popular paragon denoted by the briar in the carol is the Sir John Fogge so thoroughly associated with this rose symbolism. It is worth mentioning that roses in heraldry are usually shown without the stems, which are so prominent here.

In addition to the articles by Pearman and Conway there is good biographical information on Fogge in W. K. Jordan, 'Social Institutions in Kent 1480–1660', *Archaeologia Cantiana*, lxxv (1961), 122, and in many scattered references in the same publication.

The periwinkle of the carol is less obviously to be identified, but the same tomb appears to offer a valid clue. The writer of the carol, who uses the words 'gret tresoun', is plainly following the tradition of the periwinkle as the flower with which to crown a traitor, especially one on the way to actual execution. The same flower is used, of course, in Middle English poetry as a symbol of womanly beauty and virtue, but this quite separate tradition is well established. The *O.E.D.* notes, s.v. 'Periwinkle': 'In early times a garland of this flower was placed on the heads of persons on their way to execution, with which some have connected the It. name *fiore di morte*, flower of death.' In the grim and spirited poem on the execution of Sir Simon Fraser or Frizell in 1306 the posture of disgrace in which the traitor is brought to London includes a garland of periwinkle, apparently in addition to a garland of leaves:

> y-fetered were ys legges vnder his horse wombe;
> boþe wiþ yrn ant wiþ stel mankled were ys honde;
> A gerland of peruenke set on ys heued;
> Muche wes þe poer þat him wes byreved
> In londe.
> (B.M. MS. Harley 2253, f. 60ᵛ, *pr*. Robbins, *Hist. Poems*, p. 18, ll. 121–5)

The poem further states (ll. 179–80) that he was haled to execution 'In a curtel of burel a selkeþe wyse,/ ant a gerland on his heved of þe newe guyse', presumably of periwinkle again. Lydgate contrasts the shameful crown of periwinkle with an honourable crown of laurel in his rendering of the speech of Fortune to 'Bochas' in Book VI of *The Fall of Princes.* She tells the author that he has

> Spared [not] ther crownys nor ther purpil weedis,
> Ther goldene sceptris; but youe to them ther meedis:
> Crownid oon with laureer hih on his hed vpset,
> Other with peruynke maad for the gibet.
>
> (part iii, ed. Henry Berger, E.E.T.S., Ex. Ser., No. cxxiii, 1924, 678, ll. 123–6)

A plausible candidate for the periwinkle symbolism in Ashford would be William Malyverer, to whom on 17 August 1484 Richard III granted the valuable lands forfeited by Sir John Fogge, who had been involved in the abortive rebellion. Malyverer's enjoyment of the property was brief, for on 24 February 1485 Fogge was pardoned and given a regrant of the manors of Dymchurch, Valence, Tonford, and Dane (Agnes Ethel Conway, 'The Maidstone Sector of Buckingham's Rebellion. Oct. 18, 1483', *Archaeologia Cantiana*, xxxvii, 1925, 114). Heraldic evidence makes this identification quite plausible. For purposes of heraldic punning the name Malyverer (Mauleverer, Mallever) is associated with French *levrier* greyhound, and in Kent the family bore three greyhounds argent in their arms (James Greenstreet, 'List of the Gentry in Kent in the Time of Henry VII', *Archaeologia Cantiana*, xi, 1877, 396). Fogge's arms are recorded in the same list and are to be seen in the west window of Mersham church: Argent on a fess between 3 annulets sable 3 mullets argent (C. R. Councer, 'The Medieval Painted Glass of Mersham', *Archaeologia Cantiana*, xlviii, 1936, 81); they were apparently not used on the tomb. There is much evidence for the use of the same or very similar arms for the Yorkshire family of Mauleverer of Allerton, but I have found no record of recognized relationship with a Kentish branch (J. B. Rietstap, *Armorial Général*, Baltimore, 1965; J. W. Clay, 'Dugdale's Visitation of Yorkshire, with Additions', *The Genealogist*, x, 1893, 45–50; Ernest Spofford, ed., *Armorial Families of America*, Philadelphia, 1929, i. 237–8). There was even a legend, probably an example of folk-etymology, that the surname of the Yorkshire family meant 'Bad Hare Hunter' and that the greyhounds on the coat allude to this incident:

> A gentleman of this county [Yorkshire] being about to slip a brace of greyhounds to run for a great wager, so held them that they were more likely to strangle themselves than kill the hare; whereupon the surname was fixed on his family. (Fuller's *Worthies*, quoted by Mark Antony Lower, *Patronymica Britannica*, London, 1860, p. 220.) See note on No. 431, stza. 9, l. 1.

It is more probable that the name derives from a place, the viscounty of Maulévrier in Normandy, but the story at least indicates that the arms were well known (loc. cit.).

The presence of a sculptured greyhound, seated and apparently subdued, not lying as a footrest like the friendly dogs of so many effigies, may well have been an allusion to Fogge's eventual triumph over the man who bore the greyhounds as his arms, the triumph in the carol of the rose-briar over the flower of traitors.

burden, l. 1. *Man of mightt*: Christ.   *ydyght*: prepared, ordained.   l. 3. *wysse*: guide, direct. l. 4. *spedys*: this should possibly be emended to 'sped ws'.

stza. 1, l. 1. *ykowmbyrght*: troubled, annoyed.   l. 2. *ybent his boghe*: bent his bow, i.e. threatened. l. 3. *wendyt*: turned.   l. 5. *wed*: weed, the periwinkle.   l. 6. *leyghuys*: leaves.   l. 7. *de vysse*: guide to thyself.

stza. 2, l. 2. Have emerged out of its soil.   l. 4. *An*: if.   l. 5. *grette*: honour.   l. 6. *han naut lyme*: may not have a main branch (to hold it up).

stza. 3, l. 2. *greffit*: grafted.   l. 6. *rasse*: raze, grub out.

stza. 4, l. 1. *Dang*: thank.   l. 2. *wordes wele*: world's prosperity.   l. 3. *denk*: think.   l. 5. *ychent*: punished.

I am greatly obliged to Professor Robert R. Raymo, who first directed my attention to this carol, as well as to Dr. Felix Hull, Kent County Archivist, who gave me valuable help in the deciphering of the text.

425. Of the Death of Archbishop Scrope

Pr. F. J. Furnivall, *Hymns to the Virgin and Christ* (E.E.T.S., Or. Ser., No. 24, London, 1867), 128; Robbins, *Hist. Poems*, p. 90; M. R. James, *The Western Manuscripts in the Library of Trinity College, Cambridge* (Cambridge, 1901), ii. 148 (stza. 1 only). B.-R. 3308.

Richard le Scrope, Archbishop of York, was beheaded on 'Whitson Monday', 8 June 1405, as the result of his disaffection towards Henry IV, his conspiracy with the Percys, and his rousing of the people of York. Shakespeare's treatment of the episode (*1 Henry IV*, IV. iv, and *2 Henry IV*, I. iii, IV. i, ii) is written from the point of view of the King's policy. The carol is by a sympathizer with the Archbishop, probably a religious. It agrees strikingly with the account of the execution given by Thomas Gascoigne, who was one of those who revered Scrope as a martyr (J. E. T. Rogers, ed., *Loci e Libro Veritatum*, Oxford, 1881, pp. 225–9).

stza. 3, l. 1. *He*: i.e. the executioner.

stza. 4. Compare Gascoigne (Rogers, op. cit., p. 227): '. . . et Thomae Alman, suo decollatori . . . dixit "Fili, mortem meam Deus tibi remittat, et ego tibi remitto, rogans te intime ut des michi cum gladio tuo quinque vulnera in collo, quae intendo sustinere pro amore Domini nostri Jesu, qui, pro nobis obediens usque ad mortem, quinque vulnera principalia pacienter sustinuit."' Hall's *Chronicle* (quoted Furnivall, op. cit., p. 130) declares the report of this request a lie, written by 'sedicyous Asses'. See also the Latin poem on the same event, likewise sympathetic to Scrope, in B.M. MS. Cotton Faustina B. ix, f. 242ᵛ (*pr.* Thomas Wright, *Political Poems*, Rolls Series, London, 1859–61, ii. 114). It is significant that the 1542 and 1559 editions of Robert Fabyan's *Chronicles* omit a passage found in earlier editions:

> Then whan þe Bysshop came vnto his place of Execution, he prayed the Bowcher to gyue to hym v. strokes in the worshyp of Cristes fyue woundes / and for more penaunce, at eueryche of whiche .v. strokes kynge Henry beyng in his lodgyng had a stroke in his necke / In so moche, that he Demyd that some persone there beynge with hym present, had stryken hym *and* forth-with he was stryken with þe plage of Lepyr / So that then he knewe it was the hande of God / *and* repented hym of that hasty Iugement, without Auctoryte of the Churche. And soon after god shewyd many Myracles for the sayde Bysshop / whiche called the kynge vnto the more repen-taunce (*The Newe Cronycles*, London, 1516, f. 348ʳ).

The importance and influence of the cult which developed after the Archbishop's death and his veneration as an unofficial saint are fully and interestingly treated by J. W. McKenna, 'Popular Canonization as Political Propaganda: The Cult of Archbishop Scrope', *Speculum*, xlv (1970), 608–23. McKenna notices this carol on p. 616. Scrope's bodily relics were reputed in Yorkshire to have worked various miracles (G. G. Coulton, *Five Centuries of Religion*, Cambridge, 1936, iii. 111).

426. The Agincourt Carol

a. Music for two voices. *Pr.* Padelford, p. 101; Robbins, *Hist. Poems*, p. 91; Greene, *Selection*, p. 156; Sisam, p. 381; Davies, p. 168; with music, *E.B.M.* ii. 128, *facs.* Nos. lxvi, lxvii; Noah Greenberg, *An English Songbook* (Garden City, N.Y., 1961), p. 62, *facs.* facing p. 61; *facs.* H. Hecht and L. Schücking, *Die englische Literatur* (Potsdam, 1927), facing p. 144; etc.

b. Music for two voices. *Pr.* Padelford, p. 102; with music, Fuller Maitland, p. 15, *facs.* ibid., frontispiece; Stevens, *Med. Carols*, p. 6.

B.–R. 2716.

This stirring song, perhaps the best-known carol in English not concerned with the Nativity, was probably composed and sung by clerics rather than by minstrels and thus may be regarded as not directly in defiance of Henry V's famous interdict (R. S. Wallace and A. Hansen, eds., *Holinshed's Chronicles*, *Henry V*, Oxford, 1917, p. 43): '. . . neither would he suffer any ditties to be made and soong by minstrels of his glorious victorie, for that he would wholie have the praise and thanks altogither given to God.' The burden of the carol reflects the King's often-recorded insistence on the divine agency in the victory, and the religious sentiment of the piece might have saved it from his disapproval. Both writings of the carol are later than Henry V's lifetime.

'Deo gratias' was displayed on the tower of a conduit near St. Paul's during the splendid celebra-tion of the King's homecoming. Extracts from the descriptions of the ceremonies in the *Brut* and in a priest's diary printed by Sir Nicholas Harris Nicolas are conveniently found in Robbins, *Historical Poems*, pp. 296–7. But there is no reason to believe that this carol was actually sung on that occasion, to which stzas. 4, 5 refer as in the past. Neither can the carol be regarded, as Robbins states (p. 297), as 'clearly processional'.

Compare the long poem on Agincourt in B.M. MS. Harley 565, f. 102ʳ (*pr.* [Sir Nicholas Harris

Nicolas and Edward Tyrrell], *A Chronicle of London*, London, 1827, p. 216). This, though not a carol, has inserted at intervals the couplet:

> Wot ye right well that thus it was
> Gloria tibi, Trinitas.

Although F. M. Padelford (*Anglia*, xxxvi, 1912, 84) thought the verbal variants of the two versions to be such as showed evidence of oral transmission, the likeness of the two musical settings is such as to indicate MS. transmission, as with many other carols.

stza. 4, l. 4. Robbins pertinently quotes from the chronicle of Jehan de Waurin the cry of Henry's troops on the battlefield: 'Sire! Dieu vous doinst bonne vye et victore de vos annemis!'

There is no observable direct relation between this carol and the ballad *King Henry Fifth's Conquest of France* (Child, No. 164), which has also appeared in American versions from Vermont and Tennessee (Helen Hartness Flanders *et al.*, *The New Green Mountain Songster*, New Haven, 1939, p. 112; Mellinger Edward Henry, *Folk-Songs from the Southern Highlands*, New York, 1938, p. 106). A. L. Lloyd's curious rhetorical question finds its answer here: 'Where is the folk ballad of Magna Carta? Or of Agincourt for the matter of that? It was celebrated in upper-class poetry and song but did not engage the attention, or failed to hold the interest, of the folk' (*Folk Song in England*, London, 1967, p. 146).

427. The Rose on Branch

Pr. F. J. Furnivall, *N. & Q.*, 5th Ser., xii (1879), 124 (misplaces short lines of stanzas); Robbins, *Hist. Poems*, p. 92; Greene, *Selection*, p. 157. B.–R. 3457.

The end of the carol is missing, as two leaves have been torn from the MS.

The phrasing of the first two stanzas shows strong influence from the symbolism and poetic convention of the rose as emblem of the Virgin, which in turn draws on an enormous body of secular figurative use, with *The Romance of the Rose* pre-eminent. Not until the third stanza does it become clear that an English king is meant, as in No. 431. The allusion is to Henry V and the Agincourt campaign. The fleur-de-lis, of course, is France. Compare the song from oral tradition on the battle in Sir Nicholas Harris Nicolas, *The Battle of Agincourt* (London, 1832), Appendix, pp. 78–9, in which the French king is made to say:

> And the fairest flower in all French land,
> To the rose of England I will give free.

burden, l. 1. A good commentary on the symbolic use of the rose as a royal flower (with a verbal parallel) is given by Gerard Legh in *The Accidence of Armorie* (London, 1597), p. 99: 'This flower of al other is the beautifullest to behold, and of most comfortable smell. *Plinie* writeth that amongst all flowers of the world, the rose is chiefest, and beareth the prise.'   l. 3. *of Ryse*: on branch.

stza. 1, l. 4. *saluoure*: healer.

stza. 3, l. 4. Compare No. 428, stza. 6, l. 4.

428. In Honour of King Henry VI

Pr. J. O. Halliwell [–Phillipps], *P.S.* xiv. viii; C. & S., *M.L.R.* v. 488; Whiting, p. 193; Robbins, *Hist. Poems*, p. 108. B.–R. 822.

These verses of Audelay's on the accession of Henry VI are of greater poetical merit than two other poems in English on the same subject printed by Wright (*Political Poems*, ii. 141–8). James Ryman, the carol-writer, produced verses on the death of Henry VI, but did not give them a burden (*pr.* Zupitza, p. 268). Ryman showed himself to be a Lancastrian sympathizer and one of those who venerated Henry as a saint and martyr.

burden, l. 1. *Perles Pryns*: Christ.

stza. 1, l. 1. Henry VI was crowned on 6 November 1429, when he was ten years old. This circumstance excuses Audelay's devoting most of the carol to the exploits of the new king's father rather than to the virtues of the boy himself. There is a striking parallel to this line in the ballad *King Henry Fifth's Conquest of France* (Child, No. 164), a line that persists even in the version recorded in Vermont in 1931. In stanza 4 King Henry's little page is told by the King of France:

> Your master's young, of tender age,
> Not fit to come to my degree;
> To him I send five tennis balls
> That in French land he dare not be.

The phrase is repeated, ballad-fashion, by the page on his return to King Henry (Helen Hartness Flanders *et al.*, *The New Green Mountain Songster*, New Haven, 1939, p. 193).

stza. 3, l. 1. Audelay is, of course, historically incorrect in the motive he assigns for Henry V's invasion of France, the wooing of Katherine being a result of the war and not a cause.   l. 3. *hee*: i.e. the Dauphin. See Whiting's note.

stza. 4. The tennis-ball incident and its sequel of 'teaching the French the game' caught Audelay's imagination as it later did Shakespeare's. For a full discussion of the episode see Oskar Emmerig, '*The Bataile of Agyncourt' im Lichte geschichtlicher Quellenwerke* (Nürnberg, 1906), pp. 14–43. l. 3. *tenes-hold*: tennis, the 'hold' from Fr. *tenez. ferd*: frightened.

stza. 6, l. 4. Compare No. 427, stza. 3, l. 4.

stza. 10. l. 1. An obvious adaptation of the most hackneyed phrase of Nativity carols.

stza. 12. Both Henry IV and Henry V cherished the purpose to win back the Holy Land for Christendom, and both were thwarted by the demands of more immediate problems.   l. 4. See Whiting's note.

stza. 13. Audelay's prophecy is given a tragic irony by the events of Henry VI's reign. The last stanza, however, shows that the poet recognized the possibilities of disaster facing the new sovereign.

429. In Honour of King Edward IV

Pr. J. O. Halliwell [-Phillipps], *Archaeologia*, xxix (1842), 127; F. J. Furnivall, *Political, Religious, and Love Poems* (E.E.T.S., Or. Ser., No. 15, 1866), 4; Edward Parry, *Royal Visits and Progresses to Wales* (Chester, 1850), p. 265 (burden omitted); Robbins, *Hist. Poems*, p. 221. B.-R. 3127.

This carol must be nearly contemporary with No. 431 and the work of a jingoistic partisan of the Yorkists. In sentiment and style it resembles the poem 'Twelve Letters That Shall Save England', which is separated from it by No. 401 B. The 'R' stanza (12) reads:

> An R. for the Rose þat is fresche and wol nat fade,
>   Bothe þe rote & the stalke þat is of grete honoure,
> from Normandie vnto norway þe leues do springe,
> from irlonde vnto Estlonde me reoise þat floure.

(Furnivall, op. cit., p. 3)

It may well have been sung in the ceremonies welcoming Edward to Bristol in 1461, briefly summarized in the same MS. just before the carol text. The carol is definitely superior in quality to the sample of the recited doggerel (James Gairdner, ed., *Three Fifteenth-Century Chronicles*, Camden Society, New. Ser., xxviii, 1880, 85–6).

burden, l. 1. A fourth 'a' is probably omitted. Compare the burdens of Nos. 114, 232, 313, 414. l. 2. The first phrase of the king's official style.

stza. 2, l. 1. *stoke*: the line of York, dispossessed during the reigns of the Lancastrians, 1399–1461. In this figure of the rose from the dead stock a complimentary parallel to the rose as the type of Christ sprung from the root of Jesse is implied. Compare the flattering speeches of 'prophets' in the pageant at Coventry on the occasion of the queen's visit in 1456 (M. D. Harris, ed., *The Coventry Leet Book*, E.E.T.S., Or. Ser., Nos. 134, etc., 1907–13, 287):

'. . . furst at Bablake there was made a Jesse ouer the yate right well [arayed], and there were shewed too speches as foloweth:

YSAY . . .

Like as mankynde was gladdid by the birght of Jhesus,

So shall þis empyre ioy the birthe of your bodye; . . .

JEREMY . . .

Vn–to the rote of Jesse rote likken you well I may;

The fragrante floure sprongon of you shall so encrece & spredde,

That all the world yn ich party shall cherisshe hym, love & drede.'

stza. 3, l. 2. *birede in*: buried from.   l. 3. *rosse so white*: the famous emblem of the House of York.

stza. 4, ll. 2, 3. Edward was unmarried when he seized the throne. He married Elizabeth Woodville in 1464. The carol must have been written before the latter date.

stza. 6–8. This high-flown advice was singularly impractical, as Edward had enough difficulty in keeping his throne at home. Possibly the writer was opposing the negotiations carried on in 1464 or peace with France. 'Edward made peace treaties with Henry of Castile and John of Aragon in 1465' (Robbins).

stza. 8, l. 2. *subdeue of*: Robbins notes that *O.E.D.* does not record this phrasing and suggests as its meaning 'gain control of'.

430. Willikin's Return

Pr. first edition; Robbins, *Hist. Poems*, p. 198. B.–R. 3742.

The burden of this carol is written at the end of the text instead of at the beginning as usual. The first stanza is preceded by 'Conditor alme siderum eterna lux c', but the phrase is in a different hand and obviously not meant as a burden.

The piece is probably a close parody of a folk-song, to judge from its lilt and its use of repetitive formulas. For similar use of the figure of the ship in political verse see 'Seldom seen is soon forgot', on Edward III, his sons, and Richard II (*pr.* F. J. Furnivall, *Minor Poems of the Vernon MS.*, part ii, E.E.T.S., Or. Ser., No. 117, 715), in which the 'English ship' has a good rudder, mast, and barge; see also No. 431.1. For a full discussion of the use of the same figure in sermons from the eleventh century on see G. R. Owst, *Literature and Pulpit in Medieval England* (Cambridge, 1933), pp. 68–76.

The carol appears to date from 1470, when Warwick had broken with Edward IV and had allied himself with Margaret of Anjou. The writer is looking toward the return of the Lancastrians, which actually materialized in September of that year in the short-lived restoration of Henry VI. 'Wylekin' is probably Warwick, 'Kyng Hary', of course, Henry VI, 'my Lorde Prynce' Edward, Prince of Wales, and 'my Lorde Chaberlayne' Neville, Marquess of Montagu, who had been made Lord Chamberlain of the Household in 1459 and who declared for Henry on his landing. I am indebted to the late Dr. C. W. Previté-Orton of St. John's College, Cambridge, for a suggestion leading to this interpretation.

I am unable to identify 'my Lorde Fueryn' satisfactorily. The 'knot' that is knit is probably the re-alliance of Warwick with the Lancastrian party.

stza. 3, l. 1. *nore*: oar. l. 2. *for-sore*: heavily afflicted.

431. The Rose of Rouen

Pr. Sir Frederick Madden, *Archaeologia*, xxix (1842), 343; Edward Parry, *Royal Visits and Progresses to Wales* (Chester, 1850), p. 266; Isobel Thornley, *England under the Yorkists* (London, 1921), p. 15 (in part); Rudolph Brotanek, *Mittelenglische Dichtungen aus der Handschrift 432 des Trinity College in Dublin* (Halle, 1940), p. 138; Robbins, *Hist. Poems*, p. 215. B.–R. 1380.

The red rose of Lancaster, barbed and seeded proper, had already been one of the royal badges of Henry V (Arthur Charles Fox-Davies, *Heraldic Badges*, London, 1907, p. 110). The following notes are condensed and adapted from those of Madden, Brotanek, and Robbins.

The Battle of Towton, near York, of which this long carol gives an account, was fought in a heavy snowstorm on the eve and morning of Palm Sunday, 29 March 1461. The carol was probably written soon afterwards by a supporter of the Yorkists, perhaps by an eyewitness, as stza. 13, l. 2 suggests. Edward IV is called 'the Rose of Rouen' in allusion to his birth in that city on 29 April 1442.

burden, l. 1. Brotanek's suggestion of an intended pun with 'rone' (thicket) seems doubtful.

stza. 1, l. 3. *moued oure mone*: removed our complaint. Brotanek's emendation to 'mene' is unnecessary and gives an imprecise meaning.

stza. 3, l. 2. The 'lords of the north' were Northumberland, Westmorland, Exeter, Somerset, Devonshire, Clifford, Roos, and Dacre.

stza. 4, l. 1. *leede*: meadow. l. 2. The Yorkists had been defeated at Sandrich, near St. Albans, in the second Battle of St. Albans on Shrove Tuesday, 17 February 1460–1.

stza. 5. Queen Margaret was said to have given permission to the northern forces to spoil and ravage London, Coventry, Bristol, and Salisbury (Robbins).

stza. 6, l. 2. *Calys*: 'An important assembly area for the Yorkists when in exile in 1459' (Robbins). *loue Londone*: Brotanek's emendation to 'leue London' is inadvisable, as also in stza. 15, l. 1.

stza. 7, l. 2. *Ragged Staf*: the Earl of Warwick, from his famous heraldic badge. l. 3. *White Lyon*: the Duke of Norfolk.

stza. 8, l. 1. *Fysshe Hoke*: Lord Fauconberg. *Cornyssh Chowghe*: Lord Scrope of Bolton, wounded in the battle. l. 3. *Blak Ragged Staf*: Lord Grey of Ruthyn. *Brideld Horse*: William, Earl of Arundel, brother-in-law to the Earl of Warwick. *Watyr Bouge*: probably Henry, Viscount Bourchier, though in other accounts not included among those in the battle.

stza. 9, l. 1. *Grehound*: Sir John Mauleverer, a punning heraldic charge. Compare note on No. 424.1. Sir John was undoubtedly of the Yorkshire, not the Kentish, family. *Hertes Hede*: Thomas, Lord Stanley, later Earl of Derby. l. 2. *Harow of Caunterbury*: not the arms of Canterbury but apparently a device on a banner borne by a force from that city. *Clynton*: John, Lord Clinton, whose arms were apparently not a key but a mullet or spur-rowel. He may have used a key as a badge. ll. 3, 4. *White Ship, Blak Ram*: devices used by combatants from Bristol and Coventry respectively, in these cases taken from the arms of the cities.

stza. 10, l. 1. *The Fawcon and the Fetherlok*: both badges used by the House of York. l. 2. *Blak Bulle*: a badge used by Edward IV himself, derived from the Honour of Clare. l. 3. *Dolfyn . . . Carpis*: not yet identified by commentators. l. 4. *Libert*: Richard Neville, son of the Earl of Salisbury (Robbins). *gapid his gomes*: opened his mouth wide.

stza. 11, l. 1. *Wolf*: not yet identified by commentators. l. 2. *Dragon*: a Yorkist badge, perhaps used here to denote troops raised at Gloucester by Edward. l. 3. *Griffen*: John Neville, Lord Montague, later Earl of Northumberland, brother of the Earl of Warwick, with lands in Leicestershire. The city of Leicester bears a wyvern, perhaps here confused with a griffin. *as tyte*: swiftly. l. 4. *George*: The familiar image of St. George, perhaps here denoting Edward's brother, later King Richard III.

stza. 12, l. 1. *Boris Hede*: a well-known badge of Richard's. *Estrich Feder*: a Plantagenet badge, used by Edward. l. 3. *Wild Kat*: probably a mistaken interpretation of the lions in the arms of the city of Northampton.

stza. 13, l. 2. *vs*: Robbins suggests an 'indication of an eye-witness report'. l. 3. *Within an owre*: the battle actually lasted for some hours, perhaps ten. l. 4. *xxvii thousand*: obviously an enormous exaggeration, though the battle was a bloody one. The armies probably numbered about five thousand men each.

stza. 15, ll. 1, 2. Edward entered London on 26 June 1461 and was crowned by the Archbishop of Canterbury on 29 June.

431.1 The Ship of State

Pr. Sir Frederick Madden, *Archaeologia*, xxix (1842), 326; Robbins, *Hist. Poems*, p. 191. B.-R. 2727.

The following notes are in large part condensed and adapted from Robbins.

The allegorical figure of a ship for the nation had widespread and important use in the England of the late Middle Ages. A very full discussion of the figure as it appears in preaching and in vernacular religious and moralizing poetry appears in G. R. Owst, *Literature and Pulpit in Medieval England*, 2nd edn. (Oxford, 1961), pp. 68–76. Especially significant as a forerunner of this carol is the sermon by an anonymous monk (possibly Jo. Swetstock) in which the ship is no longer a primarily religious symbol but specifically the English nation. Owst gives liberal quotations, including the fulsome praise of Henry V and his victory at Agincourt (pp. 72–5), and notices the use of the figure in the conclusion of *Richard the Redeless* (Passus IV, ll. 71–82, ed. W. W. Skeat, Oxford, 1886, i. 628).

The ship in this poem is Henry VI. The laboured inventory of the parts of the ship which stand for various conspicuous Lancastrians shows more conscientious loyalty than poetical gift in the writer.

stza. 3, l. 1. *mast*: Prince Edward, the only son of Henry VI.

stza. 5, l. 3. *cressant*: surely an error for 'cresset', the light borne on a ship; here standing for Henry Holland, Duke of Exeter and Earl of Huntingdon.

stza. 7, l. 1. *sterne*: error for 'stere', rudder. It stands for Henry Beaufort, Duke of Somerset.

stza. 9, l. 1. *sayle-yeard*: the Earl of Pembroke, half-brother to Henry VI. l. 7. *hyeth travers*: hurries athwart.

stza. 12, l. 1. The Duke of Buckingham, the 'stay', was killed at Northampton. l. 3. The Earl of Devonshire was captured at the battle of Towton and was killed at Tewkesbury. Lord Grey of Ruthyn went over to the Yorkists and became Earl of Kent under Edward IV. *Becheham*: Lord Beauchamp of Powyk. l. 4. *Scales*: Lord Scales, killed in an attempted escape from the Tower of London.

stza. 13, l. 3. *bonet three*: the nautical term 'bonnet' for an auxiliary sail; three might well be in use.

stza. 14, l. 2. Henry Percy, Earl of Northumberland, who died at the Battle of Towton.   l. 3. *Ros*: Sir Henry Roos. John, Lord Clifford, was supposed to have murdered the Earl of Rutland, son of the Duke of York. Clifford was himself killed just before the Battle of Towton. The Earl of Egremont was Thomas Percy, third son of the third Duke of Northumberland.

stza. 15, l. 1. *toppe*: top-castle, railed platform on a mast used in the Middle Ages as a standing-place for archers.

stza. 16, l. 1. The Earl of Shrewsbury, killed at Northampton. *blame*: probably here equivalent to 'the disgrace of defeat'.   l. 3. The Earl of Wiltshire, also Earl of Ormonde, captured at Towton and beheaded at Newcastle in 1461.

stza. 17, l. 4. *stop his tyde*: 'prevent the ship [from being carried with the tide]' (*O.E.D.*, s.v. 'stop', v. 28b). This is earlier than any usage recorded by *O.E.D.*, but the idiom is exact. l. 2. Viscount Beaumont, Lord Constable of England, died at Northampton in 1460.   l. 3. Lord Welles, close friend of Henry VI, killed at Towton. Lord Rivers after Towton deserted Henry for Edward. He was the father of Elizabeth Woodville, who married Edward and became queen. Rivers was executed by the Lancastrians.

stza. 19, l. 1. The frequently used invocation. Compare No. 311. 1, burden, l. 2.   l. 5. *in hys kynde*: according to the ship's own proper requirements.

Robbins prints in eight-line stanzas, but the MS. shows that the four-line stanza, so frequent in carols, is the correct arrangement. This is a song of the kind to which some commentators would like to deny the name of carol because of its length and lack of appeal to modern taste. But the rhyming of the last line of every stanza with the burden shows how it was meant to be performed.

432. The White Rose

Music for three voices. *Pr.* Flügel, *N.L.*, p. 159; Thomas Bayne, *N. & Q.*, 8th Ser., xii (1897), 385; F. J. Furnivall, *Publications of the Ballad Society*, vii (1890), clix; G. Bullett, *The English Galaxy of Shorter Poems* (London, 1947), p. 14 (omits burden): Robbins, *Hist. Poems*, p. 93; Stevens, *M. & P.*, p. 381; Davies, p. 262; with music, J. Stafford Smith, *A Collection of English Songs* (London, [1779]), p. 8; H. B. Briggs, *A Collection of Songs and Madrigals of the Close of the 15th Century* (Plainsong and Mediaeval Music Society, London, 1891), p. 15; Stevens, *M. & P.*, p. 20 (burden only), *Early Tudor Songs*, p. 138. B.–R. 1450.

The praise of the white rose marks this carol as the work of a Yorkist sympathizer, though he may be celebrating the cessation of the strife and have ceased to be 'partisan', a term which Robbins disapproves in his notes. The garden setting is like that of the ballad 'The Rose of England' (Child, No. 166), and probably stands for England in the same way. The 'quene' or lady of stza. 1, l. 2, is possibly, although not certainly, meant for Elizabeth of York, eldest daughter of Edward IV, who was married to Henry VII in January 1486 and became the mother of Prince Arthur. See Bayne, loc. cit., and notes on No. 434.

The burden, which has no logical connection with the words of the stanzas, plainly belongs to the medieval theme of the *aube*, or lovers' reluctant parting at dawn. It is probably borrowed from some earlier and more popular song on the theme, possibly that cited in references tabulated by Stevens (*M. & P.*, p. 382): '(i) *Cokelbie Sow*, line 306; (ii) *Complaint [of Scotland]*, p. lxxxvii, song 82; (iii) Dunbar, *Merchants of Edinburgh*, line 30; (iv) Gawin Douglas's 13th Prologue to *The Aeneid*, (edn. of 1533) f. 358ᵛ; (v) [*Gude and Godlie Ballatis*], 192, a moralized version'.

stza. 1, l. 4. *betwene*: in the midst.

stza. 2, l. 3. *on rewe*: pity.

433. The Tudor Rose

Music for three voices by Sir Thomas Phelipps. *Pr.* B. Fehr, *Archiv*, cvi (1901), 58; C. & S., p. 72; F. M. Padelford, *Early Sixteenth Century Lyrics* (Boston, 1907), p. 91; Robbins, *Hist. Poems*, p. 94; Stevens, *M. & P.*, p. 364; Sisam, p. 547; Davies, p. 263; with music, J. Stafford Smith, *A Collection of English Songs*, (London, [1779]), p. 14; E. F. Rimbault, *Ancient Vocal Music* [London, 1847], part ii, No. 11; H. B. Briggs, *A Collection of Songs and Madrigals of the Close of the 15th Century* (Plainsong and Mediaeval Music Society, London, 1891), p. 27. B.–R. 1327.

This gay and spirited carol celebrates the cessation of strife between the houses of York and Lancaster, the white and red roses. It was doubtless intended to supersede such partisan carols as No. 432. Stevens plausibly dates its composition at about 1500. Compare the opening lines of Skelton's 'A Laud and Praise Made for our Sovereign Lord the King' (*The Complete Poems of John Skelton Laureate*, ed. Philip Henderson, 3rd edn., London, 1959, p. 131):

> The Rose both White and Red
> In one Rose now doth grow.

The carol preserves one of the happiest features of the medieval English lyric, the graceful use of flower-names in verse. C. & S. (p. 343) point out the likeness of stza. 3, l. 2 to the ballad refrain 'Jennifer gentle and Rosemaree' (Child, No. 1 B). With the whole image of the choice of flowers compare stzas. 4, 5 of the folk-song 'The Seeds of Love' (Cecil J. Sharp, *One Hundred English Folksongs*, Boston, 1916, pp. 76–8):

> The Violet I did not like
> Because it bloom'd so soon.
> The Lily and the Pink I really overthink
> So I vow'd that I would wait till June.
>
> In June there was a red Rose-bud,
> And that is the flow'r for me.
> I oftentimes have pluck'd that red Rose-bud
> Till I gained the willow-tree.

No other composition by this Sir Thomas Phelipps is known. C. & S. assume that he is also the author of the words and would identify him with a Thomas Phillippis, a priest at Woodstock in 1518. This must be regarded as doubtful. The division of the words among the three vocal parts is intricate and appropriate to the effects of dialogue throughout which yield to agreement in the last lines.

The variation on the strict carol form which this piece shows in concluding with a modification of the text of the initial burden (and of that written after stza. 4) may be a conscious imitation of a feature found in some Italian *ballate* and possibly of ultimately Provençal origin: 'Am Ende des ganzen Liedes setzen dann die älteren Dichter oft eine neue *ripresa* zu, welche hier statt des alten Refrains gesungen war, eine Gewohnheit, der man auch schon bei den Provenzalen begegnet' (Adolf Gaspary, *Geschichte der italienischen Literatur*, Berlin, 1885, p. 94).

burden, l. 5. *in on*: in unity.

stza. 1, l. 3. *goldis*: marigolds.

stza. 4, l. 3. *Thyn hart vnbrace*: disclose your feelings.

stza. 6, l. 5. *Oure prince*: probably Prince Arthur, born in 1486.

433.1. In Honour of King Henry VII

a. *Previously unpublished.*

b. *Repr. The Poetical Works of John Skelton*, ed. after Alexander Dyce, ii (Boston, 1856), 345; etc. B.–R. 2526 (entry erroneous).

This laborious panegyric has had a wide circulation without the burden which makes it a carol in the MS. version a, but the attribution to Skelton is highly implausible. The numerous editions based on Dyce's text (and its plates) place it in an appendix headed 'Poems Attributed to Skelton'. But there is no reason to doubt that it was 'presented', whether sung or merely recited, at the elaborate feast of St. George at Windsor in 1488, as indicated in the basic edition of b (Ashmole, *The Institution*, etc., 1672, p. 594): 'Nor was it unusual for *Poets*, in former times, to present the *Soveraign* with the issue of their Fancies, having a subject so noble as this of the *Grand Feast*; among whom, the following *Verses* were presented to King *Henry* the Seventh, at the Feast of St. *George* celebrated at *Windesor* in the 3. year of his Reign, probably by Mr. *John Skelton* (after made Poet *Laureat*) who about that time began to be of some esteem.'

In the MS. of a the text immediately preceding the carol is as follows: 'The king offerde and aftur him euery knyght aftur his estate and whan masse was doon and de profundis saide the fest was accomplished.' This is the concluding sentence of the account of the feast.

stza. 1, l. 4, stza. 3, l. 3. *ambassates*: ambassadors.

434. The Ostrich Feather

Music for three voices by Edmund Turges. *Pr.* Flügel, *N.L.*, p. 159; with music, John Stafford Smith, *A Collection of English Songs* (London, [1779]), p. 26; Stevens, *M. & P.*, p. 380, *Early Tudor Songs*, p. 135. B.-R. *Supp.* 2394.5.

E. F. Rimbault (*A Little Book of Songs and Ballads*, London, 1851, p. 21) prints the song with the note: 'The following Song is given from an ancient parchment book, consisting of early English songs in parts, in the possession of the editor. It was *written* and composed by "Maister Edmond Turges", and the MS. from which it is taken is in all probability the original. Another copy may be seen in the Fayrfax MS.' This 'ancient parchment book' I have not been able to trace. If Rimbault's statement is accurate, this book bore an extremely close relation to the Fayrfax MS., for the text which he prints agrees almost *literatim* with that here presented. It shows, in short, a higher degree of accuracy than is usual in sixteenth-century copying. As a result, Rimbault's text is in no sense a variant, and the few differences of spelling which it presents are not here recorded.

An eighteenth-century modernized version of the burden of this piece, made by Dr. B. Cooke, is in the library of the Royal College of Music, London, MS. 810. It was made from the Fayrfax MS.

Little is known of the composer Turges's life, but he may have been the son of a John Turges, harper to Queen Margaret (Grove, *Dictionary of Music and Musicians*, s.v. 'Turges'). Other pieces by him are contained in the same MS., ff. 17ᵛ, 19ᵛ, 115ᵛ (No. 436).

The ostrich feather, the heraldic badge of the Prince of Wales, here represents Prince Arthur, eldest son of Henry VII. The prayer of the carol was not answered, for the prince died in April 1502, not long after the probable date of this composition. The piece was not necessarily composed, as Grove states (loc. cit.), to celebrate the marriage of Arthur and Catherine of Aragon. For a much inferior 'balet' sung in honour of the same prince at Coventry see *The Coventry Leet Book* (ed. M. D. Harris, E.E.T.S., Or. Ser., No. 134, etc., 1907-13, 591).

435. A Prayer for Peace

Music for two and three voices. *Pr.* Fehr, p. 276; Robbins, *Hist. Poems*, p. 242; Davies, p. 262; with music, Stevens, *Med. Carols*, p. 102. B.-R. 1710.

This piece, although of only one stanza, has the carol-form. The petition for the preservation of peace would have been appropriate enough at almost any time around 1500. It may refer to the danger to the English truce with Scotland in 1499, following a clash at Norham. After negotiations of some delicacy a treaty between the two realms was signed in July of that year. The term 'neighbours' is more likely to have been applied to the Scots than to continental powers. Another possibility is that the carol is of earlier date, and that the strife of Lancaster and York is the subject of the author's concern. Robbins suggests that the carol 'more probably refers to Edward IV's negotiations with Scotland in 1479-1483' (op. cit., p. 391).

436. To King Henry VIII [?]

Music for three voices by Edmund Turges. *Pr.* B. Fehr, *Archiv*, cvi (1901), 68; with music, John Stafford Smith, *A Collection of English Songs* (London, [1779]), p. 31; *Madrigals by English Composers of the Close of the Fifteenth Century* (Plainsong and Mediaeval Music Society, London 1893), No. 3; Stevens, *M. & P.*, p. 383, *Early Tudor Songs*, p. 144. B.-R. *Supp.* 3206.5.

The text of this carol may be dated early in the reign of Henry VIII, though it is possible that it is addressed to Henry VII. The tone of the piece is more appropriate to a monarch just assuming the throne than to one who had long occupied it. The 'right of your commons' and the 'hurts of thy commonalty' are probably generalities. There is not likely to be any relationship to the revolt of Cornishmen in June 1497, as suggested in the first edition.

437.

Deleted from this edition. As Stevens points out, *M. & P.*, pp. 411-12, the music is not that of a true carol. See also Stevens, *Henry VIII*, p. 107, note on No. 66.

438. A Ballet of the King's Majesty

Pr. John Leland, *De Rebus Britannicis Collectanea*, 2nd edn. (London, 1770), iv. 319; J. Strype, *Ecclesiastical Memorials* (Oxford, 1822), ii, part ii, 329; Frederick W. Fairholt, 'The Civic Garland', *P.S.* xix (1845), 9; A. Esdaile, *The Age of Elizabeth* (London, 1915), p. 1. B.-R. *Supp.* 3118.5.

The MS. which contains this uninspired lyric gives an interesting description of the circumstances under which it was sung. As the coronation procession of the young Edward VI passed through the City of London, it encountered various pageants arranged in the streets in the manner then usual. At the 'Lytell Coundyth in Chepe' was a stage with persons representing St. George, his page, a maiden with a lamb, and a child. The child was prepared to speak a short Latin oration and St. George an English one, both of which are preserved, but, as a previous speaker had overrun his allotted time, 'yt coulde not be done. Who be yt ther was a Songe, the dyttey was thus.'

The use of the word 'ballet' in the title prefixed to this piece is of no particular force. The looseness of application of the terms 'ballad' and 'ballet' at this time is well known.

'Down-a-down' continues throughout Elizabethan song as one of the most popular phrases for burdens and refrains. The use of the refrain-syllable 'down' with its literal meaning is rare, but it occurs in No. xxxiii of John Wilbye's *The Second Set of Madrigals* (1669):

> Nor joy nor grief can make my heart contented,
> For while with joy I look on high,
> Down, down I fall with grief and die.
> (E. H. Fellowes, *English Madrigal Verse, 1588–1632*, 3rd edn., revised
> Frederick W. Sternfeld and David Greer, Oxford, 1967, p. 318)

Compare also Ophelia's use in *Hamlet*, IV. v. 169–70: 'You must sing, Down-a-down-a. Ah, how the wheel [refrain] becomes it!' Cotgrave explains *refrain* as 'The Refret, burthen, or downe of a ballade.'

An extended account of this royal entry, 'perhaps the most tawdry on record', is given by Sydney Anglo, *Spectacle, Pageantry, and Early Tudor Policy* (Oxford, 1969), pp. 282–94. Much of the ceremonial was 'cribbed' from the reports by Lydgate and Fabyan of the pageant prepared for the return of Henry VI from France in 1432.

The carol, though it had become an old-fashioned type of song, was still used in the reign of Elizabeth I for this same purpose of public tribute to a monarch. In 1578 at Norwich a carol in long lines was sung 'on the Great Stage that was next the Market-Place, by the Waytes and best voyces in the Citie' with the burden:

> The deaw of Heaven droppes this day on dry and barren ground,
> Wherefore let frutefull heartes, I saye, at drumme and trumpet sound,
> Yeelde that is due, shew that is meete, to make our joy the more,
> In our good hope, and hir great prayse, we never saw before.
> (John Nichols, *The Progresses and Public Processions of Queen Elizabeth*,
> new edn., London, 1823, ii. 182)

And in a masque performed before the Queen in 1592 'The last Songe' is a carol with the burden:

> Happie houre, happie daie,
> That Eliza came this waie!
> (Ibid. iii. 206)

The pedantic attempt at wit and the pedestrian character of the carol-writer's verse make one conjecture that the carol is the work of a schoolmaster, perhaps a follower of Ascham in view of the somewhat irrelevant practical advice of stza. 5. Such a person might well have been in charge of the choir which sang and of the coaching of the youthful (and disappointed) Latin orator.

stza. 1, l. 3. *myter*: metre.

stza. 4, l. 1. Boulogne had been captured by Henry VIII's forces in September 1544 and left in England's possession by the treaty of 1546 with France.   l. 3. *wight*: strong.

stza. 6, l. 1. *towardes*: hopeful, promising.

439. The Complaint of One Banished

Pr. Wright, *P.S.* xxiii. 5. B.–R. 4075.

This highly artificial piece shows the carol-form elaborated from a simple song-type to an involved literary metre. In its mannered extravagance it points toward some of the inferior lyrics of the next century. There is no clue to the identity of the paragon described in stza. 8.

stza. 2, l. 2. *prosyrs*: at. Lat. *proceres*, noblemen.   l. 5. *Fortunat*: perhaps the result of confusion of the names of Fortune and Fortunatus.

stza. 3, l. 4. *naysom*: noisome.

stza. 4, l. 5. *contrystant*: sorrowing.

stza. 7, l. 1. *determyne*: limit, embarrass.   l. 4. *redownd*: cause to be full of favour.

stza. 8, l. 4. *facund*: eloquent.   l. 7. *dyscuse*: make known.

440. The Loveliest Lady in Land

Pr. Ritson, *Ancient Songs* (1790), p. 26, (1829), i. 58, (1877), 50; Thomas Wright, 'Specimens of Lyric Poetry', *P.S.* iv. 51; K. Böddeker, *Altenglische Dichtungen* (Berlin, 1878), p. 168; Mary G. Segar and Emmeline Paxton, *Some Minor Poems of the Middle Ages* (London, 1917), p. 30; Carleton Brown, *English Lyrics of the XIIIth Century* (Oxford, 1932), p. 148; Sitwell, *Atlantic Book*, p. 22 (in part); G. L. Brook, *The Harley Lyrics*, 3rd edn. (Manchester, 1964), p. 48; Kaiser, *Anth.*, p. 294, *Med. Engl.*, p. 467; Sisam, p. 122; Davies, p. 88 (in part); Silverstein, p. 88; Stemmler, p. 22; etc. B.–R. 1395.

The title given to this carol by Brown is adopted here. There are significant discussions of the piece in Böddeker, pp. 167–8, Brown, Brook, Arthur K. Moore, *The Secular Lyric in Middle English* (Lexington, Kentucky, 1951), pp. 65–8, and Theo Stemmler, *Die Englischen Liebesgedichte des MS. Harley 2253* (Bonn, 1962), pp. 168–93. For French parallels to some of the epithets applied to the loved one see Otto Heider, *Untersuchungen zur mittelenglischen erotischen Lyrik* (Halle, 1905), pp. 35–7. It is among the earliest preserved secular carols and is the only piece among the contents of the important MS. to have the full carol-form, although *Alysoun*, 'Bytuene Mersh ant Aueril', has a lively burden after all stanzas (Brook, p. 33). The contrast in style between the burden and the rest of the lyric is immediately apparent and has been much commented on. To the present editor it seems obviously, as to Sir Edmund Chambers (C. & S., p. 277), to Brook (p. 6), and to Moore (p. 65) it seems probably, derived from another song, folk-song or popular song as you will, but in any event from a piece quite outside the courtly tradition of the stanzas. R. H. Robbins (*Stud. in Phil.* lvi, 1959, 577) seems to reject this view for lack of 'evidence', but it is not to be expected that Middle English scribes will attach a label 'folk-song' or even acknowledge a source in a footnote. The difference in rhythm of the burden and its use of natural imagery connected with a simple and direct expression of love-longing are evidence enough. The same image is found in the refrain of a surviving folk-song, 'The Loyal Lover' (S. Baring-Gould and H. Fleetwood Sheppard, eds., *Songs of the West*, 5th edn., London, [1913], pp. 188–9):

> Blow summer breeze, o'er the sea
> Bring my pretty love to me,

not to mention the universally known 'My Bonnie Lies over the Ocean'. It is quite probable that here, as elsewhere, we have a poem not originally designed as a carol which has been later put into carol-form by either the original author or another. It seems more likely that the stanzas were written before and independently of the burden than that, as R. M. Wilson suggests, 'In all probability the refrain of a popular *carole* has been taken as the theme of a courtly lyric, a practice found elsewhere during the Middle English period' (*Early Middle English Literature*, London, 1939, p. 262).

Carleton Brown (op. cit., pp. xxxix, xl) regards this and three other poems in the MS. as 'the work of the same person, a poet of the Welsh border'. The others are *Annot and John*, 'Ichot a burde in a bour ase beryl so bryht'; *The Lover's Complaint*, 'Wiþ longyng y am lad'; and *The Fair Maid of Ribbesdale*, 'Mosti ryden by Rybbesdale'. He lists many parallels between this piece and the Annot and Ribbesdale poems. Brook dissents: 'There are no two lyrics in the manuscript that we can with certainty assign to the same poet' (p. 26).

An elaborate literary analysis of the poem with special attention to syntax and rhetoric is given by Leo Spitzer, '*Explication de Texte* Applied to Three Great Middle English Poems', *Archivum*

Linguisticum, iii (1951), 2–22. Spitzer, who does not appear to have seen either the first edition of this work or Brook's edition, is emphatic about the character of the burden as folk-poetry. He also sees significance in the poem's having ten stanzas—'the perfect number!' In the first edition of this work the following carols on different religious subjects have ten stanzas: Nos. 53, 78, 102, 124 B, 167, 170, 204, 269, 297, 303. So has No. 399, a satire on women.

Moore thinks ill of the poem (p. 66): 'This lyric is a patchwork of redundant images and hackneyed phrases.' A more respectful discussion is given to it by Theo Stemmler (op. cit., 168–75).
stza. 1, l. 1. *Ichot*: I know. l. 3. *Menskful*: gracious. l. 4. *fonde*: take. l. 5. *wurhliche won*: goodly country. l. 8. *Lussomore*: more lovable.
stza. 2, l. 3. *monge*: mingle. l. 4. *breme*: clear, brilliant.
stza. 3, l. 1. *lure lumes*: complexion shines. l. 3. *bleo blykyeth*: face gleams. l. 5. *suyre*: neck.
stza. 4, l. 5. *lasteles*: blameless. l. 8. *Yheryed*: honoured. *heste*: vow.
stza. 5, l. 5. *murgest*: merriest. l. 7. *fi[th]ele*: Brook points out that the emendation may be unnecessary, as *fiele* is a possible form of Old French *viele*. *crouth*: crowd or 'crwth'. For a full description see Hortense Panum, *The Stringed Instruments of the Middle Ages*, revised by Jeffrey Pulver (London, 1941), pp. 239–45.
stza. 6, l. 4. *baner*. Bruce Dickins and R. M. Wilson (*Early Middle English Texts*, London, 1956, p. 228) call this 'difficult to translate' and suggest emendation to something like '*burde* "lady"' which would then balance' the *ledy* of stza. 6, l. 8. There is no difficulty in translating it as 'standard-bearer, the one in the van', which gives a personal noun to balance 'ledy'. l. 6. *paruenke*: periwinkle. l. 7. *salsecle*: heliotrope.
stzas. 7–9. In these allegorical stanzas Love is conceived as a masculine judicial personality to whom the speaker complains how Sighing, Sorrowing, and Care, three 'knights' of the lady's retinue, have threatened him in spite of a similarly personified Peace. In stza. 7, l. 1 'Hire' gives some trouble. Böddeker removes it, and Brook says that perhaps it should be removed. Spitzer reads it as 'love for her', a personification of a more special emotion than love in general. Perhaps a better interpretation is that even Love as judge is also in the lady's service.
stza. 8, l. 3. *Thoht*: Care. l. 5. *balful bende*: dire bondage.
stza. 9, l. 2. *beh*: bent. *bord*: table. l. 3. *hente*: seize. *hord*: treasure. l. 6. *fen of fote*: mud from the foot. ll. 7, 8. That she will deal honourably and helpfully with you.
stza. 10, l. 2. *dare*: crouch, hide timidly.
What seems to be a parody of this kind of alliterative love poetry is found in the Digby play of Mary Magdalene (ed. F. J. Furnivall, E.E.T.S., Ex. Ser., No. lxx, 1896, 90–1, ll. 942–9, 958–60):

> [Kyng of Marcylle speaks]
> I have a favorows fode, and fresse as the fakown,
> she is full fayer In hyr femynyte;
> whan I loke on þis lady, I am lofty as the lyon; [etc.]
>
> now godamercy, berel brytest of bewte!
> godamercy, rubu rody as þe rose!
> ye be so ple[s]avnt to my pay, ȝe put me from peyn.

441. A Lover's Plea

Music for one voice (burden only).
Pr. first edition; Robbins, *Secular Lyrics*, p. 13; Stemmler, p. 85; with music, Stevens, *Med. Carols*, p. 111 (burden only). B.-R. 2185.
stza. 2, l. 1. *beyne*: both. l. 2. *lysse*: relieve. l. 3. *geyne*: avail, serve.
stza. 3, l. 1. *myn arnde bede*: do my errand.

441.1 A Lady of High Degree

Pr. Robbins, *Secular Lyrics*, p. 145; Stemmler, p. 72. B.-R. 2232 (indexed by first line of burden).
Perhaps because this piece is written as prose in the MS., Robbins treats it as a song of four stanzas instead of as a carol of burden and three stanzas. His title is adopted here.
Such details of the lady's beauty as are mentioned are in accordance with late medieval conventions: the grey eyes (blue in modern terminology), the sides of the body long and well shaped

like Criseyde's (Chaucer, *Troilus* iii. 1248), the brows (forehead) smooth and gleaming. Compare the important article by D. S. Brewer, 'The Ideal of Feminine Beauty in Medieval Literature', *M.L.R.* 1 (1955), 257–69.

burden, l. 1. *dese*: dais, the place of honour at a dinner or other ceremony in a hall.

stza. 3, l. 3. *tray and teen*: grief and woe.

442. A Slighted Lover's Complaint

Pr. Ritson, *Ancient Songs* (1790), p. 72, (1829), i. 129, (1877), p. 111; *Rel. Ant.* i. 24; E. Arbor, *The Dunbar Anthology* (London, 1901), p. 118. B.-R. 3179.

stza. 1, l. 4. *quytt*: rewarded. *mede*: merit, desert.

stza. 7, l. 2. *nere the rathere*: none the sooner.

443. Strife over a Kiss

Pr. Reports of the Historical Manuscripts Commission, v, Appendix, p. 458 (in part); J. W. Ebsworth, *Bagford Ballads* (London, 1878), i. 519; Robbins, *Secular Lyrics*, p. 28; Sisam, p. 521; Stemmler, p. 107. B.-R. 150.

In the *Reports* the carol is said to be signed 'J. Wolstan', as also in the transcript and note in Dr. Shepard's handwriting found with the original MS. The note reads: 'The name of J. Wulstane "The Poet" does not occur in any list of the monks yet found. Therefore to the credit of the monastery [Christ Church, Canterbury], it may be presumed that he was only a novice— "*non professus nec etiam rasus*".'

Dr. Shepard misread the colophon, which is: 'Finys q*uod* wulstane p[ ]one.' The second name is damaged. I find no such name listed in the rolls of monks, but the author might be identified with 'Will: Preston', who died in 1457 (W. G. Searle, ed., *Lists of the Deans, Priors, and Monks of Christ Church Monastery*, Christ Church, Canterbury Publications, Octavo Series, No. xxxiv, Cambridge, 1902, p. 189). The last word might be 'persone' and the author's style rather than his surname.

The stanzas of the carol are written as if spoken alternately by the maid and the man, except for stza. 4, of which he speaks the first two lines, and she the last two. Charles Read Baskervill relates it to other folk-dialogues of wooing (*The Elizabethan Jig*, Chicago, 1929, p. 20).

stza. 1, l. 1. This seems to have been a current phrase, perhaps from a popular song. Compare the exchange between Cacurgus and Misogonus in the play *Misogonus* (? 1577), part of the dialogue leading up to the song mentioned in the notes to No. 134:

> Mi. Till I see my trule Ile nether singe nor say
> Ca. Alas good man he must nedes nowe be kiste
> what I praye yow for my sake a little yet stay
> (R. Warwick Bond, ed., *Early Plays from the Italian*, Oxford, 1911, p. 196, ll. 50–2)

stza. 3, l. 3. See B. J. W., *Proverbs*, W 643.

stza. 5, l. 3. *karchos nocke*: i.e. through the kerchief's opening.

444. Of Two Loving Hearts

Pr. Reports of the Historical Manuscripts Commission, v, Appendix, p. 458. B.-R. 3271.

The play on the word 'heart' in this carol is like that of Audelay on 'love' in No. 272. It is possible to interpret this piece as devotional, the two hearts being those of the author and of Christ, but in the absence of specific identification it is safer to regard it as an amorous carol of more refinement than most.

stza. 3, l. 3. *later lyne*: a reference to the refrain as the second line of the burden.

445. My Lady Is a Pretty One

Music for treble part only. *Pr.* B. Fehr, *Archiv*, cvii (1901), 57; C. & S., p. 83. B.-R. *Supp.* 3097.6.

The entry in R. H. Robbins, *Modern Language Notes*, lxxiv (1959), 202, ignores the publication of this text in the first edition of this work and mistakenly lists it as an 'addition' to the corpus of carols.

Utley (p. 204) points out its similarity to the contemporary song in the British Museum MS. Addit. 18752, f. 76ᵛ: 'My lytell prety one my prety bony one' (*pr.* Edward B. Reed, *Anglia*, xxxiii, 1910, 352).

446. In Praise of Serving-men

Pr. Ritson, *Ancient Songs* (1790), p. 92 (1829), ii. 8 (1877), p. 154; F. W. Fairholt, *P.S.* xxvii. 58; F. J. Furnivall, *Captain Cox, His Ballads and Books* (Ballad Society, London, 1871), p. cxxx; Robbins, *Secular Lyrics*, p. 32; Stemmler, p. 111. B.–R. 2654.

Furnivall (op. cit., pp. xiii, cxxix) identifies this piece with one listed among the 'ballets & songs' of Captain Cox's library as No. liv: 'So wo iz me begon, troly lo.' This is hardly safe, in view of the difference in wording and the frequent practice of using the same or similar burdens for several pieces.

burden, ll. 1, 3. *begone*: provided; 'so fortunate am I.'

stza. 1, l. 3. *mynyon trym*: daintily smart. *O.E.D.* cites the phrase for 'minion' as an adjective, but the use here is adverbial. Compare the song 'Mynyon goo trym' in British Museum Book K. 1. e. 1 (*pr.* Flügel, *Anglia*, xii, 1889, 593).

stza. 8, l. 3. *to deth depart*: till death part (us).

446.1. Uncertain, Coy, and Hard to Please

Music for three voices. *Pr.* Fehr, p. 273; Stevens, *M. & P.*, p. 350; with music, Stevens, *Med. Carols*, p. 115, *Early Tudor Songs*, p. 23. B.–R. *Supp.* 4283.5.

Stevens points out that this piece is later than the other carols in its MS. and is written in a different hand and notation (*Med. Carols*, p. 124; *M. & P.*, loc. cit.).

stza. 1, l. 3. *wrappe that yn your trayn*: Stevens (*M. & P.*) paraphrases with an engaging anachronism: 'put that in your pipe and smoke it!'

stza. 2, l. 1. *on-syttyng*: reproachful.

stza. 3, l. 3. *light credens*: fickle credulousness.

stza. 4, l. 2. See B. J. W., *Proverbs*, L 568 (an early occurrence of this very widespread saying; compare L 482, L 484, L 485, W 45). *reyne*: last, endure. l. 3. See B. J. W., *Proverbs*, S 576. All three injunctions are unique in B. J. W., although they are obviously regarded here as proverbial. Compare B. J. W., B 44.

447. A Good Use of Money

Music for bass part only. *Repr.* Flügel, *Anglia*, xii (1889), 593; Imelmann, *Shakespeare-Jahrbuch*, xxxix (1903), 131. B.–R. *Supp.* 87.5.

This is the only one of the songs in its part-book that has the true carol-form, as far as can be judged from the bass part alone. A number of the others have separate burdens and stanzas of the same verse-form throughout, but the music is varied from stanza to stanza.

stza. 2, l. 2. *mynyon*: pretty, dainty.

448. Green Groweth the Holly

Music for three voices by King Henry VIII (burden only). *Pr.* Flügel, *Anglia*, xii (1889), 237, *N.L.*, p. 135; Padelford, p. 77; Stevens, *M. & P.*, p. 398; Davies, p. 90; with music, William Chappell, *Archaeologia*, xli (1867), 374; Lady Mary Trefusis, *Songs, Ballads, and Instrumental Pieces* (Roxburghe Club, Oxford, 1912), p. 13; *Oxford Book of Carols*, Music Edn., p. 136; *facs.* H. B. Briggs, *The Musical Notation of the Middle Ages* (Plainsong and Mediaeval Music Society, London, 1890), plate xx; Stevens, *Henry VIII*, p. 28. B.–R. *Supp.* 409.5.

This famous composition, of which the words as well as the music have been generally attributed to King Henry VIII, shows a literary adaptation of the old folk-theme of the holly and the ivy. The identification of holly and ivy with man and woman persists, but the symbolism here (stzas. 2, 3) is of amity and not of opposition. The phrase forming the first two lines of the burden enjoyed currency as a folk-saying in the sense of 'for ever'. Compare the method of laying a ghost by tricking it into agreeing to stay away 'while hollies are green' (E. M. Wright, *Rustic Speech and Folk-Lore*, London, 1913, p. 193).

448.1. My Sovereign Lord

Music for three voices, by William Cornish (burden only). *Pr.* Flügel, *Anglia*, xii (1889), 242, William Chappell, *Archaeologia*, xli (1867), 378; Stevens, *M. & P.*, p. 405; with music, Stevens, *Henry VIII*, p. 40. B.-R. *Supp.* 2271.2.

There is no reason to doubt that this carol was written for performance at court, that its speaker is assumed to be Queen Catherine of Aragon, and that it reflects a real situation, Henry VIII's fondness for and success at the formal knightly tournament. The score of four out of six in the game of running at the ring, in which the contestant tries to carry away on the point of his lance a suspended metal ring, suggests reference to a particular occasion.

stza. 2, l. 1. *pure*: power.   l. 2. As a warrior who is a chieftain.   l. 3. *barryoure*: the railing separating the mounted combatants in a tourney.   l. 5. *that I sey best*: the best that I saw.

stza. 3, l. 3. *doth no comparyng*: admits no comparison.

stza. 4, l. 2. *replete*: fill.   l. 3. *behete*: promise.   l. 4. *he*: him.   *prest*: ready and willing.

stza. 5, l. 2. *one lyue*: alive.

stza. 6, l. 1. i.e. God.   l. 2. *principall*: specially.

449. Why So Unkind?

Music for tenor part only. *Pr.* Flügel, *Anglia*, xii (1889), 261. B.-R. *Supp.* 3144.5.

The phrase 'Soo to be kende to me' is written after the repetition of the burden which follows the first stanza, and is marked off from it by a bar, the only one across the stave. The music for this phrase is the same as that for the second line of the burden.

450. Now Springs the Spray

Pr. George E. Woodbine, *M.L.R.* iv (1909), 236; W. W. Skeat, *M.L.R.* v (1910), 105; Sandison, p. 47; Kenneth Sisam, *Fourteenth Century Verse and Prose* (Oxford, 1921), p. 163; Carleton Brown, *English Lyrics of the XIIIth Century* (Oxford, 1932), p. 119; Sitwell, *Atlantic Book*, p. 24; Wystan Hugh Auden and Norman Holmes Pearson, *Poets of the English Language* (New York, 1950), i. 21; Frank Kermode, *English Pastoral Poetry*, (London, 1952), p. 45 (wrongly derived from B.M. MS. Harley 2253); Kaiser, *Anth.*, p. 291, *Med. Engl.*, p. 463; Greene, *Selection*, p. 161; Sisam, p. 98; Davies, p. 77; Stemmler, p. 10; Silverstein, p. 41. B.-R. 360.

This graceful *chanson d'aventure* is one of the very earliest preserved in the carol-form. The memorandum in the same hand which follows it is dated 1302–3 (31 Edward I). On its similarity to an Old French poem beginning 'L'autrier defors Picarni', *pr.* K. Bartsch, *Altfranzösische Romanzen und Pastourellen* (Leipzig, 1870), No. ii, 7, see Brown, *English Lyrics of the XIIIth Century*, p. 214, and Sandison, pp. 47–8. R. M. Wilson comments: 'For all that the English lyric reads much more like a popular *carole* than a literary composition based on a French original' (*Early Middle English Literature*, London, 1958, p. 263).

Kermode (op. cit., p. 239) suggests that the carol 'may have concealed religious significance'. There is no evidence for this.

R. H. Robbins (*Stud. in Phil.* lvi, 1959, 577) refers to this carol as from MS. Harley 2253 and denies, without offering evidence, that it derives from popular dance.

burden, l. 1. 'Nou' is best taken as a conjunction rather than as an adverb, so that the first line can be rendered 'Now that the shoots are sprouting (i.e. now that spring is here)', as suggested by C. T. Onions, 'Two Notes on Middle English Texts', *Medium Ævum*, xvii (1948), 32–3. l. 5. May the clod cling to him! i.e. may he be buried (Skeat). This alliterative phrase appears delightfully in another amorous context used as a school exercise: 'When the clot klyngueth and þe cucko synguth & þe brome sprynguth then his tyme a ȝongelyng for to go a wowyng'. (B.M. MS. Harley 1002, *pr.* C. E. Wright, 'Late Middle English Parerga in a School Collection', *R.E.S.*, New Ser., ii, 1951, 119.)

stza. 2, ll. 1, 2. *Son*: as soon as (conjunction). This sense is suggested by C. T. Onions (loc. cit.), who points to the parallel lines in the Old French poem:

Si tost com j'oi le cri
celle part tornai.

(Brown, loc. cit.)

stza. 3, l. 3. *bihot*: promised.   . 7. *Bi this dai*. Skeat glosses 'If I can (contrive it), it shall repent him concerning this day', and does not think the line an expression of emphasis or affirmation (*M.L.R.* v, 1910, 105). But compare No. 415, burden:

> Ay, ay, be this day,
> Y wyll mak mery qwyll Y may.

450.1. Alone I Live, Alone

Music for three voices. *Pr.* John Saltmarsh, *Two Medieval Lyrics* (Cambridge, 1933), p. 8, *The Antiquaries Journal*, xv (1935), 13, *facs.* plate iii; Robbins, *Secular Lyrics*, p. 154. B.-R. *Supp.* 2293.5.

The burden of this carol occurs, about twenty years later, as the burden of the religious *chanson d'aventure* carol No. 164 in the printed collection associated with Richard Kele. The same two lines are set to music by Dr. Cooper as a round for three voices in B.M. MS. Addit. 31922 (*pr.* Stevens, *M. & P.*, p. 390, with music, *Henry VIII*, p. 17). The first line is prefixed, apparently to designate a known air, to the much earlier No. 418. The phrase is used in reference to a known song in 'A balade in commendation of our Lady' in Thynne's edition of Chaucer, 1532 (Stevens, *M. & P.*, loc. cit., with acknowledgement for the reference to P. J. Frankis).

451. A Love-Complaint

Pr. Mayer, Sheet k; Robbins, *Sec. Lyrics*, p. 16; Kaiser, *Anth.*, p. 297 (omits stza. 5), *Med. Eng.*, p. 470; Sisam, p. 375; Stemmler, p. 69. B.-R. 3418.

The changing in MS. of the gender of the pronouns throughout a medieval love-lyric is rare, if not unique to this text.

stza. 1, l. 1. *altherbest*: best of all.

stza. 2, ll. 2, 3. This line is repeated through an error in copying; it is properly l. 3. The missing line should be something like: 'He maketh haste to go me fro.'

stza. 4, l. 2. *dyrward*: dearworth, dearly beloved.

stza. 6, l. 4. A cliché frequent in love poetry in both Middle and Early Modern English. It is discussed at some length by Charles A. Huttar, ' "Forsake Me Neuer for No New": A Note on Wyatt's Poetic Diction', *N. & Q.* ccx (1965), 170–2. See also B. J. W., *Proverbs*, N 97 and note on No. 455, stza. 2, l. 2.

452. The Serving-maid's Holiday

Pr. Robbins, *Secular Lyrics*, p. 24; Greene, *Selection*, p. 162; Sisam, p. 452; Stemmler, p. 83. B.-R. 225.

The holiday in this carol is probably Midsummer Day, as in No. 453. There is nothing to prevent our supposing that Jack is the same young man in both.

burden, l. 1. *Rybbe*: scrape the flax with an iron tool. Robbins reads 'Wybbe' and glosses 'to weave', but the 'R' is clear in the MS. and is repeated after each stanza. This house-and-dairy-maid would not be carrying on the man's trade of weaving. The alliteration with 'rele' is effective.

stza. 1, l. 2. *werue*: The wharve, or whorl, the small pulley or flywheel of a spindle. *O.E.D.* cites Elyot, 1538: 'a wherue, whyche is a rounde thynge of stone, or wodde, or leadde, put on a spyndell to make it runne round'.   *vond*: found. She has been mislaying everything.

stza. 2, l. 1. *vlech*: flet, floor.   l. 2. *vnbech*: unmended.   l. 3. *vnrepe yech*: unprepared yet.

stza. 3, l. 1. *worton*: herbs.   l. 2. *Predele*: pride (v.), adorn, trim.

stza. 4, l. 2. *cherrus*: chores, domestic work.   l. 3. *solas*: make easy.   l. 4. *dowge*: douce, soft.

stza. 5, ll. 2, 3. 'All this scattering [of the milk] gets the bread out for me, except for the dough which stays under the nail.' The girl is, of course, a 'wet-hand' milker and like most old-time dairy people no doubt believes that the cow will not yield her milk unless some is first spilled on the hands ('outh' from 'outen'; 'schayl' = 'skail', scattering, spillage). Thus the dough would be rinsed off her hands, which she has not otherwise washed in her scatterbrained haste.

stza. 6, l. 3. *eyghe*: awe.

stza. 7, l. 2. *ale-schoth*: scot-ale, a festival for which the ale was provided by a forced contribution. l. 3. *sowse*: soak. *wroch*: probably written for *wrot*: snout, vulgarly used for 'nose'. See *O.E.D.*, s.v. 'Wroot, *sb.*', and compare modern slang for deep drink: 'a snoutful'.

It is dramatically suitable to have a carol presented with a milkmaid as its speaker. The custom of the milkmaid's singing while milking to soothe the cow and improve the flow has persisted into modern times. It is interesting that the milking song written by Robert Jamieson of Morayshire in imitation of actual farm-women's song is in strict carol form with initial burden (John Ord, ed., *The Bothy Songs & Ballads of Aberdeen, Banff & Moray, Angus, and the Mearns*, Paisley, 1930, p. 244).

453. Jack and the Dancing Maid

Pr. Robbins, *Secular Lyrics*, p. 22; Kaiser, *Anth.*, p. 310, *Med. Engl.*, p. 476; Greene, *Selection*, p. 164; Davies, p. 204; Silverstein, p. 134; Stemmler, p. 81. B.-R. 1849.

Midsummer Day (Nativity of St. John the Baptist, 24 June) and its eve were the occasions of so much popular custom and celebration that a separate treatise on the subject could be produced. In this carol the gathering is for the dancing of a carole, a 'ryng', and its sequel is sexual indulgence. Not much documentation is needed, but two references may be given in illustration. An Augustinian canon of Barnwell, Cambs., alleging a mistaken etymology for the place-name, writes in 1295 of the 'wakes' of the young people on St. John's Eve:

.. eo tempore appellati, eo quod pueri et adolescentes semel per annum, in vigilia scilicet Nativitatis sancti Johannis baptiste, illic convenientes more Anglorum luctamina et alia ludicria [*sic*] exercebant puerilia, et cantilenis et musicis instrumentis sibi invicem applaudebant. Unde propter turbam puerorum et puellarum illic concurrencium et ludencium mos inolevit, ut in eodem die illic conveniret negociandi gracia turba vendencium et emencium.

(John Willis Clark, *Liber Memorandorum Ecclesie de Bernewelle*, Cambridge, 1907, p. 41, quoted by F. Liebermann, *Archiv*, cxxxi (1913), 429, and in part by Arthur K. Moore, *English Studies*, xxxii, 1951, 59). A Yorkshire parallel to the episode of this carol, in which the principals, John Dogson and his serving-maid Alice Tomson, commit their sin while the St. John's fires are being kindled, is reported in the *Acts of Chapter of the Collegiate Church of SS. Peter and Wilfrid, Ripon, A.D. 1452 to A.D. 1506* under date of 1454 (Surtees Society Publications, No. lxiv, 1875, p. 39):

Interrogata an eam carnaliter cognovit, respondit quod sic. Interrogata de tempore, respondit quod in festo nativitatis Sancte [*sic*] Johannis Baptistae. Interrogata de tempore respondit quod in nocte quando ignes erant illuminati. Interrogata de loco, respondit quod primo eam carnaliter cognovit in domo praedicti Jo. Dogeson in camera basa juxta Richarson et alia vice eam cognovit in coquina dicti Jo. D. Interrogata an fama erat publica quod haberat [*sic*] eam in uxorem, respondit quod sic.

stza. 1, l. 3. *haly-watur clerk*. The carrier of the holy-water vessel, often regarded as one of rather low position. Compare Jolly Jankyn of No. 457.

stza. 4, l. 3. White gloves were apparently associated with leading the carole; compare the homily 'De Dominica in Passione Domini Nostri' in Myrc's *Festial*, ed. Theodor Erbe, part i, E.E.T.S., Ex. Ser., No. xcvi, 1905, 113, where St. Bernard 'yn Crystis person' says:

Thow man for vanyte syngyst and rowtes, and I for þe crye and wepe; þou hast on þy hed a garland of flowres, and I for þe on my hed suffyr a wreþe of stynkyng þornes; þou hast on þy hondys whyt gloues, and I for þy loue haue blody hondys; thow hast þyn armes sprad on brode ledyng carallys, and I for þy loue haue myn armes sprad on þe tre, and tachut wyth grete nayles; thow hast þy cloþe raggyd and pynchyt smale, and I haue my body for thy loue full of great walus.

The Glossarial Index offers 'carallys, *sb. pl.*, coral'! See also *A Stanzaic Life of Christ*, ed. Frances A. Foster, E.E.T.S., Or. Ser., No. 166, 1926, 200–1, ll. 5925–44, which uses the same passage from St. Bernard, who has 'gloues' only (Lat. *cyrotecas*).

The same images are found in the reproach of Christ to sinful man in a lyric from Bodl. MS. Bodley 416:

'þyn hondes streite gloved,
white & clene kept;
Myne wiþ nailes þorled,
on rode & eke my feet.

'A-cros þou berest þyn armes,
whan þou dauncest narewe.'
(Brown, *R.L. 14 C.*, No. 126, p. 225, ll. 7–12)

Compare *Quia Amore Langueo*, Lambeth 853 text, stza. 6 (ed. Frederick J. Furnivall, *Political, Religious, and Love Poems*, E.E.T.S., Or. Ser., No. 15, 1866, 182). In a carole danced at night, white gloves would be of real advantage to the gesturing leader as to a modern traffic policeman. Gloves were also a conventional gift in courtship.

There is a delightful instance from Lincolnshire, where Timothy Dennett actually met Ellen Lambert, to whom he later gave gloves, while she was milking her father's cows (Mildred Campbell, *The English Yeoman under Elizabeth and the Early Stuarts*, Yale Historical Publications: Studies, xiv, New Haven, 1942, p. 303).

stza. 7, l. 1. *rong the bell*. This phrase can hardly have its usual meaning of 'reveal the secret' or 'spread scandal'. It must mean 'achieve orgasm', as in sexual slang still current, which also has ring my chimes'. Compare Godfrey Gobylyue's reference to his mother in Stephen Hawes's *The Pastime of Pleasure* (1517):

> Her name was alyson that loued nought elles
> But euer more to rynge her blacke belles.
>
> (ed. William Edward Mead, E.E.T.S., Or. Ser., No. 173, 1928, 135, ll. 3544–5)

Compare also Spenser, *Faerie Queene*, Bk. III, canto x, stza. 48, l. 9. I am indebted to Dr. L. A. Holford-Strevens, of Christ Church, Oxford, for this reference.

l. 3. *the reaggeth deuel*. The devil was often described, pictured, and represented on the stage as ragged or shaggy. Compare the instructions to the butchers in the Banns of the Chester Plays, ed. Hermann Deimling, E.E.T.S., Ex. Ser., No. lxii, 1892, 6, ll. 121–2:

> set out as Accostomablie vsed haue yee,
> the devill in his fethers, all ragger and rente.

l. 4. Tricks or sports, here, of course, with sexual meaning as in William Forest, *The History of Grisild the Second*:

> To much Adultery dothe still florische,
> As thearin cheeif their delectation,
> Witheoute feare of Goddys indignation;
> I meane no small Byrdys of the symple sorte.
>
> (ed. W. D. Macray, London, 1875, chap. ii, stza. 20, ll. 3–6)

stza. 9, l. 1. *Ever by on and by on*: over and over again.   l. 4. A proverb: 'Ill-spun yarn will always ravel.' Compare the *Towneley Plays*, 'The Killing of Abel', l. 435: '*Garcio.* Yey, ill spon weft ay comes foule out', and 'Shepherds' Play II', l. 587: '*ijus pastor.* Ill spon weft, Iwys / ay commys foull owte' (ed. George England and A. W. Pollard, E.E.T.S., Ex. Ser., No. lxxi, 1897, 21, 135). Robbins notes (p. 236) *The Proverbs of Hendyng*, l. 272: 'Euer out comeþe euel sponne web.'

The adventure recorded in this carol exactly illustrates the warning in a sermon from B.M. MS. Harley 2398, quoted by G. R. Owst:

> Nyce [foolish] maydenhode is ylyckened to Jeptes douȝter, that walkede aboute in the monteynes twey monthes for to wepe her maydenhode. So doth nyce maydenes that walketh aboute in medes and in fayre places ledynge daunces and syngynge, as it were schewynge hem self to lese her maydenhode, and makynge sorwe that they have ybe so longe maydenes.
>
> (*Literature and Pulpit in Medieval England*, Cambridge, 1933, p. 119)

A couplet strikingly parallel to the burden of the carol is printed from B.M. MS. Addit. 33965, f. 98ʳ by Siegfried Wenzel (*Anglia*, xcii, 1974, 75):

> Weylawey þat iche ne span
> whan y to þe ringe ran.

The reference to the ring of the carole makes this version more significant than that previously published by R. H. Robbins (*Anglia*, lxxxiii, 1965, 47), which reads 'wude' instead of 'ringe'. The context introductory to the carol is a sentence of a Latin sermon which relates strikingly to stzas. 9 and 10 of No. 452: 'Sic juvencule, dum sunt virgines et caste, cantant, sed cum venter ceperit inflari, cantum mutant in lamentum.'

454. A Betrayed Maiden

Pr. James & Macaulay, p. 71; Robbins, *Secular Lyrics*, p. 18; Stemmler, p. 87. B.–R. 3594.

stza. 2, l. 1. *gramery*: magic.   l. 2. *skyll*: reason.   l. 3. *siccurly*: surely.   l. 4. *warne*: refuse.   *may*: strength, originally 'mayn' to rhyme with the burden.

stza. 3, l. 2. *lete*: allowed.   l. 4. Compare stza. 2 of a macaronic song on a similar theme in Bodl. MS. Ashmole 176, f. 98ᵛ (*c.* 1600):

> What shall I say meis parenti*bus*?
> Th*a*t w*i*th me hath laye*n* quid*am* clericus?
> They wyll me beate virgis *et* fustib*us*
> *And* me deprave cor*am* hominibus.

stza. 4, l. 2. The frequency of such a plight after pilgrimages was a common subject of medieval jest and moralizing.

455. A Forsaken Maiden's Lament

Pr. Robbins, *Secular Lyrics*, p. 17; Greene, *Selection*, p. 166; Sisam, p. 456; Tydeman, p. 60; Stemmler, p. 86. B.–R. 1330.

The line prefixed to the burden of this carol appears to be the burden of another carol, possibly on a similar theme, to the air of which this piece is written. As pointed out by Robbins (p. 234), this air cannot be that of 'Bryd on brere, brid, brid on brere!' written with music in King's College, Cambridge, Muniment Roll 2 W. 32, verso, which is not a carol (*pr.* Robbins, pp. 146–7, and previously by John Saltmarsh, *The Antiquaries Journal*, xv, 1935, 3–4, and *Two Medieval Lyrics*, Cambridge, 1933, p. 6). 'Bird on briar' is a proverbial phrase. Compare 'Ane deuoit orisoun To oure Lady The Virgin mary', B.M. MS. Arundel 285, ff. 193ᵛ–196ᵛ, ll. 11–13 (*pr.* Brown, *R.L. 15 C.*, pp. 38–41):

> Haill! cumly cristell cleir
> Aboue þe ordouris nyne
> Als blith as bird on brer,

and the burden of No. 28,

The scrap of song here written is in the same metre as the burden of the carol and has the same rhymes:

> Bryd on brere y tell yt to
> none othur y ne dar.

It is quite possible that these are the first two lines of a four-line burden which has been shortened, especially as the first words are again written and deleted after the first stanza. Compare the treatment of a four-line burden in No. 453.

This carol, to which it would be pedantic to deny the term 'popular', is, of course, on a theme familiar in the medieval French lyric, and there are many parallels to the bird-confidant of the 'Bryd on brere' lines. It undoubtedly comes from the same milieu as Nos. 452, 453. Compare No. 454, where a clerk is the betrayer, and No. 456, where Sir John (probably a priest) sins with the speaker of the carol at a well-waking.

stza. 2, l. 2. See B. J. W., *Proverbs*, N 97, and note on No. 451, stza. 6, l. 4.

stza. 3, l. 1. *sawus*: sayings, promises.

456. Waking the Well

Pr. Rel. Ant. i. 1; W. C. Hazlitt, *Faiths and Folklore* (London, 1905), ii. 617; John Brand, *Popular Antiquities* (London, 1849), ii. 379; Robbins, *Secular Lyrics*, p. 19; Stemmler, p. 70; Grigson, p. 142. B.–R. 3409.

In *Rel. Ant.* the MS. is incorrectly assigned to the beginning of the fifteenth century.

The false step related by the girl who is the speaker in this carol may be the result of her participation in a merry-making at some well, probably a 'holy' well. Hazlitt prints the piece in illustration of an article on wakes. These festivals were, of course, of pagan origin and were unsuccessfully combated and then more successfully given a Christian colouring by the Church. The *Penitential* of King Egbert, for instance, enjoined three years' penance for keeping a wake at a well or elsewhere than at a church, but the custom of well-wakes lasted none the less until modern times. St. John's Eve was a favoured time for these wakes, a time when licence was prone to occur as part of the festivities. At Kirkhampton the youths and girls jumping through the flames of the St. John's bonfires sang to the well, 'Awake, awake, for sin gales [a corruption of "St. John's"] sake'. See R. C. Hope, *The Legendary Lore of the Holy Wells of England* (London, 1893), pp. xix, 40, 42, 48.

An equally possible explanation of the carol is that the girl was observing a New Year's custom, not social, but solitary, of going to gather what was called 'the cream of the well', the first water drawn from it in the year, and that she was there surprised by the persuasive wooer. Stza. 2 suggests such an episode rather than a crowded festival.

Sir John is probably the village priest, or at any rate a cleric. Chaucer's Nun's Priest is named Sir John. Compare Audelay's account (Whiting, No. 2, ll. 144–6):

> Oure gentyl ser Ione, ioy hym mot betyde,
> He is a mere mon of mouþ among cumpane;
> He con harpe; he con syng; his orglus ben herd ful wyd.

See also F. Grose, *A Classical Dictionary of the Vulgar Tongue* (ed. E. Partridge, London, 1931), p. 311.

stza. 1, l. 2. *croke*: crock, pitcher, or jug.   l. 3. *be bel and boke*: i.e. by those used in excommunication, a common medieval oath.

stza. 2, l. 2. *burne*: spring.   l. 4. *rofe*: tore.   *bell-ey*: cloak, tunic.

stza. 4, l. 2. *copious*: plentiful. Sir John tried to make his peace with gifts.

stza. 5. The girl of this carol is more practical in her outlook than the heroines of Nos. 454, 455.

456.1. Our Sir John

Pr. Robbins, *Secular Lyrics*, p. 20; Silverstein, p. 133; Stemmler, p. 105. B.–R. 2494.

The title used by Robbins is adopted here. The Sir John of this carol is presented as being even more winning than his brother of No. 456.

stza. 3, l. 3. *box*. This use survives in modern sexual slang, although the full churchly metaphor is now uncommon, if used at all.

stza. 5, l. 1. *reluys*: glittering (Robbins's emendation and gloss).   l. 3. *othyr*: partially illegible in MS.; Robbins's reading.

457. Jolly Jankyn

Pr. Wright, *Wart. Club*, p. 100, *Songs and Carols* (London, 1836), No. xx; C. & S., p. 220; Robbins, *Secular Lyrics*, p. 21; Kaiser, *Anth.*, p. 312, *Med. Engl.*, p. 477; Wystan Hugh Auden, *The Oxford Book of Light Verse* (Oxford, 1938), p. 53; John Speirs, *Medieval English Poetry* (London, 1957), p. 82; Greene, *Selection*, p. 166; Sisam, p. 445; Davies, p. 162; Oliver, p. 122; Grigson, p. 141; Silverstein, p. 129; Tydeman, p. 59; Stemmler, p. 89. B.–R. 377.

The speaker in this lively and irreverent dramatic monologue of a flirtation during the procession and Mass on Christmas and of its consequences is one of 'þeos prude maidenes þat luuieþ ianekin', who, according to 'A lutel soth Sermun' (*An Old English Miscellany*, ed. R. Morris, E.E.T.S., Or. Ser., No. 49, 1872, 189), are among the persons destined for hell. It has elements of parody of the Mass, its refrain being the solemn formula of the *Kyrie*, but it is more essentially a kind of sacrilegious trope of parts of the sacred text. Compare its burden with the opening lines of an actual trope of the *Kyrie*:

> Kyrie,—Rex pie,—Da nobis hodie,—
> Veniae—Munus et gratiae:—Eleison.

quoted by Léon Gautier, *Histoire de la poésie liturgique au moyen âge. Les Tropes*, i, Paris, 1886, p. 148 n. II E). The piece is in much the same vein as such humorous parodies of the services as are found in Paul Lehmann, *Parodistische Texte* (Munich, 1923), pp. 59–69. In the burden there is probably a pun on the girl's name 'Alison'.

Eileen Power (*Medieval English Nunneries*, Cambridge, 1922, p. 610) quotes a 'very ribald Italian folk-song of the fourteenth or fifteenth century . . . founded upon Boccaccio's famous tale of the Abbess and the breeches', which has for burden and refrain 'Kyrie, kyrie, pregne son le monache!'

A similar frivolous use of the sacred formula as well as other phrases from the Mass occurs in the opening speech of the vice *Infidelitie* in Lewis Wager's play *The Life and Repentance of Marie Magdalene* (1566–7):

> With heigh down down and downe a down a
> *Saluator mundi Domine, Kyrieleyson*
> *Ite, Missa est*, with pipe vp *Alleluya*
> *Sed libera nos a malo*, and so let vs be at one.
>
> (ed. Frederic Ives Carpenter, Chicago, 1902, p. 6, ll. 1–4)

Robbins's note (p. 235) is confused. He attributes the Latin headings of the 'Venus Mass' to 'The Cuckoo and the Nightingale' (*pr.* W. W. Skeat, *Chaucerian and Other Pieces*, Oxford, 1897, pp. 347–58), in which the birds say their Hours and not Mass, and in which there is no Latin. The 'Venus Mass' itself (*pr.* Thomas Frederick Simmons, *The Lay Folks Mass Book*, E.E.T.S., Or. Ser., No. 71, 1879, 390–5) is divided into parts corresponding to *Introibo, Confiteor*, etc., but it bears no resemblance to the trope-like carol. See Introduction, p. lxxxiv.

The Reverend Margit Sahlin (*Étude sur la carole médiévale*, Uppsala, 1940, p. 57) attempts to use this carol in support of her theory of the derivation of '*carole*' from *Kyrie eleison* and of the form from processional songs. It is impossible to consider this carol a processional piece: only the first stanza refers to a procession, the others recounting Jankyn's part in the Mass, during which the parishioners would be kneeling and standing: 'on myn fot he trede'. What is being 'farced' is definitely the *Kyrie* of the Mass, not, as Dr. Sahlin would have it, 'le cri processionel'. Of the far-fetched assumptions involved in Dr. Sahlin's theories none is harder to accept than her claim that in continental Europe *Kyrie eleison* became the preferred or only song 'of the people' and that it was 'not understood' though it was used in the refrains of popular songs on the saints and other subjects (op. cit., pp. 132–3).

The commentary of J. D. W. Crowther is typical of a growing tendency to read into medieval lyrics more than is there: 'The poet ironically juxtaposes two births: the one bringing rejoicing and hope for all sinners, the other shame. That shame, in turn, proves the necessity for Christ's birth and for its celebration. Although the mass is parodied, it promises the true love which will bring the girl peace of mind' (*Annuale Mediaevale*, xii, 1971, 123–5). There is little peace of mind implied for the girl, nor in the use of the commonplace simile of 'wortes to the pot' does she voice 'both her admiration and her domestic hopes'.

There is a laboured 'analysis' of this carol in Lewis J. Owen and Nancy H. Owen, eds., *Middle English Poetry: An Anthology* (Indianapolis, 1971), pp. 349–51. One quotation will suffice: 'The irony here becomes sharper through the internal rhyme that first joins "Deo . . . therto . . . I go with childe," so that the linked words become a final irreverent—though unintentional—parody of the immaculate conception . . .' The editors apparently think that the last term refers to the conception of Jesus.

There must have been others besides Jankyn guilty of breaches of decorum during processions, for the Consuetudinary of St. Paul's admonishes: 'In Processions let the Clergy walk two and two, . . . with composed steps, casting their looks downward as they walk, nor let their eyes wander, the token of an irreligious heart. . . . Let them turn their eyes away from all vanitics, and walk with a pure aspect and sedate behaviour' (John David Chambers, *Divine Worship in England in the Thirteenth and Fourteenth and Nineteenth Centuries*, London, 1877, pp. 182–3). These processions used antiphons, proses, psalms, the *Te Deum*, but there is no record of such use of vernacular carols.

The duties of the parish clerk included carrying to the houses of the parish not only a censer, as does Chaucer's Absolon, but also the holy water for sprinkling the members of the households. Thus Jankyn would have had easy opportunities for amorous attentions outside the church itself (P. H. Ditchfield, *The Parish Clerk*, London, 1907, pp. 27–9).

stza. 1, l. 2. The alliterative epithet was apparently in general use, as in Skelton's *Magnificcnce*, Scene 16, where Fancy says to Courtly Abusion: 'What, whom have we here—Jenkin Jolly?' (*The Complete Poems of John Skelton Laureate*, ed. Philip Henderson, 3rd edn., London, 1959, p. 194). l. 3. 'Kerieleson' appears as the refrain of a Nativity song in B.M. MS. Harley 2942 f. 4^r, possibly a carol which has lost its burden, to which my attention was first directed by Mr. Geoffrey B. Riddehough.

Several of the pedestrian 'Goostly Psalmes and Spirituall Songes' written by Myles Coverdale about 1539 in the hope of moving 'our youth of England' to use them as replacements for 'foul and corrupt ballads' similarly have 'Kirieleyson' as external refrain (George Pearson, ed., *Remains of Myles Coverdale, Bishop of Exeter*, Parker Society, xiv, Cambridge, 1846, pp. 543, 544, 545, 549, 554, 562, 563).

The refrain may here carry the slang implication of 'a rough time' or 'a scolding', as in the listing of secular uses of ecclesiastical terms in William Tyndale's *The Obedience of a Christian Man* (1528), f. 130^v: 'He gave me a Kyrieleyson'. Compare also the speech of Dame Coye in the play *Jack Juggler* (*c.* 1553–61):

> And if I west þe fault were in him, I pray god I be ded
> But he shoulde haue such a kyrie, ere he went too bed

As he neuer had before in all his lyfe
Nor any man ells haue had of his wyfe

(ed. John S. Farmer, The Tudor Facsimile Texts [London], 1912, sig. D₁ʳ, ll. 15–18)

stza. 3, l. 2. *sel*: good fortune.

stza. 5. Compare the line from a song in the same MS. (*pr.* Wright, op. cit., p. 93): 'Therfore smale notes wil I crake'. The reference is to the rapidly sung short notes of polyphonic vocal music as opposed to the long notes of plainsong. Wycliffe and his followers objected violently and at length to this kind of 'newe song'. Compare particularly with this carol a passage from the tract 'Of feyned contemplatif lif [etc.]' (*pr.* F. D. Matthew, *The English Works of Wyclif Hitherto Unprinted*, E.E.T.S., Or. Ser., No. 74, 1880, 192):

> & þanne strumpatis & þeuys preisen sire iacke or hobbe & williem þe proude clerk, hou smale þei knacken here notis; & seyn þat þei seruen wel god & holy chirche, whanne þei dispisen god in his face, & letten oþere cristene men of here deuocion & compunccion, and stiren hem to worldly vanyte; & þus trewe seruyce of god is lettid & þis veyn knackynge for oure iolite & pride is preised abouen þe mone . . .

In 'The First Shepherds' Play', ll. 305–6 and 413–19, the shepherds admire the 'small noytys' of the angels: 'I dar say that he broght / foure & twenty to a long'; in 'The Second Shepherds' Play' the angel 'crakyd it' only 'Thre brefes to a long' (G. England and A. W. Pollard, eds., *The Towneley Plays*, E.E.T.S., Ex. Ser., No. lxxi, 1897, 110, 113, 137). Raymond Oliver glosses stza. 4, l. 2: 'I paid for his "cutting" (? of the notes)' (*Poems Without Names*, Berkeley, California, 1970, p. 122). On the simile Robbins (p. 236) cites *Liber Cure Cocorum*, l. 46: 'Hakke smalle þy wortis and persyl'. The same idiom appears in a sermon-passage condemning parents who corrupt their children: '. . . ȝe, more cruel than though they hackede here children as smal as mosselles to here pot . . .' (G. R. Owst, *Literature and Pulpit in Medieval England*, Cambridge, 1933, p. 466).

A full technical explanation of the short notes of the angels' song is given by Nan Cooke Carpenter, 'Music in the *Secunda Pastorum*', *Speculum*, xxvi (1951), 696–700.

stza. 6, l. 1. *pax-brede*: the disc of silver or gilt with a handle and a sacred symbol used in giving the 'kiss of peace' to the congregation. Its introduction is attributed to the Franciscans. See John S. Bumpus, *A Dictionary of Ecclesiastical Terms* (London, n.d.), s.v. 'Pax'. Oliver glosses ' "peace-bread", kissed during mass'! Owen and Owen make a similar blunder. l. 2. The same signal of amorous intention from a clerk appears in *A verie merie Historie of the Milner of Abington*, ll. 178, 264 (W. C. Hazlitt, *Remains of the Early Popular Poetry of England*, London, 1866, iii. 107, 110).

stza. 7, l. 1. The exclamation is a stereotyped expression; it occurs, for example, in the opening lines of the romance *Sir Gowther* in Nat. Lib. Scot. MS. Advocates 19. 3. 1 (erroneously included as part of burlesque poem, *Rel. Ant.* i. 84).

No secular carol could more plainly be of clerical origin than this one, and it is hard to understand why Oliver calls it an 'obvious folk song' (op. cit., p. 13).

458. Kit Hath Lost Her Key

Music for tenor part only. Pr. Flügel, *Anglia*, xii (1889), 261, *N.L.*, p. 138; with music, *A Collection of Songs and Madrigals by English Composers of the Close of the Fifteenth Century* (The Plainsong and Mediaeval Music Society, London, 1891), Songs, p. 1 (words only, ibid., p. xvii). B.–R. Supp. 1824.8.

J. Payne Collier's *Extracts from the Register of the Stationers' Company* (London, 1848) contains an entry for 1561–2 which may refer to a printing of this carol: 'Rd of John Tysdale, for his lycense for pryntinge of ij ballettes, Kyt hath loste hyr keye, the other, the Country hath no pere, newly moralyzed . . . viij d' (i. 55). Collier offers an erotic sequel to this carol which he claims to have transcribed 'from a MS. of a later date'. That the verses are authentically Elizabethan is highly doubtful. See Sydney Race, 'John Payne Collier and the Stationers' Registers', *N. & Q.* cc (1955), 493.

The proverbial and figurative meaning of the phrase is used by William Patton in 1548 in the catalogue of popish superstitions happily obsolete under Edward VI which appears in the 'diary' of the Duke of Somerset's expedition into Scotland: 'Oblations and offerings of meats, of otes, images of wax, bound pens and pins for deliverance of bad husbands, for a sick cow, to keep down the belly, and when "KIT had lost her key" ' (Edward Arber, ed., *An English Garner*, London,

1880, iii. 71). A marginal note lists four saints, Uncumber, Mudwin, Agnes, and Syth. See B. J. W., *Proverbs*, K 70.

stza. 2, l. 3. *Seynt Sythe*: St. Zita of Lucca (d. 1271), known in England as St. Sithe. She was patron saint of serving-maids, such as we may suppose Kit to have been, and a key was one of her emblems. On this identification see G. G. Coulton, *Art and the Reformation* (New York, 1928), p. 292, and *N. & Q.*, 12th Ser., xii. 107; also J. H. R., ibid. 180. St. Sithe was commonly appealed to in cases of the loss of keys. G. R. Owst quotes from a medieval sermon: 'and a wife lose a keye of valew of thre pens, anon she wil hete to seke seynt Sithe, and spend a noble or ten schilyngis in the iurney' (*Literature and Pulpit in Medieval England*, Cambridge, 1933, pp. 147–8). The waxen image of a key would be Kit's votive offering in accordance with the old and still current custom at shrines. 'St. Sitha, the holy waiting-maid of Lucca, had the power of finding lost articles, and her image appears, with keys at her belt, in the windows of Mells (Somerset) and carved on a tomb-chest at Croft Castle (Herefs.)' (M. D. Anderson, *The Imagery of British Churches*, London, 1955, p. 162). It is natural that St. Zita is confused at times with St. Osyth, a Saxon princess, as in a prayer by Lydgate (Derek Pearsall, *John Lydgate*, London, 1970, p. 265). The masculine pronoun 'hym' suggests that the writer of this carol was not familiar with particulars of the saint's life.

459. With Lullay, Lullay, Like a Child

Repr. Alexander Dyce, *The Poetical Works of John Skelton* (London, 1843), i. 22 (text and plates used in several other editions); *The Complete Poems of John Skelton Laureate*, ed. Philip Henderson, 3rd edn. (London, 1959), p. 22; Sitwell, *Atlantic Book*, p. 83, *Planet and Glow-worm* (London, 1944), p. 53 (in part); Davies, p. 267; Stanley Eugene Fish, *John Skelton's Poetry* (New Haven, 1967), p. 49; Robert S. Kinsman, *John Skelton: Poems*, Clarendon Medieval and Tudor Series (Oxford, 1969), p. 1; Tydeman, p. 66; Richard S. Sylvester, *The Anchor Anthology of Sixteenth Century Verse* (Garden City, N.Y., 1974), p. 95. B.-R. *Supp.* 2231.5.

No music for this carol is extant. Maurice Evans erroneously states that it was set to music by 'Cornysshe the Court musician' (*English Poetry in the Sixteenth Century*, London, 1955, p. 49). It is the only poem of Skelton's in the true carol-form. 'Woffully afraid', set to music in B.M. MS. Addit. 5465, and designated as a 'modified carol' by Stevens (*M. & P.*, p. 370), is now regarded as not by Skelton.

The 'lullay' burden is used satirically by Skelton as the repeated element in a cynical song of desertion by a mistress. Some surprising comments have been made on the carol, for example, Dame Edith Sitwell's calling it 'one of the most drowsy-sounding poems in the language' (*Atlantic Book*, p. 78). Maurice Evans (loc. cit.) calls it a beautiful lyric and sees in it 'the tale of the wife who kisses her amorous husband to sleep and then runs off to her lover'. Peter Green sees the case more clearly: '. . . the conclusion is one of grim loss and deception. This theme, of sexual disappointment and emotional betrayal, recurs again and again. Skelton's loves are either beyond his reach, or turn common strumpets' (*John Skelton*, Writers and Their Work, No. 128, London, 1960, p. 11). A good parallel to the 'lullay' of this burden is found in an unsigned poem, possibly by Wyatt, in the Devon-shire MS., B.M. Addit. 17492:

> Farewell all my welfare,
>   My shue is trod awry;
> Now may I karke and care
>   To syng *lullay by by*.
> Alas! what shall I do thereto?
> There ys no shyffte to helpe me now.

(Kenneth Muir, ed., *Collected Poems of Sir Thomas Wyatt*, London, 1949, p. 97, stza. 1)

As I have pointed out elsewhere, 'lullay, lullay' and 'lullay by by' were in use in Skelton's time 'as slang or colloquial expressions connected with misfortune in love: their meaning is a combination of "Alas!" and "Good night!" or "Farewell"' (*Medium Ævum*, xxxiii, 1963, 54). See also the notes on Nos. 322 and 396. Utley misses the already existing cynical meaning of the burden and accuses Skelton of 'demonstrating his usual sprightly malice and irreverence when he parodies the tradition [of the Virgin Mary's motherhood] to women's dispraise' (p. 197). Fish follows him in this misinterpretation.

stza. 2, l. 1. *ba, bas*: kiss. *O.E.D.* cites both as substantives, but their use as verbs is more likely here. Compare No. 60, stzas. 3, 4, l. 4.

stza. 3, l. 1. *rowth*: flow, run with force. See *O.E.D.* s.v. '† Row, *v.*⁴', citation from *Chron. Wace* of *c.* 1330, and John Jamieson, *An Etymological Dictionary of the Scottish Language* (Paisley, 1882), s.v. 'To Row *v.n.*', citation from Alexander Scott: 'Now fields convuls'd like dashing waves, / Wild *row* alang'. *wan*: lap.   l. 4. *halsyd*: embraced.   l. 6. *rowtyth*: snores. Fish (p. 52) finds an implausible association with a bull.

stza. 4, l. 3. *blynkerd blowboll*: blinded drunkard.   l. 7. *powle hachet*: i.e. pole-axe, a soldier so armed, considered as a low fellow. Kinsman (p. 212) queries: 'one as ugly as a pole-axe but shorter'. This will hardly do, as the original pole-axe is itself a very short weapon. See R. L. Greene, 'Whom Did King Hamlet Smite?' (*N. & Q.* ccxix, 1974, 128–30). *blered thyne I*: deceived, 'did in the eye'.

460. The Maid and the Miller

Repr. facs. Reed, p. 36. Grigson, p. 106. B.–R. *Supp.* 1641.5.

The traditional aptness of the miller for this kind of toll-taking is the subject of a number of broadside ballads of the next century, e.g. Bodl., Douce Ballads 2, f. 140ᵛ. It occurs in so many popular songs that a separate bibliography could be compiled. A good set of examples is given by Charles Read Baskervill, *The Elizabethan Jig* (Chicago, 1929), pp. 276–81. A modern traditional song using some of the same double meanings, including 'stones', is printed from the Cecil Sharp MSS. by James Reeves, *The Idiom of the People* (London, 1958), No. 63. Violet Alford cites this carol in a brief but interesting letter to *The Times Literary Supplement*, 1 January 1954, p. 9, which identifies the central figure with the sexually free Schöne Müllerin of German, the Meunière of French, and the Molinera of Spanish popular song, and (less plausibly) suggests a possible 'glimpse of some female corn divinity carrying out her duties'.

burden, l. 1. 'Dillum' as a refrain-word survives in an American version of 'Bangum and the Boar' (Child, No. 18): 'Dillum down dillum' (*Journal of American Folk Lore*, xxv, 1912, 175). Compare also the lampoon on Gabriel Harvey in Thomas Nashe's *Have With You to Saffron-Walden*, 1596 (*The Works of Thomas Nashe*, ed. Ronald B. McKerrow, *repr.* F. P. Wilson, Oxford, 1958, iii. 133).

stza. 1, l. 1. *brenten ars*: a term of general disparagement. Compare *O.E.D.*, s.v. 'Burnt', an older form of the now bowdlerized proverb: 'The pot calls the kettle black'.

stza. 2, l. 3. *clacke*: run, from the 'clacker' or beater of a mill, the agitator which strikes the hopper and dislodges the corn to be ground. Compare Chaucer, *Reeve's Tale*, ll. 116–19. Baskervill refers to the song of a miller in D'Urfey's *Pills to Purge Melancholy* which uses the same word in its refrain:

> His mill goes *Clack, clack, clack,*
> *How merrily, how merrily,*
> *His Mill goes* Clack.

(op. cit., p. 278)

stza. 3, l. 2. *vyce*: screw.

460.1 Puddings for Sale.

Pr. R. H. Robbins, *PMLA*, lxxxi (1966), 310. B.–R. *Supp.* 1344.5.

This uninhibited carol is undoubtedly copied, as Robbins suggests, from another manuscript rather than set down from memory, for the text is without gaps or irrelevancies. The situation implied is like that of No. 416, in which a 'chapman' offers similar ware. The piece is cancelled in the MS. by two crossed lines almost too faint to be called half-hearted.

'Pudding' in this sense is still current in 'merry' song in the eighteenth century, as Thomas D'Urfey's *Wit and Mirth: or Pills to Purge Melancholy* (London, 1719), vi, 300, 'Lumps of Pudding', and ibid. iii. 72, 'A Song'.

461. The Nun and the Friar

Repr. facs. Reed, p. 37; R. H. Robbins, 'The Bradshaw Carols', *PMLA*, xxxi (1966), 308; Grigson, p. 106. B.–R. *Supp.* 3443.5 (in error).

The burden is made by omitting the negative from a phrase of the Pater Noster: 'Et ne nos inducas in tentationem' (Luke xi. 4). Its use in No. 461.1 as well probably indicates that other very similar carols or songs were in circulation. On the history and uses in the seventeenth and later centuries of the broadside ballad-tune, obviously named for some piece of the general type, see 'The

Friar and the Nun' in Claude M. Simpson, *The British Broadside Ballad and Its Music* (New Brunswick, N.J., 1966), pp. 238–40.

stza. 3, l. 3. That is, a superior pleasure. Compare William Tyndale, *The Obedience of a Christian Man* (London, 1528), f. 130ᵛ (among examples of secular slang using ecclesiastical metaphor): 'It is a pleasure for a pope.'

461.1. The Grey Friar Teaches the Nun

Pr. R. H. Robbins, *PMLA*, lxxxi (1966), 309–10. B.–R. *Supp.* 3443.5.

Though closely similar in content and spirit to No. 461, this carol should not be treated as an expanded version of the other, as is done by Robbins in his first printing of the text and in B.–R. *Supp.* 3443.5. Apart from burden and refrains there are almost no significant verbal parallels.

Since the fragment of two leaves in which this carol is written contains two carols by the Franciscan James Ryman, it is possible that this piece, though in a different hand, was circulated within the 'order gray' to which the protagonist belongs.

burden. The burden is the same as that of No. 461, a blasphemous reversing of the phrase of the Pater Noster.

stza. 3. Robbins pertinently compares the use of the syllables of the gamut to that in a Latin and English macaronic poem in Édélestand Du Méril, *Poésies populaires latines antérieures au douzième siècle* (Paris, 1843), p. 97 n. The friar is represented as omitting the first syllable 'ut' of the medieval *gamme* or scale. See Henry Holland Carter, *A Dictionary of Middle English Musical Terms* (Bloomington, Indiana, 1961), s.v. 'Gamme'.

stza. 4, l. 1. *proper chaunt: propre-chaunt*, the hexachord on C. See Carter, op. cit., s.v. 'propre-chaunt'. *segnory*: feudal right or lordship, here satirized.

stza. 5, l. 1. *veni ad me*: a profane echo of Matthew xi. 28: 'Venite ad me omnes, qui laboratis, et onerati estis, et ego reficiam vos.' l. 3. 'And I shall put my weapon to you' ('tollum' for 'telum').

stza. 6, l. 1. *by bemoll*: with this note which is the modern B flat ('B soft'), here probably with a pun on 'be soft'.

stza. 7, l. 3. The stones have taken me by storm (with sexual pun): 'expungnaverunt' for 'expugnaverunt', probably by confusion with 'expungo', get out of the way, remove.

stza. 8, l. 4. *quoniam*: pudendum, as in Chaucer, *The Wife of Bath's Prologue*, l. 608.

462. A May-morning Encounter

Pr. Rel. Ant. ii. 39. B.–R. *Supp.* 3836.5.

Halliwell-Phillipps notes that the carol is incomplete, but he does not distinguish between the burden and the rest of the piece. The burden is probably borrowed from folk-song. On the strength of the three stanzas preserved it is impossible to say with certainty whether the carol is a religious or a secular *chanson d'aventure*.

The carol is in the same metre as a piece set for three voices by Cornish in B.M. MS. Addit. 31922, ff. 30ᵛ, 31ʳ, of which the first stanza reads:

> My love sche morneth
> For me, for me,
> My love sche morneth for me.
> Alas, pour hart,
> Sen we depart
> Morne ye no more for me.

Moralized versions using key phrases are also to be found in B.M. Book K.1.e.1 (*XX Songes*), with music by Gwynneth (*pr.* E. Flügel, *Anglia*, xii (1889), and in *A Compendious Book of Godly and Spiritual Songs*, ed., A. F. Mitchell, S.T.S., No. 39, 1897, 140).

463. The Knight and the Lady

Music for three voices, by William Cornish (burden only). *Pr.* Flügel, *Anglia*, xii (1889), 239, *N.L.*, p. 135; William Chappell, *Archaeologia*, xli (1867), 381; C. & S., p. 56; G. Bullett, *The English Galaxy of Shorter Poems* (London, 1947), p. 61; Stevens, *M. & P.*, p. 402; with music, Stevens, *Henry VIII*, p. 33. B.–R. *Supp.* 3405.5.

This piece shows a likeness to the ballad style unusual in the carols. As the burden has no connection with the subject-matter of the stanzas, it is possible that the words of the two were first joined by the composer.

On the significance of the name Amyas in the burden see C. & S., p. 337, where a historical connection between an Amyas family and both court and 'greenwood' is pointed out. In a collection of songs to be used at court the choice of the name may well have had a topical interest now only to be guessed at.

The castle is a favourite figure in medieval allegory. Compare the prose *Abbey of the Holy Ghost* (ed. George G. Perry, *Religious Pieces*, E.E.T.S., Or. Ser., No. 26, London, 1867, 53–62), where Dread is portress and Pity the 'spensere that does seruesse to gud all that scho maye'.

It seems almost certain that this piece was used in a disguising of the kind which Cornish is known to have helped to produce for the nuptial festivities of Prince Arthur and Catherine of Aragon in 1501. In one of these there were three pageants, a castle, a ship, and a mountain. 'When the ship had cast anchor, *Hope* and *Desire*, ambassadors from certain *Knights of the Mount of Love*, passed to the castle and tried to gain the favour of the ladies, who refused their advances. The ambassadors, in anger, warned the ladies that the knights would make such an assault on the castle that it would be "grevous to abyde there power and malesse". Thereupon the knights themselves entered on a third pageant which was like a mountain. The ambassadors reported the ladies' refusal, whereupon the knights hastened to the attack and soon compelled the ladies to surrender, descend from their stronghold, and join them in goodly dances' (Sydney Anglo, 'William Cornish in a Play, Pageants, Prison, and Politics', *R.E.S.*, New Ser., x, 1949, 350–2, and *Spectacle, Pageantry, and Early Tudor Policy*, Oxford, 1969). Anglo marshals an impressive array of pageant-castles, including the 'Castle of Loyaltie' in 1524, which had a 'hill' as an important property (pp. 115–16), the 'Fortresse Dangerus' on New Year's Day 1512, defended by ladies against male assault (p. 118), the 'Schatew Vert' in March 1522, which held a defender named 'Dangier' like the portress in the carol (pp. 120–1; 195, an outdoor castle in Cornhill); 198 (in Cheapside); 299; 337 (in Fleet Street). William Cornish, the composer of the music for this carol, was, of course, a leading deviser of court pageantry. The entire chapter 11, 'Music in Ceremonies, Entertainments and Plays', in Stevens, *M. & P.* should be read as background to this piece.

In Scotland 'Strangeness' appears as the porter of the 'Castle of Penance' and is destroyed by burning in the poem 'Sen that I am a Presoneir', attributed to Dunbar and written in the same style of love-allegory as this carol (*The Poems of William Dunbar*, ed. John Small, ii, S.T.S., 1893, pp. 164–7). In the same poem Good Hope bids the prisoner to 'breve a bill', and Pity is among his helpers.

stza. 2, l. 1. *blyn*: wait.
stza. 6, l. 1. *breffe a byll*: draw up a petition.

463.1. A Happy Ending

Music for three voices for burden only. *Pr.* E. Flügel, *Anglia*, xii (1889), 236, *N.L.*, p. 135; C. & S., p. 59 (burden omitted); Padelford, p. xxxix (in part); Stevens, *M. & P.*, p. 397; with music, Stevens, *Henry VIII*, p. 27. B.-R. *Supp.* 3635.5.

This *chanson d'aventure* incorporating a conventional complaint of an apparently forsaken maiden is probably representative of a class of such secular songs in the verse-form which gave the pattern to such a religious carol as No. 151. Stevens suggests that the verses were probably sung to a well-known tune not written down here (*M. & P.*, p. 398). The words of the burden were of course widely used and associated with cheerful rather than sad songs. Compare the refrain of Balthazar's song in *Much Ado About Nothing*, II. iii: 'Converting all your sounds of woe / Into Hey nonny, nonny'.

stza. 2, l. 2. without fault of hers.
stza. 3, l. 4. *rew*: repent.
stza. 4, l. 3. *sew*: seek.
stza. 5, l. 5. *To god perteynyng*: tending to my good.
stza. 6, l. 5. *yes replete*: eyes full of tears.
stza. 7, l. 2. *la bell*: Stevens queries 'but why feminine?' The 'bell' might be for 'bel ami', masculine, and the 'la' inadvertent.
stza. 8, l. 2. *at a brayde*: suddenly.
stza. 9, l. 1. *Hent*: took.   l. 2. *gent*: pleasant, with implications of aristocratic refinement, rather than merely pretty.   l. 4. *wyldernes*: country, rustic surroundings, not necessarily uncultivated.

464. I Will Love but One

Music for three voices. *Pr.* B. Fehr, *Archiv*, cvi (1901), 68; Stevens, *M. & P.*, p. 382; with music, Stevens, *Early Tudor Songs*, p. 140. B.-R. *Supp.* 2007.5.

The fifth lines of the stanzas, serving by their rhyme as links with the burden, do much to enhance the charm of this love-carol.

The first line of the burden is less irrelevant than it might otherwise seem in view of the wide currency of an English proverb, 'There are more ways to the wood than one' (J. Ray, *A Compleat Collection of English Proverbs*, London, 1768, i. 167), to which an allusion seems to be intended.

stza. 1, l. 2. *Indyfferent*: common.

stza. 2, l. 3. *fetter*: prettier.   l. 4. *buxum*: submissive.

465. The Old Forester

Deleted from this edition. As Stevens points out, *M. & P.*, p. 409, the music is not that of a true carol.

466. The Forester Still Valiant

Music for three voices (burden only). *Pr.* Flügel, xii (1889), 245, *N.L.*, p. 151; C. & S., p. 246; Stevens, *M. & P.*, p. 410; with music, Stevens, *Henry VIII*, p. 50. B.-R. *Supp.* 4068.6.

This carol is a 'reply' to No. 465 in the first edition, 'The Old Forester' (Stevens, *M. & P.*, p. 408). That refrain-song, demonstrated by Stevens not to be a true carol, is therefore deleted from this edition.

Hunter and doe standing for human sexual partners appear in a long and explicit set of erotic verses, without music but probably intended for singing, in B.M. MS. Addit. 24578, f. 88ʳ. It begins:

> It was my chance
> For to advance
>   Myself not long agoe;
> It did me good
> To range the wood
>   To seek a barren do.

The *double entente* of shooting with a bow is exploited in an epigram headed 'S*i*r Walter Raleigh to þe Lady Bend-bow' in Bodl. MS. Rawl. poet. 26, f. 2ᵗ:

> I cannot bend þe bow, wherein to shoote I sue:
> It is not made of elme, but it is made of yew.
> This bow must haue a stringe, this stringe a shafte;
> This shaft, a notch: with that the Lady laught.

The images survive into the seventeenth century in a poetical miscellany by Thomas Crosse (B.M. MS. Harley 6057, f. 4ʳ, signed 'W. Sh'.).

stza. 2, l. 1. *lynde*: here, as often in poetry, for 'tree' in general rather than specifically for 'linden'.

stza. 4, l. 2. *luge*: lodge, discover the lair of a buck, rather than as glossed by Stevens 'throw something so that it "lodges" '. *sute*: pursuit of game.

466.1. Blow Thy Horn, Hunter

a. Music for three voices (burden only) by William Cornish. *Pr.* Flügel, 'Lieder.', p. 238; Stevens, *M. & P.*, p. 400; with music, William Chappell, *Old English Popular Music*, revised H. E. Wooldridge ('London, 1893), p. 40; Noah Greenberg, *An English Songbook* (Garden City, N.Y., 1961), p. 88; Stevens, *Henry VIII*, p. 29.

b. Music for one voice by William Cornish. *Pr.* Flügel, 'Lieder.', p. 262; with music, William Chappell, *Popular Music of the Olden Time* (London, [1859]), i. 56, *Old English Popular Music*, p. 39 (in part); Stevens, *Henry VIII*, p. 29.

As Stevens points out in the notes to this piece in both his publications, it can be regarded either as a true carol with the stanzas left unset, presumably to be sung to a known tune, or as a refrain-song without a burden, the written music being used for all the stanzas. It is given the benefit of the doubt and included in this edition as a carol.

The song obviously shares the erotic double meaning of No. 466 and 'The Old Forester', No. 465 in the first edition of this work. See notes on No. 466. Stevens plausibly suggests that it may have been used in a court pageant with participants impersonating foresters like the one of which Stevens quotes Hall's account: 'When the pageaunt rested before the Quene the forenamed forsters blew their hornes, then the devise or pageant opened on all sydes, and out issued the foresaid four knyghtes' (*M. & P.*, p. 249). a has minor verbal variants in the texts for the several voices.

stza. 2, l. 2. *shoffe*: made her way.
stza. 3, l. 4. *barrayne*: not pregnant and hence fair game.
stza. 5, l. 3. *hent*: received.   l. 4. *faynte*: faintness, exhaustion.
stza. 6, ll. 3, 4: What do you take to be the second meaning of this song?

467. If It Were Not: A Carol of Anne Boleyn

Pr. A. K. Foxwell, *The Poems of Sir Thomas Wiat* (London, 1913), i. 325; Kenneth Muir, *Collected Poems of Sir Thomas Wyatt* (London, 1963), p. 136; Kenneth Muir and Patricia Thomson, *Collected Poems of Sir Thomas Wyatt* (Liverpool, 1969), p. 244; R. L. Greene, *R.E.S.*, New Ser., xxv (1974), 437. B.-R. *Supp.* 2281.5.

The notes which follow appear in large part in the article by the present editor, 'A Carol of Anne Boleyn by Wyatt' (loc. cit.).

The many critics of Wyatt's poetry have apparently not noticed that the burden of this carol has as its first line an unmistakable translation of the motto used by Anne Boleyn on her servants' liveries for a few months in 1530: 'Ainsi sera, groigne qui groigne' (Marie Louise Bruce, *Anne Boleyn*, London, 1972, pp. 168–72). Mrs. Bruce renders the motto as 'What will be, will be, grumble who may', and refers to the suggestion made by the Imperial ambassador, Eustace Chapuis, that Anne ceased to use the motto because of its similarity to that of the House of Burgundy: 'Groigne qui groigne et vive Bourgoigne'. See also Paul Friedmann, *Anne Boleyn: A Chapter of English History 1527–1536* (London, 1884), i. 128. Friedmann refers to Vienna Archives, P.C. 226, 1, f. 106, E. Chapuis to Charles V, 21 December 1530, and ibid., f. 109, E. Chapuis to Charles V, 31 December 1530. He quotes from the latter dispatch: 'Sire la dame na permis que ces serviteurs a ces festes ayent portes leurs accoustrements faytz avec la devise grognie que grognie. Je ne scais si elle attend la determination de ce parlement ou sy quelqung luy a dit que le propre et vray refrain dicelle devise est de y ajouster vive borgougne.'

The use of this motto as the burden of this carol can hardly be coincidental. The piece must be dated 1530, and the speaker of the burden and stanzas must be regarded as representing Anne herself. There is, of course, no reason to suppose that she was the actual author; she and Wyatt were on friendly terms at this time. The carol can refer to nothing else so probably as to Anne's love for King Henry, and the refrain-phrase 'If yt ware not' is then a clear reference to the yet undissolved marriage-bond with Queen Catherine which is the impediment to the 'mirthe'. It is notable that the loved man is referred to as a 'master' and as 'A frinde wiche gyvith to no man place'. The last stanza sounds a 'note' of warning which is quite in character for Anne in this year of her bristling impatience. Joost Daalder doubts Wyatt's authorship; he suggests: '. . . the writer is more likely to be Anne Boleyn or her brother George' (*Sir Thomas Wyatt: Collected Poems*, Oxford, 1975, p. xxvi n. 1). There appears to be no external evidence for the authorship of either.

When Anne had finally achieved the 'mirth' of marriage to the King, her retainers had embroidered on their liveries the phrase 'La plus Heureuse', that is, as stza. 2 of the carol puts it, 'happiest that euer was' (Bruce, op. cit., p. 219). The carol, thus viewed, becomes a striking example of the Tudor lyric which is not a general or fictitious and conventional love song, but which is connected with a real social (and here political) situation. It illustrates one important thesis of Stevens, *M. & P.*: 'The songs . . . were much more closely bound up with the life of their times than the purely "literary" lyrics of later ages' (p. 9).

It is probable that the burden of this piece was to be sung after every quatrain rather than after every other one, though without written music one cannot be certain. Miss Foxwell commented on Wyatt's use of the native medieval verse-form of the carol in *A Study of Sir Thomas Wyatt's Poems* (London, 1911), pp. 103–5. Her later designation of this piece as a '*glosa* poem' is unfortunate (*The Poems of Sir Thomas Wiat*, ii. 164). She correctly points out that No. 468 A is related to medieval English verse rather than to any Spanish *glosa*. She does not seem to realize, however, the repetitive character of the burden in the earlier carols. Later editors have rightly treated the two poems as carols. Miss Foxwell's suggestion that the woman of this piece might be Mary, 'the child-wife of the King's son, Henry Richmond', has no evidence to support it (*The Poems*, ii. xvii).

The poem from the Blage MS. beginning 'Tho some do grodge to se me joye' (Muir and Thomson, *Collected Poems*, No. clxviii) partially echoes the same sentiment in its l. 7: 'Then grodge who lyst, I shall not sease'. It is possible to read this poem as another written in the *persona* of Anne Boleyn. Muir and Thomson briefly note the parallel but with an incorrect reference (to cxx instead of ccxx) on p. 413.

stza. 2, l. 1. *skace*: scarce.

stza. 4, l. 1. *A*: he.

stza. 6, ll. 1, 2. See B. J. W., *Proverbs*, W 588.

468. Even as Ye List

A. *Pr.* G. F. Nott, *The Works of Henry Howard, Earl of Surrey and of Sir Thomas Wyatt the Elder* (London, 1816), ii. 221; A. K. Foxwell, *The Poems of Sir Thomas Wiat* (London, 1913), i. 276; Kenneth Muir, *Collected Poems of Sir Thomas Wyatt* (London, 1963), p. 106; Robert M. Bender, *Five Courtier Poets of the English Renaissance* (N.Y., 1967), p. 89; Kenneth Muir and Patricia Thomson, *Collected Poems of Sir Thomas Wyatt* (Liverpool, 1969), p. 198.

B. *Pr.* E. B. Reed, *Anglia*, xxxiii (1910), 362. B.–R. *Supp.* 813.6.

Miss Foxwell regards this as a 'doubtful poem', the MS. of A lacking the mark added to the 'fynys' which is usual with Wyatt's poems. She thinks that the poem may be either by Wyatt or by some member of his literary circle, e.g. George Boleyn, Viscount Rochford, or Francis Bryan (loc. cit.). In her notes (ii. 148) she is also doubtful but says, 'It is certainly in Wiat's style'. Critics and biographers have not so far been able to explain the personal allusions.

B. stza. 3, l. 3. *hath*: H. A. Mason reads 'hathe'. He notes the inferior and unmetrical reading 'yn contynent' in stza. 1, l. 4, but in this text even his stern critical judgement finds no grounds for comment (*Editing Wyatt*, Cambridge, 1972, p. 41).

The absence of a burden in B probably indicates that a musical setting in other than full carol-form was known or assumed for this text.

468.1. I Am as I Am

A. *Pr.* John Morford, *The Library Chronicle of the Friends of the University of Pennsylvania Library*, xxv (1959), 81, *facs.* 80; R. L. Greene, *R.E.S.*, New Ser., xv (1964), 176.

B. *Pr.* G. F. Nott, *The Works of Henry Howard, Earl of Surrey and of Sir Thomas Wyatt the Elder* (London, 1816), ii. 262; *The Poetical Works of Sir Thomas Wyatt* (London, 1831), p. 150; George Gilfillan, *The Poetical Works of Sir Thomas Wyatt* (Edinburgh, 1858), p. 138; A. K. Foxwell, *The Poems of Sir Thomas Wiat* (London, 1913), i. 354; E. M. W. Tillyard, *The Poetry of Sir Thomas Wyatt* (London, 1929), p. 126; Kenneth Muir, *Collected Poems of Sir Thomas Wyatt* (London, 1949), p. 154; Robert M. Bender, *Five Courtier Poets of the English Renaissance* (N.Y., 1967), p. 128; R. L. Greene, loc. cit.; John MacQueen, *Ballatis of Love* (Edinburgh, 1970) p. 65; Joost Daalder, *Sir Thomas Wyatt: Collected Poems* (Oxford, 1975), p. 179.

C. *Pr.* Kenneth Muir, *Unpublished Poems [by]Sir Thomas Wyatt and His Circle*, English Reprints Series, No. 18 (Liverpool, 1961), p. 81; Kenneth Muir and Patricia Thomson, *Collected Poems of Sir Thomas Wyatt* (Liverpool, 1969), p. 148.

D. *Pr. The Bannatyne Manuscript*, Hunterian Club (Glasgow, 1896), iii. 731; W. Tod Ritchie, *The Bannatyne Manuscript*, S.T.S., New Ser., No. 26, 1930, iv. 2. B.–R. *Supp.* 1270.2.

The character of D as a variant of B was pointed out by Francis Lee Utley, 'Wyatt as a Scottish Poet', *Modern Language Notes*, lx (1945), 106–11. Utley did not know of the existence of A and C. He notes the close similarity, except in dialect, of D to B and speculates on the possibility that 'Devonshire was in Scotland at one time, since it was in the possession of Margaret Douglas, and contains a poem in the hand of her son, Lord Darnley'. He rightly suggests that between B and D 'at least one copy intervened'. Daalder comments: 'It looks as though the shorter poem might underlie the other versions, among which D [here B] appears to be the most authoritative' (op. cit., p. 244).

H. A. Mason collates the four texts and offers a composite text (' "I Am As I Am" ', *R.E.S.*, New Ser., xxiii, 1972, 304–8; repeated in *Editing Wyatt*, Cambridge, 1972, pp. 122–3).

It is possible, of course, that the short version in carol-form has been made from the longer poem as found in Devonshire. But it may actually be earlier. In the article cited above I stated the case thus: '. . . the weight of probability seems to favour the interpretation that the Pennsylvania text is the earlier version, a carol (anonymous as far as we know) which Wyatt appropriated and expanded into a longer poem, eliminating both the burden and the [anomalous] "envoy". The hand of the carol appears to be definitely earlier than the hands of the Devonshire manuscript, and there would seem to be no reason for the selection by anyone of just these stanzas from the longer poem.' The article continues: 'If this view is correct, we have a new and excellent example of Wyatt's use of a medieval and native, or at least long naturalized, tradition of poetry and of his adapting it to a new influence, the encroachment upon the carol by more up-to-date forms of music and verse.' This view is supported by Winifred Maynard ('The Lyrics of Wyatt: Poems or Songs?', *R.E.S.*, New Ser., xvi, 1965, 10, n. 1).

The substance of the poem has not attracted much commentary. It may be read as a poem of the 'delivered lover' kind, as by Utley and apparently by the Scottish scribe of D. It was so understood by Nott, who regarded it as having little merit and prefixed to it the editorial title: 'The Recured Lover Exulteth in His Freedom and Voweth to Remain Free Until Death'. It can also be taken as a self-reliant and somewhat defensive expression of defiance of gossip and of enemies who circulate it. E. M. W. Tillyard's comment is a good statement of this interpretation:

> This poem seems to be a piece of personal moralising, Stoic in tone, written at a time when Wyatt was or had been in danger from his enemies. *Bond or free* in line 3 may well be a literal reference to Wyatt's own second imprisonment or to the fear of it. That Wyatt was acquainted with the Stoic philosophy is likely from his reference to Seneca.
>
> (*The Poetry of Sir Thomas Wyatt*, p. 174)

The Stoic interpretation seems preferable. Carols of like tone are found in the fifteenth century, e.g. Nos. 345, 348, 354, 381, 469.

A. burden, l. 1. In making this the key phrase of the poem, both the hypothetical author of the carol-text and Wyatt himself must have been conscious of the similarity, which some might regard as blasphemous, to the tremendous revelation by Jehovah to Moses: 'And God said unto Moses, I AM THAT I AM: and he said: Thus shalt thou say unto the children of Israel, I AM hath sent me unto you . . .' (Exodus iii. 14). The Old Testament phrase has been used more than once as a heraldic 'word' or motto, but such use is not recorded for 'I am as I am' in C. N. Elvin, *Elvin's Handbook of Mottoes*, revised R. Pinches (London, 1970).

A. stza. 3 (C. stza. 5, D. stza. 7), l. 4. *wright*: William H. Wiatt points to this homonym for 'right' as an important example of Wyatt's use of the kind of paronomasia called by classical rhetoricians *traductio* ('Sir Thomas Wyatt's Wordplay', *Annuale Mediaevale*, Duquesne Studies, i, 1960, 99–100).

469. The Delivered Lover

Pr. Rel. Ant. i. 202; Sisam, p, 489. B.–R. 3180.

The allusive and generalizing style of this carol keeps it from giving a clear picture of the situation which it treats. Utley (p. 70) is probably correct in challenging the suggestion in the first edition of this work that the 'I' of the verses is a woman. But rather than 'the perennial detractor or rival, Malebouche or Wikked Tunge', the 'wyckid creature' is more probably the classical and medieval God of Love or Eros. It is doubtful whether 'heavenly love or *caritas*' figures in the poem as Utley proposes.

The burden has a freshness and an image from nature that contrast sharply with the sophistication of the stanzas and is doubtless borrowed from folk-song.

stza. 3, l. 4. *mater*: affairs, condition.

stza. 4, l. 1. *sond*: gift.

stza. 6, l. 2. *altherbest*: best of all.

stza. 8, l. 2. Addressed to the company to whom the story is sung. Compare stza. 6, l. 3, 'fest'.

Utley comments on the note 'desor mais': '[It] may mean "henceforth I shall not love", it may be a scribe's pen name . . . or it may be a kind of motto . . . It is probably not the name of the author' (loc. cit.).

470. A Lover's Sad Plight

Pr. Robbins, *Secular Lyrics*, p. 34; Greene, *Selection*, p. 167; Sisam, p. 454; Oliver, p. 112; Stemmler, p. 84. B.–R. 1280.

This carol, found in a student's notebook, is an amusing example of the use of a humorous device which has survived to modern times in such minor classics as Goldsmith's *Elegy on Mrs. Mary Blaise* and Gilles Ménage's 'Le Fameux la Gallise' (*Menagiana*, Paris, 1729, iii. 384–91). The latter has the lines:

> Tandis qu'il ne dormoit pas,
> On tient qu'il veilloit sans cesse.

A longer and more literary, but less effective, song on this same theme is found in Balliol College, Oxford, MS. 354, f. 252ʳ (*pr.* Dyboski, p. 119) and in National Library of Wales, MS. Porkington 10 (*pr.* J. O. Halliwell[-Phillipps], *Wart. Club*, ii, 1855, p. 6; combined text of the two in C. & S., p. 217). This is probably the work of a later poet inspired by the more informal carol. It uses stza. 1, l. 3 of the carol as its refrain, and ll. 3, 4 of stzas. 2, 3 appear as follows (C. & S., stza. 4):

> In the morning when I rise shall
> Me list right well for to dine,
> But comonly I drink noon ale,
> If I may get any good wine.
>
> To make your hart to me encline
> Such tormentes to me I take;
> Singing doth me so mikell pine
> That when I slepe I may not wake.

burden. The initial phrase survives as a cliché of song into the seventeenth century. See note on No. 10, stza. 5, l. 4. It is the key phrase of the song which Coridon the countryman sings after the supper of trout in chapter iii of *The Compleat Angler* (London, 1653, pp. 85–8; in later editions ascribed to John Chalkhill):

> Then care away,
> and wend along with me.

A song in Bodl. MS. Ashmole 36–7, f. 128ʳ, begins: 'Sing care away, let us be glad' (William Henry Beach, *A Catalogue of the Manuscripts Bequeathed . . . by Elias Ashmole*, Oxford, 1845). See notes on No. 470.1.

stza. 1, l. 3. Robbins (*Secular Lyrics*, p. 238) points to the scrap of song written in Worcester Cathedral MS. F. 64, a copy of Peter Lombard's *Libri Sententiarum*, f. 8ʳ:

> He may cum to mi lef bute by þe watere wanne me lust slepen þanne mot i wakie wnder is þat hi liuie (*pr.* Bruce Dickins, *Leeds Studies in English*, iv, 1935, 44; text from MS.).

We probably have here a bit of the song of love-sickness of which the carol is a satirical reworking

470.1. The Devil Take Her

Music for one voice (burden only). *Repr. facs.* A. Hyatt King, 'The Significance of John Rastell in Early Music Printing', *The Library*, 5th Ser., xxvi (1971), facing p. 199.

This carol, which King establishes as 'the earliest broadside with music printed anywhere in Europe', is of more importance for historical bibliography than for literary content. King's article presents the authoritative account of its format and publishing history. King shows by two 'tentative reconstructions' that the composition could not have been for one voice only but might have been for either two or three voices (p. 211). Scribbled notes on the verso, deciphered by King, yield the names of several monks of Westminster, all of whom are shown by the records to have been still alive in the 1530s.

Whether Rastell himself was author as well as printer of the carol cannot be determined. King suggests that it may have been used in a musical festivity at court. In his judgement the date of printing was about 1520.

burden. Although the corner of the leaf is damaged, there can be no doubt about the first words. See notes on No. 10, stza. 5, l. 4, and No. 470, burden.

stza. 2, l. 8. *cast*: trick, fraud. l. 11. *fether*: here apparently an emblem not of triumph but of rejection, perhaps ironically.

stza. 3, l. 6. *horne.* The traditional insignia of the cuckold, here apparently assigned to a jilted unmarried lover.

stza. 4, l. 9. A reference to the proverb: 'When the moon's in the full, then wit's in the wane' (*The Oxford Dictionary of English Proverbs*, 3rd edn., Oxford, 1970, p. 542).   l. 12. *a crowe to pull*: a dispute or quarrel to settle.

471. A Lying Carol

Pr. Dyboski, p. 110; Flügel, 'Lieder.', p. 270; Grigson, p. 87. B.–R. 1350.

The burden means 'I shall prove to be the best liar'. In the Middle Ages and even into the seventeenth century it was the custom (at one time prescribed by law) to tie a whetstone about the neck of a convicted liar as he stood in the pillory. Compare Butler's *Hudibras*, part ii, canto 1, ll. 54–60. See *N. & Q.*, 1st Ser., vii (1853), 208, 8th Ser., iv (1893), 522, v (1894), 245, and B. J. W., *Proverbs*, W 216. Hence in jocular lying contests the whetstone became the symbol of victory. According to F. W. Hackwood (*Old English Sports*, London, 1907, p. 9) the whetstone was to indicate that the liar's inventiveness would need sharpening if he used it so freely.

For quotations from and references to other lying songs see G. L. Kittredge, 'Note on a Lying Song', *Journal of American Folk-Lore*, xxxix (1926), 195–9, and for a long list of references see also Utley, No. 69, pp. 133–4.

The type is widespread in French folk-song as well as in English. A good example is 'L'autre zor de me promeno', which tells of meeting two slugs ploughing a field, two hens buying salt, and a dead woman mending her apron (Julien Tiersot, *Chansons populaires recueillies dans les Alpes françaises: Savoie et Dauphiné*, Paris, 1903, p. 199). A specimen of the genre as it still survives in genuine oral tradition is 'When I Was a Little Boy', sung in 1947 in Unst, Shetland (R. Vaughan Williams and A. L. Lloyd, eds., *The Penguin Book of English Folk-Songs*, Harmondsworth, 1959, p. 101).

stza. 1, l. 1. *sowse*: pork used for pickling.

stza. 2, l. 1. *vrchyn*: hedgehog.   *shape*: cut out clothing.

stza. 3, l. 3. *pye*: magpie.

stza. 4, l. 1. *stokfysshe*: dried fish.

stza. 5, l. 2. *clewens*: balls of yarn.

stza. 6, l. 2. *plasshe*: weave.

472. Strange News

Pr. Rel. Ant. i. 239; [K.] Böddeker, *Jahrbuch für romanische und englische Sprache und Literatur*, N.F. ii (1875), 90.

Charles Read Baskervill compares this piece with other 'news songs', all of later date (*The Elizabethan Jig*, Chicago, 1929, pp. 59–63).

stza. 2, l. 4. *fat*: vat.

stza. 6, l. 1. *John*: Joan.   l. 2. *forwende*: turned into. 'I don't know what's become of her.'

473. A Nonsense Carol

Repr. Bliss, p. 53; C. & S., p. 254; *facs.* Reed, p. 38; W. H. Husk, *Songs of the Nativity* (London, 1868), p. 134; Wystan Hugh Auden, *The Oxford Book of Light Verse* (Oxford, 1938), p. 87; Denys K. Roberts, *Straw in the Hair* (London, 1953), p. 155; Greene, *Selection*, p. 168. B.–R. *Supp.* 2250.8.

The words of the burden and first stanza occur in a round or canon in Thomas Ravenscroft's *Pammelia* (1609) as follows:

> Ut, re, mi, fa, sol, la,
> La, sol, fa, mi, re, ut.
>   Hey down a down a!
>
> My heart of gold, as true as steel,
>   As I me leant unto the bowers,
> But if my lady love me well,
>   Lord, so Robin lowers.

Heave and ho,
Rumbelo.
Hey trolo, troly lo!
My lady's gone to Canterbury,
Saint Thomas, be her boot!
She met with Kate of Malmesbury,
Why weep'st thou, maple root?
O sleep'st thou or wak'st thou, Jeffery Cook?
The roast it burns; turn round about.
O Friar, how fares thy bandelow?
Friar, how fares thy sandelow?

(E. H. Fellowes, *English Madrigal Verse 1588–1632*, 3rd edn., revised Frederick W. Sternfeld
and David Greer, Oxford, 1967, p. 206)

See Reed, pp. xlix, 78.

The nonsense of this delightful piece is free-ranging, and it is hardly to be classified as a 'lying-song', as Utley suggests (p. 203). Three stanzas are printed by Roger Lancelyn Green in *The Book of Nonsense* (N.Y., 1956, p. 189), along with other examples of the traditional device of inconsequent lines.

burden, l. 2. *me lened*: O.E.D. records the reflexive use of 'lean' at the end of the sixteenth century.

stza. 1, l. 2. *the Saynt*: St. Thomas.   *bothe*: boot, help.

stza. 2, l. 1. That this line is from a popular song, probably a first line, appears from the notation which follows the poem 'to cowntar ffete a mery mode' of f. 65ᵛ of the 'Devonshire' MS., B.M. Addit. 17492:

ryme dogrel how many
myle to meghelmes
(Raymond Southall, *The Courtly Maker*, N.Y., 1964, p. 9)

The fragment is obviously intended to indicate an air suitable for the poem. Other lines of this carol are almost certainly similar borrowings from songs otherwise unknown.   l. 4. *snew*: snowed.

stza. 4, l. 3. *Jacke Napes*: a monkey.   *mow*: grimace. The line is apparently a current and stereo-typed expression. The *Vulgaria* of John Stanbridge, printed by Wynkyn de Worde in 1519, includes it:

Iacke napes maketh a mowe. Simea os distorquet.
(ed. Beatrice White, E.E.T.S., Or. Ser., No. 187, 1932, 26, 132 n.)

William Tyndale uses the image in satirizing the priest at Mass: '. . . with noddyng, beckyng, and mowyng, as it were Jackenapes when nether he Him sele, nether any man else woteth what he meneth' (*The Obedyence of a Chrysten Man*, London, 1561, f. lxxivᵛ).

stza. 7, l. 1. *Saynt Katheryn of Kent*: I am not acquainted with any records of this saint.

stza. 8, l. 1. *lauerocke*: lark.

473.1. A Nonsense Carol

Repr. facs. John S. Farmer, *The Nature of the Four Elements*, The Tudor Facsimile Texts (London, 1908).

This cheerfully incoherent composition, sung by the clownish Ignorance in John Rastell's interlude, is unique among the carols in being unrhymed, but its stanzaic character is clearly indicated in the original by a paragraph mark before each group of four lines. There are no spaces between the stanzas. That the line 'Downe downe downe etc' is definitely a burden is indicated by the dialogue which immediately precedes, as well as by its own paragraph mark.

The character Ignorance ridicules and rejects pricksong or part-singing, and adds:

But yf thou wylt haue a song that is good
I haue one of robyn hode

Humanity replies: Then a feleshyp let vs here it

Ignorance tells him:	But there is a bordon thou must bere it
	Or ellys it wyll not be
Humanity agrees:	Than begin and care not fo . . . [text damaged].

The piece does not appear to be a cento of lines borrowed from other compositions, but stza. 1, l. 4 seems to be an echo from earlier circulation of one of the Fool's snatches of song in *King Lear*: 'Sleepest or wakest thou, jolly shepherd?' (III. vi, noted by Steevens, New Variorum edn., Philadelphia, 1880, p. 209). The first two lines appear to be derived from some version of *A Gest of Robyn Hode* (Child, No. 117). In Child's texts a and b, printed by Chapman and Myllar in Edinburgh in 1508 and Wynkyn de Worde in London without date, ll. 1, 2 of stza. 3 read:

> Robyn stode in Bernesdale,
> And lenyd hym to a tre.

stza. 4, l. 2. *wrigguldy wrage*: mischief or harm. *O.E.D.* has this passage as the only citation. It compares two uses by Skelton of a personification, 'Sir Wryg Wrag', and the phrase 'at wrig-wrag', meaning at enmity, a variant used once by Nashe. 'Wrigguldy' may be, like 'wriggelty', a dialectal form of 'wriggly'.

On John Rastell see A. W. Reed, *Early Tudor Drama* (London, 1936), chap. i and *passim*, also A. Hyatt King, 'The Significance of John Rastell in Early Music Printing', *The Library*, 5th Ser., xxvi (1971), 197–214.

474. A Nonsense Carol

Repr. facs. Reed, p. 40. B.–R. *Supp.* 1605.5.

The Latin phrases of this carol are adapted from bits of the services for Christmas Day. Compare No. 29 and the song in Bodl. MS. Arch. Selden B. 26, f. 25^r, using some of the same phrases (*pr.* Padelford, p. 150; with music, Stevens, *Med. Carols*, p. 113).

burden, l. 1. A ludicrous 'farcing' of the Office of the morning Mass on Christmas Day (*Sar. Miss.*, p. 27).

stza. 1, l. 1. *mocat*: perhaps merely a typographical error, perhaps a pun on English 'mock at'. It is from an antiphon, 'Ipse invocavit me' (*Br. Sar.* i, col. clxxvii). l. 3. A frequent phrase in the Scriptures, here from Luke ii. 11, the Nativity narrative.

stza. 2, l. 1. A response in the service for Nones on Christmas Day (*Br. Sar.* i, col. cxciv).

stza. 3, l. 1. A corruption of the opening of one of the two chapters from Titus ii and iii said at Lauds and Sext, respectively, on Christmas Day, 'Apparuit gratia' and 'Apparuit benignitas' (ibid. i, cols. clxxxix, cxciii).

stza. 4, l. 2. This phrase occurs repeatedly in the Christmas services. l. 2. In the form 'A black sheep', etc., this was a proverbial saying throughout much of the sixteenth century. Compare Lyly, *Endimion*, II. ii, at close. It there appears to be much in people's mouths because of the increasing number of sheep in England and the consequent economic difficulties. Compare the burden of a carol of the late sixteenth century in Corpus Christi College, Cambridge, MS. 168 (*pr.* J. Goodwin, *P.S.* xiii, 'Six Ballads', p. 4, there wrongly interpreted):

> The blacke shepe is a perylous beast;
> Cuius contrarium falsum est.

On the whole agitation see the detailed account by Furnivall (*Ballads from Manuscripts*, Ballad Society, London, 1868–72, i. 3–37, 97) and the tract 'Certeyne causes . . .' edited by J. M. Cowper (E.E.T.S., Ex. Ser., No. xiii, 1871, 93–105).

INDEX OF FIRST LINES
OF BURDENS AND FIRST STANZAS

Italic type indicates burdens. Minor verbal variations within lines of collated texts are not recorded.